CFA® PROGRAM CURRICULUM
2013 • Level I • Volume 1

ETHICAL AND PROFESSIONAL STANDARDS AND QUANTITATIVE METHODS

CFA Institute

WILEY

John Wiley & Sons, Inc.

Cover photographs courtesy of Hector Emanuel.

ISBN 978-1-937537-00-5 (paper)
ISBN 978-1-937537-21-0 (ebk)

10 9 8 7 6 5 4 3 2 1

Please visit our website at
www.WileyGlobalFinance.com.

MIX
Paper from
responsible sources
FSC® C101537

Contents

○ indicates an optional segment

◎ indicates an optional segment

Contents

◙ indicates an optional segment

Quantitative Methods

◙ indicates an optional segment

⊙ indicates an optional segment

🔘 indicates an optional segment

How to Use the CFA Program Curriculum

Congratulations on your decision to enter the Chartered Financial Analyst (CFA®) Program. This exciting and rewarding program of study reflects your desire to become a serious investment professional. You are embarking on a program noted for its high ethical standards and the breadth of knowledge, skills, and abilities it develops. Your commitment to the CFA Program should be educationally and professionally rewarding.

The credential you seek is respected around the world as a mark of accomplishment and dedication. Each level of the program represents a distinct achievement in professional development. Successful completion of the program is rewarded with membership in a prestigious global community of investment professionals. CFA charterholders are dedicated to life-long learning and maintaining currency with the ever-changing dynamics of a challenging profession. The CFA Program represents the first step towards a career-long commitment to professional education.

The CFA examination measures your mastery of the core skills required to succeed as an investment professional. These core skills are the basis for the Candidate Body of Knowledge (CBOK™). The CBOK consists of four components:

- A broad topic outline that lists the major top-level topic areas (CBOK Topic Outline)
- Topic area weights that indicate the relative exam weightings of the top-level topic areas
- Learning outcome statements (LOS) that advise candidates about the specific knowledge, skills, and abilities they should acquire from readings covering a topic area (LOS are provided in candidate study sessions and at the beginning of each reading)
- The CFA Program curriculum, readings, and end-of-reading questions, which candidates receive upon exam registration

Therefore, the keys to your success on the CFA exam is studying and understanding the CBOK™. The following sections provide background on the CBOK, the organization of the curriculum, and tips for developing an effective study program.

CURRICULUM DEVELOPMENT PROCESS

The CFA Program is grounded in the practice of the investment profession. Using the Global Body of Investment Knowledge (GBIK) collaborative website, CFA Institute performs a continuous practice analysis with investment professionals around the world to determine the knowledge, skills, and abilities (competencies) that are relevant to the profession. Regional expert panels and targeted surveys are conducted annually to verify and reinforce the continuous feedback from the GBIK collaborative website. The practice analysis process ultimately defines the CBOK. The CBOK contains the competencies that are generally accepted and applied by investment professionals. These competencies are used in practice in a generalist context and are expected to be demonstrated by a recently qualified CFA charterholder.

A committee consisting of practicing charterholders, in conjunction with CFA Institute staff, designs the CFA Program curriculum in order to deliver the CBOK to candidates. The examinations, also written by practicing charterholders, are designed to allow you to demonstrate your mastery of the CBOK as set forth in the CFA Program curriculum. As you structure your personal study program, you should emphasize mastery of the CBOK and the practical application of that knowledge. For more information on the practice analysis, CBOK, and development of the CFA Program curriculum, please visit www.cfainstitute.org.

ORGANIZATION OF THE CURRICULUM

The Level I CFA Program curriculum is organized into 10 topic areas. Each topic area begins with a brief statement of the material and the depth of knowledge expected.

Each topic area is then divided into one or more study sessions. These study sessions—18 sessions in the Level I curriculum—should form the basic structure of your reading and preparation.

Each study session includes a statement of its structure and objective, and is further divided into specific reading assignments. An outline illustrating the organization of these 18 study sessions can be found at the front of each volume.

The reading assignments are the basis for all examination questions, and are selected or developed specifically to teach the knowledge, skills, and abilities reflected in the CBOK. These readings are drawn from CFA Institute-commissioned content, textbook chapters, professional journal articles, research analyst reports, and cases. All readings include problems and solutions to help you understand and master the topic areas.

Reading-specific Learning Outcome Statements (LOS) are listed at the beginning of each reading. These LOS indicate what you should be able to accomplish after studying the reading. The LOS, the reading, and the end-of-reading questions are dependent on each other, with the reading and questions providing context for understanding the scope of the LOS.

You should use the LOS to guide and focus your study, as each examination question is based on an assigned reading and one or more LOS. The readings provide context for the LOS and enable you to apply a principle or concept in a variety of scenarios. The candidate is responsible for the entirety of all of the required material in a study session, the assigned readings as well as the end-of-reading questions and problems.

We encourage you to review the material on LOS (http://www.cfainstitute.org/cfaprogram/courseofstudy/Pages/cfa_los.aspx), including the descriptions of LOS "command words," (www.cfainstitute.org/Documents/cfa_and_cipm_los_command_words.pdf).

FEATURES OF THE CURRICULUM

OPTIONAL
SEGMENT

END OPTIONAL
SEGMENT

- **Required vs. Optional Segments** - You should read all of an assigned reading. In some cases, however, we have reprinted an entire chapter or article and marked certain parts of the reading as "optional." The CFA examination is based only on the required segments, and the optional segments are included only when they might help you to better understand the required segments (by seeing the required material in its full context). When an optional segment begins, you will see text and a dashed vertical bar in the outside margin that will continue until the optional segment ends, accompanied by another icon. *Unless the material is specifically marked as optional, you should assume it is required.* You should rely on the required segments and the reading-specific LOS in preparing for the examination.

- **Problems/Solutions** - *All questions and problems in the readings as well as their solutions (which are provided directly following the problems) are part of the curriculum and are required material for the exam.* When appropriate, we have included problems within and after the readings to demonstrate practical application and reinforce your understanding of the concepts presented. The questions and problems are designed to help you learn these concepts and may serve as a basis for exam questions. Many of these questions are adapted from past CFA examinations.

- **Margins** - The wide margins in each volume provide space for your note-taking.

- **Six-Volume Structure** - For portability of the curriculum, the material is spread over six volumes.

- **Glossary and Index** - For your convenience, we have printed a comprehensive glossary and index in each volume. Throughout the curriculum, a **bolded blue** word in a reading denotes a term defined in the glossary.

- **Source Material** - The authorship, publisher, and copyright owners are given for each reading for your reference. We recommend that you use this CFA Institute curriculum rather than the original source materials because the curriculum may include only selected pages from outside readings, updated sections within the readings, and contains problems and solutions tailored to the CFA Program.

- **LOS Self-Check** - We have inserted checkboxes next to each LOS that you can use to track your progress in mastering the concepts in each reading.

DESIGNING YOUR PERSONAL STUDY PROGRAM

Create a Schedule - An orderly, systematic approach to examination preparation is critical. You should dedicate a consistent block of time every week to reading and studying. Complete all reading assignments and the associated problems and solutions in each study session. Review the LOS both before and after you study each reading to ensure that you have mastered the applicable content and can demonstrate the knowledge, skill, or ability described by the LOS and the assigned reading. Use the LOS self-check to track your progress and highlight areas of weakness for later review.

As you prepare for your exam, we will e-mail you important exam updates, testing policies, and study tips. Be sure to read these carefully. Curriculum errata are periodically updated and posted on the study session page at www.cfainstitute.org. You may also sign up for an RSS feed to alert you to the latest errata update.

Successful candidates report an average of over 300 hours preparing for each exam. Your preparation time will vary based on your prior education and experience. For each level of the curriculum, there are 18 study sessions, so a good plan is to devote 15–20 hours per week, for 18 weeks, to studying the material. Use the final four to six weeks before the exam to review what you've learned and practice with sample and mock exams. This recommendation, however, may underestimate the hours needed for appropriate examination preparation depending on your individual circumstances, relevant experience, and academic background. You will undoubtedly adjust your study time to conform to your own strengths and weaknesses, and your educational and professional background.

You will probably spend more time on some study sessions than on others, but on average you should plan on devoting 15-20 hours per study session. You should allow ample time for both in-depth study of all topic areas and additional concentration on those topic areas for which you feel least prepared.

Online Sample Examinations - CFA Institute online sample examinations are intended to assess your exam preparation as you progress toward the end of your study. After each question, you will receive immediate feedback noting the correct response and indicating the relevant assigned reading, so you will be able to identify areas of weakness for further study. The 120-minute sample examinations reflect the question formats, topics, and level of difficulty of the actual CFA examinations. Aggregate data indicate that the CFA examination pass rate was higher among candidates who took one or more online sample examinations than among candidates who did not take the online sample examinations. For more information on the online sample examinations, please visit www.cfainstitute.org.

Online Mock Examinations - In response to candidate requests, CFA Institute has developed mock examinations that mimic the actual CFA examinations not only in question format and level of difficulty, but also in length and topic weight. The three-hour online mock exams simulate the morning and afternoon sessions of the actual CFA exam, and are intended to be taken after you complete your study of the full curriculum, so you can test your understanding of the CBOK and your readiness for the exam. The mock exams are available in a printable PDF format with feedback provided at the end of the exam, rather than after each question as with the sample exams. CFA Institute recommends that you take these mock exams at the final stage of your preparation toward the actual CFA examination. For more information on the online mock examinations, please visit www.cfainstitute.org.

Preparatory Providers - After you enroll in the CFA Program, you may receive numerous solicitations for preparatory courses and review materials. When considering a prep course make sure the provider is in compliance with the CFA Institute Prep Provider Guidelines Program (www.cfainstitute.org/partners/examprep/Pages/cfa_prep_provider_guidelines.aspx). Just remember, there are no shortcuts to success on the CFA examinations; reading and studying the CFA curriculum is the key to success on the examination. The CFA examinations reference only the CFA Institute assigned curriculum—no preparatory course or review course materials are consulted or referenced.

SUMMARY

Every question on the CFA examination is based on the content contained in the required readings and on one or more LOS. Frequently, an examination question is based on a specific example highlighted within a reading or on a specific end-of-reading question and/or problem and its solution. To make effective use of the CFA Program curriculum, please remember these key points:

1. All pages printed in the curriculum are required reading for the examination except for occasional sections marked as optional. You may read optional pages as background, but you will not be tested on them.

2. All questions, problems, and their solutions - printed at the end of readings - are part of the curriculum and are required study material for the examination.

3. You should make appropriate use of the online sample/mock examinations and other resources available at www.cfainstitute.org.

4. You should schedule and commit sufficient study time to cover the 18 study sessions, review the materials, and take sample/mock examinations.

5. **Note:** Some of the concepts in the study sessions may be superseded by updated rulings and/or pronouncements issued after a reading was published. Candidates are expected to be familiar with the overall analytical framework contained in the assigned readings. Candidates are not responsible for changes that occur after the material was written.

FEEDBACK

At CFA Institute, we are committed to delivering a comprehensive and rigorous curriculum for the development of competent, ethically grounded investment professionals. We rely on candidate and member feedback as we work to incorporate content, design, and packaging improvements. You can be assured that we will continue to listen to your suggestions. Please send any comments or feedback to curriculum@cfainstitute.org. Ongoing improvements in the curriculum will help you prepare for success on the upcoming examinations, and for a lifetime of learning as a serious investment professional.

Index		
Japan (Nikkei)		
Seoul		
Taipei (Comp.)		
Mumbai	20,612.4	
Singapore	18,838.9	
Sydney		
Shanghai B	2971.0	1.1%
Hong Kong	4644.0	0.9%
Toronto	316.8	0.7%
Stockholm	22,700.9	0.5%
Mexico City	13,524.8	0.1%

Ethical and Professional Standards

TOPIC LEVEL LEARNING OUTCOME

The candidate should be able to explain the ethical responsibilities required by the CFA Institute Code of Ethics and Standards of Professional Conduct and to demonstrate the application of the Code and Standards. The candidate should also be able to demonstrate an understanding of the Global Investment Performance Standards.

1

Ethics and Professional Standards

ETHICAL AND PROFESSIONAL STANDARDS

The readings in this study session present a framework for ethical conduct in the investment profession by focusing on the CFA Institute Code of Ethics and Standards of Professional Conduct as well as the Global Investment Performance Standards (GIPS®).

The principles and guidance presented in the CFA Institute *Standards of Practice Handbook* (*Handbook*) form the basis for the CFA Institute self-regulatory program to maintain the highest professional standards among investment practitioners. "Guidance" in the *Handbook* addresses the practical application of the Code of Ethics and Standards of Professional Conduct. The guidance expands upon the purpose and scope of each standard, presents recommended procedures for compliance, and provides examples of the standard in practice.

The Global Investment Performance Standards (GIPS) facilitate efficient comparison of investment performance across investment managers and country borders by prescribing methodology and standards that are consistent with a clear and honest presentation of returns. Having a global standard for reporting investment performance minimizes the potential for ambiguous or misleading presentations.

READING ASSIGNMENTS

Reading 1   *Code of Ethics and Standards of Professional Conduct*
            Standards of Practice Handbook, Tenth Edition

Reading 2   *Guidance for Standards I–VII*
            Standards of Practice Handbook, Tenth Edition

Reading 3   *Introduction to the Global Investment Performance Standards (GIPS)*

Reading 4   *Global Investment Performance Standards (GIPS)*

Code of Ethics and Standards of Professional Conduct

LEARNING OUTCOMES	
Mastery	**The candidate should be able to:**
☐	**a** describe the structure of the CFA Institute Professional Conduct Program and the process for the enforcement of the Code and Standards;
☐	**b** state the six components of the Code of Ethics and the seven Standards of Professional Conduct;
☐	**c** explain the ethical responsibilities required by the Code and Standards, including the sub-sections of each Standard.

PREFACE

The *Standards of Practice Handbook* (*Handbook*) provides guidance to the people who grapple with real ethical dilemmas in the investment profession on a daily basis; the *Handbook* addresses the professional intersection where theory meets practice and where the concept of ethical behavior crosses from the abstract to the concrete. The *Handbook* is intended for a diverse and global audience: CFA Institute members navigating ambiguous ethical situations; supervisors and direct/indirect reports determining the nature of their responsibilities to each other, to existing and potential clients, and to the broader financial markets; and candidates preparing for the Chartered Financial Analyst (CFA) examinations.

Recent events in the global financial markets have tested the ethical mettle of financial market participants, including CFA Institute members. The standards taught in the CFA Program and by which CFA Institute members and candidates must abide represent timeless ethical principles and professional conduct for all market conditions. Through adherence to these standards, which continue to serve as the model for ethical behavior in the investment professional globally, each market participant does his or her part to improve the integrity and efficient operations of the financial markets.

The *Handbook* provides guidance in understanding the interconnectedness of the principles and provisions of the Code of Ethics and Standards of Professional Conduct (Code and Standards). Individually, the principles outline the high level of ethical conduct required from CFA Institute members and candidates. However, applying the principles individually may not capture the complexity of ethical requirements related to the investment industry. The Code and Standards should be viewed and interpreted as an interwoven tapestry of ethical requirements. Through members' and candidates' adherence to these principles as a whole, the integrity of and trust in the capital markets are improved.

Evolution of the CFA Institute Code of Ethics and Standards of Professional Conduct

Generally, changes to the Code and Standards over the years have been minor. CFA Institute has revised the language of the Code and Standards and occasionally added a new standard to address a prominent issue of the day. For instance, in 1992, CFA Institute added the standard addressing performance presentation to the existing list of standards.

Major changes came in 2005 with the ninth edition of the *Handbook*. CFA Institute adopted new standards, revised some existing standards, and reorganized the standards. The revisions were intended to clarify the requirements of the Code and Standards and effectively convey to its global membership what constitutes "best practice" in a number of areas relating to the investment profession.

The Code and Standards must be regularly reviewed and updated if they are to remain effective and continue to represent the highest ethical standards in the global investment industry. CFA Institute strongly believes that revisions of the Code and Standards are not undertaken for cosmetic change but to add value by addressing legitimate concerns and improving comprehension.

Changes to the Code and Standards have far-reaching implications for the CFA Institute membership, the CFA Program, and the investment industry as a whole. CFA Institute members and candidates are *required* to adhere to the Code and Standards. In addition, the Code and Standards are increasingly being adopted, in whole or in part, by firms and regulatory authorities. Their relevance goes well beyond CFA Institute members and candidates.

Standards of Practice Handbook

The periodic revisions to the Code and Standards have come in conjunction with updates of the *Standards of Practice Handbook*. The *Handbook* is the fundamental element of the ethics education effort of CFA Institute and the primary resource for guidance in interpreting and implementing the Code and Standards. The *Handbook* seeks to educate members and candidates on how to apply the Code and Standards to their professional lives and thereby benefit their clients, employers, and the investing public in general. The *Handbook* explains the purpose of the Code and Standards and how they apply in a variety of situations. The sections discuss and amplify each standard and suggest procedures to prevent violations.

Examples in the "Application of the Standard" sections are meant to illustrate how the standard applies to hypothetical but factual situations. The names contained in the examples are fictional and are not meant to refer to any actual person or entity. Unless otherwise stated, individuals in each example are CFA Institute members and holders of the CFA designation. Because factual circumstances vary so widely and often involve gray areas, the explanatory material and examples are not intended to be all inclusive. Many examples set forth in the application sections involve standards that have legal counterparts; ***members are strongly urged to discuss with their supervisors and legal and compliance departments the content of the Code and Standards and the members' general obligations under the Code and Standards***.

CFA Institute recognizes that the presence of any set of ethical standards may create a false sense of security unless the documents are fully understood, enforced, and made a meaningful part of everyday professional activities. The *Handbook* is intended to provide a useful frame of reference that suggests ethical professional behavior in the investment decision-making process. This section cannot cover every contingency or circumstance, however, and it does not attempt to do so. The development and interpretation of the Code and Standards are evolving processes; the Code and Standards will be subject to continuing refinement.

Summary of Changes in the Tenth Edition

The comprehensive review of the Code and Standards in 2005 resulted in principle requirements that remain applicable today. The review carried out for the tenth edition focused on updates to the guidance and examples within the *Handbook*. In the tenth edition, the changes relate primarily to the growing diversity of the CFA Institute membership and CFA Program candidate base and aim to make specific guidance easier to understand.

Clarification of Standard III(A)

Standard III(A) Duties to Clients—Loyalty, Prudence, and Care was shortened to improve clarity. The third sentence was deleted to avoid possible misinterpretations of the members' or candidates' required duties to their clients. The principle contained in the deleted sentence already has been established in Standard I(A) regarding the responsibility to adhere to the most strict legal, regulatory, or CFA Institute requirements.

> Deletion:
> In relationships with clients, Members and Candidates must determine applicable fiduciary duty and must comply with such duty to persons and interests to whom it is owed.

Why Ethics Matters

A new section was added to the *Handbook* to broaden the discussion of the importance of ethics to the investment profession. The chapter addresses market integrity and sustainability, the role of CFA Institute, and the importance of ongoing awareness of and education about changes in the investment industry.

Text Revisions

As the investment industry and, as a result, CFA Institute membership have become more global, the use of English that can be easily understood and translated into different languages has become critical. Therefore, in some places, CFA Institute has eliminated, modified, or added language for clarity, even though it is not the intent to change the meaning of a particular provision.

Guidance Table

To keep the *Handbook* as a primary resource for members and candidates as they tackle ethical dilemmas, bulleted tables were added to help the reader locate the guidance within a standard that is most applicable to the situations that may occur in daily professional life. The Code and Standards must not be viewed as something solely to be learned to pass the CFA examinations; its principles are intended to play an active role in everyday decision making.

Example Highlight

In a continued effort to assist readers in locating examples of situations similar to issues they are facing, this update includes a brief descriptive heading for each example in the "Application of the Standard" sections. The heading notes the principle being addressed or the nature of the example.

Cross-Standard Examples

To further highlight the applicability of multiple standards to a single set of facts, some examples are used several times. The single or slightly modified facts are accompanied by comments directed to the standard in question. The other standards using the same example are noted at the end of the comments.

CFA Institute Professional Conduct Program

All CFA Institute members and candidates enrolled in the CFA Program are required to comply with the Code and Standards. The CFA Institute Board of Governors maintains oversight and responsibility for the Professional Conduct Program (PCP), which, in conjunction with the Disciplinary Review Committee (DRC), is responsible for enforcement of the Code and Standards. The CFA Institute Bylaws and Rules of Procedure for Proceedings Related to Professional Conduct (Rules of Procedure) form the basic structure for enforcing the Code and Standards. The Rules of Procedure are based on two primary principles: 1) fair process to the member and candidate and 2) confidentiality of proceedings.

Professional Conduct staff, under the direction of the CFA Institute Designated Officer, conducts professional conduct inquiries. Several circumstances can prompt an inquiry. First, members and candidates must self-disclose on the annual Professional Conduct Statement all matters that question their professional conduct, such as involvement in civil litigation or a criminal investigation or being the subject of a written complaint. Second, written complaints received by Professional Conduct staff can bring about an investigation. Third, CFA Institute staff may become aware of questionable conduct by a member or candidate through the media or another public source. Fourth, CFA examination proctors may submit a violation report for any candidate suspected to have compromised his or her professional conduct during the examination.

When an inquiry is initiated, the Professional Conduct staff conducts an investigation that may include requesting a written explanation from the member or candidate; interviewing the member or candidate, complaining parties, and third parties; and collecting documents and records in support of its investigation. The Designated Officer, upon reviewing the material obtained during the investigation, may conclude the inquiry with no disciplinary sanction, issue a cautionary letter, or continue proceedings to discipline the member or candidate. If the Designated Officer finds that a violation of the Code and Standards occurred, the Designated Officer proposes a disciplinary sanction, which may be rejected or accepted by the member or candidate.

If the member or candidate does not accept the proposed sanction, the matter is referred to a hearing panel composed of DRC members and CFA Institute member volunteers affiliated with the DRC. The hearing panel reviews materials and presentations from the Designated Officer and from the member or candidate. The hearing panel's task is to determine whether a violation of the Code and Standards occurred and, if so, what sanction should be imposed.

Sanctions imposed by CFA Institute may have significant consequences; they include public censure, suspension of membership and use of the CFA designation, and revocation of the CFA charter. Candidates enrolled in the CFA Program who have violated the Code and Standards may be suspended from further participation in the CFA Program.

Adoption of the Code and Standards

The Code and Standards apply to individual members of CFA Institute and candidates in the CFA Program. CFA Institute does encourage firms to adopt the Code and Standards, however, as part of a firm's code of ethics. Those who claim compliance should fully understand the requirements of each of the principles of the Code and Standards.

Once a party—nonmember or firm—ensures its code of ethics meets the principles of the Code and Standards, that party should make the following statement whenever claiming compliance:

"[Insert name of party] claims compliance with the CFA Institute Code of Ethics and Standards of Professional Conduct. This claim has not been verified by CFA Institute."

CFA Institute welcomes public acknowledgement, when appropriate, that firms are complying with the CFA Institute Code of Ethics and Standards of Professional Conduct and encourages firms to notify us of the adoption plans. For firms that would like to distribute the Code and Standards to clients and potential clients, attractive one-page copies of the Code and Standards, including translations, are available on the CFA Institute website (www.cfainstitute.org).

CFA Institute has also published the Asset Manager Code of Professional Conduct (AMC), which is designed, in part, to help asset managers comply with the regulations mandating codes of ethics for investment advisers. Whereas the Code and Standards are aimed at individual investment professionals who are members of CFA Institute or candidates in the CFA Program, the AMC was drafted specifically for firms. The AMC provides specific, practical guidelines for asset managers in six areas: loyalty to clients, the investment process, trading, compliance, performance evaluation, and disclosure. The AMC and the appropriate steps to acknowledge adoption or compliance can be found on the CFA Institute website (www.cfainstitute.org).

Acknowledgments

CFA Institute is a not-for-profit organization that is heavily dependent on the expertise and intellectual contributions of member volunteers. Members devote their time as they share a mutual interest in the organization's mission to promote and achieve ethical practice in the investment profession. CFA Institute owes much to the volunteers' abundant generosity and energy in extending ethical integrity.

The CFA Institute Standards of Practice Council (SPC), a group consisting of CFA charterholder volunteers from many different countries, is charged with maintaining and interpreting the Code and Standards and ensuring that they are effective. The SPC draws its membership from a broad spectrum of organizations in the securities field, including brokers, investment advisers, banks, and insurance companies. In most instances, the SPC members have important supervisory responsibilities within their firms.

The SPC continually evaluates the Code and Standards, as well as the guidance in the *Handbook*, to ensure that they are

- representative of high standards of professional conduct;
- relevant to the changing nature of the investment profession;
- globally applicable;
- sufficiently comprehensive, practical, and specific;
- enforceable; and
- testable for the CFA Program.

The SPC has spent countless hours reviewing and discussing revisions to the Code and Standards and updates to the guidance that makes up the tenth edition of the *Handbook*. Following is a list of the current and former members of the SPC who generously donated their time and energy to this effort.

Christopher C. Loop, CFA, Chair	Toshihiko Saito, CFA, Prior Chair
Karin B. Bonding, CFA	Jinliang Li, CFA
Jean-Francois Bouilly, CFA	Lynn S. Mander, CFA
Terence E. Burns, CFA	James M. Meeth, CFA
Sharon Craggs, CFA	Brian O'Keefe, CFA

Mario Eichenberger, CFA   Guy G. Rutherfurd, Jr., CFA

James E. Hollis, CFA   Sunil B. Singhania, CFA

Samuel B. Jones, CFA   Peng Lian Wee, CFA

Ulrike Kaiser-Boeing, CFA

The chair and members of the SPC would like to thank the CFA Institute staff who supported this revision for their efforts to keep the process smooth and well organized.

This tenth edition of the *Standards of Practice Handbook* is dedicated to the late Mildred Hermann, who served in a variety of capacities with the CFA Institute predecessor organizations, the Financial Analysts Federation (FAF) and the Association for Investment Management and Research (AIMR). With a work ethic that knew no limits, she possessed an unfailing sense of fairness and uncompromising integrity—attributes she expected in all investment professionals.

As FAF/AIMR staff representative to the predecessor committees to the Standards of Practice Council, Mildred was instrumental in the development of the first edition of the *Standards of Practice Handbook* and continued her direct involvement with the four subsequent editions published up to her retirement in 1991. She proved to be a passionate and skilled technician whose prodigious intellect, range of knowledge, and seasoned judgment fused seamlessly to create a deeply informed understanding of regulatory trends and their implications for FAF/AIMR members and the investment profession at large.

Mildred's tenure was marked by her special brand of leadership, vision, and commitment in promoting the highest standards of ethical conduct and professional practice. As Rossa O'Reilly, CFA, former chair of the Board of Governors, aptly observed at her retirement, "Very few professionals have contributed as much or worked as diligently toward furthering the goals of the profession of investment analysis and portfolio management as Mildred Hermann." For those of us fortunate enough to have worked with Mildred, she is fondly remembered as a unique talent, quick wit, valued colleague, model of human decency, and a humble, beloved friend.

WHY ETHICS MATTERS

The adherence of investment professionals to ethical practices benefits all market participants and increases investor confidence in global financial markets. Clients are reassured that the investment professionals they hire operate with the clients' best interests in mind, and investment professionals benefit from the more efficient and transparent operation of the market that integrity promotes. Ethical practices instill public trust in markets and support the development of markets. Sound ethics is fundamental to capital markets and the investment profession.

The first decade of the 21st century has been but one of many times of crisis for the investment industry. This period, unfortunately, has encompassed many instances of unethical behavior—by business executives and investment professionals. The newspapers and airwaves have brimmed with a succession of accounting frauds and manipulations, Ponzi schemes, insider trading, and other misdeeds. Each case has resulted in heavy financial losses and stained reputations. Equally important has been the terrible toll these actions have taken on investors' trust. Trust is hard earned and easily lost; corporations and individuals can safeguard themselves by committing to the highest standards of ethics and professional conduct.

Ethics is not merely a virtue to be demonstrated by CFA Institute members and candidates. Ethics must permeate all levels of our profession. Serving the best interests of the investing clients and employers lies at the heart of what collectively must be done to ensure a sense of trust and integrity in the financial markets. Although the drive to achieve such a lofty collective objective is critically important, the drive must ultimately start in the workplace. It is imperative that top management foster a strong culture of ethics not just among CFA charterholders and candidates but among all staff members who are involved directly or indirectly with client relations, the investment process, record keeping, and beyond. In such a culture, all participants can see clear evidence of how extremely important ethics is when woven into the fabric of an organization, or in other words, all participants in the process will know that ethics genuinely matters.

Ethics and CFA Institute

An important goal of CFA Institute is to ensure that the organization and its members develop, promote, and follow the highest ethical standards in the investment industry. The CFA Institute Code of Ethics (Code) and Standards of Professional Conduct (Standards) are the foundation supporting the organization's quest to advance the interests of the global investment community by establishing and maintaining the highest standards of professional excellence and integrity. The Code is a set of principles that define the professional conduct CFA Institute expects from its members and candidates in the CFA Program. The Code works in tandem with the Standards, which outline conduct that constitutes fair and ethical business practices.

For more than 40 years, CFA Institute members and candidates in the CFA Program have been required to abide by the organization's Code and Standards. Periodically, CFA Institute has revised and updated its Code and Standards to ensure that they remain relevant to the changing nature of the investment profession and representative of the "highest standard" of professional conduct. Recent events have highlighted unethical actions in the areas of governance, investment ratings, financial product packaging and distribution, and outright investment fraud. Finance is a sophisticated and interconnected global industry; new investment opportunities and new financial instruments to make the most of those opportunities are constantly developing. Although the investment world has become a far more complex place since the first publication of the *Handbook*, distinguishing right from wrong remains the paramount principle of the Code and Standards.

Ethics and Market Sustainability

The increasingly interconnected nature of global finance brings to the fore an added consideration that was, perhaps, less relevant in years past. This consideration is that of *market sustainability*. In addition to committing to the highest levels of ethical behavior, today's investment professional, when making decisions, should consider the long-term health of the market as a whole. As recent events have demonstrated, the sum of apparently isolated and unrelated decisions, however innocuous when considered on an individual basis, when aggregated, can precipitate a market crisis. In an interconnected global economy and marketplace, each participant should strive to be aware of how his or her actions or products may be distributed to, used in, or have an impact on other regions or countries.

The much-discussed credit crisis that buffeted global financial markets highlights these concerns. Relying on esoteric structures, certain banks developed financial instruments that extended credit to consumers and companies that otherwise would not have had access to those monies. Clients purchased these instruments in a quest for yield in a low-interest-rate environment. But some of the higher-risk borrowers could not afford their loans and were not able to refinance them. Defaults soared, and some of the instruments collapsed. Many of the institutions that had purchased the instruments or retained stakes in them had not completed sufficient diligence on the instruments' structures and suffered horrendous losses. Established institutions toppled into ruin, wrecking lives and reputations. Had members of the investment profession considered with greater foresight the question of market sustainability in tandem with the needs and expectations of their clients, the magnitude of the crisis might have been lessened.

CFA Institute encourages all members and candidates to consider in their investment decision-making process the promotion and protection of the global financial markets as an aspect of the broader context of the application of the Code and Standards. Those in positions of authority have a special responsibility to consider the broader context of market sustainability in their development and approval of corporate policies, particularly those involving risk management and product development. In addition, corporate compensation strategies should not encourage otherwise ethically sound individuals to engage in unethical or questionable conduct for financial gain. Ethics, sustainability, and properly functioning capital markets are components of the same concept of protecting the interests of all.

Ethics and Regulation

Regulation alone will never fully anticipate and eliminate the causes of financial crises. Some individuals will try to and may well be able to circumvent the regulatory rules. Only strong ethical principles, at the level of the individual and the level of the firm, will limit abuses. Knowing the rules or regulations to apply in a particular situation, although important, is not sufficient to ensure ethical decision making. Individuals must be able both to recognize areas that are prone to ethical pitfalls and to identify those circumstances and influences that can impair ethical judgment.

The Code and Standards, as well as other voluntary ethical standards of the CFA Institute (e.g., the Global Investment Performance Standards, Soft Dollar Standards, Trade Management Guidelines, Research Objectivity Standards, and the Asset Manager Code of Professional Conduct), offer a foundation to adopt and build on in promoting an ethical corporate culture. The adoption of these standards is not limited to investment professionals and their firms affiliated with CFA Institute. National regulators might consider the *Handbook*'s guidance in fostering ethical identities within organizations and national systems.

In the future, the nature and level of regulation will depend on how companies comply with the rules already in place. Greater adherence to the spirit of current rules may well require fewer regulatory changes. Conversely, continued short-sightedness and disregard for the outcomes of particularly adverse practices may necessitate more stringent regulation. In this respect, the investment industry can have a positive effect on evolving regulation and, in that way, on its own operational environment. Through continuing education, investment professionals can reinforce and evaluate their personal ethical conduct.

Ethics Education and Awareness

New challenges will continually arise for members and candidates in applying the Code and Standards because ethical dilemmas are not unambiguously right or wrong. The dilemma exists because the choice between right and wrong is not always clear. Even well-intentioned investment professionals can find themselves in circumstances that may tempt them to cut corners. Situational influences can overpower the best of intentions.

To assist members and candidates in adhering to the principles of the Code and Standards, CFA Institute has made a significant commitment to provide members and candidates with the resources to extend and deepen their understanding of the principles' applications. The publications from CFA Institute offer a wealth of material. *CFA Magazine* contains a section on ethics in most issues. The magazine contains not only vignettes describing potentially questionable situations and guidance related to the Code and Standards but also frequent articles on broad topics relevant to current and developing ethical issues. The *Financial Analysts Journal* also publishes articles related to ethics and professional conduct. Archived issues of these publications are available on the CFA Institute website (www.cfainstitute.org).

CFA Institute includes presentations on ethics in many of its sponsored conferences. These presentations vary as widely as the articles do, from staff-led training courses to discussion of market events by outside professionals with a view toward ethical education. These presentations highlight current trends and how improved ethical decision making may lead to different or even preferred outcomes in the future.

These various resources are available to members and candidates and the investment community at large. Those unable to attend an actual conference will find podcasts, webcasts, or transcripts available on the CFA Institute website (www.cfainstitute.org). Conferences and the presentations offered in the *CFA Institute Conference Proceedings Quarterly* also provide continuing education credits for those members participating in the program.

The Research Foundation of CFA Institute, a not-for-profit organization established to promote the development and dissemination of relevant research for investment practitioners worldwide, has contributed to continued ethical education through the commission and publication in 2007 of *The Psychology of Ethics in the Finance and Investment Industry*. In this monograph, Thomas Oberlechner, professor of psychology at Webster University in Vienna, discusses the role psychology plays in individuals' ethical or unethical decision making. He concludes that understanding the dynamic nature of ethical decision making allows us to understand why unethical decisions can be made by anyone and, hence, how to manage our ethical conduct.

Markets function to an important extent on trust. Recent events have shown the fragility of this foundation and the devastating consequences that can ensue when this foundation is fundamentally questioned. Investment professionals should remain mindful of the long-term health of financial markets and incorporate this concern for the market's sustainability in their investment decision making. CFA Institute and the Standards of Practice Council hope this edition of the *Handbook* will assist and guide investment professionals in meeting the ethical demands of the highly interconnected global capital markets.

CFA INSTITUTE CODE OF ETHICS AND STANDARDS OF PROFESSIONAL CONDUCT

Preamble

The CFA Institute Code of Ethics and Standards of Professional Conduct are fundamental to the values of CFA Institute and essential to achieving its mission to lead the investment profession globally by setting high standards of education, integrity, and professional excellence. High ethical standards are critical to maintaining the public's trust in financial markets and in the investment profession. Since their creation in the 1960s, the Code and Standards have promoted the integrity of CFA Institute members and served as a model for measuring the ethics of investment professionals globally, regardless of job function, cultural differences, or local laws and regulations.

All CFA Institute members (including holders of the Chartered Financial Analyst [CFA] designation) and CFA candidates must abide by the Code and Standards and are encouraged to notify their employer of this responsibility. Violations may result in disciplinary sanctions by CFA Institute. Sanctions can include revocation of membership, revocation of candidacy in the CFA Program, and revocation of the right to use the CFA designation.

The Code of Ethics

Members of CFA Institute (including CFA charterholders) and candidates for the CFA designation ("Members and Candidates") must:

■ Act with integrity, competence, diligence, respect, and in an ethical manner with the public, clients, prospective clients, employers, employees, colleagues in the investment profession, and other participants in the global capital markets.

■ Place the integrity of the investment profession and the interests of clients above their own personal interests.

■ Use reasonable care and exercise independent professional judgment when conducting investment analysis, making investment recommendations, taking investment actions, and engaging in other professional activities.

■ Practice and encourage others to practice in a professional and ethical manner that will reflect credit on themselves and the profession.

■ Promote the integrity of and uphold the rules governing capital markets.

■ Maintain and improve their professional competence and strive to maintain and improve the competence of other investment professionals.

Standards of Professional Conduct

I. **PROFESSIONALISM**

A. **Knowledge of the Law.** Members and Candidates must understand and comply with all applicable laws, rules, and regulations (including the CFA Institute Code of Ethics and Standards of Professional Conduct) of any government, regulatory organization, licensing agency, or professional association governing their professional activities. In the event of conflict, Members and Candidates must comply with the more strict law, rule, or regulation. Members and Candidates must not knowingly participate or assist in and must dissociate from any violation of such laws, rules, or regulations.

B. **Independence and Objectivity.** Members and Candidates must use reasonable care and judgment to achieve and maintain independence and objectivity in their professional activities. Members and Candidates must not offer, solicit, or accept any gift, benefit, compensation, or consideration that reasonably could be expected to compromise their own or another's independence and objectivity.

C. **Misrepresentation.** Members and Candidates must not knowingly make any misrepresentations relating to investment analysis, recommendations, actions, or other professional activities.

D. **Misconduct.** Members and Candidates must not engage in any professional conduct involving dishonesty, fraud, or deceit or commit any act that reflects adversely on their professional reputation, integrity, or competence.

II. **INTEGRITY OF CAPITAL MARKETS**

    A. **Material Nonpublic Information.** Members and Candidates who possess material nonpublic information that could affect the value of an investment must not act or cause others to act on the information.

    B. **Market Manipulation.** Members and Candidates must not engage in practices that distort prices or artificially inflate trading volume with the intent to mislead market participants.

III. **DUTIES TO CLIENTS**

    A. **Loyalty, Prudence, and Care.** Members and Candidates have a duty of loyalty to their clients and must act with reasonable care and exercise prudent judgment. Members and Candidates must act for the benefit of their clients and place their clients' interests before their employer's or their own interests.

    B. **Fair Dealing.** Members and Candidates must deal fairly and objectively with all clients when providing investment analysis, making investment recommendations, taking investment action, or engaging in other professional activities.

    C. **Suitability.**

        1. When Members and Candidates are in an advisory relationship with a client, they must:

            a. Make a reasonable inquiry into a client's or prospective client's investment experience, risk and return objectives, and financial constraints prior to making any investment recommendation or taking investment action and must reassess and update this information regularly.

            b. Determine that an investment is suitable to the client's financial situation and consistent with the client's written objectives, mandates, and constraints before making an investment recommendation or taking investment action.

            c. Judge the suitability of investments in the context of the client's total portfolio.

        2. When Members and Candidates are responsible for managing a portfolio to a specific mandate, strategy, or style, they must make only investment recommendations or take only investment actions that are consistent with the stated objectives and constraints of the portfolio.

    D. **Performance Presentation.** When communicating investment performance information, Members and Candidates must make reasonable efforts to ensure that it is fair, accurate, and complete.

    E. **Preservation of Confidentiality.** Members and Candidates must keep information about current, former, and prospective clients confidential unless:

        1. The information concerns illegal activities on the part of the client or prospective client,

        2. Disclosure is required by law, or

        3. The client or prospective client permits disclosure of the information.

IV. **DUTIES TO EMPLOYERS**

    A. **Loyalty.** In matters related to their employment, Members and Candidates must act for the benefit of their employer and not deprive their employer of the advantage of their skills and abilities, divulge confidential information, or otherwise cause harm to their employer.

    B. **Additional Compensation Arrangements.** Members and Candidates must not accept gifts, benefits, compensation, or consideration that competes with or might reasonably be expected to create a conflict of interest with their employer's interest unless they obtain written consent from all parties involved.

    C. **Responsibilities of Supervisors.** Members and Candidates must make reasonable efforts to detect and prevent violations of applicable laws, rules, regulations, and the Code and Standards by anyone subject to their supervision or authority.

V. **INVESTMENT ANALYSIS, RECOMMENDATIONS, AND ACTIONS**

    A. **Diligence and Reasonable Basis.** Members and Candidates must:

        1. Exercise diligence, independence, and thoroughness in analyzing investments, making investment recommendations, and taking investment actions.

        2. Have a reasonable and adequate basis, supported by appropriate research and investigation, for any investment analysis, recommendation, or action.

    B. **Communication with Clients and Prospective Clients.** Members and Candidates must:

        1. Disclose to clients and prospective clients the basic format and general principles of the investment processes they use to analyze investments, select securities, and construct portfolios and must promptly disclose any changes that might materially affect those processes.

        2. Use reasonable judgment in identifying which factors are important to their investment analyses, recommendations, or actions and include those factors in communications with clients and prospective clients.

        3. Distinguish between fact and opinion in the presentation of investment analysis and recommendations.

    C. **Record Retention.** Members and Candidates must develop and maintain appropriate records to support their investment analyses, recommendations, actions, and other investment-related communications with clients and prospective clients.

VI. **CONFLICTS OF INTEREST**

    A. **Disclosure of Conflicts.** Members and Candidates must make full and fair disclosure of all matters that could reasonably be expected to impair their independence and objectivity or interfere with respective duties to their clients, prospective clients, and employer. Members and Candidates must ensure that such disclosures are prominent, are delivered in plain language, and communicate the relevant information effectively.

    B. **Priority of Transactions.** Investment transactions for clients and employers must have priority over investment transactions in which a Member or Candidate is the beneficial owner.

    C. **Referral Fees.** Members and Candidates must disclose to their employer, clients, and prospective clients, as appropriate, any compensation, consideration, or benefit received from or paid to others for the recommendation of products or services.

VII. RESPONSIBILITIES AS A CFA INSTITUTE MEMBER OR CFA CANDIDATE

A. Conduct as Members and Candidates in the CFA Program. Members and Candidates must not engage in any conduct that compromises the reputation or integrity of CFA Institute or the CFA designation or the integrity, validity, or security of the CFA examinations.

B. Reference to CFA Institute, the CFA Designation, and the CFA Program. When referring to CFA Institute, CFA Institute membership, the CFA designation, or candidacy in the CFA Program, Members and Candidates must not misrepresent or exaggerate the meaning or implications of membership in CFA Institute, holding the CFA designation, or candidacy in the CFA program.

2

Guidance for Standards I–VII

STANDARD I—PROFESSIONALISM

A. Knowledge of the Law

Members and Candidates must understand and comply with all applicable laws, rules, and regulations (including the CFA Institute Code of Ethics and Standards of Professional Conduct) of any government, regulatory organization, licensing agency, or professional association governing their professional activities. In the event of conflict, Members and Candidates must comply with the more strict law, rule, or regulation. Members and Candidates must not knowingly participate or assist in and must dissociate from any violation of such laws, rules, or regulations

Guidance

Highlights:

- *Relationship between the Code and Standards and Applicable Law*
- *Participation in or Association with Violations by Others*
- *Investment Products and Applicable Laws*

Members and candidates must understand the applicable laws and regulations of all the countries in which they trade securities or provide investment advice or other investment services. On the basis of their understanding, members and candidates must comply with the laws and regulations that directly govern their work. When questions arise, members and candidates should know their firm's policies and procedures for accessing compliance guidance. This standard does not require members and candidates to become experts, however, in compliance. Additionally, investment professionals are not required to have detailed knowledge of or be experts on all the laws that could potentially govern the member's or candidate's activities.

During times of changing regulations, members and candidates must remain vigilant in maintaining their knowledge of the requirements for their professional activities. The financial and ethical missteps in the first decade of the 21st century created an environment for swift and wide-ranging regulatory changes. As new local, regional, and global requirements are updated, members, candidates, and their firms must adjust their procedures and practices to remain in compliance.

Relationship between the Code and Standards and Applicable Law

Some members or candidates may live, work, or provide investment services to clients living in a country that has no law or regulation governing a particular action or that has laws or regulations that differ from the requirements of the Code and Standards. When applicable law and the Code and Standards require different conduct, members and candidates must follow the more strict of the applicable law or the Code and Standards.

"Applicable law" is the law that governs the member's or candidate's conduct. Which law applies will depend on the particular facts and circumstances of each case. The "more strict" law or regulation is the law or regulation that imposes greater restrictions on the action of the member or candidate or calls for the member or candidate to exert a greater degree of action that protects the interests of investors. For example, applicable law or regulation may not require members and candidates to disclose referral fees received from or paid to others for the recommendation of investment products or services. Because the Code and Standards impose this obligation, however, members and candidates must disclose the existence of such fees.

Members and candidates must adhere to the following principles:

■ Members and candidates must comply with applicable law or regulation related to their professional activities.

■ Members and candidates must not engage in conduct that constitutes a violation of the Code and Standards, even though it may otherwise be legal.

■ In the absence of any applicable law or regulation or when the Code and Standards impose a higher degree of responsibility than applicable laws and regulations, members and candidates must adhere to the Code and Standards. Applications of these principles are outlined in Exhibit 1.

CFA Institute members are obligated to abide by the CFA Institute Articles of Incorporation, Bylaws, Code of Ethics, Standards of Professional Conduct, Rules of Procedure, Membership Agreement, and other applicable rules promulgated by CFA Institute, all as amended from time to time. CFA candidates who are not members must also abide by these documents (except for the Membership Agreement) as well as rules and regulations related to the administration of the CFA examination, the Candidate Responsibility Statement, and the Candidate Pledge.

Participation in or Association with Violations by Others

Members and candidates are responsible for violations in which they *knowingly* participate or assist. Although members and candidates are presumed to have knowledge of all applicable laws, rules, and regulations, CFA Institute acknowledges that members may not recognize violations if they are not aware of all the facts giving rise to the violations. Standard I(A) applies when members and candidates know or should know that their conduct may contribute to a violation of applicable laws, rules, regulations, or the Code and Standards.

If a member or candidate has reasonable grounds to believe that imminent or ongoing client or employer activities are illegal or unethical, the member or candidate must dissociate, or separate, from the activity. In extreme cases, dissociation may require a member or candidate to leave his or her employment. Members and candidates may take the following intermediate steps to dissociate from ethical violations of others when direct discussions with the person or persons committing the violation are unsuccessful. The first step should be to attempt to stop the behavior by bringing it to the attention of the employer through a supervisor or the firm's compliance department. If this attempt is unsuccessful, then members and candidates have a responsibility to step away and dissociate from the activity. Dissociation practices will differ on the basis of the member's or candidate's role in the investment industry. It may include removing one's name from written reports or recommendations, asking for a different assignment, or refusing to accept a new client or continue to advise a current client. Inaction combined with continuing association with those involved in illegal or unethical conduct may be construed as participation or assistance in the illegal or unethical conduct.

CFA Institute strongly encourages members and candidates to report potential violations of the Code and Standards committed by fellow members and candidates. Although a failure to report is less likely to be construed as a violation than a failure to dissociate from unethical conduct, the impact of inactivity on the integrity of capital markets can be significant. Although the Code and Standards do not compel members and candidates to report violations to their governmental or regulatory organizations unless such disclosure is mandatory under applicable law, such disclosure may be prudent under certain circumstances. Members and candidates should consult their legal and compliance advisers for guidance.

Additionally, CFA Institute encourages members, nonmembers, clients, and the investing public to report violations of the Code and Standards by CFA Institute members or CFA candidates by submitting a complaint in writing to the CFA Institute Professional Conduct Program via e-mail (pcprogram@cfainstitute.org) or the CFA Institute website (www.cfainstitute.org).

Investment Products and Applicable Laws

Members and candidates involved in creating or maintaining investment services or investment products or packages of securities and/or derivatives should be mindful of where these products or packages will be sold as well as their places of origination. The applicable laws and regulations of the countries or regions of origination and expected sale should be understood by those responsible for the supervision of the services or creation and maintenance of the products or packages. Members or candidates should make reasonable efforts to review whether associated firms that are distributing products or services developed by their employing firm also abide by the laws and regulations of the countries and regions of distribution. Members and candidates should undertake the necessary due diligence when transacting cross-border business to understand the multiple applicable laws and regulations in order to protect the reputation of their firm and themselves.

Exhibit 1	Global Application of the Code and Standards

Members and candidates who practice in multiple jurisdictions may be subject to varied securities laws and regulations. If applicable law is stricter than the requirements of the Code and Standards, members and candidates must adhere

(continued)

Exhibit 1	*Continued*

to applicable law; otherwise, they must adhere to the Code and Standards. The following chart provides illustrations involving a member who may be subject to the securities laws and regulations of three different types of countries:

NS: country with no securities laws or regulations

LS: country with *less* strict securities laws and regulations than the Code and Standards

MS: country with *more* strict securities laws and regulations than the Code and Standards

Applicable Law	Duties	Explanation
Member resides in NS country, does business in LS country; LS law applies.	Member must adhere to the Code and Standards.	Because applicable law is less strict than the Code and Standards, the member must adhere to the Code and Standards.
Member resides in NS country, does business in MS country; MS law applies.	Member must adhere to the law of MS country.	Because applicable law is stricter than the Code and Standards, member must adhere to the more strict applicable law.
Member resides in LS country, does business in NS country; LS law applies.	Member must adhere to the Code and Standards.	Because applicable law is less strict than the Code and Standards, member must adhere to the Code and Standards.
Member resides in LS country, does business in MS country; MS law applies.	Member must adhere to the law of MS country.	Because applicable law is stricter than the Code and Standards, member must adhere to the more strict applicable law.
Member resides in LS country, does business in NS country; LS law applies, but it states that law of locality where business is conducted governs.	Member must adhere to the Code and Standards.	Because applicable law states that the law of the locality where the business is conducted governs and there is no local law, the member must adhere to the Code and Standards.
Member resides in LS country, does business in MS country; LS law applies, but it states that law of locality where business is conducted governs.	Member must adhere to the law of MS country.	Because applicable law of the locality where the business is conducted governs and local law is stricter than the Code and Standards, member must adhere to the more strict applicable law.
Member resides in MS country, does business in LS country; MS law applies.	Member must adhere to the law of MS country.	Because applicable law is stricter than the Code and Standards, member must adhere to the more strict applicable law.

Exhibit 1	Continued

Applicable Law	Duties	Explanation
Member resides in MS country, does business in LS country; MS law applies, but it states that law of locality where business is conducted governs.	Member must adhere to the Code and Standards.	Because applicable law states that the law of the locality where the business is conducted governs and local law is less strict than the Code and Standards, member must adhere to the Code and Standards.
Member resides in MS country, does business in LS country with a client who is a citizen of LS country; MS law applies, but it states that the law of the client's home country governs.	Member must adhere to the Code and Standards.	Because applicable law states that the law of the client's home country governs (which is less strict than the Code and Standards), member must adhere to the Code and Standards.
Member resides in MS country, does business in LS country with a client who is a citizen of MS country; MS law applies, but it states that the law of the client's home country governs.	Member must adhere to the law of MS country.	Because applicable law states that the law of the client's home country governs and the law of the client's home country is stricter than the Code and Standards, the member must adhere to the more strict applicable law.

Recommended Procedures for Compliance

Members and Candidates

Suggested methods by which members and candidates can acquire and maintain understanding of applicable laws, rules, and regulations include the following:

- *Stay informed*: Members and candidates should establish or encourage their employers to establish a procedure by which employees are regularly informed about changes in applicable laws, rules, regulations, and case law. In many instances, the employer's compliance department or legal counsel can provide such information in the form of memorandums distributed to employees in the organization. Also, participation in an internal or external continuing education program is a practical method of staying current.

- *Review procedures*: Members and candidates should review, or encourage their employers to review, the firm's written compliance procedures on a regular basis to ensure that the procedures reflect current law and provide adequate guidance to employees about what is permissible conduct under the law and/or the Code and Standards. Recommended compliance procedures for specific items of the Code and Standards are discussed in this *Handbook* in the "Guidance" sections associated with each standard.

   ■ *Maintain current files*: Members and candidates should maintain or encourage
   their employers to maintain readily accessible current reference copies of
   applicable statutes, rules, regulations, and important cases.

Distribution Area Laws

Members and candidates should make reasonable efforts to understand the applicable
laws—both country and regional—for the countries and regions where their investment products are developed and are most likely to be distributed to clients.

Legal Counsel

When in doubt about the appropriate action to undertake, it is recommended that
a member or candidate seek the advice of compliance personnel or legal counsel
concerning legal requirements. If a potential violation is being committed by a fellow
employee, it may also be prudent for the member or candidate to seek the advice of
the firm's compliance department or legal counsel.

Dissociation

When dissociating from an activity that violates the Code and Standards, members
and candidates should document the violation and urge their firms to attempt to
persuade the perpetrator(s) to cease such conduct. To dissociate from the conduct, a
member or candidate may have to resign his or her employment.

Firms

The formality and complexity of compliance procedures for firms depend on the nature
and size of the organization and the nature of its investment operations. Members
and candidates should encourage their firms to consider the following policies and
procedures to support the principles of Standard I(A):

   ■ *Develop and/or adopt a code of ethics*: The ethical culture of an organization
   starts at the top. Members and candidates should encourage their supervisors
   or managers to adopt a code of ethics. Adhering to a code of ethics facilitates
   solutions when people face ethical dilemmas and can prevent the need
   for employees to resort to a "whistleblowing" solution publicly alleging
   concealed misconduct. CFA Institute has published the *Asset Manager Code of
   Professional Conduct*, which firms may adopt or use as the basis for their codes
   (visit www.cfapubs.org/loi/ccb).

   ■ *Provide information on applicable laws*: Pertinent information that highlights
   applicable laws and regulations might be distributed to employees or made
   available in a central location. Information sources might include primary
   information developed by the relevant government, governmental agencies,
   regulatory organizations, licensing agencies, and professional associations (e.g.,
   from their websites); law firm memorandums or newsletters; and association
   memorandums or publications (e.g., *CFA Magazine*).

   ■ *Establish procedures for reporting violations*: Firms might provide written
   protocols for reporting suspected violations of laws, regulations, or company
   policies.

Application of the Standard

Example 1   (Notification of Known Violations): Michael Allen works for a brokerage firm and is responsible for an underwriting of securities. A company official gives
Allen information indicating that the financial statements Allen filed with the regulator

overstate the issuer's earnings. Allen seeks the advice of the brokerage firm's general counsel, who states that it would be difficult for the regulator to prove that Allen has been involved in any wrongdoing.

> *Comment*: Although it is recommended that members and candidates seek the advice of legal counsel, the reliance on such advice does not absolve a member or candidate from the requirement to comply with the law or regulation. Allen should report this situation to his supervisor, seek an independent legal opinion, and determine whether the regulator should be notified of the error.

Example 2 (Dissociating from a Violation): Lawrence Brown's employer, an investment banking firm, is the principal underwriter for an issue of convertible debentures by the Courtney Company. Brown discovers that the Courtney Company has concealed severe third-quarter losses in its foreign operations. The preliminary prospectus has already been distributed.

> *Comment*: Knowing that the preliminary prospectus is misleading, Brown should report his findings to the appropriate supervisory persons in his firm. If the matter is not remedied and Brown's employer does not dissociate from the underwriting, Brown should sever all his connections with the underwriting. Brown should also seek legal advice to determine whether additional reporting or other action should be taken.

Example 3 (Dissociating from a Violation): Kamisha Washington's firm advertises its past performance record by showing the 10-year return of a composite of its client accounts. Washington discovers, however, that the composite omits the performance of accounts that have left the firm during the 10-year period, whereas the description of the composite indicates the inclusion of all firm accounts. This omission has led to an inflated performance figure. Washington is asked to use promotional material that includes the erroneous performance number when soliciting business for the firm.

> *Comment*: Misrepresenting performance is a violation of the Code and Standards. Although she did not calculate the performance herself, Washington would be assisting in violating Standard I(A) if she were to use the inflated performance number when soliciting clients. She must dissociate herself from the activity. If discussing the misleading number with the person responsible is not an option for correcting the problem, she can bring the situation to the attention of her supervisor or the compliance department at her firm. If her firm is unwilling to recalculate performance, she must refrain from using the misleading promotional material and should notify the firm of her reasons. If the firm insists that she use the material, she should consider whether her obligation to dissociate from the activity requires her to seek other employment.

Example 4 (Following the Highest Requirements): James Collins is an investment analyst for a major Wall Street brokerage firm. He works in a developing country with a rapidly modernizing economy and a growing capital market. Local securities laws are minimal—in form and content—and include no punitive prohibitions against insider trading.

> *Comment*: Collins must abide by the requirements of the Codes and Standards that might be more strict than the rules of the developing country. He should be aware of the risks that a small market and the absence of a fairly regulated flow of information to the market represent to his ability to obtain information and make timely judgments. He should include this

factor in formulating his advice to clients. In handling material nonpublic information that accidentally comes into his possession, he must follow Standard II(A)–Material Nonpublic Information.

Example 5   (Following the Highest Requirements): Laura Jameson works for a multinational investment adviser based in the United States. Jameson lives and works as a registered investment adviser in the tiny, but wealthy, island nation of Karramba. Karramba's securities laws state that no investment adviser registered and working in that country can participate in initial public offerings (IPOs) for the adviser's personal account. Jameson, believing that as a U.S. citizen working for a U.S.-based company she should comply only with U.S. law, has ignored this Karrambian law. In addition, Jameson believes that, as a charterholder, as long as she adheres to the Code and Standards requirement that she disclose her participation in any IPO to her employer and clients when such ownership creates a conflict of interest, she is meeting the highest ethical requirements.

> *Comment*: Jameson is in violation of Standard I(A). As a registered investment adviser in Karramba, Jameson is prevented by Karrambian securities law from participating in IPOs regardless of the law of her home country. In addition, because the law of the country where she is working is stricter than the Code and Standards, she must follow the stricter requirements of the local law rather than the requirements of the Code and Standards.

Example 6   (Laws and Regulations Based on Religious Tenets): Amanda Janney is employed as a fixed-income portfolio manager for a large international firm. She is on a team within her firm that is responsible for creating and managing a fixed-income hedge fund to be sold throughout the firm's distribution centers to high-net-worth clients. Her firm receives expressions of interest from potential clients from the Middle East who are seeking investments that comply with Islamic law. The marketing and promotional materials for the fixed-income hedge fund do not specify whether or not the fund is a suitable investment for an investor seeking compliance with Islamic law. Because the fund is being distributed globally, Janney is concerned about the reputation of the fund and the firm and believes disclosure of whether or not the fund complies with Islamic law could help minimize potential mistakes with placing this investment.

> *Comment:* As the financial market continues to become globalized, members and candidates will need to be aware of the differences between cultural and religious laws and requirements as well as the different governmental laws and regulations. Janney and the firm could be proactive in their efforts to acknowledge areas where the new fund may not be suitable for clients.

Example 7   (Reporting Potential Unethical Actions): Krista Blume is a junior portfolio manager for high-net-worth portfolios at a large global investment manager. She observes a number of new portfolios and relationships coming from a country in Europe where the firm did not have previous business and is told that a broker in that country is responsible for this new business. At a meeting on allocation of research resources to third-party research firms, Blume notes that this broker has been added to the list and is allocated payments for research. However, she knows the portfolios do not invest in securities in the broker's country. And she has not seen any research come from this broker. Blume asks her supervisor about the name being on the list and is told that someone in marketing is receiving the research and that the name being on the list is OK. She believes that what is going on may be that the broker is being paid for new business through the inappropriate research payments and wishes to dissociate from the misconduct.

Comment: Blume should follow the firm's policies and procedures for reporting potential unethical activity, which may include discussions with her supervisor or someone in a designated compliance department. She should communicate her concerns appropriately while advocating for disclosure between the new broker relationship and the research payments.

B. Independence and Objectivity

Members and Candidates must use reasonable care and judgment to achieve and maintain independence and objectivity in their professional activities. Members and Candidates must not offer, solicit, or accept any gift, benefit, compensation, or consideration that reasonably could be expected to compromise their own or another's independence and objectivity.

Guidance

Highlights:

- *Buy-Side Clients*
- *Fund Manager Relationships*
- *Investment Banking Relationships*
- *Public Companies*
- *Credit Rating Agency Opinions*
- *Issuer-Paid Research*
- *Travel Funding*

Standard I(B) states the responsibility of CFA Institute members and candidates in the CFA Program to maintain independence and objectivity so that their clients will have the benefit of their work and opinions unaffected by any potential conflict of interest or other circumstance adversely affecting their judgment. Every member and candidate should endeavor to avoid situations that could cause or be perceived to cause a loss of independence or objectivity in recommending investments or taking investment action.

External sources may try to influence the investment process by offering analysts and portfolio managers a variety of benefits. Corporations may seek expanded research coverage; issuers and underwriters may wish to promote new securities offerings; brokers may want to increase commission business; and independent rating agencies may be influenced by the company requesting the rating. Benefits may include gifts, invitations to lavish functions, tickets, favors, or job referrals. One type of benefit is the allocation of shares in oversubscribed IPOs to investment managers for their personal accounts. This practice affords managers the opportunity to make quick profits that may not be available to their clients. Such a practice is prohibited under Standard I(B). Modest gifts and entertainment are acceptable, but special care must be taken by members and candidates to resist subtle and not-so-subtle pressures to act in conflict with the interests of their clients. Best practice dictates that members and candidates reject any offer of gift or entertainment that could be expected to threaten their independence and objectivity.

Receiving a gift, benefit, or consideration from a *client* can be distinguished from gifts given by entities seeking to influence a member or candidate to the detriment of other clients. In a client relationship, the client has already entered some type of compensation arrangement with the member, candidate, or his or her firm. A gift from a client could be considered supplementary compensation. The potential for obtaining influence to the detriment of other clients, although present, is not as great as in situations where no compensation arrangement exists. When possible, prior to accepting "bonuses" or gifts from clients, members and candidates should disclose to their employers such benefits offered by clients. If notification is not possible prior to acceptance, members and candidates must disclose to their employers benefits previously accepted from clients. Disclosure allows the employer of a member or candidate to make an independent determination about the extent to which the gift may affect the member's or candidate's independence and objectivity.

Members and candidates may also come under pressure from their own firms to, for example, issue favorable research reports or recommendations for certain companies with potential or continuing business relationships with the firm. The situation may be aggravated if an executive of the company sits on the bank or investment firm's board and attempts to interfere in investment decision making. Members and candidates acting in a sales or marketing capacity must be especially mindful of their objectivity in promoting appropriate investments for their clients.

Left unmanaged, pressures that threaten independence place research analysts in a difficult position and may jeopardize their ability to act independently and objectively. One of the ways that research analysts have coped with these pressures in the past is to use subtle and ambiguous language in their recommendations or to temper the tone of their research reports. Such subtleties are lost on some investors, however, who reasonably expect research reports and recommendations to be straightforward and transparent, and to communicate clearly an analyst's views based on unbiased analysis and independent judgment.

Members and candidates are personally responsible for maintaining independence and objectivity when preparing research reports, making investment recommendations, and taking investment action on behalf of clients. Recommendations must convey the member's or candidate's true opinions, free of bias from internal or external pressures, and be stated in clear and unambiguous language.

Members and candidates also should be aware that some of their professional or social activities within CFA Institute or its member societies may subtly threaten their independence or objectivity. When seeking corporate financial support for conventions, seminars, or even weekly society luncheons, the members or candidates responsible for the activities should evaluate both the actual effect of such solicitations on their independence and whether their objectivity might be perceived to be compromised in the eyes of their clients.

Buy-Side Clients

One source of pressure on sell-side analysts is buy-side clients. Institutional clients are traditionally the primary users of sell-side research, either directly or with soft dollar brokerage. Portfolio managers may have significant positions in the security of a company under review. A rating downgrade may adversely affect the portfolio's performance, particularly in the short term, because the sensitivity of stock prices to ratings changes has increased in recent years. A downgrade may also affect the manager's compensation, which is usually tied to portfolio performance. Moreover, portfolio performance is subject to media and public scrutiny, which may affect the manager's professional reputation. Consequently, some portfolio managers implicitly or explicitly support sell-side ratings inflation.

Portfolio managers have a responsibility to respect and foster the intellectual honesty of sell-side research. Therefore, it is improper for portfolio managers to threaten or engage in retaliatory practices, such as reporting sell-side analysts to the covered company in order to instigate negative corporate reactions. Although most portfolio managers do not engage in such practices, the perception by the research analyst that a reprisal is possible may cause concern and make it difficult for the analyst to maintain independence and objectivity.

Fund Manager Relationships

Research analysts are not the only people who must be concerned with maintaining their independence. Members and candidates who are responsible for hiring and retaining outside managers should not accepts gifts, entertainment, or travel funding that may be perceived as impairing their decisions. The use of secondary fund managers has evolved into a common practice to manage specific asset allocations. Both the primary and secondary fund managers often arrange educational and marketing events to inform others about their business strategies or investment process. Members and candidates must review the merits of each offer individually in determining whether they may attend yet maintain their independence.

Investment Banking Relationships

Some sell-side firms may exert pressure on their analysts to issue favorable research reports on current or prospective investment banking clients. For many of these firms, income from investment banking has become increasingly important to overall firm profitability because brokerage income has declined as a result of price competition. Consequently, firms offering investment banking services work hard to develop and maintain relationships with investment banking clients and prospects. These companies are often covered by the firm's research analysts because companies often select their investment banks on the basis of the reputation of their research analysts, the quality of their work, and their standing in the industry.

In some countries, research analysts frequently work closely with their investment banking colleagues to help evaluate prospective investment banking clients. In other countries, because of past abuses in managing the obvious conflicts of interest, regulators have established clear rules prohibiting the interaction of these groups. Although collaboration between research analysts and investment banking colleagues may benefit the firm and enhance market efficiency (e.g., by allowing firms to assess risks more accurately and make better pricing assumptions), it requires firms to carefully balance the conflicts of interest inherent in the collaboration. Having analysts work with investment bankers is appropriate only when the conflicts are adequately and effectively managed and disclosed. Firm managers have a responsibility to provide an environment in which analysts are neither coerced nor enticed into issuing research that does not reflect their true opinions. Firms should require public disclosure of actual conflicts of interest to investors.

Members, candidates, and their firms must adopt and follow perceived best practices in maintaining independence and objectivity in the corporate culture and protecting analysts from undue pressure by their investment banking colleagues. The "firewalls" traditionally built between these two functions must be managed to minimize conflicts of interest; indeed, enhanced firewall policies may go as far as prohibiting all communications between these groups. A key element of an enhanced firewall is separate reporting structures for personnel on the research side and personnel on the investment banking side. For example, investment banking personnel should not have any authority to approve, disapprove, or make changes to research reports or recommendations. Another element should be a compensation arrangement that minimizes the pressures on research analysts and rewards objectivity and accuracy. Compensation arrangements should not link analyst remuneration directly to investment banking assignments in which the analyst may participate as a team member. Firms should also regularly review their policies and procedures to determine whether analysts are adequately safeguarded and to improve the transparency of disclosures relating to conflicts of interest. The highest level of transparency is achieved when disclosures are prominent and specific rather than marginalized and generic.

Public Companies

Analysts may be pressured to issue favorable reports and recommendations by the companies they follow. Not every stock is a "buy," and not every research report is favorable—for many reasons, including the cyclical nature of many business activities and market fluctuations. For instance, a "good company" does not always translate into a "good stock" rating if the current stock price is fully valued. In making an investment recommendation, the analyst is responsible for anticipating, interpreting, and assessing a company's prospects and stock price performance in a factual manner. Many company managers, however, believe that their company's stock is undervalued, and these managers may find it difficult to accept critical research reports or ratings downgrades. Company managers' compensation may also be dependent on stock performance.

Due diligence in financial research and analysis involves gathering information from a wide variety of sources, including public disclosure documents (such as proxy statements, annual reports, and other regulatory filings) and also company management and investor-relations personnel, suppliers, customers, competitors, and other relevant sources. Research analysts may justifiably fear that companies will limit their ability to conduct thorough research by denying analysts who have "negative" views direct access to company managers and/or barring them from conference calls and other communication venues. Retaliatory practices include companies bringing legal action against analysts personally and/or their firms to seek monetary damages for the economic effects of negative reports and recommendations. Although few companies engage in such behavior, the perception that a reprisal is possible is a reasonable concern for analysts. This concern may make it difficult for them to conduct the comprehensive research needed to make objective recommendations. For further information and guidance, members and candidates should refer to the CFA Institute publication *Best Practice Guidelines Governing Analyst/Corporate Issuer Relations* (www.cfainstitute.org).

Credit Rating Agency Opinions

Credit rating agencies provide a service by grading the fixed-income products offered by companies. Analysts face challenges related to incentives and compensation schemes that may be tied to the final rating and successful placement of the product. Members and candidates employed at rating agencies should ensure that procedures and processes at the agencies prevent undue influences from a sponsoring company during the analysis. Members and candidates should abide by their agencies' and the industry's standards of conduct regarding the analytical process and the distribution of their reports.

The work of credit rating agencies also raises concerns similar to those inherent in investment banking relationships. Analysts may face pressure to issue ratings at a specific level because of other services the agency offers companies, namely, advising on the development of structured products. The rating agencies need to develop the necessary firewalls and protections to allow the independent operations of their different business lines.

When using information provided by credit rating agencies, members and candidates should be mindful of the potential conflicts of interest. And because of the potential conflicts, members and candidates may need to independently validate the rating granted.

Issuer-Paid Research

In light of the recent reduction of sell-side research coverage, many companies, seeking to increase visibility both in the financial markets and with potential investors, have hired analysts to produce research reports analyzing their companies. These reports bridge the gap created by the lack of coverage and can be an effective method of communicating with investors.

Issuer-paid research conducted by independent analysts, however, is fraught with potential conflicts. Depending on how the research is written and distributed, investors may be misled into believing that the research is from an independent source when, in reality, it has been paid for by the subject company.

Members and candidates must adhere to strict standards of conduct that govern how the research is to be conducted and what disclosures must be made in the report. Analysts must engage in thorough, independent, and unbiased analysis and must fully disclose potential conflicts of interest, including the nature of their compensation. Otherwise, analysts risk misleading investors.

Investors need clear, credible, and thorough information about companies, and they need research based on independent thought. At a minimum, issuer-paid research should include a thorough analysis of the company's financial statements based on publicly disclosed information, benchmarking within a peer group, and industry analysis. Analysts must exercise diligence, independence, and thoroughness in conducting their research in an objective manner. Analysts must distinguish between fact and opinion in their reports. Conclusions must have a reasonable and adequate basis and must be supported by appropriate research.

Independent analysts must also strictly limit the type of compensation that they accept for conducting issuer-paid research. Otherwise, the content and conclusions of the reports could reasonably be expected to be determined or affected by compensation from the sponsoring companies. Compensation that might influence the research report could be direct, such as payment based on the conclusions of the report, or indirect, such as stock warrants or other equity instruments that could increase in value on the basis of positive coverage in the report. In such instances, the independent analyst has an incentive to avoid including negative information or making negative conclusions. Best practice is for independent analysts, prior to writing their report, to negotiate only a flat fee for their work that is not linked to their conclusions or recommendations.

Travel Funding

The benefits related to accepting paid travel extend beyond the cost savings to the member or candidate, such as the chance to talk exclusively with the executives of a company. The problem is that members and candidates may be influenced by these discussions when flying on a corporate or chartered jet. Best practice dictates that members and candidates always use commercial transportation rather than accept paid travel arrangements from an outside company. Should commercial transportation be unavailable, members and candidates may accept modestly arranged travel to participate in appropriate information-gathering events, such as a property tour.

Recommended Procedures for Compliance

Members and candidates should adhere to the following practices and should encourage their firms to establish procedures to avoid violations of Standard I(B):

■ *Protect the integrity of opinions*: Members, candidates, and their firms should establish policies stating that every research report concerning the securities of a corporate client should reflect the unbiased opinion of the analyst. Firms should also design compensation systems that protect the integrity of the investment decision process by maintaining the independence and objectivity of analysts.

■ *Create a restricted list*: If the firm is unwilling to permit dissemination of adverse opinions about a corporate client, members and candidates should encourage the firm to remove the controversial company from the research universe and put it on a restricted list so that the firm disseminates only factual information about the company.

■ *Restrict special cost arrangements*: When attending meetings at an issuer's headquarters, members and candidates should pay for commercial transportation and hotel charges. No corporate issuer should reimburse members or candidates for air transportation. Members and candidates should encourage issuers to limit the use of corporate aircraft to situations in which commercial transportation is not available or in which efficient movement could not otherwise be arranged. Members and candidates should take particular care that when frequent meetings are held between an individual issuer and an individual member or candidate, the issuer should not always host the member or candidate.

■ *Limit gifts*: Members and candidates must limit the acceptance of gratuities and/or gifts to token items. Standard I(B) does not preclude customary, ordinary business-related entertainment as long as its purpose is not to influence or reward members or candidates. Firms should consider a strict value limit for acceptable gifts that is based on the local or regional customs and should address whether the limit is per gift or an aggregate annual value.

■ *Restrict investments*: Members and candidates should encourage their investment firms to develop formal polices related to employee purchases of equity or equity-related IPOs. Firms should require prior approval for employee participation in IPOs, with prompt disclosure of investment actions taken following the offering. Strict limits should be imposed on investment personnel acquiring securities in private placements.

■ *Review procedures*: Members and candidates should encourage their firms to implement effective supervisory and review procedures to ensure that analysts and portfolio managers comply with policies relating to their personal investment activities.

■ *Independence policy*: Members, candidates, and their firms should establish a formal written policy on the independence and objectivity of research and implement reporting structures and review procedures to ensure that research analysts do not report to and are not supervised or controlled by any department of the firm that could compromise the independence of the analyst. More detailed recommendations related to a firm's policies regarding research objectivity are set forth in the CFA Institute statement *Research Objectivity Standards* (www.cfainstitute.org).

■ *Appointed officer*: Firms should appoint a senior officer with oversight responsibilities for compliance with the firm's code of ethics and all regulations concerning its business. Firms should provide every employee with the procedures and policies for reporting potentially unethical behavior, violations of regulations, or other activities that may harm the firm's reputation.

Application of the Standard

Example 1   (Travel Expenses): Steven Taylor, a mining analyst with Bronson Brokers, is invited by Precision Metals to join a group of his peers in a tour of mining facilities in several western U.S. states. The company arranges for chartered group flights from

accommodations in Spartan Motels, the only chain with accom-
mine mines, for three nights. Taylor allows Precision Metals to pick
to the other analysts, with one exception—John Adams, an employee
trust company who insists on following his company's policy and paying
hotel room himself.

> *Comment*: The policy of the company where Adams works complies closely
> with Standard I(B) by avoiding even the appearance of a conflict of interest,
> but Taylor and the other analysts were not necessarily violating Standard
> I(B). In general, when allowing companies to pay for travel and/or accom-
> modations in these circumstances, members and candidates must use their
> judgment. They must be on guard that such arrangements not impinge on
> a member's or candidate's independence and objectivity. In this example,
> the trip was strictly for business and Taylor was not accepting irrelevant or
> lavish hospitality. The itinerary required chartered flights, for which ana-
> lysts were not expected to pay. The accommodations were modest. These
> arrangements are not unusual and did not violate Standard I(B) as long as
> Taylor's independence and objectivity were not compromised. In the final
> analysis, members and candidates should consider both whether they can
> remain objective and whether their integrity might be perceived by their
> clients to have been compromised.

Example 2 (Research Independence): Susan Dillon, an analyst in the corporate finance
department of an investment services firm, is making a presentation to a potential
new business client that includes the promise that her firm will provide full research
coverage of the potential client.

> *Comment*: Dillon may agree to provide research coverage, but she must
> not commit her firm's research department to providing a favorable recom-
> mendation. The firm's recommendation (favorable, neutral, or unfavorable)
> must be based on an independent and objective investigation and analysis
> of the company and its securities.

Example 3 (Research Independence and Intrafirm Pressure): Walter Fritz is
an equity analyst with Hilton Brokerage who covers the mining industry. He has
concluded that the stock of Metals & Mining is overpriced at its current level,
but he is concerned that a negative research report will hurt the good relationship between Metals & Mining and the investment banking division of his firm.
In fact, a senior manager of Hilton Brokerage has just sent him a copy of a proposal his firm has made to Metals & Mining to underwrite a debt offering. Fritz
needs to produce a report right away and is concerned about issuing a less-than-
favorable rating.

> *Comment*: Fritz's analysis of Metals & Mining must be objective and based
> solely on consideration of company fundamentals. Any pressure from
> other divisions of his firm is inappropriate. This conflict could have been
> eliminated if, in anticipation of the offering, Hilton Brokerage had placed
> Metals & Mining on a restricted list for its sales force.

Example 4 (Research Independence and Issuer Relationship Pressure): As in
Example 3, Walter Fritz has concluded that Metals & Mining stock is overvalued at
its current level, but he is concerned that a negative research report might jeopardize
a close rapport that he has nurtured over the years with Metals & Mining's CEO,
chief finance officer, and investment relations officer. Fritz is concerned that a negative report might result also in management retaliation—for instance, cutting him
off from participating in conference calls when a quarterly earnings release is made,

denying him the ability to ask questions on such calls, and/or denying him access to top management for arranging group meetings between Hilton Brokerage clients with top Metals & Mining managers.

> *Comment:* As in Example 3, Fritz's analysis must be objective and based solely on consideration of company fundamentals. Any pressure from Metals & Mining is inappropriate. Fritz should reinforce the integrity of his conclusions by stressing that his investment recommendation is based on relative valuation, which may include qualitative issues with respect to Metals & Mining's management.

Example 5   (Research Independence and Sales Pressure): As support for the sales effort of her corporate bond department, Lindsey Warner offers credit guidance to purchasers of fixed-income securities. Her compensation is closely linked to the performance of the corporate bond department. Near the quarter's end, Warner's firm has a large inventory position in the bonds of Milton, Ltd., and has been unable to sell the bonds because of Milton's recent announcement of an operating problem. Salespeople have asked her to contact large clients to push the bonds.

> *Comment:* Unethical sales practices create significant potential violations of the Code and Standards. Warner's opinion of the Milton bonds must not be affected by internal pressure or compensation. In this case, Warner must refuse to push the Milton bonds unless she is able to justify that the market price has already adjusted for the operating problem.

Example 6   (Research Independence and Prior Coverage): Jill Jorund is a securities analyst following airline stocks and a rising star at her firm. Her boss has been carrying a "buy" recommendation on International Airlines and asks Jorund to take over coverage of that airline. He tells Jorund that under no circumstances should the prevailing buy recommendation be changed.

> *Comment:* Jorund must be independent and objective in her analysis of International Airlines. If she believes that her boss's instructions have compromised her, she has two options: Tell her boss that she cannot cover the company under these constraints or take over coverage of the company, reach her own independent conclusions, and if they conflict with her boss's opinion, share the conclusions with her boss or other supervisors in the firm so that they can make appropriate recommendations. Jorund must issue only recommendations that reflect her independent and objective opinion.

Example 7   (Gifts and Entertainment from Related Party): Edward Grant directs a large amount of his commission business to a New York-based brokerage house. In appreciation for all the business, the brokerage house gives Grant two tickets to the World Cup in South Africa, two nights at a nearby resort, several meals, and transportation via limousine to the game. Grant fails to disclose receiving this package to his supervisor.

> *Comment:* Grant has violated Standard I(B) because accepting these substantial gifts may impede his independence and objectivity. Every member and candidate should endeavor to avoid situations that might cause or be perceived to cause a loss of independence or objectivity in recommending investments or taking investment action. By accepting the trip, Grant has opened himself up to the accusation that he may give the broker favored treatment in return.

Example 8   (Gifts and Entertainment from Client): Theresa Green manages the portfolio of Ian Knowlden, a client of Tisbury Investments. Green achieves an annual return for Knowlden that is consistently better than that of the benchmark she and the client previously agreed to. As a reward, Knowlden offers Green two tickets to Wimbledon and the use of Knowlden's flat in London for a week. Green discloses this gift to her supervisor at Tisbury.

> *Comment*: Green is in compliance with Standard I(B) because she disclosed the gift from one of her clients in accordance with the firm's policies. Members and candidates may accept bonuses or gifts from clients as long as they disclose them to their employers, because gifts in a client relationship are deemed less likely to affect a member's or candidate's objectivity and independence than gifts in other situations. Disclosure is required, however, so that supervisors can monitor such situations to guard against employees favoring a gift-giving client to the detriment of other fee-paying clients (such as by allocating a greater proportion of IPO stock to the gift-giving client's portfolio).
>
> Best practices for monitoring include comparing the transaction costs of the Knowlden account with the costs of other accounts managed by Green and other similar accounts within Tisbury. The supervisor could also compare the performance returns with the returns of other clients with the same mandate. This comparison will assist in determining whether a pattern of favoritism by Green is disadvantaging other Tisbury clients or the possibility that this favoritism could affect her future behavior.

Example 9 (Travel Expenses from External Manager): Tom Wayne is the investment manager of the Franklin City Employees Pension Plan. He recently completed a successful search for a firm to manage the foreign equity allocation of the plan's diversified portfolio. He followed the plan's standard procedure of seeking presentations from a number of qualified firms and recommended that his board select Penguin Advisors because of its experience, well-defined investment strategy, and performance record. The firm claims compliance with the Global Investment Performance Standards (GIPS) and has been verified. Following the selection of Penguin, a reporter from the *Franklin City Record* calls to ask if there was any connection between this action and the fact that Penguin was one of the sponsors of an "investment fact-finding trip to Asia" that Wayne made earlier in the year. The trip was one of several conducted by the Pension Investment Academy, which had arranged the itinerary of meetings with economic, government, and corporate officials in major cities in several Asian countries. The Pension Investment Academy obtains support for the cost of these trips from a number of investment managers, including Penguin Advisors; the Academy then pays the travel expenses of the various pension plan managers on the trip and provides all meals and accommodations. The president of Penguin Advisors was also one of the travelers on the trip.

> *Comment*: Although Wayne can probably put to good use the knowledge he gained from the trip in selecting portfolio managers and in other areas of managing the pension plan, his recommendation of Penguin Advisors may be tainted by the possible conflict incurred when he participated in a trip partly paid for by Penguin Advisors and when he was in the daily company of the president of Penguin Advisors. To avoid violating Standard I(B), Wayne's basic expenses for travel and accommodations should have been paid by his employer or the pension plan; contact with the president of Penguin Advisors should have been limited to informational or educational events only; and the trip, the organizer, and the sponsor should have been made a matter of public record. Even if his actions were not in violation of Standard I(B), Wayne should have been sensitive to the public perception of the trip when reported in the newspaper and the extent to which the

subjective elements of his decision might have been affected by the familiarity that the daily contact of such a trip would encourage. This advantage would probably not be shared by firms competing with Penguin Advisors.

Example 10 (Research Independence and Compensation Arrangements): Javier Herrero recently left his job as a research analyst for a large investment adviser. While looking for a new position, he was hired by an investor-relations firm to write a research report on one of its clients, a small educational software company. The investor-relations firm hopes to generate investor interest in the technology company. The firm will pay Herrero a flat fee plus a bonus if any new investors buy stock in the company as a result of Herrero's report.

> *Comment*: If Herrero accepts this payment arrangement, he will be in violation of Standard I(B) because the compensation arrangement can reasonably be expected to compromise his independence and objectivity. Herrero will receive a bonus for attracting investors, which provides an incentive to draft a positive report regardless of the facts and to ignore or play down any negative information about the company. Herrero should accept only a flat fee that is not tied to the conclusions or recommendations of the report. Issuer-paid research that is objective and unbiased can be done under the right circumstances as long as the analyst takes steps to maintain his or her objectivity and includes in the report proper disclosures regarding potential conflicts of interest.

Example 11 (Recommendation Objectivity and Service Fees): Two years ago, Bob Wade, trust manager for Central Midas Bank, was approached by Western Funds about promoting its family of funds, with special interest in the service-fee class of funds. To entice Central to promote this class, Western Funds offered to pay the bank a service fee of 0.25 percent. Without disclosing the fee being offered to the bank, Wade asked one of the investment managers to review Western's funds to determine whether they were suitable for clients of Central Midas Bank. The manager completed the normal due diligence review and determined that the new funds were fairly valued in the market with fee structures on a par with competitors. Wade decided to accept Western's offer and instructed the team of portfolio managers to exclusively promote these funds and the service-fee class to clients seeking to invest new funds or transfer from their current investments.

Now, two years later, the funds managed by Western begin to underperform their peers. Wade is counting on the fees to reach his profitability targets and continues to push these funds as acceptable investments for Central's clients.

> *Comment*: Wade is violating Standard I(B) because the fee arrangement has affected the objectivity of his recommendations. Wade is relying on the fee as a component of the department's profitability and is unwilling to offer other products that may affect the fees received.
>
> See also Standard VI(A)–Disclosure of Conflicts.

Example 12 (Recommendation Objectivity): Bob Thompson has been doing research for the portfolio manager of the fixed-income department. His assignment is to do sensitivity analysis on securitized subprime mortgages. He has discussed with the manager possible scenarios to use to calculate expected returns. A key assumption in such calculations is housing price appreciation (HPA) because it drives "prepays" (prepayments of mortgages) and losses. Thompson is concerned with the significant appreciation experienced over the previous five years as a result of the increased availability of funds from subprime mortgages. Thompson insists that the analysis should include a scenario run with negative 10 percent for the first year, negative 5 percent for the second year, and then (to project a worst-case scenario) 0 percent for Years 3 through 5. The manager replies that these assumptions are too dire because there has never been a time in their available database when HPA was negative.

Thompson conducts his research to better understand the risks inherent in these securities and evaluates these securities in the worst-case scenario, an unlikely but possible environment. Based on the results of the enhanced scenarios, Thompson does not recommend the purchase of the securitization. Against the general market trends, the manager follows Thompson's recommendation and does not invest. The following year, the housing market collapses. In avoiding the subprime investments, the manager's portfolio outperforms its peer group that year.

> *Comment*: Thompson's actions in running the worst-case scenario against the protests of the portfolio manager are in alignment with the principles of Standard I(B). Thompson did not allow his research to be pressured by the general trends of the market or the manager's desire to limit the research to historical norms.
> See also Standard V(A)—Diligence and Reasonable Basis.

C. Misrepresentation

Members and Candidates must not knowingly make any misrepresentations relating to investment analysis, recommendations, actions, or other professional activities.

Guidance

Highlights:

- *Impact on Investment Practice*
- *Plagiarism*
- *Work Completed for Employer*

Trust is the foundation of the investment profession. Investors must be able to rely on the statements and information provided to them by those with whom the investors have trusted their financial well-being. Investment professionals who make false or misleading statements not only harm investors but also reduce the level of investor confidence in the investment profession and threaten the integrity of capital markets as a whole.

A misrepresentation is any untrue statement or omission of a fact or any statement that is otherwise false or misleading. A member or candidate must not knowingly omit or misrepresent information or give a false impression of a firm, organization, or security in the member's or candidate's oral representations, advertising (whether in the press or through brochures), electronic communications, or written materials (whether publicly disseminated or not). In this context, "knowingly" means that the member or candidate either knows or should have known that the misrepresentation was being made or that omitted information could alter the investment decision-making process.

Written materials include, but are not limited to, research reports, underwriting documents, company financial reports, market letters, newspaper columns, and books. Electronic communications include, but are not limited to, internet communications, webpages, chat rooms, and e-mails. Members and candidates who use webpages should regularly monitor materials posted on the site to ensure that the site contains current information. Members and candidates should also ensure that all reasonable precautions have been taken to protect the site's integrity and security and that the site does not misrepresent any information and does provide full disclosure.

The omission of a fact or outcome has increased in importance because of the growing use of technical analysis. Many members and candidates rely on models to scan for new investment opportunities, to develop investment vehicles, and to produce investment recommendations and ratings. Although not every model can test for every factor or outcome, members and candidates should ensure that their analyses incorporate a broad range of assumptions—from very positive scenarios to extremely negative scenarios. The omission from the analysis of potentially negative outcomes or of levels of risk outside the norm may misrepresent the true economic value of the investment.

Impact on Investment Practice

Members and candidates must not misrepresent any aspect of their practice, including (but not limited to) their qualifications or credentials, the qualifications or services provided by their firm, their performance record and the record of their firm, and the characteristics of an investment. Any misrepresentation made by a member or candidate relating to the member's or candidate's professional activities is a breach of this standard.

Members and candidates should exercise care and diligence when incorporating third-party information. Misrepresentations resulting from the use of the credit ratings, research, testimonials, or marketing materials of these outside parties become the responsibility of the investment professional when it affects that professional's business practices.

Investing through outside managers continues to expand as an acceptable method of investing in areas outside a firm's core competencies. Members and candidates must disclose their intended use of external managers and must not represent those managers' investment practices as their own. Although the level of involvement of outside managers may change over time, appropriate disclosures by members and candidates are important to avoiding misrepresentations, especially if the primary activity is to invest directly with a single external manager. Standard V(B)—Communication with Clients and Prospective Clients discusses in further detail communicating the firm's investment practices.

Standard I(C) prohibits members and candidates from guaranteeing clients any specific return on volatile investments. Most investments contain some element of risk that makes their return inherently unpredictable. For these investments, guaranteeing either a particular rate of return or a guaranteed preservation of investment capital (e.g., "I can guarantee that you will earn 8 percent on equities this year" or "I can guarantee that you will not lose money on this investment") is misleading to investors. Standard I(C) does not prohibit members and candidates from providing clients with information on investment products that have guarantees built into the structure of the product itself or for which an institution has agreed to cover any losses.

Plagiarism

Standard I(C) also prohibits plagiarism in the preparation of material for distribution to employers, associates, clients, prospects, or the general public. Plagiarism is defined as copying or using in substantially the same form materials prepared by others without acknowledging the source of the material or identifying the author and publisher of such material. Members and candidates must not copy (or represent as their own) original ideas or material without permission and must acknowledge and identify the source of ideas or material that is not their own.

The investment profession uses a myriad of financial, economic, and statistical data in the investment decision-making process. Through various publications and presentations, the investment professional is constantly exposed to the work of others and to the temptation to use that work without proper acknowledgment.

Misrepresentation through plagiarism in investment management can take various forms. The simplest and most flagrant example is to take a research report or study done by another firm or person, change the names, and release the material as one's own original analysis. This action is a clear violation of Standard I(C). Other practices include 1) using excerpts from articles or reports prepared by others either verbatim or with only slight changes in wording without acknowledgment, 2) citing specific quotations as attributable to "leading analysts" and "investment experts" without naming the specific references, 3) presenting statistical estimates of forecasts prepared by others and identifying the sources but without including the qualifying statements or caveats that may have been used, 4) using charts and graphs without stating their sources, and 5) copying proprietary computerized spreadsheets or algorithms without seeking the cooperation or authorization of their creators.

In the case of distributing third-party, outsourced research, members and candidates may use and distribute these reports as long as they do not represent themselves as the authors of such a report. Indeed, the member or candidate may add value for the client by sifting through research and repackaging it for clients. In such cases, clients should be fully informed that they are paying for the ability of the member or candidate to find the best research from a wide variety of sources. Members and candidates must not misrepresent their abilities, the extent of their expertise, or the extent of their work in a way that would mislead their clients or prospective clients. Members and candidates should disclose whether the research being presented to clients comes from another source, from either within or outside the member's or candidate's firm. This allows clients to understand who has the expertise behind the report or if the work is being done by the analyst, other members of the firm, or an outside party.

Standard 1(C) also applies to plagiarism in oral communications, such as through group meetings; visits with associates, clients, and customers; use of audio/video media (which is rapidly increasing); and telecommunications, including electronic data transfer and the outright copying of electronic media.

One of the most egregious practices in violation of this standard is the preparation of research reports based on multiple sources of information without acknowledging the sources. Examples of information from such sources include ideas, statistical compilations, and forecasts combined to give the appearance of original work. Although there is no monopoly on ideas, members and candidates must give credit where it is clearly due. Analysts should not use undocumented forecasts, earnings projections, asset values, and so on. Sources must be revealed to bring the responsibility directly back to the author of the report or the firm involved.

Work Completed for Employer

The preceding paragraphs address actions that would constitute a violation of Standard I(C). In some situations, however, members or candidates may use research conducted or models developed by others within the same firm without committing a violation. The most common example relates to the situation in which one (or more) of the original analysts is no longer with the firm. Research and models developed while employed by a firm are the property of the firm. The firm retains the right to continue using the work completed after a member or candidate has left the organization. The firm may issue future reports without providing attribution to the prior analysts. A member or candidate cannot, however, reissue a previously released report solely under his or her name.

Recommended Procedures for Compliance

Factual Presentations

Members and candidates can prevent unintentional misrepresentations of the qualifications or services they or their firms provide if each member and candidate understands the limit of the firm's or individual's capabilities and the need to be accurate and complete in presentations. Firms can provide guidance for employees who make written or oral presentations to clients or potential clients by providing a written list of the firm's available services and a description of the firm's qualifications. This list should suggest ways of describing the firm's services, qualifications, and compensation that are both accurate and suitable for client or customer presentations. Firms can also help prevent misrepresentation by specifically designating which employees are authorized to speak on behalf of the firm. Whether or not the firm provides guidance, members and candidates should make certain that they understand the services the firm can perform and its qualifications.

Qualification Summary

In addition, to ensure accurate presentations to clients, each member and candidate should prepare a summary of his or her own qualifications and experience and a list of the services the member or candidate is capable of performing. Firms can assist member and candidate compliance by periodically reviewing employee correspondence and documents that contain representations of individual or firm qualifications.

Verify Outside Information

When providing information to clients from third parties, members and candidates share a responsibility for the accuracy of the marketing and distribution materials that pertain to the third party's capabilities, services, and products. Misrepresentation by third parties can damage the member's or candidate's reputation, the reputation of the firm, and the integrity of the capital markets. Members and candidates should encourage their employers to develop procedures for verifying information of third-party firms.

Maintain Webpages

Members and candidates who publish webpages should regularly monitor materials posted on the site to ensure that the site contains current information. Members and candidates should also ensure that all reasonable precautions have been taken to protect the site's integrity, confidentiality, and security and that the site does not misrepresent any information and provides full disclosure.

Plagiarism Policy

To avoid plagiarism in preparing research reports or conclusions of analysis, members and candidates should take the following steps:

- *Maintain copies*: Keep copies of all research reports, articles containing research ideas, material with new statistical methodologies, and other materials that were relied on in preparing the research report.

- *Attribute quotations*: Attribute to their sources any direct quotations, including projections, tables, statistics, model/product ideas, and new methodologies prepared by persons other than recognized financial and statistical reporting services or similar sources.

- *Attribute summaries*: Attribute to their sources any paraphrases or summaries of material prepared by others. For example, to support his analysis of Brown Company's competitive position, the author of a research report on Brown might summarize another analyst's report on Brown's chief competitor, but the author of the Brown report must acknowledge in his own report the reliance on the other analyst's report.

Application of the Standard

Example 1   (Representing the Firm's Abilities): Allison Rogers is a partner in the firm of Rogers and Black, a small firm offering investment advisory services. She assures a prospective client who has just inherited US$1 million that "we can perform all the financial and investment services you need." Rogers and Black is well equipped to provide investment advice but, in fact, cannot provide asset allocation assistance or a full array of financial and investment services.

> *Comment*: Rogers has violated Standard I(C) by orally misrepresenting the services her firm can perform for the prospective client. She must limit herself to describing the range of investment advisory services Rogers and Black can provide and offer to help the client obtain elsewhere the financial and investment services that her firm cannot provide.

Example 2   (Disclosure of Issuer-Paid Research): Anthony McGuire is an issuer-paid analyst hired by publicly traded companies to electronically promote their stocks. McGuire creates a website that promotes his research efforts as a seemingly independent analyst. McGuire posts a profile and a strong buy recommendation for each company on the website indicating that the stock is expected to increase in value. He does not disclose the contractual relationships with the companies he covers on his website, in the research reports he issues, or in the statements he makes about the companies in internet chat rooms.

> *Comment*: McGuire has violated Standard I(C) because the internet site is misleading to potential investors. Even if the recommendations are valid and supported with thorough research, his omissions regarding the true relationship between himself and the companies he covers constitute a misrepresentation. McGuire has also violated Standard VI(A)—Disclosure of Conflicts by not disclosing the existence of an arrangement with the companies through which he receives compensation in exchange for his services.

Example 3   (Correction of Unintentional Errors): Hijan Yao is responsible for the creation and distribution of the marketing materials for his firm, which claims compliance with the GIPS standards. Yao creates and distributes a presentation of performance by the firm's Asian equity composite that states the composite has ¥350 billion in assets. In fact, the composite has only ¥35 billion in assets, and the higher figure on the presentation is a result of a typographical error. Nevertheless, the erroneous material is distributed to a number of clients before Yao catches the mistake.

> *Comment*: Once the error is discovered, Yao must take steps to cease distribution of the incorrect material and correct the error by informing those who have received the erroneous information. Because Yao did not knowingly make the misrepresentation, however, he did not violate Standard I(C). Since his firm claims compliance with the GIPS standards, it must also comply with the GIPS Guidance Statement on Error Correction in relation to the error.

Example 4   (Noncorrection of Known Errors): Syed Muhammad is the president of an investment management firm. The promotional material for the firm, created by the firm's marketing department, incorrectly claims that Muhammad has an advanced degree in finance from a prestigious business school in addition to the CFA designation. Although Muhammad attended the school for a short period of time, he did not receive a degree. Over the years, Muhammad and others in the firm have distributed this material to numerous prospective clients and consultants.

> *Comment*: Even though Muhammad may not have been directly responsible for the misrepresentation of his credentials in the firm's promotional material, he used this material numerous times over an extended period and should have known of the misrepresentation. Thus, Muhammad has violated Standard I(C).

Example 5   (Plagiarism): Cindy Grant, a research analyst for a Canadian brokerage firm, has specialized in the Canadian mining industry for the past 10 years. She recently read an extensive research report on Jefferson Mining, Ltd., by Jeremy Barton, another analyst. Barton provided extensive statistics on the mineral reserves, production capacity, selling rates, and marketing factors affecting Jefferson's operations. He also noted that initial drilling results on a new ore body, which had not been made public, might show the existence of mineral zones that could increase the life of Jefferson's main mines, but Barton cited no specific data as to the initial drilling results. Grant called an officer of Jefferson, who gave her the initial drilling results over the telephone. The data indicated that the expected life of the main mines would be tripled. Grant added these statistics to Barton's report and circulated it as her own report within her firm.

> *Comment*: Grant plagiarized Barton's report by reproducing large parts of it in her own report without acknowledgment.

Example 6   (Misrepresentation of Information): When Ricki Marks sells mortgage-backed derivatives called "interest-only strips" (IOs) to public pension plan clients, she describes them as "guaranteed by the U.S. government." Purchasers of the IOs are entitled only to the interest stream generated by the mortgages, however, not the notional principal itself. One particular municipality's investment policies and local law require that securities purchased by its public pension plans be guaranteed by the U.S. government. Although the underlying mortgages are guaranteed, neither the investor's investment nor the interest stream on the IOs is guaranteed. When interest rates decline, causing an increase in prepayment of mortgages, interest payments to the IOs' investors decline, and these investors lose a portion of their investment.

> *Comment*: Marks violated Standard I(C) by misrepresenting the terms and character of the investment.

Example 7   (Potential Information Misrepresentation): Khalouck Abdrabbo manages the investments of several high-net-worth individuals in the United States who are approaching retirement. Abdrabbo advises these individuals that a portion of their investments be moved from equity to bank-sponsored certificates of deposit and money market accounts so that the principal will be "guaranteed" up to a certain amount. The interest is not guaranteed.

> *Comment*: Although there is risk that the institution offering the certificates of deposits and money market accounts could go bankrupt, in the United States, these accounts are insured by the U.S. government through the Federal Deposit Insurance Corporation. Therefore, using the term "guaranteed" in this context is not inappropriate as long as the amount is within the government-insured limit. Abdrabbo should explain these facts to the clients.

Example 8   (Plagiarism): Steve Swanson is a senior analyst in the investment research department of Ballard and Company. Apex Corporation has asked Ballard to assist in acquiring the majority ownership of stock in the Campbell Company, a financial consulting firm, and to prepare a report recommending that stockholders of Campbell agree to the acquisition. Another investment firm, Davis and Company, had already prepared a report for Apex analyzing both Apex and Campbell and recommending an exchange ratio. Apex has given the Davis report to Ballard officers, who have passed it on to Swanson. Swanson reviews the Davis report and other available material on Apex and Campbell companies. From his analysis, he concludes that the common stocks of Campbell and Apex represent good value at their current prices; he believes, however, that the Davis report does not consider all the factors a Campbell stockholder would need to know to make a decision. Swanson reports his conclusions to the partner in charge, who tells him to "use the Davis report, change a few words, sign your name, and get it out."

> *Comment*: If Swanson does as requested, he will violate Standard I(C). He could refer to those portions of the Davis report that he agrees with if he identifies Davis as the source; he could then add his own analysis and conclusions to the report before signing and distributing it.

Example 9 (Plagiarism): Claude Browning, a quantitative analyst for Double Alpha, Inc., returns in great excitement from a seminar. In that seminar, Jack Jorrely, a well-publicized quantitative analyst at a national brokerage firm, discussed one of his new models in great detail, and Browning is intrigued by the new concepts. He proceeds to test the model, making some minor mechanical changes but retaining the concepts, until he produces some very positive results. Browning quickly announces to his supervisors at Double Alpha that he has discovered a new model and that clients and prospective clients should be informed of this positive finding as ongoing proof of Double Alpha's continuing innovation and ability to add value.

> *Comment*: Although Browning tested Jorrely's model on his own and even slightly modified it, he must still acknowledge the original source of the idea. Browning can certainly take credit for the final, practical results; he can also support his conclusions with his own test. The credit for the innovative thinking, however, must be awarded to Jorrely.

Example 10 (Plagiarism): Fernando Zubia would like to include in his firm's marketing materials some "plain-language" descriptions of various concepts, such as the price-to-earnings (P/E) multiple and why standard deviation is used as a measure of risk. The descriptions come from other sources, but Zubia wishes to use them without reference to the original authors. Would this use of material be a violation of Standard I(C)?

> *Comment*: Copying verbatim any material without acknowledgement, including plain-language descriptions of the P/E multiple and standard deviation, violates Standard I(C). Even though these concepts are general, best practice would be for Zubia to describe them in his own words or cite the sources from which the descriptions are quoted. Members and candidates would be violating Standard I(C) if they were either responsible for creating marketing materials without attribution or knowingly use plagiarized materials.

Example 11 (Plagiarism): Through a mainstream media outlet, Erika Schneider learns about a study that she would like to cite in her research. Should she cite both the mainstream intermediary source as well as the author of the study itself when using that information?

> *Comment*: In all instances, a member or candidate must cite the actual source of the information. Best practice for Schneider would be to obtain the information directly from the author and review it before citing it in

a report. In that case, Schneider would not need to report how she found out about the information. For example, suppose Schneider read in the *Financial Times* about a study issued by CFA Institute; best practice for Schneider would be to obtain a copy of the study from CFA Institute, review it, and then cite it in her report. If she does not use any interpretation of the report from the *Financial Times* and the newspaper does not add value to the report itself, the newspaper is merely a conduit to the original information and does not need to be cited. If she does not obtain the report and review the information, Schneider runs the risk of relying on second-hand information that may misstate facts. If, for example, the *Financial Times* erroneously reported some information from the original CFA Institute study and Schneider copied that erroneous information without acknowledging CFA Institute, she could be the object of complaints. Best practice would be either to obtain the complete study from its original author and cite only that author or to use the information provided by the intermediary and cite both sources.

Example 12   (Misrepresentation of Information): Paul Ostrowski runs a two-person investment management firm. Ostrowski's firm subscribes to a service from a large investment research firm that provides research reports that can be repackaged by smaller firms for those firms' clients. Ostrowski's firm distributes these reports to clients as its own work.

> *Comment*: Ostrowski can rely on third-party research that has a reasonable and adequate basis, but he cannot imply that he is the author of such research. If he does, Ostrowski is misrepresenting the extent of his work in a way that misleads the firm's clients or prospective clients.

Example 13   (Misrepresentation of Information): Tom Stafford is part of a team within Appleton Investment Management responsible for managing a pool of assets for Open Air Bank, which distributes structured securities to offshore clients. He becomes aware that Open Air is promoting the structured securities as a much less risky investment than the investment management policy followed by him and the team to manage the original pool of assets. Also, Open Air has procured an independent rating for the pool that significantly overstates the quality of the investments. Stafford communicates his concerns to his team leader and supervisor, who responds that Open Air owns the product and is responsible for all marketing and distribution. Stafford's supervisor goes on to say that the product is outside of the U.S. regulatory regime that Appleton follows and that all risks of the product are disclosed at the bottom of page 184 of the prospectus.

> *Comment:* As a member of the investment team, Stafford is qualified to recognize the degree of accuracy of the materials that characterize the portfolio, and he is correct to be worried about Appleton's responsibility for a misrepresentation of the risks. Thus, he should continue to pursue the issue of Open Air's inaccurate promotion of the portfolio according to the firm's policies and procedures.
>
> The Code and Standards stress protecting the reputation of the firm and the sustainability and integrity of the capital markets. Misrepresenting the quality and risks associated with the investment pool may lead to negative consequences for others well beyond the direct investors.

Example 14   (Avoiding a Misrepresentation): Trina Smith is a fixed-income portfolio manager at a pension fund. She has observed that the market for highly structured mortgages is the focus of salespeople she meets and that these products represent a significant number of trading opportunities. In discussions about this topic with her team, Smith learns that calculating yields on changing cash flows within the deal structure requires very specialized vendor software. After more research, they find out that each deal is unique and that deals can have more than a dozen layers and changing cash flow priorities. Smith comes to the conclusion that, because of the complexity of these securities, the team cannot effectively distinguish between potentially good and bad investment options. To avoid misrepresenting their understanding, the team decides that the highly structured mortgage segment of the securitized market should not become part of the core of the fund's portfolio; they will allow some of the less complex securities to be part of the core.

> *Comment:* Smith is in compliance with Standard 1(C) by not investing in securities that she and her team cannot effectively understand. Because she is not able to describe the risk and return profile of the securities to the pension fund beneficiaries and trustees, she appropriately limits the fund's exposure to this sector.

D. Misconduct

Members and Candidates must not engage in any professional conduct involving dishonesty, fraud, or deceit or commit any act that reflects adversely on their professional reputation, integrity, or competence.

Guidance

Whereas Standard I(A) addresses the obligation of members and candidates to comply with applicable law that governs their professional activities, Standard I(D) addresses *all* conduct that reflects poorly on the professional integrity, good reputation, or competence of members and candidates. Any act that involves lying, cheating, stealing, or other dishonest conduct is a violation of this standard if the offense reflects adversely on a member's or candidate's professional activities. Although CFA Institute discourages any sort of unethical behavior by members and candidates, the Code and Standards are primarily aimed at conduct and actions related to a member's or candidate's professional life.

Conduct that damages trustworthiness or competence may include behavior that, although it is not illegal, nevertheless negatively affects a member's or candidate's ability to perform his or her responsibilities. For example, abusing alcohol during business hours might constitute a violation of this standard because it could have a detrimental effect on the member's or candidate's ability to fulfill his or her professional responsibilities. Personal bankruptcy may not reflect on the integrity or trustworthiness of the person declaring bankruptcy, but if the circumstances of the bankruptcy involve fraudulent or deceitful business conduct, the bankruptcy may be a violation of this standard.

In some cases, the absence of appropriate conduct or the lack of sufficient effort may be a violation of Standard I(D). The integrity of the investment profession is built on trust. A member or candidate—whether an investment banker, rating or research analyst, or portfolio manager—is expected to conduct the necessary due diligence to properly understand the nature and risks of an investment before making an investment recommendation. By not taking these steps and, instead, relying on someone else in the process to have performed them, members or candidates may violate the trust their clients have placed in them. This loss of trust may have a significant impact on the reputation of the member or candidate and the operations of the financial market as a whole.

Individuals may attempt to abuse the CFA Institute Professional Conduct Program by actively seeking CFA Institute enforcement of the Code and Standards, and Standard I(D) in particular, as a method of settling personal, political, or other disputes unrelated to professional ethics. CFA Institute is aware of this issue, and appropriate disciplinary policies, procedures, and enforcement mechanisms are in place to address misuse of the Code and Standards and the Professional Conduct Program in this way.

Recommended Procedures for Compliance

In addition to ensuring that their own behavior is consistent with Standard I(D), to prevent general misconduct, members and candidates should encourage their firms to adopt the following policies and procedures to support the principles of Standard I(D):

- *Code of ethics*: Develop and/or adopt a code of ethics to which every employee must subscribe and make clear that any personal behavior that reflects poorly on the individual involved, the institution as a whole, or the investment industry will not be tolerated.
- *List of violations*: Disseminate to all employees a list of potential violations and associated disciplinary sanctions, up to and including dismissal from the firm.
- *Employee references*: Check references of potential employees to ensure that they are of good character and not ineligible to work in the investment industry because of past infractions of the law.

Application of the Standard

Example 1   (Professionalism and Competence): Simon Sasserman is a trust investment officer at a bank in a small affluent town. He enjoys lunching every day with friends at the country club, where his clients have observed him having numerous drinks. Back at work after lunch, he clearly is intoxicated while making investment decisions. His colleagues make a point of handling any business with Sasserman in the morning because they distrust his judgment after lunch.

> *Comment*: Sasserman's excessive drinking at lunch and subsequent intoxication at work constitute a violation of Standard I(D) because this conduct has raised questions about his professionalism and competence. His behavior reflects poorly on him, his employer, and the investment industry.

Example 2   (Fraud and Deceit): Howard Hoffman, a security analyst at ATZ Brothers, Inc., a large brokerage house, submits reimbursement forms over a two-year period to ATZ's self-funded health insurance program for more than two dozen bills, most of which have been altered to increase the amount due. An investigation by the firm's director of employee benefits uncovers the inappropriate conduct. ATZ subsequently terminates Hoffman's employment and notifies CFA Institute.

> *Comment*: Hoffman violated Standard I(D) because he engaged in intentional conduct involving fraud and deceit in the workplace that adversely reflected on his integrity.

Example 3   (Fraud and Deceit): Jody Brink, an analyst covering the automotive industry, volunteers much of her spare time to local charities. The board of one of the charitable institutions decides to buy five new vans to deliver hot lunches to low-income elderly people. Brink offers to donate her time to handle purchasing agreements. To pay a long-standing debt to a friend who operates an automobile dealership—and to compensate herself for her trouble—she agrees to a price 20 percent higher than normal and splits the surcharge with her friend. The director of the charity ultimately discovers the scheme and tells Brink that her services, donated or otherwise, are no longer required.

> *Comment*: Brink engaged in conduct involving dishonesty, fraud, and misrepresentation and has violated Standard I(D).

Example 4   (Personal Actions and Integrity): Carmen Garcia manages a mutual fund dedicated to socially responsible investing. She is also an environmental activist. As the result of her participation in nonviolent protests, Garcia has been arrested on numerous occasions for trespassing on the property of a large petrochemical plant that is accused of damaging the environment.

> *Comment*: Generally, Standard I(D) is not meant to cover legal transgressions resulting from acts of civil disobedience in support of personal beliefs because such conduct does not reflect poorly on the member's or candidate's professional reputation, integrity, or competence.

Example 5   (Professional Misconduct): Meredith Rasmussen works on a buy-side trading desk of an investment management firm and concentrates on in-house trades for a hedge fund subsidiary managed by a team at the investment management firm. The hedge fund has been very successful and is marketed globally by the firm. From her experience as the trader for much of the activity of the fund, Rasmussen has become quite knowledgeable about the hedge fund's strategy, tactics, and performance. When a distinct break in the market occurs, however, and many of the securities involved in the hedge fund's strategy decline markedly in value, Rasmussen observes that the reported performance of the hedge fund does not reflect this decline. In her experience, the lack of effect is a very unlikely occurrence. She approaches the head of trading about her concern and is told that she should not ask any questions, that the fund is big and successful and is not her concern. She is fairly sure something is not right, so she contacts the compliance officer, who also tells her to stay away from the issue of the hedge fund's reporting.

> *Comment:* Rasmussen has clearly come upon an error in policies, procedures, and compliance practices within the firm's operations. According to the firm's procedures for reporting potentially unethical activity, she should pursue the issue by gathering some proof of her reason for doubt. Should all internal communications within the firm not satisfy her concerns, Rasmussen should consider reporting the potential unethical activity to the appropriate regulator.
>
> See also Standard IV(A) for guidance on whistleblowing and Standard IV(C) for the duties of a supervisor.

STANDARD II—INTEGRITY OF CAPITAL MARKETS

A. Material Nonpublic Information

Members and Candidates who possess material nonpublic information that could affect the value of an investment must not act or cause others to act on the information.

Guidance

Highlights:

■ *What Is "Material" Information?*

■ *What Constitutes "Nonpublic" Information?*

■ *Mosaic Theory*

■ *Investment Research Reports*

Trading or inducing others to trade on material nonpublic information erodes confidence in capital markets, institutions, and investment professionals by supporting the idea that those with inside information and special access can take unfair advantage of the general investing public. Although trading on inside information may lead to short-term profits, in the long run, individuals and the profession as a whole will suffer from such trading. It will cause investors to avoid capital markets because the markets are perceived to be "rigged" in favor of the knowledgeable insider. Standard II(A) promotes and maintains a high level of confidence in market integrity, which is one of the foundations of the investment profession.

The prohibition on using this information goes beyond the direct buying and selling of individual securities or bonds. Members and candidates must not use material nonpublic information to influence their investment actions related to derivatives (e.g., swaps or option contracts), mutual funds, or other alternative investments. *Any* trading based on material nonpublic information constitutes a violation of Standard II(A). The expansion of financial products and the increasing interconnectivity of financial markets globally have resulted in new potential opportunities for trading on material nonpublic information.

What Is "Material" Information?

Information is "material" if its disclosure would probably have an impact on the price of a security or if reasonable investors would want to know the information before making an investment decision. In other words, information is material if it would significantly alter the total mix of information currently available about a security in such a way that the price of the security would be affected.

The specificity of the information, the extent of its difference from public information, its nature, and its reliability are key factors in determining whether a particular piece of information fits the definition of material. For example, material information may include, but is not limited to, information on the following:

■ earnings;

■ mergers, acquisitions, tender offers, or joint ventures;

■ changes in assets or asset quality;

■ innovative products, processes, or discoveries;

■ new licenses, patents, registered trademarks, or regulatory approval/rejection of a product;

■ developments regarding customers or suppliers (e.g., the acquisition or loss of a contract);

■ changes in management;

■ change in auditor notification or the fact that the issuer may no longer rely on an auditor's report or qualified opinion;

■ events regarding the issuer's securities (e.g., defaults on senior securities, calls of securities for redemption, repurchase plans, stock splits, changes in dividends, changes to the rights of security holders, public or private sales of additional securities, and changes in credit ratings);

- bankruptcies;

- significant legal disputes;

- government reports of economic trends (employment, housing starts, currency information, etc.);

- orders for large trades before they are executed.

In addition to the substance and specificity of the information, the source or relative reliability of the information also determines materiality. The less reliable a source, the less likely the information provided would be considered material. For example, factual information from a corporate insider regarding a significant new contract for a company is likely to be material, whereas an assumption based on speculation by a competitor about the same contract is likely to be less reliable and, therefore, not material.

Also, the more ambiguous the effect of the information on price, the less material that information is considered. If it is unclear whether the information will affect the price of a security and to what extent, the information may not be considered material. The passage of time may also render information that was once important immaterial.

What Constitutes "Nonpublic" Information?

Information is "nonpublic" until it has been disseminated or is available to the marketplace in general (as opposed to a select group of investors). Dissemination can be defined as "made known to." For example, a company report of profits that is posted on the internet and distributed widely through a press release or accompanied by a filing has been effectively disseminated to the marketplace. Members and candidates must have a reasonable expectation that people have received the information before it can be considered public. It is not necessary, however, to wait for the slowest method of delivery. Once the information is disseminated to the market, it is public information that is no longer covered by this standard.

Members and candidates must be particularly aware of information that is selectively disclosed by corporations to a small group of investors, analysts, or other market participants. Information that is made available to analysts remains nonpublic until it is made available to investors in general. Corporations that disclose information on a limited basis create the potential for insider-trading violations.

Issues of selective disclosure often arise when a corporate insider provides material information to analysts in a briefing or conference call before that information is released to the public. Analysts must be aware that a disclosure made to a room full of analysts does not necessarily make the disclosed information "public." Analysts should also be alert to the possibility that they are selectively receiving material nonpublic information when a company provides them with guidance or interpretation of such publicly available information as financial statements or regulatory filings.

Mosaic Theory

A financial analyst gathers and interprets large quantities of information from many sources. The analyst may use significant conclusions derived from the analysis of public and nonmaterial nonpublic information as the basis for investment recommendations and decisions even if those conclusions would have been material inside information had they been communicated directly to the analyst by a company. Under the "mosaic theory," financial analysts are free to act on this collection, or mosaic, of information without risking violation.

The practice of financial analysis depends on the free flow of information. For the fair and efficient operation of the capital markets, analysts and investors must have the greatest amount of information possible to facilitate making well-informed investment decisions about how and where to invest capital. Accurate, timely, and intelligible communication are essential if analysts and investors are to obtain the data needed to make informed decisions about how and where to invest capital. These disclosures must go beyond the information mandated by the reporting requirements of the securities laws and should include specific business information about items used to guide a company's future growth, such as new products, capital projects, and the competitive environment. Analysts seek and use such information to compare and contrast investment alternatives.

Much of the information used by analysts comes directly from companies. Analysts often receive such information through contacts with corporate insiders, especially investor-relations staff and financial officers. Information may be disseminated in the form of press releases, through oral presentations by company executives in analysts' meetings or conference calls, or during analysts' visits to company premises. In seeking to develop the most accurate and complete picture of a company, analysts should also reach beyond contacts with companies themselves and collect information from other sources, such as customers, contractors, suppliers, and the companies' competitors.

Analysts are in the business of formulating opinions and insights that are not obvious to the general investing public about the attractiveness of particular securities. In the course of their work, analysts actively seek out corporate information not generally known to the market for the express purpose of analyzing that information, forming an opinion on its significance, and informing their clients, who can be expected to trade on the basis of the recommendation. Analysts' initiatives to discover and analyze information and communicate their findings to their clients significantly enhance market efficiency, thus benefiting all investors (see *Dirks v. Securities and Exchange Commission*). Accordingly, violations of Standard II(A) will *not* result when a perceptive analyst reaches a conclusion about a corporate action or event through an analysis of public information and items of nonmaterial nonpublic information.

Investment professionals should note, however, that although analysts are free to use mosaic information in their research reports, they should save and document all their research [see Standard V(C)—Record Retention]. Evidence of the analyst's knowledge of public and nonmaterial nonpublic information about a corporation strengthens the assertion that the analyst reached his or her conclusions solely through appropriate methods rather than through the use of material nonpublic information.

Investment Research Reports

When a particularly well-known or respected analyst issues a report or makes changes to his or her recommendation, that information alone may have an effect on the market and thus may be considered material. Theoretically, under Standard II(A), such a report would have to be made public before it was distributed to clients. The analyst is not a company insider, however, and does not have access to inside information. Presumably, the analyst created the report from information available to the public (mosaic theory) and by using his or her expertise to interpret the information. The analyst's hard work, paid for by the client, generated the conclusions. Simply because the public in general would find the conclusions material does not require that the analyst make his or her work public. Investors who are not clients of the analyst can either do the work themselves or become clients of the analyst for access to the analyst's expertise.

Recommended Procedures for Compliance

Achieve Public Dissemination

If a member or candidate determines that information is material, the member or candidate should make reasonable efforts to achieve public dissemination of the information. This effort usually entails encouraging the issuer company to make the information public. If public dissemination is not possible, the member or candidate must communicate the information only to the designated supervisory and compliance personnel within the member's or candidate's firm and must not take investment action or alter current investment recommendations on the basis of the information. Moreover, members and candidates must not knowingly engage in any conduct that may induce company insiders to privately disclose material nonpublic information.

Adopt Compliance Procedures

Members and candidates should encourage their firms to adopt compliance procedures to prevent the misuse of material nonpublic information. Particularly important is improving compliance in such areas as the review of employee and proprietary trading, documentation of firm procedures, and the supervision of interdepartmental communications in multiservice firms. Compliance procedures should suit the particular characteristics of a firm, including its size and the nature of its business.

Adopt Disclosure Procedures

Members and candidates should encourage their firms to develop and follow disclosure policies designed to ensure that information is disseminated to the marketplace in an equitable manner. For example, analysts from small firms should receive the same information and attention from a company as analysts from large firms receive. Similarly, companies should not provide certain information to buy-side analysts but not to sell-side analysts, or vice versa. Furthermore, a company should not discriminate among analysts in the provision of information or "blackball" particular analysts who have given negative reports on the company in the past.

Issue Press Releases

Companies should consider issuing press releases prior to analyst meetings and conference calls and scripting those meetings and calls to decrease the chance that further information will be disclosed. If material nonpublic information is disclosed for the first time in an analyst meeting or call, the company should promptly issue a press release or otherwise make the information publicly available.

Firewall Elements

An information barrier commonly referred to as a "firewall" is the most widely used approach to preventing the communication of material nonpublic information within firms. It restricts the flow of confidential information to those who need to know the information to perform their jobs effectively. The minimum elements of such a system include, but are not limited to, the following:

- substantial control of relevant interdepartmental communications, preferably through a clearance area within the firm in either the compliance or legal department;
- review of employee trading through the maintenance of "watch," "restricted," and "rumor" lists;
- documentation of the procedures designed to limit the flow of information between departments and of the actions taken to enforce those procedures;
- heightened review or restriction of proprietary trading while a firm is in possession of material nonpublic information.

Appropriate Interdepartmental Communications

Although documentation requirements must, for practical reasons, take into account the differences between the activities of small firms and those of large, multiservice firms, firms of all sizes and types benefit by improving the documentation of their internal enforcement of firewall procedures. Therefore, even at small firms, procedures concerning interdepartmental communication, the review of trading activity, and the investigation of possible violations should be compiled and formalized.

Physical Separation of Departments

As a practical matter, to the extent possible, firms should consider the physical separation of departments and files to prevent the communication of sensitive information that should not be shared. For example, the investment banking and corporate finance areas of a brokerage firm should be separated from the sales and research departments, and a bank's commercial lending department should be segregated from its trust and research departments.

Prevention of Personnel Overlap

There should be no overlap of personnel between the investment banking and corporate finance areas of a brokerage firm and the sales and research departments or between a bank's commercial lending department and its trust and research departments. For a firewall to be effective in a multiservice firm, an employee can be allowed to be on only one side of the firewall at any time. Inside knowledge may not be limited to information about a specific offering or the current financial condition of a company. Analysts may be exposed to much information about the company, including new product developments or future budget projections that clearly constitute inside knowledge and thus preclude the analyst from returning to his or her research function. For example, an analyst who follows a particular company may provide limited assistance to the investment bankers under carefully controlled circumstances when the firm's investment banking department is involved in a deal with the company. That analyst must then be treated as though he or she were an investment banker; the analyst must remain on the investment banking side of the wall until any information he or she learns is publicly disclosed. In short, the analyst cannot use any information learned in the course of the project for research purposes and cannot share that information with colleagues in the research department.

A Reporting System

A primary objective of an effective firewall procedure is to establish a reporting system in which authorized people review and approve communications between departments. If an employee behind a firewall believes that he or she needs to share confidential information with someone on the other side of the wall, the employee should consult a designated compliance officer to determine whether sharing the information is necessary and how much information should be shared. If the sharing is necessary, the compliance officer should coordinate the process of "looking over the wall" so that the necessary information will be shared and the integrity of the procedure will be maintained.

A single supervisor or compliance officer should have the specific authority and responsibility of deciding whether or not information is material and whether it is sufficiently public to be used as the basis for investment decisions. Ideally, the supervisor or compliance officer responsible for communicating information to a firm's research or brokerage area would not be a member of that area.

Personal Trading Limitations

Firms should consider restrictions or prohibitions on personal trading by employees and should carefully monitor both proprietary trading and personal trading by employees. Firms should require employees to make periodic reports (to the extent that such reporting is not already required by securities laws) of their own transactions and transactions made for the benefit of family members. Securities should be placed on a restricted list when a firm has or may have material nonpublic information. The broad distribution of a restricted list often triggers the sort of trading the list was developed to avoid. Therefore, a watch list shown to only the few people responsible for compliance should be used to monitor transactions in specified securities. The use of a watch list in combination with a restricted list is an increasingly common means of ensuring effective control of personal trading.

Record Maintenance

Multiservice firms should maintain written records of the communications between various departments. Firms should place a high priority on training and should consider instituting comprehensive training programs, particularly for employees in sensitive areas.

Proprietary Trading Procedures

Procedures concerning the restriction or review of a firm's proprietary trading while it possesses material nonpublic information will necessarily depend on the types of proprietary trading in which a firm may engage. A prohibition on all types of proprietary activity when a firm comes into possession of material nonpublic information is *not* appropriate. For example, when a firm acts as a market maker, a prohibition on proprietary trading may be counterproductive to the goals of maintaining the confidentiality of information and market liquidity. This concern is particularly important in the relationships between small, regional broker/dealers and small issuers. In many situations, a firm will take a small issuer public with the understanding that the firm will continue to be a market maker in the stock. In such instances, a withdrawal by the firm from market-making acts would be a clear tip to outsiders. Firms that continue market-making activity while in the possession of material nonpublic information should, however, instruct their market makers to remain passive to the market—that is, to take only the contra side of unsolicited customer trades.

In risk-arbitrage trading, the case for a trading prohibition is more compelling than it is in the case of market making. The impetus for arbitrage trading is neither passive nor reactive, and the potential for illegal profits is greater than in market making. The most prudent course for firms is to suspend arbitrage activity when a security is placed on the watch list. Those firms that continue arbitrage activity face a high hurdle in proving the adequacy of their internal procedures for preventing trading on material nonpublic information and must demonstrate a stringent review and documentation of firm trades.

Communication to All Employees

Written compliance policies and guidelines should be circulated to all employees of a firm. Policies and guidelines should be used in conjunction with training programs aimed at enabling employees to recognize material nonpublic information. Such information is not always clearly identifiable. Employees must be given sufficient training to either make an informed decision or to realize they need to consult a supervisor or compliance officer before engaging in questionable transactions.

Application of the Standard

Example 1 (Acting on Nonpublic Information): Frank Barnes, the president and controlling shareholder of the SmartTown clothing chain, decides to accept a tender offer and sell the family business at a price almost double the market price of its shares. He describes this decision to his sister (SmartTown's treasurer), who conveys it to her daughter (who owns no stock in the family company at present), who tells her husband, Staple. Staple, however, tells his stockbroker, Alex Halsey, who immediately buys SmartTown stock for himself.

> *Comment*: The information regarding the pending sale is both material and nonpublic. Staple has violated Standard II(A) by communicating the inside information to his broker. Halsey also has violated the standard by buying the shares on the basis of material nonpublic information.

Example 2   (Acting on Nonpublic Information): Josephine Walsh is riding an elevator up to her office when she overhears the chief financial officer (CFO) for the Swan Furniture Company tell the president of Swan that he has just calculated the company's earnings for the past quarter and they have unexpectedly and significantly dropped. The CFO adds that this drop will not be released to the public until next week. Walsh immediately calls her broker and tells him to sell her Swan stock.

> *Comment*: Walsh has sufficient information to determine that the information is both material and nonpublic. By trading on the inside information, she has violated Standard II(A).

Example 3   (Controlling Nonpublic Information): Samuel Peter, an analyst with Scotland and Pierce Incorporated, is assisting his firm with a secondary offering for Bright Ideas Lamp Company. Peter participates, via telephone conference call, in a meeting with Scotland and Pierce investment banking employees and Bright Ideas' CEO. Peter is advised that the company's earnings projections for the next year have significantly dropped. Throughout the telephone conference call, several Scotland and Pierce salespeople and portfolio managers walk in and out of Peter's office, where the telephone call is taking place. As a result, they are aware of the drop in projected earnings for Bright Ideas. Before the conference call is concluded, the salespeople trade the stock of the company on behalf of the firm's clients and other firm personnel trade the stock in a firm proprietary account and in employee personal accounts.

> *Comment*: Peter has violated Standard II(A) because he failed to prevent the transfer and misuse of material nonpublic information to others in his firm. Peter's firm should have adopted information barriers to prevent the communication of nonpublic information between departments of the firm. The salespeople and portfolio managers who traded on the information have also violated Standard II(A) by trading on inside information.

Example 4   (Acting on Nonpublic Information): Madison & Lambeau, a well-respected broker/dealer, submits a weekly column to *Securities Weekly* magazine. Once published, the column usually affects the value of the stocks discussed. Ron George, an employee of Madison & Lambeau, knows that *Securities Weekly* is published by Ziegler Publishing, for which his nephew is the night foreman. George's nephew faxes him an advance copy of the weekly column before it is printed. George regularly trades in the securities mentioned in the Madison & Lambeau column prior to its distribution, and to date, he has realized a personal profit of US$42,000 as well as significant profits for his clients.

> *Comment*: George has violated Standard II(A) by trading on material nonpublic information. The Madison & Lambeau article is considered nonpublic until the magazine is distributed through the normal channels.

Example 5   (Acting on Nonpublic Information): Greg Newman and his wife, Nancy Newman, volunteer at a local charitable organization that delivers meals to the elderly. One morning, Nancy Newman receives a telephone call from Betsy Sterling, another volunteer, who asks if the Newmans can fill in for her and her husband that afternoon. Betsy Sterling indicates that her husband is busy at work because his company has just fired its chief financial officer for misappropriation of funds. Nancy Newman agrees to perform the volunteer work for the Sterlings and advises her husband of the situation. Greg Newman knows that Betsy Sterling's husband is the CEO at O'Hara Brothers Incorporated, and he determines that this information is not public. Then, he sells his entire holding of 3,000 shares of O'Hara Brothers. Three days later, the firing is announced and O'Hara Brothers stock drops in value.

> *Comment*: Because the information is material and nonpublic, Greg Newman has violated Standard II(A) by trading on this information.

Example 6 (Selective Disclosure of Material Information): Elizabeth Levenson is based in Taipei and covers the Taiwanese market for her firm, which is based in Singapore. She is invited, together with the other 10 largest shareholders of a manufacturing company, to meet the finance director of that company. During the meeting, the finance director states that the company expects its workforce to strike next Friday, which will cripple productivity and distribution. Can Levenson use this information as a basis to change her rating on the company from "buy" to "sell"?

> *Comment*: Levenson must first determine whether the material information is public. According to Standard II(A), if the company has not made this information public (a small-group forum does not qualify as a method of public dissemination), she cannot use the information.

Example 7 (Determining Materiality): Leah Fechtman is trying to decide whether to hold or sell shares of an oil-and-gas exploration company that she owns in several of the funds she manages. Although the company has underperformed the index for some time already, the trends in the industry sector signal that companies of this type might become takeover targets. While she is considering her decision, her doctor, who casually follows the markets, mentions that she thinks that the company in question will soon be bought out by a large multinational conglomerate and that it would be a good idea to buy the stock right now. After talking to various investment professionals and checking their opinions on the company as well as checking industry trends, Fechtman decides the next day to accumulate more stock in the oil-and-gas exploration company.

> *Comment*: Although information on an expected takeover bid may be of the type that is generally material and nonpublic, in this case, the source of information is unreliable, so the information cannot be considered material. Therefore, Fechtman is not prohibited from trading the stock on the basis of this information.

Example 8 (Applying the Mosaic Theory): Jagdish Teja is a buy-side analyst covering the furniture industry. Looking for an attractive company to recommend as a buy, he analyzes several furniture makers by studying their financial reports and visiting their operations. He also talks to some designers and retailers to find out which furniture styles are trendy and popular. Although none of the companies that he analyzes are a clear buy, he discovers that one of them, Swan Furniture Company (SFC), may be in trouble financially. Swan's extravagant new designs have been introduced at substantial cost. Even though these designs initially attracted attention, in the long run, the public is buying more conservative furniture from other makers. Based on this information and on a profit-and-loss analysis, Teja believes that Swan's next quarter's earnings will drop substantially. He issues a sell recommendation for SFC. Immediately after receiving that recommendation, investment managers start reducing the SFC stock in their portfolios.

Comment: Information on quarterly earnings data is material and nonpublic. Teja arrived at his conclusion about the earnings drop on the basis of public information and on pieces of nonmaterial nonpublic information (such as opinions of designers and retailers). Therefore, trading based on Teja's correct conclusion is not prohibited by Standard II(A).

Example 9   (Applying the Mosaic Theory): Roger Clement is a senior financial analyst who specializes in the European automobile sector at Rivoli Capital. Because he has been repeatedly nominated by many leading industry magazines and newsletters as "best analyst" for the automobile industry, he is widely regarded as an authority on the sector. After speaking with representatives of Turgot Chariots, a European auto manufacturer with sales primarily in South Korea, as well as interviews with salespeople, labor leaders, his firm's Korean currency analysts, and banking officials, Clement has analyzed Turgot Chariots and concluded that 1) its newly introduced model will probably not meet sales anticipation, 2) its corporate restructuring strategy may well face serious opposition from the unions, 3) the depreciation of the Korean won should lead to pressure on margins for the industry in general and Turgot's market segment in particular, and 4) banks could take a tougher-than-expected stance in the upcoming round of credit renegotiations with the company. For these reasons, he changes his conclusion about the company from "market outperform" to "market underperform."

> *Comment*: To reach a conclusion about the value of the company, Clement has pieced together a number of nonmaterial or public bits of information that affect Turgot Chariots. Therefore, under the mosaic theory, Clement has not violated Standard II(A) in drafting the report.

Example 10   (Analyst Recommendations as Material Nonpublic Information): The next day, Clement is preparing to be interviewed on a global financial news television program where he will discuss his changed recommendation on Turgot Chariots for the first time in public. While preparing for the program, he mentions to the show's producers and Mary Zito, the journalist who will be interviewing him, the information he will be discussing. Just prior to going on the air, Zito sells her holdings in Turgot Chariots.

> *Comment*: When Zito receives advance notice of Clement's change of opinion, she knows it will have a material impact on the stock price, even if she is not totally aware of Clement's underlying reasoning. She is not a client of Clement but obtains early access to the material nonpublic information prior to publication. Her trades are thus based on material nonpublic information and violate Standard II(A).

Example 11   (Acting on Nonpublic Information): Timothy Holt is a portfolio manager for the Toro Aggressive Growth Fund, a large mutual fund with an aggressive-growth mandate. Because of its mandate, the fund is heavily invested in small-cap companies with strong growth potential. Based on an unfavorable analysis of McCardell Industries by his research department, Holt decides to liquidate the fund's holdings in this company. Holt knows that this action will be widely viewed as negative by the market and that the company's stock is likely to plunge. He contacts several family members to tell them to liquidate any of their holdings before Toro's holdings are sold.

> *Comment*: When Holt tells his family to sell stock in advance of Toro's trade, he is violating Standard II(A) by causing others to trade on material nonpublic information.

Example 12 (Acting on Nonpublic Information): Holt executes his sell order of McCardell Industries with Toro's broker, Karim Ahmed. Ahmed immediately recognizes the likely effect this order will have on the stock price of McCardell and sells his own holdings in the company prior to placing the order.

> *Comment*: Ahmed has violated Standard II(A) by trading on material nonpublic information.

Example 13 (Acting on Nonpublic Information): Ashton Kellogg is a retired investment professional who manages his own portfolio. He owns shares in National Savings, a large local bank. A close friend and golfing buddy, John Mayfield, is a senior executive at National. National has seen its stock drop considerably, and the news and outlook are not good. In a conversation about the economy and the banking industry on the golf course, Mayfield drops the information that National will surprise the investment community in a few days when it announces excellent earnings for the quarter. Kellogg is pleasantly surprised by this information, and thinking that Mayfield, as a senior executive, knows the law and would not disclose inside information, he doubles his position in the bank. Subsequently, National announces that it had good operating earnings but had to set aside reserves for anticipated significant losses on its loan portfolio. The combined news causes the stock to go down 60 percent.

> *Comment*: Even though Kellogg believes that Mayfield would not break the law by disclosing insider information and money was lost on the purchase, Kellogg should not have purchased additional shares of National. It is the member's or candidate's responsibility to make sure, before executing investment actions, that comments about earnings are not material nonpublic information. Kellogg has violated Standard II(A).

B. Market Manipulation

Members and Candidates must not engage in practices that distort prices or artificially inflate trading volume with the intent to mislead market participants.

Guidance

Highlights:

- *Information-Based Manipulation*
- *Transaction-Based Manipulation*

Standard II(B) requires that members and candidates uphold market integrity by prohibiting market manipulation. Market manipulation includes practices that distort security prices or trading volume with the intent to deceive people or entities that rely on information in the market. Market manipulation damages the interests of all investors by disrupting the smooth functioning of financial markets and lowering investor confidence. Although market manipulation may be less likely to occur in mature financial markets than in emerging markets, cross-border investing increasingly exposes all global investors to the potential for such practices.

Market manipulation includes 1) the dissemination of false or misleading information and 2) transactions that deceive or would be likely to mislead market participants by distorting the price-setting mechanism of financial instruments. The development of new products and technologies increases the incentives, means, and opportunities for market manipulation.

Information-Based Manipulation

Information-based manipulation includes, but is not limited to, spreading false rumors to induce trading by others. For example, members and candidates must refrain from "pumping up" the price of an investment by issuing misleading positive information or overly optimistic projections of a security's worth only to later "dump" the investment (sell ownership in it) once the price of the stock, fueled by the misleading information's effect on other market participants, reaches an artificially high level.

Transaction-Based Manipulation

Transaction-based manipulation involves instances where the member or candidate knew or should have known that his or her actions could very well affect the pricing of a security. This includes, but is not limited to, the following:

- transactions that artificially affect prices or volume to give the impression of activity or price movement in a financial instrument, which represent a diversion from the expectations of a fair and efficient market; and

- securing a controlling, dominant position in a financial instrument to exploit and manipulate the price of a related derivative and/or the underlying asset.

Standard II(B) is not intended to preclude transactions undertaken on legitimate trading strategies based on perceived market inefficiencies. The intent of the action is critical to determining whether it is a violation of this standard.

Application of the Standard

Example 1   (Independent Analysis and Company Promotion): The principal owner of Financial Information Services (FIS) entered into an agreement with two micro-cap companies to promote the companies' stock in exchange for stock and cash compensation. The principal owner caused FIS to disseminate e-mails, design and maintain several internet sites, and distribute an online investment newsletter—all of which recommended investment in the two companies. The systematic publication of purportedly independent analyses and recommendations containing inaccurate and highly promotional and speculative statements increased public investment in the companies and led to dramatically higher stock prices.

> *Comment*: The principal owner of FIS violated Standard II(B) by using inaccurate reporting and misleading information under the guise of independent analysis to artificially increase the stock price of the companies. Furthermore, the principal owner violated Standard V(A)—Diligence and Reasonable Basis by not having a reasonable and adequate basis for recommending the two companies and violated Standard VI(A)—Disclosure of Conflicts by not disclosing to investors the compensation agreements (which constituted a conflict of interest).

Example 2   (Personal Trading Practices and Price): An employee of a broker/dealer acquired a significant ownership interest in several publicly traded microcap stocks and held the stock in various brokerage accounts in which the broker/dealer had a controlling interest. The employee orchestrated the manipulation of the stock price by artificially increasing the bid price for the stock through transactions among the various accounts.

> *Comment*: The employee of the broker/dealer violated Standard II(B) by distorting the price of the stock through false trading and manipulative sales practices.

Example 3 (Creating Artificial Price Volatility): Matthew Murphy is an analyst at Divisadero Securities & Co., which has a significant number of hedge funds among its most important brokerage clients. Some of the hedge funds hold short positions on Wirewolf Semiconductor. Two trading days before the publication of the quarter-end report, Murphy alerts his sales force that he is about to issue a research report on Wirewolf that will include the following opinion:

- quarterly revenues are likely to fall short of management's guidance,

- earnings will be as much as 5 cents per share (or more than 10 percent) below consensus, and

- Wirewolf's highly respected chief financial officer may be about to join another company.

Knowing that Wirewolf has already entered its declared quarter-end "quiet period" before reporting earnings (and thus would be reluctant to respond to rumors), Murphy times the release of his research report specifically to sensationalize the negative aspects of the message in order to create significant downward pressure on Wirewolf's stock—to the distinct advantage of Divisadero's hedge fund clients. The report's conclusions are based on speculation, not on fact. The next day, the research report is broadcast to all of Divisadero's clients and to the usual newswire services.

Before Wirewolf's investor-relations department can assess the damage on the final trading day of the quarter and refute Murphy's report, its stock opens trading sharply lower, allowing Divisadero's clients to cover their short positions at substantial gains.

> *Comment*: Murphy violated Standard II(B) by aiming to create artificial price volatility designed to have a material impact on the price of an issuer's stock. Moreover, by lacking an adequate basis for the recommendation, Murphy also violated Standard V(A)—Diligence and Reasonable Basis.

Example 4 (Personal Trading and Volume): Rajesh Sekar manages two funds—an equity fund and a balanced fund—whose equity components are supposed to be managed in accordance with the same model. According to that model, the funds' holdings in stock of Digital Design Inc. (DD) are excessive. Reduction of the DD holdings would not be easy, however, because the stock has low liquidity in the stock market. Sekar decides to start trading larger portions of DD stock back and forth between his two funds to slowly increase the price; he believes market participants will see growing volume and increasing price and become interested in the stock. If other investors are willing to buy the DD stock because of such interest, then Sekar will be able to get rid of at least some of his overweight position without inducing price decreases. In this way, the whole transaction will be for the benefit of fund participants, even if additional brokers' commissions are incurred.

> *Comment*: Sekar's plan would be beneficial for his funds' participants but is based on artificial distortion of both trading volume and the price of the DD stock and thus constitutes a violation of Standard II(B).

Example 5 ("Pump-Priming" Strategy): Sergei Gonchar is chairman of the ACME Futures Exchange, which is launching a new bond futures contract. To convince investors, traders, arbitrageurs, hedgers, and so on, to use its contract, the exchange attempts to demonstrate that it has the best liquidity. To do so, it enters into agreements with members in which they commit to a substantial minimum trading volume on the new contract over a specific period in exchange for substantial reductions of their regular commissions.

> *Comment*: The formal liquidity of a market is determined by the obligations set on market makers, but the actual liquidity of a market is better estimated by the actual trading volume and bid–ask spreads. Attempts to

mislead participants about the actual liquidity of the market constitute a violation of Standard II(B). In this example, investors have been intentionally misled to believe they chose the most liquid instrument for some specific purpose, but they could eventually see the actual liquidity of the contract significantly reduced after the term of the agreement expires. If the ACME Futures Exchange fully discloses its agreement with members to boost transactions over some initial launch period, it will not violate Standard II(B). ACME's intent is not to harm investors but, on the contrary, to give them a better service. For that purpose, it may engage in a liquidity-pumping strategy, but the strategy must be disclosed.

Example 6 (Creating Artificial Price Volatility): Emily Gordon, an analyst of household products companies, is employed by a research boutique, Picador & Co. Based on information that she has gathered during a trip through Latin America, she believes that Hygene, Inc., a major marketer of personal care products, has generated better-than-expected sales from its new product initiatives in South America. After modestly boosting her projections for revenue and for gross profit margin in her worksheet models for Hygene, Gordon estimates that her earnings projection of US$2.00 per diluted share for the current year may be as much as 5 percent too low. She contacts the chief financial officer (CFO) of Hygene to try to gain confirmation of her findings from her trip and to get some feedback regarding her revised models. The CFO declines to comment and reiterates management's most recent guidance of US$1.95 to US$2.05 for the year.

Gordon decides to try to force a comment from the company by telling Picador & Co. clients who follow a momentum investment style that consensus earnings projections for Hygene are much too low; she explains that she is considering raising her published estimate by an ambitious US$0.15 to US$2.15 per share. She believes that when word of an unrealistically high earnings projection filters back to Hygene's investor-relations department, the company will feel compelled to update its earnings guidance. Meanwhile, Gordon hopes that she is at least correct with respect to the earnings direction and that she will help clients who act on her insights to profit from a quick gain by trading on her advice.

Comment: By exaggerating her earnings projections in order to try to fuel a quick gain in Hygene's stock price, Gordon is in violation of Standard II(B). Furthermore, by virtue of previewing her intentions of revising upward her earnings projections to only a select group of clients, she is in violation of Standard III(B)—Fair Dealing. Instead of what she did, it would have been acceptable for Gordon to write a report that:

- framed her earnings projection in a range of possible outcomes,
- outlined clearly the assumptions used in her Hygene models that took into consideration the findings from her trip through Latin America; and
- distributed the report to all Picador & Co. clients in an equitable manner.

Example 7 (Pump and Dump Strategy): In an effort to pump up the price of his holdings in Moosehead & Belfast Railroad Company, Steve Weinberg logs on to several investor chat rooms on the internet to start rumors that the company is about to expand its rail network in anticipation of receiving a large contract for shipping lumber.

Comment: Weinberg has violated Standard II(B) by disseminating false information about Moosehead & Belfast with the intent to mislead market participants.

Example 8 (Manipulating Model Inputs): Bill Mandeville supervises a structured financing team for Superior Investment Bank. His responsibilities include packaging new structured investment products and managing Superior's relationship with relevant rating agencies. To achieve the best rating possible, Mandeville uses mostly positive scenarios as model inputs—scenarios that reflect minimal downside risk in the assets underlying the structured products. The resulting output statistics in the rating request and underwriting prospectus support the idea that the new structured products have minimal potential downside risk. Additionally, Mandeville's compensation from Superior is partially based on both the level of the rating assigned and the successful sale of new structured investment products but does not have a link to the long-term performance of the instruments.

Mandeville is extremely successful and leads Superior as the top originator of structured investment products for the next two years. In the third year, the economy experiences difficulties and the values of the assets underlying structured products significantly decline. The subsequent defaults lead to major turmoil in the capital markets, the demise of Superior Investment Bank, and Mandeville's loss of employment.

> *Comment:* Mandeville manipulates the inputs of a model to minimize associated risk to achieve higher ratings. His understanding of structured products allows him to skillfully decide which inputs to include in support of the desired rating and price. This information manipulation for short-term gain, which is in violation of Standard II(B), ultimately causes significant damage to many parties and the capital markets as a whole. Mandeville should have realized that promoting a rating and price with inaccurate information could cause not only a loss of price confidence in the particular structured product but also a loss of investor trust in the system. Such loss of confidence affects the ability of the capital markets to operate efficiently.

STANDARD III—DUTIES TO CLIENTS

A. Loyalty, Prudence, and Care

Members and Candidates have a duty of loyalty to their clients and must act with reasonable care and exercise prudent judgment. Members and Candidates must act for the benefit of their clients and place their clients' interests before their employer's or their own interests.

Guidance

Highlights:

- *Identifying the Actual Investment Client*
- *Developing the Client's Portfolio*
- *Soft Commission Policies*
- *Proxy Voting Policies*

Standard III(A) clarifies that client interests are paramount. A member's or candidate's responsibility to a client includes a duty of loyalty and a duty to exercise reasonable care. Investment actions must be carried out for the sole benefit of the client and in a manner the member or candidate believes, given the known facts and circumstances, to be in the best interest of the client. Members and candidates must exercise the same level of prudence, judgment, and care that they would apply in the management and disposition of their own interests in similar circumstances.

Prudence requires caution and discretion. The exercise of prudence by invest-ment professionals requires that they act with the care, skill, and diligence in the circumstances that a reasonable person acting in a like capacity and familiar with such matters would use. In the context of managing a client's portfolio, prudence requires following the investment parameters set forth by the client and balancing risk and return. Acting with care requires members and candidates to act in a prudent and judicious manner in avoiding harm to clients.

Standard III(A) sets minimum expectations for members and candidates when fulfilling their responsibilities to their clients. Regulatory and legal requirements for such duties can vary across the investment industry depending on a variety of factors, including job function of the investment professional, the existence of an adviser/client relationship, and the nature of the recommendations being offered. From the perspec-tive of the end user of financial services, these different standards can be arcane and confusing, leaving investors unsure of what level of service to expect from investment professionals they employ. The single standard of conduct described in Standard III(A) benefits investors by establishing a benchmark for the duties of loyalty, prudence, and care and clarifies that all CFA Institute members and candidates, regardless of job title, local laws, or cultural differences, are required to comply with these fundamental responsibilities. Investors hiring members or candidates who must adhere to the duty of loyalty, prudence, and care set forth in this standard can be confident that these responsibilities are a requirement regardless of any legally imposed fiduciary duties.

Standard III(A), however, is not a substitute for a member's or candidate's legal or regulatory obligations. Members and candidates must also understand and adhere to any legally imposed fiduciary responsibility they assume with each client. Fiduciary duties are often imposed by law or regulation when an individual or institution is charged with the duty of acting for the benefit of another party, such as manag-ing investment assets. The duty required in fiduciary relationships exceeds what is acceptable in many other business relationships because a fiduciary is in an enhanced position of trust.

As stated in Standard I(A), members and candidates must abide by the most strict requirements imposed on them by regulators or the Code and Standards, including any legally imposed fiduciary duty. Standard III(A) establishes a minimum benchmark for the duties of loyalty, prudence, and care that are required of all members and candidates regardless of whether a legal fiduciary duty applies.

Members and candidates must also be aware of whether they have "custody" or effective control of client assets. If so, a heightened level of responsibility arises. Members and candidates are considered to have custody if they have any direct or indirect access to client funds. Members and candidates must manage any pool of assets in their control in accordance with the terms of the governing documents (such as trust documents and investment management agreements), which are the primary determinant of the manager's powers and duties. Whenever their actions are contrary to provisions of those instruments or applicable law, members and candidates are at risk of violating Standard III(A).

Identifying the Actual Investment Client

The first step for members and candidates in fulfilling their duty of loyalty to clients is to determine the identity of the "client" to whom the duty of loyalty is owed. In the context of an investment manager managing the personal assets of an individual, the client is easily identified. When the manager is responsible for the portfolios of pension plans or trusts, however, the client is not the person or entity who hires the manager but, rather, the beneficiaries of the plan or trust. The duty of loyalty is owed to the ultimate beneficiaries.

In some situations, an actual client or group of beneficiaries may not exist. Members and candidates managing a fund to an index or an expected mandate owe the duty of loyalty, prudence, and care to invest in a manner consistent with the stated mandate. The decisions of a fund's manager, although benefitting all fund investors, do not have to be based on an individual investor's requirements and risk profile. Client loyalty and care for those investing in the fund are the responsibility of members and candidates who have an advisory relationship with those individuals.

Situations involving potential conflicts of interest with respect to responsibilities to clients may be extremely complex because they may involve a number of competing interests. The duty of loyalty, prudence, and care applies to a large number of persons in varying capacities, but the exact duties may differ in many respects in accord with the relationship with each client or each type of account in which the assets are managed. Members and candidates must not only put their obligations to clients first in all dealings but must also endeavor to avoid all real or potential conflicts of interest.

Members and candidates with positions whose responsibilities do not include direct investment management also have "clients" that must be considered. Just as there are various types of advisory relationships, members and candidates must look at their roles and responsibilities when making a determination of who their clients are. Sometimes the client is easily identifiable; such is the case in the relationship between a company executive and the firm's public shareholders. At other times, the client may be the investing public as a whole, in which case, the goals of independence and objectivity of research surpass the goal of loyalty to a single organization.

Developing the Client's Portfolio

The duty of loyalty, prudence, and care owed to the individual client is especially important because the professional investment manager typically possesses greater knowledge in the investment arena than the client does. This disparity places the individual client in a vulnerable position; the client must trust the manager. The manager in these situations should ensure that the client's objectives and expectations for the performance of the account are realistic and suitable to the client's circumstances and that the risks involved are appropriate. In most circumstances, recommended investment strategies should relate to the long-term objectives and circumstances of the client.

Particular care must be taken to detect whether the goals of the investment manager or the firm in placing business, selling products, and executing security transactions potentially conflict with the best interests and objectives of the client. When members and candidates cannot avoid potential conflicts between their firm and clients' interests, they must provide clear and factual disclosures of the circumstances to the clients.

Members and candidates must follow any guidelines set by their clients for the management of their assets. Some clients, such as charitable organizations and pension plans, have strict investment policies that limit investment options to certain types or classes of investment or prohibit investment in certain securities. Other organizations have aggressive policies that do not prohibit investments by type but, instead, set criteria on the basis of the portfolio's total risk and return.

Investment decisions must be judged in the context of the total portfolio rather than by individual investment within the portfolio. The member's or candidate's duty is satisfied with respect to a particular investment if the individual has thoroughly considered the investment's place in the overall portfolio, the risk of loss and opportunity for gains, tax implications, and the diversification, liquidity, cash flow, and overall return requirements of the assets or the portion of the assets for which the manager is responsible.

Soft Commission Policies

An investment manager often has discretion over the selection of brokers executing transactions. Conflicts arise when an investment manager uses client brokerage to purchase research services that benefit the investment manager, a practice commonly called "soft dollars" or "soft commissions." Whenever members or candidates use client brokerage to purchase goods or services that do not benefit the client, they should disclose to clients the methods or policies followed in addressing the potential conflict. A member or candidate who pays a higher commission than he or she would normally pay to purchase goods or services, without corresponding benefit to the client, violates the duty of loyalty to the client.

From time to time, a client will direct a manager to use the client's brokerage to purchase goods or services for the client, a practice that is commonly called "directed brokerage." Because brokerage commission is an asset of the client and is used to benefit that client, not the manager, such a practice does not violate any duty of loyalty. A member or candidate is obligated to seek "best price" and "best execution," however, and be assured by the client that the goods or services purchased from the brokerage will benefit the account beneficiaries. "Best execution" refers to a trading process that seeks to maximize the value of the client's portfolio within the client's stated investment objectives and constraints. In addition, the member or candidate should disclose to the client that the client may not be getting best execution from the directed brokerage.

Proxy Voting Policies

The duty of loyalty, prudence, and care may apply in a number of situations facing the investment professional other than issues related directly to investing assets.

Part of a member's or candidate's duty of loyalty includes voting proxies in an informed and responsible manner. Proxies have economic value to a client, and members and candidates must ensure that they properly safeguard and maximize this value. An investment manager who fails to vote, casts a vote without considering the impact of the question, or votes blindly with management on nonroutine governance issues (e.g., a change in company capitalization) may violate this standard. Voting of proxies is an integral part of the management of investments.

A cost–benefit analysis may show that voting all proxies may not benefit the client, so voting proxies may not be necessary in all instances. Members and candidates should disclose to clients their proxy voting policies.

Recommended Procedures for Compliance

Regular Account Information

Members and candidates with control of client assets should submit to each client, at least quarterly, an itemized statement showing the funds and securities in the custody or possession of the member or candidate plus all debits, credits, and transactions that occurred during the period; should disclose to the client where the assets are to be maintained, as well as where or when they are moved; and should separate the client's assets from any other party's assets, including the member's or candidate's own assets.

Client Approval

If a member or candidate is uncertain about the appropriate course of action with respect to a client, the member or candidate should ask what he or she would expect or demand if the member or candidate were the client. If in doubt, a member or candidate should disclose the questionable matter in writing to the client and obtain client approval.

Firm Policies

Members and candidates should address and encourage their firms to address the following topics when drafting the statements or manuals containing their policies and procedures regarding responsibilities to clients:

- *Follow all applicable rules and laws*: Members and candidates must follow all legal requirements and applicable provisions of the Code and Standards.

- *Establish the investment objectives of the client*: Make a reasonable inquiry into a client's investment experience, risk and return objectives, and financial constraints prior to making investment recommendations or taking investment actions.

- *Consider all the information when taking actions*: When taking investment actions, members and candidates must consider the appropriateness and suitability of the investment relative to 1) the client's needs and circumstances, 2) the investment's basic characteristics, and 3) the basic characteristics of the total portfolio.

- *Diversify*: Members and candidates should diversify investments to reduce the risk of loss, unless diversification is not consistent with plan guidelines or is contrary to the account objectives.

- *Carry out regular reviews*: Members and candidates should establish regular review schedules to ensure that the investments held in the account adhere to the terms of the governing documents.

- *Deal fairly with all clients with respect to investment actions*: Members and candidates must not favor some clients over others and should establish policies for allocating trades and disseminating investment recommendations.

- *Disclose conflicts of interest*: Members and candidates must disclose all actual and potential conflicts of interest so that clients can evaluate those conflicts.

- *Disclose compensation arrangements*: Members and candidates should make their clients aware of all forms of manager compensation.

- *Vote proxies*: In most cases, members and candidates should determine who is authorized to vote shares and vote proxies in the best interests of the clients and ultimate beneficiaries.

- *Maintain confidentiality*: Members and candidates must preserve the confidentiality of client information.

- *Seek best execution*: Unless directed by the client as ultimate beneficiary, members and candidates must seek best execution for their clients. (Best execution is defined in the preceding text.)

- *Place client interests first*: Members and candidates must serve the best interests of clients.

Application of the Standard

Example 1   (Identifying the Client—Plan Participants): First Country Bank serves as trustee for the Miller Company's pension plan. Miller is the target of a hostile takeover attempt by Newton, Inc. In attempting to ward off Newton, Miller's managers persuade Julian Wiley, an investment manager at First Country Bank, to purchase Miller common stock in the open market for the employee pension plan. Miller's officials indicate that such action would be favorably received and would probably result in other accounts being placed with the bank. Although Wiley believes the stock to be overvalued and would not ordinarily buy it, he purchases the stock to support Miller's managers, to maintain Miller's good favor toward the bank, and to realize additional new business. The heavy stock purchases cause Miller's market price to rise to such a level that Newton retracts its takeover bid.

> *Comment*: Standard III(A) requires that a member or candidate, in evaluating a takeover bid, act prudently and solely in the interests of plan participants and beneficiaries. To meet this requirement, a member or candidate

must carefully evaluate the long-term prospects of the company against the short-term prospects presented by the takeover offer and by the ability to invest elsewhere. In this instance, Wiley, acting on behalf of his employer, which was the trustee for a pension plan, clearly violated Standard III(A). He used the pension plan to perpetuate existing management, perhaps to the detriment of plan participants and the company's shareholders, and to benefit himself. Wiley's responsibilities to the plan participants and beneficiaries should have taken precedence over any ties of his bank to corporate managers and over his self-interest. Wiley had a duty to examine the takeover offer on its own merits and to make an independent decision. The guiding principle is the appropriateness of the investment decision to the pension plan, not whether the decision benefitted Wiley or the company that hired him.

Example 2   (Client Commission Practices): JNI, a successful investment counseling firm, serves as investment manager for the pension plans of several large regionally based companies. Its trading activities generate a significant amount of commission-related business. JNI uses the brokerage and research services of many firms, but most of its trading activity is handled through a large brokerage company, Thompson, Inc. The reason is that the executives of the two firms have a close friendship. Thompson's commission structure is high in comparison with charges for similar brokerage services from other firms. JNI considers Thompson's research services and execution capabilities average. In exchange for JNI directing its brokerage to Thompson, Thompson absorbs a number of JNI overhead expenses, including those for rent.

> *Comment*: JNI executives are breaching their responsibilities by using client brokerage for services that do not benefit JNI clients and by not obtaining best price and best execution for their clients. Because JNI executives are not upholding their duty of loyalty, they are violating Standard III(A).

Example 3   (Brokerage Arrangements): Charlotte Everett, a struggling independent investment adviser, serves as investment manager for the pension plans of several companies. One of her brokers, Scott Company, is close to consummating management agreements with prospective new clients whereby Everett would manage the new client accounts and trade the accounts exclusively through Scott. One of Everett's existing clients, Crayton Corporation, has directed Everett to place securities transactions for Crayton's account exclusively through Scott. But to induce Scott to exert efforts to send more new accounts to her, Everett also directs transactions to Scott from other clients without their knowledge.

> *Comment*: Everett has an obligation at all times to seek best price and best execution on all trades. Everett may direct new client trades exclusively through Scott Company as long as Everett receives best price and execution on the trades or receives a written statement from new clients that she is *not* to seek best price and execution and that they are aware of the consequence for their accounts. Everett may trade other accounts through Scott as a reward for directing clients to Everett only if the accounts receive best price and execution and the practice is disclosed to the accounts. Because Everett does not disclose the directed trading, Everett has violated Standard III(A).

Example 4   (Brokerage Arrangements): Emilie Rome is a trust officer for Paget Trust Company. Rome's supervisor is responsible for reviewing Rome's trust account transactions and her monthly reports of personal stock transactions. Rome has been using Nathan Gray, a broker, almost exclusively for trust account brokerage transactions.

When Gray makes a market in stocks, he has been giving Rome a lower price for personal purchases and a higher price for sales than he gives to Rome's trust accounts and other investors.

> *Comment*: Rome is violating her duty of loyalty to the bank's trust accounts by using Gray for brokerage transactions simply because Gray trades Rome's personal account on favorable terms. Rome is placing her own interests before those of her clients.

Example 5 (Client Commission Practices): Lauren Parker, an analyst with Provo Advisors, covers South American equities for her firm. She likes to travel to the markets for which she is responsible and decides to go on a trip to Chile, Argentina, and Brazil. The trip is sponsored by SouthAM, Inc., a research firm with a small broker/dealer affiliate that uses the clearing facilities of a larger New York brokerage house. SouthAM specializes in arranging South American trips for analysts during which they can meet with central bank officials, government ministers, local economists, and senior executives of corporations. SouthAM accepts commission dollars at a ratio of 2 to 1 against the hard dollar costs of the research fee for the trip. Parker is not sure that SouthAM's execution is competitive, but without informing her supervisor, she directs the trading desk at Provo to start giving commission business to SouthAM so she can take the trip. SouthAM has conveniently timed the briefing trip to coincide with the beginning of Carnival season, so Parker also decides to spend five days of vacation in Rio de Janeiro at the end of the trip. Parker uses commission dollars to pay for the five days of hotel expenses.

> *Comment*: Parker is violating Standard III(A) by not exercising her duty of loyalty to her clients. She should have determined whether the commissions charged by SouthAM are reasonable in relation to the benefit of the research provided by the trip. She also should have determined whether best execution and prices could be received from SouthAM. In addition, the five extra days are not part of the research effort because they do not assist in the investment decision making. Thus, the hotel expenses for the five days should not be paid for with client assets.

Example 6 (Excessive Trading): Vida Knauss manages the portfolios of a number of high-net-worth individuals. A major part of her investment management fee is based on trading commissions. Knauss engages in extensive trading for each of her clients to ensure that she attains the minimum commission level set by her firm. Although the securities purchased and sold for the clients are appropriate and fall within the acceptable asset classes for the clients, the amount of trading for each account exceeds what is necessary to accomplish the client's investment objectives.

> *Comment*: Knauss has violated Standard III(A) because she is using the assets of her clients to benefit her firm and herself.

Example 7 (Managing Family Accounts): Adam Dill recently joined New Investments Asset Managers. To assist Dill in building a book of clients, both his father and brother opened new fee-paying accounts. Dill followed all the firm's procedures in noting his relationships with these clients and in developing their investment policy statements.

After several years, the number of Dill's clients has grown, but he still manages the original accounts of his family members. An IPO is coming to market that is a suitable investment for many of his clients, including his brother. Dill does not receive the amount of stock he requested, so to avoid any appearance of a conflict of interest, he does not allocate any shares to his brother's account.

> *Comment:* Dill has violated Standard III(A) because he is not acting for the benefit of his brother's account as well as his other accounts. The brother's

account is a regular fee-paying account comparable to the accounts of his other clients. By not allocating the shares proportionately across *all* accounts for which he thought the IPO was suitable, Dill is disadvantaging specific clients.

Dill would have been correct in not allocating shares to his brother's account if that account was being managed outside the normal fee structure of the firm.

Example 8   (Identifying the Client): Donna Hensley has been hired by a law firm to testify as an expert witness. Although the testimony is intended to represent impartial advice, she is concerned that her work may have negative consequences for the law firm. If the law firm is Hensley's client, how does she ensure that her testimony will not violate the required duty of loyalty, prudence, and care to one's client?

> *Comment:* In this situation, the law firm represents Hensley's employer and the aspect of "who is the client" is not well defined. When acting as an expert witness, Hensley is bound by the standard of independence and objectivity in the same manner as an independent research analyst would be bound. Hensley must not let the law firm influence the testimony she is to provide in the legal proceedings.

Example 9   (Identifying the Client): Jon Miller is a mutual fund portfolio manager. The fund is focused on the global financial services sector. Wanda Spears is a private wealth manager in the same city as Miller and is a friend of Miller. At a local CFA Institute society meeting, Spears mentions to Miller that her new client is an investor in Miller's fund. She states that the two of them now share a responsibility to this client.

> *Comment:* Spears' statement is not totally correct. Because she provides the advisory services to her new client, she alone is bound by the duty of loyalty to this client. Miller's responsibility is to manage the fund according to the investment policy statement of the fund. His actions should not be influenced by the needs of any particular fund investor.

B. Fair Dealing

Members and Candidates must deal fairly and objectively with all clients when providing investment analysis, making investment recommendations, taking investment action, or engaging in other professional activities

Guidance

Highlights:

- *Investment Recommendations*
- *Investment Action*

Standard III(B) requires members and candidates to treat all clients fairly when disseminating investment recommendations or making material changes to prior investment recommendations or when taking investment action with regard to general purchases, new issues, or secondary offerings. Only through the fair treatment of all parties can the investment management profession maintain the confidence of the investing public.

When an investment adviser has multiple clients, the potential exists for the adviser to favor one client over another. This favoritism may take various forms—from the quality and timing of services provided to the allocation of investment opportunities.

The term "fairly" implies that the member or candidate must take care not to discriminate against any clients when disseminating investment recommendations or taking investment action. Standard III(B) does not state "equally" because members and candidates could not possibly reach all clients at exactly the same time—whether by printed mail, telephone (including text messaging), computer (including internet updates and e-mail distribution), facsimile (fax), or wire. Each client has unique needs, investment criteria, and investment objectives, so not all investment opportunities are suitable for all clients. In addition, members and candidates may provide more personal, specialized, or in-depth service to clients who are willing to pay for premium services through higher management fees or higher levels of brokerage. Members and candidates may differentiate their services to clients, but different levels of service must not disadvantage or negatively affect clients. In addition, the different service levels should be disclosed to clients and prospective clients and should be available to everyone (i.e., different service levels should not be offered selectively).

Standard III(B) covers conduct in two broadly defined categories—investment recommendations and investment action.

Investment Recommendations

The first category of conduct involves members and candidates whose primary function is the preparation of investment recommendations to be disseminated either to the public or within a firm for the use of others in making investment decisions. This group includes members and candidates employed by investment counseling, advisory, or consulting firms as well as banks, brokerage firms, and insurance companies. The criterion is that the member's or candidate's primary responsibility is the preparation of recommendations to be acted on by others, including those in the member's or candidate's organization.

An investment recommendation is any opinion expressed by a member or candidate in regard to purchasing, selling, or holding a given security or other investment. The opinion may be disseminated to customers or clients through an initial detailed research report, through a brief update report, by addition to or deletion from a list of recommended securities, or simply by oral communication. A recommendation that is distributed to anyone outside the organization is considered a communication for general distribution under Standard III(B).

Standard III(B) addresses the manner in which investment recommendations or changes in prior recommendations are disseminated to clients. Each member or candidate is obligated to ensure that information is disseminated in such a manner that all clients have a fair opportunity to act on every recommendation. Communicating with all clients on a uniform basis presents practical problems for members and candidates because of differences in timing and methods of communication with various types of customers and clients. Members and candidates should encourage their firms to design an equitable system to prevent selective or discriminatory disclosure and should inform clients about what kind of communications they will receive.

The duty to clients imposed by Standard III(B) may be more critical when members or candidates change their recommendations than when they make initial recommendations. Material changes in a member's or candidate's prior investment recommendations because of subsequent research should be communicated to all current clients; particular care should be taken that the information reaches those clients who the member or candidate knows have acted on or been affected by the earlier advice. Clients who do not know that the member or candidate has changed a recommendation and who, therefore, place orders contrary to a current recommendation should be advised of the changed recommendation before the order is accepted.

Investment Action

The second category of conduct includes those members and candidates whose primary function is taking investment action (portfolio management) on the basis of recommendations prepared internally or received from external sources. Investment action, like investment recommendations, can affect market value. Consequently, Standard III(B) requires that members or candidates treat all clients fairly in light of their investment objectives and circumstances. For example, when making investments in new offerings or in secondary financings, members and candidates should distribute the issues to all customers for whom the investments are appropriate in a manner consistent with the policies of the firm for allocating blocks of stock. If the issue is oversubscribed, then the issue should be prorated to all subscribers. This action should be taken on a round-lot basis to avoid odd-lot distributions. In addition, if the issue is oversubscribed, members and candidates should forgo any sales to themselves or their immediate families in order to free up additional shares for clients. If the investment professional's family-member accounts are managed similarly to the accounts of other clients of the firm, however, the family-member accounts should not be excluded from buying such shares.

Members and candidates must make every effort to treat all individual and institutional clients in a fair and impartial manner. A member or candidate may have multiple relationships with an institution; for example, the member or candidate may be a corporate trustee, pension fund manager, manager of funds for individuals employed by the customer, loan originator, or creditor. A member or candidate must exercise care to treat all clients fairly.

Members and candidates should disclose to clients and prospective clients the documented allocation procedures they or their firms have in place and how the procedures would affect the client or prospect. The disclosure should be clear and complete so that the client can make an informed investment decision. Even when complete disclosure is made, however, members and candidates must put client interests ahead of their own. A member's or candidate's duty of fairness and loyalty to clients can never be overridden by client consent to patently unfair allocation procedures.

Treating clients fairly also means that members and candidates should not take advantage of their position in the industry to the detriment of clients. For instance, in the context of IPOs, members and candidates must make bona fide public distributions of "hot issue" securities (defined as securities of a public offering that are trading at a premium in the secondary market whenever such trading commences because of the great demand for the securities). Members and candidates are prohibited from withholding such securities for their own benefit and must not use such securities as a reward or incentive to gain benefit.

Recommended Procedures for Compliance

Develop Firm Policies

Although Standard III(B) refers to a member's or candidate's responsibility to deal fairly and objectively with clients, members and candidates should also encourage their firms to establish compliance procedures requiring all employees who disseminate investment recommendations or take investment actions to treat customers and clients fairly. At the very least, a member or candidate should recommend appropriate procedures to management if none are in place. And the member or candidate should make management aware of possible violations of fair-dealing practices within the firm when they come to the attention of the member or candidate.

The extent of the formality and complexity of such compliance procedures depends on the nature and size of the organization and the type of securities involved. An investment adviser who is a sole proprietor and handles only discretionary accounts might not disseminate recommendations to the public, but that adviser should have formal written procedures to ensure that all clients receive fair investment action.

Good business practice dictates that initial recommendations be made available to all customers who indicate an interest. Although a member or candidate need not communicate a recommendation to all customers, the selection process by which customers receive information should be based on suitability and known interest, not on any preferred or favored status. A common practice to assure fair dealing is to communicate recommendations simultaneously within the firm and to customers.

Members and candidates should consider the following points when establishing fair-dealing compliance procedures:

- *Limit the number of people involved*: Members and candidates should make reasonable efforts to limit the number of people who are privy to the fact that a recommendation is going to be disseminated.

- *Shorten the time frame between decision and dissemination*: Members and candidates should make reasonable efforts to limit the amount of time that elapses between the decision to make an investment recommendation and the time the actual recommendation is disseminated. If a detailed institutional recommendation is in preparation that might take two or three weeks to publish, a short summary report including the conclusion might be published in advance. In an organization where both a research committee and an investment policy committee must approve a recommendation, the meetings should be held on the same day if possible. The process of reviewing, printing, and mailing reports or faxing or distributing them by e-mail necessarily involves the passage of time, sometimes long periods of time. In large firms with extensive review processes, the time factor is usually not within the control of the analyst who prepares the report. Thus, many firms and their analysts communicate to customers and firm personnel the new or changed recommendations by an update or "flash" report. The communication technique might be fax, e-mail, wire, or short written report.

- *Publish guidelines for pre-dissemination behavior*: Guidelines are needed that prohibit personnel who have prior knowledge of an investment recommendation from discussing or taking any action on the pending recommendation.

- *Simultaneous dissemination*: Members and candidates should establish procedures for the timing of dissemination of investment recommendations so that all clients are treated fairly—that is, are informed at approximately the same time. For example, if a firm is going to announce a new recommendation, supervisory personnel should time the announcement to avoid placing any client or group of clients at unfair advantage relative to other clients. A communication to all branch offices should be sent at the time of the general announcement. (When appropriate, the firm should accompany the announcement of a new recommendation with a statement that trading restrictions for the firm's employees are now in effect.) The trading restrictions should stay in effect until the recommendation is widely distributed to all relevant clients. Once this distribution has occurred, the member or candidate may follow up separately with individual clients, but members and candidates should not give favored clients advance information when such advance notification may disadvantage other clients.

- *Maintain a list of clients and their holdings*: Members and candidates should maintain a list of all clients and the securities or other investments each client holds in order to facilitate notification of customers or clients of a change in an investment recommendation. If a particular security or other investment is to be sold, such a list can be used to ensure that all holders are treated fairly in the liquidation of that particular investment.

- *Develop and document trade allocation procedures*: When formulating procedures for allocating trades, members and candidates should develop a set of guiding principles that ensure
  - fairness to advisory clients, both in priority of execution of orders and in the allocation of the price obtained in execution of block orders or trades,
  - timeliness and efficiency in the execution of orders; and
  - accuracy of the member's or candidate's records as to trade orders and client account positions.

With these principles in mind, members and candidates should develop or encourage their firm to develop written allocation procedures, with particular attention to procedures for block trades and new issues. Procedures to consider are as follows:

- requiring orders and modifications or cancellations of orders to be documented and time stamped;
- processing and executing orders on a first-in, first-out basis with consideration of bundling orders for efficiency as appropriate for the asset class or the security;
- developing a policy to address such issues as calculating execution prices and "partial fills" when trades are grouped, or in a block, for efficiency;
- giving all client accounts participating in a block trade the same execution price and charging the same commission;
- when the full amount of the block order is not executed, allocating partially executed orders among the participating client accounts pro rata on the basis of order size while not going below an established minimum lot size for some securities (e.g., bonds);
- when allocating trades for new issues, obtaining advance indications of interest, allocating securities by client (rather than portfolio manager), and providing a method for calculating allocations.

Disclose Trade Allocation Procedures

Members and candidates should disclose to clients and prospective clients how they select accounts to participate in an order and how they determine the amount of securities each account will buy or sell. Trade allocation procedures must be fair and equitable, and disclosure of inequitable allocation methods does not relieve the member or candidate of this obligation.

Establish Systematic Account Review

Member and candidate supervisors should review each account on a regular basis to ensure that no client or customer is being given preferential treatment and that the investment actions taken for each account are suitable for each account's objectives. Because investments should be based on individual needs and circumstances, an investment manager may have good reasons for placing a given security or other investment in one account while selling it from another account and should fully document the reasons behind both sides of the transaction. Members and candidates should encourage firms to establish review procedures, however, to detect whether trading in one account is being used to benefit a favored client.

Disclose Levels of Service

Members and candidates should disclose to all clients whether the organization offers different levels of service to clients for the same fee or different fees. Different levels of service should not be offered to clients selectively.

Application of the Standard

Example 1 (Selective Disclosure): Bradley Ames, a well-known and respected analyst, follows the computer industry. In the course of his research, he finds that a small, relatively unknown company whose shares are traded over the counter has just signed significant contracts with some of the companies he follows. After a considerable amount of investigation, Ames decides to write a research report on the small company and recommend purchase of its shares. While the report is being reviewed by the company for factual accuracy, Ames schedules a luncheon with several of his best clients to discuss the company. At the luncheon, he mentions the purchase recommendation scheduled to be sent early the following week to all the firm's clients.

> *Comment*: Ames has violated Standard III(B) by disseminating the purchase recommendation to the clients with whom he has lunch a week before the recommendation is sent to all clients.

Example 2 (Fair Dealing between Funds): Spencer Rivers, president of XYZ Corporation, moves his company's growth-oriented pension fund to a particular bank primarily because of the excellent investment performance achieved by the bank's commingled fund for the prior five-year period. Later, Rivers compares the results of his pension fund with those of the bank's commingled fund. He is startled to learn that, even though the two accounts have the same investment objectives and similar portfolios, his company's pension fund has significantly underperformed the bank's commingled fund. Questioning this result at his next meeting with the pension fund's manager, Rivers is told that, as a matter of policy, when a new security is placed on the recommended list, Morgan Jackson, the pension fund manager, first purchases the security for the commingled account and then purchases it on a pro rata basis for all other pension fund accounts. Similarly, when a sale is recommended, the security is sold first from the commingled account and then sold on a pro rata basis from all other accounts. Rivers also learns that if the bank cannot get enough shares (especially of hot issues) to be meaningful to all the accounts, its policy is to place the new issues only in the commingled account.

Seeing that Rivers is neither satisfied nor pleased by the explanation, Jackson quickly adds that nondiscretionary pension accounts and personal trust accounts have a lower priority on purchase and sale recommendations than discretionary pension fund accounts. Furthermore, Jackson states, the company's pension fund had the opportunity to invest up to 5 percent in the commingled fund.

> *Comment*: The bank's policy does not treat all customers fairly, and Jackson has violated her duty to her clients by giving priority to the growth-oriented commingled fund over all other funds and to discretionary accounts over nondiscretionary accounts. Jackson must execute orders on a systematic basis that is fair to all clients. In addition, trade allocation procedures should be disclosed to all clients when they become clients. Of course, in this case, disclosure of the bank's policy would not change the fact that the policy is unfair.

Example 3 (Fair Dealing and IPO Distribution): Dominic Morris works for a small regional securities firm. His work consists of corporate finance activities and investing for institutional clients. Arena, Ltd., is planning to go public. The partners have secured rights to buy an arena football league franchise and are planning to use the funds from the issue to complete the purchase. Because arena football is the current rage, Morris believes he has a hot issue on his hands. He has quietly negotiated some options for himself for helping convince Arena to do the financing through his securities firm. When he seeks expressions of interest, the institutional buyers oversubscribe the issue. Morris, assuming that the institutions have the financial clout to drive the stock up, then fills all orders (including his own) and decreases the institutional blocks.

> *Comment*: Morris has violated Standard III(B) by not treating all customers fairly. He should not have taken any shares himself and should have prorated the shares offered among all clients. In addition, he should have disclosed to his firm and to his clients that he received options as part of the deal [see Standard VI(A)—Disclosure of Conflicts].

Example 4 (Fair Dealing and Transaction Allocation): Eleanor Preston, the chief investment officer of Porter Williams Investments (PWI), a medium-sized money management firm, has been trying to retain a client, Colby Company. Management at Colby, which accounts for almost half of PWI's revenues, recently told Preston that if the performance of its account did not improve, it would find a new money manager. Shortly after this threat, Preston purchases mortgage-backed securities (MBS) for several accounts, including Colby's. Preston is busy with a number of transactions that day, so she fails to allocate the trades immediately or write up the trade tickets. A few days later, when Preston is allocating trades, she notes that some of the MBS have significantly increased in price and some have dropped. Preston decides to allocate the profitable trades to Colby and spread the losing trades among several other PWI accounts.

> *Comment*: Preston has violated Standard III(B) by failing to deal fairly with her clients in taking these investment actions. Preston should have allocated the trades prior to executing the orders, or she should have had a systematic approach to allocating the trades, such as pro rata, as soon as practical after they were executed. Among other things, Preston must disclose to the client that the adviser may act as broker for, receive commissions from, and have a potential conflict of interest regarding both parties in agency cross-transactions. After the disclosure, she should obtain from the client consent authorizing such transactions in advance.

Example 5 (Selective Disclosure): Saunders Industrial Waste Management (SIWM) publicly indicates to analysts that it is comfortable with the somewhat disappointing earnings per share projection of US$1.16 for the quarter. Bernard Roberts, an analyst at Coffey Investments, is confident that SIWM management has understated the forecasted earnings so that the real announcement will cause an "upside surprise" and boost the price of SIWM stock. The "whisper number" (rumored) estimate based on extensive research and discussed among knowledgeable analysts is higher than US$1.16. Roberts repeats the US$1.16 figure in his research report to all Coffey clients but informally tells his large clients that he expects the earnings per share to be higher, making SIWM a good buy.

> *Comment*: By not sharing his opinion regarding the potential for a significant upside earnings surprise with all clients, Roberts is not treating all clients fairly and has violated Standard III(B).

Example 6 (Additional Services for Select Clients): Jenpin Weng uses e-mail to issue a new recommendation to all his clients. He then calls his three largest institutional clients to discuss the recommendation in detail.

Comment: Weng has not violated Standard III(B) because he widely disseminated the recommendation and provided the information to all his clients prior to discussing it with a select few. Weng's largest clients received additional personal service because they presumably pay higher fees or because they have a large amount of assets under Weng's management. If Weng had discussed the report with a select group of clients prior to distributing it to all his clients, he would have violated Standard III(B).

Example 7 (Minimum Lot Allocations): Lynn Hampton is a well-respected private wealth manager in her community with a diversified client base. She determines that a new 10-year bond being offered by Healthy Pharmaceuticals is appropriate for five of her clients. Three clients request to purchase US$10,000 each, and the other two request US$50,000 each. The minimum lot size is established at US$5,000, and the issue is oversubscribed at the time of placement. Her firm's policy is that odd-lot allocations, especially those below the minimum, should be avoided because they may affect the liquidity of the security at the time of sale.

Hampton is informed she will receive only US$55,000 of the offering for all accounts. Hampton distributes the bond investments as follows: The three accounts that requested US$10,000 are allocated US$5,000 each, and the two accounts that requested US$50,000 are allocated US$20,000 each.

Comment: Hampton has not violated Standard III(B), even though the distribution is not on a complete pro rata basis because of the required minimum lot size. With the total allocation being significantly below the amount requested, Hampton ensured that each client received at least the minimum lot size of the issue. This approach allowed the clients to efficiently sell the bond later if necessary.

C. Suitability

1. When Members and Candidates are in an advisory relationship with a client, they must:

   a. Make a reasonable inquiry into a client's or prospective client's investment experience, risk and return objectives, and financial constraints prior to making any investment recommendation or taking investment action and must reassess and update this information regularly.

   b. Determine that an investment is suitable to the client's financial situation and consistent with the client's written objectives, mandates, and constraints before making an investment recommendation or taking investment action.

   c. Judge the suitability of investments in the context of the client's total portfolio.

2. When Members and Candidates are responsible for managing a portfolio to a specific mandate, strategy, or style, they must make only investment recommendations or take only investment actions that are consistent with the stated objectives and constraints of the portfolio.

Guidance

Highlights:

- *Developing an Investment Policy*
- *Understanding the Client's Risk Profile*

- *Updating an Investment Policy*
- *The Need for Diversification*
- *Managing to an Index or Mandate*

Standard III(C) requires that members and candidates who are in an investment advisory relationship with clients consider carefully the needs, circumstances, and objectives of the clients when determining the appropriateness and suitability of a given investment or course of investment action. An appropriate suitability determination will not, however, prevent some investments or investment actions from losing value.

In judging the suitability of a potential investment, the member or candidate should review many aspects of the client's knowledge, experience related to investing, and financial situation. These aspects include, but are not limited to, the risk profile of the investment as compared with the constraints of the client, the impact of the investment on the diversity of the portfolio, and whether the client has the means or net worth to assume the associated risk. The investment professional's determination of suitability should reflect only the investment recommendations or actions that a prudent person would be willing to undertake. Not every investment opportunity will be suitable for every portfolio, regardless of the potential return being offered.

The responsibilities of members and candidates to gather information and make a suitability analysis prior to making a recommendation or taking investment action fall on those members and candidates who provide investment advice in the course of an advisory relationship with a client. Other members and candidates may be simply executing specific instructions for retail clients when buying or selling securities, such as shares in mutual funds. These members and candidates and some others, such as sell-side analysts, may not have the opportunity to judge the suitability of a particular investment for the ultimate client. In cases of unsolicited trade requests that a member or candidate knows are unsuitable for the client, the member or candidate should refrain from making the trade or should seek an affirmative statement from the client that suitability is not a consideration.

Developing an Investment Policy

When an advisory relationship exists, members and candidates must gather client information at the inception of the relationship. Such information includes the client's financial circumstances, personal data (such as age and occupation) that are relevant to investment decisions, attitudes toward risk, and objectives in investing. This information should be incorporated into a written investment policy statement (IPS) that addresses the client's risk tolerance, return requirements, and all investment constraints (including time horizon, liquidity needs, tax concerns, legal and regulatory factors, and unique circumstances). Without identifying such client factors, members and candidates cannot judge whether a particular investment or strategy is suitable for a particular client. The IPS also should identify and describe the roles and responsibilities of the parties to the advisory relationship and investment process, as well as schedules for review and evaluation of the IPS. After formulating long-term capital market expectations, members and candidates can assist in developing an appropriate strategic asset allocation and investment program for the client, whether these are presented in separate documents or incorporated in the IPS or in appendices to the IPS.

Understanding the Client's Risk Profile

One of the most important factors to be considered in matching appropriateness and suitability of an investment with a client's needs and circumstances is measuring that client's tolerance for risk. The investment professional must consider the possibilities of rapidly changing investment environments and their likely impact on a client's holdings, both individual securities and the collective portfolio. The risk of many investment strategies can and should be analyzed and quantified in advance.

The use of synthetic investment vehicles and derivative investment products has introduced particular issues of risk. Members and candidates should pay careful attention to the leverage inherent in many of these vehicles or products when considering them for use in a client's investment program. Such leverage and limited liquidity, depending on the degree to which they are hedged, bear directly on the issue of suitability for the client.

Updating an Investment Policy

Updating the IPS should be repeated at least annually and also prior to material changes to any specific investment recommendations or decisions on behalf of the client. The effort to determine the needs and circumstances of each client is not a one-time occurrence. Investment recommendations or decisions are usually part of an ongoing process that takes into account the diversity and changing nature of portfolio and client characteristics. The passage of time is bound to produce changes that are important with respect to investment objectives.

For an individual client, important changes might include the number of dependents, personal tax status, health, liquidity needs, risk tolerance, amount of wealth beyond that represented in the portfolio, and extent to which compensation and other income provide for current-income needs. With respect to an institutional client, such changes might relate to the magnitude of unfunded liabilities in a pension fund, the withdrawal privileges in an employee savings plan, or the distribution requirements of a charitable foundation. Without efforts to update information concerning client factors, one or more factors could change without the investment manager's knowledge.

Suitability review can be done effectively only if the client fully discloses his or her complete financial portfolio, including those portions not managed by the member or candidate. If clients withhold information about their financial portfolio, the suitability analysis conducted by members and candidates cannot be expected to be complete; it must be based on the information provided.

The Need for Diversification

The investment profession has long recognized that the combination of several different investments is likely to provide a more acceptable level of risk exposure than having all assets in a single investment. The unique characteristics (or risks) of an individual investment may become partially or entirely neutralized when it is combined with other individual investments within a portfolio. Some reasonable amount of diversification is thus the norm for many portfolios, especially those managed by individuals or institutions that have some degree of legal fiduciary responsibility.

An investment with high relative risk on its own may be a suitable investment in the context of the entire portfolio or when the client's stated objectives contemplate speculative or risky investments. The manager may be responsible for only a portion of the client's total portfolio, or the client may not have provided a full financial picture. Members and candidates can be responsible for assessing the suitability of an investment only on the basis of the information and criteria actually provided by the client.

Managing to an Index or Mandate

Some members and candidates do not manage money for individuals but are responsible for managing a fund to an index or an expected mandate. The responsibility of these members and candidates is to invest in a manner consistent with the stated mandate. For example, a member or candidate who serves as the fund manager for a large-cap income fund would not be following the fund mandate by investing heavily in small-cap or start-up companies whose stock is speculative in nature. Members and candidates who manage pooled assets to a specific mandate are not responsible for determining the suitability of the fund as an investment for investors who may be purchasing shares in the fund. The responsibility for determining the suitability of an investment for clients can only be conferred on members and candidates who have an advisory relationship with clients.

Recommended Procedures for Compliance

Investment Policy Statement

To fulfill the basic provisions of Standard III(C), a member or candidate should put the needs and circumstances of each client and the client's investment objectives into a written investment policy statement. In formulating an investment policy for the client, the member or candidate should take the following into consideration:

- client identification—1) type and nature of client, 2) the existence of separate beneficiaries, and 3) approximate portion of total client assets that the member or candidate is managing;

- investor objectives—1) return objectives (income, growth in principal, maintenance of purchasing power) and 2) risk tolerance (suitability, stability of values);

- investor constraints—1) liquidity needs, 2) expected cash flows (patterns of additions and/or withdrawals), 3) investable funds (assets and liabilities or other commitments), 4) time horizon, 5) tax considerations, 6) regulatory and legal circumstances, 7) investor preferences, prohibitions, circumstances, and unique needs, and 8) proxy voting responsibilities and guidance;

- performance measurement benchmarks.

Regular Updates

The investor's objectives and constraints should be maintained and reviewed periodically to reflect any changes in the client's circumstances. Members and candidates should regularly compare client constraints with capital market expectations to arrive at an appropriate asset allocation. Changes in either factor may result in a fundamental change in asset allocation. Annual review is reasonable unless business or other reasons, such as a major change in market conditions, dictate more frequent review. Members and candidates should document attempts to carry out such a review if circumstances prevent it.

Suitability Test Policies

With the increase in regulatory required suitability tests, members and candidates should encourage their firms to develop related policies and procedures. The procedures will differ according to the size of the firm and scope of the services offered to its clients.

The test procedures should require the investment professional to look beyond the potential return of the investment and include the following:

- an analysis on the impact on the portfolio's diversification;

- a comparison of the investment risks with the client's assessed risk tolerance; and

- the fit of the investment with the required investment strategy.

Application of the Standard

Example 1   (Investment Suitability—Risk Profile): Caleb Smith, an investment adviser, has two clients: Larry Robertson, 60 years old, and Gabriel Lanai, 40 years old. Both clients earn roughly the same salary, but Robertson has a much higher risk tolerance because he has a large asset base. Robertson is willing to invest part of his assets very aggressively; Lanai wants only to achieve a steady rate of return with low volatility to pay for his children's education. Smith recommends investing 20 percent of both portfolios in zero-yield, small-cap, high-technology equity issues.

> *Comment*: In Robertson's case, the investment may be appropriate because of his financial circumstances and aggressive investment position, but this investment is not suitable for Lanai. Smith is violating Standard III(C) by applying Robertson's investment strategy to Lanai because the two clients' financial circumstances and objectives differ.

Example 2 (Investment Suitability—Entire Portfolio): Jessica Walters, an investment adviser, suggests to Brian Crosby, a risk-averse client, that covered call options be used in his equity portfolio. The purpose would be to enhance Crosby's income and partially offset any untimely depreciation in the portfolio's value should the stock market or other circumstances affect his holdings unfavorably. Walters educates Crosby about all possible outcomes, including the risk of incurring an added tax liability if a stock rises in price and is called away and, conversely, the risk of his holdings losing protection on the downside if prices drop sharply.

> *Comment*: When determining suitability of an investment, the primary focus should be on the characteristics of the client's entire portfolio, not the characteristics of single securities on an issue-by-issue basis. The basic characteristics of the entire portfolio will largely determine whether investment recommendations are taking client factors into account. Therefore, the most important aspects of a particular investment are those that will affect the characteristics of the total portfolio. In this case, Walters properly considers the investment in the context of the entire portfolio and thoroughly explains the investment to the client.

Example 3 (IPS Updating): In a regular meeting with client Seth Jones, the portfolio managers at Blue Chip Investment Advisors are careful to allow some time to review his current needs and circumstances. In doing so, they learn that some significant changes have recently taken place in his life. A wealthy uncle left Jones an inheritance that increased his net worth fourfold, to US$1,000,000.

> *Comment*: The inheritance has significantly increased Jones's ability (and possibly his willingness) to assume risk and has diminished the average yield required to meet his current-income needs. Jones's financial circumstances have definitely changed, so Blue Chip managers must update Jones's investment policy statement to reflect how his investment objectives have changed. Accordingly, the Blue Chip portfolio managers should consider a somewhat higher equity ratio for his portfolio than was called for by the previous circumstances, and the managers' specific common stock recommendations might be heavily tilted toward low-yield, growth-oriented issues.

Example 4 (Following an Investment Mandate): Louis Perkowski manages a high-income mutual fund. He purchases zero-dividend stock in a financial services company because he believes the stock is undervalued and is in a potential growth industry, which makes it an attractive investment.

> *Comment*: A zero-dividend stock does not seem to fit the mandate of the fund that Perkowski is managing. Unless Perkowski's investment fits within the mandate or is within the realm of allowable investments the fund has made clear in its disclosures, Perkowski has violated Standard III(C).

Example 5 (IPS Requirements and Limitations): Max Gubler, chief investment officer of a property/casualty insurance subsidiary of a large financial conglomerate, wants to improve the diversification of the subsidiary's investment portfolio and increase its returns. The subsidiary's investment policy statement provides for highly liquid investments, such as large-cap equities and government, supranational, and corporate bonds with a minimum credit rating of AA and maturity of no more than five years. In a recent presentation, a venture capital group offered very attractive prospective returns on some of its private equity funds that provide seed capital to ventures. An exit strategy was already contemplated, but investors would have to observe a minimum three-year lock-up period and a subsequent laddered exit option for a maximum of one-third of their shares per year. Gubler does not want to miss this opportunity. After extensive analysis, with the intent to optimize the return on the equity assets within the subsidiary's current portfolio, he invests 4 percent in this seed fund, leaving the portfolio's total equity exposure still well below its upper limit.

> *Comment*: Gubler is violating Standard III(A)—Loyalty, Prudence, and Care as well as Standard III(C). His new investment locks up part of the subsidiary's assets for at least three years and up to as many as five years and possibly beyond. The IPS requires investments in highly liquid investments and describes accepted asset classes; private equity investments with a lock-up period certainly do not qualify. Even without a lock-up period, an asset class with only an occasional, and thus implicitly illiquid, market may not be suitable for the portfolio. Although an IPS typically describes objectives and constraints in great detail, the manager must also make every effort to understand the client's business and circumstances. Doing so should enable the manager to recognize, understand, and discuss with the client other factors that may be or may become material in the investment management process.

Example 6 (Submanager and IPS Reviews): Paul Ostrowski's investment management business has grown significantly over the past couple of years, and some clients want to diversify internationally. Ostrowski decides to find a submanager to handle the expected international investments. Because this will be his first subadviser, Ostrowski uses the CFA Institute model "request for proposal" to design a questionnaire for his search. By his deadline, he receives seven completed questionnaires from a variety of domestic and international firms trying to gain his business. Ostrowski reviews all the applications in detail and decides to select the firm that charges the lowest fees because doing so will have the least impact on his firm's bottom line.

> *Comment:* When selecting an external or subadviser, Ostrowski needs to ensure that the new manager's services are appropriate for his clients. This due diligence includes comparing the risk profile of the clients with the investment strategy of the manager. In basing the decision on the fee structure alone, Ostrowski may be violating Standard III(C).
>
> When clients ask to diversify into international products, it is an appropriate time to review and update the clients' IPS. Ostrowski's review may determine that the risk of international investments modifies the risk profiles of the clients or does not represent an appropriate investment.
>
> See also Standard V(A)—Diligence and Reasonable Basis for further discussion of the review process needed in selecting appropriate submanagers.

Example 7 (Investment Suitability—Risk Profile): Samantha Snead, a portfolio manager for Thomas Investment Counsel, Inc., specializes in managing public retirement funds and defined-benefit pension plan accounts, all of which have long-term investment objectives. A year ago, Snead's employer, in an attempt to motivate and retain key investment professionals, introduced a bonus compensation system that rewards portfolio managers on the basis of quarterly performance relative to their peers and to certain benchmark indices. In an attempt to improve the short-term performance of her accounts, Snead changes her investment strategy and purchases several high-beta stocks for client portfolios. These purchases are seemingly contrary to the clients' investment policy statements. Following their purchase, an officer of Griffin Corporation, one of Snead's pension fund clients, asks why Griffin Corporation's portfolio seems to be dominated by high-beta stocks of companies that often appear among the most actively traded issues. No change in objective or strategy has been recommended by Snead during the year.

>Comment: Snead violated Standard III(C) by investing the clients' assets in high-beta stocks. These high-risk investments are contrary to the long-term risk profile established in the clients' IPS. Snead has changed the investment strategy of the clients in an attempt to reap short-term rewards offered by her firm's new compensation arrangement, not in response to changes in clients' investment policy statements.
>
>See also Standard VI(A)—Disclosure of Conflicts.

Example 8 (Investment Suitability): Andre Shrub owns and operates Conduit, an investment advisory firm. Prior to opening Conduit, Shrub was an account manager with Elite Investment, a hedge fund managed by his good friend Adam Reed. To attract clients to a new Conduit fund, Shrub offers lower-than-normal management fees. He can do so because the fund consists of two top-performing funds managed by Reed. Given his personal friendship with Reed and the prior performance record of these two funds, Shrub believes this new fund is a winning combination for all parties. Clients quickly invest with Conduit to gain access to the Elite funds. No one is turned away because Conduit is seeking to expand its assets under management.

>Comment: Shrub has violated Standard III(C) because the risk profile of the new fund may not be suitable for every client. As an investment adviser, Shrub needs to establish an investment policy statement for each client and recommend only investments that match that client's risk and return profile in that client's IPS. Shrub is required to act as more than a simple sales agent for Elite.
>
>Although Shrub cannot disobey the direct request of a client to purchase a specific security, he should fully discuss the risks of a planned purchase and provide reasons why it might not be suitable for a client. This requirement may lead members and candidates to decline new customers if those customers' requested investment decisions are significantly out of line with their stated requirements.
>
>See also Standard V(A)—Diligence and Reasonable Basis.

D. Performance Presentation

When communicating investment performance information, Members and Candidates must make reasonable efforts to ensure that it is fair, accurate, and complete.

Guidance

Standard III(D) requires members and candidates to provide credible performance information to clients and prospective clients and to avoid misstating performance or misleading clients and prospective clients about the investment performance of members or candidates or their firms. This standard encourages full disclosure of investment performance data to clients and prospective clients.

Standard III(D) covers any practice that would lead to misrepresentation of a member's or candidate's performance record, whether the practice involves performance presentation or performance measurement. This standard prohibits misrepresentations of past performance or reasonably expected performance. A member or candidate must give a fair and complete presentation of performance information whenever communicating data with respect to the performance history of individual accounts, composites or groups of accounts, or composites of an analyst's or firm's performance results. Furthermore, members and candidates should not state or imply that clients will obtain or benefit from a rate of return that was generated in the past.

The requirements of this standard are not limited to members and candidates managing separate accounts. Whenever a member or candidate provides performance information for which the manager is claiming responsibility, such as for pooled funds, the history must be accurate. Research analysts promoting the success or accuracy of their recommendations must ensure that their claims are fair, accurate, and complete.

If the presentation is brief, the member or candidate must make available to clients and prospects, on request, the detailed information supporting that communication. Best practice dictates that brief presentations include a reference to the limited nature of the information provided.

Recommended Procedures for Compliance

Apply GIPS Standards. For members and candidates who are showing the performance history of the assets they manage, compliance with the GIPS standards is the best method to meet their obligations under Standard III(D). Members and candidates should encourage their firms to comply with the GIPS standards.

Compliance without Applying GIPS Standards

Members and candidates can also meet their obligations under Standard III(D) by:

- considering the knowledge and sophistication of the audience to whom a performance presentation is addressed;
- presenting the performance of the weighted composite of similar portfolios rather than using a single representative account;
- including terminated accounts as part of performance history with a clear indication of when the accounts were terminated;
- including disclosures that fully explain the performance results being reported (for example, stating, when appropriate, that results are simulated when model results are used, clearly indicating when the performance record is that of a prior entity, or disclosing whether the performance is gross of fees, net of fees, or after tax); and
- maintaining the data and records used to calculate the performance being presented.

Application of the Standard

Example 1   (Performance Calculation and Length of Time): Kyle Taylor of Taylor Trust Company, noting the performance of Taylor's common trust fund for the past two years, states in a brochure sent to his potential clients, "You can expect steady 25 percent annual compound growth of the value of your investments over the year." Taylor Trust's common trust fund did increase at the rate of 25 percent per year for the past year, which mirrored the increase of the entire market. The fund has never averaged that growth for more than one year, however, and the average rate of growth of all of its trust accounts for five years is 5 percent per year.

> *Comment*: Taylor's brochure is in violation of Standard III(D). Taylor should have disclosed that the 25 percent growth occurred only in one year. Additionally, Taylor did not include client accounts other than those in the firm's common trust fund. A general claim of firm performance should take into account the performance of all categories of accounts. Finally, by stating that clients can expect a steady 25 percent annual compound growth rate, Taylor is also violating Standard I(C)—Misrepresentation, which prohibits assurances or guarantees regarding an investment.

Example 2 (Performance Calculation and Asset Weighting): Anna Judd, a senior partner of Alexander Capital Management, circulates a performance report for the capital appreciation accounts for the years 1988 through 2004. The firm claims compliance with the GIPS standards. Returns are not calculated in accordance with the requirements of the GIPS standards, however, because the composites are not asset weighted.

> *Comment*: Judd is in violation of Standard III(D). When claiming compliance with GIPS standards, firms must meet all of the requirements, make mandatory disclosures, and meet any other requirements that apply to that firm's specific situation. Judd's violation is not from any misuse of the data but from a false claim of GIPS compliance.

Example 3 (Performance Presentation and Prior Fund/Employer): Aaron McCoy is vice president and managing partner of the equity investment group of Mastermind Financial Advisors, a new business. Mastermind recruited McCoy because he had a proven six-year track record with G&P Financial. In developing Mastermind's advertising and marketing campaign, McCoy prepares an advertisement that includes the equity investment performance he achieved at G&P Financial. The advertisement for Mastermind does not identify the equity performance as being earned while at G&P. The advertisement is distributed to existing clients and prospective clients of Mastermind.

> *Comment*: McCoy has violated Standard III(D) by distributing an advertisement that contains material misrepresentations about the historical performance of Mastermind. Standard III(D) requires that members and candidates make every reasonable effort to ensure that performance information is a fair, accurate, and complete representation of an individual's or firm's performance. As a general matter, this standard does not prohibit showing past performance of funds managed at a prior firm as part of a performance track record as long as showing that record is accompanied by appropriate disclosures about where the performance took place and the person's specific role in achieving that performance. If McCoy chooses to use his past performance from G&P in Mastermind's advertising, he should make full disclosure of the source of the historical performance.

Example 4 (Performance Presentation and Simulated Results): Jed Davis has developed a mutual fund selection product based on historical information from the 1990–95 period. Davis tested his methodology by applying it retroactively to data from the 1996–2003 period, thus producing simulated performance results for those years. In January 2004, Davis's employer decided to offer the product and Davis began promoting it through trade journal advertisements and direct dissemination to clients. The advertisements included the performance results for the 1996–2003 period but did not indicate that the results were simulated.

Comment: Davis violated Standard III(D) by failing to clearly identify simulated performance results. Standard III(D) prohibits members and candidates from making any statements that misrepresent the performance achieved by them or their firms and requires members and candidates to make every reasonable effort to ensure that performance information presented to clients is fair, accurate, and complete. Use of simulated results should be accompanied by full disclosure as to the source of the performance data, including the fact that the results from 1995 through 2003 were the result of applying the model retroactively to that time period.

Example 5 (Performance Calculation and Selected Accounts Only): In a presentation prepared for prospective clients, William Kilmer shows the rates of return realized over a five-year period by a "composite" of his firm's discretionary accounts that have a "balanced" objective. This composite consisted of only a few of the accounts, however, that met the balanced criterion set by the firm, excluded accounts under a certain asset level without disclosing the fact of their exclusion, and included accounts that did not have the balanced mandate because those accounts would boost the investment results. In addition, to achieve better results, Kilmer manipulated the narrow range of accounts included in the composite by changing the accounts that made up the composite over time.

Comment: Kilmer violated Standard III(D) by misrepresenting the facts in the promotional material sent to prospective clients, distorting his firm's performance record, and failing to include disclosures that would have clarified the presentation.

E. Preservation of Confidentiality

Members and Candidates must keep information about current, former, and prospective clients confidential unless:

1. The information concerns illegal activities on the part of the client;
2. Disclosure is required by law; or
3. The client or prospective client permits disclosure of the information.

Guidance

Highlights:

- *Status of Client*
- *Compliance with Laws*
- *Electronic Information and Security*
- *Professional Conduct Investigations by CFA Institute*

Standard III(E) requires that members and candidates preserve the confidentiality of information communicated to them by their clients, prospective clients, and former clients. This standard is applicable when 1) the member or candidate receives information because of his or her special ability to conduct a portion of the client's business or personal affairs and 2) the member or candidate receives information that arises from or is relevant to that portion of the client's business that is the subject of the special or confidential relationship. If disclosure of the information is required by law or the information concerns illegal activities by the client, however, the member or candidate may have an obligation to report the activities to the appropriate authorities.

Status of Client

This standard protects the confidentiality of client information even if the person or entity is no longer a client of the member or candidate. Therefore, members and candidates must continue to maintain the confidentiality of client records even after the client relationship has ended. If a client or former client expressly authorizes the member or candidate to disclose information, however, the member or candidate may follow the terms of the authorization and provide the information.

Compliance with Laws

As a general matter, members and candidates must comply with applicable law. If applicable law requires disclosure of client information in certain circumstances, members and candidates must comply with the law. Similarly, if applicable law requires members and candidates to maintain confidentiality, even if the information concerns illegal activities on the part of the client, members and candidates should not disclose such information. When in doubt, members and candidates should consult with their employer's compliance personnel or legal counsel before disclosing confidential information about clients.

Electronic Information and Security

Because of the ever increasing volume of electronically stored information, members and candidates need to be particularly aware of possible accidental disclosures. Many employers have strict policies about storing client information on personal laptops or portable drives. Standard III(E) does not require members or candidates to become experts in information security technology, but they should have a thorough understanding of the policies of their employers. The size and operations of the firm will lead to differing policies for ensuring the security of confidential information maintained within the firm.

Professional Conduct Investigations by CFA Institute

The requirements of Standard III(E) are not intended to prevent members and candidates from cooperating with an investigation by the CFA Institute Professional Conduct Program (PCP). When permissible under applicable law, members and candidates shall consider the PCP an extension of themselves when requested to provide information about a client in support of a PCP investigation into their own conduct. Members and candidates are encouraged to cooperate with investigations into the conduct of others. Any information turned over to the PCP is kept in the strictest confidence. Members and candidates will not be considered in violation of this standard by forwarding confidential information to the PCP.

Recommended Procedures for Compliance

The simplest, most conservative, and most effective way to comply with Standard III(E) is to avoid disclosing any information received from a client except to authorized fellow employees who are also working for the client. In some instances, however, a member or candidate may want to disclose information received from clients that is outside the scope of the confidential relationship and does not involve illegal activities. Before making such a disclosure, a member or candidate should ask the following:

- In what context was the information disclosed? If disclosed in a discussion of work being performed for the client, is the information relevant to the work?
- Is the information background material that, if disclosed, will enable the member or candidate to improve service to the client?

Members and candidates need to understand and follow their firm's electronic information storage procedures. If the firm does not have procedures in place, members and candidates should encourage the development of procedures that appropriately reflect the firm's size and business operations.

Application of the Standard

Example 1 (Possessing Confidential Information): Sarah Connor, a financial analyst employed by Johnson Investment Counselors, Inc., provides investment advice to the trustees of City Medical Center. The trustees have given her a number of internal reports concerning City Medical's needs for physical plant renovation and expansion. They have asked Connor to recommend investments that would generate capital appreciation in endowment funds to meet projected capital expenditures. Connor is approached by a local businessman, Thomas Kasey, who is considering a substantial contribution either to City Medical Center or to another local hospital. Kasey wants to find out the building plans of both institutions before making a decision, but he does not want to speak to the trustees.

> *Comment*: The trustees gave Connor the internal reports so she could advise them on how to manage their endowment funds. Because the information in the reports is clearly both confidential and within the scope of the confidential relationship, Standard III(E) requires that Connor refuse to divulge information to Kasey.

Example 2 (Disclosing Confidential Information): Lynn Moody is an investment officer at the Lester Trust Company. She has an advisory customer who has talked to her about giving approximately US$50,000 to charity to reduce her income taxes. Moody is also treasurer of the Home for Indigent Widows (HIW), which is planning its annual giving campaign. HIW hopes to expand its list of prospects, particularly those capable of substantial gifts. Moody recommends that HIW's vice president for corporate gifts call on her customer and ask for a donation in the US$50,000 range.

> *Comment*: Even though the attempt to help the Home for Indigent Widows was well intended, Moody violated Standard III(E) by revealing confidential information about her client.

Example 3 (Disclosing Possible Illegal Activity): Government officials approach Casey Samuel, the portfolio manager for Garcia Company's pension plan, to examine pension fund records. They tell her that Garcia's corporate tax returns are being audited and the pension fund is being reviewed. Two days earlier, Samuel had learned in a regular investment review with Garcia officers that potentially excessive and improper charges were being made to the pension plan by Garcia. Samuel consults her employer's general counsel and is advised that Garcia has probably violated tax and fiduciary regulations and laws.

> *Comment*: Samuel should inform her supervisor of these activities, and her employer should take steps, with Garcia, to remedy the violations. If that approach is not successful, Samuel and her employer should seek advice of legal counsel to determine the appropriate steps to be taken. Samuel may well have a duty to disclose the evidence she has of the continuing legal violations and to resign as asset manager for Garcia.

Example 4 (Disclosing Possible Illegal Activity): David Bradford manages money for a family-owned real estate development corporation. He also manages the individual portfolios of several of the family members and officers of the corporation, including the chief financial officer (CFO). Based on the financial records of the corporation and some questionable practices of the CFO that Bradford has observed, Bradford believes that the CFO is embezzling money from the corporation and putting it into his personal investment account.

> *Comment*: Bradford should check with his firm's compliance department or appropriate legal counsel to determine whether applicable securities regulations require reporting the CFO's financial records.

STANDARD IV—DUTIES TO EMPLOYERS

A. Loyalty

In matters related to their employment, Members and Candidates must act for the benefit of their employer and not deprive their employer of the advantage of their skills and abilities, divulge confidential information, or otherwise cause harm to their employer.

Guidance

Highlights:

- *Employer Responsibilities*
- *Independent Practice*
- *Leaving an Employer*
- *Whistleblowing*
- *Nature of Employment*

Standard IV(A) requires members and candidates to protect the interests of their firm by refraining from any conduct that would injure the firm, deprive it of profit, or deprive it of the member's or candidate's skills and ability. Members and candidates must always place the interests of clients above the interests of their employer but should also consider the effects of their conduct on the sustainability and integrity of the employer firm. In matters related to their employment, members and candidates must not engage in conduct that harms the interests of their employer. Implicit in this standard is the obligation of members and candidates to comply with the policies and procedures established by their employers that govern the employer–employee relationship—to the extent that such policies and procedures do not conflict with applicable laws, rules, regulations, or the Code and Standards.

This standard is not meant to be a blanket requirement to place employer interests ahead of personal interests in all matters. The standard does not require members and candidates to subordinate important personal and family obligations to their work. Members and candidates should enter into a dialogue with their employer about balancing personal and employment obligations when personal matters may interfere with their work on a regular or significant basis.

Employer Responsibilities

The employer–employee relationship imposes duties and responsibilities on both parties. Employers must recognize the duties and responsibilities that they owe to their employees if they expect to have contented and productive employees.

Members and candidates are encouraged to provide their employers with a copy of the Code and Standards. These materials will inform the employer of the responsibilities of a CFA Institute member or candidate in the CFA Program. The Code and Standards also serve as a basis for questioning employer policies and practices that conflict with these responsibilities.

Employers are not obligated to adhere to the Code and Standards. In expecting to retain competent employees who are members and candidates, however, they should not develop conflicting policies and procedures. The employer is responsible for a positive working environment, which includes an ethical workplace. Senior management has the additional responsibility to devise compensation structures and incentive arrangements that do not encourage unethical behavior.

Independent Practice

Included in Standard IV(A) is the requirement that members and candidates abstain from independent competitive activity that could conflict with the interests of their employer. Although Standard IV(A) does not preclude members or candidates from entering into an independent business while still employed, members and candidates who plan to engage in independent practice for compensation must notify their employer and describe the types of services the members or candidates will render to prospective independent clients, the expected duration of the services, and the compensation for the services. Members and candidates should not render services until they receive consent from their employer to all of the terms of the arrangement. "Practice" means any service that the employer currently makes available for remuneration. "Undertaking independent practice" means engaging in competitive business, as opposed to making preparations to begin such practice.

Leaving an Employer

When members and candidates are planning to leave their current employer, they must continue to act in the employer's best interest. They must not engage in any activities that would conflict with this duty until their resignation becomes effective. It is difficult to define specific guidelines for those members and candidates who are planning to compete with their employer as part of a new venture. The circumstances of each situation must be reviewed to distinguish permissible preparations from violations of duty. Activities that might constitute a violation, especially in combination, include the following:

- misappropriation of trade secrets;
- misuse of confidential information;
- solicitation of employer's clients prior to cessation of employment;
- self-dealing (appropriating for one's own property a business opportunity or information belonging to one's employer); and
- misappropriation of clients or client lists.

A departing employee is generally free to make arrangements or preparations to go into a competitive business before terminating the relationship with his or her employer as long as such preparations do not breach the employee's duty of loyalty. Members and candidates who are contemplating seeking other employment must not contact existing clients or potential clients prior to leaving their employer for purposes of soliciting their business for the new employer. Once notice is provided to the employer of the intent to resign, the member or candidate must follow the employer's policies and procedures related to notifying clients of his or her planned departure. In addition, the member or candidate must not take records or files to a new employer without the written permission of the previous employer.

Once an employee has left the firm, the skills and experience that an employee obtained while employed are not "confidential" or "privileged" information. Similarly, simple knowledge of the names and existence of former clients is generally not confidential information unless deemed such by an agreement or by law. Standard IV(A) does not prohibit experience or knowledge gained at one employer from being used at another employer. Firm records, however, or work performed on behalf of the firm that is stored in paper copy or electronically for the member's or candidate's convenience while employed should be erased or returned to the employer unless the firm gives permission to keep those records after employment ends.

The standard does not prohibit former employees from contacting clients of their previous firm as long as the contact information does not come from the records of the former employer or violate an applicable "noncompete agreement." Members and candidates are free to use public information after departing to contact former clients without violating Standard IV(A) as long as there is no specific agreement not to do so.

Employers often require employees to sign noncompete agreements that preclude a departing employee from engaging in certain conduct. Members and candidates should take care to review the terms of any such agreement when leaving their employer to determine what, if any, conduct those agreements may prohibit.

Whistleblowing

A member's or candidate's personal interests, as well as the interests of his or her employer, are secondary to protecting the integrity of capital markets and the interests of clients. Therefore, circumstances may arise (e.g., when an employer is engaged in illegal or unethical activity) in which members and candidates must act contrary to their employer's interests in order to comply with their duties to the market and clients. In such instances, activities that would normally violate a member's or candidate's duty to his or her employer (such as contradicting employer instructions, violating certain policies and procedures, or preserving a record by copying employer records) may be justified. Such action would be permitted only if the intent is clearly aimed at protecting clients or the integrity of the market, not for personal gain.

Nature of Employment

A wide variety of business relationships exists within the investment industry. For instance, a member or candidate may be an employee or an independent contractor. Members and candidates must determine whether they are employees or independent contractors in order to determine the applicability of Standard IV(A). This issue will be decided largely by the degree of control exercised by the employing entity over the member or candidate. Factors determining control include whether the member's or candidate's hours, work location, and other parameters of the job are set; whether facilities are provided to the member or candidate; whether the member's or candidate's expenses are reimbursed; whether the member or candidate seeks work from other employers; and the number of clients or employers the member or candidate works for.

A member's or candidate's duties within an independent contractor relationship are governed by the oral or written agreement between the member and the client. Members and candidates should take care to define clearly the scope of their responsibilities and the expectations of each client within the context of each relationship. Once the member or candidate establishes a relationship with a client, the member or candidate has a duty to abide by the terms of the agreement.

Recommended Procedures for Compliance

Employers may establish codes of conduct and operating procedures for their employees to follow. Members and candidates should fully understand the policies to ensure that they are not in conflict with the Code and Standards. The following topics identify policies that members and candidates should encourage their firms to adopt if the policies are not currently in their procedures.

Competition Policy

Members and candidates must understand any restrictions placed by the employer on offering similar services outside the firm while employed by the firm. The policy may outline the procedures for requesting approval to undertake the outside service or may be a strict prohibition of such service. If a member's or candidate's employer elects to have its employees sign a noncompete agreement as part of the employment agreement, members and candidates should ensure that the details are clear and fully explained prior to signing the agreement.

Termination Policy

Members and candidates should clearly understand the termination policies of their employer. The policy should establish clear procedures regarding the resignation process, including addressing how the termination will be disclosed to clients and staff. The firm's policy may also outline the procedures for transferring responsibilities of ongoing research responsibilities and account management.

Incident-Reporting Procedures

Members and candidates should be aware of their firm's policies related to whistle-blowing and encourage their firms to adopt industry best practices in this area. Many firms are required by regulatory mandates to establish confidential and anonymous reporting procedures that allow employees to report potentially unethical and illegal activities in the firm.

Employee Classification

Members and candidates should understand their status within their employer firm. Firms are encouraged to adopt a standardized classification structure—e.g., part time, full time, outside contractor—for their employees and indicate how each of the firm's policies applies to each employee class.

Application of the Standard

Example 1   (Soliciting Former Clients): Samuel Magee manages pension accounts for Trust Assets, Inc., but has become frustrated with the working environment and has been offered a position with Fiduciary Management. Before resigning from Trust Assets, Magee asks four big accounts to leave that firm and open accounts with Fiduciary. Magee also persuades several prospective clients to sign agreements with Fiduciary Management. Magee had previously made presentations to these prospects on behalf of Trust Assets.

> *Comment*: Magee violated the employee–employer principle requiring him to act solely for his employer's benefit. Magee's duty is to Trust Assets as long as he is employed there. The solicitation of Trust Assets' current clients and prospective clients is unethical and violates Standard IV(A).

Example 2   (Former Employer's Documents and Files): James Hightower has been employed by Jason Investment Management Corporation for 15 years. He began as an analyst but assumed increasing responsibilities and is now a senior portfolio manager and a member of the firm's investment policy committee. Hightower has decided to leave Jason Investment and start his own investment management business. He has been careful not to tell any of Jason's clients that he is leaving; he does not want to be accused of breaching his duty to Jason by soliciting Jason's clients before his departure. Hightower is planning to copy and take with him the following documents and information he developed or worked on while at Jason: 1) the client list, with addresses, telephone numbers, and other pertinent client information; 2) client account statements; 3) sample marketing presentations to prospective clients containing Jason's performance record; 4) Jason's recommended list of securities; 5) computer models to determine asset allocations for accounts with various objectives; 6) computer models for stock selection; and 7) personal computer spreadsheets for Hightower's major corporate recommendations, which he developed when he was an analyst.

> *Comment*: Except with the consent of their employer, departing members and candidates may not take employer property, which includes books, records, reports, and other materials, because taking such materials may interfere with their employer's business opportunities. Taking any employer records, even those the member or candidate prepared, violates Standard IV(A). Employer records include items stored in hard copy or any other medium (e.g., home computers, portable storage devices, cell phones).

Example 3 (Addressing Rumors): Reuben Winston manages all-equity portfolios at Target Asset Management (TAM), a large, established investment counselor. Ten years previously, Philpott & Company, which manages a family of global bond mutual funds, acquired TAM in a diversification move. After the merger, the combined operations prospered in the fixed-income business but the equity management business at TAM languished. Lately, a few of the equity pension accounts that had been with TAM before the merger have terminated their relationships with TAM. One day, Winston finds on his voice mail a message from a concerned client, "Hey! I just heard that Philpott is close to announcing the sale of your firm's equity management business to Rugged Life. What is going on?" Not being aware of any such deal, Winston and his associates are stunned. Their internal inquiries are met with denials from Philpott management, but the rumors persist. Feeling left in the dark, Winston contemplates leading an employee buyout of TAM's equity management business.

> *Comment*: An employee-led buyout of TAM's equity asset management business would be consistent with Standard IV(A) because it would rest on the permission of the employer and, ultimately, the clients. In this case, however, in which employees suspect the senior managers or principals are not truthful or forthcoming, Winston should consult legal counsel to determine appropriate action.

Example 4 (Ownership of Completed Prior Work): Laura Clay, who is unemployed, wants part-time consulting work while seeking a full-time analyst position. During an interview at Bradley Associates, a large institutional asset manager, Clay is told that the firm has no immediate research openings but would be willing to pay her a flat fee to complete a study of the wireless communications industry within a given period of time. Clay would be allowed unlimited access to Bradley's research files and would be welcome to come to the offices and use whatever support facilities are available during normal working hours. Bradley's research director does not seek any exclusivity for Clay's output, and the two agree to the arrangement on a handshake. As Clay nears completion of the study, she is offered an analyst job in the research department of Winston & Company, a brokerage firm, and she is pondering submitting the draft of her wireless study for publication by Winston.

> *Comment*: Although she is under no written contractual obligation to Bradley, Clay has an obligation to let Bradley act on the output of her study before Winston & Company or Clay use the information to their advantage. That is, unless Bradley gives permission to Clay and waives its rights to her

wireless report, Clay would be in violation of Standard IV(A) if she were to immediately recommend to Winston the same transactions recommended in the report to Bradley. Furthermore, Clay must not take from Bradley any research file material or other property that she may have used.

Example 5 (Ownership of Completed Prior Work): Emma Madeline, a recent college graduate and a candidate in the CFA Program, spends her summer as an unpaid intern at Murdoch and Lowell. The senior managers at Murdoch are attempting to bring the firm into compliance with the GIPS standards, and Madeline is assigned to assist in its efforts. Two months into her internship, Madeline applies for a job at McMillan & Company, which has plans to become GIPS compliant. Madeline accepts the job with McMillan. Before leaving Murdoch, she copies the firm's software that she helped develop because she believes this software will assist her in her new position.

> *Comment*: Even though Madeline does not receive monetary compensation for her services at Murdoch, she has used firm resources in creating the software and is considered an employee because she receives compensation and benefits in the form of work experience and knowledge. By copying the software, Madeline violated Standard IV(A) because she misappropriated Murdoch's property without permission.

Example 6 (Soliciting Former Clients): Dennis Elliot has hired Sam Chisolm, who previously worked for a competing firm. Chisolm left his former firm after 18 years of employment. When Chisolm begins working for Elliot, he wants to contact his former clients because he knows them well and is certain that many will follow him to his new employer. Is Chisolm in violation of Standard IV(A) if he contacts his former clients?

> *Comment*: Because client records are the property of the firm, contacting former clients for any reason through the use of client lists or other information taken from a former employer without permission would be a violation of Standard IV(A). In addition, the nature and extent of the contact with former clients may be governed by the terms of any noncompete agreement signed by the employee and the former employer that covers contact with former clients after employment.
>
> Simple knowledge of the names and existence of former clients is not confidential information, just as skills or experience that an employee obtains while employed are not "confidential" or "privileged" information. The Code and Standards do not impose a prohibition on the use of experience or knowledge gained at one employer from being used at another employer. The Code and Standards also do not prohibit former employees from contacting clients of their previous firm, in the absence of a noncompete agreement. Members and candidates are free to use public information about their former firm after departing to contact former clients without violating Standard IV(A).
>
> In the absence of a noncompete agreement, as long as Chisolm maintains his duty of loyalty to his employer before joining Elliot's firm, does not take steps to solicit clients until he has left his former firm, and does not make use of material from his former employer without its permission after he has left, he is not in violation of the Code and Standards.

Example 7 (Starting a New Firm): Geraldine Allen currently works at a registered investment company as an equity analyst. Without notice to her employer, she registers with government authorities to start an investment company that will compete with her employer, but she does not actively seek clients. Does registration of this competing company with the appropriate regulatory authorities constitute a violation of Standard IV(A)?

Comment: Allen's preparation for the new business by registering with the regulatory authorities does not conflict with the work for her employer if the preparations have been done on Allen's own time outside the office and if Allen will not be soliciting clients for the business or otherwise operating the new company until she has left her current employer.

Example 8   (Competing with Current Employer): Several employees are planning to depart their current employer within a few weeks and have been careful to not engage in any activities that would conflict with their duty to their current employer. They have just learned that one of their employer's clients has undertaken a request for proposal (RFP) to review and possibly hire a new investment consultant. The RFP has been sent to the employer and all of its competitors. The group believes that the new entity to be formed would be qualified to respond to the RFP and be eligible for the business. The RFP submission period is likely to conclude before the employees' resignations are effective. Is it permissible for the group of departing employees to respond to the RFP for their anticipated new firm?

Comment: A group of employees responding to an RFP that their employer is also responding to would lead to direct competition between the employees and the employer. Such conduct violates Standard IV(A) unless the group of employees receives permission from their employer as well as the entity sending out the RFP.

Example 9   (Externally Compensated Assignments): Alfonso Mota is a research analyst with Tyson Investments. He works part time as a mayor for his hometown, a position for which he receives compensation. Must Mota seek permission from Tyson to serve as mayor?

Comment: If Mota's mayoral duties are so extensive and time-consuming that they might detract from his ability to fulfill his responsibilities at Tyson, he should discuss his outside activities with his employer and come to a mutual agreement regarding how to manage his personal commitments with his responsibilities to his employer.

Example 10   (Soliciting Former Clients): After leaving her employer, Shawna McQuillen establishes her own money management business. While with her former employer, she did not sign a noncompete agreement that would have prevented her from soliciting former clients. Upon her departure, she does not take any of her client lists or contact information and she clears her personal computer of any employer records, including client contact information. She obtains the phone numbers of her former clients through public records and contacts them to solicit their business.

Comment: McQuillen is not in violation of Standard IV(A) because she has not used information or records from her former employer and is not prevented by an agreement with her former employer from soliciting her former clients.

Example 11   (Whistleblowing Actions): Meredith Rasmussen works on a buy-side trading desk and concentrates on in-house trades for a hedge fund subsidiary managed by a team at the investment management firm. The hedge fund has been very successful and is marketed globally by the firm. From her experience as the trader for much of the activity of the fund, Rasmussen has become quite knowledgeable about the hedge fund's strategy, tactics, and performance. When a distinct break in the market occurs, however, and many of the securities involved in the hedge fund's strategy decline markedly in value, Rasmussen observes that the reported performance of the hedge fund does not reflect this decline. In her experience, the lack of any effect is a very unlikely occurrence. She approaches the head of trading about her concern and is told that she should not ask any questions, that the fund is big and successful and is not her concern. She is fairly sure something is not right, so she contacts the compliance officer, who also tells her to stay away from the issue of this hedge fund's reporting.

> *Comment*: Rasmussen has clearly come upon an error in policies, procedures, and compliance practices in the firm's operations. Having been unsuccessful in finding a resolution with her supervisor and the compliance officer, Rasmussen should consult the firm's whistleblowing policy to determine the appropriate next step toward informing management of her concerns. The potentially unethical actions of the investment management division are appropriate grounds for further disclosure, so Rasmussen's whistleblowing would not represent a violation of Standard IV(A).
>
> See also Standard I(D)—Misconduct and Standard IV(C)—Responsibilities of Supervisors.

Example 12   (Soliciting Former Clients): Angel Crome has been a private banker for YBSafe Bank for the past eight years. She has been very successful and built a considerable client portfolio during that time but is extremely frustrated by the recent loss of reputation by her current employer and subsequent client insecurity. A locally renowned headhunter contacted Crome a few days ago and offered her an interesting job with a competing private bank. This bank offers a substantial signing bonus for advisers with their own client portfolios. Crome figures that she can solicit at least 70 percent of her clients to follow her and gladly enters into the new employment contract.

> *Comment*: Crome may contact former clients upon termination of her employment with YBSafe Bank, but she is prohibited from using client records built and kept with her in her capacity as an employee of YBSafe Bank. Client lists are proprietary information of her former employer and must not be used for her or her new employer's benefit. The use of written, electronic, or any other form of records, other than publicly available information, to contact her former clients at YBSafe Bank will be a violation of Standard IV(A).

Example 13   (Notification of Code and Standards): Krista Smith is a relatively new assistant trader for the fixed-income desk of a major investment bank. She is on a team responsible for structuring collateralized debt obligations (CDOs) made up of securities in the inventory of the trading desk. At a meeting of the team, senior executives explain the opportunity to eventually separate the CDO into various risk-rated tranches to be sold to the clients of the firm. After the senior executives leave the meeting, the head trader announces various responsibilities of each member of the team and then says, "This is a good time to unload some of the junk we have been stuck with for a while and disguise it with ratings and a thick, unreadable prospectus, so don't be shy in putting this CDO together. Just kidding." Smith is worried by this remark and asks some of her colleagues what the head trader meant. They all respond that he was just kidding but that there is some truth in the remark because the CDO is seen by management as an opportunity to improve the quality of the securities in the firm's inventory.

Concerned about the ethical environment of the workplace, Smith decides to talk to her supervisor about her concerns and provides the head trader with a copy of the Code and Standards. Smith discusses the principle of placing the client above the interest of the firm and the possibility that the development of the new CDO will not adhere to this responsibility. The head trader assures Smith that the appropriate analysis will be conducted when determining the appropriate securities for collateral. Furthermore, the ratings are assigned by an independent firm and the prospectus will include full and factual disclosures. Smith is reassured by the meeting, but she also reviews the company's procedures and requirements for reporting potential violations of company policy and securities laws.

> *Comment*: Smith's review of the company policies and procedures for reporting violations allows her to be prepared to report through the appropriate whistleblower process if she decides that the CDO development process involves unethical actions by others. Smith's actions comply with the Code and Standards principles of placing the clients' interests first and being loyal to her employer. In providing her supervisor with a copy of the Code and Standards, Smith is highlighting the high level of ethical conduct she is required to adhere to in her professional activities.

B. Additional Compensation Arrangements

Members and Candidates must not accept gifts, benefits, compensation, or consideration that competes with or might reasonably be expected to create a conflict of interest with their employer's interest unless they obtain written consent from all parties involved.

Guidance

Standard IV(B) requires members and candidates to obtain permission from their employer before accepting compensation or other benefits from third parties for the services rendered to the employer or for any services that might create a conflict with their employer's interest. Compensation and benefits include direct compensation by the client and any indirect compensation or other benefits received from third parties. "Written consent" includes any form of communication that can be documented (for example, communication via computer e-mail that can be retrieved and documented).

Members and candidates must obtain permission for additional compensation/benefits because such arrangements may affect loyalties and objectivity and create potential conflicts of interest. Disclosure allows an employer to consider the outside arrangements when evaluating the actions and motivations of members and candidates. Moreover, the employer is entitled to have full knowledge of all compensation/benefit arrangements so as to be able to assess the true cost of the services members or candidates are providing.

Recommended Procedures for Compliance

Members and candidates should make an immediate written report to their employer specifying any compensation they propose to receive for services in addition to the compensation or benefits received from their employer. The details of the report should be confirmed by the party offering the additional compensation, including performance incentives offered by clients. This written report should state the terms of any agreement under which a member or candidate will receive additional compensation; "terms" include the nature of the compensation, the approximate amount of compensation, and the duration of the agreement.

Application of the Standard

Example 1 (Notification of Client Bonus Compensation): Geoff Whitman, a portfolio analyst for Adams Trust Company, manages the account of Carol Cochran, a client. Whitman is paid a salary by his employer, and Cochran pays the trust company a standard fee based on the market value of assets in her portfolio. Cochran proposes to Whitman that "any year that my portfolio achieves at least a 15 percent return before taxes, you and your wife can fly to Monaco at my expense and use my condominium during the third week of January." Whitman does not inform his employer of the arrangement and vacations in Monaco the following January as Cochran's guest.

> *Comment*: Whitman violated Standard IV(B) by failing to inform his employer in writing of this supplemental, contingent compensation arrangement. The nature of the arrangement could have resulted in partiality to Cochran's account, which could have detracted from Whitman's performance with respect to other accounts he handles for Adams Trust. Whitman must obtain the consent of his employer to accept such a supplemental benefit.

Example 2   (Notification of Outside Compensation): Terry Jones sits on the board of directors of Exercise Unlimited, Inc. In return for his services on the board, Jones receives unlimited membership privileges for his family at all Exercise Unlimited facilities. Jones purchases Exercise Unlimited stock for the client accounts for which it is appropriate. Jones does not disclose this arrangement to his employer because he does not receive monetary compensation for his services to the board.

> *Comment*: Jones has violated Standard IV(B) by failing to disclose to his employer benefits received in exchange for his services on the board of directors. The nonmonetary compensation may create a conflict of interest in the same manner as being paid to serve as a director.

Example 3   (Prior Approval for Outside Compensation): Jonathan Hollis is an analyst of oil-and-gas companies for Specialty Investment Management. He is currently recommending the purchase of ABC Oil Company shares and has published a long, well-thought-out research report to substantiate his recommendation. Several weeks after publishing the report, Hollis received a call from the investor-relations office of ABC Oil saying that Thomas Andrews, CEO of the company, saw the report and really liked the analyst's grasp of the business and his company. The investor-relations officer invited Hollis to visit ABC Oil to discuss the industry further. ABC Oil offers to send a company plane to pick Hollis up and arrange for his accommodations while visiting. Hollis, after gaining the appropriate approvals, accepts the meeting with the CEO but declines the offered travel arrangements.

Several weeks later, Andrews and Hollis meet to discuss the oil business and Hollis's report. Following the meeting, Hollis joins Andrews and the investment relations officer for dinner at an upscale restaurant near ABC Oil's headquarters.

Upon returning to Specialty Investment Management, Hollis provides a full review of the meeting to the director of research, including a disclosure of the dinner attended.

> *Comment*: Hollis's actions did not violate Standard IV(B). Through gaining approval before accepting the meeting and declining the offered travel arrangements, Hollis sought to avoid any potential conflicts of interest between his company and ABC Oil. Because the location of the dinner was not available prior to arrival and Hollis notified his company of the dinner upon his return, accepting the dinner should not impair his objectivity. By disclosing the dinner, Hollis has enabled Specialty Investment Management to assess whether it has any impact on future reports and recommendations by Hollis related to ABC Oil.

C. Responsibilities of Supervisors

Members and Candidates must make reasonable efforts to detect and prevent violations of applicable laws, rules, regulations, and the Code and Standards by anyone subject to their supervision or authority.

Guidance

Highlights:

- *Detection Procedures*
- *Compliance Procedures*
- *Inadequate Procedures*
- *Enforcement of Non-Investment-Related Policies*

Standard IV(C) states that members and candidates must take steps to prevent persons acting under their supervision from violating laws, rules, regulations, firm policies, or the Code and Standards.

Any investment professional who has employees subject to her or his control or influence—whether or not the employees are CFA Institute members, CFA charterholders, or candidates in the CFA Program—exercises supervisory responsibility. Members and candidates acting as supervisors must also have in-depth knowledge of the Code and Standards so that they can apply this knowledge in discharging their supervisory responsibilities.

The conduct that constitutes reasonable supervision in a particular case depends on the number of employees supervised and the work performed by those employees. Members and candidates who supervise large numbers of employees cannot personally evaluate the conduct of their employees on a continuing basis. Although these members and candidates may delegate supervisory duties, such delegation does not relieve them of their supervisory responsibility. Their responsibilities under Standard IV(C) include instructing those subordinates to whom supervision is delegated about methods to prevent and detect violations of laws, rules, regulations, firm policies, and the Code and Standards.

Detection Procedures

Members and candidates with supervisory responsibility must make reasonable efforts to detect violations of laws, rules, regulations, firm policies, and the Code and Standards. They exercise reasonable supervision by establishing and implementing written compliance procedures and ensuring that those procedures are followed through periodic review. If a member or candidate has adopted reasonable procedures and taken steps to institute an effective compliance program, then the member or candidate may not be in violation of Standard IV(C) if he or she does not detect violations that occur despite these efforts. The fact that violations do occur may indicate, however, that the compliance procedures are inadequate. In addition, in some cases, merely enacting such procedures may not be sufficient to fulfill the duty required by Standard IV(C). A member or candidate may be in violation of Standard IV(C) if he or she knows or should know that the procedures designed to detect and prevent violations are not being followed.

Compliance Procedures

Members and candidates with supervisory responsibility must understand what constitutes an adequate compliance system for their firms and make reasonable efforts to see that appropriate compliance procedures are established, documented, communicated to covered personnel, and followed. "Adequate" procedures are those designed to meet industry standards, regulatory requirements, the requirements of the Code and Standards, and the circumstances of the firm. Once compliance procedures are established, the supervisor must also make reasonable efforts to ensure that the procedures are monitored and enforced.

To be effective, compliance procedures must be in place prior to the occurrence of a violation of the law or the Code and Standards. Although compliance procedures cannot be designed to anticipate every potential violation, they should be designed to anticipate the activities most likely to result in misconduct. Each compliance program must be appropriate for the size and nature of the organization. The member or candidate should review model compliance procedures or other industry programs to ensure that the firm's procedures meet the minimum industry standards.

Once a supervisor learns that an employee has violated or may have violated the law or the Code and Standards, the supervisor must promptly initiate an investigation to ascertain the extent of the wrongdoing. Relying on an employee's statements about the extent of the violation or assurances that the wrongdoing will not recur is not enough. Reporting the misconduct up the chain of command and warning the employee to cease the activity are also not enough. Pending the outcome of the investigation, a supervisor should take steps to ensure that the violation will not be repeated, such as placing limits on the employee's activities or increasing the monitoring of the employee's activities.

Inadequate Procedures

A member or candidate with supervisory responsibility should bring an inadequate compliance system to the attention of the firm's senior managers and recommend corrective action. If the member or candidate clearly cannot discharge supervisory responsibilities because of the absence of a compliance system or because of an inadequate compliance system, the member or candidate should decline in writing to accept supervisory responsibility until the firm adopts reasonable procedures to allow adequate exercise of supervisory responsibility.

Enforcement of Non-Investment-Related Policies

A member or candidate with supervisory responsibility should enforce policies related to investment and non-investment-related activities equally. Firms regularly establish policies related to attendance and acceptable workplace actions, such as mandatory vacations for specific positions. The equal enforcement of all firm policies assists in creating a strong ethical work environment where all rules are demonstrated to be important.

Recommended Procedures for Compliance

Codes of Ethics or Compliance Procedures

Members and candidates are encouraged to recommend that their employers adopt a code of ethics. Adoption of a code of ethics is critical to establishing a strong ethical foundation for investment advisory firms and their employees. Codes of ethics formally emphasize and reinforce the client loyalty responsibilities of investment firm personnel, protect investing clients by deterring misconduct, and protect the firm's reputation for integrity.

There is a distinction, however, between codes of ethics and the specific policies and procedures needed to ensure compliance with the codes and with securities laws and regulations. Although both are important, codes of ethics should consist of fundamental, principle-based ethical and fiduciary concepts that are applicable to all of the firm's employees. In this way, firms can best convey to employees and clients the ethical ideals that investment advisers strive to achieve. These concepts need to be implemented, however, by detailed, firmwide compliance policies and procedures. Compliance procedures assist the firm's personnel in fulfilling the responsibilities enumerated in the code of ethics and make probable that the ideals expressed in the code of ethics will be adhered to in the day-to-day operation of the firm.

Stand-alone codes of ethics should be written in plain language and should address general fiduciary concepts. They should be unencumbered by numerous detailed procedures. Codes presented in this way are the most effective in stressing to employees that they are in positions of trust and must act with integrity at all times. Mingling compliance procedures in the firm's code of ethics goes against the goal of reinforcing the ethical obligations of employees.

Separating the code of ethics from compliance procedures will also reduce, if not eliminate, the legal terminology and "boilerplate" language that can make the underlying ethical principles incomprehensible to the average person. Above all, to ensure that a culture of ethics and integrity is created rather than merely a focus on following the rules, the principles in the code of ethics must be stated in a way that is accessible and understandable to everyone in the firm.

Members and candidates should encourage their employers to provide their codes of ethics to clients. In this case also, a simple, straightforward code of ethics will be best understood by clients. Unencumbered by the compliance procedures, the code of ethics will be effective in conveying that the firm is committed to conducting business in an ethical manner and in the best interests of the clients.

Adequate Compliance Procedures

A supervisor complies with Standard IV(C) by identifying situations in which legal violations or violations of the Code and Standards are likely to occur and by establishing and enforcing compliance procedures to prevent such violations. Adequate compliance procedures should:

- be contained in a clearly written and accessible manual that is tailored to the firm's operations;
- be drafted so that the procedures are easy to understand;
- designate a compliance officer whose authority and responsibility are clearly defined and who has the necessary resources and authority to implement the firm's compliance procedures;
- describe the hierarchy of supervision and assign duties among supervisors;
- implement a system of checks and balances;
- outline the scope of the procedures;
- outline procedures to document the monitoring and testing of compliance procedures;
- outline permissible conduct; and
- delineate procedures for reporting violations and sanctions.

Once a compliance program is in place, a supervisor should:

- disseminate the contents of the program to appropriate personnel;
- periodically update procedures to ensure that the measures are adequate under the law;

- continually educate personnel regarding the compliance procedures;
- issue periodic reminders of the procedures to appropriate personnel;
- incorporate a professional conduct evaluation as part of an employee's performance review;
- review the actions of employees to ensure compliance and identify violators; and
- take the necessary steps to enforce the procedures once a violation has occurred.

Once a violation is discovered, a supervisor should:

- respond promptly;
- conduct a thorough investigation of the activities to determine the scope of the wrongdoing; and
- increase supervision or place appropriate limitations on the wrongdoer pending the outcome of the investigation.

Application of the Standard

Example 1   (Supervising Research Activities): Jane Mattock, senior vice president and head of the research department of H&V, Inc., a regional brokerage firm, has decided to change her recommendation for Timber Products from buy to sell. In line with H&V's procedures, she orally advises certain other H&V executives of her proposed actions before the report is prepared for publication. As a result of Mattock's conversation with Dieter Frampton, one of the executives of H&V accountable to Mattock, Frampton immediately sells Timber's stock from his own account and from certain discretionary client accounts. In addition, other personnel inform certain institutional customers of the changed recommendation before it is printed and disseminated to all H&V customers who have received previous Timber reports.

> *Comment*: Mattock has violated Standard IV(C) by failing to reasonably and adequately supervise the actions of those accountable to her. She did not prevent or establish reasonable procedures designed to prevent dissemination of or trading on the information by those who knew of her changed recommendation. She must ensure that her firm has procedures for reviewing or recording any trading in the stock of a corporation that has been the subject of an unpublished change in recommendation. Adequate procedures would have informed the subordinates of their duties and detected sales by Frampton and selected customers.

Example 2   (Supervising Research Activities): Deion Miller is the research director for Jamestown Investment Programs. The portfolio managers have become critical of Miller and his staff because the Jamestown portfolios do not include any stock that has been the subject of a merger or tender offer. Georgia Ginn, a member of Miller's staff, tells Miller that she has been studying a local company, Excelsior, Inc., and recommends its purchase. Ginn adds that the company has been widely rumored to be the subject of a merger study by a well-known conglomerate and discussions between them are under way. At Miller's request, Ginn prepares a memo recommending the stock. Miller passes along Ginn's memo to the portfolio managers prior to leaving for vacation, and he notes that he has not reviewed the memo. As a result of the memo, the portfolio managers buy Excelsior stock immediately. The day Miller returns to the office, he learns that Ginn's only sources for the report were her brother, who is an acquisitions analyst with Acme Industries, the "well-known conglomerate," and that the merger discussions were planned but not held.

Comment: Miller violated Standard IV(C) by not exercising reasonable supervision when he disseminated the memo without checking to ensure that Ginn had a reasonable and adequate basis for her recommendations and that Ginn was not relying on material nonpublic information.

Example 3 (Supervising Trading Activities): David Edwards, a trainee trader at Wheeler & Company, a major national brokerage firm, assists a customer in paying for the securities of Highland, Inc., by using anticipated profits from the immediate sale of the same securities. Despite the fact that Highland is not on Wheeler's recommended list, a large volume of its stock is traded through Wheeler in this manner. Roberta Ann Mason is a Wheeler vice president responsible for supervising compliance with the securities laws in the trading department. Part of her compensation from Wheeler is based on commission revenues from the trading department. Although she notices the increased trading activity, she does nothing to investigate or halt it.

Comment: Mason's failure to adequately review and investigate purchase orders in Highland stock executed by Edwards and her failure to supervise the trainee's activities violate Standard IV(C). Supervisors should be especially sensitive to actual or potential conflicts between their own self-interests and their supervisory responsibilities.

Example 4 (Supervising Trading Activities and Record Keeping): Samantha Tabbing is senior vice president and portfolio manager for Crozet, Inc., a registered investment advisory and registered broker/dealer firm. She reports to Charles Henry, the president of Crozet. Crozet serves as the investment adviser and principal underwriter for ABC and XYZ public mutual funds. The two funds' prospectuses allow Crozet to trade financial futures for the funds for the limited purpose of hedging against market risks. Henry, extremely impressed by Tabbing's performance in the past two years, directs Tabbing to act as portfolio manager for the funds. For the benefit of its employees, Crozet has also organized the Crozet Employee Profit-Sharing Plan (CEPSP), a defined-contribution retirement plan. Henry assigns Tabbing to manage 20 percent of the assets of CEPSP. Tabbing's investment objective for her portion of CEPSP's assets is aggressive growth. Unbeknownst to Henry, Tabbing frequently places S&P 500 Index purchase and sale orders for the funds and the CEPSP without providing the futures commission merchants (FCMs) who take the orders with any prior or simultaneous designation of the account for which the trade has been placed. Frequently, neither Tabbing nor anyone else at Crozet completes an internal trade ticket to record the time an order was placed or the specific account for which the order was intended. FCMs often designate a specific account only after the trade, when Tabbing provides such designation. Crozet has no written operating procedures or compliance manual concerning its futures trading, and its compliance department does not review such trading. After observing the market's movement, Tabbing assigns to CEPSP the S&P 500 positions with more-favorable execution prices and assigns positions with less-favorable execution prices to the funds.

Comment: Henry violated Standard IV(C) by failing to adequately supervise Tabbing with respect to her S&P 500 trading. Henry further violated Standard IV(C) by failing to establish record-keeping and reporting procedures to prevent or detect Tabbing's violations.

Example 5 (Accepting Responsibility): Meredith Rasmussen works on a buy-side trading desk and concentrates on in-house trades for a hedge fund subsidiary managed by a team at the investment management firm. The hedge fund has been very successful and is marketed globally by the firm. From her experience as the trader for much of the activity of the fund, Rasmussen has become quite knowledgeable about the hedge fund's strategy, tactics, and performance. When a distinct break in the market occurs and many of the securities involved in the hedge fund's strategy decline markedly in value, however, Rasmussen observes that the reported performance of the hedge fund does not at all reflect this decline. From her experience, this lack of an effect is a very unlikely occurrence. She approaches the head of trading about her concern and is told that she should not ask any questions, that the fund is too big and successful and is not her concern. She is fairly sure something is not right, so she contacts the compliance officer and is again told to stay away from the hedge fund reporting issue.

> *Comment:* Rasmussen has clearly come upon an error in policies, procedures, and compliance practices within the firm's operations. According to Standard IV(C), the supervisor and the compliance officer have the responsibility to review the concerns brought forth by Rasmussen. Supervisors have the responsibility of establishing and encouraging an ethical culture in the firm. The dismissal of Rasmussen's question violates Standard IV(C) and undermines the firm's ethical operations.
>
> See also Standard I(D)—Misconduct and, for guidance on whistleblowing, Standard IV(A)—Loyalty.

Example 6   (Inadequate Procedures): Brendan Witt, a former junior sell-side technology analyst, decided to return to school to earn an MBA. To keep his research skills and industry knowledge sharp, Witt accepted a position with On-line and Informed, an independent internet-based research company. The position requires the publication of a recommendation and report on a different company every month. Initially, Witt is a regular contributor of new research and a participant in the associated discussion boards that generally have positive comments on the technology sector. Over time, his ability to manage his educational requirements and his work requirements begin to conflict with one another. Knowing a recommendation is due the next day for On-line, Witt creates a report based on a few news articles and what the conventional wisdom of the markets has deemed the "hot" security of the day.

> *Comment*: Allowing the report submitted by Witt to be posted highlights a lack of compliance procedures by the research firm. Witt's supervisor needs to work with the management of On-line to develop an appropriate review process to ensure that all contracted analysts comply with the requirements.
>
> See also Standard V(A)—Diligence and Reasonable Basis, as it relates to Witt's responsibility for substantiating a recommendation.

Example 7   (Inadequate Supervision): Michael Papis is the chief investment officer of his state's retirement fund. The fund has always used outside advisers for the real estate allocation, and this information is clearly presented in all fund communications. Thomas Nagle, a recognized sell-side research analyst and Papis's business school classmate, recently left the investment bank he worked for to start his own asset management firm, Accessible Real Estate. Nagle is trying to build his assets under management and contacts Papis about gaining some of the retirement fund's allocation. In the previous few years, the performance of the retirement fund's real estate investments was in line with the fund's benchmark but was not extraordinary. Papis decides to help out his old friend and also to seek better returns by moving the real estate allocation to Accessible. The only notice of the change in adviser appears in the next annual report in the listing of associated advisers.

> *Comment*: Papis's actions highlight the need for supervision and review at all levels in an organization. His responsibilities may include the selection of external advisers, but the decision to change advisers appears arbitrary. Members and candidates should ensure that their firm has appropriate policies and procedures in place to detect inappropriate actions such as the action taken by Papis.

See also Standard V(A)—Diligence and Reasonable Basis, Standard V(B)—Communication with Clients and Prospective Clients, and Standard VI(A)—Disclosure of Conflicts.

STANDARD V—INVESTMENT ANALYSIS, RECOMMENDATIONS, AND ACTIONS

A. Diligence and Reasonable Basis

Members and Candidates must:

1. Exercise diligence, independence, and thoroughness in analyzing investments, making investment recommendations, and taking investment actions.

2. Have a reasonable and adequate basis, supported by appropriate research and investigation, for any investment analysis, recommendation, or action.

Guidance

Highlights:

- *Defining Diligence and Reasonable Basis*
- *Using Secondary or Third-Party Research*
- *Quantitatively Oriented Research*
- *Selecting External Advisers and Subadvisers*
- *Group Research and Decision Making*

The application of Standard V(A) depends on the investment philosophy the member, candidate, or firm is following, the role of the member or candidate in the investment decision-making process, and the support and resources provided by the member's or candidate's employer. These factors will dictate the nature of the diligence and thoroughness of the research and the level of investigation required by Standard V(A).

The requirements for issuing conclusions based on research will vary in relation to the member's or candidate's role in the investment decision-making process, but the member or candidate must make reasonable efforts to cover all pertinent issues when arriving at a recommendation. Members and candidates enhance transparency by providing or offering to provide supporting information to clients when recommending a purchase or sale or when changing a recommendation.

Defining Diligence and Reasonable Basis

Every investment decision is based on a set of facts known and understood at the time. Clients turn to members and candidates for advice and expect these advisers to have more information and knowledge than they do. This information and knowledge is the basis from which members and candidates apply their professional judgment in taking investment actions and making recommendations.

At a basic level, clients want assurance that members and candidates are putting forth the necessary effort to support the recommendations they are making. Communicating the level and thoroughness of the information reviewed before the member or candidate makes a judgment allows clients to understand the reasonableness of the recommended investment actions.

As with determining the suitability of an investment for the client, the necessary level of research and analysis will differ with the product, security, or service being offered. In providing an investment service, members and candidates typically use a variety of resources, including company reports, third-party research, and results from quantitative models. A reasonable basis is formed through a balance of these resources appropriate for the security or decision being analyzed.

The following list provides some, but definitely not all, examples of attributes to consider while forming the basis for a recommendation:

- company's operating and financial history;
- current stage of the industry's business cycle;
- mutual fund's fee structure and management history;
- output and potential limitations of quantitative models;
- quality of the assets included in a securitization; and
- appropriateness of selected peer-group comparisons.

Even though an investment recommendation may be well-informed, downside risk remains for any investment. Members and candidates can base their decision only on the information available at the time the decision is made. The steps taken in developing a diligent and reasonable recommendation should minimize unexpected downside events.

Using Secondary or Third-Party Research

If members and candidates rely on secondary or third-party research, they must make reasonable and diligent efforts to determine whether such research is sound. Secondary research is defined as research conducted by someone else in the member's or candidate's firm. Third-party research is research conducted by entities outside the member's or candidate's firm, such as a brokerage firm, bank, or research firm. If a member or candidate has reason to suspect that either secondary or third-party research or information comes from a source that lacks a sound basis, the member or candidate must not rely on that information. Criteria that a member or candidate can use in forming an opinion on whether research is sound include the following:

- assumptions used;
- rigor of the analysis performed;
- date/timeliness of the research; and
- evaluation of the objectivity and independence of the recommendations.

A member or candidate may rely on others in his or her firm to determine whether secondary or third-party research is sound and use the information in good faith unless the member or candidate has reason to question its validity or the processes and procedures used by those responsible for the research. For example, a portfolio manager may not have a choice of a data source because the firm's senior managers conducted due diligence to determine which vendor would provide services; the member or candidate can use the information in good faith assuming the due diligence process was deemed adequate.

A member or candidate should verify that the firm has a policy about the timely and consistent review of approved research providers to ensure that the quality of the research continues to meet the necessary standards. If such a policy is not in place at the firm, the member or candidate should encourage the development and adoption of a formal review practice.

Quantitatively Oriented Research

Standard V(A) applies to the rapidly expanding use of quantitatively oriented research models, such as computer-generated screening and ranking of equity securities and the creation or valuation of derivative instruments. Models are being used for more than the back testing of investment strategies, and the continued development of models is an important part of capital market developments.

The importance and limitations of financial models became clear as the credit crisis unfolded in 2007 and 2008. In many cases the financial models used to value collateralized debt securities and related derivative products were poorly understood. Members and candidates need to have an understanding of the parameters used in the model or quantitative research. Although they are not required to become experts in the technical aspects of the models, they must be able to explain to their clients the importance of the quantitative research and how the results were used in the decision-making process.

Members and candidates need to consider the time horizon of the data used as inputs in financial models. The information from many commercially available databases may not effectively incorporate both positive and negative market cycles. In the development of a recommendation, the member or candidate may need to test the models by using volatility and performance expectations that represent scenarios outside the observable databases. In reviewing the computer models or the resulting output, members and candidates need to pay particular attention to the assumptions used in the analysis and the rigor of the analysis to ensure that the model incorporates negative market events.

Selecting External Advisers and Subadvisers

Financial instruments and asset allocation techniques continue to develop and evolve. This progression has led to the use of specialized managers to invest in specific asset classes or diversification strategies that complement a firm's in-house expertise. Standard V(A) applies to the level of review necessary in selecting an external adviser or subadviser.

Members and candidates need to ensure that their firms have standardized criteria for reviewing external advisers. Such criteria would include, but would not be limited to, the following:

- reviewing the adviser's established code of ethics;
- understanding the adviser's compliance and internal control procedures;
- assessing the quality of the published return information; and
- reviewing the adviser's adherence to its stated strategy.

CFA Institute published codes, standards, and guides to best practice provide members and candidates with examples of acceptable practices for external advisers and advice in selecting a new adviser. The following guides are available at the CFA Institute website (www.cfainstitute.org): Asset Manager Code of Professional Conduct, Global Investment Performance Standards, and Model Request for Proposal (for equity, credit, or real estate managers).

Group Research and Decision Making

Commonly, members and candidates are part of a group or team that is collectively responsible for producing investment analysis or research. The conclusions or recommendations of the group report represent the consensus of the group and are not necessarily the views of the member or candidate, even though the name of the member or candidate is included on the report. In some instances, the member or candidate will not agree with the view of the group. If, however, the member or candidate believes that the consensus opinion has a reasonable and adequate basis and is independent and objective, the member or candidate need not decline to be identified with the report. If the member or candidate is confident in the process, the member or candidate does not need to dissociate from the report even if it does not reflect his or her opinion.

Recommended Procedures for Compliance

Members and candidates should encourage their firms to consider the following policies and procedures to support the principles of Standard V(A):

■ Establish a policy requiring that research reports, credit ratings, and investment recommendations have a basis that can be substantiated as reasonable and adequate. An individual employee (a supervisory analyst) or a group of employees (a review committee) should be appointed to review and approve such items prior to external circulation to determine whether the criteria established in the policy have been met.

■ Develop detailed, written guidance for analysts (research, investment, or credit), supervisory analysts, and review committees that establishes the due diligence procedures for judging whether a particular recommendation has a reasonable and adequate basis.

■ Develop measurable criteria for assessing the quality of research, the reasonableness and adequacy of the basis for any recommendation or rating, and the accuracy of recommendations over time. In some cases, firms may consider implementing compensation arrangements that depend on these measurable criteria and that are applied consistently to all related analysts.

■ Develop detailed, written guidance that establishes minimum levels of scenario testing of all computer-based models used in developing, rating, and evaluating financial instruments. The policy should contain criteria related to the breadth of the scenarios tested, the accuracy of the output over time, and the analysis of cash flow sensitivity to inputs.

■ Develop measurable criteria for assessing outside providers, including the quality of information being provided, the reasonableness and adequacy of the provider's collection practices, and the accuracy of the information over time. The established policy should outline how often the provider's products are reviewed.

■ Adopt a standardized set of criteria for evaluating the adequacy of external advisers. The policy should include how often and on what basis the allocation of funds to the adviser will be reviewed.

Application of the Standard

Example 1   (Sufficient Due Diligence): Helen Hawke manages the corporate finance department of Sarkozi Securities, Ltd. The firm is anticipating that the government will soon close a tax loophole that currently allows oil-and-gas exploration companies to pass on drilling expenses to holders of a certain class of shares. Because market demand for this tax-advantaged class of stock is currently high, Sarkozi convinces several companies to undertake new equity financings at once before the loophole closes. Time is of the essence, but Sarkozi lacks sufficient resources to conduct adequate research on all the prospective issuing companies. Hawke decides to estimate the IPO prices on the basis of the relative size of each company and to justify the pricing later when her staff has time.

> *Comment*: Sarkozi should have taken on only the work that it could adequately handle. By categorizing the issuers by general size, Hawke has bypassed researching all the other relevant aspects that should be considered when pricing new issues and thus has not performed sufficient due diligence. Such an omission can result in investors purchasing shares at prices that have no actual basis. Hawke has violated Standard V(A).

Example 2 (Sufficient Scenario Testing): Babu Dhaliwal works for Heinrich Brokerage in the corporate finance group. He has just persuaded Feggans Resources, Ltd., to allow his firm to do a secondary equity financing at Feggans Resources' current stock price. Because the stock has been trading at higher multiples than similar companies with equivalent production, Dhaliwal presses the Feggans Resources managers to project what would be the maximum production they could achieve in an optimal scenario. Based on these numbers, he is able to justify the price his firm will be asking for the secondary issue. During a sales pitch to the brokers, Dhaliwal then uses these numbers as the base-case production levels that Feggans Resources will achieve.

> *Comment*: When presenting information to the brokers, Dhaliwal should have given a range of production scenarios and the probability of Feggans Resources achieving each level. By giving the maximum production level as the likely level of production, he has misrepresented the chances of achieving that production level and seriously misled the brokers. Dhaliwal has violated Standard V(A).

Example 3 (Developing a Reasonable Basis): Brendan Witt, a former junior sell-side technology analyst, decided to return to school to earn an MBA. To keep his research skills and industry knowledge sharp, Witt accepted a position with On-line and Informed, an independent internet-based research company. The position requires the publication of a recommendation and report on a different company every month. Initially, Witt is a regular contributor of new research and a participant in the associated discussion boards that generally have positive comments on the technology sector. Over time, his ability to manage his educational requirements and his work requirements begin to conflict with one another. Knowing a recommendation is due the next day for On-line, Witt creates a report based on a few news articles and what the conventional wisdom of the markets has deemed the "hot" security of the day.

> *Comment*: Witt's knowledge of and exuberance for technology stocks, a few news articles, and the conventional wisdom of the markets do not constitute, without more information, a reasonable and adequate basis for a stock recommendation that is supported by appropriate research and investigation. Therefore, Witt has violated Standard V(A).
>
> See also Standard IV(C)—Responsibilities of Supervisors as it relates to the firm's inadequate procedures.

Example 4 (Timely Client Updates): Kristen Chandler is an investment consultant in the London office of Dalton Securities, a major global investment consultant firm. One of her U.K. pension funds has decided to appoint a specialist U.S. equity manager. Dalton's global manager of research relies on local consultants to cover managers within their regions and, after conducting thorough due diligence, puts their views and ratings in Dalton's manager database. Chandler accesses Dalton's global manager research database and conducts a screen of all U.S. equity managers on the basis of a match with the client's desired philosophy/style, performance, and tracking-error targets. She selects the five managers that meet these criteria and puts them in a briefing report that is delivered to the client 10 days later. Between the time of Chandler's database search and the delivery of the report to the client, Chandler is told that Dalton has updated the database with the information that one of the firms that Chandler has recommended for consideration lost its chief investment officer, the head of its U.S. equity research, and the majority of its portfolio managers on the U.S. equity product—all of whom have left to establish their own firm. Chandler does not revise her report with this updated information.

> *Comment*: Chandler has failed to satisfy the requirement of Standard V(A). Although Dalton updated the manager ratings to reflect the personnel turnover at one of the firms, Chandler did not update her report to reflect the new information.

Example 5   (Group Research Opinions): Evelyn Mastakis is a junior analyst who has been asked by her firm to write a research report predicting the expected interest rate for residential mortgages over the next six months. Mastakis submits her report to the fixed-income investment committee of her firm for review, as required by firm procedures. Although some committee members support Mastakis's conclusion, the majority of the committee disagrees with her conclusion, and the report is significantly changed to indicate that interest rates are likely to increase more than originally predicted by Mastakis. Should Mastakis ask that her name be taken off the report when it is disseminated?

> *Comment*: The results of research are not always clear, and different people may have different opinions based on the same factual evidence. In this case, the committee may have valid reasons for issuing a report that differs from the analyst's original research. The firm can issue a report that is different from the original report of an analyst as long as there is a reasonable or adequate basis for its conclusions.
>
> Generally, analysts must write research reports that reflect their own opinion and can ask the firm not to put their name on reports that ultimately differ from that opinion. When the work is a group effort, however, not all members of the team may agree with all aspects of the report. Ultimately, members and candidates can ask to have their names removed from the report, but if they are satisfied that the process has produced results or conclusions that have a reasonable or adequate basis, members or candidates do not have to dissociate from the report even when they do not agree with its contents. If Mastakis is confident in the process, she does not need to dissociate from the report even if it does not reflect her opinion.

Example 6   (Reliance on Third-Party Research): Gary McDermott runs a two-person investment management firm. McDermott's firm subscribes to a service from a large investment research firm that provides research reports. McDermott's firm makes investment recommendations on the basis of these reports.

> *Comment*: Members and candidates can rely on third-party research but must make reasonable and diligent efforts to determine that such research is sound. If McDermott undertakes due diligence efforts on a regular basis to ensure that the research produced by the large firm is objective and reasonably based, McDermott can rely on that research when making investment recommendations to clients.

Example 7   (Due Diligence in Submanager Selection): Paul Ostrowski's business has grown significantly over the past couple of years, and some clients want to diversify internationally. Ostrowski decides to find a submanager to handle the expected international investments. Because this will be his first subadviser, Ostrowski uses the CFA Institute model "request for proposal" to design a questionnaire for his search. By his deadline, he receives seven completed questionnaires from a variety of domestic and international firms trying to gain his business. Ostrowski reviews all the applications in detail and decides to select the firm that charges the lowest fees because doing so will have the least impact on his firm's bottom line.

> *Comment:* The selection of an external adviser or subadviser should be based on a full and complete review of the advisers' services, performance history, and cost structure. In basing the decision on the fee structure alone, Ostrowski may be violating Standard V(A).
>
> See also Standard III(C)—Suitability as it relates to the ability of the selected adviser to meet the needs of the clients.

Example 8   (Sufficient Due Diligence): Michael Papis is the chief investment officer of his state's retirement fund. The fund has always used outside advisers for the real estate allocation, and this information is clearly presented in all fund communications. Thomas Nagle, a recognized sell-side research analyst and Papis's business school classmate, recently left the investment bank he worked for to start his own asset management firm, Accessible Real Estate. Nagle is trying to build his assets under management and contacts Papis about gaining some of the retirement fund's allocation. In the previous few years, the performance of the retirement fund's real estate investments was in line with the fund's benchmark but was not extraordinary. Papis decides to help out his old friend and also to seek better returns by moving the real estate allocation to Accessible. The only notice of the change in adviser appears in the next annual report in the listing of associated advisers.

> *Comment*: Papis violated Standard V(A) in this example. His responsibilities may include the selection of the external advisers, but the decision to change investers appears to have been arbitrary. If Papis was dissatisfied with the current real estate adviser, he should have conducted a proper solicitation to select the most appropriate adviser.
>
> See also Standard IV(C)—Responsibilities of Supervisors, Standard V(B)—Communication with Clients and Prospective Clients, and Standard VI(A)—Disclosure of Conflicts.

Example 9   (Sufficient Due Diligence): Andre Shrub owns and operates Conduit, an investment advisory firm. Prior to opening Conduit, Shrub was an account manager with Elite Investment, a hedge fund managed by his good friend Adam Reed. To attract clients to a new Conduit fund, Shrub offers lower-than-normal management fees. He can do so because the fund consists of two top-performing funds managed by Reed. Given his personal friendship with Reed and the prior performance record of these two funds, Shrub believes this new fund is a winning combination for all parties. Clients quickly invest with Conduit to gain access to the Elite funds. No one is turned away because Conduit is seeking to expand its assets under management.

> *Comment:* Shrub violated Standard V(A) by not conducting a thorough analysis of the funds managed by Reed before developing the new Conduit fund. Due diligence must be applied more deeply than review of a single security. It includes a review of outside managers and investment funds. Shrub's reliance on his personal relationship with Reed and his prior knowledge of Elite are insufficient justification for the investments. The funds may be appropriately considered, but a full review of their operating procedures, reporting practices, and transparency are some elements of the necessary due diligence.
>
> See also Standard III(C)—Suitability.

Example 10   (Sufficient Due Diligence): Bob Thompson has been doing research for the portfolio manager of the fixed-income department. His assignment is to do sensitivity analysis on securitized subprime mortgages. He has discussed with the manager possible scenarios to use to calculate expected returns. A key assumption in such calculations is housing price appreciation (HPA) because it drives "prepays" (prepayments of mortgages) and losses. Thompson is concerned with the significant appreciation experienced over the previous five years as a result of the increased availability of funds from subprime mortgages. Thompson insists that the analysis should include a scenario run with negative 10 percent for the first year, negative 5 percent for the second year, and then (to project a worst-case scenario) 0 percent for Years 3 through 5. The manager replies that these assumptions are too dire because there has never been a time in their available database when HPA was negative.

Thompson conducts his research to better understand the risks inherent in these securities and evaluates these securities in the worst-case scenario, an unlikely but possible environment. Based on the results of the enhanced scenarios, Thompson does not recommend the purchase of the securitization. Against the general market trends, the manager follows Thompson's recommendation and does not invest. The following year, the housing market collapses. In avoiding the subprime investments, the manager's portfolio outperforms its peer group that year.

> *Comment*: Thompson's actions in running the scenario test with inputs beyond the historical trends available in the firm's databases adheres to the principles of Standard V(A). His concerns over recent trends provide a sound basis for further analysis. Thompson understands the limitations of his model, when combined with the limited available historical information, to accurately predict the performance of the funds if market conditions change negatively.
> See also Standard I(B)—Independence and Objectivity.

Example 11   (Use of Quantitatively Oriented Models): Espacia Liakos works in sales for Hellenica Securities, a firm specializing in developing intricate derivative strategies to profit from particular views on market expectations. One of her clients is Eugenie Carapalis, who has become convinced that commodity prices will become more volatile over the coming months. Carapalis asks Liakos to quickly engineer a strategy that will benefit from this expectation. Liakos turns to Hellenica's modelling group to fulfil this request. Because of the tight deadline, the modelling group outsources parts of the work to several trusted third parties. Liakos implements the disparate components of the strategy as the firms complete them.

Within a month, Carapalis is proven correct: Volatility across a range of commodities increases sharply. But her derivatives position with Hellenica returns huge losses, and the losses increase daily. Liakos investigates and realizes that, although each of the various components of the strategy had been validated, they had never been evaluated as an integrated whole. In extreme conditions, portions of the model worked at cross-purposes with other portions, causing the overall strategy to fail dramatically.

> *Comment:* Liakos violated Standard V(A). Members and candidates must understand the statistical significance of the results of the models they recommend and must be able to explain them to clients. Liakos did not take adequate care to ensure a thorough review of the whole model; its components were evaluated only individually. Because Carapalis clearly intended to implement the strategy as a whole rather than as separate parts, Liakos should have tested how the components of the strategy interacted as well as how they performed individually.

Example 12   (Successful Due Diligence/Failed Investment): Alton Newbury is an investment adviser to high-net-worth clients. A client with an aggressive risk profile in his investment policy statement asks about investing in the Top Shelf hedge fund.

This fund, based in Calgary, Alberta, Canada, has reported 20 percent returns for the first three years. The fund prospectus states that its strategy involves long and short positions in the energy sector and extensive leverage. Based on his analysis of the fund's track record, the principals involved in managing the fund, the fees charged, and the fund's risk profile, Newbury recommends the fund to the client and secures a position in it. The next week, the fund announces that it has suffered a loss of 60 percent of its value and is suspending operations and redemptions until after a regulatory review. Newbury's client calls him in a panic and asks for an explanation.

> *Comment:* Newbury's actions were consistent with Standard V(A). Analysis of an investment that results in a reasonable basis for recommendation does not guarantee that the investment will have no downside risk. Newbury should discuss the analysis process with the client while reminding him or her that past performance does not lead to guaranteed future gains and that losses in an aggressive investment portfolio should be expected.

B. Communication with Clients and Prospective Clients

Members and Candidates must:

1. Disclose to clients and prospective clients the basic format and general principles of the investment processes they use to analyze investments, select securities, and construct portfolios and must promptly disclose any changes that might materially affect those processes.

2. Use reasonable judgment in identifying which factors are important to their investment analyses, recommendations, or actions and include those factors in communications with clients and prospective clients.

3. Distinguish between fact and opinion in the presentation of investment analyses and recommendations.

Guidance

Highlights:

- *Informing Clients of the Investment Process*
- *Different Forms of Communication*
- *Identifying Limitations of Analysis*
- *Distinction between Facts and Opinions in Reports*

Standard V(B) addresses member and candidate conduct with respect to communicating with clients. Developing and maintaining clear, frequent, and thorough communication practices is critical to providing high-quality financial services to clients. When clients understand the information communicated to them, they also can understand exactly how members and candidates are acting on their behalf, which gives clients the opportunity to make well-informed decisions about their investments. Such understanding can be accomplished only through clear communication.

Standard V(B) states that members and candidates should communicate in a recommendation the factors that were instrumental in making the investment recommendation. A critical part of this requirement is to distinguish clearly between opinions and facts. In preparing a research report, the member or candidate must present the basic characteristics of the security(ies) being analyzed, which will allow the reader to evaluate the report and incorporate information the reader deems relevant to his or her investment decision-making process.

Similarly, in preparing a recommendation about, for example, an asset allocation strategy, alternative investment vehicle, or structured investment product, the member or candidate should include factors that are relevant to whatever asset classes are being discussed. In all cases, the upside potential and downside risk expressed in terms of expected total returns should be among the factors communicated. Follow-on communication of any changes in the risk characteristics of a security or asset strategy would also be advisable.

Informing Clients of the Investment Process

Members and candidates must adequately describe to clients and prospective clients the manner in which the member or candidate conducts the investment decision-making process. The member or candidate must keep clients and other interested parties informed on an ongoing basis about changes to the investment process. Only by thoroughly understanding the nature of the investment product or service can a client determine whether changes to that product or service could materially affect his or her investment objectives.

Understanding the basic characteristics of an investment is of great importance in judging the suitability of that investment on a stand-alone basis, but it is especially important in determining the impact each investment will have on the characteristics of a portfolio. Although the risk and return characteristics of a common stock might seem to be essentially the same for any investor when the stock is viewed in isolation, the effects of those characteristics greatly depend on the other investments held. For instance, if the particular stock will represent 90 percent of an individual's investments, the stock's importance in the portfolio is vastly different from what it would be to an investor with a highly diversified portfolio for whom the stock will represent only 2 percent of the holdings.

A firm's investment policy may include the use of outside advisers to manage various portions of the clients' assets under management. Members and candidates should inform the clients about the specialization or diversification expertise provided by the external adviser(s). This information allows clients to understand the full mix of products and strategies being applied that may affect their investment objectives.

Different Forms of Communication

For purposes of Standard V(B), communication is not confined to a written report of the type traditionally generated by an analyst researching a security, company, or industry. A presentation of information can be made via any means of communication, including in-person recommendation or description, telephone conversation, media broadcast, or transmission by computer (e.g., on the internet). Furthermore, the nature of these communications is highly diverse—from one word ("buy" or "sell") to in-depth reports of more than 100 pages.

A communication may contain a general recommendation about the market, asset allocations, or classes of investments (e.g., stocks, bonds, real estate) or may relate to a specific security. If recommendations are contained in capsule form (such as a recommended stock list), members and candidates should notify clients that additional information and analyses are available from the producer of the report.

Identifying Limitations of Analysis

Investment advice based on quantitative research and analysis must be supported by readily available reference material and should be applied in a manner consistent with previously applied methodology; if changes in methodology are made, they should be highlighted. Members and candidates should outline known limitations of the analysis and conclusions contained in their investment advice. In evaluating the basic characteristics of the investment being recommended, members and candidates should consider in the report the potential total returns and the principal risks inherent in the expected returns, which may include credit risk, financial risk (specifically, the use of leverage or financial derivatives), and overall market risk.

Once the process has been completed, the member or candidate who prepares the report must include those elements that are important to the analysis and conclusions of the report so that the reader can follow and challenge the report's reasoning. A report writer who has done adequate investigation may emphasize certain areas, touch briefly on others, and omit certain aspects deemed unimportant. For instance, a report may dwell on a quarterly earnings release or new-product introduction and omit other matters as long as the analyst clearly stipulates the limits to the scope of the report.

Distinction between Facts and Opinions in Reports

Standard V(B) requires that opinion be separated from fact. Violations often occur when reports fail to separate the past from the future by not indicating that earnings estimates, changes in the outlook for dividends, and/or future market price information are *opinions* subject to future circumstances. In the case of complex quantitative analyses, analysts must clearly separate fact from statistical conjecture and should identify the known limitations of an analysis. Analysts may violate Standard V(B) by failing to identify the limits of statistically developed projections, because this omission leaves readers unaware of the limits of the published projections.

Recommended Procedures for Compliance

Because the selection of relevant factors is an analytical skill, determination of whether a member or candidate has used reasonable judgment in excluding and including information in research reports depends heavily on case-by-case review rather than a specific checklist. To assist in the after-the-fact review of a report, the member or candidate must maintain records indicating the nature of the research and should, if asked, be able to supply additional information to the client (or any user of the report) covering factors not included in the report.

Application of the Standard

Example 1   (Sufficient Disclosure of Investment System): Sarah Williamson, director of marketing for Country Technicians, Inc., is convinced that she has found the perfect formula for increasing Country Technician's income and diversifying its product base. Williamson plans to build on Country Technician's reputation as a leading money manager by marketing an exclusive and expensive investment advice letter to high-net-worth individuals. One hitch in the plan is the complexity of Country Technician's investment system—a combination of technical trading rules (based on historical price and volume fluctuations) and portfolio construction rules designed to minimize risk. To simplify the newsletter, she decides to include only each week's top-five "buy" and "sell" recommendations and to leave out details of the valuation models and the portfolio structuring scheme.

> *Comment*: Williamson's plans for the newsletter violate Standard V(B). Williamson need not describe the investment system in detail in order to implement the advice effectively, but she must inform clients of Country Technician's basic process and logic. Without understanding the basis for a recommendation, clients cannot possibly understand its limitations or its inherent risks.

Example 2   (Providing Opinions as Facts): Richard Dox is a mining analyst for East Bank Securities. He has just finished his report on Boisy Bay Minerals. Included in his report is his own assessment of the geological extent of mineral reserves likely to be found on the company's land. Dox completed this calculation on the basis of the core samples from the company's latest drilling. According to Dox's calculations, the company has more than 500,000 ounces of gold on the property. Dox concludes his research report as follows: "Based on the fact that the company has 500,000 ounces of gold to be mined, I recommend a strong BUY."

> *Comment*: If Dox issues the report as written, he will violate Standard V(B). His calculation of the total gold reserves for the property is an opinion, not a fact. Opinion must be distinguished from fact in research reports.

Example 3   (Proper Description of a Security): Olivia Thomas, an analyst at Government Brokers, Inc., which is a brokerage firm specializing in government bond trading, has produced a report that describes an investment strategy designed to benefit from an expected decline in U.S. interest rates. The firm's derivative products group has designed a structured product that will allow the firm's clients to benefit from this strategy. Thomas's report describing the strategy indicates that high returns are possible if various scenarios for declining interest rates are assumed. Citing the proprietary nature of the structured product underlying the strategy, the report does not describe in detail how the firm is able to offer such returns or the related risks in the scenarios, nor does the report address the likely returns of the strategy if, contrary to expectations, interest rates rise.

> *Comment*: Thomas has violated Standard V(B) because her report fails to describe properly the basic characteristics of the actual and implied risks of the investment strategy, including how the structure was created and the degree to which leverage was embedded in the structure. The report should include a balanced discussion of how the strategy would perform in the case of rising as well as falling interest rates, preferably illustrating how the strategies might be expected to perform in the event of a reasonable variety of interest rate and credit-risk-spread scenarios. If liquidity issues are relevant with regard to the valuation of either the derivatives or the underlying securities, provisions the firm has made to address those risks should also be disclosed.

Example 4   (Notification of Fund Mandate Change): May & Associates is an aggressive-growth manager that has represented itself since its inception as a specialist at investing in small-cap U.S. stocks. One of May's selection criteria is a maximum capitalization of US$250 million for any given company. After a string of successful years of superior performance relative to its peers, May has expanded its client base significantly, to the point at which assets under management now exceed $3 billion. For liquidity purposes, May's chief investment officer (CIO) decides to lift the maximum permissible market-cap ceiling to US$500 million and change the firm's sales and marketing literature accordingly to inform prospective clients and third-party consultants.

> *Comment*: Although May's CIO is correct about informing potentially interested parties as to the change in investment process, he must also notify May's existing clients. Among the latter group might be a number of clients who not only retained May as a small-cap manager but also retained midcap and large-cap specialists in a multiple-manager approach. Such clients could regard May's change of criteria as a style change that distorts their overall asset allocations.

Example 5 (Notification of Fund Mandate Change): Rather than lifting the ceiling for its universe from US$250 million to US$500 million, May & Associates extends its small-cap universe to include a number of non-U.S. companies.

> *Comment*: Standard V(B) requires that May's CIO advise May's clients of this change because the firm may have been retained by some clients specifically for its prowess at investing in U.S. small-cap stocks. Other changes that require client notification are introducing derivatives to emulate a certain market sector or relaxing various other constraints, such as portfolio beta. In all such cases, members and candidates must disclose changes to all interested parties.

Example 6 (Notification of Changes to the Investment Process): RJZ Capital Management is an active value-style equity manager that selects stocks by using a combination of four multifactor models. The firm has found favorable results when back testing the most recent 10 years of available market data in a new dividend discount model (DDM) designed by the firm. This model is based on projected inflation rates, earnings growth rates, and interest rates. The president of RJZ decides to replace its simple model that uses price to trailing 12-months earnings with the new DDM.

> *Comment*: Because the introduction of a new and different valuation model represents a material change in the investment process, RJZ's president must communicate the change to the firm's clients. RJZ is moving away from a model based on hard data toward a new model that is at least partly dependent on the firm's forecasting skills. Clients would likely view such a model as a significant change rather than a mere refinement of RJZ's process.

Example 7 (Notification of Changes to the Investment Process): RJZ Capital Management loses the chief architect of its multifactor valuation system. Without informing its clients, the president of RJZ decides to redirect the firm's talents and resources toward developing a product for passive equity management—a product that will emulate the performance of a major market index.

> *Comment*: By failing to disclose to clients a substantial change to its investment process, the president of RJZ has violated Standard V(B).

Example 8 (Notification of Changes to the Investment Process): At Fundamental Asset Management, Inc., the responsibility for selecting stocks for addition to the firm's "approved" list has just shifted from individual security analysts to a committee consisting of the research director and three senior portfolio managers. Eleanor Morales, a portfolio manager with Fundamental Asset Management, thinks this change is not important enough to communicate to her clients.

> *Comment*: Morales must disclose the process change to all her clients. Some of Fundamental's clients might be concerned about the morale and motivation among the firm's best research analysts after such a change. Moreover, clients might challenge the stock-picking track record of the portfolio managers and might even want to monitor the situation closely.

Example 9 (Sufficient Disclosure of Investment System): Amanda Chinn is the investment director for Diversified Asset Management, which manages the endowment of a charitable organization. Because of recent staff departures, Diversified has decided to limit its direct investment focus to large-cap securities and supplement the needs for small-cap and midcap management by hiring outside fund managers. In describing the planned strategy change to the charity, Chinn's update letter states,

"As investment director, I will directly oversee the investment team managing the endowment's large-capitalization allocation. I will coordinate the selection and ongoing review of external managers responsible for allocations to other classes." The letter also describes the reasons for the change and the characteristics external managers must have to be considered.

> *Comment*: Standard V(B) requires the disclosure of the investment process used to construct the portfolio of the fund. Changing the investment process from managing all classes of investments within the firm to the use of external managers is one example of information that needs to be communicated to clients. Chinn and her firm have embraced the principles of Standard V(B) by providing their client with relevant information. The charity can now make a reasonable decision about whether Diversified Asset Management remains the appropriate manager for its fund.

Example 10   (Notification of Changes to the Investment Process): Michael Papis is the chief investment officer of his state's retirement fund. The fund has always used outside advisers for the real estate allocation, and this information is clearly presented in all fund communications. Thomas Nagle, a recognized sell-side research analyst and Papis's business school classmate, recently left the investment bank he worked for to start his own asset management firm, Accessible Real Estate. Nagle is trying to build his assets under management and contacts Papis about gaining some of the retirement fund's allocation. In the previous few years, the performance of the retirement fund's real estate investments was in line with the fund's benchmark but was not extraordinary. Papis decides to help out his old friend and also to seek better returns by moving the real estate allocation to Accessible. The only notice of the change in adviser appears in the next annual report in the listing of associated advisers.

> *Comment*: Papis has violated Standard V(B). He attempted to hide the nature of his decision to change external managers by making only a limited disclosure. The plan recipients and the fund's trustees need to be aware when changes are made to ensure that operational procedures are being followed.
>
>   See also Standard IV(C)—Responsibilities of Supervisors, Standard V(A)—Diligence and Reasonable Basis, and Standard VI(A)—Disclosure of Conflicts.

C. Record Retention

Members and Candidates must develop and maintain appropriate records to support their investment analyses, recommendations, actions, and other investment-related communications with clients and prospective clients.

Guidance

Highlights:

- *Records Are Property of the Firm*
- *Local Requirements*

Members and candidates must retain records that substantiate the scope of their research and reasons for their actions or conclusions. Which records are required to support recommendations and/or investment actions depends on the role of the member or candidate in the investment decision-making process. Records may be maintained either in hard copy or electronic form.

Some examples of supporting documentation that assists the member or candidate in meeting the requirements for retention are as follows:

- personal notes from meetings with the covered company;
- press releases or presentations issued by the covered company;
- computer-based model outputs and analyses;
- computer-based model input parameters;
- risk analyses of securities' impacts on a portfolio;
- selection criteria for external advisers;
- notes from clients from meetings to review investment policy statements;
- outside research reports.

Records Are Property of the Firm

As a general matter, records created as part of a member's or candidate's professional activity on behalf of his or her employer are the property of the firm. When a member or candidate leaves a firm to seek other employment, the member or candidate cannot take the property of the firm, including originals or copies of supporting records of the member's or candidate's work, to the new employer without the express consent of the previous employer. The member or candidate cannot use historical recommendations or research reports created at the previous firm because the supporting documentation is unavailable. For future use, the member or candidate must re-create the supporting records at the new firm with information gathered through public sources or directly from the covered company and not from memory or sources obtained at the previous employer.

Local Requirements

Local regulators often impose requirements on members, candidates, and their firms related to record retention that must be followed. Fulfilling such regulatory requirements also may satisfy the requirements of Standard V(C), but members and candidates should explicitly determine whether it does. In the absence of regulatory guidance, CFA Institute recommends maintaining records for at least seven years.

Recommended Procedures for Compliance

The responsibility to maintain records that support investment action generally falls with the firm rather than individuals. Members and candidates must, however, archive research notes and other documents, either electronically or in hard copy, that support their current investment-related communications. Doing so will assist their firms in complying with requirements for preservation of internal or external records.

Application of the Standard

Example 1　(Record Retention and IPS Objectives and Recommendations): One of Nikolas Lindstrom's clients is upset by the negative investment returns in his equity portfolio. The investment policy statement for the client requires that the portfolio manager follow a benchmark-oriented approach. The benchmark for the client includes a 35 percent investment allocation in the technology sector. The client acknowledges that this allocation was appropriate, but over the past three years, technology stocks have suffered severe losses. The client complains to the investment manager that so much money was allocated to this sector.

> *Comment*: For Lindstrom, having appropriate records is important to show that over the past three years the percentage of technology stocks in the

benchmark index was 35 percent as called for in the IPS. Lindstrom should also have the IPS for the client stating that the benchmark was appropriate for the client's investment objectives. He should also have records indicating that the investment has been explained appropriately to the client and that the IPS was updated on a regular basis. Taking these actions, Lindstrom would be in compliance with Standard V(C).

Example 2   (Record Retention and Research Process): Malcolm Young is a research analyst who writes numerous reports rating companies in the luxury retail industry. His reports are based on a variety of sources, including interviews with company managers, manufacturers, and economists; onsite company visits; customer surveys; and secondary research from analysts covering related industries.

> *Comment*: Young must carefully document and keep copies of all the information that goes into his reports, including the secondary or third-party research of other analysts. Failure to maintain such files would violate Standard V(C).

Example 3   (Records as Firm, Not Employee, Property): Martin Blank develops an analytical model while he is employed by Grosse Point Investment Management, LLP (GPIM). While at the firm, he systematically documents the assumptions that make up the model as well as his reasoning behind the assumptions. As a result of the success of his model, Blank is hired to be the head of the research department of one of GPIM's competitors. Blank takes copies of the records supporting his model to his new firm.

> *Comment*: The records created by Blank supporting the research model he developed at GPIM are the records of GPIM. Taking the documents with him to his new employer without GPIM's permission violates Standard V(C). To use the model in the future, Blank must re-create the records supporting his model at the new firm.

STANDARD VI—CONFLICTS OF INTEREST

A. Disclosure of Conflicts

Members and Candidates must make full and fair disclosure of all matters that could reasonably be expected to impair their independence and objectivity or interfere with respective duties to their clients, prospective clients, and employer. Members and Candidates must ensure that such disclosures are prominent, are delivered in plain language, and communicate the relevant information effectively.

Guidance

Highlights:

- *Disclosure of Conflicts to Employers*
- *Disclosure to Clients*
- *Cross-Departmental Conflicts*
- *Conflicts with Stock Ownership*
- *Conflicts as a Director*

Best practice is to avoid actual conflicts or the appearance of conflicts of interest when possible. Conflicts of interest often arise in the investment profession. Conflicts can occur between the interests of clients, the interests of employers, and the member's or candidate's own personal interests. Common sources for conflict are compensation structures, especially incentive and bonus structures that provide immediate returns for members and candidates with little or no consideration of long-term value creation.

Identifying and managing these conflicts is a critical part of working in the investment industry and can take many forms. When conflicts cannot be reasonably avoided, clear and complete disclosure of their existence is necessary.

Standard VI(A) protects investors and employers by requiring members and candidates to fully disclose to clients, potential clients, and employers all actual and potential conflicts of interest. Once a member or candidate has made full disclosure, the member's or candidate's employer, clients, and prospective clients will have the information needed to evaluate the objectivity of the investment advice or action taken on their behalf.

To be effective, disclosures must be prominent and must be made in plain language and in a manner designed to effectively communicate the information. Members and candidates have the responsibility of determining how often, in what manner, and in what particular circumstances the disclosure of conflicts must be made. Best practices dictate updating disclosures when the nature of a conflict of interest changes materially—for example, if the nature of a conflict of interest deepens through the introduction of bonuses based on each quarter's profits as opposed to the previous review based on annual profits. In making and updating disclosures of conflicts of interest, members and candidates should err on the side of caution to ensure that conflicts are effectively communicated.

Disclosure of Conflicts to Employers

Disclosure of conflicts to employers may be appropriate in many instances. When reporting conflicts of interest to employers, members and candidates should give their employers enough information to assess the impact of the conflict. By complying with employer guidelines, members and candidates allow their employers to avoid potentially embarrassing and costly ethical or regulatory violations.

Reportable situations include conflicts that would interfere with rendering unbiased investment advice and conflicts that would cause a member or candidate to act not in the employer's best interest. The same circumstances that generate conflicts to be reported to clients and prospective clients also would dictate reporting to employers. Ownership of stocks analyzed or recommended, participation on outside boards, and financial or other pressures that could influence a decision are to be promptly reported to the employer so that their impact can be assessed and a decision made on how to resolve the conflict.

The mere appearance of a conflict of interest may create problems for members, candidates, and their employers. Therefore, many of the conflicts previously mentioned could be explicitly prohibited by an employer. For example, many employers restrict personal trading, outside board membership, and related activities to prevent situations that might not normally be considered problematic from a conflict-of-interest point of view but that could give the appearance of a conflict of interest. Members and candidates must comply with these restrictions. Members and candidates must take reasonable steps to avoid conflicts and, if they occur inadvertently, must report them promptly so that the employer and the member or candidate can resolve them as quickly and effectively as possible.

Standard VI(A) also deals with a member's or candidate's conflicts of interest that might be detrimental to the employer's business. Any potential conflict situation that could prevent clear judgment about or full commitment to the execution of the member's or candidate's duties to the employer should be reported to the member's or candidate's employer and promptly resolved.

Disclosure to Clients

Members and candidates must maintain their objectivity when rendering investment advice or taking investment action. Investment advice or actions may be perceived to be tainted in numerous situations. Can a member or candidate remain objective if, on behalf of the firm, the member or candidate obtains or assists in obtaining fees for services? Can a member or candidate give objective advice if he or she owns stock in the company that is the subject of an investment recommendation or if the member or candidate has a close personal relationship with the company managers? Requiring members and candidates to disclose all matters that reasonably could be expected to impair the member's or candidate's objectivity allows clients and prospective clients to judge motives and possible biases for themselves.

Often in the investment industry, a conflict, or the perception of a conflict, cannot be avoided. The most obvious conflicts of interest, which should always be disclosed, are relationships between an issuer and the member, candidate, or their firm (such as a directorship or consultancy by a member; investment banking, underwriting, and financial relationships; broker/dealer market-making activities; and material beneficial ownership of stock). For the purposes of Standard VI(A), members and candidates beneficially own securities or other investments if they have a direct or indirect pecuniary interest in the securities; have the power to vote or direct the voting of the shares of the securities or investments; or have the power to dispose or direct the disposition of the security or investment.

A member or candidate must take reasonable steps to determine whether a conflict of interest exists and disclose to clients any known conflicts of the member's or candidate's firm. Disclosure of broker/dealer market-making activities alerts clients that a purchase or sale might be made from or to the firm's principal account and that the firm has a special interest in the price of the stock.

Additionally, disclosures should be made to clients of fee arrangements, subadvisory agreements, or other situations involving nonstandard fee structures. Equally important is the disclosure of arrangements in which the firm benefits directly from investment recommendations. An obvious conflict of interest is the rebate of a portion of the service fee some classes of mutual funds charge to investors. Members and candidates should ensure that their firms disclose such relationships so clients can fully understand the costs of their investments and the benefits received by their investment manager's employer.

Cross-Departmental Conflicts

Other circumstances can give rise to actual or potential conflicts of interest. For instance, a sell-side analyst working for a broker/dealer may be encouraged, not only by members of her or his own firm but by corporate issuers themselves, to write research reports about particular companies. The buy-side analyst is likely to be faced with similar conflicts as banks exercise their underwriting and security-dealing powers. The marketing division may ask an analyst to recommend the stock of a certain company in order to obtain business from that company.

The potential for conflicts of interest also exists with broker-sponsored limited partnerships formed to invest venture capital. Increasingly, members and candidates are expected not only to follow issues from these partnerships once they are offered to the public but also to promote the issues in the secondary market after public offerings. Members, candidates, and their firms should attempt to resolve situations presenting potential conflicts of interest or disclose them in accordance with the principles set forth in Standard VI(A).

Conflicts with Stock Ownership

The most prevalent conflict requiring disclosure under Standard VI(A) is a member's or candidate's ownership of stock in companies that he or she recommends to clients and/or that clients hold. Clearly, the easiest method for preventing a conflict is to prohibit members and candidates from owning any such securities, but this approach is overly burdensome and discriminates against members and candidates.

Therefore, sell-side members and candidates should disclose any materially beneficial ownership interest in a security or other investment that the member or candidate is recommending. Buy-side members and candidates should disclose their procedures for reporting requirements for personal transactions. Conflicts arising from personal investing are discussed more fully in the guidance for Standard VI(B).

Conflicts as a Director

Service as a director poses three basic conflicts of interest. First, a conflict may exist between the duties owed to clients and the duties owed to shareholders of the company. Second, investment personnel who serve as directors may receive the securities or options to purchase securities of the company as compensation for serving on the board, which could raise questions about trading actions that might increase the value of those securities. Third, board service creates the opportunity to receive material nonpublic information involving the company. Even though the information is confidential, the perception could be that information not available to the public is being communicated to a director's firm—whether a broker, investment adviser, or other type of organization. When members or candidates providing investment services also serve as directors, they should be isolated from those making investment decisions by the use of firewalls or similar restrictions.

Recommended Procedures for Compliance

Members or candidates should disclose special compensation arrangements with the employer that might conflict with client interests, such as bonuses based on short-term performance criteria, commissions, incentive fees, performance fees, and referral fees. If the member's or candidate's firm does not permit such disclosure, the member or candidate should document the request and may consider dissociating from the activity.

Members' and candidates' firms are encouraged to include information on compensation packages in firms' promotional literature. If a member or candidate manages a portfolio for which the fee is based on capital gains or capital appreciation (a performance fee), this information should be disclosed to clients. If a member, candidate, or a member's or candidate's firm has outstanding agent options to buy stock as part of the compensation package for corporate financing activities, the amount and expiration date of these options should be disclosed as a footnote to any research report published by the member's or candidate's firm.

Application of the Standard

Example 1   (Conflict of Interest and Business Relationships): Hunter Weiss is a research analyst with Farmington Company, a broker and investment banking firm. Farmington's merger and acquisition department has represented Vimco, a conglomerate, in all of Vimco's acquisitions for 20 years. From time to time, Farmington officers sit on the boards of directors of various Vimco subsidiaries. Weiss is writing a research report on Vimco.

> *Comment*: Weiss must disclose in his research report Farmington's special relationship with Vimco. Broker/dealer management of and participation

in public offerings must be disclosed in research reports. Because the position of underwriter to a company entails a special past and potential future relationship with a company that is the subject of investment advice, it threatens the independence and objectivity of the report writer and must be disclosed.

Example 2   (Conflict of Interest and Business Stock Ownership): The investment management firm of Dover & Roe sells a 25 percent interest in its partnership to a multinational bank holding company, First of New York. Immediately after the sale, Margaret Hobbs, president of Dover & Roe, changes her recommendation for First of New York's common stock from "sell" to "buy" and adds First of New York's commercial paper to Dover & Roe's approved list for purchase.

> *Comment*: Hobbs must disclose the new relationship with First of New York to all Dover & Roe clients. This relationship must also be disclosed to clients by the firm's portfolio managers when they make specific investment recommendations or take investment actions with respect to First of New York's securities.

Example 3   (Conflict of Interest and Personal Stock Ownership): Carl Fargmon, a research analyst who follows firms producing office equipment, has been recommending purchase of Kincaid Printing because of its innovative new line of copiers. After his initial report on the company, Fargmon's wife inherits from a distant relative US$3 million of Kincaid stock. He has been asked to write a follow-up report on Kincaid.

> *Comment*: Fargmon must disclose his wife's ownership of the Kincaid stock to his employer and in his follow-up report. Best practice would be to avoid the conflict by asking his employer to assign another analyst to draft the follow-up report.

Example 4   (Conflict of Interest and Personal Stock Ownership): Betty Roberts is speculating in penny stocks for her own account and purchases 100,000 shares of Drew Mining, Inc., for 30 cents a share. She intends to sell these shares at the sign of any substantial upward price movement of the stock. A week later, her employer asks her to write a report on penny stocks in the mining industry to be published in two weeks. Even without owning the Drew stock, Roberts would recommend it in her report as a "buy." A surge in the price of the stock to the US$2 range is likely to result once the report is issued.

> *Comment*: Although this holding may not be material, Roberts must disclose it in the report and to her employer before writing the report because the gain for her will be substantial if the market responds strongly to her recommendation. The fact that she has only recently purchased the stock adds to the appearance that she is not entirely objective.

Example 5   (Conflict of Interest and Compensation Arrangement): Samantha Snead, a portfolio manager for Thomas Investment Counsel, Inc., specializes in managing public retirement funds and defined-benefit pension plan accounts, all of which have long-term investment objectives. A year ago, Snead's employer, in an attempt to motivate and retain key investment professionals, introduced a bonus compensation system that rewards portfolio managers on the basis of quarterly performance relative to their peers and to certain benchmark indices. In an attempt to improve the short-term performance of her accounts, Snead changes her investment strategy and purchases several high-beta stocks for client portfolios. These purchases are seemingly contrary to the clients' investment policy statements. Following their purchase, an officer of Griffin Corporation, one of Snead's pension fund clients, asks why Griffin

Corporation's portfolio seems to be dominated by high-beta stocks of companies that often appear among the most actively traded issues. No change in objective or strategy has been recommended by Snead during the year.

> *Comment*: Snead has violated Standard VI(A) by failing to inform her clients of the changes in her compensation arrangement with her employer, which created a conflict of interest between her compensation and her clients' IPS. Firms may pay employees on the basis of performance, but pressure by Thomas Investment Counsel to achieve short-term performance goals is in basic conflict with the objectives of Snead's accounts.
>
> See also Standard III(C)—Suitability.

Example 6 (Conflict of Interest and Options and Compensation Arrangements): Wayland Securities works with small companies doing IPOs and/or secondary offerings. Typically, these deals are in the US$10 million to US$50 million range, and as a result, the corporate finance fees are quite small. To compensate for the small fees, Wayland Securities usually takes "agents options"—that is, rights (exercisable within a two-year time frame) to acquire up to an additional 10 percent of the current offering. Following an IPO performed by Wayland for Falk Resources, Ltd., Darcy Hunter, the head of corporate finance at Wayland, is concerned about receiving value for her Falk Resources options. The options are one month from expiring, and the stock is not doing well. She contacts John Fitzpatrick in the research department of Wayland Securities, reminds him that he is eligible for 30 percent of these options, and indicates that now would be a good time to give some additional coverage to Falk Resources. Fitzpatrick agrees and immediately issues a favorable report.

> *Comment*: For Fitzpatrick to avoid being in violation of Standard VI(A), he must indicate in the report the volume and expiration date of agent options outstanding. Furthermore, because he is personally eligible for some of the options, Fitzpatrick must disclose the extent of this compensation. He also must be careful that he does not violate his duty of independence and objectivity under Standard I(B).

Example 7 (Conflict of Interest and Compensation Arrangements): Gary Carter is a representative with Bengal International, a registered broker/dealer. Carter is approached by a stock promoter for Badger Company, who offers to pay Carter additional compensation for sales of Badger Company's stock to Carter's clients. Carter accepts the stock promoter's offer but does not disclose the arrangements to his clients or to his employer. Carter sells shares of the stock to his clients.

> *Comment*: Carter has violated Standard VI(A) by failing to disclose to clients that he is receiving additional compensation for recommending and selling Badger stock. Because he did not disclose the arrangement with Badger to his clients, the clients were unable to evaluate whether Carter's recommendations to buy Badger were affected by this arrangement. Carter's conduct also violated Standard VI(A) by failing to disclose to his employer monetary compensation received in addition to the compensation and benefits conferred by his employer. Carter was required by Standard VI(A) to disclose the arrangement with Badger to his employer so that his employer could evaluate whether the arrangement affected Carter's objectivity and loyalty.

Example 8 (Conflict of Interest and Directorship): Carol Corky, a senior portfolio manager for Universal Management, recently became involved as a trustee with the Chelsea Foundation, a large not-for-profit foundation in her hometown. Universal is a small money manager (with assets under management of approximately

US$100 million) that caters to individual investors. Chelsea has assets in excess of US$2 billion. Corky does not believe informing Universal of her involvement with Chelsea is necessary.

> *Comment*: By failing to inform Universal of her involvement with Chelsea, Corky violated Standard VI(A). Given the large size of the endowment at Chelsea, Corky's new role as a trustee can reasonably be expected to be time-consuming, to the possible detriment of Corky's portfolio responsibilities with Universal. Also, as a trustee, Corky may become involved in the investment decisions at Chelsea. Therefore, Standard VI(A) obligates Corky to discuss becoming a trustee at Chelsea with her compliance officer or supervisor at Universal before accepting the position, and she should have disclosed the degree to which she would be involved in investment decisions at Chelsea.

Example 9   (Conflict of Interest and Personal Trading): Bruce Smith covers East European equities for Marlborough Investments, an investment management firm with a strong presence in emerging markets. While on a business trip to Russia, Smith learns that investing in Russian equity directly is difficult but that equity-linked notes that replicate the performance of the underlying Russian equity can be purchased from a New York–based investment bank. Believing that his firm would not be interested in such a security, Smith purchases a note linked to a Russian telecommunications company for his own account without informing Marlborough. A month later, Smith decides that the firm should consider investing in Russian equities by way of the equity-linked notes. He prepares a write-up on the market that concludes with a recommendation to purchase several of the notes. One note he recommends is linked to the same Russian telecom company that Smith holds in his personal account.

> *Comment*: Smith has violated Standard VI(A) by failing to disclose his purchase and ownership of the note linked to the Russian telecom company. Smith is required by the standard to disclose the investment opportunity to his employer and look to his company's policies on personal trading to determine whether it was proper for him to purchase the note for his own account. By purchasing the note, Smith may or may not have impaired his ability to make an unbiased and objective assessment of the appropriateness of the derivative instrument for his firm, but Smith's failure to disclose the purchase to his employer impaired his employer's ability to decide whether his ownership of the security is a conflict of interest that might affect Smith's future recommendations. Then, when he recommended the particular telecom notes to his firm, Smith compounded his problems by not disclosing that he owned the notes in his personal account—a clear conflict of interest.

Example 10   (Conflict of Interest and Requested Favors): Michael Papis is the chief investment officer of his state's retirement fund. The fund has always used outside advisers for the real estate allocation, and this information is clearly presented in all fund communications. Thomas Nagle, a recognized sell-side research analyst and Papis's business school classmate, recently left the investment bank he worked for to start his own asset management firm, Accessible Real Estate. Nagle is trying to build his assets under management and contacts Papis about gaining some of the retirement fund's allocation. In the previous few years, the performance of the retirement fund's real estate investments was in line with the fund's benchmark but was not extraordinary. Papis decides to help out his old friend and also to seek better returns by moving the real estate allocation to Accessible. The only notice of the change in adviser appears in the next annual report in the listing of associated advisers.

Comment: Papis has violated Standard VI(A) by not disclosing to his employer his personal relationship with Nagle. Disclosure of his past history with Nagle would allow his firm to determine whether the conflict may have impaired Papis's independence in deciding to change managers.

See also Standard IV(C)—Responsibilities of Supervisors, Standard V(A)—Diligence and Reasonable Basis, and Standard V(B)—Communication with Clients and Prospective Clients.

Example 11 (Conflict of Interest and Business Relationships): Bob Wade, trust manager for Central Midas Bank, was approached by Western Funds about promoting its family of funds, with special interest in the service-fee class. To entice Central to promote this class, Western Funds offered to pay the bank a service fee of 0.25 percent. Without disclosing the fee being offered to the bank, Wade asked one of the investment managers to review the Western Funds family of funds to determine whether they were suitable for clients of Central. The manager completed the normal due diligence review and determined that the funds were fairly valued in the market with fee structures on a par with their competitors. Wade decided to accept Western's offer and instructed the team of portfolio managers to exclusively promote these funds and the service-fee class to clients seeking to invest new funds or transfer from their current investments. So as to not influence the investment managers, Wade did not disclose the fee offer and allowed that income to flow directly to the bank.

Comment: Wade is violating Standard VI(A) by not disclosing the portion of the service fee being paid to Central. Although the investment managers may not be influenced by the fee, neither they nor the client have the proper information about Wade's decision to exclusively market this fund family and class of investments. Central may come to rely on the new fee as a component of the firm's profitability and may be unwilling to offer other products in the future that could affect the fees received.

See also Standard I(B)—Independence and Objectivity.

B. Priority of Transactions

Investment transactions for clients and employers must have priority over investment transactions in which a Member or Candidate is the beneficial owner.

Guidance

Highlights:

■ *Avoiding Potential Conflicts*
■ *Personal Trading Secondary to Trading for Clients*
■ *Standards for Nonpublic Information*
■ *Impact on All Accounts with Beneficial Ownership*

Standard VI(B) reinforces the responsibility of members and candidates to give the interests of their clients and employers priority over their personal financial interests. This standard is designed to prevent any potential conflict of interest or the appearance of a conflict of interest with respect to personal transactions. Client interests have priority. Client transactions must take precedence over transactions made on behalf of the member's or candidate's firm or personal transactions.

Avoiding Potential Conflicts

Conflicts between the client's interest and an investment professional's personal interest may occur. Although conflicts of interest exist, nothing is inherently unethical about individual managers, advisers, or mutual fund employees making money from personal investments as long as 1) the client is not disadvantaged by the trade, 2) the investment professional does not benefit personally from trades undertaken for clients, and 3) the investment professional complies with applicable regulatory requirements.

Some situations occur where a member or candidate may need to enter a personal transaction that runs counter to current recommendations or what the portfolio manager is doing for client portfolios. For example, a member or candidate may be required at some point to sell an asset to make a college tuition payment or a down payment on a home, to meet a margin call, or so on. The sale may be contrary to the long-term advice the member or candidate is currently providing to clients. In these situations, the same three criteria given in the preceding paragraph should be applied in the transaction so as to not violate Standard VI(B).

Personal Trading Secondary to Trading for Clients

Standard VI(B) states that transactions for clients and employers must have priority over transactions in securities or other investments of which a member or candidate is the beneficial owner. The objective of the standard is to prevent personal transactions from adversely affecting the interests of clients or employers. A member or candidate having the same investment positions or being co-invested with clients does not always create a conflict. Some clients in certain investment situations require members or candidates to have aligned interests. Personal investment positions or transactions of members or candidates or their firm should never, however, adversely affect client investments.

Standards for Nonpublic Information

Standard VI(B) covers the activities of members and candidates who have knowledge of pending transactions that may be made on behalf of their clients or employers, who have access to nonpublic information during the normal preparation of research recommendations, or who take investment actions. Members and candidates are prohibited from conveying nonpublic information to any person whose relationship to the member or candidate makes the member or candidate a beneficial owner of the person's securities. Members and candidates must not convey this information to any other person if the nonpublic information can be deemed material.

Impact on All Accounts with Beneficial Ownership

Members or candidates may undertake transactions in accounts for which they are a beneficial owner only after their clients and employers have had adequate opportunity to act on a recommendation. Personal transactions include those made for the member's or candidate's own account, for family (including spouse, children, and other immediate family members) accounts, and for accounts in which the member or candidate has a direct or indirect pecuniary interest, such as a trust or retirement account. Family accounts that are client accounts should be treated like any other firm account and should neither be given special treatment nor be disadvantaged because of the family relationship. If a member or candidate has a beneficial ownership in the account, however, the member or candidate may be subject to preclearance or reporting requirements of the employer or applicable law.

Recommended Procedures for Compliance

Policies and procedures designed to prevent potential conflicts of interest, and even the appearance of a conflict of interest, with respect to personal transactions are critical to establishing investor confidence in the securities industry. Therefore, members and candidates should urge their firms to establish such policies and procedures. Because investment firms vary greatly in assets under management, types of clients, number of employees, and so on, each firm should have policies regarding personal investing that are best suited to the firm. Members and candidates should then prominently disclose these policies to clients and prospective clients.

The specific provisions of each firm's standards will vary, but all firms should adopt certain basic procedures to address the conflict areas created by personal investing. These procedures include the following:

- *Limited participation in equity IPOs*: Some eagerly awaited IPOs rise significantly in value shortly after the issue is brought to market. Because the new issue may be highly attractive and sought after, the opportunity to participate in the IPO may be limited. Therefore, purchases of IPOs by investment personnel create conflicts of interest in two principal ways. First, participation in an IPO may have the appearance of taking away an attractive investment opportunity from clients for personal gain—a clear breach of the duty of loyalty to clients. Second, personal purchases in IPOs may have the appearance that the investment opportunity is being bestowed as an incentive to make future investment decisions for the benefit of the party providing the opportunity. Members and candidates can avoid these conflicts or appearances of conflicts of interest by not participating in IPOs.

  Reliable and systematic review procedures should be established to ensure that conflicts relating to IPOs are identified and appropriately dealt with by supervisors. Members and candidates should preclear their participation in IPOs, even in situations without any conflict of interest between a member's or candidate's participation in an IPO and the client's interests. Members and candidates should not benefit from the position that their clients occupy in the marketplace—through preferred trading, the allocation of limited offerings, and/or oversubscription.

- *Restrictions on private placements*: Strict limits should be placed on investment personnel acquiring securities in private placements, and appropriate supervisory and review procedures should be established to prevent noncompliance.

  Firms do not routinely use private placements for clients (e.g., venture capital deals) because of the high risk associated with them. Conflicts related to private placements are more significant to members and candidates who manage large pools of assets or act as plan sponsors because these managers may be offered special opportunities, such as private placements, as a reward or an enticement for continuing to do business with a particular broker.

  Participation in private placements raises conflict-of-interest issues that are similar to issues surrounding IPOs. Investment personnel should not be involved in transactions, including (but not limited to) private placements that could be perceived as favors or gifts that seem designed to influence future judgment or to reward past business deals.

  Whether the venture eventually proves to be good or bad, managers have an immediate conflict concerning private placement opportunities. If and when the investments go public, participants in private placements have an incentive to recommend the investments to clients regardless of the suitability of the investments for their clients. Doing so increases the value of the participants' personal portfolios.

- *Establish blackout/restricted periods*: Investment personnel involved in the investment decision-making process should establish blackout periods prior to trades for clients so that managers cannot take advantage of their knowledge of client activity by "front-running" client trades (trading for one's personal account before trading for client accounts).

Individual firms must decide who within the firm should be required to comply with the trading restrictions. At a minimum, all individuals who are involved in the investment decision-making process should be subject to the same restricted period. Each firm must determine specific requirements related to blackout and restricted periods that are most relevant to the firm while ensuring that the procedures are governed by the guiding principles set forth in the Code and Standards. Size of firm and type of securities purchased are relevant factors. For example, in a large firm, a blackout requirement is, in effect, a total trading ban because the firm is continually trading in most securities. In a small firm, the blackout period is more likely to prevent the investment manager from front-running.

■ *Reporting requirements*: Supervisors should establish reporting procedures for investment personnel, including disclosure of personal holdings/beneficial ownerships, confirmations of trades to the firm and the employee, and preclearance procedures. Once trading restrictions are in place, they must be enforced. The best method for monitoring and enforcing procedures to eliminate conflicts of interest in personal trading is through reporting requirements, including the following:

   ● **Disclosure of holdings in which the employee has a beneficial interest**. Disclosure by investment personnel to the firm should be made upon commencement of the employment relationship and at least annually thereafter. To address privacy considerations, disclosure of personal holdings should be handled in a confidential manner by the firm.

   ● **Providing duplicate confirmations of transactions**. Investment personnel should be required to direct their brokers to supply to firms duplicate copies or confirmations of all their personal securities transactions and copies of periodic statements for all securities accounts. The duplicate confirmation requirement has two purposes: 1) The requirement sends a message that there is independent verification, which reduces the likelihood of unethical behavior, and 2) it enables verification of the accounting of the flow of personal investments that cannot be determined from merely looking at holdings.

   ● **Preclearance procedures**. Investment personnel should examine all planned personal trades to identify possible conflicts prior to the execution of the trades. Preclearance procedures are designed to identify possible conflicts before a problem arises.

■ *Disclosure of policies*: Upon request, members and candidates should fully disclose to investors their firm's policies regarding personal investing. The information about employees' personal investment activities and policies will foster an atmosphere of full and complete disclosure and calm the public's legitimate concerns about the conflicts of interest posed by investment personnel's personal trading. The disclosure must provide helpful information to investors; it should not be simply boilerplate language such as "investment personnel are subject to policies and procedures regarding their personal trading."

Application of the Standard

Example 1   (Personal Trading): Research analyst Marlon Long does not recommend purchase of a common stock for his employer's account because he wants to purchase the stock personally and does not want to wait until the recommendation is approved and the stock purchased by his employer.

> *Comment*: Long has violated Standard VI(B) by taking advantage of his knowledge of the stock's value before allowing his employer to benefit from that information.

Example 2 (Trading for Family Member Account): Carol Baker, the portfolio manager of an aggressive-growth mutual fund, maintains an account in her husband's name at several brokerage firms with which the fund and a number of Baker's other individual clients do a substantial amount of business. Whenever a hot issue becomes available, she instructs the brokers to buy it for her husband's account. Because such issues normally are scarce, Baker often acquires shares in hot issues but her clients are not able to participate in them.

> *Comment*: To avoid violating Standard VI(B), Baker must acquire shares for her mutual fund first and acquire them for her husband's account only after doing so, even though she might miss out on participating in new issues via her husband's account. She also must disclose the trading for her husband's account to her employer because this activity creates a conflict between her personal interests and her employer's interests.

Example 3 (Family Accounts as Equals): Erin Toffler, a portfolio manager at Esposito Investments, manages the retirement account established with the firm by her parents. Whenever IPOs become available, she first allocates shares to all her other clients for whom the investment is appropriate; only then does she place any remaining portion in her parents' account, if the issue is appropriate for them. She has adopted this procedure so that no one can accuse her of favoring her parents.

> *Comment*: Toffler has violated Standard VI(B) by breaching her duty to her parents by treating them differently from her other accounts simply because of the family relationship. As fee-paying clients of Esposito Investments, Toffler's parents are entitled to the same treatment as any other client of the firm. If Toffler has beneficial ownership in the account, however, and Esposito Investments has preclearance and reporting requirements for personal transactions, she may have to preclear the trades and report the transactions to Esposito.

Example 4 (Personal Trading and Disclosure): Gary Michaels is an entry-level employee who holds a low-paying job serving both the research department and the investment management department of an active investment management firm. He purchases a sports car and begins to wear expensive clothes after only a year of employment with the firm. The director of the investment management department, who has responsibility for monitoring the personal stock transactions of all employees, investigates and discovers that Michaels has made substantial investment gains by purchasing stocks just before they were put on the firm's recommended "buy" list. Michaels was regularly given the firm's quarterly personal transaction form but declined to complete it.

> *Comment*: Michaels violated Standard VI(B) by placing personal transactions ahead of client transactions. In addition, his supervisor violated the Standard IV(C)—Responsibilities of Supervisors by permitting Michaels to continue to perform his assigned tasks without having signed the quarterly personal transaction form. Note also that if Michaels had communicated information about the firm's recommendations to a person who traded the security, that action would be a misappropriation of the information and a violation of Standard II(A)—Material Nonpublic Information.

Example 5 (Trading Prior to Report Dissemination): A brokerage's insurance analyst, Denise Wilson, makes a closed-circuit TV report to her firm's branches around the country. During the broadcast, she includes negative comments about a major company in the insurance industry. The following day, Wilson's report is printed and distributed to the sales force and public customers. The report recommends that both short-term traders and intermediate investors take profits by selling that insurance company's stock. Seven minutes after the broadcast, however, Ellen Riley, head of the firm's trading department, had closed out a long "call" position in the stock. Then, shortly thereafter, Riley established a sizable "put" position in the stock. When asked about her activities, Riley claimed she took the actions to facilitate anticipated sales by institutional clients.

> *Comment*: Riley did not give customers an opportunity to buy or sell in the options market before the firm itself did. By taking action before the report was disseminated, Riley's firm may have depressed the price of the calls and increased the price of the puts. The firm could have avoided a conflict of interest if it had waited to trade for its own account until its clients had an opportunity to receive and assimilate Wilson's recommendations. As it is, Riley's actions violated Standard VI(B).

C. Referral Fees

Members and Candidates must disclose to their employer, clients, and prospective clients, as appropriate, any compensation, consideration, or benefit received from or paid to others for the recommendation of products or services

Guidance

Standard VI(C) states the responsibility of members and candidates to inform their employer, clients, and prospective clients of any benefit received for referrals of customers and clients. Such disclosures allow clients or employers to evaluate 1) any partiality shown in any recommendation of services and 2) the full cost of the services. Members and candidates must disclose when they pay a fee or provide compensation to others who have referred prospective clients to the member or candidate.

Appropriate disclosure means that members and candidates must advise the client or prospective client, before entry into any formal agreement for services, of any benefit given or received for the recommendation of any services provided by the member or candidate. In addition, the member or candidate must disclose the nature of the consideration or benefit—for example, flat fee or percentage basis; one-time or continuing benefit; based on performance; benefit in the form of provision of research or other noncash benefit—together with the estimated dollar value. Consideration includes all fees, whether paid in cash, in soft dollars, or in kind.

Recommended Procedures for Compliance

Members and candidates should encourage their employers to develop procedures related to referral fees. The firm may completely restrict such fees. If the firm does not adopt a strict prohibition of such fees, the procedures should indicate the appropriate steps for requesting approval.

Employers should have investment professionals provide to the clients notification of approved referral fee programs and provide the employer regular (at least quarterly) updates on the amount and nature of compensation received.

Application of the Standard

Example 1   (Disclosure of Referral Arrangements and Outside Parties): Brady Securities, Inc., a broker/dealer, has established a referral arrangement with Lewis Brothers, Ltd., an investment counseling firm. In this arrangement, Brady Securities refers all prospective tax-exempt accounts, including pension, profit-sharing, and endowment accounts, to Lewis Brothers. In return, Lewis Brothers makes available to Brady Securities on a regular basis the security recommendations and reports of its research staff, which registered representatives of Brady Securities use in serving customers. In addition, Lewis Brothers conducts monthly economic and market reviews for Brady Securities personnel and directs all stock commission business generated by referral accounts to Brady Securities.

Willard White, a partner in Lewis Brothers, calculates that the incremental costs involved in functioning as the research department of Brady Securities are US$20,000 annually.

Referrals from Brady Securities last year resulted in fee income of US$200,000 for Lewis Brothers, and directing all stock trades through Brady Securities resulted in additional costs to Lewis Brothers' clients of US$10,000.

Diane Branch, the chief financial officer of Maxwell Inc., contacts White and says that she is seeking an investment manager for Maxwell's profit-sharing plan. She adds, "My friend Harold Hill at Brady Securities recommended your firm without qualification, and that's good enough for me. Do we have a deal?" White accepts the new account but does not disclose his firm's referral arrangement with Brady Securities.

> *Comment*: White has violated Standard VI(C) by failing to inform the prospective customer of the referral fee payable in services and commissions for an indefinite period to Brady Securities. Such disclosure could have caused Branch to reassess Hill's recommendation and make a more critical evaluation of Lewis Brothers' services.

Example 2   (Disclosure of Interdepartmental Referral Arrangements): James Handley works for the trust department of Central Trust Bank. He receives compensation for each referral he makes to Central Trust's brokerage department and personal financial management department that results in a sale. He refers several of his clients to the personal financial management department but does not disclose the arrangement within Central Trust to his clients.

> *Comment*: Handley has violated Standard VI(C) by not disclosing the referral arrangement at Central Trust Bank to his clients. Standard VI(C) does not distinguish between referral payments paid by a third party for referring clients to the third party and internal payments paid within the firm to attract new business to a subsidiary. Members and candidates must disclose all such referral fees. Therefore, Handley is required to disclose, at the time of referral, any referral fee agreement in place among Central Trust Bank's departments. The disclosure should include the nature and the value of the benefit and should be made in writing.

Example 3   (Disclosure of Referral Arrangements and Informing Firm): Katherine Roberts is a portfolio manager at Katama Investments, an advisory firm specializing in managing assets for high-net-worth individuals. Katama's trading desk uses a variety of brokerage houses to execute trades on behalf of its clients. Roberts asks the trading desk to direct a large portion of its commissions to Naushon, Inc., a small broker/dealer run by one of Roberts' business school classmates. Katama's traders have found that Naushon is not very competitive on pricing, and although Naushon generates some research for its trading clients, Katama's other analysts have found most of Naushon's research to be not especially useful. Nevertheless, the traders do as Roberts asks, and in return for receiving a large portion of Katama's business, Naushon recommends the investment services of Roberts and Katama to its wealthiest clients. This arrangement is not disclosed to either Katama or the clients referred by Naushon.

> *Comment*: Roberts is violating Standard VI(C) by failing to inform her employer of the referral arrangement.

Example 4   (Disclosure of Referral Arrangements and Employer Compensation): Yeshao Wen is a portfolio manager for a bank. He receives additional monetary compensation from his employer when he is successful in assisting in the sales process and generation of assets under management. The assets in question will be invested in proprietary products, such as affiliate company mutual funds.

> *Comment*: Standard VI(C) is meant to address instances where the investment advice provided by a member or candidate appears to be objective and independent but in fact is influenced by an unseen referral arrangement. It is not meant to cover compensation by employers to employees for generating new business when it would be obvious to potential clients that the employees are "referring" potential clients to the services of their employers.
>
> If Wen is selling the bank's investment management services in general, he does not need to disclose to potential clients that he will receive a bonus for finding new clients and acquiring new assets under management for the bank. Potential clients are probably aware that it would be financially beneficial both to the portfolio manager and the manager's firm for the portfolio manager to sell the services of the firm and attract new clients.
>
> In this example, however, the assets will be managed in "proprietary product offerings" of the manager's company (for example, an in-house mutual fund) and Wen will receive additional compensation for selling firm products. Some sophisticated investors may realize that it would be financially beneficial to the portfolio manager and the manager's firm if the investor were to buy the product offerings of the firm. Best practice dictates, however, that members or candidates acting as portfolio managers disclose to clients that they are compensated for selling firm products to clients. Such disclosure will meet the purpose of Standard VI(C), which is to allow investors to determine whether there is any partiality on the part of the portfolio manager making investment advice.

Example 5   (Disclosure of Referral Arrangements and Outside Organizations): Alex Burl is a portfolio manager at Helpful Investments, a local investment advisory firm. Burl is on the advisory board of his child's school, which is looking for ways to raise money to purchase new playground equipment for the school. Burl discusses a plan with his supervisor in which he will donate to the school a portion of his service fee from new clients referred by the parents of students at the school. Upon getting the approval from Helpful, Burl presents the idea to the school's advisory board and directors. The school agrees to announce the program at the next parent event and asks Burl to provide the appropriate written materials to be distributed. A week following the distribution of the flyers, Burl receives the first school-related referral. In establishing the client's investment policy statement, Burl clearly discusses the school's referral and outlines the plans for distributing the donation back to the school.

> *Comment*: Burl has not violated Standard VI(C) because he secured the permission of his employer, Helpful Investments, and the school prior to beginning the program and because he discussed the arrangement with the client at the time the investment policy statement was designed.

Example 6 (Disclosure of Referral Arrangements and Outside Parties): The sponsor of a state employee pension is seeking to hire a firm to manage the pension plan's emerging market allocation. To assist in the review process, the sponsor has hired Thomas Arrow as a consultant to solicit proposals from various advisers. Arrow is contracted by the sponsor to represent its best interest in selecting the most appropriate new manager. The process runs smoothly, and Overseas Investments is selected as the new manager.

The following year, news breaks that Arrow is under investigation by the local regulator for accepting kickbacks from investment managers after they are awarded new pension allocations. Overseas Investments is included in the list of firms allegedly making these payments. Although the sponsor is happy with the performance of Overseas since it has been managing the pension plan's emerging market funds, the sponsor still decides to have an independent review of the proposals and the selection process to ensure that Overseas was the appropriate firm for its needs. This review confirms that, even though Arrow was being paid by both parties, the recommendation of Overseas appeared to be objective and appropriate.

> *Comment*: Arrow has violated Standard VI(C) because he did not disclose the fee being paid by Overseas. Withholding this information raises the question of a potential lack of objectivity in the recommendations Overseas is making; this aspect is in addition to questions about the legality of having firms pay to be considered for an allocation.
>
> Regulators and governmental agencies may adopt requirements concerning allowable consultant activities. Local regulations sometimes include having a consultant register with the regulatory agency's ethics board. Regulator policies may include a prohibition on acceptance of payments from investment managers receiving allocations and require regular reporting of contributions made to political organizations and candidates. Arrow would have to adhere to these requirements as well as the Code and Standards.

STANDARD VII—RESPONSIBILITIES AS A CFA INSTITUTE MEMBER OR CFA CANDIDATE

A. Conduct as Members and Candidates in the CFA Program

Members and Candidates must not engage in any conduct that compromises the reputation or integrity of CFA Institute or the CFA designation or the integrity, validity, or security of the CFA examinations.

Guidance

Highlights:

- *Confidential Program Information*
- *Additional CFA Program Restrictions*
- *Expressing an Opinion*

Standard VII(A) covers the conduct of CFA Institute members and candidates involved with the CFA Program and prohibits any conduct that undermines the public's confidence that the CFA charter represents a level of achievement based on merit and ethical conduct. The standard's function is to hold members and candidates to a high ethical criterion while they are participating in or involved with the CFA Program. Conduct covered includes but is not limited to

- cheating or assisting others on the CFA examination or any other CFA Institute examination;
- disregarding the rules and policies of the CFA Program related to exam administration;
- providing confidential program or exam information to candidates or the public;
- disregarding or attempting to circumvent security measures established by CFA Institute for the CFA exam;
- improperly using the CFA designation in any form of communication;
- improperly using an association with CFA Institute to further personal or professional goals;
- misrepresenting information on the Professional Conduct Statement or in the CFA Institute Continuing Education Program.

Confidential Program Information

CFA Institute is vigilant about protecting the integrity of the CFA Program content and examination process. The CFA Program prohibits candidates from disclosing confidential material gained during the exam process.

Examples of information that cannot be disclosed by candidates sitting for an exam include but are not limited to

- specific details of questions appearing on the exam, and
- broad topical areas and formulas tested or not tested on the exam.

All aspects of the exam, including questions, broad topical areas, and formulas, tested or not tested, are considered confidential until such time as CFA Institute elects to release them publicly. This confidentiality requirement allows CFA Institute to maintain the integrity and rigor of the exam for future candidates. Standard VII(A) does not prohibit candidates from discussing nonconfidential information or curriculum material with others or in study groups in preparation for the exam.

Candidates increasingly use online forums and new technology as part of their exam preparations. CFA Institute actively polices blogs, forums, and related social networking groups for information considered confidential. The organization works with both individual candidates and the sponsors of online or offline services to promptly remove any and all violations. As noted in the discussion of Standard I(A)—Knowledge of the Law, candidates, members, and the public are encouraged to report suspected violations to CFA Institute.

Additional CFA Program Restrictions

The CFA Program examination administration policies define additional allowed and disallowed actions concerning the exams. Violating any of the testing policies, such as the calculator policy, personal belongings policy, or the Candidate Pledge, constitutes a violation of Standard VII(A). Candidates will find all of these policies on the CFA Program portion of the CFA Institute website (www.cfainstitute.org). Exhibit 2 provides the Candidate Pledge, which highlights the respect candidates must have for the integrity, validity, and security of the CFA exam.

Members may participate as volunteers in various aspects of the CFA Program. Standard VII(A) prohibits members from disclosing and/or soliciting confidential material gained prior to or during the exam and grading processes with those outside the CFA exam development process.

Examples of information that cannot be shared by members involved in developing, administering, or grading the exams include but are not limited to

- questions appearing on the exam or under consideration,
- deliberation related to the exam process, and
- information related to the scoring of questions.

Expressing an Opinion

Standard VII(A) does *not* cover expressing opinions regarding the CFA Program or CFA Institute. Members and candidates are free to disagree and express their disagreement with CFA Institute on its policies, procedures, or any advocacy positions taken by the organization. When expressing a personal opinion, a candidate is prohibited from disclosing content-specific information, including any actual exam question and the information as to subject matter covered or not covered in the exam.

Exhibit 2	**Sample of CFA Program Testing Policies**
Candidate Pledge	As a candidate in the CFA Program, I am obligated to follow Standard VII(A) of the CFA Institute Standards of Professional Conduct, which states that members and candidates must not engage in any conduct that compromises the reputation or integrity of CFA Institute or the CFA designation or the integrity, validity, or security of the CFA exam.
	■ Prior to this exam, I have not given or received information regarding the content of this exam. During this exam, I will not give or receive any information regarding the content of this exam.
	■ After this exam, I will not **disclose any portion of this exam** and I will not remove **any exam materials** from the testing room in original or copied form. I understand that all exam materials, including my answers, are the property of CFA Institute and will not be returned to me in any form.
	■ I will follow **all** rules of the CFA Program as stated on the CFA Institute website and the back cover of the exam book. My violation of any rules of the CFA Program will result in CFA Institute voiding my exam results and may lead to suspension or termination of my candidacy in the CFA Program.

Application of the Standard

Example 1 (Sharing Exam Questions): Travis Nero serves as a proctor for the administration of the CFA examination in his city. In the course of his service, he reviews a copy of the Level II exam on the evening prior to the exam's administration and provides information concerning the exam questions to two candidates who use it to prepare for the exam.

Comment: Nero and the two candidates have violated Standard VII(A). By giving information about the exam questions to two candidates, Nero provided an unfair advantage to the two candidates and undermined the integrity and validity of the Level II exam as an accurate measure of the knowledge, skills, and abilities necessary to earn the right to use the CFA designation. By accepting the information, the candidates also compromised the integrity and validity of the Level II exam and undermined the ethical framework that is a key part of the designation.

Example 2   (Bringing Written Material into Exam Room): Loren Sullivan is enrolled to take the Level II CFA examination. He has been having difficulty remembering a particular formula, so prior to entering the exam room, he writes the formula on the palm of his hand. During the afternoon section of the exam, a proctor notices Sullivan looking at the palm of his hand. She asks to see his hand and finds the formula to be readable.

Comment: Because Sullivan wrote down information from the Candidate Body of Knowledge (CBOK) and took that written information into the exam room, his conduct compromised the validity of his exam performance and violated Standard VII(A). Sullivan's conduct was also in direct contradiction of the rules and regulations of the CFA Program, the Candidate Pledge, and the CFA Institute Code and Standards.

Example 3   (Writing after Exam Period End): At the conclusion of the morning section of the Level I CFA examination, the proctors announce that all candidates are to stop writing immediately. John Davis has not completed the exam, so he continues to randomly fill in ovals on his answer sheet. A proctor approaches Davis's desk and reminds him that he should stop writing immediately. Davis, however, continues to complete the answer sheet. After the proctor asks him to stop writing two additional times, Davis finally puts down his pencil.

Comment: By continuing to complete his exam after time was called, Davis has violated Standard VII(A). By continuing to write, Davis took unfair advantage of other candidates, and his conduct compromised the validity of his exam performance. Additionally, by not heeding the proctor's repeated instructions, Davis violated the rules and regulations of the CFA Program.

Example 4   (Sharing Exam Content): After completing Level II of the CFA Exam, Annabelle Rossi writes in her blog about her experience. She posts the following: "Level II is complete! I think I did fairly well on the exam. It was really difficult, but fair. I think I did especially well on the derivatives questions. And there were tons of them! I think I counted 18! The ethics questions were really hard. I'm glad I spent so much time on the Code and Standards. I was surprised to see there were no questions at all about IPO allocations. I expected there to be a couple. Well, off to celebrate getting through it. See you tonight?"

Comment: Rossi did not violate Standard VII(A) when she wrote about how difficult she found the exam or how well she thinks she may have done. By revealing portions of the CBOK covered on the exam and areas not covered, however, she did violate Standard VII(A) and the Candidate Pledge. Depending on the time frame in which the comments were posted, Rossi not only may have assisted future candidates but also may have provided an unfair advantage to candidates sitting for the same exam, thereby undermining the integrity and validity of the Level II exam.

Example 5   (Sharing Exam Content): Level I candidate Etienne Gagne has been a frequent visitor to an internet forum designed specifically for CFA Program candidates.

The week after completing the Level I examination, Gagne and several others begin a discussion thread on the forum about the most challenging questions and attempt to determine the correct answers.

> *Comment*: Gagne has violated Standard VII(A) by providing and soliciting confidential exam information, which compromises the integrity of the exam process and violates the Candidate Pledge. In trying to determine correct answers to specific questions, the group's discussion included question-specific details considered to be confidential to the CFA Program. CFA Institute works with candidates and the sponsors of such online discussion boards and forums to remove information of this specific nature from these websites.

Example 6 (Sharing Exam Content): CFA4Sure is a company that produces test-preparation materials for CFA Program candidates. Many candidates register for and use the company's products. The day after the CFA examination, CFA4Sure sends an e-mail to all its customers asking them to share with the company the hardest questions from the exam so that CFA4Sure can better prepare its customers for the next exam administration. Marisol Pena e-mails a summary of the questions she found most difficult on the exam.

> *Comment*: Pena has violated Standard VII(A) by disclosing a portion of the exam questions. The information provided is considered confidential until publicly released by CFA Institute. CFA4Sure is likely to use such feedback to refine its review materials for future candidates. Pena's sharing of the specific questions undermines the integrity of the exam while potentially making the exam easier for future candidates.
>
> If the CFA4Sure employees who participated in the solicitation of confidential CFA Program information are CFA Institute members or candidates, they also have violated Standard VII(A).

Example 7 (Sharing Exam Questions): Ashlie Hocking is in London writing Level II of the CFA examination. After completing the exam, she immediately attempts to contact her friend in Sydney, Australia, to tip him off about specific questions on the exam.

> *Comment*: Hocking has violated Standard VII(A) by attempting to give her friend an unfair advantage, thereby compromising the integrity of the CFA exam process.

Example 8 (Discussion of Exam Grading Guidelines and Results): Prior to participating in grading CFA examinations, Wesley Whitcomb is required to sign a CFA Institute Grader Agreement. As part of the Grader Agreement, Whitcomb agrees not to reveal or discuss the exam materials with anyone except CFA Institute staff or other graders. Several weeks after the conclusion of the CFA exam grading, Whitcomb tells several colleagues who are candidates in the CFA Program which question he graded. He also discusses the guideline answer and adds that few candidates scored well on the question.

> *Comment*: Whitcomb violated Standard VII(A) by breaking the Grader Agreement and disclosing information related to a specific question on the exam, which compromised the integrity of the exam process.

Example 9 (Compromising CFA Institute Integrity as a Volunteer): Jose Ramirez is an investor-relations consultant for several small companies that are seeking greater exposure to investors. He is also the program chair for the CFA Institute society in the city where he works. Ramirez schedules only companies that are his clients to make presentations to the society and excludes other companies.

Comment: Ramirez, by using his volunteer position at CFA Institute to benefit himself and his clients, compromises the reputation and integrity of CFA Institute and thus violates Standard VII(A).

Example 10 (Compromising CFA Institute Integrity as a Volunteer): Marguerite Warrenski is a member of the CFA Institute GIPS Executive Committee, which oversees the creation, implementation, and revision of the GIPS standards. As a member of the Executive Committee, she has advance knowledge of confidential information regarding the GIPS standards, including any new or revised standards the committee is considering. She tells her clients that her Executive Committee membership will allow her to better assist her clients in keeping up with changes to the Standards and facilitating their compliance with the changes.

Comment: Warrenski is using her association with the GIPS Executive Committee to promote her firm's services to clients and potential clients. In defining her volunteer position at CFA Institute as a strategic business advantage over competing firms and implying to clients that she would use confidential information to further their interests, Warrenski is compromising the reputation and integrity of CFA Institute and thus violating Standard VII(A). She may factually state her involvement with the Executive Committee but cannot infer any special advantage to her clients from such participation.

B. Reference to CFA Institute, the CFA Designation, and the CFA Program

When referring to CFA Institute, CFA Institute membership, the CFA designation, or candidacy in the CFA Program, Members and Candidates must not misrepresent or exaggerate the meaning or implications of membership in CFA Institute, holding the CFA designation, or candidacy in the CFA Program.

Guidance

Highlights:

- *CFA Institute Membership*
- *Using the CFA Designation*
- *Referring to Candidacy in the CFA Program*
- *Proper Usage of the CFA Marks*

Standard VII(B) is intended to prevent promotional efforts that make promises or guarantees that are tied to the CFA designation. Individuals may refer to their CFA designation, CFA Institute membership, or candidacy in the CFA Program but must not exaggerate the meaning or implications of membership in CFA Institute, holding the CFA designation, or candidacy in the CFA Program.

Standard VII(B) is not intended to prohibit factual statements related to the positive benefit of earning the CFA designation. However, statements referring to CFA Institute, the CFA designation, or the CFA Program that overstate the competency of an individual or imply, either directly or indirectly, that superior performance can be expected from someone with the CFA designation are not allowed under the standard.

Statements that highlight or emphasize the commitment of CFA Institute members, CFA charterholders, and CFA candidates to ethical and professional conduct or mention the thoroughness and rigor of the CFA Program are appropriate. Members and candidates may make claims about the relative merits of CFA Institute, the CFA Program, or the Code and Standards as long as those statements are implicitly or explicitly stated as the opinion of the speaker. Statements that do not express opinions have to be supported by facts.

Standard VII(B) applies to any form of communication, including but not limited to communications made in electronic or written form (such as on firm letterhead, business cards, professional biographies, directory listings, printed advertising, firm brochures, or personal resumes) and oral statements made to the public, clients, or prospects.

CFA Institute Membership

The term "CFA Institute member" refers to "regular" and "affiliate" members of CFA Institute who have met the membership requirements as defined in the CFA Institute Bylaws. Once accepted as a CFA Institute member, the member must satisfy the following requirements to maintain his or her status:

- remit annually to CFA Institute a completed Professional Conduct Statement, which renews the commitment to abide by the requirements of the Code and Standards and the CFA Institute Professional Conduct Program, and
- pay applicable CFA Institute membership dues on an annual basis.

If a CFA Institute member fails to meet any of these requirements, the individual is no longer considered an active member. Until membership is reactivated, individuals must not present themselves to others as active members. They may state, however, that they were CFA Institute members in the past or refer to the years when their membership was active.

Using the CFA Designation

Those who have earned the right to use the Chartered Financial Analyst designation may use the trademarks or registered marks "Chartered Financial Analyst" or "CFA" and are encouraged to do so but only in a manner that does not misrepresent or exaggerate the meaning or implications of the designation. The use of the designation may be accompanied by an accurate explanation of the requirements that have been met to earn the right to use the designation.

"CFA charterholders" are those individuals who have earned the right to use the CFA designation granted by CFA Institute. These people have satisfied certain requirements, including completion of the CFA Program and required years of acceptable work experience. Once granted the right to use the designation, individuals must also satisfy the CFA Institute membership requirements (see above) to maintain their right to use the designation.

If a CFA charterholder fails to meet any of the membership requirements, he or she forfeits the right to use the CFA designation. Until membership is reactivated, individuals must not present themselves to others as CFA charterholders. They may state, however, that they were charterholders in the past.

Referring to Candidacy in the CFA Program

Candidates in the CFA Program may refer to their participation in the CFA Program, but the reference must clearly state that an individual is a candidate in the CFA Program and must not imply that the candidate has achieved any type of partial designation. A person is a candidate in the CFA Program if:

- the person's application for registration in the CFA Program has been accepted by CFA Institute, as evidenced by issuance of a notice of acceptance, and the person is enrolled to sit for a specified examination; or

■ the registered person has sat for a specified examination but exam results have not yet been received.

If an individual is registered for the CFA Program but declines to sit for an exam or otherwise does not meet the definition of a candidate as described in the CFA Institute Bylaws, then that individual is no longer considered an active candidate. Once the person is enrolled to sit for a future examination, his or her CFA candidacy resumes.

CFA candidates must never state or imply that they have a partial designation as a result of passing one or more levels or cite an expected completion date of any level of the CFA Program. Final award of the charter is subject to meeting the CFA Program requirements and approval by the CFA Institute Board of Governors.

If a candidate passes each level of the exam in consecutive years and wants to state that he or she did so, that is not a violation of Standard VII(B) because it is a statement of fact. If the candidate then goes on to claim or imply superior ability by obtaining the designation in only three years, however, he or she is in violation of Standard VII(B).

Exhibit 3 provides examples of proper and improper references to the CFA designation.

Exhibit 3	Proper and Improper References to the CFA Designation

Proper References	Improper References
"Completion of the CFA Program has enhanced my portfolio management skills."	"CFA charterholders achieve better performance results."
"John Smith passed all three CFA examinations in three consecutive years."	"John Smith is among the elite, having passed all three CFA examinations in three consecutive attempts."
"The CFA designation is globally recognized and attests to a charterholder's success in a rigorous and comprehensive study program in the field of investment management and research analysis."	"As a CFA charterholder, I am the most qualified to manage client investments."
"The credibility that the CFA designation affords and the skills the CFA Program cultivates are key assets for my future career development."	"As a CFA charterholder, Jane White provides the best value in trade execution."
"I enrolled in the CFA Program to obtain the highest set of credentials in the global investment management industry."	"Enrolling as a candidate in the CFA Program ensures one of becoming better at valuing debt securities."
"I passed Level I of the CFA exam."	"CFA, Level II"
"I am a 2010 Level III CFA candidate."	"CFA, Expected 2011"
"I passed all three levels of the CFA Program and will be eligible for the CFA charter upon completion of the required work experience."	
"As a CFA charterholder, I am committed to the highest ethical standards."	

Proper Usage of the CFA Marks

Upon obtaining the CFA charter from CFA Institute, charterholders are given the right to use the CFA marks, including Chartered Financial Analyst®, CFA®, and the CFA Logo (a certification mark):

These marks are registered by CFA Institute in countries around the world.

The Chartered Financial Analyst and CFA marks must always be used either after a charterholder's name or as adjectives (never as nouns) in written documents or oral conversations. For example, to refer to oneself as "a CFA" or "a Chartered Financial Analyst" is improper.

The CFA Logo certification mark is used by charterholders as a distinctive visual symbol of the CFA designation that can be easily recognized by employers, colleagues, and clients. As a certification mark, it must be used only to directly refer to an individual charterholder or group of charterholders.

Exhibit 4 provides examples of correct and incorrect use of the marks. CFA charterholders should refer to the complete guidelines published by CFA Institute for additional and up-to-date information and examples illustrating proper and improper use of the CFA Logo, Chartered Financial Analyst mark, and CFA mark. These guidelines and the CFA logo are available on the CFA Institute website at www.cfainstitute.org.

Exhibit 4	Correct and Incorrect Use of the Chartered Financial Analyst and CFA Marks	
Correct	**Incorrect**	**Principle**
He is one of two CFA charterholders in the company. He earned the right to use the Chartered Financial Analyst designation.	He is one of two CFAs in the company. He is a Chartered Financial Analyst.	The CFA and Chartered Financial Analyst designations must always be used as adjectives, never as nouns or common names.
Jane Smith, CFA	Jane Smith, C.F.A. John Doe, cfa	No periods. Always capitalize the letters "CFA".
John Jones, CFA	John, a CFA-type portfolio manager. The focus is on Chartered Financial Analysis. CFA-equivalent program. Swiss-CFA	Do not alter the designation to create new words or phrases.
John Jones, Chartered Financial Analyst	Jones Chartered Financial Analysts, Inc.	The designation must not be used as part of the name of a firm.
Jane Smith, CFA John Doe, Chartered Financial Analyst	Jane Smith, **CFA** John Doe, **Chartered Financial Analyst**	The CFA designation should not be given more prominence (e.g., larger, bold) than the charterholder's name.
Level I candidate in the CFA Program.	Chartered Financial Analyst (CFA), September 2011.	Candidates in the CFA Program must not cite the expected date of exam completion and award of charter.
Passed Level I of the CFA examination in 2010.	CFA Level I. CFA degree expected in 2011.	No designation exists for someone who has passed Level I, Level II, or Level III of the exam. The CFA designation should not be referred to as a degree.

(continued)

Exhibit 4	*Continued*	

Correct	Incorrect	Principle
I have passed all three levels of the CFA Program and may be eligible for the CFA charter upon completion of the required work experience.	CFA (Passed Finalist)	A candidate who has passed Level III but has not yet received his or her charter cannot use the CFA or Chartered Financial Analyst designation.
CFA, 2009, CFA Institute, (optional: Charlottesville, Virginia, USA)	CFA, 2009, CFA Society of the UK	In citing the designation in a resume, a charterholder should use the date that he or she received the designation and should cite CFA Institute as the conferring body.

Recommended Procedures for Compliance

Misuse of a member's CFA designation or CFA candidacy or improper reference to it is common by those in a member's or candidate's firm who do not possess knowledge of the requirements of Standard VII(B). As an appropriate step to reduce this risk, members and candidates should disseminate written information about Standard VII(B) and the accompanying guidance to their firm's legal, compliance, public relations, and marketing departments (see www.cfainstitute.org/).

For materials that refer to employees' affiliation with CFA Institute, members and candidates should encourage their firms to create templates that are approved by a central authority (such as the compliance department) as being consistent with Standard VII(B). This practice promotes consistency and accuracy in the firm of references to CFA Institute membership, the CFA designation, and CFA candidacy.

Application of the Standard

Example 1   (Passing Exams in Consecutive Years): An advertisement for AZ Investment Advisors states that all the firm's principals are CFA charterholders and all passed the three examinations on their first attempt. The advertisement prominently links this fact to the notion that AZ's mutual funds have achieved superior performance.

> *Comment*: AZ may state that all principals passed the three examinations on the first try as long as this statement is true, but it must not be linked to performance or imply superior ability. Implying that 1) CFA charterholders achieve better investment results and 2) those who pass the exams on the first try may be more successful than those who do not violates Standard VII(B).

Example 2   (Right to Use CFA Designation): Five years after receiving his CFA charter, Louis Vasseur resigns his position as an investment analyst and spends the next two years traveling abroad. Because he is not actively engaged in the investment profession, he does not file a completed Professional Conduct Statement with CFA Institute and does not pay his CFA Institute membership dues. At the conclusion of his travels, Vasseur becomes a self-employed analyst accepting assignments as an independent contractor. Without reinstating his CFA Institute membership by filing his Professional Conduct Statement and paying his dues, he prints business cards that display "CFA" after his name.

> *Comment*: Vasseur has violated Standard VII(B) because his right to use the CFA designation was suspended when he failed to file his Professional Conduct Statement and stopped paying dues. Therefore, he no longer is able to state or imply that he is an active CFA charterholder. When Vasseur files his Professional Conduct Statement, resumes paying CFA Institute dues to activate his membership, and completes the CFA Institute reinstatement procedures he will be eligible to use the CFA designation.

Example 3   ("Retired" CFA Institute Membership Status): After a 25-year career, James Simpson retires from his firm. Because he is not actively engaged in the investment profession, he does not file a completed Professional Conduct Statement with CFA Institute and does not pay his CFA Institute membership dues. Simpson designs a plain business card (without a corporate logo) to hand out to friends with his new contact details, and he continues to put "CFA" after his name.

> *Comment*: Simpson has violated Standard VII(B). Because he failed to file his Professional Conduct Statement and ceased paying dues, his membership has been suspended and he must give up the right to use the CFA designation. CFA Institute has procedures, however, for reclassifying a member and charterholder as "retired" and reducing the annual dues. If he wants to obtain retired status, he needs to file the appropriate paperwork with CFA Institute. When Simpson receives his notification from CFA Institute that his membership has been reclassified as retired and he resumes paying reduced dues, his membership will be reactivated and his right to use the CFA designation will be reinstated.

Example 4   (CFA Logo—Individual Use Only): Asia Futures Ltd is a small quantitative investment advisory firm. The firm takes great pride in the fact that all its employees are CFA charterholders. To underscore this fact, the firm's senior partner is proposing to change the firm's letterhead to include the following:

Asia Futures Ltd.

> *Comment*: The CFA Logo is a certification mark intended to identify *individual* charterholders and must not be incorporated in a company name, confused with a company logo, or placed in such close proximity to a company name or logo as to give the reader the idea that the certification mark certifies the company. The only appropriate use of the CFA logo is on the business card or letterhead of each individual CFA charterholder.

Example 5   (Stating Facts about CFA Designation and Program): Rhonda Reese has been a CFA charterholder since 2000. In a conversation with a friend who is considering enrolling in the CFA Program, she states that she has learned a great deal from the CFA Program and that many firms require their employees to be CFA charterholders. She would recommend the CFA Program to anyone pursuing a career in investment management.

> *Comment*: Reese's comments comply with Standard VII(B). Her statements refer to facts: The CFA Program enhanced her knowledge, and many firms require the CFA designation for their investment professionals.

Example 6   (Order of Professional and Academic Designations): Tatiana Prittima has earned both her CFA designation and a PhD in finance. She would like to cite both her accomplishments on her business card but is unsure of the proper method for doing so.

> *Comment*: The order of designations cited on such items as resumes and business cards is a matter of personal preference. Prittima is free to cite the CFA designation either before or after citing her PhD.

PRACTICE PROBLEMS FOR READING 2

Unless otherwise stated in the question, all individuals in the following questions are CFA Institute members or candidates in the CFA Program and, therefore, are subject to the CFA Institute Code of Ethics and Standards of Professional Conduct.

1. Smith, a research analyst with a brokerage firm, decides to change his recommendation for the common stock of Green Company, Inc., from a "buy" to a "sell." He mails this change in investment advice to all the firm's clients on Wednesday. The day after the mailing, a client calls with a buy order for 500 shares of Green Company. In this circumstance, Smith should:

    A. accept the order.

    B. advise the customer of the change in recommendation before accepting the order.

    C. not accept the order because it is contrary to the firm's recommendation.

2. Which statement about a manager's use of client brokerage commissions violates the Code and Standards?

    A. A client may direct a manager to use that client's brokerage commissions to purchase goods and services for that client.

    B. Client brokerage commissions should be used to benefit the client and should be commensurate with the value of the brokerage and research services received.

    C. Client brokerage commissions may be directed to pay for the investment manager's operating expenses.

3. Jamison is a junior research analyst with Howard & Howard, a brokerage and investment banking firm. Howard & Howard's mergers and acquisitions department has represented the Britland Company in all of its acquisitions for the past 20 years. Two of Howard & Howard's senior officers are directors of various Britland subsidiaries. Jamison has been asked to write a research report on Britland. What is the best course of action for her to follow?

    A. Jamison may write the report but must refrain from expressing any opinions because of the special relationships between the two companies.

    B. Jamison should not write the report because the two Howard & Howard officers serve as directors for subsidiaries of Britland.

    C. Jamison may write the report if she discloses the special relationships with the company in the report.

4. Which of the following statements clearly *conflicts* with the recommended procedures for compliance presented in the CFA Institute *Standards of Practice Handbook*?

    A. Firms should disclose to clients the personal investing policies and procedures established for their employees.

    B. Prior approval must be obtained for the personal investment transactions of all employees.

    C. For confidentiality reasons, personal transactions and holdings should not be reported to employers unless mandated by regulatory organizations.

5. Bronson provides investment advice to the board of trustees of a private university endowment fund. The trustees have provided Bronson with the fund's financial information, including planned expenditures. Bronson receives a phone call on Friday afternoon from Murdock, a prominent alumnus,

requesting that Bronson fax him comprehensive financial information about the fund. According to Murdock, he has a potential contributor but needs the information that day to close the deal and cannot contact any of the trustees. Based on the CFA Institute Standards, Bronson should:

A. send Murdock the information because disclosure would benefit the client.

B. not send Murdock the information to preserve confidentiality.

C. send Murdock the information, provided Bronson promptly notifies the trustees.

6. Miller heads the research department of a large brokerage firm. The firm has many analysts, some of whom are subject to the Code and Standards. If Miller delegates some supervisory duties, which statement best describes her responsibilities under the Code and Standards?

A. Miller's supervisory responsibilities do not apply to those subordinates who are not subject to the Code and Standards.

B. Miller no longer has supervisory responsibility for those duties delegated to her subordinates.

C. Miller retains supervisory responsibility for all subordinates despite her delegation of some duties.

7. Willier is the research analyst responsible for following Company X. All the information he has accumulated and documented suggests that the outlook for the company's new products is poor, so the stock should be rated a weak "hold." During lunch, however, Willier overhears a financial analyst from another firm whom he respects offer opinions that conflict with Willier's forecasts and expectations. Upon returning to his office, Willier releases a strong "buy" recommendation to the public. Willier:

A. violated the Standards by failing to distinguish between facts and opinions in his recommendation.

B. violated the Standards because he did not have a reasonable and adequate basis for his recommendation.

C. was in full compliance with the Standards.

8. An investment management firm has been hired by ETV Corporation to work on an additional public offering for the company. The firm's brokerage unit now has a "sell" recommendation on ETV, but the head of the investment banking department has asked the head of the brokerage unit to change the recommendation from "sell" to "buy." According to the Standards, the head of the brokerage unit would be permitted to:

A. increase the recommendation by no more than one increment (in this case, to a "hold" recommendation).

B. place the company on a restricted list and give only factual information about the company.

C. assign a new analyst to decide if the stock deserves a higher rating.

9. Albert and Tye, who recently started their own investment advisory business, have registered to take the Level III CFA examination. Albert's business card reads, "Judy Albert, CFA Level II." Tye has not put anything about the CFA designation on his business card, but promotional material that he designed for the business describes the CFA requirements and indicates that Tye participates in the CFA Program and has completed Levels I and II. According to the Standards:

A. Albert has violated the Standards but Tye has not.

B. Tye has violated the Standards but Albert has not.

C. Both Albert and Tye have violated the Standards.

10. Scott works for a regional brokerage firm. He estimates that Walkton Industries will increase its dividend by US$1.50 a share during the next year. He realizes that this increase is contingent on pending legislation that would, if enacted, give Walkton a substantial tax break. The U.S. representative for Walkton's home district has told Scott that, although she is lobbying hard for the bill and prospects for its passage are favorable, concern of the U.S. Congress over the federal deficit could cause the tax bill to be voted down. Walkton Industries has not made any statements about a change in dividend policy. Scott writes in his research report, "We expect Walkton's stock price to rise by at least US$8.00 a share by the end of the year because the dividend will increase by US$1.50 a share. Investors buying the stock at the current time should expect to realize a total return of at least 15 percent on the stock." According to the Standards:

   A. Scott violated the Standards because he used material inside information.

   B. Scott violated the Standards because he failed to separate opinion from fact.

   C. Scott violated the Standards by basing his research on uncertain predictions of future government action.

11. Which *one* of the following actions will help to ensure the fair treatment of brokerage firm clients when a new investment recommendation is made?

   A. Informing all people in the firm in advance that a recommendation is to be disseminated.

   B. Distributing recommendations to institutional clients prior to individual accounts.

   C. Minimizing the time between the decision and the dissemination of a recommendation.

12. The mosaic theory holds that an analyst:

   A. violates the Code and Standards if the analyst fails to have knowledge of and comply with applicable laws.

   B. can use material public information and nonmaterial nonpublic information in the analyst's analysis.

   C. should use all available and relevant information in support of an investment recommendation.

13. Jurgen is a portfolio manager. One of her firm's clients has told Jurgen that he will compensate her beyond the compensation provided by her firm on the basis of the capital appreciation of his portfolio each year. Jurgen should:

   A. turn down the additional compensation because it will result in conflicts with the interests of other clients' accounts.

   B. turn down the additional compensation because it will create undue pressure on her to achieve strong short-term performance.

   C. obtain permission from her employer prior to accepting the compensation arrangement.

14. One of the discretionary accounts managed by Farnsworth is the Jones Corporation employee profit-sharing plan. Jones, the company president, recently asked Farnsworth to vote the shares in the profit-sharing plan in favor of the slate of directors nominated by Jones Corporation and against the directors sponsored by a dissident stockholder group. Farnsworth does not want to lose this account because he directs all the account's trades to a brokerage firm that provides Farnsworth with useful information about tax-free investments. Although this information is not of value in managing the Jones Corporation account, it does help in managing several other accounts. The brokerage firm providing this information also offers the lowest commissions

for trades and provides best execution. Farnsworth investigates the director issue, concludes that the management-nominated slate is better for the long-run performance of the company than the dissident group's slate, and votes accordingly. Farnsworth:

A. violated the Standards in voting the shares in the manner requested by Jones but not in directing trades to the brokerage firm.

B. did not violate the Standards in voting the shares in the manner requested by Jones or in directing trades to the brokerage firm.

C. violated the Standards in directing trades to the brokerage firm but not in voting the shares as requested by Jones.

15. Brown works for an investment counseling firm. Green, a new client of the firm, is meeting with Brown for the first time. Green used another counseling firm for financial advice for years, but she has switched her account to Brown's firm. After spending a few minutes getting acquainted, Brown explains to Green that she has discovered a highly undervalued stock that offers large potential gains. She recommends that Green purchase the stock. Brown has committed a violation of the Standards. What should she have done differently?

A. Brown should have determined Green's needs, objectives, and tolerance for risk before making a recommendation of any type of security.

B. Brown should have thoroughly explained the characteristics of the company to Green, including the characteristics of the industry in which the company operates.

C. Brown should have explained her qualifications, including her education, training, experience, and the meaning of the CFA designation.

16. Grey recommends the purchase of a mutual fund that invests solely in long-term U.S. Treasury bonds. He makes the following statements to his clients:

Statement 1. "The payment of the bonds is guaranteed by the U.S. government; therefore, the default risk of the bonds is virtually zero."

Statement 2. "If you invest in the mutual fund, you will earn a 10 percent rate of return each year for the next several years based on historical performance of the market."

Did Grey's statements violate the CFA Institute Code and Standards?

A. Neither statement violated the Code and Standards.

B. Only statement 1 violated the Code and Standards.

C. Only statement 2 violated the Code and Standards.

17. Anderb, a portfolio manager for XYZ Investment Management Company—a registered investment organization that advises investment firms and private accounts—was promoted to that position three years ago. Bates, her supervisor, is responsible for reviewing Anderb's portfolio account transactions and her required monthly reports of personal stock transactions. Anderb has been using Jonelli, a broker, almost exclusively for brokerage transactions for the portfolio account. For securities in which Jonelli's firm makes a market, Jonelli has been giving Anderb lower prices for personal purchases and higher prices for personal sales than Jonelli gives to Anderb's portfolio accounts and other investors. Anderb has been filing monthly reports with Bates only for those months in which she has no personal transactions, which is about every fourth month. Which of the following is *most likely* to be a violation of the Code and Standards?

A. Anderb failed to disclose to her employer her personal transactions.

B. Anderb owned the same securities as those of her clients.

    C. Bates allowed Anderb to use Jonelli as her broker for personal trades.

18. Which of the following is a correct statement of a member's or candidate's duty under the Code and Standards?

    A. In the absence of specific applicable law or other regulatory requirements, the Code and Standards govern the member's or candidate's actions.

    B. A member or candidate is required to comply only with applicable local laws, rules, regulations, or customs, even though the Code and Standards may impose a higher degree of responsibility or a higher duty on the member or candidate.

    C. A member or candidate who trades securities in a securities market where no applicable local laws or stock exchange rules regulate the use of material nonpublic information may take investment action based on material nonpublic information.

19. Ward is scheduled to visit the corporate headquarters of Evans Industries. Ward expects to use the information he obtains there to complete his research report on Evans stock. Ward learns that Evans plans to pay all of Ward's expenses for the trip, including costs of meals, hotel room, and air transportation. Which of the following actions would be the *best* course for Ward to take under the Code and Standards?

    A. Accept the expense-paid trip and write an objective report.

    B. Pay for all travel expenses, including costs of meals and incidental items.

    C. Accept the expense-paid trip but disclose the value of the services accepted in the report.

20. Which of the following statements is *correct* under the Code and Standards?

    A. CFA Institute members and candidates are prohibited from undertaking independent practice in competition with their employer.

    B. Written consent from the employer is necessary to permit independent practice that could result in compensation or other benefits in competition with a member's or candidate's employer.

    C. Members and candidates are prohibited from making arrangements or preparations to go into a competitive business before terminating their relationship with their employer.

21. Smith is a financial analyst with XYZ Brokerage Firm. She is preparing a purchase recommendation on JNI Corporation. Which of the following situations is *most likely* to represent a conflict of interest for Smith that would have to be disclosed?

    A. Smith frequently purchases items produced by JNI.

    B. XYZ holds for its own account a substantial common stock position in JNI.

    C. Smith's brother-in-law is a supplier to JNI.

22. Michelieu tells a prospective client, "I may not have a long-term track record yet, but I'm sure that you'll be very pleased with my recommendations and service. In the three years that I've been in the business, my equity-oriented clients have averaged a total return of more than 26 percent a year." The statement is true, but Michelieu only has a few clients, and one of his clients took a large position in a penny stock (against Michelieu's advice) and realized a huge gain. This large return caused the average of all of Michelieu's clients to exceed 26 percent a year. Without this one investment, the average gain would have been 8 percent a year. Has Michelieu violated the Standards?

    A. No.

    B. Yes, because the statement misrepresents Michelieu's track record.

    C. Yes, because the standards prohibit members from guaranteeing future results.

23. An investment banking department of a brokerage firm often receives material nonpublic information that could have considerable value if used in advising the firm's brokerage clients. In order to conform to the Code and Standards, which one of the following is the best policy for the brokerage firm?

    A. Permanently prohibit both "buy" and "sell" recommendations of the stocks of clients of the investment banking department.

    B. Establish physical and informational barriers within the firm to prevent the exchange of information between the investment banking and brokerage operations.

    C. Monitor the exchange of information between the investment banking department and the brokerage operation.

24. Stewart has been hired by Goodner Industries, Inc., to manage its pension fund. Stewart's duty of loyalty, prudence, and care is owed to:

    A. the management of Goodner.

    B. the participants and beneficiaries of Goodner's pension plan.

    C. the shareholders of Goodner.

25. Which of the following statements is a stated purpose of disclosure in Standard VI(C)—Referral Fees?

    A. Disclosure will allow the client to request discounted service fees.

    B. Disclosure will help the client evaluate any possible partiality shown in the recommendation of services.

    C. Disclosure means advising a prospective client about the referral arrangement once a formal client relationship has been established.

26. Rose, a portfolio manager for a local investment advisory firm, is planning to sell a portion of his personal investment portfolio to cover the costs of his child's academic tuition. Rose wants to sell a portion of his holdings in Household Products, but his firm recently upgraded the stock to "strong buy." Which of the following describes Rose's options under the Code and Standards?

    A. Based on his firm's "buy" recommendation, Rose cannot sell the shares because he would be improperly prospering from the inflated recommendation.

    B. Rose is free to sell his personal holdings once his firm is properly informed of his intentions.

    C. Rose can sell his personal holdings but only when a client of the firm places an order to buy shares of Household.

27. A former hedge fund manager, Jackman, has decided to launch a new private wealth management firm. From his prior experiences, he believes the new firm needs to achieve US$1 million in assets under management in the first year. Jackman offers a $10,000 incentive to any adviser who joins his firm with the minimum of $200,000 in committed investments. Jackman places notice of the opening on several industry web portals and career search sites. Which of the following is *correct* according to the Code and Standards?

    A. A member or candidate is eligible for the new position and incentive if he or she can arrange for enough current clients to switch to the new firm and if the member or candidate discloses the incentive fee.

    B. A member or candidate may not accept employment with the new firm because Jackman's incentive offer violates the Code and Standards.

C. A member or candidate is not eligible for the new position unless he or she is currently unemployed because soliciting the clients of the member's or candidate's current employer is prohibited.

28. Carter works for Invest Today, a local asset management firm. A broker that provides Carter with proprietary research through client brokerage arrangements is offering a new trading service. The broker is offering low-fee, execution-only trades to complement its traditional full-service, execution-and-research trades. To entice Carter and other asset managers to send additional business its way, the broker will apply the commissions paid on the new service toward satisfying the brokerage commitment of the prior full-service arrangements. Carter has always been satisfied with the execution provided on the full-service trades, and the new low-fee trades are comparable to the fees of other brokers currently used for the accounts that prohibit soft dollar arrangements.

A. Carter can trade for his accounts that prohibit soft dollar arrangements under the new low-fee trading scheme.

B. Carter cannot use the new trading scheme because the commissions are prohibited by the soft dollar restrictions of the accounts.

C. Carter should trade only through the new low-fee scheme and should increase his trading volume to meet his required commission commitment.

29. Rule has worked as a portfolio manager for a large investment management firm for the past 10 years. Rule earned his CFA charter last year and has decided to open his own investment management firm. After leaving his current employer, Rule creates some marketing material for his new firm. He states in the material, "In earning the CFA charter, a highly regarded credential in the investment management industry, I further enhanced the portfolio management skills learned during my professional career. While completing the examination process in three consecutive years, I consistently received the highest possible scores on the topics of Ethics, Alternative Investments, and Portfolio Management." Has Rule violated Standard VII(B)—Reference to CFA Institute, the CFA Designation, and the CFA Program in his marketing material?

A. Rule violated Standard VII(B) in stating that he completed the exams in three consecutive years.

B. Rule violated Standard VII(B) in stating that he received the highest scores in the topics of Ethics, Alternative Investments, and Portfolio Management.

C. Rule did not violate Standard VII(B).

30. Stafford is a portfolio manager for a specialized real estate mutual fund. Her firm clearly describes in the fund's prospectus its soft dollar policies. Stafford decides that entering the CFA Program will enhance her investment decision-making skill and decides to use the fund's soft dollar account to pay the registration and exam fees for the CFA Program. Which of the following statements is *most likely* correct?

A. Stafford did not violate the Code and Standards because the prospectus informed investors of the fund's soft dollar policies.

B. Stafford violated the Code and Standards because improving her investment skills is not a reasonable use of the soft dollar account.

C. Stafford violated the Code and Standards because the CFA Program does not meet the definition of research allowed to be purchased with brokerage commissions.

31. Long has been asked to be the keynote speaker at an upcoming investment conference. The event is being hosted by one of the third-party investment

managers currently used by his pension fund. The manager offers to cover all conference and travel costs for Long and make the conference registrations free for three additional members of his investment management team. To ensure that the conference obtains the best speakers, the host firm has arranged for an exclusive golf outing for the day following the conference on a local championship-caliber course. Which of the following is *least likely* to violate Standard I(B)?

- **A.** Long may accept only the offer to have his conference-related expenses paid by the host firm.
- **B.** Long may accept the offer to have his conference-related expenses paid and may attend the exclusive golf outing at the expense of the hosting firm.
- **C.** Long may accept the entire package of incentives offered to speak at this conference.

32. Andrews, a private wealth manager, is conducting interviews for a new research analyst for his firm. One of the candidates is Wright, an analyst with a local investment bank. During the interview, while Wright is describing his analytical skills, he mentions a current merger in which his firm is acting as the adviser. Andrews has heard rumors of a possible merger between the two companies, but no releases have been made by the companies concerned. Which of the following actions by Andrews is *least likely* a violation of the Code and Standards?

- **A.** Waiting until the next day before trading on the information to allow time for it to become public.
- **B.** Notifying all investment managers in his firm of the new information so none of their clients are disadvantaged.
- **C.** Placing the securities mentioned as part of the merger on the firm's restricted trading list.

33. Pietro, president of Local Bank, has hired the bank's market maker, Vogt, to seek a merger partner. Local is currently not listed on a stock exchange and has not reported that it is seeking strategic alternatives. Vogt has discussed the possibility of a merger with several firms, but they have all decided to wait until after the next period's financial data are available. The potential buyers believe the results will be worse than the results of prior periods and will allow them to pay less for Local Bank.

Pietro wants to increase the likelihood of structuring a merger deal quickly. Which of the following actions would *most likely* be a violation of the Code and Standards?

- **A.** Pietro could instruct Local Bank to issue a press release announcing that it has retained Vogt to find a merger partner.
- **B.** Pietro could place a buy order for 2,000 shares (or four times the average weekly volume) through Vogt for his personal account.
- **C.** After confirming with Local's chief financial officer, Pietro could instruct Local to issue a press release reaffirming the firm's prior announced earnings guidance for the full fiscal year.

34. ABC Investment Management acquires a new, very large account with two concentrated positions. The firm's current policy is to add new accounts for the purpose of performance calculation after the first full month of management. Cupp is responsible for calculating the firm's performance returns. Before the end of the initial month, Cupp notices that one of the significant holdings of the new accounts is acquired by another company, causing the value of the investment to double. Because of this holding, Cupp decides to account for the new portfolio as of the date of transfer, thereby allowing ABC Investment to reap the positive impact of that month's portfolio return.

A. Cupp did not violate the Code and Standards because the GIPS standards allow composites to be updated on the date of large external cash flows.

B. Cupp did not violate the Code and Standards because companies are allowed to determine when to incorporate new accounts into their composite calculation.

C. Cupp violated the Code and Standards because the inclusion of the new account produces an inaccurate calculation of the monthly results according to the firm's stated policies.

35. Cannan has been working from home on weekends and occasionally saves correspondence with clients and completed work on her home computer. Because of worsening market conditions, Cannan is one of several employees released by her firm. While Cannan is looking for a new job, she uses the files she saved at home to request letters of recommendation from former clients. She also provides to prospective clients some of the reports as examples of her abilities.

A. Cannan is violating the Code and Standards because she did not receive permission from her former employer to keep or use the files after her employment ended.

B. Cannan did not violate the Code and Standards because the files were created and saved on her own time and computer.

C. Cannan violated the Code and Standards because she is prohibited from saving files on her home computer.

36. Quinn sat for the Level III CFA exam this past weekend. He updates his resume with the following statement: "In finishing the CFA Program, I improved my skills related to researching investments and managing portfolios. I will be eligible for the CFA charter upon completion of the required work experience."

A. Quinn violated the Code and Standards by claiming he improved his skills through the CFA Program.

B. Quinn violated the Code and Standards by incorrectly stating that he is eligible for the CFA charter.

C. Quinn did not violate the Code and Standards with his resume update.

37. During a round of golf, Rodriguez, chief financial officer of Mega Retail, mentions to Hart, a local investment adviser and long-time personal friend, that Mega is having an exceptional sales quarter. Rodriguez expects the results to be almost 10 percent above the current estimates. The next day, Hart initiates the purchase of a large stake in the local exchange-traded retail fund for her personal account.

A. Hart violated the Code and Standards by investing in the exchange-traded fund that included Mega Retail.

B. Hart did not violate the Code and Standards because she did not invest directly in securities of Mega Retail.

C. Rodriguez did not violate the Code and Standards because the comments made to Hart were not intended to solicit an investment in Mega Retail.

38. Park is very frustrated after taking her Level II exam. While she was studying for the exam, to supplement the curriculum provided, she ordered and used study material from a third-party provider. Park believes the additional material focused her attention on specific topic areas that were not tested while ignoring

other areas. She posts the following statement on the provider's discussion board: "I am very dissatisfied with your firm's CFA Program Level II material. I found the exam extremely difficult and myself unprepared for specific questions after using your product. How could your service provide such limited instructional resources on the analysis of inventories and taxes when the exam had multiple questions about them? I will not recommend your products to other candidates."

A. Park violated the Code and Standards by purchasing third-party review material.

B. Park violated the Code and Standards by providing her opinion on the difficulty of the exam.

C. Park violated the Code and Standards by providing specific information on topics tested on the exam.

39. Paper was recently terminated as one of a team of five managers of an equity fund. The fund had two value-focused managers and terminated one of them to reduce costs. In a letter sent to prospective employers, Paper presents, with written permission of the firm, the performance history of the fund to demonstrate his past success.

A. Paper did not violate the Code and Standards.

B. Paper violated the Code and Standards by claiming the performance of the entire fund as his own.

C. Paper violated the Code and Standards by including the historical results of his prior employer.

40. Townsend was recently appointed to the board of directors of a youth golf program that is the local chapter of a national not-for-profit organization. The program is beginning a new fund-raising campaign to expand the number of annual scholarships it provides. Townsend believes many of her clients make annual donations to charity. The next week in her regular newsletter to all clients, she includes a small section discussing the fund-raising campaign and her position on the organization's board.

A. Townsend did not violate the Code and Standards.

B. Townsend violated the Code and Standards by soliciting donations from her clients through the newsletter.

C. Townsend violated the Code and Standards by not getting approval of the organization before soliciting her clients.

SOLUTIONS FOR READING 2

1. B is correct. This question involves Standard III(B)—Fair Dealing. Smith disseminated a change in the stock recommendation to his clients but then received a request contrary to that recommendation from a client who probably had not yet received the recommendation. Prior to executing the order, Smith should take additional steps to ensure that the customer has received the change of recommendation. Answer A is incorrect because the client placed the order prior to receiving the recommendation and, therefore, does not have the benefit of Smith's most recent recommendation. Answer C is also incorrect; simply because the client request is contrary to the firm's recommendation does not mean a member can override a direct request by a client. After Smith contacts the client to ensure that the client has received the changed recommendation, if the client still wants to place a buy order for the shares, Smith is obligated to comply with the client's directive.

2. C is correct. This question involves Standard III(A)—Loyalty, Prudence, and Care and the specific topic of soft dollars or soft commissions. Answer C is the correct choice because client brokerage commissions may not be directed to pay for the investment manager's operating expenses. Answer B describes how members and candidates should determine how to use brokerage commissions—that is, if the use is in the best interests of clients and is commensurate with the value of the services provided. Answer A describes a practice that is commonly referred to as "directed brokerage." Because brokerage is an asset of the client and is used to benefit the client, not the manager, such practice does not violate a duty of loyalty to the client. Members and candidates are obligated in all situations to disclose to clients their practices in the use of client brokerage commissions.

3. C is correct. This question involves Standard VI(A)—Disclosure of Conflicts. The question establishes a conflict of interest in which an analyst, Jamison, is asked to write a research report on a company that is a client of the analyst's employer. In addition, two directors of the company are senior officers of Jamison's employer. Both facts establish that there are conflicts of interest that must be disclosed by Jamison in her research report. Answer B is incorrect because an analyst is not prevented from writing a report simply because of the special relationship the analyst's employer has with the company as long as that relationship is disclosed. Answer A is incorrect because whether or not Jamison expresses any opinions in the report is irrelevant to her duty to disclose a conflict of interest. Not expressing opinions does not relieve the analyst of the responsibility to disclose the special relationships between the two companies.

4. C is correct. This question asks about compliance procedures relating to personal investments of members and candidates. The statement in answer C clearly conflicts with the recommended procedures in the *Standards of Practice Handbook*. Employers should compare personal transactions of employees with those of clients on a regular basis regardless of the existence of a requirement by any regulatory organization. Such comparisons ensure that employees' personal trades do not conflict with their duty to their clients, and the comparisons can be conducted in a confidential manner. The statement in answer A does not conflict with the procedures in the *Handbook*. Disclosure of such policies will give full information to clients regarding potential conflicts of interest on the part of those entrusted to manage their money. Answer B is incorrect because firms are encouraged to establish policies whereby employees clear their personal holdings and transactions with their employers.

5. B is correct. This question relates to Standard III(A)—Loyalty, Prudence, and Care and Standard III(E)—Preservation of Confidentiality. In this case, the member manages funds of a private endowment. Clients, who are, in this case, the trustees of the fund, must place some trust in members and candidates. Bronson cannot disclose confidential financial information to anyone without the permission of the fund, regardless of whether the disclosure may benefit the fund. Therefore, answer A is incorrect. Answer C is incorrect because Bronson must notify the fund and obtain the fund's permission before publicizing the information.

6. C is correct. Under Standard IV(C)—Responsibilities of Supervisors, members and candidates may delegate supervisory duties to subordinates but such delegation does not relieve members or candidates of their supervisory responsibilities. As a result, answer B is incorrect. Moreover, whether or not Miller's subordinates are subject to the Code and Standards is irrelevant to her supervisory responsibilities. Therefore, answer A is incorrect.

7. B is correct. This question relates to Standard V(A)—Diligence and Reasonable Basis. The opinion of another financial analyst is not an adequate basis for Willier's action in changing the recommendation. Answer C is thus incorrect. So is answer A because, although it is true that members and candidates must distinguish between facts and opinions in recommendations, the question does not illustrate a violation of that nature. If the opinion overheard by Willier had sparked him to conduct additional research and investigation that justified a change of opinion, then a changed recommendation would be appropriate.

8. B is correct. This question relates to Standard I(B)—Independence and Objectivity. When asked to change a recommendation on a company stock to gain business for the firm, the head of the brokerage unit must refuse in order to maintain his independence and objectivity in making recommendations. He must not yield to pressure by the firm's investment banking department. To avoid the appearance of a conflict of interest, the firm should discontinue issuing recommendations about the company. Answer A is incorrect; changing the recommendation in any manner that is contrary to the analyst's opinion violates the duty to maintain independence and objectivity. Answer C is incorrect because merely assigning a new analyst to decide whether the stock deserves a higher rating will not address the conflict of interest.

9. A is correct. Standard VII(B)—Reference to CFA Institute, the CFA Designation, and the CFA Program is the subject of this question. The reference on Albert's business card implies that there is a "CFA Level II" designation; Tye merely indicates in promotional material that he is participating in the CFA Program and has completed Levels I and II. Candidates may not imply that there is some sort of partial designation earned after passing a level of the CFA exam. Therefore, Albert has violated Standard VII(B). Candidates may communicate that they are participating in the CFA Program, however, and may state the levels that they have completed. Therefore, Tye has not violated Standard VII(B).

10. B is correct. This question relates to Standard V(B)—Communication with Clients and Prospective Clients. Scott has issued a research report stating that he expects the price of Walkton Industries stock to rise by US$8 a share "because the dividend will increase" by US$1.50 per share. He has made this statement knowing that the dividend will increase only if Congress enacts certain legislation, an uncertain prospect. By stating that the dividend will increase, Scott failed to separate fact from opinion.

The information regarding passage of legislation is not material nonpublic information because it is conjecture, and the question does not state whether the U.S. Representative gave Scott her opinion on the passage of the legislation in confidence. She could have been offering this opinion to anyone who asked. Therefore, statement A is incorrect. It may be acceptable to base a recommendation, in part, on an expectation of future events, even though they may be uncertain. Therefore, answer C is incorrect.

11. C is correct. This question, which relates to Standard III(B)—Fair Dealing, tests the knowledge of the procedures that will assist members and candidates in treating clients fairly when making investment recommendations. The steps listed in C will all help ensure the fair treatment of clients. Answer A may have negative effects on the fair treatment of clients. The more people who know about a pending change, the greater the chance that someone will inform some clients before the information's release. The firm should establish policies that limit the number of people who are aware in advance that a recommendation is to be disseminated. Answer B, distributing recommendations to institutional clients before distributing them to individual accounts, discriminates among clients on the basis of size and class of assets and is a violation of Standard III(B).

12. B is correct. This question deals with Standard II(A)—Material Nonpublic Information. The mosaic theory states that an analyst may use material public information and nonmaterial nonpublic information in creating a larger picture than shown by any individual piece of information and the conclusions the analyst reaches become material only after the pieces are assembled. Answers A and C are accurate statements relating to the Code and Standards but do not describe the mosaic theory.

13. C is correct. This question involves Standard IV(B)—Additional Compensation Arrangements. The arrangement described in the question—whereby Jurgen would be compensated beyond the compensation provided by her firm, on the basis of an account's performance—is not a violation of the Standards as long as Jurgen discloses the arrangement in writing to her employer and obtains permission from her employer prior to entering into the arrangement. Answers A and B are incorrect; although the private compensation arrangement could conflict with the interests of other clients and lead to short-term performance pressures, members and candidates may enter into such agreements as long as they have disclosed the arrangements to their employer and obtained permission for the arrangement from their employer.

14. B is correct. This question relates to Standard III(A)—Loyalty, Prudence, and Care—specifically, a member's or candidate's responsibility for voting proxies and the use of client brokerage. According to the facts stated in the question, Farnsworth did not violate Standard III(A). Although the company president asked Farnsworth to vote the shares of the Jones Corporation profit-sharing plan a certain way, Farnsworth investigated the issue and concluded, independently, the best way to vote. Therefore, even though his decision coincided with the wishes of the company president, Farnsworth is not in violation of his responsibility to be loyal and to provide care to his clients. In this case, the participants and the beneficiaries of the profit-sharing plan are the clients, not the company's management. Had Farnsworth not investigated the issue or had he yielded to the president's wishes and voted for a slate of directors that he had determined was not in the best interest of the company, Farnsworth would have violated his responsibilities to the beneficiaries of the plan. In addition, because the brokerage firm provides the lowest commissions and best execution for securities transactions, Farnsworth has met his obligations to the client in using this brokerage firm. It does not matter that the brokerage firm also provides research information that is not useful for the

account generating the commission, because Farnsworth is not paying extra money of the client's for that information.

15. A is correct. In this question, Brown is providing investment recommendations before making inquiries about the client's financial situation, investment experience, or investment objectives. Brown is thus violating Standard III(C)—Suitability. Answers B and C provide examples of information members and candidates should discuss with their clients at the outset of the relationship, but these answers do not constitute a complete list of those factors. Answer A is the best answer.

16. C is correct. This question involves Standard I(C)—Misrepresentation. Statement 1 is a factual statement that discloses to clients and prospects accurate information about the terms of the investment instrument. Statement 2, which guarantees a specific rate of return for a mutual fund, is an opinion stated as a fact and, therefore, violates Standard I(C). If statement 2 were rephrased to include a qualifying statement, such as "in my opinion, investors may earn...," it would not be in violation of the Standards.

17. A is correct. This question involves three of the Standards. Anderb, the portfolio manager, has been obtaining more favorable prices for her personal securities transactions than she gets for her clients, which is a breach of Standard III(A)—Loyalty, Prudence, and Care. In addition, she violated Standard I(D)—Misconduct by failing to adhere to company policy and by hiding her personal transactions from her firm. Anderb's supervisor, Bates, violated Standard IV(C)—Responsibilities of Supervisors; although the company had requirements for reporting personal trading, Bates failed to adequately enforce those requirements. Answer B does not represent a violation because Standard VI(B)—Priority of Transactions requires that personal trading in a security be conducted after the trading in that security of clients and the employer. The Code and Standards do not prohibit owning such investments, although firms may establish policies that limit the investment opportunities of members and candidates. Answer C does not represent a violation because the Code and Standards do not contain a prohibition against employees using the same broker they use for their personal accounts that they also use for their client accounts. This arrangement should be disclosed to the employer so that the employer may determine whether a conflict of interest exists.

18. A is correct. This question relates to Standard I(A)—Knowledge of the Law—specifically, global application of the Code and Standards. Members and candidates who practice in multiple jurisdictions may be subject to various securities laws and regulations. If applicable law is more strict than the requirements of the Code and Standards, members and candidates must adhere to applicable law; otherwise, members and candidates must adhere to the Code and Standards. Therefore, answer A is correct. Answer B is incorrect because members and candidates must adhere to the higher standard set by the Code and Standards if local applicable law is less strict. Answer C is incorrect because when no applicable law exists, members and candidates are required to adhere to the Code and Standards, and the Code and Standards prohibit the use of material nonpublic information.

19. B is correct. The best course of action under Standard I(B)—Independence and Objectivity is to avoid a conflict of interest whenever possible. Therefore, for Ward to pay for all his expenses is the correct answer. Answer C details a course of action in which the conflict would be disclosed, but the solution is not as appropriate as avoiding the conflict of interest. Answer A would not be the best course because it would not remove the appearance of a conflict of

interest; even though the report would not be affected by the reimbursement of expenses, it could appear to be.

20. B is correct. Under Standard IV(A)—Loyalty, members and candidates may undertake independent practice that may result in compensation or other benefit in competition with their employer as long as they obtain consent from their employer. Answer C is not consistent with the Standards because the Standards allow members and candidates to make arrangements or preparations to go into competitive business as long as those arrangements do not interfere with their duty to their current employer. Answer A is not consistent with the Standards because the Standards do not include a complete prohibition against undertaking independent practice.

21. B is correct. This question involves Standard VI(A)—Disclosure of Conflicts— specifically, the holdings of an analyst's employer in company stock. Answers A and C do not describe conflicts of interest that Smith would have to disclose. Answer A describes the use of a firm's products, which would not be a required disclosure. In answer C, the relationship between the analyst and the company through a relative is so tangential that it does not create a conflict of interest necessitating disclosure.

22. B is correct. This question relates to Standard I(C)—Misrepresentation. Although Michelieu's statement about the total return of his clients' accounts on average may be technically true, it is misleading because the majority of the gain resulted from one client's large position taken against Michelieu's advice. Therefore, this statement misrepresents the investment performance the member is responsible for. He has not taken steps to present a fair, accurate, and complete presentation of performance. Answer A is incorrect because Michelieu's statement is a misrepresentation of his performance history. Answer C is incorrect because Michelieu does not guarantee future results.

23. B is correct. The best policy to prevent violation of Standard II(A)— Material Nonpublic Information is the establishment of firewalls in a firm to prevent exchange of insider information. The physical and informational barrier of a firewall between the investment banking department and the brokerage operation prevents the investment banking department from providing information to analysts on the brokerage side who may be writing recommendations on a company stock. Prohibiting recommendations of the stock of companies that are clients of the investment banking department is an alternative, but answer A states that this prohibition would be permanent, which is not the best answer. Once an offering is complete and the material nonpublic information obtained by the investment banking department becomes public, resuming publishing recommendations on the stock is not a violation of the Code and Standards because the information of the investment banking department no longer gives the brokerage operation an advantage in writing the report. Answer C is incorrect because no exchange of information should be occurring between the investment banking department and the brokerage operation, so monitoring of such exchanges is not an effective compliance procedure for preventing the use of material nonpublic information.

24. B is correct. Under Standard III(A)—Loyalty, Prudence, and Care, members and candidates who manage a company's pension fund owe these duties to the participants and beneficiaries of the pension plan, not the management of the company or the company's shareholders.

25. B is correct. Answer B gives one of the two primary reasons listed in the *Handbook* for disclosing referral fees to clients under Standard VI(C)—Referral Fees. (The other is to allow clients and employers to evaluate the full cost of the

services.) Answer A is inconsistent because Standard VI(C) does not require members or candidates to discount their fees when they receive referral fees. Answer C is inconsistent with Standard VI(C) because disclosure of referral fees, to be effective, should be made to prospective clients before entering into a formal client relationship with them.

26. B is correct. Standard VI(B)—Priority of Transactions does not limit transactions of company employees that differ from current recommendations as long as the sale does not disadvantage current clients. Thus, answer A is incorrect. Answer C is incorrect because the Standard does not require the matching of personal and client trades.

27. C is correct. Standard IV(A)—Loyalty discusses activities permissible to members and candidates when they are leaving their current employer; soliciting clients is strictly prohibited. Thus, answer A is inconsistent with the Code and Standards even with the required disclosure. Answer B is incorrect because the offer does not directly violate the Code and Standards. There may be out-of-work members and candidates who can arrange the necessary commitments without violating the Code and Standards.

28. A is correct. The question relates to Standard III(A)—Loyalty, Prudence, and Care. Carter believes the broker offers effective execution at a fee that is comparable with those of other brokers, so he is free to use the broker for all accounts. Answer B is incorrect because the accounts that prohibit soft dollar arrangements do not want to fund the purchase of research by Carter. The new trading scheme does not incur additional commissions from clients, so it would not go against the prohibitions. Answer C is incorrect because Carter should not incur unnecessary or excessive "churning" of the portfolios (excessive trading) for the purpose of meeting the brokerage commitments of soft dollar arrangements.

29. B is correct. According to Standard VII(B)—Reference to CFA Institute, the CFA Designation, and the CFA Program, CFA Program candidates do not receive their actual scores on the exam. Topic and subtopic results are grouped into three broad categories, and the exam is graded only as "pass" or "fail." Although a candidate may have achieved a topical score of "above 70 percent," she or he cannot factually state that she or he received the highest possible score because that information is not reported. Thus, answer C is incorrect. Answer A is incorrect as long as the member or candidate actually completed the exams consecutively. Standard VII(B) does not prohibit the communication of factual information about completing the CFA Program in three consecutive years.

30. C is correct. According to Standard III(A)—Loyalty, Prudence, and Care, the CFA Program would be considered a personal or firm expense and should not be paid for with the fund's brokerage commissions. Soft dollar accounts should be used only to purchase research services that directly assist the investment manager in the investment decision-making process, not to assist the management of the firm or to further education. Thus, answer A is incorrect. Answer B is incorrect because the reasonableness of how the money is used is not an issue; the issue is that educational expense is not research.

31. A is correct. Standard I(B)—Independence and Objectivity emphasizes the need for members and candidates to maintain their independence and objectivity. Best practices dictate that firms adopt a strict policy not to accept compensation for travel arrangements. At times, however, accepting paid travel would not compromise one's independence and objectivity. Answers B and C are incorrect because the added benefits—free conference admission

for additional staff members and an exclusive golf retreat for the speaker—could be viewed as inducements related to the firm's working arrangements and not solely related to the speaking engagement. Should Long wish to bring other team members or participate in the golf outing, he or his firm should be responsible for the associated fees.

32. C is correct. The guidance to Standard II(A)—Material Nonpublic Information recommends adding securities to the firm's restricted list when the firm has or may have material nonpublic information. By adding these securities to this list, Andrews would uphold this standard. Because waiting until the next day will not ensure that news of the merger is made public, answer A is incorrect. Negotiations may take much longer between the two companies, and the merger may never happen. Andrews must wait until the information is disseminated to the market before he trades on that information. Answer B is incorrect because Andrews should not disclose the information to other managers; no trading is allowed on material nonpublic information.

33. B is correct. Through placing a personal purchase order that is significantly greater than the average volume, Pietro is violating Standard IIB—Market Manipulation. He is attempting to manipulate an increase in the share price and thus bring a buyer to the negotiating table. The news of a possible merger and confirmation of the firm's earnings guidance may also have positive effects on the price of Local Bank, but Pietro's actions in instructing the release of the information does not represent a violation through market manipulation. Announcements of this nature are common and practical to keep investors informed. Thus, answers A and C are incorrect.

34. C is correct. Cupp violated Standard III(D)—Performance Presentations when he deviated from the firm's stated policies solely to capture the gain from the holding being acquired. Answer A is incorrect because the firm does not claim GIPS compliance and the GIPS standards require external cash flows to be treated in a consistent manner with the firm's documented policies. Answer B is incorrect because the firm does not state that it is updating its composite policies. If such a change were to occur, all cash flows for the month would have to be reviewed to ensure their consistent treatment under the new policy.

35. A is correct. According to Standard V(C)—Record Retention, Cannan needed the permission of her employer to maintain the files at home after her employment ended. Without that permission, she should have deleted the files. All files created as part of a member's or candidate's professional activity are the property of the firm, even those created outside normal work hours. Thus, answer B is incorrect. Answer C is incorrect because the Code and Standards do not prohibit using one's personal computer to complete work for one's employer.

36. B is correct. According to Standard VII(B)—Reference to CFA Institute, the CFA Designation, and the CFA Program, Quinn cannot claim to have finished the CFA Program or be eligible for the CFA charter until he officially learns that he has passed the Level III exam. Until the results for the most recent exam are released, those who sat for the exam should continue to refer to themselves as "candidates." Thus, answer C is incorrect. Answer A is incorrect because members and candidates may discuss areas of practice in which they believe the CFA Program improved their personal skills.

37. A is correct. Hart's decision to invest in the retail fund appears directly correlated with Rodriguez's statement about the successful quarter of Mega Retail and thus violates Standard II(A)—Material Nonpublic Information. Rodriguez's information would be considered material because it would

influence the share price of Mega Retail and probably influence the price of the entire exchange-traded retail fund. Thus, answer B is incorrect. Answer C is also incorrect because Rodriguez shared information that was both material and nonpublic. Company officers regularly have such knowledge about their firms, which is not a violation. The sharing of such information, however, even in a conversation between friends, does violate Standard II(A).

38. C is correct. Standard VII(A)—Conduct as Members and Candidates in the CFA Program prohibits providing information to candidates or the public that is considered confidential to the CFA Program. In revealing that questions related to the analysis of inventories and analysis of taxes were on the exam, Park has violated this standard. Answer B is incorrect because the guidance for the standard explicitly acknowledges that members and candidates are allowed to offer their opinions about the CFA Program. Answer A is incorrect because candidates are not prohibited from using outside resources.

39. B is correct. Paper has violated Standard III(D)—Performance Presentation by not disclosing that he was part of a team of managers that achieved the results shown. If he had also included the return of the portion he directly managed, he would not have violated the standard. Thus, answer A is incorrect. Answer C is incorrect because Paper received written permission from his prior employer to include the results.

40. A is correct. Townsend has not provided any information about her clients to the leaders or managers of the golf program; thus, she has not violated Standard III(E)—Preservation of Confidentiality. Providing contact information about her clients for a direct-mail solicitation would have been a violation. Answer B is incorrect because the notice in the newsletter does not violate Standard III(E). Answer C is incorrect because the golf program's fund-raising campaign had already begun, so discussing the opportunity to donate was appropriate.

Introduction to the Global Investment Performance Standards (GIPS)

The objective of this reading is to orient the Level I candidate approaching the assigned sections of the GIPS standards. It explains why the GIPS standards were created, who can claim compliance, and who benefits from compliance. It also introduces the key notion of composites, states the purpose of verification, and previews the structure of the Standards.

WHY WERE THE GIPS STANDARDS CREATED?

Institutions and individuals are constantly scrutinizing past investment performance returns in search of the best manager to achieve their investment objectives.

In the past, the investment community had great difficulty making meaningful comparisons on the basis of accurate investment performance data. Several performance measurement practices hindered the comparability of performance returns from one firm to another, while others called into question the accuracy and credibility of performance reporting overall. Misleading practices included:

- <u>Representative Accounts</u>: Selecting a top-performing portfolio to represent the firm's overall investment results for a specific mandate.

- <u>Survivorship Bias</u>: Presenting an "average" performance history that *excludes* portfolios whose poor performance was weak enough to result in termination of the firm.

- <u>Varying Time Periods</u>: Presenting performance for a selected time period during which the mandate produced excellent returns or out-performed its benchmark—making comparison with other firms' results difficult or impossible.

Making a valid comparison of investment performance among even the most ethical investment management firms was problematic. For example, a pension fund seeking to hire an investment management firm might receive proposals from several firms, all using different methodologies for calculating their results.

The GIPS standards are a practitioner-driven set of ethical principles that establish a standardized, industry-wide approach for investment firms to follow in calculating and presenting their historical investment results to prospective clients. The GIPS standards ensure fair representation and full disclosure of investment performance. In other words, the GIPS standards lead investment management firms to avoid misrepresentations of performance and to communicate all relevant information that prospective clients should know in order to evaluate past results.

II WHO CAN CLAIM COMPLIANCE?

First, any investment management firm may choose to comply with the GIPS standards. Complying with the GIPS standards is voluntary. Compliance with the GIPS standards is not typically required by legal or regulatory authorities.

Second, only investment management firms that *actually manage* assets can claim compliance with the Standards. Plan sponsors and consultants cannot make a claim of compliance unless they actually manage assets for which they are making a claim of compliance. They can claim to endorse the Standards and/or require that their investment managers comply with the Standards. Similarly, software (and the vendors who supply software) cannot be "compliant." Software can assist firms in achieving compliance with the GIPS standards (e.g., by calculating performance in a manner consistent with the calculation requirements of the Standards) but only an investment management firm can claim compliance once the firm has satisfied all requirements of the Standards.

Third, compliance is a firm-wide process that cannot be achieved on a single product or composite. A firm has only two options with regard to compliance with the GIPS standards: fully comply with *all* requirements of the GIPS standards and claim compliance through the use of the GIPS Compliance Statement; or not comply with all requirements of the GIPS standards and not claim compliance with, or make any reference to, the GIPS standards.

III WHO BENEFITS FROM COMPLIANCE?

The GIPS standards benefit two main groups: investment management firms and prospective clients.

- By choosing to comply with the GIPS standards, investment management firms assure prospective clients that the historical "track record" they report is both complete and fairly presented. Compliance enables the GIPS-compliant firm to participate in competitive bids against other compliant firms throughout the world. Achieving and maintaining compliance may also strengthen the firm's internal controls over performance-related processes and procedures.

- Investors have a greater level of confidence in the integrity of performance presentations of a GIPS-compliant firm and can more easily compare performance presentations from different investment management firms. While the GIPS standards certainly do not eliminate the need for in-depth due diligence on the part of the investor, compliance with the Standards enhances the credibility of investment management firms that have chosen to undertake this responsibility.

COMPOSITES

One of the key concepts of the Standards is the required use of composites. A composite is an aggregation of one or more portfolios managed according to a similar investment mandate, objective, or strategy. A composite must include all actual, fee-paying, discretionary portfolios managed in accordance with the same investment mandate, objective, or strategy. For example, if a GIPS-compliant firm presents its track record for a Global Equity Composite (the Composite), the Composite must include all portfolios that are managed, or have historically been managed, in the firm's Global Equity strategy. The firm may not subjectively select which Global Equity portfolios will be included in or excluded from the calculation and presentation of the Global Equity Composite. The determination of which portfolios to include in the Composite should be done according to pre-established criteria (i.e., on an ex-ante basis), not after the fact. This prevents a firm from including only their best-performing portfolios in the Composite.

VERIFICATION

Firms that claim compliance with the GIPS standards are responsible for their claim of compliance and for maintaining that compliance. That is, firms self-regulate their claim of compliance. Once a firm claims compliance with the Standards, they may voluntarily hire an independent third party to perform a verification in order to increase confidence in the firm's claim of compliance. Verification may also increase the knowledge of the firm's performance measurement team and improve the consistency and quality of the firm's compliant presentations.

Verification is performed with respect to an entire firm, not on specific composites. Verification does not ensure the accuracy of any specific composite presentation. Verification tests:

- whether the investment firm has complied with all the composite construction requirements of the GIPS standards on a firm-wide basis, and

- whether the firm's policies and procedures are designed to calculate and present performance in compliance with the GIPS standards.

Verification must be performed by an independent third party. A firm cannot perform its own verification.

Third-party verification brings additional credibility to a firm's claim of compliance. A verified firm may provide existing and prospective clients with greater assurance about its claim of compliance with the GIPS standards. Verification may also provide improved internal processes and procedures as well as marketing advantages to the firm.

THE STRUCTURE OF THE GIPS STANDARDS

The provisions within the 2010 edition of the GIPS standards are divided into nine sections: Fundamentals of Compliance, Input Data, Calculation Methodology, Composite Construction, Disclosure, Presentation and Reporting, Real Estate, Private Equity, and Wrap Free/Separately Managed Account (SMA) Portfolios. The provisions are further categorized into requirements and recommendations.

Index			
Tokyo (Nikkei)			
Seoul			
Taipei (Comp.)			
Mumbai			
Singapore			
Sydney			
Shanghai B	397.0	1.0%	-4.7%
Hong Kong	16,440	0.9%	-10.5%
Toronto	316.8	0.7%	-6.9%
Stockholm	22,700.9	0.5%	-4.2%
Mexico City	13,524.8	0.1%	4.1%

4

Global Investment Performance Standards (GIPS)

LEARNING OUTCOMES

Mastery	The candidate should be able to:
☐	**a** describe the key features of the GIPS standards and the fundamentals of compliance;
☐	**b** describe the scope of the GIPS standards with respect to an investment firm's definition and historical performance record;
☐	**c** explain how the GIPS standards are implemented in countries with existing standards for performance reporting and describe the appropriate response when the GIPS standards and local regulations conflict;
☐	**d** describe the nine major sections of the GIPS standards.

OPTIONAL
SEGMENT

PREFACE

CFA Institute is a global not-for-profit association of investment professionals with the mission of leading the investment profession globally by setting the highest standards of ethics, education, and professional excellence. CFA Institute has a long-standing history of and commitment to establishing a broadly accepted ethical standard for calculating and presenting investment performance based on the principles of fair representation and full disclosure. The goals in developing and evolving the Global Investment Performance Standards (GIPS) are to establish them as the recognized standard for calculating and presenting investment performance around the world and for the GIPS standards to become a firm's "passport" to market investment management services globally. As of January 2010, CFA Institute has partnered with organizations in 32 countries that contribute to the development and promotion of the GIPS standards.

History

- In 1995, CFA Institute, formerly known as the Association for Investment Management and Research (AIMR), sponsored and funded the Global Investment Performance Standards Committee to develop global standards for calculating and presenting investment performance, based on the existing AIMR Performance Presentation Standards (AIMR-PPS®).

- In 1998, the proposed GIPS standards were posted on the CFA Institute website and circulated for comment to more than 4,000 individuals who had expressed interest. The result was the first Global Investment Performance Standards, published in April 1999.

- The initial edition of the GIPS standards was designed to create a minimum global investment performance standard that would:

  - Permit and facilitate acceptance and adoption in developing markets;

  - Give the global investment management industry one commonly accepted approach for calculating and presenting performance; and

  - Address liquid asset classes (equity, fixed income, and cash).

- In 1999, the Global Investment Performance Standards Committee was replaced by the Investment Performance Council (IPC) to further develop and promote the GIPS standards. The development of the GIPS standards was a global industry initiative with participation from individuals and organizations from more than 15 countries.

- The IPC was charged with developing provisions for other asset classes (e.g., real estate, private equity) and addressing other performance-related issues (e.g., fees, advertising) to broaden the scope and applicability of the GIPS standards. This was accomplished when the second edition of the GIPS standards was published in February 2005.

- With the release of the 2005 edition of the GIPS standards and growing adoption and expansion of the GIPS standards, the IPC decided to move to a single global investment performance standard and eliminate the need for local variations of the GIPS standards. All country-specific performance standards converged with the GIPS standards, resulting in 25 countries adopting a single, global standard for the calculation and presentation of investment performance.

- In 2005, with the convergence of country-specific versions to the GIPS standards and the need to reorganize the governance structure to facilitate involvement from GIPS country sponsors, CFA Institute dissolved the IPC and created the GIPS Executive Committee and the GIPS Council. The GIPS Executive Committee serves as the decision-making authority for the GIPS standards, and the GIPS Council facilitates the involvement of all country sponsors in the ongoing development and promotion of the GIPS standards.

- To maintain global relevance, and in recognition of the dynamic nature of the investment industry, the GIPS standards must be continually updated through interpretations, guidance, and new provisions. In 2008, the GIPS Executive Committee began its review of the GIPS standards in an effort to further refine the provisions as well as eliminate provisions that are no longer necessary and add new requirements and recommendations that promote best practice. The GIPS Executive Committee worked in close collaboration with its technical subcommittees, specially formed working groups, and GIPS country sponsors. These groups reviewed the existing provisions and guidance and conducted surveys and other research as part of the efforts to produce the 2010 edition of the GIPS standards.

**END OPTIONAL
SEGMENT**

GLOBAL INVESTMENT PERFORMANCE STANDARDS

Introduction
Preamble—Why Is a Global Investment Performance Standard Needed?

Standardized Investment Performance: Financial markets and the investment management industry have become increasingly global in nature. The growth in the types and number of financial entities, the globalization of the investment process, and the increased competition among investment management firms demonstrate the need to standardize the calculation and presentation of investment performance.

Global Passport: Asset managers and both existing and prospective clients benefit from an established global standard for calculating and presenting investment performance. Investment practices, regulation, performance measurement, and reporting of performance vary considerably from country to country. By adhering to a global standard, firms in countries with minimal or no investment performance standards will be able to compete for business on an equal footing with firms from countries with more developed standards. Firms from countries with established practices will have more confidence in being fairly compared with local firms when competing for business in countries that have not previously adopted performance standards. Performance standards that are accepted globally enable investment firms to measure and present their investment performance so that investors can readily compare investment performance among firms.

Investor Confidence: Investment managers that adhere to investment performance standards help assure investors that the firm's investment performance is complete and fairly presented. Both prospective and existing clients of investment firms benefit from a global investment performance standard by having a greater degree of confidence in the performance information presented to them.

Objectives

The establishment of a voluntary global investment performance standard leads to an accepted set of best practices for calculating and presenting investment performance that is readily comparable among investment firms, regardless of geographic location. These standards also facilitate a dialogue between investment firms and their existing and prospective clients regarding investment performance.

The goals of the GIPS Executive Committee are:

- To establish investment industry best practices for calculating and presenting investment performance that promote investor interests and instill investor confidence;

- To obtain worldwide acceptance of a single standard for the calculation and presentation of investment performance based on the principles of fair representation and full disclosure;

- To promote the use of accurate and consistent investment performance data;

- To encourage fair, global competition among investment firms without creating barriers to entry; and

- To foster the notion of industry "self-regulation" on a global basis.

Overview

Key features of the Global Investment Performance Standards include the following:

■ The GIPS standards are ethical standards for investment performance presentation to ensure fair representation and full disclosure of investment performance. In order to claim compliance, firms must adhere to the requirements included in the GIPS standards.

■ Meeting the objectives of fair representation and full disclosure is likely to require more than simply adhering to the minimum requirements of the GIPS standards. Firms should also adhere to the recommendations to achieve best practice in the calculation and presentation of performance.

■ The GIPS standards require firms to include all actual, discretionary, fee-paying portfolios in at least one composite defined by investment mandate, objective, or strategy in order to prevent firms from cherry-picking their best performance.

■ The GIPS standards rely on the integrity of input data. The accuracy of input data is critical to the accuracy of the performance presentation. The underlying valuations of portfolio holdings drive the portfolio's performance. It is essential for these and other inputs to be accurate. The GIPS standards require firms to adhere to certain calculation methodologies and to make specific disclosures along with the firm's performance.

■ Firms must comply with all requirements of the GIPS standards, including any updates, Guidance Statements, interpretations, Questions & Answers (Q&As), and clarifications published by CFA Institute and the GIPS Executive Committee, which are available on the GIPS website (www.gipsstandards.org) as well as in the *GIPS Handbook*.

The GIPS standards do not address every aspect of performance measurement or cover unique characteristics of each asset class. The GIPS standards will continue to evolve over time to address additional areas of investment performance. Understanding and interpreting investment performance requires consideration of both risk and return. Historically, the GIPS standards focused primarily on returns. In the spirit of fair representation and full disclosure, and in order to provide investors with a more comprehensive view of a firm's performance, the 2010 edition of the GIPS standards includes new provisions related to risk.

Historical Performance Record

■ A firm is required to initially present, at a minimum, five years of annual investment performance that is compliant with the GIPS standards. If the firm or the composite has been in existence less than five years, the firm must present performance since the firm's inception or the composite inception date.

■ After a firm presents a minimum of five years of GIPS-compliant performance (or for the period since the firm's inception or the composite inception date if the firm or the composite has been in existence less than five years), the firm must present an additional year of performance each year, building up to a minimum of 10 years of GIPS-compliant performance.

■ Firms may link non-GIPS-compliant performance to their GIPS-compliant performance provided that only GIPS-compliant performance is presented for periods after 1 January 2000 and the firm discloses the periods of non-compliance. Firms must not link non-GIPS-compliant performance for periods beginning on or after 1 January 2000 to their GIPS-compliant performance. Firms that manage private equity, real estate, and/or wrap fee/separately managed account (SMA) portfolios must also comply with Sections 6, 7, and 8, respectively, of the Provisions of the GIPS standards that became effective as of 1 January 2006.

Compliance

Firms must take all steps necessary to ensure that they have satisfied all the requirements of the GIPS standards before claiming compliance. Firms are strongly encouraged to perform periodic internal compliance checks. Implementing adequate internal controls during all stages of the investment performance process—from data input to preparing performance presentations—will instill confidence in the validity of performance presented as well as in the claim of compliance.

Firms may choose to have an independent third-party verification that tests the construction of the firm's composites as well as the firm's policies and procedures as they relate to compliance with the GIPS standards. The value of verification is widely recognized, and being verified is considered to be best practice. The GIPS Executive Committee strongly recommends that firms be verified. In addition to verification, firms may also choose to have specifically focused composite testing (performance examination) performed by an independent third-party verifier to provide additional assurance regarding a particular composite.

Effective Date

The effective date for the 2010 edition of the GIPS standards is 1 January 2011. Compliant presentations that include performance for periods that begin on or after 1 January 2011 must be prepared in accordance with the 2010 edition of the GIPS standards. Prior editions of the GIPS standards may be found on the GIPS website (www.gipsstandards.org).

Implementing a Global Standard

The presence of a local sponsoring organization for investment performance standards is essential for effective implementation and ongoing support of the GIPS standards within a country. Such country sponsors also provide an important link between the GIPS Executive Committee, the governing body for the GIPS standards, and the local markets in which investment managers operate.

The country sponsor, by actively supporting the GIPS standards and the work of the GIPS Executive Committee, ensures that the country's interests are taken into account as the GIPS standards are developed. Compliance with the GIPS standards is voluntary, and support from the local country sponsor helps to drive the adoption of the GIPS standards.

The GIPS Executive Committee strongly encourages countries without an investment performance standard to promote the GIPS standards as the local standard and translate them into the local language when necessary. Although the GIPS standards may be translated into many languages, if a discrepancy arises, the English version of the GIPS standards is the official governing version.

The GIPS Executive Committee will continue to promote the principles of fair representation and full disclosure and develop the GIPS standards so that they maintain their relevance within the changing investment management industry.

The self-regulatory nature of the GIPS standards necessitates a strong commitment to ethical integrity. Self-regulation also assists regulators in exercising their responsibility for ensuring the fair disclosure of information within financial markets. The GIPS Executive Committee encourages regulators to:

■ Recognize the benefit of voluntary compliance with standards that represent global best practices;

■ Give consideration to taking enforcement actions on firms that falsely claim compliance with the GIPS standards; and

■ Recognize and encourage independent third-party verification.

Where existing laws, regulations, or industry standards already impose requirements related to the calculation and presentation of investment performance, firms are strongly encouraged to comply with the GIPS standards in addition to applicable regulatory requirements. Compliance with applicable law and/or regulation does not necessarily lead to compliance with the GIPS standards. In cases in which laws and/or regulations conflict with the GIPS standards, firms are required to comply with the laws and regulations and make full disclosure of the conflict in the compliant presentation.

Country Sponsors

OPTIONAL
SEGMENT

The presence of a local sponsoring organization for investment performance standards, known as a "country sponsor," is essential for effective implementation of the GIPS standards and ongoing support within a country. Country sponsors collectively form the GIPS Council, which provides a formal role in the ongoing development and oversight of the GIPS standards. Country sponsors:

■ Promote the GIPS standards locally;

■ Provide local market support and input for the GIPS standards;

■ Present country-specific issues to the GIPS Executive Committee; and

■ Participate in the governance of the GIPS standards via membership in the GIPS Council and Regional Investment Performance Subcommittees.

Each organization undergoes a formal review before being endorsed as a country sponsor. Additional information and a current list of country sponsors can be found on the GIPS website (www.gipsstandards.org).

Endorsed GIPS Country Sponsors (as of 1 January 2010)

Australia   Investment and Financial Services Association Limited—Performance Analyst Group

Austria   1) Österreichische Vereinigung für Finanzanalyse und Asset Management and 2) Vereinigung Österreichischer Investmentgesellschaften

Belgium   Belgian Asset Managers Association

Canada   Canadian Investment Performance Committee

Denmark   The Danish Society of Financial Analysts and CFA Denmark

France   1) Société Française des Analystes Financiers and 2) Association Française de la Gestion Financière

Germany   German Asset Management Standards Committee: 1) Bundesverband Investment und Asset Management e.V., 2) Deutsche Vereinigung für Finanzanalyse und Asset Management, and 3) German CFA Society

Greece   Hellenic CFA Society

Hong Kong   Local Sponsor: The Hong Kong Society of Financial Analysts

Hungary   1) CFA Society of Hungary and 2) the Association of Hungarian Investment Fund and Asset Management Companies

Ireland   Irish Association of Investment Managers

Italy   Italian Investment Performance Committee: 1) L'Associazione Bancaria Italiana, 2) L'Associazione Italiana degli Analisti Finanziari, 3) Assogestioni, 4) Sviluppo Mercato Fondi Pensione, 5) Assirevi, and 6) Italian CFA Society

Japan   The Security Analysts Association of Japan

Kazakhstan   Kazakhstan Association of Financial and Investment Analysts

Liechtenstein   Liechtenstein Bankers' Association

Micronesia   Asia Pacific Association for Fiduciary Studies

The Netherlands   The Netherlands Beroepsvereniging van Beleggingsprofessionals

New Zealand   CFA Society of New Zealand

Norway   The Norwegian Society of Financial Analysts

Pakistan   CFA Association of Pakistan

Portugal   Associação Portuguesa de Analista Financeiros

Russia   National League of Management Companies

Singapore   Investment Management Association of Singapore

South Africa   Association for Savings and Investment, South Africa

South Korea   Korea GIPS Committee

Spain   Asociación Española de Presentación de Resultados de Gestión

Sri Lanka   CFA Sri Lanka

Sweden   Swedish Society of Financial Analysts

Switzerland   Swiss Bankers Association

Ukraine   The Ukrainian Association of Investment Business

United Kingdom   U.K. Investment Performance Committee: 1) Association of British Insurers, 2) Investment Management Association, and 3) National Association of Pension Funds

United States   CFA Institute—U.S. Investment Performance Committee

END OPTIONAL SEGMENT

PROVISIONS OF THE GLOBAL INVESTMENT PERFORMANCE STANDARDS

The provisions within the GIPS standards are divided into the following nine sections: Fundamentals of Compliance, Input Data, Calculation Methodology, Composite Construction, Disclosure, Presentation and Reporting, Real Estate, Private Equity, and Wrap Fee/Separately Managed Account (SMA) Portfolios.

The provisions for each section are categorized into requirements and recommendations. Firms must meet all the requirements to claim compliance with the GIPS standards. Firms are encouraged to implement as many of the recommendations as possible. These recommended provisions are considered to be industry best practice and assist firms in fully adhering to the spirit and intent of the GIPS standards.

0. **Fundamentals of Compliance:** Several core principles create the foundation for the GIPS standards, including properly defining the firm, providing compliant presentations to all prospective clients, adhering to applicable laws and regulations, and ensuring that information presented is not false or misleading. Two important issues that a firm must consider when becoming compliant with the GIPS standards are the definition of the firm and the firm's definition of discretion. The definition of the firm is the foundation for firm-wide compliance and creates defined boundaries whereby total firm assets can be determined. The firm's definition of discretion establishes criteria to judge which portfolios must be included in a composite and is based on the firm's ability to implement its investment strategy.

1. **Input Data:** Consistency of input data used to calculate performance is critical to effective compliance with the GIPS standards and establishes the foundation for full, fair, and comparable investment performance presentations. For periods beginning on or after 1 January 2011, all portfolios must be valued in accordance with the definition of fair value and the GIPS Valuation Principles.

2. **Calculation Methodology:** Achieving comparability among investment management firms' performance presentations requires uniformity in methods used to calculate returns. The GIPS standards mandate the use of certain calculation methodologies to facilitate comparability.

3. **Composite Construction:** A composite is an aggregation of one or more portfolios managed according to a similar investment mandate, objective, or strategy. The composite return is the asset-weighted average of the performance of all portfolios in the composite. Creating meaningful composites is essential to the fair presentation, consistency, and comparability of performance over time and among firms.

4. **Disclosure:** Disclosures allow firms to elaborate on the data provided in the presentation and give the reader the proper context in which to understand the performance. To comply with the GIPS standards, firms must disclose certain information in all compliant presentations regarding their performance and the policies adopted by the firm. Although some disclosures are required for all firms, others are specific to certain circumstances and may not be applicable in all situations. Firms are not required to make negative assurance disclosures (e.g., if the firm does not use leverage in a particular composite strategy, no disclosure of the use of leverage is required). One of the essential disclosures for every firm is the claim of compliance. Once a firm meets all the requirements of the GIPS standards, it must appropriately use the claim of compliance to indicate compliance with the GIPS standards. The 2010 edition of the GIPS standards includes a revised compliance statement that indicates if the firm has or has not been verified.

5. **Presentation and Reporting:** After constructing the composites, gathering the input data, calculating returns, and determining the necessary disclosures, the firm must incorporate this information in presentations based on the requirements in the GIPS standards for presenting investment performance. No finite set of requirements can cover all potential situations or anticipate future developments in investment industry structure, technology, products, or practices. When appropriate, firms have the responsibility to include in GIPS-compliant presentations information not addressed by the GIPS standards.

6. **Real Estate:** Unless otherwise noted, this section supplements all of the required and recommended provisions in Sections 0–5. Real estate provisions were first included in the 2005 edition of the GIPS standards and became effective 1 January 2006. The 2010 edition of the GIPS standards includes new provisions for closed-end real estate funds. Firms should note that certain provisions of Sections 0–5 do not apply to real estate investments or are superseded by provisions within Section 6. The provisions that do not apply have been noted within Section 6.

7. **Private Equity:** Unless otherwise noted, this section supplements all of the required and recommended provisions in Sections 0–5. Private equity provisions were first included in the 2005 edition of the GIPS standards and became effective 1 January 2006. Firms should note that certain provisions in Sections 0–5 do not apply to private equity investments or are superseded by provisions within Section 7. The provisions that do not apply have been noted within Section 7.

8. **Wrap Fee/Separately Managed Account (SMA) Portfolios:** Unless otherwise noted, this section supplements all of the required and recommended provisions in Sections 0–5. Firms should note that certain provisions in Sections 0–5 of the GIPS standards do not apply to wrap fee/SMA portfolios or are superseded by provisions within Section 8. The provisions that do not apply have been noted within Section 8.

Defined Terms: Words appearing in capital letters in the GIPS standards are defined in the GIPS Glossary, which is located at the end of this reading.

0. Fundamentals of Compliance

I.0.1 Fundamentals of Compliance—Requirements

0.A.1. FIRMS MUST comply with all the REQUIREMENTS of the GIPS standards, including any updates, Guidance Statements, interpretations, Questions & Answers (Q&As), and clarifications published by CFA Institute and the GIPS Executive Committee, which are available on the GIPS standards website (www.gipsstandards.org) as well as in the *GIPS Handbook*.

0.A.2. FIRMS MUST comply with all applicable laws and regulations regarding the calculation and presentation of performance.

0.A.3. FIRMS MUST NOT present performance or performance-related information that is false or misleading.

0.A.4. The GIPS standards MUST be applied on a FIRM-wide basis.

0.A.5. FIRMS MUST document their policies and procedures used in establishing and maintaining compliance with the GIPS standards, including ensuring the existence and ownership of client assets, and MUST apply them consistently.

0.A.6. If the FIRM does not meet all the REQUIREMENTS of the GIPS standards, the FIRM MUST NOT represent or state that it is "in compliance with the Global Investment Performance Standards except for . . ." or make any other statements that may indicate partial compliance with the GIPS standards.

0.A.7. Statements referring to the calculation methodology as being "in accordance," "in compliance," or "consistent" with the Global Investment Performance Standards, or similar statements, are prohibited.

0.A.8. Statements referring to the performance of a single, existing client PORTFOLIO as being "calculated in accordance with the Global Investment Performance Standards" are prohibited, except when a GIPS-compliant FIRM reports the performance of an individual client's PORTFOLIO to that client.

0.A.9. FIRMS MUST make every reasonable effort to provide a COMPLIANT PRESENTATION to all PROSPECTIVE CLIENTS. FIRMS MUST NOT choose to whom they present a COMPLIANT PRESENTATION. As long as a PROSPECTIVE CLIENT has received a COMPLIANT PRESENTATION within the previous 12 months, the FIRM has met this REQUIREMENT.

0.A.10. FIRMS MUST provide a complete list of COMPOSITE DESCRIPTIONS to any PROSPECTIVE CLIENT that makes such a request. FIRMS MUST include terminated COMPOSITES on the FIRM'S list of COMPOSITE DESCRIPTIONS for at least five years after the COMPOSITE TERMINATION DATE.

0.A.11. FIRMS MUST provide a COMPLIANT PRESENTATION for any COMPOSITE listed on the FIRM'S list of COMPOSITE DESCRIPTIONS to any PROSPECTIVE CLIENT that makes such a request.

0.A.12. FIRMS MUST be defined as an investment firm, subsidiary, or division held out to clients or PROSPECTIVE CLIENTS as a DISTINCT BUSINESS ENTITY.

0.A.13. For periods beginning on or after 1 January 2011, TOTAL FIRM ASSETS MUST be the aggregate FAIR VALUE of all discretionary and non-discretionary assets managed by the FIRM. This includes both fee-paying and non-fee-paying PORTFOLIOS.[1]

0.A.14. TOTAL FIRM ASSETS MUST include assets assigned to a SUB-ADVISOR provided the FIRM has discretion over the selection of the SUB-ADVISOR.

0.A.15. Changes in a FIRM'S organization MUST NOT lead to alteration of historical COMPOSITE performance.

0.A.16. When the FIRM jointly markets with other firms, the FIRM claiming compliance with the GIPS standards MUST be sure that it is clearly defined and separate relative to other firms being marketed, and that it is clear which FIRM is claiming compliance.

I.0.2 Fundamentals of Compliance—Recommendations

0.B.1. FIRMS SHOULD comply with the RECOMMENDATIONS of the GIPS standards, including RECOMMENDATIONS in any updates, Guidance Statements, interpretations, Questions & Answers (Q&As), and clarifications published by CFA Institute and the GIPS Executive Committee, which will be made available on the GIPS website (www.gipsstandards.org) as well as in the *GIPS Handbook.*

---

1 For periods prior to 1 January 2011, TOTAL FIRM ASSETS MUST be the aggregate of the MARKET VALUE of all discretionary and non-discretionary assets under management within the defined FIRM.

0.B.2. FIRMS SHOULD be verified.

0.B.3. FIRMS SHOULD adopt the broadest, most meaningful definition of the FIRM. The scope of this definition SHOULD include all geographical (country, regional, etc.) offices operating under the same brand name regardless of the actual name of the individual investment management company.

0.B.4. FIRMS SHOULD provide to each existing client, on an annual basis, a COMPLIANT PRESENTATION of the COMPOSITE in which the client's PORTFOLIO is included.

1. Input Data

I.0.3 Input Data—Requirements

1.A.1. All data and information necessary to support all items included in a COMPLIANT PRESENTATION MUST be captured and maintained.

1.A.2. For periods beginning on or after 1 January 2011, PORTFOLIOS MUST be valued in accordance with the definition of FAIR VALUE and the GIPS Valuation Principles.[2]

1.A.3. FIRMS MUST value PORTFOLIOS in accordance with the COMPOSITE-specific valuation policy. PORTFOLIOS MUST be valued:

  a. For periods beginning on or after 1 January 2001, at least monthly.[3]

  b. For periods beginning on or after 1 January 2010, on the date of all LARGE CASH FLOWS. FIRMS MUST define LARGE CASH FLOW for each COMPOSITE to determine when PORTFOLIOS in that COMPOSITE MUST be valued.

  c. No more frequently than required by the valuation policy.

1.A.4. For periods beginning on or after 1 January 2010, FIRMS MUST value PORTFOLIOS as of the calendar month end or the last business day of the month.

1.A.5. For periods beginning on or after 1 January 2005, FIRMS MUST use TRADE DATE ACCOUNTING.

1.A.6. ACCRUAL ACCOUNTING MUST be used for fixed-income securities and all other investments that earn interest income. The value of fixed-income securities MUST include accrued income.

1.A.7. For periods beginning on or after 1 January 2006, COMPOSITES MUST have consistent beginning and ending annual valuation dates. Unless the COMPOSITE is reported on a non-calendar fiscal year, the beginning and ending valuation dates MUST be at calendar year end or on the last business day of the year.

I.0.4 Input Data—Recommendations

1.B.1. FIRMS SHOULD value PORTFOLIOS on the date of all EXTERNAL CASH FLOWS.

1.B.2. Valuations SHOULD be obtained from a qualified independent third party.

---

2 For periods prior to 1 January 2011, PORTFOLIO valuations MUST be based on MARKET VALUES (not cost basis or book values).

3 For periods prior to 1 January 2001, PORTFOLIOS MUST be valued at least quarterly.

1.B.3. ACCRUAL ACCOUNTING SHOULD be used for dividends (as of the ex-dividend date).

1.B.4. FIRMS SHOULD accrue INVESTMENT MANAGEMENT FEES.

2. Calculation Methodology

I.0.5 Calculation Methodology—Requirements

2.A.1. TOTAL RETURNS MUST be used.

2.A.2. FIRMS MUST calculate TIME-WEIGHTED RATES OF RETURN that adjust for EXTERNAL CASH FLOWS. Both periodic and sub-period returns MUST be geometrically LINKED. EXTERNAL CASH FLOWS MUST be treated according to the FIRM'S COMPOSITE-specific policy. At a minimum:

  a. For periods beginning on or after 1 January 2001, FIRMS MUST calculate PORTFOLIO returns at least monthly.

  b. For periods beginning on or after 1 January 2005, FIRMS MUST calculate PORTFOLIO returns that adjust for daily-weighted EXTERNAL CASH FLOWS.

2.A.3. Returns from cash and cash equivalents held in PORTFOLIOS MUST be included in all return calculations.

2.A.4. All returns MUST be calculated after the deduction of the actual TRADING EXPENSES incurred during the period. FIRMS MUST NOT use estimated TRADING EXPENSES.

2.A.5. If the actual TRADING EXPENSES cannot be identified and segregated from a BUNDLED FEE:

  a. When calculating GROSS-OF-FEES returns, returns MUST be reduced by the entire BUNDLED FEE or the portion of the BUNDLED FEE that includes the TRADING EXPENSES. FIRMS MUST NOT use estimated TRADING EXPENSES.

  b. When calculating NET-OF-FEES returns, returns MUST be reduced by the entire BUNDLED FEE or the portion of the BUNDLED FEE that includes the TRADING EXPENSES and the INVESTMENT MANAGEMENT FEE. FIRMS MUST NOT use estimated TRADING EXPENSES.

2.A.6. COMPOSITE returns MUST be calculated by asset-weighting the individual PORTFOLIO returns using beginning-of-period values or a method that reflects both beginning-of-period values and EXTERNAL CASH FLOWS.

2.A.7. COMPOSITE returns MUST be calculated:

  a. For periods beginning on or after 1 January 2006, by asset-weighting the individual PORTFOLIO returns at least quarterly.

  b. For periods beginning on or after 1 January 2010, by asset-weighting the individual PORTFOLIO returns at least monthly.

I.0.6 Calculation Methodology—Recommendations

2.B.1. Returns SHOULD be calculated net of non-reclaimable withholding taxes on dividends, interest, and capital gains. Reclaimable withholding taxes SHOULD be accrued.

2.B.2. For periods prior to 1 January 2010, FIRMS SHOULD calculate COMPOSITE returns by asset-weighting the individual PORTFOLIO returns at least monthly.

3. Composite Construction

I.0.7 Composite Construction—Requirements

3.A.1. All actual, fee-paying, discretionary PORTFOLIOS MUST be included in at least one COMPOSITE. Although non-fee-paying discretionary PORTFOLIOS may be included in a COMPOSITE (with appropriate disclosure), non-discretionary PORTFOLIOS MUST NOT be included in a FIRM'S COMPOSITES.

3.A.2. COMPOSITES MUST include only actual assets managed by the FIRM.

3.A.3. FIRMS MUST NOT LINK performance of simulated or model PORTFOLIOS with actual performance.

3.A.4. COMPOSITES MUST be defined according to investment mandate, objective, or strategy. COMPOSITES MUST include all PORTFOLIOS that meet the COMPOSITE DEFINITION. Any change to a COMPOSITE DEFINITION MUST NOT be applied retroactively. The COMPOSITE DEFINITION MUST be made available upon request.

3.A.5. COMPOSITES MUST include new PORTFOLIOS on a timely and consistent basis after each PORTFOLIO comes under management.

3.A.6. Terminated PORTFOLIOS MUST be included in the historical performance of the COMPOSITE up to the last full measurement period that each PORTFOLIO was under management.

3.A.7. PORTFOLIOS MUST NOT be switched from one COMPOSITE to another unless documented changes to a PORTFOLIO'S investment mandate, objective, or strategy or the redefinition of the COMPOSITE makes it appropriate. The historical performance of the PORTFOLIO MUST remain with the original COMPOSITE.

3.A.8. For periods beginning on or after 1 January 2010, a CARVE-OUT MUST NOT be included in a COMPOSITE unless the CARVE-OUT is managed separately with its own cash balance.[4]

3.A.9. If the FIRM sets a minimum asset level for PORTFOLIOS to be included in a COMPOSITE, the FIRM MUST NOT include PORTFOLIOS below the minimum asset level in that COMPOSITE. Any changes to a COMPOSITE-specific minimum asset level MUST NOT be applied retroactively.

3.A.10. FIRMS that wish to remove PORTFOLIOS from COMPOSITES in cases of SIGNIFICANT CASH FLOWS MUST define "significant" on an EX-ANTE, COMPOSITE-specific basis and MUST consistently follow the COMPOSITE-specific policy.

I.0.8 Composite Construction—Recommendations

3.B.1. If the FIRM sets a minimum asset level for PORTFOLIOS to be included in a COMPOSITE, the FIRM SHOULD NOT present a COMPLIANT PRESENTATION of the COMPOSITE to a PROSPECTIVE CLIENT known not to meet the COMPOSITE'S minimum asset level.

3.B.2. To remove the effect of a SIGNIFICANT CASH FLOW, the FIRM SHOULD use a TEMPORARY NEW ACCOUNT.

---

4 For periods prior to 1 January 2010, if CARVE-OUTS were included in a COMPOSITE, cash MUST have been allocated to the CARVE-OUT in a timely and consistent manner.

4. Disclosure

I.0.9 Disclosure—Requirements

4.A.1.   Once a FIRM has met all the REQUIREMENTS of the GIPS standards, the FIRM MUST disclose its compliance with the GIPS standards using one of the following compliance statements. The claim of compliance MUST only be used in a COMPLIANT PRESENTATION.

For FIRMS that are verified:

> "[Insert name of FIRM] claims compliance with the Global Investment Performance Standards (GIPS®) and has prepared and presented this report in compliance with the GIPS standards. [Insert name of FIRM] has been independently verified for the periods [insert dates]. The verification report(s) is/are available upon request.
>
> Verification assesses whether (1) the firm has complied with all the composite construction requirements of the GIPS standards on a firm-wide basis and (2) the firm's policies and procedures are designed to calculate and present performance in compliance with the GIPS standards. Verification does not ensure the accuracy of any specific composite presentation."

For COMPOSITES of a verified FIRM that have also had a PERFORMANCE EXAMINATION:

> "[Insert name of FIRM] claims compliance with the Global Investment Performance Standards (GIPS®) and has prepared and presented this report in compliance with the GIPS standards. [Insert name of FIRM] has been independently verified for the periods [insert dates].
>
> Verification assesses whether (1) the firm has complied with all the composite construction requirements of the GIPS standards on a firm-wide basis and (2) the firm's policies and procedures are designed to calculate and present performance in compliance with the GIPS standards. The [insert name of COMPOSITE] composite has been examined for the periods [insert dates]. The verification and performance examination reports are available upon request."

For FIRMS that have not been verified:

> "[Insert name of FIRM] claims compliance with the Global Investment Performance Standards (GIPS®) and has prepared and presented this report in compliance with the GIPS standards. [Insert name of FIRM] has not been independently verified."

4.A.2.   FIRMS MUST disclose the definition of the FIRM used to determine TOTAL FIRM ASSETS and FIRM-wide compliance.

4.A.3.   FIRMS MUST disclose the COMPOSITE DESCRIPTION.

4.A.4.   FIRMS MUST disclose the BENCHMARK DESCRIPTION.

4.A.5.   When presenting GROSS-OF-FEES returns, FIRMS MUST disclose if any other fees are deducted in addition to the TRADING EXPENSES.

4.A.6.   When presenting NET-OF-FEES returns, FIRMS MUST disclose:

   a.   If any other fees are deducted in addition to the INVESTMENT MANAGEMENT FEES and TRADING EXPENSES;

   b.   If model or actual INVESTMENT MANAGEMENT FEES are used; and

   c.   If returns are net of any PERFORMANCE-BASED FEES.

4.A.7. FIRMS MUST disclose the currency used to express performance.

4.A.8. FIRMS MUST disclose which measure of INTERNAL DISPERSION is presented.

4.A.9. FIRMS MUST disclose the FEE SCHEDULE appropriate to the COMPLIANT PRESENTATION.

4.A.10. FIRMS MUST disclose the COMPOSITE CREATION DATE.

4.A.11. FIRMS MUST disclose that the FIRM'S list of COMPOSITE DESCRIPTIONS is available upon request.

4.A.12. FIRMS MUST disclose that policies for valuing PORTFOLIOS, calculating performance, and preparing COMPLIANT PRESENTATIONS are available upon request.

4.A.13. FIRMS MUST disclose the presence, use, and extent of leverage, derivatives, and short positions, if material, including a description of the frequency of use and characteristics of the instruments sufficient to identify risks.

4.A.14. FIRMS MUST disclose all significant events that would help a PROSPECTIVE CLIENT interpret the COMPLIANT PRESENTATION.

4.A.15. For any performance presented for periods prior to 1 January 2000 that does not comply with the GIPS standards, FIRMS MUST disclose the periods of non-compliance.

4.A.16. If the FIRM is redefined, the FIRM MUST disclose the date of, description of, and reason for the redefinition.

4.A.17. If a COMPOSITE is redefined, the FIRM MUST disclose the date of, description of, and reason for the redefinition.

4.A.18. FIRMS MUST disclose changes to the name of a COMPOSITE.

4.A.19. FIRMS MUST disclose the minimum asset level, if any, below which PORTFOLIOS are not included in a COMPOSITE. FIRMS MUST also disclose any changes to the minimum asset level.

4.A.20. FIRMS MUST disclose relevant details of the treatment of withholding taxes on dividends, interest income, and capital gains, if material. FIRMS MUST also disclose if BENCHMARK returns are net of withholding taxes if this information is available.

4.A.21. For periods beginning on or after 1 January 2011, FIRMS MUST disclose and describe any known material differences in exchange rates or valuation sources used among the PORTFOLIOS within a COMPOSITE, and between the COMPOSITE and the BENCHMARK.[5]

4.A.22. If the COMPLIANT PRESENTATION conforms with laws and/or regulations that conflict with the REQUIREMENTS of the GIPS standards, FIRMS MUST disclose this fact and disclose the manner in which the laws and/or regulations conflict with the GIPS standards.

4.A.23. For periods prior to 1 January 2010, if CARVE-OUTS are included in a COMPOSITE, FIRMS MUST disclose the policy used to allocate cash to CARVE-OUTS.

4.A.24. If a COMPOSITE contains PORTFOLIOS with BUNDLED FEES, FIRMS MUST disclose the types of fees that are included in the BUNDLED FEE.

4.A.25. For periods beginning on or after 1 January 2006, FIRMS MUST disclose the use of a SUB-ADVISOR and the periods a SUB-ADVISOR was used.

---

5 For periods prior to 1 January 2011, FIRMS MUST disclose and describe any known inconsistencies in the exchange rates used among the PORTFOLIOS within a COMPOSITE and between the COMPOSITE and the BENCHMARK.

4.A.26. For periods prior to 1 January 2010, FIRMS MUST disclose if any PORTFOLIOS were not valued at calendar month end or on the last business day of the month.

4.A.27. For periods beginning on or after 1 January 2011, FIRMS MUST disclose the use of subjective unobservable inputs for valuing PORTFOLIO investments (as described in the GIPS Valuation Principles) if the PORTFOLIO investments valued using subjective unobservable inputs are material to the COMPOSITE.

4.A.28. For periods beginning on or after 1 January 2011, FIRMS MUST disclose if the COMPOSITE'S valuation hierarchy materially differs from the RECOMMENDED hierarchy in the GIPS Valuation Principles.

4.A.29. If the FIRM determines no appropriate BENCHMARK for the COMPOSITE exists, the FIRM MUST disclose why no BENCHMARK is presented.

4.A.30. If the FIRM changes the BENCHMARK, the FIRM MUST disclose the date of, description of, and reason for the change.

4.A.31. If a custom BENCHMARK or combination of multiple BENCHMARKS is used, the FIRM MUST disclose the BENCHMARK components, weights, and rebalancing process.

4.A.32. If the FIRM has adopted a SIGNIFICANT CASH FLOW policy for a specific COMPOSITE, the FIRM MUST disclose how the FIRM defines a SIGNIFICANT CASH FLOW for that COMPOSITE and for which periods.

4.A.33. FIRMS MUST disclose if the three-year annualized EX-POST STANDARD DEVIATION of the COMPOSITE and/or BENCHMARK is not presented because 36 monthly returns are not available.

4.A.34. If the FIRM determines that the three-year annualized EX-POST STANDARD DEVIATION is not relevant or appropriate, the FIRM MUST:

a. Describe why EX-POST STANDARD DEVIATION is not relevant or appropriate; and

b. Describe the additional risk measure presented and why it was selected.

4.A.35. FIRMS MUST disclose if the performance from a past firm or affiliation is LINKED to the performance of the FIRM.

I.0.10 Disclosure—Recommendations

4.B.1. FIRMS SHOULD disclose material changes to valuation policies and/or methodologies.

4.B.2. FIRMS SHOULD disclose material changes to calculation policies and/or methodologies.

4.B.3. FIRMS SHOULD disclose material differences between the BENCHMARK and the COMPOSITE'S investment mandate, objective, or strategy.

4.B.4. FIRMS SHOULD disclose the key assumptions used to value PORTFOLIO investments.

4.B.5. If a parent company contains multiple firms, each FIRM within the parent company SHOULD disclose a list of the other firms contained within the parent company.

4.B.6. For periods prior to 1 January 2011, FIRMS SHOULD disclose the use of subjective unobservable inputs for valuing PORTFOLIO investments (as described in the GIPS Valuation Principles) if the PORTFOLIO investments valued using subjective unobservable inputs are material to the COMPOSITE.

4.B.7. For periods prior to 1 January 2006, FIRMS SHOULD disclose the use of a SUB-ADVISOR and the periods a SUB-ADVISOR was used.

4.B.8. FIRMS SHOULD disclose if a COMPOSITE contains PROPRIETARY ASSETS.

5. Presentation and Reporting

I.0.11 Presentation and Reporting—Requirements

5.A.1. The following items MUST be presented in each COMPLIANT PRESENTATION:

    a. At least five years of performance (or for the period since the FIRM'S inception or the COMPOSITE INCEPTION DATE if the FIRM or the COMPOSITE has been in existence less than five years) that meets the REQUIREMENTS of the GIPS standards. After a FIRM presents a minimum of five years of GIPS-compliant performance (or for the period since the FIRM'S inception or the COMPOSITE INCEPTION DATE if the FIRM or the COMPOSITE has been in existence less than five years), the FIRM MUST present an additional year of performance each year, building up to a minimum of 10 years of GIPS-compliant performance.

    b. COMPOSITE returns for each annual period. COMPOSITE returns MUST be clearly identified as GROSS-OF-FEES or NET-OF-FEES.

    c. For COMPOSITES with a COMPOSITE INCEPTION DATE of 1 January 2011 or later, when the initial period is less than a full year, returns from the COMPOSITE INCEPTION DATE through the initial annual period end.

    d. For COMPOSITES with a COMPOSITE TERMINATION DATE of 1 January 2011 or later, returns from the last annual period end through the COMPOSITE TERMINATION DATE.

    e. The TOTAL RETURN for the BENCHMARK for each annual period. The BENCHMARK MUST reflect the investment mandate, objective, or strategy of the COMPOSITE.

    f. The number of PORTFOLIOS in the COMPOSITE as of each annual period end. If the COMPOSITE contains five or fewer PORTFOLIOS at period end, the number of PORTFOLIOS is not REQUIRED.

    g. COMPOSITE assets as of each annual period end.

    h. Either TOTAL FIRM ASSETS or COMPOSITE assets as a percentage of TOTAL FIRM ASSETS, as of each annual period end.

    i. A measure of INTERNAL DISPERSION of individual PORTFOLIO returns for each annual period. If the COMPOSITE contains five or fewer PORTFOLIOS for the full year, a measure of INTERNAL DISPERSION is not REQUIRED.

5.A.2. For periods ending on or after 1 January 2011, FIRMS MUST present, as of each annual period end:

    a. The three-year annualized EX-POST STANDARD DEVIATION (using monthly returns) of both the COMPOSITE and the BENCHMARK; and

    b. An additional three-year EX-POST risk measure for the BENCHMARK (if available and appropriate) and the COMPOSITE, if the FIRM determines that the three-year annualized EX-POST STANDARD

DEVIATION is not relevant or appropriate. The PERIODICITY of the COMPOSITE and the BENCHMARK MUST be identical when calculating the EX-POST risk measure.

5.A.3.   FIRMS MUST NOT LINK non-GIPS-compliant performance for periods beginning on or after 1 January 2000 to their GIPS-compliant performance. FIRMS may LINK non-GIPS-compliant performance to GIPS-compliant performance provided that only GIPS-compliant performance is presented for periods beginning on or after 1 January 2000.

5.A.4.   Returns for periods of less than one year MUST NOT be annualized.

5.A.5.   For periods beginning on or after 1 January 2006 and ending prior to 1 January 2011, if a COMPOSITE includes CARVE-OUTS, the FIRM MUST present the percentage of COMPOSITE assets represented by CARVE-OUTS as of each annual period end.

5.A.6.   If a COMPOSITE includes non-fee-paying PORTFOLIOS, the FIRM MUST present the percentage of COMPOSITE assets represented by non-fee-paying PORTFOLIOS as of each annual period end.

5.A.7.   If a COMPOSITE includes PORTFOLIOS with BUNDLED FEES, the FIRM MUST present the percentage of COMPOSITE assets represented by PORTFOLIOS with BUNDLED FEES as of each annual period end.

5.A.8.   **a.**   Performance of a past firm or affiliation MUST be LINKED to or used to represent the historical performance of a new or acquiring FIRM if, on a COMPOSITE-specific basis:

   i.   Substantially all of the investment decision makers are employed by the new or acquiring FIRM (e.g., research department staff, portfolio managers, and other relevant staff);

   ii.   The decision-making process remains substantially intact and independent within the new or acquiring FIRM; and

   iii.   The new or acquiring FIRM has records that document and support the performance.

   b.   If a FIRM acquires another firm or affiliation, the FIRM has one year to bring any non-compliant assets into compliance.

I.0.12   Presentation and Reporting—Recommendations

5.B.1.   FIRMS SHOULD present GROSS-OF-FEES returns.

5.B.2.   FIRMS SHOULD present the following items:

   a.   Cumulative returns of the COMPOSITE and the BENCHMARK for all periods;

   b.   Equal-weighted mean and median COMPOSITE returns;

   c.   Quarterly and/or monthly returns; and

   d.   Annualized COMPOSITE and BENCHMARK returns for periods longer than 12 months.

5.B.3.   For periods prior to 1 January 2011, FIRMS SHOULD present the three-year annualized EX-POST STANDARD DEVIATION (using monthly returns) of the COMPOSITE and the BENCHMARK as of each annual period end.

5.B.4.   For each period for which an annualized EX-POST STANDARD DEVIATION of the COMPOSITE and the BENCHMARK are presented, the corresponding annualized return of the COMPOSITE and the BENCHMARK SHOULD also be presented.

5.B.5. For each period for which an annualized return of the COMPOSITE and the BENCHMARK are presented, the corresponding annualized EX-POST STANDARD DEVIATION (using monthly returns) of the COMPOSITE and the BENCHMARK SHOULD also be presented.

5.B.6. FIRMS SHOULD present additional relevant COMPOSITE-level EX-POST risk measures.

5.B.7. FIRMS SHOULD present more than 10 years of annual performance in the COMPLIANT PRESENTATION.

5.B.8. FIRMS SHOULD comply with the GIPS standards for all historical periods.

5.B.9. FIRMS SHOULD update COMPLIANT PRESENTATIONS quarterly.

6. Real Estate

Unless otherwise noted, the following REAL ESTATE provisions supplement the REQUIRED and RECOMMENDED provisions of the GIPS standards in Sections 0–5.

REAL ESTATE provisions were first included in the GIPS standards in 2005 and became effective 1 January 2006. All COMPLIANT PRESENTATIONS that included REAL ESTATE performance for periods beginning on or after 1 January 2006 were REQUIRED to meet all the REQUIREMENTS of the REAL ESTATE provisions of the 2005 edition of the GIPS standards. The following REAL ESTATE provisions are effective 1 January 2011. All REAL ESTATE COMPOSITES that include performance for periods beginning on or after 1 January 2011 MUST comply with all the REQUIREMENTS and SHOULD adhere to the RECOMMENDATIONS of the following REAL ESTATE provisions.

The following investment types are not considered REAL ESTATE and, therefore, MUST follow Sections 0–5 in Provisions of the Global Investment Performance Standards:

- Publicly traded REAL ESTATE securities;
- Commercial mortgage-backed securities (CMBS); and
- Private debt investments, including commercial and residential loans where the expected return is solely related to contractual interest rates without any participation in the economic performance of the underlying REAL ESTATE.

Real Estate—Requirements

I.0.13 Input Data—Requirements (the following provisions do not apply: 1.A.3.a, 1.A.3.b, and 1.A.4)

6.A.1. For periods beginning on or after 1 January 2011, REAL ESTATE investments MUST be valued in accordance with the definition of FAIR VALUE and the GIPS Valuation Principles.[6]

6.A.2. For periods beginning on or after 1 January 2008, REAL ESTATE investments MUST be valued at least quarterly.[7]

6.A.3. For periods beginning on or after 1 January 2010, FIRMS MUST value PORTFOLIOS as of each quarter end or the last business day of each quarter.

---

6 For periods prior to 1 January 2011, REAL ESTATE investments MUST be valued at MARKET VALUE (as previously defined for REAL ESTATE in the 2005 edition of the GIPS standards).
7 For periods prior to 1 January 2008, REAL ESTATE investments MUST be valued at least once every 12 months.

6.A.4. REAL ESTATE investments MUST have an EXTERNAL VALUATION:

    a. For periods prior to 1 January 2012, at least once every 36 months.

    b. For periods beginning on or after 1 January 2012, at least once every 12 months unless client agreements stipulate otherwise, in which case REAL ESTATE investments MUST have an EXTERNAL VALUATION at least once every 36 months or per the client agreement if the client agreement requires EXTERNAL VALUATIONS more frequently than every 36 months.

6.A.5. EXTERNAL VALUATIONS must be performed by an independent external PROFESSIONALLY DESIGNATED, CERTIFIED, OR LICENSED COMMERCIAL PROPERTY VALUER/APPRAISER. In markets where these professionals are not available, the FIRM MUST take necessary steps to ensure that only well-qualified independent property valuers or appraisers are used.

I.0.14 Calculation Methodology—Requirements (the following provisions do not apply: 2.A.2.a, 2.A.4, and 2.A.7)

6.A.6. FIRMS MUST calculate PORTFOLIO returns at least quarterly.

6.A.7. All returns MUST be calculated after the deduction of actual TRANSACTION EXPENSES incurred during the period.

6.A.8. For periods beginning on or after 1 January 2011, INCOME RETURNS and CAPITAL RETURNS (component returns) MUST be calculated separately using geometrically LINKED TIME-WEIGHTED RATES OF RETURN.

6.A.9. COMPOSITE TIME-WEIGHTED RATES OF RETURN, including component returns, MUST be calculated by asset-weighting the individual PORTFOLIO returns at least quarterly.

I.0.15 Disclosure—Requirements (the following provisions do not apply: 4.A.5, 4.A.6.a, 4.A.15, 4.A.26, 4.A.33, and 4.A.34)

6.A.10. The following items MUST be disclosed in each COMPLIANT PRESENTATION:

    a. The FIRM'S description of discretion;

    b. The INTERNAL VALUATION methodologies used to value REAL ESTATE investments for the most recent period;

    c. For periods beginning on or after 1 January 2011, material changes to valuation policies and/or methodologies;

    d. For periods beginning on or after 1 January 2011, material differences between an EXTERNAL VALUATION and the valuation used in performance reporting and the reason for the differences;

    e. The frequency REAL ESTATE investments are valued by an independent external PROFESSIONALLY DESIGNATED, CERTIFIED, OR LICENSED COMMERCIAL PROPERTY VALUER/APPRAISER;

    f. When component returns are calculated separately using geometrically LINKED TIME-WEIGHTED RATES OF RETURN; and

    g. For periods prior to 1 January 2011, if component returns are adjusted such that the sum of the INCOME RETURN and the CAPITAL RETURN equals the TOTAL RETURN.

6.A.11. For any performance presented for periods prior to 1 January 2006 that does not comply with the GIPS standards, FIRMS MUST disclose the periods of non-compliance.

6.A.12. When presenting GROSS-OF-FEES returns, FIRMS MUST disclose if any other fees are deducted in addition to the TRANSACTION EXPENSES.

6.A.13. When presenting NET-OF-FEES returns, FIRMS MUST disclose if any other fees are deducted in addition to the INVESTMENT MANAGEMENT FEES and TRANSACTION EXPENSES.

I.0.16 Presentation and Reporting—Requirements (the following provisions do not apply: 5.A.1.i, 5.A.2, and 5.A.3)

6.A.14. FIRMS MUST present component returns in addition to TOTAL RETURNS. COMPOSITE component returns MUST be clearly identified as GROSS-OF-FEES or NET-OF-FEES.

6.A.15. FIRMS MUST NOT LINK non-GIPS-compliant performance for periods beginning on or after 1 January 2006 to their GIPS-compliant performance. FIRMS may LINK non-GIPS-compliant performance to their GIPS-compliant performance provided that only GIPS-compliant performance is presented for periods beginning on or after 1 January 2006.

6.A.16. The following items MUST be presented in each COMPLIANT PRESENTATION:

   a. As a measure of INTERNAL DISPERSION, high and low annual TIME-WEIGHTED RATES OF RETURN for the individual PORTFOLIOS in the COMPOSITE. If the COMPOSITE contains five or fewer PORTFOLIOS for the full year, a measure of INTERNAL DISPERSION is not REQUIRED.

   b. As of each annual period end, the percentage of COMPOSITE assets valued using an EXTERNAL VALUATION during the annual period.

The following provisions are additional REQUIREMENTS for REAL ESTATE CLOSED-END FUND COMPOSITES:

I.0.17 Calculation Methodology—Requirements

6.A.17. FIRMS MUST calculate annualized SINCE INCEPTION INTERNAL RATES OF RETURN (SI-IRR).

6.A.18. The SI-IRR MUST be calculated using quarterly cash flows at a minimum.

I.0.18 Composite Construction—Requirements

6.A.19. COMPOSITES MUST be defined by VINTAGE YEAR and investment mandate, objective, or strategy. The COMPOSITE DEFINITION MUST remain consistent throughout the life of the COMPOSITE.

I.0.19 Disclosure—Requirements

6.A.20. FIRMS MUST disclose the FINAL LIQUIDATION DATE for liquidated COMPOSITES.

6.A.21. FIRMS MUST disclose the frequency of cash flows used in the SI-IRR calculation.

6.A.22. FIRMS MUST disclose the VINTAGE YEAR of the COMPOSITE and how the VINTAGE YEAR is defined.

I.0.20 Presentation and Reporting—Requirements

6.A.23. The following items MUST be presented in each COMPLIANT PRESENTATION:

    a. FIRMS MUST present the NET-OF-FEES SI-IRR of the COMPOSITE through each annual period end. FIRMS MUST initially present at least five years of performance (or for the period since the FIRM'S inception or the COMPOSITE INCEPTION DATE if the FIRM or the COMPOSITE has been in existence less than five years) that meets the REQUIREMENTS of the GIPS standards. Each subsequent year, FIRMS MUST present an additional year of performance.

    b. For periods beginning on or after 1 January 2011, when the initial period is less than a full year, FIRMS MUST present the non-annualized NET-OF-FEES SI-IRR through the initial annual period end.

    c. For periods ending on or after 1 January 2011, FIRMS MUST present the NET-OF-FEES SI-IRR through the COMPOSITE FINAL LIQUIDATION DATE.

6.A.24. If the GROSS-OF-FEES SI-IRR of the COMPOSITE is presented in the COMPLIANT PRESENTATION, FIRMS MUST present the GROSS-OF-FEES SI-IRR of the COMPOSITE for the same periods as the NET-OF-FEES SI-IRR is presented.

6.A.25. FIRMS MUST present, as of each annual period end:

    a. COMPOSITE SINCE INCEPTION PAID-IN CAPITAL;

    b. COMPOSITE SINCE INCEPTION DISTRIBUTIONS;

    c. COMPOSITE cumulative COMMITTED CAPITAL;

    d. TOTAL VALUE to SINCE INCEPTION PAID-IN CAPITAL (INVESTMENT MULTIPLE or TVPI);

    e. SINCE INCEPTION DISTRIBUTIONS to SINCE INCEPTION PAID-IN CAPITAL (REALIZATION MULTIPLE or DPI);

    f. SINCE INCEPTION PAID-IN CAPITAL to cumulative COMMITTED CAPITAL (PIC MULTIPLE); and

    g. RESIDUAL VALUE to SINCE INCEPTION PAID-IN CAPITAL (UNREALIZED MULTIPLE or RVPI).

6.A.26. FIRMS MUST present the SI-IRR of the BENCHMARK through each annual period end. The BENCHMARK MUST:

    a. Reflect the investment mandate, objective, or strategy of the COMPOSITE;

    b. Be presented for the same time period as presented for the COMPOSITE; and

    c. Be the same VINTAGE YEAR as the COMPOSITE.

REAL ESTATE—RECOMMENDATIONS

I.0.21 Input Data—Recommendations (the following provision does not apply: 1.B.1)

6.B.1. For periods prior to 1 January 2012, REAL ESTATE investments SHOULD be valued by an independent external PROFESSIONALLY DESIGNATED, CERTIFIED, OR LICENSED COMMERCIAL PROPERTY VALUER/ APPRAISER at least once every 12 months.

6.B.2. REAL ESTATE investments SHOULD be valued as of the annual period end by an independent external PROFESSIONALLY DESIGNATED, CERTIFIED, OR LICENSED COMMERCIAL PROPERTY VALUER/APPRAISER.

I.0.22 Disclosure—Recommendations

6.B.3. FIRMS SHOULD disclose the basis of accounting for the PORTFOLIOS in the COMPOSITE (e.g., U.S. GAAP, IFRS).

6.B.4. FIRMS SHOULD explain and disclose material differences between the valuation used in performance reporting and the valuation used in financial reporting as of each annual period end.

6.B.5. For periods prior to 1 January 2011, FIRMS SHOULD disclose material changes to valuation policies and/or methodologies.

I.0.23 Presentation and Reporting—Recommendations (the following provisions do not apply: 5.B.3, 5.B.4, and 5.B.5)

6.B.6. FIRMS SHOULD present both GROSS-OF-FEES and NET-OF-FEES returns.

6.B.7. FIRMS SHOULD present the percentage of the total value of COMPOSITE assets that are not REAL ESTATE as of each annual period end.

6.B.8. FIRMS SHOULD present the component returns of the BENCHMARK, if available.

The following provision is an additional RECOMMENDATION for REAL ESTATE CLOSED-END FUND COMPOSITES:

I.0.24 Calculation Methodology—Recommendations

6.B.9. The SI-IRR SHOULD be calculated using daily cash flows.

7. Private Equity

Unless otherwise noted, the following PRIVATE EQUITY provisions supplement the REQUIRED and RECOMMENDED provisions of the GIPS standards in Sections 0–5.

PRIVATE EQUITY provisions were first included in the GIPS standards in 2005 and became effective 1 January 2006. All COMPLIANT PRESENTATIONS that included PRIVATE EQUITY performance for periods ending on or after 1 January 2006 were REQUIRED to meet all the REQUIREMENTS of the PRIVATE EQUITY provisions of the 2005 edition of the GIPS standards. The following PRIVATE EQUITY provisions are effective 1 January 2011. All PRIVATE EQUITY COMPOSITES that include performance for periods ending on or after 1 January 2011 MUST comply with all the REQUIREMENTS and SHOULD comply with the RECOMMENDATIONS of the following PRIVATE EQUITY provisions.

The following are provisions that apply to the calculation and presentation of PRIVATE EQUITY investments made by fixed life, fixed commitment PRIVATE EQUITY investment vehicles including PRIMARY FUNDS and FUNDS OF FUNDS. These provisions also apply to fixed life, fixed commitment SECONDARY FUNDS, which MUST apply either the provisions applicable to PRIMARY FUNDS or the provisions applicable to FUNDS OF FUNDS depending on which form the SECONDARY FUND uses to make investments. PRIVATE EQUITY OPEN-END and EVERGREEN FUNDS MUST follow Sections 0–5 in the Provisions of the Global Investment Performance Standards. REAL ESTATE CLOSED-END FUNDS MUST follow Section 6 in the Provisions of the Global Investment Performance Standards.

Private Equity—Requirements

I.0.25 Input Data—Requirements (the following provisions do not apply: 1.A.3.a, 1.A.3.b, and 1.A.4)

7.A.1. For periods ending on or after 1 January 2011, PRIVATE EQUITY investments MUST be valued in accordance with the definition of FAIR VALUE and the GIPS Valuation Principles.[8]

7.A.2. PRIVATE EQUITY investments MUST be valued at least annually.

I.0.26 Calculation Methodology—Requirements (the following provisions do not apply: 2.A.2, 2.A.4, 2.A.6, and 2.A.7)

7.A.3. FIRMS MUST calculate annualized SINCE INCEPTION INTERNAL RATES OF RETURN (SI-IRR).

7.A.4. For periods ending on or after 1 January 2011, the SI-IRR MUST be calculated using daily cash flows. Stock DISTRIBUTIONS MUST be included as cash flows and MUST be valued at the time of DISTRIBUTION.[9]

7.A.5. All returns MUST be calculated after the deduction of actual TRANSACTION EXPENSES incurred during the period.

7.A.6. NET-OF-FEES returns MUST be net of actual INVESTMENT MANAGEMENT FEES (including CARRIED INTEREST).

7.A.7. For FUNDS OF FUNDS, all returns MUST be net of all underlying partnership and/or fund fees and expenses, including CARRIED INTEREST.

I.0.27 Composite Construction—Requirements (the following provision does not apply: 3.A.10)

7.A.8. COMPOSITE DEFINITIONS MUST remain consistent throughout the life of the COMPOSITE.

7.A.9. PRIMARY FUNDS MUST be included in at least one COMPOSITE defined by VINTAGE YEAR and investment mandate, objective, or strategy.

7.A.10. FUNDS OF FUNDS MUST be included in at least one COMPOSITE defined by VINTAGE YEAR of the FUND OF FUNDS and/or investment mandate, objective, or strategy.

I.0.28 Disclosure—Requirements (the following provisions do not apply: 4.A.5, 4.A.6.a, 4.A.6.b, 4.A.8, 4.A.15, 4.A.26, 4.A.32, 4.A.33, and 4.A.34)

7.A.11. FIRMS MUST disclose the VINTAGE YEAR of the COMPOSITE and how the VINTAGE YEAR is defined.

7.A.12. FIRMS MUST disclose the FINAL LIQUIDATION DATE for liquidated COMPOSITES.

7.A.13. FIRMS MUST disclose the valuation methodologies used to value PRIVATE EQUITY investments for the most recent period.

7.A.14. For periods ending on or after 1 January 2011, FIRMS MUST disclose material changes to valuation policies and/or methodologies.

---

8 For periods ending prior to 1 January 2011, PRIVATE EQUITY investments MUST be valued according to either the GIPS Private Equity Valuation Principles in Appendix D of the 2005 edition of the GIPS standards or the GIPS Valuation Principles in the 2010 edition of the GIPS standards.

9 For periods ending prior to 1 January 2011, the SI-IRR MUST be calculated using either daily or monthly cash flows.

7.A.15. If the FIRM adheres to any industry valuation guidelines in addition to the GIPS Valuation Principles, the FIRM MUST disclose which guidelines have been applied.

7.A.16. FIRMS MUST disclose the calculation methodology used for the BENCHMARK. If FIRMS present the PUBLIC MARKET EQUIVALENT of a COMPOSITE as a BENCHMARK, FIRMS MUST disclose the index used to calculate the PUBLIC MARKET EQUIVALENT.

7.A.17. FIRMS MUST disclose the frequency of cash flows used in the SI-IRR calculation if daily cash flows are not used for periods prior to 1 January 2011.

7.A.18. For GROSS-OF-FEES returns, FIRMS MUST disclose if any other fees are deducted in addition to the TRANSACTION EXPENSES.

7.A.19. For NET-OF-FEES returns, FIRMS MUST disclose if any other fees are deducted in addition to the INVESTMENT MANAGEMENT FEES and TRANSACTION EXPENSES.

7.A.20. For any performance presented for periods ending prior to 1 January 2006 that does not comply with the GIPS standards, FIRMS MUST disclose the periods of non-compliance.

I.0.29 Presentation and Reporting—Requirements (the following provisions do not apply: 5.A.1.a, 5.A.1.b, 5.A.1.c, 5.A.1.d, 5.A.1.e, 5.A.1.i, 5.A.2, and 5.A.3)

7.A.21. The following items MUST be presented in each COMPLIANT PRESENTATION:

   a. FIRMS MUST present both the NET-OF-FEES and GROSS-OF-FEES SI-IRR of the COMPOSITE through each annual period end. FIRMS MUST initially present at least five years of performance (or for the period since the FIRM'S inception or the COMPOSITE INCEPTION DATE if the FIRM or the COMPOSITE has been in existence less than five years) that meets the REQUIREMENTS of the GIPS standards. Each subsequent year, FIRMS MUST present an additional year of performance. COMPOSITE returns MUST be clearly identified as GROSS-OF-FEES or NET-OF-FEES.

   b. For periods beginning on or after 1 January 2011, when the initial period is less than a full year, FIRMS MUST present the non-annualized NET-OF-FEES and GROSS-OF-FEES SI-IRR through the initial annual period end.

   c. For periods ending on or after 1 January 2011, FIRMS MUST present the NET-OF-FEES and GROSS-OF-FEES SI-IRR through the COMPOSITE FINAL LIQUIDATION DATE.

7.A.22. For periods ending on or after 1 January 2011, for FUND OF FUNDS COMPOSITES, if the COMPOSITE is defined only by investment mandate, objective, or strategy, FIRMS MUST also present the SI-IRR of the underlying investments aggregated by VINTAGE YEAR as well as other measures as REQUIRED in 7.A.23. These measures MUST be presented gross of the FUND OF FUNDS INVESTMENT MANAGEMENT FEES and MUST be presented as of the most recent annual period end.

7.A.23. FIRMS MUST present as of each annual period end:

   a. COMPOSITE SINCE INCEPTION PAID-IN CAPITAL;

   b. COMPOSITE SINCE INCEPTION DISTRIBUTIONS;

   c. COMPOSITE cumulative COMMITTED CAPITAL;

      d. TOTAL VALUE to SINCE INCEPTION PAID-IN CAPITAL (INVESTMENT MULTIPLE or TVPI);

      e. SINCE INCEPTION DISTRIBUTIONS to SINCE INCEPTION PAID-IN CAPITAL (REALIZATION MULTIPLE or DPI);

      f. SINCE INCEPTION PAID-IN CAPITAL to cumulative COMMITTED CAPITAL (PIC MULTIPLE); and

      g. RESIDUAL VALUE to SINCE INCEPTION PAID-IN CAPITAL (UNREALIZED MULTIPLE or RVPI).

7.A.24. FIRMS MUST present the SI-IRR for the BENCHMARK through each annual period end. The BENCHMARK MUST:

      a. Reflect the investment mandate, objective, or strategy of the COMPOSITE;

      b. Be presented for the same time periods as presented for the COMPOSITE; and

      c. Be the same VINTAGE YEAR as the COMPOSITE.

7.A.25. For FUND OF FUNDS COMPOSITES, if the COMPOSITE is defined only by investment mandate, objective, or strategy and a BENCHMARK is presented for the underlying investments, the BENCHMARK MUST be the same VINTAGE YEAR and investment mandate, objective, or strategy as the underlying investments.

7.A.26. For periods ending on or after 1 January 2011, for FUND OF FUNDS COMPOSITES, FIRMS MUST present the percentage, if any, of COMPOSITE assets that is invested in DIRECT INVESTMENTS (rather than in fund investment vehicles) as of each annual period end.

7.A.27. For periods ending on or after 1 January 2011, for PRIMARY FUND COMPOSITES, FIRMS MUST present the percentage, if any, of COMPOSITE assets that is invested in fund investment vehicles (rather than in DIRECT INVESTMENTS) as of each annual period end.

7.A.28. FIRMS MUST NOT present non-GIPS-compliant performance for periods ending on or after 1 January 2006. For periods ending prior to 1 January 2006, FIRMS may present non-GIPS-compliant performance.

Private Equity—Recommendations

I.0.30 Input Data—Recommendations (the following provision does not apply: 1.B.1)

7.B.1. PRIVATE EQUITY investments SHOULD be valued at least quarterly.

I.0.31 Calculation Methodology—Recommendations (the following provision does not apply: 2.B.2)

7.B.2. For periods ending prior to 1 January 2011, the SI-IRR SHOULD be calculated using daily cash flows.

Composite Construction—Recommendations (the following provision does not apply: 3.B.2)

I.0.32 Disclosure—Recommendations

7.B.3. FIRMS SHOULD explain and disclose material differences between the valuations used in performance reporting and the valuations used in financial reporting as of each annual period end.

7.B.4. For periods prior to 1 January 2011, FIRMS SHOULD disclose material changes to valuation policies and/or methodologies.

I.0.33 Presentation and Reporting—Recommendations (the following provisions do not apply: 5.B.2, 5.B.3, 5.B.4, and 5.B.5)

7.B.5. For periods ending on or after 1 January 2011, for FUND OF FUNDS COMPOSITES, if the COMPOSITE is defined only by VINTAGE YEAR of the FUND OF FUNDS, FIRMS SHOULD also present the SI-IRR of the underlying investments aggregated by investment mandate, objective, or strategy and other measures as listed in 7.A.23. These measures SHOULD be presented gross of the FUND OF FUNDS INVESTMENT MANAGEMENT FEES.

7.B.6. For periods ending prior to 1 January 2011, for FUND OF FUNDS COMPOSITES, FIRMS SHOULD present the percentage, if any, of COMPOSITE assets that is invested in DIRECT INVESTMENTS (rather than in fund investment vehicles) as of each annual period end.

7.B.7. For periods ending prior to 1 January 2011, for PRIMARY FUND COMPOSITES, FIRMS SHOULD present the percentage, if any, of COMPOSITE assets that is invested in fund investment vehicles (rather than in DIRECT INVESTMENTS) as of each annual period end.

8. Wrap Fee/Separately Managed Account (SMA) Portfolios

The following provisions apply to the calculation and presentation of performance when presenting a COMPLIANT PRESENTATION to a WRAP FEE/SMA PROSPECTIVE CLIENT (which includes prospective WRAP FEE/SMA sponsors, prospective WRAP FEE/SMA clients, and existing WRAP FEE/SMA sponsors). Unless otherwise noted, the following WRAP FEE/SMA provisions supplement all the REQUIRED and RECOMMENDED provisions of the GIPS standards in Sections 0–5.

Although there are different types of WRAP FEE/SMA structures, these provisions apply to all WRAP FEE/SMA PORTFOLIOS where there are BUNDLED FEES and the WRAP FEE/SMA sponsor serves as an intermediary between the FIRM and the end user of the investment services. These provisions are not applicable to PORTFOLIOS defined as other types of BUNDLED FEE PORTFOLIOS. These provisions are also not applicable to model PORTFOLIOS that are provided by a FIRM to a WRAP FEE/SMA sponsor if the FIRM does not have discretionary PORTFOLIO management responsibility for the individual WRAP FEE/SMA PORTFOLIOS. Similarly, a FIRM or overlay manager in a Multiple Strategy Portfolio (MSP) or similar program is also excluded from applying these provisions to such PORTFOLIOS if they do not have discretion.

All WRAP FEE/SMA COMPLIANT PRESENTATIONS that include performance results for periods beginning on or after 1 January 2006 MUST meet all the REQUIREMENTS of the following WRAP FEE/SMA provisions.

Wrap Fee/SMA Requirements

I.0.34 Composite Construction—Requirements

8.A.1. FIRMS MUST include the performance record of actual WRAP FEE/SMA PORTFOLIOS in appropriate COMPOSITES in accordance with the FIRM'S established PORTFOLIO inclusion policies. Once established, these COMPOSITES (containing actual WRAP FEE/SMA PORTFOLIOS) MUST be used in the FIRM'S COMPLIANT PRESENTATIONS presented to WRAP FEE/SMA PROSPECTIVE CLIENTS.

I.0.35 Disclosure—Requirements (the following provision does not apply: 4.A.15)

8.A.2. For all WRAP FEE/SMA COMPLIANT PRESENTATIONS that include periods prior to the inclusion of an actual WRAP FEE/SMA PORTFOLIO in the COMPOSITE, the FIRM MUST disclose, for each period presented, that the COMPOSITE does not contain actual WRAP FEE/SMA PORTFOLIOS.

8.A.3. For any performance presented for periods prior to 1 January 2006 that does not comply with the GIPS standards, FIRMS MUST disclose the periods of non-compliance.

8.A.4. When FIRMS present COMPOSITE performance to an existing WRAP FEE/SMA sponsor that includes only that sponsor's WRAP FEE/SMA PORTFOLIOS (resulting in a "sponsor-specific COMPOSITE"):

    a. FIRMS MUST disclose the name of the WRAP FEE/SMA sponsor represented by the sponsor-specific COMPOSITE; and

    b. If the sponsor-specific COMPOSITE COMPLIANT PRESENTATION is intended for the purpose of generating WRAP FEE/SMA business and does not include performance net of the entire WRAP FEE, the COMPLIANT PRESENTATION MUST disclose that the named sponsor-specific COMPLIANT PRESENTATION is only for the use of the named WRAP FEE/SMA sponsor.

I.0.36 Presentation and Reporting—Requirements (the following provision does not apply: 5.A.3)

8.A.5. When FIRMS present performance to a WRAP FEE/SMA PROSPECTIVE CLIENT, the COMPOSITE presented MUST include the performance of all actual WRAP FEE/SMA PORTFOLIOS, if any, managed according to the COMPOSITE investment mandate, objective, or strategy, regardless of the WRAP FEE/SMA sponsor (resulting in a "style-defined COMPOSITE").

8.A.6. When FIRMS present performance to a WRAP FEE/SMA PROSPECTIVE CLIENT, performance MUST be presented net of the entire WRAP FEE.

8.A.7. FIRMS MUST NOT LINK non-GIPS-compliant performance for periods beginning on or after 1 January 2006 to their GIPS-compliant performance. FIRMS may LINK non-GIPS-compliant performance to their GIPS-compliant performance provided that only GIPS-compliant performance is presented for periods beginning on or after 1 January 2006.

II. GIPS VALUATION PRINCIPLES

The GIPS standards are based on the ethical principles of fair representation and full disclosure. In order for the performance calculations to be meaningful, the valuations of PORTFOLIO investments must have integrity and fairly reflect their value. Effective 1 January 2011, the GIPS standards REQUIRE FIRMS to apply a FAIR VALUE methodology following the definition and REQUIREMENTS listed below. The GIPS Valuation Principles, including the definition of FAIR VALUE, were developed with consideration of the work done by the International Accounting Standards Board (IASB) and the Financial Accounting Standards Board (FASB) as well as other organizations.

The shift to a broader FAIR VALUE REQUIREMENT has implications for all FIRMS claiming compliance with the GIPS standards. For liquid securities in active markets, the change to FAIR VALUE from MARKET VALUE will typically not result in a change to valuations. FIRMS MUST use the objective, observable, unadjusted quoted market prices for identical investments on the measurement date, if available.

Markets are not always liquid and investment prices are not always objective and/or observable. For illiquid or hard to value investments, or for investments where no observable MARKET VALUE or market price is available, additional steps are necessary. A FIRM'S valuation policies and procedures MUST address situations where the market prices may be available for similar but not identical investments, inputs to valuations are subjective rather than objective, and/or markets are inactive instead of active. There is a RECOMMENDED valuation hierarchy in Section C below. FIRMS MUST disclose if the COMPOSITE'S valuation hierarchy materially differs from the RECOMMENDED valuation hierarchy.

Although a FIRM may use external third parties to value investments, the FIRM still retains responsibility for compliance with the GIPS standards, including the GIPS Valuation Principles.

FIRMS claiming compliance with the GIPS standards MUST adhere to all the REQUIREMENTS and SHOULD comply with the RECOMMENDATIONS below.

A. Fair Value Definition

FAIR VALUE is defined as the amount at which an investment could be exchanged in a current arm's length transaction between willing parties in which the parties each act knowledgeably and prudently. The valuation MUST be determined using the objective, observable, unadjusted quoted market price for an identical investment in an active market on the measurement date, if available. In the absence of an objective, observable, unadjusted quoted market price for an identical investment in an active market on the measurement date, the valuation MUST represent the FIRM'S best estimate of the MARKET VALUE. FAIR VALUE MUST include accrued income.

B. Valuation Requirements

FIRMS MUST comply with the following valuation REQUIREMENTS:

1. For periods beginning on or after 1 January 2011, PORTFOLIOS MUST be valued in accordance with the definition of FAIR VALUE and the GIPS Valuation Principles (Provision 1.A.2).

2. FIRMS MUST value investments using objective, observable, unadjusted quoted market prices for identical investments in active markets on the measurement date, if available.

3. FIRMS MUST comply with all applicable laws and regulations regarding the calculation and presentation of performance (Provision 0.A.2). Accordingly, FIRMS MUST comply with applicable laws and regulations relating to valuation.

4. If the COMPLIANT PRESENTATION conforms with laws and/or regulations that conflict with the REQUIREMENTS of the GIPS standards, FIRMS MUST disclose this fact and disclose the manner in which the laws and/or regulations conflict with the GIPS standards (Provision 4.A.22). This includes any conflicts between laws and/or regulations and the GIPS Valuation Principles.

5. FIRMS MUST document their policies and procedures used in establishing and maintaining compliance with the GIPS standards, including ensuring the existence and ownership of client assets, and MUST apply them consistently (Provision 0.A.5). Accordingly, FIRMS MUST document their valuation policies, procedures, methodologies, and hierarchy, including any changes, and MUST apply them consistently.

6. FIRMS MUST disclose that policies for valuing PORTFOLIOS, calculating performance, and preparing COMPLIANT PRESENTATIONS are available upon request (Provision 4.A.12).

7. For periods beginning on or after 1 January 2011, FIRMS MUST disclose the use of subjective unobservable inputs for valuing PORTFOLIO investments (as described in the GIPS Valuation Principles) if the PORTFOLIO investments valued using subjective unobservable inputs are material to the COMPOSITE (Provision 4.A.27).

8. For periods beginning on or after 1 January 2011, FIRMS MUST disclose if the COMPOSITE'S valuation hierarchy materially differs from the RECOMMENDED hierarchy in the GIPS Valuation Principles (Provision 4.A.28).

Additional Real Estate Valuation Requirements:

9. REAL ESTATE investments MUST have an EXTERNAL VALUATION (Provision 6.A.4).

10. The EXTERNAL VALUATION process MUST adhere to practices of the relevant valuation governing and standard setting body.

11. The FIRM MUST NOT use EXTERNAL VALUATIONS where the valuer's or appraiser's fee is contingent upon the investment's appraised value.

12. EXTERNAL VALUATIONS must be performed by an independent external PROFESSIONALLY DESIGNATED, CERTIFIED, OR LICENSED COMMERCIAL PROPERTY VALUER/APPRAISER. In markets where these professionals are not available, the FIRM MUST take necessary steps to ensure that only well-qualified independent property valuers or appraisers are used (Provision 6.A.5).

13. FIRMS MUST disclose the INTERNAL VALUATION methodologies used to value REAL ESTATE investments for the most recent period (Provision 6.A.10.b).

14. For periods beginning on or after 1 January 2011, FIRMS MUST disclose material changes to valuation policies and/or methodologies (Provision 6.A.10.c).

15. For periods beginning on or after 1 January 2011, FIRMS MUST disclose material differences between an EXTERNAL VALUATION and the valuation used in performance reporting and the reason for the differences (Provision 6.A.10.d).

16. FIRMS MUST present, as of each annual period end, the percentage of COMPOSITE assets valued using an EXTERNAL VALUATION during the annual period (Provision 6.A.16.b).

Additional Private Equity Valuation Requirements:

17. The valuation methodology selected MUST be the most appropriate for a particular investment based on the nature, facts, and circumstances of the investment.

18. FIRMS MUST disclose the valuation methodologies used to value PRIVATE EQUITY investments for the most recent period (Provision 7.A.13).

19. For periods ending on or after 1 January 2011, FIRMS MUST disclose material changes to valuation policies and/or methodologies (Provision 7.A.14).

20. If the FIRM adheres to any industry valuation guidelines in addition to the GIPS Valuation Principles, the FIRM MUST disclose which guidelines have been applied (Provision 7.A.15).

C. Valuation Recommendations

FIRMS SHOULD comply with the following valuation RECOMMENDATIONS:

1. **Valuation Hierarchy**: FIRMS SHOULD incorporate the following hierarchy into the policies and procedures for determining FAIR VALUE for PORTFOLIO investments on a COMPOSITE-specific basis.

    a. Investments MUST be valued using objective, observable, unadjusted quoted market prices for identical investments in active markets on the measurement date, if available. If not available, then investments SHOULD be valued using;

    b. Objective, observable quoted market prices for similar investments in active markets. If not available or appropriate, then investments SHOULD be valued using;

    c. Quoted prices for identical or similar investments in markets that are not active (markets in which there are few transactions for the investment, the prices are not current, or price quotations vary substantially over time and/or between market makers). If not available or appropriate, then investments SHOULD be valued based on;

    d. Market-based inputs, other than quoted prices, that are observable for the investment. If not available or appropriate, then investments SHOULD be valued based on;

    e. Subjective unobservable inputs for the investment where markets are not active at the measurement date. Unobservable inputs SHOULD only be used to measure FAIR VALUE to the extent that observable inputs and prices are not available or appropriate. Unobservable inputs reflect the FIRM'S own assumptions about the assumptions that market participants would use in pricing the investment and SHOULD be developed based on the best information available under the circumstances.

2. FIRMS SHOULD disclose material changes to valuation policies and/or methodologies (Provision 4.B.1).

3. FIRMS SHOULD disclose the key assumptions used to value PORTFOLIO investments (Provision 4.B.4).

4. For periods prior to 1 January 2011, FIRMS SHOULD disclose the use of subjective unobservable inputs for valuing PORTFOLIO investments (as described in the GIPS Valuation Principles) if the PORTFOLIO investments valued using subjective unobservable inputs are material to the COMPOSITE (Provision 4.B.6).

5. Valuations SHOULD be obtained from a qualified independent third party (Provision 1.B.2).

Additional Real Estate Valuation Recommendations:

6. Although appraisal standards may allow for a range of estimated values, it is RECOMMENDED that a single value be obtained from external valuers or appraisers because only one value is used in performance reporting.

7. It is RECOMMENDED that the external appraisal firm be rotated every three to five years.

8. FIRMS SHOULD explain and disclose material differences between the valuation used in performance reporting and the valuation used in financial reporting as of each annual period end (Provision 6.B.4).

9. For periods prior to 1 January 2011, FIRMS SHOULD disclose material changes to valuation policies and/or methodologies (Provision 6.B.5).

Additional Private Equity Valuation Recommendations:

10. FIRMS SHOULD explain and disclose material differences between the valuations used in performance reporting and the valuations used in financial reporting as of each annual period end (Provision 7.B.3).

11. For periods prior to 1 January 2011, FIRMS SHOULD disclose material changes to valuation policies and/or methodologies (Provision 7.B.4).

12. The following considerations SHOULD be incorporated into the valuation process:

    a. The quality and reliability of the data used in each methodology;

    b. The comparability of enterprise or transaction data;

    c. The stage of development of the enterprise; and

    d. Any additional considerations unique to the enterprise.

III. GIPS ADVERTISING GUIDELINES

A. Purpose of the GIPS Advertising Guidelines

The GIPS Advertising Guidelines provide FIRMS with options for advertising performance when mentioning the FIRM'S claim of compliance. The GIPS Advertising Guidelines do not replace the GIPS standards, nor do they absolve FIRMS from presenting a COMPLIANT PRESENTATION as REQUIRED by the GIPS standards. These guidelines only apply to FIRMS that already satisfy all the REQUIREMENTS of the GIPS standards on a FIRM-wide basis and claim compliance with the GIPS standards in an advertisement. FIRMS that choose to claim compliance in an advertisement MUST follow the GIPS Advertising Guidelines or include a COMPLIANT PRESENTATION in the advertisement.

Definition of Advertisement

For the purposes of these guidelines, an advertisement includes any materials that are distributed to or designed for use in newspapers, magazines, FIRM brochures, letters, media, websites, or any other written or electronic material addressed to more than one PROSPECTIVE CLIENT. Any written material, other than one-on-one presentations and individual client reporting, distributed to maintain existing clients or solicit new clients for a FIRM is considered an advertisement.

Relationship of GIPS Advertising Guidelines to Regulatory Requirements

FIRMS advertising performance MUST adhere to all applicable laws and regulations governing advertisements. FIRMS are encouraged to seek legal or regulatory counsel because additional disclosures may be REQUIRED. In cases where applicable laws and/or regulations conflict with the REQUIREMENTS of the GIPS standards and/or the GIPS Advertising Guidelines, FIRMS are REQUIRED to comply with the law or regulation.

The calculation and advertisement of pooled unitized investment vehicles, such as mutual funds and open-ended investment companies, are regulated in most markets. The GIPS Advertising Guidelines are not intended to replace applicable laws and/or regulations when a FIRM is advertising performance solely for a pooled unitized investment vehicle.

Other Information

The advertisement may include other information beyond what is REQUIRED under the GIPS Advertising Guidelines provided the information is shown with equal or lesser prominence relative to the information REQUIRED by the GIPS Advertising Guidelines and the information does not conflict with the REQUIREMENTS of the GIPS standards and/or the GIPS Advertising Guidelines. FIRMS MUST adhere to the principles of fair representation and full disclosure when advertising and MUST NOT present performance or performance-related information that is false or misleading.

B. Requirements of the GIPS Advertising Guidelines

All advertisements that include a claim of compliance with the GIPS standards by following the GIPS Advertising Guidelines MUST disclose the following:

1. The definition of the FIRM.

2. How a PROSPECTIVE CLIENT can obtain a COMPLIANT PRESENTATION and/or the FIRM'S list of COMPOSITE DESCRIPTIONS.

3. The GIPS compliance statement for advertisements:

> "[Insert name of FIRM] claims compliance with the Global Investment Performance Standards (GIPS®)."

All advertisements that include a claim of compliance with the GIPS standards by following the GIPS Advertising Guidelines and that present performance MUST also disclose the following information, which MUST be taken or derived from a COMPLIANT PRESENTATION:

4. The COMPOSITE DESCRIPTION.

5. COMPOSITE TOTAL RETURNS according to one of the following:

    a. One-, three-, and five-year annualized COMPOSITE returns through the most recent period with the period-end date clearly identified. If the COMPOSITE has been in existence for less than five years, FIRMS MUST also present the annualized returns since the COMPOSITE INCEPTION DATE. (For example, if a COMPOSITE has been in existence for four years, FIRMS MUST present one-, three-, and four-year annualized returns through the most recent period.) Returns for periods of less than one year MUST NOT be annualized.

    b. Period-to-date COMPOSITE returns in addition to one-, three-, and five-year annualized COMPOSITE returns through the same period of time as presented in the corresponding COMPLIANT PRESENTATION with the period end date clearly identified. If the COMPOSITE has been in existence for less than five years, FIRMS MUST also present the annualized returns since the COMPOSITE INCEPTION DATE (For example, if a COMPOSITE has been in existence for four years, FIRMS MUST present one-, three-, and four-year annualized returns in addition to the period-to-date COMPOSITE return.) Returns for periods of less than one year MUST NOT be annualized.

    c. Period-to-date COMPOSITE returns in addition to five years of annual COMPOSITE returns (or for each annual period since the COMPOSITE INCEPTION DATE if the COMPOSITE has been in existence for less than five years) with the period end date clearly identified. The annual returns MUST be calculated through the same period of time as presented in the corresponding COMPLIANT PRESENTATION.

6. Whether returns are presented GROSS-OF-FEES and/or NET-OF-FEES.

7. The TOTAL RETURN for the BENCHMARK for the same periods for which the COMPOSITE return is presented. FIRMS MUST present TOTAL RETURNS for the same BENCHMARK as presented in the corresponding COMPLIANT PRESENTATION.

8. The BENCHMARK DESCRIPTION.

9. If the FIRM determines no appropriate BENCHMARK for the COMPOSITE exists, the FIRM MUST disclose why no BENCHMARK is presented.

10. The currency used to express performance.

11. The presence, use, and extent of leverage, derivatives, and short positions, if material, including a description of the frequency of use and characteristics of the instruments sufficient to identify risks.

12. For any performance presented in an advertisement for periods prior to 1 January 2000 that does not comply with the GIPS standards, FIRMS MUST disclose the periods of non-compliance.

13. If the advertisement conforms with laws and/or regulations that conflict with the REQUIREMENTS of the GIPS standards and/or the GIPS Advertising Guidelines, FIRMS MUST disclose this fact and disclose the manner in which the laws and/or regulations conflict with the GIPS standards and/or the GIPS Advertising Guidelines.

IV. VERIFICATION

VERIFICATION is intended to provide a FIRM and its existing clients and PROSPECTIVE CLIENTS additional confidence in the FIRM'S claim of compliance with the GIPS standards. VERIFICATION may increase the knowledge of the FIRM'S performance measurement team and improve the consistency and quality of the FIRM'S COMPLIANT PRESENTATIONS. VERIFICATION may also provide improved internal processes and procedures as well as marketing advantages to the FIRM. Verification does not ensure the accuracy of any specific COMPOSITE presentation.

The GIPS standards RECOMMEND that FIRMS be verified. VERIFICATION brings additional credibility to the claim of compliance and supports the overall guiding principles of fair representation and full disclosure of a FIRM'S investment performance.

The VERIFICATION procedures attempt to strike a balance between ensuring the quality, accuracy, and relevance of performance presentations and minimizing the cost to FIRMS.

A. Scope and Purpose of Verification

1. VERIFICATION MUST be performed by a qualified independent third party.

2. VERIFICATION assesses whether:

   a. The FIRM has complied with all the COMPOSITE construction REQUIREMENTS of the GIPS standards on a FIRM-wide basis, and

   b. The FIRM'S policies and procedures are designed to calculate and present performance in compliance with the GIPS standards.

3. A single VERIFICATION REPORT is issued with respect to the whole FIRM. VERIFICATION cannot be carried out on a COMPOSITE and, accordingly, does not provide assurance about the performance of any specific

COMPOSITE. FIRMS MUST NOT state that a particular COMPOSITE has been "verified" or make any claim to that effect.

4. The initial minimum period for which VERIFICATION can be performed is one year (or from FIRM inception date through period end if less than one year) of a FIRM'S presented performance. The RECOMMENDED period over which VERIFICATION is performed is that part of the FIRM'S performance for which compliance with the GIPS standards is claimed.

5. A VERIFICATION REPORT MUST opine that:

   a. The FIRM has complied with all the COMPOSITE construction REQUIREMENTS of the GIPS standards on a FIRM-wide basis, and

   b. The FIRM'S policies and procedures are designed to calculate and present performance in compliance with the GIPS standards.

   The FIRM MUST NOT state that it has been verified unless a VERIFICATION REPORT has been issued.

6. A principal verifier may accept the work of another verifier as part of the basis for the principal verifier's opinion. A principal verifier may also choose to rely on the audit and/or internal control work of a qualified and reputable independent third party. In addition, a principal verifier may choose to rely on the other audit and/or internal control work performed by the VERIFICATION firm. If reliance on another party's work is planned, the scope of work, including time period covered, results of procedures performed, qualifications, competency, objectivity, and reputation of the other party, MUST be assessed by the principal verifier when making the determination as to whether to place any reliance on such work. Reliance considerations and conclusions MUST be documented by the principal verifier. The principal verifier MUST use professional skepticism when deciding whether to place reliance on work performed by another independent third party.

7. Sample PORTFOLIO Selection: Verifiers MUST subject the entire FIRM to testing when performing VERIFICATION procedures unless reliance is placed on work performed by a qualified and reputable independent third party or appropriate alternative control procedures have been performed by the verifier. Verifiers may use a sampling methodology when performing such procedures. Verifiers MUST consider the following criteria when selecting samples:

   a. Number of COMPOSITES at the FIRM;

   b. Number of PORTFOLIOS in each COMPOSITE;

   c. Type of COMPOSITE;

   d. TOTAL FIRM ASSETS;

   e. Internal control structure at the FIRM (system of checks and balances in place);

   f. Number of years being verified; and

   g. Computer applications, software used in the construction and maintenance of COMPOSITES, the use of external performance measurers, and the method of calculating performance.

   This list is not all-inclusive and contains only the minimum criteria that MUST be considered in the selection and evaluation of a sample. For example, one potentially useful approach would be to include in the sample a PORTFOLIO that has the largest impact on COMPOSITE performance because of its size or because of extremely good or bad performance. Missing or incomplete documents, or the presence of errors, would normally be expected to warrant selecting a larger sample or applying additional VERIFICATION procedures.

8. After performing the VERIFICATION, the verifier may conclude that the FIRM is not in compliance with the GIPS standards or that the records of the FIRM cannot support a VERIFICATION. In such situations, the verifier MUST issue a statement to the FIRM clarifying why a VERIFICATION REPORT could not be issued. A VERIFICATION REPORT MUST NOT be issued when the verifier knows that the FIRM is not in compliance with the GIPS standards or the records of the FIRM cannot support a VERIFICATION.

9. The minimum VERIFICATION procedures are described below in Section B. The VERIFICATION REPORT MUST state that the VERIFICATION has been conducted in accordance with these VERIFICATION procedures.

B. Required Verification Procedures

The following are the minimum procedures that verifiers MUST follow when conducting a VERIFICATION. Verifiers MUST complete the VERIFICATION in accordance with these procedures prior to issuing a VERIFICATION REPORT to the FIRM:

1. Pre-VERIFICATION Procedures:
   a. Knowledge of the GIPS Standards: Verifiers MUST understand all the REQUIREMENTS and RECOMMENDATIONS of the GIPS standards, including any updates, Guidance Statements, interpretations, Questions & Answers (Q&As), and clarifications published by CFA Institute and the GIPS Executive Committee, which are available on the GIPS standards website (www.gipsstandards.org) as well as in the *GIPS Handbook*.
   b. Knowledge of Regulations: Verifiers MUST be knowledgeable of applicable laws and regulations regarding the calculation and presentation of performance and MUST consider any differences between these laws and regulations and the GIPS standards.
   c. Knowledge of the FIRM: Verifiers MUST gain an understanding of the FIRM, including the corporate structure of the FIRM and how it operates.
   d. Knowledge of the FIRM'S Policies and Procedures: Verifiers MUST understand the FIRM'S policies and procedures for establishing and maintaining compliance with all the applicable REQUIREMENTS and adopted RECOMMENDATIONS of the GIPS standards. The verifier MUST obtain a copy of the FIRM'S policies and procedures used in establishing and maintaining compliance with the GIPS standards and ensure that all applicable policies and procedures are properly included and adequately documented.
   e. Knowledge of Valuation Basis and Performance Calculations: Verifiers MUST understand the policies, procedures, and methodologies used to value PORTFOLIOS and compute investment performance.

2. VERIFICATION Procedures:
   a. Fundamentals of Compliance: Verifiers MUST perform sufficient procedures to determine that:
      i. The FIRM is, and has been, appropriately defined;
      ii. The FIRM has defined and maintained COMPOSITES in compliance with the GIPS standards;
      iii. All the FIRM'S actual, fee-paying, discretionary PORTFOLIOS are included in at least one COMPOSITE;
      iv. The FIRM'S definition of discretion has been consistently applied over time;

    v. At all times, all PORTFOLIOS are included in their respective COMPOSITES and no PORTFOLIOS that belong in a particular COMPOSITE have been excluded;

    vi. The FIRM'S policies and procedures for ensuring the existence and ownership of client assets are appropriate and have been consistently applied;

    vii. The COMPOSITE BENCHMARK reflects the investment mandate, objective, or strategy of the COMPOSITE;

    viii. The FIRM'S policies and procedures for creating and maintaining COMPOSITES have been consistently applied;

    ix. The FIRM'S list of COMPOSITE DESCRIPTIONS is complete; and

    x. TOTAL FIRM ASSETS are appropriately calculated and disclosed.

b. Determination of Discretionary Status of PORTFOLIOS: Verifiers MUST obtain a list of all PORTFOLIOS. Verifiers MUST select PORTFOLIOS from this list and perform sufficient procedures to determine that the FIRM'S classification of the PORTFOLIOS as discretionary or non-discretionary is appropriate by referring to the PORTFOLIO'S investment management agreement and/or investment guidelines and the FIRM'S policies and procedures for determining investment discretion.

c. Allocation of PORTFOLIOS to COMPOSITES: Verifiers MUST obtain lists of all open (both new and existing) and closed PORTFOLIOS for all COMPOSITES for the periods being verified. Verifiers MUST select PORTFOLIOS from these lists and perform sufficient procedures to determine that:

    i. The timing of inclusion in the COMPOSITE is in accordance with policies and procedures of the FIRM.

    ii. The timing of exclusion from the COMPOSITE is in accordance with policies and procedures of the FIRM.

    iii. The PORTFOLIO'S investment mandate, objective, or strategy, as indicated by the PORTFOLIO'S investment management agreement, investment guidelines, PORTFOLIO summary, and/or other appropriate documentation, is consistent with the COMPOSITE DEFINITION.

    iv. PORTFOLIOS are completely and accurately included in COMPOSITES by tracing selected PORTFOLIOS from:

        a. The PORTFOLIO'S investment management agreement and/or investment management guidelines to the COMPOSITE(S); and

        b. The COMPOSITE(S) to the PORTFOLIO'S investment management agreement and/or investment guidelines.

    v. PORTFOLIOS sharing the same investment mandate, objective, or strategy are included in the same COMPOSITE.

    vi. Movements from one COMPOSITE to another are appropriate and consistent with documented changes to a PORTFOLIO'S investment mandate, objective, or strategy or the redefinition of the COMPOSITE.

d. Data Review: For selected PORTFOLIOS, verifiers MUST perform sufficient procedures to determine that the treatment of the following items is consistent with the FIRM'S policy:

    i. Classification of PORTFOLIO flows (e.g., receipts, disbursements, dividends, interest, fees, and taxes);

    ii. Accounting treatment of income, interest, and dividend accruals and receipts;

    iii. Accounting treatment of taxes, tax reclaims, and tax accruals;

    iv. Accounting treatment of purchases, sales, and the opening and closing of other positions; and

    v. Accounting treatment and valuation methodologies for investments, including derivatives.

e. Performance Measurement Calculation: Recognizing that VERIFICATION does not provide assurance that specific COMPOSITE returns are correctly calculated and presented, verifiers MUST determine that the FIRM has calculated and presented performance in accordance with the FIRM'S policies and procedures. Verifiers MUST perform the following procedures:

    i. Recalculate rates of return for a sample of PORTFOLIOS, determine that an acceptable return formula as REQUIRED by the GIPS standards is used, and determine that the FIRM'S calculations are in accordance with the FIRM'S policies and procedures. The verifier MUST also determine that any fees and expenses are treated in accordance with the GIPS standards and the FIRM'S policies and procedures.

    ii. Take a sample of COMPOSITE and BENCHMARK calculations to determine the accuracy of all required numerical data (e.g., risk measures, INTERNAL DISPERSION).

    iii. If a custom BENCHMARK or combination of multiple BENCHMARKS is used, take a sample of the BENCHMARK data used by the FIRM to determine that the calculation methodology has been correctly applied and the data used are consistent with the BENCHMARK disclosure in the COMPLIANT PRESENTATION.

f. COMPLIANT PRESENTATIONS: Verifiers MUST perform sufficient procedures on a sample of COMPLIANT PRESENTATIONS to determine that the presentations include all the information and disclosures REQUIRED by the GIPS standards. The information and disclosures MUST be consistent with the FIRM'S records, the FIRM'S documented policies and procedures, and the results of the verifier's procedures.

g. Maintenance of Records: The verifier MUST maintain sufficient documentation to support all procedures performed supporting the issuance of the VERIFICATION REPORT, including all significant judgments and conclusions made by the verifier.

h. Representation Letter: The verifier MUST obtain a representation letter from the FIRM confirming that policies and procedures used in establishing and maintaining compliance with the GIPS standards are as described in the FIRM'S policies and procedures documents and have been consistently applied throughout the periods being verified. The representation letter MUST confirm that the FIRM complies with the GIPS standards for the period being verified. The representation letter MUST also contain any other specific representations made to the verifier during the VERIFICATION.

C. Performance Examinations

In addition to a VERIFICATION, a FIRM may choose to have a specifically focused PERFORMANCE EXAMINATION of a particular COMPOSITE COMPLIANT PRESENTATION. However, a PERFORMANCE EXAMINATION REPORT MUST NOT be issued unless a VERIFICATION REPORT has also been issued. The PERFORMANCE EXAMINATION may be performed concurrently with the VERIFICATION.

A PERFORMANCE EXAMINATION is not REQUIRED for a FIRM to be verified. The FIRM MUST NOT state that a COMPOSITE has been examined unless the PERFORMANCE EXAMINATION REPORT has been issued for the specific COMPOSITE.

Please see the Guidance Statement on PERFORMANCE EXAMINATIONS for additional guidance.

END OPTIONAL
SEGMENT

GIPS GLOSSARY

V.

ACCRUAL ACCOUNTING	The recording of financial transactions as they come into existence rather than when they are paid or settled.
ADDITIONAL INFORMATION	Information that is REQUIRED or RECOMMENDED under the GIPS standards and is not considered SUPPLEMENTAL INFORMATION.
ADMINISTRATIVE FEE	All fees other than TRADING EXPENSES and the INVESTMENT MANAGEMENT FEE. ADMINISTRATIVE FEES include CUSTODY FEES, accounting fees, auditing fees, consulting fees, legal fees, performance measurement fees, and other related fees. (See "BUNDLED FEE")
ALL-IN FEE	A type of BUNDLED FEE that can include any combination of INVESTMENT MANAGEMENT FEES, TRADING EXPENSES, CUSTODY FEES, and ADMINISTRATIVE FEES. ALL-IN-FEES are client specific and typically offered in certain jurisdictions where asset management, brokerage, and custody services are offered by the same company.
BENCHMARK	A point of reference against which the COMPOSITE'S performance and/or risk is compared.
BENCHMARK DESCRIPTION	General information regarding the investments, structure, and/or characteristics of the BENCHMARK. The description MUST include the key features of the BENCHMARK, or the name of the BENCHMARK for a readily recognized index or other point of reference.
BUNDLED FEE	A fee that combines multiple fees into one total or "bundled" fee. BUNDLED FEES can include any combination of INVESTMENT MANAGEMENT FEES, TRADING EXPENSES, CUSTODY FEES, and/or ADMINISTRATIVE FEES. Two examples of BUNDLED FEES are WRAP FEES and ALL-IN-FEES.
CAPITAL EMPLOYED (REAL ESTATE)	The denominator of the return calculations and is defined as the "weighted-average equity" (weighted-average capital) during the measurement period. CAPITAL EMPLOYED does not include any INCOME RETURN or CAPITAL RETURN earned during the measurement period. Beginning capital is adjusted by weighting the EXTERNAL CASH FLOWS that occurred during the period.

CAPITAL RETURN (REAL ESTATE)	The change in value of the REAL ESTATE investments and cash and/or cash equivalent assets held throughout the measurement period, adjusted for all capital expenditures (subtracted) and net proceeds from sales (added). The CAPITAL RETURN is computed as a percentage of the CAPITAL EMPLOYED. Also known as "capital appreciation return" or "appreciation return."
CARRIED INTEREST (REAL ESTATE and PRIVATE EQUITY)	The profits that GENERAL PARTNERS are allocated from the profits on the investments made by the investment vehicle. Also known as "carry" or "promote."
CARVE-OUT	A portion of a PORTFOLIO that is by itself representative of a distinct investment strategy. It is used to create a track record for a narrower mandate from a multiple-strategy PORTFOLIO managed to a broader mandate. For periods beginning on or after 1 January 2010, a CARVE-OUT MUST be managed separately with its own cash balance.
CLOSED-END FUND (REAL ESTATE and PRIVATE EQUITY)	A type of investment vehicle where the number of investors, total COMMITTED CAPITAL, and life are fixed and not open for subscriptions and/or redemptions. CLOSED-END FUNDS have a capital call (drawdown) process in place that is controlled by the GENERAL PARTNER.
COMMITTED CAPITAL (REAL ESTATE and PRIVATE EQUITY)	Pledges of capital to an investment vehicle by investors (LIMITED PARTNERS and the GENERAL PARTNER) or by the FIRM. COMMITTED CAPITAL is typically not drawn down at once but drawn down over a period of time. Also known as "commitments."
COMPLIANT PRESENTATION	A presentation for a COMPOSITE that contains all the information REQUIRED by the GIPS standards and may also include ADDITIONAL INFORMATION or SUPPLEMENTAL INFORMATION. (See Sample COMPLIANT PRESENTATIONS in Appendix 4A)
COMPOSITE	An aggregation of one or more PORTFOLIOS managed according to a similar investment mandate, objective, or strategy.
COMPOSITE CREATION DATE	The date when the FIRM first groups one or more PORTFOLIOS to create a COMPOSITE. The COMPOSITE CREATION DATE is not necessarily the same as the COMPOSITE INCEPTION DATE.
COMPOSITE DEFINITION	Detailed criteria that determine the assignment of PORTFOLIOS to COMPOSITES. Criteria may include investment mandate, style or strategy, asset class, the use of derivatives, leverage and/or hedging, targeted risk metrics, investment constraints or restrictions, and/or PORTFOLIO type (e.g., segregated or pooled, taxable versus tax exempt.)
COMPOSITE DESCRIPTION	General information regarding the investment mandate, objective, or strategy of the COMPOSITE. The COMPOSITE DESCRIPTION may be more abbreviated than the COMPOSITE DEFINITION but MUST include all key features of the COMPOSITE and MUST include enough information to allow a PROSPECTIVE CLIENT to understand the key characteristics of the COMPOSITE'S investment mandate, objective, or strategy. (See the Sample List of Composite Descriptions in Appendix 4C)

COMPOSITE INCEPTION DATE	The initial date of the COMPOSITE'S performance record. The COMPOSITE INCEPTION DATE is not necessarily the same as the COMPOSITE CREATION DATE.
COMPOSITE TERMINATION DATE	The date that the last PORTFOLIO exits a COMPOSITE.
CUSTODY FEE	The fees payable to the custodian for the safekeeping of PORTFOLIO assets. CUSTODY FEES are considered to be ADMINISTRATIVE FEES and typically contain an asset-based portion and a transaction-based portion. The CUSTODY FEE may also include charges for additional services, including accounting, securities lending, and/or performance measurement. Custodial fees that are charged per transaction SHOULD be included in the CUSTODY FEE and not included as part of TRADING EXPENSES.
DIRECT INVESTMENTS (PRIVATE EQUITY)	Investments made directly in PRIVATE EQUITY investments rather than investments made in fund investment vehicles or cash and/or cash equivalents.
DISTINCT BUSINESS ENTITY	A unit, division, department, or office that is organizationally and functionally segregated from other units, divisions, departments, or offices and that retains discretion over the assets it manages and that should have autonomy over the investment decision-making process. Possible criteria that can be used to determine this include: ■ being a legal entity, ■ having a distinct market or client type (e.g., institutional, retail, private client, etc.), and ■ using a separate and distinct investment process.
DISTRIBUTION (REAL ESTATE and PRIVATE EQUITY)	Cash or stock distributed to LIMITED PARTNERS (or investors) from an investment vehicle. DISTRIBUTIONS are typically at the discretion of the GENERAL PARTNER (or the FIRM). DISTRIBUTIONS include both recallable and non-recallable DISTRIBUTIONS.
DPI (REAL ESTATE and PRIVATE EQUITY)	SINCE INCEPTION DISTRIBUTIONS divided by SINCE INCEPTION PAID-IN CAPITAL. (See "REALIZATION MULTIPLE")
EVERGREEN FUND (PRIVATE EQUITY)	An OPEN-END FUND that allows for on-going subscriptions and/or redemptions by investors.
EX-ANTE	Before the fact.
EX-POST	After the fact.
EXTERNAL CASH FLOW	Capital (cash or investments) that enters or exits a PORTFOLIO.
EXTERNAL VALUATION (REAL ESTATE)	An assessment of value performed by an independent external third party who is a qualified, PROFESSIONALLY DESIGNATED, CERTIFIED, OR LICENSED COMMERCIAL PROPERTY VALUER/APPRAISER.

FAIR VALUE	The amount at which an investment could be exchanged in a current arm's length transaction between willing parties in which the parties each act knowledgeably and prudently. The valuation MUST be determined using the objective, observable, unadjusted quoted market price for an identical investment in an active market on the measurement date, if available. In the absence of an objective, observable, unadjusted quoted market price for an identical investment in an active market on the measurement date, the valuation MUST represent the FIRM'S best estimate of the MARKET VALUE. FAIR VALUE MUST include accrued income.
FEE SCHEDULE	The FIRM'S current schedule of INVESTMENT MANAGEMENT FEES or BUNDLED FEES relevant to the particular COMPLIANT PRESENTATION.
FINAL LIQUIDATION DATE (REAL ESTATE and PRIVATE EQUITY)	The date when the last PORTFOLIO in a COMPOSITE is fully distributed.
FIRM	The entity defined for compliance with the GIPS standards. (See "DISTINCT BUSINESS ENTITY")
FUND OF FUNDS (PRIVATE EQUITY)	An investment vehicle that invests in underlying investment vehicles. PRIVATE EQUITY FUNDS OF FUNDS predominately invest in CLOSED-END FUNDS and may make opportunistic DIRECT INVESTMENTS.
GENERAL PARTNER (REAL ESTATE and PRIVATE EQUITY)	A class of partner in a LIMITED PARTNERSHIP. The GENERAL PARTNER retains liability for the actions of the LIMITED PARTNERSHIP. The GENERAL PARTNER is typically the fund manager, and the LIMITED PARTNERS (LPs) are the other investors in the LIMITED PARTNERSHIP. The GENERAL PARTNER earns an INVESTMENT MANAGEMENT FEE that typically includes a percentage of the LIMITED PARTNERSHIP'S profits. (See "CARRIED INTEREST")
GROSS-OF-FEES	The return on investments reduced by any TRADING EXPENSES incurred during the period.
GROSS-OF-FEES (REAL ESTATE and PRIVATE EQUITY)	The return on investments reduced by any TRANSACTION EXPENSES incurred during the period.
INCOME RETURN (REAL ESTATE)	The investment income earned on all investments (including cash and cash equivalents) during the measurement period net of all non-recoverable expenditures, interest expense on debt, and property taxes. The INCOME RETURN is computed as a percentage of the CAPITAL EMPLOYED.
INTERNAL DISPERSION	A measure of the spread of the annual returns of individual PORTFOLIOS within a COMPOSITE. Measures may include, but are not limited to, high/low, range, or STANDARD DEVIATION (asset weighted or equal weighted) of PORTFOLIO returns.

INTERNAL VALUATION (REAL ESTATE)	A FIRM'S best estimate of value based on the most current and accurate information available under the circumstances. INTERNAL VALUATION methodologies include applying a discounted cash flow model, using a sales comparison or replacement cost approach, or conducting a review of all significant events (both general market and asset specific) that could have a material impact on the investment.
INVESTMENT MANAGEMENT FEE	A fee payable to the FIRM for the management of a PORTFOLIO. INVESTMENT MANAGEMENT FEES are typically asset based (percentage of assets), performance based (see "PERFORMANCE-BASED FEE"), or a combination of the two but may take different forms as well. INVESTMENT MANAGEMENT FEES also include CARRIED INTEREST.
INVESTMENT MULTIPLE (TVPI) (REAL ESTATE and PRIVATE EQUITY)	TOTAL VALUE divided by SINCE INCEPTION PAID-IN CAPITAL.
LARGE CASH FLOW	The level at which the FIRM determines that an EXTERNAL CASH FLOW may distort performance if the PORTFOLIO is not valued. FIRMS MUST define the amount in terms of the value of cash/asset flow or in terms of a percentage of the PORTFOLIO assets or the COMPOSITE assets.
LIMITED PARTNER (REAL ESTATE and PRIVATE EQUITY)	An investor in a LIMITED PARTNERSHIP. The GENERAL PARTNER is liable for the actions of the LIMITED PARTNERSHIP, and the LIMITED PARTNERS are generally protected from legal actions and any losses beyond their COMMITTED CAPITAL.
LIMITED PARTNERSHIP (REAL ESTATE and PRIVATE EQUITY)	The legal structure used by most PRIVATE EQUITY and REAL ESTATE CLOSED-END FUNDS. LIMITED PARTNERSHIPS are usually fixed life investment vehicles. The GENERAL PARTNER manages the LIMITED PARTNERSHIP pursuant to the partnership agreement.
LINK	1. <u>Mathematical Linking</u>: The method by which sub-period returns are geometrically combined to calculate the period return using the following formula: Period return = $[(1+R_1) \times (1+R_2)...(1+R_n)] - 1$ where $R_1, R_2...R_n$ are the sub-period returns for sub-period 1 through n, respectively. 2. <u>Presentational Linking</u>: To be visually connected or otherwise associated within a COMPLIANT PRESENTATION (e.g., two pieces of information are LINKED by placing them next to each other).
MARKET VALUE	The price at which investors can buy or sell an investment at a given time multiplied by the quantity held plus any accrued income.
MUST	A provision, task, or action that is mandatory or REQUIRED to be followed or performed. (See "REQUIRE/REQUIREMENT")
MUST NOT	A task or action that is forbidden or prohibited.

NET-OF-FEES	The GROSS-OF-FEES return reduced by INVESTMENT MANAGEMENT FEES (including PERFORMANCE-BASED FEES and CARRIED INTEREST).
OPEN-END FUND (REAL ESTATE and PRIVATE EQUITY)	A type of investment vehicle where the number of investors and the total COMMITTED CAPITAL is not fixed and is open for subscriptions and/or redemptions. (See "EVERGREEN FUND")
PAID-IN CAPITAL (REAL ESTATE and PRIVATE EQUITY)	Capital inflows to an investment vehicle. COMMITTED CAPITAL is typically drawn down from LIMITED PARTNERS (or investors) over a period of time through a series of capital calls, which are at the discretion of the GENERAL PARTNER or FIRM. PAID-IN CAPITAL is equal to the amount of COMMITTED CAPITAL that has been drawn down SINCE INCEPTION. PAID-IN CAPITAL includes DISTRIBUTIONS that are subsequently recalled by the GENERAL PARTNER or FIRM and reinvested into the investment vehicle.
PERFORMANCE-BASED FEE	A type of INVESTMENT MANAGEMENT FEE that is typically based on the performance of the PORTFOLIO on an absolute basis or relative to a BENCHMARK.
PERFORMANCE EXAMINATION	A detailed examination of a specific COMPOSITE'S COMPLIANT PRESENTATION by an independent verifier.
PERFORMANCE EXAMINATION REPORT	A PERFORMANCE EXAMINATION REPORT is issued after a PERFORMANCE EXAMINATION has been performed and opines that a particular COMPOSITE'S COMPLIANT PRESENTATION has been prepared and presented in compliance with the GIPS standards.
PERIODICITY	The length of the time period over which a variable is measured (e.g., a variable that is measured at a monthly PERIODICITY consists of observations for each month).
PIC MULTIPLE (REAL ESTATE and PRIVATE EQUITY)	SINCE INCEPTION PAID-IN CAPITAL divided by cumulative COMMITTED CAPITAL.
PORTFOLIO	An individually managed group of investments. A PORTFOLIO may be an account or pooled investment vehicle.
PRIMARY FUND (PRIVATE EQUITY)	An investment vehicle that makes DIRECT INVESTMENTS rather than investing in other investment vehicles.
PRIVATE EQUITY	Investment strategies include, but are not limited to, venture capital, leveraged buyouts, consolidations, mezzanine and distressed debt investments, and a variety of hybrids, such as venture leasing and venture factoring.
PROFESSIONALLY DESIGNATED, CERTIFIED, OR LICENSED COMMERCIAL PROPERTY VALUER/ APPRAISER (REAL ESTATE)	In Europe, Canada, and parts of Southeast Asia, the predominant professional designation is that of the Royal Institution of Chartered Surveyors (RICS). In the United States, the professional designation is Member [of the] Appraisal Institute (MAI). In addition, each state regulates REAL ESTATE appraisers and registers, licenses, or certifies them based on their experience and test results.

PROPRIETARY ASSETS	Investments owned by the FIRM, the FIRM'S management, and/or the FIRM'S parent company that are managed by the FIRM.
PROSPECTIVE CLIENT	Any person or entity that has expressed interest in one of the FIRM'S COMPOSITE strategies and qualifies to invest in the COMPOSITE. Existing clients may also qualify as PROSPECTIVE CLIENTS for any strategy that is different from their current investment strategy. Investment consultants and other third parties are included as PROSPECTIVE CLIENTS if they represent investors that qualify as PROSPECTIVE CLIENTS.
PUBLIC MARKET EQUIVALENT (PME) (PRIVATE EQUITY)	The performance of a public market index expressed in terms of an internal rate of return (IRR), using the same cash flows and timing as those of the COMPOSITE over the same time period. A PME can be used as a BENCHMARK by comparing the IRR of a PRIVATE EQUITY COMPOSITE with the PME of a public market index.
REAL ESTATE	Investments in:

Investments in:

- Wholly owned or partially owned properties,
- Commingled funds, property unit trusts, and insurance company separate accounts,
- Unlisted, private placement securities issued by private REAL ESTATE investment trusts (REITs) and REAL ESTATE operating companies (REOCs); and
- Equity-oriented debt (e.g., participating mortgage loans) or any private interest in a property where some portion of return to the investor at the time of investment is related to the performance of the underlying REAL ESTATE.

REALIZATION MULTIPLE (DPI) (REAL ESTATE and PRIVATE EQUITY)	SINCE INCEPTION DISTRIBUTIONS divided by SINCE INCEPTION PAID-IN CAPITAL.
RECOMMEND/ RECOMMENDATION	A suggested provision, task, or action that SHOULD be followed or performed. A RECOMMENDATION is considered to be best practice but is not a REQUIREMENT. (See "SHOULD")
REQUIRE/REQUIREMENT	A provision, task, or action that MUST be followed or performed. (See "MUST")
RESIDUAL VALUE (PRIVATE EQUITY and REAL ESTATE)	The remaining equity that LIMITED PARTNERS (or investors) have in an investment vehicle at the end of the performance reporting period.
RVPI (REAL ESTATE and PRIVATE EQUITY)	RESIDUAL VALUE divided by SINCE INCEPTION PAID-IN CAPITAL. (See "UNREALIZED MULTIPLE")
SECONDARY FUND (PRIVATE EQUITY)	An investment vehicle that buys interests in existing investment vehicles.
SETTLEMENT DATE ACCOUNTING	Recognizing the asset or liability on the date when the exchange of cash and investments is completed.

SHOULD	A provision, task, or action that is RECOMMENDED to be followed or performed and is considered to be best practice, but is not REQUIRED. (See "RECOMMEND/RECOMMENDATION")
SIGNIFICANT CASH FLOW	The level at which the FIRM determines that a client-directed EXTERNAL CASH FLOW may temporarily prevent the FIRM from implementing the COMPOSITE strategy. The measure of significance MUST be determined as either a specific monetary amount (e.g., €50,000,000) or a percentage of PORTFOLIO assets (based on the most recent valuation).
SINCE INCEPTION (REAL ESTATE and PRIVATE EQUITY)	From the initial cash flow of a COMPOSITE.
SINCE INCEPTION INTERNAL RATE OF RETURN (SI-IRR) (REAL ESTATE and PRIVATE EQUITY)	The internal rate of return (IRR) is the implied discount rate or effective compounded rate of return that equates the present value of cash outflows with the present value of cash inflows. The SI-IRR is a special case of the IRR that equates the present value of all cash flows (capital calls and DISTRIBUTIONS) with the period end value. The SI-IRR is always annualized except when the reporting period is less than one year, in which case the SI-IRR is not annualized.
STANDARD DEVIATION	A measure of the variability of returns. As a measure of INTERNAL DISPERSION, STANDARD DEVIATION quantifies the distribution of the returns of the individual PORTFOLIOS within the COMPOSITE. As a measure of historical risk, STANDARD DEVIATION quantifies the variability of the COMPOSITE and/or BENCHMARK returns over time. Also referred to as "external STANDARD DEVIATION."
SUB-ADVISOR	A third-party investment manager hired by the FIRM to manage some or all of the assets for which a FIRM has investment management responsibility.
SUPPLEMENTAL INFORMATION	Any performance-related information included as part of a COMPLIANT PRESENTATION that supplements or enhances the REQUIRED and/or RECOMMENDED provisions of the GIPS standards.
TEMPORARY NEW ACCOUNT	An account for temporarily holding client-directed EXTERNAL CASH FLOWS until they are invested according to the COMPOSITE strategy or disbursed. FIRMS can use a TEMPORARY NEW ACCOUNT to remove the effect of a SIGNIFICANT CASH FLOW on a PORTFOLIO. When a SIGNIFICANT CASH FLOW occurs in a PORTFOLIO, the FIRM may direct the EXTERNAL CASH FLOW to a TEMPORARY NEW ACCOUNT according to the COMPOSITE'S SIGNIFICANT CASH FLOW policy.
TIME-WEIGHTED RATE OF RETURN	A method of calculating period-by-period returns that negates the effects of EXTERNAL CASH FLOWS.

TOTAL FIRM ASSETS	All discretionary and non-discretionary assets for which a FIRM has investment management responsibility. TOTAL FIRM ASSETS includes assets assigned to a SUB-ADVISOR provided the FIRM has discretion over the selection of the SUB-ADVISOR.
TOTAL RETURN	The rate of return that includes the realized and unrealized gains and losses plus income for the measurement period.
TOTAL RETURN (REAL ESTATE)	The rate of return, including all CAPITAL RETURN and INCOME RETURN components, expressed as a percentage of the CAPITAL EMPLOYED over the measurement period.
TOTAL VALUE (REAL ESTATE and PRIVATE EQUITY)	RESIDUAL VALUE plus DISTRIBUTIONS.
TRADE DATE ACCOUNTING	Recognizing the asset or liability on the date of the purchase or sale and not on the settlement date. Recognizing the asset or liability within three days of the date the transaction is entered into (trade date, T+1, T+2, or T+3) satisfies the TRADE DATE ACCOUNTING REQUIREMENT for purposes of the GIPS standards. (See "SETTLEMENT DATE ACCOUNTING")
TRADING EXPENSES	The actual costs of buying or selling investments. These costs typically take the form of brokerage commissions, exchange fees and/or taxes, and/or bid–offer spreads from either internal or external brokers. Custodial fees charged per transaction SHOULD be considered CUSTODY FEES and not TRADING EXPENSES.
TRANSACTION EXPENSES (REAL ESTATE and PRIVATE EQUITY)	All actual legal, financial, advisory, and investment banking fees related to buying, selling, restructuring, and/or recapitalizing PORTFOLIO investments as well as TRADING EXPENSES, if any.
TVPI (REAL ESTATE and PRIVATE EQUITY)	TOTAL VALUE divided by SINCE INCEPTION PAID-IN CAPITAL. (See "INVESTMENT MULTIPLE")
UNREALIZED MULTIPLE (RVPI) (REAL ESTATE and PRIVATE EQUITY)	RESIDUAL VALUE divided by SINCE INCEPTION PAID-IN CAPITAL.
VERIFICATION	A process by which an independent verifier assesses whether 1) the FIRM has complied with all the COMPOSITE construction REQUIREMENTS of the GIPS standards on a FIRM-wide basis and 2) the FIRM'S policies and procedures are designed to calculate and present performance in compliance with the GIPS standards.
VERIFICATION REPORT	A VERIFICATION REPORT is issued after a VERIFICATION has been performed and opines that the FIRM has complied with all the COMPOSITE construction REQUIREMENTS of the GIPS standards on a FIRM-wide basis and that the FIRM'S policies and procedures are designed to calculate and present performance in compliance with the GIPS standards.

VINTAGE YEAR
(REAL ESTATE and PRIVATE EQUITY)

Two methods used to determine VINTAGE YEAR are:

1. The year of the investment vehicle's first drawdown or capital call from its investors; or

2. The year when the first COMMITTED CAPITAL from outside investors is closed and legally binding.

WRAP FEE

WRAP FEES are a type of BUNDLED FEE and are specific to a particular investment product. The WRAP FEE is charged by a WRAP FEE sponsor for investment management services and typically includes associated TRADING EXPENSES that cannot be separately identified. WRAP FEES can be all-inclusive, asset-based fees and may include a combination of INVESTMENT MANAGEMENT FEES, TRADING EXPENSES, CUSTODY FEES, and/or ADMINISTRATIVE FEES. A WRAP FEE PORTFOLIO is sometimes referred to as a "separately managed account" (SMA) or "managed account."

APPENDIX 4A: SAMPLE COMPLIANT PRESENTATIONS

Sample 1

Investment Firm Balanced Growth Composite

1 January 2002 through 31 December 2011

Year	Composite Gross Return (%)	Composite Net Return (%)	Custom Benchmark Return (%)	Composite 3-Yr St Dev (%)	Benchmark 3-Yr St Dev (%)	Number of Portfolios	Internal Dispersion (%)	Composite Assets ($ M)	Firm Assets ($ M)
2002	−10.5	−11.4	−11.8			31	4.5	165	236
2003	16.3	15.1	13.2			34	2.0	235	346
2004	7.5	6.4	8.9			38	5.7	344	529
2005	1.8	0.8	0.3			45	2.8	445	695
2006	11.2	10.1	12.2			48	3.1	520	839
2007	6.1	5.0	7.1			49	2.8	505	1,014
2008	−21.3	−22.1	−24.9			44	2.9	475	964
2009	16.5	15.3	14.7			47	3.1	493	983
2010	10.6	9.5	13.0			51	3.5	549	1,114
2011	2.7	1.7	0.4	7.1	7.4	54	2.5	575	1,236

Sample 1 Investment Firm claims compliance with the Global Investment Performance Standards (GIPS®) and has prepared and presented this report in compliance with the GIPS standards. Sample 1 Investment Firm has been independently verified for the periods 1 January 2000 through 31 December 2010. The verification report is available upon request. Verification assesses whether 1) the firm has complied with all the composite construction requirements of the GIPS standards on a firm-wide basis and 2) the firm's policies and procedures are designed to calculate and present performance in compliance with the GIPS standards. Verification does not ensure the accuracy of any specific composite presentation.

Notes:

1. Sample 1 Investment Firm is a balanced portfolio investment manager that invests solely in U.S.-based securities. Sample 1 Investment Firm is defined as an independent investment management firm that is not affiliated with any parent organization. Policies for valuing portfolios, calculating performance, and preparing compliant presentations are available upon request.

2. The Balanced Growth Composite includes all institutional balanced portfolios that invest in large-cap U.S. equities and investment-grade bonds with the goal of providing long-term capital growth and steady income from a well-diversified strategy. Although the strategy allows for equity exposure ranging between 50–70%, the typical allocation is between 55–65%. The account minimum for the composite is $5 million.

3. The custom benchmark is 60% YYY U.S. Equity Index and 40% ZZZ U.S. Aggregate Bond Index. The benchmark is rebalanced monthly.

4. Valuations are computed and performance is reported in U.S. dollars.

5. Gross-of-fees returns are presented before management and custodial fees but after all trading expenses. Composite and benchmark returns are presented net of non-reclaimable withholding taxes. Net-of-fees returns are calculated by deducting the highest fee of 0.83% from the monthly gross composite return. The management fee schedule is as follows: 1.00% on the first $25 million; 0.60% thereafter.

6. This composite was created in February 2000. A complete list of composite descriptions is available upon request.

7. Internal dispersion is calculated using the equal-weighted standard deviation of annual gross returns of those portfolios that were included in the composite for the entire year.

8. The three-year annualized standard deviation measures the variability of the composite and the benchmark returns over the preceding 36-month period. The standard deviation is not presented for 2002 through 2010 because monthly composite and benchmark returns were not available and is not required for periods prior to 2011.

Sample 2

Asset Management Company

	Active World Equity Composite Creation Date: 1 July 2005 Reporting Currency: EUR					
Year	Gross Return (%)	XYZ World Index Return (%)	Dispersion (Range) (%)	# of Portfolios	Composite Assets (€ M)	% of Firm Assets (%)
2011	−1.9	−0.5	0.2	6	224.9	2.1
2010	16.3	13.5	0.7	8	256.7	2.0
2009	29.0	25.8	1.5	8	205.6	1.9
2008	−39.8	−36.4	1.3	7	164.1	1.5
2007	−2.8	−2.7	n/a	≤ 5	143.7	1.2
2006	9.3	7.5	n/a	≤ 5	62.8	0.4
2005*	14.2	12.6	n/a	≤ 5	16.1	< 0.1

*Returns are for the period from 1 July 2005 (inception date) through 31 December 2005.

Compliance Statement

Sample 2 Asset Management Company claims compliance with the Global Investment Performance Standards (GIPS®) and has prepared and presented this report in compliance with the GIPS standards. Sample 2 Asset Management Company has not been independently verified.

Definition of the Firm

Sample 2 Asset Management Company is an independent investment management firm that was established in 1997. Sample 2 Asset Management Company manages a variety of equity, fixed-income, and balanced assets for primarily European clients.

Policies

Sample 2 Asset Management Company's policies for valuing portfolios, calculating performance, and preparing compliant presentations are available upon request.

Composite Description

The Active World Equity Composite includes accounts whose objective is to exceed the XYZ World Index by 2% over a rolling three-year period. Securities are selected using the firm's proprietary analytics tool, which selects securities expected to be the top performers from within the XYZ World Index universe. Portfolios are more concentrated, typically holding approximately 100–120 securities, versus the benchmark, which reflects the performance of more than 500 holdings. Composite returns may, therefore, have a lower correlation with the benchmark than a more diversified global equity strategy.

Benchmark

The benchmark is the XYZ World Index, which is designed to measure the equity market performance of developed market countries. The benchmark is market-cap weighted and is composed of all XYZ country-specific developed market indices. Sources of foreign exchange rates may be different between the composite and the benchmark; however, there have not been material differences to date. Benchmark returns are net of withholding taxes.

Fees

Returns are presented gross of management fees, custodial fees, and withholding taxes but net of all trading expenses.

List of Composites

A list of all composite descriptions is available upon request.

Fee Schedule

The standard fixed management fee for accounts with assets under management of up to €50 million is 0.35% per annum; 0.25% thereafter.

Minimum Account Size

The minimum portfolio size for inclusion in the composite is €1 million.

Internal Dispersion

Internal dispersion is calculated using the asset-weighted standard deviation of annual gross-of-fees returns of those portfolios that were included in the composite for the entire year. For those years when less than six portfolios were included in the composite for the full year, no dispersion measure is presented.

Ex-Post Standard Deviation

The three-year annualized ex-post standard deviation of the composite and benchmark as of each year end is as follows:

Year	Composite 3-Yr St Dev (%)	Benchmark 3-Yr St Dev (%)
2011	12.9	14.6
2010	13.2	14.1
2009	17.0	16.3
2008	15.6	14.2

Sample 3

Real Estate: Open-End Funds/Separate Accounts

Real Estate Advisors
Value-Added Strategy Composite
Schedule of Performance Results 1 January 2002 through 31 December 2011

	Composite Gross-of-Fees Returns					Composite Net-of-Fees Returns	Value-Added Benchmark Returns (Open-End Funds/Separate Accounts)			Composite Statistics at Year End				
Year	Income Return (%)	Capital Return (%)	Total Return (%)	Low (%)	High (%)	Total Return (%)	Income Return (%)	Capital Return (%)	Total Return (%)	# of Portfolios	Composite Assets (HKD Million)	External Appraisal % of Composite Assets	Total Firm Assets (HKD Million)	Non-Real Estate % of Composite Assets
2002	7.9	1.9	9.9	n/a	n/a	8.8	8.4	−1.6	7.1	≤ 5	3,085	25	13,919	0
2003	8.5	2.9	11.7	5.8	20.4	10.5	8.0	1.0	9.2	6	3,294	25	14,911	0
2004	8.2	2.6	10.9	5.5	19.2	8.3	7.5	6.7	14.4	7	3,348	44	15,144	0
2005	6.6	11.2	18.1	9.0	31.6	16.6	6.8	12.7	19.7	7	3,728	72	19,794	0
2006	6.1	7.9	14.2	7.1	24.9	12.5	6.2	9.9	16.3	8	4,022	46	20,482	0
2007	5.4	8.0	13.7	6.8	23.9	11.8	5.6	9.9	15.6	7	4,348	33	24,219	0
2008	5.2	−11.4	−6.6	−9.8	−1.6	−8.2	5.1	−11.1	−5.9	7	3,836	100	21,447	0
2009	7.5	2.7	10.3	5.2	18.1	7.4	7.3	3.2	10.8	7	3,371	52	16,601	0
2010	7.2	1.7	9.0	4.2	19.5	6.9	7.8	3.1	11.1	7	2,852	38	4,516	0
2011	7.2	2.8	10.2	5.1	17.8	8.1	7.1	3.2	10.6	7	3,457	50	17,414	5

			Annualized Returns (%)											
3 Year	7.3	1.9	9.8			7.5	7.4	3.2	10.8					
5 Year	6.5	2.9	7.1			5.0	6.6	1.4	8.2					
7 Year	6.4	2.6	9.6			7.6	6.6	4.2	10.9					
10 Year	7.0	11.2	10.0			8.1	7.0	3.5	10.7					
Since Inception	7.0	7.9	10.0			8.1	7.0	3.5	10.7					

Disclosures

Compliance Statement

Sample 3 Real Estate Advisors claims compliance with the Global Investment Performance Standards (GIPS®) and has prepared and presented this report in compliance with the GIPS standards. Sample 3 Real Estate Advisors has been independently verified for the periods 1 January 2006 through 31 December 2011. The verification reports are available upon request.

Verification assesses whether 1) the firm has complied with all the composite construction requirements of the GIPS standards on a firm-wide basis and 2) the firm's policies and procedures are designed to calculate and present performance in compliance with the GIPS standards. Verification does not ensure the accuracy of any specific composite presentation.

The Firm

Sample 3 Real Estate Advisors (the "Firm"), a subsidiary of Sample 3 Capital, Inc., is based in Hong Kong and manages international real estate strategies. A list of the Firm's composite descriptions is available upon request.

The Composite

The Value-Added Strategy Composite consists of all discretionary open-end funds and separate accounts managed by the Firm using a value-added investment strategy with an equal income and appreciation focus and having a minimum portfolio size of HKD 10 million. Portfolio management will invest in only Asian multi-family, office, industrial, and retail property types that require correction or mitigation of the investments' operating, financial, redevelopment, and/or management risk (s). A moderate level of leverage ranging between 30% and 40% is used. Real estate investments are generally illiquid, and the investment outlook may change given the availability of credit or other financing sources.

The composite was created on 1 January 2006. The returns presented for periods prior to 2006 are not in compliance with the GIPS standards. Annual internal dispersion is presented using the high and low gross total returns for those portfolios that have been in the composite for the entire year.

Description of Discretion

The Firm has responsibility for sourcing, valuing, and managing the acquisition and disposition of assets. Although some of the Firm's separate accounts require client approval for the acquisition and disposition of assets, the Firm defines such portfolios as discretionary because its recommendations are consistent with the investment strategy and such client approvals are typically perfunctory.

Valuation

Real estate assets are internally valued by the Firm quarterly. For periods prior to 1 January 2011, assets were externally appraised by an independent appraiser at least every 36 months. Beginning 1 January 2011, assets are externally appraised annually unless client agreements stipulate otherwise, in which case such assets are appraised at least every 36 months or per the client agreement if the client agreement requires external valuation more frequently than every 36 months. The percentage of composite assets valued using an external valuation is shown for each annual period. When market circumstances dictate, the Firm may increase the frequency of external appraisals. All valuations are performed as of calendar quarter-ends.

Internal property valuations are determined by applying market discount rates to future projections of gross cash flows and capitalized terminal values over the expected holding period for each asset. To the extent leverage (debt) is used, the debt is valued separately from the real estate. Property mortgages, notes, and loans are marked to market using prevailing interest rates for comparable property loans if the terms of existing loans preclude the immediate repayment of such loans. Due to the nature of real estate investments, valuations are based upon subjective unobservable inputs.

Basis of Accounting

All funds in the composite report their assets and liabilities on a fair value basis using International Financial Reporting Standards (IFRS).

Calculation of Performance Returns

Returns are presented in Hong Kong dollars and are net of leverage. Net-of-fee returns are net of actual investment management fees including incentive fees, which are recorded on an accrual basis. Returns include cash and cash equivalents and related interest income.

Capital expenditures, tenant improvements, and lease commissions are capitalized, included in the cost of property, and reflected in the capital return component. Income and capital returns may not equal total returns due to the compounding linking of quarterly returns. Composite returns are calculated quarterly on an asset-weighted basis using beginning-of-period values. Annual returns are calculated by linking quarterly composite returns.

Policies for valuing portfolios, calculating performance, and preparing compliant presentations are available upon request.

Investment Management Fees

Some of the funds in the composite pay incentive fees ranging between 10% and 20% of profits in excess of a targeted SI-IRR. The standard annual investment management fee schedule for separately managed institutional accounts is as follows:

Up to HKD 30 million:	1.6%
HKD 30 – 50 million:	1.3%
Over HKD 50 million:	1.0%

Benchmark

The benchmark is the Value-Added Open-End Fund/Separate Account Index (the "Benchmark"). The Benchmark returns have been taken from published sources. The Benchmark is leveraged, includes various real estate property types, and excludes cash, cash equivalents, and other non-property-related assets, liabilities, income, and expenses. The extent of leverage used by the Benchmark may be different from that of the portfolios in the composite. As of 31 December 2011, the Benchmark leverage was 52%.

Sample 4

Real Estate: Closed-End Fund

2006 Value-Added Strategy Closed-End Fund Composite
Schedule of Performance Results 1 April 2006 through 31 December 2011

	Composite Gross TWR			Composite NET TWR	Benchmark			Composite at Year-End						
Year	Income Return (%)	Capital Return (%)	Total Return (%)	Total Return (%)	Income Return (%)	Capital Return (%)	Total Return (%)	# of Portfolios	Composite Assets (U.S. Million)	Leverage (%)	External Appraisal % of Composite Assets	Total Firm Assets (U.S. Million)	% of Firm Assets	Non-Real Estate % of Composite Assets
4/06–12/06	–3.2	0.8	–2.5	–4.0	4.9	2.2	7.2	1	70	40	35	2,641	20	0
2007	2.5	3.4	6.0	4.5	5.8	1.1	7.1	1	164	45	28	3,125	18	0
2008	6.2	1.9	8.2	6.7	6.9	3.8	10.9	1	215	50	100	2,754	18	0
2009	7.4	30.7	38.6	36.1	7.0	10.2	17.4	1	256	53	44	2,142	21	0
2010	6.6	–13.7	–7.3	–8.8	6.1	–8.8	–2.5	1	111	57	28	1,873	19	0
2011	5.8	-1.5	4.3	2.8	5.4	–2.6	3.0	1	112	60	85	2,247	20	15

Underlying Partnership Investments by Strategy
Results Reported as of 31 December 2012

Investment Strategy	SI-IRR Gross-of-Fees (%)	Benchmark Return (%)	Committed Capital ($ Mil)	Paid-In Capital ($ Mil)	Cumulative Distributions ($ Mil)	Assets ($ Mil)	TVPI Multiple	DPI Multiple	RVPI Multiple	PIC Multiple
Venture Capital	65.3	32.6	8.0	8.0	16.0	2.0	2.3	2.0	0.3	1.0
Buyout	11.3	10.2	12.0	12.0	13.0	4.5	1.5	1.1	0.4	1.0

TVPI (investment multiple) = total value to paid-in capital
DPI (realization multiple) = cumulative distributions to paid-in capital
RVPI (unrealized multiple) = residual value to paid-in capital
PIC (PIC multiple) = paid-in capital to committed capital

Disclosures

Compliance Statement

Sample 4 Real Estate Managers claims compliance with the Global Investment Performance Standards (GIPS®) and has prepared and presented this report in compliance with the GIPS standards. Sample 4 Real Estate Managers has been independently verified for the periods 1 January 2006 through 31 December 2011. The verification reports are available upon request.

Verification assesses whether 1) the firm has complied with all the composite construction requirements of the GIPS standards on a firm-wide basis and 2) the firm's policies and procedures are designed to calculate and present performance in compliance with the GIPS standards. Verification does not ensure the accuracy of any specific composite presentation.

The Firm

Sample 4 Real Estate Managers (the "Firm") is a registered investment adviser under the Investment Advisers Act of 1940. A list of the Firm's composite descriptions is available upon request.

The Composite

The 2006 Value-Added Strategy Closed-End Fund Composite includes a single closed-end commingled fund managed by the Firm using a value-added investment strategy with a focus on both income and appreciation. Portfolio management intends to invest in properties located in major markets within the United States with higher operational risk than traditional property types. The target level of leverage is 50% with a maximum allowable level of 60%. Real estate investments are generally illiquid, and the investment outlook may change given the availability of credit or other financing sources. If investment opportunities and/or exit strategies become limited, the life of the fund may be extended and capital calls and distributions may be delayed. The composite was created on 1 January 2006. The composite vintage year is 2006, which was determined based on the fund's first capital call in April 2006.

Description of Discretion

The Firm has complete discretion for all investment activities within the fund.

Valuation

Real estate investments are internally valued by the Firm quarterly. For periods prior to 1 January 2011, investments were externally appraised by an independent appraiser at least every 36 months. Beginning 1 January 2011, assets are externally appraised annually. The percentage of composite assets valued using an external valuation is shown for each annual period. When market circumstances dictate, the Firm may increase the frequency of external appraisals. All valuations are performed as of calendar quarter-ends. Internal investment valuations are determined by applying market discount rates to future projections of net cash flows (gross real estate cash flows less debt service) and capitalized terminal values over the expected holding period for each asset. Due to the nature of real estate investments, valuations are based upon subjective unobservable inputs.

Basis of Accounting

All assets and liabilities are reported on a fair value basis using U.S. Generally Accepted Accounting Principles for non-operating companies.

Calculation of Performance Returns and Metrics

Returns are presented in U.S. dollars and are net of leverage. Net-of-fee returns are net of actual investment management fees, including incentive fees, which are recorded on an accrual basis.

Capital expenditures, tenant improvements, and lease commissions are capitalized, included in the cost of property, and reflected in the capital return component. Income and capital returns may not equal total returns due to the compounding linking of quarterly returns. Composite time-weighted returns are calculated quarterly on an asset-weighted basis using beginning-of-period values. Annual returns are calculated by linking quarterly composite returns.

SI-IRRs are calculated using quarterly cash flows through 2010 and daily cash flows starting in 2011.

Policies for valuing portfolios, calculating performance, and preparing presentations are available upon request.

Investment Management Fees

The fund pays an incentive fee of 15% of profits if the SI-IRR exceeds a preferred return to investors of 11%. The incentive fee is calculated annually. The standard annual investment management fee schedule for separately managed institutional accounts is as follows:

Up to $100 million:	1.50%
Over $100 million:	1.25%

Benchmark

The benchmark is the Value-Added Closed-End Fund Index (the "Benchmark"). The Benchmark is a time-weighted return index and returns have been taken from published sources. The Benchmark is leveraged and includes various real estate investment and property types, cash and other non-property-related assets, liabilities, income, and expenses. The extent of leverage used by the Benchmark may be different from that of the fund in the composite. As of 31 December 2011, the Benchmark leverage was 60%. There is no SI-IRR benchmark available for the 2006 vintage year.

Sample 5

Private Equity: Fund of Funds by Investment Strategy

ABC Fund of Funds Manager, LLC
2006 Buyout Strategy Fund of Funds Composite
Results Reported as of Calendar Year End

Year End	# of Portfolios	Gross-of-Fees SI-IRR (%)	Net-of-Fees SI-IRR (%)	Benchmark SI-IRR (%)	Composite Assets ($ Mil)	Composite % of Firm Assets
2006*	8	26.9	26.4	17.2	2,336	80.8
2007	10	18.5	17.8	10.2	2,512	83.6
2008	11	18.7	18.1	11.0	3,227	84.2
2009	13	19.6	18.9	11.5	4,518	84.8
2010	13	20.7	20.1	11.8	6,330	85.2
2011	13	21.9	21.3	11.8	9,269	86.0
2012	14	22.2	21.7	12.3	12,286	86.4
2013	14	15.1	14.4	9.6	12,346	87.7

*Partial year from 15 April 2006 (inception) through 31 December 2006.

Year End	Paid-In Capital ($ Mil)	Cumulative Committed Capital ($ Mil)	Since Inception Distributions	Investment Multiple (TVPI)	Realization Multiple (DPI)	Unrealized Multiple (RVPI)	PIC Multiple (PIC)
2006	1,556	3,177	1,205	1.5	0.8	0.7	0.48
2007	1,908	3,675	1,341	1.3	0.7	0.6	0.51
2008	2,371	5,166	1,623	1.4	0.7	0.7	0.45
2009	3,254	6,401	2,186	1.4	0.7	0.7	0.50
2010	4,400	8,370	2,950	1.4	0.7	0.8	0.51
2011	6,303	11,344	4,138	1.5	0.7	0.8	0.54
2012	8,167	13,713	6,513	1.5	0.8	0.7	0.69
2013	9,651	15,290	7,091	1.3	0.7	0.5	0.71

Aggregate Performance of Underlying Investments by Vintage Year Results Reported as of 31 December 2013		
Vintage Year	**Gross-of-Fees Annualized SI-IRR (%)**	**Benchmark SI-IRR (%)**
2006	22.3	2.5
2007	13.4	1.9
2008	26.0	7.1
2009	18.1	3.9
2010	0.7	1.0
2011	−16.2	−7.5
2012	−25.6	−19.9
2013	−49.9	−40.3

Vintage Year	Paid-In Capital ($ Mil)	Cumulative Committed Capital ($ Mil)	Since Inception Distributions ($ Mil)	Investment Multiple(TVPI)	Realization Multiple (DPI)	Unrealized Multiple (RVPI)	PIC Multiple (PIC)
2006	731	724	939	3.0	1.3	1.7	1.0
2007	710	234	294	1.8	0.4	1.3	3.0
2008	1,475	1,220	1,442	2.0	1.0	1.0	1.2
2009	1,640	1,048	1,156	1.9	0.7	1.2	1.6
2010	1,896	3,695	1,124	1.9	0.6	1.4	0.5
2011	1,984	4,518	1,100	2.1	0.6	1.5	0.4
2012	680	1,998	938	2.2	1.4	0.8	0.3
2013	535	1,853	100	1.1	0.2	0.9	0.3

TVPI (investment multiple) = total value to paid-in capital
DPI (realization multiple) = cumulative distributions to paid-in capital
RVPI (unrealized multiple) = residual value to paid-in capital
PIC (PIC multiple) = paid-in capital to committed capital

Compliance Statement

ABC Fund of Funds Manager, LLC, claims compliance with the Global Investment Performance Standards (GIPS®) and has prepared and presented this report in compliance with the GIPS standards. ABC Fund of Funds Manager, LLC, has been independently verified for the periods 15 April 2006 through 31 December 2012.

Verification assesses whether 1) the firm has complied with all the composite construction requirements of the GIPS standards on a firm-wide basis and 2) the firm's policies and procedures are designed to calculate and present performance in compliance with the GIPS standards. Verification does not ensure the accuracy of any specific composite presentation. The verification report is available upon request.

The Firm

ABC Fund of Funds Manager, LLC, is an independent private equity investment firm with offices in New York, London, and Tokyo. The firm's list of composite descriptions, as well as information regarding the firm's policies for valuing investments, calculating performance, and preparing compliant presentations, are available upon request.

The Composite

The 2006 Buyout Strategy Fund of Funds Composite includes primary and secondary partnership investments with strategies focused on leveraged and growth-oriented buyouts primarily in the United States. Managers of partnerships are expected to focus on reducing costs, preparing companies for downturn, and providing operational improvement rather than financial engineering. Investments may be in small, medium, and large buyout partnerships, aiming to make selective commitments diversifying across stages, industries, and vintage years. Secondary deals take advantage of distressed primary partnership sales providing access to an increased mix of assets. The underlying funds are leveraged between 100–300%. Private equity investments are illiquid and, therefore, if investment opportunities and/or exit strategies become limited, the life of the fund may be extended and capital calls and distributions may be delayed. The composite was created on 31 December 2006. The vintage year is 2006 and was determined by the initial subscription date of the fund of funds.

Valuation

The firm uses valuations reported by the general partner of the investment partnerships. Given the nature of the investments, all valuations are determined using both subjective observable and subjective unobservable inputs.

Calculation of Performance Returns

The fund's SI-IRR calculation uses daily cash flows. All cash flows and values used to calculate returns are in, or have been converted to, U.S. dollars. Gross returns are net of all underlying investment partnership expenses, management fees, and carried interest but gross of ABC Fund of Funds Manager's management fees. Net returns are net of all underlying partnership fees and expenses, including ABC Fund of Funds Manager's management fees.

Investment Management Fee

ABC Fund of Funds Manager's management fee varies based on the size of the commitment and structure of the program. The management fee is 100 basis points, based on the total commitment to a fund of funds, plus a 10% carry on total gains. Net returns are calculated using actual management fees of the fund of funds and underlying funds, including performance fees.

Benchmark

The benchmark is derived from private equity dollar-weighted IRRs, and the calculation is based on the overall market return for buyout fund of funds as determined by benchmark provider GHI. Individual vintage year benchmarks are the median SI-IRR for the applicable vintage years, at 31 December 2013.

Sample 6

Private Equity: Fund of Funds by Vintage Year

			Investments 2002 Fund of Funds Composite Results Reported as of Calendar Year End			
Calendar Year	Gross-of-Fees SI-IRR (%)	Net-of-Fees SI-IRR (%)	Benchmark SI-IRR (%)	Composite Assets ($ Mil)	Total Firm Assets ($ Mil)	# of Portfolios
2002*	2.5	−5.5	8.5	2.6	250	≤ 5
2003	−4.2	−12.3	−3.8	4.7	300	≤ 5
2004	12.5	6.5	14.4	7.5	350	≤ 5
2005	45.8	40.8	42.7	24.2	400	≤ 5
2006	35.6	31.5	30.2	21.6	450	≤ 5
2007	22.2	19.3	13.5	14.7	500	≤ 5
2008	17.4	15.5	8.1	11.8	550	≤ 5
2009	17.3	15.3	7.5	11.0	600	≤ 5
2010	16.5	14.8	8.0	9.3	650	≤ 5
2011	15.9	13.5	8.5	8.1	700	≤ 5
2012	16.8	14.0	10.3	6.5	750	≤ 5

*Returns are for the period from 1 May 2002 (inception date) through 31 December 2002.

Calendar Year	Cumulative Committed Capital ($ Mil)	Paid-In Capital ($ Mil)	Cumulative Distributions ($ Mil)	DPI	RVPI	TVPI	PIC
2002	20	3	0	0.00	1.04	1.04	0.15
2003	20	5	0	0.00	0.93	0.93	0.25
2004	20	8	2	0.22	0.94	1.16	0.40
2005	20	15	4	0.23	1.62	1.85	0.75
2006	20	17	12	0.71	1.25	1.96	0.85
2007	20	18	16	0.89	0.82	1.71	0.90
2008	20	19	17	0.89	0.62	1.51	0.95
2009	20	19	19	0.99	0.57	1.56	0.96
2010	20	20	23	1.18	0.47	1.65	0.98
2011	20	20	25	1.25	0.41	1.66	1.00
2012	20	20	29	1.45	0.33	1.78	1.00

Underlying Partnership Investments by Strategy

Results Reported as of 31 December 2012

Investment Strategy	SI-IRR Gross-of-Fees (%)	Benchmark Return (%)	Committed Capital ($ Mil)	Paid-In Capital ($ Mil)	Cumulative Distributions ($ Mil)	Assets ($ Mil)	TVPI Multiple	DPI Multiple	RVPI Multiple	PIC Multiple
Venture Capital	65.3	32.6	8.0	8.0	16.0	2.0	2.3	2.0	0.3	1.0
Buyout	11.3	10.2	12.0	12.0	13.0	4.5	1.5	1.1	0.4	1.0

Disclosures

Sample 6 Investments claims compliance with the Global Investment Performance Standards (GIPS®) and has prepared and presented this report in compliance with the GIPS standards. Sample 6 Investments has not been independently verified.

Sample 6 Investments is an independent private equity manager of fund of funds strategies with offices in Zurich, Menlo Park, New York, and Hong Kong. The composite was created in May 2002 and includes one closed-end fund that invests in buyout and venture capital funds. The fund of funds has an 8–10 year investment time horizon, but it may be longer based on the life of the underlying funds, which may be extended due to changes in investment and/or exit opportunities. As more fully described in the fund's offering memorandum, primary risks include industry and geographic concentration depending on investment opportunities, and liquidity risks due to the nature of the fund's investments.

The composite's vintage year is 2002, which was determined using the date of the initial capital call of the fund of funds. Returns are presented in U.S. dollars.

The 2002 Fund of Funds Composite complies with PQR's valuation guidelines, which are consistent with the GIPS Valuation Principles. Valuations are normally based on valuations provided by the manager of the underlying investments' partnerships. Because fund investments are not publicly traded, all investments are considered to be valued using subjective unobservable inputs.

All returns for the 2002 Fund of Funds Composite reflect the deduction of administrative expenses (legal, auditing, etc.) of the closed-end fund. Gross returns do not reflect the deduction of Sample 6 Investments' management fees. Net returns reflect the deduction of actual management fees and accrued carried interest, if any.

The fund's SI-IRR calculation incorporates daily cash flows. Sample 6 Investments' annual management fee is 1% on the total committed capital.

The Vendor ABC Private Equity Fund of Funds Index (vintage year 2002) is used as the benchmark.

A complete list of the firm's composite descriptions is available upon request, as are policies for valuing portfolios, calculating performance, and preparing compliant presentations.

Private Equity: Primary Fund Vehicle

	Private Equity Capital Management 2001 Venture Capital Composite Results Reported as of 31 December				
Year End	Paid-In Capital (AUD Mil)	Since Inception Distributions (AUD Mil)	Cumulative Committed Capital (AUD Mil)	Composite Assets (AUD Mil)	% of Firm Assets
2001*	40.3	0.0	175.0	38.5	64.2
2002	82.3	1.0	175.0	78.8	52.5
2003	129.5	29.9	175.0	105.0	58.3
2004	143.5	42.3	175.0	120.8	41.6
2005	157.5	97.0	175.0	119.0	37.8
2006	166.2	129.3	175.0	112.0	31.1
2007	171.5	184.7	175.0	98.0	28.0
2008	182.5	184.7	175.0	78.8	21.0
2009	182.5	184.7	175.0	49.0	11.9
2010	182.5	184.7	175.0	31.5	7.5
2011	182.5	205.8	175.0	5.2	1.1

*Returns are for the period from 3 February 2001 (inception date) through 31 December 2001.

Year End	TVPI	DPI	RVPI	PIC	Composite Gross-of-Fees SI-IRR (%)	Composite Net-of-Fees SI-IRR (%)	Benchmark SI-IRR (%)
2001	0.96	0.00	0.96	0.23	−7.5	−9.5	−12.5
2002	0.97	0.01	0.96	0.47	0.3	−1.6	−3.5
2003	1.04	0.23	0.81	0.74	4.1	2.3	1.2
2004	1.14	0.29	0.84	0.82	8.2	6.4	7.4
2005	1.37	0.62	0.76	0.90	11.0	9.3	8.2
2006	1.45	0.78	0.67	0.95	13.0	10.1	9.7
2007	1.65	1.08	0.57	0.98	18.1	12.3	11.4
2008	1.44	1.01	0.43	1.04	16.9	10.4	10.1
2009	1.28	1.01	0.27	1.04	14.9	8.7	7.2
2010	1.18	1.01	0.17	1.04	14.0	7.7	6.8
2011	1.16	1.13	0.03	1.04	11.2	6.2	5.5

TVPI = Total Value to Since Inception Paid-In Capital
DPI = Since Inception Distributions to Since Inception Paid-In Capital
PIC = Since Inception Paid-In Capital to Cumulative Committed Capital
RVPI = Residual Value to Since Inception Paid-In Capital

Disclosures

Compliance Statement

Private Equity Capital Management claims compliance with the Global Investment Performance Standards (GIPS®) and has prepared and presented this report in compliance with the GIPS standards. Private Equity Capital Management has been independently verified for the periods 3 February 2001 through 31 December 2010.

Verification assesses whether 1) the firm has complied with all the composite construction requirements of the GIPS standards on a firm-wide basis and 2) the firm's policies and procedures are designed to calculate and present performance in compliance with the GIPS standards. The 2001 Venture Capital Composite has been examined for the periods 1 January 2005 through 31 December 2010. The verification and performance examination reports are available upon request.

Firm & Composite

Private Equity Capital Management ("PECM") is an independent private equity investment firm with offices in New York, London, and Sydney. The 2001 Venture Capital Composite includes one fund, whose objective is to seek long-term capital appreciation by acquiring minority interests in early-stage technology companies. The fund invests in technology companies in Europe, Asia Pacific, and emerging markets. European venture investments are more concentrated than in the other regions and are focused in a few high quality companies. Exit opportunities include IPOs, trade sales, and secondary sales. Opportunities in China and India will be targeted for investment, and an allocation to Chinese high-tech will be at least 10% of the invested capital over the life of the fund. International venture capital investments are generally illiquid and are subject to currency risk. If investment opportunities and/or exit strategies become limited, the life of the fund may be extended and capital calls and distributions may be delayed. The 2001 Venture Capital Composite was created in 2001. The vintage year of the composite is 2001 and was determined by the year of the first drawdown. The firm's list of composite descriptions and the firm's policies for calculating performance and preparing compliant presentation are available upon request.

Input Data & Calculation

The 2001 Venture Capital Composite complies with the LMN Venture Capital Association's valuation guidelines as well as the GIPS Valuation Principles. Valuations are prepared by PECM's valuation committee and reviewed by an independent advisory board. All investments within the composite are valued using either a most recent transaction or an earnings multiple. Policies for valuing investments are available upon request. Due to the nature of private equity investments, all investments are valued using subjective unobservable inputs.

The SI-IRR calculation incorporates monthly cash flows for periods prior to 31 December 2009 and daily cash flows thereafter. Performance is expressed in Australian dollars (AUD).

Gross returns are net of transaction expenses and all administrative expenses. Net returns are net of transaction expenses, administrative expenses, management fees, and carried interest. The standard fee schedule currently in effect is as follows:

> The manager will receive an annual management fee equal to 2% of capital commitments. The manager's participation in profits (carried interest) begins after the limited partners have been provided an 8% preferred return. The manager collects 20% of the distributed profits from that point forward. Subsequently, if the amount of cumulative carried interest exceeds 20% of the net cumulative gains, the manager will repay the excess amount to the fund for distribution to the limited partners.

There is only one fund in the composite for all periods; therefore, the internal dispersion of portfolio returns is not applicable.

Benchmark

The benchmark return is derived from private equity dollar-weighted IRRs, and the calculation is based on the overall market return for international venture capital funds as published by Benchmark Provider GHI. Vintage year benchmarks are median returns for the applicable vintage year, as of each year end.

Investments Large-Cap SMA Composite

1 January 2001 through 31 December 31, 2010

| | | | | | As of 31 December | | |
Year	Net Return (%)	XYZ Index Return (%)	Internal Dispersion (%)	Number of Portfolios	Composite Assets ($ Millions)	Firm Assets ($ Millions)	% of SMA Portfolios
2010	8.4	10.2	0.7	1,834	2,125	18,222	100
2009	21.1	21.1	1.1	1,730	2,130	17,635	100
2008	−39.7	−39.8	1.0	1,631	2,141	19,246	100
2007	1.4	6.2	1.2	1,532	2,127	14,819	100
2006	11.4	10.5	0.9	1,428	2,116	12,362	100
2005	1.0	4.3	0.8	68	1,115	12,051	0
2004	6.8	4.9	1.0	52	1,110	13,419	0
2003	23.9	27.0	1.1	46	990	10,612	0
2002	−24.4	−19.1	0.9	38	975	9,422	0
2001	−17.7	−12.8	0.8	41	870	8,632	0

Notes:

1. Sample 8 Investments claims compliance with the Global Investment Performance Standards (GIPS®) and has prepared and presented this report in compliance with the GIPS standards. Sample 8 Investments has been independently verified for the period from 1 April 1996 through 31 December 2009.

   Verification assesses whether 1) the firm has complied with all the composite construction requirements of the GIPS standards on a firm-wide basis and 2) the firm's policies and procedures are designed to calculate and present performance in compliance with the GIPS standards. The Large Cap SMA Composite has been examined for the period from 1 January 2006 through 31 December 2009. The verification and performance examination reports are available upon request.

2. Sample 8 Investments is an independent investment adviser registered under the Investment Advisers Act of 1940, was founded in March 1996, and manages global large-cap equity, fixed-income, and balanced strategies.

3. Beginning 1 January 2006, the composite includes only wrap fee (SMA) portfolios benchmarked to the XYZ Index. Performance results prior to 2006 are based on the Large-Cap Institutional Composite returns.

4. The Large-Cap SMA Composite is comprised of portfolios invested in U.S. equities which have a market capitalization greater than $5 billion.

5. The composite was created in February 2006. A list of composite descriptions is available upon request.

6. All returns are expressed in U.S. dollars. Policies for valuing portfolios, calculating performance, and preparing compliant presentations are available upon request.

7. The XYZ Index returns are provided to represent the investment environment existing during the time periods shown. For comparison purposes, the index is fully invested and includes the reinvestment of income. The returns for the index do not include any trading costs, management fees, or other costs. Index returns have been taken from published sources.

8. "Pure" gross returns, presented below as supplemental information, from 2006 through 2010 do not reflect the deduction of any trading costs, fees, or expenses and are presented for comparison purposes only. "Pure" gross returns prior to 2006 reflect the deduction of trading costs. The SMA fee includes all charges for trading costs, portfolio management, custody, and other administrative fees. Net returns are calculated by subtracting the highest applicable SMA fee (2.50% on an annual basis, or 0.21% monthly) on a monthly basis from the "pure" gross composite monthly return. The standard fee schedule in effect is as follows: 2.50% on total assets.

9. The dispersion is measured by the equal-weighted standard deviation of annual returns of those portfolios that are included in the composite for the full year.

10. At 31 December 2010, the three-year annualized ex-post standard deviation of the composite and the benchmark are 12.3% and 13.2%, respectively.

11. Past performance is not an indicator of future results.

Year	"Pure" Gross Return* (%)	Supplemental Information	
		Net Return (%) Assuming 3% SMA Fees	Net Return (%) Assuming 2% SMA Fees
2010	11.1	7.9	9.0
2009	24.0	20.5	21.7
2008	−38.0	−40.1	−39.4
2007	4.0	0.9	2.0
2006	14.1	10.8	11.9
2005	3.5	0.5	1.5
2004	9.5	6.3	7.4
2003	26.9	23.3	24.5
2002	−22.3	−24.8	−23.9
2001	−15.5	−18.1	−17.2

* "Pure" gross-of-fees returns do not reflect the deduction of any expenses, including trading costs. "Pure" gross-of-fees returns are supplemental to net returns.

APPENDIX 4B: SAMPLE ADVERTISEMENTS FOR READING 4

OPTIONAL SEGMENT

1. Sample Advertisement without Performance

Generic Asset Management

Generic Asset Management is the institutional asset management division of Generic Inc. and is a registered investment advisory firm specializing in qualitative growth-oriented investment management.

Generic Asset Management claims compliance with the Global Investment Performance Standards (GIPS®). To receive a list of composite descriptions of Generic Asset Management and/or a presentation that complies with the GIPS standards, contact Jean Paul at (123) 456-7890, or write to Generic Asset Management, 123 Main Street, Returnsville 12345, or jpaul@genericassetmanagment.com.

2. Sample Advertisement Including One-, Three-, and Five-Year Annualized Returns

Generic Asset Management: Global Equity Growth Composite			
		Ending 31 Mar 2012	
	1-Year	3-Year Annualized	5-Year Annualized
Global Equity Growth Composite	−0.3%	13.7%	0.1%
XYZ World Index	−0.5%	13.8%	−0.6%

Note: Returns are shown in U.S. dollars net of fees.

Generic Asset Management is the institutional asset management subsidiary of Generic Inc. and is a registered investment adviser specializing in qualitative growth-oriented investment management. The Global Equity Growth strategy focuses on earnings, growth of earnings, and key valuation metrics. The benchmark is the XYZ World Index, which is designed to measure the equity market performance of developed market countries. The benchmark is market-cap weighted and is composed of all XYZ developed market indices.

Generic Asset Management claims compliance with the Global Investment Performance Standards (GIPS®). To receive a list of composite descriptions of Generic Asset Management and/or a presentation that complies with the GIPS standards, contact Jean Paul at (123) 456-7890, or write Generic Asset Management, One Plain Street, Returnsville 12345, or jpaul@genericassetmanagement.com.

3. Sample Advertisement Including Period-to-Date and One-, Three-, and Five-Year Annualized Returns

Generic Asset Management: Global Equity Growth Composite				
	Ending 31 Mar 2012		Ending 31 Dec 2011	
	Period to Date (3 months)	1-Year	3-Year Annualized	5-Year Annualized
Global Equity Growth Composite	−3.84%	1.3%	15.0%	−1.2%
XYZ World Index	−4.94%	1.5%	14.1%	−0.7%

Note: Returns are shown in U.S. dollars net of fees.

Generic Asset Management is the institutional asset management subsidiary of Generic Inc. and is a registered investment adviser specializing in qualitative growth-oriented investment management. The Global Equity Growth strategy focuses on earnings, growth of earnings, and key valuation metrics. The benchmark is the XYZ World Index, which is designed to measure the equity market performance of developed market countries. The benchmark is market-cap weighted and is composed of all XYZ developed market indices.

Generic Asset Management claims compliance with the Global Investment Performance Standards (GIPS®). To receive a list of composite descriptions of Generic Asset Management and/or a presentation that complies with the GIPS standards, contact Jean Paul at (123) 456-7890, or write Generic Asset Management, One Plain Street, Returnsville 12345, or jpaul@genericassetmanagement .com.

4. Sample Advertisement Including Five Years of Annual Returns

Generic Asset Management: Global Equity Growth Composite

	Period to Date (3 months to 31 Mar 2012)	Annual Returns Periods Ended 31 December				
		2011	2010	2009	2008	2007
Global Equity Growth Composite	−3.84%	1.3%	13.0%	33.0%	−40.6%	9.6%
XYZ World Index	−4.94%	1.5%	11.8%	30.8%	−40.3%	9.6%

Note: Returns are shown in U.S. dollars net of fees.

Generic Asset Management is the institutional asset management subsidiary of Generic Inc. and is a registered investment adviser specializing in qualitative, growth-oriented investment management. The Global Equity Growth strategy focuses on earnings, growth of earnings, and key valuation metrics. The benchmark is the XYZ World Index, which is designed to measure the equity market performance of developed market countries. The benchmark is market-cap weighted and is composed of all XYZ developed market indices.

Generic Asset Management claims compliance with the Global Investment Performance Standards (GIPS®).

To receive a list of composite descriptions of Generic Asset Management and/or a presentation that complies with the GIPS standards, contact Jean Paul at (123) 456-7890, or write to Generic Asset Management, 123 Main Street, Returnsville 12345, or jpaul@genericassetmanagment.com.

END OPTIONAL SEGMENT

APPENDIX 4C: SAMPLE LIST OF COMPOSITE DESCRIPTIONS

Sample Asset Management Firm

V.0.1 List of Composite Descriptions

1. **Unconstrained Activist U.K. Equity Composite**

   The Unconstrained Activist U.K. Equity Composite includes all institutional portfolios invested in both listed and unlisted U.K. equities that pursue an activist investment policy; there is no restriction on the market capitalization of companies held. Portfolios within this composite are highly concentrated, holding approximately 15 securities, so returns may have lower correlation with the benchmark than a fully diversified strategy. In times of increased market volatility, the composite characteristics may change significantly and stock liquidity could be reduced. Due to their more concentrated nature, portfolios will tend to have more stock-specific risk than a more diversified strategy. Portfolios can use both exchange-traded and OTC derivative contracts for efficient portfolio management, which may expose the strategy to counterparty risk. The benchmark is the FTSE All Share® Index.

2. **Emerging Market High Yield Fixed Income Composite**

   The Emerging Market High Yield Fixed Income Composite includes all institutional and retail portfolios invested in high yield debt securities issued by countries outside the OECD. The strategy allows for investment in foreign currency denominated assets over which the manager has full discretion on hedging. The strategy aims to deliver a total return primarily through income but with some capital growth. High yield bonds carry increased levels of credit and default risk and are less liquid than government and investment grade bonds. Investment in less regulated markets carries increased political, economic, and issuer risk. The benchmark is the J.P. Morgan Emerging Market Bond Index (EMBI+).

3. **U.K. Liquidity Plus Composite**

   The U.K. Liquidity Plus Composite includes all institutional portfolios invested in a broad range of short-dated interest-bearing deposits, cash equivalents, short-term commercial paper, and other money market investments issued by major U.K. clearing banks and lending institutions. The strategy has a targeted modified duration of less than one year. The principal investment objectives are preservation of capital, maintenance of liquidity, and provision of yield greater than that available for the benchmark, the three-month LIBOR rate. The U.K. Liquidity Plus strategy differs from more conventional cash strategies in that it additionally holds short-term commercial paper, which has a greater exposure to credit risk.

4. **Socially Responsible Investment (SRI) Composite**

   The Socially Responsible Investment Composite includes all segregated institutional and pooled portfolios that invest in global equity securities issued by companies that make a positive contribution to society and the environment through sustainable and socially responsible practices. The strategy aims to provide long term capital appreciation together with a growing income stream through investment in a portfolio of core equity holdings diversified by economic sector, industry group, and geographic business concentration. All foreign currency exposures are fully hedged back to U.S. dollars.

The SRI process tends to screen out certain companies and sectors, which may result in a more concentrated strategy than a fully diversified strategy. Changes in legislation, scientific thinking, national and supra-national policies, and behaviors could significantly affect the stocks of companies held within the strategy. The benchmark is the Morningstar Ethical/SRI Global GIF Sector peer group.

5. **Leveraged Bond Composite**

   The Leveraged Bond Composite includes all institutional segregated portfolios invested in a diversified range of high yield corporate and government bonds with the aim of providing investors with a high level of income while seeking to maximize the total return. The portfolios are invested in domestic and international fixed income securities of varying maturities. The strategy allows investment in exchange-traded and OTC derivative contracts (including, but not limited to, options, futures, swaps, and forward currency contracts) for the purposes of risk, volatility, and currency exposure management. The strategy allows leverage up to but not exceeding twice the value of a portfolio's investments through the use of repurchase financing arrangements with counterparties. Inherent in derivative instrument investments is the risk of counterparty default. Leverage may also magnify losses as well as gains to the extent that leverage is employed. The benchmark is the Barclays Capital Global Aggregate Bond Index.

6. **Global Commodity Composite**

   The Global Commodity Composite includes institutional portfolios that globally invest in a diversified range of companies that provide exposure to commodities, energy, and materials. Investment is primarily through the common or ordinary stock of these companies. Investment directly in raw materials is allowable to a maximum exposure of 10%. Exchange-traded funds and exchange-traded commodity securities up to a maximum 20% exposure are also allowed. The base currency is U.S. dollars, and any or all of the currency risk associated with investments in currencies other than dollars may be hedged between 0% and 100% at the manager's discretion. The strategy cannot gear or otherwise deploy leverage but may use exchange-traded derivative instruments for efficient portfolio management.

   Investments directly or indirectly in commodities may add to portfolio volatility. Global commodity prices can be affected by changes in legislation, national and supra-national policies, and behaviors. In times of commodity price volatility, the liquidity of directly held commodities and the correlation with the broad market can change quickly. The benchmark is the Dow Jones–UBS Commodity Index Total Return[SM].

7. **Large Cap Equity Growth Composite**

   The Large Cap Equity Growth Composite includes all institutional portfolios that invest in large capitalization U.S. stocks that are considered to have growth in earnings prospects that is superior to that of the average company within the benchmark, the Russell 3000® Growth Index. The targeted tracking error between the composite and the benchmark is less than 3%.

8. **Balanced Growth Composite**

   The Balanced Growth Composite includes all institutional balanced portfolios that invest in large-cap U.S. equities and investment-grade bonds with the goal of providing long-term capital growth and steady income from a well-diversified strategy. Although the strategy allows for equity exposure ranging between 50–70%, the typical allocation is between 55–65%.

9. **Currency Overlay Composite**

The Currency Overlay Composite includes all institutional and retail portfolios invested in a broad range of foreign-currency-denominated deposits or instruments such as forward contracts, futures, or foreign exchange derivatives. The principal investment objective is alpha generation through currency appreciation and/or risk mitigation from adverse movements in exchange rates where the original currency exposure stems from a global or international portfolio. Hedging strategies may range from passive to fully active. Currency-related investing carries inherent risks due to changes in macroeconomic policy, which can be amplified in the case of emerging markets where political regime shifts and changes in the control of capital may be more prevalent. In volatile periods, liquidity and correlations between currencies may change expected returns drastically. Foreign exchange forwards and derivatives traded over the counter have counterparty default risk.

10. **Asian Market Neutral Composite**

The Asian Market Neutral Composite includes a single hedge fund with a market neutral strategy that invests in publically traded Asian equities with a market capitalization greater than $500 million. The strategy uses a risk controlled quantitative screening and optimization process that invests at least 85% of the net asset value in long equity positions and at least 85% of the net asset value in short equity positions. The long portion of the strategy will overweight those securities that have been quantitatively identified as potentially exhibiting superior and sustainable earnings growth compared with the market; conversely, the short portion of the strategy will consist of securities that have been identified as having inferior growth prospects or that may also be adversely affected by either specific events or by momentum considerations. The principal objective of the strategy is to outperform the return on three-month U.S. Treasury Bills through active trading of long and short equity positions.

The Asian Market Neutral strategy seeks to dollar balance exposures between long and short positions so that broad market movements are neutralized. In certain market conditions, the investment process behind the strategy can give rise to unmatched country, sector, industry, market capitalization, and/or style bias exposures in the portfolio. The active trading strategy will involve significantly greater stock turnover when compared with passive strategies.

11. **2001 Venture Capital Composite**

The 2001 Venture Capital Composite includes one fund, whose objective is to seek long-term capital appreciation by acquiring minority interests in early-stage technology companies. The fund invests in technology companies in Europe, Asia Pacific, and emerging markets. European venture investments are more concentrated than in the other regions and are focused in a few high-quality companies. Exit opportunities include IPOs, trade sales, and secondary sales. Opportunities in China and India will be targeted for investment, and an allocation to Chinese high-tech will be at least 10% of the invested capital over the life of the fund. International venture capital investments are generally illiquid and are subject to currency risk. If investment opportunities and/or exit strategies become limited, the life of the fund may be extended and capital calls and distributions may be delayed.

12. 2006 Buyout Strategy Fund of Funds Composite

The 2006 Buyout Strategy Fund of Funds Composite includes primary and secondary partnership investments with strategies focused on leveraged and growth-oriented buyouts primarily in the United States. Managers of partnerships are expected to focus on reducing costs, preparing companies for downturn, and providing operational improvement rather than financial engineering. Investments may be in small, medium, and large buyout partnerships, aiming to make selective commitments diversifying across stages, industries, and vintage years. Secondary deals take advantage of distressed primary partnership sales providing access to an increased mix of assets. The underlying funds are leveraged between 100–300%. Private equity investments are illiquid and, therefore, if investment opportunities and/or exit strategies become limited, the life of the fund may be extended and capital calls and distributions may be delayed.

13. Value-Added Strategy Non-Closed-End Real Estate Composite

The Value-Added Strategy Composite consists of all discretionary open-end funds and separate accounts managed by the Firm using a value-added investment strategy with an equal income and appreciation focus and having a minimum portfolio size of $10 million. Portfolio management will invest in multi-family, office, industrial, and retail property types only within Asia that require correction or mitigation of the investments' operating, financial, redevelopment, and/or management risk(s). A moderate level of leverage ranging between 30% and 40% is used. Real estate investments are generally illiquid, and the investment outlook may change given the availability of credit or other financing sources.

14. Value-Added Strategy Closed-End Real Estate Composite

The Value-Added Strategy Composite includes a single closed-end commingled fund managed by the Firm using a value-added investment strategy with a focus on both income and appreciation. Portfolio management intends to invest in properties located in major markets within the United States with higher operational risk than traditional property types. The target level of leverage is 50% with a maximum allowable level of 60%. Real estate investments are generally illiquid, and the investment outlook may change given the availability of credit or other financing sources. If investment opportunities and/or exit strategies become limited, the life of the fund may be extended and capital calls and distributions may be delayed.

15. U.S. Core Equity Composite (Terminated Composites)

The U.S. Core Equity Composite includes all institutional portfolios and pooled funds managed to a GARP (growth at a reasonable price) strategy through investment in a high-quality, focused portfolio of domestic, large capitalization stocks that are expected to generate returns above the S&P 500® Index over a market cycle. Sample Asset Management Firm uses a quantitative screening process together with fundamental research and then overlays macroeconomic factors and economic sector exposures to construct portfolios. The benchmark is the S&P 500 Index. Quantitative-driven investment screening relies on historical stock correlations, which can be adversely affected during periods of severe market volatility. The composite terminated in March 2009.

Detailed composite definitions are available upon request.

PRACTICE PROBLEMS FOR READING 4

1. With respect to the Global Investment Performance Standards, which of the following is one of the nine sections containing investment performance provisions?

    A. Real Estate.

    B. Derivatives.

    C. Legal and Ethical Considerations.

2. According to the Fundamentals of Compliance section of the Global Investment Performance Standards, issues that a firm must consider when claiming compliance include all of the following *except*:

    A. replicating performance.

    B. properly defining the firm.

    C. documenting firm policies and procedures used in establishing and maintaining compliance with the Standards.

3. G&F Advisors claims compliance with the Global Investment Performance Standards (GIPS) in its marketing materials. The compliant presentation includes a footnote which indicates that the firm has been verified by an independent third party. An additional note states that G&F is in compliance with the GIPS standards except for its private equity investments. It is *likely* that G&F violated the GIPS standards?

    A. No, because the footnotes meet the requirements of the Standards.

    B. No, because the provisions do not apply to the private equity investments.

    C. Yes, because they cannot claim compliance unless all requirements of the Standard are met.

SOLUTIONS FOR READING 4

1. A is correct. Real Estate is one of the nine sections in the 2010 edition of the GIPS standards. Derivatives and Legal and Ethical Considerations are not sections of the Standards.

2. A is correct. Replication of performance is not included in the Fundaments of Compliance section within the GIPS standards.

3. C is correct. Firms must meet all the requirements set forth in the GIPS standards and cannot claim partial compliance.

Quantitative Methods

TOPIC LEVEL LEARNING OUTCOME

The candidate should be able to explain and demonstrate the use of elementary statistics, data collection and analysis, probability theory, distributions theory, and the time value of money in financial decision-making.

2

Quantitative Methods:

Basic Concepts

This introductory study session presents the fundamentals of some quantitative techniques essential in financial analysis. These techniques are used throughout the CFA Program curriculum. This session introduces two main tools of quantitative analysis: the time value of money and probability and descriptive statistics.

Time value of money techniques are used throughout financial analysis. Time value of money calculations are the basic tools used to support corporate finance decisions and to estimate the fair value of fixed income, equity, and other types of securities or investments.

Similarly, statistics and probability theory are essential tools for describing and estimating risk.

READING ASSIGNMENTS

Reading 5   **The Time Value of Money**

               Quantitative Methods for Investment Analysis, Second Edition, by Richard A. DeFusco, CFA, Dennis W. McLeavey, CFA, Jerald E. Pinto, CFA, and David E. Runkle, CFA

Reading 6   **Discounted Cash Flow Applications**

               Quantitative Methods for Investment Analysis, Second Edition, by Richard A. DeFusco, CFA, Dennis W. McLeavey, CFA, Jerald E. Pinto, CFA, and David E. Runkle, CFA

Reading 7   *Statistical Concepts and Market Returns*

Quantitative Methods for Investment Analysis, Second Edition, by Richard A. DeFusco, CFA, Dennis W. McLeavey, CFA, Jerald E. Pinto, CFA, and David E. Runkle, CFA

Reading 8   *Probability Concepts*

Quantitative Methods for Investment Analysis, Second Edition, by Richard A. DeFusco, CFA, Dennis W. McLeavey, CFA, Jerald E. Pinto, CFA, and David E. Runkle, CFA

The Time Value of Money

by Richard A. DeFusco, CFA, Dennis W. McLeavey, CFA, Jerald E. Pinto, CFA, and David E. Runkle, CFA

INTRODUCTION

As individuals, we often face decisions that involve saving money for a future use, or borrowing money for current consumption. We then need to determine the amount we need to invest, if we are saving, or the cost of borrowing, if we are shopping for a loan. As investment analysts, much of our work also involves evaluating transactions with present and future cash flows. When we place a value on any security, for example, we are attempting to determine the worth of a stream of future cash flows. To carry out all the above tasks accurately, we must understand the mathematics of time value of money problems. Money has time value in that individuals value a given amount of money more highly the earlier it is received. Therefore, a smaller amount of money now may be equivalent in value to a larger amount received at a future date. The **time value of money** as a topic in investment mathematics deals with equivalence relationships between cash flows with different dates. Mastery of time value of money concepts and techniques is essential for investment analysts.

Quantitative Methods for Investment Analysis, Second Edition, by Richard A. DeFusco, CFA, Dennis W. McLeavey, CFA, Jerald E. Pinto, CFA, and David E. Runkle, CFA. Copyright © 2004 by CFA Institute.

The reading is organized as follows: Section 2 introduces some terminology used throughout the reading and supplies some economic intuition for the variables we will discuss. Section 3 tackles the problem of determining the worth at a future point in time of an amount invested today. Section 4 addresses the future worth of a series of cash flows. These two sections provide the tools for calculating the equivalent value at a future date of a single cash flow or series of cash flows. Sections 5 and 6 discuss the equivalent value today of a single future cash flow and a series of future cash flows, respectively. In Section 7, we explore how to determine other quantities of interest in time value of money problems.

INTEREST RATES: INTERPRETATION

In this reading, we will continually refer to interest rates. In some cases, we assume a particular value for the interest rate; in other cases, the interest rate will be the unknown quantity we seek to determine. Before turning to the mechanics of time value of money problems, we must illustrate the underlying economic concepts. In this section, we briefly explain the meaning and interpretation of interest rates.

Time value of money concerns equivalence relationships between cash flows occurring on different dates. The idea of equivalence relationships is relatively simple. Consider the following exchange: You pay $10,000 today and in return receive $9,500 today. Would you accept this arrangement? Not likely. But what if you received the $9,500 today and paid the $10,000 one year from now? Can these amounts be considered equivalent? Possibly, because a payment of $10,000 a year from now would probably be worth less to you than a payment of $10,000 today. It would be fair, therefore, to **discount** the $10,000 received in one year; that is, to cut its value based on how much time passes before the money is paid. An **interest rate**, denoted r, is a rate of return that reflects the relationship between differently dated cash flows. If $9,500 today and $10,000 in one year are equivalent in value, then $10,000 – $9,500 = $500 is the required compensation for receiving $10,000 in one year rather than now. The interest rate—the required compensation stated as a rate of return—is $500/$9,500 = 0.0526 or 5.26 percent.

Interest rates can be thought of in three ways. First, they can be considered required rates of return—that is, the minimum rate of return an investor must receive in order to accept the investment. Second, interest rates can be considered discount rates. In the example above, 5.26 percent is that rate at which we discounted the $10,000 future amount to find its value today. Thus, we use the terms "interest rate" and "discount rate" almost interchangeably. Third, interest rates can be considered opportunity costs. An **opportunity cost** is the value that investors forgo by choosing a particular course of action. In the example, if the party who supplied $9,500 had instead decided to spend it today, he would have forgone earning 5.26 percent on the money. So we can view 5.26 percent as the opportunity cost of current consumption.

Economics tells us that interest rates are set in the marketplace by the forces of supply and demand, where investors are suppliers of funds and borrowers are demanders of funds. Taking the perspective of investors in analyzing market-determined interest rates, we can view an interest rate r as being composed of a real risk-free interest rate plus a set of four premiums that are required returns or compensation for bearing distinct types of risk:

r = Real risk-free interest rate + Inflation premium
    + Default risk premium + Liquidity premium + Maturity premium

▪ The **real risk-free interest rate** is the single-period interest rate for a completely risk-free security if no inflation were expected. In economic theory, the real risk-free rate reflects the time preferences of individuals for current versus future real consumption.

- The **inflation premium** compensates investors for expected inflation and reflects the average inflation rate expected over the maturity of the debt. Inflation reduces the purchasing power of a unit of currency—the amount of goods and services one can buy with it. The sum of the real risk-free interest rate and the inflation premium is the **nominal risk-free interest rate**.[1] Many countries have governmental short-term debt whose interest rate can be considered to represent the nominal risk-free interest rate in that country. The interest rate on a 90-day U.S. Treasury bill (T-bill), for example, represents the nominal risk-free interest rate over that time horizon.[2] U.S. T-bills can be bought and sold in large quantities with minimal transaction costs and are backed by the full faith and credit of the U.S. government.

- The **default risk premium** compensates investors for the possibility that the borrower will fail to make a promised payment at the contracted time and in the contracted amount.

- The **liquidity premium** compensates investors for the risk of loss relative to an investment's fair value if the investment needs to be converted to cash quickly. U.S. T-bills, for example, do not bear a liquidity premium because large amounts can be bought and sold without affecting their market price. Many bonds of small issuers, by contrast, trade infrequently after they are issued; the interest rate on such bonds includes a liquidity premium reflecting the relatively high costs (including the impact on price) of selling a position.

- The **maturity premium** compensates investors for the increased sensitivity of the market value of debt to a change in market interest rates as maturity is extended, in general (holding all else equal). The difference between the interest rate on longer-maturity, liquid Treasury debt and that on short-term Treasury debt reflects a positive maturity premium for the longer-term debt (and possibly different inflation premiums as well).

Using this insight into the economic meaning of interest rates, we now turn to a discussion of solving time value of money problems, starting with the future value of a single cash flow.

THE FUTURE VALUE OF A SINGLE CASH FLOW   3

In this section, we introduce time value associated with a single cash flow or lump-sum investment. We describe the relationship between an initial investment or **present value (PV)**, which earns a rate of return (the interest rate per period) denoted as r, and its **future value (FV)**, which will be received N years or periods from today.

---

1 Technically, 1 plus the nominal rate equals the product of 1 plus the real rate and 1 plus the inflation rate. As a quick approximation, however, the nominal rate is equal to the real rate plus an inflation premium. In this discussion we focus on approximate additive relationships to highlight the underlying concepts.

2 Other developed countries issue securities similar to U.S. Treasury bills. The French government issues BTFs or negotiable fixed-rate discount Treasury bills (*Bons du Trésor à taux fixe et à intérêts précomptés*) with maturities of 3, 6, and 12 months. The Japanese government issues a short-term Treasury bill with maturities of 6 and 12 months. The German government issues at discount both Treasury financing paper (*Finanzierungsschätze des Bundes* or, for short, *Schätze*) and Treasury discount paper (*Bubills*) with maturities up to 24 months. In the United Kingdom, the British government issues gilt-edged Treasury bills with maturities ranging from 1 to 364 days. The Canadian government bond market is closely related to the U.S. market; Canadian Treasury bills have maturities of 3, 6, and 12 months.

The following example illustrates this concept. Suppose you invest $100 (PV = $100) in an interest-bearing bank account paying 5 percent annually. At the end of the first year, you will have the $100 plus the interest earned, 0.05 × $100 = $5, for a total of $105. To formalize this one-period example, we define the following terms:

PV = present value of the investment
FV_N = future value of the investment N periods from today
r = rate of interest per period

For N = 1, the expression for the future value of amount PV is

$$FV_1 = PV(1 + r)$$ (1)

For this example, we calculate the future value one year from today as FV_1 = $100(1.05) = $105.

Now suppose you decide to invest the initial $100 for two years with interest earned and credited to your account annually (annual compounding). At the end of the first year (the beginning of the second year), your account will have $105, which you will leave in the bank for another year. Thus, with a beginning amount of $105 (PV = $105), the amount at the end of the second year will be $105(1.05) = $110.25. Note that the $5.25 interest earned during the second year is 5 percent of the amount invested at the beginning of Year 2.

Another way to understand this example is to note that the amount invested at the beginning of Year 2 is composed of the original $100 that you invested plus the $5 interest earned during the first year. During the second year, the original principal again earns interest, as does the interest that was earned during Year 1. You can see how the original investment grows:

Original investment	$100.00
Interest for the first year ($100 × 0.05)	5.00
Interest for the second year based on original investment ($100 × 0.05)	5.00
Interest for the second year based on interest earned in the first year (0.05 × $5.00 interest on interest)	0.25
Total	$110.25

The $5 interest that you earned each period on the $100 original investment is known as **simple interest** (the interest rate times the principal). **Principal** is the amount of funds originally invested. During the two-year period, you earn $10 of simple interest. The extra $0.25 that you have at the end of Year 2 is the interest you earned on the Year 1 interest of $5 that you reinvested.

The interest earned on interest provides the first glimpse of the phenomenon known as **compounding**. Although the interest earned on the initial investment is important, for a given interest rate it is fixed in size from period to period. The compounded interest earned on reinvested interest is a far more powerful force because, for a given interest rate, it grows in size each period. The importance of compounding increases with the magnitude of the interest rate. For example, $100 invested today would be worth about $13,150 after 100 years if compounded annually at 5 percent, but worth more than $20 million if compounded annually over the same time period at a rate of 13 percent.

To verify the $20 million figure, we need a general formula to handle compounding for any number of periods. The following general formula relates the present value of an initial investment to its future value after N periods:

$$FV_N = PV(1 + r)^N$$ (2)

where r is the stated interest rate per period and N is the number of compounding periods. In the bank example, $FV_2 = \$100(1 + 0.05)^2 = \$110.25$. In the 13 percent investment example, $FV_{100} = \$100(1.13)^{100} = \$20,316,287.42$.

The most important point to remember about using the future value equation is that the stated interest rate, r, and the number of compounding periods, N, must be compatible. Both variables must be defined in the same time units. For example, if N is stated in months, then r should be the one-month interest rate, unannualized.

A time line helps us to keep track of the compatibility of time units and the interest rate per time period. In the time line, we use the time index t to represent a point in time a stated number of periods from today. Thus the present value is the amount available for investment today, indexed as $t = 0$. We can now refer to a time N periods from today as $t = N$. The time line in Figure 1 shows this relationship.

Figure 1	The Relationship between an Initial Investment, PV, and Its Future Value, FV

In Figure 1, we have positioned the initial investment, PV, at $t = 0$. Using Equation 2, we move the present value, PV, forward to $t = N$ by the factor $(1 + r)^N$. This factor is called a future value factor. We denote the future value on the time line as FV and position it at $t = N$. Suppose the future value is to be received exactly 10 periods from today's date ($N = 10$). The present value, PV, and the future value, FV, are separated in time through the factor $(1 + r)^{10}$.

The fact that the present value and the future value are separated in time has important consequences:

- We can add amounts of money only if they are indexed at the same point in time.
- For a given interest rate, the future value increases with the number of periods.
- For a given number of periods, the future value increases with the interest rate.

To better understand these concepts, consider three examples that illustrate how to apply the future value formula.

Example 1

The Future Value of a Lump Sum with Interim Cash Reinvested at the Same Rate

You are the lucky winner of your state's lottery of $5 million after taxes. You invest your winnings in a five-year certificate of deposit (CD) at a local financial institution. The CD promises to pay 7 percent per year compounded annually. This institution also lets you reinvest the interest at that rate for the duration of the CD. How much will you have at the end of five years if your money remains invested at 7 percent for five years with no withdrawals?

Solution:

To solve this problem, compute the future value of the $5 million investment using the following values in Equation 2:

$$PV = \$5,000,000$$
$$r = 7\% = 0.07$$
$$N = 5$$
$$FV_N = PV(1+r)^N$$
$$= \$5,000,000(1.07)^5$$
$$= \$5,000,000(1.402552)$$
$$= \$7,012,758.65$$

At the end of five years, you will have $7,012,758.65 if your money remains invested at 7 percent with no withdrawals.

In this and most examples in this reading, note that the factors are reported at six decimal places but the calculations may actually reflect greater precision. For example, the reported 1.402552 has been rounded up from 1.40255173 (the calculation is actually carried out with more than eight decimal places of precision by the calculator or spreadsheet). Our final result reflects the higher number of decimal places carried by the calculator or spreadsheet.[3]

Example 2

The Future Value of a Lump Sum with No Interim Cash

An institution offers you the following terms for a contract: For an investment of ¥2,500,000, the institution promises to pay you a lump sum six years from now at an 8 percent annual interest rate. What future amount can you expect?

Solution:

Use the following data in Equation 2 to find the future value:

$$PV = ¥2,500,000$$
$$r = 8\% = 0.08$$
$$N = 6$$
$$FV_N = PV(1+r)^N$$
$$= ¥2,500,000(1.08)^6$$
$$= ¥2,500,000(1.586874)$$
$$= ¥3,967,186$$

You can expect to receive ¥3,967,186 six years from now.

Our third example is a more complicated future value problem that illustrates the importance of keeping track of actual calendar time.

---

3 We could also solve time value of money problems using tables of interest rate factors. Solutions using tabled values of interest rate factors are generally less accurate than solutions obtained using calculators or spreadsheets, so practitioners prefer calculators or spreadsheets.

Example 3

The Future Value of a Lump Sum

A pension fund manager estimates that his corporate sponsor will make a $10 million contribution five years from now. The rate of return on plan assets has been estimated at 9 percent per year. The pension fund manager wants to calculate the future value of this contribution 15 years from now, which is the date at which the funds will be distributed to retirees. What is that future value?

Solution:

By positioning the initial investment, PV, at $t = 5$, we can calculate the future value of the contribution using the following data in Equation 2:

$$PV = \$10 \text{ million}$$
$$r = 9\% = 0.09$$
$$N = 10$$
$$FV_N = PV(1+r)^N$$
$$= \$10,000,000(1.09)^{10}$$
$$= \$10,000,000(2.367364)$$
$$= \$23,673,636.75$$

This problem looks much like the previous two, but it differs in one important respect: its timing. From the standpoint of today ($t = 0$), the future amount of $23,673,636.75 is 15 years into the future. Although the future value is 10 years from its present value, the present value of $10 million will not be received for another five years.

Figure 2	The Future Value of a Lump Sum, Initial Investment Not at $t = 0$

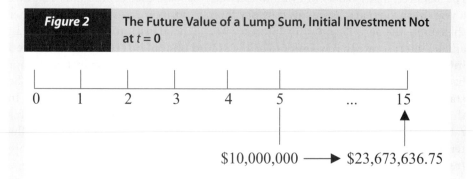

As Figure 2 shows, we have followed the convention of indexing today as $t = 0$ and indexing subsequent times by adding 1 for each period. The additional contribution of $10 million is to be received in five years, so it is indexed as $t = 5$ and appears as such in the figure. The future value of the investment in 10 years is then indexed at $t = 15$; that is, 10 years following the receipt of the $10 million contribution at $t = 5$. Time lines like this one can be extremely useful when dealing with more-complicated problems, especially those involving more than one cash flow.

In a later section of this reading, we will discuss how to calculate the value today of the $10 million to be received five years from now. For the moment, we can use Equation 2. Suppose the pension fund manager in Example 3 above were to receive $6,499,313.86 today from the corporate sponsor. How much will that sum be worth at the end of five years? How much will it be worth at the end of 15 years?

$$PV = \$6,499,313.86$$
$$r = 9\% = 0.09$$
$$N = 5$$
$$FV_N = PV(1+r)^N$$
$$= \$6,499,313.86(1.09)^5$$
$$= \$6,499,313.86(1.538624)$$
$$= \$10,000,000 \text{ at the five-year mark}$$

and

$$PV = \$6,499,313.86$$
$$r = 9\% = 0.09$$
$$N = 15$$
$$FV_N = PV(1+r)^N$$
$$= \$6,499,313.86(1.09)^{15}$$
$$= \$6,499,313.86(3.642482)$$
$$= \$23,673,636.74 \text{ at the 15-year mark}$$

These results show that today's present value of about $6.5 million becomes $10 million after five years and $23.67 million after 15 years.

3.1 The Frequency of Compounding

In this section, we examine investments paying interest more than once a year. For instance, many banks offer a monthly interest rate that compounds 12 times a year. In such an arrangement, they pay interest on interest every month. Rather than quote the periodic monthly interest rate, financial institutions often quote an annual interest rate that we refer to as the **stated annual interest rate** or **quoted interest rate**. We denote the stated annual interest rate by r_s. For instance, your bank might state that a particular CD pays 8 percent compounded monthly. The stated annual interest rate equals the monthly interest rate multiplied by 12. In this example, the monthly interest rate is $0.08/12 = 0.0067$ or 0.67 percent.[4] This rate is strictly a quoting convention because $(1 + 0.0067)^{12} = 1.083$, not 1.08; the term $(1 + r_s)$ is not meant to be a future value factor when compounding is more frequent than annual.

With more than one compounding period per year, the future value formula can be expressed as

$$FV_N = PV\left(1+\frac{r_s}{m}\right)^{mN} \tag{3}$$

where r_s is the stated annual interest rate, m is the number of compounding periods per year, and N now stands for the number of years. Note the compatibility here between the interest rate used, r_s/m, and the number of compounding periods, mN. The periodic rate, r_s/m, is the stated annual interest rate divided by the number of compounding periods per year. The number of compounding periods, mN, is the number of compounding periods in one year multiplied by the number of years. The periodic rate, r_s/m, and the number of compounding periods, mN, must be compatible.

---

[4] To avoid rounding errors when using a financial calculator, divide 8 by 12 and then press the *%i* key, rather than simply entering 0.67 for *%i*, so we have $(1 + 0.08/12)12 = 1.083000$.

Example 4

The Future Value of a Lump Sum with Quarterly Compounding

Continuing with the CD example, suppose your bank offers you a CD with a two-year maturity, a stated annual interest rate of 8 percent compounded quarterly, and a feature allowing reinvestment of the interest at the same interest rate. You decide to invest $10,000. What will the CD be worth at maturity?

Solution:

Compute the future value with Equation 3 as follows:

$$PV = \$10,000$$
$$r_s = 8\% = 0.08$$
$$m = 4$$
$$r_s/m = 0.08/4 = 0.02$$
$$N = 2$$
$$mN = 4(2) = 8 \text{ interest periods}$$

$$FV_N = PV\left(1 + \frac{r_s}{m}\right)^{mN}$$
$$= \$10,000(1.02)^8$$
$$= \$10,000(1.171659)$$
$$= \$11,716.59$$

At maturity, the CD will be worth $11,716.59.

The future value formula in Equation 3 does not differ from the one in Equation 2. Simply keep in mind that the interest rate to use is the rate per period and the exponent is the number of interest, or compounding, periods.

Example 5

The Future Value of a Lump Sum with Monthly Compounding

An Australian bank offers to pay you 6 percent compounded monthly. You decide to invest A$1 million for one year. What is the future value of your investment if interest payments are reinvested at 6 percent?

Solution:

Use Equation 3 to find the future value of the one-year investment as follows:

$$PV = A\$1,000,000$$
$$r_s = 6\% = 0.06$$
$$m = 12$$
$$r_s/m = 0.06/12 = 0.0050$$
$$N = 1$$
$$mN = 12(1) = 12 \text{ interest periods}$$

$$FV_N = PV\left(1 + \frac{r_s}{m}\right)^{mN}$$
$$= A\$1,000,000(1.005)^{12}$$
$$= A\$1,000,000(1.061678)$$
$$= A\$1,061,677.81$$

> If you had been paid 6 percent with annual compounding, the future amount would be only A\$1,000,000(1.06) = A\$1,060,000 instead of A\$1,061,677.81 with monthly compounding.

3.2 Continuous Compounding

The preceding discussion on compounding periods illustrates discrete compounding, which credits interest after a discrete amount of time has elapsed. If the number of compounding periods per year becomes infinite, then interest is said to compound continuously. If we want to use the future value formula with continuous compounding, we need to find the limiting value of the future value factor for $m \to \infty$ (infinitely many compounding periods per year) in Equation 3. The expression for the future value of a sum in N years with continuous compounding is

$$\text{FV}_N = \text{PV}e^{r_s N} \tag{4}$$

The term $e^{r_s N}$ is the transcendental number $e \approx 2.7182818$ raised to the power $r_s N$. Most financial calculators have the function e^x.

Example 6

The Future Value of a Lump Sum with Continuous Compounding

Suppose a \$10,000 investment will earn 8 percent compounded continuously for two years. We can compute the future value with Equation 4 as follows:

$$PV = \$10,000$$
$$r_s = 8\% = 0.08$$
$$N = 2$$
$$\text{FV}_N = \text{PV}e^{r_s N}$$
$$= \$10,000e^{0.08(2)}$$
$$= \$10,000(1.173511)$$
$$= \$11,735.11$$

With the same interest rate but using continuous compounding, the \$10,000 investment will grow to \$11,735.11 in two years, compared with \$11,716.59 using quarterly compounding as shown in Example 4.

Table 1 shows how a stated annual interest rate of 8 percent generates different ending dollar amounts with annual, semiannual, quarterly, monthly, daily, and continuous compounding for an initial investment of \$1 (carried out to six decimal places).

As Table 1 shows, all six cases have the same stated annual interest rate of 8 percent; they have different ending dollar amounts, however, because of differences in the frequency of compounding. With annual compounding, the ending amount is \$1.08. More frequent compounding results in larger ending amounts. The ending dollar amount with continuous compounding is the maximum amount that can be earned with a stated annual rate of 8 percent.

Table 1		The Effect of Compounding Frequency on Future Value		
Frequency	r_s/m	mN	**Future Value of $1**	
Annual	8%/1 = 8%	1 × 1 = 1	$1.00(1.08)	= $1.08
Semiannual	8%/2 = 4%	2 × 1 = 2	$1.00(1.04)^2$	= $1.081600
Quarterly	8%/4 = 2%	4 × 1 = 4	$1.00(1.02)^4$	= $1.082432
Monthly	8%/12 = 0.6667%	12 × 1 = 12	$1.00(1.006667)^{12}$	= $1.083000
Daily	8%/365 = 0.0219%	365 × 1 = 365	$1.00(1.000219)^{365}$	= $1.083278
Continuous			$1.00e^{0.08(1)}$	= $1.083287

Table 1 also shows that a $1 investment earning 8.16 percent compounded annually grows to the same future value at the end of one year as a $1 investment earning 8 percent compounded semiannually. This result leads us to a distinction between the stated annual interest rate and the **effective annual rate** (EAR).[5] For an 8 percent stated annual interest rate with semiannual compounding, the EAR is 8.16 percent.

3.3 Stated and Effective Rates

The stated annual interest rate does not give a future value directly, so we need a formula for the EAR. With an annual interest rate of 8 percent compounded semiannually, we receive a periodic rate of 4 percent. During the course of a year, an investment of $1 would grow to $1(1.04)^2$ = $1.0816, as illustrated in Table 1. The interest earned on the $1 investment is $0.0816 and represents an effective annual rate of interest of 8.16 percent. The effective annual rate is calculated as follows:

$$\text{EAR} = (1 + \text{Periodic interest rate})^m - 1 \qquad (5)$$

The periodic interest rate is the stated annual interest rate divided by m, where m is the number of compounding periods in one year. Using our previous example, we can solve for EAR as follows: $(1.04)^2 - 1$ = 8.16 percent.

The concept of EAR extends to continuous compounding. Suppose we have a rate of 8 percent compounded continuously. We can find the EAR in the same way as above by finding the appropriate future value factor. In this case, a $1 investment would grow to $1e^{0.08(1.0)}$ = $1.0833. The interest earned for one year represents an effective annual rate of 8.33 percent and is larger than the 8.16 percent EAR with semiannual compounding because interest is compounded more frequently. With continuous compounding, we can solve for the effective annual rate as follows:

$$\text{EAR} = e^{r_s} - 1 \qquad (6)$$

We can reverse the formulas for EAR with discrete and continuous compounding to find a periodic rate that corresponds to a particular effective annual rate.

---

5 Among the terms used for the effective annual return on interest-bearing bank deposits are annual percentage yield (APY) in the United States and equivalent annual rate (EAR) in the United Kingdom. By contrast, the **annual percentage rate** (APR) measures the cost of borrowing expressed as a yearly rate. In the United States, the APR is calculated as a periodic rate times the number of payment periods per year and, as a result, some writers use APR as a general synonym for the stated annual interest rate. Nevertheless, APR is a term with legal connotations; its calculation follows regulatory standards that vary internationally. Therefore, "stated annual interest rate" is the preferred general term for an annual interest rate that does not account for compounding within the year.

Suppose we want to find the appropriate periodic rate for a given effective annual rate of 8.16 percent with semiannual compounding. We can use Equation 5 to find the periodic rate:

$$0.0816 = (1 + \text{Periodic rate})^2 - 1$$
$$1.0816 = (1 + \text{Periodic rate})^2$$
$$(1.0816)^{1/2} - 1 = \text{Periodic rate}$$
$$(1.04) - 1 = \text{Periodic rate}$$
$$4\% = \text{Periodic rate}$$

To calculate the continuously compounded rate (the stated annual interest rate with continuous compounding) corresponding to an effective annual rate of 8.33 percent, we find the interest rate that satisfies Equation 6:

$$0.0833 = e^{r_s} - 1$$
$$1.0833 = e^{r_s}$$

To solve this equation, we take the natural logarithm of both sides. (Recall that the natural log of e^{r_s} is ln $e^{r_s} = r_s$.) Therefore, ln $1.0833 = r_s$, resulting in r_s = 8 percent. We see that a stated annual rate of 8 percent with continuous compounding is equivalent to an EAR of 8.33 percent.

4 THE FUTURE VALUE OF A SERIES OF CASH FLOWS

In this section, we consider series of cash flows, both even and uneven. We begin with a list of terms commonly used when valuing cash flows that are distributed over many time periods.

- An **annuity** is a finite set of level sequential cash flows.
- An **ordinary annuity** has a first cash flow that occurs one period from now (indexed at $t = 1$).
- An **annuity due** has a first cash flow that occurs immediately (indexed at $t = 0$).
- A **perpetuity** is a perpetual annuity, or a set of level never-ending sequential cash flows, with the first cash flow occurring one period from now.

4.1 Equal Cash Flows—Ordinary Annuity

Consider an ordinary annuity paying 5 percent annually. Suppose we have five separate deposits of $1,000 occurring at equally spaced intervals of one year, with the first payment occurring at $t = 1$. Our goal is to find the future value of this ordinary annuity after the last deposit at $t = 5$. The increment in the time counter is one year, so the last payment occurs five years from now. As the time line in Figure 3 shows, we find the future value of each $1,000 deposit as of $t = 5$ with Equation 2, $FV_N = PV(1 + r)^N$. The arrows in Figure 3 extend from the payment date to $t = 5$. For instance, the first $1,000 deposit made at $t = 1$ will compound over four periods. Using Equation 2, we find that the future value of the first deposit at $t = 5$ is $1,000(1.05)^4 = $1,215.51. We calculate the future value of all other payments in a similar fashion. (Note that we are finding the future value at $t = 5$, so the last payment does not earn any interest.) With all values now at $t = 5$, we can add the future values to arrive at the future value of the annuity. This amount is $5,525.63.

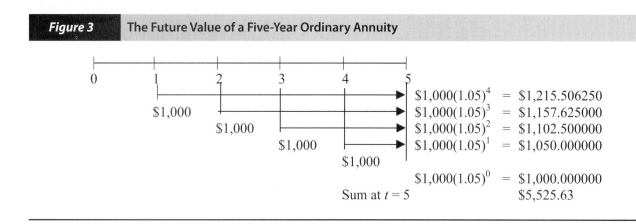

Figure 3 The Future Value of a Five-Year Ordinary Annuity

We can arrive at a general annuity formula if we define the annuity amount as A, the number of time periods as N, and the interest rate per period as r. We can then define the future value as

$$FV_N = A\left[(1+r)^{N-1} + (1+r)^{N-2} + (1+r)^{N-3} + \ldots + (1+r)^{1} + (1+r)^{0}\right]$$

which simplifies to

$$FV_N = A\left[\frac{(1+r)^{N}-1}{r}\right] \tag{7}$$

The term in brackets is the future value annuity factor. This factor gives the future value of an ordinary annuity of \$1 per period. Multiplying the future value annuity factor by the annuity amount gives the future value of an ordinary annuity. For the ordinary annuity in Figure 3, we find the future value annuity factor from Equation 7 as

$$\left[\frac{(1.05)^{5}-1}{0.05}\right] = 5.525631$$

With an annuity amount $A = \$1,000$, the future value of the annuity is $\$1,000(5.525631)$ = \$5,525.63, an amount that agrees with our earlier work.

The next example illustrates how to find the future value of an ordinary annuity using the formula in Equation 7.

Example 7

The Future Value of an Annuity

Suppose your company's defined contribution retirement plan allows you to invest up to €20,000 per year. You plan to invest €20,000 per year in a stock index fund for the next 30 years. Historically, this fund has earned 9 percent per year on average. Assuming that you actually earn 9 percent a year, how much money will you have available for retirement after making the last payment?

Solution:

Use Equation 7 to find the future amount:

$$A = €20,000$$
$$r = 9\% = 0.09$$
$$N = 30$$

$$\text{FV annuity factor} = \frac{(1+r)^{N}-1}{r} = \frac{(1.09)^{30}-1}{0.09} = 136.307539$$

$$FV_N = €20,000(136.307539)$$
$$= €2,726,150.77$$

Assuming the fund continues to earn an average of 9 percent per year, you will have €2,726,150.77 available at retirement.

4.2 Unequal Cash Flows

In many cases, cash flow streams are unequal, precluding the simple use of the future value annuity factor. For instance, an individual investor might have a savings plan that involves unequal cash payments depending on the month of the year or lower savings during a planned vacation. One can always find the future value of a series of unequal cash flows by compounding the cash flows one at a time. Suppose you have the five cash flows described in Table 2, indexed relative to the present ($t = 0$).

Table 2	A Series of Unequal Cash Flows and Their Future Values at 5 Percent		

Time	Cash Flow ($)	Future Value at Year 5	
$t = 1$	1,000	$\$1,000(1.05)^4$ =	\$1,215.51
$t = 2$	2,000	$\$2,000(1.05)^3$ =	\$2,315.25
$t = 3$	4,000	$\$4,000(1.05)^2$ =	\$4,410.00
$t = 4$	5,000	$\$5,000(1.05)^1$ =	\$5,250.00
$t = 5$	6,000	$\$6,000(1.05)^0$ =	\$6,000.00
		Sum =	\$19,190.76

All of the payments shown in Table 2 are different. Therefore, the most direct approach to finding the future value at $t = 5$ is to compute the future value of each payment as of $t = 5$ and then sum the individual future values. The total future value at Year 5 equals \$19,190.76, as shown in the third column. Later in this reading, you will learn shortcuts to take when the cash flows are close to even; these shortcuts will allow you to combine annuity and single-period calculations.

THE PRESENT VALUE OF A SINGLE CASH FLOW

5.1 Finding the Present Value of a Single Cash Flow

Just as the future value factor links today's present value with tomorrow's future value, the present value factor allows us to discount future value to present value. For example, with a 5 percent interest rate generating a future payoff of \$105 in one year, what current amount invested at 5 percent for one year will grow to \$105? The answer is \$100; therefore, \$100 is the present value of \$105 to be received in one year at a discount rate of 5 percent.

Given a future cash flow that is to be received in N periods and an interest rate per period of r, we can use the formula for future value to solve directly for the present value as follows:

$$FV_N = PV(1+r)^N$$

$$PV = FV_N \left[\frac{1}{(1+r)^N} \right]$$

$$PV = FV_N (1+r)^{-N}$$

(8)

We see from Equation 8 that the present value factor, $(1 + r)^{-N}$, is the reciprocal of the future value factor, $(1 + r)^N$.

Example 8

The Present Value of a Lump Sum

An insurance company has issued a Guaranteed Investment Contract (GIC) that promises to pay $100,000 in six years with an 8 percent return rate. What amount of money must the insurer invest today at 8 percent for six years to make the promised payment?

Solution:

We can use Equation 8 to find the present value using the following data:

$$FV_N = \$100,000$$
$$r = 8\% = 0.08$$
$$N = 6$$
$$PV = FV_N (1+r)^{-N}$$
$$= \$100,000 \left[\frac{1}{(1.08)^6} \right]$$
$$= \$100,000(0.6301696)$$
$$= \$63,016.96$$

We can say that $63,016.96 today, with an interest rate of 8 percent, is equivalent to $100,000 to be received in six years. Discounting the $100,000 makes a future $100,000 equivalent to $63,016.96 when allowance is made for the time value of money. As the time line in Figure 4 shows, the $100,000 has been discounted six full periods.

Figure 4	**The Present Value of a Lump Sum to Be Received at Time $t = 6$**

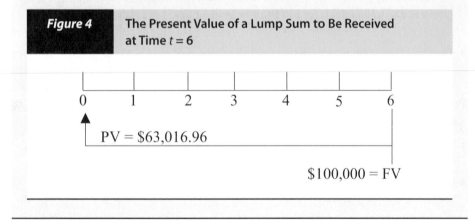

Example 9

The Projected Present Value of a More Distant Future Lump Sum

Suppose you own a liquid financial asset that will pay you $100,000 in 10 years from today. Your daughter plans to attend college four years from today, and you want to know what the asset's present value will be at that time. Given an 8 percent discount rate, what will the asset be worth four years from today?

Solution:

The value of the asset is the present value of the asset's promised payment. At $t = 4$, the cash payment will be received six years later. With this information, you can solve for the value four years from today using Equation 8:

$$\begin{aligned}
FV_N &= \$100{,}000 \\
r &= 8\% = 0.08 \\
N &= 6 \\
PV &= FV_N(1+r)^{-N} \\
&= \$100{,}000\frac{1}{(1.08)^6} \\
&= \$100{,}000(0.6301696) \\
&= \$63{,}016.96
\end{aligned}$$

Figure 5	The Relationship between Present Value and Future Value

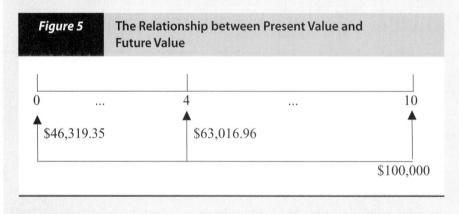

The time line in Figure 5 shows the future payment of \$100,000 that is to be received at $t = 10$. The time line also shows the values at $t = 4$ and at $t = 0$. Relative to the payment at $t = 10$, the amount at $t = 4$ is a projected present value, while the amount at $t = 0$ is the present value (as of today).

Present value problems require an evaluation of the present value factor, $(1 + r)^{-N}$. Present values relate to the discount rate and the number of periods in the following ways:

■ For a given discount rate, the farther in the future the amount to be received, the smaller that amount's present value.

■ Holding time constant, the larger the discount rate, the smaller the present value of a future amount.

5.2 The Frequency of Compounding

Recall that interest may be paid semiannually, quarterly, monthly, or even daily. To handle interest payments made more than once a year, we can modify the present value formula (Equation 8) as follows. Recall that r_s is the quoted interest rate and equals the periodic interest rate multiplied by the number of compounding periods in each year. In general, with more than one compounding period in a year, we can express the formula for present value as

$$PV = FV_N\left(1 + \tfrac{r_s}{m}\right)^{-mN} \tag{9}$$

where

m = number of compounding periods per year
r_s = quoted annual interest rate
N = number of years

The formula in Equation 9 is quite similar to that in Equation 8. As we have already noted, present value and future value factors are reciprocals. Changing the frequency of compounding does not alter this result. The only difference is the use of the periodic interest rate and the corresponding number of compounding periods.

The following example illustrates Equation 9.

Example 10

The Present Value of a Lump Sum with Monthly Compounding

The manager of a Canadian pension fund knows that the fund must make a lump-sum payment of C$5 million 10 years from now. She wants to invest an amount today in a GIC so that it will grow to the required amount. The current interest rate on GICs is 6 percent a year, compounded monthly. How much should she invest today in the GIC?

Solution:

Use Equation 9 to find the required present value:

$$FV_N = C\$5,000,000$$
$$r_s = 6\% = 0.06$$
$$m = 12$$
$$r_s/m = 0.06/12 = 0.005$$
$$N = 10$$
$$mN = 12(10) = 120$$
$$PV = FV_N \left(1 + \tfrac{r_s}{m}\right)^{-mN}$$
$$= C\$5,000,000(1.005)^{-120}$$
$$= C\$5,000,000(0.549633)$$
$$= C\$2,748,163.67$$

In applying Equation 9, we use the periodic rate (in this case, the monthly rate) and the appropriate number of periods with monthly compounding (in this case, 10 years of monthly compounding, or 120 periods).

THE PRESENT VALUE OF A SERIES OF CASH FLOWS

Many applications in investment management involve assets that offer a series of cash flows over time. The cash flows may be highly uneven, relatively even, or equal. They may occur over relatively short periods of time, longer periods of time, or even stretch on indefinitely. In this section, we discuss how to find the present value of a series of cash flows.

6.1 The Present Value of a Series of Equal Cash Flows

We begin with an ordinary annuity. Recall that an ordinary annuity has equal annuity payments, with the first payment starting one period into the future. In total, the annuity makes N payments, with the first payment at $t = 1$ and the last at $t = N$. We can express the present value of an ordinary annuity as the sum of the present values of each individual annuity payment, as follows:

$$PV = \frac{A}{(1+r)} + \frac{A}{(1+r)^2} + \frac{A}{(1+r)^3} + \ldots + \frac{A}{(1+r)^{N-1}} + \frac{A}{(1+r)^N} \tag{10}$$

where

A = the annuity amount
r = the interest rate per period corresponding to the frequency of annuity payments (for example, annual, quarterly, or monthly)
N = the number of annuity payments

Because the annuity payment (A) is a constant in this equation, it can be factored out as a common term. Thus the sum of the interest factors has a shortcut expression:

$$PV = A \left[\frac{1 - \frac{1}{(1+r)^N}}{r} \right] \tag{11}$$

In much the same way that we computed the future value of an ordinary annuity, we find the present value by multiplying the annuity amount by a present value annuity factor (the term in brackets in Equation 11).

Example 11

The Present Value of an Ordinary Annuity

Suppose you are considering purchasing a financial asset that promises to pay €1,000 per year for five years, with the first payment one year from now. The required rate of return is 12 percent per year. How much should you pay for this asset?

Solution:

To find the value of the financial asset, use the formula for the present value of an ordinary annuity given in Equation 11 with the following data:

A = €1,000
r = 12% = 0.12
N = 5

$$PV = A \left[\frac{1 - \frac{1}{(1+r)^N}}{r} \right]$$

$$= €1,000 \left[\frac{1 - \frac{1}{(1.12)^5}}{0.12} \right]$$

$$= €1,000 (3.604776)$$
$$= €3,604.78$$

The series of cash flows of €1,000 per year for five years is currently worth €3,604.78 when discounted at 12 percent.

Keeping track of the actual calendar time brings us to a specific type of annuity with level payments: the annuity due. An annuity due has its first payment occurring today ($t = 0$). In total, the annuity due will make N payments. Figure 6 presents the time line for an annuity due that makes four payments of $100.

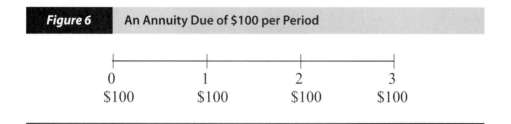

Figure 6   An Annuity Due of $100 per Period

0	1	2	3
$100	$100	$100	$100

As Figure 6 shows, we can view the four-period annuity due as the sum of two parts: a $100 lump sum today and an ordinary annuity of $100 per period for three periods. At a 12 percent discount rate, the four $100 cash flows in this annuity due example will be worth $340.18.[6]

Expressing the value of the future series of cash flows in today's dollars gives us a convenient way of comparing annuities. The next example illustrates this approach.

Example 12

An Annuity Due as the Present Value of an Immediate Cash Flow Plus an Ordinary Annuity

You are retiring today and must choose to take your retirement benefits either as a lump sum or as an annuity. Your company's benefits officer presents you with two alternatives: an immediate lump sum of $2 million or an annuity with 20 payments of $200,000 a year with the first payment starting today. The interest rate at your bank is 7 percent per year compounded annually. Which option has the greater present value? (Ignore any tax differences between the two options.)

Solution:

To compare the two options, find the present value of each at time $t = 0$ and choose the one with the larger value. The first option's present value is $2 million, already expressed in today's dollars. The second option is an annuity due. Because the first payment occurs at $t = 0$, you can separate the annuity benefits into two pieces: an immediate $200,000 to be paid today ($t = 0$) and an ordinary annuity of $200,000 per year for 19 years. To value this option, you need to find the present value of the ordinary annuity using Equation 11 and then add $200,000 to it.

---

6 There is an alternative way to calculate the present value of an annuity due. Compared to an ordinary annuity, the payments in an annuity due are each discounted one less period. Therefore, we can modify Equation 11 to handle annuities due by multiplying the right-hand side of the equation by $(1 + r)$:

$$PV(\text{Annuity due}) = A\left\{\left[1-(1+r)^{-N}\right]/r\right\}(1+r)$$

$$A = \$200,000$$
$$N = 19$$
$$r = 7\% = 0.07$$

$$PV = A\left[\frac{1-\frac{1}{(1+r)^N}}{r}\right]$$

$$= \$200,000\left[\frac{1-\frac{1}{(1.07)^{19}}}{0.07}\right]$$

$$= \$200,000(10.335595)$$
$$= \$2,067,119.05$$

The 19 payments of \$200,000 have a present value of \$2,067,119.05. Adding the initial payment of \$200,000 to \$2,067,119.05, we find that the total value of the annuity option is \$2,267,119.05. The present value of the annuity is greater than the lump sum alternative of \$2 million.

We now look at another example reiterating the equivalence of present and future values.

Example 13

The Projected Present Value of an Ordinary Annuity

A German pension fund manager anticipates that benefits of €1 million per year must be paid to retirees. Retirements will not occur until 10 years from now at time $t = 10$. Once benefits begin to be paid, they will extend until $t = 39$ for a total of 30 payments. What is the present value of the pension liability if the appropriate annual discount rate for plan liabilities is 5 percent compounded annually?

Solution:

This problem involves an annuity with the first payment at $t = 10$. From the perspective of $t = 9$, we have an ordinary annuity with 30 payments. We can compute the present value of this annuity with Equation 11 and then look at it on a time line.

$$A = €1,000,000$$
$$r = 5\% = 0.05$$
$$N = 30$$

$$PV = A\left[\frac{1-\frac{1}{(1+r)^N}}{r}\right]$$

$$= €1,000,000\left[\frac{1-\frac{1}{(1.05)^{30}}}{0.05}\right]$$

$$= €1,000,000(15.372451)$$
$$= €15,372,451.03$$

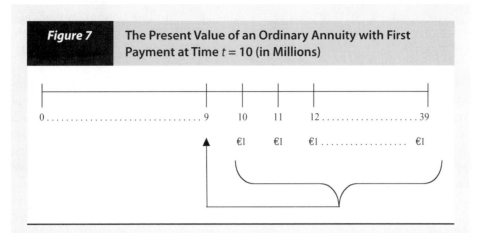

Figure 7 | The Present Value of an Ordinary Annuity with First Payment at Time $t = 10$ (in Millions)

On the time line, we have shown the pension payments of €1 million extending from $t = 10$ to $t = 39$. The bracket and arrow indicate the process of finding the present value of the annuity, discounted back to $t = 9$. The present value of the pension benefits as of $t = 9$ is €15,372,451.03. The problem is to find the present value today (at $t = 0$).

Now we can rely on the equivalence of present value and future value. As Figure 7 shows, we can view the amount at $t = 9$ as a future value from the vantage point of $t = 0$. We compute the present value of the amount at $t = 9$ as follows:

$$\text{FV}_N = €15{,}372{,}451.03 \, (\text{the present value at } t = 9)$$
$$N = 9$$
$$r = 5\% = 0.05$$
$$\text{PV} = \text{FV}_N \left(1 + r\right)^{-N}$$
$$= €15{,}372{,}451.03 \left(1.05\right)^{-9}$$
$$= €15{,}372{,}451.03 \left(0.644609\right)$$
$$= €9{,}909{,}219.00$$

The present value of the pension liability is €9,909,219.00.

Example 13 illustrates three procedures emphasized in this reading:

- finding the present or future value of any cash flow series;
- recognizing the equivalence of present value and appropriately discounted future value; and
- keeping track of the actual calendar time in a problem involving the time value of money.

6.2 The Present Value of an Infinite Series of Equal Cash Flows—Perpetuity

Consider the case of an ordinary annuity that extends indefinitely. Such an ordinary annuity is called a perpetuity (a perpetual annuity). To derive a formula for the present value of a perpetuity, we can modify Equation 10 to account for an infinite series of cash flows:

$$\text{PV} = A \sum_{t=1}^{\infty} \left[\frac{1}{\left(1 + r\right)^t} \right]$$

(12)

As long as interest rates are positive, the sum of present value factors converges and

$$PV = \frac{A}{r} \tag{13}$$

To see this, look back at Equation 11, the expression for the present value of an ordinary annuity. As N (the number of periods in the annuity) goes to infinity, the term $1/(1 + r)^N$ approaches 0 and Equation 11 simplifies to Equation 13. This equation will reappear when we value dividends from stocks because stocks have no predefined life span. (A stock paying constant dividends is similar to a perpetuity.) With the first payment a year from now, a perpetuity of $10 per year with a 20 percent required rate of return has a present value of $10/0.2 = $50.

Equation 13 is valid only for a perpetuity with level payments. In our development above, the first payment occurred at $t = 1$; therefore, we compute the present value as of $t = 0$.

Other assets also come close to satisfying the assumptions of a perpetuity. Certain government bonds and preferred stocks are typical examples of financial assets that make level payments for an indefinite period of time.

Example 14

The Present Value of a Perpetuity

The British government once issued a type of security called a consol bond, which promised to pay a level cash flow indefinitely. If a consol bond paid £100 per year in perpetuity, what would it be worth today if the required rate of return were 5 percent?

Solution:

To answer this question, we can use Equation 13 with the following data:

$$A = £100$$
$$r = 5\% = 0.05$$
$$PV = A/r$$
$$= £100/0.05$$
$$= £2,000$$

The bond would be worth £2,000.

6.3 Present Values Indexed at Times Other than $t = 0$

In practice with investments, analysts frequently need to find present values indexed at times other than $t = 0$. Subscripting the present value and evaluating a perpetuity beginning with $100 payments in Year 2, we find $PV_1 = $100/0.05 = $2,000$ at a 5 percent discount rate. Further, we can calculate today's PV as $PV_0 = $2,000/1.05 = $1,904.76$.

Consider a similar situation in which cash flows of $6 per year begin at the end of the 4th year and continue at the end of each year thereafter, with the last cash flow at the end of the 10th year. From the perspective of the end of the third year, we are facing a typical seven-year ordinary annuity. We can find the present value of the annuity from the perspective of the end of the third year and then discount that present value back to the present. At an interest rate of 5 percent, the cash flows of $6 per year starting at the end of the fourth year will be worth $34.72 at the end of the third year ($t = 3$) and $29.99 today ($t = 0$).

The next example illustrates the important concept that an annuity or perpetuity beginning sometime in the future can be expressed in present value terms one period prior to the first payment. That present value can then be discounted back to today's present value.

Example 15

The Present Value of a Projected Perpetuity

Consider a level perpetuity of £100 per year with its first payment beginning at $t = 5$. What is its present value today (at $t = 0$), given a 5 percent discount rate?

Solution:

First, we find the present value of the perpetuity at $t = 4$ and then discount that amount back to $t = 0$. (Recall that a perpetuity or an ordinary annuity has its first payment one period away, explaining the $t = 4$ index for our present value calculation.)

i. Find the present value of the perpetuity at $t = 4$:

$$A = £100$$
$$r = 5\% = 0.05$$
$$PV = A/r$$
$$= £100/0.05$$
$$= £2,000$$

ii. Find the present value of the future amount at $t = 4$. From the perspective of $t = 0$, the present value of £2,000 can be considered a future value. Now we need to find the present value of a lump sum:

$$FV_N = £2,000 \text{ (the present value at } t = 4)$$
$$r = 5\% = 0.05$$
$$N = 4$$
$$PV = FV_N (1+r)^{-N}$$
$$= £2,000(1.05)^{-4}$$
$$= £2,000(0.822702)$$
$$= £1,645.40$$

Today's present value of the perpetuity is £1,645.40.

As discussed earlier, an annuity is a series of payments of a fixed amount for a specified number of periods. Suppose we own a perpetuity. At the same time, we issue a perpetuity obligating us to make payments; these payments are the same size as those of the perpetuity we own. However, the first payment of the perpetuity we issue is at $t = 5$; payments then continue on forever. The payments on this second perpetuity exactly offset the payments received from the perpetuity we own at $t = 5$ and all subsequent dates. We are left with level nonzero net cash flows at $t = 1, 2, 3,$ and 4. This outcome exactly fits the definition of an annuity with four payments. Thus we can construct an annuity as the difference between two perpetuities with equal, level payments but differing starting dates. The next example illustrates this result.

Example 16

The Present Value of an Ordinary Annuity as the Present Value of a Current Minus Projected Perpetuity

Given a 5 percent discount rate, find the present value of a four-year ordinary annuity of £100 per year starting in Year 1 as the difference between the following two level perpetuities:

Perpetuity 1   £100 per year starting in Year 1 (first payment at $t = 1$)
Perpetuity 2   £100 per year starting in Year 5 (first payment at $t = 5$)

Solution:

If we subtract Perpetuity 2 from Perpetuity 1, we are left with an ordinary annuity of £100 per period for four years (payments at $t = 1, 2, 3, 4$). Subtracting the present value of Perpetuity 2 from that of Perpetuity 1, we arrive at the present value of the four-year ordinary annuity:

   i. $PV_0(\text{Perpetuity 1}) = £100/0.05 = £2,000$

   ii. $PV_4(\text{Perpetuity 2}) = £100/0.05 = £2,000$

   iii. $PV_0(\text{Perpetuity 2}) = £2,000/(1.05)^4 = £1,645.40$

   iv. $PV_0(\text{Annuity}) = PV_0(\text{Perpetuity 1}) - PV_0(\text{Perpetuity 2})$
$$= £2,000 - £1,645.40$$
$$= £354.60$$

The four-year ordinary annuity's present value is equal to £2,000 – £1,645.40 = £354.60.

6.4 The Present Value of a Series of Unequal Cash Flows

When we have unequal cash flows, we must first find the present value of each individual cash flow and then sum the respective present values. For a series with many cash flows, we usually use a spreadsheet. Table 3 lists a series of cash flows with the time periods in the first column, cash flows in the second column, and each cash flow's present value in the third column. The last row of Table 3 shows the sum of the five present values.

Table 3	A Series of Unequal Cash Flows and Their Present Values at 5 Percent	
Time Period	**Cash Flow ($)**	**Present Value at Year 0**
1	1,000	$\$1,000(1.05)^{-1}$ = $952.38
2	2,000	$\$2,000(1.05)^{-2}$ = $1,814.06
3	4,000	$\$4,000(1.05)^{-3}$ = $3,455.35
4	5,000	$\$5,000(1.05)^{-4}$ = $4,113.51
5	6,000	$\$6,000(1.05)^{-5}$ = $4,701.16
		Sum = $15,036.46

We could calculate the future value of these cash flows by computing them one at a time using the single-payment future value formula. We already know the present value of this series, however, so we can easily apply time-value equivalence. The future value of the series of cash flows from Table 2, $19,190.76, is equal to the single $15,036.46 amount compounded forward to $t = 5$:

$$PV = \$15,036.46$$
$$N = 5$$
$$r = 5\% = 0.05$$
$$FV_N = PV(1+r)^N$$
$$= \$15,036.46(1.05)^5$$
$$= \$15,036.46(1.276282)$$
$$= \$19,190.76$$

SOLVING FOR RATES, NUMBER OF PERIODS, OR SIZE OF ANNUITY PAYMENTS

In the previous examples, certain pieces of information have been made available. For instance, all problems have given the rate of interest, r, the number of time periods, N, the annuity amount, A, and either the present value, PV, or future value, FV. In real-world applications, however, although the present and future values may be given, you may have to solve for either the interest rate, the number of periods, or the annuity amount. In the subsections that follow, we show these types of problems.

7.1 Solving for Interest Rates and Growth Rates

Suppose a bank deposit of €100 is known to generate a payoff of €111 in one year. With this information, we can infer the interest rate that separates the present value of €100 from the future value of €111 by using Equation 2, $FV_N = PV(1 + r)^N$, with $N = 1$. With PV, FV, and N known, we can solve for r directly:

$$1 + r = FV/PV$$
$$1 + r = €111/€100 = 1.11$$
$$r = 0.11, \text{ or } 11\%$$

The interest rate that equates €100 at $t = 0$ to €111 at $t = 1$ is 11 percent. Thus we can state that €100 grows to €111 with a growth rate of 11 percent.

As this example shows, an interest rate can also be considered a growth rate. The particular application will usually dictate whether we use the term "interest rate" or "growth rate." Solving Equation 2 for r and replacing the interest rate r with the growth rate g produces the following expression for determining growth rates:

$$g = (FV_N/PV)^{1/N} - 1 \tag{14}$$

Below are two examples that use the concept of a growth rate.

Example 17

Calculating a Growth Rate (1)

For 1998, Limited Brands, Inc., recorded net sales of $8,436 million. For 2002, Limited Brands recorded net sales of $8,445 million, only slightly higher than in 1998. Over the four-year period from the end of 1998 to the end of 2002, what was the rate of growth of Limited Brands' net sales?

Solution:

To solve this problem, we can use Equation 14, $g = (FV_N/PV)^{1/N} - 1$. We denote net sales in 1998 as PV and net sales in 2002 as FV_4. We can then solve for the growth rate as follows:

$$g = \sqrt[4]{\$8,445/\$8,436} - 1$$
$$= \sqrt[4]{1.001067} - 1$$
$$= 1.000267 - 1$$
$$= 0.000267$$

The calculated growth rate of approximately 0.03 percent a year, barely more than zero, confirms the initial impression that Limited Brands' net sales were essentially flat during the 1998–2002 period.

Example 18

Calculating a Growth Rate (2)

In Example 17, we found that Limited Brands' compound growth rate of net sales was close to zero for 1998 to 2002. As a retailer, Limited Brands' sales depend both on the number of stores (or selling square feet or meters) and sales per store (or sales per average selling square foot or meter). In fact, Limited Brands decreased its number of stores during the 1998–2002 period. In 1998, Limited Brands operated 5,382 stores, whereas in 2002 it operated 4,036 stores. In this case, we can speak of a positive compound rate of decrease or a negative compound growth rate. What was the growth rate in number of stores operated?

Solution:

Using Equation 14, we find

$$g = \sqrt[4]{4{,}036/5{,}382} - 1$$
$$= \sqrt[4]{0.749907} - 1$$
$$= 0.930576 - 1$$
$$= -0.069424$$

The rate of growth in stores operated was approximately –6.9 percent during the 1998–2002 period. Note that we can also refer to –6.9 percent as the compound annual growth rate because it is the single number that compounds the number of stores in 1998 forward to the number of stores in 2002. Table 4 lists the number of stores operated by Limited Brands from 1998 to 2002.

Table 4	**Number of Limited Brands Stores, 1998–2002**		
Year	**Number of Stores**	**$(1 + g)_t$**	**t**
1998	5,382		0
1999	5,023	5,023/5,382 = 0.933296	1
2000	5,129	5,129/5,023 = 1.021103	2
2001	4,614	4,614/5,129 = 0.899591	3
2002	4,036	4,036/4,614 = 0.874729	4

Source: www.limited.com.

Table 4 also shows 1 plus the one-year growth rate in number of stores. We can compute the 1 plus four-year cumulative growth in number of stores from 1998 to 2002 as the product of quantities (1 + one-year growth rate). We arrive at the same result as when we divide the ending number of stores, 4,036, by the beginning number of stores, 5,382:

$$\frac{4{,}036}{5{,}382} = \left(\frac{5{,}023}{5{,}382}\right)\left(\frac{5{,}129}{5{,}023}\right)\left(\frac{4{,}614}{5{,}129}\right)\left(\frac{4{,}036}{4{,}614}\right)$$
$$= (1+g_1)(1+g_2)(1+g_3)(1+g_4)$$
$$0.749907 = (0.933296)(1.021103)(0.899591)(0.874729)$$

The right-hand side of the equation is the product of 1 plus the one-year growth rate in number of stores operated for each year. Recall that, using Equation 14, we took the fourth root of 4,036/5,382 = 0.749907. In effect, we were solving for the single value of g which, when compounded over four periods, gives the correct product of 1 plus the one-year growth rates.[7]

In conclusion, we do not need to compute intermediate growth rates as in Table 4 to solve for a compound growth rate g. Sometimes, however, the intermediate growth rates are interesting or informative. For example, during one year (2000), Limited Brands increased its number of stores. We can also analyze the variability in growth rates when we conduct an analysis as in Table 4. How did Limited Brands maintain approximately the same revenues during the period although it operated increasingly fewer stores? Elsewhere in Limited Brands' disclosures, the company noted that its sales per average selling square foot increased during the period.

The compound growth rate is an excellent summary measure of growth over multiple time periods. In our Limited Brands example, the compound growth rate of –6.9 percent is the single growth rate that, when added to 1, compounded over four years, and multiplied by the 1998 number of stores operated, yields the 2002 number of stores operated.

7.2 Solving for the Number of Periods

In this section, we demonstrate how to solve for the number of periods given present value, future value, and interest or growth rates.

Example 19

The Number of Annual Compounding Periods Needed for an Investment to Reach a Specific Value

You are interested in determining how long it will take an investment of €10,000,000 to double in value. The current interest rate is 7 percent compounded annually. How many years will it take €10,000,000 to double to €20,000,000?

Solution:

Use Equation 2, $FV_N = PV(1 + r)^N$, to solve for the number of periods, N, as follows:

$$(1+r)^N = FV_N/PV = 2$$
$$N \ln(1+r) = \ln(2)$$
$$N = \ln(2)/\ln(1+r)$$
$$= \ln(2)/\ln(1.07) = 10.24$$

With an interest rate of 7 percent, it will take approximately 10 years for the initial €10,000,000 investment to grow to €20,000,000. Solving for N in the expression $(1.07)^N = 2.0$ requires taking the natural logarithm of both sides and using the rule that $\ln(x^N) = N \ln(x)$. Generally, we find that $N = [\ln(FV/PV)]/\ln(1 + r)$. Here, $N = \ln(€20,000,000/ €10,000,000)/\ln(1.07) = \ln(2)/\ln(1.07) = 10.24$.[8]

---

7 The compound growth rate that we calculate here is an example of a geometric mean, specifically the geometric mean of the growth rates. We define the geometric mean in the reading on statistical concepts.
8 To quickly approximate the number of periods, practitioners sometimes use an ad hoc rule called the **Rule of 72**: Divide 72 by the stated interest rate to get the approximate number of years it would take to double an investment at the interest rate. Here, the approximation gives $72/7 = 10.3$ years. The Rule of 72 is loosely based on the observation that it takes 12 years to double an amount at a 6 percent interest rate, giving $6 \times 12 = 72$. At a 3 percent rate, one would guess it would take twice as many years, $3 \times 24 = 72$.

7.3 Solving for the Size of Annuity Payments

In this section, we discuss how to solve for annuity payments. Mortgages, auto loans, and retirement savings plans are classic examples of applications of annuity formulas.

Example 20

The Annuity Payments Needed to Reach a Future Value with Monthly Compounding

You are planning to purchase a $120,000 house by making a down payment of $20,000 and borrowing the remainder with a 30-year fixed-rate mortgage with monthly payments. The first payment is due at $t = 1$. Current mortgage interest rates are quoted at 8 percent with monthly compounding. What will your monthly mortgage payments be?

Solution:

The bank will determine the mortgage payments such that at the stated periodic interest rate, the present value of the payments will be equal to the amount borrowed (in this case, $100,000). With this fact in mind, we can use Equation 11,

$$PV = A \left[\frac{1 - \dfrac{1}{(1+r)^N}}{r} \right], \text{ to solve for the annuity amount, } A, \text{ as the present value}$$

divided by the present value annuity factor:

$$PV = \$100,000$$
$$r_s = 8\% = 0.08$$
$$m = 12$$
$$r_s/m = 0.08/12 = 0.006667$$
$$N = 30$$
$$mN = 12 \times 30 = 360$$

$$\text{Present value annuity factor} = \frac{1 - \dfrac{1}{\left[1 + (r_s/m)\right]^{mN}}}{r_s/m} = \frac{1 - \dfrac{1}{(1.006667)^{360}}}{0.006667}$$

$$= 136.283494$$

$$A = PV/\text{Present value annuity factor}$$
$$= \$100,000/136.283494$$
$$= \$733.76$$

The amount borrowed, $100,000, is equivalent to 360 monthly payments of $733.76 with a stated interest rate of 8 percent. The mortgage problem is a relatively straightforward application of finding a level annuity payment.

Next, we turn to a retirement-planning problem. This problem illustrates the complexity of the situation in which an individual wants to retire with a specified retirement income. Over the course of a life cycle, the individual may be able to save only a small amount during the early years but then may have the financial resources to save more during later years. Savings plans often involve uneven cash flows, a topic we will examine in the last part of this reading. When dealing with uneven cash flows, we take maximum advantage of the principle that dollar amounts indexed at the same point in time are additive—the **cash flow additivity principle**.

Example 21

The Projected Annuity Amount Needed to Fund a Future-Annuity Inflow

Jill Grant is 22 years old (at $t = 0$) and is planning for her retirement at age 63 (at $t = 41$). She plans to save $2,000 per year for the next 15 years ($t = 1$ to $t = 15$). She wants to have retirement income of $100,000 per year for 20 years, with the first retirement payment starting at $t = 41$. How much must Grant save each year from $t = 16$ to $t = 40$ in order to achieve her retirement goal? Assume she plans to invest in a diversified stock-and-bond mutual fund that will earn 8 percent per year on average.

Solution:

To help solve this problem, we set up the information on a time line. As Figure 8 shows, Grant will save $2,000 (an outflow) each year for Years 1 to 15. Starting in Year 41, Grant will start to draw retirement income of $100,000 per year for 20 years. In the time line, the annual savings is recorded in parentheses ($2) to show that it is an outflow. The problem is to find the savings, recorded as X, from Year 16 to Year 40.

Figure 8	Solving for Missing Annuity Payments (in Thousands)

Solving this problem involves satisfying the following relationship: the present value of savings (outflows) equals the present value of retirement income (inflows). We could bring all the dollar amounts to $t = 40$ or to $t = 15$ and solve for X.

Let us evaluate all dollar amounts at $t = 15$ (we encourage the reader to repeat the problem by bringing all cash flows to $t = 40$). As of $t = 15$, the first payment of X will be one period away (at $t = 16$). Thus we can value the stream of Xs using the formula for the present value of an ordinary annuity.

This problem involves three series of level cash flows. The basic idea is that the present value of the retirement income must equal the present value of Grant's savings. Our strategy requires the following steps:

1. Find the future value of the savings of $2,000 per year and index it at $t = 15$. This value tells us how much Grant will have saved.

2. Find the present value of the retirement income at $t = 15$. This value tells us how much Grant needs to meet her retirement goals (as of $t = 15$). Two substeps are necessary. First, calculate the present value of the annuity of $100,000 per year at $t = 40$. Use the formula for the present value of an annuity. (Note that the present value is indexed at $t = 40$ because the first payment is at $t = 41$.) Next, discount the present value back to $t = 15$ (a total of 25 periods).

3. Now compute the difference between the amount Grant has saved (Step 1) and the amount she needs to meet her retirement goals (Step 2). Her savings from $t = 16$ to $t = 40$ must have a present value equal to the difference between the future value of her savings and the present value of her retirement income.

Our goal is to determine the amount Grant should save in each of the 25 years from $t = 16$ to $t = 40$. We start by bringing the $2,000 savings to $t = 15$, as follows:

$$A = \$2,000$$
$$r = 8\% = 0.08$$
$$N = 15$$

$$FV = A\left[\frac{(1+r)^N - 1}{r}\right]$$

$$= \$2,000\left[\frac{(1.08)^{15} - 1}{0.08}\right]$$

$$= \$2,000(27.152114)$$

$$= \$54,304.23$$

At $t = 15$, Grant's initial savings will have grown to $54,304.23.

Now we need to know the value of Grant's retirement income at $t = 15$. As stated earlier, computing the retirement present value requires two substeps. First, find the present value at $t = 40$ with the formula in Equation 11; second, discount this present value back to $t = 15$. Now we can find the retirement income present value at $t = 40$:

$$A = \$100,000$$
$$r = 8\% = 0.08$$
$$N = 20$$

$$PV = A\left[\frac{1 - \dfrac{1}{(1+r)^N}}{r}\right]$$

$$= \$100,000\left[\frac{1 - \dfrac{1}{(1.08)^{20}}}{0.08}\right]$$

$$= \$100,000(9.818147)$$

$$= \$981,814.74$$

The present value amount is as of $t = 40$, so we must now discount it back as a lump sum to $t = 15$:

$$FV_N = \$981,814.74$$
$$N = 25$$
$$r = 8\% = 0.08$$

$$PV = FV_N(1+r)^{-N}$$

$$= \$981,814.74(1.08)^{-25}$$

$$= \$981,814.74(0.146018)$$

$$= \$143,362.53$$

Now recall that Grant will have saved $54,304.23 by $t = 15$. Therefore, in present value terms, the annuity from $t = 16$ to $t = 40$ must equal the difference between the amount already saved ($54,304.23) and the amount required for retirement ($143,362.53). This amount is equal to $143,362.53 − $54,304.23 = $89,058.30. Therefore, we must now find the annuity payment, A, from $t = 16$

to $t = 40$ that has a present value of \$89,058.30. We find the annuity payment as follows:

$$PV = \$89{,}058.30$$
$$r = 8\% = 0.08$$
$$N = 25$$

$$\text{Present value annuity factor} = \left[\frac{1 - \dfrac{1}{(1+r)^N}}{r}\right]$$

$$= \left[\frac{1 - \dfrac{1}{(1.08)^{25}}}{0.08}\right]$$

$$= 10.674776$$

$$A = PV/\text{Present value annuity factor}$$
$$= \$89{,}058.30/10.674776$$
$$= \$8{,}342.87$$

Grant will need to increase her savings to \$8,342.87 per year from $t = 16$ to $t = 40$ to meet her retirement goal of having a fund equal to \$981,814.74 after making her last payment at $t = 40$.

7.4 Review of Present and Future Value Equivalence

As we have demonstrated, finding present and future values involves moving amounts of money to different points on a time line. These operations are possible because present value and future value are equivalent measures separated in time. Table 5 illustrates this equivalence; it lists the timing of five cash flows, their present values at $t = 0$, and their future values at $t = 5$.

To interpret Table 5, start with the third column, which shows the present values. Note that each \$1,000 cash payment is discounted back the appropriate number of periods to find the present value at $t = 0$. The present value of \$4,329.48 is exactly equivalent to the series of cash flows. This information illustrates an important point: A lump sum can actually generate an annuity. If we place a lump sum in an account that earns the stated interest rate for all periods, we can generate an annuity that is equivalent to the lump sum. Amortized loans, such as mortgages and car loans, are examples of this principle.

Table 5	The Equivalence of Present and Future Values		
Time	**Cash Flow ($)**	**Present Value at $t = 0$**	**Future Value at $t = 5$**
1	1,000	$\$1{,}000(1.05)^{-1}$ = \$952.38	$\$1{,}000(1.05)^{4}$ = \$1,215.51
2	1,000	$\$1{,}000(1.05)^{-2}$ = \$907.03	$\$1{,}000(1.05)^{3}$ = \$1,157.63
3	1,000	$\$1{,}000(1.05)^{-3}$ = \$863.84	$\$1{,}000(1.05)^{2}$ = \$1,102.50
4	1,000	$\$1{,}000(1.05)^{-4}$ = \$822.70	$\$1{,}000(1.05)^{1}$ = \$1,050.00
5	1,000	$\$1{,}000(1.05)^{-5}$ = \$783.53	$\$1{,}000(1.05)^{0}$ = \$1,000.00
		Sum: \$4,329.48	Sum: \$5,525.64

To see how a lump sum can fund an annuity, assume that we place $4,329.48 in the bank today at 5 percent interest. We can calculate the size of the annuity payments by using Equation 11. Solving for A, we find

$$A = \frac{PV}{\frac{1-\left[1/(1+r)^N\right]}{r}}$$
$$= \frac{\$4,329.48}{\frac{1-\left[1/(1.05)^5\right]}{0.05}}$$
$$= \$1,000$$

Table 6 shows how the initial investment of $4,329.48 can actually generate five $1,000 withdrawals over the next five years.

To interpret Table 6, start with an initial present value of $4,329.48 at $t = 0$. From $t = 0$ to $t = 1$, the initial investment earns 5 percent interest, generating a future value of $4,329.48(1.05) = $4,545.95. We then withdraw $1,000 from our account, leaving $4,545.95 − $1,000 = $3,545.95 (the figure reported in the last column for time period 1). In the next period, we earn one year's worth of interest and then make a $1,000 withdrawal. After the fourth withdrawal, we have $952.38, which earns 5 percent. This amount then grows to $1,000 during the year, just enough for us to make the last withdrawal. Thus the initial present value, when invested at 5 percent for five years, generates the $1,000 five-year ordinary annuity. The present value of the initial investment is exactly equivalent to the annuity.

Now we can look at how future value relates to annuities. In Table 5, we reported that the future value of the annuity was $5,525.64. We arrived at this figure by compounding the first $1,000 payment forward four periods, the second $1,000 forward three periods, and so on. We then added the five future amounts at $t = 5$. The annuity is equivalent to $5,525.64 at $t = 5$ and $4,329.48 at $t = 0$. These two dollar measures are thus equivalent. We can verify the equivalence by finding the present value of $5,525.64, which is $5,525.64 × (1.05)^{-5} = $4,329.48. We found this result above when we showed that a lump sum can generate an annuity.

Table 6	How an Initial Present Value Funds an Annuity			
Time Period	Amount Available at the Beginning of the Time Period ($)	Ending Amount before Withdrawal		Withdrawal ($)	Amount Available after Withdrawal ($)
1	4,329.48	$4,329.48(1.05) =	$4,545.95	1,000	3,545.95
2	3,545.95	$3,545.95(1.05) =	$3,723.25	1,000	2,723.25
3	2,723.25	$2,723.25(1.05) =	$2,859.41	1,000	1,859.41
4	1,859.41	$1,859.41(1.05) =	$1,952.38	1,000	952.38
5	952.38	$952.38(1.05) =	$1,000	1,000	0

To summarize what we have learned so far: A lump sum can be seen as equivalent to an annuity, and an annuity can be seen as equivalent to its future value. Thus present values, future values, and a series of cash flows can all be considered equivalent as long as they are indexed at the same point in time.

7.5 The Cash Flow Additivity Principle

The cash flow additivity principle—the idea that amounts of money indexed at the same point in time are additive—is one of the most important concepts in time value of money mathematics. We have already mentioned and used this principle; this section provides a reference example for it.

Consider the two series of cash flows shown on the time line in Figure 9. The series are denoted A and B. If we assume that the annual interest rate is 2 percent, we can find the future value of each series of cash flows as follows. Series A's future value is $100(1.02) + \$100 = \$202$. Series B's future value is $200(1.02) + \$200 = \$404$. The future value of (A + B) is $202 + \$404 = \$606$ by the method we have used up to this point. The alternative way to find the future value is to add the cash flows of each series, A and B (call it A + B), and then find the future value of the combined cash flow, as shown in Figure 9.

The third time line in Figure 9 shows the combined series of cash flows. Series A has a cash flow of $100 at $t = 1$, and Series B has a cash flow of $200 at $t = 1$. The combined series thus has a cash flow of $300 at $t = 1$. We can similarly calculate the cash flow of the combined series at $t = 2$. The future value of the combined series (A + B) is $300(1.02) + \$300 = \$606$—the same result we found when we added the future values of each series.

The additivity and equivalence principles also appear in another common situation. Suppose cash flows are $4 at the end of the first year and $24 (actually separate payments of $4 and $20) at the end of the second year. Rather than finding present values of the first year's $4 and the second year's $24, we can treat this situation as a $4 annuity for two years and a second-year $20 lump sum. If the discount rate were 6 percent, the $4 annuity would have a present value of $7.33 and the $20 lump sum a present value of $17.80, for a total of $25.13.

Figure 9	The Additivity of Two Series of Cash Flows

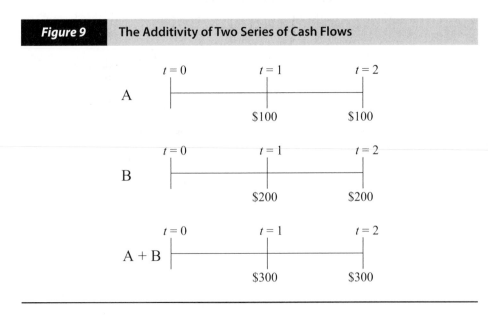

SUMMARY

In this reading, we have explored a foundation topic in investment mathematics, the time value of money. We have developed and reviewed the following concepts for use in financial applications:

- The interest rate, r, is the required rate of return; r is also called the discount rate or opportunity cost.

- An interest rate can be viewed as the sum of the real risk-free interest rate and a set of premiums that compensate lenders for risk: an inflation premium, a default risk premium, a liquidity premium, and a maturity premium.

- The future value, FV, is the present value, PV, times the future value factor, $(1 + r)^N$.

- The interest rate, r, makes current and future currency amounts equivalent based on their time value.

- The stated annual interest rate is a quoted interest rate that does not account for compounding within the year.

- The periodic rate is the quoted interest rate per period; it equals the stated annual interest rate divided by the number of compounding periods per year.

- The effective annual rate is the amount by which a unit of currency will grow in a year with interest on interest included.

- An annuity is a finite set of level sequential cash flows.

- There are two types of annuities, the annuity due and the ordinary annuity. The annuity due has a first cash flow that occurs immediately; the ordinary annuity has a first cash flow that occurs one period from the present (indexed at $t = 1$).

- On a time line, we can index the present as 0 and then display equally spaced hash marks to represent a number of periods into the future. This representation allows us to index how many periods away each cash flow will be paid.

- Annuities may be handled in a similar fashion as single payments if we use annuity factors instead of single-payment factors.

- The present value, PV, is the future value, FV, times the present value factor, $(1 + r)^{-N}$.

- The present value of a perpetuity is A/r, where A is the periodic payment to be received forever.

- It is possible to calculate an unknown variable, given the other relevant variables in time value of money problems.

- The cash flow additivity principle can be used to solve problems with uneven cash flows by combining single payments and annuities.

PRACTICE PROBLEMS FOR READING 5

1. The table below gives current information on the interest rates for two two-year and two eight-year maturity investments. The table also gives the maturity, liquidity, and default risk characteristics of a new investment possibility (Investment 3). All investments promise only a single payment (a payment at maturity). Assume that premiums relating to inflation, liquidity, and default risk are constant across all time horizons.

Investment	Maturity (in Years)	Liquidity	Default Risk	Interest Rate (%)
1	2	High	Low	2.0
2	2	Low	Low	2.5
3	7	Low	Low	r_3
4	8	High	Low	4.0
5	8	Low	High	6.5

Based on the information in the above table, address the following:

A. Explain the difference between the interest rates on Investment 1 and Investment 2.

B. Estimate the default risk premium.

C. Calculate upper and lower limits for the interest rate on Investment 3, r_3.

2. A client has a $5 million portfolio and invests 5 percent of it in a money market fund projected to earn 3 percent annually. Estimate the value of this portion of his portfolio after seven years.

3. A client invests $500,000 in a bond fund projected to earn 7 percent annually. Estimate the value of her investment after 10 years.

4. For liquidity purposes, a client keeps $100,000 in a bank account. The bank quotes a stated annual interest rate of 7 percent. The bank's service representative explains that the stated rate is the rate one would earn if one were to cash out rather than invest the interest payments. How much will your client have in his account at the end of one year, assuming no additions or withdrawals, using the following types of compounding?

A. Quarterly.

B. Monthly.

C. Continuous.

5. A bank quotes a rate of 5.89 percent with an effective annual rate of 6.05 percent. Does the bank use annual, quarterly, or monthly compounding?

6. A bank pays a stated annual interest rate of 8 percent. What is the effective annual rate using the following types of compounding?

A. Quarterly.

B. Monthly.

C. Continuous.

7. A couple plans to set aside $20,000 per year in a conservative portfolio projected to earn 7 percent a year. If they make their first savings contribution one year from now, how much will they have at the end of 20 years?

8. Two years from now, a client will receive the first of three annual payments of $20,000 from a small business project. If she can earn 9 percent annually on her investments and plans to retire in six years, how much will the three business project payments be worth at the time of her retirement?

9. To cover the first year's total college tuition payments for his two children, a father will make a $75,000 payment five years from now. How much will he need to invest today to meet his first tuition goal if the investment earns 6 percent annually?

10. A client has agreed to invest €100,000 one year from now in a business planning to expand, and she has decided to set aside the funds today in a bank account that pays 7 percent compounded quarterly. How much does she need to set aside?

11. A client can choose between receiving 10 annual $100,000 retirement payments, starting one year from today, or receiving a lump sum today. Knowing that he can invest at a rate of 5 percent annually, he has decided to take the lump sum. What lump sum today will be equivalent to the future annual payments?

12. A perpetual preferred stock position pays quarterly dividends of $1,000 indefinitely (forever). If an investor has a required rate of return of 12 percent per year compounded quarterly on this type of investment, how much should he be willing to pay for this dividend stream?

13. At retirement, a client has two payment options: a 20-year annuity at €50,000 per year starting after one year or a lump sum of €500,000 today. If the client's required rate of return on retirement fund investments is 6 percent per year, which plan has the higher present value and by how much?

14. You are considering investing in two different instruments. The first instrument will pay nothing for three years, but then it will pay $20,000 per year for four years. The second instrument will pay $20,000 for three years and $30,000 in the fourth year. All payments are made at year-end. If your required rate of return on these investments is 8 percent annually, what should you be willing to pay for:

   A. The first instrument?

   B. The second instrument (use the formula for a four-year annuity)?

15. Suppose you plan to send your daughter to college in three years. You expect her to earn two-thirds of her tuition payment in scholarship money, so you estimate that your payments will be $10,000 a year for four years. To estimate whether you have set aside enough money, you ignore possible inflation in tuition payments and assume that you can earn 8 percent annually on your investments. How much should you set aside now to cover these payments?

16. A client is confused about two terms on some certificate-of-deposit rates quoted at his bank in the United States. You explain that the stated annual interest rate is an annual rate that does not take into account compounding within a year. The rate his bank calls APY (annual percentage yield) is the effective annual rate taking into account compounding. The bank's customer service representative mentioned monthly compounding, with $1,000 becoming $1,061.68 at the end of a year. To prepare to explain the terms to your client, calculate the stated annual interest rate that the bank must be quoting.

17. A client seeking liquidity sets aside €35,000 in a bank account today. The account pays 5 percent compounded monthly. Because the client is concerned about the fact that deposit insurance covers the account for only up to €100,000, calculate how many months it will take to reach that amount.

18. A client plans to send a child to college for four years starting 18 years from now. Having set aside money for tuition, she decides to plan for room and board also. She estimates these costs at $20,000 per year, payable at the beginning of each year, by the time her child goes to college. If she starts next year and makes 17 payments into a savings account paying 5 percent annually, what annual payments must she make?

19. A couple plans to pay their child's college tuition for 4 years starting 18 years from now. The current annual cost of college is C$7,000, and they expect this cost to rise at an annual rate of 5 percent. In their planning, they assume that they can earn 6 percent annually. How much must they put aside each year, starting next year, if they plan to make 17 equal payments?

20. You are analyzing the last five years of earnings per share data for a company. The figures are $4.00, $4.50, $5.00, $6.00, and $7.00. At what compound annual rate did EPS grow during these years?

21. An analyst expects that a company's net sales will double and the company's net income will triple over the next five-year period starting now. Based on the analyst's expectations, which of the following *best* describes the expected compound annual growth?

    A. Net sales will grow 15% annually and net income will grow 25% annually.

    B. Net sales will grow 20% annually and net income will grow 40% annually.

    C. Net sales will grow 25% annually and net income will grow 50% annually.

SOLUTIONS FOR READING 5

1. **A.** Investment 2 is identical to Investment 1 except that Investment 2 has low liquidity. The difference between the interest rate on Investment 2 and Investment 1 is 0.5 percentage point. This amount represents the liquidity premium, which represents compensation for the risk of loss relative to an investment's fair value if the investment needs to be converted to cash quickly.

    B. To estimate the default risk premium, find the two investments that have the same maturity but different levels of default risk. Both Investments 4 and 5 have a maturity of eight years. Investment 5, however, has low liquidity and thus bears a liquidity premium. The difference between the interest rates of Investments 5 and 4 is 2.5 percentage points. The liquidity premium is 0.5 percentage point (from Part A). This leaves 2.5 – 0.5 = 2.0 percentage points that must represent a default risk premium reflecting Investment 5's high default risk.

    C. Investment 3 has liquidity risk and default risk comparable to Investment 2, but with its longer time to maturity, Investment 3 should have a higher maturity premium. The interest rate on Investment 3, r_3, should thus be above 2.5 percent (the interest rate on Investment 2). If the liquidity of Investment 3 were high, Investment 3 would match Investment 4 except for Investment 3's shorter maturity. We would then conclude that Investment 3's interest rate should be less than the interest rate on Investment 4, which is 4 percent. In contrast to Investment 4, however, Investment 3 has low liquidity. It is possible that the interest rate on Investment 3 exceeds that of Investment 4 despite 3's shorter maturity, depending on the relative size of the liquidity and maturity premiums. However, we expect r_3 to be less than 4.5 percent, the expected interest rate on Investment 4 if it had low liquidity. Thus 2.5 percent $< r_3 <$ 4.5 percent.

2. **i.** Draw a time line.

    ii. Identify the problem as the future value of a lump sum.

    iii. Use the formula for the future value of a lump sum.

    $$PV = 0.05 \times \$5,000,000 = \$250,000$$
    $$FV_N = PV(1+r)^N$$
    $$= \$250,000(1.03)^7$$
    $$= \$307,468.47$$

    The future value in seven years of $250,000 received today is $307,468.47 if the interest rate is 3 percent compounded annually.

3. **i.** Draw a time line.

ii. Identify the problem as the future value of a lump sum.

iii. Use the formula for the future value of a lump sum.

$$FV_N = PV(1+r)^N$$
$$= \$500,000(1.07)^{10}$$
$$= \$983,575.68$$

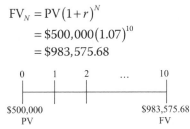

Your client will have $983,575.68 in 10 years if she invests $500,000 today and earns 7 percent annually.

4. A. To solve this problem, take the following steps:

i. Draw a time line and recognize that a year consists of four quarterly periods.

ii. Recognize the problem as the future value of a lump sum with quarterly compounding.

iii. Use the formula for the future value of a lump sum with periodic compounding, where m is the frequency of compounding within a year and N is the number of years.

$$FV_N = PV\left(1+\frac{r_s}{m}\right)^{mN}$$
$$= \$100,000\left(1+\frac{0.07}{4}\right)^{4(1)}$$
$$= \$107,185.90$$

iv. As an alternative to Step iii, use a financial calculator. Most of the equations in this reading can be solved using a financial calculator. Calculators vary in the exact keystrokes required (see your calculator's manual for the appropriate keystrokes), but the following table illustrates the basic variables and algorithms. Remember, however, that a financial calculator is only a shortcut way of performing the mechanics and is not a substitute for setting up the problem or knowing which equation is appropriate.

Time Value of Money Variable	Notation Used on Most Calculators	Numerical Value for This Problem
Number of periods or payments	N	4
Interest rate per period	%i	7/4
Present value	PV	$100,000
Future value	FV **compute**	X
Payment size	PMT	n/a (= 0)

In summary, your client will have $107,185.90 in one year if he deposits $100,000 today in a bank account paying a stated interest rate of 7 percent compounded quarterly.

B. To solve this problem, take the following steps:

i. Draw a time line and recognize that with monthly compounding, we need to express all values in monthly terms. Therefore, we have 12 periods.

ii. Recognize the problem as the future value of a lump sum with monthly compounding.

iii. Use the formula for the future value of a lump sum with periodic compounding, where m is the frequency of compounding within a year and N is the number of years.

$$FV_N = PV\left(1 + \frac{r_s}{m}\right)^{mN}$$

$$= \$100,000\left(1 + \frac{0.07}{12}\right)^{12(1)}$$

$$= \$107,229.01$$

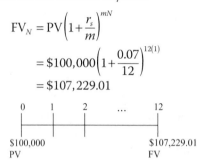

iv. As an alternative to Step iii, use a financial calculator.

Notation Used on Most Calculators	Numerical Value for This Problem
N	12
$\%i$	7/12
PV	$100,000
FV **compute**	X
PMT	n/a (= 0)

Using your calculator's financial functions, verify that the future value, X, equals $107,229.01.

In summary, your client will have $107,229.01 at the end of one year if he deposits $100,000 today in his bank account paying a stated interest rate of 7 percent compounded monthly.

C. To solve this problem, take the following steps:

i. Draw a time line and recognize that with continuous compounding, we need to use the formula for the future value with continuous compounding.

ii. Use the formula for the future value with continuous compounding (N is the number of years in the expression).

$$FV_N = PVe^{r_s N}$$

$$= \$100,000e^{0.07(1)}$$

$$= \$107,250.82$$

The notation $e^{0.07(1)}$ is the exponential function, where e is a number approximately equal to 2.718282. On most calculators, this function is on the key marked e^x. First calculate the value of X. In this problem, X is 0.07(1) = 0.07. Key 0.07 into the calculator. Next press the e^x key. You should get 1.072508. If you cannot get this figure, check your calculator's manual.

In summary, your client will have $107,250.82 at the end of one year if he deposits $100,000 today in his bank account paying a stated interest rate of 7 percent compounded continuously.

5. Stated annual interest rate = 5.89 percent.

Effective annual rate on bank deposits = 6.05 percent.

$$1 + \text{EAR} = \left(1 + \frac{\text{Stated interest rate}}{m}\right)^m$$

$$1.0605 = \left(1 + \frac{0.0589}{m}\right)^m$$

For annual compounding, with $m = 1$, $1.0605 \neq 1.0589$.

For quarterly compounding, with $m = 4$, $1.0605 \neq 1.060214$.

For monthly compounding, with $m = 12$, $1.0605 \approx 1.060516$.

Hence, the bank uses monthly compounding.

6. **A.** Use the formula for the effective annual rate.

Effective annual rate = $(1 + \text{Periodic interest rate})^m - 1$

$$\left(1 + \frac{0.08}{4}\right)^{4(1)} - 1 = 0.0824 \text{ or } 8.24\%$$

B. Use the formula for the effective annual rate.

Effective annual rate = $(1 + \text{Periodic interest rate})^m - 1$

$$\left(1 + \frac{0.08}{12}\right)^{12(1)} - 1 = 0.0830 \text{ or } 8.30\%$$

C. Use the formula for the effective annual rate with continuous compounding.

Effective annual rate = $e^{r_s} - 1$

$$e^{0.08} - 1 = 0.0833 \text{ or } 8.33\%$$

7. **i.** Draw a time line.

ii. Identify the problem as the future value of an annuity.

iii. Use the formula for the future value of an annuity.

$$FV_N = A\left[\frac{(1+r)^N - 1}{r}\right]$$

$$= \$20,000\left[\frac{(1+0.07)^{20} - 1}{0.07}\right]$$

$$= \$819,909.85$$

FV = $819,909.85

iv. Alternatively, use a financial calculator.

Notation Used on Most Calculators	Numerical Value for This Problem
N	20
$\%i$	7
PV	n/a (=0)
FV **compute**	X
PMT	$20,000

Enter 20 for N, the number of periods. Enter 7 for the interest rate and 20,000 for the payment size. The present value is not needed, so enter 0. Calculate the future value. Verify that you get $819,909.85 to make sure you have mastered your calculator's keystrokes.

In summary, if the couple sets aside $20,000 each year (starting next year), they will have $819,909.85 in 20 years if they earn 7 percent annually.

8. **i.** Draw a time line.

ii. Recognize the problem as the future value of a delayed annuity. Delaying the payments requires two calculations.

iii. Use the formula for the future value of an annuity (Equation 7).

$$FV_N = A\left[\frac{(1+r)^N - 1}{r}\right]$$

to bring the three $20,000 payments to an equivalent lump sum of $65,562.00 four years from today.

Notation Used on Most Calculators	Numerical Value for This Problem
N	3
$\%i$	9
PV	n/a (=0)
FV **compute**	X
PMT	$20,000

iv. Use the formula for the future value of a lump sum (Equation 2), $FV_N = PV(1 + r)^N$, to bring the single lump sum of $65,562.00 to an equivalent lump sum of $77,894.21 six years from today.

Notation Used on Most Calculators	Numerical Value for This Problem
N	2
$\%i$	9
PV	$65,562.00
FV **compute**	X
PMT	n/a (=0)

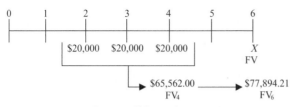

In summary, your client will have $77,894.21 in six years if she receives three yearly payments of $20,000 starting in Year 2 and can earn 9 percent annually on her investments.

9. i. Draw a time line.

ii. Identify the problem as the present value of a lump sum.

iii. Use the formula for the present value of a lump sum.

$$PV = FV_N (1+r)^{-N}$$
$$= \$75,000(1+0.06)^{-5}$$
$$= \$56,044.36$$

In summary, the father will need to invest $56,044.36 today in order to have $75,000 in five years if his investments earn 6 percent annually.

10. i. Draw a time line and recognize that a year consists of four quarterly periods.

ii. Recognize the problem as the present value of a lump sum with quarterly compounding.

iii. Use the formula for the present value of a lump sum with periodic compounding, where m is the frequency of compounding within a year and N is the number of years.

$$PV = FV_N \left(1+\frac{r_s}{m}\right)^{-mN}$$
$$= €100,000\left(1+\frac{0.07}{4}\right)^{-4(1)}$$
$$= €93,295.85$$

iv. Alternatively, use a financial calculator.

Notation Used on Most Calculators	Numerical Value for This Problem
N	4
$\%i$	7/4
PV **compute**	X
FV	€100,000
PMT	n/a (=0)

Use your calculator's financial functions to verify that the present value, *X*, equals €93,295.85.

In summary, your client will have to deposit €93,295.85 today to have €100,000 in one year if her bank account pays 7 percent compounded quarterly.

11. i. Draw a time line for the 10 annual payments.

  ii. Identify the problem as the present value of an annuity.

  iii. Use the formula for the present value of an annuity.

$$PV = A\left[\frac{1 - \frac{1}{(1+r)^N}}{r}\right]$$

$$= \$100,000\left[\frac{1 - \frac{1}{(1+0.05)^{10}}}{0.05}\right]$$

$$= \$772,173.49$$

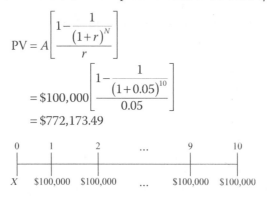

PV = $772,173.49

  iv. Alternatively, use a financial calculator.

Notation Used on Most Calculators	Numerical Value for This Problem
N	10
%i	5
PV **compute**	X
FV	n/a (=0)
PMT	$100,000

In summary, the present value of 10 payments of $100,000 is $772,173.49 if the first payment is received in one year and the rate is 5 percent compounded annually. Your client should accept no less than this amount for his lump sum payment.

12. i. Draw a time line.

  ii. Recognize the problem as the present value of a perpetuity.

  iii. Use the formula for the present value of a perpetuity.

$$PV = \left(\frac{A}{r}\right) = \left(\frac{\$1,000}{0.03}\right) = \$33,333.33$$

PV = $33,333.33

The investor will have to pay $33,333.33 today to receive $1,000 per quarter forever if his required rate of return is 3 percent per quarter (12 percent per year).

13. **i.** Draw a time line to compare the lump sum and the annuity.

    ii. Recognize that we have to compare the present values of a lump sum and an annuity.

    iii. Use the formula for the present value of an annuity (Equation 11).

$$PV = €50,000 \left[\frac{1 - \dfrac{1}{(1.06)^{20}}}{0.06} \right] = €573,496$$

Notation Used on Most Calculators	Numerical Value for This Problem
N	20
$\%i$	6
PV **compute**	X
FV	n/a (=0)
PMT	$50,000

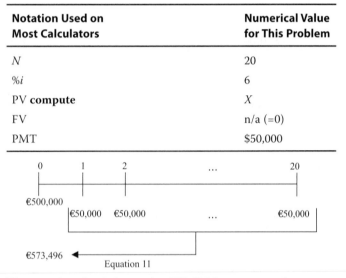

The annuity plan is better by €73,496 in present value terms (€573,496 − €500,000).

14. A. To evaluate the first instrument, take the following steps:

    i. Draw a time line.

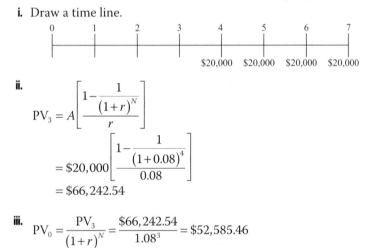

    ii.

$$PV_3 = A \left[\frac{1 - \dfrac{1}{(1+r)^N}}{r} \right]$$

$$= \$20,000 \left[\frac{1 - \dfrac{1}{(1+0.08)^4}}{0.08} \right]$$

$$= \$66,242.54$$

    iii. $$PV_0 = \frac{PV_3}{(1+r)^N} = \frac{\$66,242.54}{1.08^3} = \$52,585.46$$

You should be willing to pay $52,585.46 for this instrument.

B. To evaluate the second instrument, take the following steps:

   i. Draw a time line.

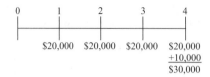

$20,000 $20,000 $20,000 $20,000
                            +10,000
                             $30,000

The time line shows that this instrument can be analyzed as an ordinary annuity of $20,000 with four payments (valued in Step ii below) and a $10,000 payment to be received at $t = 4$ (valued in Step iii below).

   ii.

$$PV = A\left[\frac{1-\frac{1}{(1+r)^N}}{r}\right]$$

$$= \$20,000\left[\frac{1-\frac{1}{(1+0.08)^4}}{0.08}\right]$$

$$= \$66,242.54$$

   iii. $$PV = \frac{FV_4}{(1+r)^N} = \frac{\$10,000}{(1+0.08)^4} = \$7,350.30$$

   iv. Total = $66,242.54 + $7,350.30 = $73,592.84

   You should be willing to pay $73,592.84 for this instrument.

15. **i.** Draw a time line.

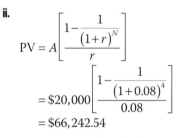

X
PV $10,000 $10,000 $10,000 $10,000

   ii. Recognize the problem as a delayed annuity. Delaying the payments requires two calculations.

   iii. Use the formula for the present value of an annuity (Equation 11).

$$PV = A\left[\frac{1-\frac{1}{(1+r)^N}}{r}\right]$$

to bring the four payments of $10,000 back to a single equivalent lump sum of $33,121.27 at $t = 2$. Note that we use $t = 2$ because the first annuity payment is then one period away, giving an ordinary annuity.

Notation Used on Most Calculators	Numerical Value for This Problem
N	4
%i	8
PV **compute**	X
PMT	$10,000

   iv. Then use the formula for the present value of a lump sum (Equation 8), $PV = FV_N(1 + r)^{-N}$, to bring back the single payment of $33,121.27 (at $t = 2$) to an equivalent single payment of $28,396.15 (at $t = 0$).

Notation Used on Most Calculators	Numerical Value for This Problem
N	2
%i	8
PV compute	X
FV	$33,121.27
PMT	n/a (=0)

In summary, you should set aside $28,396.15 today to cover four payments of $10,000 starting in three years if your investments earn a rate of 8 percent annually.

16. i. Draw a time line.

ii. Recognize the problem as the future value of a lump sum with monthly compounding.

iii. Use the formula for the future value of a lump sum with periodic compounding

$$FV_N = PV[1 + (r_s/m)]^{mN}$$

and solve for r_s, the stated annual interest rate:

$$\$1,061.68 = \$1,000[1 + (r_s/12)]^{12(1)} \text{ so } r_s = 0.06$$

iv. Alternatively, use a financial calculator to solve for r.

Notation Used on Most Calculators	Numerical Value for This Problem
N	12
%i compute	X
PV	$1,000
FV	$1,061.68
PMT	n/a (=0)

Use your calculator's financial functions to verify that the stated interest rate of the savings account is 6 percent with monthly compounding.

17. i. Draw a time line.

```
0        1        2      ...      X
|--------|--------|---------------|
€35,000                      €100,000
  PV                            FV
```

ii. Recognize the problem as the future value of a lump sum with monthly compounding.

iii. Use the formula for the future value of a lump sum, $FV_N = PV[1 + (r_s/m)]^{mN}$, where m is the frequency of compounding within a year and N is the number of years. Solve for mN, the number of months.

$€100,000 = €35,000[1 + (0.05/12)]^{12N}$ so $12N = 252.48$ months

iv. Alternatively, use a financial calculator.

Notation Used on Most Calculators	Numerical Value for This Problem
Ncompute	X
$\%i$	5/12
PV	€35,000
FV	€100,000
PMT	n/a (=0)

Use your calculator's financial functions to verify that your client will have to wait 252.48 months to have €100,000 if he deposits €35,000 today in a bank account paying 5 percent compounded monthly. (Some calculators will give 253 months.)

18. **i.** Draw a time line.

ii. Recognize that you need to equate the values of two annuities.

iii. Equate the value of the four $20,000 payments to a single payment in Period 17 using the formula for the present value of an annuity (Equation 11), with $r = 0.05$. The present value of the college costs as of $t = 17$ is $70,919.

$$PV = \$20,000 \left[\frac{1 - \dfrac{1}{(1.05)^4}}{0.05} \right] = \$70,919$$

Notation Used on Most Calculators	Numerical Value for This Problem
N	4
$\%i$	5
PV **compute**	X
FV	n/a (=0)
PMT	$20,000

iv. Equate the value of the 17 investments of X to the amount calculated in Step iii, college costs as of $t = 17$, using the formula for the future value of an annuity (Equation 7). Then solve for X.

$$\$70,919 = \left[\frac{(1.05)^{17} - 1}{0.05} \right] = 25.840366X$$

$$X = \$2,744.50$$

Notation Used on Most Calculators	Numerical Value for This Problem
N	17
$\%i$	5
PV	n/a (=0)
FV	$70,919
PMT **compute**	X

In summary, your client will have to save $2,744.50 each year if she starts next year and makes 17 payments into a savings account paying 5 percent annually.

19. **i.** Draw a time line.

ii. Recognize that the payments in Years 18, 19, 20, and 21 are the future values of a lump sum of C$7,000 in Year 0.

iii. With $r = 5\%$, use the formula for the future value of a lump sum (Equation 2), $FV_N = PV (1 + r)^N$, four times to find the payments. These future values are shown on the time line below.

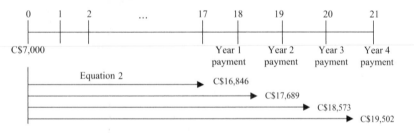

iv. Using the formula for the present value of a lump sum ($r = 6\%$), equate the four college payments to single payments as of $t = 17$ and add them together.
C$16,846$(1.06)^{-1}$ + C$17,689$(1.06)^{-2}$ + C$18,573$(1.06)^{-3}$ + C$19,502$(1.06)^{-4}$ = C$62,677

v. Equate the sum of C$62,677 at $t = 17$ to the 17 payments of X, using the formula for the future value of an annuity (Equation 7). Then solve for X.

$$C\$62,677 = X\left[\frac{(1.06)^{17} - 1}{0.06}\right] = 28.21288X$$
$$X = C\$2,221.58$$

Notation Used on Most Calculators	Numerical Value for This Problem
N	17
$\%i$	6
PV	n/a (=0)
FV	C\$62,677
PMT **compute**	X

In summary, the couple will need to put aside C\$2,221.58 each year if they start next year and make 17 equal payments.

20. To compute the compound growth rate, we only need the beginning and ending EPS values of \$4.00 and \$7.00 respectively, and use the following equation:

$$FV_N = PV(1+r)^N$$
$$7 = 4(1+r)^4$$
$$1+r = (7/4)^{1/4}$$
$$r = (7/4)^{1/4} - 1$$
$$= 0.1502 = 15.02\%$$

EPS grew at an annual rate of 15.02 percent during the four years.

21. A is correct. Using the general time value of money formula, for sales, solve for r in the equation $2 = 1 \times (1 + r)^5$. For income, solve $3 = 1 \times (1 + r)^5$. Alternatively, using a financial calculator, for sales, enter $N=5$, PV=1, PMT=0, FV=−2 and compute I/Y. For income, change the FV to −3 and again solve for I/Y. The solution for sales is 14.87%; and for income is 24.57%.

READING

Discounted Cash Flow Applications

by Richard A. DeFusco, CFA, Dennis W. McLeavey, CFA, Jerald E. Pinto, CFA, and David E. Runkle, CFA

LEARNING OUTCOMES

Mastery	The candidate should be able to:
☐	**a** calculate and interpret the net present value (NPV) and the internal rate of return (IRR) of an investment;
☐	**b** contrast the NPV rule to the IRR rule, and identify problems associated with the IRR rule;
☐	**c** calculate and interpret a holding period return (total return);
☐	**d** calculate and compare the money-weighted and time-weighted rates of return of a portfolio and evaluate the performance of portfolios based on these measures;
☐	**e** calculate and interpret the bank discount yield, holding period yield, effective annual yield, and money market yield for U.S. Treasury bills and other money market instruments;
☐	**f** convert among holding period yields, money market yields, effective annual yields, and bond equivalent yields.

INTRODUCTION

1

As investment analysts, much of our work includes evaluating transactions involving present and future cash flows. In the reading on the time value of money (TVM), we presented the mathematics needed to solve those problems and illustrated the techniques for the major problem types. In this reading we turn to applications. Analysts must master the numerous applications of TVM or discounted cash flow analysis in equity, fixed income, and derivatives analysis as they study each of those topics individually. In this reading, we present a selection of important TVM applications: net present value and internal rate of return as tools for evaluating cash flow streams, portfolio return measurement, and the calculation of money market yields. Important in themselves, these applications also introduce concepts that reappear in many other investment contexts.

The reading is organized as follows. Section 2 introduces two key TVM concepts, net present value and internal rate of return. Building on these concepts, Section 3 discusses a key topic in investment management, portfolio return measurement. Investment managers often face the task of investing funds for the short term; to understand the choices available, they need to understand the calculation of money market yields. The reading thus concludes with a discussion of that topic in Section 4.

Quantitative Methods for Investment Analysis, Second Edition, by Richard A. DeFusco, CFA, Dennis W. McLeavey, CFA, Jerald E. Pinto, CFA, and David E. Runkle, CFA. Copyright © 2004 by CFA Institute.

NET PRESENT VALUE AND INTERNAL RATE OF RETURN

In applying discounted cash flow analysis in all fields of finance, we repeatedly encounter two concepts, net present value and internal rate of return. In the following sections we present these keystone concepts.

We could explore the concepts of net present value and internal rate of return in many contexts, because their scope of application covers all areas of finance. Capital budgeting, however, can serve as a representative starting point. Capital budgeting is important not only in corporate finance but also in security analysis, because both equity and fixed income analysts must be able to assess how well managers are investing the assets of their companies. There are three chief areas of financial decision-making in most businesses. **Capital budgeting** is the allocation of funds to relatively long-range projects or investments. From the perspective of capital budgeting, a company is a portfolio of projects and investments. **Capital structure** is the choice of long-term financing for the investments the company wants to make. **Working capital management** is the management of the company's short-term assets (such as inventory) and short-term liabilities (such as money owed to suppliers).

2.1 Net Present Value and the Net Present Value Rule

Net present value (NPV) describes a way to characterize the value of an investment, and the net present value rule is a method for choosing among alternative investments. The **net present value** of an investment is the present value of its cash inflows minus the present value of its cash outflows. The word "net" in net present value refers to subtracting the present value of the investment's outflows (costs) from the present value of its inflows (benefits) to arrive at the net benefit.

The steps in computing NPV and applying the NPV rule are as follows:

1. Identify all cash flows associated with the investment—all inflows and outflows.[1]

2. Determine the appropriate discount rate or opportunity cost, r, for the investment project.[2]

3. Using that discount rate, find the present value of each cash flow. (Inflows have a positive sign and increase NPV; outflows have a negative sign and decrease NPV.)

4. Sum all present values. The sum of the present values of all cash flows (inflows and outflows) is the investment's net present value.

5. Apply the **NPV rule**: If the investment's NPV is positive, an investor should undertake it; if the NPV is negative, the investor should not undertake it. If an investor has two candidates for investment but can only invest in one (i.e., **mutually exclusive projects**), the investor should choose the candidate with the higher positive NPV.

What is the meaning of the NPV rule? In calculating the NPV of an investment proposal, we use an estimate of the opportunity cost of capital as the discount rate. The

---

1 In developing cash flow estimates, we observe two principles. First, we include only the **incremental cash flows** resulting from undertaking the project; we do not include sunk costs (costs that have been committed prior to the project). Second, we account for tax effects by using after-tax cash flows. For a full discussion of these and other issues in capital budgeting, see Brealey and Myers (2003).

2 The **weighted-average cost of capital** (WACC) is often used to discount cash flows. This value is a weighted average of the after-tax required rates of return on the company's common stock, preferred stock, and long-term debt, where the weights are the fraction of each source of financing in the company's target capital structure. For a full discussion of the issues surrounding the cost of capital, see Brealey and Myers (2003).

opportunity cost of capital is the alternative return that investors forgo in undertaking the investment. When NPV is positive, the investment adds value because it more than covers the opportunity cost of the capital needed to undertake it. So a company undertaking a positive NPV investment increases shareholders' wealth. An individual investor making a positive NPV investment increases personal wealth, but a negative NPV investment decreases wealth.

When working problems using the NPV rule, it will be helpful to refer to the following formula:

$$NPV = \sum_{t=0}^{N} \frac{CF_t}{(1+r)^t}$$ (1)

where

CF_t = the expected net cash flow at time t

N = the investment's projected life

r = the discount rate or opportunity cost of capital

As always, we state the inputs on a compatible time basis: If cash flows are annual, N is the project's life in years and r is an annual rate. For instance, suppose you are reviewing a proposal that requires an initial outlay of $2 million ($CF_0$ = –$2 million). You expect that the proposed investment will generate net positive cash flows of CF_1 = $0.50 million at the end of Year 1, CF_2 = $0.75 million at the end of Year 2, and CF_3 = $1.35 million at the end of Year 3. Using 10 percent as a discount rate, you calculate the NPV as follows:

$$NPV = -\$2 + \$0.50/(1.10) + \$0.75/(1.10)^2 + \$1.35/(1.10)^3$$
$$= -\$2 + \$0.454545 + \$0.619835 + \$1.014275$$
$$= \$0.088655 \text{ million}$$

Because the NPV of $88,655 is positive, you accept the proposal under the NPV rule.

Consider an example in which a research and development program is evaluated using the NPV rule.

Example 1

Evaluating a Research and Development Program Using the NPV Rule

As an analyst covering the RAD Corporation, you are evaluating its research and development (R&D) program for the current year. Management has announced that it intends to invest $1 million in R&D. Incremental net cash flows are forecasted to be $150,000 per year in perpetuity. RAD Corporation's opportunity cost of capital is 10 percent.

1. State whether RAD's R&D program will benefit shareholders, as judged by the NPV rule.

2. Evaluate whether your answer to Part 1 changes if RAD Corporation's opportunity cost of capital is 15 percent rather than 10 percent.

Solution to 1:

The constant net cash flows of $150,000, which we can denote as $\overline{CF}$, form a perpetuity. The present value of the perpetuity is $\overline{CF}/r$, so we calculate the project's NPV as

$$NPV = CF_0 + \overline{CF}/r = -\$1,000,000 + 150,000/0.10 = \$500,000$$

With an opportunity cost of 10 percent, the present value of the program's cash inflows is $1.5 million. The program's cost is an immediate outflow of $1 million; therefore, its net present value is $500,000. As NPV is positive, you conclude that RAD Corporation's R&D program will benefit shareholders.

Solution to 2:

With an opportunity cost of capital of 15 percent, you compute the NPV as you did above, but this time you use a 15 percent discount rate:

$$NPV = -\$1,000,000 + \$150,000/0.15 = \$0$$

With a higher opportunity cost of capital, the present value of the inflows is smaller and the program's NPV is smaller: At 15 percent, the NPV exactly equals $0. At NPV = 0, the program generates just enough cash flow to compensate shareholders for the opportunity cost of making the investment. When a company undertakes a zero-NPV project, the company becomes larger but shareholders' wealth does not increase.

2.2 The Internal Rate of Return and the Internal Rate of Return Rule

Financial managers often want a single number that represents the rate of return generated by an investment. The rate of return computation most often used in investment applications (including capital budgeting) is the internal rate of return (IRR). The internal rate of return rule is a second method for choosing among investment proposals. The **internal rate of return** is the discount rate that makes net present value equal to zero. It equates the present value of the investment's costs (outflows) to the present value of the investment's benefits (inflows). The rate is "internal" because it depends only on the cash flows of the investment; no external data are needed. As a result, we can apply the IRR concept to any investment that can be represented as a series of cash flows. In the study of bonds, we encounter IRR under the name of yield to maturity. Later in this reading, we will explore IRR as the money-weighted rate of return for portfolios.

Before we continue, however, we must add a note of caution about interpreting IRR: Even if our cash flow projections are correct, we will realize a compound rate of return that is equal to IRR over the life of the investment *only if* we can reinvest all interim cash flows at exactly the IRR. Suppose the IRR for a project is 15 percent but we consistently reinvest the cash generated by the project at a lower rate. In this case, we will realize a return that is less than 15 percent. (This principle can work in our favor if we can reinvest at rates above 15 percent.)

To return to the definition of IRR, in mathematical terms we said the following:

$$NPV = CF_0 + \frac{CF_1}{(1+IRR)^1} + \frac{CF_2}{(1+IRR)^2} + \ldots + \frac{CF_N}{(1+IRR)^N} = 0 \qquad (2)$$

Again, the IRR in Equation 2 must be compatible with the timing of the cash flows. If the cash flows are quarterly, we have a quarterly IRR in Equation 2. We can then state the IRR on an annual basis. For some simple projects, the cash flow at $t = 0$, CF_0, captures the single capital outlay or initial investment; cash flows after $t = 0$ are the positive returns to the investment. In such cases, we can say $CF_0 = -$Investment (the negative sign indicates an outflow). Thus we can rearrange Equation 2 in a form that is helpful in those cases:

$$Investment = \frac{CF_1}{(1+IRR)^1} + \frac{CF_2}{(1+IRR)^2} + \ldots + \frac{CF_N}{(1+IRR)^N}$$

For most real-life problems, financial analysts use software, spreadsheets, or financial calculators to solve this equation for IRR, so you should familiarize yourself with such tools.[3]

The investment decision rule using IRR, the **IRR rule**, states the following: "Accept projects or investments for which the IRR is greater than the opportunity cost of capital." The IRR rule uses the opportunity cost of capital as a **hurdle rate**, or rate that a project's IRR must exceed for the project to be accepted. Note that if the opportunity cost of capital is equal to the IRR, then the NPV is equal to 0. If the project's opportunity cost is less than the IRR, the NPV is greater than 0 (using a discount rate less than the IRR will make the NPV positive). With these comments in mind, we work through two examples that involve the internal rate of return.

Example 2

Evaluating a Research and Development Program Using the IRR Rule

In the previous RAD Corporation example, the initial outlay is $1 million and the program's cash flows are $150,000 in perpetuity. Now you are interested in determining the program's internal rate of return. Address the following:

1. Write the equation for determining the internal rate of return of this R&D program.

2. Calculate the IRR.

Solution to 1:

Finding the IRR is equivalent to finding the discount rate that makes the NPV equal to 0. Because the program's cash flows are a perpetuity, you can set up the NPV equation as

$$\text{NPV} = -\text{Investment} + \overline{\text{CF}}/\text{IRR} = 0$$
$$\text{NPV} = -\$1,000,000 + \$150,000/\text{IRR} = 0$$

or as

$$\text{Investment} = \overline{\text{CF}}/\text{IRR}$$
$$\$1,000,000 = \$150,000/\text{IRR}$$

Solution to 2:

We can solve for IRR as IRR = $150,000/$1,000,000 = 0.15 or 15 percent. The solution of 15 percent accords with the definition of IRR. In Example 1, you found that a discount rate of 15 percent made the program's NPV equal to 0. By definition, therefore, the program's IRR must be 15 percent. If the opportunity cost of capital is also 15 percent, the R&D program just covers its opportunity costs and neither increases nor decreases shareholder wealth. If it is less than 15 percent, the IRR rule indicates that management should invest in the program because it more than covers its opportunity cost. If the opportunity cost is greater than 15 percent, the IRR rule tells management to reject the R&D program. For a given opportunity cost, the IRR rule and the NPV rule lead to the same decision in this example.

---

3 In some real-world capital budgeting problems, the initial investment (which has a minus sign) may be followed by subsequent cash inflows (which have plus signs) and outflows (which have minus signs). In these instances, the project can have more than one IRR. The possibility of multiple solutions is a theoretical limitation of IRR.

Example 3

The IRR and NPV Rules Side by Side

The Japanese company Kageyama Ltd. is considering whether or not to open a new factory to manufacture capacitors used in cell phones. The factory will require an investment of ¥1,000 million. The factory is expected to generate level cash flows of ¥294.8 million per year in each of the next five years. According to information in its financial reports, Kageyama's opportunity cost of capital for this type of project is 11 percent.

1. Determine whether the project will benefit Kageyama's shareholders using the NPV rule.

2. Determine whether the project will benefit Kageyama's shareholders using the IRR rule.

Solution to 1:

The cash flows can be grouped into an initial outflow of ¥1,000 million and an ordinary annuity of five inflows of ¥294.8 million. The expression for the present value of an annuity is $A[1 - (1 + r)^{-N}]/r$, where A is the level annuity payment. Therefore, with amounts shown in millions of Japanese yen,

$$\text{NPV} = -1,000 + 294.8\left[1 - (1.11)^{-5}\right]/0.11$$
$$\text{NPV} = -1,000 + 1,089.55 = 89.55$$

Because the project's NPV is positive ¥89.55 million, it should benefit Kageyama's shareholders.

Solution to 2:

The IRR of the project is the solution to

$$\text{NPV} = -1,000 + 294.8\left[1 - (1 + \text{IRR})^{-5}\right]/\text{IRR} = 0$$

This project's positive NPV tells us that the internal rate of return must be greater than 11 percent. Using a calculator, we find that IRR is 0.145012 or 14.50 percent. Table 1 gives the keystrokes on most financial calculators.

Table 1	Computing IRR
Notation Used on Most Calculators	**Numerical Value for This Problem**
N	5
%i compute	X
PV	−1,000
PMT	294.8
FV	n/a (=0)

Because the IRR of 14.50 percent is greater than the opportunity cost of the project, the project should benefit Kageyama's shareholders. Whether it uses the IRR rule or the NPV rule, Kageyama makes the same decision: Build the factory.

In the previous example, value creation is evident: For a single ¥1,000 million payment, Kageyama creates a project worth ¥1,089.55 million, a value increase of ¥89.55 million. Another perspective on value creation comes from converting the initial investment into a capital charge against the annual operating cash flows that the project generates. Recall that the project generates an annual operating cash flow of ¥294,800,000. If we subtract a capital charge of ¥270,570,310 (the amount of a five-year annuity having a present value of ¥1,000 million at 11 percent), we find ¥294,800,000 − ¥270,570,310 = ¥24,229,690. The amount of ¥24,229,690 represents the profit in each of the next five years after taking into account opportunity costs. The present value of a five-year annuity of ¥24,229,690 at an 11 percent cost of capital is exactly what we calculated as the project's NPV: ¥89.55 million. Therefore, we can also calculate NPV by converting the initial investment to an annual capital charge against cash flow.

2.3 Problems with the IRR Rule

The IRR and NPV rules give the same accept or reject decision when projects are independent—that is, when the decision to invest in one project does not affect the decision to undertake another. When a company cannot finance all the projects it would like to undertake—that is, when projects are mutually exclusive—it must rank the projects from most profitable to least. However, rankings according to IRR and NPV may not be the same. The IRR and NPV rules rank projects differently when

- the size or scale of the projects differs (measuring size by the investment needed to undertake the project), or
- the timing of the projects' cash flows differs.

When the IRR and NPV rules conflict in ranking projects, we should take directions from the NPV rule. Why that preference? The NPV of an investment represents the expected addition to shareholder wealth from an investment, and we take the maximization of shareholder wealth to be a basic financial objective of a company. To illustrate the preference for the NPV rule, consider first the case of projects that differ in size. Suppose that a company has only €30,000 available to invest.[4] The company has available two one-period investment projects described as A and B in Table 2.

Table 2	IRR and NPV for Mutually Exclusive Projects of Different Size			
Project	Investment at $t = 0$	Cash Flow at $t = 1$	IRR (%)	NPV at 8%
A	−€10,000	€15,000	50	€3,888.89
B	−€30,000	€42,000	40	€8,888.89

Project A requires an immediate investment of €10,000. This project will make a single cash payment of $15,000 at $t = 1$. Because the IRR is the discount rate that equates the present value of the future cash flow with the cost of the investment, the IRR equals 50 percent. If we assume that the opportunity cost of capital is 8 percent, then the NPV of Project A is €3,888.89. We compute the IRR and NPV of Project B as 40 percent and €8,888.89, respectively. The IRR and NPV rules indicate that we should undertake both projects, but to do so we would need €40,000—more money than is available. So we need to rank the projects. How do the projects rank according to IRR and NPV?

---

4 Or suppose the two projects require the same physical or other resources, so that only one can be undertaken.

The IRR rule ranks Project A, with the higher IRR, first. The NPV rule, however, ranks Project B, with the higher NPV, first—a conflict with the IRR rule's ranking. Choosing Project A because it has the higher IRR would not lead to the largest increase in shareholders' wealth. Investing in Project A effectively leaves €20,000 (€30,000 minus A's cost) uninvested. Project A increases wealth by almost €4,000, but Project B increases wealth by almost €9,000. The difference between the two projects' scale creates the inconsistency in the ranking between the two rules.

IRR and NPV can also rank projects of the same scale differently when the timing of cash flows differs. We can illustrate this principle with Projects A and D, presented in Table 3.

Table 3	IRR and NPV for Mutually Exclusive Projects with Different Timing of Cash Flows					
Project	CF0 (€)	CF1 (€)	CF2 (€)	CF3 (€)	IRR (%)	NPV at 8%
A	−10,000	15,000	0	0	50.0	€3,888.89
D	−10,000	0	0	21,220	28.5	€6,845.12

The terms CF_0, CF_1, CF_2, and CF_3 represent the cash flows at time periods 0, 1, 2, and 3. The IRR for Project A is the same as it was in the previous example. The IRR for Project D is found as follows:

$$-10,000 + \frac{21,220}{(1+\text{IRR})^3} = 0$$

The IRR for Project D is 28.5 percent, compared with 50 percent for Project A. IRRs and IRR rankings are not affected by any external interest rate or discount rate because a project's cash flows alone determine the internal rate of return. The IRR calculation furthermore assumes reinvestment at the IRR, so we generally cannot interpret them as achievable rates of return. For Project D, for example, to achieve a 28.5 percent return we would need to earn 28.5 percent on €10,000 for the first year, earn 28.5 percent on €10,000(1.285) = €12,850 the second year, and earn 28.5 percent on €10,000(1.285)² = €16,512.25 the third year.[5] A reinvestment rate such as 50 percent or 28.5 percent may be quite unrealistic. By contrast, the calculation of NPV uses an external market-determined discount rate, and reinvestment is assumed to take place at that discount rate. NPV rankings can depend on the external discount rate chosen. Here, Project D has a larger but more distant cash inflow (€21,220 versus €15,000). As a result, Project D has a higher NPV than Project A at lower discount rates.[6] The NPV rule's assumption about reinvestment rates is more realistic and more economically relevant because it incorporates the market-determined opportunity cost of capital as a discount rate. As a consequence, the NPV is the expected addition to shareholder wealth from an investment.

In summary, when dealing with mutually exclusive projects, choose among them using the NPV rule when the IRR rule and NPV rule conflict.[7]

---

[5] The ending amount €10,000(1.285)3 = €21,218 differs from the €21,220 amount listed in Table 3 because we rounded IRR.

[6] There is a crossover discount rate above which Project A has a higher NPV than Project D. This crossover rate is 18.94 percent.

[7] Technically, different reinvestment rate assumptions account for this conflict between the IRR and NPV rules. The IRR rule assumes that the company can earn the IRR on all reinvested cash flows, but the NPV rule assumes that cash flows are reinvested at the company's opportunity cost of capital. The NPV assumption is far more realistic. For further details on this and other topics in capital budgeting, see Brealey and Myers (2003).

PORTFOLIO RETURN MEASUREMENT

Suppose you are an investor and you want to assess the success of your investments. You face two related but distinct tasks. The first is **performance measurement**, which involves calculating returns in a logical and consistent manner. Accurate performance measurement provides the basis for your second task, **performance appraisal**.[8] Performance measurement is thus of great importance for all investors and investment managers because it is the foundation for all further analysis.

In our discussion of portfolio return measurement, we will use the fundamental concept of **holding period return (HPR)**, the return that an investor earns over a specified holding period. For an investment that makes one cash payment at the end of the holding period, HPR $= (P_1 - P_0 + D_1)/P_0$, where P_0 is the initial investment, P_1 is the price received at the end of the holding period, and D_1 is the cash paid by the investment at the end of the holding period.

Particularly when we measure performance over many periods, or when the portfolio is subject to additions and withdrawals, portfolio performance measurement is a challenging task. Two of the measurement tools available are the money-weighted rate of return measure and the time-weighted rate of return measure. The first measure we discuss, the money-weighted rate of return, implements a concept we have already covered in the context of capital budgeting: internal rate of return.

3.1 Money-Weighted Rate of Return

The first performance measurement concept that we will discuss is an internal rate of return calculation. In investment management applications, the internal rate of return is called the money-weighted rate of return because it accounts for the timing and amount of all dollar flows into and out of the portfolio.[9]

To illustrate the money-weighted return, consider an investment that covers a two-year horizon. At time $t = 0$, an investor buys one share at $200. At time $t = 1$, he purchases an additional share at $225. At the end of Year 2, $t = 2$, he sells both shares for $235 each. During both years, the stock pays a per-share dividend of $5. The $t = 1$ dividend is not reinvested. Table 4 shows the total cash inflows and outflows.

Table 4	Cash Flows	
Time	**Outlay**	
0	$200 to purchase the first share	
1	$225 to purchase the second share	
	Proceeds	
1	$5 dividend received from first share (and not reinvested)	
2	$10 dividend ($5 per share × 2 shares) received	
2	$470 received from selling two shares at $235 per share	

The money-weighted return on this portfolio is its internal rate of return for the two-year period. The portfolio's internal rate of return is the rate, r, for which the present value of the cash inflows minus the present value of the cash outflows equals 0, or

PV (outflows) = PV (inflows)

$$\$200 + \frac{\$225}{(1+r)} = \frac{\$5}{(1+r)} + \frac{\$480}{(1+r)^2}$$

The left-hand side of this equation details the outflows: $200 at time $t = 0$ and $225 at time $t = 1$. The $225 outflow is discounted back one period because it occurs at $t = 1$. The right-hand side of the equation shows the present value of the inflows: $5 at time $t = 1$ (discounted back one period) and $480 (the $10 dividend plus the $470 sale proceeds) at time $t = 2$ (discounted back two periods).

To solve for the money-weighted return, we use either a financial calculator that allows us to enter cash flows or a spreadsheet with an IRR function.[10] The first step is to group net cash flows by time. For this example, we have –$200 for the $t = 0$ net cash flow, –$220 = –$225 + $5 for the $t = 1$ net cash flow, and $480 for the $t = 2$ net cash flow. After entering these cash flows, we use the spreadsheet's or calculator's IRR function to find that the money-weighted rate of return is 9.39 percent.[11]

Now we take a closer look at what has happened to the portfolio during each of the two years. In the first year, the portfolio generated a one-period holding period return of ($5 + $225 – $200)/$200 = 15 percent. At the beginning of the second year, the amount invested is $450, calculated as $225 (per share price of stock) × 2 shares, because the $5 dividend was spent rather than reinvested. At the end of the second year, the proceeds from the liquidation of the portfolio are $470 (as detailed in Table 4) plus $10 in dividends (as also detailed in Table 4). So in the second year the portfolio produced a holding period return of ($10 + $470 – $450)/$450 = 6.67 percent. The mean holding period return was (15% + 6.67%)/2 = 10.84 percent. The money-weighted rate of return, which we calculated as 9.39 percent, puts a greater weight on the second year's relatively poor performance (6.67 percent) than the first year's relatively good performance (15 percent), as more money was invested in the second year than in the first. That is the sense in which returns in this method of calculating performance are "money weighted."

As a tool for evaluating investment managers, the money-weighted rate of return has a serious drawback. Generally, the investment manager's clients determine when money is given to the investment manager and how much money is given. As we have seen, those decisions may significantly influence the investment manager's money-weighted rate of return. A general principle of evaluation, however, is that a person or entity should be judged only on the basis of their own actions, or actions under their control. An evaluation tool should isolate the effects of the investment manager's actions. The next section presents a tool that is effective in that respect.

3.2 Time-Weighted Rate of Return

An investment measure that is not sensitive to the additions and withdrawals of funds is the time-weighted rate of return. In the investment management industry, the time-weighted rate of return is the preferred performance measure. The **time-weighted rate of return** measures the compound rate of growth of $1 initially invested in the portfolio over a stated measurement period. In contrast to the money-weighted rate of return, the time-weighted rate of return is not affected by cash withdrawals or

---

10 In this particular case we could solve for r by solving the quadratic equation $480x^2 - 220x - 200 = 0$ with $x = 1/(1 + r)$, using standard results from algebra. In general, however, we rely on a calculator or spreadsheet software to compute a money-weighted rate of return.

11 Note that the calculator or spreadsheet will give the IRR as a periodic rate. If the periods are not annual, we annualize the periodic rate.

additions to the portfolio. The term "time-weighted" refers to the fact that returns are averaged over time. To compute an exact time-weighted rate of return on a portfolio, take the following three steps:

1. Price the portfolio immediately prior to any significant addition or withdrawal of funds. Break the overall evaluation period into subperiods based on the dates of cash inflows and outflows.

2. Calculate the holding period return on the portfolio for each subperiod.

3. Link or compound holding period returns to obtain an annual rate of return for the year (the time-weighted rate of return for the year). If the investment is for more than one year, take the geometric mean of the annual returns to obtain the time-weighted rate of return over that measurement period.

Let us return to our money-weighted example and calculate the time-weighted rate of return for that investor's portfolio. In that example, we computed the holding period returns on the portfolio, Step 2 in the procedure for finding the time-weighted rate of return. Given that the portfolio earned returns of 15 percent during the first year and 6.67 percent during the second year, what is the portfolio's time-weighted rate of return over an evaluation period of two years?

We find this time-weighted return by taking the geometric mean of the two holding period returns, Step 3 in the procedure above. The calculation of the geometric mean exactly mirrors the calculation of a compound growth rate. Here, we take the product of 1 plus the holding period return for each period to find the terminal value at $t = 2$ of \$1 invested at $t = 0$. We then take the square root of this product and subtract 1 to get the geometric mean. We interpret the result as the annual compound growth rate of \$1 invested in the portfolio at $t = 0$. Thus we have

$$\left(1 + \text{Time-weighted return}\right)^2 = (1.15)(1.0667)$$

$$\text{Time-weighted return} = \sqrt{(1.15)(1.0667)} - 1 = 10.76\%$$

The time-weighted return on the portfolio was 10.76 percent, compared with the money-weighted return of 9.39 percent, which gave larger weight to the second year's return. We can see why investment managers find time-weighted returns more meaningful. If a client gives an investment manager more funds to invest at an unfavorable time, the manager's money-weighted rate of return will tend to be depressed. If a client adds funds at a favorable time, the money-weighted return will tend to be elevated. The time-weighted rate of return removes these effects.

In defining the steps to calculate an exact time-weighted rate of return, we said that the portfolio should be valued immediately prior to any significant addition or withdrawal of funds. With the amount of cash flow activity in many portfolios, this task can be costly. We can often obtain a reasonable approximation of the time-weighted rate of return by valuing the portfolio at frequent, regular intervals, particularly if additions and withdrawals are unrelated to market movements. The more frequent the valuation, the more accurate the approximation. Daily valuation is commonplace. Suppose that a portfolio is valued daily over the course of a year. To compute the time-weighted return for the year, we first compute each day's holding period return:

$$r_t = \frac{\text{MVE}_t - \text{MVB}_t}{\text{MVB}_t}$$

where MVB_t equals the market value at the beginning of day t and MVE_t equals the market value at the end of day t. We compute 365 such daily returns, denoted $r_1, r_2, \ldots, r_{365}$. We obtain the annual return for the year by linking the daily holding period returns in the following way: $(1 + r_1) \times (1 + r_2) \times \ldots \times (1 + r_{365}) - 1$. If withdrawals and additions to the portfolio happen only at day's end, this annual return is a precise time-weighted rate of return for the year. Otherwise, it is an approximate time-weighted return for the year.

If we have a number of years of data, we can calculate a time-weighted return for each year individually, as above. If r_i is the time-weighted return for year i, we calculate an annualized time-weighted return as the geometric mean of N annual returns, as follows:

$$r_{TW} = \left[(1+r_1) \times (1+r_2) \times \ldots \times (1+r_N) \right]^{1/N} - 1$$

Example 4 illustrates the calculation of the time-weighted rate of return.

Example 4

Time-Weighted Rate of Return

Strubeck Corporation sponsors a pension plan for its employees. It manages part of the equity portfolio in-house and delegates management of the balance to Super Trust Company. As chief investment officer of Strubeck, you want to review the performance of the in-house and Super Trust portfolios over the last four quarters. You have arranged for outflows and inflows to the portfolios to be made at the very beginning of the quarter. Table 5 summarizes the inflows and outflows as well as the two portfolios' valuations. In the table, the ending value is the portfolio's value just prior to the cash inflow or outflow at the beginning of the quarter. The amount invested is the amount each portfolio manager is responsible for investing.

Table 5	Cash Flows for the In-House Strubeck Account and the Super Trust Account			
	Quarter			
	1 ($)	**2 ($)**	**3 ($)**	**4 ($)**
In-House Account				
Beginning value	4,000,000	6,000,000	5,775,000	6,720,000
Beginning of period inflow (outflow)	1,000,000	(500,000)	225,000	(600,000)
Amount invested	5,000,000	5,500,000	6,000,000	6,120,000
Ending value	6,000,000	5,775,000	6,720,000	5,508,000
Super Trust Account				
Beginning value	10,000,000	13,200,000	12,240,000	5,659,200
Beginning of period inflow (outflow)	2,000,000	(1,200,000)	(7,000,000)	(400,000)
Amount invested	12,000,000	12,000,000	5,240,000	5,259,200
Ending value	13,200,000	12,240,000	5,659,200	5,469,568

Based on the information given, address the following.

1. Calculate the time-weighted rate of return for the in-house account.
2. Calculate the time-weighted rate of return for the Super Trust account.

Solution to 1:

To calculate the time-weighted rate of return for the in-house account, we compute the quarterly holding period returns for the account and link them into an annual return. The in-house account's time-weighted rate of return is 27 percent, calculated as follows:

1Q HPR: $r_1 = (\$6,000,000 - \$5,000,000) / \$5,000,000 = 0.20$
2Q HPR: $r_2 = (\$5,775,000 - \$5,500,000) / \$5,500,000 = 0.05$
3Q HPR: $r_3 = (\$6,720,000 - \$6,000,000) / \$6,000,000 = 0.12$
4Q HPR: $r_4 = (\$5,508,000 - \$6,120,000) / \$6,120,000 = -0.10$

$$(1+r_1)(1+r_2)(1+r_3)(1+r_4)-1=(1.20)(1.05)(1.12)(0.90)-1=0.27 \text{ or } 27\%$$

Solution to 2:

The account managed by Super Trust has a time-weighted rate of return of 26 percent, calculated as follows:

1Q HPR: $r_1 = (\$13,200,000 - \$12,000,000)/\$12,000,000 = 0.10$

2Q HPR: $r_2 = (\$12,240,000 - \$12,000,000)/\$12,000,000 = 0.02$

3Q HPR: $r_3 = (\$5,659,200 - \$5,240,000)/\$5,240,000 = 0.08$

4Q HPR: $r_4 = (\$5,469,568 - \$5,259,200)/\$5,259,200 = 0.04$

$$(1+r_1)(1+r_2)(1+r_3)(1+r_4)-1=(1.10)(1.02)(1.08)(1.04)-1=0.26 \text{ or } 26\%$$

The in-house portfolio's time-weighted rate of return is higher than the Super Trust portfolio's by 100 basis points.

Having worked through this exercise, we are ready to look at a more detailed case.

Example 5

Time-Weighted and Money-Weighted Rates of Return Side by Side

Your task is to compute the investment performance of the Walbright Fund during 2003. The facts are as follows:

- On 1 January 2003, the Walbright Fund had a market value of $100 million.

- During the period 1 January 2003 to 30 April 2003, the stocks in the fund showed a capital gain of $10 million.

- On 1 May 2003, the stocks in the fund paid a total dividend of $2 million. All dividends were reinvested in additional shares.

- Because the fund's performance had been exceptional, institutions invested an additional $20 million in Walbright on 1 May 2003, raising assets under management to $132 million ($100 + $10 + $2 + $20).

- On 31 December 2003, Walbright received total dividends of $2.64 million. The fund's market value on 31 December 2003, not including the $2.64 million in dividends, was $140 million.

- The fund made no other interim cash payments during 2003.

Based on the information given, address the following.

1. Compute the Walbright Fund's time-weighted rate of return.

2. Compute the Walbright Fund's money-weighted rate of return.

3. Interpret the differences between the time-weighted and money-weighted rates of return.

Solution to 1:

Because interim cash flows were made on 1 May 2003, we must compute two interim total returns and then link them to obtain an annual return. Table 6 lists the relevant market values on 1 January, 1 May, and 31 December as well as the associated interim four-month (1 January to 1 May) and eight-month (1 May to 31 December) holding period returns.

Table 6	Cash Flows for the Walbright Fund

1 January 2003	Beginning portfolio value = $100 million
1 May 2003	Dividends received before additional investment = $2 million
	Ending portfolio value = $110 million
	Holding period return $= \dfrac{\$2+\$10}{\$100} = 12\%$
	New investment = $20 million
	Beginning market value for last 2/3 of year = $132 million
31 December 2003	Dividends received = $2.64 million
	Ending portfolio value = $140 million
	Holding period return $= \dfrac{\$2.64+\$140-\$132}{\$132}$
	$= 8.06\%$

Now we must geometrically link the four- and eight-month returns to compute an annual return. We compute the time-weighted return as follows:

$$\text{Time-weighted return} = 1.12 \times 1.0806 - 1 = 0.2103$$

In this instance, we compute a time-weighted rate of return of 21.03 percent for one year. The four-month and eight-month intervals combine to equal one year. (Taking the square root of the product 1.12×1.0806 would be appropriate only if 1.12 and 1.0806 each applied to one full year.)

Solution to 2:

To calculate the money-weighted return, we find the discount rate that sets the present value of the outflows (purchases) equal to the present value of the inflows (dividends and future payoff). The initial market value of the fund and all additions to it are treated as cash outflows. (Think of them as expenditures.) Withdrawals, receipts, and the ending market value of the fund are counted as inflows. (The ending market value is the amount investors receive on liquidating the fund.) Because interim cash flows have occurred at four-month intervals, we must solve for the four-month internal rate of return. Table 6 details the cash flows and their timing.

The present value equation (in millions) is as follows:

$$\text{PV}(\text{outflows}) = \text{PV}(\text{inflows})$$
$$\$100 + \frac{\$2}{(1+r)^1} + \frac{\$20}{(1+r)^1} = \frac{\$2}{(1+r)^1} + \frac{\$2.64}{(1+r)^3} + \frac{\$140}{(1+r)^3}$$

The left-hand side of the equation shows the investments in the fund or outflows: a $100 million initial investment followed by the $2 million dividend reinvested and an additional $20 million of new investment (both occurring at the end of the first four-month interval, which makes the exponent in the denominator 1). The right-hand side of the equation shows the payoffs or inflows: the $2 million dividend at the first four-month interval followed by the $2.64 million dividend and the terminal market value of $140 million (both occurring at the end of the third four-month interval, which makes the exponent in the denominator 3).

The second four-month interval has no cash flow. We can bring all the terms to the right of the equal sign, arranging them in order of time. After simplification,

$$0 = -\$100 - \frac{\$20}{(1+r)^1} + \frac{\$142.64}{(1+r)^3}$$

Using a spreadsheet or IRR-enabled calculator, we use −100, −20, 0, and $142.64 for the $t = 0$, $t = 1$, $t = 2$, and $t = 3$ net cash flows, respectively.[12] Using either tool, we get a four-month IRR of 6.28 percent. The quick way to annualize this is to multiply by 3. A more accurate way is $(1.0628)^3 - 1 = 0.20$ or 20 percent.

Solution to 3:

In this example, the time-weighted return (21.03 percent) is greater than the money-weighted return (20 percent). The Walbright Fund's performance was relatively poorer during the eight-month period, when the fund owned more shares, than it was overall. This fact is reflected in a lower money-weighted rate of return compared with time-weighted rate of return, as the money-weighted return is sensitive to the timing and amount of withdrawals and additions to the portfolio.

The accurate measurement of portfolio returns is important to the process of evaluating portfolio managers. In addition to considering returns, however, analysts must also weigh risk. When we worked through Example 4, we stopped short of suggesting that in-house management was superior to Super Trust because it earned a higher time-weighted rate of return. With risk in focus, we can talk of risk-adjusted performance and make comparisons—but only cautiously. In other readings, we will discuss the Sharpe ratio, an important risk-adjusted performance measure that we might apply to an investment manager's time-weighted rate of return. For now, we have illustrated the major tools for measuring the return on a portfolio.

MONEY MARKET YIELDS   **4**

In our discussion of internal rate of return and net present value, we referred to the opportunity cost of capital as a market-determined rate. In this section, we begin a discussion of discounted cash flow analysis in actual markets by considering short-term debt markets.

To understand the various ways returns are presented in debt markets, we must discuss some of the conventions for quoting yields on money-market instruments. The **money market** is the market for short-term debt instruments (one-year maturity or less). Some instruments require the issuer to repay the lender the amount borrowed plus interest. Others are **pure discount instruments** that pay interest as the difference between the amount borrowed and the amount paid back.

In the U.S. money market, the classic example of a pure discount instrument is the U.S. Treasury bill (T-bill) issued by the federal government. The **face value** of a T-bill is the amount the U.S. government promises to pay back to a T-bill investor. In buying a T-bill, investors pay the face amount less the discount, and receive the face amount at maturity. The **discount** is the reduction from the face amount that gives the price for the T-bill. This discount becomes the interest that accumulates, because the investor receives the face amount at maturity. Thus, investors earn a dollar return equal to the discount if they hold the instrument to maturity. T-bills are by far the most important class of money-market instruments in the United States.

---

12 By convention, we denote outflow with a negative sign, and we need 0 as a placeholder for the $t = 2$.

Other types of money-market instruments include commercial paper and bankers' acceptances, which are discount instruments, and negotiable certificates of deposit, which are interest-bearing instruments. The market for each of these instruments has its own convention for quoting prices or yields. The remainder of this section examines the quoting conventions for T-bills and other money-market instruments. In most instances, the quoted yields must be adjusted for use in other present value problems.

Pure discount instruments such as T-bills are quoted differently from U.S. government bonds. T-bills are quoted on a **bank discount basis**, rather than on a price basis. The bank discount basis is a quoting convention that annualizes, based on a 360-day year, the discount as a percentage of face value. Yield on a bank discount basis is computed as follows:

$$r_{BD} = \frac{D}{F}\frac{360}{t} \tag{3}$$

where

> r_{BD} = the annualized yield on a bank discount basis
> D = the dollar discount, which is equal to the difference between the face value of the bill, F, and its purchase price, P_0
> F = the face value of the T-bill
> t = the actual number of days remaining to maturity
> 360 = bank convention of the number of days in a year

The bank discount yield (often called simply the discount yield) takes the dollar discount from par, D, and expresses it as a fraction of the face value (not the price) of the T-bill. This fraction is then multiplied by the number of periods of length t in one year (that is, $360/t$), where the year is assumed to have 360 days. Annualizing in this fashion assumes simple interest (no compounding). Consider the following example.

Example 6

The Bank Discount Yield

Suppose a T-bill with a face value (or par value) of $100,000 and 150 days until maturity is selling for $98,000. What is its bank discount yield?

Solution:

For this example, the dollar discount, D, is $2,000. The yield on a bank discount basis is 4.8 percent, as computed with Equation 3:

$$r_{BD} = \frac{\$2,000}{\$100,000}\frac{360}{150} = 4.8\%$$

The bank discount formula takes the T-bill's dollar discount from face or par as a fraction of face value, 2 percent, and then annualizes by the factor $360/150 = 2.4$. The price of discount instruments such as T-bills is quoted using discount yields, so we typically translate discount yield into price.

Suppose we know the bank discount yield of 4.8 percent but do not know the price. We solve for the dollar discount, D, as follows:

$$D = r_{BD}F\frac{t}{360}$$

With r_{BD} = 4.8 percent, the dollar discount is $D = 0.048 \times \$100,000 \times 150/360 = \$2,000$. Once we have computed the dollar discount, the purchase price for the T-bill is its face value minus the dollar discount, $F - D = \$100,000 - \$2,000 = \$98,000$.

Yield on a bank discount basis is not a meaningful measure of investors' return, for three reasons. First, the yield is based on the face value of the bond, not on its purchase price. Returns from investments should be evaluated relative to the amount that is invested. Second, the yield is annualized based on a 360-day year rather than a 365-day year. Third, the bank discount yield annualizes with simple interest, which ignores the opportunity to earn interest on interest (compound interest).

We can extend Example 6 to discuss three often-used alternative yield measures. The first is the holding period return over the remaining life of the instrument (150 days in the case of the T-bill in Example 6). It determines the return that an investor will earn by holding the instrument to maturity; as used here, this measure refers to an unannualized rate of return (or periodic rate of return). In fixed income markets, this holding period return is also called a **holding period yield (HPY)**.[13] For an instrument that makes one cash payment during its life, HPY is

$$HPY = \frac{P_1 - P_0 + D_1}{P_0} \qquad (4)$$

where
  P_0 = the initial purchase price of the instrument
  P_1 = the price received for the instrument at its maturity
  D_1 = the cash distribution paid by the instrument at its maturity (i.e., interest)

When we use this expression to calculate the holding period yield for an interest-bearing instrument (for example, coupon-bearing bonds), we need to observe an important detail: The purchase and sale prices must include any **accrued interest** added to the trade price because the bond was traded between interest payment dates. Accrued interest is the coupon interest that the seller earns from the last coupon date but does not receive as a coupon, because the next coupon date occurs after the date of sale.[14]

For pure discount securities, all of the return is derived by redeeming the bill for more than its purchase price. Because the T-bill is a pure discount instrument, it makes no interest payment and thus $D_1 = 0$. Therefore, the holding period yield is the dollar discount divided by the purchase price, $HPY = D/P_0$, where $D = P_1 - P_0$. The holding period yield is the amount that is annualized in the other measures. For the T-bill in Example 6, the investment of $98,000 will pay $100,000 in 150 days. The holding period yield on this investment using Equation 4 is ($100,000 – $98,000)/$98,000 = $2,000/$98,000 = 2.0408 percent. For this example, the periodic return of 2.0408 percent is associated with a 150-day period. If we were to use the T-bill rate of return as the opportunity cost of investing, we would use a discount rate of 2.0408 percent for the 150-day T-bill to find the present value of any other cash flow to be received in 150 days. As long as the other cash flow has risk characteristics similar to those of the T-bill, this approach is appropriate. If the other cash flow were riskier than the T-bill, then we could use the T-bill's yield as a base rate, to which we would add a risk premium. The formula for the holding period yield is the same regardless of the currency of denomination.

The second measure of yield is the **effective annual yield (EAY)**. The EAY takes the quantity 1 plus the holding period yield and compounds it forward to one year,

---

13 Bond-market participants often use the term "yield" when referring to total returns (returns incorporating both price change and income), as in yield to maturity. In other cases, yield refers to returns from income alone (as in current yield, which is annual interest divided by price). As used in this volume and by many writers, holding period yield is a bond market synonym for holding period return, total return, and horizon return.

14 The price with accrued interest is called the **full price**. Trade prices are quoted "clean" (without accrued interest), but accrued interest, if any, is added to the purchase price. For more on accrued interest, see Fabozzi (2004).

then subtracts 1 to recover an annualized return that accounts for the effect of interest-on-interest.[15]

$$EAY = (1 + HPY)^{365/t} - 1 \qquad\qquad (5)$$

In our example, we can solve for EAY as follows:

$$EAY = (1.020408)^{365/150} - 1 = 1.050388 - 1 = 5.0388\%$$

This example illustrates a general rule: The bank discount yield is less than the effective annual yield.

The third alternative measure of yield is the **money market yield** (also known as the **CD equivalent yield**). This convention makes the quoted yield on a T-bill comparable to yield quotations on interest-bearing money-market instruments that pay interest on a 360-day basis. In general, the money market yield is equal to the annualized holding period yield; assuming a 360-day year, r_{MM} = (HPY)(360/t). Compared to the bank discount yield, the money market yield is computed on the purchase price, so $r_{MM} = (r_{BD})(F/P_0)$. This equation shows that the money market yield is larger than the bank discount yield. In practice, the following expression is more useful because it does not require knowing the T-bill price:

$$r_{MM} = \frac{360 r_{BD}}{360 - (t)(r_{BD})} \qquad\qquad (6)$$

For the T-bill example, the money market yield is r_{MM} = (360)(0.048)/[360 − (150)(0.048)] = 4.898 percent.[16]

Table 7 summarizes the three yield measures we have discussed.

Table 7	Three Commonly Used Yield Measures	
Holding Period Yield (HPY)	**Effective Annual Yield (EAY)**	**Money Market Yield (CD Equivalent Yield)**
$HPY = \dfrac{P_1 - P_0 + D_1}{P_0}$	$EAY = (1 + HPY)^{365/t} - 1$	$r_{MM} = \dfrac{360 r_{BD}}{360 - (t)(r_{BD})}$

The next example will help you consolidate your knowledge of these yield measures.

Example 7

Using the Appropriate Discount Rate

You need to find the present value of a cash flow of $1,000 that is to be received in 150 days. You decide to look at a T-bill maturing in 150 days to determine the relevant interest rate for calculating the present value. You have found a variety of yields for the 150-day bill. Table 8 presents this information.

---

15 Effective annual yield was called the effective annual rate (Equation 5) in the reading on the time value of money.

16 Some national markets use the money market yield formula, rather than the bank discount yield formula, to quote the yields on discount instruments such as T-bills. In Canada, the convention is to quote Treasury bill yields using the money market formula assuming a 365-day year. Yields for German Treasury discount paper with a maturity less than one year and French BTFs (T-bills) are computed with the money market formula assuming a 360-day year.

Table 8	Short-Term Money Market Yields
Holding period yield	2.0408%
Bank discount yield	4.8%
Money market yield	4.898%
Effective annual yield	5.0388%

Which yield or yields are appropriate for finding the present value of the $1,000 to be received in 150 days?

Solution:

The holding period yield is appropriate, and we can also use the money market yield and effective annual yield after converting them to a holding period yield.

- *Holding period yield* (2.0408 percent). This yield is exactly what we want. Because it applies to a 150-day period, we can use it in a straightforward fashion to find the present value of the $1,000 to be received in 150 days. (Recall the principle that discount rates must be compatible with the time period.) The present value is

$$PV = \frac{\$1,000}{1.020408} = \$980.00$$

Now we can see why the other yield measures are inappropriate or not as easily applied.

- *Bank discount yield* (4.8 percent). We should not use this yield measure to determine the present value of the cash flow. As mentioned earlier, the bank discount yield is based on the face value of the bill and not on its price.

- *Money market yield* (4.898 percent). To use the money market yield, we need to convert it to the 150-day holding period yield by dividing it by (360/150). After obtaining the holding period yield 0.04898/(360/150) = 0.020408, we use it to discount the $1,000 as above.

- *Effective annual yield* (5.0388 percent). This yield has also been annualized, so it must be adjusted to be compatible with the timing of the cash flow. We can obtain the holding period yield from the EAY as follows:

$$(1.050388)^{150/365} - 1 = 0.020408$$

Recall that when we found the effective annual yield, the exponent was 365/150, or the number of 150-day periods in a 365-day year. To shrink the effective annual yield to a 150-day yield, we use the reciprocal of the exponent that we used to annualize.

In Example 7, we converted two short-term measures of annual yield to a holding period yield for a 150-day period. That is one type of conversion. We frequently also need to convert periodic rates to annual rates. The issue can arise both in money markets and in longer-term debt markets. As an example, many bonds (long-term debt instruments) pay interest semiannually. Bond investors compute IRRs for bonds, known as yields to maturity (YTM). If the semiannual yield to maturity is 4 percent, how do we annualize it? An exact approach, taking account of compounding, would be to compute $(1.04)^2 - 1 = 0.0816$ or 8.16 percent. This is what we have been calling an effective annual yield. An approach used in U.S. bond markets, however, is to double the semiannual YTM: 4% × 2 = 8%. The yield to maturity calculated this way, ignoring compounding, has been called a **bond-equivalent yield**. Annualizing a semi-annual yield by doubling is putting the yield on a bond-equivalent basis. In practice the result, 8 percent, would be referred to simply as the bond's yield to maturity. In money markets, if we annualized a six-month period yield by doubling it, in order to make the result comparable to bonds' YTMs we would also say that the result was a bond-equivalent yield.

SUMMARY

In this reading, we applied the concepts of present value, net present value, and internal rate of return to the fundamental problem of valuing investments. We applied these concepts first to corporate investment, the well-known capital budgeting problem. We then examined the fundamental problem of calculating the return on a portfolio subject to cash inflows and outflows. Finally we discussed money market yields and basic bond market terminology. The following summarizes the reading's key concepts:

- The net present value (NPV) of a project is the present value of its cash inflows minus the present value of its cash outflows. The internal rate of return (IRR) is the discount rate that makes NPV equal to 0. We can interpret IRR as an expected compound return only when all interim cash flows can be reinvested at the internal rate of return and the investment is maintained to maturity.

- The NPV rule for decision making is to accept all projects with positive NPV or, if projects are mutually exclusive, to accept the project with the higher positive NPV. With mutually exclusive projects, we rely on the NPV rule. The IRR rule is to accept all projects with an internal rate of return exceeding the required rate of return. The IRR rule can be affected by problems of scale and timing of cash flows.

- Money-weighted rate of return and time-weighted rate of return are two alternative methods for calculating portfolio returns in a multiperiod setting when the portfolio is subject to additions and withdrawals. Time-weighted rate of return is the standard in the investment management industry. Money-weighted rate of return can be appropriate if the investor exercises control over additions and withdrawals to the portfolio.

- The money-weighted rate of return is the internal rate of return on a portfolio, taking account of all cash flows.

- The time-weighted rate of return removes the effects of timing and amount of withdrawals and additions to the portfolio and reflects the compound rate of growth of one unit of currency invested over a stated measurement period.

- The bank discount yield for U.S. Treasury bills (and other money-market instruments sold on a discount basis) is given by $r_{BD} = (F - P_0)/F \times 360/t = D/F \times 360/t$, where F is the face amount to be received at maturity, P_0 is the price of the Treasury bill, t is the number of days to maturity, and D is the dollar discount.

- For a stated holding period or horizon, holding period yield (HPY) = (Ending price – Beginning price + Cash distributions)/(Beginning price). For a U.S. Treasury bill, HPY = D/P_0.

- The effective annual yield (EAY) is $(1 + HPY)^{365/t} - 1$.

- The money market yield is given by $r_{MM} = \text{HPY} \times 360/t$, where t is the number of days to maturity.

- For a Treasury bill, money market yield can be obtained from the bank discount yield using $r_{MM} = (360 \times r_{BD})/(360 - t \times r_{BD})$.

- We can convert back and forth between holding period yields, money market yields, and effective annual yields by using the holding period yield, which is common to all the calculations.

- The bond-equivalent yield of a yield stated on a semiannual basis is that yield multiplied by 2.

PRACTICE PROBLEMS FOR READING 6

1. Waldrup Industries is considering a proposal for a joint venture that will require an investment of C$13 million. At the end of the fifth year, Waldrup's joint venture partner will buy out Waldrup's interest for C$10 million. Waldrup's chief financial officer has estimated that the appropriate discount rate for this proposal is 12 percent. The expected cash flows are given below.

Year	Cash Flow (C$)
0	−13,000,000
1	3,000,000
2	3,000,000
3	3,000,000
4	3,000,000
5	10,000,000

  A. Calculate this proposal's NPV.

  B. Make a recommendation to the CFO (chief financial officer) concerning whether Waldrup should enter into this joint venture.

2. Waldrup Industries has committed to investing C$5,500,000 in a project with expected cash flows of C$1,000,000 at the end of Year 1, C$1,500,000 at the end of Year 4, and C$7,000,000 at the end of Year 5.

  A. Demonstrate that the internal rate of return of the investment is 13.51 percent.

  B. State how the internal rate of return of the investment would change if Waldrup's opportunity cost of capital were to increase by 5 percentage points.

3. Bestfoods, Inc. is planning to spend $10 million on advertising. The company expects this expenditure to result in annual incremental cash flows of $1.6 million in perpetuity. The corporate opportunity cost of capital for this type of project is 12.5 percent.

  A. Calculate the NPV for the planned advertising.

  B. Calculate the internal rate of return.

  C. Should the company go forward with the planned advertising? Explain.

4. Trilever is planning to establish a new factory overseas. The project requires an initial investment of $15 million. Management intends to run this factory for six years and then sell it to a local entity. Trilever's finance department has estimated the following yearly cash flows:

Year	Cash Flow ($)
0	−15,000,000
1	4,000,000
2	4,000,000
3	4,000,000
4	4,000,000
5	4,000,000
6	7,000,000

Practice Problems and Solutions: *Quantitative Methods for Investment Analysis*, Second Edition, by Richard A. DeFusco, CFA, Dennis W. McLeavey, CFA, Jerald E. Pinto, CFA, and David E. Runkle, CFA. Copyright © 2004 by CFA Institute.

Trilever's CFO decides that the company's cost of capital of 19 percent is an appropriate hurdle rate for this project.

A. Calculate the internal rate of return of this project.

B. Make a recommendation to the CFO concerning whether to undertake this project.

5. Westcott–Smith is a privately held investment management company. Two other investment counseling companies, which want to be acquired, have contacted Westcott–Smith about purchasing their business. Company A's price is £2 million. Company B's price is £3 million. After analysis, Westcott–Smith estimates that Company A's profitability is consistent with a perpetuity of £300,000 a year. Company B's prospects are consistent with a perpetuity of £435,000 a year. Westcott–Smith has a budget that limits acquisitions to a maximum purchase cost of £4 million. Its opportunity cost of capital relative to undertaking either project is 12 percent.

A. Determine which company or companies (if any) Westcott–Smith should purchase according to the NPV rule.

B. Determine which company or companies (if any) Westcott–Smith should purchase according to the IRR rule.

C. State which company or companies (if any) Westcott–Smith should purchase. Justify your answer.

6. John Wilson buys 150 shares of ABM on 1 January 2002 at a price of $156.30 per share. A dividend of $10 per share is paid on 1 January 2003. Assume that this dividend is not reinvested. Also on 1 January 2003, Wilson sells 100 shares at a price of $165 per share. On 1 January 2004, he collects a dividend of $15 per share (on 50 shares) and sells his remaining 50 shares at $170 per share.

A. Write the formula to calculate the money-weighted rate of return on Wilson's portfolio.

B. Using any method, compute the money-weighted rate of return.

C. Calculate the time-weighted rate of return on Wilson's portfolio.

D. Describe a set of circumstances for which the money-weighted rate of return is an appropriate return measure for Wilson's portfolio.

E. Describe a set of circumstances for which the time-weighted rate of return is an appropriate return measure for Wilson's portfolio.

7. Mario Luongo and Bob Weaver both purchase the same stock for €100. One year later, the stock price is €110 and it pays a dividend of €5 per share. Weaver decides to buy another share at €110 (he does not reinvest the €5 dividend, however). Luongo also spends the €5 per share dividend but does not transact in the stock. At the end of the second year, the stock pays a dividend of €5 per share but its price has fallen back to €100. Luongo and Weaver then decide to sell their entire holdings of this stock. The performance for Luongo and Weaver's investments are as follows:

Luongo: Time-weighted return = 4.77 percent

Money-weighted return = 5.00 percent

Weaver: Money-weighted return = 1.63 percent

Briefly explain any similarities and differences between the performance of Luongo's and Weaver's investments.

8. A Treasury bill with a face value of $100,000 and 120 days until maturity is selling for $98,500.

    A. What is the T-bill's bank discount yield?

    B. What is the T-bill's money market yield?

    C. What is the T-bill's effective annual yield?

9. Jane Cavell has just purchased a 90-day U.S. Treasury bill. She is familiar with yield quotes on German Treasury discount paper but confused about the bank discount quoting convention for the U.S. T-bill she just purchased.

    A. Discuss three reasons why bank discount yield is not a meaningful measure of return.

    B. Discuss the advantage of money market yield compared with bank discount yield as a measure of return.

    C. Explain how the bank discount yield can be converted to an estimate of the holding period return Cavell can expect if she holds the T-bill to maturity.

SOLUTIONS FOR READING 6

1. We can calculate the present value of the cash inflows in several ways. We can discount each cash inflow separately at the required rate of return of 12 percent and then sum the present values. We can also find the present value of a four-year annuity of C$3 million, add to it the present value of the $t = 5$ cash flow of C$10 million, and subtract the $t = 0$ outflow of C$13 million. Or we can compute the present value of a five-year annuity of C$3 million, add to it the present value of a cash inflow of C$7 million = C$10 million – C$3 million dated $t = 5$, and subtract the $t = 0$ outflow of C$13 million. For this last approach, we illustrate the keystrokes for many financial calculators.

Notation Used on Most Calculators	Numerical Value for This Problem
N	5
$\%i$	12
PV **compute**	X
PMT	3,000,000
FV	7,000,000

We find that the PV of the inflows is C$14,786,317.

   A. Therefore, NPV = C$14,786,317 – C$13,000,000 = C$1,786,317.

   B. Waldrup should undertake this project because it has a positive NPV.

2. **A.** The internal rate of return is the discount rate that makes the NPV equal zero:

$$\text{NPV} = \text{CF}_0 + \frac{\text{CF}_1}{(1+\text{IRR})^1} + \frac{\text{CF}_2}{(1+\text{IRR})^2} + \ldots + \frac{\text{CF}_N}{(1+\text{IRR})^N} = 0$$

   To show that the investment project has an IRR of 13.51 percent we need to show that its NPV equals zero, ignoring rounding errors. Substituting the project's cash flows and IRR = 0.1351 into the above equation,

$$\text{NPV} = -\text{C}\$5,500,000 + \frac{\text{C}\$1,000,000}{(1.1351)^1} + \frac{\text{C}\$1,500,000}{(1.1351)^4} + \frac{\text{C}\$7,000,000}{(1.1351)^5}$$

$$= -\text{C}\$5,500,000 + \text{C}\$5,499,266 = -\text{C}\$734$$

   Given that the cash flows were of the magnitude of millions, the amount C$734 differs negligibly from 0.

   B. The internal rate of return is unaffected by any change in any external rate, including the increase in Waldrup's opportunity cost of capital.

3. **A.** NPV is the sum of the present values of all the cash flows associated with the investment, where inflows are signed positive and outflows are signed negative. This problem has only one outflow, an initial expenditure of $10 million at $t = 0$. The projected cash inflows from this advertising project form a perpetuity. We calculate the present value of a perpetuity as $\overline{\text{CF}}/r$, where $\overline{\text{CF}}$ is the level annual cash flow and r is the discount rate. Using the opportunity cost of capital of 12.5 percent as the discount rate, we have

$$\text{NPV} = -\$10,000,000 + 1,600,000/0.125 = -\$10,000,000 + 12,800,000$$

$$= \$2,800,000$$

B. In this case, the cash inflows are a perpetuity. Therefore, we can solve for the internal rate of return as follows:

$$\text{Initial investment} = (\text{Annual cash inflow})/\text{IRR}$$
$$10,000,000 = 1,600,000/\text{IRR}$$
$$\text{IRR} = 16 \text{ percent}$$

C. Yes, Bestfoods should spend $10 million on advertising. The NPV of $2.8 million is positive. The IRR of 16 percent is also in excess of the 12.5 percent opportunity cost of capital.

4. Using the IRR function in a spreadsheet or an IRR-enabled financial calculator, we enter the individual cash flows and apply the IRR function. We illustrate how we can solve for IRR in this particular problem using a financial calculator without a dedicated IRR function. The cash flows from $t = 1$ through $t = 6$ can be treated as a six-year, $4 million annuity with $7 million – $4 million = $3 million, entered as a future amount at $t = 6$.

Notation Used on Most Calculators	Numerical Value for This Problem
N	6
$\%i$ **compute**	X
PV	−15,000,000
PMT	4,000,000
FV	3,000,000

A. The IRR of the project is 18.25 percent.

B. Because the project's IRR is less than the hurdle rate of 19 percent, the company should not undertake the project.

5. **A.** *Company A*. Let $\overline{CF}$ = £300,000 be the amount of the perpetuity. Then with $r = 0.12$, the NPV in acquiring Company A would be

$$\text{NPV} = \text{CF}_0 + \overline{CF}/r = -£2,000,000 + £300,000/0.12 = £500,000$$

Company B. Let $\overline{CF}$ = £435,000 be the amount of the perpetuity. Then with $r = 0.12$, the NPV in acquiring Company B would be

$$\text{NPV} = \text{CF}_0 + \overline{CF}/r = -£3,000,000 + £435,000/0.12 = £625,000$$

Both Company A and Company B would be positive NPV acquisitions, but Westcott–Smith cannot purchase both because the total purchase price of £5 million exceeds its budgeted amount of £4 million. Because Company B's NPV of £625,000 is higher than Company A's NPV of £500,000, Westcott–Smith should purchase Company B according to the NPV rule.

B. *Company A*. Using the notation from Part A, IRR is defined by the expression NPV = −Investment + $\overline{CF}$/IRR = 0. Thus −£2,000,000 + £300,000/IRR = 0 and solving for IRR,

$$\text{IRR} = £300,000/£2,000,000 = 0.15 \text{ or } 15 \text{ percent}$$

Company B.

$$\text{IRR} = £435,000/£3,000,000 = 0.145 \text{ or } 14.5 \text{ percent}$$

Both Company A and Company B have IRRs that exceed Westcott–Smith's opportunity cost of 12 percent, but Westcott–Smith cannot purchase both because of its budget constraint. According to the IRR rule, Westcott–Smith should purchase Company A because its IRR of 15 percent is higher than Company B's IRR of 14.5 percent.

C. Westcott–Smith should purchase Company B. When the NPV and IRR rules conflict in ranking mutually exclusive investments, we should follow the NPV rule because it directly relates to shareholder wealth maximization.

6. A. The money-weighted rate of return is the discount rate that equates the present value of inflows to the present value of outflows.

Outflows:

At $t = 0$ (1 January 2002):
  150 shares purchased × \$156.30 per share = \$23,455

Inflows:

At $t = 1$ (1 January 2003):
  150 shares × \$10 dividend per share = \$1,500
  100 shares sold × \$165 per share = \$16,500
At $t = 2$ (1 January 2004):
  50 shares purchased × \$15 dividend per share = \$750
  50 shares sold × \$170 per share = \$8,500

$$\text{PV(Outflows)} = \text{PV(Inflows)}$$
$$23,445 = \frac{1,500+16,500}{1+r} + \frac{750+8,500}{(1+r)^2}$$
$$= \frac{18,000}{1+r} + \frac{9,250}{(1+r)^2}$$

The last line is the equation for calculating the money-weighted rate of return on Wilson's portfolio.

B. We can solve for the money-weighted return by entering −23,445, 18,000, and 9,250 in a spreadsheet or calculator with an IRR function. In this case, we can also solve for money-weighted rate of return as the real root of the quadratic equation $18,000x + 9,250x^2 - 23,445 = 0$, where $x = 1/(1 + r)$. By any method, the solution is $r = 0.120017$ or approximately 12 percent.

C. The time-weighted rate of return is the solution to $(1 + \text{Time-weighted rate of return})^2 = (1 + r_1)(1 + r_2)$, where r_1 and r_2 are the holding period returns in the first and second years, respectively. The value of the portfolio at $t = 0$ is \$23,445. At $t = 1$, there are inflows of sale proceeds of \$16,500 and \$1,500 in dividends, or \$18,000 in total. The balance of 50 shares is worth \$8,250 = 50 shares × \$165 per share. So at $t = 1$ the valuation is \$26,250 = \$18,000 + \$8,250. Thus

$$r_1 = (\$26,250 - \$23,445)/\$23,445 = 0.119642 \text{ for the first year}$$

The amount invested at $t = 1$ is \$8,250 = (50 shares)(\$165 per share). At $t = 2$, \$750 in dividends are received, as well as sale proceeds of \$8,500 (50 shares sold × \$170 per share). So at $t = 2$, the valuation is \$9,250 = \$750 + \$8,500. Thus

$$r_2 = (\$9,250 - \$8,250)/\$8,250 = 0.121212 \text{ for the second year}$$

Time-weighted rate of return = $\sqrt{(1.119642)(1.121212)} - 1 = 0.1204$ or approximately 12 percent.

D. If Wilson is a private investor with full discretionary control over the timing and amount of withdrawals and additions to his portfolios, then the money-weighted rate of return is an appropriate measure of portfolio returns.

E. If Wilson is an investment manager whose clients exercise discretionary control over the timing and amount of withdrawals and additions to the portfolio, then the time-weighted rate of return is the appropriate measure of portfolio returns. Time-weighted rate of return is standard in the investment management industry.

7. *Similarities.* The time-weighted returns for Luongo's and Weaver's investments will be equal, because the time-weighted return is not sensitive to additions or withdrawals of funds. Even though Weaver purchased another share at €110, the return earned by Luongo and Weaver each year for the time-weighted return calculation is the same.

Differences. The money-weighted returns for Luongo and Weaver will differ because they take into account the timing of additions and withdrawals. During the two-year period, Weaver owned more shares of the stock during the year that it did poorly (the stock return for Year 1 is (110 + 5 − 100)/100 = 15 percent and for Year 2 it is (100 + 5 − 110)/110 = −4.55 percent). As a consequence, the money-weighted return for Weaver (1.63 percent) is less than that of Luongo (5.00 percent). The money-weighted return reflects the timing of additions and withdrawals. Note, the cash flows for the money-weighted returns for Luongo and Weaver are (for t = 0, 1, and 2) Luongo: −100, +5, +105; Weaver: −100, −105, +210.

8. In this solution, F stands for face value, P stands for price, and D stands for the discount from face value ($D = F − P$).

A. Use the discount yield formula (Equation 3), $r_{BD} = D/F \times 360/t$:

$$r_{BD} = (\$1{,}500/\$100{,}000) \times (360/120) = 0.0150 \times 3 = 0.045$$

The T-bill's bank discount yield is 4.5 percent a year.

B. Use your answer from Part A and the money market yield formula (Equation 6), $r_{MM} = (360 \times r_{BD})/(360 − t \times r_{BD})$:

$$r_{MM} = (360 \times 0.045)/(360 − 120 \times 0.045) = 0.04568$$

The T-bill's money market yield is 4.57 percent a year.

C. Calculate the holding period yield (using Equation 4), then compound it forward to one year. First, the holding period yield (HPY) is

$$HPY = \frac{P_1 − P + D_1}{P_0} = (100{,}000 − 98{,}500)/98{,}500 = 0.015228$$

Next, compound the 120-day holding period yield, a periodic rate, forward to one year using Equation 5:

$$\text{Effective annual yield} = (1 + HPY)^{360/t} − 1$$
$$\text{Effective annual yield} = (1.015228)^{360/120} − 1 = 0.047044$$

The T-bill's effective annual yield is 4.7 percent a year.

9. A. In the United States, T-bill yields are quoted on a bank discount basis. The bank discount yield is not a meaningful measure of the return for three reasons: First, the yield is based on the face value of the bond, not on its purchase price. Returns from investments should be evaluated relative to the amount that is invested. Second, the yield is annualized based on a 360-day year rather than a 365-day year. Third, the bank discount yield annualizes with simple interest, which ignores the opportunity to earn interest on interest (compound interest).

B. The money market yield is superior to the bank discount yield because the money market yield is computed relative to the purchase price (not the face value).

C. The T-bill yield can be restated on a money market basis by multiplying the bank discount yield by the ratio of the face value to the purchase price. Cavell could divide the annualized yield by 4 to compute the 90-day holding period yield. This is a more meaningful measure of the return that she will actually earn over 90 days (assuming that she holds the T-bill until it matures).

7

Statistical Concepts and Market Returns

by Richard A. DeFusco, CFA, Dennis W. McLeavey, CFA, Jerald E. Pinto, CFA, and David E. Runkle, CFA

LEARNING OUTCOMES

Mastery	The candidate should be able to:
☐	**a** distinguish between descriptive statistics and inferential statistics, between a population and a sample, and among the types of measurement scales;
☐	**b** define a parameter, a sample statistic, and a frequency distribution;
☐	**c** calculate and interpret relative frequencies and cumulative relative frequencies, given a frequency distribution;
☐	**d** describe the properties of a data set presented as a histogram or a frequency polygon;
☐	**e** calculate and interpret measures of central tendency, including the population mean, sample mean, arithmetic mean, weighted average or mean, geometric mean, harmonic mean, median, and mode;
☐	**f** calculate and interpret quartiles, quintiles, deciles, and percentiles;
☐	**g** calculate and interpret 1) a range and a mean absolute deviation and 2) the variance and standard deviation of a population and of a sample;
☐	**h** calculate and interpret the proportion of observations falling within a specified number of standard deviations of the mean using Chebyshev's inequality;
☐	**i** calculate and interpret the coefficient of variation and the Sharpe ratio;
☐	**j** explain skewness and the meaning of a positively or negatively skewed return distribution;
☐	**k** describe the relative locations of the mean, median, and mode for a unimodal, nonsymmetrical distribution;
☐	**l** explain measures of sample skewness and kurtosis;
☐	**m** explain the use of arithmetic and geometric means when analyzing investment returns.

Quantitative Methods for Investment Analysis, Second Edition, by Richard A. DeFusco, CFA, Dennis W. McLeavey, CFA, Jerald E. Pinto, CFA, and David E. Runkle, CFA. Copyright © 2004 by CFA Institute.

INTRODUCTION

Statistical methods provide a powerful set of tools for analyzing data and drawing conclusions from them. Whether we are analyzing asset returns, earnings growth rates, commodity prices, or any other financial data, statistical tools help us quantify and communicate the data's important features. This reading presents the basics of describing and analyzing data, the branch of statistics known as descriptive statistics. The reading supplies a set of useful concepts and tools, illustrated in a variety of investment contexts. One theme of our presentation, reflected in the reading's title, is the demonstration of the statistical methods that allow us to summarize return distributions.[1] We explore four properties of return distributions:

■ where the returns are centered (central tendency);

■ how far returns are dispersed from their center (dispersion);

■ whether the distribution of returns is symmetrically shaped or lopsided (skewness); and

■ whether extreme outcomes are likely (kurtosis).

These same concepts are generally applicable to the distributions of other types of data, too.

The reading is organized as follows. After defining some basic concepts in Section 2, in Sections 3 and 4 we discuss the presentation of data: Section 3 describes the organization of data in a table format, and Section 4 describes the graphic presentation of data. We then turn to the quantitative description of how data are distributed: Section 5 focuses on measures that quantify where data are centered, or measures of central tendency. Section 6 presents other measures that describe the location of data. Section 7 presents measures that quantify the degree to which data are dispersed. Sections 8 and 9 describe additional measures that provide a more accurate picture of data. Section 10 provides investment applications of concepts introduced in Section 5.

SOME FUNDAMENTAL CONCEPTS

Before starting the study of statistics with this reading, it may be helpful to examine a picture of the overall field. In the following, we briefly describe the scope of statistics and its branches of study. We explain the concepts of population and sample. Data come in a variety of types, affecting the ways they can be measured and the appropriate statistical methods for analyzing them. We conclude by discussing the basic types of data measurement.

2.1 The Nature of Statistics

The term **statistics** can have two broad meanings, one referring to data and the other to method. A company's average earnings per share (EPS) for the last 20 quarters, or its average returns for the past 10 years, are statistics. We may also analyze historical EPS to forecast future EPS, or use the company's past returns to infer its risk. The totality of methods we employ to collect and analyze data is also called statistics.

---

1 Ibbotson Associates (www.ibbotson.com) generously provided much of the data used in this reading. We also draw on Dimson, Marsh, and Staunton's (2002) history and study of world markets as well as other sources.

Statistical methods include descriptive statistics and statistical inference (inferential statistics). **Descriptive statistics** is the study of how data can be summarized effectively to describe the important aspects of large data sets. By consolidating a mass of numerical details, descriptive statistics turns data into information. **Statistical inference** involves making forecasts, estimates, or judgments about a larger group from the smaller group actually observed. The foundation for statistical inference is probability theory, and both statistical inference and probability theory will be discussed in later readings. Our focus in this reading is solely on descriptive statistics.

2.2 Populations and Samples

Throughout the study of statistics we make a critical distinction between a population and a sample. In this section, we explain these two terms as well as the related terms "parameter" and "sample statistic."[2]

- **Definition of Population.** A **population** is defined as all members of a specified group.

Any descriptive measure of a population characteristic is called a **parameter**. Although a population can have many parameters, investment analysts are usually concerned with only a few, such as the mean value, the range of investment returns, and the variance.

Even if it is possible to observe all the members of a population, it is often too expensive in terms of time or money to attempt to do so. For example, if the population is all telecommunications customers worldwide and an analyst is interested in their purchasing plans, she will find it too costly to observe the entire population. The analyst can address this situation by taking a sample of the population.

- **Definition of Sample.** A **sample** is a subset of a population.

In taking a sample, the analyst hopes it is characteristic of the population. The field of statistics known as sampling deals with taking samples in appropriate ways to achieve the objective of representing the population well. A later reading addresses the details of sampling.

Earlier, we mentioned statistics in the sense of referring to data. Just as a parameter is a descriptive measure of a population characteristic, a sample statistic (statistic, for short) is a descriptive measure of a sample characteristic.

- **Definition of Sample Statistic.** A **sample statistic** (or **statistic**) is a quantity computed from or used to describe a sample.

We devote much of this reading to explaining and illustrating the use of statistics in this sense. The concept is critical also in statistical inference, which addresses such problems as estimating an unknown population parameter using a sample statistic.

2.3 Measurement Scales

To choose the appropriate statistical methods for summarizing and analyzing data, we need to distinguish among different **measurement scales** or levels of measurement. All data measurements are taken on one of four major scales: nominal, ordinal, interval, or ratio.

Nominal scales represent the weakest level of measurement: They categorize data but do not rank them. If we assigned integers to mutual funds that follow different investment strategies, the number 1 might refer to a small-cap value fund, the number 2 to a large-cap value fund, and so on for each possible style. This nominal scale categorizes the funds according to their style but does not rank them.

---

2 This reading introduces many statistical concepts and formulas. To make it easy to locate them, we have set off some of the more important ones with bullet points.

Ordinal scales reflect a stronger level of measurement. Ordinal scales sort data into categories that are ordered with respect to some characteristic. For example, the Morningstar and Standard & Poor's star ratings for mutual funds represent an ordinal scale in which one star represents a group of funds judged to have had relatively the worst performance, with two, three, four, and five stars representing groups with increasingly better performance, as evaluated by those services.

An ordinal scale may also involve numbers to identify categories. For example, in ranking balanced mutual funds based on their five-year cumulative return, we might assign the number 1 to the top 10 percent of funds, and so on, so that the number 10 represents the bottom 10 percent of funds. The ordinal scale is stronger than the nominal scale because it reveals that a fund ranked 1 performed better than a fund ranked 2. The scale tells us nothing, however, about the difference in performance between funds ranked 1 and 2 compared with the difference in performance between funds ranked 3 and 4, or 9 and 10.

Interval scales provide not only ranking but also assurance that the differences between scale values are equal. As a result, scale values can be added and subtracted meaningfully. The Celsius and Fahrenheit scales are interval measurement scales. The difference in temperature between 10°C and 11°C is the same amount as the difference between 40°C and 41°C. We can state accurately that 12°C = 9°C + 3°C, for example. Nevertheless, the zero point of an interval scale does not reflect complete absence of what is being measured; it is not a true zero point or natural zero. Zero degrees Celsius corresponds to the freezing point of water, not the absence of temperature. As a consequence of the absence of a true zero point, we cannot meaningfully form ratios on interval scales.

As an example, 50°C, although five times as large a number as 10°C, does not represent five times as much temperature. Also, questionnaire scales are often treated as interval scales. If an investor is asked to rank his risk aversion on a scale from 1 (extremely risk-averse) to 7 (extremely risk-loving), the difference between a response of 1 and a response of 2 is sometimes assumed to represent the same difference in risk aversion as the difference between a response of 6 and a response of 7. When that assumption can be justified, the data are measured on an interval scale.

Ratio scales represent the strongest level of measurement. They have all the characteristics of interval measurement scales as well as a true zero point as the origin. With ratio scales, we can meaningfully compute ratios as well as meaningfully add and subtract amounts within the scale. As a result, we can apply the widest range of statistical tools to data measured on a ratio scale. Rates of return are measured on a ratio scale, as is money. If we have twice as much money, then we have twice the purchasing power. Note that the scale has a natural zero—zero means no money.

Now that we have addressed the important preliminaries, we can discuss summarizing and describing data.

Example 1

Identifying Scales of Measurement

State the scale of measurement for each of the following:

1. Credit ratings for bond issues.[3]

2. Cash dividends per share.

---

[3] Credit ratings for a bond issue gauge the bond issuer's ability to meet the promised principal and interest payments on the bond. For example, one rating agency, Standard & Poor's, assigns bond issues to one of the following ratings, given in descending order of credit quality (increasing probability of default): AAA, AA+, AA, AA−, A+, A, A−, BBB+, BBB, BBB−, BB+, BB, BB−, B, CCC+, CCC−, CC, C, CI, D. For more information on credit risk and credit ratings, see Fabozzi (2004a).

3. Hedge fund classification types.[4]

4. Bond maturity in years.

Solution to 1:

Credit ratings are measured on an ordinal scale. A rating places a bond issue in a category, and the categories are ordered with respect to the expected probability of default. But the difference in the expected probability of default between AA– and A+, for example, is not necessarily equal to that between BB– and B+. In other words, letter credit ratings are not measured on an interval scale.

Solution to 2:

Cash dividends per share are measured on a ratio scale. For this variable, 0 represents the complete absence of dividends; it is a true zero point.

Solution to 3:

Hedge fund classification types are measured on a nominal scale. Each type groups together hedge funds with similar investment strategies. In contrast to credit ratings for bonds, however, hedge fund classification schemes do not involve a ranking. Thus such classification schemes are not measured on an ordinal scale.

Solution to 4:

Bond maturity is measured on a ratio scale.

SUMMARIZING DATA USING FREQUENCY DISTRIBUTIONS

In this section, we discuss one of the simplest ways to summarize data—the frequency distribution.

- **Definition of Frequency Distribution.** A **frequency distribution** is a tabular display of data summarized into a relatively small number of intervals.

Frequency distributions help in the analysis of large amounts of statistical data, and they work with all types of measurement scales.

Rates of return are the fundamental units that analysts and portfolio managers use for making investment decisions and we can use frequency distributions to summarize rates of return. When we analyze rates of return, our starting point is the holding period return (also called the total return).

- **Holding Period Return Formula.** The holding period return for time period t, R_t is

$$R_t = \frac{P_t - P_{t-1} + D_t}{P_{t-1}} \qquad (1)$$

where

P_t = price per share at the end of time period t

P_{t-1} = price per share at the end of time period $t - 1$, the time period immediately preceding time period t

D_t = cash distributions received during time period t

---

4 "Hedge fund" refers to investment vehicles with legal structures that result in less regulatory oversight than other pooled investment vehicles such as mutual funds. Hedge fund classification types group hedge funds by the kind of investment strategy they pursue.

Thus the holding period return for time period *t* is the capital gain (or loss) plus distributions divided by the beginning-period price. (For common stocks, the distribution is a dividend; for bonds, the distribution is a coupon payment.) Equation 1 can be used to define the holding period return on any asset for a day, week, month, or year simply by changing the interpretation of the time interval between successive values of the time index, *t*.

The holding period return, as defined in Equation 1, has two important characteristics. First, it has an element of time attached to it. For example, if a monthly time interval is used between successive observations for price, then the rate of return is a monthly figure. Second, rate of return has no currency unit attached to it. For instance, suppose that prices are denominated in euros. The numerator and denominator of Equation 1 would be expressed in euros, and the resulting ratio would not have any units because the units in the numerator and denominator would cancel one another. This result holds regardless of the currency in which prices are denominated.[5]

With these concerns noted, we now turn to the frequency distribution of the holding period returns on the S&P 500 Index.[6] First, we examine annual rates of return; then we look at monthly rates of return. The annual rates of return on the S&P 500 calculated with Equation 1 span the period January 1926 to December 2002, for a total of 77 annual observations. Monthly return data cover the period January 1926 to December 2002, for a total of 924 monthly observations.

We can state a basic procedure for constructing a frequency distribution as follows.

▪ **Construction of a Frequency Distribution.**

1. Sort the data in ascending order.
2. Calculate the range of the data, defined as Range = Maximum value – Minimum value.
3. Decide on the number of intervals in the frequency distribution, *k*.
4. Determine interval width as Range/*k*.
5. Determine the intervals by successively adding the interval width to the minimum value, to determine the ending points of intervals, stopping after reaching an interval that includes the maximum value.
6. Count the number of observations falling in each interval.
7. Construct a table of the intervals listed from smallest to largest that shows the number of observations falling in each interval.

In Step 4, when rounding the interval width, round up rather than down, to ensure that the final interval includes the maximum value of the data.

As the above procedure makes clear, a frequency distribution groups data into a set of intervals.[7] An **interval** is a set of values within which an observation falls. Each observation falls into only one interval, and the total number of intervals covers all the values represented in the data. The actual number of observations in a given interval is called the **absolute frequency**, or simply the frequency. The frequency distribution is the list of intervals together with the corresponding measures of frequency.

To illustrate the basic procedure, suppose we have 12 observations sorted in ascending order: –4.57, –4.04, –1.64, 0.28, 1.34, 2.35, 2.38, 4.28, 4.42, 4.68, 7.16, and 11.43. The minimum observation is –4.57 and the maximum observation is +11.43, so the range is +11.43 – (–4.57) = 16. If we set *k* = 4, the interval width is 16/4 = 4. Table 1 shows the repeated addition of the interval width of 4 to determine the endpoints for the intervals (Step 5).

5 Note, however, that if price and cash distributions in the expression for holding period return were not in one's home currency, one would generally convert those variables to one's home currency before calculating the holding period return. Because of exchange rate fluctuations during the holding period, holding period returns on an asset computed in different currencies would generally differ.
6 We use the total return series on the S&P 500 from January 1926 to December 2002 provided by Ibbotson Associates.
7 Intervals are also sometimes called classes, ranges, or bins.

Table 1		Endpoints of Intervals		
−4.57	+	4.00	=	−0.57
−0.57	+	4.00	=	3.43
3.43	+	4.00	=	7.43
7.4	+	4.00	=	11.43

Thus the intervals are [−4.57 to −0.57), [−0.57 to 3.43), [3.43 to 7.43), and [7.43 to 11.43].[8] Table 2 summarizes Steps 5 through 7.

Table 2	Frequency Distribution			Absolute Frequency
Interval				
A	−4.57	≤ observation <	−0.57	3
B	−0.57	≤ observation <	3.43	4
C	3.43	≤ observation <	7.43	4
D	7.43	≤ observation ≤	11.43	1

Note that the intervals do not overlap, so each observation can be placed uniquely into one interval.

In practice, we may want to refine the above basic procedure. For example, we may want the intervals to begin and end with whole numbers for ease of interpretation. We also need to explain the choice of the number of intervals, k. We turn to these issues in discussing the construction of frequency distributions for the S&P 500.

We first consider the case of constructing a frequency distribution for the annual returns on the S&P 500 over the period 1926 to 2002. During that period, the return on the S&P 500 had a minimum value of −43.34 percent (in 1931) and a maximum value of +53.99 percent (in 1933). Thus the range of the data was +54% − (−43%) = 97%, approximately. The question now is the number k of intervals into which we should group observations. Although some guidelines for setting k have been suggested in statistical literature, the setting of a useful value for k often involves inspecting the data and exercising judgment. How much detail should we include? If we use too few intervals, we will summarize too much and lose pertinent characteristics. If we use too many intervals, we may not summarize enough.

We can establish an appropriate value for k by evaluating the usefulness of the resulting interval width. A large number of empty intervals may indicate that we are trying to organize the data to present too much detail. Starting with a relatively small interval width, we can see whether or not the intervals are mostly empty and whether or not the value of k associated with that interval width is too large. If intervals are mostly empty or k is very large, we can consider increasingly larger intervals (smaller values of k) until we have a frequency distribution that effectively summarizes the distribution. For the annual S&P 500 series, return intervals of 1 percent width would result in 97 intervals and many of them would be empty because we have only 77 annual observations. We need to keep in mind that the purpose of a frequency distribution is to *summarize* the data. Suppose that for ease of interpretation we want to use an interval width stated in whole rather than fractional percents. A 2 percent interval width would have many fewer empty intervals than a 1 percent interval width and effectively summarize the data. A 2 percent interval width would be associated with

---

8 The notation [−4.57 to −0.57) means −4.57 ≤ observation < −0.57. In this context, a square bracket indicates that the endpoint is included in the interval.

97/2 = 48.5 intervals, which we can round up to 49 intervals. That number of intervals will cover 2% × 49 = 98%. We can confirm that if we start the smallest 2 percent interval at the whole number –44.0 percent, the final interval ends at –44.0% + 98% = 54% and includes the maximum return in the sample, 53.99 percent. In so constructing the frequency distribution, we will also have intervals that end and begin at a value of 0 percent, allowing us to count the negative and positive returns in the data. Without too much work, we have found an effective way to summarize the data. We will use return intervals of 2 percent, beginning with $-44\% \leq R_t < -42\%$ (given as "–44% to –42%" in the table) and ending with $52\% \leq R_t \leq 54\%$. Table 3 shows the frequency distribution for the annual total returns on the S&P 500.

Table 3 includes three other useful ways to present data, which we can compute once we have established the frequency distribution: the relative frequency, the cumulative frequency (also called the cumulative absolute frequency), and the cumulative relative frequency.

- **Definition of Relative Frequency.** The **relative frequency** is the absolute frequency of each interval divided by the total number of observations.

The **cumulative relative frequency** cumulates (adds up) the relative frequencies as we move from the first to the last interval. It tells us the fraction of observations that are less than the upper limit of each interval. Examining the frequency distribution given in Table 3, we see that the first return interval, –44 percent to –42 percent, has one observation; its relative frequency is 1/77 or 1.30 percent. The cumulative frequency for this interval is 1 because only one observation is less than –42 percent. The cumulative relative frequency is thus 1/77 or 1.30 percent. The next return interval has zero observations; therefore, its cumulative frequency is 0 plus 1 and its cumulative relative frequency is 1.30 percent (the cumulative relative frequency from the previous interval). We can find the other cumulative frequencies by adding the (absolute) frequency to the previous cumulative frequency. The cumulative frequency, then, tells us the number of observations that are less than the upper limit of each return interval.

As Table 3 shows, return intervals have frequencies from 0 to 7 in this sample. The interval encompassing returns between –10 percent and –8 percent ($-10\% \leq R_t < -8\%$) has the most observations, seven. Next most frequent are returns between 18 percent and 20 percent ($18\% \leq R_t < 20\%$), with six observations. From the cumulative frequency column, we see that the number of negative returns is 23. The number of positive returns must then be equal to 77 – 23, or 54. We can express the number of positive and negative outcomes as a percentage of the total to get a sense of the risk inherent in investing in the stock market. During the 77-year period, the S&P 500 had negative annual returns 29.9 percent of the time (that is, 23/77). This result appears in the fifth column of Table 3, which reports the cumulative relative frequency.

The frequency distribution gives us a sense of not only where most of the observations lie but also whether the distribution is evenly distributed, lopsided, or peaked. In the case of the S&P 500, we can see that more than half of the outcomes are positive and most of those annual returns are larger than 10 percent. (Only 11 of the 54 positive annual returns—about 20 percent—were between 0 and 10 percent.)

Table 3 permits us to make an important further point about the choice of the number of intervals related to equity returns in particular. From the frequency distribution in Table 3, we can see that only five outcomes fall between –44 percent to –16 percent and between 38 percent to 54 percent. Stock return data are frequently characterized by a few very large or small outcomes. We could have collapsed the return intervals in the tails of the frequency distribution by choosing a smaller value of k, but then we would have lost the information about how extremely poorly or well the stock market had performed. A risk manager may need to know the worst possible outcomes and thus may want to have detailed information on the tails (the extreme values). A frequency distribution with a relatively large value of k is useful for that.

Table 3 Frequency Distribution for the Annual Total Return on the S&P 500, 1926–2002

Return Interval (%)	Frequency	Relative Frequency (%)	Cumulative Frequency	Cumulative Relative Frequency (%)
−44.0 to −42.0	1	1.30	1	1.30
−42.0 to −40.0	0	0.00	1	1.30
−40.0 to −38.0	0	0.00	1	1.30
−38.0 to −36.0	0	0.00	1	1.30
−36.0 to −34.0	1	1.30	2	2.60
−34.0 to −32.0	0	0.00	2	2.60
−32.0 to −30.0	0	0.00	2	2.60
−30.0 to −28.0	0	0.00	2	2.60
−28.0 to −26.0	1	1.30	3	3.90
−26.0 to −24.0	1	1.30	4	5.19
−24.0 to −22.0	1	1.30	5	6.49
−22.0 to −20.0	0	0.00	5	6.49
−20.0 to −18.0	0	0.00	5	6.49
−18.0 to −16.0	0	0.00	5	6.49
−16.0 to −14.0	1	1.30	6	7.79
−14.0 to −12.0	0	0.00	6	7.79
−12.0 to −10.0	4	5.19	10	12.99
−10.0 to −8.0	7	9.09	17	22.08
−8.0 to −6.0	1	1.30	18	23.38
−6.0 to −4.0	1	1.30	19	24.68
−4.0 to −2.0	1	1.30	20	25.97
−2.0 to 0.0	3	3.90	23	29.87
0.0 to 2.0	2	2.60	25	32.47
2.0 to 4.0	0	0.00	25	32.47
4.0 to 6.0	4	5.19	29	37.66
6.0 to 8.0	4	5.19	33	42.86
8.0 to 10.0	1	1.30	34	44.16
10.0 to 12.0	3	3.90	37	48.05
12.0 to 14.0	1	1.30	38	49.35
14.0 to 16.0	1	1.30	39	50.65
16.0 to 18.0	2	2.60	41	53.25
18.0 to 20.0	6	7.79	47	61.04
20.0 to 22.0	3	3.90	50	64.94
22.0 to 24.0	5	6.49	55	71.43
24.0 to 26.0	2	2.60	57	74.03
26.0 to 28.0	1	1.30	58	75.32
28.0 to 30.0	1	1.30	59	76.62
30.0 to 32.0	5	6.49	64	83.12
32.0 to 34.0	4	5.19	68	88.31
34.0 to 36.0	0	0.00	68	88.31
36.0 to 38.0	4	5.19	72	93.51
38.0 to 40.0	0	0.00	72	93.51
40.0 to 42.0	0	0.00	72	93.51
42.0 to 44.0	2	2.60	74	96.10
44.0 to 46.0	0	0.00	74	96.10
46.0 to 48.0	1	1.30	75	97.40
48.0 to 50.0	0	0.00	75	97.40
50.0 to 52.0	0	0.00	75	97.40
52.0 to 54.0	2	2.60	77	100.00

Note: The lower class limit is the weak inequality ($\leq$) and the upper class limit is the strong inequality ($<$).
Source: Frequency distribution generated with Ibbotson Associates EnCorr Analyzer.

A portfolio manager or analyst may be equally interested in detailed information on the tails; however, if the manager or analyst wants a picture only of where most of the observations lie, he might prefer to use an interval width of 4 percent (25 intervals beginning at –44 percent), for example.

The frequency distribution for monthly returns on the S&P 500 looks quite different from that for annual returns. The monthly return series from January 1926 to December 2002 has 924 observations. Returns range from a minimum of approximately –30 percent to a maximum of approximately +43 percent. With such a large quantity of monthly data we must summarize to get a sense of the distribution, and so we group the data into 37 equally spaced return intervals of 2 percent. The gains from summarizing in this way are substantial. Table 4 presents the resulting frequency distribution. The absolute frequencies appear in the second column, followed by the relative frequencies. The relative frequencies are rounded to two decimal places. The cumulative absolute and cumulative relative frequencies appear in the fourth and fifth columns, respectively.

Table 4	Frequency Distribution for the Monthly Total Return on the S&P 500, January 1926 to December 2002			
Return Interval (%)	Absolute Frequency	Relative Frequency (%)	Cumulative Absolute Frequency	Cumulative Relative Frequency (%)
–30.0 to –28.0	1	0.11	1	0.11
–28.0 to –26.0	0	0.00	1	0.11
–26.0 to –24.0	1	0.11	2	0.22
–24.0 to –22.0	1	0.11	3	0.32
–22.0 to –20.0	2	0.22	5	0.54
–20.0 to –18.0	2	0.22	7	0.76
–18.0 to –16.0	2	0.22	9	0.97
–16.0 to –14.0	3	0.32	12	1.30
–14.0 to –12.0	5	0.54	17	1.84
–12.0 to –10.0	6	0.65	23	2.49
–10.0 to –8.0	20	2.16	43	4.65
–8.0 to –6.0	30	3.25	73	7.90
–6.0 to –4.0	54	5.84	127	13.74
–4.0 to –2.0	90	9.74	217	23.48
–2.0 to 0.0	138	14.94	355	38.42
0.0 to 2.0	182	19.70	537	58.12
2.0 to 4.0	153	16.56	690	74.68
4.0 to 6.0	126	13.64	816	88.31
6.0 to 8.0	58	6.28	874	94.59
8.0 to 10.0	21	2.27	895	96.86
10.0 to 12.0	14	1.52	909	98.38
12.0 to 14.0	6	0.65	915	99.03
14.0 to 16.0	2	0.22	917	99.24
16.0 to 18.0	3	0.32	920	99.57
18.0 to 20.0	0	0.00	920	99.57
20.0 to 22.0	0	0.00	920	99.57
22.0 to 24.0	0	0.00	920	99.57

| | | Relative | Cumulative | Cumulative |
Return Interval (%)	Absolute Frequency	Frequency (%)	Absolute Frequency	Relative Frequency (%)
24.0 to 26.0	1	0.11	921	99.68
26.0 to 28.0	0	0.00	921	99.68
28.0 to 30.0	0	0.00	921	99.68
30.0 to 32.0	0	0.00	921	99.68
32.0 to 34.0	0	0.00	921	99.68
34.0 to 36.0	0	0.00	921	99.68
36.0 to 38.0	0	0.00	921	99.68
38.0 to 40.0	2	0.22	923	99.89
40.0 to 42.0	0	0.00	923	99.89
42.0 to 44.0	1	0.11	924	100.00

Note: The lower class limit is the weak inequality ($\leq$) and the upper class limit is the strong inequality ($<$). The relative frequency is the absolute frequency or cumulative frequency divided by the total number of observations.
Source: Frequency distribution generated with Ibbotson Associates EnCorr Analyzer.

The advantage of a frequency distribution is evident in Table 4, which tells us that the vast majority of observations (599/924 = 65 percent) lie in the four intervals spanning −2 percent to +6 percent. Altogether, we have 355 negative returns and 569 positive returns. Almost 62 percent of the monthly outcomes are positive. Looking at the cumulative relative frequency in the last column, we see that the interval −2 percent to 0 percent shows a cumulative frequency of 38.42 percent, for an upper return limit of 0 percent. This means that 38.42 percent of the observations lie below the level of 0 percent. We can also see that not many observations are greater than +12 percent or less than −12 percent. Note that the frequency distributions of annual and monthly returns are not directly comparable. On average, we should expect the returns measured at shorter intervals (for example, months) to be smaller than returns measured over longer periods (for example, years).

Next, we construct a frequency distribution of average inflation-adjusted returns over 1900–2000 for 16 major equity markets.

Example 2

Constructing a Frequency Distribution

How have equities rewarded investors in different countries in the long run? To answer this question, we could examine the average annual returns directly.[9] The worth of a nominal level of return depends on changes in the purchasing power of money, however, and internationally there have been a variety of experiences with price inflation. It is preferable, therefore, to compare the average real or inflation-adjusted returns earned by investors in different countries. Dimson, Marsh, and Staunton (2002) presented authoritative evidence on asset returns in 16 countries for the 101 years 1900–2000. Table 5 excerpts their findings for average inflation-adjusted returns.

---

9 The average or arithmetic mean of a set of values equals the sum of the values divided by the number of values summed. To find the arithmetic mean of 101 annual returns, for example, we sum the 101 annual returns and then divide the total by 101. Among the most familiar of statistical concepts, the arithmetic mean is explained in more detail later in the reading.

Table 5	Real (Inflation-Adjusted) Equity Returns: Sixteen Major Equity Markets, 1900–2000

Country	Arithmetic Mean (%)
Australia	9.0
Belgium	4.8
Canada	7.7
Denmark	6.2
France	6.3
Germany	8.8
Ireland	7.0
Italy	6.8
Japan	9.3
Netherlands	7.7
South Africa	9.1
Spain	5.8
Sweden	9.9
Switzerland	6.9
United Kingdom	7.6
United States	8.7

Source: Dimson, Marsh, and Staunton (2002), Table 9-3. Swiss equities date from 1911.

Table 6 summarizes the data in Table 5 into six intervals spanning 4 percent to 10 percent.

Table 6	Frequency Distribution of Average Real Equity Returns

Return Interval (%)	Absolute Frequency	Relative Frequency (%)	Cumulative Absolute Frequency	Cumulative Relative Frequency (%)
4.0 to 5.0	1	6.25	1	6.25
5.0 to 6.0	1	6.25	2	12.50
6.0 to 7.0	4	25.00	6	37.50
7.0 to 8.0	4	25.00	10	62.50
8.0 to 9.0	2	12.50	12	75.00
9.0 to 10	4	25.00	16	100.00

Note: Relative frequencies are rounded to sum to 100%.

As Table 6 shows, there is substantial variation internationally of average real equity returns. Three-fourths of the observations fall in one of three intervals: 6.0 to 7.0 percent, 7.0 to 8.0 percent, or 9.0 to 10.0 percent. Most average real equity returns are between 6.0 percent and 10 percent; the cumulative relative frequency of returns less than 6.0 percent was only 12.50 percent.

THE GRAPHIC PRESENTATION OF DATA

A graphical display of data allows us to visualize important characteristics quickly. For example, we may see that the distribution is symmetrically shaped, and this finding may influence which probability distribution we use to describe the data. In this section, we discuss the histogram, the frequency polygon, and the cumulative frequency distribution as methods for displaying data graphically. We construct all of these graphic presentations with the information contained in the frequency distribution of the S&P 500 shown in either Table 3 or Table 4.

4.1 The Histogram

A histogram is the graphical equivalent of a frequency distribution.

■ **Definition of Histogram.** A **histogram** is a bar chart of data that have been grouped into a frequency distribution.

The advantage of the visual display is that we can see quickly where most of the observations lie. To see how a histogram is constructed, look at the return interval $18\% \leq R_t < 20\%$ in Table 3. This interval has an absolute frequency of 6. Therefore, we erect a bar or rectangle with a height of 6 over that return interval on the horizontal axis. Continuing with this process for all other return intervals yields a histogram. Figure 1 presents the histogram of the annual total return series on the S&P 500 from 1926 to 2002.

| Figure 1 | Histogram of S&P 500 Annual Total Returns: 1926 to 2002 |

Source: Ibbotson EnCorr Analyzer™.

In the histogram in Figure 1, the height of each bar represents the absolute frequency for each return interval. The return interval $-10\% \leq R_t < -8\%$ has a frequency of 7 and is represented by the tallest bar in the histogram. Because there are no gaps between the interval limits, there are no gaps between the bars of the histogram. Many of the return intervals have zero frequency; therefore, they have no height in the histogram.

Figure 2 presents the histogram for the distribution of monthly returns on the S&P 500. Somewhat more symmetrically shaped than the histogram of annual returns shown in Figure 1, this histogram also appears more bell-shaped than the distribution of annual returns.

Figure 2	Histogram of S&P 500 Monthly Total Returns: January 1926 to December 2002

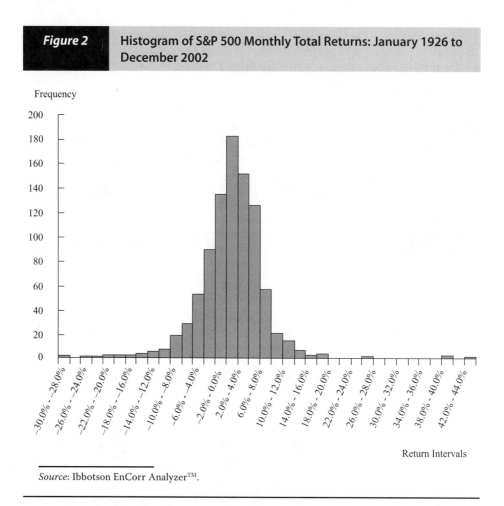

Source: Ibbotson EnCorr Analyzer™.

4.2 The Frequency Polygon and the Cumulative Frequency Distribution

Two other graphical tools for displaying data are the frequency polygon and the cumulative frequency distribution. To construct a **frequency polygon**, we plot the midpoint of each interval on the *x*-axis and the absolute frequency for that interval on the *y*-axis; we then connect neighboring points with a straight line. Figure 3 shows the frequency polygon for the 924 monthly returns for the S&P 500 from January 1926 to December 2002.

Figure 3	Frequency Polygon of S&P 500 Monthly Total Returns: January 1926 to December 2002

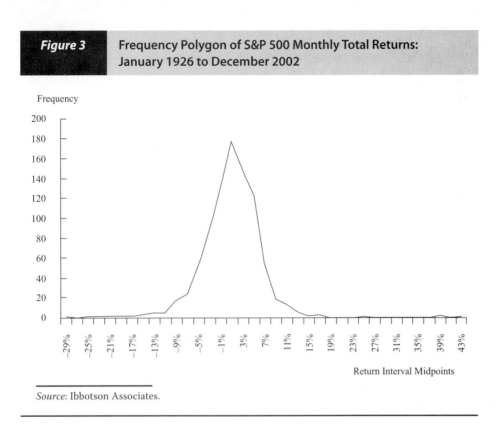

Source: Ibbotson Associates.

In Figure 3, we have replaced the bars in the histogram with points connected with straight lines. For example, the return interval 0 percent to 2 percent has an absolute frequency of 182. In the frequency polygon, we plot the return-interval midpoint of 1 percent and a frequency of 182. We plot all other points in a similar way.[10] This form of visual display adds a degree of continuity to the representation of the distribution.

Another form of line graph is the cumulative frequency distribution. Such a graph can plot either the cumulative absolute or cumulative relative frequency against the upper interval limit. The cumulative frequency distribution allows us to see how many or what percent of the observations lie below a certain value. To construct the cumulative frequency distribution, we graph the returns in the fourth or fifth column of Table 4 against the upper limit of each return interval. Figure 4 presents a graph of the cumulative absolute distribution for the monthly returns on the S&P 500. Notice that the cumulative distribution tends to flatten out when returns are extremely negative or extremely positive. The steep slope in the middle of Figure 4 reflects the fact that most of the observations lie in the neighborhood of −2 percent to 6 percent.

---

10 Even though the upper limit on the interval is not a return falling in the interval, we still average it with the lower limit to determine the midpoint.

| Figure 4 | Cumulative Absolute Frequency Distribution of S&P 500 Monthly Total Returns: January 1926 to December 2002 |

Source: Ibbotson Associates.

We can further examine the relationship between the relative frequency and the cumulative relative frequency by looking at the two return intervals reproduced in Table 7. The first return interval (0 percent to 2 percent) has a cumulative relative frequency of 58.12 percent. The next return interval (2 percent to 4 percent) has a cumulative relative frequency of 74.68 percent. The change in the cumulative relative frequency as we move from one interval to the next is the next interval's relative frequency. For instance, as we go from the first return interval (0 percent to 2 percent) to the next return interval (2 percent to 4 percent), the change in the cumulative relative frequency is 74.68% − 58.12% = 16.56%. (Values in the table have been rounded to two decimal places.) The fact that the slope is steep indicates that these frequencies are large. As you can see in the graph of the cumulative distribution, the slope of the curve changes as we move from the first return interval to the last. A fairly small slope for the cumulative distribution for the first few return intervals tells us that these return intervals do not contain many observations. You can go back to the frequency distribution in Table 4 and verify that the cumulative absolute frequency is only 23 observations (the cumulative relative frequency is 2.49 percent) up to the 10th return interval (−12 percent to −10 percent). In essence, the slope of the cumulative absolute distribution at any particular interval is proportional to the number of observations in that interval.

| Table 7 | Selected Class Frequencies for the S&P 500 Monthly Returns |

Return Interval (%)	Absolute Frequency	Relative Frequency (%)	Cumulative Absolute Frequency	Cumulative Relative Frequency (%)
0.0 to 2.0	182	19.70	537	58.12
2.0 to 4.0	153	16.56	690	74.68

MEASURES OF CENTRAL TENDENCY

So far, we have discussed methods we can use to organize and present data so that they are more understandable. The frequency distribution of an asset class's return series, for example, reveals the nature of the risks that investors may encounter in a particular asset class. As an illustration, the histogram for the annual returns on the S&P 500 clearly shows that large positive and negative annual returns are common. Although frequency distributions and histograms provide a convenient way to summarize a series of observations, these methods are just a first step toward describing the data. In this section we discuss the use of quantitative measures that explain characteristics of data. Our focus is on measures of central tendency and other measures of location or location parameters. A **measure of central tendency** specifies where the data are centered. Measures of central tendency are probably more widely used than any other statistical measure because they can be computed and applied easily. **Measures of location** include not only measures of central tendency but other measures that illustrate the location or distribution of data.

In the following subsections we explain the common measures of central tendency—the arithmetic mean, the median, the mode, the weighted mean, and the geometric mean. We also explain other useful measures of location, including quartiles, quintiles, deciles, and percentiles.

5.1 The Arithmetic Mean

Analysts and portfolio managers often want one number that describes a representative possible outcome of an investment decision. The arithmetic mean is by far the most frequently used measure of the middle or center of data.

■ **Definition of Arithmetic Mean.** The **arithmetic mean** is the sum of the observations divided by the number of observations.

We can compute the arithmetic mean for both populations and samples, known as the population mean and the sample mean, respectively.

5.1.1 *The Population Mean*

The population mean is the arithmetic mean computed for a population. If we can define a population adequately, then we can calculate the population mean as the arithmetic mean of all the observations or values in the population. For example, analysts examining the fiscal 2002 year-over-year growth in same-store sales of major U.S. wholesale clubs might define the population of interest to include only three companies: BJ's Wholesale Club (NYSE: BJ), Costco Wholesale Corporation (NASDAQ: COST), and Sam's Club, part of Wal-Mart Stores (NYSE: WMT).[11] As another example, if a portfolio manager's investment universe (the set of securities she must choose from) is the Nikkei–Dow Jones Average, the relevant population is the 225 shares on the First Section of the Tokyo Stock Exchange that compose the Nikkei.

■ **Population Mean Formula.** The **population mean**, μ, is the arithmetic mean value of a population. For a finite population, the population mean is

$$\mu = \frac{\sum_{i=1}^{N} X_i}{N} \qquad (2)$$

where N is the number of observations in the entire population and X_i is the ith observation.

---

11 A wholesale club implements a store format dedicated mostly to bulk sales in warehouse-sized stores to customers who pay membership dues. As of the early 2000s, those three wholesale clubs dominated the segment in the United States.

The population mean is an example of a parameter. The population mean is unique; that is, a given population has only one mean. To illustrate the calculation, we can take the case of the population mean of current price-to-earnings ratio (P/E) of stocks of U.S. companies running major wholesale clubs as of the beginning of September 2003. As of that date, the current P/Es for BJ, COST, and WMT were 16.73, 22.02, and 29.30, respectively, according to First Call/Thomson Financial. Thus the population mean current P/E on that date was μ = (16.73 + 22.02 + 29.30)/3 = 68.05/3 = 22.68.

5.1.2 *The Sample Mean*

The sample mean is the arithmetic mean computed for a sample. Many times we cannot observe every member of a set; instead, we observe a subset or sample of the population. The concept of the mean can be applied to the observations in a sample with a slight change in notation.

- **Sample Mean Formula.** The **sample mean** or average, $\overline{X}$ (read "X-bar"), is the arithmetic mean value of a sample:

$$\overline{X} = \frac{\sum_{i=1}^{n} X_i}{n} \tag{3}$$

where n is the number of observations in the sample.

Equation 3 tells us to sum the values of the observations (X_i) and divide the sum by the number of observations. For example, if the sample of P/E multiples contains the values 35, 30, 22, 18, 15, and 12, the sample mean P/E is 132/6 = 22. The sample mean is also called the arithmetic average.[12] As we discussed earlier, the sample mean is a statistic (that is, a descriptive measure of a sample).

Means can be computed for individual units or over time. For instance, the sample might be the 2003 return on equity (ROE) for the 300 companies in the Financial Times Stock Exchange (FTSE) Eurotop 300, an index of Europe's 300 largest companies. In this case, we calculate mean ROE in 2003 as an average across 300 individual units. When we examine the characteristics of some units at a specific point in time (such as ROE for the FTSE Eurotop 300), we are examining **cross-sectional data**. The mean of these observations is called a cross-sectional mean. On the other hand, if our sample consists of the historical monthly returns on the FTSE Eurotop 300 for the past five years, then we have **time-series data**. The mean of these observations is called a time-series mean. We will examine specialized statistical methods related to the behavior of time series in the reading on times-series analysis.

Next, we show an example of finding the sample mean return for equities in 16 European countries for 2002. In this case, the mean is cross-sectional because we are averaging individual country returns.

Example 3

Calculating a Cross-Sectional Mean

The MSCI EAFE (Europe, Australasia, and Far East) Index is a free float-adjusted market capitalization index designed to measure developed-market equity performance excluding the United States and Canada.[13] As of the end of 2002, the EAFE consisted of 21 developed market country indexes, including indexes for 16 European markets, 2 Australasian markets (Australia and New Zealand), and 3 Far Eastern markets (Hong Kong, Japan, and Singapore).

---

12 Statisticians prefer the term "mean" to "average." Some writers refer to all measures of central tendency (including the median and mode) as averages. The term "mean" avoids any possibility of confusion.
13 The term "free float adjusted" means that the weights of companies in the index reflect the value of the shares actually available for investment.

Suppose we are interested in the local currency performance of the 16 European markets in the EAFE in 2002, a severe bear market year. We want to find the sample mean total return for 2002 across these 16 markets. The return series reported in Table 8 are in local currency (that is, returns are for investors living in the country). Because this return is not stated in any single investor's home currency, it is not a return any single investor would earn. Rather, it is an average of returns in 16 local currencies.

Table 8	Total Returns for European Equity Markets, 2002
Market	**Total Return in Local Currency (%)**
Austria	−2.97
Belgium	−29.71
Denmark	−29.67
Finland	−41.65
France	−33.99
Germany	−44.05
Greece	−39.06
Ireland	−38.97
Italy	−23.64
Netherlands	−34.27
Norway	−29.73
Portugal	−28.29
Spain	−29.47
Sweden	−43.07
Switzerland	−25.84
United Kingdom	−25.66

Source: www.mscidata.com.

Using the data in Table 8, calculate the sample mean return for the 16 equity markets in 2002.

Solution:

The calculation applies Equation 3 to the returns in Table 8: (−2.97 − 29.71 − 29.67 − 41.65 − 33.99 − 44.05 − 39.06 − 38.97 − 23.64 − 34.27 − 29.73 − 28.29 − 29.47 − 43.07 − 25.84 − 25.66)/16 = −500.04/16 = −31.25 percent.

In Example 3, we can verify that seven markets had returns less than the mean and nine had returns that were greater. We should not expect any of the actual observations to equal the mean, because sample means provide only a summary of the data being analyzed. As an analyst, you will often need to find a few numbers that describe the characteristics of the distribution. The mean is generally the statistic that you will use as a measure of the typical outcome for a distribution. You can then use the mean to compare the performance of two different markets. For example, you might be interested in comparing the stock market performance of investments in Pacific Rim countries with investments in European countries. You can use the mean returns in these markets to compare investment results.

5.1.3 *Properties of the Arithmetic Mean*

The arithmetic mean can be likened to the center of gravity of an object. Figure 5 expresses this analogy graphically by plotting nine hypothetical observations on a bar. The nine observations are 2, 4, 4, 6, 10, 10, 12, 12, and 12; the arithmetic mean is 72/9 = 8. The observations are plotted on the bar with various heights based on their frequency (that is, 2 is one unit high, 4 is two units high, and so on). When the bar is placed on a fulcrum, it balances only when the fulcrum is located at the point on the scale that corresponds to the arithmetic mean.

| **Figure 5** | **Center of Gravity Analogy for the Arithmetic Mean** |

When the fulcrum is placed at 8, the bar is perfectly balanced.

As analysts, we often use the mean return as a measure of the typical outcome for an asset. As in the example above, however, some outcomes are above the mean and some are below it. We can calculate the distance between the mean and each outcome and call it a deviation. Mathematically, it is always true that the sum of the deviations around the mean equals 0. We can see this by using the definition of the arithmetic mean shown in Equation 3, multiplying both sides of the equation by n: $n\overline{X} = \sum_{i=1}^{n} X_i$. The sum of the deviations from the mean can thus be calculated as follows:

$$\sum_{i=1}^{n}\left(X_i - \overline{X}\right) = \sum_{i=1}^{n} X_i - \sum_{i=1}^{n} \overline{X} = \sum_{i=1}^{n} X_i - n\overline{X} = 0$$

Deviations from the arithmetic mean are important information because they indicate risk. The concept of deviations around the mean forms the foundation for the more complex concepts of variance, skewness, and kurtosis, which we will discuss later in this reading.

An advantage of the arithmetic mean over two other measures of central tendency, the median and mode, is that the mean uses all the information about the size and magnitude of the observations. The mean is also easy to work with mathematically.

A property and potential drawback of the arithmetic mean is its sensitivity to extreme values. Because all observations are used to compute the mean, the arithmetic mean can be pulled sharply upward or downward by extremely large or small observations, respectively. For example, suppose we compute the arithmetic mean of the following seven numbers: 1, 2, 3, 4, 5, 6, and 1,000. The mean is 1,021/7 = 145.86 or approximately 146. Because the magnitude of the mean, 146, is so much larger than that of the bulk of the observations (the first six), we might question how well it represents the location of the data. In practice, although an extreme value or outlier in a financial dataset may only represent a rare value in the population, it may also reflect an error in recording the value of an observation, or an observation generated from a different population from that producing the other observations in the sample. In the latter two cases in particular, the arithmetic mean could be misleading. Perhaps the most common approach in such cases is to report the median in place of or in addition to the mean.[14] We discuss the median next.

5.2 The Median

A second important measure of central tendency is the median.

■ **Definition of Median.** The **median** is the value of the middle item of a set of items that has been sorted into ascending or descending order. In an odd-numbered sample of n items, the median occupies the $(n + 1)/2$ position. In an even-numbered sample, we define the median as the mean of the values of items occupying the $n/2$ and $(n + 2)/2$ positions (the two middle items).[15]

Earlier we gave the current P/Es of three wholesale clubs as 16.73, 22.02, and 29.30. With an odd number of observations ($n = 3$), the median occupies the $(n + 1)/2 = 4/2 = 2$nd position. The median P/E was 22.02. The P/E value of 22.02 is the "middlemost" observation: One lies above it, and one lies below it. Whether we use the calculation for an even- or odd-numbered sample, an equal number of observations lie above and below the median. A distribution has only one median.

A potential advantage of the median is that, unlike the mean, extreme values do not affect it. The median, however, does not use all the information about the size and magnitude of the observations; it focuses only on the relative position of the ranked observations. Calculating the median is also more complex; to do so, we need to order the observations from smallest to largest, determine whether the sample size is even or odd and, on that basis, apply one of two calculations. Mathematicians express this disadvantage by saying that the median is less mathematically tractable than the mean.

To demonstrate finding the median, we use the data from Example 3, reproduced in Table 9 in ascending order of the 2002 total return for European equities. Because this sample has 16 observations, the median is the mean of the values in the sorted array that occupy the $16/2 = 8$th and $18/2 = 9$th positions. Norway's return occupies the eighth position with a return of −29.73 percent, and Belgium's return occupies the ninth position with a return of −29.71 percent. The median, as the mean of these

---

14 Other approaches to handling extreme values involve variations of the arithmetic mean. The **trimmed mean** is computed by excluding a stated small percentage of the lowest and highest values and then computing an arithmetic mean of the remaining values. For example, a 5 percent trimmed mean discards the lowest 2.5 percent and the largest 2.5 percent of values and computes the mean of the remaining 95 percent of values. A trimmed mean is used in sports competitions when judges' lowest and highest scores are discarded in computing a contestant's score. A **Winsorized mean** assigns a stated percent of the lowest values equal to one specified low value, and a stated percent of the highest values equal to one specified high value, then computes a mean from the restated data. For example, a 95 percent Winsorized mean sets the bottom 2.5 percent of values equal to the 2.5th percentile value and the upper 2.5 percent of values equal to the 97.5th percentile value. (Percentile values are defined later.)

15 The notation M_d is occasionally used for the median. Just as for the mean, we may distinguish between a population median and a sample median. With the understanding that a population median divides a population in half while a sample median divides a sample in half, we follow general usage in using the term "median" without qualification, for the sake of brevity.

two returns, is (−29.73 − 29.71)/2 = −29.72 percent. Note that the median is not influenced by extremely large or small outcomes. Had Germany's total return been a much lower value or Austria's total return a much larger value, the median would not have changed. Using a context that arises often in practice, Example 4 shows how to use the mean and median in a sample with extreme values.

Table 9	Total Returns for European Equity Markets, 2002 (in Ascending Order)	
No.	Market	Total Return in Local Currency (%)
1	Germany	−44.05
2	Sweden	−43.07
3	Finland	−41.65
4	Greece	−39.06
5	Ireland	−38.97
6	Netherlands	−34.27
7	France	−33.99
8	Norway	−29.73
9	Belgium	−29.71
10	Denmark	−29.67
11	Spain	−29.47
12	Portugal	−28.29
13	Switzerland	−25.84
14	United Kingdom	−25.66
15	Italy	−23.64
16	Austria	−2.97

Source: www.mscidata.com.

Example 4

Median and Arithmetic Mean: The Case of the Price–Earnings Ratio

Suppose a client asks you for a valuation analysis on the seven-stock U.S. common stock portfolio given in Table 10. The stocks are equally weighted in the portfolio. One valuation measure that you use is P/E, the ratio of share price to earnings per share (EPS). Many variations exist for the denominator in the P/E, but you are examining P/E defined as current price divided by the current mean of all analysts' EPS estimates for the company for the current fiscal year ("Consensus Current EPS" in the table).[16] The values in Table 10 are as of 11 September 2003. For comparison purposes, the consensus current P/E on the S&P 500 was 23.63 at that time.

---

16 For more information on price multiples, see Stowe, Robinson, Pinto, and McLeavey (2002).

Table 10	P/Es for a Client Portfolio	
Stock	**Consensus Current EPS**	**Consensus Current P/E**
Exponent Inc. (NASDAQ: EXPO)	1.23	13.68
Express Scripts (NASDAQ: ESRX)	3.19	19.07
General Dynamics (NYSE: GD)	4.95	17.56
Limited Brands (NYSE: LTD)	1.06	15.60
Merant plc (NASDAQ: MRNT)	0.03	443.33
Microsoft Corporation (NASDAQ: MSFT)	1.11	25.61
O'Reilly Automotive, Inc. (NASDAQ: ORLY)	1.84	21.01

Source: First Call/Thomson Financial.

Using the data in Table 10, address the following:

1. Calculate the arithmetic mean P/E.
2. Calculate the median P/E.
3. Evaluate the mean and median P/Es as measures of central tendency for the above portfolio.

Solution to 1:

The mean P/E is (13.68 + 19.07 + 17.56 + 15.60 + 443.33 + 25.61 + 21.01)/7 = 555.86/7 = 79.41.

Solution to 2:

The P/Es listed in ascending order are:

13.68	15.60	17.56	19.07	21.01	25.61	443.33

The sample has an odd number of observations with $n = 7$, so the median occupies the $(n + 1)/2 = 8/2 = 4$th position in the sorted list. Therefore, the median P/E is 19.07.

Solution to 3:

Merant's P/E of approximately 443 tremendously influences the value of the portfolio's arithmetic mean P/E. The mean P/E of 79 is much larger than the P/E of six of the seven stocks in the portfolio. The mean P/E also misleadingly suggests an orientation to stocks with high P/Es. The mean P/E of the stocks excluding Merant, or excluding the largest- and smallest-P/E stocks (Merant and Exponent), is below the S&P 500's P/E of 23.63. The median P/E of 19.07 appears to better represent the central tendency of the P/Es.

It frequently happens that when a company's EPS is close to zero—at a low point in the business cycle, for example—its P/E is extremely high. The high P/E in those circumstances reflects an anticipated future recovery of earnings. Extreme P/E values need to be investigated and handled with care. For reasons related to this example, analysts often use the median of price multiples to characterize the valuation of industry groups.

5.3 The Mode

The third important measure of central tendency is the mode.

■ **Definition of Mode.** The **mode** is the most frequently occurring value in a distribution.[17]

A distribution can have more than one mode, or even no mode. When a distribution has one most frequently occurring value, the distribution is said to be unimodal. If a distribution has two most frequently occurring values, then it has two modes and we say it is bimodal. If the distribution has three most frequently occurring values, then it is trimodal. When all the values in a data set are different, the distribution has no mode because no value occurs more frequently than any other value.

Stock return data and other data from continuous distributions may not have a modal outcome. When such data are grouped into intervals, however, we often find an interval (possibly more than one) with the highest frequency: the **modal interval** (or intervals). For example, the frequency distribution for the monthly returns on the S&P 500 has a modal interval of 0 percent to 2 percent, as shown in Figure 2; this return interval has 182 observations out of a total of 924. The modal interval always has the highest bar in the histogram.

The mode is the only measure of central tendency that can be used with nominal data. When we categorize mutual funds into different styles and assign a number to each style, the mode of these categorized data is the most frequent mutual fund style.

5.4 Other Concepts of Mean

Earlier we explained the arithmetic mean, which is a fundamental concept for describing the central tendency of data. Other concepts of mean are very important in investments, however. In the following, we discuss such concepts.

Example 5

Calculating a Mode

Table 11 gives the credit ratings on senior unsecured debt as of September 2002 of nine U.S. department stores rated by Moody's Investors Service. In descending order of credit quality (increasing expected probability of default), Moody's ratings are Aaa, Aa1, Aa2, Aa3, A1, A2, A3, Baa1, Baa2, Baa3, Ba1, Ba2, Ba3, B1, B2, B3, Caa, Ca, and C.[18]

Table 11	Senior Unsecured Debt Ratings: U.S. Department Stores, September 2002
Company	**Credit Rating**
Dillards, Inc.	Ba3
Federated Department Stores, Inc.	Baa1
Kohl's Corporation	A3
May's Department Stores Company	A2
Neiman Marcus Group, Inc.	Baa2

---

[17] The notation M_o is occasionally used for the mode. Just as for the mean and the median, we may distinguish between a population mode and a sample mode. With the understanding that a population mode is the value with the greatest probability of occurrence, while a sample mode is the most frequently occurring value in the sample, we follow general usage in using the term "mode" without qualification, for the sake of brevity.
[18] For more information on credit risk and credit ratings, see Fabozzi (2004a).

Table 11	Continued
Company	**Credit Rating**
Nordstom, Inc.	Baa1
Penney, JC, Company, Inc.	Ba2
Saks Incorporated	B1
Sears, Roebuck and Co.	Baa1

Source: Moody's Investors Service.

Using the data in Table 11, address the following concerning the senior unsecured debt of U.S. department stores:

1. State the modal credit rating.
2. State the median credit rating.

Solution to 1:

The group of companies represents seven distinct credit ratings, ranging from A2 to B1. To make our task easy, we first organize the ratings into a frequency distribution.

Table 12	Senior Unsecured Debt Ratings: U.S. Department Stores, Distribution of Credit Ratings
Credit Rating	**Frequency**
A2	1
A3	1
Baa1	3
Baa2	1
Ba2	1
Ba3	1
B1	1

All credit ratings have a frequency of 1 except for Baa1, which has a frequency of 3. Therefore, the modal credit rating of U.S. department stores as of the date of the Moody's report was Baa1. Moody's considers bonds rated Baa1 to be medium-grade obligations—they are neither highly protected nor poorly secured.

Solution to 2:

For the group $n = 9$, an odd number. The group's median occupies the $(n + 1)/2 = 10/2 = 5$th position. We see from Table 12 that Baa1 occupies the fifth position. Therefore the median credit rating at September 2002 was Baa1.

5.4.1 The Weighted Mean

The concept of weighted mean arises repeatedly in portfolio analysis. In the arithmetic mean, all observations are equally weighted by the factor $1/n$ (or $1/N$). In working with portfolios, we need the more general concept of weighted mean to allow different weights on different observations.

To illustrate the weighted mean concept, an investment manager with $100 million to invest might allocate $70 million to equities and $30 million to bonds. The portfolio has a weight of 0.70 on stocks and 0.30 on bonds. How do we calculate the return on this portfolio? The portfolio's return clearly involves an averaging of the returns on the stock and bond investments. The mean that we compute, however, must reflect the fact that stocks have a 70 percent weight in the portfolio and bonds have a 30 percent weight. The way to reflect this weighting is to multiply the return on the stock investment by 0.70 and the return on the bond investment by 0.30, then sum the two results. This sum is an example of a weighted mean. It would be incorrect to take an arithmetic mean of the return on the stock and bond investments, equally weighting the returns on the two asset classes.

Consider a portfolio invested in Canadian stocks and bonds in which the stock component is indexed on the S&P/TSX Composite Index and the bond component is indexed on the RBC Capital Markets Canadian Bond Market Index. These indexes represent the broad Canadian equity and bond markets, respectively. The portfolio manager allocates 60 percent of the portfolio to Canadian stocks and 40 percent to Canadian bonds. Table 13 presents total returns for these indexes for 1998 to 2002.

Table 13	Total Returns for Canadian Equities and Bonds, 1998–2002	
Year	Equities (%)	Bonds (%)
1998	−1.6	9.1
1999	31.7	−1.1
2000	7.4	10.3
2001	−12.6	8.0
2002	−12.4	8.7

Source: www.fidelity.ca and www.money.msn.ca.

■ **Weighted Mean Formula.** The **weighted mean** $\bar{X}_w$ (read "X-bar sub-w"), for a set of observations $X_1, X_2, \ldots, X_n$ with corresponding weights of $w_1, w_2, \ldots, w_n$ is computed as

$$\bar{X}_w = \sum_{i=1}^{n} w_i X_i \tag{4}$$

where the sum of the weights equals 1; that is, $\sum_i w_i = 1$.

In the context of portfolios, a positive weight represents an asset held long and a negative weight represents an asset held short.[19]

The return on the portfolio under consideration is the weighted average of the return on Canadian stocks and Canadian bonds (the weight on stocks is 0.60; that on bonds is 0.40). Apart from expenses, if the portfolio tracks the indexes perfectly, we find, using Equation 4, that

$$\begin{aligned}
\text{Portfolio return for 1998} &= w_{\text{stock}} R_{\text{stock}} + w_{\text{bonds}} R_{\text{bonds}} \\
&= 0.60(-1.6\%) + 0.40(9.1\%) \\
&= 2.7\%
\end{aligned}$$

It should be clear that the correct mean to compute in this example is the weighted mean and not the arithmetic mean. If we had computed the arithmetic mean for 1998, we would have calculated a return equal to ½(−1.6%) + ½(9.1%) = (−1.6% +

---

[19] The formula for the weighted mean can be compared to the formula for the arithmetic mean. For a set of observations $X_1, X_2, \ldots, X_n$, let the weights $w_1, w_2, \ldots, w_n$ all equal $1/n$. Under this assumption, the formula for the weighted mean is $(1/n)\sum_{i=1}^{n} X_i$. This is the formula for the arithmetic mean. Therefore, the arithmetic mean is a special case of the weighted mean in which all the weights are equal.

9.1%)/2 = 3.8%. Given that the portfolio manager invested 60 percent in stocks and 40 percent in bonds, the arithmetic mean would underweight the investment in stocks and overweight the investment in bonds, resulting in a number for portfolio return that is too high by 1.1 percentage points (3.8% − 2.7%).

Now suppose that the portfolio manager maintains constant weights of 60 percent in stocks and 40 percent in bonds for all five years. This method is called a constant-proportions strategy. Because value is price multiplied by quantity, price fluctuation causes portfolio weights to change. As a result, the constant-proportions strategy requires rebalancing to restore the weights in stocks and bonds to their target levels. Assuming that the portfolio manager is able to accomplish the necessary rebalancing, we can compute the portfolio returns in 1999, 2000, 2001, and 2002 with Equation 4 as follows:

Portfolio return for 1999 = 0.60(31.7) + 0.40(−1.1) = 18.6%

Portfolio return for 2000 = 0.60(7.4) + 0.40(1.03) = 8.6%

Portfolio return for 2001 = 0.60(−12.6) + 0.40(8.0) = −4.4%

Portfolio return for 2002 = 0.60(−12.4) + 0.40(8.7) = −4.0%

We can now find the time-series mean of the returns for 1998 through 2002 using Equation 3 for the arithmetic mean. The time-series mean total return for the portfolio is (2.7 + 18.6 + 8.6 − 4.4 − 4.0)/5 = 21.5/5 = 4.3 percent.

Instead of calculating the portfolio time-series mean return from portfolio annual returns, we can calculate the arithmetic mean bond and stock returns for the five years and then apply the portfolio weights of 0.60 and 0.40, respectively, to those values. The mean stock return is (−1.6 + 31.7 + 7.4 − 12.6 − 12.4)/5 = 12.5/5 = 2.5 percent. The mean bond return is (9.1 − 1.1 + 10.3 + 8.0 + 8.7)/ 5 = 35.0/5 = 7.0 percent. Therefore, the mean total return for the portfolio is 0.60(2.5) + 0.40(7.0) = 4.3 percent, which agrees with our previous calculation.

Example 6

Portfolio Return as a Weighted Mean

Table 14 gives information on the estimated average asset allocation of Canadian pension funds as well as four-year asset class returns.[20]

Table 14	Asset Allocation for Average Canadian Pension Fund, as of 31 March 2003	
Asset Class	**Asset Allocation (Weight)**	**Asset Class Return (%)**
Equities	34.6	0.6
U.S. equities	10.8	−9.3
International equities	6.4	−10.5
Bonds	34.0	6.0
Mortgages	1.3	9.0
Real estate	4.5	10.2
Cash and equivalents	8.4	4.2

Source: Standard Life Investments, Inc.

---

20 In Table 14, equities are represented by the S&P/TSX Composite Index, U.S. equities by the S&P 500, international (non-North American) equities by the MSCI EAFE Index, bonds by the Scotia Capital Markets Universe Bond Index, mortgages by the Scotia Capital Markets Mortgage Index, real estate by the Standard Life Investments pooled real estate fund, and cash and equivalents by 91-day T-bills.

Using the information in Table 14, calculate the mean return earned by the average Canadian pension fund over the four years ending 31 March 2003.

Solution:

Converting the percent asset allocation to decimal form, we find the mean return as a weighted average of the asset class returns. We have

$$
\begin{aligned}
\text{Mean portfolio return} = & \ 0.346(0.6\%) + 0.108(-9.3\%) + \\
& \ 0.064(-10.5\%) + 0.340(6.0\%) + \\
& \ 0.013(9.0\%) + 0.045(10.2\%) + 0.084(4.2\%) \\
= & \ 0.208\% - 1.004\% - 0.672\% + 2.040\% + \\
& \ 0.117\% + 0.459\% + 0.353\% \\
= & \ 1.5 \text{ percent}
\end{aligned}
$$

The previous examples illustrate the general principle that a portfolio return is a weighted sum. Specifically, a portfolio's return is the weighted average of the returns on the assets in the portfolio; the weight applied to each asset's return is the fraction of the portfolio invested in that asset.

Market indexes are computed as weighted averages. For market-capitalization indexes such as the CAC-40 in France or the S&P 500 in the United States, each included stock receives a weight corresponding to its outstanding market value divided by the total market value of all stocks in the index.

Our illustrations of weighted mean use past data, but they might just as well use forward-looking data. When we take a weighted average of forward-looking data, the weighted mean is called **expected value**. Suppose we make one forecast for the year-end level of the S&P 500 assuming economic expansion and another forecast for the year-end level of the S&P 500 assuming economic contraction. If we multiply the first forecast by the probability of expansion and the second forecast by the probability of contraction and then add these weighted forecasts, we are calculating the expected value of the S&P 500 at year-end. If we take a weighted average of possible future returns on the S&P 500, we are computing the S&P 500's expected return. The probabilities must sum to 1, satisfying the condition on the weights in the expression for weighted mean, Equation 4.

5.4.2 *The Geometric Mean*

The geometric mean is most frequently used to average rates of change over time or to compute the growth rate of a variable. In investments, we frequently use the geometric mean to average a time series of rates of return on an asset or a portfolio, or to compute the growth rate of a financial variable such as earnings or sales. In the reading on the time value of money, for instance, we computed a sales growth rate (Example 17). That growth rate was a geometric mean. Because of the subject's importance, in a later section we will return to the use of the geometric mean and offer practical perspectives on its use. The geometric mean is defined by the following formula.

■ **Geometric Mean Formula.** The **geometric mean**, G, of a set of observations $X_1, X_2, \ldots, X_n$ is

$$
G = \sqrt[n]{X_1 X_2 X_3 \ldots X_n}
$$

(5)

with $X_i \geq 0$ for $i = 1, 2, \ldots, n$.

Equation 5 has a solution, and the geometric mean exists, only if the product under the radical sign is non-negative. We impose the restriction that all the observations X_i in Equation 5 are greater than or equal to zero. We can solve for the geometric mean using Equation 5 directly with any calculator that has an exponentiation key (on most calculators, y^x). We can also solve for the geometric mean using natural logarithms. Equation 5 can also be stated as

$$\ln\ G = \frac{1}{n}\ln\left(X_1 X_2 X_3 \ldots X_n\right)$$

or as

$$\ln\ G = \frac{\sum\limits_{i=1}^{n}\ln X_i}{n}$$

When we have computed $\ln G$, then $G = e^{\ln G}$ (on most calculators, the key for this step is e^x).

Risky assets can have negative returns up to −100 percent (if their price falls to zero), so we must take some care in defining the relevant variables to average in computing a geometric mean. We cannot just use the product of the returns for the sample and then take the nth root because the returns for any period could be negative. We must redefine the returns to make them positive. We do this by adding 1.0 to the returns expressed as decimals. The term $(1 + R_t)$ represents the year-ending value relative to an initial unit of investment at the beginning of the year. As long as we use $(1 + R_t)$, the observations will never be negative because the biggest negative return is −100 percent. The result is the geometric mean of $1 + R_t$; by then subtracting 1.0 from this result, we obtain the geometric mean of the individual returns R_t. For example, the returns on Canadian stocks as represented by the S&P/TSX Composite Index during the 1998–2002 period were given in Table 13 as −0.016, 0.317, 0.074, −0.126, and −0.124, putting the returns into decimal form. Adding 1.0 to those returns produces 0.9840, 1.317, 1.074, 0.874, and 0.876. Using Equation 5 we have $\sqrt[5]{(0.9840)(1.317)(1.074)(0.874)(0.876)} = \sqrt[5]{1.065616} = 1.012792$. This number is 1 plus the geometric mean rate of return. Subtracting 1.0 from this result, we have 1.012792 − 1.0 = 0.012792 or approximately 1.3 percent. The geometric mean return for Canadian stocks during the 1998–2002 period was 1.3 percent.

An equation that summarizes the calculation of the geometric mean return, R_G, is a slightly modified version of Equation 5 in which the X_i represent "1 + return in decimal form." Because geometric mean returns use time series, we use a subscript t indexing time as well.

$$1 + R_G = \sqrt[T]{(1 + R_1)(1 + R_2)\ldots(1 + R_T)}$$

$$1 + R_G = \left[\prod_{t=1}^{T}(1 + R_t)\right]^{\frac{1}{T}}$$

which leads to the following formula.

- **Geometric Mean Return Formula.** Given a time series of holding period returns R_t, $t = 1, 2, \ldots, T$, the geometric mean return over the time period spanned by the returns R_1 through R_T is

$$R_G = \left[\prod_{t=1}^{T}(1 + R_t)\right]^{\frac{1}{T}} - 1 \qquad\qquad\qquad \textbf{(6)}$$

We can use Equation 6 to solve for the geometric mean return for any return data series. Geometric mean returns are also referred to as compound returns. If the returns being averaged in Equation 6 have a monthly frequency, for example, we may call the geometric mean monthly return the compound monthly return. The next example illustrates the computation of the geometric mean while contrasting the geometric and arithmetic means.

Example 7

Geometric and Arithmetic Mean Returns (1)

As a mutual fund analyst, you are examining, as of early 2003, the most recent five years of total returns for two U.S. large-cap value equity mutual funds.

	Table 15	Total Returns for Two Mutual Funds, 1998–2002

Year	Selected American Shares (SLASX)	T. Rowe Price Equity Income (PRFDX)
1998	16.2%	9.2%
1999	20.3	3.8
2000	9.3	13.1
2001	−11.1	1.6
2002	−17.0	−13.0

Source: American Association of Individual Investors (AAII).

Based on the data in Table 15, address the following:

1. Calculate the geometric mean return of SLASX.

2. Calculate the arithmetic mean return of SLASX and contrast it to the fund's geometric mean return.

3. Calculate the geometric mean return of PRFDX.

4. Calculate the arithmetic mean return of PRFDX and contrast it to the fund's geometric mean return.

Solution to 1:

Converting the returns on SLASX to decimal form and adding 1.0 to each return produces 1.162, 1.203, 1.093, 0.889, and 0.830. We use Equation 6 to find SLASX's geometric mean return:

$$R_G = \sqrt[5]{(1.162)(1.203)(1.093)(0.889)(0.830)} - 1$$
$$= \sqrt[5]{1.127384} - 1 = 1.024270 - 1 = 0.024270$$
$$= 2.43\%$$

Solution to 2:

For SLASX, $\bar{R}$ = (16.2 + 20.3 + 9.3 − 11.1 − 17.0)/ 5 = 17.7/5 = 3.54%. The arithmetic mean return for SLASX exceeds the geometric mean return by 3.54 − 2.43 = 1.11% or 111 basis points.

Solution to 3:

Converting the returns on PRFDX to decimal form and adding 1.0 to each return produces 1.092, 1.038, 1.131, 1.016, and 0.870. We use Equation 6 to find PRFDX's geometric mean return:

$$R_G = \sqrt[5]{(1.092)(1.038)(1.131)(1.016)(0.870)} - 1$$
$$= \sqrt[5]{1.133171} - 1 = 1.025319 - 1 = 0.025319$$
$$= 2.53\%$$

Solution to 4:

PRFDX, $\bar{R}$ = (9.2 + 3.8 + 13.1 + 1.6 − 13.0)/5 = 14.7/5 = 2.94%. The arithmetic mean for PRFDX exceeds the geometric mean return by 2.94 − 2.53 = 0.41% or 41 basis points. The table below summarizes the findings.

Table 16	Mutual Fund Arithmetic and Geometric Mean Returns: Summary of Findings	
Fund	**Arithmetic Mean (%)**	**Geometric Mean (%)**
SLASX	3.54	2.43
PRFDX	2.94	2.53

In Example 7, for both mutual funds, the geometric mean return was less than the arithmetic mean return. In fact, the geometric mean is always less than or equal to the arithmetic mean.[21] The only time that the two means will be equal is when there is no variability in the observations—that is, when all the observations in the series are the same.[22] In Example 7, there was variability in the funds' returns; thus for both funds, the geometric mean was strictly less than the arithmetic mean. In general, the difference between the arithmetic and geometric means increases with the variability in the period-by-period observations.[23] This relationship is also illustrated by Example 7. Even casual inspection reveals that the returns of SLASX are more variable than those of PRFDX, and consequently, the spread between the arithmetic and geometric mean returns is larger for SLASX (111 basis points) than for PRFDX (41 basis points).[24] The arithmetic and geometric mean also rank the two funds differently. Although SLASX has the higher arithmetic mean return, PRFDX has the higher geometric mean return. How should the analyst interpret this result?

The geometric mean return represents the growth rate or compound rate of return on an investment. One dollar invested in SLASX at the beginning of 1998 would have grown to (1.162)(1.203)(1.093)(0.889)(0.830) = $1.127, which is equal to 1 plus the geometric mean return compounded over five periods: $(1.0243)^5$ = $1.127, confirming that the geometric mean is the compound rate of return. For PRFDX, one dollar would have grown to a larger amount, (1.092)(1.038)(1.131)(1.016)(0.870) = $1.133, equal to $(1.0253)^5$. With its focus on the profitability of an investment over a multiperiod horizon, the geometric mean is of key interest to investors. The arithmetic mean return, focusing on average single-period performance, is also of interest. Both arithmetic and geometric means have a role to play in investment management, and both are often reported for return series. Example 8 highlights these points in a simple context.

---

21 This statement can be proved using Jensen's inequality that the average value of a function is less than or equal to the function evaluated at the mean if the function is concave from below—the case for $\ln(X)$.

22 For instance, suppose the return for each of the three years is 10 percent. The arithmetic mean is 10 percent. To find the geometric mean, we first express the returns as $(1 + R_t)$ and then find the geometric mean: $[(1.10)(1.10)(1.10)]1/3 − 1.0$ = 10 percent. The two means are the same.

23 We will soon introduce standard deviation as a measure of variability. Holding the arithmetic mean return constant, the geometric mean return decreases for an increase in standard deviation.

24 We will introduce formal measures of variability later. But note, for example, the 20.4 percentage point swing in returns between 2000 and 2001 for SLASX versus the 11.5 percentage point for PRFDX.

Example 8

Geometric and Arithmetic Mean Returns (2)

A hypothetical investment in a single stock initially costs €100. One year later, the stock is trading at €200. At the end of the second year, the stock price falls back to the original purchase price of €100. No dividends are paid during the two-year period. Calculate the arithmetic and geometric mean annual returns.

Solution:

First, we need to find the Year 1 and Year 2 annual returns with Equation 1.

   Return in Year 1 = 200/100 − 1 = 100%

   Return in Year 2 = 100/200 − 1 = −50%

The arithmetic mean of the annual returns is (100% − 50%)/2 = 25%.

Before we find the geometric mean, we must convert the percentage rates of return to $(1 + R_t)$. After this adjustment, the geometric mean from Equation 6 is $\sqrt{2.0 \times 0.50} - 1 = 0$ percent.

The geometric mean return of 0 percent accurately reflects that the ending value of the investment in Year 2 equals the starting value in Year 1. The compound rate of return on the investment is 0 percent. The arithmetic mean return reflects the average of the one-year returns.

5.4.3 The Harmonic Mean

The arithmetic mean, the weighted mean, and the geometric mean are the most frequently used concepts of mean in investments. A fourth concept, the **harmonic mean**, $\bar{X}_H$, is appropriate in a limited number of applications.[25]

■ **Harmonic Mean Formula.** The **harmonic mean** of a set of observations $X_1, X_2, \ldots, X_n$ is

$$\bar{X}_H = n \bigg/ \sum_{i=1}^{n} (1/X_i)$$
(7)

with $X_i > 0$ for $i = 1, 2, \ldots, n$

The harmonic mean is the value obtained by summing the reciprocals of the observations—terms of the form $1/X_i$—then averaging that sum by dividing it by the number of observations n, and, finally, taking the reciprocal of the average.

The harmonic mean may be viewed as a special type of weighted mean in which an observation's weight is inversely proportional to its magnitude. The harmonic mean is a relatively specialized concept of the mean that is appropriate when averaging ratios ("amount per unit") when the ratios are repeatedly applied to a fixed quantity to yield a variable number of units. The concept is best explained through an illustration. A well-known application arises in the investment strategy known as **cost averaging**, which involves the periodic investment of a fixed amount of money. In this application, the ratios we are averaging are prices per share at purchases dates, and we are applying those prices to a constant amount of money to yield a variable number of shares.

Suppose an investor purchases €1,000 of a security each month for $n = 2$ months. The share prices are €10 and €15 at the two purchase dates. What is the average price paid for the security?

---

[25] The terminology "harmonic" arises from its use relative to a type of series involving reciprocals known as a harmonic series.

In this example, in the first month we purchase €1,000/€10 = 100 shares and in the second month we purchase €1,000/€15 = 66.67, or 166.67 shares in total. Dividing the total euro amount invested, €2,000, by the total number of shares purchased, 166.67, gives an average price paid of €2,000/166.67 = €12. The average price paid is in fact the harmonic mean of the asset's prices at the purchase dates. Using Equation 7, the harmonic mean price is 2/[(1/10) + (1/15)] = €12. The value €12 is less than the arithmetic mean purchase price (€10 + €15)/2 = €12.5. However, we could find the correct value of €12 using the weighted mean formula, where the weights on the purchase prices equal the shares purchased at a given price as a proportion of the total shares purchased. In our example, the calculation would be (100/166.67)€10.00 + (66.67/166.67)€15.00 = €12. If we had invested varying amounts of money at each date, we could not use the harmonic mean formula. We could, however, still use the weighted mean formula in a manner similar to that just described.

A mathematical fact concerning the harmonic, geometric, and arithmetic means is that unless all the observations in a data set have the same value, the harmonic mean is less than the geometric mean, which in turn is less than the arithmetic mean. In the illustration given, the harmonic mean price was indeed less than the arithmetic mean price.

OTHER MEASURES OF LOCATION: QUANTILES

6

Having discussed measures of central tendency, we now examine an approach to describing the location of data that involves identifying values at or below which specified proportions of the data lie. For example, establishing that 25, 50, and 75 percent of the annual returns on a portfolio are at or below the values –0.05, 0.16, and 0.25, respectively, provides concise information about the distribution of portfolio returns. Statisticians use the word **quantile** (or **fractile**) as the most general term for a value at or below which a stated fraction of the data lies. In the following, we describe the most commonly used quantiles—quartiles, quintiles, deciles, and percentiles—and their application in investments.

6.1 Quartiles, Quintiles, Deciles, and Percentiles

We know that the median divides a distribution in half. We can define other dividing lines that split the distribution into smaller sizes. **Quartiles** divide the distribution into quarters, **quintiles** into fifths, deciles into tenths, and **percentiles** into hundredths. Given a set of observations, the yth percentile is the value at or below which y percent of observations lie. Percentiles are used frequently, and the other measures can be defined with respect to them. For example, the first quartile (Q_1) divides a distribution such that 25 percent of the observations lie at or below it; therefore, the first quartile is also the 25th percentile. The second quartile (Q_2) represents the 50th percentile, and the third quartile (Q_3) represents the 75th percentile because 75 percent of the observations lie at or below it.

When dealing with actual data, we often find that we need to approximate the value of a percentile. For example, if we are interested in the value of the 75th percentile, we may find that no observation divides the sample such that exactly 75 percent of the observations lie at or below that value. The following procedure, however, can help us determine or estimate a percentile. The procedure involves first locating the position of the percentile within the set of observations and then determining (or estimating) the value associated with that position.

Let P_y be the value at or below which y percent of the distribution lies, or the yth percentile. (For example, P_{18} is the point at or below which 18 percent of the observations lie; $100 - 18 = 82$ percent are greater than P_{18}.) The formula for the position of a percentile in an array with n entries sorted in ascending order is

$$L_y = (n+1)\frac{y}{100} \tag{8}$$

where y is the percentage point at which we are dividing the distribution and L_y is the location (L) of the percentile (P_y) in the array sorted in ascending order. The value of L_y may or may not be a whole number. In general, as the sample size increases, the percentile location calculation becomes more accurate; in small samples it may be quite approximate.

As an example of the case in which L_y is not a whole number, suppose that we want to determine the third quartile of returns for 2002 (Q_3 or P_{75}) for the 16 European equity markets given in Table 8. According to Equation 8, the position of the third quartile is $L_{75} = (16 + 1)75/100 = 12.75$, or between the 12th and 13th items in Table 9, which ordered the returns into ascending order. The 12th item in Table 9 is the return to equities in Portugal in 2002, −28.29 percent. The 13th item is the return to equities in Switzerland in 2002, −25.84 percent. Reflecting the "0.75" in "12.75," we would conclude that P_{75} lies 75 percent of the distance between −28.29 percent and −25.84 percent.

To summarize:

■ When the location, L_y, is a whole number, the location corresponds to an actual observation. For example, if Italy had not been included in the sample, then $n + 1$ would have been 16 and, with $L_{75} = 12$, the third quartile would be $P_{75} = X_{12}$, where X_i is defined as the value of the observation in the ith ($i = L_{75}$) position of the data sorted in ascending order (i.e., $P_{75} = -28.29$).

■ When L_y is not a whole number or integer, L_y lies between the two closest integer numbers (one above and one below), and we use **linear interpolation** between those two places to determine P_y. Interpolation means estimating an unknown value on the basis of two known values that surround it (lie above and below it); the term "linear" refers to a straight-line estimate. Returning to the calculation of P_{75} for the equity returns, we found that $L_y = 12.75$; the next lower whole number is 12 and the next higher whole number is 13. Using linear interpolation, $P_{75} \approx X_{12} + (12.75 - 12)(X_{13} - X_{12})$. As above, in the 12th position is the return to equities in Portugal, so $X_{12} = -28.29$ percent; $X_{13} = -25.84$ percent, the return to equities in Switzerland. Thus our estimate is $P_{75} \approx X_{12} + (12.75 - 12)(X_{13} - X_{12}) = -28.29 + 0.75 [-25.84 - (-28.29)] = -28.29 + 0.75(2.45) = -28.29 + 1.84 = -26.45$ percent. In words, −28.29 and −25.84 bracket P_{75} from below and above, respectively. Because $12.75 - 12 = 0.75$, using linear interpolation we move 75 percent of the distance from −28.29 to −25.84 as our estimate of P_{75}. We follow this pattern whenever L_y is a non-integer: The nearest whole numbers below and above L_y establish the positions of observations that bracket P_y and then interpolate between the values of those two observations.

Example 9 illustrates the calculation of various quantiles for the dividend yield on the components of a major European equity index.

Example 9

Calculating Percentiles, Quartiles, and Quintiles

The DJ EuroSTOXX 50 is an index of Europe's 50 largest publicly traded companies as measured by market capitalization. Table 17 shows the dividend yields on the 50 component stocks in the index as of mid-2003, ranked in ascending order.

Table 17	Dividend Yields on the Components of the DJ EuroSTOXX 50				
No.	Company	Dividend Yield (%)	No.	Company	Dividend Yield (%)
1	AstraZeneca	0.00	8	Roche Holding	1.33
2	BP	0.00	9	Munich Re Group	1.36
3	Deutsche Telekom	0.00	10	General Assicurazioni	1.39
4	HSBC Holdings	0.00	11	Vodafone Group	1.41
5	Credit Suisse Group	0.26	12	Carrefour	1.51
6	L'Oréal	1.09	13	Nokia	1.75
7	SwissRe	1.27	33	Santander Central Hispano	3.66
14	Novartis	1.81	34	Banco Bilbao Vizcaya Argentaria	3.67
15	Allianz	1.92	35	Diageo	3.68
16	Koninklije Philips Electronics	2.01	36	HBOS	3.78
17	Siemens	2.16	37	E.ON	3.87
18	Deutsche Bank	2.27	38	Shell Transport and Co.	3.88
19	Telecom Italia	2.27	39	Barclays	4.06
20	AXA	2.39	40	Royal Dutch Petroleum Co.	4.27
21	Telefonica	2.49	41	Fortis	4.28
22	Nestlé	2.55	42	Bayer	4.45
23	Royal Bank of Scotland Group	2.60	43	DaimlerChrysler	4.68
24	ABN-AMRO Holding	2.65	44	Suez	5.13
25	BNP Paribas	2.65	45	Aviva	5.15
26	UBS	2.65	46	Eni	5.66
27	Tesco	2.95	47	ING Group	6.16
28	Total	3.11	48	Prudential	6.43
29	GlaxoSmithKline	3.31	49	Lloyds TSB	7.68
30	BT Group	3.34	50	AEGON	8.14
31	Unilever	3.53			
32	BASF	3.59			

Source: france.finance.yahoo.com accessed 8 July 2003.

Using the data in Table 17, address the following:

1. Calculate the 10th and 90th percentiles.
2. Calculate the first, second, and third quartiles.
3. State the value of the median.

Reading 7 ■ Statistical Concepts and Market Returns

4. How many quintiles are there, and to what percentiles do the quintiles correspond?

5. Calculate the value of the first quintile.

Solution to 1:

In this example, $n = 50$. Using Equation 8, $L_y = (n + 1)y/100$ for position of the yth percentile, so for the 10th percentile we have

$$L_{10} = (50 + 1)(10/100) = 5.1$$

L_{10} is between the fifth and sixth observations with values $X_5 = 0.26$ and $X_6 = 1.09$. The estimate of the 10th percentile (first decile) for dividend yield is

$$P_{10} \approx X_5 + (5.1 - 5)(X_6 - X_5) = 0.26 + 0.1(1.09 - 0.26)$$
$$= 0.26 + 0.1(0.83) = 0.34\%$$

For the 90th percentile,

$$L_{90} = (50 + 1)(90/100) = 45.9$$

L_{90} is between the 45th and 46th observations with values $X_{45} = 5.15$ and $X_{46} = 5.66$, respectively. The estimate of the 90th percentile (ninth decile) is

$$P_{90} \approx X_{45} + (45.9 - 45)(X_{46} - X_{45}) = 5.15 + 9.9(5.66 - 5.15)$$
$$= 5.15 + 0.9(0.51) = 5.61\%$$

Solution to 2:

The first, second, and third quartiles correspond to P_{25}, P_{50}, and P_{75}, respectively.

$L_{25} = (51)(25/100) = 12.75$ L_{25} is between the 12th and 13th entries with values $X_{12} = 1.51$ and $X_{13} = 1.75$.

$$P_{25} = Q_1 \approx X_{12} + (12.75 - 12)(X_{13} - X_{12})$$
$$= 1.51 + 0.75(1.75 - 1.51)$$
$$= 1.51 + 0.75(0.24) = 1.69\%$$

$L_{50} = (50)(50/100) = 25.5$ L_{50} is between the 25th and 26th entries. But these entries share the same value, $X_{25} = X_{26} = 2.65$, so no interpolation is needed.

$$P_{50} = Q_2 = 2.65\%$$

$L_{75} = (51)(75/100) = 38.25$ L_{75} is between the 38th and 39th entries with values $X_{38} = 3.88$ and $X_{39} = 4.06$.

$$P_{75} = Q_3 \approx X_{38} + (38.25 - 38)(X_{39} - X_{38})$$
$$= 3.88 + 0.25(4.06 - 3.88)$$
$$= 3.88 + 0.25(0.18) = 3.93\%$$

Solution to 3:

The median is the 50th percentile, 2.65 percent. This is the same value that we would obtain by taking the mean of the $n/2 = 50/2 = 25$th item and $(n + 2)/2 = 52/2 = 26$th items, consistent with the procedure given earlier for the median of an even-numbered sample.

Solution to 4:

There are five quintiles, and they are specified by P_{20}, P_{40}, P_{60}, and P_{80}.

Solution to 5:

The first quintile is P_{20}.

$L_{20} = (50 + 1)(20/100) = 10.2$ L_{20} is between the 10th and 11th observations with values $X_{10} = 1.39$ and $X_{11} = 1.41$.

The estimate of the first quintile is

$$P_{20} \approx X_{10} + (10.2 - 10)(X_{11} - X_{10})$$
$$= 1.39 + 0.2(1.41 - 1.39)$$
$$= 1.39 + 0.2(0.02) = 1.394\% \text{ or } 1.39\%.$$

6.2 Quantiles in Investment Practice

In this section, we discuss the use of quantiles in investments. Quantiles are used in portfolio performance evaluation as well as in investment strategy development and research.

Investment analysts use quantiles every day to rank performance—for example, the performance of portfolios. The performance of investment managers is often characterized in terms of the quartile in which they fall relative to the performance of their peer group of managers. The Morningstar mutual fund star rankings, for example, associates the number of stars with percentiles of performance relative to similar-style mutual funds.

Another key use of quantiles is in investment research. Analysts refer to a group defined by a particular quantile as that quantile. For example, analysts often refer to the set of companies with returns falling below the 10th percentile cutoff point as the bottom return decile. Dividing data into quantiles based on some characteristic allows analysts to evaluate the impact of that characteristic on a quantity of interest. For instance, empirical finance studies commonly rank companies based on the market value of their equity and then sort them into deciles. The 1st decile contains the portfolio of those companies with the smallest market values, and the 10th decile contains those companies with the largest market value. Ranking companies by decile allows analysts to compare the performance of small companies with large ones.

We can illustrate the use of quantiles, in particular quartiles, in investment research using the example of Bauman, Conover, and Miller (1998). That study compared the performance of international growth stocks to value stocks. Typically, value stocks are defined as those for which the market price is relatively low in relation to earnings per share, book value per share, or dividends per share. Growth stocks, on the other hand, have comparatively high prices in relation to those same measures. The Bauman et al. classification criteria were the following valuation measures: price-to-earnings (P/E), price-to-cash flow (P/CF), price-to-book value (P/B), and dividend yield (D/P). They assigned one-fourth of the total sample with the lowest P/E on 30 June of each year from 1986 to 1996 (the value group) to Quartile 1, and the one-fourth with the highest P/E of each year (the growth group) to Quartile 4. The stocks with the second-highest P/E formed Quartile 3, and the stocks with the second-lowest P/E, Quartile 2. The authors repeated this process for each of the four fundamental factors. Treating each quartile group as a portfolio composed of equally weighted stocks, they were able to compare the performance of the various value/growth quartiles. Table 1 from their study is reproduced as Table 18 on the previous page.

Table 18 reports each valuation factor's median, mean return, and standard deviation for each quartile grouping. Moving from Quartile 1 to Quartile 4, P/E, P/CF, and P/B increase, but D/P decreases. Regardless of the selection criteria, international value stocks outperformed international growth stocks during the sample period.

| Table 18 | Mean Annual Returns of Value and Growth Stocks Based on Selected Characteristics, 1986–1996 |

Selection Criteria	Total Observations	Q_1 (Value)	Q_2	Q_3	Q_4 (Growth)	Spread in Return, Q_1 to Q_4
Classification by P/E	28,463					
Median P/E		8.7	15.2	24.2	72.5	
Return		15.0%	13.6%	13.5%	10.6%	+4.4%
Standard deviation		46.5	38.3	42.5	50.4	
Classification by P/CF	30,240					
Median P/CF		4.4	8.2	13.3	34.2	
Return		15.5%	13.7%	12.9%	11.2%	+4.3%
Standard deviation		48.7	41.2	41.9	51.4	
Classification by P/B	32,265					
Median P/B		0.8	1.4	2.2	4.3	
Return		18.1%	14.4%	12.6%	12.4%	+5.7%
Standard deviation		69.6	45.9	45.1	57.0	
Classification by D/P	25,394					
Median D/P		5.6%	3.2%	1.9%	0.6%	
Return		14.1%	14.1%	12.5%	9.3%	+4.8%
Standard deviation		40.5	38.7	38.9	42.0	

Source: Bauman et al.

Bauman, Conover, and Miller also divided companies into one of four quartiles based on market value of equity. Then they examined the returns to the stocks in the quartiles. Table 7 from their article is reproduced here as Table 19. As the table shows, the small-company portfolio had a median market value of $46.6 million and the large company portfolio had a median value of $2,472.3 million. Large companies were more than 50 times larger than small companies, yet their mean stock returns were less than half those of the small companies (small, 22.0 percent; large, 10.8 percent). Overall, Bauman et al. found two effects. First, international value stocks (as the authors defined them) outperformed international growth stocks. Second, international small stocks outperformed international large stocks.

| Table 19 | Mean Annual Returns of International Stocks Grouped by Market Capitalization, 1986–1996 |

Selection Criteria	Total Observations	Q_1 (Small)	Q_2	Q_3	Q_4 (Large)	Spread in Return, Q_1 to Q_4
Classification by size	32,555					
Median size (millions)		$46.6	$209.9%	$583.7	$2,472.3	
Return		22.0%	13.6%	11.1%	10.8%	+11.2%
Standard deviation		87.8	45.2	39.5	34.0	

Source: Bauman et al.

The authors' next step was to examine how value and growth stocks performed while controlling for size. This step involved constructing 16 different value/growth and size portfolios (4 × 4 = 16) and investigating the interaction between these two fundamental factors. They found that international value stocks outperformed international growth stocks except when market capitalization was very small. For portfolio managers, these findings suggest that value stocks offered investors relatively more favorable returns than did growth stocks in international markets during the specific time period studied.

MEASURES OF DISPERSION

As the well-known researcher Fischer Black has written, "[t]he key issue in investments is estimating expected return."[26] Few would disagree with the importance of expected return or mean return in investments: The mean return tells us where returns, and investment results, are centered. To completely understand an investment, however, we also need to know how returns are dispersed around the mean. **Dispersion** is the variability around the central tendency. If mean return addresses reward, dispersion addresses risk.

In this section, we examine the most common measures of dispersion: range, mean absolute deviation, variance, and standard deviation. These are all measures of **absolute dispersion**. Absolute dispersion is the amount of variability present without comparison to any reference point or benchmark.

These measures are used throughout investment practice. The variance or standard deviation of return is often used as a measure of risk pioneered by Nobel laureate Harry Markowitz. William Sharpe, another winner of the Nobel Prize in economics, developed the Sharpe ratio, a measure of risk-adjusted performance. That measure makes use of standard deviation of return. Other measures of dispersion, mean absolute deviation and range, are also useful in analyzing data.

7.1 The Range

We encountered range earlier when we discussed the construction of frequency distribution. The simplest of all the measures of dispersion, range can be computed with interval or ratio data.

■ **Definition of Range.** The **range** is the difference between the maximum and minimum values in a data set:

Range = Maximum value − Minimum value   (9)

As an illustration of range, the largest monthly return for the S&P 500 in the period from January 1926 to December 2002 is 42.56 percent (in April 1933) and the smallest is −29.73 percent (in September 1931). The range of returns is thus 72.29 percent [42.56 percent − (−29.73 percent)]. An alternative definition of range reports the maximum and minimum values. This alternative definition provides more information than does the range as defined in Equation 9.

One advantage of the range is ease of computation. A disadvantage is that the range uses only two pieces of information from the distribution. It cannot tell us how the data are distributed (that is, the shape of the distribution). Because the range is the difference between the maximum and minimum returns, it can reflect extremely large or small outcomes that may not be representative of the distribution.[27]

---

26 Black (1993).

27 Another distance measure of dispersion that we may encounter, the interquartile range, focuses on the middle rather than the extremes. The **interquartile range** (IQR) is the difference between the third and first quartiles of a data set: IQR = $Q_3 − Q_1$. The IQR represents the length of the interval containing the middle 50 percent of the data, with a larger interquartile range indicating greater dispersion, all else equal.

7.2 The Mean Absolute Deviation

Measures of dispersion can be computed using all the observations in the distribution rather than just the highest and lowest. The question is, how should we measure dispersion? Our previous discussion on properties of the arithmetic mean introduced the notion of distance or deviation from the mean $(X_i - \bar{X})$ as a fundamental piece of information used in statistics. We could compute measures of dispersion as the arithmetic average of the deviations around the mean, but we would encounter a problem: The deviations around the mean always sum to 0. If we computed the mean of the deviations, the result would also equal 0. Therefore, we need to find a way to address the problem of negative deviations canceling out positive deviations.

One solution is to examine the absolute deviations around the mean as in the mean absolute deviation.

■ **Mean Absolute Deviation Formula.** The **mean absolute deviation** (MAD) for a sample is

$$\text{MAD} = \frac{\sum\limits_{i=1}^{n} \left| X_i - \bar{X} \right|}{n} \tag{10}$$

where $\bar{X}$ is the sample mean and n is the number of observations in the sample.

In calculating MAD, we ignore the signs of the deviations around the mean. For example, if $X_i = -11.0$ and $\bar{X} = 4.5$, the absolute value of the difference is $|-11.0 - 4.5| = |-15.5| = 15.5$. The mean absolute deviation uses all of the observations in the sample and is thus superior to the range as a measure of dispersion. One technical drawback of MAD is that it is difficult to manipulate mathematically compared with the next measure we will introduce, variance.[28] Example 10 illustrates the use of the range and the mean absolute deviation in evaluating risk.

Example 10

The Range and the Mean Absolute Deviation

Having calculated mean returns for the two mutual funds in Example 7, the analyst is now concerned with evaluating risk.

Table 15	(Repeated) Total Returns for Two Mutual Funds, 1998–2002	
Year	**Selected American Shares (SLASX)**	**T. Rowe Price Equity Income (PRFDX)**
1998	16.2%	9.2%
1999	20.3	3.8
2000	9.3	13.1
2001	−11.1	1.6
2002	−17.0	−13.0

Source: AAII.

---

[28] In some analytic work such as optimization, the calculus operation of differentiation is important. Variance as a function can be differentiated, but absolute value cannot.

Based on the data in Table 15 repeated on the previous page, answer the following:

1. Calculate the range of annual returns for (A) SLASX and (B) PRFDX, and state which mutual fund appears to be riskier based on these ranges.

2. Calculate the mean absolute deviation of returns on (A) SLASX and (B) PRFDX, and state which mutual fund appears to be riskier based on MAD.

Solution to 1:

A. For SLASX, the largest return was 20.3 percent and the smallest was −17.0 percent. The range is thus 20.3 − (−17.0) = 37.3%.

B. For PFRDX, the range is 13.1 − (−13.0) = 26.1%. With a larger range of returns than PRFDX, SLASX appeared to be the riskier fund during the 1998–2002 period.

Solution to 2:

A. The arithmetic mean return for SLASX as calculated in Example 7 is 3.54 percent. The MAD of SLASX returns is

$$\text{MAD} = \frac{|16.2-3.54|+|20.3-3.54|+|9.3-3.54|+|-11.1-3.54|+|-17.0-3.54|}{5}$$

$$= \frac{12.66+16.76+5.76+14.64+20.54}{5}$$

$$= \frac{70.36}{5} = 14.1\%$$

B. The arithmetic mean return for PRFDX as calculated in Example 7 is 2.94 percent. The MAD of PRFDX returns is

$$\text{MAD} = \frac{|9.2-2.94|+|3.8-2.94|+|13.1-2.94|+|1.6-2.94|+|-13.0-2.94|}{5}$$

$$= \frac{6.26+0.86+10.16+1.34+15.94}{5}$$

$$= \frac{34.56}{5} = 6.9\%$$

SLASX, with a MAD of 14.1 percent, appears to be much riskier than PRFDX, with a MAD of 6.9 percent.

7.3 Population Variance and Population Standard Deviation

The mean absolute deviation addressed the issue that the sum of deviations from the mean equals zero by taking the absolute value of the deviations. A second approach to the treatment of deviations is to square them. The variance and standard deviation, which are based on squared deviations, are the two most widely used measures of dispersion. **Variance** is defined as the average of the squared deviations around the mean. **Standard deviation** is the positive square root of the variance. The following discussion addresses the calculation and use of variance and standard deviation.

7.3.1 *Population Variance*

If we know every member of a population, we can compute the **population variance**. Denoted by the symbol σ^2, the population variance is the arithmetic average of the squared deviations around the mean.

■ **Population Variance Formula.** The **population variance** is

$$\sigma^2 = \frac{\sum_{i=1}^{N}(X_i - \mu)^2}{N}$$
(11)

where μ is the population mean and N is the size of the population.

Given knowledge of the population mean, μ, we can use Equation 11 to calculate the sum of the squared differences from the mean, taking account of all N items in the population, and then to find the mean squared difference by dividing the sum by N. Whether a difference from the mean is positive or negative, squaring that difference results in a positive number. Thus variance takes care of the problem of negative deviations from the mean canceling out positive deviations by the operation of squaring those deviations. The P/Es for BJ, COST, and WMT were given earlier as 16.73, 22.02, and 29.30, respectively. We calculated the mean P/E as 22.68. Therefore, the population variance of the P/Es is $(1/3)[(16.73 - 22.68)^2 + (22.02 - 22.68)^2 + (29.30 - 22.68)^2] = (1/3)(-5.95^2 + -0.66^2 + 6.62^2) = (1/3)(35.4025 + 0.4356 + 43.8244) = (1/3)(79.6625) = 26.5542$.

7.3.2 *Population Standard Deviation*

Because the variance is measured in squared units, we need a way to return to the original units. We can solve this problem by using standard deviation, the square root of the variance. Standard deviation is more easily interpreted than the variance because standard deviation is expressed in the same unit of measurement as the observations.

■ **Population Standard Deviation Formula.** The **population standard deviation**, defined as the positive square root of the population variance, is

$$\sigma = \sqrt{\frac{\sum_{i=1}^{N}(X_i - \mu)^2}{N}}$$
(12)

where μ is the population mean and N is the size of the population.

Using the example of the P/Es for BJ, COST, and WMT, according to Equation 12 we would calculate the variance, 26.5542, then take the square root: $\sqrt{26.5542} = 5.1531$ or approximately 5.2.

Both the population variance and standard deviation are examples of parameters of a distribution. In later readings, we will introduce the notion of variance and standard deviation as risk measures.

In investments, we often do not know the mean of a population of interest, usually because we cannot practically identify or take measurements from each member of the population. We then estimate the population mean with the mean from a sample drawn from the population, and we calculate a sample variance or standard deviation using formulas different from Equations 11 and 12. We shall discuss these calculations in subsequent sections. However, in investments we sometimes have a defined group that we can consider to be a population. With well-defined populations, we use Equations 11 and 12, as in the following example.

Example 11

Calculating the Population Standard Deviation

Table 20 gives the yearly portfolio turnover for the 10 U.S. equity funds that composed the 2002 Forbes Magazine Honor Roll.[29] Portfolio turnover, a measure of trading activity, is the lesser of the value of sales or purchases over a year

---

[29] *Forbes* magazine annually selects U.S. equity mutual funds meeting certain criteria for its Honor Roll. The criteria relate to capital preservation (performance in bear markets), continuity of management (the fund must have a manager with at least six years' tenure), diversification, accessibility (disqualifying funds that are closed to new investors), and after-tax long-term performance.

divided by average net assets during the year. The number and identity of the funds on the Forbes Honor Roll changes from year to year.

Table 20	Portfolio Turnover: 2002 Forbes Honor Roll Mutual Funds

Fund	Yearly Portfolio Turnover (%)
FPA Capital Fund (FPPTX)	23
Mairs & Power Growth Fund (MPGFX)	8
Muhlenkamp Fund (MUHLX)	11
Longleaf Partners Fund (LLPFX)	18
Heartland Value Fund (HRTVX)	56
Scudder–Dreman High Return Equity-A (KDHAX)	29
Clipper Fund (CFIMX)	23
Weitz Value Fund (WVALX)	13
Third Avenue Value Fund (TAVFX)	16
Dodge & Cox Stock Fund (DODGX)	10

Source: Forbes (2003).

Based on the data in Table 20, address the following:

1. Calculate the population mean portfolio turnover for the period used by *Forbes* for the ten 2002 Honor Roll funds.

2. Calculate the population variance and population standard deviation of portfolio turnover.

3. Explain the use of the population formulas in this example.

Solution to 1:

$\mu = (23 + 8 + 11 + 18 + 56 + 29 + 23 + 13 + 16 + 10)/10 = 207/10 = 20.7$ percent.

Solution to 2:

Having established that $\mu = 20.7$, we can calculate $\sigma^2 = \dfrac{\sum\limits_{i=1}^{N}(X_i - \mu)^2}{N}$ by first calculating the numerator in the expression and then dividing by $N = 10$. The numerator (the sum of the squared differences from the mean) is

$(23 - 20.7)^2 + (8 - 20.7)^2 + (11 - 20.7)^2 + (18 - 20.7)^2 +$
$(56 - 20.7)^2 + (29 - 20.7)^2 + (23 - 20.7)^2 + (13 - 20.7)^2 +$
$(16 - 20.7)^2 + (10 - 20.7)^2 = 1,784.1$

Thus $\sigma^2 = 1,784.1/10 = 178.41$.

To calculate standard deviation, $\sigma = \sqrt{178.41} = 13.357$ percent. (The unit of variance is percent squared so the unit of standard deviation is percent.)

Solution to 3:

If the population is clearly defined to be the Forbes Honor Roll funds in one specific year (2002), and if portfolio turnover is understood to refer to the specific one-year period reported upon by *Forbes*, the application of the population formulas to variance and standard deviation is appropriate. The results of 178.41 and 13.357 are, respectively, the cross-sectional variance and standard deviation in yearly portfolio turnover for the 2002 Forbes Honor Roll Funds.[30]

7.4 Sample Variance and Sample Standard Deviation

7.4.1 *Sample Variance*

In many instances in investment management, a subset or sample of the population is all that we can observe. When we deal with samples, the summary measures are called statistics. The statistic that measures the dispersion in a sample is called the sample variance.

■ **Sample Variance Formula.** The **sample variance** is

$$s^2 = \frac{\sum_{i=1}^{n}(X_i - \bar{X})^2}{n-1}$$
(13)

where $\bar{X}$ is the sample mean and n is the number of observations in the sample.

Equation 13 tells us to take the following steps to compute the sample variance:

i. Calculate the sample mean, $\bar{X}$.

ii. Calculate each observation's squared deviation from the sample mean, $(X_i - \bar{X})^2$.

iii. Sum the squared deviations from the mean: $\sum_{i=1}^{n}(X_i - \bar{X})^2$.

iv. Divide the sum of squared deviations from the mean by $n - 1$:

$$\sum_{i=1}^{n}(X_i - \bar{X})^2 \big/ (n-1).$$

We will illustrate the calculation of the sample variance and the sample standard deviation in Example 12.

We use the notation s^2 for the sample variance to distinguish it from population variance, σ^2. The formula for sample variance is nearly the same as that for population variance except for the use of the sample mean, $\bar{X}$, in place of the population mean, μ, and a different divisor. In the case of the population variance, we divide by the size of the population, N. For the sample variance, however, we divide by the sample size minus 1, or $n - 1$. By using $n - 1$ (rather than n) as the divisor, we improve the statistical properties of the sample variance. In statistical terms, the sample variance defined in Equation 13 is an unbiased estimator of the population variance.[31] The quantity $n - 1$ is also known as the number of degrees of freedom in estimating the population variance. To estimate the population variance with s^2, we must first calculate the mean. Once we have computed the sample mean, there are only $n - 1$ independent deviations from it.

---

30 In fact, we could not properly use the Honor Roll funds to estimate the population variance of portfolio turnover (for example) of any other differently defined population, because the Honor Roll funds are not a random sample from any larger population of U.S. equity mutual funds.

31 We discuss this concept further in the reading on sampling.

7.4.2 *Sample Standard Deviation*

Just as we computed a population standard deviation, we can compute a sample standard deviation by taking the positive square root of the sample variance.

■ **Sample Standard Deviation Formula.** The **sample standard deviation**, *s*, is

$$s = \sqrt{\frac{\sum_{i=1}^{n}(X_i - \bar{X})^2}{n-1}} \tag{14}$$

where $\bar{X}$ is the sample mean and *n* is the number of observations in the sample.

To calculate the sample standard deviation, we first compute the sample variance using the steps given. We then take the square root of the sample variance. Example 12 illustrates the calculation of the sample variance and standard deviation for the two mutual funds introduced earlier.

Example 12

Calculating Sample Variance and Sample Standard Deviation

After calculating the geometric and arithmetic mean returns of two mutual funds in Example 7, we calculated two measures of dispersions for those funds, the range and mean absolute deviation of returns, in Example 10. We now calculate the sample variance and sample standard deviation of returns for those same two funds.

Table 15	(Repeated) Total Returns for Two Mutual Funds, 1998–2002	
Year	**Selected American Shares (SLASX)**	**T. Rowe Price Equity Income (PRFDX)**
1998	16.2%	9.2%
1999	20.3	3.8
2000	9.3	13.1
2001	−11.1	1.6
2002	−17.0	−13.0

Source: AAII.

Based on the data in Table 15 repeated above, answer the following:

1. Calculate the sample variance of return for (A) SLASX and (B) PRFDX.
2. Calculate sample standard deviation of return for (A) SLASX and (B) PRFDX.
3. Contrast the dispersion of returns as measured by standard deviation of return and mean absolute deviation of return for each of the two funds.

Solution to 1:

To calculate the sample variance, we use Equation 13. (Deviation answers are all given in percent squared.)

A. SLASX

 i. The sample mean is

$$\bar{R} = (16.2 + 20.3 + 9.3 - 11.1 - 17.0)/5 = 17.7/5 = 3.54\%.$$

 ii. The squared deviations from the mean are

$$(16.2 - 3.54)^2 = (12.66)^2 = 160.2756$$

$$(20.3 - 3.54)^2 = (16.76)^2 = 280.8976$$

$$(9.3 - 3.54)^2 = (5.76)^2 = 33.1776$$

$$(-11.1 - 3.54)^2 = (-14.64)^2 = 214.3296$$

$$(-17.0 - 3.54)^2 = (-20.54)^2 = 421.8916$$

 iii. The sum of the squared deviations from the mean is 160.2756 + 280.8976 + 33.1776 + 214.3296 + 421.8916 = 1,110.5720.

 iv. Divide the sum of the squared deviations from the mean by $n - 1$: 1,110.5720/(5 − 1) = 1,110.5720/4 = 277.6430

B. PRFDX

 i. The sample mean is

$$\bar{R} = (9.2 + 3.8 + 13.1 + 1.6 - 13.0)/5 = 14.7/5 = 2.94\%.$$

 ii. The squared deviations from the mean are

$$(9.2 - 2.94)^2 = (6.26)^2 = 39.1876$$

$$(3.8 - 2.94)^2 = (0.86)^2 = 0.7396$$

$$(13.1 - 2.94)^2 = (10.16)^2 = 103.2256$$

$$(1.6 - 2.94)^2 = (-1.34)^2 = 1.7956$$

$$(-13.0 - 2.94)^2 = (-15.94)^2 = 254.0836$$

 iii. The sum of the squared deviations from the mean is 39.1876 + 0.7396 + 103.2256 + 1.7956 + 254.0836 = 399.032.

 iv. Divide the sum of the squared deviations from the mean by $n - 1$: 399.032/4 = 99.758

Solution to 2:

To find the standard deviation, we take the positive square root of variance.

A. For SLASX, $s = \sqrt{277.6430} = 16.66\%$ or 16.7 percent.

B. For PRFDX, $s = \sqrt{99.758} = 9.99\%$ or 10.0 percent.

Solution to 3:

Table 21 summarizes the results from Part 2 for standard deviation and incorporates the results for MAD from Example 10.

Table 21	Two Mutual Funds: Comparison of Standard Deviation and Mean Absolute Deviation	
Fund	**Standard Deviation (%)**	**Mean Absolute Deviation (%)**
SLASX	16.7	14.1
PRFDX	10.0	6.9

Note that the mean absolute deviation is less than the standard deviation. The mean absolute deviation will always be less than or equal to the standard deviation because the standard deviation gives more weight to large deviations than to small ones (remember, the deviations are squared).

Because the standard deviation is a measure of dispersion about the arithmetic mean, we usually present the arithmetic mean and standard deviation together when summarizing data. When we are dealing with data that represent a time series of percent changes, presenting the geometric mean—representing the compound rate of growth—is also very helpful. Table 22 presents the historical geometric and arithmetic mean returns, along with the historical standard deviation of returns, for various equity return series. We present these statistics for nominal (rather than inflation-adjusted) returns so we can observe the original magnitudes of the returns.

Table 22	Equity Market Returns: Means and Standard Deviations		
Return Series	**Geometric Mean (%)**	**Arithmetic Mean (%)**	**Standard Deviation**
I. Ibbotson Associates Series: 1926–2002			
S&P 500 (Annual)	10.20	12.20	20.49
S&P 500 (Monthly)	0.81	0.97	5.65
II. Dimson et al. (2002) Series (Annual): 1900–2000			
Australia	11.9	13.3	18.2
Belgium	8.2	10.5	24.1
Canada	9.7	11.0	16.6
Denmark	8.9	10.7	21.7
France	12.1	14.5	24.6
Germany	9.7	15.2	36.4
Ireland	9.5	11.5	22.8
Italy	12.0	16.1	34.2
Japan	12.5	15.9	29.5
Netherlands	9.0	11.0	22.7
South Africa	12.0	14.2	23.7
Spain	10.0	12.1	22.8
Sweden	11.6	13.9	23.5
Switzerland	7.6	9.3	19.7
United Kingdom	10.1	11.9	21.8
United States	10.1	12.0	19.9

Source: Ibbotson EnCorr Analyzer™; Dimson et al.

7.5 Semivariance, Semideviation, and Related Concepts

An asset's variance or standard deviation of returns is often interpreted as a measure of the asset's risk. Variance and standard deviation of returns take account of returns above and below the mean, but investors are concerned only with downside risk, for example, returns below the mean. As a result, analysts have developed semivariance, semidevia-tion, and related dispersion measures that focus on downside risk. **Semivariance** is defined as the average squared deviation below the mean. **Semideviation** (sometimes called semistandard deviation) is the positive square root of semivariance. To compute the sample semivariance, for example, we take the following steps:

i. Calculate the sample mean.

ii. Identify the observations that are smaller than or equal to the mean (discarding observations greater than the mean).

iii. Compute the sum of the squared negative deviations from the mean (using the observations that are smaller than or equal to the mean).

iv. Divide the sum of the squared negative deviations from Step iii by $n - 1$. A formula for semivariance approximating the unbiased estimator is

$$\sum_{\text{for all } X_i \leq \bar{X}} \left(X_i - \bar{X}\right)^2 \Big/ (n-1)$$

To take the case of Selected American Shares with returns (in percent) of 16.2, 20.3, 9.3, −11.1, and −17.0, we earlier calculated a mean return of 3.54 percent. Two returns, −11.1 and −17.0, are smaller than 3.54. We compute the sum of the squared negative deviations from the mean as $(-11.1 - 3.54)^2 + (-17.0 - 3.54)^2 = -14.64^2 + -20.54^2 = 214.3296 + 421.8916 = 636.2212$. With $n - 1 = 4$, we conclude that semivariance is $636.2212/4 = 159.0553$ and that semideviation is $\sqrt{159.0553} = 12.6$ percent, approximately. The semideviation of 12.6 percent is less than the standard deviation of 16.7 percent. From this downside risk perspective, therefore, standard deviation overstates risk.

In practice, we may be concerned with values of return (or another variable) below some level other than the mean. For example, if our return objective is 10 percent annually, we may be concerned particularly with returns below 10 percent a year. We can call 10 percent the target. The name **target semivariance** has been given to average squared deviation below a stated target, and **target semideviation** is its positive square root. To calculate a sample target semivariance, we specify the target as a first step. After identifying observations below the target, we find the sum of the squared negative deviations from the target and divide that sum by the number of observations minus 1. A formula for target semivariance is

$$\sum_{\text{for all } X_i \leq B} \left(X_i - B\right)^2 \Big/ (n-1)$$

where B is the target and n is the number of observations. With a target return of 10 percent, we find in the case of Selected American Shares that three returns (9.3, −11.1, and −17.0) were below the target. The target semivariance is $[(9.3 - 10.0)^2 + (-11.1 - 10.0)^2 + (-17.0 - 10.0)^2]/(5 - 1) = 293.675$, and the target semideviation is $\sqrt{293.675} = 17.14$ percent, approximately.

When return distributions are symmetric, semivariance and variance are effectively equivalent. For asymmetric distributions, variance and semivariance rank prospects' risk differently.[32] Semivariance (or semideviation) and target semivariance (or target semideviation) have intuitive appeal, but they are harder to work with mathematically than variance.[33] Variance or standard deviation enters into the definition of many of the most commonly used finance risk concepts, such as the Sharpe ratio and beta. Perhaps because of these reasons, variance (or standard deviation) is much more frequently used in investment practice.

---

32 See Estrada (2003). We discuss skewness later in this reading.

33 As discussed in the reading on probability concepts and the various readings on portfolio concepts, we can find a portfolio's variance as a straightforward function of the variances and correlations of the component securities. There is no similar procedure for semivariance and target semivariance. We also cannot take the derivative of semivariance or target semivariance.

7.6 Chebyshev's Inequality

The Russian mathematician Pafnuty Chebyshev developed an inequality using standard deviation as a measure of dispersion. The inequality gives the proportion of values within k standard deviations of the mean.

■ **Definition of Chebyshev's Inequality.** According to Chebyshev's inequality, for any distribution with finite variance, the proportion of the observations within k standard deviations of the arithmetic mean is at least $1 - 1/k^2$ for all $k > 1$.

Table 23 illustrates the proportion of the observations that must lie within a certain number of standard deviations around the sample mean.

Table 23	Proportions from Chebyshev's Inequality	
k	**Interval around the Sample Mean**	**Proportion (%)**
1.25	$\bar{X} \pm 1.25s$	36
1.50	$\bar{X} \pm 1.50s$	56
2.00	$\bar{X} \pm 2s$	75
2.50	$\bar{X} \pm 2.50s$	84
3.00	$\bar{X} \pm 3s$	89
4.00	$\bar{X} \pm 4s$	94

Note: Standard deviation is denoted as s.

When $k = 1.25$, for example, the inequality states that the minimum proportion of the observations that lie within $\pm 1.25s$ is $1 - 1/(1.25)^2 = 1 - 0.64 = 0.36$ or 36 percent.

The most frequently cited facts that result from Chebyshev's inequality are that a two-standard-deviation interval around the mean must contain at least 75 percent of the observations, and a three-standard-deviation interval around the mean must contain at least 89 percent of the observations, no matter how the data are distributed.

The importance of Chebyshev's inequality stems from its generality. The inequality holds for samples and populations and for discrete and continuous data regardless of the shape of the distribution. As we shall see in the reading on sampling, we can make much more precise interval statements if we can assume that the sample is drawn from a population that follows a specific distribution called the normal distribution. Frequently, however, we cannot confidently assume that distribution.

The next example illustrates the use of Chebyshev's inequality.

Example 13

Applying Chebyshev's Inequality

According to Table 22, the arithmetic mean monthly return and standard deviation of monthly returns on the S&P 500 were 0.97 percent and 5.65 percent, respectively, during the 1926–2002 period, totaling 924 monthly observations. Using this information, address the following:

1. Calculate the endpoints of the interval that must contain at least 75 percent of monthly returns according to Chebyshev's inequality.

2. What are the minimum and maximum number of observations that must lie in the interval computed in Part 1, according to Chebyshev's inequality?

Solution to 1:

According to Chebyshev's inequality, at least 75 percent of the observations must lie within two standard deviations of the mean, $\bar{X} \pm 2s$. For the monthly S&P 500 return series, we have 0.97% ± 2(5.65%) = 0.97% ± 11.30%. Thus the lower endpoint of the interval that must contain at least 75 percent of the observations is 0.97% − 11.30% = −10.33%, and the upper endpoint is 0.97% + 11.30% = 12.27%.

Solution to 2:

For a sample size of 924, at least 0.75(924) = 693 observations must lie in the interval from −10.33% to 12.27% that we computed in Part 1. Chebyshev's inequality gives the minimum percentage of observations that must fall within a given interval around the mean, but it does not give the maximum percentage. Table 4, which gave the frequency distribution of monthly returns on the S&P 500, is excerpted below. The data in the excerpted table are consistent with the prediction of Chebyshev's inequality. The set of intervals running from −10.0% to 12.0% is just slightly narrower than the two-standard-deviation interval −10.33% to 12.27%. A total of 886 observations (approximately 96 percent of observations) fall in the range from −10.0% to 12.0%.

Table 4	Frequency Distribution for the Monthly Total Return on the S&P 500, January 1926 to December 2002 (Excerpt)
Return Interval (%)	**Absolute Frequency**
−10.0 to −8.0	20
−8.0 to −6.0	30
−6.0 to −4.0	54
−4.0 to −2.0	90
−2.0 to 0.0	138
0.0 to 2.0	182
2.0 to 4.0	153
4.0 to 6.0	126
6.0 to 8.0	58
8.0 to 10.0	21
10.0 to 12.0	14
	886

7.7 Coefficient of Variation

We noted earlier that standard deviation is more easily interpreted than variance because standard deviation uses the same units of measurement as the observations. We may sometimes find it difficult to interpret what standard deviation means in terms of the relative degree of variability of different sets of data, however, either because the data sets have markedly different means or because the data sets have different units of measurement. In this section we explain a measure of relative dispersion, the coefficient of variation that can be useful in such situations. **Relative dispersion** is the amount of dispersion relative to a reference value or benchmark.

We can illustrate the problem of interpreting the standard deviation of data sets with markedly different means using two hypothetical samples of companies. The first sample, composed of small companies, includes companies with 2003 sales of €50 million, €75 million, €65 million, and €90 million. The second sample, composed of large companies, includes companies with 2003 sales of €800 million, €825 million, €815 million, and €840 million. We can verify using Equation 14 that the standard deviation of sales in both samples is €16.8 million.[34] In the first sample, the largest observation, €90 million, is 80 percent larger than the smallest observation, €50 million. In the second sample, the largest observation is only 5 percent larger than the smallest observation. Informally, a standard deviation of €16.8 million represents a high degree of variability relative to the first sample, which reflects mean 2003 sales of €70 million, but a small degree of variability relative to the second sample, which reflects mean 2003 sales of €820 million.

The coefficient of variation is helpful in situations such as that just described.

■ **Coefficient of Variation Formula.** The **coefficient of variation**, CV, is the ratio of the standard deviation of a set of observations to their mean value:[35]

$$CV = s / \bar{X} \tag{15}$$

where s is the sample standard deviation and $\bar{X}$ is the sample mean.

When the observations are returns, for example, the coefficient of variation measures the amount of risk (standard deviation) per unit of mean return. Expressing the magnitude of variation among observations relative to their average size, the coefficient of variation permits direct comparisons of dispersion across different data sets. Reflecting the correction for scale, the coefficient of variation is a scale-free measure (that is, it has no units of measurement).

We can illustrate the application of the coefficient of variation using our earlier example of two samples of companies. The coefficient of variation for the first sample is (€16.8 million)/(€70 million) = 0.24; the coefficient of variation for the second sample is (€16.8 million)/(€820 million) = 0.02. This confirms our intuition that the first sample had much greater variability in sales than the second sample. Note that 0.24 and 0.02 are pure numbers in the sense that they are free of units of measurement (because we divided the standard deviation by the mean, which is measured in the same units as the standard deviation). If we need to compare the dispersion among data sets stated in different units of measurement, the coefficient of variation can be useful because it is free from units of measurement. Example 14 illustrates the calculation of the coefficient of variation.

Example 14

Calculating the Coefficient of Variation

Table 24 summarizes annual mean returns and standard deviations for several major U.S. asset classes, using an option in Ibbotson Encorr Analyzer to convert monthly return statistics to annual ones.

---

[34] The second sample was created by adding €750 million to each observation in the first sample. Standard deviation (and variance) has the property of remaining unchanged if we add a constant amount to each observation.

[35] The reader will also encounter CV defined as $100(s / \bar{X})$, which states CV as a percentage.

Table 24	Arithmetic Mean Annual Return and Standard Deviation of Returns, U.S. Asset Classes, 1926–2002	
Asset Class	**Arithmetic Mean Return (%)**	**Standard Deviation of Return (%)**
S&P 500	12.3	21.9
U.S. small stock	16.9	35.1
U.S. long-term corporate	6.1	7.2
U.S. long-term government	5.8	8.2
U.S. 30-day T-bill	3.8	0.9

Source: Ibbotson EnCorr Analyzer™.

Using the information in Table 24, address the following:

1. Calculate the coefficient of variation for each asset class given.

2. Rank the asset classes from most risky to least risky using CV as a measure of relative dispersion.

3. Determine whether there is more difference between the absolute or the relative riskiness of the S&P 500 and U.S. small stocks. Use the standard deviation as a measure of absolute risk and CV as a measure of relative risk.

Solution to 1:

S&P 500: CV = 21.9%/12.3% = 1.780

U.S. small stock: CV = 35.1%/16.9% = 2.077

U.S. long-term corporate: CV = 7.2%/6.1% = 1.180

U.S. long-term government: CV = 8.2%/5.8% = 1.414

U.S. 30-day T-bill: CV = 0.9%/3.8% = 0.237

Solution to 2:

Based on CV, the ranking is U.S. small stocks (most risky), S&P 500, U.S. long-term governments, U.S. long-term corporates, and U.S. 30-day T-bills (least risky).

Solution to 3:

As measured both by standard deviation and CV, U.S. small stocks were riskier than the S&P 500. However, the CVs reveal less difference between small-stock and S&P 500 return variability than that suggested by the standard deviations alone. The standard deviation of small stock returns was (35.1 − 21.9)/21.9 = 0.603 or about 60 percent larger than S&P 500 returns, compared with a difference in the CV of (2.077 − 1.780)/1.780 = 0.167 or 17 percent.

7.8 The Sharpe Ratio

Although CV was designed as a measure of relative dispersion, its inverse reveals something about return per unit of risk because the standard deviation of returns is commonly used as a measure of investment risk. For example, a portfolio with a mean monthly return of 1.19 percent and a standard deviation of 4.42 percent has an inverse CV of 1.19%/4.42% = 0.27. This result indicates that each unit of standard deviation represents a 0.27 percent return.

A more precise return–risk measure recognizes the existence of a risk-free return, a return for virtually zero standard deviation. With a risk-free asset, an investor can choose a risky portfolio, p, and then combine that portfolio with the risk-free asset to achieve any desired level of absolute risk as measured by standard deviation of return, s_p. Consider a graph with mean return on the vertical axis and standard deviation of return on the horizontal axis. Any combination of portfolio p and the risk-free asset lies on a ray (line) with slope equal to the quantity (Mean return – Risk-free return) divided by s_p. The ray giving investors choices offering the most reward (return in excess of the risk-free rate) per unit of risk is the one with the highest slope. The ratio of excess return to standard deviation of return for a portfolio p—the slope of the ray passing through p—is a single-number measure of a portfolio's performance known as the Sharpe ratio, after its developer, William F. Sharpe.

- **Sharpe Ratio Formula.** The **Sharpe ratio** for a portfolio p, based on historical returns, is defined as

$$S_h = \frac{\overline{R}_p - \overline{R}_F}{s_p} \tag{16}$$

  where $\overline{R}_p$ is the mean return to the portfolio, $\overline{R}_F$ is the mean return to a risk-free asset, and s_p is the standard deviation of return on the portfolio.[36]

The numerator of the Sharpe measure is the portfolio's mean return minus the mean return on the risk-free asset over the sample period. The $\overline{R}_p - \overline{R}_F$ term measures the extra reward that investors receive for the added risk taken. We call this difference the **mean excess return** on portfolio p. Thus the Sharpe ratio measures the reward, in terms of mean excess return, per unit of risk, as measured by standard deviation of return. Those risk-averse investors who make decisions only in terms of mean return and standard deviation of return prefer portfolios with larger Sharpe ratios to those with smaller Sharpe ratios.

To illustrate the calculation of the Sharpe ratio, consider the performance of the S&P 500 and U.S. small stocks during the 1926–2002 period, as given previously in Table 24. Using the mean U.S. T-bill return to represent the risk-free rate, we find

$$\text{S\&P 500: } S_h = \frac{12.3 - 3.8}{21.9} = 0.39$$

$$\text{U.S. small stocks: } S_h = \frac{16.9 - 3.8}{35.1} = 0.37$$

Although U.S. small stocks earned higher mean returns, they performed slightly less well than the S&P 500, as measured by the Sharpe ratio.

The Sharpe ratio is a mainstay of performance evaluation. We must issue two cautions concerning its use, one related to interpreting negative Sharpe ratios and the other to conceptual limitations.

Finance theory tells us that in the long run, investors should be compensated with additional mean return above the risk-free rate for bearing additional risk, at least if

---

[36] The equation presents the *ex post* or historical Sharpe ratio. We can also think of the Sharpe ratio for a portfolio going forward based on our expectations for mean return, the risk-free return, and the standard deviation of return; this would be the *ex ante* Sharpe ratio. One may also encounter an alternative calculation for the Sharpe ratio in which the denominator is the standard deviation of the series (Portfolio return – Risk-free return) rather than the standard deviation of portfolio return; in practice, the two standard deviation calculations generally yield very similar results. For more information on the Sharpe ratio (which has also been called the Sharpe measure, the reward-to-variability ratio, and the excess return to variability measure), see Elton, Gruber, Brown, and Goetzmann (2003) and Sharpe (1994).

the risky portfolio is well diversified. If investors are so compensated, the numerator of the Sharpe ratio will be positive. Nevertheless, we often find that portfolios exhibit negative Sharpe ratios when the ratio is calculated over periods in which bear markets for equities dominate. This raises a caution when dealing with negative Sharpe ratios. With positive Sharpe ratios, a portfolio's Sharpe ratio decreases if we increase risk, all else equal. That result is intuitive for a risk-adjusted performance measure. With negative Sharpe ratios, however, increasing risk results in a numerically larger Sharpe ratio (for example, doubling risk may increase the Sharpe ratio from −1 to −0.5). Therefore, in a comparison of portfolios with negative Sharpe ratios, we cannot generally interpret the larger Sharpe ratio (the one closer to zero) to mean better risk-adjusted performance.[37] Practically, to make an interpretable comparison in such cases using the Sharpe ratio, we may need to increase the evaluation period such that one or more of the Sharpe ratios becomes positive; we might also consider using a different performance evaluation metric.

The conceptual limitation of the Sharpe ratio is that it considers only one aspect of risk, standard deviation of return. Standard deviation is most appropriate as a risk measure for portfolio strategies with approximately symmetric return distributions. Strategies with option elements have asymmetric returns. Relatedly, an investment strategy may produce frequent small gains but have the potential for infrequent but extremely large losses.[38] Such a strategy is sometimes described as picking up coins in front of a bulldozer; for example, some hedge fund strategies tend to produce that return pattern. Calculated over a period in which the strategy is working (a large loss has not occurred), this type of strategy would have a high Sharpe ratio. In this case, the Sharpe ratio would give an overly optimistic picture of risk-adjusted performance because standard deviation would incompletely measure the risk assumed.[39] Therefore, before applying the Sharpe ratio to evaluate a manager, we should judge whether standard deviation adequately describes the risk of the manager's investment strategy.

Example 15 illustrates the calculation of the Sharpe ratio in a portfolio performance evaluation context.

Example 15

Calculating the Sharpe Ratio

In earlier examples, we computed the various statistics for two mutual funds, Selected American Shares (SLASX) and T. Rowe Price Equity Income (PRFDX), for a five-year period ending in December 2002. Table 25 summarizes selected statistics for these two mutual funds for a longer period, the 10-year period ending in 2002.

Table 25	Mutual Fund Mean Return and Standard Deviation of Return, 1993–2002	
Fund	**Arithmetic Mean (%)**	**Standard Deviation of Return (%)**
SLASX	12.58	19.44
PRFDX	11.64	13.65

Source: AAII.

---

37 If the standard deviations are equal, however, the portfolio with the negative Sharpe ratio closer to zero is superior.

38 This statement describes a return distribution with negative skewness. We discuss skewness later in this reading.

39 For more information, see Amin and Kat (2003).

The U.S. 30-day T-bill rate is frequently used as a proxy for the risk-free rate. Table 26 gives the annual return on T-bills for the 1993–2002 period.

Table 26	Annualized U.S. 30-Day T-Bill Rates of Return, 1993–2002
Year	**Return (%)**
1993	2.90
1994	3.90
1995	5.60
1996	5.21
1997	5.26
1998	4.86
1999	4.68
2000	5.89
2001	3.83
2002	1.65

Source: Ibbotson Associates.

Using the information in Tables 25 and 26, address the following:

1. Calculate the Sharpe ratios for SLASX and PRFDX during the 1993–2002 period.

2. State which fund had superior risk-adjusted performance during this period, as measured by the Sharpe ratio.

Solution to 1:

We already have in hand the means of the portfolio return and standard deviations of returns. The mean annual risk-free rate of return from 1993 to 2002, using U.S. T-bills as a proxy, is (2.90 + 3.90 + 5.60 + 5.21 + 5.26 + 4.86 + 4.68 + 5.89 + 3.83 + 1.65)/10 = 43.78/10 = 4.38 percent.

$$\text{SLASX: } S_{h,\text{SLASX}} = \frac{12.58 - 4.38}{19.44} = 0.42$$

$$\text{PRFDX: } S_{h,\text{PRFDX}} = \frac{11.64 - 4.38}{13.65} = 0.53$$

Solution to 2:

PRFDX had a higher positive Sharpe ratio than SLASX during the period. As measured by the Sharpe ratio, PRFDX's performance was superior.

SYMMETRY AND SKEWNESS IN RETURN DISTRIBUTIONS

Mean and variance may not adequately describe an investment's distribution of returns. In calculations of variance, for example, the deviations around the mean are squared, so we do not know whether large deviations are likely to be positive or negative. We need to go beyond measures of central tendency and dispersion to reveal other important characteristics of the distribution. One important characteristic of interest to analysts is the degree of symmetry in return distributions.

If a return distribution is symmetrical about its mean, then each side of the distribution is a mirror image of the other. Thus equal loss and gain intervals exhibit the same frequencies. Losses from –5 percent to –3 percent, for example, occur with about the same frequency as gains from 3 percent to 5 percent.

One of the most important distributions is the normal distribution, depicted in Figure 6. This symmetrical, bell-shaped distribution plays a central role in the mean–variance model of portfolio selection; it is also used extensively in financial risk management. The normal distribution has the following characteristics:

- Its mean and median are equal.

- It is completely described by two parameters—its mean and variance.

- Roughly 68 percent of its observations lie between plus and minus one standard deviation from the mean; 95 percent lie between plus and minus two standard deviations; and 99 percent lie between plus and minus three standard deviations.

A distribution that is not symmetrical is called **skewed**. A return distribution with positive skew has frequent small losses and a few extreme gains. A return distribution with negative skew has frequent small gains and a few extreme losses. Figure 7 shows positively and negatively skewed distributions. The positively skewed distribution shown has a long tail on its right side; the negatively skewed distribution has a long tail on its left side. For the positively skewed unimodal distribution, the mode is less than the median, which is less than the mean. For the negatively skewed unimodal distribution, the mean is less than the median, which is less than the mode.[40] Investors should be attracted by a positive skew because the mean return falls above the median. Relative to the mean return, positive skew amounts to a limited, though frequent, downside compared with a somewhat unlimited, but less frequent, upside.

---

[40] As a mnemonic, in this case the mean, median, and mode occur in the same order as they would be listed in a dictionary.

Figure 6 Properties of a Normal Distribution (EV 5 Expected Value)

Figure 7   Properties of a Skewed Distribution

Distribution Skewed to the Right (Positively Skewed)   Distribution Skewed to the Left (Negatively Skewed)

Source: Reprinted from *Fixed Income Analysis*. Copyright CFA Institute.

Skewness is the name given to a statistical measure of skew. (The word "skewness" is also sometimes used interchangeably for "skew.") Like variance, skewness is computed using each observation's deviation from its mean. **Skewness** (sometimes referred to as relative skewness) is computed as the average cubed deviation from the mean standardized by dividing by the standard deviation cubed to make the measure free of scale.[41] A symmetric distribution has skewness of 0, a positively skewed distribution has positive skewness, and a negatively skewed distribution has negative skewness, as given by this measure.

We can illustrate the principle behind the measure by focusing on the numerator. Cubing, unlike squaring, preserves the sign of the deviations from the mean. If a distribution is positively skewed with a mean greater than its median, then more than half of the deviations from the mean are negative and less than half are positive. In order for the sum to be positive, the losses must be small and likely, and the gains less likely but more extreme. Therefore, if skewness is positive, the average magnitude of positive deviations is larger than the average magnitude of negative deviations.

A simple example illustrates that a symmetrical distribution has a skewness measure equal to 0. Suppose we have the following data: 1, 2, 3, 4, 5, 6, 7, 8, and 9. The mean outcome is 5, and the deviations are −4, −3, −2, −1, 0, 1, 2, 3, and 4. Cubing the deviations yields −64, −27, −8, −1, 0, 1, 8, 27, and 64, with a sum of 0. The numerator of skewness (and so skewness itself) is thus equal to 0, supporting our claim. Below we give the formula for computing skewness from a sample.

■ **Sample Skewness Formula. Sample skewness** (also called sample relative skewness), S_K, is

$$S_K = \left[\frac{n}{(n-1)(n-2)} \right] \frac{\sum_{i=1}^{n} (X_i - \bar{X})^3}{s^3} \tag{17}$$

where n is the number of observations in the sample and s is the sample standard deviation.[42]

The algebraic sign of Equation 17 indicates the direction of skew, with a negative S_K indicating a negatively skewed distribution and a positive S_K indicating a positively skewed distribution. Note that as n becomes large, the expression reduces to the mean cubed deviation, $S_K \approx \left(\dfrac{1}{n}\right) \dfrac{\sum\limits_{i=1}^{n}\left(X_i - \bar{X}\right)^3}{s^3}$. As a frame of reference, for a sample size of 100 or larger taken from a normal distribution, a skewness coefficient of ±0.5 would be considered unusually large.

Table 27 shows several summary statistics for the annual and monthly returns on the S&P 500. Earlier we discussed the arithmetic mean return and standard deviation of return, and we shall shortly discuss kurtosis.

Table 27	S&P 500 Annual and Monthly Total Returns, 1926–2002: Summary Statistics				
Return Series	**Number of Periods**	**Arithmetic Mean (%)**	**Standard Deviation (%)**	**Skewness**	**Excess Kurtosis**
S&P 500 (Annual)	77	12.20	20.49	−0.2943	−0.2207
S&P 500 (Monthly)	924	0.97	5.65	0.3964	9.4645

Source: Ibbotson EnCorr Analyzer™.

Table 27 reveals that S&P 500 annual returns during this period were negatively skewed while monthly returns were positively skewed, and the magnitude of skewness was greater for the monthly series. We would find for other market series that the shape of the distribution of returns often depends on the holding period examined.

Some researchers believe that investors should prefer positive skewness, all else equal—that is, they should prefer portfolios with distributions offering a relatively large frequency of unusually large payoffs.[43] Different investment strategies may tend to introduce different types and amounts of skewness into returns. Example 16 illustrates the calculation of skewness for a managed portfolio.

Example 16

Calculating Skewness for a Mutual Fund

Table 28 presents 10 years of annual returns on the T. Rowe Price Equity Income Fund (PRFDX).

Table 28	Annual Rates of Return: T. Rowe Price Equity Income, 1993–2002
Year	**Return (%)**
1993	14.8
1994	4.5
1995	33.3
1996	20.3
1997	28.8
1998	9.2
1999	3.8
2000	13.1
2001	1.6
2002	−13.0

Source: AAII.

---

[43] For more on the role of skewness in portfolio selection, see Reilly and Brown (2003) and Elton et al. (2003) and the references therein.

Using the information in Table 28, address the following:

1. Calculate the skewness of PRFDX showing two decimal places.
2. Characterize the shape of the distribution of PRFDX returns based on your answer to Part 1.

Solution to 1:

To calculate skewness, we find the sum of the cubed deviations from the mean, divide by the standard deviation cubed, and then multiply that result by $n/[(n-1)(n-2)]$. Table 29 gives the calculations.

Table 29	Calculating Skewness for PRFDX		
Year	R_t	$R_t - \bar{R}$	$\left(R_t - \bar{R}\right)^3$
1993	14.8%	3.16	31.554
1994	4.5%	−7.14	−363.994
1995	33.3%	21.66	10,161.910
1996	20.3%	8.66	649.462
1997	28.8%	17.16	5,053.030
1998	9.2%	−2.44	−14.527
1999	3.8%	−7.84	−481.890
2000	13.1%	1.46	3.112
2001	1.6%	−10.04	−1,012.048
2002	−13.0%	−24.64	−14,959.673
$n =$	10		
$\bar{R} =$	11.64%		
		Sum =	−933.064
$s =$	13.65%	$s^3 =$	2,543.302
		Sum/s^3 =	−0.3669
		$n/[(n-1)(n-2)] =$	0.1389
		Skewness =	**−0.05**

Source: AAII.

Using Equation 17, the calculation is:

$$S_K = \left[\frac{10}{(9)(8)}\right]\frac{-933.064}{13.65^3} = -0.05$$

In this example, five deviations are negative and five are positive. Two large positive deviations, in 1995 and 1997, are more than offset by a very large negative deviation in 2002 and a moderately large negative deviation in 2001, both bear market years. The result is that skewness is a very small negative number.

Solution to 2:

Based on this small sample, the distribution of annual returns for the fund appears to be approximately symmetric (or very slightly negatively skewed). The negative and positive deviations from the mean are equally frequent, and large positive deviations approximately offset large negative deviations.

KURTOSIS IN RETURN DISTRIBUTIONS

In the previous section, we discussed how to determine whether a return distribution deviates from a normal distribution because of skewness. One other way in which a return distribution might differ from a normal distribution is by having more returns clustered closely around the mean (being more peaked) and more returns with large deviations from the mean (having fatter tails). Relative to a normal distribution, such a distribution has a greater percentage of small deviations from the mean return (more small surprises) and a greater percentage of extremely large deviations from the mean return (more big surprises). Most investors would perceive a greater chance of extremely large deviations from the mean as increasing risk.

Kurtosis is the statistical measure that tells us when a distribution is more or less peaked than a normal distribution. A distribution that is more peaked than normal is called **leptokurtic** (*lepto* from the Greek word for slender); a distribution that is less peaked than normal is called **platykurtic** (*platy* from the Greek word for broad); and a distribution identical to the normal distribution in this respect is called **mesokurtic** (*meso* from the Greek word for middle). The situation of more-frequent extremely large surprises that we described is one of leptokurtosis.[44]

Figure 8 illustrates a leptokurtic distribution. It is more peaked and has fatter tails than the normal distribution.

Figure 8	**Leptokurtic: Fat Tailed**

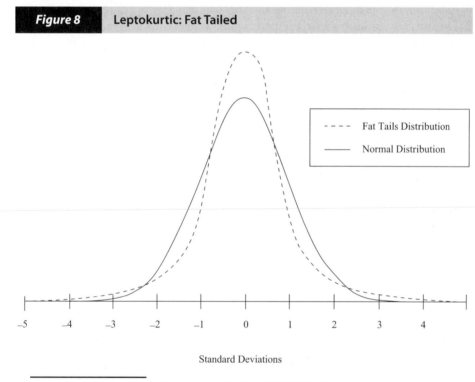

Standard Deviations

Source: Reprinted from *Fixed Income Analysis*. Copyright CFA Institute.

The calculation for kurtosis involves finding the average of deviations from the mean raised to the fourth power and then standardizing that average by dividing by the standard deviation raised to the fourth power.[45] For all normal distributions, kurtosis is equal to 3. Many statistical packages report estimates of **excess kurtosis**, which is

---

44 Kurtosis has been described as an illness characterized by episodes of extremely rude behavior.
45 This measure is free of scale. It is always positive because the deviations are raised to the fourth power.

kurtosis minus 3.[46] Excess kurtosis thus characterizes kurtosis relative to the normal distribution. A normal or other mesokurtic distribution has excess kurtosis equal to 0. A leptokurtic distribution has excess kurtosis greater than 0, and a platykurtic distribution has excess kurtosis less than 0. A return distribution with positive excess kurtosis—a leptokurtic return distribution—has more frequent extremely large deviations from the mean than a normal distribution. Below is the expression for computing kurtosis from a sample.

■ **Sample Excess Kurtosis Formula.** The **sample excess kurtosis** is

$$K_E = \left(\frac{n(n+1)}{(n-1)(n-2)(n-3)} \frac{\sum_{i=1}^{n}(X_i - \bar{X})^4}{s^4} \right) - \frac{3(n-1)^2}{(n-2)(n-3)} \tag{18}$$

where n is the sample size and s is the sample standard deviation.

In Equation 18, **sample kurtosis** is the first term. Note that as n becomes large, Equation 18 approximately equals $\frac{n^2}{n^3} \frac{\sum(X - \bar{X})^4}{s^4} - \frac{3n^2}{n^2} = \frac{1}{n} \frac{\sum(X - \bar{X})^4}{s^4} - 3$. For a sample of 100 or larger taken from a normal distribution, a sample excess kurtosis of 1.0 or larger would be considered unusually large.

Most equity return series have been found to be leptokurtic. If a return distribution has positive excess kurtosis (leptokurtosis) and we use statistical models that do not account for the fatter tails, we will underestimate the likelihood of very bad or very good outcomes. For example, the return on the S&P 500 for 19 October 1987 was 20 standard deviations away from the mean daily return. Such an outcome is possible with a normal distribution, but its likelihood is almost equal to 0. If daily returns are drawn from a normal distribution, a return four standard deviations or more away from the mean is expected once every 50 years; a return greater than five standard deviations away is expected once every 7,000 years. The return for October 1987 is more likely to have come from a distribution that had fatter tails than from a normal distribution. Looking at Table 27 given earlier, the monthly return series for the S&P 500 has very large excess kurtosis, approximately 9.5. It is extremely fat-tailed relative to the normal distribution. By contrast, the annual return series has very slightly negative excess kurtosis (roughly −0.2). The results for excess kurtosis in the table are consistent with research findings that the normal distribution is a better approximation for U.S. equity returns for annual holding periods than for shorter ones (such as monthly).[47]

The following example illustrates the calculations for sample excess kurtosis for one of the two mutual funds we have been examining.

Example 17

Calculating Sample Excess Kurtosis

Having concluded in Example 16 that the annual returns on T. Rowe Price Equity Income Fund were approximately symmetrically distributed during the 1993–2002 period, what can we say about the kurtosis of the fund's return distribution? Table 28 (repeated below) recaps the annual returns for the fund.

---

46 Ibbotson and some software packages, such as Microsoft Excel, label "excess kurtosis" as simply "kurtosis." This highlights the fact that one should familiarize oneself with the description of statistical quantities in any software packages that one uses.
47 See Campbell, Lo, and MacKinlay (1997) for more details.

Table 28	Annual Rates of Return: T. Rowe Price Equity Income, 1993–2002 (Repeated)

Year	Return (%)
1993	14.8
1994	4.5
1995	33.3
1996	20.3
1997	28.8
1998	9.2
1999	3.8
2000	13.1
2001	1.6
2002	−13.0

Source: AAII.

Using the information from Table 28 repeated above, address the following:

1. Calculate the sample excess kurtosis of PRFDX showing two decimal places.

2. Characterize the shape of the distribution of PRFDX returns based on your answer to Part 1 as leptokurtic, mesokurtic, or platykurtic.

Solution to 1:

To calculate excess kurtosis, we find the sum of the deviations from the mean raised to the fourth power, divide by the standard deviation raised to the fourth power, and then multiply that result by $n(n+1)/[(n-1)(n-2)(n-3)]$. This calculation determines kurtosis. Excess kurtosis is kurtosis minus $3(n-1)^2/[(n-2)(n-3)]$. Table 30 gives the calculations.

Table 30	Calculating Kurtosis for PRFDX		
Year	R_t	$R_t - \bar{R}$	$\left(R_t - \bar{R}\right)^4$
1993	14.8%	3.16	99.712
1994	4.5%	−7.14	2,598.920
1995	33.3%	21.66	220,106.977
1996	20.3%	8.66	5,624.340
1997	28.8%	17.16	86,709.990
1998	9.2%	−2.44	35.445
1999	3.8%	−7.84	3,778.020
2000	13.1%	1.46	4.544
2001	1.6%	−10.04	10,160.963
2002	−13.0%	−24.64	368,606.351
$n =$	10		

(continued)

Table 30	Continued		
Year	R_t	$R_t - \bar{R}$	$(R_t - \bar{R})^4$
$\bar{R} =$	11.64%		
		Sum =	697,725.261
$s =$	13.65%	$s^4 =$	34,716.074
		Sum/s^4 =	20.098
		$n(n+1)/[(n-1)(n-2)(n-3)] =$	0.2183
		Kurtosis =	**4.39**
		$3(n-1)^2/[(n-2)(n-3)] =$	4.34
		Excess Kurtosis =	**0.05**

Source: AAII.

Using Equation 18, the calculation is

$$K_E = \left[\frac{110}{(9)(8)(7)} \frac{697,725.261}{13.65^4} \right] - \frac{3(9)^2}{(8)(7)}$$
$$= 4.39 - 4.34$$
$$= 0.05$$

Solution to 2:

The distribution of PRFDX's annual returns appears to be mesokurtic, based on a sample excess kurtosis close to zero. With skewness and excess kurtosis both close to zero, PRFDX's annual returns appear to have been approximately normally distributed during the period.[48]

10   USING GEOMETRIC AND ARITHMETIC MEANS

With the concepts of descriptive statistics in hand, we will see why the geometric mean is appropriate for making investment statements about past performance. We will also explore why the arithmetic mean is appropriate for making investment statements in a forward-looking context.

For reporting historical returns, the geometric mean has considerable appeal because it is the rate of growth or return we would have had to earn each year to match the actual, cumulative investment performance. In our simplified Example 8, for instance, we purchased a stock for €100 and two years later it was worth €100, with an intervening year at €200. The geometric mean of 0 percent is clearly the compound rate of growth during the two years. Specifically, the ending amount is the beginning amount times $(1 + R_G)^2$. The geometric mean is an excellent measure of past performance.

---

48 It is useful to know that we can conduct a Jarque–Bera (JB) statistical test of normality based on sample size n, sample skewness, and sample excess kurtosis. We can conclude that a distribution is not normal with no more than a 5 percent chance of being wrong if the quantity $\text{JB} = n\left[\left(S_K^2/6\right) + \left(K_E^2/24\right)\right]$ is 6 or greater for a sample with at least 30 observations. In this mutual fund example, we have only 10 observations and the test described is only correct based on large samples (as a guideline, for $n \geq 30$). Gujarati (2003) provides more details on this test.

Example 8 illustrated how the arithmetic mean can distort our assessment of historical performance. In that example, the total performance for the two-year period was unambiguously 0 percent. With a 100 percent return for the first year and –50 percent for the second, however, the arithmetic mean was 25 percent. As we noted previously, the arithmetic mean is always greater than or equal to the geometric mean. If we want to estimate the average return over a one-period horizon, we should use the arithmetic mean because the arithmetic mean is the average of one-period returns. If we want to estimate the average returns over more than one period, however, we should use the geometric mean of returns because the geometric mean captures how the total returns are linked over time.

As a corollary to using the geometric mean for performance reporting, the use of **semilogarithmic** rather than arithmetic scales is more appropriate when graphing past performance.[49] In the context of reporting performance, a semilogarithmic graph has an arithmetic scale on the horizontal axis for time and a logarithmic scale on the vertical axis for the value of the investment. The vertical axis values are spaced according to the differences between their logarithms. Suppose we want to represent £1, £10, £100, and £1,000 as values of an investment on the vertical axis. Note that each successive value represents a 10-fold increase over the previous value, and each will be equally spaced on the vertical axis because the difference in their logarithms is roughly 2.30; that is, $\ln 10 - \ln 1 = \ln 100 - \ln 10 = \ln 1,000 - \ln 100 = 2.30$. On a semilogarithmic scale, equal movements on the vertical axis reflect equal percentage changes, and growth at a constant compound rate plots as a straight line. A plot curving upward reflects increasing growth rates over time. The slopes of a plot at different points may be compared in order to judge relative growth rates.

In addition to reporting historical performance, financial analysts need to calculate expected equity risk premiums in a forward-looking context. For this purpose, the arithmetic mean is appropriate.

We can illustrate the use of the arithmetic mean in a forward-looking context with an example based on an investment's future cash flows. In contrasting the geometric and arithmetic means for discounting future cash flows, the essential issue concerns uncertainty. Suppose an investor with $100,000 faces an equal chance of a 100 percent return or a –50 percent return, represented on the tree diagram as a 50/50 chance of a 100 percent return or a –50 percent return per period. With 100 percent return in one period and –50 percent return in the other, the geometric mean return is $\sqrt{2(0.5)} - 1 = 0$.

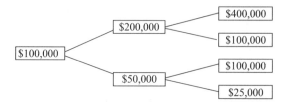

The geometric mean return of 0 percent gives the mode or median of ending wealth after two periods and thus accurately predicts the modal or median ending wealth of $100,000 in this example. Nevertheless, the arithmetic mean return better predicts the arithmetic mean ending wealth. With equal chances of 100 percent or –50 percent returns, consider the four equally likely outcomes of $400,000, $100,000, $100,000, and $25,000 as if they actually occurred. The arithmetic mean ending wealth would be $156,250 = ($400,000 + $100,000 + $100,000 + $25,000)/4. The actual returns would be 300 percent, 0 percent, 0 percent, and –75 percent for a two-period arithmetic mean return of (300 + 0 + 0 –75)/4 = 56.25 percent. This arithmetic mean return

---

49 See Campbell (1974) for more information.

predicts the arithmetic mean ending wealth of $100,000 × 1.5625 = $156,250. Noting that 56.25 percent for two periods is 25 percent per period, we then must discount the expected terminal wealth of $156,250 at the 25 percent arithmetic mean rate to reflect the uncertainty in the cash flows.

Uncertainty in cash flows or returns causes the arithmetic mean to be larger than the geometric mean. The more uncertain the returns, the more divergence exists between the arithmetic and geometric means. The geometric mean return approximately equals the arithmetic return minus half the variance of return.[50] Zero variance or zero uncertainty in returns would leave the geometric and arithmetic return approximately equal, but real-world uncertainty presents an arithmetic mean return larger than the geometric. For example, Dimson et al. (2002) reported that from 1900 to 2000, U.S. equities had nominal annual returns with an arithmetic mean of 12 percent and standard deviation of 19.9 percent. They reported the geometric mean as 10.1 percent. We can see the geometric mean is approximately the arithmetic mean minus half of the variance of returns: $R_G \approx 0.12 - (1/2)(0.199^2) = 0.10$.

SUMMARY

In this reading, we have presented descriptive statistics, the set of methods that permit us to convert raw data into useful information for investment analysis.

- A population is defined as all members of a specified group. A sample is a subset of a population.

- A parameter is any descriptive measure of a population. A sample statistic (statistic, for short) is a quantity computed from or used to describe a sample.

- Data measurements are taken using one of four major scales: nominal, ordinal, interval, or ratio. Nominal scales categorize data but do not rank them. Ordinal scales sort data into categories that are ordered with respect to some characteristic. Interval scales provide not only ranking but also assurance that the differences between scale values are equal. Ratio scales have all the characteristics of interval scales as well as a true zero point as the origin. The scale on which data are measured determines the type of analysis that can be performed on the data.

- A frequency distribution is a tabular display of data summarized into a relatively small number of intervals. Frequency distributions permit us to evaluate how data are distributed.

- The relative frequency of observations in an interval is the number of observations in the interval divided by the total number of observations. The cumulative relative frequency cumulates (adds up) the relative frequencies as we move from the first interval to the last, thus giving the fraction of the observations that are less than the upper limit of each interval.

- A histogram is a bar chart of data that have been grouped into a frequency distribution. A frequency polygon is a graph of frequency distributions obtained by drawing straight lines joining successive points representing the class frequencies.

- Sample statistics such as measures of central tendency, measures of dispersion, skewness, and kurtosis help with investment analysis, particularly in making probabilistic statements about returns.

---

50 See Bodie, Kane, and Marcus (2001).

- Measures of central tendency specify where data are centered and include the (arithmetic) mean, median, and mode (most frequently occurring value). The mean is the sum of the observations divided by the number of observations. The median is the value of the middle item (or the mean of the values of the two middle items) when the items in a set are sorted into ascending or descending order. The mean is the most frequently used measure of central tendency. The median is not influenced by extreme values and is most useful in the case of skewed distributions. The mode is the only measure of central tendency that can be used with nominal data.

- A portfolio's return is a weighted mean return computed from the returns on the individual assets, where the weight applied to each asset's return is the fraction of the portfolio invested in that asset.

- The geometric mean, G, of a set of observations $X_1, X_2, \ldots X_n$ is $G = \sqrt[n]{X_1 X_2 X_3 \ldots X_n}$ with $X_i \geq 0$ for $i = 1, 2, \ldots, n$. The geometric mean is especially important in reporting compound growth rates for time series data.

- Quantiles such as the median, quartiles, quintiles, deciles, and percentiles are location parameters that divide a distribution into halves, quarters, fifths, tenths, and hundredths, respectively.

- Dispersion measures such as the variance, standard deviation, and mean absolute deviation (MAD) describe the variability of outcomes around the arithmetic mean.

- Range is defined as the maximum value minus the minimum value. Range has only a limited scope because it uses information from only two observations.

- MAD for a sample is $\dfrac{\sum_{i=1}^{n} \left| X_i - \bar{X} \right|}{n}$ where $\bar{X}$ is the sample mean and n is the number of observations in the sample.

- The variance is the average of the squared deviations around the mean, and the standard deviation is the positive square root of variance. In computing sample variance (s^2) and sample standard deviation, the average squared deviation is computed using a divisor equal to the sample size minus 1.

- The semivariance is the average squared deviation below the mean; semideviation is the positive square root of semivariance. Target semivariance is the average squared deviation below a target level; target semideviation is its positive square root. All these measures quantify downside risk.

- According to Chebyshev's inequality, the proportion of the observations within k standard deviations of the arithmetic mean is at least $1 - 1/k^2$ for all $k > 1$. Chebyshev's inequality permits us to make probabilistic statements about the proportion of observations within various intervals around the mean for any distribution with finite variance. As a result of Chebyshev's inequality, a two-standard-deviation interval around the mean must contain at least 75 percent of the observations, and a three-standard-deviation interval around the mean must contain at least 89 percent of the observations, no matter how the data are distributed.

- The coefficient of variation, CV, is the ratio of the standard deviation of a set of observations to their mean value. A scale-free measure of relative dispersion, by expressing the magnitude of variation among observations relative to their average size, the CV permits direct comparisons of dispersion across different data sets.

- The Sharpe ratio for a portfolio, p, based on historical returns, is defined as $S_h = \dfrac{\bar{R}_p - \bar{R}_F}{s_p}$, where $\bar{R}_p$ is the mean return to the portfolio, $\bar{R}_F$ is the mean return to a risk-free and asset, and s_p is the standard deviation of return on the portfolio.

■ Skew describes the degree to which a distribution is not symmetric about its mean. A return distribution with positive skewness has frequent small losses and a few extreme gains. A return distribution with negative skewness has frequent small gains and a few extreme losses. Zero skewness indicates a symmetric distribution of returns.

■ Kurtosis measures the peakedness of a distribution and provides information about the probability of extreme outcomes. A distribution that is more peaked than the normal distribution is called leptokurtic; a distribution that is less peaked than the normal distribution is called platykurtic; and a distribution identical to the normal distribution in this respect is called mesokurtic. The calculation for kurtosis involves finding the average of deviations from the mean raised to the fourth power and then standardizing that average by the standard deviation raised to the fourth power. Excess kurtosis is kurtosis minus 3, the value of kurtosis for all normal distributions.

PRACTICE PROBLEMS FOR READING 7

1. Identify each of the following groups as a population or a sample. If the group is a sample, identify the population to which the sample is related.

   A. The S&P MidCap 400 Index viewed as representing U.S. stocks with market capitalization falling within a stated range.

   B. U.K. shares that traded on 11 August 2003 and that also closed above £100/share as of the close of the London Stock Exchange on that day.

   C. Marsh & McLennan Companies, Inc. (NYSE: MMC) and AON Corporation (NYSE: AOC). This group is part of Standard & Poor's Insurance Brokers Index.

   D. The set of 31 estimates for Microsoft EPS for fiscal year 2003, as of the 4 June 2003 date of a First Call/Thomson Financial report.

2. State the type of scale used to measure the following sets of data.

   A. Sales in euros.

   B. The investment style of mutual funds.

   C. An analyst's rating of a stock as *underweight, market weight,* or *overweight,* referring to the analyst's suggested weighting of the stock in a portfolio.

   D. A measure of the risk of portfolios on a scale of whole numbers from 1 (very conservative) to 5 (very risky) where the difference between 1 and 2 represents the same increment in risk as the difference between 4 and 5.

The table below gives the deviations of a hypothetical portfolio's annual total returns (gross of fees) from its benchmark's annual returns, for a 12-year period ending in 2003. Use this information to answer Questions 3–4.

Portfolio's Deviations from Benchmark Return, 1992–2003 (%)	
1992	−7.14
1993	1.62
1994	2.48
1995	−2.59
1996	9.37
1997	−0.55
1998	−0.89
1999	−9.19
2000	−5.11
2001	−0.49
2002	6.84
2003	3.04

3. A. Calculate the frequency, cumulative frequency, relative frequency, and cumulative relative frequency for the portfolio's deviations from benchmark return, given the set of intervals in the table that follows.

Practice Problems and Solutions: 1–19 taken from *Quantitative Methods for Investment Analysis,* Second Edition, by Richard A. DeFusco, CFA, Dennis W. McLeavey, CFA, Jerald E. Pinto, CFA, and David E. Runkle, CFA. Copyright © 2004 by CFA Institute. All other problems and solutions copyright © CFA Institute.

Return Interval	Frequency	Cumulative Frequency	Relative Frequency (%)	Cumulative Relative Frequency (%)
−9.19 ≤ A < −4.55				
−4.55 ≤ B < 0.09				
0.09 ≤ C < 4.73				
4.73 ≤ D ≤ 9.37				

    B. Construct a histogram using the data.

    C. Identify the modal interval of the grouped data.

4. Tracking risk (also called tracking error) is the standard deviation of the deviation of a portfolio's gross-of-fees total returns from benchmark return. Calculate the tracking risk of the portfolio, stated in percent (give the answer to two decimal places).

The table below gives the annual total returns on the MSCI Germany Index from 1993 to 2002. The returns are in the local currency. Use the information in this table to answer Questions 5–10.

MSCI Germany Index Total Returns, 1993–2002	
Year	**Return (%)**
1993	46.21
1994	−6.18
1995	8.04
1996	22.87
1997	45.90
1998	20.32
1999	41.20
2000	−9.53
2001	−17.75
2002	−43.06

Source: Ibbotson EnCorr Analyzer™.

5. To describe the distribution of observations, perform the following:

    A. Create a frequency distribution with five equally spaced classes (round up at the second decimal place in computing the width of class intervals).

    B. Calculate the cumulative frequency of the data.

    C. Calculate the relative frequency and cumulative relative frequency of the data.

    D. State whether the frequency distribution is symmetric or asymmetric. If the distribution is asymmetric, characterize the nature of the asymmetry.

6. To describe the central tendency of the distribution, perform the following:

    A. Calculate the sample mean return.

    B. Calculate the median return.

    C. Identify the modal interval (or intervals) of the grouped returns.

7. To describe the compound rate of growth of the MSCI Germany Index, calculate the geometric mean return.

8. To describe the values at which certain returns fall, calculate the 30th percentile.

9. To describe the dispersion of the distribution, perform the following:

   A. Calculate the range.

   B. Calculate the mean absolute deviation (MAD).

   C. Calculate the variance.

   D. Calculate the standard deviation.

   E. Calculate the semivariance.

   F. Calculate the semideviation.

10. To describe the degree to which the distribution may depart from normality, perform the following:

    A. Calculate the skewness.

    B. Explain the finding for skewness in terms of the location of the median and mean returns.

    C. Calculate excess kurtosis.

    D. Contrast the distribution of annual returns on the MSCI Germany Index to a normal distribution model for returns.

11. A. Explain the relationship among arithmetic mean return, geometric mean return, and variability of returns.

    B. Contrast the use of the arithmetic mean return to the geometric mean return of an investment from the perspective of an investor concerned with the investment's terminal value.

    C. Contrast the use of the arithmetic mean return to the geometric mean return of an investment from the perspective of an investor concerned with the investment's average one-year return.

   The following table repeats the annual total returns on the MSCI Germany Index previously given and also gives the annual total returns on the JP Morgan Germany five- to seven-year government bond index (JPM 5–7 Year GBI, for short). During the period given in the table, the International Monetary Fund Germany Money Market Index (IMF Germany MMI, for short) had a mean annual total return of 4.33 percent. Use that information and the information in the table to answer Questions 12–14.

Year	MSCI Germany Index (%)	JPM Germany 5–7 Year GBI (%)
1993	46.21	15.74
1994	−6.18	−3.40
1995	8.04	18.30
1996	22.87	8.35
1997	45.90	6.65
1998	20.32	12.45
1999	41.20	−2.19
2000	−9.53	7.44
2001	−17.75	5.55
2002	−43.06	10.27

Source: Ibbotson EnCorr Analyzer™.

12. Calculate the annual returns and the mean annual return on a portfolio 60 percent invested in the MSCI Germany Index and 40 percent invested in the JPM Germany GBI.

13. A. Calculate the coefficient of variation for:

    i. the 60/40 equity/bond portfolio described in Problem 12.

    ii. the MSCI Germany Index.

    iii. the JPM Germany 5–7 Year GBI.

    B. Contrast the risk of the 60/40 equity/bond portfolio, the MSCI Germany Index, and the JPM Germany 5–7 Year GBI, as measured by the coefficient of variation.

14. A. Using the IMF Germany MMI as a proxy for the risk-free return, calculate the Sharpe ratio for:

    i. the 60/40 equity/bond portfolio described in Problem 12.

    ii. the MSCI Germany Index.

    iii. the JPM Germany 5–7 Year GBI.

    B. Contrast the risk-adjusted performance of the 60/40 equity/bond portfolio, the MSCI Germany Index, and the JPM Germany 5–7 Year GBI, as measured by the Sharpe ratio.

15. Suppose a client asks you for a valuation analysis on the eight-stock U.S. common stock portfolio given in the table below. The stocks are equally weighted in the portfolio. You are evaluating the portfolio using three price multiples. The trailing 12 months (TTM) price-to-earnings ratio (P/E) is current price divided by diluted EPS over the past four quarters.[1] The TTM price-to-sales ratio (P/S) is current price divided by sales per share over the last four quarters. The price-to-book ratio (P/B) is the current price divided by book value per share as given in the most recent quarterly statement. The data in the table are as of 12 September 2003.

Client Portfolio

Common Stock	TTM P/E	TTM P/S	P/B
Abercrombie & Fitch (NYSE: AFN)	13.67	1.66	3.43
Albemarle Corporation (NYSE: ALB)	14.43	1.13	1.96
Avon Products, Inc. (NYSE: AVP)	28.06	2.45	382.72
Berkshire Hathaway (NYSE: BRK.A)	18.46	2.39	1.65
Everest Re Group Ltd (NYSE: RE)	11.91	1.34	1.30
FPL Group, Inc. (NYSE: FPL)	15.80	1.04	1.70
Johnson Controls, Inc. (NYSE: JCI)	14.24	0.40	2.13
Tenneco Automotive, Inc. (NYSE: TEN)	6.44	0.07	41.31

Source: www.multexinvestor.com.

---

1 In particular, diluted EPS is for continuing operations and before extraordinary items and accounting changes.

Based only on the information in the above table, calculate the following for the portfolio:

A.   **i.** Arithmetic mean P/E.

     ii. Median P/E.

B.   **i.** Arithmetic mean P/S.

     ii. Median P/S.

C.   **i.** Arithmetic mean P/B.

     ii. Median P/B.

D. Based on your answers to Parts A, B, and C, characterize the appropriateness of using the following valuation measures:

     i. Mean and median P/E.

     ii. Mean and median P/S.

     iii. Mean and median P/B.

16. The table below gives statistics relating to a hypothetical 10-year record of two portfolios.

	Mean Annual Return (%)	Standard Deviation of Return (%)	Skewness
Portfolio A	8.3	19.5	−1.9
Portfolio B	8.3	18.0	3.0

Based only on the information in the above table, perform the following:

A. Contrast the distributions of returns of Portfolios A and B.

B. Evaluate the relative attractiveness of Portfolios A and B.

17. The table below gives statistics relating to a hypothetical three-year record of two portfolios.

	Mean Monthly Return (%)	Standard Deviation (%)	Skewness	Excess Kurtosis
Portfolio A	1.1994	5.5461	−2.2603	6.2584
Portfolio B	1.1994	6.4011	−2.2603	8.0497

Based only on the information in the above table, perform the following:

A. Contrast the distributions of returns of Portfolios A and B.

B. Evaluate the relative attractiveness of Portfolios A and B.

18. The table below gives statistics relating to a hypothetical five-year record of two portfolios.

	Mean Monthly Return (%)	Standard Deviation (%)	Skewness	Excess Kurtosis
Portfolio A	1.6792	5.3086	−0.1395	−0.0187
Portfolio B	1.8375	5.9047	0.4934	−0.8525

Based only on the information in the above table, perform the following:

A. Contrast the distributions of returns of Portfolios A and B.

B. Evaluate the relative attractiveness of Portfolios A and B.

19. At the UXI Foundation, portfolio managers are normally kept on only if their annual rate of return meets or exceeds the mean annual return for portfolio managers of a similar investment style. Recently, the UXI Foundation has also been considering two other evaluation criteria: the median annual return of funds with the same investment style, and two-thirds of the return performance of the top fund with the same investment style.

The table below gives the returns for nine funds with the same investment style as the UXI Foundation.

Fund	Return (%)
1	17.8
2	21.0
3	38.0
4	19.2
5	2.5
6	24.3
7	18.7
8	16.9
9	12.6

With the above distribution of fund performance, which of the three evaluation criteria is the most difficult to achieve?

20. If the observations in a data set have different values, is the geometric mean for that data set less than that data set's:

	harmonic mean?	arithmetic mean?
A.	No	No
B.	No	Yes
C.	Yes	No

21. Is a return distribution characterized by frequent small losses and a few large gains *best* described as having:

	negative skew?	a mean that is greater than the median?
A.	No	No
B.	No	Yes
C.	Yes	No

22. An analyst gathered the following information about the return distributions for two portfolios during the same time period:

Portfolio	Skewness	Kurtosis
A	−1.3	2.2
B	0.5	3.5

The analyst stated that the distribution for Portfolio A is more peaked than a normal distribution and that the distribution for Portfolio B has a long tail on the left side of the distribution. Which of the following is *most* true?

A. The statement is not correct in reference to either portfolio.

B. The statement is correct in reference to Portfolio A, but the statement is not correct in reference to Portfolio B.

C. The statement is not correct in reference to Portfolio A, but the statement is correct in reference to Portfolio B.

23. The coefficient of variation is useful in determining the relative degree of variability of different data sets if those data sets have different:

A. means or different units of measurement.

B. means, but not different units of measurement.

C. units of measurement, but not different means.

24. An analyst gathered the following information:

Portfolio	Mean Return (%)	Standard Deviation of Returns (%)
1	9.8	19.9
2	10.5	20.3
3	13.3	33.9

If the risk-free rate of return is 3.0 percent, the portfolio that had the *best* risk-adjusted performance based on the Sharpe ratio is:

A. Portfolio 1.

B. Portfolio 2.

C. Portfolio 3.

25. An analyst gathered the following information about a portfolio's performance over the past ten years:

Mean annual return	11.8%
Standard deviation of annual returns	15.7%
Portfolio beta	1.2

If the mean return on the risk-free asset over the same period was 5.0%, the coefficient of variation and Sharpe ratio, respectively, for the portfolio are *closest* to:

	Coefficient of variation	Sharpe ratio
A.	0.75	0.43
B.	1.33	0.36
C.	1.33	0.43

SOLUTIONS FOR READING 7

1. **A.** The S&P MidCap 400 Index represents a sample of all U.S. stocks in the mid-cap or medium capitalization range. The related population is "all U.S. mid-cap stocks."

   B. The statement tells us to enumerate all members of a group and is sufficiently precise to allow us to do that. The statement defines a population.

   C. The two companies constitute a sample of U.S. insurance brokers. The related population is "U.S. insurance brokers."

   D. The statement defines a population. The 31 estimates for Microsoft EPS are the population of publicly available U.S. analyst estimates of Microsoft's FY2003 EPS, as of the report's date.

2. **A.** Sales in euros are measured on a ratio scale.

   B. Mutual fund investment styles are measured on a nominal scale. We can count the number of funds following a particular style, but whatever classification scheme we use, we cannot order styles into "greater than" or "less than" relationships.

   C. The ratings are measured on an ordinal scale. An analyst's rating of a stock as underweight, market weight, or overweight orders the rated securities in terms of levels of expected investment performance.

   D. The risk measurements are measured on an interval scale because not only do the measurements involve a ranking, but differences between adjacent values represent equal differences in risk. Because the measurement scale does not have a true zero, they are not measured on a ratio scale.

3. **A.** The entries in the table are as follows.

Return Interval	Frequency	Cumulative Frequency	Relative Frequency (%)	Cumulative Relative Frequency (%)
$-9.19\% \le A < -4.55\%$	3	3	25.00	25.00
$-4.55\% \le B < 0.09\%$	4	7	33.33	58.33
$0.09\% \le C < 4.73\%$	3	10	25.00	83.33
$4.73\% \le D \le 9.37\%$	2	12	16.67	100.00

   The frequency column provides the count of the observations falling in each return interval. The cumulative frequency adds up (cumulates) the frequencies. For example, the cumulative frequency of 7 for Interval B is the sum of the frequency of 3 for Interval A and the frequency of 4 for Interval B. The cumulative frequency for the last interval, D, equals the total number of observations, 12. The relative frequency column gives the frequency of an interval as a percentage of the total number of observations. The relative frequency for Interval B, for example, is 4/12 = 33.33 percent. The cumulative relative frequency column cumulates the relative frequencies. After reaching the last interval, the cumulative relative frequency should be 100 percent, ignoring rounding errors.

B. The histogram for these data is shown below.

**Absolute
Frequency**

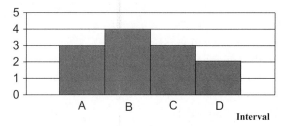

Interval

C. From the frequency distribution in Part A or the histogram in Part B, we can see that Interval B (−4.55 to 0.09) has the most members, 4. Interval B is thus the modal interval.

4. To calculate tracking risk of the portfolio, we use the sample standard deviation of the data in the table. We use the expression for sample standard deviation rather than population standard deviation because we are estimating the portfolio's tracking risk based on a sample. We use Equation 14,

$$s = \sqrt{\frac{\sum_{i=1}^{n}\left(X_i - \bar{X}\right)^2}{n-1}}$$

where X_i is the ith entry in the table of return deviations. The calculation in detail is as follows:

i. $\bar{X}$ = (−7.14 + 1.62 + 2.48 − 2.59 + 9.37 − 0.55 − 0.89 − 9.19 − 5.11 − 0.49 + 6.84 + 3.04)/12 = −2.61/12 = −0.2175 percent.

ii. Having established that the mean deviation from the benchmark was $\bar{X}$ = −0.2175, we calculate the squared deviations from the mean as follows:

$$\left[-7.14-(-0.2175)\right]^2 = (-6.9225)^2 = 47.921006$$
$$\left[1.62-(-0.2175)\right]^2 = (1.8375)^2 = 3.376406$$
$$\left[2.48-(-0.2175)\right]^2 = (2.6975)^2 = 7.276506$$
$$\left[-2.59-(-0.2175)\right]^2 = (-2.3725)^2 = 5.628756$$
$$\left[9.37-(-0.2175)\right]^2 = (9.5875)^2 = 91.920156$$
$$\left[-0.55-(-0.2175)\right]^2 = (-0.3325)^2 = 0.110556$$
$$\left[-0.89-(-0.2175)\right]^2 = (-0.6725)^2 = 0.452256$$
$$\left[-9.19-(-0.2175)\right]^2 = (-8.9725)^2 = 80.505756$$
$$\left[-5.11-(-0.2175)\right]^2 = (-4.8925)^2 = 23.936556$$
$$\left[-0.49-(-0.2175)\right]^2 = (-0.2725)^2 = 0.074256$$
$$\left[6.84-(-0.2175)\right]^2 = (7.0575)^2 = 49.808306$$
$$\left[3.04-(-0.2175)\right]^2 = (3.2575)^2 = 10.611306$$

iii. The sum of the squared deviations from the mean is

$$\sum_{i=1}^{12}\left(X_i - \bar{X}\right)^2 = 321.621825$$

Note that the sum is given with full precision. You may also get 321.621822, adding the terms rounded at the sixth decimal place. The solution is not affected.

iv. Divide the sum of the squared deviations from the mean by $n-1$: 321.621825/(12 − 1) = 321.621825/11 = 29.238347

v. Take the square root: $s = \sqrt{29.238347} = 5.41$ percent. Thus the portfolio's tracking risk was 5.41 percent a year.

5. A. A frequency distribution is a tabular display of data summarized into a relatively small number of equally sized intervals. In this example, we want five equally sized intervals. To make the frequency distribution table, we take the following seven steps.

i. Sort the data in ascending order.

−43.06%
−17.75%
−9.53%
−6.18%
8.04%
20.32%
22.87%
41.20%
45.90%
46.21%

ii. Calculate the range. Recall that the range formula is

Range = Maximum value − Minimum value.

In this case, the range is 46.21 − (−43.06) = 89.27.

iii. Decide on the number of intervals in the frequency distribution, k. This number was specified as $k = 5$ in the statement of the problem.

iv. Determine the interval width as Range/k = 89.27/5 = 17.854 or 17.86, rounding up at the second decimal place as instructed in the statement of the problem. Note that if we rounded down to 17.85, the final class would terminate at 46.19 and not capture the largest return, 46.21.

v. Determine the intervals by successively adding the interval width to the minimum value, to determine the ending points of intervals, stopping after we reach an interval that includes the maximum value.

−43.06 + 17.86 = −25.20
−25.20 + 17.86 = −7.34
−7.34 + 17.86 = 10.52
10.52 + 17.86 = 28.38
28.38 + 17.86 = 46.24

Thus the intervals are from −43.06 up to (but not including) −25.20, −25.20 to −7.34, −7.34 to 10.52, 10.52 to 28.38, and 28.38 to (including) 46.24.

vi. Count the number of observations falling in each interval. The count is one observation in −43.06 to −25.20, two observations in −25.20 to −7.34, two observations in −7.34 to 10.52, two observations in 10.52 to 28.38, and three observations in 28.38 to 46.24.

vii. Construct a table of the intervals listed from smallest to largest that shows the number of observations falling in each interval. The heading of the last column may be "frequency" or "absolute frequency."

Interval		Frequency
A	$-43.06 \leq$ observation < -25.20	1
B	$-25.20 \leq$ observation < -7.34	2
C	$-7.34 \leq$ observation < 10.52	2
D	$10.52 \leq$ observation < 28.38	2
E	$28.38 \leq$ observation ≤ 46.24	3

B. We find the cumulative frequencies by adding the absolute frequencies as we move from the first interval to the last interval.

Interval		Absolute Frequency	Calculations for Cumulative Frequency	Cumulative Frequency
A	$-43.06 \leq$ observation < -25.20	1		1
B	$-25.20 \leq$ observation < -7.34	2	$1 + 2 =$	3
C	$-7.34 \leq$ observation < 10.52	2	$3 + 2 =$	5
D	$10.52 \leq$ observation < 28.38	2	$5 + 2 =$	7
E	$28.38 \leq$ observation ≤ 46.24	3	$7 + 3 =$	10

The cumulative frequency is a running total of the absolute frequency, and the cumulative frequency for the last interval equals the total number of observations, 10.

C. The relative frequency of an interval is the frequency of the interval divided by the total number of observations. The cumulative relative frequency sums the relative frequencies. The cumulative relative frequency for the last interval is 100 percent.

Intervals		Absolute Frequency	Relative Frequency (%)	Calculations for Cumulative Frequency (%)	Cumulative Relative Frequency (%)
A	$-43.06 \leq$ observation < -25.20	1	$1/10 = 10$		10
B	$-25.20 \leq$ observation < -7.34	2	$2/10 = 20$	$10 + 20 =$	30
C	$-7.34 \leq$ observation < 10.52	2	$2/10 = 20$	$30 + 20 =$	50
D	$10.52 \leq$ observation < 28.38	2	$2/10 = 20$	$50 + 20 =$	70
E	$28.38 \leq$ observation ≤ 46.24	3	$3/10 = 30$	$70 + 30 =$	100
		10			

D. The last interval in the frequency distribution contains 30 percent of the observations, whereas the first interval contains 10 percent of the observations. The middle three intervals each contain 20 percent of the observations. The last two intervals thus contain 50 percent of the observations. The distribution is asymmetric. With most observations somewhat concentrated to the right but with one extreme negative observation (in the first interval), we conclude that the distribution is negatively skewed.

6. **A.** We calculate the sample mean by finding the sum of the 10 values in the table and then dividing by 10. According to Equation 3, the sample mean return, $\bar{R}$, is

$$\bar{R} = \frac{\sum_{i=1}^{10} R_i}{10}$$

using a common notation for returns, R_i. Thus $\bar{R}$ = (46.21 − 6.18 + 8.04 + 22.87 + 45.90 + 20.32 + 41.20 − 9.53 − 17.75 − 43.06)/10 = 108.02/10 = 10.802 or 10.80 percent.

B. The median is defined as the value of the middle item of a group that has been sorted into ascending or descending order. In a sample of n items, where n is an odd number, the median is the value of the item in the sorted data set occupying the $(n + 1)/2$ position. When the data set has an even number of observations (as in this example), the median is the mean of the values of the items occupying the $n/2$ and $(n + 2)/2$ positions (the two middle items). With $n = 10$, these are the fifth and sixth positions.

To find the median, the first step is to rank the data. We previously sorted the returns in ascending order in Solution 5A(i).

Returns (%)	Position
−43.06	1
−17.75	2
−9.53	3
−6.18	4
8.04	5
20.32	6
22.87	7
41.20	8
45.90	9
46.21	10

The value of the item in the fifth position is 8.04, and the value of the item in the sixth position is 20.32. The median return is then (8.04 + 20.32)/2 = 28.36/2 = 14.18 percent.

C. The modal return interval, as noted in Solution 5A, is Interval E, running from 28.38 percent to 46.24 percent.

7. The geometric mean requires that all the numbers be greater than or equal to 0. To ensure that the returns satisfy this requirement, after converting the returns to decimal form we add 1 to each return. We then use Equation 6 for the geometric mean return, R_G:

$$R_G = \left[\prod_{t=1}^{10} (1 + R_t) \right]^{(1/10)} - 1$$

which can also be written as

$$R_G = \sqrt[10]{(1 + R_1)(1 + R_2)\ldots(1 + R_{10})} - 1$$

To find the geometric mean in this example, we take the following five steps:

i. Divide each figure in the table by 100 to put the returns into decimal representation.

ii. Add 1 to each return to obtain the terms $1 + R_t$.

Return (%)	Return in Decimal Form	1 + Return
46.21	0.4621	1.4621
−6.18	−0.0618	0.9382
8.04	0.0804	1.0804
22.87	0.2287	1.2287
45.90	0.4590	1.4590
20.32	0.2032	1.2032
41.20	0.4120	1.4120
−9.53	−0.0953	0.9047
−17.75	−0.1775	0.8225
−43.06	−0.4306	0.5694

iii. Multiply together all the numbers in the third column to get 1.9124.

iv. Take the 10th root of 1.9124 to get $\sqrt[10]{1.9124} = 1.0670$. On most calculators, we evaluate $\sqrt[10]{1.9124}$ using the y^x key. Enter 1.9124 with the y^x key. Next, enter 1/10 = 0.10. Then press the = key to get 1.0670.

v. Subtract 1 to get 0.0670, or 6.70 percent a year. The geometric mean return is 6.70 percent. This result means that the compound annual rate of growth of the MSCI Germany Index was 6.7 percent annually during the 1993–2002 period. Note that this value is much less than the arithmetic mean of 10.80 percent that we calculated in the solution to Problem 6A.

8. Recall the formula for the location of the percentile (Equation 8):

$$L_y = (n+1)\frac{y}{100}$$

where L_y is the location or position of the yth percentile, P_y, and y is the percentage point at which we want to divide the distribution.

If we apply the percentile location formula, we find $L_{30} = (10+1)\frac{30}{100} = 3.3$, which is not a whole number. To find the 30th percentile from the sorted data, we interpolate by taking the value in the third position, −9.53, and adding 30 percent of the difference between the items in fourth and third position. The estimate of the 30th percentile is $P_{30} \approx -9.53 + 0.3[-6.18 - (-9.53)] = -9.53 + 0.3(3.35) = -9.53 + 1.005 = -8.53$.

Therefore, the 30th percentile is −8.53. By definition, the 30th percentile is that value at or below which 30 percent of the observations lie. In this problem, 3 observations out of 10 lie below −8.53.

9. **A.** In the solution to Problem 5A, we calculated the range as Maximum value − Minimum value = 46.21 − (−43.06) = 89.27.

B. The mean absolute deviation is defined in Equation 10 as

$$\text{MAD} = \frac{\sum_{i=1}^{10}|R_i - \bar{R}|}{10}$$

To find the MAD for this example, we take the following four steps:

i. Calculate the arithmetic mean of the original values.

ii. Subtract the arithmetic mean from each value.

iii. Take the absolute value of each deviation from the mean.

iv. Sum the absolute values of the deviations and divide by the total number of observations. The mean absolute deviation in this case is 24.50 percent.

The following table summarizes the calculation.

Original Data R_i	Deviation from Mean $R_i - \bar{R}$	Absolute Value of Deviation from Mean $\lvert R_i - \bar{R} \rvert$
46.21	35.41	35.41
−6.18	−16.98	16.98
8.04	−2.76	2.76
22.87	12.07	12.07
45.90	35.10	35.10
20.32	9.52	9.52
41.20	30.40	30.40
−9.53	−20.33	20.33
−17.75	−28.55	28.55
−43.06	−53.86	53.86
$\bar{R} = 10.8$		

$$\sum_{i=1}^{10} \lvert R_i - \bar{R} \rvert = 244.98$$

$$MAD = \frac{\sum_{i=1}^{10} \lvert R_i - \bar{R} \rvert}{10} = 24.50$$

C. Variance is defined as the mean of the squared deviations around the mean. We find the sample variance with Equation 13:

$$s^2 = \frac{\sum_{i=1}^{10} \left(R_i - \bar{R} \right)^2}{10 - 1}$$

To calculate the variance, we take the following four steps:

i. Calculate the arithmetic mean of the original values.

ii. Subtract the arithmetic mean from each value.

iii. Square each deviation from the mean.

iv. Sum the squared deviations and divide by the total number of observations minus 1. The variance, in this case, is 896.844711.

The following table summarizes the calculation.

Original Data R_i	Deviation from Mean $R_i - \bar{R}$	Squared Value of Deviation from Mean $\left(R_i - \bar{R} \right)^2$
46.21	35.41	1253.8681
−6.18	−16.98	288.3204
8.04	−2.76	7.6176
22.87	12.07	145.6849
45.90	35.10	1232.0100
20.32	9.52	90.6304
41.20	30.40	924.1600
−9.53	−20.33	413.3089

Original Data R_i	Deviation from Mean $R_i - \bar{R}$	Squared Value of Deviation from Mean $(R_i - \bar{R})^2$
−17.75	−28.55	815.1025
−43.06	−53.86	2900.8996

$\bar{R} = 10.8$

$$\sum_{i=1}^{10}(R_i - \bar{R})^2 = 8{,}071.6024$$

$$s^2 = \frac{\sum_{i=1}^{10}(R_i - \bar{R})^2}{9} = 896.844711$$

Recall that the units of variance are the squared units of the underlying variable, so to be precise we say that the sample variance is 896.844711 percent squared. To have a result in the original units of measurement, we calculate the standard deviation.

D. The standard deviation is the positive square root of the variance. We calculate the standard deviation with Equation 14:

$$s = \sqrt{896.844711} = 29.9474 \text{ or } 29.95\%$$

The standard deviation is thus 29.95 percent.

E. Semivariance is the average squared deviation below the mean. Five observations (−43.06, −17.75, −9.53, −6.18, and 8.04) lie below the mean return of 10.8. We compute the sum of the squared deviations from the mean as $(-43.06 - 10.8)^2 + (-17.75 - 10.8)^2 + (-9.53 - 10.8)^2 + (-6.18 - 10.8)^2 + (8.04 - 10.8)^2 = 4{,}425.2490$. Semivariance equals $4{,}425.2490/(10 - 1) = 491.6943$.

F. Semideviation equals $\sqrt{491.6943} = 22.174$ or 22.17%.

10. A. According to Equation 17, sample skewness S_K is

$$S_K = \left[\frac{n}{(n-1)(n-2)}\right]\frac{\sum_{i=1}^{n}(R_i - \bar{R})^3}{s^3}$$

The sample size, n, is 10. We previously calculated $\bar{R} = 10.8$ and deviations from the mean (see the tables in the solution to Problems 9B and 9C). We also calculated $s = 29.9474$ (showing four decimal places) in the solution to 9D. Thus $s^3 = 26{,}858.2289$. Using these results, we calculate the sum of the cubed deviations from the mean as follows:

$$\begin{aligned}
\sum_{i=1}^{10}(R_i - \bar{R})^3 = \sum_{i=1}^{10}(R_i - 10.8)^3 &= 35.41^3 + (-16.98)^3 + (-2.76)^3 + 12.07^3 \\
&\quad + 35.1^3 + 9.52^3 + 30.4^3 + (-20.33)^3 + (-28.55)^3 + (-53.86)^3 \\
&= 44{,}399.4694 - 4{,}895.6804 - 21.0246 + 1{,}758.4167 \\
&\quad + 43{,}243.551 + 862.8014 + 28{,}094.464 - 8{,}402.5699 \\
&\quad - 23{,}271.1764 - 156{,}242.4525 \\
&= -74{,}474.2012
\end{aligned}$$

So finally we have

$$S_K = \frac{10}{(9)(8)}\frac{-74{,}474.2012}{26{,}858.2289} = -0.39$$

In the sample period, the returns on the MSCI Germany Index were slightly negatively skewed.

B. For a negatively skewed distribution, the median is greater than the arithmetic mean. In our sample, the median return of 14.18 percent is greater than the mean return of 10.80.

C. According to Equation 18, sample excess kurtosis, K_E, is

$$K_E = \left\{ \left[\frac{n(n+1)}{(n-1)(n-2)(n-3)} \right] \frac{\sum_{i=1}^{n}(R_i - \bar{R})^4}{s^4} \right\} - \frac{3(n-1)^2}{(n-2)(n-3)}$$

The sample size, n, is 10. We previously calculated $\bar{R} = 10.8$ and deviations from the mean (see the tables in the solution to Problems 9B and 9C). We also calculated $s = 29.9474$ (showing four decimal places) in the answer to 9D. Thus $s^4 = 804,334.1230$. Using these results, we calculate the sum of the deviations from the mean raised to the fourth power as follows:

$$\sum_{i=1}^{10}(R_i - \bar{R})^4 = \sum_{i=1}^{10}(R_i - 10.8)^4 = 35.41^4 + (-16.98)^4 + (-2.76)^4 + 12.07^4$$

$$+ 35.1^4 + 9.52^4 + 30.4^4 + (-20.33)^4 + (-28.55)^4 + (-53.86)^4$$
$$= 1,572,185.212 + 83,128.6531 + 58.0278 + 21,224.0901$$
$$+ 1,517,848.64 + 8,213.8694 + 854,071.7056 + 170,824.2468$$
$$+ 664,392.0855 + 8,415,218.489$$
$$= 13,307,165.02$$

Thus we have

$$\left\{ \left[\frac{10(11)}{(9)(8)(7)} \right] \frac{13,307,165.02}{804,334.123} \right\} - \frac{3(9)^2}{(8)(7)} = 3.6109 - 4.3393 = -0.73$$

In the sample period, the returns on the MSCI Germany Index were slightly platykurtic. This means that there were fewer observations in the tails of the distribution than we would expect based on a normal distribution model for returns.

D. In contrast to a normal distribution, the distribution of returns on the MSCI Germany Index is somewhat asymmetric in direction of negative skew and is somewhat platykurtic (less peaked).

11. A. So long as a return series has any variability, the geometric mean return must be less than the arithmetic mean return. As one illustration of this relationship, in the solution to Problem 6A, we computed the arithmetic mean annual return on the MSCI Germany Index as 10.80 percent. In the solution to Problem 7, we computed the geometric mean annual return as 6.7 percent. In general, the difference between the geometric and arithmetic means increases with the variability of the period-by-period observations.

B. The geometric mean return is more meaningful than the arithmetic mean return for an investor concerned with the terminal value of an investment. The geometric mean return is the compound rate of growth, so it directly relates to the terminal value of an investment. By contrast, a higher arithmetic mean return does not necessarily imply a higher terminal value for an investment.

C. The arithmetic mean return is more meaningful than the geometric mean return for an investor concerned with the average one-period performance of an investment. The arithmetic mean return is a direct representation of the average one-period return. In contrast, the geometric mean return, as a compound rate of growth, aims to summarize what a return series means for the growth rate of an investment over many periods.

12. The following table shows the calculation of the portfolio's annual returns, and the mean annual return.

Year	Weighted Mean Calculation	Portfolio Return (%)
1993	0.60(46.21) + 0.40(15.74) =	34.02
1994	0.60(−6.18) + 0.40(−3.40) =	−5.07
1995	0.60(8.04) + 0.40(18.30) =	12.14
1996	0.60(22.87) + 0.40(8.35) =	17.06
1997	0.60(45.90) + 0.40(6.65) =	30.20
1998	0.60(20.32) + 0.40(12.45) =	17.17
1999	0.60(41.20) + 0.40(−2.19) =	23.84
2000	0.60(−9.53) + 0.40(7.44) =	−2.74
2001	0.60(−17.75) + 0.40(5.55) =	−8.43
2002	0.60(−43.06) + 0.40(10.27) =	−21.73
	Sum =	96.46
	Mean Annual Return =	9.65

Note: The sum of the portfolio returns carried without rounding is 96.48.

13. A. **i.** For the 60/40 equity/bond portfolio, the mean return (as computed in Problem 12) was 9.65 percent. We can compute the sample standard deviation of returns as $s = 18.31$ percent using Equation 14. The coefficient of variation for the 60/40 portfolio was $CV = s/\bar{R} = 18.31/9.65 = 1.90$.

  ii. For the MSCI Germany Index, $CV = s/\bar{R} = 29.95/10.80 = 2.77$.

  iii. For the JPM Germany 5–7 Year GBI, $CV = s/\bar{R} = 6.94/7.92 = 0.88$.

  B. The coefficient of variation is a measure of relative dispersion. For returns, it measures the amount of risk per unit of mean return. The MSCI Germany Index portfolio, the JPM Germany GBI, and the 60/40 equity/bond portfolio, were respectively most risky, least risky, and intermediate in risk, based on their values of CV.

Portfolio	CV	Risk
MSCI Germany Index	2.77	Highest
60/40 Equity/bond portfolio	1.90	
JPM Germany GBI	0.88	Lowest

14. A. **i.** For the 60/40 equity/bond portfolio, we earlier computed a mean return and standard deviation of return of 9.65 percent and 18.31, respectively. The statement of the problem gave the mean annual return on the proxy for the risk-free rate, the IMF Germany MMI, as 4.33 percent. We compute the Sharpe ratio as

$$S_h = \frac{\bar{R}_p - \bar{R}_F}{s_p} = \frac{9.65 - 4.33}{18.31} = 0.29$$

  ii. For the MSCI Germany Index,

$$S_h = \frac{\bar{R}_p - \bar{R}_F}{s_p} = \frac{10.80 - 4.33}{29.95} = 0.22$$

iii. For the JPM Germany 5–7 Year GBI,

$$S_h = \frac{\overline{R}_p - \overline{R}_F}{s_p} = \frac{7.92 - 4.33}{6.94} = 0.52$$

B. The Sharpe ratio measures excess return per unit of risk as measured by standard deviation. Because we are comparing positive Sharpe ratios, a larger Sharpe ratio reflects better risk-adjusted performance. During the period, the JPM Germany GBI had the best risk-adjusted performance and the MSCI Germany Index had the worst risk-adjusted performance, as measured by the Sharpe ratio. The 60/40 equity/bond portfolio was intermediate in risk-adjusted performance.

Portfolio	Sharpe Ratio	Performance
JPM Germany GBI	0.52	Best
60/40 Equity/bond portfolio	0.29	
MSCI Germany Index	0.22	Worst

15. A. **i.** The arithmetic mean P/E is (13.67 + 14.43 + 28.06 + 18.46 + 11.91 + 15.80 + 14.24 + 6.44)/8 = 15.38.

ii. Because the portfolio has an even number of stocks (eight), the median P/E is the mean of the P/Es in the $n/2 = 8/2 = $ 4th and $(n + 2)/2 = 10/2 = $ 5th positions in the data sorted in ascending order. (These are the middle two P/Es.) The fourth position P/E is 14.24, and the fifth position P/E is 14.43. The median P/E is (14.24 + 14.43)/2 = 14.34.

B. **i.** The arithmetic mean P/S is (1.66 + 1.13 + 2.45 + 2.39 + 1.34 + 1.04 + 0.40 + 0.07)/8 = 1.31.

ii. The median P/S is the mean of the P/Ss in the fourth and fifth positions in the data sorted in ascending order. The fourth position P/S is 1.13, and the fifth position P/S is 1.34. The median P/S is (1.13 + 1.34)/2 = 1.24.

C. **i.** The arithmetic mean P/B is (3.43 + 1.96 + 382.72 + 1.65 + 1.30 + 1.70 + 2.13 + 41.31)/8 = 54.53.

ii. The median P/B is the mean of the P/Bs in the fourth and fifth positions in the data sorted in ascending order. The fourth position P/B is 1.96, and the fifth position P/B is 2.13. The median P/B is (1.96 + 2.13)/2 = 2.05.

D. **i.** The distribution of P/Es is not characterized by outliers (extreme values) and the mean P/E and median P/E at 15.38 and 14.34, respectively, are similar in magnitude. Both the mean P/E and the median P/E are appropriate measures of central tendency. Because the mean P/E uses all the information in the sample and is mathematically simpler than the median, however, we might give it preference.

ii. Both the mean P/S and the median P/S are appropriate measures of central tendency. The mean P/S and median P/S at 1.31 and 1.24, respectively, are similar in magnitude. The P/S of 0.07 for Tenneco Automotive, Inc. is very small, yet it has only a moderate influence on the mean. As price is bounded from below at zero and sales are non-negative, the lowest possible P/S is 0. By contrast, there is no upper limit in theory on any price ratio. It is extremely high rather than extremely low P/Ss that would be the greater concern in using an arithmetic mean P/S. Note, too, that the P/E of about 6.4 for Tenneco, the lowest P/E observation, is not inconsistent with the P/S of 0.07 as long as the P/S is a valid observation (rather than a recording error).

   iii. The median P/B, but not the mean P/B, is an appropriate measure of central tendency. The mean P/B of 54.53 is unduly influenced by the extreme P/Bs of roughly 383 for Avon Products and roughly 41 for Tenneco Automotive. The case of Tenneco is interesting. The P/E and the P/S in particular appear to indicate that the stock is cheap in terms of the earnings and sales that a dollar buys; the P/B appears to indicate the reverse. Because book value is an accounting number subject to such decisions as write-downs, we might investigate whether book value per share for Tenneco and Avon reflects such actions.

16. A. With identical means, the two return distributions are similarly centered. Portfolio B's distribution has somewhat less dispersion, as measured by standard deviation. Both return distributions are asymmetric but in different ways. The return distribution for Portfolio A is negatively skewed; Portfolio B's distribution is positively skewed.

   B. Most investors would prefer the return distribution of Portfolio B, which has the same mean return as Portfolio A but less risk as measured by standard deviation of return. Furthermore, Portfolio B's returns are positively skewed, indicating a higher frequency of very large positive returns relative to Portfolio A. In contrast, Portfolio A's returns are negatively skewed.

17. A. With identical means, the two return distributions are similarly centered. Portfolio B's distribution has somewhat more dispersion, as measured by standard deviation. Both return distributions are negatively skewed to the same degree. Both portfolios have very large excess kurtosis, indicating much more frequent returns at the extremes, both positive and negative, than for a normal distribution.

   B. With identical mean returns and skewness, the comparison reduces to risk. Portfolio B is riskier as measured by standard deviation. Furthermore, risk-averse investors might view Portfolio B's more frequent extreme returns (both negative and positive), as indicated by greater kurtosis, as an additional risk element. Consequently, Portfolio A has the better risk–reward profile.

18. A. Portfolio B's returns are centered to the right of Portfolio A's, as indicated by mean return. Portfolio B's distribution has somewhat more dispersion than A's. Both return distributions are asymmetric but in different ways. The return distribution for Portfolio A is slightly negatively skewed. Portfolio B's distribution is moderately positively skewed. Portfolio A's return distribution is mesokurtic, and Portfolio B's return distribution is slightly platykurtic.

   B. We cannot know which portfolio particular investors would prefer without knowing their exact preferences for risk and return. Portfolio B has a higher mean return and moderately positive skewness, but it also has more risk as measured by standard deviation of return.

19. To determine which evaluation criterion is the most difficult to achieve, we need to i) calculate the mean return of the nine funds, ii) calculate the median return of the nine funds, iii) calculate two-thirds of the return of the best-performing fund, and iv) compare the results.

   i. Calculate the mean return of the nine funds.

   Find the sum of the values in the table and divide by 9.

$$\bar{X} = (17.8 + 21.0 + 38.0 + 19.2 + 2.5 + 24.3 + 18.7 + 16.9 + 12.6)/9$$
$$= 171/9 = 19.0$$

   ii. Calculate the median return of the nine funds. The first step is to sort the returns from largest to smallest.

Return (%)	Ranking
38.0	9
24.3	8
21.0	7
19.2	6
18.7	5
17.8	4
16.9	3
12.6	2
2.5	1

The median is the middle item, which occupies the $(n + 1)/2 = 5$th position in this odd-numbered sample. We conclude that the median is 18.7.

iii. Calculate two-thirds of the return of the best-performing fund. The top return is 38.0; therefore, two-thirds of the top return is $(2/3)38.0 = 25.33$.

iv. The following table summarizes what we have learned about these funds.

Criterion 1	Criterion 2	Criterion 3
19.0	18.7	25.3

Criterion 3, two-thirds of the return on the top fund, is the most difficult to meet.

In analyzing this problem, note that Criterion 3 is very sensitive to the value of the maximum observation. For example, if we were to subtract 10 from the maximum (to make it 28) and add 10 to the minimum (to make it 12.5), the mean and median would be unchanged. Criterion 3 would fall to two-thirds of 28, or 18.67. In this case, the mean, at 19.0, would be the most difficult criterion to achieve.

20. B is correct. Unless all the values of the observations in a data set have the same value, the harmonic mean is less than the corresponding geometric mean, which in turn is less than the corresponding arithmetic mean. In other words, regarding means, typically harmonic mean < geometric mean < arithmetic mean.

21. B is correct. A distribution with frequent small losses and a few large gains has positive skew (long tail on the right side) and the mean is greater than the median.

22. A is correct. The analyst's statement is not correct in reference to either portfolio. Portfolio A has a kurtosis of less than 3 meaning that it is less peaked than a normal distribution (platykurtic). Portfolio B is positively skewed (long tail on the right side of the distribution).

23. A is correct. The coefficient of variation is a relative measure of risk (dispersion) and is useful for both data sets that have different means and for data sets that do not have the same unit of measurement.

24. B is correct. The Sharpe ratio is the mean excess return (mean return less risk-free rate of 3.0 percent) divided by the standard deviation of the portfolio. It is highest for portfolio 2 with a Sharpe ratio of $7.5/20.3 = 0.3695$. For portfolio 1, the Sharpe ratio is $6.8/19.9 = 0.3417$ and for portfolio 3 the Sharpe ratio is $10.3/33.9 = 0.3038$.

25. C is correct. The coefficient of variation measures total risk per unit of return or standard deviation/mean return, or $15.7/11.8 = 1.33$. The Sharpe ratio is excess return per unit of risk or excess return/standard deviation. The mean excess return is $11.8\% - 5.0\% = 6.8\%$, so the Sharpe ratio is $6.8/15.7 = 0.43$.

Probability Concepts

by Richard A. DeFusco, CFA, Dennis W. McLeavey, CFA, Jerald E. Pinto, CFA, and David E. Runkle, CFA

LEARNING OUTCOMES

Mastery	The candidate should be able to:
☐	**a** define a random variable, an outcome, an event, mutually exclusive events, and exhaustive events;
☐	**b** state the two defining properties of probability and distinguish among empirical, subjective, and a priori probabilities;
☐	**c** state the probability of an event in terms of odds for and against the event;
☐	**d** distinguish between unconditional and conditional probabilities;
☐	**e** explain the multiplication, addition, and total probability rules;
☐	**f** calculate and interpret 1) the joint probability of two events, 2) the probability that at least one of two events will occur, given the probability of each and the joint probability of the two events, and 3) a joint probability of any number of independent events;
☐	**g** distinguish between dependent and independent events;
☐	**h** calculate and interpret an unconditional probability using the total probability rule;
☐	**i** explain the use of conditional expectation in investment applications;
☐	**j** explain the use of a tree diagram to represent an investment problem;
☐	**k** calculate and interpret covariance and correlation;
☐	**l** calculate and interpret the expected value, variance, and standard deviation of a random variable and of returns on a portfolio;
☐	**m** calculate and interpret covariance given a joint probability function;
☐	**n** calculate and interpret an updated probability using Bayes' formula;
☐	**o** identify the most appropriate method to solve a particular counting problem, and solve counting problems using the factorial, combination, and permutation notations.

INTRODUCTION

All investment decisions are made in an environment of risk. The tools that allow us to make decisions with consistency and logic in this setting come under the heading of probability. This reading presents the essential probability tools needed to frame and address many real-world problems involving risk. We illustrate how these tools apply to such issues as predicting investment manager performance, forecasting financial variables, and pricing bonds so that they fairly compensate bondholders for default risk. Our focus is practical. We explore in detail the concepts that are most important to investment research and practice. One such concept is independence, as it relates to the predictability of returns and financial variables. Another is expectation, as analysts continually look to the future in their analyses and decisions. Analysts and investors must also cope with variability. We present variance, or dispersion around expectation, as a risk concept important in investments. The reader will acquire specific skills in using portfolio expected return and variance.

The basic tools of probability, including expected value and variance, are set out in Section 2 of this reading. Section 3 introduces covariance and correlation (measures of relatedness between random quantities) and the principles for calculating portfolio expected return and variance. Two topics end the reading: Bayes' formula and outcome counting. Bayes' formula is a procedure for updating beliefs based on new information. In several areas, including a widely used option-pricing model, the calculation of probabilities involves defining and counting outcomes. The reading ends with a discussion of principles and shortcuts for counting.

PROBABILITY, EXPECTED VALUE, AND VARIANCE

The probability concepts and tools necessary for most of an analyst's work are relatively few and simple but require thought to apply. This section presents the essentials for working with probability, expectation, and variance, drawing on examples from equity and fixed income analysis.

An investor's concerns center on returns. The return on a risky asset is an example of a **random variable**, a quantity whose **outcomes** (possible values) are uncertain. For example, a portfolio may have a return objective of 10 percent a year. The portfolio manager's focus at the moment may be on the likelihood of earning a return that is less than 10 percent over the next year. Ten percent is a particular value or outcome of the random variable "portfolio return." Although we may be concerned about a single outcome, frequently our interest may be in a set of outcomes: The concept of "event" covers both.

■ **Definition of Event.** An **event** is a specified set of outcomes.

We may specify an event to be a single outcome—for example, *the portfolio earns a return of 10 percent.* (We use italics to highlight statements that define events.) We can capture the portfolio manager's concerns by defining the event as *the portfolio earns a return below 10 percent.* This second event, referring as it does to all possible returns greater than or equal to −100 percent (the worst possible return) but less than 10 percent, contains an infinite number of outcomes. To save words, it is common to use a capital letter in italics to represent a defined event. We could define *A = the portfolio earns a return of 10 percent* and *B = the portfolio earns a return below 10 percent.*

To return to the portfolio manager's concern, how likely is it that the portfolio will earn a return below 10 percent?

The answer to this question is a **probability**: a number between 0 and 1 that measures the chance that a stated event will occur. If the probability is 0.40 that the portfolio earns a return below 10 percent, there is a 40 percent chance of that event happening. If an event is impossible, it has a probability of 0. If an event is certain to happen, it has a probability of 1. If an event is impossible or a sure thing, it is not random at all. So, 0 and 1 bracket all the possible values of a probability.

Probability has two properties, which together constitute its definition.

- ■ **Definition of Probability.** The two defining properties of a probability are as follows:

    1. The probability of any event E is a number between 0 and 1: $0 \le P(E) \le 1$.

    2. The sum of the probabilities of any set of mutually exclusive and **exhaustive** events equals 1.

P followed by parentheses stands for "the probability of (the event in parentheses)," as in $P(E)$ for "the probability of event E." We can also think of P as a rule or function that assigns numerical values to events consistent with Properties 1 and 2.

In the above definition, the term mutually exclusive means that only one event can occur at a time; **exhaustive** means that the events cover all possible outcomes. The events A = *the portfolio earns a return of 10 percent* and B = *the portfolio earns a return below 10 percent* are mutually exclusive because A and B cannot both occur at the same time. For example, a return of 8.1 percent means that B has occurred and A has not occurred. Although events A and B are mutually exclusive, they are not exhaustive because they do not cover outcomes such as a return of 11 percent. Suppose we define a third event: C = *the portfolio earns a return above 10 percent.* Clearly, A, B, and C are mutually exclusive and exhaustive events. Each of $P(A)$, $P(B)$, and $P(C)$ is a number between 0 and 1, and $P(A) + P(B) + P(C) = 1$.

The most basic kind of mutually exclusive and exhaustive events is the set of all the distinct possible outcomes of the random variable. If we know both that set and the assignment of probabilities to those outcomes—the probability distribution of the random variable—we have a complete description of the random variable, and we can assign a probability to any event that we might describe.[1] The probability of any event is the sum of the probabilities of the distinct outcomes included in the definition of the event. Suppose the event of interest is D = *the portfolio earns a return above the risk-free rate,* and we know the probability distribution of portfolio returns. Assume the risk-free rate is 4 percent. To calculate $P(D)$, the probability of D, we would sum the probabilities of the outcomes that satisfy the definition of the event; that is, we would sum the probabilities of portfolio returns greater than 4 percent.

Earlier, to illustrate a concept, we assumed a probability of 0.40 for a portfolio earning less than 10 percent, without justifying the particular assumption. We also talked about using a probability distribution of outcomes to calculate the probability of events, without explaining how a probability distribution might be estimated. Making actual financial decisions using inaccurate probabilities might have grave consequences. How, in practice, do we estimate probabilities? This topic is a field of study in itself, but there are three broad approaches to estimating probabilities. In investments, we often estimate the probability of an event as a relative frequency of occurrence based on historical data. This method produces an **empirical probability**. For example, Amihud and Li (2002) report that of their sample of 16,189 dividend changes for NYSE and AMEX stocks during the years 1962 to 2000, 14,911 were increases and 1,278 were decreases. The empirical probability that a dividend change is a dividend decrease for U.S. stocks is thus 1,278/16,189 = 0.08, approximately. We will point out empirical probabilities in several places as they appear in this reading.

---

[1] In the reading on common probability distributions, we describe some of the probability distributions most frequently used in investment applications.

Relationships must be stable through time for empirical probabilities to be accurate. We cannot calculate an empirical probability of an event not in the historical record or a reliable empirical probability for a very rare event. There are cases, then, in which we may adjust an empirical probability to account for perceptions of changing relationships. In other cases, we have no empirical probability to use at all. We may also make a personal assessment of probability without reference to any particular data. Each of these three types of probability is a **subjective probability**, one drawing on personal or subjective judgment. Subjective probabilities are of great importance in investments. Investors, in making buy and sell decisions that determine asset prices, often draw on subjective probabilities. Subjective probabilities appear in various places in this reading, notably in our discussion of Bayes' formula.

In a more narrow range of well-defined problems, we can sometimes deduce probabilities by reasoning about the problem. The resulting probability is an **a priori probability**, one based on logical analysis rather than on observation or personal judgment. We will use this type of probability in Example 6. The counting methods we discuss later are particularly important in calculating an a priori probability. Because a priori and empirical probabilities generally do not vary from person to person, they are often grouped as **objective probabilities**.

In business and elsewhere, we often encounter probabilities stated in terms of odds—for instance, "the odds for *E*" or the "odds against *E*." For example, as of mid-2003, analysts' fiscal year 2004 EPS forecasts for one Toronto Stock Exchange-listed company ranged from C\$3.98 to C\$4.25. Nevertheless, one analyst asserts that the odds for the company beating the highest estimate, C\$4.25, are 1 to 7. A second analyst argues that the odds against that happening are 15 to 1. What do those statements imply about the probability of the company's EPS beating the highest estimate? We interpret probabilities stated in terms of odds as follows:

- ▪ **Probability Stated as Odds.** Given a probability $P(E)$,

  1. Odds for $E = P(E)/[1 - P(E)]$. The odds for E are the probability of E divided by 1 minus the probability of E. Given odds for E of "a to b," the implied probability of E is $a/(a + b)$.

In the example, the statement that the odds for *the company's EPS for FY2004 beating C\$4.25* are 1 to 7 means that the speaker believes the probability of the event is $1/(1 + 7) = 1/8 = 0.125$.

  2. Odds against $E = [1 - P(E)]/P(E)$, the reciprocal of odds for E. Given odds against E of "a to b," the implied probability of E is $b/(a + b)$.

The statement that the odds against *the company's EPS for FY2004 beating C\$4.25* are 15 to 1 is consistent with a belief that the probability of the event is $1/(1 + 15) = 1/16 = 0.0625$.

To further explain odds for an event, if $P(E) = 1/8$, the odds for E are $(1/8)/(7/8) = (1/8)(8/7) = 1/7$, or "1 to 7." For each occurrence of E, we expect seven cases of non-occurrence; out of eight cases in total, therefore, we expect E to happen once, and the probability of E is 1/8. In wagering, it is common to speak in terms of the odds against something, as in Statement 2. For odds of "15 to 1" against E (an implied probability of E of 1/16), a \$1 wager on E, if successful, returns \$15 in profits plus the \$1 staked in the wager. We can calculate the bet's anticipated profit as follows:

Win:	Probability = 1/16; Profit =\$15
Loss:	Probability = 15/16; Profit =−\$1

Anticipated profit = (1/16)(\$15) + (15/16)(−\$1) =\$0

Weighting each of the wager's two outcomes by the respective probability of the outcome, if the odds (probabilities) are accurate, the anticipated profit of the bet is \$0.

Example 1

Profiting from Inconsistent Probabilities

You are examining the common stock of two companies in the same industry in which an important antitrust decision will be announced next week. The first company, SmithCo Corporation, will benefit from a governmental decision that there is no antitrust obstacle related to a merger in which it is involved. You believe that SmithCo's share price reflects a 0.85 probability of such a decision. A second company, Selbert Corporation, will equally benefit from a "go ahead" ruling. Surprisingly, you believe Selbert stock reflects only a 0.50 probability of a favorable decision. Assuming your analysis is correct, what investment strategy would profit from this pricing discrepancy?

Consider the logical possibilities. One is that the probability of 0.50 reflected in Selbert's share price is accurate. In that case, Selbert is fairly valued but SmithCo is overvalued, as its current share price overestimates the probability of a "go ahead" decision. The second possibility is that the probability of 0.85 is accurate. In that case, SmithCo shares are fairly valued, but Selbert shares, which build in a lower probability of a favorable decision, are undervalued. You diagram the situation as shown in Table 1.

Table 1	Worksheet for Investment Problem	
	True Probability of a "Go Ahead" Decision	
	0.50	**0.85**
SmithCo	Shares Overvalued	Shares Fairly Valued
Selbert	Shares Fairly Valued	Shares Undervalued

The 0.50 probability column shows that Selbert shares are a better value than SmithCo shares. Selbert shares are also a better value if a 0.85 probability is accurate. Thus SmithCo shares are overvalued relative to Selbert shares.

Your investment actions depend on your confidence in your analysis and on any investment constraints you face (such as constraints on selling stock short).[2] A conservative strategy would be to buy Selbert shares and reduce or eliminate any current position in SmithCo. The most aggressive strategy is to short SmithCo stock (relatively overvalued) and simultaneously buy the stock of Selbert (relatively undervalued). This strategy is known as **pairs arbitrage trade**: a trade in two closely related stocks involving the short sale of one and the purchase of the other.

The prices of SmithCo and Selbert shares reflect probabilities that are not **consistent**. According to one of the most important probability results for investments, the **Dutch Book Theorem**,[3] inconsistent probabilities create profit opportunities. In our example, investors, by their buy and sell decisions to exploit the inconsistent probabilities, should eliminate the profit opportunity and inconsistency.

---

2 *Selling short* or *shorting stock* means selling borrowed shares in the hope of repurchasing them later at a lower price.

3 The theorem's name comes from the terminology of wagering. Suppose someone places a $100 bet on X at odds of 10 to 1 against X, and later he is able to place a $600 bet against X at odds of 1 to 1 against X. Whatever the outcome of X, that person makes a riskless profit (equal to $400 if X occurs or $500 if X does not occur) because the implied probabilities are inconsistent. He is said to have made a *Dutch book* in X. Ramsey (1931) presented the problem of inconsistent probabilities. See also Lo (1999).

To understand the meaning of a probability in investment contexts, we need to distinguish between two types of probability: unconditional and conditional. Both unconditional and conditional probabilities satisfy the definition of probability stated earlier, but they are calculated or estimated differently and have different interpretations. They provide answers to different questions.

The probability in answer to the straightforward question "What is the probability of this event A?" is an **unconditional probability**, denoted $P(A)$. Unconditional probabilities are also frequently referred to as **marginal probabilities**.[4]

Suppose the question is "What is the probability that *the stock earns a return above the risk-free rate* (event A)?" The answer is an unconditional probability that can be viewed as the ratio of two quantities. The numerator is the sum of the probabilities of stock returns above the risk-free rate. Suppose that sum is 0.70. The denominator is 1, the sum of the probabilities of all possible returns. The answer to the question is $P(A) = 0.70$.

Contrast the question "What is the probability of A?" with the question "What is the probability of A, given that B has occurred?" The probability in answer to this last question is a **conditional probability**, denoted $P(A \mid B)$ (read: "the probability of A given B").

Suppose we want to know the probability that *the stock earns a return above the risk-free rate* (event A), given that *the stock earns a positive return* (event B). With the words "given that," we are restricting returns to those larger than 0 percent—a new element in contrast to the question that brought forth an unconditional probability. The conditional probability is calculated as the ratio of two quantities. The numerator is the sum of the probabilities of stock returns above the risk-free rate; in this particular case, the numerator is the same as it was in the unconditional case, which we gave as 0.70. The denominator, however, changes from 1 to the sum of the probabilities for all outcomes (returns) above 0 percent. Suppose that number is 0.80, a larger number than 0.70 because returns between 0 and the risk-free rate have some positive probability of occurring. Then $P(A \mid B) = 0.70/0.80 = 0.875$. If we observe that the stock earns a positive return, the probability of a return above the risk-free rate is greater than the unconditional probability, which is the probability of the event given no other information. The result is intuitive.[5] To review, an unconditional probability is the probability of an event without any restriction; it might even be thought of as a stand-alone probability. A conditional probability, in contrast, is a probability of an event given that another event has occurred.

In discussing approaches to calculating probability, we gave one empirical estimate of the probability that a change in dividends is a dividend decrease. That probability was an unconditional probability. Given additional information on company characteristics, could an investor refine that estimate? Investors continually seek an information edge that will help improve their forecasts. In mathematical terms, they are attempting to frame their view of the future using probabilities conditioned on relevant information or events. Investors do not ignore useful information; they adjust their probabilities to reflect it. Thus, the concepts of conditional probability (which we analyze in more detail below), as well as related concepts discussed further on, are extremely important in investment analysis and financial markets.

To state an exact definition of conditional probability, we first need to introduce the concept of joint probability. Suppose we ask the question "What is the probability of both A and B happening?" The answer to this question is a **joint probability**, denoted $P(AB)$ (read: "the probability of A and B"). If we think of the probability of A and the probability of B as sets built of the outcomes of one or more random variables, the

---

4 In analyses of probabilities presented in tables, unconditional probabilities usually appear at the ends or *margins* of the table, hence the term *marginal probability*. Because of possible confusion with the way *marginal* is used in economics (roughly meaning *incremental*), we use the term *unconditional probability* throughout this discussion.

5 In this example, the conditional probability is greater than the unconditional probability. The conditional probability of an event may, however, be greater than, equal to, or less than the unconditional probability, depending on the facts. For instance, the probability that *the stock earns a return above the risk-free rate* given that *the stock earns a negative return* is 0.

joint probability of A and B is the sum of the probabilities of the outcomes they have in common. For example, consider two events: *the stock earns a return above the risk-free rate* (A) and *the stock earns a positive return* (B). The outcomes of A are contained within (a subset of) the outcomes of B, so $P(AB)$ equals $P(A)$. We can now state a formal definition of conditional probability that provides a formula for calculating it.

- **Definition of Conditional Probability.** The conditional probability of A given that B has occurred is equal to the joint probability of A and B divided by the probability of B (assumed not to equal 0).

$$P(A\,|\,B) = P(AB)\,/\,P(B),\, P(B) \neq 0 \tag{1}$$

Sometimes we know the conditional probability $P(A\mid B)$ and we want to know the joint probability $P(AB)$. We can obtain the joint probability from the following **multiplication rule for probabilities**, which is Equation 1 rearranged.

- **Multiplication Rule for Probability.** The joint probability of A and B can be expressed as

$$P(AB) = P(A\,|\,B)\,P(B) \tag{2}$$

Example 2

Conditional Probabilities and Predictability of Mutual Fund Performance (1)

Kahn and Rudd (1995) examined whether historical performance predicts future performance for a sample of mutual funds that included 300 actively managed U.S. domestic equity funds. One approach they used involved calculating each fund's exposure to a set of style indexes (the term "style" captures the distinctions of growth/value and large-capitalization/mid-capitalization/small-capitalization). After establishing a style benchmark (a comparison portfolio matched to the fund's style) for each fund, Kahn and Rudd computed the fund's selection return for two periods. They defined selection return as fund return minus the fund's style-benchmark return. The first period was October 1990 to March 1992. The top 50 percent of funds by selection return for that period were labeled winners; the bottom 50 percent were labeled losers. Based on selection return in the next period, April 1992 to September 1993, the top 50 percent of funds were tagged as winners and the bottom 50 percent as losers for that period. An excerpt from their results is given in Table 2. The winner-winner entry, for example, shows that 79 of the 150 first-period winner funds were also winners in the second period (52.7% = 79/150). Note that the four entries in parentheses in the table can be viewed as conditional probabilities.

Table 2	Equity Selection Returns Period 1: October 1990 to March 1992 Period 2: April 1992 to September 1993

Entries are number of funds (percent of row total in parentheses)

	Period 2 Winner	Period 2 Loser
Period 1 winner	79 (52.7%)	71 (47.3%)
Period 1 loser	71 (47.3%)	79 (52.7%)

Source: Kahn and Rudd (1995), Table 3.

Based on the data in Table 2, answer the following questions:

1. State the four events needed to define the four conditional probabilities.

2. State the four entries of the table as conditional probabilities using the form $P(\textit{this event} \mid \textit{that event})$ = number.

3. Are the conditional probabilities in Part 2 empirical, a priori, or subjective probabilities?

4. Using information in the table, calculate the probability of the event a *fund is a loser in both Period 1 and Period 2.* (Note that because 50 percent of funds are categorized as losers in each period, the unconditional probability that a fund is labeled a loser in either period is 0.5.)

Solution to 1:

The four events needed to define the conditional probabilities are as follows:

> *Fund is a Period 1 winner*
>
> *Fund is a Period 1 loser*
>
> *Fund is a Period 2 loser*
>
> *Fund is a Period 2 winner*

Solution to 2:

From Row 1:

> $P(\textit{fund is a Period 2 winner} \mid \textit{fund is a Period 1 winner})$ = 0.527
>
> $P(\textit{fund is a Period 2 loser} \mid \textit{fund is a Period 1 winner})$ = 0.473

From Row 2:

> $P(\textit{fund is a Period 2 winner} \mid \textit{fund is a Period 1 loser})$ = 0.473
>
> $P(\textit{fund is a Period 2 loser} \mid \textit{fund is a Period 1 loser})$ = 0.527

Solution to 3:

These probabilities are calculated from data, so they are empirical probabilities.

Solution to 4:

The estimated probability is 0.264. With A the event that a *fund is a Period 2 loser* and B the event that a *fund is a Period 1 loser*, AB is the event that a *fund is a loser in both Period 1 and Period 2.* From Table 2, $P(A|B)$ = 0.527 and $P(B)$ = 0.50. Thus, using Equation 2, we find that

> $P(AB) = P(A \mid B)P(B) = 0.527(0.50) = 0.2635$

or a probability of approximately 0.264.

Equation 2 states that the joint probability of A and B equals the probability of A given B times the probability of B. Because $P(AB) = P(BA)$, the expression $P(AB) = P(BA) = P(B \mid A)P(A)$ is equivalent to Equation 2.

When we have two events, A and B, that we are interested in, we often want to know the probability that either A or B occurs. Here the word "or" is inclusive, meaning that either A or B occurs or that both A and B occur. Put another way, the probability of A or B is the probability that at least one of the two events occurs. Such probabilities are calculated using the **addition rule for probabilities**.

- **Addition Rule for Probabilities.** Given events A and B, the probability that A or B occurs, or both occur, is equal to the probability that A occurs, plus the probability that B occurs, minus the probability that both A and B occur.

$$P(A \text{ or } B) = P(A) + P(B) - P(AB) \tag{3}$$

If we think of the individual probabilities of A and B as sets built of outcomes of one or more random variables, the first step in calculating the probability of A or B is to sum the probabilities of the outcomes in A to obtain $P(A)$. If A and B share any outcomes, then if we now added $P(B)$ to $P(A)$, we would count twice the probabilities of those shared outcomes. So we add to $P(A)$ the quantity $[P(B) - P(AB)]$, which is the probability of outcomes in B net of the probability of any outcomes already counted when we computed $P(A)$. Figure 1 illustrates this process; we avoid double-counting the outcomes in the intersection of A and B by subtracting $P(AB)$. As an example of the calculation, if $P(A) = 0.50$, $P(B) = 0.40$, and $P(AB) = 0.20$, then $P(A \text{ or } B) = 0.50 + 0.40 - 0.20 = 0.70$. Only if the two events A and B were mutually exclusive, so that $P(AB) = 0$, would it be correct to state that $P(A \text{ or } B) = P(A) + P(B)$.

| Figure 1 | Addition Rule for Probabilities |

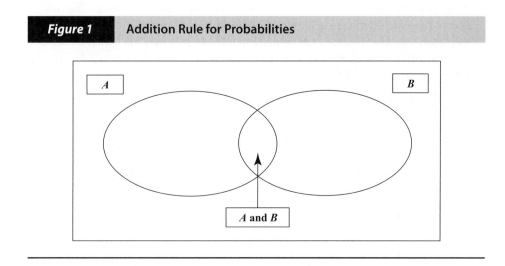

The next example shows how much useful information can be obtained using the few probability rules presented to this point.

Example 3

Probability of a Limit Order Executing

You have two buy limit orders outstanding on the same stock. A limit order to buy stock at a stated price is an order to buy at that price or lower. A number of vendors, including an internet service that you use, supply the estimated probability that a limit order will be filled within a stated time horizon, given the current stock price and the price limit. One buy order (Order 1) was placed at a price limit of $10. The probability that it will execute within one hour is 0.35. The second buy order (Order 2) was placed at a price limit of $9.75; it has a 0.25 probability of executing within the same one-hour time frame.

1. What is the probability that either Order 1 or Order 2 will execute?
2. What is the probability that Order 2 executes, given that Order 1 executes?

Solution to 1:

The probability is 0.35. The two probabilities that are given are *P(Order 1 executes)* = 0.35 and *P(Order 2 executes)* = 0.25. Note that if Order 2 executes, it is certain that Order 1 also executes because the price must pass through $10 to reach $9.75. Thus,

P(Order 1 executes | Order 2 executes) = 1

and

P(Order 1 executes and *Order 2 executes)* = *P(Order 1 executes | Order 2 executes)P(Order 2 executes)* = 1(0.25) = 0.25

To answer the question, we use the addition rule for probabilities:

P(Order 1 executes or *Order 2 executes)* = *P(Order 1 executes)* + *P(Order 2 executes)* − *P(Order 1 executes* and *Order 2 executes)* = 0.35 + 0.25 − 0.25 = 0.35

Note that the outcomes for which Order 2 executes are a subset of the outcomes for which Order 1 executes. After you count the probability that Order 1 executes, you have counted the probability of the outcomes for which Order 2 also executes. Therefore, the answer to the question is the probability that Order 1 executes, 0.35.

Solution to 2:

If the first order executes, the probability that the second order executes is 0.714. In the solution to Part 1, you found that *P(Order 1 executes* and *Order 2 executes)* = *P(Order 1 executes | Order 2 executes)P(Order 2 executes)* = 1(0.25) = 0.25. An equivalent way to state this joint probability is useful here:

P(Order 1 executes and *Order 2 executes)* = 0.25 = *P(Order 2 executes | Order 1 executes)P(Order 1 executes)*

Because *P(Order 1 executes)* = 0.35 was a given, you have one equation with one unknown:

0.25 = *P(Order 2 executes | Order 1 executes)*(0.35)

You conclude that *P(Order 2 executes | Order 1 executes)* = 0.25/0.35 = 5/7, or about 0.714. You can also use Equation 1 to obtain this answer.

Of great interest to investment analysts are the concepts of independence and dependence. These concepts bear on such basic investment questions as which financial variables are useful for investment analysis, whether asset returns can be predicted, and whether superior investment managers can be selected based on their past records.

Two events are independent if the occurrence of one event does not affect the probability of occurrence of the other event.

■ **Definition of Independent Events.** Two events *A* and *B* are **independent** if and only if $P(A \mid B) = P(A)$ or, equivalently, $P(B \mid A) = P(B)$.

When two events are not independent, they are **dependent**: The probability of occurrence of one is related to the occurrence of the other. If we are trying to forecast one event, information about a dependent event may be useful, but information about an independent event will not be useful.

When two events are independent, the multiplication rule for probabilities, Equation 2, simplifies because $P(A|B)$ in that equation then equals $P(A)$.

■ **Multiplication Rule for Independent Events.** When two events are independent, the joint probability of A and B equals the product of the individual probabilities of A and B.

$$P(AB) = P(A)P(B) \qquad\qquad (4)$$

Therefore, if we are interested in two independent events with probabilities of 0.75 and 0.50, respectively, the probability that both will occur is 0.375 = 0.75(0.50). The multiplication rule for independent events generalizes to more than two events; for example, if A, B, and C are independent events, then $P(ABC) = P(A)P(B)P(C)$.

Example 4

BankCorp's Earnings per Share (1)

As part of your work as a banking industry analyst, you build models for forecasting earnings per share of the banks you cover. Today you are studying BankCorp. The historical record shows that in 55 percent of recent quarters BankCorp's EPS has increased sequentially, and in 45 percent of quarters EPS has decreased or remained unchanged sequentially.[6] At this point in your analysis, you are assuming that changes in sequential EPS are independent.

Earnings per share for 2Q:2004 (that is, EPS for the second quarter of 2004) were larger than EPS for 1Q:2004.

1. What is the probability that 3Q:2004 EPS will be larger than 2Q:2004 EPS (a positive change in sequential EPS)?

2. What is the probability that EPS decreases or remains unchanged in the next two quarters?

Solution to 1:

Under the assumption of independence, the probability that 3Q:2004 EPS will be larger than 2Q:2004 EPS is the unconditional probability of positive change, 0.55. The fact that 2Q:2004 EPS was larger than 1Q:2004 EPS is not useful information, as the next change in EPS is independent of the prior change.

Solution to 2:

The probability is 0.2025 = 0.45(0.45).

The following example illustrates how difficult it is to satisfy a set of independent criteria even when each criterion by itself is not necessarily stringent.

Example 5

Screening Stocks for Investment

You have developed a stock screen—a set of criteria for selecting stocks. Your investment universe (the set of securities from which you make your choices) is the Russell 1000 Index, an index of 1,000 large-capitalization U.S. equities. Your criteria capture different aspects of the selection problem; you believe that the criteria are independent of each other, to a close approximation.

---

6 *Sequential* comparisons of quarterly EPS are with the immediate prior quarter. A sequential comparison stands in contrast to a comparison with the same quarter one year ago (another frequent type of comparison).

Criterion	Fraction of Russell 1000 Stocks Meeting Criterion
First valuation criterion	0.50
Second valuation criterion	0.50
Analyst coverage criterion	0.25
Profitability criterion for company	0.55
Financial strength criterion for company	0.67

How many stocks do you expect to pass your screen?

Only 23 stocks out of 1,000 pass through your screen. If you define five events—*the stock passes the first valuation criterion, the stock passes the second valuation criterion, the stock passes the analyst coverage criterion, the company passes the profitability criterion, the company passes the financial strength criterion* (say events *A, B, C, D,* and *E,* respectively)—then the probability that a stock will pass all five criteria, under independence, is

$$P(ABCDE) = P(A)P(B)P(C)P(D)P(E) = (0.50)(0.50)(0.25)(0.55)(0.67)$$
$$= 0.023031$$

Although only one of the five criteria is even moderately strict (the strictest lets 25 percent of stocks through), the probability that a stock can pass all five is only 0.023031, or about 2 percent. The size of the list of candidate investments is 0.023031(1,000) = 23.031, or 23 stocks.

An area of intense interest to investment managers and their clients is whether records of past performance are useful in identifying repeat winners and losers. The following example shows how this issue relates to the concept of independence.

Example 6

Conditional Probabilities and Predictability of Mutual Fund Performance (2)

The purpose of the Kahn and Rudd (1995) study, introduced in Example 2, was to address the question of repeat mutual fund winners and losers. If the status of a fund as a winner or a loser in one period is independent of whether it is a winner in the next period, the practical value of performance ranking is questionable. Using the four events defined in Example 2 as building blocks, we can define the following events to address the issue of predictability of mutual fund performance:

Fund is a Period 1 winner and *fund is a Period 2 winner*

Fund is a Period 1 winner and *fund is a Period 2 loser*

Fund is a Period 1 loser and *fund is a Period 2 winner*

Fund is a Period 1 loser and *fund is a Period 2 loser*

In Part 4 of Example 2, you calculated that

P(fund is a Period 2 loser and *fund is a Period 1 loser)* = 0.264

If the ranking in one period is independent of the ranking in the next period, what will you expect *P(fund is a Period 2 loser* and *fund is a Period 1 loser)* to be? Interpret the empirical probability 0.264.

By the multiplication rule for independent events, P(*fund is a Period 2 loser* and *fund is a Period 1 loser*) = P(*fund is a Period 2 loser*)P(*fund is a Period 1 loser*). Because 50 percent of funds are categorized as losers in each period, the unconditional probability that a fund is labeled a loser in either period is 0.50. Thus P(*fund is a Period 2 loser*)P(*fund is a Period 1 loser*) = 0.50(0.50) = 0.25. If the status of a fund as a loser in one period is independent of whether it is a loser in the prior period, we conclude that P(*fund is a Period 2 loser* and *fund is a Period 1 loser*) = 0.25. This probability is a priori because it is obtained from reasoning about the problem. You could also reason that the four events described above define categories and that if funds are randomly assigned to the four categories, there is a 1/4 probability of *fund is a Period 1 loser* and *fund is a Period 2 loser*. If the classifications in Period 1 and Period 2 were dependent, then the assignment of funds to categories would not be random. The empirical probability of 0.264 is only slightly above 0.25. Is this apparent slight amount of predictability the result of chance? A test conducted by Kahn and Rudd indicated a 35.6 percent chance of observing the tabled data if the Period 1 and Period 2 rankings were independent.

In investments, the question of whether one event (or characteristic) provides information about another event (or characteristic) arises in both time-series settings (through time) and cross-sectional settings (among units at a given point in time). Examples 4 and 6 illustrated independence in a time-series setting. Example 5 illustrated independence in a cross-sectional setting. Independence/dependence relationships are often also explored in both settings using regression analysis, a technique we discuss in a later reading.

In many practical problems, we logically analyze a problem as follows: We formulate scenarios that we think affect the likelihood of an event that interests us. We then estimate the probability of the event, given the scenario. When the scenarios (conditioning events) are mutually exclusive and exhaustive, no possible outcomes are left out. We can then analyze the event using the **total probability rule**. This rule explains the unconditional probability of the event in terms of probabilities conditional on the scenarios.

The total probability rule is stated below for two cases. Equation 5 gives the simplest case, in which we have two scenarios. One new notation is introduced: If we have an event or scenario S, the event not-S, called the **complement** of S, is written S^C.[7] Note that $P(S) + P(S^C) = 1$, as either S or not-S must occur. Equation 6 states the rule for the general case of n mutually exclusive and exhaustive events or scenarios.

- **The Total Probability Rule.**

$$P(A) = P(AS) + P(AS^C)$$
$$= P(A|S)P(S) + P(A|S^C)P(S^C)$$

(5)

$$P(A) = P(AS_1) + P(AS_2) + \dots + P(AS_n)$$
$$= P(A|S_1)P(S_1) + P(A|S_2)P(S_2) + \dots + P(A|S_n)P(S_n)$$

(6)

where $S_1, S_2, \dots, S_n$ are mutually exclusive and exhaustive scenarios or events.

Equation 6 states the following: The probability of any event [$P(A)$] can be expressed as a weighted average of the probabilities of the event, given scenarios [terms such

---

7 For readers familiar with mathematical treatments of probability, S, a notation usually reserved for a concept called the sample space, is being appropriated to stand for *scenario*.

$P(A|S_1)$]; the weights applied to these conditional probabilities are the respective probabilities of the scenarios [terms such as $P(S_1)$ multiplying $P(A|S_1)$], and the scenarios must be mutually exclusive and exhaustive. Among other applications, this rule is needed to understand Bayes' formula, which we discuss later in the reading.

In the next example, we use the total probability rule to develop a consistent set of views about BankCorp's earnings per share.

Example 7

BankCorp's Earnings per Share (2)

You are continuing your investigation into whether you can predict the direction of changes in BankCorp's quarterly EPS. You define four events:

Event	Probability
A = Change in sequential EPS is positive next quarter	0.55
A^C = *Change in sequential EPS is 0 or negative next quarter*	0.45
S = Change in sequential EPS is positive in the prior quarter	0.55
S^C = *Change in sequential EPS is 0 or negative in the prior quarter*	0.45

On inspecting the data, you observe some persistence in EPS changes: Increases tend to be followed by increases, and decreases by decreases. The first probability estimate you develop is P(*change in sequential EPS is positive next quarter | change in sequential EPS is 0 or negative in the prior quarter*) = $P(A|S^C)$ = 0.40. The most recent quarter's EPS (2Q:2004) is announced, and the change is a positive sequential change (the event *S*). You are interested in forecasting EPS for 3Q:2004.

1. Write this statement in probability notation: "the probability that the change in sequential EPS is positive next quarter, given that the change in sequential EPS is positive the prior quarter."

2. Calculate the probability in Part 1. (Calculate the probability that is consistent with your other probabilities or beliefs.)

Solution to 1:

In probability notation, this statement is written $P(A \mid S)$.

Solution to 2:

The probability is 0.673 that the change in sequential EPS is positive for 3Q:2004, given the positive change in sequential EPS for 2Q:2004, as shown on the following page.

According to Equation 5, $P(A) = P(A \mid S)P(S) + P(A \mid S^C)P(S^C)$. The values of the probabilities needed to calculate $P(A \mid S)$ are already known: $P(A)$ = 0.55, $P(S)$ = 0.55, $P(S^C)$ = 0.45, and $P(A \mid S^C)$ = 0.40. Substituting into Equation 5,

$$0.55 = P(A|S)(0.55) + 0.40(0.45)$$

Solving for the unknown, $P(A \mid S)$ = [0.55 − 0.40(0.45)]/0.55 = 0.672727, or 0.673.

You conclude that P(*change in sequential EPS is positive next quarter | change in sequential EPS is positive the prior quarter*) = 0.673. Any other probability is not consistent with your other estimated probabilities. Reflecting the persistence in EPS changes, this conditional probability of a positive EPS change, 0.673, is greater than the unconditional probability of an EPS increase, 0.55.

In the reading on statistical concepts and market returns, we discussed the concept of a weighted average or weighted mean. The example highlighted in that reading was that portfolio return is a weighted average of the returns on the individual assets in the portfolio, where the weight applied to each asset's return is the fraction of the portfolio invested in that asset. The total probability rule, which is a rule for stating an unconditional probability in terms of conditional probabilities, is also a weighted average. In that formula, probabilities of scenarios are used as weights. Part of the definition of weighted average is that the weights sum to 1. The probabilities of mutually exclusive and exhaustive events do sum to 1 (this is part of the definition of probability). The next weighted average we discuss, the expected value of a random variable, also uses probabilities as weights.

The expected value of a random variable is an essential quantitative concept in investments. Investors continually make use of expected values—in estimating the rewards of alternative investments, in forecasting EPS and other corporate financial variables and ratios, and in assessing any other factor that may affect their financial position. The expected value of a random variable is defined as follows:

- **Definition of Expected Value.** The **expected value** of a random variable is the probability-weighted average of the possible outcomes of the random variable. For a random variable X, the expected value of X is denoted $E(X)$.

Expected value (for example, expected stock return) looks either to the future, as a forecast, or to the "true" value of the mean (the population mean, discussed in the reading on statistical concepts and market returns). We should distinguish expected value from the concepts of historical or sample mean. The sample mean also summarizes in a single number a central value. However, the sample mean presents a central value for a particular set of observations as an equally weighted average of those observations. To summarize, the contrast is forecast versus historical, or population versus sample.

Example 8

BankCorp's Earnings per Share (3)

You continue with your analysis of BankCorp's EPS. In Table 3, you have recorded a probability distribution for BankCorp's EPS for the current fiscal year.

Table 3	Probability Distribution for BankCorp's EPS
Probability	**EPS ($)**
0.15	2.60
0.45	2.45
0.24	2.20
0.16	2.00
1.00	

What is the expected value of BankCorp's EPS for the current fiscal year? Following the definition of expected value, list each outcome, weight it by its probability, and sum the terms.

$$E(\text{EPS}) = 0.15(\$2.60) + 0.45(\$2.45) + 0.24(\$2.20) + 0.16(\$2.00)$$
$$= \$2.3405$$

The expected value of EPS is $2.34.

An equation that summarizes your calculation in Example 8 is

$$E(X) = P(X_1)X_1 + P(X_2)X_2 + \ldots + P(X_n)X_n = \sum_{i=1}^{n} P(X_i)X_i \qquad (7)$$

where X_i is one of n possible outcomes of the random variable X.[8]

The expected value is our forecast. Because we are discussing random quantities, we cannot count on an individual forecast being realized (although we hope that, on average, forecasts will be accurate). It is important, as a result, to measure the risk we face. Variance and standard deviation measure the dispersion of outcomes around the expected value or forecast.

■ **Definition of Variance.** The **variance** of a random variable is the expected value (the probability-weighted average) of squared deviations from the random variable's expected value:

$$\sigma^2(X) = E\left\{\left[X - E(X)\right]^2\right\} \qquad (8)$$

The two notations for variance are $\sigma^2(X)$ and $\mathrm{Var}(X)$.

Variance is a number greater than or equal to 0 because it is the sum of squared terms. If variance is 0, there is no dispersion or risk. The outcome is certain, and the quantity X is not random at all. Variance greater than 0 indicates dispersion of outcomes. Increasing variance indicates increasing dispersion, all else equal. Variance of X is a quantity in the squared units of X. For example, if the random variable is return in percent, variance of return is in units of percent squared. Standard deviation is easier to interpret than variance, as it is in the same units as the random variable. If the random variable is return in percent, standard deviation of return is also in units of percent.

■ **Definition of Standard Deviation.** **Standard deviation** is the positive square root of variance.

The best way to become familiar with these concepts is to work examples.

Example 9

BankCorp's Earnings per Share (4)

In Example 8, you calculated the expected value of BankCorp's EPS as $2.34, which is your forecast. Now you want to measure the dispersion around your forecast. Table 4 shows your view of the probability distribution of EPS for the current fiscal year.

Table 4	Probability Distribution for BankCorp's EPS
Probability	**EPS ($)**
0.15	2.60
0.45	2.45
0.24	2.20
0.16	2.00
1.00	

---

[8] For simplicity, we model all random variables in this reading as discrete random variables, which have a countable set of outcomes. For continuous random variables, which are discussed along with discrete random variables in the reading on common probability distributions, the operation corresponding to summation is integration.

What are the variance and standard deviation of BankCorp's EPS for the current fiscal year?

The order of calculation is always expected value, then variance, then standard deviation. Expected value has already been calculated. Following the definition of variance above, calculate the deviation of each outcome from the mean or expected value, square each deviation, weight (multiply) each squared deviation by its probability of occurrence, and then sum these terms.

$$\sigma^2(\text{EPS}) = P(\$2.60)\big[\$2.60 - E(\text{EPS})\big]^2 + P(\$2.45)\big[\$2.45 - E(\text{EPS})\big]^2$$
$$+ P(\$2.20)\big[\$2.20 - E(\text{EPS})\big]^2 + P(\$2.00)\big[\$2.00 - E(\text{EPS})\big]^2$$
$$= 0.15(2.60 - 2.34)^2 + 0.45(2.45 - 2.34)^2$$
$$+ 0.24(2.20 - 2.34)^2 + 0.16(2.00 - 2.34)^2$$
$$= 0.01014 + 0.005445 + 0.004704 + \$0.018496 = \$0.038785$$

Standard deviation is the positive square root of $0.038785:

$$\sigma(\text{EPS}) = \$0.038785^{1/2} = \$0.196939, \text{ or approximately } \$0.20.$$

An equation that summarizes your calculation of variance in Example 9 is

$$\sigma^2(X) = P(X_1)\big[X_1 - E(X)\big]^2 + P(X_2)\big[X_2 - E(X)\big]^2$$
$$+ \dots + P(X_n)\big[X_n - E(X)\big]^2 = \sum_{i=1}^{n} P(X_i)\big[X_i - E(X)\big]^2 \tag{9}$$

where X_i is one of n possible outcomes of the random variable X.

In investments, we make use of any relevant information available in making our forecasts. When we refine our expectations or forecasts, we are typically making adjustments based on new information or events; in these cases we are using **conditional expected values**. The expected value of a random variable X given an event or scenario S is denoted $E(X \mid S)$. Suppose the random variable X can take on any one of n distinct outcomes $X_1, X_2, \dots, X_n$ (these outcomes form a set of mutually exclusive and exhaustive events). The expected value of X conditional on S is the first outcome, X_1, times the probability of the first outcome given S, $P(X_1 \mid S)$, plus the second outcome, X_2, times the probability of the second outcome given S, $P(X_2 \mid S)$, and so forth.

$$E(X \mid S) = P(X_1 \mid S)X_1 + P(X_2 \mid S)X_2 + \dots + P(X_n \mid S)X_n \tag{10}$$

We will illustrate this equation shortly.

Parallel to the total probability rule for stating unconditional probabilities in terms of conditional probabilities, there is a principle for stating (unconditional) expected values in terms of conditional expected values. This principle is the **total probability rule for expected value**.

■ **The Total Probability Rule for Expected Value.**

$$E(X) = E(X \mid S)P(S) + E(X \mid S^c)P(S^c) \tag{11}$$

$$E(X) = E(X \mid S_1)P(S_1) + E(X \mid S_2)P(S_2) + \dots + E(X \mid S_n)P(S_n) \tag{12}$$

where $S_1, S_2, \dots, S_n$ are mutually exclusive and exhaustive scenarios or events.

The general case, Equation 12, states that the expected value of X equals the expected value of X given Scenario 1, $E(X \mid S_1)$, times the probability of Scenario 1, $P(S_1)$, plus the expected value of X given Scenario 2, $E(X \mid S_2)$, times the probability of Scenario 2, $P(S_2)$, and so forth.

To use this principle, we formulate mutually exclusive and exhaustive scenarios that are useful for understanding the outcomes of the random variable. This approach was employed in developing the probability distribution of BankCorp's EPS in Examples 8 and 9, as we now discuss.

The earnings of BankCorp are interest rate sensitive, benefiting from a declining interest rate environment. Suppose there is a 0.60 probability that BankCorp will operate in a *declining interest rate environment* in the current fiscal year and a 0.40 probability that it will operate in a *stable interest rate environment* (assessing the chance of an increasing interest rate environment as negligible). If a *declining interest rate environment* occurs, the probability that EPS will be $2.60 is estimated at 0.25, and the probability that EPS will be $2.45 is estimated at 0.75. Note that 0.60, the probability of *declining interest rate environment*, times 0.25, the probability of $2.60 EPS given a *declining interest rate environment*, equals 0.15, the (unconditional) probability of $2.60 given in the table in Examples 8 and 9. The probabilities are consistent. Also, 0.60(0.75) = 0.45, the probability of $2.45 EPS given in Tables 3 and 4. The **tree diagram** in Figure 2 shows the rest of the analysis.

Figure 2	**BankCorp's Forecasted EPS**

A declining interest rate environment points us to the **node** of the tree that branches off into outcomes of $2.60 and $2.45. We can find expected EPS given a declining interest rate environment as follows, using Equation 10:

$$E(\text{EPS} \mid declining\ interest\ rate\ environment) = 0.25(\$2.60) + 0.75(\$2.45)$$
$$= \$2.4875$$

If interest rates are stable,

$$E(\text{EPS} \mid stable\ interest\ rate\ environment) = 0.60(\$2.20) + 0.40(\$2.00)$$
$$= \$2.12$$

Once we have the new piece of information that interest rates are stable, for example, we revise our original expectation of EPS from $2.34 downward to $2.12. Now using the total probability rule for expected value,

$$E(\text{EPS}) = E(\text{EPS} \mid declining\ interest\ rate\ environment)$$
$$P(declining\ interest\ rate\ environment)$$
$$+ E(\text{EPS} \mid stable\ interest\ rate\ environment)$$
$$P(stable\ interest\ rate\ environment)$$

So $E(\text{EPS}) = \$2.4875\,(0.60) + \$2.12\,(0.40) = \$2.3405$ or about $2.34.

This amount is identical to the estimate of the expected value of EPS calculated directly from the probability distribution in Example 8. Just as our probabilities must be consistent, so must our expected values, unconditional and conditional; otherwise our investment actions may create profit opportunities for other investors at our expense.

To review, we first developed the factors or scenarios that influence the outcome of the event of interest. After assigning probabilities to these scenarios, we formed expectations conditioned on the different scenarios. Then we worked backward to formulate an expected value as of today. In the problem just worked, EPS was the event of interest, and the interest rate environment was the factor influencing EPS.

We can also calculate the variance of EPS given each scenario:

$$\sigma^2\left(\text{EPS} \mid \textit{declining interest rate environment}\right)$$
$$= P\left(\$2.60 \mid \textit{declining interest rate environment}\right)$$
$$\times \left[\$2.60 - E\left(\text{EPS} \mid \textit{declining interest rate environment}\right)\right]^2$$
$$+ P\left(\$2.45 \mid \textit{declining interest rate environment}\right)$$
$$\times \left[\$2.45 - E\left(\text{EPS} \mid \textit{declining interest rate environment}\right)\right]^2$$
$$= 0.25\left(\$2.60 - \$2.4875\right)^2 + 0.75\left(\$2.45 - \$2.4875\right)^2$$
$$= 0.004219$$

$$\sigma^2(\text{EPS} \mid \textit{stable interest rate environment})$$
$$= P\left(\$2.20 \mid \textit{stable interest rate environment}\right)$$
$$\times \left[\$2.20 - E\left(\text{EPS} \mid \textit{stable interest rate environment}\right)\right]^2$$
$$+ P\left(\$2.00 \mid \textit{stable interest rate environment}\right)$$
$$\times \left[\$2.00 - E\left(\text{EPS} \mid \textit{stable interest rate environment}\right)\right]^2$$
$$= 0.60\left(\$2.20 - \$2.12\right)^2 + 0.40\left(\$2.00 - \$2.12\right)^2 = 0.0096$$

These are **conditional variances**, the variance of EPS given a *declining interest rate environment* and the variance of EPS given a *stable interest rate environment*. The relationship between unconditional variance and conditional variance is a relatively advanced topic.[9] The main points are 1) that variance, like expected value, has a conditional counterpart to the unconditional concept and 2) that we can use conditional variance to assess risk given a particular scenario.

Example 10

BankCorp's Earnings per Share (5)

Continuing with BankCorp, you focus now on BankCorp's cost structure. One model you are researching for BankCorp's operating costs is

$$\hat{Y} = a + bX$$

---

9 The unconditional variance of EPS is the sum of two terms: 1) the expected value (probability-weighted average) of the conditional variances (parallel to the total probability rules) and 2) the variance of conditional expected values of EPS. The second term arises because the variability in conditional expected value is a source of risk. Term 1 is $\sigma2(\text{EPS}) = P(\textit{declining interest rate environment})\ \sigma2(\text{EPS} \mid \textit{declining interest rate environment}) + P(\textit{stable interest rate environment})\ \sigma^2(\text{EPS} \mid \textit{stable interest rate environment}) = 0.60(0.004219) + 0.40(0.0096) = 0.006371$. Term 2 is $\sigma^2[E(\text{EPS} \mid \text{interest rate environment})] = 0.60(\$2.4875 - \$2.34)^2 + 0.40(\$2.12 - \$2.34)^2 = 0.032414$. Summing the two terms, unconditional variance equals $0.006371 + 0.032414 = 0.038785$.

where $\widehat{Y}$ is a forecast of operating costs in millions of dollars and X is the number of branch offices. $\widehat{Y}$ represents the expected value of Y given X, or $E(Y \mid X)$. ($\widehat{Y}$ is a notation used in regression analysis, which we discuss in a later reading.) You interpret the intercept a as fixed costs and b as variable costs. You estimate the equation as

$$\widehat{Y} = 12.5 + 0.65X$$

BankCorp currently has 66 branch offices, and the equation estimates that $12.5 + 0.65(66) = \$55.4$ million. You have two scenarios for growth, pictured in the tree diagram in Figure 3.

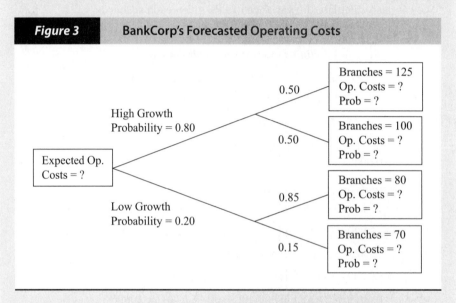

Figure 3   BankCorp's Forecasted Operating Costs

1. Compute the forecasted operating costs given the different levels of operating costs, using $\widehat{Y} = 12.5 + 0.65X$. State the probability of each level of the number of branch offices. These are the answers to the questions in the terminal boxes of the tree diagram.

2. Compute the expected value of operating costs under the high growth scenario. Also calculate the expected value of operating costs under the low growth scenario.

3. Answer the question in the initial box of the tree: What are BankCorp's expected operating costs?

Solution to 1:

Using $\widehat{Y} = 12.5 + 0.65X$, from top to bottom, we have

Operating Costs	Probability
$\widehat{Y} = 12.5 + 0.65(125) = \$93.75$ million	$0.80(0.50) = 0.40$
$\widehat{Y} = 12.5 + 0.65(100) = \$77.50$ million	$0.80(0.50) = 0.40$
$\widehat{Y} = 12.5 + 0.65(80) = \$64.50$ million	$0.20(0.85) = 0.17$
$\widehat{Y} = 12.5 + 0.65(70) = \$58.00$ million	$0.20(0.15) = 0.03$
	Sum = 1.00

Solution to 2:

Dollar amounts are in millions.

$$E(\text{operating costs}\,|\,high\ growth) = 0.50(\$93.75) + 0.50(\$77.50)$$
$$= \$85.625$$

$$E(\text{operating costs}\,|\,low\ growth) = 0.85(\$64.50) + 0.15(\$58.00)$$
$$= \$63.525$$

Solution to 3:

Dollar amounts are in millions.

$$E(\text{operating costs}) = E(\text{operating costs}\,|\,high\ growth)P(high\ growth)$$
$$+ E(\text{operating costs}\,|\,low\ growth)P(low\ growth)$$
$$= \$85.625(0.80) + \$63.525(0.20) = \$81.205$$

BankCorp's expected operating costs are $81.205 million.

We will see conditional probabilities again when we discuss Bayes' formula. This section has introduced a few problems that can be addressed using probability concepts. The following problem draws on these concepts, as well as on analytical skills.

Example 11

The Default Risk Premium for a One-Period Debt Instrument

As the co-manager of a short-term bond portfolio, you are reviewing the pricing of a speculative-grade, one-year-maturity, zero-coupon bond. For this type of bond, the return is the difference between the amount paid and the principal value received at maturity. Your goal is to estimate an appropriate default risk premium for this bond. You define the default risk premium as the extra return above the risk-free return that will compensate investors for default risk. If R is the promised return (yield-to-maturity) on the debt instrument and R_F is the risk-free rate, the default risk premium is $R - R_F$. You assess the probability that the bond defaults as $P(the\ bond\ defaults) = 0.06$. Looking at current money market yields, you find that one-year U.S. Treasury bills (T-bills) are offering a return of 5.8 percent, an estimate of R_F. As a first step, you make the simplifying assumption that bondholders will recover nothing in the event of a default. What is the minimum default risk premium you should require for this instrument?

The challenge in this type of problem is to find a starting point. In many problems, including this one, an effective first step is to divide up the possible outcomes into mutually exclusive and exhaustive events in an economically logical way. Here, from the viewpoint of a bondholder, the two events that affect returns are *the bond defaults* and *the bond does not default*. These two events cover all outcomes. How do these events affect a bondholder's returns? A second step is to compute the value of the bond for the two events. We have no specifics on bond **face value**, but we can compute value per $1 or one unit of currency invested.

	The Bond Defaults	The Bond Does Not Default
Bond value	$0	$(1 + R)

The third step is to find the expected value of the bond (per \$1 invested).

$$E(\text{bond}) = \$0 \times P(\text{the bond defaults})$$
$$+ \$(1+R)\big[1 - P(\text{the bond defaults})\big]$$

So $E(\text{bond}) = \$(1 + R)[1 - P(\text{the bond defaults})]$. The expected value of the T-bill per \$1 invested is $(1 + R_F)$. In fact, this value is certain because the T-bill is risk free. The next step requires economic reasoning. You want the default premium to be large enough so that you expect to at least break even compared with investing in the T-bill. This outcome will occur if the expected value of the bond equals the expected value of the T-bill per \$1 invested.

$$\begin{array}{ccc} \textit{Expected Value of Bond} & = & \textit{Expected Value of T-Bill} \\ \$(1+R)\big[1 - P(\text{the bond defaults})\big] & = & (1+R_F) \end{array}$$

Solving for the promised return on the bond, you find $R = \{(1 + R_F)/[1 - P(\text{the bond defaults})]\} - 1$. Substituting in the values in the statement of the problem, $R = [1.058/(1 - 0.06)] - 1 = 1.12553 - 1 = 0.12553$ or about 12.55 percent, and default risk premium is $R - R_F = 12.55\% - 5.8\% = 6.75\%$.

You require a default risk premium of at least 675 basis points. You can state the matter as follows: If the bond is priced to yield 12.55 percent, you will earn a 675 basis-point spread and receive the bond principal with 94 percent probability. If the bond defaults, however, you will lose everything. With a premium of 675 basis points, you expect to just break even relative to an investment in T-bills. Because an investment in the zero-coupon bond has variability, if you are risk averse you will demand that the premium be larger than 675 basis points.

This analysis is a starting point. Bondholders usually recover part of their investment after a default. A next step would be to incorporate a recovery rate.

In this section, we have treated random variables such as EPS as stand-alone quantities. We have not explored how descriptors such as expected value and variance of EPS may be functions of other random variables. Portfolio return is one random variable that is clearly a function of other random variables, the random returns on the individual securities in the portfolio. To analyze a portfolio's expected return and variance of return, we must understand these quantities are a function of characteristics of the individual securities' returns. Looking at the dispersion or variance of portfolio return, we see that the way individual security returns move together or covary is important. To understand the significance of these movements, we need to explore some new concepts, covariance and correlation. The next section, which deals with portfolio expected return and variance of return, introduces these concepts.

PORTFOLIO EXPECTED RETURN AND VARIANCE OF RETURN

Modern portfolio theory makes frequent use of the idea that investment opportunities can be evaluated using expected return as a measure of reward and variance of return as a measure of risk. The calculation and interpretation of portfolio expected return and variance of return are fundamental skills. In this section, we will develop an understanding of portfolio expected return and variance of return.[10] Portfolio return is determined by the returns on the individual holdings. As a result, the calculation of portfolio variance, as a function of the individual asset returns, is more complex than the variance calculations illustrated in the previous section.

We work with an example of a portfolio that is 50 percent invested in an S&P 500 Index fund, 25 percent invested in a U.S. long-term corporate bond fund, and 25 percent invested in a fund indexed to the MSCI EAFE Index (representing equity markets in Europe, Australasia, and the Far East). Table 5 shows these weights.

Table 5	Portfolio Weights
Asset Class	**Weights**
S&P 500	0.50
U.S. long-term corporate bonds	0.25
MSCI EAFE	0.25

We first address the calculation of the expected return on the portfolio. In the previous section, we defined the expected value of a random variable as the probability-weighted average of the possible outcomes. Portfolio return, we know, is a weighted average of the returns on the securities in the portfolio. Similarly, the expected return on a portfolio is a weighted average of the expected returns on the securities in the portfolio, using exactly the same weights. When we have estimated the expected returns on the individual securities, we immediately have portfolio expected return. This convenient fact follows from the properties of expected value.

- **Properties of Expected Value.** Let w_i be any constant and R_i be a random variable.

  1. The expected value of a constant times a random variable equals the constant times the expected value of the random variable.

  $$E(w_i R_i) = w_i E(R_i)$$

  2. The expected value of a weighted sum of random variables equals the weighted sum of the expected values, using the same weights.

  $$E(w_1 R_1 + w_2 R_2 + \ldots + w_n R_n) = w_1 E(R_1) + w_2 E(R_2) \\ + \ldots + w_n E(R_n) \tag{13}$$

Suppose we have a random variable with a given expected value. If we multiply each outcome by 2, for example, the random variable's expected value is multiplied by 2 as well. That is the meaning of Part 1. The second statement is the rule that directly leads to the expression for portfolio expected return. A portfolio with n securities is defined by its portfolio weights, w_1, w_2, ..., w_n, which sum to 1. So portfolio return, R_p, is $R_p = w_1 R_1 + w_2 R_2 + \ldots + w_n R_n$. We can state the following principle:

- **Calculation of Portfolio Expected Return.** Given a portfolio with n securities, the expected return on the portfolio is a weighted average of the expected returns on the component securities:

  $$E(R_p) = E(w_1 R_1 + w_2 R_2 + \ldots + w_n R_n) \\ = w_1 E(R_1) + w_2 E(R_2) + \ldots + w_n E(R_n)$$

---

10 Although we outline a number of basic concepts in this section, we do not present mean–variance analysis per se. For a presentation of mean–variance analysis, see the readings on portfolio concepts, as well as the extended treatments in standard investment textbooks such as Bodie, Kane, and Marcus (2001), Elton, Gruber, Brown, and Goetzmann (2003), Reilly and Brown (2003), and Sharpe, Alexander, and Bailey (1999).

Suppose we have estimated expected returns on the assets in the portfolio, as given in Table 6.

Table 6	Weights and Expected Returns	
Asset Class	**Weight**	**Expected Return (%)**
S&P 500	0.50	13
U.S. long-term corporate bonds	0.25	6
MSCI EAFE	0.25	15

We calculate the expected return on the portfolio as 11.75 percent:

$$E(R_p) = w_1 E(R_1) + w_2 E(R_2) + w_3 E(R_3)$$
$$= 0.50(13\%) + 0.25(6\%) + 0.25(15\%) = 11.75\%$$

In the previous section, we studied variance as a measure of dispersion of outcomes around the expected value. Here we are interested in portfolio variance of return as a measure of investment risk. Letting R_p stand for the return on the portfolio, portfolio variance is $\sigma^2(R_p) = E\{[R_p - E(R_p)]^2\}$ according to Equation 8. How do we implement this definition? In the reading on statistical concepts and market returns, we learned how to calculate a historical or sample variance based on a sample of returns. Now we are considering variance in a forward-looking sense. We will use information about the individual assets in the portfolio to obtain portfolio variance of return. To avoid clutter in notation, we write ER_p for $E(R_p)$. We need the concept of covariance.

▪ **Definition of Covariance.** Given two random variables R_i and R_j, the covariance between R_i and R_j is

$$\text{Cov}(R_i, R_j) = E\left[(R_i - ER_i)(R_j - ER_j)\right] \qquad (14)$$

Alternative notations are $\sigma(R_i, R_j)$ and σ_{ij}.

Equation 14 states that the covariance between two random variables is the probability-weighted average of the cross-products of each random variable's deviation from its own expected value. We will return to discuss covariance after we establish the need for the concept. Working from the definition of variance, we find

$$\sigma^2(R_p) = E\left[(R_p - ER_p)^2\right]$$
$$= E\left\{\left[w_1 R_1 + w_2 R_2 + w_3 R_3 - E(w_1 R_1 + w_2 R_2 + w_3 R_3)\right]^2\right\}$$
$$= E\left\{\left[w_1 R_1 + w_2 R_2 + w_3 R_3 - w_1 ER_1 - w_2 ER_2 - w_3 ER_3\right]^2\right\}$$
(using Equation 13)
$$= E\left\{\left[w_1(R_1 - ER_1) + w_2(R_2 - ER_2) + w_3(R_3 - ER_3)\right]^2\right\}$$
(rearranging)
$$= E\left\{\left[w_1(R_1 - ER_1) + w_2(R_2 - ER_2) + w_3(R_3 - ER_3)\right]\right.$$
$$\left. \times \left[w_1(R_1 - ER_1) + w_2(R_2 - ER_2) + w_3(R_3 - ER_3)\right]\right\}$$
(what squaring means)
$$= E\left[w_1 w_1(R_1 - ER_1)(R_1 - ER_1) + w_1 w_2(R_1 - ER_1)(R_2 - ER_2)\right.$$
$$+ w_1 w_3(R_1 - ER_1)(R_3 - ER_3) + w_2 w_1(R_2 - ER_2)(R_1 - ER_1)$$
$$+ w_2 w_2(R_2 - ER_2)(R_2 - ER_2) + w_2 w_3(R_2 - ER_2)(R_3 - ER_3)$$
$$+ w_3 w_1(R_3 - ER_3)(R_1 - ER_1) + w_3 w_2(R_3 - ER_3)(R_2 - ER_2)$$
$$\left. + w_3 w_3(R_3 - ER_3)(R_3 - ER_3)\right] \qquad \text{(doing the multiplication)}$$

$$= w_1^2 E\left[\left(R_1 - ER_1\right)^2\right] + w_1 w_2 E\left[\left(R_1 - ER_1\right)\left(R_2 - ER_2\right)\right]$$
$$\quad + w_1 w_3 E\left[\left(R_1 - ER_1\right)\left(R_3 - ER_3\right)\right] + w_2 w_1 E\left[\left(R_2 - ER_2\right)\left(R_1 - ER_1\right)\right]$$
$$\quad + w_2^2 E\left[\left(R_2 - ER_2\right)^2\right] + w_2 w_3 E\left[\left(R_2 - ER_2\right)\left(R_3 - ER_3\right)\right]$$
$$\quad + w_3 w_1 E\left[\left(R_3 - ER_3\right)\left(R_1 - ER_1\right)\right] + w_3 w_2 E\left[\left(R_3 - ER_3\right)\left(R_2 - ER_2\right)\right]$$
$$\quad + w_3^2 E\left[\left(R_3 - ER_3\right)^2\right] \qquad \left(\text{recalling that the } w_i \text{ terms are constants}\right)$$

$$= w_1^2 \sigma^2\left(R_1\right) + w_1 w_2 \text{Cov}\left(R_1, R_2\right) + w_1 w_3 \text{Cov}\left(R_1, R_3\right)$$
$$\quad + w_1 w_2 Cov\left(R_1, R_2\right) + w_2^2 \sigma^2\left(R_2\right) + w_2 w_3 \text{Cov}\left(R_2, R_3\right) \qquad \textbf{(15)}$$
$$\quad + w_1 w_3 Cov\left(R_1, R_3\right) + w_2 w_3 Cov\left(R_2, R_3\right) + w_3^2 \sigma^2\left(R_3\right)$$

The last step follows from the definitions of variance and covariance.[11] For the italicized covariance terms in Equation 15, we used the fact that the order of variables in covariance does not matter: $\text{Cov}(R_2, R_1) = \text{Cov}(R_1, R_2)$, for example. As we will show, the diagonal variance terms $\sigma^2(R_1)$, $\sigma^2(R_2)$, and $\sigma^2(R_3)$ can be expressed as $\text{Cov}(R_1, R_1)$, $\text{Cov}(R_2, R_2)$, and $\text{Cov}(R_3, R_3)$, respectively. Using this fact, the most compact way to state Equation 15 is $\sigma^2\left(R_p\right) = \sum_{i=1}^{3} \sum_{j=1}^{3} w_i w_j \text{Cov}\left(R_i, R_j\right)$. The double summation signs say: "Set $i = 1$ and let j run from 1 to 3; then set $i = 2$ and let j run from 1 to 3; next set $i = 3$ and let j run from 1 to 3; finally, add the nine terms." This expression generalizes for a portfolio of any size n to

$$\sigma^2\left(R_p\right) = \sum_{i=1}^{n} \sum_{j=1}^{n} w_i w_j \text{Cov}\left(R_i, R_j\right) \qquad \textbf{(16)}$$

We see from Equation 15 that individual variances of return constitute part, but not all, of portfolio variance. The three variances are actually outnumbered by the six covariance terms off the diagonal. For three assets, the ratio is 1 to 2, or 50 percent. If there are 20 assets, there are 20 variance terms and $20(20) - 20 = 380$ off-diagonal covariance terms. The ratio of variance terms to off-diagonal covariance terms is less than 6 to 100, or 6 percent. A first observation, then, is that as the number of holdings increases, covariance[12] becomes increasingly important, all else equal.

What exactly is the effect of covariance on portfolio variance? The covariance terms capture how the co-movements of returns affect portfolio variance. For example, consider two stocks: One tends to have high returns (relative to its expected return) when the other has low returns (relative to its expected return). The returns on one stock tend to offset the returns on the other stock, lowering the variability or variance of returns on the portfolio. Like variance, the units of covariance are hard to interpret, and we will introduce a more intuitive concept shortly. Meanwhile, from the definition of covariance, we can establish two essential observations about covariance.

1. We can interpret the sign of covariance as follows:

    Covariance of returns is negative if, when the return on one asset is above its expected value, the return on the other asset tends to be below its expected value (an average inverse relationship between returns).

    Covariance of returns is 0 if returns on the assets are unrelated.

    Covariance of returns is positive when the returns on both assets tend to be on the same side (above or below) their expected values at the same time (an average positive relationship between returns).

---

11 Useful facts about variance and covariance include: 1) The variance of a constant *times* a random variable equals the constant squared times the variance of the random variable, or $\sigma^2(wR) = w^2\sigma^2(R)$; 2) The variance of a constant *plus* a random variable equals the variance of the random variable, or $\sigma^2(w + R) = \sigma^2(R)$ because a constant has zero variance; 3) The covariance between a constant and a random variable is zero.
12 When the meaning of covariance as "off-diagonal covariance" is obvious, as it is here, we omit the qualifying words. Covariance is usually used in this sense.

2. The covariance of a random variable with itself (*own covariance*) is its own variance: $\text{Cov}(R, R) = E\{[R - E(R)][R - E(R)]\} = E\{[R - E(R)]^2\} = \sigma^2(R)$.

A complete list of the covariances constitutes all the statistical data needed to compute portfolio variance of return. Covariances are often presented in a square format called a **covariance matrix**. Table 7 summarizes the inputs for portfolio expected return and variance of return.

Table 7	Inputs to Portfolio Expected Return and Variance

A. Inputs to Portfolio Expected Return

Asset	A	B	C
	$E(R_A)$	$E(R_B)$	$E(R_C)$

B. Covariance Matrix: The Inputs to Portfolio Variance of Return

Asset	A	B	C
A	$\text{Cov}(R_A, R_A)$	$\text{Cov}(R_A, R_B)$	$\text{Cov}(R_A, R_C)$
B	$\text{Cov}(R_B, R_A)$	$\text{Cov}(R_B, R_B)$	$\text{Cov}(R_B, R_C)$
C	$\text{Cov}(R_C, R_A)$	$\text{Cov}(R_C, R_B)$	$\text{Cov}(R_C, R_C)$

With three assets, the covariance matrix has $3^2 = 3 \times 3 = 9$ entries, but it is customary to treat the diagonal terms, the variances, separately from the off-diagonal terms. These diagonal terms are bolded in Table 7. This distinction is natural, as security variance is a single-variable concept. So there are $9 - 3 = 6$ covariances, excluding variances. But $\text{Cov}(R_B, R_A) = \text{Cov}(R_A, R_B)$, $\text{Cov}(R_C, R_A) = \text{Cov}(R_A, R_C)$, and $\text{Cov}(R_C, R_B) = \text{Cov}(R_B, R_C)$. The covariance matrix below the diagonal is the mirror image of the covariance matrix above the diagonal. As a result, there are only $6/2 = 3$ distinct covariance terms to estimate. In general, for n securities, there are $n(n - 1)/2$ distinct covariances to estimate and n variances to estimate.

Suppose we have the covariance matrix shown in Table 8. We will be working in returns stated as percents and the table entries are in units of percent squared (%²). The terms 38%² and 400%² are 0.0038 and 0.0400, respectively, stated as decimals; correctly working in percents and decimals leads to identical answers.

Table 8	Covariance Matrix

	S&P 500	U.S. Long-Term Corporate Bonds	MSCI EAFE
S&P 500	400	45	189
U.S. long-term corporate bonds	45	81	38
MSCI EAFE	189	38	441

Taking Equation 15 and grouping variance terms together produces the following:

$$\sigma^2(R_p) = w_1^2\sigma^2(R_1) + w_2^2\sigma^2(R_2) + w_3^2\sigma^2(R_3) + 2w_1w_2\text{Cov}(R_1, R_2)$$
$$+ 2w_1w_3\text{Cov}(R_1, R_3) + 2w_2w_3\text{Cov}(R_2, R_3)$$
$$= (0.50)^2(400) + (0.25)^2(81) + (0.25)^2(441) \tag{17}$$
$$+ 2(0.50)(0.25)(45) + 2(0.50)(0.25)(189)$$
$$+ 2(0.25)(0.25)(38)$$
$$= 100 + 5.0625 + 27.5625 + 11.25 + 47.25 + 4.75 = 195.875$$

The variance is 195.875. Standard deviation of return is $195.875^{1/2} = 14$ percent. To summarize, the portfolio has an expected annual return of 11.75 percent and a standard deviation of return of 14 percent.

Let us look at the first three terms in the calculation above. Their sum, $100 + 5.0625 + 27.5625 = 132.625$, is the contribution of the individual variances to portfolio variance. If the returns on the three assets were independent, covariances would be 0 and the standard deviation of portfolio return would be $132.625^{1/2} = 11.52$ percent as compared to 14 percent before. The portfolio would have less risk. Suppose the covariance terms were negative. Then a negative number would be added to 132.625, so portfolio variance and risk would be even smaller. At the same time, we have not changed expected return. For the same expected portfolio return, the portfolio has less risk. This risk reduction is a diversification benefit, meaning a risk-reduction benefit from holding a portfolio of assets. The diversification benefit increases with decreasing covariance. This observation is a key insight of modern portfolio theory. It is even more intuitively stated when we can use the concept of **correlation**. Then we can say that as long as security returns are not perfectly positively correlated, diversification benefits are possible. Furthermore, the smaller the correlation between security returns, the greater the cost of not diversifying (in terms of risk-reduction benefits forgone), all else equal.

- **Definition of Correlation.** The correlation between two random variables, R_i and R_j, is defined as $\rho(R_i, R_j) = \text{Cov}(R_i, R_j)/\sigma(R_i)\sigma(R_j)$. Alternative notations are $\text{Corr}(R_i, R_j)$ and ρ_{ij}.

Frequently, covariance is substituted out using the relationship $\text{Cov}(R_i, R_j) = \rho(R_i, R_j) \sigma(R_i)\sigma(R_j)$. The division indicated in the definition makes correlation a pure number (one without a unit of measurement) and places bounds on its largest and smallest possible values. Using the above definition, we can state a correlation matrix from data in the covariance matrix alone. Table 9 shows the correlation matrix.

Table 9	Correlation Matrix of Returns		
	S&P 500	U.S. Long-Term Corporate Bonds	MSCI EAFE
S&P 500	1.00	0.25	0.45
U.S. long-term corporate bonds	0.25	1.00	0.20
MSCI EAFE	0.45	0.20	1.00

For example, the covariance between long-term bonds and MSCI EAFE is 38, from Table 8. The standard deviation of long-term bond returns is $81^{1/2} = 9$ percent, that of MSCI EAFE returns is $441^{1/2} = 21$ percent, from diagonal terms in Table 8. The correlation ρ(Return on long-term bonds, Return on EAFE) is $38/(9\%)(21\%) = 0.201$, rounded to 0.20. The correlation of the S&P 500 with itself equals 1: The calculation is its own covariance divided by its standard deviation squared.

- **Properties of Correlation.**

    1. Correlation is a number between -1 and $+1$ for two random variables, X and Y:

        $$-1 \le \rho(X,Y) \le +1$$

    2. A correlation of 0 (uncorrelated variables) indicates an absence of any linear (straight-line) relationship between the variables.[13] Increasingly positive

---

13 If the correlation is 0, $R_1 = a + bR_2 + \text{error}$, with $b = 0$.

correlation indicates an increasingly strong positive linear relationship (up to 1, which indicates a perfect linear relationship). Increasingly negative correlation indicates an increasingly strong negative (inverse) linear relationship (down to −1, which indicates a perfect inverse linear relationship).[14]

Example 12

Portfolio Expected Return and Variance of Return

You have a portfolio of two mutual funds, A and B, 75 percent invested in A, as shown in Table 10.

Table 10	Mutual Fund Expected Returns, Return Variances, and Covariances	
Fund	**A** $E(R_A) = 20\%$	**B** $E(R_B) = 12\%$
Covariance Matrix		
Fund	A	B
A	625	120
B	120	196

1. Calculate the expected return of the portfolio.
2. Calculate the correlation matrix for this problem. Carry out the answer to two decimal places.
3. Compute portfolio standard deviation of return.

Solution to 1:

$E(R_p) = w_A E(R_A) + (1 - w_A)E(R_B) = 0.75(20\%) + 0.25(12\%) = 18\%$. Portfolio weights must sum to 1: $w_B = 1 - w_A$.

Solution to 2:

$\sigma(R_A) = 625^{1/2} = 25$ percent $\sigma(R_B) = 196^{1/2} = 14$ percent. There is one distinct covariance and thus one distinct correlation: $\rho(R_A, R_B) = \text{Cov}(R_A, R_B)/\sigma(R_A)\sigma(R_B) = 120/25(14) = 0.342857$, or 0.34 Table 11 shows the correlation matrix.

Table 11	Correlation Matrix	
	A	**B**
A	1.00	0.34
B	0.34	1.00

Diagonal terms are always equal to 1 in a correlation matrix.

---

14 If the correlation is positive, $R_1 = a + bR_2 +$ error, with $b > 0$. If the correlation is negative, $b < 0$.

Solution to 3:

$$\sigma^2(R_p) = w_A^2\sigma^2(R_A) + w_B^2\sigma^2(R_B) + 2w_Aw_B\text{Cov}(R_A, R_B)$$
$$= (0.75)^2(625) + (0.25)^2(196) + 2(0.75)(0.25)(120)$$
$$= 351.5625 + 12.25 + 45 = 408.8125$$
$$\sigma(R_p) = 408.8125^{1/2} = 20.22 \text{ percent}$$

How do we estimate return covariance and correlation? Frequently, we make forecasts on the basis of historical covariance or use other methods based on historical return data, such as a market model regression.[15] We can also calculate covariance using the **joint probability function** of the random variables, if that can be estimated. The joint probability function of two random variables X and Y, denoted $P(X, Y)$, gives the probability of joint occurrences of values of X and Y. For example, $P(3, 2)$, is the probability that X equals 3 and Y equals 2.

Suppose that the joint probability function of the returns on BankCorp stock (R_A) and the returns on NewBank stock (R_B) has the simple structure given in Table 12.

Table 12	Joint Probability Function of BankCorp and NewBank Returns (Entries Are Joint Probabilities)		
	$R_B = 20\%$	$R_B = 16\%$	$R_B = 10\%$
$R_A = 25\%$	0.20	0	0
$R_A = 12\%$	0	0.50	0
$R_A = 10\%$	0	0	0.30

The expected return on BankCorp stock is $0.20(25\%) + 0.50(12\%) + 0.30(10\%) = 14\%$. The expected return on NewBank stock is $0.20(20\%) + 0.50(16\%) + 0.30(10\%) = 15\%$. The joint probability function above might reflect an analysis based on whether banking industry conditions are good, average, or poor. Table 13 presents the calculation of covariance.

Table 13	Covariance Calculations				
Banking Industry Condition	Deviations BankCorp	Deviations NewBank	Product of Deviations	Probability of Condition	Probability-Weighted Product
Good	25−14	20−15	55	0.20	11
Average	12−14	16−15	−2	0.50	−1
Poor	10−14	10−15	20	0.30	6
					$\text{Cov}(R_A, R_B) = 16$

Note: Expected return for BankCorp is 14% and for NewBank, 15%.

---

15 See any of the textbooks mentioned in Footnote 10.

The first and second columns of numbers show, respectively, the deviations of BankCorp and NewBank returns from their mean or expected value. The next column shows the product of the deviations. For example, for good industry conditions, $(25 - 14)(20 - 15) = 11(5) = 55$. Then 55 is multiplied or weighted by 0.20, the probability that banking industry conditions are good: $55(0.20) = 11$. The calculations for average and poor banking conditions follow the same pattern. Summing up these probability-weighted products, we find that $\mathrm{Cov}(R_A, R_B) = 16$.

A formula for computing the covariance between random variables R_A and R_B is

$$\mathrm{Cov}(R_A, R_B) = \sum_i \sum_j P(R_{A,i}, R_{B,j})(R_{A,i} - ER_A)(R_{B,j} - ER_B) \tag{18}$$

The formula tells us to sum all possible deviation cross-products weighted by the appropriate joint probability. In the example we just worked, as Table 12 shows, only three joint probabilities are nonzero. Therefore, in computing the covariance of returns in this case, we need to consider only three cross-products:

$$
\begin{aligned}
\mathrm{Cov}(R_A, R_B) &= P(25,20)\big[(25-14)(20-15)\big] + P(12,16)\big[(12-14) \\
&\quad (16-15)\big] + P(10,10)\big[(10-14)(10-15)\big] \\
&= 0.20(11)(5) + 0.50(-2)(1) + 0.30(-4)(-5) \\
&= 11 - 1 + 6 = 16
\end{aligned}
$$

One theme of this reading has been independence. Two random variables are independent when every possible pair of events—one event corresponding to a value of X and another event corresponding to a value of Y—are independent events. When two random variables are independent, their joint probability function simplifies.

- **Definition of Independence for Random Variables.** Two random variables X and Y are independent if and only if $P(X, Y) = P(X)P(Y)$.

For example, given independence, $P(3, 2) = P(3)P(2)$. We multiply the individual probabilities to get the joint probabilities. *Independence* is a stronger property than *uncorrelatedness* because correlation addresses only linear relationships. The following condition holds for independent random variables and, therefore, also holds for uncorrelated random variables.

- **Multiplication Rule for Expected Value of the Product of Uncorrelated Random Variables.** The expected value of the product of uncorrelated random variables is the product of their expected values.

$E(XY) = E(X)E(Y)$ if X and Y are uncorrelated.

Many financial variables, such as revenue (price times quantity), are the product of random quantities. When applicable, the above rule simplifies calculating expected value of a product of random variables.[16]

TOPICS IN PROBABILITY

In the remainder of the reading we discuss two topics that can be important in solving investment problems. We start with Bayes' formula: what probability theory has to say about learning from experience. Then we move to a discussion of shortcuts and principles for counting.

---

16 Otherwise, the calculation depends on conditional expected value; the calculation can be expressed as $E(XY) = E(X) E(Y \mid X)$.

4.1 Bayes' Formula

When we make decisions involving investments, we often start with viewpoints based on our experience and knowledge. These viewpoints may be changed or confirmed by new knowledge and observations. Bayes' formula is a rational method for adjusting our viewpoints as we confront new information.[17] Bayes' formula and related concepts have been applied in many business and investment decision-making contexts, including the evaluation of mutual fund performance.[18]

Bayes' formula makes use of Equation 6, the total probability rule. To review, that rule expressed the probability of an event as a weighted average of the probabilities of the event, given a set of scenarios. Bayes' formula works in reverse; more precisely, it reverses the "given that" information. Bayes' formula uses the occurrence of the event to infer the probability of the scenario generating it. For that reason, Bayes' formula is sometimes called an inverse probability. In many applications, including the one illustrating its use in this section, an individual is updating his beliefs concerning the causes that may have produced a new observation.

■ **Bayes' Formula.** Given a set of prior probabilities for an event of interest, if you receive new information, the rule for updating your probability of the event is

Updated probability of event given the new information

$$= \frac{\text{Probability of the new information given event}}{\text{Unconditional probability of the new information}} \times \text{Prior probability of event}$$

In probability notation, this formula can be written concisely as:

$$P(\text{Event} \mid \text{Information}) = \frac{P(\text{Information} \mid \text{Event})}{P(\text{Information})} P(\text{Event})$$

To illustrate Bayes' formula, we work through an investment example that can be adapted to any actual problem. Suppose you are an investor in the stock of DriveMed, Inc. Positive earnings surprises relative to consensus EPS estimates often result in positive stock returns, and negative surprises often have the opposite effect. DriveMed is preparing to release last quarter's EPS result, and you are interested in which of these three events happened: *last quarter's EPS exceeded the consensus EPS estimate*, or *last quarter's EPS exactly met the consensus EPS estimate*, or *last quarter's EPS fell short of the consensus EPS estimate.* This list of the alternatives is mutually exclusive and exhaustive.

On the basis of your own research, you write down the following **prior probabilities** (or priors, for short) concerning these three events:

■ *P(EPS exceeded consensus)* = 0.45

■ *P(EPS met consensus)* = 0.30

■ *P(EPS fell short of consensus)* = 0.25

These probabilities are "prior" in the sense that they reflect only what you know now, before the arrival of any new information.

The next day, DriveMed announces that it is expanding factory capacity in Singapore and Ireland to meet increased sales demand. You assess this new information. The decision to expand capacity relates not only to current demand but probably also to the prior quarter's sales demand. You know that sales demand is positively related to EPS. So now it appears more likely that last quarter's EPS will exceed the consensus.

The question you have is, "In light of the new information, what is the updated probability that the prior quarter's EPS exceeded the consensus estimate?"

---

17 Named after the Reverend Thomas Bayes (1702–61).
18 See Baks, Metrick, and Wachter (2001).

Bayes' formula provides a rational method for accomplishing this updating. We can abbreviate the new information as *DriveMed expands*. The first step in applying Bayes' formula is to calculate the probability of the new information (here: *DriveMed expands*), given a list of events or scenarios that may have generated it. The list of events should cover all possibilities, as it does here. Formulating these conditional probabilities is the key step in the updating process. Suppose your view is

P(*DriveMed expands* | *EPS exceeded consensus*) = 0.75
P(*DriveMed expands* | *EPS met consensus*) = 0.20
P(*DriveMed expands* | *EPS fell short of consensus*) = 0.05

Conditional probabilities of an observation (here: *DriveMed expands*) are sometimes referred to as **likelihoods**. Again, likelihoods are required for updating the probability.

Next, you combine these conditional probabilities or likelihoods with your prior probabilities to get the unconditional probability for DriveMed expanding, P(*DriveMed expands*), as follows:

$$
\begin{aligned}
&P\left(DriveMed\ expands\right)\\
&= P\left(DriveMed\ expands \mid EPS\ exceeded\ consensus\right)\\
&\qquad \times P\left(EPS\ exceeded\ consensus\right)\\
&+ P\left(DriveMed\ expands \mid EPS\ met\ consensus\right)\\
&\qquad \times P\left(EPS\ met\ consensus\right)\\
&+ P\left(DriveMed\ expands \mid EPS\ fell\ short\ of\ consensus\right)\\
&\qquad \times P\left(EPS\ fell\ short\ of\ consensus\right)\\
&= 0.75\left(0.45\right)+0.20\left(0.30\right)+0.05\left(0.25\right)=0.41,\ or\ 41\%
\end{aligned}
$$

This is Equation 6, the total probability rule, in action. Now you can answer your question by applying Bayes' formula:

$$
\begin{aligned}
&P\left(EPS\ exceeded\ consensus \mid DriveMed\ expands\right)\\
&= \frac{P\left(DriveMed\ expands \mid EPS\ exceeded\ consensus\right)}{P\left(DriveMed\ expands\right)}P\left(EPS\ exceeded\ consensus\right)\\
&= \left(0.75/0.41\right)\left(0.45\right)=1.829268\left(0.45\right)=0.823171
\end{aligned}
$$

Prior to DriveMed's announcement, you thought the probability that DriveMed would beat consensus expectations was 45 percent. On the basis of your interpretation of the announcement, you update that probability to 82.3 percent. This updated probability is called your **posterior probability** because it reflects or comes after the new information.

The Bayes' calculation takes the prior probability, which was 45 percent, and multiplies it by a ratio—the first term on the right-hand side of the equal sign. The denominator of the ratio is the probability that DriveMed expands, as you view it without considering (conditioning on) anything else. Therefore, this probability is unconditional. The numerator is the probability that DriveMed expands, if last quarter's EPS actually exceeded the consensus estimate. This last probability is larger than unconditional probability in the denominator, so the ratio (1.83 roughly) is greater than 1. As a result, your updated or posterior probability is larger than your prior probability. Thus, the ratio reflects the impact of the new information on your prior beliefs.

Example 13

Inferring whether DriveMed's EPS Met Consensus EPS

You are still an investor in DriveMed stock. To review the givens, your prior probabilities are P(*EPS exceeded consensus*) = 0.45, P(*EPS met consensus*) = 0.30, and P(*EPS fell short of consensus*) = 0.25. You also have the following conditional probabilities:

P(*DriveMed expands | EPS exceeded consensus*) = 0.75
P(*DriveMed expands | EPS met consensus*) = 0.20
P(*DriveMed expands | EPS fell short of consensus*) = 0.05

Recall that you updated your probability that last quarter's EPS exceeded the consensus estimate from 45 percent to 82.3 percent after DriveMed announced it would expand. Now you want to update your other priors.

1. Update your prior probability that DriveMed's EPS met consensus.

2. Update your prior probability that DriveMed's EPS fell short of consensus.

3. Show that the three updated probabilities sum to 1. (Carry each probability to four decimal places.)

4. Suppose, because of lack of prior beliefs about whether DriveMed would meet consensus, you updated on the basis of prior probabilities that all three possibilities were equally likely: P(*EPS exceeded consensus*) = P(*EPS met consensus*) = P(*EPS fell short of consensus*) = 1/3. What is your estimate of the probability P(*EPS exceeded consensus | DriveMed expands*)?

Solution to 1:

The probability is P(*EPS met consensus | DriveMed expands*) =

$$\frac{P\big(DriveMed\ expands\,|\,EPS\ met\ consensus\big)}{P\big(DriveMed\ expands\big)}P\big(EPS\ met\ consensus\big)$$

The probability P(*DriveMed expands*) is found by taking each of the three conditional probabilities in the statement of the problem, such as P(*DriveMed expands | EPS exceeded consensus*); multiplying each one by the prior probability of the conditioning event, such as P(*EPS exceeded consensus*); then adding the three products. The calculation is unchanged from the problem in the text above: P(*DriveMed expands*) = 0.75(0.45) + 0.20(0.30) + 0.05(0.25) = 0.41, or 41 percent. The other probabilities needed, P(*DriveMed expands | EPS met consensus*) = 0.20 and P(*EPS met consensus*) = 0.30, are givens. So

> P(*EPS met consensus | DriveMed expands*) = [P(*DriveMed expands | EPS met consensus*)/P(*DriveMed expands*)]P(*EPS met consensus*)
> = (0.20/0.41)(0.30) = 0.487805(0.30) = 0.146341

After taking account of the announcement on expansion, your updated probability that last quarter's EPS for DriveMed just met consensus is 14.6 percent compared with your prior probability of 30 percent.

Solution to 2:

P(*DriveMed expands*) was already calculated as 41 percent. Recall that P(*DriveMed expands | EPS fell short of consensus*) = 0.05 and P(*EPS fell short of consensus*) = 0.25 are givens.

> P(*EPS fell short of consensus | DriveMed expands*)
> = [P(*DriveMed expands | EPS fell short of consensus*)/
> P(*DriveMed expands*)]P(*EPS fell short of consensus*)
> = (0.05 / 0.41)(0.25) = 0.121951(0.25) = 0.030488

As a result of the announcement, you have revised your probability that DriveMed's EPS fell short of consensus from 25 percent (your prior probability) to 3 percent.

Solution to 3:

The sum of the three updated probabilities is

$$P(\text{EPS exceeded consensus} | \text{DriveMed expands}) + P(\text{EPS met consensus} |$$
$$\text{DriveMed expands}) + P(\text{EPS fell short of consensus} | \text{DriveMed expands}$$
$$= 0.8232 + 0.1463 + 0.0305 = 1.0000$$

The three events (*EPS exceeded consensus*, *EPS met consensus*, *EPS fell short of consensus*) are mutually exclusive and exhaustive: One of these events or statements must be true, so the conditional probabilities must sum to 1. Whether we are talking about conditional or unconditional probabilities, whenever we have a complete set of the distinct possible events or outcomes, the probabilities must sum to 1. This calculation serves as a check on your work.

Solution to 4:

Using the probabilities given in the question,

$$P(\text{DriveMed expands})$$
$$= P(\text{DriveMed expands} | \text{EPS exceeded consensus})$$
$$P(\text{EPS exceeded consensus}) + P(\text{DriveMed expands} |$$
$$\text{EPS met consensus}) P(\text{EPS met consensus}) + P(\text{DriveMed expands} |$$
$$\text{EPS fell short of consensus}) P(\text{EPS fell short of consensus})$$
$$= 0.75(1/3) + 0.20(1/3) + 0.05(1/3) = 1/3$$

Not surprisingly, the probability of DriveMed expanding is 1/3 because the decision maker has no prior beliefs or views regarding how well EPS performed relative to the consensus estimate. Now we can use Bayes' formula to find $P(\text{EPS exceeded consensus} | \text{DriveMed expands}) = [P(\text{DriveMed expands} | \text{EPS exceeded consensus})/P(\text{DriveMed expands})] P(\text{EPS exceeded consensus}) = [(0.75/(1/3)](1/3) = 0.75$ or 75 percent. This probability is identical to your estimate of $P(\text{DriveMed expands} | \text{EPS exceeded consensus})$.

When the prior probabilities are equal, the probability of information given an event equals the probability of the event given the information. When a decision-maker has equal prior probabilities (called **diffuse priors**), the probability of an event is determined by the information.

4.2 Principles of Counting

The first step in addressing a question often involves determining the different logical possibilities. We may also want to know the number of ways that each of these possibilities can happen. In the back of our mind is often a question about probability. How likely is it that I will observe this particular possibility? Records of success and failure are an example. When we evaluate a market timer's record, one well-known evaluation method uses counting methods presented in this section.[19] An important investment model, the binomial option pricing model, incorporates the combination formula that we will cover shortly. We can also use the methods in this section to calculate what we called a priori probabilities in Section 2. When we can assume that the possible outcomes of a random variable are equally likely, the probability of an event equals the number of possible outcomes favorable for the event divided by the total number of outcomes.

---

19 Henriksson and Merton (1981).

In counting, enumeration (counting the outcomes one by one) is of course the most basic resource. What we discuss in this section are shortcuts and principles. Without these shortcuts and principles, counting the total number of outcomes can be very difficult and prone to error. The first and basic principle of counting is the multiplication rule.

■ **Multiplication Rule of Counting.** If one task can be done in n_1 ways, and a second task, given the first, can be done in n_2 ways, and a third task, given the first two tasks, can be done in n_3 ways, and so on for k tasks, then the number of ways the k tasks can be done is $(n_1)(n_2)(n_3) \dots (n_k)$.

Suppose we have three steps in an investment decision process. The first step can be done in two ways, the second in four ways, and the third in three ways. Following the multiplication rule, there are $(2)(4)(3) = 24$ ways in which we can carry out the three steps.

Another illustration is the assignment of members of a group to an equal number of positions. For example, suppose you want to assign three security analysts to cover three different industries. In how many ways can the assignments be made? The first analyst may be assigned in three different ways. Then two industries remain. The second analyst can be assigned in two different ways. Then one industry remains. The third and last analyst can be assigned in only one way. The total number of different assignments equals $(3)(2)(1) = 6$. The compact notation for the multiplication we have just performed is 3! (read: 3 factorial). If we had n analysts, the number of ways we could assign them to n tasks would be

$$n! = n(n-1)(n-2)(n-3) \dots 1$$

or n **factorial**. (By convention, 0! = 1.) To review, in this application we repeatedly carry out an operation (here, job assignment) until we use up all members of a group (here, three analysts). With n members in the group, the multiplication formula reduces to n factorial.[20]

The next type of counting problem can be called labeling problems.[21] We want to give each object in a group a label, to place it in a category. The following example illustrates this type of problem.

A mutual fund guide ranked 18 bond mutual funds by total returns for the year 2000. The guide also assigned each fund one of five risk labels: *high risk* (four funds), *above-average risk* (four funds), *average risk* (three funds), *below-average risk* (four funds), and *low risk* (three funds); as $4 + 4 + 3 + 4 + 3 = 18$, all the funds are accounted for. How many different ways can we take 18 mutual funds and label 4 of them high risk, 4 above-average risk, 3 average risk, 4 below-average risk, and 3 low risk, so that each fund is labeled?

The answer is close to 13 billion. We can label any of 18 funds *high risk* (the first slot), then any of 17 remaining funds, then any of 16 remaining funds, then any of 15 remaining funds (now we have 4 funds in the *high risk* group); then we can label any of 14 remaining funds *above-average risk*, then any of 13 remaining funds, and so forth. There are 18! possible sequences. However, order of assignment within a category does not matter. For example, whether a fund occupies the first or third slot of the four funds labeled *high risk*, the fund has the same label (*high risk*). Thus there are 4! ways to assign a given group of four funds to the four *high risk* slots. Making the same argument for the other categories, in total there are $(4!)(4!)(3!)(4!)(3!)$ equivalent sequences. To eliminate such redundancies from the 18! total, we divide 18! by $(4!)(4!)$

20　The shortest explanation of n factorial is that it is the number of ways to order n objects in a row. In all the problems to which we apply this counting method, we must use up all the members of a group (sampling without replacement).

21　This discussion follows Kemeny, Schleifer, Snell, and Thompson (1972) in terminology and approach.

(3!)(4!)(3!). We have 18!/(4!)(4!)(3!)(4!)(3!) = 18!/(24)(24)(6)(24)(6) = 12,864,852,000. This procedure generalizes as follows.

- **Multinomial Formula (General Formula for Labeling Problems).** The number of ways that n objects can be labeled with k different labels, with n_1 of the first type, n_2 of the second type, and so on, with $n_1 + n_2 + \ldots + n_k = n$, is given by

$$\frac{n!}{n_1!n_2! \ldots n_k!}$$

The multinomial formula with two different labels ($k = 2$) is especially important. This special case is called the combination formula. A **combination** is a listing in which the order of the listed items does not matter. We state the combination formula in a traditional way, but no new concepts are involved. Using the notation in the formula below, the number of objects with the first label is $r = n_1$ and the number with the second label is $n - r = n_2$ (there are just two categories, so $n_1 + n_2 = n$). Here is the formula:

- **Combination Formula (Binomial Formula).** The number of ways that we can choose r objects from a total of n objects, when the order in which the r objects are listed does not matter, is

$$_nC_r = \binom{n}{r} = \frac{n!}{(n-r)!r!}$$

Here $_nC_r$ and $\binom{n}{r}$ are shorthand notations for $n!/(n-r)!r!$ (read: n choose r, or n combination r).

If we label the r objects as *belongs to the group* and the remaining objects as *does not belong to the group*, whatever the group of interest, the combination formula tells us how many ways we can select a group of size r. We can illustrate this formula with the binomial option pricing model. This model describes the movement of the underlying asset as a series of moves, price up (U) or price down (D). For example, two sequences of five moves containing three up moves, such as UUUDD and UDUUD, result in the same final stock price. At least for an option with a payoff dependent on final stock price, the number but not the order of up moves in a sequence matters. How many sequences of five moves *belong to the group with three up moves?* The answer is 10, calculated using the combination formula ("5 choose 3"):

$$_5C_3 = 5!/(5-3)!3!$$
$$= (5)(4)(3)(2)(1)/(2)(1)(3)(2)(1) = 120/12 = 10 \text{ ways}$$

A useful fact can be illustrated as follows: $_5C_3 = 5!/2!3!$ equals $_5C_2 = 5!/3!2!$, as 3 + 2 = 5; $_5C_4 = 5!/1!4!$ equals $_5C_1 = 5!/4!1!$, as 4 + 1 = 5. This symmetrical relationship can save work when we need to calculate many possible combinations.

Suppose jurors want to select three companies out of a group of five to receive the first-, second-, and third-place awards for the best annual report. In how many ways can the jurors make the three awards? Order does matter if we want to distinguish among the three awards (the rank within the group of three); clearly the question makes order important. On the other hand, if the question were "In how many ways can the jurors choose three winners, without regard to place of finish?" we would use the combination formula.

To address the first question above, we need to count ordered listings such as *first place, New Company; second place, Fir Company; third place, Well Company.* An ordered listing is known as a **permutation**, and the formula that counts the number of permutations is known as the permutation formula.[22]

---

22 A more formal definition states that a permutation is an ordered subset of n distinct objects.

■ **Permutation Formula.** The number of ways that we can choose r objects from a total of n objects, when the order in which the r objects are listed does matter, is

$$_nP_r = \frac{n!}{(n-r)!}$$

So the jurors have $_5P_3 = 5!/(5-3)! = (5)(4)(3)(2)(1)/(2)(1) = 120/2 = 60$ ways in which they can make their awards. To see why this formula works, note that $(5)(4)(3)(2)(1)/(2)(1)$ reduces to $(5)(4)(3)$, after cancellation of terms. This calculation counts the number of ways to fill three slots choosing from a group of five people, according to the multiplication rule of counting. This number is naturally larger than it would be if order did not matter (compare 60 to the value of 10 for "5 choose 3" that we calculated above). For example, *first place, Well Company*; *second place, Fir Company*; *third place, New Company* contains the same three companies as *first place, New Company*; *second place, Fir Company*; *third place, Well Company*. If we were concerned only with award winners (without regard to place of finish), the two listings would count as one combination. But when we are concerned with the order of finish, the listings count as two permutations.

Answering the following questions may help you apply the counting methods we have presented in this section.

1. Does the task that I want to measure have a finite number of possible outcomes? If the answer is yes, you may be able to use a tool in this section, and you can go to the second question. If the answer is no, the number of outcomes is infinite, and the tools in this section do not apply.

2. Do I want to assign every member of a group of size n to one of n slots (or tasks)? If the answer is yes, use n factorial. If the answer is no, go to the third question.

3. Do I want to count the number of ways to apply one of three or more labels to each member of a group? If the answer is yes, use the multinomial formula. If the answer is no, go to the fourth question.

4. Do I want to count the number of ways that I can choose r objects from a total of n, when the order in which I list the r objects does not matter (can I give the r objects a label)? If the answer to these questions is yes, the combination formula applies. If the answer is no, go to the fifth question.

5. Do I want to count the number of ways I can choose r objects from a total of n, when the order in which I list the r objects is important? If the answer is yes, the permutation formula applies. If the answer is no, go to question 6.

6. Can the multiplication rule of counting be used? If it cannot, you may have to count the possibilities one by one, or use more advanced techniques than those presented here.[23]

SUMMARY

In this reading, we have discussed the essential concepts and tools of probability. We have applied probability, expected value, and variance to a range of investment problems.

■ A random variable is a quantity whose outcome is uncertain.

■ Probability is a number between 0 and 1 that describes the chance that a stated event will occur.

---

23 Feller (1957) contains a very full treatment of counting problems and solution methods.

- An event is a specified set of outcomes of a random variable.

- Mutually exclusive events can occur only one at a time. Exhaustive events cover or contain all possible outcomes.

- The two defining properties of a probability are, first, that $0 \leq P(E) \leq 1$ (where $P(E)$ denotes the probability of an event E), and second, that the sum of the probabilities of any set of mutually exclusive and exhaustive events equals 1.

- A probability estimated from data as a relative frequency of occurrence is an empirical probability. A probability drawing on personal or subjective judgment is a subjective probability. A probability obtained based on logical analysis is an a priori probability.

- A probability of an event E, $P(E)$, can be stated as odds for $E = P(E)/[1 - P(E)]$ or odds against $E = [1 - P(E)]/P(E)$.

- Probabilities that are inconsistent create profit opportunities, according to the Dutch Book Theorem.

- A probability of an event *not* conditioned on another event is an unconditional probability. The unconditional probability of an event A is denoted $P(A)$. Unconditional probabilities are also called marginal probabilities.

- A probability of an event given (conditioned on) another event is a conditional probability. The probability of an event A given an event B is denoted $P(A \mid B)$.

- The probability of both A and B occurring is the joint probability of A and B, denoted $P(AB)$.

- $P(A \mid B) = P(AB)/P(B)$, $P(B) \neq 0$.

- The multiplication rule for probabilities is $P(AB) = P(A \mid B)P(B)$.

- The probability that A or B occurs, or both occur, is denoted by $P(A \text{ or } B)$.

- The addition rule for probabilities is $P(A \text{ or } B) = P(A) + P(B) - P(AB)$.

- When events are independent, the occurrence of one event does not affect the probability of occurrence of the other event. Otherwise, the events are dependent.

- The multiplication rule for independent events states that if A and B are independent events, $P(AB) = P(A)P(B)$. The rule generalizes in similar fashion to more than two events.

- According to the total probability rule, if $S_1, S_2, ..., S_n$ are mutually exclusive and exhaustive scenarios or events, then $P(A) = P(A \mid S_1)P(S_1) + P(A \mid S_2)P(S_2) + ... + P(A \mid S_n)P(S_n)$.

- The expected value of a random variable is a probability-weighted average of the possible outcomes of the random variable. For a random variable X, the expected value of X is denoted $E(X)$.

- The total probability rule for expected value states that $E(X) = E(X \mid S_1)P(S_1) + E(X \mid S_2)P(S_2) + ... + E(X \mid S_n)P(S_n)$, where $S_1, S_2, ..., S_n$ are mutually exclusive and exhaustive scenarios or events.

- The variance of a random variable is the expected value (the probability-weighted average) of squared deviations from the random variable's expected value $E(X)$: $\sigma^2(X) = E\{[X - E(X)]^2\}$, where $\sigma^2(X)$ stands for the variance of X.

- Variance is a measure of dispersion about the mean. Increasing variance indicates increasing dispersion. Variance is measured in squared units of the original variable.

- Standard deviation is the positive square root of variance. Standard deviation measures dispersion (as does variance), but it is measured in the same units as the variable.

- Covariance is a measure of the co-movement between random variables.

- The covariance between two random variables R_i and R_j is the expected value of the cross-product of the deviations of the two random variables from their respective means: $\text{Cov}(R_i, R_j) = E\{[R_i - E(R_i)][R_j - E(R_j)]\}$. The covariance of a random variable with itself is its own variance.

- Correlation is a number between -1 and $+1$ that measures the co-movement (linear association) between two random variables: $\rho(R_i, R_j) = \text{Cov}(R_i, R_j)/[\sigma(R_i)\sigma(R_j)]$.

- To calculate the variance of return on a portfolio of n assets, the inputs needed are the n expected returns on the individual assets, n variances of return on the individual assets, and $n(n-1)/2$ distinct covariances.

- Portfolio variance of return is $\sigma^2(R_p) = \sum_{i=1}^{n}\sum_{j=1}^{n} w_i w_j \text{Cov}(R_i, R_j)$.

- The calculation of covariance in a forward-looking sense requires the specification of a joint probability function, which gives the probability of joint occurrences of values of the two random variables.

- When two random variables are independent, the joint probability function is the product of the individual probability functions of the random variables.

- Bayes' formula is a method for updating probabilities based on new information.

- Bayes' formula is expressed as follows: Updated probability of event given the new information = [(Probability of the new information given event)/(Unconditional probability of the new information)] × Prior probability of event.

- The multiplication rule of counting says, for example, that if the first step in a process can be done in 10 ways, the second step, given the first, can be done in 5 ways, and the third step, given the first two, can be done in 7 ways, then the steps can be carried out in $(10)(5)(7) = 350$ ways.

- The number of ways to assign every member of a group of size n to n slots is $n!$ $= n(n-1)(n-2)(n-3) \ldots 1$. (By convention, $0! = 1$.)

- The number of ways that n objects can be labeled with k different labels, with n_1 of the first type, n_2 of the second type, and so on, with $n_1 + n_2 + \ldots + n_k = n$, is given by $n!/(n_1!n_2! \ldots n_k!)$. This expression is the multinomial formula.

- A special case of the multinomial formula is the combination formula. The number of ways to choose r objects from a total of n objects, when the order in which the r objects are listed does not matter, is

$$_nC_r = \binom{n}{r} = \frac{n!}{(n-r)!r!}$$

- The number of ways to choose r objects from a total of n objects, when the order in which the r objects are listed does matter, is

$$_nP_r = \frac{n!}{(n-r)!}$$

This expression is the permutation formula.

PRACTICE PROBLEMS FOR READING 8

1. Define the following terms:

   A. Probability.

   B. Conditional probability.

   C. Event.

   D. Independent events.

   E. Variance.

2. State three mutually exclusive and exhaustive events describing the reaction of a company's stock price to a corporate earnings announcement on the day of the announcement.

3. Label each of the following as an empirical, a priori, or subjective probability.

   A. The probability that U.S. stock returns exceed long-term corporate bond returns over a 10-year period, based on Ibbotson Associates data.

   B. An updated (posterior) probability of an event arrived at using Bayes' formula and the perceived prior probability of the event.

   C. The probability of a particular outcome when exactly 12 equally likely possible outcomes exist.

   D. A historical probability of default for double-B rated bonds, adjusted to reflect your perceptions of changes in the quality of double-B rated issuance.

4. You are comparing two companies, BestRest Corporation and Relaxin, Inc. The exports of both companies stand to benefit substantially from the removal of import restrictions on their products in a large export market. The price of BestRest shares reflects a probability of 0.90 that the restrictions will be removed within the year. The price of Relaxin stock, however, reflects a 0.50 probability that the restrictions will be removed within that time frame. By all other information related to valuation, the two stocks appear comparably valued. How would you characterize the implied probabilities reflected in share prices? Which stock is relatively overvalued compared to the other?

5. Suppose you have two limit orders outstanding on two different stocks. The probability that the first limit order executes before the close of trading is 0.45. The probability that the second limit order executes before the close of trading is 0.20. The probability that the two orders both execute before the close of trading is 0.10. What is the probability that at least one of the two limit orders executes before the close of trading?

6. Suppose that 5 percent of the stocks meeting your stock-selection criteria are in the telecommunications (telecom) industry. Also, dividend-paying telecom stocks are 1 percent of the total number of stocks meeting your selection criteria. What is the probability that a stock is dividend paying, given that it is a telecom stock that has met your stock selection criteria?

7. You are using the following three criteria to screen potential acquisition targets from a list of 500 companies:

Criterion	Fraction of the 500 Companies Meeting the Criterion
Product lines compatible	0.20
Company will increase combined sales growth rate	0.45
Balance sheet impact manageable	0.78

If the criteria are independent, how many companies will pass the screen?

8. You apply both valuation criteria and financial strength criteria in choosing stocks. The probability that a randomly selected stock (from your investment universe) meets your valuation criteria is 0.25. Given that a stock meets your valuation criteria, the probability that the stock meets your financial strength criteria is 0.40. What is the probability that a stock meets both your valuation and financial strength criteria?

9. A report from Fitch data service states the following two facts:[1]

- In 2002, the volume of defaulted U.S. high-yield debt was $109.8 billion. The average market size of the high-yield bond market during 2002 was $669.5 billion.

- The average recovery rate for defaulted U.S. high-yield bonds in 2002 (defined as average price one month after default) was $0.22 on the dollar.

Address the following three tasks:

A. On the basis of the first fact given above, calculate the default rate on U.S. high-yield debt in 2002. Interpret this default rate as a probability.

B. State the probability computed in Part A as an odds against default.

C. The quantity 1 minus the recovery rate given in the second fact above is the expected loss per $1 of principal value, given that default has occurred. Suppose you are told that an institution held a diversified high-yield bond portfolio in 2002. Using the information in both facts, what was the institution's expected loss in 2002, per $1 of principal value of the bond portfolio?

10. You are given the following probability distribution for the annual sales of ElStop Corporation:

Probability Distribution for ElStop Annual Sales	
Probability	Sales ($ Millions)
0.20	275
0.40	250
0.25	200
0.10	190
0.05	180
Sum = 1.00	

1 "High Yield Defaults 2002: The Perfect Storm," 19 February, 2003.

    A. Calculate the expected value of ElStop's annual sales.

    B. Calculate the variance of ElStop's annual sales.

    C. Calculate the standard deviation of ElStop's annual sales.

11. Suppose the prospects for recovering principal for a defaulted bond issue depend on which of two economic scenarios prevails. Scenario 1 has probability 0.75 and will result in recovery of $0.90 per $1 principal value with probability 0.45, or in recovery of $0.80 per $1 principal value with probability 0.55. Scenario 2 has probability 0.25 and will result in recovery of $0.50 per $1 principal value with probability 0.85, or in recovery of $0.40 per $1 principal value with probability 0.15.

    A. Compute the probability of each of the four possible recovery amounts: $0.90, $0.80, $0.50, and $0.40.

    B. Compute the expected recovery, given the first scenario.

    C. Compute the expected recovery, given the second scenario.

    D. Compute the expected recovery.

    E. Graph the information in a tree diagram.

12. Suppose we have the expected daily returns (in terms of U.S. dollars), standard deviations, and correlations shown in the table below.

U.S., German, and Italian Bond Returns

U.S. Dollar Daily Returns in Percent

	U.S. Bonds	German Bonds	Italian Bonds
Expected Return	0.029	0.021	0.073
Standard Deviation	0.409	0.606	0.635

Correlation Matrix

	U.S. Bonds	German Bonds	Italian Bonds
U.S. Bonds	1	0.09	0.10
German Bonds		1	0.70
Italian Bonds			1

Source: Kool (2000), Table 1 (excerpted and adapted).

    A. Using the data given above, construct a covariance matrix for the daily returns on U.S., German, and Italian bonds.

    B. State the expected return and variance of return on a portfolio 70 percent invested in U.S. bonds, 20 percent in German bonds, and 10 percent in Italian bonds.

    C. Calculate the standard deviation of return for the portfolio in Part B.

13. The variance of a stock portfolio depends on the variances of each individual stock in the portfolio and also the covariances among the stocks in the portfolio. If you have five stocks, how many unique covariances (excluding variances) must you use in order to compute the variance of return on your portfolio? (Recall that the covariance of a stock with itself is the stock's variance.)

14. Calculate the covariance of the returns on Bedolf Corporation (R_B) with the returns on Zedock Corporation (R_Z), using the following data.

Probability Function of Bedolf and Zedock Returns			
	$R_Z = 15\%$	$R_Z = 10\%$	$R_Z = 5\%$
$R_B = 30\%$	0.25	0	0
$R_B = 15\%$	0	0.50	0
$R_B = 10\%$	0	0	0.25

Note: Entries are joint probabilities.

15. You have developed a set of criteria for evaluating distressed credits. Companies that do not receive a passing score are classed as likely to go bankrupt within 12 months. You gathered the following information when validating the criteria:

- Forty percent of the companies to which the test is administered will go bankrupt within 12 months: P(*nonsurvivor*) = 0.40.

- Fifty-five percent of the companies to which the test is administered pass it: P(*pass test*) = 0.55.

- The probability that a company will pass the test given that it will subsequently survive 12 months, is 0.85: P(*pass test | survivor*) = 0.85.

   A. What is P(*pass test | nonsurvivor*)?

   B. Using Bayes' formula, calculate the probability that a company is a survivor, given that it passes the test; that is, calculate P(survivor | pass test).

   C. What is the probability that a company is a *nonsurvivor*, given that it fails the test?

   D. Is the test effective?

16. On one day in March, 3,292 issues traded on the NYSE: 1,303 advanced, 1,764 declined, and 225 were unchanged. In how many ways could this set of outcomes have happened? (Set up the problem but do not solve it.)

17. Your firm intends to select 4 of 10 vice presidents for the investment committee. How many different groups of four are possible?

18. As in Example 11, you are reviewing the pricing of a speculative-grade, one-year-maturity, zero-coupon bond. Your goal is to estimate an appropriate default risk premium for this bond. The default risk premium is defined as the extra return above the risk-free return that will compensate investors for default risk. If R is the promised return (yield-to-maturity) on the debt instrument and R_F is the risk-free rate, the default risk premium is $R - R_F$. You assess that the probability that the bond defaults is 0.06: P(*the bond defaults*) = 0.06. One-year U.S. T-bills are offering a return of 5.8 percent, an estimate of R_F. In contrast to your approach in Example 11, you no longer make the simplifying assumption that bondholders will recover nothing in the event of a default. Rather, you now assume that recovery will be $0.35 on the dollar, given default.

   A. Denote the fraction of principal and interest recovered in default as θ. Following the model of Example 11, develop a general expression for the promised return R on this bond.

   B. Given your expression for R and the estimate of R_F, state the minimum default risk premium you should require for this instrument.

19. An analyst developed two scenarios with respect to the recovery of $100,000 principal from defaulted loans:

Scenario	Probability of Scenario (%)	Amount Recovered ($)	Probability of Amount (%)
1	40	50,000	60
		30,000	40
2	60	80,000	90
		60,000	10

The amount of the expected recovery is *closest* to:

A. $36,400.

B. $63,600.

C. $81,600.

20. The correlation coefficient that indicates the weakest linear relationship between variables is:

A. −0.75.

B. −0.22.

C. 0.35.

SOLUTIONS FOR READING 8

1. **A.** Probability is defined by the following two properties: 1) the probability of any event is a number between 0 and 1 inclusive, and 2) the sum of the probabilities of any set of mutually exclusive and exhaustive events equals 1.

   B. Conditional probability is the probability of a stated event, given that another event has occurred. For example $P(A \mid B)$ is the probability of A, given that B has occurred.

   C. An event is any specified outcome or set of outcomes of a random variable.

   D. Two events are independent if the occurrence of one event does not affect the probability of occurrence of the other event. In symbols, two events A and B are independent if and only if $P(A \mid B) = P(A)$ or, equivalently, $P(B \mid A) = P(B)$.

   E. The variance of a random variable is the expected value (the probability-weighted average) of squared deviations from the random variable's expected value. In symbols, $\sigma^2(X) = E\{[X - E(X)]^2\}$.

2. One logical set of three mutually exclusive and exhaustive events for the reaction of a company's stock price on the day of a corporate earnings announcement is as follows (wording may vary):

   - Stock price increases on the day of the announcement.

   - Stock price does not change on the day of the announcement.

   - Stock price decreases on the day of the announcement.

   In fact, there are an unlimited number of ways to split up the possible outcomes into three mutually exclusive and exhaustive events. For example, the following list also answers this question satisfactorily:

   - Stock price increases by more than 4 percent on the day of the announcement.

   - Stock price increases by 0 percent to 4 percent on the day of the announcement.

   - Stock price decreases on the day of the announcement.

3. **A.** The probability is an empirical probability.

   B. The probability is a subjective probability.

   C. The probability is an a priori probability.

   D. The probability is a subjective probability.

4. The implied probabilities of 0.90 and 0.50 are inconsistent in that they create a potential profit opportunity. Compared with Relaxin shares, the shares of BestRest are relatively overvalued because their price incorporates a much higher probability of the favorable event (lifting of the trade restriction) than the shares of Relaxin.

5. The probability that at least one of the two orders executes is given by the addition rule for probabilities. Let A stand for the event that *the first limit order executes before the close of trading* [$P(A) = 0.45$] and let B stand for the event that *the second limit order executes before the close of trading* [$P(B) = 0.20$]. $P(AB)$ is given as 0.10. Therefore, $P(A \text{ or } B) = P(A) + P(B) - P(AB) = 0.45 + 0.20 - 0.10 = 0.55$. The probability that at least one of the two orders executes before the close of trading is 0.55.

6. Use Equation 1 to find this conditional probability: P(*stock is dividend paying* | *telecom stock that meets criteria*) = P(*stock is dividend paying and telecom stock that meets criteria*)/P(*telecom stock that meets criteria*) = 0.01/0.05 = 0.20.

7. According to the multiplication rule for independent events, the probability of a company meeting all three criteria is the product of the three probabilities. Labeling the event that a company passes the first, second, and third criteria, A, B, and C, respectively $P(ABC) = P(A)P(B)P(C) = (0.20)(0.45)(0.78) = 0.0702$. As a consequence, $(0.0702)(500) = 35.10$, so 35 companies pass the screen.

8. Use Equation 2, the multiplication rule for probabilities $P(AB) = P(A \mid B)P(B)$, defining A as the event that *a stock meets the financial strength criteria* and defining B as the event that *a stock meets the valuation criteria*. Then $P(AB) = P(A \mid B)P(B) = 0.40 \times 0.25 = 0.10$. The probability that a stock meets both the financial and valuation criteria is 0.10.

9. **A.** The default rate was ($109.8 billion)/($669.5 billion) = 0.164 or 16.4 percent. This result can be interpreted as the probability that $1 invested in a market-value-weighted portfolio of U.S. high-yield bonds was subject to default in 2002.

   B. The odds against an event are denoted $E = [1 - P(E)]/P(E)$. In this case, the odds against default are $(1 - 0.164)/0.164 = 5.098$, or "5.1 to 1."

   C. First, note that $E(loss \mid bond\ defaults) = 1 - \$0.22 = \$0.78$. According to the total probability rule for expected value, $E(loss) = E(loss \mid bond\ defaults)P(bond\ defaults) + E(loss \mid bond\ does\ not\ default)P(bond\ does\ not\ default) = (\$0.78)(0.164) + (\$0.0)(0.836) = 0.128$, or $0.128. Thus, the institution's expected loss was approximately 13 cents per dollar of principal value invested.

10. **A.** Using Equation 7 for the expected value of a random variable (dollar amounts are in millions),

$$E(\text{Sales}) = 0.20(\$275) + 0.40(\$250) + 0.25(\$200) + 0.10(\$190)$$
$$+ 0.50(\$180) = \$233$$

   B. Using Equation 9 for variance,

$$\sigma^2(\text{Sales}) = P(\$275)\big[\$275 - E(\text{Sales})\big]^2 + P(\$250)\big[\$250 - E(\text{Sales})\big]^2$$
$$+ P(\$200)\big[\$200 - E(\text{Sales})\big]^2 + P(\$190)$$
$$\big[\$190 - E(\text{Sales})\big]^2 + P(\$180)\big[\$180 - E(\text{Sales})\big]^2$$
$$= 0.20(\$275 - \$233)^2 + 0.40(\$250 - \$233)^2$$
$$+ 0.25(\$200 - \$233)^2 + 0.10(\$190 - \$233)^2$$
$$+ 0.05(\$180 - \$233)^2$$
$$= \$352.80 + \$115.60 + \$272.25 + \$184.90 + \$140.45$$
$$= \$1,066(\text{million})^2$$

   C. The standard deviation of annual sales is $[\$1,066\ (\text{million})^2]^{1/2} = \$32.649655$ million, or $32.65 million.

11. **A.** *Outcomes associated with Scenario 1:* With a 0.45 probability of a $0.90 recovery per $1 principal value, given Scenario 1, and with the probability of Scenario 1 equal to 0.75, the probability of recovering $0.90 is 0.45 (0.75) = 0.3375. By a similar calculation, the probability of recovering $0.80 is 0.55(0.75) = 0.4125.

   Outcomes associated with Scenario 2: With a 0.85 probability of a $0.50 recovery per $1 principal value, given Scenario 2, and with the probability of Scenario 2 equal to 0.25, the probability of recovering $0.50 is 0.85(0.25) = 0.2125. By a similar calculation, the probability of recovering $0.40 is 0.15(0.25) = 0.0375.

B. $E(recovery \mid Scenario\ 1) = 0.45(\$0.90) + 0.55(\$0.80) = \$0.845$

C. $E(recovery \mid Scenario\ 2) = 0.85(\$0.50) + 0.15(\$0.40) = \$0.485$

D. $E(recovery) = 0.75(\$0.845) + 0.25(\$0.485) = \$0.755$

E.

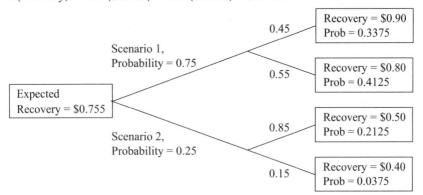

12. A. The diagonal entries in the covariance matrix are the variances, found by squaring the standard deviations.

Var(U.S. bond returns) = 0.409^2 = 0.167281
Var(German bond returns) = 0.606^2 = 0.367236
Var(Italian bond returns) = 0.635^2 = 0.403225

The covariances are found using the relationship $Cov(R_i, R_j) = \rho(R_i, R_j)\ \sigma(R_i)\ \sigma(R_j)$.

There are three distinct covariances:

- Cov(U.S. bond returns, German bond returns) = ρ(U.S. bond returns, German bond returns)σ(U.S. bond returns)σ(German bond returns) = $0.09 \times 0.409 \times 0.606 = 0.022307$

- Cov(U.S. bond returns, Italian bond returns) = ρ(U.S. bond returns, Italian bond returns)σ(U.S. bond returns)σ(Italian bond returns) = $0.10 \times 0.409 \times 0.635 = 0.025972$

- Cov(German bond returns, Italian bond returns) = ρ(German bond returns, Italian bond returns)σ(German bond returns)σ(Italian bond returns) = $0.70 \times 0.606 \times 0.635 = 0.269367$

Covariance Matrix of Returns

	U.S. Bonds	German Bonds	Italian Bonds
U.S. Bonds	0.167281	0.022307	0.025972
German Bonds	0.022307	0.367236	0.269367
Italian Bonds	0.025972	0.269367	0.403225

B. Using Equations 13 and 16, we find

$E(R_P) = 0.70 \times 0.029 + 0.20 \times 0.021 + 0.10 \times 0.073 = 0.0318$.

$$\begin{aligned}
\sigma^2(R_P) &= w_1^2\sigma^2(R_1) + w_2^2\sigma^2(R_2) + w_3^2\sigma^2(R_3) + 2w_1w_2Cov(R_1, R_2) \\
&\quad + 2w_1w_3Cov(R_1, R_3) + 2w_2w_3Cov(R_2, R_3) \\
&= (0.70)^2(0.167281) + (0.20)^2(0.367236) + (0.10)^2(0.403225) \\
&\quad + 2(0.70)(0.20)(0.022307) + 2(0.70)(0.10)(0.025972) \\
&\quad + 2(0.20)(0.10)(0.269367) \\
&= (0.081968 + 0.014689 + 0.004032 + 0.006246 + 0.003636 \\
&\quad + 0.010775) \\
&= 0.121346
\end{aligned}$$

    C. The standard deviation of this portfolio is $\sqrt{\sigma^2\left(R_p\right)}=(0.121346)^{1/2}=0.348348$.

13. A covariance matrix for five assets has $5 \times 5 = 25$ entries. Subtracting the five diagonal variance terms, we have $25 - 5 = 20$ off-diagonal entries. Because the covariance matrix is symmetric, only 10 entries are unique ($10 = 20/2$). Hence, you must use 10 unique covariances in your five-stock portfolio variance calculation.

14. The covariance is 25, computed as follows. First, we calculate expected values:

$$E\left(R_B\right)=(0.25\times30\%)+(0.50\times15\%)+(0.25\times10\%)=17.5\%$$
$$E\left(R_Z\right)=(0.25\times15\%)+(0.50\times10\%)+(0.25\times5\%)=10\%$$

Then we find the covariance as follows:

$$\begin{aligned}
\text{Cov}\left(R_B,R_Z\right)=\ &P(30,15)\times\left[(30-17.5)\times(15-10)\right]+P(15,10)\\
&\times\left[(15-17.5)\times(10-10)\right]+P(10,5)\times\left[(10-17.5)\right.\\
&\left.\times(5-10)\right]\\
=\ &(0.25\times12.5\times5)+\left[0.50\times(-2.5)\times0\right]+\left[0.25\right.\\
&\left.\times(-7.5)\times(-5)\right]\\
=\ &15.625+0+9.375=25
\end{aligned}$$

15. A. We can set up the equation using the total probability rule:
$$P(\text{pass test})=P(\text{pass test}\mid\text{survivor})P(\text{survivor})$$
$$+P(\text{pass test}\mid\text{nonsurvivor})P(\text{nonsurvivor})$$

We know that $P(\text{survivor})=1-P(\text{nonsurvivor})=1-0.40=0.60$. Therefore, $P(\text{pass test})=0.55=0.85(0.60)+P(\text{pass test}\mid \text{nonsurvivor})(0.40)$. Thus $P(\text{pass test}\mid\text{nonsurvivor})=[0.55-0.85(0.60)]/0.40=0.10$.

    B. $$P(\text{survivor}\mid\text{pass test})=\left[P(\text{pass test}\mid\text{survivor})/P(\text{pass test})\right]P(\text{survivor})$$
$$=(0.85/0.55)0.60=0.927273$$

The information that a company passes the test causes you to update your probability that it is a survivor from 0.60 to approximately 0.927.

    C. According to Bayes' formula, P(nonsurvivor | fail test) = [P(fail test | nonsurvivor)/ P(fail test)]P(nonsurvivor) = [P(fail test | nonsurvivor)/0.45]0.40.

We can set up the following equation to obtain P(fail test | nonsurvivor):

$$P(\text{fail test})=P(\text{fail test}\mid\text{nonsurvivor})P(\text{nonsurvivor})$$
$$+P(\text{fail test}\mid\text{survivor})P(\text{survivor})$$
$$0.45=P(\text{fail test}\mid\text{nonsurvivor})0.40+0.15(0.60)$$

where P(fail test | survivor) = 1 − P(pass test | survivor) = 1 − 0.85 = 0.15. So P(fail test | nonsurvivor) = [0.45 − 0.15(0.60)]/0.40 = 0.90. Using this result with the formula above, we find P(nonsurvivor | fail test) = (0.90/0.45)0.40 = 0.80. Seeing that a company fails the test causes us to update the probability that it is a nonsurvivor from 0.40 to 0.80.

    D. A company passing the test greatly increases our confidence that it is a survivor. A company failing the test doubles the probability that it is a nonsurvivor. Therefore, the test appears to be useful.

16. This is a labeling problem in which we assign each NYSE issue a label: advanced, declined, or unchanged. The expression to count the number of ways

3,292 issues can be assigned to these three categories such that 1,303 advanced, 1,764 declined, and 225 remained unchanged is $3{,}292!/(1{,}303!)(1{,}764!)(225!)$.

17. We find the answer using the combination formula $\binom{n}{r} = n!/[(n-r)!r!]$.

Here, $n = 10$ and $r = 4$, so the answer is $10!/[(10-4)!4!] = 3{,}628{,}800/(720)(24) = 210$.

18. **A.** The two events that affect a bondholder's returns are *the bond defaults* and *the bond does not default*. First, compute the value of the bond for the two events per $1 invested.

	The Bond Defaults	*The Bond Does Not Default*
Bond value	$\theta \times \$(1 + R)$	$\$(1 + R)$

Second, find the expected value of the bond (per $1 invested):

$$E(\text{bond}) = \theta \times \$(1+R) \times P(\text{the bond defaults}) + \$(1+R)$$
$$\times \left[1 - P(\text{the bond defaults})\right]$$

On the other hand, the expected value of the T-bill is the certain value $(1 + R_F)$. Setting the expected value of the bond to the expected value of the T-bill permits us to find the promised return on the bond such that bondholders expect to break even.

$$\theta \times \$(1+R) \times P(\text{the bond defaults}) + \$(1+R)$$
$$\times \left[1 - P(\text{the bond defaults})\right] = \$(1 + R_F)$$

Rearranging the left-hand side,

$$(1+R) \times \left\{\theta \times P(\text{the bond defaults}) + \left[1 - P(\text{the bond defaults})\right]\right\}$$
$$= (1 + R_F)$$

$$R = (1 + R_F)/\left\{\theta \times P(\text{the bond defaults})\right.$$
$$+ \left.\left[1 - P(\text{the bond defaults})\right]\right\} - 1$$

B. For this problem, $R_F = 0.058$, $P(\textit{the bond defaults}) = 0.06$, $1 - P(\textit{the bond defaults}) = 0.94$, and $\theta = 0.35$.

$$R = \left[1.058/(0.35(0.06) + 0.94)\right] - 1 = 0.100937, \text{ or } 10.1 \text{ percent}$$

With a recovery rate of 35 cents on the dollar, a minimum default risk premium of about 430 basis points is required, calculated as 4.3% = 10.1% − 5.8%.

19. B is correct. If Scenario 1 occurs, the expected recovery is 60% ($50,000) + 40% ($30,000) = $42,000, and if Scenario 2 occurs, the expected recovery is 90% ($80,000) + 10%($60,000) = $78,000. Weighting by the probability of each scenario, the expected recovery is 40%($42,000) + 60%($78,000) = $63,600. Alternatively, first calculating the probability of each amount occurring, the expected recovery is (40%)(60%)($50,000) + (40%)(40%)($30,000) + (60%)(90%) ($80,000) + (60%)(10%)($60,000) = $63,600.

20. B is correct. Correlations near positive 1.00 exhibit strong positive linearity; correlations near negative 1.00 exhibit strong negative linearity. Correlations of zero indicate no linear relation between variables. The closer the correlation is to zero, the weaker is the linear relationship.

STUDY SESSION

3

Quantitative Methods:

Application

This study session introduces some of the discrete and continuous probability distributions most commonly used to describe the behavior of random variables. Probability theory and calculations are widely applied in finance, for example, in the field of investment and project valuation and in financial risk management.

Furthermore, this session explains how to estimate different parameters (e.g., mean and standard deviation) of a population if only a sample, rather than the whole population, can be observed. Hypothesis testing is a closely related topic. This session presents the techniques that can be applied to accept or reject an assumed hypothesis (null hypothesis) about various parameters of a population.

The last reading introduces the fundamentals of technical analysis and illustrates how it is used to analyze securities and securities markets.

READING ASSIGNMENTS

Reading 9 **_Common Probability Distributions_**

Quantitative Methods for Investment Analysis, Second Edition, by Richard A. DeFusco, CFA, Dennis W. McLeavey, CFA, Jerald E. Pinto, CFA, and David E. Runkle, CFA

Reading 10 **_Sampling and Estimation_**

Quantitative Methods for Investment Analysis, Second Edition, by Richard A. DeFusco, CFA, Dennis W. McLeavey, CFA, Jerald E. Pinto, CFA, and David E. Runkle, CFA

Common Probability Distributions

by Richard A. DeFusco, CFA, Dennis W. McLeavey, CFA, Jerald E. Pinto, CFA, and David E. Runkle, CFA

LEARNING OUTCOMES

Mastery	The candidate should be able to:
☐	**a** define a probability distribution and distinguish between discrete and continuous random variables and their probability functions;
☐	**b** describe the set of possible outcomes of a specified discrete random variable;
☐	**c** interpret a cumulative distribution function;
☐	**d** calculate and interpret probabilities for a random variable, given its cumulative distribution function;
☐	**e** define a discrete uniform random variable, a Bernoulli random variable, and a binomial random variable;
☐	**f** calculate and interpret probabilities given the discrete uniform and the binomial distribution functions;
☐	**g** construct a binomial tree to describe stock price movement;
☐	**h** calculate and interpret tracking error;
☐	**i** define the continuous uniform distribution and calculate and interpret probabilities, given a continuous uniform distribution;
☐	**j** explain the key properties of the normal distribution;
☐	**k** distinguish between a univariate and a multivariate distribution, and explain the role of correlation in the multivariate normal distribution;
☐	**l** determine the probability that a normally distributed random variable lies inside a given interval;
☐	**m** define the standard normal distribution, explain how to standardize a random variable, and calculate and interpret probabilities using the standard normal distribution;
☐	**n** define shortfall risk, calculate the safety-first ratio, and select an optimal portfolio using Roy's safety-first criterion;
☐	**o** explain the relationship between normal and lognormal distributions and why the lognormal distribution is used to model asset prices;

Quantitative Methods for Investment Analysis, Second Edition, by Richard A. DeFusco, CFA, Dennis W. McLeavey, CFA, Jerald E. Pinto, CFA, and David E. Runkle, CFA. Copyright © 2004 by CFA Institute.

Mastery	The candidate should be able to:
☐	**p** distinguish between discretely and continuously compounded rates of return, and calculate and interpret a continuously compounded rate of return, given a specific holding period return;
☐	**q** explain Monte Carlo simulation and describe its major applications and limitations;
☐	**r** compare Monte Carlo simulation and historical simulation.

1 INTRODUCTION TO COMMON PROBABILITY DISTRIBUTIONS

In nearly all investment decisions we work with random variables. The return on a stock and its earnings per share are familiar examples of random variables. To make probability statements about a random variable, we need to understand its probability distribution. A **probability distribution** specifies the probabilities of the possible outcomes of a random variable.

In this reading, we present important facts about four probability distributions and their investment uses. These four distributions—the uniform, binomial, normal, and lognormal—are used extensively in investment analysis. They are used in such basic valuation models as the Black–Scholes–Merton option pricing model, the binomial option pricing model, and the capital asset pricing model. With the working knowledge of probability distributions provided in this reading, you will also be better prepared to study and use other quantitative methods such as hypothesis testing, regression analysis, and time-series analysis.

After discussing probability distributions, we end the reading with an introduction to Monte Carlo simulation, a computer-based tool for obtaining information on complex problems. For example, an investment analyst may want to experiment with an investment idea without actually implementing it. Or she may need to price a complex option for which no simple pricing formula exists. In these cases and many others, Monte Carlo simulation is an important resource. To conduct a Monte Carlo simulation, the analyst must identify risk factors associated with the problem and specify probability distributions for them. Hence, Monte Carlo simulation is a tool that requires an understanding of probability distributions.

Before we discuss specific probability distributions, we define basic concepts and terms. We then illustrate the operation of these concepts through the simplest distribution, the uniform distribution. That done, we address probability distributions that have more applications in investment work but also greater complexity.

2 DISCRETE RANDOM VARIABLES

A **random variable** is a quantity whose future outcomes are uncertain. The two basic types of random variables are discrete random variables and continuous random variables. A **discrete random variable** can take on at most a countable number of possible values. For example, a discrete random variable X can take on a limited number of outcomes $x_1, x_2, ..., x_n$ (n possible outcomes), or a discrete random variable Y can take on an unlimited number of outcomes y_1, y_2, ... (without end).[1] Because we can count all the possible outcomes of X and Y (even if we go on forever in the case of Y), both X and Y satisfy the definition of a discrete random variable. By contrast, we cannot count the outcomes of a **continuous random variable**. We cannot describe the possible outcomes of a continuous random variable Z with a list z_1, z_2, ... because the outcome $(z_1 + z_2)/2$, not in the list, would always be possible. Rate of return is an example of a continuous random variable.

In working with a random variable, we need to understand its possible outcomes. For example, stocks traded on the New York Stock Exchange and NASDAQ are quoted in ticks of $0.01. Quoted stock price is thus a discrete random variable with possible values $0, $0.01, $0.02, ... But we can also model stock price as a continuous random variable (as a lognormal random variable, to look ahead). In many applications, we have a choice between using a discrete or a continuous distribution. We are usually guided by which distribution is most efficient for the task we face. This opportunity for choice is not surprising, as many discrete distributions can be approximated with a continuous distribution, and vice versa. In most practical cases, a probability distribution is only a mathematical idealization, or approximate model, of the relative frequencies of a random variable's possible outcomes.

Example 1

The Distribution of Bond Price

You are researching a probability model for bond price, and you begin by thinking about the characteristics of bonds that affect price. What are the lowest and the highest possible values for bond price? Why? What are some other characteristics of bonds that may affect the distribution of bond price?

The lowest possible value of bond price is 0, when the bond is worthless. Identifying the highest possible value for bond price is more challenging. The promised payments on a coupon bond are the coupons (interest payments) plus the face amount (principal). The price of a bond is the present discounted value of these promised payments. Because investors require a return on their investments, 0 percent is the lower limit on the discount rate that investors would use to discount a bond's promised payments. At a discount rate of 0 percent, the price of a bond is the sum of the face value and the remaining coupons without any discounting. The discount rate thus places the upper limit on bond price. Suppose, for example, that face value is $1,000 and two $40 coupons remain; the interval $0 to $1,080 captures all possible values of the bond's price. This upper limit decreases through time as the number of remaining payments decreases.

Other characteristics of a bond also affect its price distribution. Pull to par value is one such characteristic: As the maturity date approaches, the standard deviation of bond price tends to grow smaller as bond price converges to par value. Embedded options also affect bond price. For example, with bonds that are currently callable, the issuer may retire the bonds at a prespecified premium above par; this option of the issuer cuts off part of the bond's upside. Modeling bond price distribution is a challenging problem.

---

1 We follow the convention that an uppercase letter represents a random variable and a lowercase letter represents an outcome or specific value of the random variable. Thus X refers to the random variable, and x refers to an outcome of X. We subscript outcomes, as in x_1 and x_2, when we need to distinguish among different outcomes in a list of outcomes of a random variable.

Every random variable is associated with a probability distribution that describes the variable completely. We can view a probability distribution in two ways. The basic view is the **probability function**, which specifies the probability that the random variable takes on a specific value: $P(X = x)$ is the probability that a random variable X takes on the value x. (Note that capital X represents the random variable and lowercase x represents a specific value that the random variable may take.) For a discrete random variable, the shorthand notation for the probability function is $p(x) = P(X = x)$. For continuous random variables, the probability function is denoted $f(x)$ and called the **probability density function** (pdf), or just the density.[2]

A probability function has two key properties (which we state, without loss of generality, using the notation for a discrete random variable):

■ $0 \le p(x) \le 1$, because probability is a number between 0 and 1.

■ The sum of the probabilities $p(x)$ over all values of X equals 1. If we add up the probabilities of all the distinct possible outcomes of a random variable, that sum must equal 1.

We are often interested in finding the probability of a range of outcomes rather than a specific outcome. In these cases, we take the second view of a probability distribution, the cumulative distribution function (cdf). The **cumulative distribution function**, or distribution function for short, gives the probability that a random variable X is less than or equal to a particular value x, $P(X \le x)$. For both discrete and continuous random variables, the shorthand notation is $F(x) = P(X \le x)$. How does the cumulative distribution function relate to the probability function? The word "cumulative" tells the story. To find $F(x)$, we sum up, or cumulate, values of the probability function for all outcomes less than or equal to x. The function of the cdf is parallel to that of cumulative relative frequency, which we discussed in the reading on statistical concepts and market returns.

Next, we illustrate these concepts with examples and show how we use discrete and continuous distributions. We start with the simplest distribution, the discrete uniform.

2.1 The Discrete Uniform Distribution

The simplest of all probability distributions is the discrete uniform distribution. Suppose that the possible outcomes are the integers (whole numbers) 1 to 8, inclusive, and the probability that the random variable takes on any of these possible values is the same for all outcomes (that is, it is uniform). With eight outcomes, $p(x) = 1/8$, or 0.125, for all values of X ($X = 1, 2, 3, 4, 5, 6, 7, 8$); the statement just made is a complete description of this discrete uniform random variable. The distribution has a finite number of specified outcomes, and each outcome is equally likely. Table 1 summarizes the two views of this random variable, the probability function and the cumulative distribution function.

Table 1	Probability Function and Cumulative Distribution Function for a Discrete Uniform Random Variable	
X = x	**Probability Function** $p(x) = P(X = x)$	**Cumulative Distribution Function** $F(x) = P(X \le x)$
1	0.125	0.125
2	0.125	0.250

---

[2] The technical term for the probability function of a discrete random variable, probability mass function (pmf), is used less frequently.

Table 1	Continued	

X = x	Probability Function $p(x) = P(X = x)$	Cumulative Distribution Function $F(x) = P(X \leq x)$
3	0.125	0.375
4	0.125	0.500
5	0.125	0.625
6	0.125	0.750
7	0.125	0.875
8	0.125	1.000

We can use Table 1 to find three probabilities: $P(X \leq 7)$, $P(4 \leq X \leq 6)$, and $P(4 < X \leq 6)$. The following examples illustrate how to use the cdf to find the probability that a random variable will fall in any interval (for any random variable, not only the uniform).

- The probability that X is less than or equal to 7, $P(X \leq 7)$, is the next-to-last entry in the third column, 0.875 or 87.5 percent.

- To find $P(4 \leq X \leq 6)$, we need to find the sum of three probabilities: $p(4)$, $p(5)$, and $p(6)$. We can find this sum in two ways. We can add $p(4)$, $p(5)$, and $p(6)$ from the second column. Or we can calculate the probability as the difference between two values of the cumulative distribution function:

$$F(6) = P(X \leq 6) = p(6) + p(5) + p(4) + p(3) + p(2) + p(1)$$
$$F(3) = P(X \leq 3) = p(3) + p(2) + p(1)$$

so

$$P(4 \leq X \leq 6) = F(6) - F(3) = p(6) + p(5) + p(4) = 3/8$$

So we calculate the second probability as $F(6) - F(3) = 3/8$.

- The third probability, $P(4 < X \leq 6)$, the probability that X is less than or equal to 6 but greater than 4, is $p(5) + p(6)$. We compute it as follows, using the cdf:

$$P(4 < X \leq 6) = P(X \leq 6) - P(X \leq 4) = F(6) - F(4) = p(6) + p(5) = 2/8$$

So we calculate the third probability as $F(6) - F(4) = 2/8$.

Suppose we want to check that the discrete uniform probability function satisfies the general properties of a probability function given earlier. The first property is $0 \leq p(x) \leq 1$. We see that $p(x) = 1/8$ for all x in the first column of the table. (Note that $p(x)$ equals 0 for numbers x such as −14 or 12.215 that are not in that column.) The first property is satisfied. The second property is that the probabilities sum to 1. The entries in the second column of Table 1 do sum to 1.

The cdf has two other characteristic properties:

- The cdf lies between 0 and 1 for any x: $0 \leq F(x) \leq 1$.

- As we increase x, the cdf either increases or remains constant.

Check these statements by looking at the third column in Table 1.

We now have some experience working with probability functions and cdfs for discrete random variables. Later in this reading, we will discuss Monte Carlo simulation, a methodology driven by random numbers. As we will see, the uniform distribution has an important technical use: It is the basis for generating random numbers, which in turn produce random observations for all other probability distributions.[3]

2.2 The Binomial Distribution

In many investment contexts, we view a result as either a success or a failure, or as binary (twofold) in some other way. When we make probability statements about a record of successes and failures, or about anything with binary outcomes, we often use the binomial distribution. What is a good model for how a stock price moves through time? Different models are appropriate for different uses. Cox, Ross, and Rubinstein (1979) developed an option pricing model based on binary moves, price up or price down, for the asset underlying the option. Their binomial option pricing model was the first of a class of related option pricing models that have played an important role in the development of the derivatives industry. That fact alone would be sufficient reason for studying the binomial distribution, but the binomial distribution has uses in decision-making as well.

The building block of the binomial distribution is the **Bernoulli random variable**, named after the Swiss probabilist Jakob Bernoulli (1654–1704). Suppose we have a trial (an event that may repeat) that produces one of two outcomes. Such a trial is a **Bernoulli trial**. If we let Y equal 1 when the outcome is success and Y equal 0 when the outcome is failure, then the probability function of the Bernoulli random variable Y is

$$p(1) = P(Y = 1) = p$$
$$p(0) = P(Y = 0) = 1 - p$$

where p is the probability that the trial is a success. Our next example is the very first step on the road to understanding the binomial option pricing model.

Example 2

One-Period Stock Price Movement as a Bernoulli Random Variable

Suppose we describe stock price movement in the following way. Stock price today is S. Next period stock price can move up or down. The probability of an up move is p, and the probability of a down move is $1 - p$. Thus, stock price is a Bernoulli random variable with probability of success (an up move) equal to p. When the stock moves up, ending price is uS, with u equal to 1 plus the rate of return if the stock moves up. For example, if the stock earns 0.01 or 1 percent on an up move, $u = 1.01$. When the stock moves down, ending price is dS, with d equal to 1 plus the rate of return if the stock moves down. For example, if the stock earns –0.01 or –1 percent on a down move, $d = 0.99$. Figure 1 shows a diagram of this model of stock price dynamics.

---

3 See Hillier and Lieberman (2000). Random numbers initially generated by computers are usually random positive integer numbers that are converted to approximate continuous uniform random numbers between 0 and 1. Then the continuous uniform random numbers are used to produce random observations on other distributions, such as the normal, using various techniques. We will discuss random observation generation further in the section on Monte Carlo simulation.

Figure 1	**One-Period Stock Price as a Bernoulli Random Variable**

End-of-Period Stock Price

Probability = p

Stock Price Moves Up:
Stock Price Equals uS

Stock Price Today, S

Probability = 1 – p

Stock Price Moves Down:
Stock Price Equals dS

We will continue with the above example later. In the model of stock price movement in Example 2, success and failure at a given trial relate to up moves and down moves, respectively. In the following example, success is a profitable trade and failure is an unprofitable one.

Example 3

A Trading Desk Evaluates Block Brokers (1)

You work in equities trading at an institutional money manager that regularly trades with a number of block brokers. Blocks are orders to sell or buy that are too large for the liquidity ordinarily available in dealer networks or stock exchanges. Your firm has known interests in certain kinds of stock. Block brokers call your trading desk when they want to sell blocks of stocks that they think your firm may be interested in buying. You know that these transactions have definite risks. For example, if the broker's client (the seller of the shares) has unfavorable information on the stock, or if the total amount he is selling through all channels is not truthfully communicated to you, you may see an immediate loss on the trade. From time to time, your firm audits the performance of block brokers. Your firm calculates the post-trade, market-risk-adjusted dollar returns on stocks purchased from block brokers. On that basis, you classify each trade as unprofitable or profitable. You have summarized the performance of the brokers in a spreadsheet, excerpted in Table 2 for November 2003. (The broker names are coded BB001 and BB002.)

Table 2	**Block Trading Gains and Losses**	

	November 2003	
	Profitable Trades	**Losing Trades**
BB001	3	9
BB002	5	3

> View each trade as a Bernoulli trial. Calculate the percentage of profitable trades with the two block brokers for November 2003. These are estimates of p, the underlying probability of a successful (profitable) trade with each broker.
>
> Your firm has logged $3 + 9 = 12$ trades (the row total) with block broker BB001. Because 3 of the 12 trades were profitable, the percentage of profitable trades was 3/12 or 25 percent. With broker BB002, the percentage of profitable trades was 5/8 or 62.5 percent. A trade is a Bernoulli trial, and the above calculations provide estimates of the underlying probability of a profitable trade (success) with the two brokers. For broker BB001, your estimate is $\hat{p} = 0.25$; for broker BB002, your estimate is $\hat{p} = 0.625$.[4]

In n Bernoulli trials, we can have 0 to n successes. If the outcome of an individual trial is random, the total number of successes in n trials is also random. A **binomial random variable** X is defined as the number of successes in n Bernoulli trials. A binomial random variable is the sum of Bernoulli random variables Y_i, $i = 1, 2, ..., n$:

$$X = Y_1 + Y_2 + ... + Y_n$$

where Y_i is the outcome on the ith trial (1 if a success, 0 if a failure). We know that a Bernoulli random variable is defined by the parameter p. The number of trials, n, is the second parameter of a binomial random variable. The binomial distribution makes these assumptions:

- The probability, p, of success is constant for all trials.
- The trials are independent.

The second assumption has great simplifying force. If individual trials were correlated, calculating the probability of a given number of successes in n trials would be much more complicated.

Under the above two assumptions, a binomial random variable is completely described by two parameters, n and p. We write

$$X \sim B(n, p)$$

which we read as "X has a binomial distribution with parameters n and p." You can see that a Bernoulli random variable is a binomial random variable with $n = 1$: $Y \sim B(1, p)$.

Now we can find the general expression for the probability that a binomial random variable shows x successes in n trials. We can think in terms of a model of stock price dynamics that can be generalized to allow any possible stock price movements if the periods are made extremely small. Each period is a Bernoulli trial: With probability p, the stock price moves up; with probability $1 - p$, the price moves down. A success is an up move, and x is the number of up moves or successes in n periods (trials). With each period's moves independent and p constant, the number of up moves in n periods is a binomial random variable. We now develop an expression for $P(X = x)$, the probability function for a binomial random variable.

Any sequence of n periods that shows exactly x up moves must show $n - x$ down moves. We have many different ways to order the up moves and down moves to get a total of x up moves, but given independent trials, any sequence with x up moves must occur with probability $p^x(1 - p)^{n-x}$. Now we need to multiply this probability by the number of different ways we can get a sequence with x up moves. Using a basic result in counting from the reading on probability concepts, there are

$$\frac{n!}{(n-x)!x!}$$

---

4 The "hat" over p indicates that it is an estimate of p, the underlying probability of a profitable trade with the broker.

different sequences in n trials that result in x up moves (or successes) and $n - x$ down moves (or failures). Recall from the reading on probability concepts that n factorial ($n!$) is defined as $n(n - 1)(n - 2) \ldots 1$ (and $0! = 1$ by convention). For example, $5! = (5)(4)(3)(2)(1) = 120$. The combination formula $n!/[(n - x)!x!]$ is denoted by

$$\binom{n}{x}$$

(read "n combination x" or "n choose x"). For example, over three periods, exactly three different sequences have two up moves: UUD, UDU, and DUU. We confirm this by

$$\binom{3}{2} = \frac{3!}{(3-2)!2!} = \frac{(3)(2)(1)}{(1)(2)(1)} = 3$$

If, hypothetically, each sequence with two up moves had a probability of 0.15, then the total probability of two up moves in three periods would be $3 \times 0.15 = 0.45$. This example should persuade you that for X distributed $B(n, p)$, the probability of x successes in n trials is given by

$$p(x) = P(X = x) = \binom{n}{x} p^x (1 - p)^{n-x} = \frac{n!}{(n - x)!x!} p^x (1 - p)^{n-x} \qquad \text{(1)}$$

Some distributions are always symmetric, such as the normal, and others are always asymmetric or skewed, such as the lognormal. The binomial distribution is symmetric when the probability of success on a trial is 0.50, but it is asymmetric or skewed otherwise.

We illustrate Equation 1 (the probability function) and the cdf through the symmetrical case. Consider a random variable distributed $B(n = 5, p = 0.50)$. Table 3 contains a complete description of this random variable. The fourth column of Table 3 is Column 2, n combination x, times Column 3, $p^x(1 - p)^{n-x}$; Column 4 gives the probability for each value of the number of up moves from the first column. The fifth column, cumulating the entries in the fourth column, is the cumulative distribution function.

Table 3   Binomial Probabilities, $p = 0.50$ and $n = 5$

Number of Up Moves, x (1)	Number of Possible Ways to Reach x Up Moves (2)	Probability for Each Way (3)	Probability for x, $p(x)$ (4) = (2) × (3)	$F(x) = P(X \leq x)$ (5)
0	1	$0.50^0(1 - 0.50)^5 = 0.03125$	0.03125	0.03125
1	5	$0.50^1(1 - 0.50)^4 = 0.03125$	0.15625	0.18750
2	10	$0.50^2(1 - 0.50)^3 = 0.03125$	0.31250	0.50000
3	10	$0.50^3(1 - 0.50)^2 = 0.03125$	0.31250	0.81250
4	5	$0.50^4(1 - 0.50)^1 = 0.03125$	0.15625	0.96875
5	1	$0.50^5(1 - 0.50)^0 = 0.03125$	0.03125	1.00000

What would happen if we kept $n = 5$ but sharply lowered the probability of success on a trial to 10 percent? "Probability for Each Way" for $X = 0$ (no up moves) would then be about 59 percent: $0.10^0(1 - 0.10)^5 = 0.59049$. Because zero successes could still happen one way (Column 2), $p(0) = 59$ percent. You may want to check that given $p = 0.10$, $P(X \leq 2) = 99.14$ percent: The probability of two or fewer up moves would be more than 99 percent. The random variable's probability would be massed on 0, 1, and 2 up moves, and the probability of larger outcomes would be minute. The outcomes of 3 and larger would be the long right tail, and the distribution would be right skewed. On the other hand, if we set $p = 0.90$, we would have the mirror image of the distribution with $p = 0.10$. The distribution would be left skewed.

With an understanding of the binomial probability function in hand, we can continue with our example of block brokers.

Example 4

A Trading Desk Evaluates Block Brokers (2)

You now want to evaluate the performance of the block brokers in Example 3. You begin with two questions:

1. If you are paying a fair price on average in your trades with a broker, what should be the probability of a profitable trade?

2. Did each broker meet or miss that expectation on probability?

You also realize that the brokers' performance has to be evaluated in light of the sample's size, and for that you need to use the binomial probability function (Equation 1). You thus address the following (referring to the data in Example 3):

3. Under the assumption that the prices of trades were fair,
    A. calculate the probability of three or fewer profitable trades with broker BB001.
    B. calculate the probability of five or more profitable trades with broker BB002.

Solution to 1 and 2:

If the price you trade at is fair, 50 percent of the trades you do with a broker should be profitable.[5] The rate of profitable trades with broker BB001 was 25 percent. Therefore, broker BB001 missed your performance expectation. Broker BB002, at 62.5 percent profitable trades, exceeded your expectation.

Solution to 3:

A. For broker BB001, the number of trades (the trials) was $n = 12$, and 3 were profitable. You are asked to calculate the probability of three or fewer profitable trades, $F(3) = p(3) + p(2) + p(1) + p(0)$.

Suppose the underlying probability of a profitable trade with BB001 is $p = 0.50$. With $n = 12$ and $p = 0.50$, according to Equation 1 the probability of three profitable trades is

$$p(3) = \binom{n}{x} p^x (1-p)^{n-x} = \binom{12}{3}(0.50^3)(0.50^9)$$

$$= \frac{12!}{(12-3)!3!}0.50^{12} = 220(0.000244) = 0.053711$$

The probability of exactly 3 profitable trades out of 12 is 5.4 percent if broker BB001 were giving you fair prices. Now you need to calculate the other probabilities:

$$p(2) = \left[12!/(12-2)!2!\right](0.50^2)(0.50^{10}) = 66(0.000244) = 0.016113$$

$$p(1) = \left[12!/(12-1)!1!\right](0.50^1)(0.50^{11}) = 12(0.000244) = 0.00293$$

$$p(0) = \left[12!/(12-0)!0!\right](0.50^0)(0.50^{12}) = 1(0.000244) = 0.000244$$

---

[5] Of course, you need to adjust for the direction of the overall market after the trade (any broker's record will be helped by a bull market) and perhaps make other risk adjustments. Assume that these adjustments have been made.

Adding all the probabilities, $F(3) = 0.053711 + 0.016113 + 0.00293 + 0.000244 = 0.072998$ or 7.3 percent. The probability of doing 3 or fewer profitable trades out of 12 would be 7.3 percent if your trading desk were getting fair prices from broker BB001.

B. For broker BB002, you are assessing the probability that the underlying probability of a profitable trade with this broker was 50 percent, despite the good results. The question was framed as the probability of doing five or more profitable trades if the underlying probability is 50 percent: $1 - F(4) = p(5) + p(6) + p(7) + p(8)$. You could calculate $F(4)$ and subtract it from 1, but you can also calculate $p(5) + p(6) + p(7) + p(8)$ directly.

You begin by calculating the probability that exactly 5 out of 8 trades would be profitable if BB002 were giving you fair prices:

$$p(5) = \binom{8}{5}(0.50^5)(0.50^3)$$

$$= 56(0.003906) = 0.21875$$

The probability is about 21.9 percent. The other probabilities are

$$p(6) = 28(0.003906) = 0.109375$$
$$p(7) = 8(0.003906) = 0.03125$$
$$p(8) = 1(0.003906) = 0.003906$$

So $p(5) + p(6) + p(7) + p(8) = 0.21875 + 0.109375 + 0.03125 + 0.003906 = 0.363281$ or 36.3 percent.[6] A 36.3 percent probability is substantial; the underlying probability of executing a fair trade with BB002 might well have been 0.50 despite your success with BB002 in November 2003. If one of the trades with BB002 had been reclassified from profitable to unprofitable, exactly half the trades would have been profitable. In summary, your trading desk is getting at least fair prices from BB002; you will probably want to accumulate additional evidence before concluding that you are trading at better-than-fair prices.

The magnitude of the profits and losses in these trades is another important consideration. If all profitable trades had small profits but all unprofitable trades had large losses, for example, you might lose money on your trades even if the majority of them were profitable.

In the next example, the binomial distribution helps in evaluating the performance of an investment manager.

Example 5

Meeting a Tracking Error Objective

You work for a pension fund sponsor. You have assigned a new money manager to manage a $500 million portfolio indexed on the MSCI EAFE (Europe, Australasia, and Far East) Index, which is designed to measure developed-market equity performance excluding the United States and Canada. After research, you believe it is reasonable to expect that the manager will keep tracking error within a band of 75 basis points (bps) of the benchmark's return, on a quarterly

---

[6] In this example all calculations were worked through by hand, but binomial probability and cdf functions are also available in computer spreadsheet programs.

basis.[7] **Tracking error** is the total return on the portfolio (gross of fees) minus the total return on the benchmark index—here, the EAFE.[8] To quantify this expectation further, you will be satisfied if tracking error is within the 75 bps band 90 percent of the time. The manager meets the objective in six out of eight quarters. Of course, six out of eight quarters is a 75 percent success rate. But how does the manager's record precisely relate to your expectation of a 90 percent success rate and the sample size, 8 observations? To answer this question, you must find the probability that, given an assumed true or underlying success rate of 90 percent, performance could be as bad as or worse than that delivered. Calculate the probability (by hand or with a spreadsheet).

Specifically, you want to find the probability that tracking error is within the 75 bps band in six or fewer quarters out of the eight in the sample. With $n = 8$ and $p = 0.90$, this probability is $F(6) = p(6) + p(5) + p(4) + p(3) + p(2) + p(1) + p(0)$. Start with

$$p(6) = (8!/6!2!)(0.90^6)(0.10^2) = 28(0.005314) = 0.148803$$

and work through the other probabilities:

$$p(5) = (8!/5!3!)(0.90^5)(0.10^3) = 56(0.00059) = 0.033067$$
$$p(4) = (8!/4!4!)(0.90^4)(0.10^4) = 70(0.000066) = 0.004593$$
$$p(3) = (8!/3!5!)(0.90^3)(0.10^5) = 56(0.000007) = 0.000408$$
$$p(2) = (8!/2!6!)(0.90^2)(0.10^6) = 28(0.000001) = 0.000023$$
$$p(1) = (8!/1!7!)(0.90^1)(0.10^7) = 8(0.00000009) = 0.00000072$$
$$p(0) = (8!/0!8!)(0.90^0)(0.10^8) = 1(0.00000001) = 0.00000001$$

Summing all these probabilities, you conclude that $F(6) = 0.148803 + 0.033067 + 0.004593 + 0.000408 + 0.000023 + 0.00000072 + 0.00000001 = 0.186895$ or 18.7 percent. There is a moderate 18.7 percent probability that the manager would show the record he did (or a worse record) if he had the skill to meet your expectations 90 percent of the time.

You can use other evaluation concepts such as tracking risk, defined as the standard deviation of tracking error, to assess the manager's performance. The calculation above would be only one input into any conclusions that you reach concerning the manager's performance. But to answer problems involving success rates, you need to be skilled in using the binomial distribution.

Two descriptors of a distribution that are often used in investments are the mean and the variance (or the standard deviation, the positive square root of variance).[9] Table 4 gives the expressions for the mean and variance of binomial random variables.

Table 4	Mean and Variance of Binomial Random Variables	
	Mean	**Variance**
Bernoulli, $B(1, p)$	p	$p(1 - p)$
Binomial, $B(n, p)$	np	$np(1 - p)$

[7] A basis point is one-hundredth of 1 percent (0.01 percent).
[8] Some practitioners use tracking error to describe what we later call tracking risk, the standard deviation of the differences between the portfolio's and benchmark's returns.
[9] The mean (or arithmetic mean) is the sum of all values in a distribution or dataset, divided by the number of values summed. The variance is a measure of dispersion about the mean. See the reading on statistical concepts and market returns for further details on these concepts.

Because a single Bernoulli random variable, $Y \sim B(1, p)$, takes on the value 1 with probability p and the value 0 with probability $1 - p$, its mean or weighted-average outcome is p. Its variance is $p(1 - p)$.[10] A general binomial random variable, $B(n, p)$, is the sum of n Bernoulli random variables, and so the mean of a $B(n, p)$ random variable is np. Given that a $B(1, p)$ variable has variance $p(1 - p)$, the variance of a $B(n, p)$ random variable is n times that value, or $np(1 - p)$, assuming that all the trials (Bernoulli random variables) are independent. We can illustrate the calculation for two binomial random variables with differing probabilities as follows:

Random Variable	Mean	Variance
$B(n = 5, p = 0.50)$	$2.50 = 5(0.50)$	$1.25 = 5(0.50)(0.50)$
$B(n = 5, p = 0.10)$	$0.50 = 5(0.10)$	$0.45 = 5(0.10)(0.90)$

For a $B(n = 5, p = 0.50)$ random variable, the expected number of successes is 2.5 with a standard deviation of $1.118 = (1.25)^{1/2}$; for a $B(n = 5, p = 0.10)$ random variable, the expected number of successes is 0.50 with a standard deviation of $0.67 = (0.45)^{1/2}$.

Example 6

The Expected Number of Defaults in a Bond Portfolio

Suppose as a bond analyst you are asked to estimate the number of bond issues expected to default over the next year in an unmanaged high-yield bond portfolio with 25 U.S. issues from distinct issuers. The credit ratings of the bonds in the portfolio are tightly clustered around Moody's B2/Standard & Poor's B, meaning that the bonds are speculative with respect to the capacity to pay interest and repay principal. The estimated annual default rate for B2/B rated bonds is 10.7 percent.

1. Over the next year, what is the expected number of defaults in the portfolio, assuming a **binomial model** for defaults?

2. Estimate the standard deviation of the number of defaults over the coming year.

3. Critique the use of the binomial probability model in this context.

Solution to 1:

For each bond, we can define a Bernoulli random variable equal to 1 if the bond defaults during the year and zero otherwise. With 25 bonds, the expected number of defaults over the year is $np = 25(0.107) = 2.675$ or approximately 3.

Solution to 2:

The variance is $np(1 - p) = 25(0.107)(0.893) = 2.388775$. The standard deviation is $(2.388775)^{1/2} = 1.55$. Thus a two standard deviation confidence interval about the expected number of defaults would run from approximately 0 to approximately 6, for example.

---

10 We can show that $p(1 - p)$ is the variance of a Bernoulli random variable as follows, noting that a Bernoulli random variable can take on only one of two values, 1 or 0: $\sigma^2(Y) = E[(Y - EY)^2] = E[(Y - p)^2] = (1 - p)^2 p + (0 - p)^2 (1 - p) = (1 - p)[(1 - p)p + p^2] = p(1 - p)$.

Solution to 3:

An assumption of the binomial model is that the trials are independent. In this context, a trial relates to whether an individual bond issue will default over the next year. Because the issuing companies probably share exposure to common economic factors, the trials may not be independent. Nevertheless, for a quick estimate of the expected number of defaults, the binomial model may be adequate.

Earlier, we looked at a simple one-period model for stock price movement. Now we extend the model to describe stock price movement on three consecutive days. Each day is an independent trial. The stock moves up with constant probability p (the **up transition probability**); if it moves up, u is 1 plus the rate of return for an up move. The stock moves down with constant probability $1 - p$ (the **down transition probability**); if it moves down, d is 1 plus the rate of return for a down move. We graph stock price movement in Figure 2, where we now associate each of the $n = 3$ stock price moves with time indexed by t. The shape of the graph suggests why it is a called a **binomial tree**. Each boxed value from which successive moves or outcomes branch in the tree is called a **node**; in this example, a node is potential value for the stock price at a specified time.

Figure 2	A Binomial Model of Stock Price Movement

We see from the tree that the stock price at $t = 3$ has four possible values: $uuuS$, $uudS$, $uddS$, and $dddS$. The probability that the stock price equals *any* one of these four values is given by the binomial distribution. For example, three sequences of moves result in a final stock price of $uudS$: These are uud, udu, and duu. These sequences have two up moves out of three moves in total; the combination formula confirms that the number of ways to get two up moves (successes) in three periods (trials) is $3!/(3 - 2)!2! = 3$. Next note that each of these sequences, uud, udu, and duu, has probability $p^2(1 - p)$. So $P(S_3 = uudS) = 3p^2(1 - p)$, where S_3 indicates the stock's price after three moves.

The binomial random variable in this application is the number of up moves. Final stock price distribution is a function of the initial stock price, the *number* of up moves, and the *size* of the up moves and down moves. We cannot say that stock price itself is a binomial random variable; rather, it is a function of a binomial random variable, as well as of u and d, and initial price. This richness is actually one key to why this way of modeling stock price is useful: It allows us to choose values of these parameters to approximate various distributions for stock price (using a large number of time periods).[11] One distribution that can be approximated is the lognormal, an important continuous distribution model for stock price that we will discuss later. The flexibility extends further. In the tree shown above, the transition probabilities are the same at each node: p for an up move and $1 - p$ for a down move. That standard formula describes a process in which stock return volatility is constant through time. Option experts, however, sometimes model changing volatility through time using a binomial tree in which the probabilities for up and down moves differ at different nodes.

The binomial tree also supplies the possibility of testing a condition or contingency at any node. This flexibility is useful in investment applications such as option pricing. Consider an American call option on a dividend-paying stock. (Recall that an American option can be exercised at any time before expiration, at any node on the tree.) Just before an ex-dividend date, it may be optimal to exercise an American call option on stock to buy the stock and receive the dividend.[12] If we model stock price with a binomial tree, we can test, at each node, whether exercising the option is optimal. Also, if we know the value of the call at the four terminal nodes at $t = 3$ and we have a model for discounting values by one period, we can step backward one period to $t = 2$ to find the call's value at the three nodes there. Continuing back recursively, we can find the call's value today. This type of recursive operation is easily programmed on a computer. As a result, binomial trees can value options even more complex than American calls on stock.[13]

CONTINUOUS RANDOM VARIABLES

3

In the previous section, we considered discrete random variables (i.e., random variables whose set of possible outcomes is countable). In contrast, the possible outcomes of continuous random variables are never countable. If 1.250 is one possible value of a continuous random variable, for example, we cannot name the next higher or lower possible value. Technically, the range of possible outcomes of a continuous random variable is the real line (all real numbers between $-\infty$ and $+\infty$) or some subset of the real line.

In this section, we focus on the two most important continuous distributions in investment work, the normal and lognormal. As we did with discrete distributions, we introduce the topic through the uniform distribution.

3.1 Continuous Uniform Distribution

The continuous uniform distribution is the simplest continuous probability distribution. The uniform distribution has two main uses. As the basis of techniques for generating random numbers, the uniform distribution plays a role in Monte Carlo simulation. As the probability distribution that describes equally likely outcomes, the uniform distribution is an appropriate probability model to represent a particular kind of uncertainty in beliefs in which all outcomes appear equally likely.

---

11 For example, we can split 20 days into 100 subperiods, taking care to use compatible values for u and d.
12 Cash dividends represent a reduction of a company's assets. Early exercise may be optimal because the exercise price of options is typically not reduced by the amount of cash dividends, so cash dividends negatively affect the position of an American call option holder.
13 See Chance (2003) for more information on option pricing models.

The pdf for a uniform random variable is

$$f(x) = \begin{cases} \dfrac{1}{b-a} & \text{for } a < x < b \\ 0 & \text{otherwise} \end{cases}$$

For example, with $a = 0$ and $b = 8$, $f(x) = 1/8$ or 0.125. We graph this density in Figure 3.

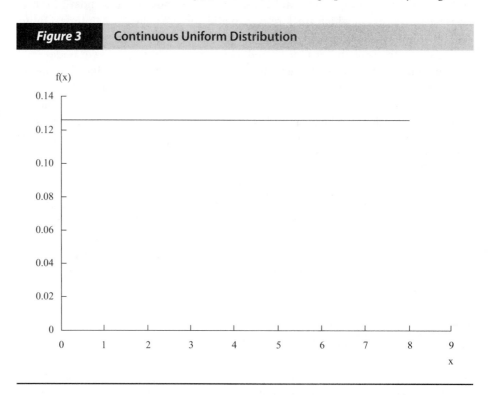

Figure 3   Continuous Uniform Distribution

The graph of the density function plots as a horizontal line with a value of 0.125.

What is the probability that a uniform random variable with limits $a = 0$ and $b = 8$ is less than or equal to 3, or $F(3) = P(X \leq 3)$? When we were working with the discrete uniform random variable with possible outcomes 1, 2, ..., 8, we summed individual probabilities: $p(1) + p(2) + p(3) = 0.375$. In contrast, the probability that a continuous uniform random variable, or any continuous random variable, assumes any given fixed value is 0. To illustrate this point, consider the narrow interval 2.510 to 2.511. Because that interval holds an infinity of possible values, the sum of the probabilities of values in that interval alone would be infinite if each individual value in it had a positive probability. To find the probability $F(3)$, we find the area under the curve graphing the pdf, between 0 to 3 on the x axis. In calculus, this operation is called integrating the probability function $f(x)$ from 0 to 3. This area under the curve is a rectangle with base $3 - 0 = 3$ and height 1/8. The area of this rectangle equals base times height: $3(1/8) = 3/8$ or 0.375. So $F(3) = 3/8$ or 0.375.

The interval from 0 to 3 is three-eighths of the total length between the limits of 0 and 8, and $F(3)$ is three-eighths of the total probability of 1. The middle line of the expression for the cdf captures this relationship.

$$F(x) = \begin{cases} 0 & \text{for } x \leq a \\ \dfrac{x-a}{b-a} & \text{for } a < x < b \\ 1 & \text{for } x \geq b \end{cases}$$

For our problem, $F(x) = 0$ for $x \leq 0$, $F(x) = x/8$ for $0 < x < 8$, and $F(x) = 1$ for $x \geq 8$. We graph this cdf in Figure 4.

Figure 4   Continuous Uniform Cumulative Distribution

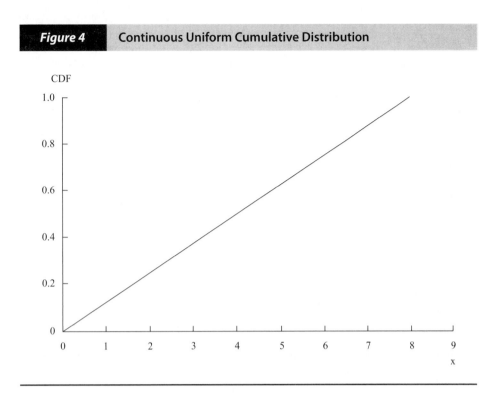

The mathematical operation that corresponds to finding the area under the curve of a pdf $f(x)$ from a to b is the integral of $f(x)$ from a to b:

$$P(a \le X \le b) = \int_a^b f(x)\,dx \tag{2}$$

where $\int dx$ is the symbol for summing $\int$ over small changes dx, and the limits of integration (a and b) can be any real numbers or $-\infty$ and $+\infty$. All probabilities of continuous random variables can be computed using Equation 2. For the uniform distribution example considered above, $F(7)$ is Equation 2 with lower limit $a = 0$ and upper limit $b = 7$. The integral corresponding to the cdf of a uniform distribution reduces to the three-line expression given previously. To evaluate Equation 2 for nearly all other continuous distributions, including the normal and lognormal, we rely on spreadsheet functions, computer programs, or tables of values to calculate probabilities. Those tools use various numerical methods to evaluate the integral in Equation 2.

Recall that the probability of a continuous random variable equaling any fixed point is 0. This fact has an important consequence for working with the cumulative distribution function of a continuous random variable: For any continuous random variable X, $P(a \le X \le b) = P(a < X \le b) = P(a \le X < b) = P(a < X < b)$, because the probabilities at the endpoints a and b are 0. For discrete random variables, these relations of equality are not true, because probability accumulates at points.

Example 7

Probability That a Lending Facility Covenant Is Breached

You are evaluating the bonds of a below-investment-grade borrower at a low point in its business cycle. You have many factors to consider, including the terms of the company's bank lending facilities. The contract creating a bank lending facility such as an unsecured line of credit typically has clauses known as covenants. These covenants place restrictions on what the borrower can do. The company will be in breach of a covenant in the lending facility if the interest coverage ratio, EBITDA/interest, calculated on EBITDA over the four trailing quarters, falls below 2.0. EBITDA is earnings before interest, taxes, depreciation, and amortization.[14] Compliance with the covenants will be checked at the end of the current quarter. If the covenant is breached, the bank can demand immediate repayment of all borrowings on the facility. That action would probably trigger a liquidity crisis for the company. With a high degree of confidence, you forecast interest charges of $25 million. Your estimate of EBITDA runs from $40 million on the low end to $60 million on the high end.

Address two questions (treating projected interest charges as a constant):

1. If the outcomes for EBITDA are equally likely, what is the probability that EBITDA/interest will fall below 2.0, breaching the covenant?

2. Estimate the mean and standard deviation of EBITDA/interest. For a continuous uniform random variable, the mean is given by $\mu = (a + b)/2$ and the variance is given by $\sigma^2 = (b - a)^2/12$.

Solution to 1:

EBITDA/interest is a continuous uniform random variable because all outcomes are equally likely. The ratio can take on values between 1.6 = ($40 million)/($25 million) on the low end and 2.4 = ($60 million/$25 million) on the high end. The range of possible values is 2.4 − 1.6 = 0.8. What fraction of the possible values falls below 2.0, the level that triggers default? The distance between 2.0 and 1.6 is 0.40; the value 0.40 is one-half the total length of 0.8, or 0.4/0.8 = 0.50. So the probability that the covenant will be breached is 50 percent.

Solution to 2:

In Solution 1, we found that the lower limit of EBITDA/interest is 1.6. This lower limit is a. We found that the upper limit is 2.4. This upper limit is b. Using the formula given above,

$$\mu = (a + b)/2 = (1.6 + 2.4)/2 = 2.0$$

The variance of the interest coverage ratio is

$$\sigma^2 = (b - a)^2/12 = (2.4 - 1.6)^2/12 = 0.053333$$

The standard deviation is the positive square root of the variance, 0.230940 = $(0.053333)^{1/2}$. The standard deviation is not particularly useful as a risk measure for a uniform distribution, however. The probability that lies within various standard deviation bands around the mean is sensitive to different specifications of the upper and lower limits (although Chebyshev's inequality is always satisfied).[15] Here, a one standard deviation interval around the mean of 2.0 runs from 1.769 to 2.231 and captures 0.462/0.80 = 0.5775 or 57.8 percent of the probability. A two standard deviation interval runs from 1.538 to 2.462, which extends past both the lower and upper limits of the random variable.

---

14 For a detailed discussion on the use and misuse of EBITDA, see Moody's Investors Service Global Credit Research, *Putting EBITDA in Perspective* (June 2000).

15 Chebyshev's inequality is discussed in the reading on statistical concepts and market returns.

3.2 The Normal Distribution

The normal distribution may be the most extensively used probability distribution in quantitative work. It plays key roles in modern portfolio theory and in a number of risk management technologies. Because it has so many uses, the normal distribution must be thoroughly understood by investment professionals.

The role of the normal distribution in statistical inference and regression analysis is vastly extended by a crucial result known as the central limit theorem. The central limit theorem states that the sum (and mean) of a large number of independent random variables is approximately normally distributed.[16]

The French mathematician Abraham de Moivre (1667–1754) introduced the normal distribution in 1733 in developing a version of the central limit theorem. As Figure 5 shows, the normal distribution is symmetrical and bell-shaped. The range of possible outcomes of the normal distribution is the entire real line: all real numbers lying between $-\infty$ and $+\infty$. The tails of the bell curve extend without limit to the left and to the right.

Figure 5	Two Normal Distributions

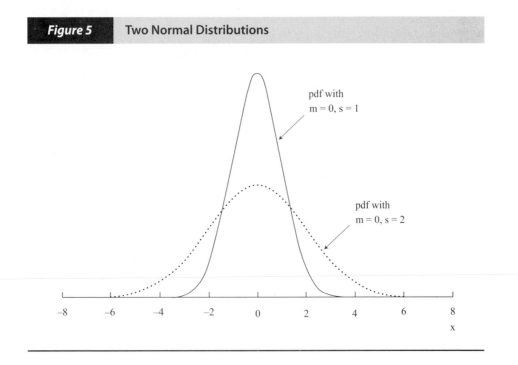

The defining characteristics of a normal distribution are as follows:

- The normal distribution is completely described by two parameters—its mean, μ, and variance, σ^2. We indicate this as $X \sim N(\mu, \sigma^2)$ (read "X follows a normal distribution with mean μ and variance σ^2"). We can also define a normal distribution in terms of the mean and the standard deviation, σ (this is often convenient because σ is measured in the same units as X and μ). As a consequence, we can answer any probability question about a normal random variable if we know its mean and variance (or standard deviation).

---

16 The central limit theorem is discussed further in the reading on sampling.

■ The normal distribution has a skewness of 0 (it is symmetric). The normal distribution has a kurtosis (measure of peakedness) of 3; its excess kurtosis (kurtosis – 3.0) equals 0.[17] As a consequence of symmetry, the mean, median, and the mode are all equal for a normal random variable.

■ A linear combination of two or more normal random variables is also normally distributed.

These bullet points concern a single variable or univariate normal distribution: the distribution of one normal random variable. A **univariate distribution** describes a single random variable. A **multivariate distribution** specifies the probabilities for a group of related random variables. You will encounter the **multivariate normal distribution** in investment work and reading and should know the following about it.

When we have a group of assets, we can model the distribution of returns on each asset individually, or the distribution of returns on the assets as a group. "As a group" means that we take account of all the statistical interrelationships among the return series. One model that has often been used for security returns is the multivariate normal distribution. A multivariate normal distribution for the returns on n stocks is completely defined by three lists of parameters:

■ the list of the mean returns on the individual securities (n means in total);

■ the list of the securities' variances of return (n variances in total); and

■ the list of all the distinct pairwise return correlations: $n(n-1)/2$ distinct correlations in total.[18]

The need to specify correlations is a distinguishing feature of the multivariate normal distribution in contrast to the univariate normal distribution.

The statement "assume returns are normally distributed" is sometimes used to mean a joint normal distribution. For a portfolio of 30 securities, for example, portfolio return is a weighted average of the returns on the 30 securities. A weighted average is a linear combination. Thus, portfolio return is normally distributed if the individual security returns are (joint) normally distributed. To review, in order to specify the normal distribution for portfolio return, we need the means, variances, and the distinct pairwise correlations of the component securities.

With these concepts in mind, we can return to the normal distribution for one random variable. The curves graphed in Figure 5 are the normal density function:

$$f(x) = \frac{1}{\sigma\sqrt{2\pi}} \exp\left(\frac{-(x-\mu)^2}{2\sigma^2}\right) \text{ for } -\infty < x < +\infty \tag{3}$$

The two densities graphed in Figure 5 correspond to a mean of $\mu = 0$ and standard deviations of $\sigma = 1$ and $\sigma = 2$. The normal density with $\mu = 0$ and $\sigma = 1$ is called the **standard normal distribution** (or **unit normal distribution**). Plotting two normal distributions with the same mean and different standard deviations helps us appreciate why standard deviation is a good measure of dispersion for the normal distribution: Observations are much more concentrated around the mean for the normal distribution with $\sigma = 1$ than for the normal distribution with $\sigma = 2$.

---

17 If we have a sample of size n from a normal distribution, we may want to know the possible variation in sample skewness and kurtosis. For a normal random variable, the standard deviation of sample skewness is $6/n$ and the standard deviation of sample kurtosis is $24/n$.

18 For example, a distribution with two stocks (a bivariate normal distribution) has two means, two variances, and one correlation: $2(2-1)/2$. A distribution with 30 stocks has 30 means, 30 variances, and 435 distinct correlations: $30(30-1)/2$. The return correlation of Dow Chemical with American Express stock is the same as the correlation of American Express with Dow Chemical stock, so these are counted as one distinct correlation.

Although not literally accurate, the normal distribution can be considered an approximate model for returns. Nearly all the probability of a normal random variable is contained within three standard deviations of the mean. For realistic values of mean return and return standard deviation for many assets, the normal probability of outcomes below –100 percent is very small. Whether the approximation is useful in a given application is an empirical question. For example, the normal distribution is a closer fit for quarterly and yearly holding period returns on a diversified equity portfolio than it is for daily or weekly returns.[19] A persistent departure from normality in most equity return series is kurtosis greater than 3, the fat-tails problem. So when we approximate equity return distributions with the normal distribution, we should be aware that the normal distribution tends to underestimate the probability of extreme returns.[20] Option returns are skewed. Because the normal is a symmetrical distribution, we should be cautious in using the normal distribution to model the returns on portfolios containing significant positions in options.

The normal distribution, however, is less suitable as a model for asset prices than as a model for returns. A normal random variable has no lower limit. This characteristic has several implications for investment applications. An asset price can drop only to 0, at which point the asset becomes worthless. As a result, practitioners generally do not use the normal distribution to model the distribution of asset prices. Also note that moving from any level of asset price to 0 translates into a return of –100 percent. Because the normal distribution extends below 0 without limit, it cannot be literally accurate as a model for asset returns.

Having established that the normal distribution is the appropriate model for a variable of interest, we can use it to make the following probability statements:

- Approximately 50 percent of all observations fall in the interval $\mu \pm (2/3)\,\sigma$.

- Approximately 68 percent of all observations fall in the interval $\mu \pm \sigma$.

- Approximately 95 percent of all observations fall in the interval $\mu \pm 2\sigma$.

- Approximately 99 percent of all observations fall in the interval $\mu \pm 3\sigma$.

One, two, and three standard deviation intervals are illustrated in Figure 6. The intervals indicated are easy to remember but are only approximate for the stated probabilities. More-precise intervals are $\mu \pm 1.96\sigma$ for 95 percent of the observations and $\mu \pm 2.58\sigma$ for 99 percent of the observations.

Figure 6	Units of Standard Deviation

---

[19] See Fama (1976) and Campbell, Lo, and MacKinlay (1997).
[20] Fat tails can be modeled by a mixture of normal random variables or by a Student's t-distribution with a relatively small number of degrees of freedom. See Kon (1984) and Campbell, Lo, and MacKinlay (1997). We discuss the Student's t-distribution in the reading on sampling and estimation.

In general, we do not observe the population mean or the population standard deviation of a distribution, so we need to estimate them.[21] We estimate the population mean, μ, using the sample mean, $\bar{X}$ (sometimes denoted as $\hat{\mu}$), and estimate the population standard deviation, σ, using the sample standard deviation, s (sometimes denoted as $\hat{\sigma}$).

There are as many different normal distributions as there are choices for mean (μ) and variance (σ^2). We can answer all of the above questions in terms of any normal distribution. Spreadsheets, for example, have functions for the normal cdf for any specification of mean and variance. For the sake of efficiency, however, we would like to refer all probability statements to a single normal distribution. The standard normal distribution (the normal distribution with μ = 0 and σ = 1) fills that role.

There are two steps in **standardizing** a random variable X: Subtract the mean of X from X, then divide that result by the standard deviation of X. If we have a list of observations on a normal random variable, X, we subtract the mean from each observation to get a list of deviations from the mean, then divide each deviation by the standard deviation. The result is the standard normal random variable, Z. (Z is the conventional symbol for a standard normal random variable.) If we have $X \sim N(\mu, \sigma^2)$ (read "X follows the normal distribution with parameters μ and σ^2"), we standardize it using the formula

$$Z = (X - \mu)/\sigma \tag{4}$$

Suppose we have a normal random variable, X, with μ = 5 and σ = 1.5. We standardize X with Z = (X − 5)/1.5. For example, a value X = 9.5 corresponds to a standardized value of 3, calculated as Z = (9.5 − 5)/1.5 = 3. The probability that we will observe a value as small as or smaller than 9.5 for $X \sim N(5, 1.5)$ is exactly the same as the probability that we will observe a value as small as or smaller than 3 for $Z \sim N(0, 1)$. We can answer all probability questions about X using standardized values and probability tables for Z. We generally do not know the population mean and standard deviation, so we often use the sample mean $\bar{X}$ for μ and the sample standard deviation s for σ.

Standard normal probabilities can also be computed with spreadsheets, statistical and econometric software, and programming languages. Tables of the cumulative distribution function for the standard normal random variable are in the back of this book. Table 5 shows an excerpt from those tables. N(x) is a conventional notation for the cdf of a standard normal variable.[22]

Table 5	$P(Z \le x) = N(x)$ for $x \ge 0$ or $P(Z \le z) = N(z)$ for $z \ge 0$								
x or z	0	0.01	0.02	0.03	0.04	0.05	0.06	0.07	0.08	0.09
0.00	0.5000	0.5040	0.5080	0.5120	0.5160	0.5199	0.5239	0.5279	0.5319	0.5359
0.10	0.5398	0.5438	0.5478	0.5517	0.5557	0.5596	0.5636	0.5675	0.5714	0.5753
0.20	0.5793	0.5832	0.5871	0.5910	0.5948	0.5987	0.6026	0.6064	0.6103	0.6141
0.30	0.6179	0.6217	0.6255	0.6293	0.6331	0.6368	0.6406	0.6443	0.6480	0.6517
0.40	0.6554	0.6591	0.6628	0.6664	0.6700	0.6736	0.6772	0.6808	0.6844	0.6879
0.50	0.6915	0.6950	0.6985	0.7019	0.7054	0.7088	0.7123	0.7157	0.7190	0.7224

---

21 A population is all members of a specified group, and the population mean is the arithmetic mean computed for the population. A sample is a subset of a population, and the sample mean is the arithmetic mean computed for the sample. For more information on these concepts, see the reading on statistical concepts and market returns.

22 Another often-seen notation for the cdf of a standard normal variable is $\Phi(x)$.

To find the probability that a standard normal variable is less than or equal to 0.24, for example, locate the row that contains 0.20, look at the 0.04 column, and find the entry 0.5948. Thus, $P(Z \leq 0.24) = 0.5948$ or 59.48 percent.

The following are some of the most frequently referenced values in the standard normal table:

- The 90th percentile point is 1.282: $P(Z \leq 1.282) = N(1.282) = 0.90$ or 90 percent, and 10 percent of values remain in the right tail.

- The 95th percentile point is 1.65: $P(Z \leq 1.65) = N(1.65) = 0.95$ or 95 percent, and 5 percent of values remain in the right tail. Note the difference between the use of a percentile point when dealing with one tail rather than two tails. Earlier, we used 1.65 standard deviations for the 90 percent confidence interval, where 5 percent of values lie outside that interval on each of the two sides. Here we use 1.65 because we are concerned with the 5 percent of values that lie only on one side, the right tail.

- The 99th percentile point is 2.327: $P(Z \leq 2.327) = N(2.327) = 0.99$ or 99 percent, and 1 percent of values remain in the right tail.

The tables that we give for the normal cdf include probabilities for $x \leq 0$. Many sources, however, give tables only for $x \geq 0$. How would one use such tables to find a normal probability? Because of the symmetry of the normal distribution, we can find all probabilities using tables of the cdf of the standard normal random variable, $P(Z \leq x) = N(x)$, for $x \geq 0$. The relations below are helpful for using tables for $x \geq 0$, as well as in other uses:

- For a non-negative number x, use $N(x)$ from the table. Note that for the probability to the right of x, we have $P(Z \geq x) = 1.0 - N(x)$.

- For a negative number $-x$, $N(-x) = 1.0 - N(x)$: Find $N(x)$ and subtract it from 1. All the area under the normal curve to the left of x is $N(x)$. The balance, $1.0 - N(x)$, is the area and probability to the right of x. By the symmetry of the normal distribution around its mean, the area and the probability to the right of x are equal to the area and the probability to the left of $-x$, $N(-x)$.

- For the probability to the right of $-x$, $P(Z \geq -x) = N(x)$.

Example 8

Probabilities for a Common Stock Portfolio

Assume the portfolio mean return is 12 percent and the standard deviation of return estimate is 22 percent per year.

You want to calculate the following probabilities, assuming that a normal distribution describes returns. (You can use the excerpt from the table of normal probabilities to answer these questions.)

1. What is the probability that portfolio return will exceed 20 percent?

2. What is the probability that portfolio return will be between 12 percent and 20 percent? In other words, what is $P(12\% \leq \text{Portfolio return} \leq 20\%)$?

3. You can buy a one-year T-bill that yields 5.5 percent. This yield is effectively a one-year risk-free interest rate. What is the probability that your portfolio's return will be equal to or less than the risk-free rate?

If X is portfolio return, standardized portfolio return is $Z = (X - \bar{X})/s = (X - 12\%)/22\%$. We use this expression throughout the solutions.

Solution to 1:

For $X = 20\%$, $Z = (20\% - 12\%)/22\% = 0.363636$. You want to find $P(Z > 0.363636)$. First note that $P(Z > x) = P(Z \geq x)$ because the normal is a continuous distribution. Recall that $P(Z \geq x) = 1.0 - P(Z \leq x)$ or $1 - N(x)$. Rounding 0.363636 to 0.36, according to the table, $N(0.36) = 0.6406$. Thus, $1 - 0.6406 = 0.3594$. The probability that portfolio return will exceed 20 percent is about 36 percent if your normality assumption is accurate.

Solution to 2:

$P(12\% \leq \text{Portfolio return} \leq 20\%) = N(Z \text{ corresponding to } 20\%) - N(Z \text{ corresponding to } 12\%)$. For the first term, $Z = (20\% - 12\%)/22\% = 0.36$ approximately, and $N(0.36) = 0.6406$ (as in Solution 1). To get the second term immediately, note that 12 percent is the mean, and for the normal distribution 50 percent of the probability lies on either side of the mean. Therefore, $N(Z \text{ corresponding to } 12\%)$ must equal 50 percent. So $P(12\% \leq \text{Portfolio return} \leq 20\%) = 0.6406 - 0.50 = 0.1406$ or approximately 14 percent.

Solution to 3:

If X is portfolio return, then we want to find $P(\text{Portfolio return} \leq 5.5\%)$. This question is more challenging than Parts 1 or 2, but when you have studied the solution below you will have a useful pattern for calculating other shortfall probabilities.

There are three steps, which involve standardizing the portfolio return: First, subtract the portfolio mean return from each side of the inequality: $P(\text{Portfolio return} - 12\% \leq 5.5\% - 12\%)$. Second, divide each side of the inequality by the standard deviation of portfolio return: $P[(\text{Portfolio return} - 12\%)/22\% \leq (5.5\% - 12\%)/22\%] = P(Z \leq -0.295455) = N(-0.295455)$. Third, recognize that on the left-hand side we have a standard normal variable, denoted by Z. As we pointed out above, $N(-x) = 1 - N(x)$. Rounding -0.29545 to -0.30 for use with the excerpted table, we have $N(-0.30) = 1 - N(0.30) = 1 - 0.6179 = 0.3821$, roughly 38 percent. The probability that your portfolio will underperform the one-year risk-free rate is about 38 percent.

We can get the answer above quickly by subtracting the mean portfolio return from 5.5 percent, dividing by the standard deviation of portfolio return, and evaluating the result (-0.295455) with the standard normal cdf.

3.3 Applications of the Normal Distribution

Modern portfolio theory (MPT) makes wide use of the idea that the value of investment opportunities can be meaningfully measured in terms of mean return and variance of return. In economic theory, **mean–variance analysis** holds exactly when investors are risk averse; when they choose investments so as to maximize expected utility, or satisfaction; and when either 1) returns are normally distributed, or 2) investors have quadratic utility functions.[23] Mean–variance analysis can still be useful, however—that is, it can hold approximately—when either assumption 1 or 2 is violated. Because practitioners prefer to work with observables such as returns, the proposition that returns are at least approximately normally distributed has played a key role in much of MPT.

Mean–variance analysis generally considers risk symmetrically in the sense that standard deviation captures variability both above and below the mean.[24] An alternative

---

23 Utility functions are mathematical representations of attitudes toward risk and return.
24 We shall discuss mean–variance analysis in detail in the readings on portfolio concepts.

approach evaluates only downside risk. We discuss one such approach, safety-first rules, as it provides an excellent illustration of the application of normal distribution theory to practical investment problems. **Safety-first rules** focus on **shortfall risk**, the risk that portfolio value will fall below some minimum acceptable level over some time horizon. The risk that the assets in a defined benefit plan will fall below plan liabilities is an example of a shortfall risk.

Suppose an investor views any return below a level of R_L as unacceptable. Roy's safety-first criterion states that the optimal portfolio minimizes the probability that portfolio return, R_p, falls below the threshold level, R_L.[25] In symbols, the investor's objective is to choose a portfolio that minimizes $P(R_p < R_L)$. When portfolio returns are normally distributed, we can calculate $P(R_p < R_L)$ using the number of standard deviations that R_L lies below the expected portfolio return, $E(R_p)$. The portfolio for which $E(R_p) - R_L$ is largest relative to standard deviation minimizes $P(R_p < R_L)$. Therefore, if returns are normally distributed, the safety-first optimal portfolio *maximizes* the safety-first ratio (SFRatio):

$$\text{SFRatio} = \left[E(R_p) - R_L \right] / \sigma_P$$

The quantity $E(R_p) - R_L$ is the distance from the mean return to the shortfall level. Dividing this distance by σ_P gives the distance in units of standard deviation. There are two steps in choosing among portfolios using Roy's criterion (assuming normality):[26]

1. Calculate each portfolio's SFRatio.

2. Choose the portfolio with the highest SFRatio.

For a portfolio with a given safety-first ratio, the probability that its return will be less than R_L is $N(-\text{SFRatio})$, and the safety-first optimal portfolio has the lowest such probability. For example, suppose an investor's threshold return, R_L, is 2 percent. He is presented with two portfolios. Portfolio 1 has an expected return of 12 percent with a standard deviation of 15 percent. Portfolio 2 has an expected return of 14 percent with a standard deviation of 16 percent. The SFRatios are $0.667 = (12 - 2)/15$ and $0.75 = (14 - 2)/16$ for Portfolios 1 and 2, respectively. For the superior Portfolio 2, the probability that portfolio return will be less than 2 percent is $N(-0.75) = 1 - N(0.75) = 1 - 0.7734 = 0.227$ or about 23 percent, assuming that portfolio returns are normally distributed.

You may have noticed the similarity of SFRatio to the Sharpe ratio. If we substitute the risk-free rate, R_F, for the critical level R_L, the SFRatio becomes the Sharpe ratio. The safety-first approach provides a new perspective on the Sharpe ratio: When we evaluate portfolios using the Sharpe ratio, the portfolio with the highest Sharpe ratio is the one that minimizes the probability that portfolio return will be less than the risk-free rate (given a normality assumption).

Example 9

The Safety-First Optimal Portfolio for a Client

You are researching asset allocations for a client with an $800,000 portfolio. Although her investment objective is long-term growth, at the end of a year she may want to liquidate $30,000 of the portfolio to fund educational expenses. If that need arises, she would like to be able to take out the $30,000 without invading the initial capital of $800,000. Table 6 shows three alternative allocations.

---

25 A.D. Roy (1952) introduced this criterion.
26 If there is an asset offering a risk-free return over the time horizon being considered, and if R_L is less than or equal to that risk-free rate, then it is optimal to be fully invested in the risk-free asset. Holding the risk-free asset in this case eliminates the chance that the threshold return is not met.

Table 6	Mean and Standard Deviation for Three Allocations (in Percent)		
	A	B	C
Expected annual return	25	11	14
Standard deviation of return	27	8	20

Address these questions (assume normality for Parts 2 and 3):

1. Given the client's desire not to invade the $800,000 principal, what is the shortfall level, R_L? Use this shortfall level to answer Part 2.
2. According to the safety-first criterion, which of the three allocations is the best?
3. What is the probability that the return on the safety-first optimal portfolio will be less than the shortfall level?

Solution to 1:

Because $30,000/$800,000 is 3.75 percent, for any return less than 3.75 percent the client will need to invade principal if she takes out $30,000. So R_L = 3.75 percent.

Solution to 2:

To decide which of the three allocations is safety-first optimal, select the alternative with the highest ratio $[E(R_p) - R_L]/\sigma_p$:

Allocation A: $0.787037 = (25 - 3.75)/27$

Allocation B: $0.90625 = (11 - 3.75)/8$

Allocation C: $0.5125 = (14 - 3.75)/20$

Allocation B, with the largest ratio (0.90625), is the best alternative according to the safety-first criterion.

Solution to 3:

To answer this question, note that $P(R_B < 3.75) = N(-0.90625)$. We can round 0.90625 to 0.91 for use with tables of the standard normal cdf. First, we calculate $N(-0.91) = 1 - N(0.91) = 1 - 0.8186 = 0.1814$ or about 18.1 percent. Using a spreadsheet function for the standard normal cdf on −0.90625 without rounding, we get 18.24 percent or about 18.2 percent. The safety-first optimal portfolio has a roughly 18 percent chance of not meeting a 3.75 percent return threshold.

Several points are worth noting. First, if the inputs were even slightly different, we could get a different ranking. For example, if the mean return on B were 10 rather than 11 percent, A would be superior to B. Second, if meeting the 3.75 percent return threshold were a necessity rather than a wish, $830,000 in one year could be modeled as a liability. Fixed income strategies such as cash flow matching could be used to offset or immunize the $830,000 quasi-liability.

Roy's safety-first rule was the earliest approach to addressing shortfall risk. The standard mean-variance portfolio selection process can also accommodate a shortfall risk constraint.[27]

---

[27] See Leibowitz and Henriksson (1989), for example.

In many investment contexts besides Roy's safety-first criterion, we use the normal distribution to estimate a probability. For example, Kolb, Gay, and Hunter (1985) developed an expression based on the standard normal distribution for the probability that a futures trader will exhaust his liquidity because of losses in a futures contract. Another arena in which the normal distribution plays an important role is financial risk management. Financial institutions such as investment banks, security dealers, and commercial banks have formal systems to measure and control financial risk at various levels, from trading positions to the overall risk for the firm.[28] Two mainstays in managing financial risk are Value at Risk (VAR) and stress testing/scenario analysis. **Stress testing/scenario analysis**, a complement to VAR, refers to a set of techniques for estimating losses in extremely unfavorable combinations of events or scenarios. **Value at Risk (VAR)** is a money measure of the minimum value of losses expected over a specified time period (for example, a day, a quarter, or a year) at a given level of probability (often 0.05 or 0.01). Suppose we specify a one-day time horizon and a level of probability of 0.05, which would be called a 95 percent one-day VAR.[29] If this VAR equaled €5 million for a portfolio, there would be a 0.05 probability that the portfolio would lose €5 million or more in a single day (assuming our assumptions were correct). One of the basic approaches to estimating VAR, the variance-covariance or analytical method, assumes that returns follow a normal distribution. For more information on VAR, see Chance (2003).

3.4 The Lognormal Distribution

Closely related to the normal distribution, the lognormal distribution is widely used for modeling the probability distribution of share and other asset prices. For example, the lognormal appears in the Black–Scholes–Merton option pricing model. The Black–Scholes–Merton model assumes that the price of the asset underlying the option is lognormally distributed.

A random variable Y follows a lognormal distribution if its natural logarithm, ln Y, is normally distributed. The reverse is also true: If the natural logarithm of random variable Y, ln Y, is normally distributed, then Y follows a lognormal distribution. If you think of the term lognormal as "the log is normal," you will have no trouble remembering this relationship.

The two most noteworthy observations about the lognormal distribution are that it is bounded below by 0 and it is skewed to the right (it has a long right tail). Note these two properties in the graphs of the pdfs of two lognormal distributions in Figure 7. Asset prices are bounded from below by 0. In practice, the lognormal distribution has been found to be a usefully accurate description of the distribution of prices for many financial assets. On the other hand, the normal distribution is often a good approximation for returns. For this reason, both distributions are very important for finance professionals.

---

28 **Financial risk** is risk relating to asset prices and other financial variables. The contrast is to other, non-financial risks (for example, relating to operations and technology), which require different tools to manage.
29 In 95 percent one-day VAR, the 95 percent refers to the confidence in the value of VAR and is equal to 1 – 0.05; this is a traditional way to state VAR.

Figure 7	Two Lognormal Distributions

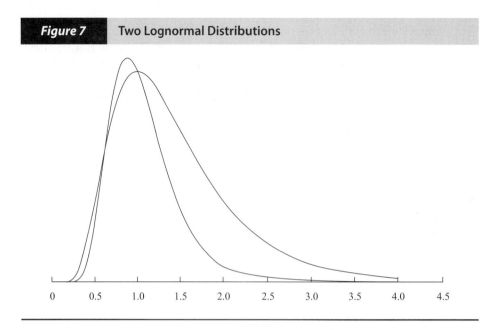

Like the normal distribution, the lognormal distribution is completely described by two parameters. Unlike the other distributions we have considered, a lognormal distribution is defined in terms of the parameters of a *different* distribution. The two parameters of a lognormal distribution are the mean and standard deviation (or variance) of its associated normal distribution: the mean and variance of ln Y, given that Y is lognormal. Remember, we must keep track of two sets of means and standard deviations (or variances): the mean and standard deviation (or variance) of the associated normal distribution (these are the parameters), and the mean and standard deviation (or variance) of the lognormal variable itself.

The expressions for the mean and variance of the lognormal variable itself are challenging. Suppose a normal random variable X has expected value μ and variance σ^2. Define $Y = \exp(X)$. Remember that the operation indicated by $\exp(X)$ or e^X is the opposite operation from taking logs.[30] Because ln Y = ln $[\exp(X)]$ = X is normal (we assume X is normal), Y is lognormal. What is the expected value of $Y = \exp(X)$? A guess might be that the expected value of Y is $\exp(\mu)$. The expected value is actually $\exp(\mu + 0.50\sigma^2)$, which is larger than $\exp(\mu)$ by a factor of $\exp(0.50\sigma^2) > 1$.[31] To get some insight into this concept, think of what happens if we increase σ^2. The distribution spreads out; it can spread upward, but it cannot spread downward past 0. As a result, the center of its distribution is pushed to the right—the distribution's mean increases.[32]

The expressions for the mean and variance of a lognormal variable are summarized below, where μ and σ^2 are the mean and variance of the associated normal distribution (refer to these expressions as needed, rather than memorizing them):

■ Mean (μ_L) of a lognormal random variable = $\exp(\mu + 0.50\sigma^2)$

■ Variance (σ_L^2) of a lognormal random variable = $\exp(2\mu + \sigma^2) \times [\exp(\sigma^2) - 1]$

We now explore the relationship between the distribution of stock return and stock price. In the following we show that if a stock's continuously compounded return is normally distributed, then future stock price is necessarily lognormally distributed.[33]

---

30 The quantity $e \approx 2.7182818$.

31 Note that $\exp(0.50\sigma^2) > 1$ because $\sigma^2 > 0$.

32 Luenberger (1998) is the source of this explanation.

33 Continuous compounding treats time as essentially continuous or unbroken, in contrast to discrete compounding, which treats time as advancing in discrete finite intervals. Continuously compounded returns are the model for returns in so-called **continuous time** finance models such as the Black–Scholes–Merton option pricing model. See the reading on the time value of money for more information on compounding.

Furthermore, we show that stock price may be well described by the lognormal distribution even when continuously compounded returns do not follow a normal distribution. These results provide the theoretical foundation for using the lognormal distribution to model prices.

To outline the presentation that follows, we first show that the stock price at some future time T, S_T, equals the current stock price, S_0, multiplied by e raised to power $r_{0,T}$, the continuously compounded return from 0 to T; this relationship is expressed as $S_T = S_0\exp(r_{0,T})$. We then show that we can write $r_{0,T}$ as the sum of shorter-term continuously compounded returns and that if these shorter-period returns are normally distributed, then $r_{0,T}$ is normally distributed (given certain assumptions) or approximately normally distributed (not making those assumptions). As S_T is proportional to the log of a normal random variable, S_T is lognormal.

To supply a framework for our discussion, suppose we have a series of equally spaced observations on stock price: $S_0, S_1, S_2, ..., S_T$. Current stock price, S_0, is a known quantity and so is nonrandom. The future prices (such as S_1), however, are random variables. The **price relative**, S_1/S_0, is an ending price, S_1, over a beginning price, S_0; it is equal to 1 plus the holding period return on the stock from $t = 0$ to $t = 1$:

$$S_1/S_0 = 1 + R_{0,1}$$

For example, if $S_0 = \$30$ and $S_1 = \$34.50$, then $S_1/S_0 = \$34.50/\$30 = 1.15$. Therefore, $R_{0,1} = 0.15$ or 15 percent. In general, price relatives have the form

$$S_{t+1}/S_t = 1 + R_{t,t+1}$$

where $R_{t,t+1}$ is the rate of return from t to $t + 1$.

An important concept is the continuously compounded return associated with a holding period return such as $R_{0,1}$. The **continuously compounded return** associated with a holding period is the natural logarithm of 1 plus that holding period return, or equivalently, the natural logarithm of the ending price over the beginning price (the price relative).[34] For example, if we observe a one-week holding period return of 0.04, the equivalent continuously compounded return, called the one-week continuously compounded return, is $\ln(1.04) = 0.039221$; €1.00 invested for one week at 0.039221 continuously compounded gives €1.04, equivalent to a 4 percent one-week holding period return. The continuously compounded return from t to $t + 1$ is

$$r_{t,t+1} = \ln(S_{t+1}/S_t) = \ln(1 + R_{t,t+1}) \tag{5}$$

For our example, $r_{0,1} = \ln(S_1/S_0) = \ln(1 + R_{0,1}) = \ln(\$34.50/\$30) = \ln(1.15) = 0.139762$. Thus, 13.98 percent is the continuously compounded return from $t = 0$ to $t = 1$. The continuously compounded return is smaller than the associated holding period return. If our investment horizon extends from $t = 0$ to $t = T$, then the continuously compounded return to T is

$$r_{0,T} = \ln(S_T/S_0)$$

Applying the function exp to both sides of the equation, we have $\exp(r_{0,T}) = \exp[\ln(S_T/S_0)] = S_T/S_0$, so

$$S_T = S_0 \exp(r_{0,T})$$

We can also express S_T/S_0 as the product of price relatives:

$$S_T/S_0 = (S_T/S_{T-1})(S_{T-1}/S_{T-2})...(S_1/S_0)$$

Taking logs of both sides of this equation, we find that continuously compounded return to time T is the sum of the one-period continuously compounded returns:

$$r_{0,T} = r_{T-1,T} + r_{T-2,T-1} + ...r_{0,1} \tag{6}$$

---

34 In this reading we use lowercase r to refer specifically to continuously compounded returns.

Using holding period returns to find the ending value of a $1 investment involves the multiplication of quantities (1 + holding period return). Using continuously compounded returns involves addition.

A key assumption in many investment applications is that returns are **independently and identically distributed (IID)**. Independence captures the proposition that investors cannot predict future returns using past returns (i.e., weak-form market efficiency). Identical distribution captures the assumption of stationarity.[35]

Assume that the one-period continuously compounded returns (such as $r_{0,1}$) are IID random variables with mean μ and variance σ^2 (but making no normality or other distributional assumption). Then

$$E(r_{0,T}) = E(r_{T-1,T}) + E(r_{T-2,T-1}) + \ldots + E(r_{0,1}) = \mu T \qquad (7)$$

(we add up μ for a total of T times) and

$$\sigma^2(r_{0,T}) = \sigma^2 T \qquad (8)$$

(as a consequence of the independence assumption). The variance of the T holding period continuously compounded return is T multiplied by the variance of the one-period continuously compounded return; also, $\sigma(r_{0,T}) = \sigma\sqrt{T}$. If the one-period continuously compounded returns on the right-hand side of Equation 6 are normally distributed, then the T holding period continuously compounded return, $r_{0,T}$, is also normally distributed with mean μT and variance $\sigma^2 T$. This relationship is so because a linear combination of normal random variables is also normal. But even if the one-period continuously compounded returns are not normal, their sum, $r_{0,T}$, is approximately normal according to a result in statistics known as the central limit theorem.[36] Now compare $S_T = S_0 \exp(r_{0,T})$ to $Y = \exp(X)$, where X is normal and Y is lognormal (as we discussed above). Clearly, we can model future stock price S_T as a lognormal random variable because $r_{0,T}$ should be at least approximately normal. This assumption of normally distributed returns is the basis in theory for the lognormal distribution as a model for the distribution of prices of shares and other assets.

Continuously compounded returns play a role in many option pricing models, as mentioned earlier. An estimate of volatility is crucial for using option pricing models such as the Black–Scholes–Merton model. **Volatility** measures the standard deviation of the continuously compounded returns on the underlying asset.[37] In practice, we very often estimate volatility using a historical series of continuously compounded daily returns. We gather a set of daily holding period returns and then use Equation 5 to convert them into continuously compounded daily returns. We then compute the standard deviation of the continuously compounded daily returns and annualize that number using Equation 8.[38] (By convention, volatility is stated as an annualized measure.)[39] Example 10 illustrates the estimation of volatility for the shares of Michelin.

---

35 Stationarity implies that the mean and variance of return do not change from period to period.

36 We mentioned the central limit theorem earlier in our discussion of the normal distribution. To give a somewhat fuller statement of it, according to the central limit theorem the sum (as well as the mean) of a set of independent, identically distributed random variables with finite variances is normally distributed, whatever distribution the random variables follow. We discuss the central limit theorem in the reading on sampling.

37 Volatility is also called the instantaneous standard deviation, and as such is denoted σ. The underlying asset, or simply the underlying, is the asset underlying the option. For more information on these concepts, see Chance (2003).

38 To compute the standard deviation of a set or sample of n returns, we sum the squared deviation of each return from the mean return and then divide that sum by $n - 1$. The result is the sample variance. Taking the square root of the sample variance gives the sample standard deviation. To review the calculation of standard deviation, see the reading on statistical concepts and market returns.

39 Annualizing is often done on the basis of 250 days in a year, the approximate number of days markets are open for trading. The 250-day number may lead to a better estimate of volatility than the 365-day number. Thus if daily volatility were 0.01, we would state volatility (on an annual basis) as $0.01\sqrt{250} = 0.1581$.

Example 10

Volatility as Used in Option Pricing Models

Suppose you are researching Michelin (Euronext: MICP.PA) and are interested in Michelin's price action in a week in which a number of international events affected stock markets. You decide to use volatility as a measure of the variability of Michelin shares during that week. Table 7 shows closing prices during that week.

Table 7	Michelin Daily Closing Prices
Date	**Closing Price (€)**
31 March 2003	25.20
01 April 2003	25.21
02 April 2003	25.52
03 April 2003	26.10
04 April 2003	26.14

Source: http://fr.finance.yahoo.com.

Use the data in Table 7 to do the following:

1. Estimate the volatility of Michelin shares. (Annualize volatility based on 250 days in a year.)

2. Identify the probability distribution for Michelin share prices if continuously compounded daily returns follow the normal distribution.

Solution to 1:

First, use Equation 5 to calculate the continuously compounded daily returns; then find their standard deviation in the usual way. (In the calculation of sample variance to get sample standard deviation, use a divisor of 1 less than the sample size.)

$$\ln(25.21/25.20) = 0.000397, \ln(25.52/25.21) = 0.012222$$
$$\ln(26.10/25.52) = 0.022473, \ln(26.14/26.10) = 0.001531$$
$$\text{Sum} = 0.036623, \text{Mean} = 0.009156, \text{Variance} = 0.000107,$$
$$\text{Standard Deviation} = 0.010354$$

The standard deviation of continuously compounded daily returns is 0.010354. Equation 8 states that $\hat{\sigma}(r_{0,T}) = \hat{\sigma}\sqrt{T}$. In this example, $\hat{\sigma}$ is the sample standard deviation of one-period continuously compounded returns. Thus, $\hat{\sigma}$ refers to 0.010354. We want to annualize, so the horizon T corresponds to one year. As $\hat{\sigma}$ is in days, we set T equal to the number of trading days in a year (250).

We find that annualized volatility for Michelin stock that week was 16.4 percent, calculated as $0.010354\sqrt{250} = 0.163711$.

Note that the sample mean, 0.009156, is a possible estimate of the mean, μ, of the continuously compounded one-period or daily returns. The sample mean can be translated into an estimate of the expected continuously compounded annual return using Equation 7 $\hat{\mu}T = 0.009156(250)$ (using 250 to be consistent

> with the calculation of volatility). But four observations are far too few to estimate expected returns. The variability in the daily returns overwhelms any information about expected return in a series this short.
>
> **Solution to 2:**
>
> Michelin share prices should follow the lognormal distribution if the continuously compounded daily returns on Michelin shares follow the normal distribution.

We have shown that the distribution of stock price is lognormal, given certain assumptions. What are the mean and variance of S_T if S_T follows the lognormal distribution? Earlier in this section, we gave bullet-point expressions for the mean and variance of a lognormal random variable. In the bullet-point expressions, the $\hat{\mu}$ and $\hat{\sigma}^2$ would refer, in the context of this discussion, to the mean and variance of the T horizon (not the one-period) continuously compounded returns (assumed to follow a normal distribution), compatible with the horizon of S_T.[40] Related to the use of mean and variance (or standard deviation), earlier in this reading we used those quantities to construct intervals in which we expect to find a certain percentage of the observations of a normally distributed random variable. Those intervals were symmetric about the mean. Can we state similar, symmetric intervals for a lognormal random variable? Unfortunately, we cannot. Because the lognormal distribution is not symmetric, such intervals are more complicated than for the normal distribution, and we will not discuss this specialist topic here.[41]

Finally, we have presented the relation between the mean and variance of continuously compounded returns associated with different time horizons (see Equations 7 and 8), but how are the means and variances of holding period returns and continuously compounded returns related? As analysts, we typically think in terms of holding period returns rather than continuously compounded returns, and we may desire to convert means and standard deviations of holding period returns to means and standard deviations of continuously compounded returns for an option application, for example. To effect such conversions (and those in the other direction, from a continuous compounding to a holding period basis), we can use the expressions in Ferguson (1993).

4   MONTE CARLO SIMULATION

With an understanding of probability distributions, we are now prepared to learn about a computer-based technique in which probability distributions play an integral role. The technique is called Monte Carlo simulation. **Monte Carlo simulation** in finance involves the use of a computer to represent the operation of a complex financial system. A characteristic feature of Monte Carlo simulation is the generation of a large number of random samples from a specified probability distribution or distributions to represent the role of risk in the system.

Monte Carlo simulation has several quite distinct uses. One use is in planning. Stanford University researcher Sam Savage provided the following neat picture of that role: "What is the last thing you do before you climb on a ladder? You shake it, and that is Monte Carlo simulation."[42] Just as shaking a ladder helps us assess the risks in

---

40 The expression for the mean is $E(S_T) = S_0 \exp[E(r_{0,T}) + 0.5\sigma^2(r_{0,T})]$, for example.
41 See Hull (2003) for a discussion of lognormal confidence intervals.
42 *Business Week*, 22 January 2001.

climbing it, Monte Carlo simulation allows us to experiment with a proposed policy before actually implementing it. For example, investment performance can be evaluated with reference to a benchmark or a liability. Defined benefit pension plans often invest assets with reference to plan liabilities. Pension liabilities are a complex random process. In a Monte Carlo asset-liability financial planning study, the functioning of pension assets and liabilities is simulated over time, given assumptions about how assets are invested, the work force, and other variables. A key specification in this and all Monte Carlo simulations is the probability distributions of the various sources of risk (including interest rates and security market returns, in this case). The implications of different investment policy decisions on the plan's funded status can be assessed through simulated time. The experiment can be repeated for another set of assumptions. We can view Example 11 below as coming under this heading. In that example, market return series are not long enough to address researchers' questions on stock market timing, so the researchers simulate market returns to find answers to their questions.

Monte Carlo simulation is also widely used to develop estimates of VAR. In this application, we simulate the portfolio's profit and loss performance for a specified time horizon. Repeated trials within the simulation (each trial involving a draw of random observations from a probability distribution) produce a frequency distribution for changes in portfolio value. The point that defines the cutoff for the least favorable 5 percent of simulated changes is an estimate of 95 percent VAR, for example.

In an extremely important use, Monte Carlo simulation is a tool for valuing complex securities, particularly European-style options for which no analytic pricing formula is available.[43] For other securities, such as mortgage-backed securities with complex embedded options, Monte Carlo simulation is also an important modeling resource.

Researchers use Monte Carlo simulation to test their models and tools. How critical is a particular assumption to the performance of a model? Because we control the assumptions when we do a simulation, we can run the model through a Monte Carlo simulation to examine a model's sensitivity to a change in our assumptions.

To understand the technique of Monte Carlo simulation, let us present the process as a series of steps.[44] To illustrate the steps, we take the case of using Monte Carlo simulation to value a type of option for which no analytic pricing formula is available, an Asian call option on a stock. An **Asian call option** is a European-style option with a value at maturity equal to the difference between the stock price at maturity and the average stock price during the life of the option, or $0, whichever is greater. For instance, if the final stock price is $34 with an average value of $31 over the life of the option, the value of the option at maturity is $3 (the greater of $34 – $31 = $3 and $0). Steps 1 through 3 of the process describe specifying the simulation; Steps 4 through 7 describe running the simulation.

1. Specify the quantities of interest (option value, for example, or the funded status of a pension plan) in terms of underlying variables. The underlying variable or variables could be stock price for an equity option, the market value of pension assets, or other variables relating to the pension benefit obligation for a pension plan. Specify the starting values of the underlying variables.

   To illustrate the steps, we are using the case of valuing an Asian call option on stock. We use C_{iT} to represent the value of the option at maturity T. The subscript i in C_{iT} indicates that C_{iT} is a value resulting from the ith **simulation trial**, each simulation trial involving a drawing of random values (an iteration of Step 4).

---

43 A **European-style option** or **European option** is an option exercisable only at maturity.
44 The steps should be viewed as providing an overview of Monte Carlo simulation rather than as a detailed recipe for implementing a Monte Carlo simulation in its many varied applications.

2. Specify a time grid. Take the horizon in terms of calendar time and split it into a number of subperiods, say K in total. Calendar time divided by the number of subperiods, K, is the time increment, Δt.

3. Specify distributional assumptions for the risk factors that drive the underlying variables. For example, stock price is the underlying variable for the Asian call, so we need a model for stock price movement. Say we choose the following model for changes in stock price, where Z_k stands for the standard normal random variable:

$$\Delta(\text{Stock price}) = (\mu \times \text{Prior stock price} \times \Delta t) + (\sigma \times \text{Prior stock price} \times Z_k)$$

In the way that we are using the term, Z_k is a risk factor in the simulation. Through our choice of μ and σ, we control the distribution of stock price. Although this example has one risk factor, a given simulation may have multiple risk factors.

4. Using a computer program or spreadsheet function, draw K random values of each risk factor. In our example, the spreadsheet function would produce a draw of K values of the standard normal variable Z_k: Z_1, Z_2, Z_3, ..., Z_K.

5. Calculate the underlying variables using the random observations generated in Step 4. Using the above model of stock price dynamics, the result is K observations on changes in stock price. An additional calculation is needed to convert those changes into K stock prices (using initial stock price, which is given). Another calculation produces the average stock price during the life of the option (the sum of K stock prices divided by K).

6. Compute the quantities of interest. In our example, the first calculation is the value of an Asian call at maturity, C_{iT}. A second calculation discounts this terminal value back to the present to get the call value as of today, C_{i0}. We have completed one simulation trial. (The subscript i in C_{i0} stands for the ith simulation trial, as it does in C_{iT}.) In a Monte Carlo simulation, a running tabulation is kept of statistics relating to the distribution of the quantities of interest, including their mean value and standard deviation, over the simulation trials to that point.

7. Iteratively go back to Step 4 until a specified number of trials, I, is completed. Finally, produce statistics for the simulation. The key value for our example is the mean value of C_{i0} for the total number of simulation trials. This mean value is the Monte Carlo estimate of the value of the Asian call.

How many simulation trials should be specified? In general, we need to increase the number of trials by a factor of 100 to get each extra digit of accuracy. Depending on the problem, tens of thousands of trials may be needed to obtain accuracy to two decimal places (as required for option value, for example). Conducting a large number of trials is not necessarily a problem, given today's computing power. The number of trials needed can be reduced using variance reduction procedures, a topic outside the scope of this reading.[45]

In Step 4 of our example, a computer function produced a set of random observations on a standard normal random variable. Recall that for a uniform distribution, all possible numbers are equally likely. The term **random number generator** refers to an algorithm that produces uniformly distributed random numbers between 0

---

45 For details on this and other technical aspects of Monte Carlo simulation, see Hillier and Lieberman (2000).

and 1. In the context of computer simulations, the term **random number** refers to an observation drawn from a uniform distribution.[46] For other distributions, the term "random observation" is used in this context.

It is a remarkable fact that random observations from any distribution can be produced using the uniform random variable with endpoints 0 and 1. To see why this is so, consider the inverse transformation method of producing random observations. Suppose we are interested in obtaining random observations for a random variable, X, with cumulative distribution function $F(x)$. Recall that $F(x)$ evaluated at x is a number between 0 and 1. Suppose a random outcome of this random variable is 3.21 and that $F(3.21) = 0.25$ or 25 percent. Define an inverse of F, call it F^{-1}, that can do the following: Substitute the probability 0.25 into F^{-1} and it returns the random outcome 3.21. In other words, $F^{-1}(0.25) = 3.21$. To generate random observations on X, the steps are 1) generate a uniform random number, r, between 0 and 1 using the random number generator and 2) evaluate $F^{-1}(r)$ to obtain a random observation on X. Random observation generation is a field of study in itself, and we have briefly discussed the inverse transformation method here just to illustrate a point. As a generalist you do not need to address the technical details of converting random numbers into random observations, but you do need to know that random observations from any distribution can be generated using a uniform random variable.

In Examples 11 and 12, we give an application of Monte Carlo simulation to a question of great interest to investment practice: the potential gains from market timing.

Example 11

Potential Gains from Market Timing: A Monte Carlo Simulation (1)

All active investors want to achieve superior performance. One possible source of superior performance is market timing ability. How accurate does an investor need to be as a bull- and bear-market forecaster for market timing to be profitable? What size gains compared with a buy-and-hold strategy accrue to a given level of accuracy? Because of the variability in asset returns, a huge amount of return data is needed to find statistically reliable answers to these questions. Chua, Woodward, and To (1987) thus selected Monte Carlo simulation to address the potential gains from market timing. They were interested in the perspective of a Canadian investor.

To understand their study, suppose that at the beginning of a year, an investor predicts that the next year will see either a bull market or bear market. If the prediction is *bull market,* the investor puts all her money in stocks and earns the market return for that year. On the other hand, if the prediction is *bear market,* the investor holds T-bills and earns the T-bill return. After the fact, a market is categorized as *bull market* if the stock market return, R_{Mt}, minus T-bill return, R_{Ft}, is positive for the year; otherwise, the market is classed as *bear market.* The investment results of a market timer can be compared with those

---

46 The numbers that random number generators produce depend on a seed or initial value. If the same seed is fed to the same generator, it will produce the same sequence. All sequences eventually repeat. Because of this predictability, the technically correct name for the numbers produced by random number generators is **pseudo-random numbers**. Pseudo-random numbers have sufficient qualities of randomness for most practical purposes.

of a buy-and-hold investor. A buy-and-hold investor earns the market return every year. For Chua et al., one quantity of interest was the gain from market timing. They defined this quantity as the market timer's average return minus the average return to a buy-and-hold investor.

To simulate market returns, Chua et al. generated 10,000 random standard normal observations, Z_t. At the time of the study, Canadian stocks had a historical mean annual return of 12.95 percent with a standard deviation of 18.30 percent. To reflect these parameters, the simulated market returns are $R_{Mt} = 0.1830Z_t + 0.1295$, $t = 1, 2, ..., 10,000$. Using a second set of 10,000 random standard normal observations, historical return parameters for Canadian T-bills, as well as the historical correlation of T-bill and stock returns, the authors generated 10,000 T-bill returns.

An investor can have different skills in forecasting bull and bear markets. Chua et al. characterized market timers by accuracy in forecasting bull markets and accuracy in forecasting bear markets. For example, bull market forecasting accuracy of 50 percent means that when the timer forecasts *bull market* for the next year, she is right just half the time, indicating no skill. Suppose an investor has 60 percent accuracy in forecasting *bull market* and 80 percent accuracy in forecasting *bear market* (a 60–80 timer). We can simulate how an investor would fare. After generating the first observation on $R_{Mt} - R_{Ft}$, we know whether that observation is a bull or bear market. If the observation is *bull market*, then 0.60 (forecast accuracy for bull markets) is compared with a random number (between 0 and 1). If the random number is less than 0.60, which occurs with a 60 percent probability, then the market timer is assumed to have correctly predicted *bull market* and her return for that first observation is the market return. If the random number is greater than 0.60, then the market timer is assumed to have made an error and predicted *bear market*; her return for that observation is the risk-free rate. In a similar fashion, if that first observation is *bear market*, the timer has an 80 percent chance of being right in forecasting *bear market* based on a random number draw. In either case, her return is compared with the market return to record her gain versus a buy-and-hold strategy. That process is one simulation trial. The simulated mean return earned by the timer is the average return earned by the timer over all trials in the simulation.

To increase our understanding of the process, consider a hypothetical Monte Carlo simulation with four trials for the 60–80 timer (who, to reiterate, has 60 percent accuracy in forecasting bull markets and 80 percent accuracy in forecasting bear markets). Table 8 gives data for the simulation. Let us look at Trials 1 and 2. In Trial 1, the first random number drawn leads to a market return of 0.121. Because the market return, 0.121, exceeded the T-bill return, 0.050, we have a bull market. We generate a random number, 0.531, which we then compare with the timer's bull market accuracy, 0.60. Because 0.531 is less than 0.60, the timer is assumed to have made a correct bull market forecast and thus to have invested in stocks. Thus the timer earns the stock market return, 0.121, for that trial. In the second trial we observe another bull market, but because the random number 0.725 is greater than 0.60, the timer is assumed to have made an error and predicted a bear market; therefore, the timer earned the T-bill return, 0.081, rather than higher stock market return.

| Table 8 | Hypothetical Simulation for a 60–80 Market Timer | | | | |

| | After Draws for Z_t and for the T-bill Return | | | Simulation Results | | |
| | | | Bull or Bear Market? | Value of X | Timer's Prediction Correct? | Return Earned by Timer |
Trial	R_{Mt}	R_{Ft}				
1	0.121	0.050	Bull	0.531	Yes	0.121
2	0.092	0.081	Bull	0.725	No	0.081
3	−0.020	0.034	Bear	0.786	Yes	0.034
4	0.052	0.055	*A*	0.901	*B*	*C*
						$\bar{R} = $ D

Note: $\bar{R}$ is the mean return earned by the timer over the four simulation trials.

Using the data in Table 8, determine the values of A, B, C, and D.

Solution:

The value of A is *Bear* because the stock market return was less than the T-bill return in Trial 4. The value of B is *No*. Because we observe a bear market, we compare the random number 0.901 with 0.80, the timer's bear-market forecasting accuracy. Because 0.901 is greater than 0.8, the timer is assumed to have made an error. The value of C is 0.052, the return on the stock market, because the timer made an error and invested in the stock market and earned 0.052 rather than the higher T-bill return of 0.055. The value of D is $\bar{R}$ = (0.121 + 0.081 + 0.034 + 0.052) = 0.288/4 = 0.072. Note that we could calculate other statistics besides the mean, such as the standard deviation of the returns earned by the timer over the four trials in the simulation.

Example 12

Potential Gains from Market Timing: A Monte Carlo Simulation (2)

Having discussed the plan of the Chua et al. study and illustrated the method for a hypothetical Monte Carlo simulation with four trials, we conclude our presentation of the study.

The hypothetical simulation in Example 11 had four trials, far too few to reach statistically precise conclusions. The simulation of Chua et al. incorporated 10,000 trials. Chua et al. specified bull- and bear-market prediction skill levels of 50, 60, 70, 80, 90, and 100 percent. Table 9 presents a very small excerpt from their simulation results for the no transaction costs case (transaction costs were also examined). Reading across the row, the timer with 60 percent bull market and 80 percent bear market forecasting accuracy had a mean annual gain from market timing of −1.12 percent per year. On average, the buy-and-hold investor out-earned this skillful timer by 1.12 percentage points. There was substantial variability in gains across the simulation trials, however: The standard deviation of the gain was 14.77 percent, so in many trials (but not on average) the gain was positive. Row 3 (win/loss) is the ratio of profitable switches between stocks and T-bills to unprofitable switches. This ratio was a favorable 1.2070 for the 60–80 timer. (When transaction costs were considered, however, fewer switches are profitable: The win–loss ratio was 0.5832 for the 60–80 timer.)

Table 9	Gains from Stock Market Timing (No Transaction Costs)					
Bull Market Accuracy (%)	**Bear Market Accuracy (%)**					
	50	**60**	**70**	**80**	**90**	**100**
60 Mean (%)	−2.50	−1.99	−1.57	−1.12	−0.68	−0.22
S.D. (%)	13.65	14.11	14.45	14.77	15.08	15.42
Win/Loss	0.7418	0.9062	1.0503	1.2070	1.3496	1.4986

Source: Chua, Woodward, and To (1987), Table II (excerpt).

The authors concluded that the cost of not being invested in the market during bull market years is high. Because a buy-and-hold investor never misses a bull market year, she has 100 percent forecast accuracy for bull markets (at the cost of 0 percent accuracy for bear markets). Given their definitions and assumptions, the authors also concluded that successful market timing requires a minimum accuracy of 80 percent in forecasting both bull and bear markets. Market timing is a continuing area of interest and study, and other perspectives exist. However, this example illustrates how Monte Carlo simulation is used to address important investment issues.

The analyst chooses the probability distributions in Monte Carlo simulation. By contrast, **historical simulation** samples from a historical record of returns (or other underlying variables) to simulate a process. The concept underlying historical simulation (also called **back simulation**) is that the historical record provides the most direct evidence on distributions (and that the past applies to the future). For example, refer back to Step 2 in the outline of Monte Carlo simulation above and suppose the time increment is one day. Further, suppose we base the simulation on the record of daily stock returns over the last five years. In one type of historical simulation, we randomly draw K returns from that record to generate one simulation trial. We put back the observations into the sample, and in the next trial we again randomly sample with replacement. The simulation results directly reflect frequencies in the data. A drawback of this approach is that any risk not represented in the time period selected (for example, a stock market crash) will not be reflected in the simulation. Compared with Monte Carlo simulation, historical simulation does not lend itself to "what if" analyses. Nevertheless, historic simulation is an established alternative simulation methodology.

Monte Carlo simulation is a complement to analytical methods. It provides only statistical estimates, not exact results. Analytical methods, where available, provide more insight into cause-and-effect relationships. For example, the Black–Scholes–Merton option pricing model for the value of a European call option is an analytical method, expressed as a formula. It is a much more efficient method for valuing such a call than is Monte Carlo simulation. As an analytical expression, the Black–Scholes–Merton model permits the analyst to quickly gauge the sensitivity of call value to changes in current stock price and the other variables that determine call value. In contrast, Monte Carlo simulations do not directly provide such precise insights. However, only some types of options can be priced with analytical expressions. As financial product innovations proceed, the field of applications for Monte Carlo simulation continues to grow.

SUMMARY

In this reading, we have presented the most frequently used probability distributions in investment analysis and the Monte Carlo simulation.

- A probability distribution specifies the probabilities of the possible outcomes of a random variable.

- The two basic types of random variables are discrete random variables and continuous random variables. Discrete random variables take on at most a countable number of possible outcomes that we can list as $x_1, x_2, \ldots$ In contrast, we cannot describe the possible outcomes of a continuous random variable Z with a list $z_1, z_2, \ldots$ because the outcome $(z_1 + z_2)/2$, not in the list, would always be possible.

- The probability function specifies the probability that the random variable will take on a specific value. The probability function is denoted $p(x)$ for a discrete random variable and $f(x)$ for a continuous random variable. For any probability function $p(x)$, $0 \le p(x) \le 1$, and the sum of $p(x)$ over all values of X equals 1.

- The cumulative distribution function, denoted $F(x)$ for both continuous and discrete random variables, gives the probability that the random variable is less than or equal to x.

- The discrete uniform and the continuous uniform distributions are the distributions of equally likely outcomes.

- The binomial random variable is defined as the number of successes in n Bernoulli trials, where the probability of success, p, is constant for all trials and the trials are independent. A Bernoulli trial is an experiment with two outcomes, which can represent success or failure, an up move or a down move, or another binary (two-fold) outcome.

- A binomial random variable has an expected value or mean equal to np and variance equal to $np(1 - p)$.

- A binomial tree is the graphical representation of a model of asset price dynamics in which, at each period, the asset moves up with probability p or down with probability $(1 - p)$. The binomial tree is a flexible method for modeling asset price movement and is widely used in pricing options.

- The normal distribution is a continuous symmetric probability distribution that is completely described by two parameters: its mean, μ, and its variance, σ^2.

- A univariate distribution specifies the probabilities for a single random variable. A multivariate distribution specifies the probabilities for a group of related random variables.

- To specify the normal distribution for a portfolio when its component securities are normally distributed, we need the means, standard deviations, and all the distinct pairwise correlations of the securities. When we have those statistics, we have also specified a multivariate normal distribution for the securities.

■ For a normal random variable, approximately 68 percent of all possible outcomes are within a one standard deviation interval about the mean, approximately 95 percent are within a two standard deviation interval about the mean, and approximately 99 percent are within a three standard deviation interval about the mean.

■ A normal random variable, X, is standardized using the expression $Z = (X - \mu)/\sigma$, where μ and σ are the mean and standard deviation of X. Generally, we use the sample mean $\bar{X}$ as an estimate of μ and the sample standard deviation s as an estimate of σ in this expression.

■ The standard normal random variable, denoted Z, has a mean equal to 0 and variance equal to 1. All questions about any normal random variable can be answered by referring to the cumulative distribution function of a standard normal random variable, denoted $N(x)$ or $N(z)$.

■ Shortfall risk is the risk that portfolio value will fall below some minimum acceptable level over some time horizon.

■ Roy's safety-first criterion, addressing shortfall risk, asserts that the optimal portfolio is the one that minimizes the probability that portfolio return falls below a threshold level. According to Roy's safety-first criterion, if returns are normally distributed, the safety-first optimal portfolio P is the one that maximizes the quantity $[E(R_P) - R_L]/\sigma_P$, where R_L is the minimum acceptable level of return.

■ A random variable follows a lognormal distribution if the natural logarithm of the random variable is normally distributed. The lognormal distribution is defined in terms of the mean and variance of its associated normal distribution. The lognormal distribution is bounded below by 0 and skewed to the right (it has a long right tail).

■ The lognormal distribution is frequently used to model the probability distribution of asset prices because it is bounded below by zero.

■ Continuous compounding views time as essentially continuous or unbroken; discrete compounding views time as advancing in discrete finite intervals.

■ The continuously compounded return associated with a holding period is the natural log of 1 plus the holding period return, or equivalently, the natural log of ending price over beginning price.

■ If continuously compounded returns are normally distributed, asset prices are lognormally distributed. This relationship is used to move back and forth between the distributions for return and price. Because of the central limit theorem, continuously compounded returns need not be normally distributed for asset prices to be reasonably well described by a lognormal distribution.

■ Monte Carlo simulation involves the use of a computer to represent the operation of a complex financial system. A characteristic feature of Monte Carlo simulation is the generation of a large number of random samples from specified probability distribution(s) to represent the operation of risk in the system. Monte Carlo simulation is used in planning, in financial risk management, and in valuing complex securities. Monte Carlo simulation is a complement to analytical methods but provides only statistical estimates, not exact results.

■ Historical simulation is an established alternative to Monte Carlo simulation that in one implementation involves repeated sampling from a historical data series. Historical simulation is grounded in actual data but can reflect only risks represented in the sample historical data. Compared with Monte Carlo simulation, historical simulation does not lend itself to "what if" analyses.

PRACTICE PROBLEMS FOR READING 9

1. A European put option on stock conveys the right to sell the stock at a prespecified price, called the exercise price, at the maturity date of the option. The value of this put at maturity is (exercise price – stock price) or $0, whichever is greater. Suppose the exercise price is $100 and the underlying stock trades in ticks of $0.01. At any time before maturity, the terminal value of the put is a random variable.

   A. Describe the distinct possible outcomes for terminal put value. (Think of the put's maximum and minimum values and its minimum price increments.)

   B. Is terminal put value, at a time before maturity, a discrete or continuous random variable?

   C. Letting Y stand for terminal put value, express in standard notation the probability that terminal put value is less than or equal to $24. No calculations or formulas are necessary.

2. Suppose X, Y, and Z are discrete random variables with these sets of possible outcomes: $X = \{2, 2.5, 3\}$, $Y = \{0, 1, 2, 3\}$, and $Z = \{10, 11, 12\}$. For each of the functions $f(X)$, $g(Y)$, and $h(Z)$, state whether the function satisfies the conditions for a probability function.

   A. $f(2) = -0.01\ f(2.5) = -0.50\ f(3) = -0.51$

   B. $g(0) = 0.25\ g(1) = 0.50\ g(2) = 0.125\ g(3) = 0.125$

   C. $h(10) = 0.35\ h(11) = 0.15\ h(12) = 0.52$

3. Define the term "binomial random variable." Describe the types of problems for which the binomial distribution is used.

4. Over the last 10 years, a company's annual earnings increased year over year seven times and decreased year over year three times. You decide to model the number of earnings increases for the next decade as a binomial random variable.

   A. What is your estimate of the probability of success, defined as an increase in annual earnings?

   For Parts B, C, and D of this problem, assume the estimated probability is the actual probability for the next decade.

   B. What is the probability that earnings will increase in exactly 5 of the next 10 years?

   C. Calculate the expected number of yearly earnings increases during the next 10 years.

   D. Calculate the variance and standard deviation of the number of yearly earnings increases during the next 10 years.

   E. The expression for the probability function of a binomial random variable depends on two major assumptions. In the context of this problem, what must you assume about annual earnings increases to apply the binomial distribution in Part B? What reservations might you have about the validity of these assumptions?

5. You are examining the record of an investment newsletter writer who claims a 70 percent success rate in making investment recommendations that are profitable over a one-year time horizon. You have the one-year record

Practice Problems and Solutions: 1–18 taken from *Quantitative Methods for Investment Analysis*, Second Edition, by Richard A. DeFusco, CFA, Dennis W. McLeavey, CFA, Jerald E. Pinto, CFA, and David E. Runkle, CFA. Copyright © 2004 by CFA Institute. All other problems and solutions copyright © CFA Institute.

of the newsletter's seven most recent recommendations. Four of those recommendations were profitable. If all the recommendations are independent and the newsletter writer's skill is as claimed, what is the probability of observing four or fewer profitable recommendations out of seven in total?

6. By definition, a down-and-out call option on stock becomes worthless and terminates if the price of the underlying stock moves down and touches a prespecified point during the life of the call. If the prespecified level is $75, for example, the call expires worthless if and when the stock price falls to $75. Describe, without a diagram, how a binomial tree can be used to value a down-and-out call option.

7. You are forecasting sales for a company in the fourth quarter of its fiscal year. Your low-end estimate of sales is €14 million, and your high-end estimate is €15 million. You decide to treat all outcomes for sales between these two values as equally likely, using a continuous uniform distribution.

  A. What is the expected value of sales for the fourth quarter?

  B. What is the probability that fourth-quarter sales will be less than or equal to €14,125,000?

8. State the approximate probability that a normal random variable will fall within the following intervals:

  A. Mean plus or minus one standard deviation.

  B. Mean plus or minus two standard deviations.

  C. Mean plus or minus three standard deviations.

9. Find the area under the normal curve up to $z = 0.36$; that is, find $P(Z \leq 0.36)$. Interpret this value.

10. In futures markets, profits or losses on contracts are settled at the end of each trading day. This procedure is called marking to market or daily resettlement. By preventing a trader's losses from accumulating over many days, marking to market reduces the risk that traders will default on their obligations. A futures markets trader needs a liquidity pool to meet the daily mark to market. If liquidity is exhausted, the trader may be forced to unwind his position at an unfavorable time.

  Suppose you are using financial futures contracts to hedge a risk in your portfolio. You have a liquidity pool (cash and cash equivalents) of λ dollars per contract and a time horizon of T trading days. For a given size liquidity pool, λ, Kolb, Gay, and Hunter (1985) developed an expression for the probability stating that you will exhaust your liquidity pool within a T-day horizon as a result of the daily mark to market. Kolb et al. assumed that the expected change in futures price is 0 and that futures price changes are normally distributed. With σ representing the standard deviation of daily futures price changes, the standard deviation of price changes over a time horizon to day T is $\sigma\sqrt{T}$, given continuous compounding. With that background, the Kolb et al. expression is

  Probability of exhausting liquidity pool $= 2\big[1 - N(x)\big]$

  where $x = \lambda / \big(\sigma\sqrt{T}\big)$. Here x is a standardized value of λ. $N(x)$ is the standard normal cumulative distribution function. For some intuition about $1 - N(x)$ in the expression, note that the liquidity pool is exhausted if losses exceed the size of the liquidity pool at any time up to and including T; the probability of that event happening can be shown to be proportional to an area in the right tail of a standard normal distribution, $1 - N(x)$.

Using the Kolb et al. expression, answer the following questions:

A. Your hedging horizon is five days, and your liquidity pool is $2,000 per contract. You estimate that the standard deviation of daily price changes for the contract is $450. What is the probability that you will exhaust your liquidity pool in the five-day period?

B. Suppose your hedging horizon is 20 days, but all the other facts given in Part A remain the same. What is the probability that you will exhaust your liquidity pool in the 20-day period?

The following information relates to Questions 11–13

As reported by Liang (1999), U.S. equity funds in three style categories had the following mean monthly returns, standard deviations of return, and Sharpe ratios during the period January 1994 to December 1996:

Strategy	January 1994 to December 1996		
	Mean Return (%)	Standard Deviation (%)	Sharpe Ratio
Large-cap growth	1.15	2.89	0.26
Large-cap value	1.08	2.20	0.31
Large-cap blend	1.07	2.38	0.28

Source: Liang (1999), Table 5 (excerpt).

11. Basing your estimate of future-period monthly return parameters on the sample mean and standard deviation for the period January 1994 to December 1996, construct a 90 percent confidence interval for the monthly return on a large-cap blend fund. Assume fund returns are normally distributed.

12. Basing your estimate of future-period monthly return parameters on the sample mean and standard deviation for the period January 1994 to December 1996, calculate the probability that a large-cap growth fund will earn a monthly return of 0 percent or less. Assume fund returns are normally distributed.

13. Assuming fund returns are normally distributed, which fund category minimized the probability of earning less than the risk-free rate for the period January 1994 to December 1996?

14. A client has a portfolio of common stocks and fixed-income instruments with a current value of £1,350,000. She intends to liquidate £50,000 from the portfolio at the end of the year to purchase a partnership share in a business. Furthermore, the client would like to be able to withdraw the £50,000 without reducing the initial capital of £1,350,000. The following table shows four alternative asset allocations.

Mean and Standard Deviation for Four Allocations (in Percent)				
	A	B	C	D
Expected annual return	16	12	10	9
Standard deviation of return	24	17	12	11

Address the following questions (assume normality for Parts B and C):

A. Given the client's desire not to invade the £1,350,000 principal, what is the shortfall level, R_L? Use this shortfall level to answer Part B.

B. According to the safety-first criterion, which of the allocations is the best?

C. What is the probability that the return on the safety-first optimal portfolio will be less than the shortfall level, R_L?

15. A. Describe two important characteristics of the lognormal distribution.

B. Compared with the normal distribution, why is the lognormal distribution a more reasonable model for the distribution of asset prices?

C. What are the two parameters of a lognormal distribution?

16. The basic calculation for volatility (denoted σ) as used in option pricing is the annualized standard deviation of continuously compounded daily returns. Calculate volatility for Dollar General Corporation (NYSE: DG) based on its closing prices for two weeks, given in the table below. (Annualize based on 250 days in a year.)

Dollar General Corporation Daily Closing Stock Price	
Date	**Closing Price ($)**
27 January 2003	10.68
28 January 2003	10.87
29 January 2003	11.00
30 January 2003	10.95
31 January 2003	11.26
3 February 2003	11.31
4 February 2003	11.23
5 February 2003	10.91
6 February 2003	10.80
7 February 2003	10.47

Source: http://finance.yahoo.com.

17. A. Define Monte Carlo simulation and explain its use in finance.

B. Compared with analytical methods, what are the strengths and weaknesses of Monte Carlo simulation for use in valuing securities?

18. A standard lookback call option on stock has a value at maturity equal to (Value of the stock at maturity – Minimum value of stock during the life of the option prior to maturity) or $0, whichever is greater. If the minimum value reached prior to maturity was $20.11 and the value of the stock at maturity is $23, for example, the call is worth $23 – $20.11 = $2.89. Briefly discuss how you might use Monte Carlo simulation in valuing a lookback call option.

19. At the end of the current year, an investor wants to make a donation of $20,000 to charity but does not want the year-end market value of her portfolio to fall below $600,000. If the shortfall level is equal to the risk-free rate of return and returns from all portfolios considered are normally distributed, will the portfolio that minimizes the probability of failing to achieve the investor's objective *most likely* have the:

	highest safety-first ratio?	highest Sharpe ratio?
A.	No	Yes
B.	Yes	No
C.	Yes	Yes

20. An analyst stated that normal distributions are suitable for describing asset returns and that lognormal distributions are suitable for describing distributions of asset prices. The analyst's statement is correct in regard to:

    A. both normal distributions and lognormal distributions.

    B. normal distributions, but incorrect in regard to lognormal distributions.

    C. lognormal distributions, but incorrect in regard to normal distributions.

SOLUTIONS FOR READING 9

1. **A.** The put's minimum value is $0. The put's value is $0 when the stock price is at or above $100 at the maturity date of the option. The put's maximum value is $100 = $100 (the exercise price) – $0 (the lowest possible stock price). The put's value is $100 when the stock is worthless at the option's maturity date. The put's minimum price increments are $0.01. The possible outcomes of terminal put value are thus $0.00, $0.01, $0.02, . . . , $100.

   B. The price of the underlying has minimum price fluctuations of $0.01: These are the minimum price fluctuations for terminal put value. For example, if the stock finishes at $98.20, the payoff on the put is $100 – $98.20 = $1.80. We can specify that the nearest values to $1.80 are $1.79 and $1.81. With a continuous random variable, we cannot specify the nearest values. So, we must characterize terminal put value as a discrete random variable.

   C. The probability that terminal put value is less than or equal to $24 is $P(Y \leq 24)$ or $F(24)$, in standard notation, where F is the cumulative distribution function for terminal put value.

2. **A.** Because $f(2) = -0.01$ is negative, $f(X)$ cannot be a probability function. Probabilities are numbers between 0 and 1.

   B. The function $g(Y)$ does satisfy the conditions of a probability function:

   All the values of $g(Y)$ are between 0 and 1, and the values of $g(Y)$ sum to 1.

   C. The function $h(Z)$ cannot be a probability function: The values of $h(Z)$ sum to 1.02, which is more than 1.

3. A binomial random variable is defined as the number of successes in n Bernoulli trials (a trial that produces one of two outcomes). The binomial distribution is used to make probability statements about a record of successes and failures or about anything with binary (twofold) outcomes.

4. **A.** The probability of an earnings increase (success) in a year is estimated as $7/10 = 0.70$ or 70 percent, based on the record of the past 10 years.

   B. The probability that earnings will increase in 5 out of the next 10 years is about 10.3 percent. Define a binomial random variable X, counting the number of earnings increases over the next 10 years. From Part A, the probability of an earnings increase in a given year is $p = 0.70$ and the number of trials (years) is $n = 10$. Equation 1 gives the probability that a binomial random variable has x successes in n trials, with the probability of success on a trial equal to p.

   $$P(X = x) = \binom{n}{x} p^x (1-p)^{n-x} = \frac{n!}{(n-x)!x!} p^x (1-p)^{n-x}$$

   For this example,

   $$\binom{10}{5} 0.7^5 0.3^{10-5} = \frac{10!}{(10-5)!5!} 0.7^5 0.3^{10-5}$$
   $$= 252 \times 0.16807 \times 0.00243 = 0.102919$$

   We conclude that the probability that earnings will increase in exactly 5 of the next 10 years is 0.1029, or approximately 10.3 percent.

   C. The expected number of yearly increases is $E(X) = np = 10 \times 0.70 = 7$.

   D. The variance of the number of yearly increases over the next 10 years is $\sigma^2 = np(1-p) = 10 \times 0.70 \times 0.30 = 2.1$. The standard deviation is 1.449 (the positive square root of 2.1).

E. You must assume that 1) the probability of an earnings increase (success) is constant from year to year and 2) earnings increases are independent trials. If current and past earnings help forecast next year's earnings, Assumption 2 is violated. If the company's business is subject to economic or industry cycles, neither assumption is likely to hold.

5. The observed success rate is $4/7 = 0.571$, or 57.1 percent. The probability of four or fewer successes is $F(4) = p(4) + p(3) + p(2) + p(1) + p(0)$, where $p(4)$, $p(3)$, $p(2)$, $p(1)$, and $p(0)$ are respectively the probabilities of 4, 3, 2, 1, and 0 successes, according to the binomial distribution with $n = 7$ and $p = 0.70$. We have

$$p(4) = (7!/4!3!)(0.70^4)(0.30^3) = 35(0.006483) = 0.226895$$
$$p(3) = (7!/3!4!)(0.70^3)(0.30^4) = 35(0.002778) = 0.097241$$
$$p(2) = (7!/2!5!)(0.70^2)(0.30^5) = 21(0.001191) = 0.025005$$
$$p(1) = (7!/1!6!)(0.70^1)(0.30^6) = 7(0.000510) = 0.003572$$
$$p(0) = (7!/0!7!)(0.70^0)(0.30^7) = 1(0.000219) = 0.000219$$

Summing all these probabilities, you conclude that $F(4) = 0.226895 + 0.097241 + 0.025005 + 0.003572 + 0.000219 = 0.352931$, or 35.3 percent.

6. At each node of a binomial tree, we can test the condition that stock price is at or below the prespecified level. As in Figure 2, we calculate stock price at all nodes of the tree. We calculate the value of the call at the terminal nodes as a function of the terminal price of the stock. Using a model for discounting values by one period, we calculate call value one period earlier, and so forth, to reach $t = 0$. But at any node at which stock price is at or below the prespecified level, we automatically set call value to $0.

7. A. The expected value of fourth-quarter sales is €14,500,000, calculated as (€14,000,000 + €15,000,000)/2. With a continuous uniform random variable, the mean or expected value is the midpoint between the smallest and largest values. (See Example 7.)

   B. The probability that fourth-quarter sales will be less than €14,125,000 is 0.125 or 12.5 percent, calculated as (€14,125,000 − €14,000,000)/(€15,000,000 − €14,000,000).

8. A. Approximately 68 percent of all outcomes of a normal random variable fall within plus or minus one standard deviation of the mean.

   B. Approximately 95 percent of all outcomes of a normal random variable fall within plus or minus two standard deviations of the mean.

   C. Approximately 99 percent of all outcomes of a normal random variable fall within plus or minus three standard deviations of the mean.

9. The area under the normal curve for $z = 0.36$ is 0.6406 or 64.06 percent. The following table presents an excerpt from the tables of the standard normal cumulative distribution function in the back of this volume. To locate $z = 0.36$, find 0.30 in the fourth row of numbers, then look at the column for 0.06 (the second decimal place of 0.36). The entry is 0.6406.

					$P(Z \leq x) = N(x)$ for $x \geq 0$ or $P(Z \leq z) = N(z)$ for $z \geq 0$				
x or *z*	0	0.01	0.02	0.03	0.04	0.05	0.06	0.07	0.08	0.09
0.00	0.5000	0.5040	0.5080	0.5120	0.5160	0.5199	0.5239	0.5279	0.5319	0.5359
0.10	0.5398	0.5438	0.5478	0.5517	0.5557	0.5596	0.5636	0.5675	0.5714	0.5753
0.20	0.5793	0.5832	0.5871	0.5910	0.5948	0.5987	0.6026	0.6064	0.6103	0.6141

x or z	0	0.01	0.02	0.03	0.04	0.05	0.06	0.07	0.08	0.09
					$P(Z \le x) = N(x)$ for $x \ge 0$ or $P(Z \le z) = N(z)$ for $z \ge 0$					
0.30	0.6179	0.6217	0.6255	0.6293	0.6331	0.6368	**0.6406**	0.6443	0.6480	0.6517
0.40	0.6554	0.6591	0.6628	0.6664	0.6700	0.6736	0.6772	0.6808	0.6844	0.6879
0.50	0.6915	0.6950	0.6985	0.7019	0.7054	0.7088	0.7123	0.7157	0.7190	0.7224

The interpretation of 64.06 percent for $z = 0.36$ is that 64.06 percent of observations on a standard normal random variable are smaller than or equal to the value 0.36. (So 100% − 64.06% = 35.94% of the values are greater than 0.36.)

10. **A.** The probability of exhausting the liquidity pool is 4.7 percent. First calculate $x = \lambda/(\sigma\sqrt{T}) = \$2{,}000/(\$450\sqrt{5}) = 1.987616$. We can round this value to 1.99 to use the standard normal tables in the back of this book. Using those tables, we find that $N(1.99) = 0.9767$. Thus, the probability of exhausting the liquidity pool is $2[1 − N(1.99)] = 2(1 − 0.9767) = 0.0466$ or about 4.7 percent.

B. The probability of exhausting the liquidity pool is now 32.2 percent. The calculation follows the same steps as those in Part A. We calculate $x = \lambda/(\sigma\sqrt{T}) = \$2{,}000/(\$450\sqrt{20}) = 0.993808$. We can round this value to 0.99 to use the standard normal tables in the back of this book. Using those tables, we find that $N(0.99) = 0.8389$. Thus, the probability of exhausting the liquidity pool is $2[1 − N(0.99)] = 2(1 − 0.8389) = 0.3222$ or about 32.2 percent. This is a substantial probability that you will run out of funds to meet mark to market.

In their paper, Kolb et al. call the probability of exhausting the liquidity pool the probability of ruin, a traditional name for this type of calculation.

11. A 90 percent confidence interval for returns on large-cap blend funds is the interval [−2.857%, 4.997%]. An exact 90 percent confidence interval is equal to the mean plus and minus 1.65 standard deviations. The lower limit is 1.07% − 1.65(2.38%) = −2.857%. The upper limit is 1.07% + 1.65(2.38%) = 4.997%.

12. Under a normality assumption, the probability that the average large-cap growth fund will earn a negative monthly return is 34.5 percent. We calculate the standardized value as (0% − 1.15%)/2.89% = −0.397924. Rounding this value to −0.40 to use the standard normal tables in the back of the book, we find that $N(−0.40) = 0.3446$. If you use a spreadsheet function on −0.397924, you will find $N(−0.397924) = 0.345343$.

13. The large-cap value fund category minimized the probability of earning a return less than the risk-free rate of return for the period. Large-cap value funds achieved the highest Sharpe ratio during the period. Recall from our discussion of Roy's safety-first criterion that the Sharpe ratio is equivalent to using the risk-free rate as the shortfall level in SFRatio, and the alternative with the largest SFRatio minimizes the probability of earning a return less than the shortfall level (under a normality assumption). Therefore, to answer the question, we select the alternative with the highest Sharpe ratio, the large-cap value fund.

14. **A.** Because £50,000/£1,350,000 is 3.7 percent, for any return less than 3.7 percent the client will need to invade principal if she takes out £50,000. So R_L = 3.7 percent.

B. To decide which of the allocations is safety-first optimal, select the alternative with the highest ratio $[E(R_p) − R_L]/\sigma_p$:

Allocation A : $0.5125 = (16 - 3.7)/24$

Allocation B : $0.488235 = (12 - 3.7)/17$

Allocation C : $0.525 = (10 - 3.7)/12$

Allocation D : $0.481818 = (9 - 3.7)/11$

Allocation C, with the largest ratio (0.525), is the best alternative according to the safety-first criterion.

C. To answer this question, note that $P(R_C < 3.7) = N(-0.525)$. We can round 0.525 to 0.53 for use with tables of the standard normal cdf. First, we calculate $N(-0.53) = 1 - N(0.53) = 1 - 0.7019 = 0.2981$ or about 30 percent. The safety-first optimal portfolio has a roughly 30 percent chance of not meeting a 3.7 percent return threshold.

15. A. Two important features of the lognormal distribution are that it is bounded below by 0 and it is right-skewed.

B. Normal random variables can be negative (the bell curve extends to the left without limit). In contrast, lognormal random variables cannot be negative. Asset prices also cannot be negative. So the lognormal distribution is superior to the normal as a probability model for asset prices.

C. The two parameters of a lognormal distribution are the mean and variance (or standard deviation) of the associated normal distribution. If Y is lognormal and $X = \ln Y$, the two parameters of the distribution of Y are the mean and variance (or standard deviation) of X.

16. To compute volatility for Dollar General Corporation, we begin by calculating the continuously compounded daily returns using Equation 5:

$$r_{t,t+1} = \ln\left(S_{t+1}/S_t\right) = \ln\left(1 + R_{t,t+1}\right)$$

Then we find the variance of those continuously compounded returns, the sum of the squared deviations from the mean divided by 8 (the sample size of 9 continuously compounded returns minus 1). We take the square root of the variance to find the standard deviation. Finally, we multiply the standard deviation by $\sqrt{250}$ to annualize it.

The continuously compounded daily returns are (reading across the line, then down):

$\ln(10.87/10.68) = 0.017634$, $\ln(11.00/10.87) = 0.011889$,

$\ln(10.95/11.00) = -0.004556$, $\ln(11.26/10.95) = 0.027917$,

$\ln(11.31/11.26) = 0.004431$, $\ln(11.23/11.31) = -0.007099$,

$\ln(10.91/11.23) = -0.028909$, $\ln(10.80/10.91) = -0.010134$,

$\ln(10.47/10.80) = -0.031032$.

Sum = -0.019859, Mean = -0.002207, Variance = 0.000398, Standard deviation = 0.019937

The standard deviation of continuously compounded daily returns is 0.019937. Then $\sigma\sqrt{T} = 0.019937\sqrt{250} = 0.315232$ or 31.5 percent.

17. A. Elements that should appear in a definition of Monte Carlo simulation are that it makes use of a computer; that it is used to represent the operation of a complex system, or in some applications, to find an approximate solution to a problem; and that it involves the generation of a large number of random samples from a specified probability distribution. The exact wording can vary, but one definition follows:

Monte Carlo simulation in finance involves the use of a computer to represent the operation of a complex financial system. In some important applications, Monte Carlo simulation is used to find an approximate solution to a complex financial problem. An integral part of Monte Carlo simulation is the generation of a large number of random samples from a probability distribution.

B. *Strengths.* Monte Carlo simulation can be used to price complex securities for which no analytic expression is available, particularly European-style options.

Weaknesses. Monte Carlo simulation provides only statistical estimates, not exact results. Analytic methods, when available, provide more insight into cause-and-effect relationships than does Monte Carlo simulation.

18. In the text, we described how we could use Monte Carlo simulation to value an Asian option, a complex European-style option. Just as we can calculate the average value of the stock over a simulation trial to value an Asian option, we can also calculate the minimum value of the stock over a simulation trial. Then, for a given simulation trial, we can calculate the terminal value of the call, given the minimum value of the stock for the simulation trial. We can then discount back this terminal value to the present to get the value of the call today ($t = 0$). The average of these $t = 0$ values over all simulation trials is the Monte Carlo simulated value of the lookback call option.

19. C is correct. The portfolio with the highest safety-first ratio minimizes the probability that the portfolio return will be less than the shortfall level (given normality). In this problem, the shortfall level is equal to the risk-free rate of return and thus the highest safety-first ratio portfolio will be the same as the highest Sharpe ratio portfolio.

20. A is correct. A normal distribution is suitable for describing asset returns. However, the normal distribution is not suitable for asset prices because asset prices cannot be negative. The lognormal distribution is bounded by zero (skewed to the right) and is suitable for describing distributions of asset prices.

READING

10

Sampling and Estimation

by Richard A. DeFusco, CFA, Dennis W. McLeavey, CFA, Jerald E. Pinto, CFA, and David E. Runkle, CFA

LEARNING OUTCOMES

Mastery	The candidate should be able to:
☐	**a** define simple random sampling and a sampling distribution;
☐	**b** explain sampling error;
☐	**c** distinguish between simple random and stratified random sampling;
☐	**d** distinguish between time-series and cross-sectional data;
☐	**e** explain the central limit theorem and its importance;
☐	**f** calculate and interpret the standard error of the sample mean;
☐	**g** identify and describe desirable properties of an estimator;
☐	**h** distinguish between a point estimate and a confidence interval estimate of a population parameter;
☐	**i** describe the properties of Student's *t*-distribution and calculate and interpret its degrees of freedom;
☐	**j** calculate and interpret a confidence interval for a population mean, given a normal distribution with 1) a known population variance, 2) an unknown population variance, or 3) an unknown variance and a large sample size;
☐	**k** describe the issues regarding selection of the appropriate sample size, data-mining bias, sample selection bias, survivorship bias, look-ahead bias, and time-period bias.

INTRODUCTION

1

Each day, we observe the high, low, and close of stock market indexes from around the world. Indexes such as the S&P 500 Index and the Nikkei-Dow Jones Average are samples of stocks. Although the S&P 500 and the Nikkei do not represent the populations of U.S. or Japanese stocks, we view them as valid indicators of the whole population's behavior. As analysts, we are accustomed to using this sample information to assess how various markets from around the world are performing. Any statistics that we compute with sample information, however, are only estimates of the under-lying population parameters. A sample, then, is a subset of the population—a subset studied to infer conclusions about the population itself.

Quantitative Methods for Investment Analysis, Second Edition, by Richard A. DeFusco, CFA, Dennis W. McLeavey, CFA, Jerald E. Pinto, CFA, and David E. Runkle, CFA. Copyright © 2004 by CFA Institute.

This reading explores how we sample and use sample information to estimate population parameters. In the next section, we discuss **sampling**—the process of obtaining a sample. In investments, we continually make use of the mean as a measure of central tendency of random variables, such as return and earnings per share. Even when the probability distribution of the random variable is unknown, we can make probability statements about the population mean using the central limit theorem. In Section 3, we discuss and illustrate this key result. Following that discussion, we turn to statistical estimation. Estimation seeks precise answers to the question "What is this parameter's value?"

The central limit theorem and estimation are the core of the body of methods presented in this reading. In investments, we apply these and other statistical techniques to financial data; we often interpret the results for the purpose of deciding what works and what does not work in investments. We end this reading with a discussion of the interpretation of statistical results based on financial data and the possible pitfalls in this process.

SAMPLING

In this section, we present the various methods for obtaining information on a population (all members of a specified group) through samples (part of the population). The information on a population that we try to obtain usually concerns the value of a **parameter**, a quantity computed from or used to describe a population of data. When we use a sample to estimate a parameter, we make use of sample statistics (statistics, for short). A **statistic** is a quantity computed from or used to describe a sample of data.

We take samples for one of two reasons. In some cases, we cannot possibly examine every member of the population. In other cases, examining every member of the population would not be economically efficient. Thus, savings of time and money are two primary factors that cause an analyst to use sampling to answer a question about a population. In this section, we discuss two methods of random sampling: simple random sampling and stratified random sampling. We then define and illustrate the two types of data an analyst uses: cross-sectional data and time-series data.

2.1 Simple Random Sampling

Suppose a telecommunications equipment analyst wants to know how much major customers will spend on average for equipment during the coming year. One strategy is to survey the population of telecom equipment customers and inquire what their purchasing plans are. In statistical terms, the characteristics of the population of customers' planned expenditures would then usually be expressed by descriptive measures such as the mean and variance. Surveying all companies, however, would be very costly in terms of time and money.

Alternatively, the analyst can collect a representative sample of companies and survey them about upcoming telecom equipment expenditures. In this case, the analyst will compute the sample mean expenditure, $\bar{X}$, a statistic. This strategy has a substantial advantage over polling the whole population because it can be accomplished more quickly and at lower cost.

Sampling, however, introduces error. The error arises because not all the companies in the population are surveyed. The analyst who decides to sample is trading time and money for sampling error.

When an analyst chooses to sample, he must formulate a sampling plan. A **sampling plan** is the set of rules used to select a sample. The basic type of sample from which we can draw statistically sound conclusions about a population is the **simple random sample** (random sample, for short).

■ **Definition of Simple Random Sample.** A simple random sample is a subset of a larger population created in such a way that each element of the population has an equal probability of being selected to the subset.

The procedure of drawing a sample to satisfy the definition of a simple random sample is called **simple random sampling**. How is simple random sampling carried out? We need a method that ensures randomness—the lack of any pattern—in the selection of the sample. For a finite (limited) population, the most common method for obtaining a random sample involves the use of random numbers (numbers with assured properties of randomness). First, we number the members of the population in sequence. For example, if the population contains 500 members, we number them in sequence with three digits, starting with 001 and ending with 500. Suppose we want a simple random sample of size 50. In that case, using a computer random-number generator or a table of random numbers, we generate a series of three-digit random numbers. We then match these random numbers with the number codes of the population members until we have selected a sample of size 50.

Sometimes we cannot code (or even identify) all the members of a population. We often use **systematic sampling** in such cases. With systematic sampling, we select every *k*th member until we have a sample of the desired size. The sample that results from this procedure should be approximately random. Real sampling situations may require that we take an approximately random sample.

Suppose the telecommunications equipment analyst polls a random sample of telecom equipment customers to determine the average equipment expenditure. The sample mean will provide the analyst with an estimate of the population mean expenditure. Any difference between the sample mean and the population mean is called **sampling error**.

■ **Definition of Sampling Error.** Sampling error is the difference between the observed value of a statistic and the quantity it is intended to estimate.

A random sample reflects the properties of the population in an unbiased way, and sample statistics, such as the sample mean, computed on the basis of a random sample are valid estimates of the underlying population parameters.

A sample statistic is a random variable. In other words, not only do the original data from the population have a distribution but so does the sample statistic.

This distribution is the statistic's **sampling distribution**.

■ **Definition of Sampling Distribution of a Statistic.** The sampling distribution of a statistic is the distribution of all the distinct possible values that the statistic can assume when computed from samples of the same size randomly drawn from the same population.

In the case of the sample mean, for example, we refer to the "sampling distribution of the sample mean" or the distribution of the sample mean. We will have more to say about sampling distributions later in this reading. Next, however, we look at another sampling method that is useful in investment analysis.

2.2 Stratified Random Sampling

The simple random sampling method just discussed may not be the best approach in all situations. One frequently used alternative is stratified random sampling.

■ **Definition of Stratified Random Sampling.** In stratified random sampling, the population is divided into subpopulations (strata) based on one or more classification criteria. Simple random samples are then drawn from each stratum in sizes proportional to the relative size of each stratum in the population. These samples are then pooled to form a stratified random sample.

In contrast to simple random sampling, stratified random sampling guarantees that population subdivisions of interest are represented in the sample. Another advantage is that estimates of parameters produced from stratified sampling have greater precision—that is, smaller variance or dispersion—than estimates obtained from simple random sampling.

Bond indexing is one area in which stratified sampling is frequently applied. **Indexing** is an investment strategy in which an investor constructs a portfolio to mirror the performance of a specified index. In pure bond indexing, also called the full-replication approach, the investor attempts to fully replicate an index by owning all the bonds in the index in proportion to their market value weights. Many bond indexes consist of thousands of issues, however, so pure bond indexing is difficult to implement. In addition, transaction costs would be high because many bonds do not have liquid markets. Although a simple random sample could be a solution to the cost problem, the sample would probably not match the index's major risk factors—interest rate sensitivity, for example. Because the major risk factors of fixed-income portfolios are well known and quantifiable, stratified sampling offers a more effective approach. In this approach, we divide the population of index bonds into groups of similar duration (interest rate sensitivity), cash flow distribution, sector, credit quality, and call exposure. We refer to each group as a stratum or cell (a term frequently used in this context).[1] Then, we choose a sample from each stratum proportional to the relative market weighting of the stratum in the index to be replicated.

Example 1

Bond Indexes and Stratified Sampling

Suppose you are the manager of a mutual fund indexed to the Lehman Brothers Government Index. You are exploring several approaches to indexing, including a stratified sampling approach. You first distinguish agency bonds from U.S. Treasury bonds. For each of these two groups, you define 10 maturity intervals—1 to 2 years, 2 to 3 years, 3 to 4 years, 4 to 6 years, 6 to 8 years, 8 to 10 years, 10 to 12 years, 12 to 15 years, 15 to 20 years, and 20 to 30 years—and also separate the bonds with coupons (annual interest rates) of 6 percent or less from the bonds with coupons of more than 6 percent.

1. How many cells or strata does this sampling plan entail?
2. If you use this sampling plan, what is the minimum number of issues the indexed portfolio can have?
3. Suppose that in selecting among the securities that qualify for selection within each cell, you apply a criterion concerning the liquidity of the security's market. Is the sample obtained random? Explain your answer.

Solution to 1:

We have 2 issuer classifications, 10 maturity classifications, and 2 coupon classifications. So, in total, this plan entails 2(10)(2) = 40 different strata or cells. (This answer is an application of the multiplication rule of counting discussed in the reading on probability concepts.)

---

[1] See Fabozzi (2004b).

Solution to 2:

You cannot have fewer than one issue for each cell, so the portfolio must include at least 40 issues.

Solution to 3:

If you apply any additional criteria to the selection of securities for the cells, not every security that might be included has an equal probability of being selected. As a result, the sampling is not random. In practice, indexing using stratified sampling usually does not strictly involve random sampling because the selection of bond issues within cells is subject to various additional criteria. Because the purpose of sampling in this application is not to make an inference about a population parameter but rather to index a portfolio, lack of randomness is not in itself a problem in this application of stratified sampling.

In the next section, we discuss the kinds of data used by financial analysts in sampling and practical issues that arise in selecting samples.

2.3 Time-Series and Cross-Sectional Data

Investment analysts commonly work with both time-series and cross-sectional data. A time series is a sequence of returns collected at discrete and equally spaced intervals of time (such as a historical series of monthly stock returns). Cross-sectional data are data on some characteristic of individuals, groups, geographical regions, or companies at a single point in time. The 2003 year-end book value per share for all New York Stock Exchange-listed companies is an example of cross-sectional data.

Economic or financial theory offers no basis for determining whether a long or short time period should be selected to collect a sample. As analysts, we might have to look for subtle clues. For example, combining data from a period of fixed exchange rates with data from a period of floating exchange rates would be inappropriate. The variance of exchange rates when exchange rates were fixed would certainly be less than when rates were allowed to float. As a consequence, we would not be sampling from a population described by a single set of parameters.[2] Tight versus loose **monetary policy** also influences the distribution of returns to stocks; thus, combining data from tight-money and loose-money periods would be inappropriate. Example 2 illustrates the problems that can arise when sampling from more than one distribution.

Example 2

Calculating Sharpe Ratios: One or Two Years of Quarterly Data

Analysts often use the Sharpe ratio to evaluate the performance of a managed portfolio. The **Sharpe ratio** is the average return in excess of the risk-free rate divided by the standard deviation of returns. This ratio measures the excess return earned per unit of standard deviation of return.

To compute the Sharpe ratio, suppose that an analyst collects eight quarterly excess returns (i.e., total return in excess of the risk-free rate). During the first year, the investment manager of the portfolio followed a low-risk strategy, and

---

2 When the mean or variance of a time series is not constant through time, the time series is not stationary.

during the second year, the manager followed a high-risk strategy. For each of these years, the analyst also tracks the quarterly excess returns of some benchmark against which the manager will be evaluated. For each of the two years, the Sharpe ratio for the benchmark is 0.21. Table 1 gives the calculation of the Sharpe ratio of the portfolio.

Table 1	Calculation of Sharpe Ratios: Low-Risk and High-Risk Strategies	
Quarter/Measure	**Year 1 Excess Returns**	**Year 2 Excess Returns**
Quarter 1	−3%	−12%
Quarter 2	5	20
Quarter 3	−3	−12
Quarter 4	5	20
Quarterly average	1%	4%
Quarterly standard deviation	4.62%	18.48%
Sharpe ratio = 0.22 = 1/4.62 = 4/18.48		

For the first year, during which the manager followed a low-risk strategy, the average quarterly return in excess of the risk-free rate was 1 percent with a standard deviation of 4.62 percent. The Sharpe ratio is thus 1/4.62 = 0.22. The second year's results mirror the first year except for the higher average return and volatility. The Sharpe ratio for the second year is 4/18.48 = 0.22. The Sharpe ratio for the benchmark is 0.21 during the first and second years. Because larger Sharpe ratios are better than smaller ones (providing more return per unit of risk), the manager appears to have outperformed the benchmark.

Now, suppose the analyst believes a larger sample to be superior to a small one. She thus decides to pool the two years together and calculate a Sharpe ratio based on eight quarterly observations. The average quarterly excess return for the two years is the average of each year's average excess return. For the two-year period, the average excess return is (1 + 4)/2 = 2.5 percent per quarter. The standard deviation for all eight quarters measured from the sample mean of 2.5 percent is 12.57 percent. The portfolio's Sharpe ratio for the two-year period is now 2.5/12.57 = 0.199; the Sharpe ratio for the benchmark remains 0.21. Thus, when returns for the two-year period are pooled, the manager appears to have provided less return per unit of risk than the benchmark and less when compared with the separate yearly results.

The problem with using eight quarters of return data is that the analyst has violated the assumption that the sampled returns come from the same population. As a result of the change in the manager's investment strategy, returns in Year 2 followed a different distribution than returns in Year 1. Clearly, during Year 1, returns were generated by an underlying population with lower mean and variance than the population of the second year. Combining the results for the first and second years yielded a sample that was representative of no population. Because the larger sample did not satisfy model assumptions, any conclusions the analyst reached based on the larger sample are incorrect. For this example, she was better off using a smaller sample than a larger sample because the smaller sample represented a more homogeneous distribution of returns.

The second basic type of data is cross-sectional data.[3] With cross-sectional data, the observations in the sample represent a characteristic of individuals, groups, geographical regions, or companies at a single point in time. The telecommunications analyst discussed previously is essentially collecting a cross-section of planned capital expenditures for the coming year.

Whenever we sample cross-sectionally, certain assumptions must be met if we wish to summarize the data in a meaningful way. Again, a useful approach is to think of the observation of interest as a random variable that comes from some underlying population with a given mean and variance. As we collect our sample and begin to summarize the data, we must be sure that all the data do, in fact, come from the same underlying population. For example, an analyst might be interested in how efficiently companies use their inventory assets. Some companies, however, turn over their inventory more quickly than others because of differences in their operating environments (e.g., grocery stores turn over inventory more quickly than automobile manufacturers, in general). So the distribution of inventory turnover rates may not be characterized by a single distribution with a given mean and variance. Therefore, summarizing inventory turnover across all companies might be inappropriate. If random variables are generated by different underlying distributions, the sample statistics computed from combined samples are not related to one underlying population parameter. The size of the sampling error in such cases is unknown.

In instances such as these, analysts often summarize company-level data by industry. Attempting to summarize by industry partially addresses the problem of differing underlying distributions, but large corporations are likely to be in more than one industrial sector, so analysts should be sure they understand how companies are assigned to the industry groups.

Whether we deal with time-series data or cross-sectional data, we must be sure to have a random sample that is representative of the population we wish to study. With the objective of inferring information from representative samples, we now turn to the next part of this reading, which focuses on the central limit theorem as well as point and interval estimates of the population mean.

DISTRIBUTION OF THE SAMPLE MEAN   3

Earlier in this reading, we presented a telecommunications equipment analyst who decided to sample in order to estimate mean planned capital expenditures by his customers. Supposing that the sample is representative of the underlying population, how can the analyst assess the sampling error in estimating the population mean? Viewed as a formula that takes a function of the random outcomes of a random variable, the sample mean is itself a random variable with a probability distribution. That probability distribution is called the statistic's sampling distribution.[4] To estimate how

---

3 The reader may also encounter two types of datasets that have both time-series and cross-sectional aspects. **Panel data** consist of observations through time on a single characteristic of multiple observational units. For example, the annual inflation rate of the Eurozone countries over a five-year period would represent panel data. **Longitudinal data** consist of observations on characteristic(s) of the same observational unit through time. Observations on a set of financial ratios for a single company over a 10-year period would be an example of longitudinal data. Both panel and longitudinal data may be represented by arrays (matrixes) in which successive rows represent the observations for successive time periods.

4 Sometimes confusion arises because "sample mean" is also used in another sense. When we calculate the sample mean for a particular sample, we obtain a definite number, say 8. If we state that "the sample mean is 8" we are using "sample mean" in the sense of a particular outcome of sample mean as a random variable. The number 8 is of course a constant and does not have a probability distribution. In this discussion, we are not referring to "sample mean" in the sense of a constant number related to a particular sample.

closely the sample mean can be expected to match the underlying population mean, the analyst needs to understand the sampling distribution of the mean. Fortunately, we have a result, the central limit theorem, that helps us understand the sampling distribution of the mean for many of the estimation problems we face.

3.1 The Central Limit Theorem

One of the most practically useful theorems in probability theory, the central limit theorem has important implications for how we construct confidence intervals and test hypotheses. Formally, it is stated as follows:

- **The Central Limit Theorem.** Given a population described by any probability distribution having mean μ and finite variance σ^2, the sampling distribution of the sample mean $\overline{X}$ computed from samples of size n from this population will be approximately normal with mean μ (the population mean) and variance σ^2/n (the population variance divided by n) when the sample size n is large.

The central limit theorem allows us to make quite precise probability statements about the population mean by using the sample mean, *whatever the distribution of the population* (so long as it has finite variance), because the sample mean follows an approximate normal distribution for large-size samples. The obvious question is, "When is a sample's size large enough that we can assume the sample mean is normally distributed?" In general, when sample size n is greater than or equal to 30, we can assume that the sample mean is approximately normally distributed.[5]

The central limit theorem states that the variance of the distribution of the sample mean is σ^2/n. The positive square root of variance is standard deviation. The standard deviation of a sample statistic is known as the standard error of the statistic. The standard error of the sample mean is an important quantity in applying the central limit theorem in practice.

- **Definition of the Standard Error of the Sample Mean.** For sample mean $\overline{X}$ calculated from a sample generated by a population with standard deviation σ, the standard error of the sample mean is given by one of two expressions:

$$\sigma_{\overline{X}} = \frac{\sigma}{\sqrt{n}} \tag{1}$$

when we know σ, the population standard deviation, or by

$$s_{\overline{X}} = \frac{s}{\sqrt{n}} \tag{2}$$

when we do not know the population standard deviation and need to use the sample standard deviation, s, to estimate it.[6]

---

5 When the underlying population is very nonnormal, a sample size well in excess of 30 may be required for the normal distribution to be a good description of the sampling distribution of the mean.

6 We need to note a technical point: When we take a sample of size n from a finite population of size N, we apply a shrinkage factor to the estimate of the standard error of the sample mean that is called the finite population correction factor (fpc). The fpc is equal to $[(N-n)/(N-1)]^{1/2}$. Thus, if $N = 100$ and $n = 20$, $[(100-20)/(100-1)]^{1/2} = 0.898933$. If we have estimated a standard error of, say, 20, according to Equation 1 or Equation 2, the new estimate is $20(0.898933) = 17.978663$. The fpc applies only when we sample from a finite population without replacement; most practitioners also do not apply the fpc if sample size n is very small relative to N (say, less than 5 percent of N). For more information on the finite population correction factor, see Daniel and Terrell (1995).

In practice, we almost always need to use Equation 2. The estimate of s is given by the square root of the sample variance, s^2, calculated as follows:

$$s^2 = \frac{\sum_{i=1}^{n}\left(X_i - \bar{X}\right)^2}{n-1}$$

(3)

We will soon see how we can use the sample mean and its standard error to make probability statements about the population mean by using the technique of confidence intervals. First, however, we provide an illustration of the central limit theorem's force.

Example 3

The Central Limit Theorem

It is remarkable that the sample mean for large sample sizes will be distributed normally regardless of the distribution of the underlying population. To illustrate the central limit theorem in action, we specify in this example a distinctly non-normal distribution and use it to generate a large number of random samples of size 100. We then calculate the sample mean for each sample. The frequency distribution of the calculated sample means is an approximation of the sampling distribution of the sample mean for that sample size. Does that sampling distribution look like a normal distribution?

We return to the telecommunications analyst studying the capital expenditure plans of telecom businesses. Suppose that capital expenditures for communications equipment form a continuous uniform random variable with a **lower bound** equal to $0 and an upper bound equal to $100—for short, call this a uniform (0, 100) random variable. The probability function of this continuous uniform random variable has a rather simple shape that is anything but normal. It is a horizontal line with a vertical intercept equal to 1/100. Unlike a normal random variable, for which outcomes close to the mean are most likely, all possible outcomes are equally likely for a uniform random variable.

To illustrate the power of the central limit theorem, we conduct a Monte Carlo simulation to study the capital expenditure plans of telecom businesses.[7] In this simulation, we collect 200 random samples of the capital expenditures of 100 companies (200 random draws, each consisting of the capital expenditures of 100 companies with $n = 100$). In each simulation trial, 100 values for capital expenditure are generated from the uniform (0, 100) distribution. For each random sample, we then compute the sample mean. We conduct 200 simulation trials in total. Because we have specified the distribution generating the samples, we know that the population mean capital expenditure is equal to ($0 + $100 million)/2 = $50 million; the population variance of capital expenditures is equal to $(100 - 0)^2/12 = 833.33$; thus, the standard deviation is $28.87 million and the standard error is $28.87/\sqrt{100} = 2.887$ under the central limit theorem.[8]

---

7 Monte Carlo simulation involves the use of a computer to represent the operation of a system subject to risk. An integral part of Monte Carlo simulation is the generation of a large number of random samples from a specified probability distribution or distributions.

8 If a is the lower limit of a uniform random variable and b is the upper limit, then the random variable's mean is given by $(a + b)/2$ and its variance is given by $(b - a)^2/12$. The reading on common probability distributions fully describes continuous uniform random variables.

The results of this Monte Carlo experiment are tabulated in Table 2 in the form of a frequency distribution. This distribution is the estimated sampling distribution of the sample mean.

Table 2	Frequency Distribution: 200 Random Samples of a Uniform (0,100) Random Variable	
Range of Sample Means ($ Million)		**Absolute Frequency**
$42.5 \leq \overline{X} < 44$		1
$44 \leq \overline{X} < 45.5$		6
$45.5 \leq \overline{X} < 47$		22
$47 \leq \overline{X} < 48.5$		39
$48.5 \leq \overline{X} < 50$		41
$50 \leq \overline{X} < 51.5$		39
$51.5 \leq \overline{X} < 53$		23
$53 \leq \overline{X} < 54.5$		12
$54.5 \leq \overline{X} < 56$		12
$56 \leq \overline{X} < 57.5$		5

Note: $\overline{X}$ is the mean capital expenditure for each sample.

The frequency distribution can be described as bell-shaped and centered close to the population mean of 50. The most frequent, or modal, range, with 41 observations, is 48.5 to 50. The overall average of the sample means is $49.92, with a standard error equal to $2.80. The calculated standard error is close to the value of 2.887 given by the central limit theorem. The discrepancy between calculated and expected values of the mean and standard deviation under the central limit theorem is a result of random chance (sampling error).

In summary, although the distribution of the underlying population is very nonnormal, the simulation has shown that a normal distribution well describes the estimated sampling distribution of the sample mean, with mean and standard error consistent with the values predicted by the central limit theorem.

To summarize, according to the central limit theorem, when we sample from any distribution, the distribution of the sample mean will have the following properties as long as our sample size is large:

■ The distribution of the sample mean $\overline{X}$ will be approximately normal.

■ The mean of the distribution of $\overline{X}$ will be equal to the mean of the population from which the samples are drawn.

■ The variance of the distribution of $\overline{X}$ will be equal to the variance of the population divided by the sample size.

We next discuss the concepts and tools related to estimating the population parameters, with a special focus on the population mean. We focus on the population mean because analysts are more likely to meet interval estimates for the population mean than any other type of interval estimate.

POINT AND INTERVAL ESTIMATES OF THE POPULATION MEAN

Statistical inference traditionally consists of two branches, hypothesis testing and estimation. Hypothesis testing addresses the question "Is the value of this parameter (say, a population mean) equal to some specific value (0, for example)?" In this process, we have a hypothesis concerning the value of a parameter, and we seek to determine whether the evidence from a sample supports or does not support that hypothesis. We discuss hypothesis testing in detail in the reading on hypothesis testing.

The second branch of statistical inference, and the focus of this reading, is estimation. Estimation seeks an answer to the question "What is this parameter's (for example, the population mean's) value?" In estimating, unlike in hypothesis testing, we do not start with a hypothesis about a parameter's value and seek to test it. Rather, we try to make the best use of the information in a sample to form one of several types of estimates of the parameter's value. With estimation, we are interested in arriving at a rule for best calculating a single number to estimate the unknown population parameter (a point estimate). Together with calculating a point estimate, we may also be interested in calculating a range of values that brackets the unknown population parameter with some specified level of probability (a confidence interval). In Section 4.1 we discuss point estimates of parameters and then, in Section 4.2, the formulation of confidence intervals for the population mean.

4.1 Point Estimators

An important concept introduced in this reading is that sample statistics viewed as formulas involving random outcomes are random variables. The formulas that we use to compute the sample mean and all the other sample statistics are examples of estimation formulas or **estimators**. The particular value that we calculate from sample observations using an estimator is called an **estimate**. An estimator has a sampling distribution; an estimate is a fixed number pertaining to a given sample and thus has no sampling distribution. To take the example of the mean, the calculated value of the sample mean in a given sample, used as an estimate of the population mean, is called a **point estimate** of the population mean. As Example 3 illustrated, the formula for the sample mean can and will yield different results in repeated samples as different samples are drawn from the population.

In many applications, we have a choice among a number of possible estimators for estimating a given parameter. How do we make our choice? We often select estimators because they have one or more desirable statistical properties. Following is a brief description of three desirable properties of estimators: unbiasedness (lack of bias), efficiency, and consistency.[9]

- **Definition of Unbiasedness.** An unbiased estimator is one whose expected value (the mean of its sampling distribution) equals the parameter it is intended to estimate.

For example, the expected value of the sample mean, $\bar{X}$, equals μ, the population mean, so we say that the sample mean is an unbiased estimator (of the population mean). The sample variance, s^2, which is calculated using a divisor of $n - 1$ (Equation 3), is an unbiased estimator of the population variance, σ^2. If we were to calculate the sample variance using a divisor of n, the estimator would be biased: Its expected value would be smaller than the population variance. We would say that sample variance calculated with a divisor of n is a biased estimator of the population variance.

---

9 See Daniel and Terrell (1995) or Greene (2003) for a thorough treatment of the properties of estimators.

Whenever one unbiased estimator of a parameter can be found, we can usually find a large number of other unbiased estimators. How do we choose among alternative unbiased estimators? The criterion of efficiency provides a way to select from among unbiased estimators of a parameter.

■ **Definition of Efficiency.** An unbiased estimator is efficient if no other unbiased estimator of the same parameter has a sampling distribution with smaller variance.

To explain the definition, in repeated samples we expect the estimates from an efficient estimator to be more tightly grouped around the mean than estimates from other unbiased estimators. Efficiency is an important property of an estimator.[10] Sample mean $\bar{X}$ is an efficient estimator of the population mean; sample variance s^2 is an efficient estimator of σ^2.

Recall that a statistic's sampling distribution is defined for a given sample size. Different sample sizes define different sampling distributions. For example, the variance of sampling distribution of the sample mean is smaller for larger sample sizes. Unbiasedness and efficiency are properties of an estimator's sampling distribution that hold for any size sample. An unbiased estimator is unbiased equally in a sample of size 10 and in a sample of size 1,000. In some problems, however, we cannot find estimators that have such desirable properties as unbiasedness in small samples.[11] In this case, statisticians may justify the choice of an estimator based on the properties of the estimator's sampling distribution in extremely large samples, the estimator's so-called asymptotic properties. Among such properties, the most important is consistency.

■ **Definition of Consistency.** A consistent estimator is one for which the probability of estimates close to the value of the population parameter increases as sample size increases.

Somewhat more technically, we can define a consistent estimator as an estimator whose sampling distribution becomes concentrated on the value of the parameter it is intended to estimate as the sample size approaches infinity. The sample mean, in addition to being an efficient estimator, is also a consistent estimator of the population mean: As sample size n goes to infinity, its standard error, $\sigma/\sqrt{n}$, goes to 0 and its sampling distribution becomes concentrated right over the value of population mean, μ. To summarize, we can think of a consistent estimator as one that tends to produce more and more accurate estimates of the population parameter as we increase the sample's size. If an estimator is consistent, we may attempt to increase the accuracy of estimates of a population parameter by calculating estimates using a larger sample. For an inconsistent estimator, however, increasing sample size does not help to increase the probability of accurate estimates.

4.2 Confidence Intervals for the Population Mean

When we need a single number as an estimate of a population parameter, we make use of a point estimate. However, because of sampling error, the point estimate is not likely to equal the population parameter in any given sample. Often, a more useful approach than finding a point estimate is to find a range of values that we expect to bracket the parameter with a specified level of probability—an interval estimate of the parameter. A confidence interval fulfills this role.

---

10 An efficient estimator is sometimes referred to as the best unbiased estimator.
11 Such problems frequently arise in regression and time-series analyses.

- **Definition of Confidence Interval.** A confidence interval is a range for which one can assert with a given probability $1 - \alpha$, called the **degree of confidence**, that it will contain the parameter it is intended to estimate. This interval is often referred to as the $100(1 - \alpha)\%$ confidence interval for the parameter.

The endpoints of a confidence interval are referred to as the lower and upper confidence limits. In this reading, we are concerned only with two-sided confidence intervals—confidence intervals for which we calculate both lower and upper limits.[12]

Confidence intervals are frequently given either a probabilistic interpretation or a practical interpretation. In the probabilistic interpretation, we interpret a 95 percent confidence interval for the population mean as follows. In repeated sampling, 95 percent of such confidence intervals will, in the long run, include or bracket the population mean. For example, suppose we sample from the population 1,000 times, and based on each sample, we construct a 95 percent confidence interval using the calculated sample mean. Because of random chance, these confidence intervals will vary from each other, but we expect 95 percent, or 950, of these intervals to include the unknown value of the population mean. In practice, we generally do not carry out such repeated sampling. Therefore, in the practical interpretation, we assert that we are 95 percent confident that a single 95 percent confidence interval contains the population mean. We are justified in making this statement because we know that 95 percent of all possible confidence intervals constructed in the same manner will contain the population mean. The confidence intervals that we discuss in this reading have structures similar to the following basic structure:

- **Construction of Confidence Intervals.** A $100(1 - \alpha)\%$ confidence interval for a parameter has the following structure.

    Point estimate ± Reliability factor × Standard error

where

Point estimate	= a point estimate of the parameter (a value of a sample statistic)
Reliability factor	= a number based on the assumed distribution of the point estimate and the degree of confidence $(1 - \alpha)$ for the confidence interval
Standard error	= the standard error of the sample statistic providing the point estimate[13]

The most basic confidence interval for the population mean arises when we are sampling from a normal distribution with known variance. The reliability factor in this case is based on the standard normal distribution, which has a mean of 0 and a variance of 1. A standard normal random variable is conventionally denoted by Z. The notation z_α denotes the point of the standard normal distribution such that α of the probability remains in the right tail. For example, 0.05 or 5 percent of the possible values of a standard normal random variable are larger than $z_{0.05} = 1.65$.

---

12 It is also possible to define two types of one-sided confidence intervals for a population parameter. A lower one-sided confidence interval establishes a lower limit only. Associated with such an interval is an assertion that with a specified degree of confidence the population parameter equals or exceeds the lower limit. An upper one-sided confidence interval establishes an upper limit only; the related assertion is that the population parameter is less than or equal to that upper limit, with a specified degree of confidence. Investment researchers rarely present one-sided confidence intervals, however.

13 The quantity (reliability factor) × (standard error) is sometimes called the precision of the estimator; larger values of the product imply lower precision in estimating the population parameter.

Suppose we want to construct a 95 percent confidence interval for the population mean and, for this purpose, we have taken a sample of size 100 from a normally distributed population with known variance of $\sigma^2 = 400$ (so, $\sigma = 20$). We calculate a sample mean of $\bar{X} = 25$. Our point estimate of the population mean is, therefore, 25. If we move 1.96 standard deviations above the mean of a normal distribution, 0.025 or 2.5 percent of the probability remains in the right tail; by symmetry of the normal distribution, if we move 1.96 standard deviations below the mean, 0.025 or 2.5 percent of the probability remains in the left tail. In total, 0.05 or 5 percent of the probability is in the two tails and 0.95 or 95 percent lies in between. So, $z_{0.025} = 1.96$ is the reliability factor for this 95 percent confidence interval. Note the relationship $100(1 - \alpha)\%$ for the confidence interval and the $z_{\alpha/2}$ for the reliability factor. The standard error of the sample mean, given by Equation 1, is $\sigma_{\bar{X}} = 20/\sqrt{100} = 2$. The confidence interval, therefore, has a lower limit of $\bar{X} - 1.96\sigma_{\bar{X}} = 25 - 1.96(2) = 25 - 3.92 = 21.08$. The upper limit of the confidence interval is $\bar{X} + 1.96\sigma_{\bar{X}} = 25 + 1.96(2) = 25 + 3.92 = 28.92$. The 95 percent confidence interval for the population mean spans 21.08 to 28.92.

- **Confidence Intervals for the Population Mean (Normally Distributed Population with Known Variance).** A $100(1 - \alpha)\%$ confidence interval for population mean μ when we are sampling from a normal distribution with known variance σ^2 is given by

$$\bar{X} \pm z_{\alpha/2} \frac{\sigma}{\sqrt{n}} \tag{4}$$

The reliability factors for the most frequently used confidence intervals are as follows.

- **Reliability Factors for Confidence Intervals Based on the Standard Normal Distribution.** We use the following reliability factors when we construct confidence intervals based on the standard normal distribution:[14]
  - 90 percent confidence intervals: Use $z_{0.05} = 1.65$
  - 95 percent confidence intervals: Use $z_{0.025} = 1.96$
  - 99 percent confidence intervals: Use $z_{0.005} = 2.58$

These reliability factors highlight an important fact about all confidence intervals. As we increase the degree of confidence, the confidence interval becomes wider and gives us less precise information about the quantity we want to estimate. "The surer we want to be, the less we have to be sure of."[15]

In practice, the assumption that the sampling distribution of the sample mean is at least approximately normal is frequently reasonable, either because the underlying distribution is approximately normal or because we have a large sample and the central limit theorem applies. However, rarely do we know the population variance in practice. When the population variance is unknown but the sample mean is at least approximately normally distributed, we have two acceptable ways to calculate the confidence interval for the population mean. We will soon discuss the more conservative approach, which is based on Student's t-distribution (the t-distribution, for short).[16] In investment literature, it is the most frequently used approach in both estimation and hypothesis tests concerning the mean when the population variance is not known, whether sample size is small or large.

14 Most practitioners use values for $z_{0.05}$ and $z_{0.005}$ that are carried to two decimal places. For reference, more exact values for $z_{0.05}$ and $z_{0.005}$ are 1.645 and 2.575, respectively. For a quick calculation of a 95 percent confidence interval, $z_{0.025}$ is sometimes rounded from 1.96 to 2.
15 Freund and Williams (1977), p. 266.
16 The distribution of the statistic t is called Student's t-distribution after the pen name "Student" used by W. S. Gosset, who published his work in 1908.

A second approach to confidence intervals for the population mean, based on the standard normal distribution, is the z-alternative. It can be used only when sample size is large. (In general, a sample size of 30 or larger may be considered large.) In contrast to the confidence interval given in Equation 4, this confidence interval uses the sample standard deviation, s, in computing the standard error of the sample mean (Equation 2).

- **Confidence Intervals for the Population Mean—The z-Alternative (Large Sample, Population Variance Unknown).** A $100(1 - \alpha)$% confidence interval for population mean μ when sampling from any distribution with unknown variance and when sample size is large is given by

$$\bar{X} \pm z_{\alpha/2} \frac{s}{\sqrt{n}} \tag{5}$$

Because this type of confidence interval appears quite often, we illustrate its calculation in Example 4.

Example 4

Confidence Interval for the Population Mean of Sharpe Ratios—z-Statistic

Suppose an investment analyst takes a random sample of U.S. equity mutual funds and calculates the average Sharpe ratio. The sample size is 100, and the average Sharpe ratio is 0.45. The sample has a standard deviation of 0.30. Calculate and interpret the 90 percent confidence interval for the population mean of all U.S. equity mutual funds by using a reliability factor based on the standard normal distribution.

The reliability factor for a 90 percent confidence interval, as given earlier, is $z_{0.05} = 1.65$. The confidence interval will be

$$\bar{X} \pm z_{0.05} \frac{s}{\sqrt{n}} = 0.45 \pm 1.65 \frac{0.30}{\sqrt{100}} = 0.45 \pm 1.65(0.03) = 0.45 \pm 0.0495$$

The confidence interval spans 0.4005 to 0.4995, or 0.40 to 0.50, carrying two decimal places. The analyst can say with 90 percent confidence that the interval includes the population mean.

In this example, the analyst makes no specific assumption about the probability distribution describing the population. Rather, the analyst relies on the central limit theorem to produce an approximate normal distribution for the sample mean.

As Example 4 shows, even if we are unsure of the underlying population distribution, we can still construct confidence intervals for the population mean as long as the sample size is large because we can apply the central limit theorem.

We now turn to the conservative alternative, using the t-distribution, for constructing confidence intervals for the population mean when the population variance is not known. For confidence intervals based on samples from normally distributed populations with unknown variance, the theoretically correct reliability factor is based on the t-distribution. Using a reliability factor based on the t-distribution is essential for a small sample size. Using a t reliability factor is appropriate when the population variance is unknown, even when we have a large sample and could use the central limit theorem to justify using a z reliability factor. In this large sample case, the t-distribution provides more-conservative (wider) confidence intervals.

The *t*-distribution is a symmetrical probability distribution defined by a single parameter known as **degrees of freedom (df)**. Each value for the number of degrees of freedom defines one distribution in this family of distributions. We will shortly compare *t*-distributions with the standard normal distribution, but first we need to understand the concept of degrees of freedom. We can do so by examining the calculation of the sample variance.

Equation 3 gives the unbiased estimator of the sample variance that we use. The term in the denominator, $n - 1$, which is the sample size minus 1, is the number of degrees of freedom in estimating the population variance when using Equation 3. We also use $n - 1$ as the number of degrees of freedom for determining reliability factors based on the *t*-distribution. The term "degrees of freedom" is used because in a random sample, we assume that observations are selected independently of each other. The numerator of the sample variance, however, uses the sample mean. How does the use of the sample mean affect the number of observations collected independently for the sample variance formula? With a sample of size 10 and a mean of 10 percent, for example, we can freely select only 9 observations. Regardless of the 9 observations selected, we can always find the value for the 10th observation that gives a mean equal to 10 percent. From the standpoint of the sample variance formula, then, there are 9 degrees of freedom. Given that we must first compute the sample mean from the total of n independent observations, only $n - 1$ observations can be chosen independently for the calculation of the sample variance. The concept of degrees of freedom comes up frequently in statistics, and you will see it often in later readings.

Suppose we sample from a normal distribution. The ratio $z = \left(\bar{X} - \mu \right) / \left(\sigma / \sqrt{n} \right)$ is distributed normally with a mean of 0 and standard deviation of 1; however, the ratio $t = \left(\bar{X} - \mu \right) / \left(s / \sqrt{n} \right)$ follows the *t*-distribution with a mean of 0 and $n - 1$ degrees of freedom. The ratio represented by t is not normal because t is the ratio of two random variables, the sample mean and the sample standard deviation. The definition of the standard normal random variable involves only one random variable, the sample mean. As degrees of freedom increase, however, the *t*-distribution approaches the standard normal distribution. Figure 1 shows the standard normal distribution and two *t*-distributions, one with df = 2 and one with df = 8.

Figure 1	Student's *t*-Distribution versus the Standard Normal Distribution

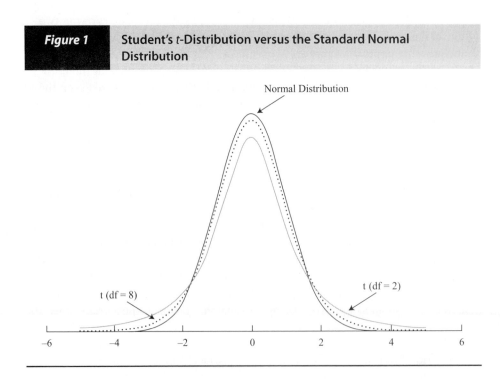

Of the three distributions shown in Figure 1, the standard normal distribution has tails that approach zero faster than the tails of the two t-distributions. The t-distribution is also symmetrically distributed around its mean value of zero, just like the normal distribution. As the degrees of freedom increase, the t-distribution approaches the standard normal. The t-distribution with df = 8 is closer to the standard normal than the t-distribution with df = 2.

Beyond plus and minus four standard deviations from the mean, the area under the standard normal distribution appears to approach 0; both t-distributions continue to show some area under each curve beyond four standard deviations, however. The t-distributions have fatter tails, but the tails of the t-distribution with df = 8 more closely resemble the normal distribution's tails. As the degrees of freedom increase, the tails of the t-distribution become less fat.

Frequently referred to values for the t-distribution are presented in tables at the end of the book. For each degree of freedom, five values are given: $t_{0.10}$, $t_{0.05}$, $t_{0.025}$, $t_{0.01}$, and $t_{0.005}$. The values for $t_{0.10}$, $t_{0.05}$, $t_{0.025}$, $t_{0.01}$, and $t_{0.005}$ are such that, respectively, 0.10, 0.05, 0.025, 0.01, and 0.005 of the probability remains in the right tail, for the specified number of degrees of freedom.[17] For example, for df = 30, $t_{0.10}$ = 1.310, $t_{0.05}$ = 1.697, $t_{0.025}$ = 2.042, $t_{0.01}$ = 2.457, and $t_{0.005}$ = 2.750.

We now give the form of confidence intervals for the population mean using the t-distribution.

- **Confidence Intervals for the Population Mean (Population Variance Unknown)—t-Distribution.** If we are sampling from a population with unknown variance and either of the conditions below holds:

  - the sample is large, or

  - the sample is small but the population is normally distributed, or approximately normally distributed,

  then a $100(1 - \alpha)\%$ confidence interval for the population mean μ is given by

  $$\bar{X} \pm t_{\alpha/2} \frac{s}{\sqrt{n}} \tag{6}$$

  where the number of degrees of freedom for $t_{\alpha/2}$ is $n - 1$ and n is the sample size.

Example 5 reprises the data of Example 4 but uses the t-statistic rather than the z-statistic to calculate a confidence interval for the population mean of Sharpe ratios.

Example 5

Confidence Interval for the Population Mean of Sharpe Ratios—t-Statistic

As in Example 4, an investment analyst seeks to calculate a 90 percent confidence interval for the population mean Sharpe ratio of U.S. equity mutual funds based on a random sample of 100 U.S. equity mutual funds. The sample mean Sharpe ratio is 0.45, and the sample standard deviation of the Sharpe ratios is 0.30. Now recognizing that the population variance of the distribution of Sharpe ratios is unknown, the analyst decides to calculate the confidence interval using the theoretically correct t-statistic.

Because the sample size is 100, df = 99. In the tables in the back of the book, the closest value is df = 100. Using df = 100 and reading down the 0.05 column,

---

17 The values $t_{0.10}$, $t_{0.05}$, $t_{0.025}$, $t_{0.01}$, and $t_{0.005}$ are also referred to as one-sided critical values of t at the 0.10, 0.05, 0.025, 0.01, and 0.005 significance levels, for the specified number of degrees of freedom.

we find that $t_{0.05} = 1.66$. This reliability factor is slightly larger than the reliability factor $z_{0.05} = 1.65$ that was used in Example 4. The confidence interval will be

$$\bar{X} \pm t_{0.05}\frac{s}{\sqrt{n}} = 0.45 \pm 1.66\frac{0.30}{\sqrt{100}} = 0.45 \pm 1.66(0.03) = 0.45 \pm 0.0498$$

The confidence interval spans 0.4002 to 0.4998, or 0.40 to 0.50, carrying two decimal places. To two decimal places, the confidence interval is unchanged from the one computed in Example 4.

Table 3 summarizes the various reliability factors that we have used.

Table 3	Basis of Computing Reliability Factors	
Sampling from:	**Statistic for Small Sample Size**	**Statistic for Large Sample Size**
Normal distribution with known variance	z	z
Normal distribution with unknown variance	t	t^*
Nonnormal distribution with known variance	not available	z
Nonnormal distribution with unknown variance	not available	t^*

*Use of z also acceptable.

4.3 Selection of Sample Size

What choices affect the width of a confidence interval? To this point we have discussed two factors that affect width: the choice of statistic (t or z) and the choice of degree of confidence (affecting which specific value of t or z we use). These two choices determine the reliability factor. (Recall that a confidence interval has the structure Point estimate ± Reliability factor × Standard error.)

The choice of sample size also affects the width of a confidence interval. All else equal, a larger sample size decreases the width of a confidence interval. Recall the expression for the standard error of the sample mean:

$$\text{Standard error of the sample mean} = \frac{\text{Sample standard deviation}}{\sqrt{\text{Sample size}}}$$

We see that the standard error varies inversely with the square root of sample size. As we increase sample size, the standard error decreases and consequently the width of the confidence interval also decreases. The larger the sample size, the greater precision with which we can estimate the population parameter.[18] All else equal, larger samples are good, in that sense. In practice, however, two considerations may operate against increasing sample size. First, as we saw in Example 2 concerning the Sharpe ratio, increasing the size of a sample may result in sampling from more than

---

18 A formula exists for determining the sample size needed to obtain a desired width for a confidence interval. Define E = Reliability factor × Standard error. The smaller E is, the smaller the width of the confidence interval, because $2E$ is the confidence interval's width. The sample size to obtain a desired value of E at a given degree of confidence $(1 - \alpha)$ is $n = [(t_{\alpha/2}s)/E]^2$.

one population. Second, increasing sample size may involve additional expenses that outweigh the value of additional precision. Thus three issues that the analyst should weigh in selecting sample size are the need for precision, the risk of sampling from more than one population, and the expenses of different sample sizes.

Example 6

A Money Manager Estimates Net Client Inflows

A money manager wants to obtain a 95 percent confidence interval for fund inflows and outflows over the next six months for his existing clients. He begins by calling a random sample of 10 clients and inquiring about their planned additions to and withdrawals from the fund. The manager then computes the change in cash flow for each client sampled as a percentage change in total funds placed with the manager. A positive percentage change indicates a net cash inflow to the client's account, and a negative percentage change indicates a net cash outflow from the client's account. The manager weights each response by the relative size of the account within the sample and then computes a weighted average.

As a result of this process, the money manager computes a weighted average of 5.5 percent. Thus, a point estimate is that the total amount of funds under management will increase by 5.5 percent in the next six months. The standard deviation of the observations in the sample is 10 percent. A histogram of past data looks fairly close to normal, so the manager assumes the population is normal.

1. Calculate a 95 percent confidence interval for the population mean and interpret your findings.

The manager decides to see what the confidence interval would look like if he had used a sample size of 20 or 30 and found the same mean (5.5 percent) and standard deviation (10 percent).

2. Using the sample mean of 5.5 percent and standard deviation of 10 percent, compute the confidence interval for sample sizes of 20 and 30. For the sample size of 30, use Equation 6.

3. Interpret your results from Parts 1 and 2.

Solution to 1:

Because the population is unknown and the sample size is small, the manager must use the t-statistic in Equation 6 to calculate the confidence interval. Based on the sample size of 10, df $= n - 1 = 10 - 1 = 9$. For a 95 percent confidence interval, he needs to use the value of $t_{0.025}$ for df $= 9$. According to the tables in Appendix B at the end of this volume, this value is 2.262. Therefore, a 95 percent confidence interval for the population mean is

$$\bar{X} \pm t_{0.025}\frac{s}{\sqrt{n}} = 5.5\% \pm 2.262\frac{10\%}{\sqrt{10}}$$
$$= 5.5\% \pm 2.262(3.162)$$
$$= 5.5\% \pm 7.15\%$$

The confidence interval for the population mean spans −1.65 percent to +12.65 percent.[19] The manager can be confident at the 95 percent level that this range includes the population mean.

---

[19] We assumed in this example that sample size is sufficiently small compared with the size of the client base that we can disregard the finite population correction factor (mentioned in Footnote 6).

Solution to 2:

Table 4 gives the calculations for the three sample sizes.

Table 4	The 95 Percent Confidence Interval for Three Sample Sizes			
Distribution	**95% Confidence Interval**	**Lower Bound**	**Upper Bound**	**Relative Size**
$t(n = 10)$	5.5% ± 2.262(3.162)	−1.65%	12.65%	100.0%
$t(n = 20)$	5.5% ± 2.093(2.236)	0.82	10.18	65.5
$t(n = 30)$	5.5% ± 2.045(1.826)	1.77	9.23	52.2

Solution to 3:

The width of the confidence interval decreases as we increase the sample size. This decrease is a function of the standard error becoming smaller as n increases. The reliability factor also becomes smaller as the number of degrees of freedom increases. The last column of Table 4 shows the relative size of the width of confidence intervals based on $n = 10$ to be 100 percent. Using a sample size of 20 reduces the confidence interval's width to 65.5 percent of the interval width for a sample size of 10. Using a sample size of 30 cuts the width of the interval almost in half. Comparing these choices, the money manager would obtain the most precise results using a sample of 30.

Having covered many of the fundamental concepts of sampling and estimation, we are in a good position to focus on sampling issues of special concern to analysts. The quality of inferences depends on the quality of the data as well as on the quality of the sampling plan used. Financial data pose special problems, and sampling plans frequently reflect one or more biases. The next section of this reading discusses these issues.

5 MORE ON SAMPLING

We have already seen that the selection of sample period length may raise the issue of sampling from more than one population. There are, in fact, a range of challenges to valid sampling that arise in working with financial data. In this section we discuss four such sampling-related issues: data-mining bias, sample selection bias, look-ahead bias, and time-period bias. All of these issues are important for point and interval estimation and hypothesis testing. As we will see, if the sample is biased in any way, then point and interval estimates and any other conclusions that we draw from the sample will be in error.

5.1 Data-Mining Bias

Data mining relates to overuse of the same or related data in ways that we shall describe shortly. Data-mining bias refers to the errors that arise from such misuse of data. Investment strategies that reflect data-mining biases are often not successful in the future. Nevertheless, both investment practitioners and researchers have frequently engaged in data mining. Analysts thus need to understand and guard against this problem.

Data-mining is the practice of determining a model by extensive searching through a dataset for statistically significant patterns (that is, repeatedly "drilling" in the same data until finding something that appears to work).[20] In exercises involving statistical significance we set a significance level, which is the probability of rejecting the hypothesis we are testing when the hypothesis is in fact correct.[21] Because rejecting a true hypothesis is undesirable, the investigator often sets the significance level at a relatively small number such as 0.05 or 5 percent.[22] Suppose we test the hypothesis that a variable does not predict stock returns, and we test in turn 100 different variables. Let us also suppose that in truth none of the 100 variables has the ability to predict stock returns. Using a 5 percent significance level in our tests, we would still expect that 5 out of 100 variables would appear to be significant predictors of stock returns because of random chance alone. We have mined the data to find some apparently significant variables. In essence, we have explored the same data again and again until we found some after-the-fact pattern or patterns in the dataset. This is the sense in which data mining involves overuse of data. If we were to just report the significant variables, without also reporting the total number of variables that we tested that were unsuccessful as predictors, we would be presenting a very misleading picture of our findings. Our results would appear to be far more significant than they actually were, because a series of tests such as the one just described invalidates the conventional interpretation of a given significance level (such as 5 percent), according to the theory of inference.

How can we investigate the presence of data-mining bias? With most financial data, the most ready means is to conduct out-of-sample tests of the proposed variable or strategy. An **out-of-sample test** uses a sample that does not overlap the time period(s) of the sample(s) on which a variable, strategy, or model, was developed. If a variable or investment strategy is the result of data mining, it should generally not be significant in out-of-sample tests. A variable or investment strategy that is statistically and economically significant in out-of-sample tests, and that has a plausible economic basis, may be the basis for a valid investment strategy. Caution is still warranted, however. The most crucial out-of-sample test is future investment success. If the strategy becomes known to other investors, prices may adjust so that the strategy, however well tested, does not work in the future. To summarize, the analyst should be aware that many apparently profitable investment strategies may reflect data-mining bias and thus be cautious about the future applicability of published investment research results.

Untangling the extent of data mining can be complex. To assess the significance of an investment strategy, we need to know how many unsuccessful strategies were tried not only by the current investigator but also by *previous* investigators using the same or related datasets. Much research, in practice, closely builds on what other investigators have done, and so reflects intergenerational data mining, to use the terminology of McQueen and Thorley (1999). **Intergenerational data mining** involves using information developed by previous researchers using a dataset to guide current research using the same or a related dataset.[23] Analysts have accumulated many

---

20 Some researchers use the term "data snooping" instead of data mining.
21 To convey an understanding of data mining, it is very helpful to introduce some basic concepts related to hypothesis testing. The reading on hypothesis testing contains further discussion of significance levels and tests of significance.
22 In terms of our previous discussion of confidence intervals, significance at the 5 percent level corresponds to a hypothesized value for a population statistic falling outside a 95 percent confidence interval based on an appropriate sample statistic (e.g., the sample mean, when the hypothesis concerns the population mean).
23 The term "intergenerational" comes from viewing each round of researchers as a generation. Campbell, Lo, and MacKinlay (1997) have called intergenerational data mining "data snooping." The latter phrase, however, is sommonly used as a synonym of data mining; thus McQueen and Thorley's terminology is less ambiguous. The term "intragenerational data mining" is available when we want to highlight that the reference is to an investigator's new or independent data mining.

observations about the peculiarities of many financial datasets, and other analysts may develop models or investment strategies that will tend to be supported within a dataset based on their familiarity with the prior experience of other analysts. As a consequence, the importance of those new results may be overstated. Research has suggested that the magnitude of this type of data-mining bias may be considerable.[24]

With the background of the above definitions and explanations, we can understand McQueen and Thorley's (1999) cogent exploration of data mining in the context of the popular Motley Fool "Foolish Four" investment strategy. The Foolish Four strategy, first presented in 1996, was a version of the Dow Dividend Strategy that was tuned by its developers to exhibit an even higher arithmetic mean return than the Dow Dividend Strategy over 1973 to 1993.[25] From 1973 to 1993, the Foolish Four portfolio had an average annual return of 25 percent, and the claim was made in print that the strategy should have similar returns in the future. As McQueen and Thorley discussed, however, the Foolish Four strategy was very much subject to data-mining bias, including bias from intergenerational data mining, as the strategy's developers exploited observations about the dataset made by earlier workers. McQueen and Thorley highlighted the data-mining issues by taking the Foolish Four portfolio one step further. They mined the data to create a "Fractured Four" portfolio that earned nearly 35 percent over 1973 to 1996, beating the Foolish Four strategy by almost 8 percentage points. Observing that all of the Foolish Four stocks did well in even years but not odd years and that the second-to-lowest-priced high-yielding stock was relatively the best-performing stock in odd years, the strategy of the Fractured Four portfolio was to hold the Foolish Four stocks with equal weights in even years and hold only the second-to-lowest-priced stock in odd years. How likely is it that a performance difference between even and odd years reflected underlying economic forces, rather than a chance pattern of the data over the particular time period? Probably, very unlikely. Unless an investment strategy reflected underlying economic forces, we would not expect it to have any value in a forward-looking sense. Because the Foolish Four strategy also partook of data mining, the same issues applied to it. McQueen and Thorley found that in an out-of-sample test over the 1949–72 period, the Foolish Four strategy had about the same mean return as buying and holding the DJIA, but with higher risk. If the higher taxes and transaction costs of the Foolish Four strategy were accounted for, the comparison would have been even more unfavorable.

McQueen and Thorley presented two signs that can warn analysts about the potential existence of data mining:

▪ *Too much digging/too little confidence.* The testing of many variables by the researcher is the "too much digging" warning sign of a data-mining problem. Unfortunately, many researchers do not disclose the number of variables examined in developing a model. Although the number of variables examined may not be reported, we should look closely for verbal hints that the researcher searched over many variables. The use of terms such as "we noticed (or noted) that" or "someone noticed (or noted) that," with respect to a pattern in a dataset, should raise suspicions that the researchers were trying out variables based on their own or others' observations of the data.

---

24 For example, Lo and MacKinlay (1990) concluded that the magnitude of this type of bias on tests of the capital asset pricing model was considerable.

25 The Dow Dividend Strategy, also known as Dogs of the Dow Strategy,Ç consists of holding an equally weighted portfolio of the 10 highest-yielding DJIA stocks as of the beginning of a year. At the time of McQueen and Thorley's research, the Foolish Four strategy was as follows: At the beginning of each year, the Foolish Four portfolio purchases a 4-stock portfolio from the 5 lowest-sriced stocks of the 10 highest-yielding DJIA stocks. The lowest-priced stock of the five is excluded, and 40 percent is invested in the second-to-lowest-priced stock, with 20 percent weights in the remaining three.

■ *No story/no future.* The absence of an explicit economic rationale for a variable or trading strategy is the "no story" warning sign of a data-mining problem. Without a plausible economic rationale or story for why a variable should work, the variable is unlikely to have predictive power. In a demonstration exercise using an extensive search of variables in an international financial database, Leinweber (1997) found that butter production in a particular country remote from the United States explained 75 percent of the variation in U.S. stock returns as represented by the S&P 500. Such a pattern, with no plausible economic rationale, is highly likely to be a random pattern particular to a specific time period.[26] What if we do have a plausible economic explanation for a significant variable? McQueen and Thorley caution that a plausible economic rationale is a necessary but not a sufficient condition for a trading strategy to have value. As we mentioned earlier, if the strategy is publicized, market prices may adjust to reflect the new information as traders seek to exploit it; as a result, the strategy may no longer work.

5.2 Sample Selection Bias

When researchers look into questions of interest to analysts or portfolio managers, they may exclude certain stocks, bonds, portfolios, or time periods from the analysis for various reasons—perhaps because of data availability. When data availability leads to certain assets being excluded from the analysis, we call the resulting problem **sample selection bias**. For example, you might sample from a database that tracks only companies currently in existence. Many mutual fund databases, for instance, provide historical information about only those funds that currently exist. Databases that report historical balance sheet and income statement information suffer from the same sort of bias as the mutual fund databases: Funds or companies that are no longer in business do not appear there. So, a study that uses these types of databases suffers from a type of sample selection bias known as **survivorship bias**.

Dimson, Marsh, and Staunton (2002) raised the issue of survivorship bias in international indexes:

> An issue that has achieved prominence is the impact of market survival on estimated long-run returns. Markets can experience not only disappointing performance but also total loss of value through confiscation, hyperinflation, nationalization, and market failure. By measuring the performance of markets that survive over long intervals, we draw inferences that are conditioned on survival. Yet, as pointed out by Brown, Goetzmann, and Ross (1995) and Jorion and Goetzmann (1999), one cannot determine in advance which markets will survive and which will perish. (p. 41)

Survivorship bias sometimes appears when we use both stock price and accounting data. For example, many studies in finance have used the ratio of a company's market price to book equity per share (i.e., the price-to-book ratio, P/B) and found that P/B is inversely related to a company's returns (see Fama and French 1992, 1993). P/B is also used to create many popular value and growth indexes. If the database that we use to collect accounting data excludes failing companies, however, a survivorship bias might result. Kothari, Shanken, and Sloan (1995) investigated just this question and argued that failing stocks would be expected to have low returns and low P/Bs. If we exclude failing stocks, then those stocks with low P/Bs that are included will have returns that are higher on average than if all stocks with low P/Bs were included.

---

26 In the finance literature, such a random but irrelevant-to-the-future pattern is sometimes called an artifact of the dataset.

Kothari, Shanken, and Sloan suggested that this bias is responsible for the previous findings of an inverse relationship between average return and P/B.[27] The only advice we can offer at this point is to be aware of any biases potentially inherent in a sample. Clearly, sample selection biases can cloud the results of any study.

A sample can also be biased because of the removal (or delisting) of a company's stock from an exchange.[28] For example, the Center for Research in Security Prices at the University of Chicago is a major provider of return data used in academic research. When a delisting occurs, CRSP attempts to collect returns for the delisted company, but many times, it cannot do so because of the difficulty involved; CRSP must simply list delisted company returns as missing. A study in the *Journal of Finance* by Shumway and Warther (1999) documented the bias caused by delisting for CRSP NASDAQ return data. The authors showed that delistings associated with poor company performance (e.g., bankruptcy) are missed more often than delistings associated with good or neutral company performance (e.g., merger or moving to another exchange). In addition, delistings occur more frequently for small companies.

Sample selection bias occurs even in markets where the quality and consistency of the data are quite high. Newer asset classes such as hedge funds may present even greater problems of sample selection bias. Hedge funds are a heterogeneous group of investment vehicles typically organized so as to be free from regulatory oversight. In general, hedge funds are not required to publicly disclose performance (in contrast to, say, mutual funds). Hedge funds themselves decide whether they want to be included in one of the various databases of hedge fund performance. Hedge funds with poor track records clearly may not wish to make their records public, creating a problem of self-selection bias in hedge fund databases. Further, as pointed out by Fung and Hsieh (2002), because only hedge funds with good records will volunteer to enter a database, in general, overall past hedge fund industry performance will tend to appear better than it really is. Furthermore, many hedge fund databases drop funds that go out of business, creating survivorship bias in the database. Even if the database does not drop defunct hedge funds, in the attempt to eliminate survivorship bias, the problem remains of hedge funds that stop reporting performance because of poor results.[29]

5.3 Look-Ahead Bias

A test design is subject to **look-ahead bias** if it uses information that was not available on the test date. For example, tests of trading rules that use stock market returns and accounting balance sheet data must account for look-ahead bias. In such tests, a company's book value per share is commonly used to construct the P/B variable. Although the market price of a stock is available for all market participants at the same point in time, fiscal year-end book equity per share might not become publicly available until sometime in the following quarter.

5.4 Time-Period Bias

A test design is subject to **time-period bias** if it is based on a time period that may make the results time-period specific. A short time series is likely to give period specific results that may not reflect a longer period. A long time series may give a more accurate picture of true investment performance; its disadvantage lies in the potential for a structural change occurring during the time frame that would result

---

27 See Fama and French (1996, p. 80) for discussion of data snooping and survivorship bias in their tests.
28 Delistings occur for a variety of reasons: merger, bankruptcy, liquidation, or migration to another exchange.
29 See Ackerman, McEnally, and Ravenscraft (1999) and Fung and Hsieh (2002) for more details on the problems of interpreting hedge fund performance. Note that an offsetting type of bias may occur if successful funds stop reporting performance because they no longer want new cash inflows.

in two different return distributions. In this situation, the distribution that would reflect conditions before the change differs from the distribution that would describe conditions after the change.

Example 7

Biases in Investment Research

An analyst is reviewing the empirical evidence on historical U.S. equity returns. She finds that value stocks (i.e., those with low P/Bs) outperformed growth stocks (i.e., those with high P/Bs) in some recent time periods. After reviewing the U.S. market, the analyst wonders whether value stocks might be attractive in the United Kingdom. She investigates the performance of value and growth stocks in the U.K. market from January 1990 to December 2003. To conduct this research, the analyst does the following:

- obtains the current composition of the Financial Times Stock Exchange (FTSE) All Share Index, which is a market-capitalization-weighted index;

- eliminates the few companies that do not have December fiscal year-ends;

- uses year-end book values and market prices to rank the remaining universe of companies by P/Bs at the end of the year;

- based on these rankings, divides the universe into 10 portfolios, each of which contains an equal number of stocks;

- calculates the equal-weighted return of each portfolio and the return for the FTSE All Share Index for the 12 months following the date each ranking was made; and

- subtracts the FTSE returns from each portfolio's returns to derive excess returns for each portfolio.

Describe and discuss each of the following biases introduced by the analyst's research design:

- survivorship bias;

- look-ahead bias; and

- time-period bias.

Survivorship Bias.

A test design is subject to survivorship bias if it fails to account for companies that have gone bankrupt, merged, or otherwise departed the database. In this example, the analyst used the current list of FTSE stocks rather than the actual list of stocks that existed at the start of each year. To the extent that the computation of returns excluded companies removed from the index, the performance of the portfolios with the lowest P/B is subject to survivorship bias and may be overstated. At some time during the testing period, those companies not currently in existence were eliminated from testing. They would probably have had low prices (and low P/Bs) and poor returns.

Look-Ahead Bias.

A test design is subject to look-ahead bias if it uses information unavailable on the test date. In this example, the analyst conducted the test under the assumption that the necessary accounting information was available at the end of the fiscal year. For example, the analyst assumed that book value per share for fiscal 1990 was available on 31 December 1990. Because this information is not released until several months after the close of a fiscal year, the test may have contained look-ahead bias. This bias would make a strategy based on the information appear successful, but it assumes perfect forecasting ability.

Time-Period Bias.

A test design is subject to time-period bias if it is based on a time period that may make the results time-period specific. Although the test covered a period extending more than 10 years, that period may be too short for testing an anomaly. Ideally, an analyst should test market anomalies over several business cycles to ensure that results are not period specific. This bias can favor a proposed strategy if the time period chosen was favorable to the strategy.

SUMMARY

In this reading, we have presented basic concepts and results in sampling and estimation. We have also emphasized the challenges faced by analysts in appropriately using and interpreting financial data. As analysts, we should always use a critical eye when evaluating the results from any study. The quality of the sample is of the utmost importance: If the sample is biased, the conclusions drawn from the sample will be in error.

■ To draw valid inferences from a sample, the sample should be random.

■ In simple random sampling, each observation has an equal chance of being selected. In stratified random sampling, the population is divided into subpopulations, called strata or cells, based on one or more classification criteria; simple random samples are then drawn from each stratum.

■ Stratified random sampling ensures that population subdivisions of interest are represented in the sample. Stratified random sampling also produces more-precise parameter estimates than simple random sampling.

■ Time-series data are a collection of observations at equally spaced intervals of time. Cross-sectional data are observations that represent individuals, groups, geographical regions, or companies at a single point in time.

■ The central limit theorem states that for large sample sizes, for any underlying distribution for a random variable, the sampling distribution of the sample mean for that variable will be approximately normal, with mean equal to the population mean for that random variable and variance equal to the population variance of the variable divided by sample size.

■ Based on the central limit theorem, when the sample size is large, we can compute confidence intervals for the population mean based on the normal distribution regardless of the distribution of the underlying population. In general, a sample size of 30 or larger can be considered large.

■ An estimator is a formula for estimating a parameter. An estimate is a particular value that we calculate from a sample by using an estimator.

■ Because an estimator or statistic is a random variable, it is described by some probability distribution. We refer to the distribution of an estimator as its sampling distribution. The standard deviation of the sampling distribution of the sample mean is called the standard error of the sample mean.

■ The desirable properties of an estimator are unbiasedness (the expected value of the estimator equals the population parameter), efficiency (the estimator has the smallest variance), and consistency (the probability of accurate estimates increases as sample size increases).

- The two types of estimates of a parameter are point estimates and interval estimates. A point estimate is a single number that we use to estimate a parameter. An interval estimate is a range of values that brackets the population parameter with some probability.

- A confidence interval is an interval for which we can assert with a given probability $1 - \alpha$, called the degree of confidence, that it will contain the parameter it is intended to estimate. This measure is often referred to as the $100(1 - \alpha)\%$ confidence interval for the parameter.

- A $100(1 - \alpha)\%$ confidence interval for a parameter has the following structure: Point estimate ± Reliability factor × Standard error, where the reliability factor is a number based on the assumed distribution of the point estimate and the degree of confidence $(1 - \alpha)$ for the confidence interval and where standard error is the standard error of the sample statistic providing the point estimate.

- A $100(1 - \alpha)\%$ confidence interval for population mean μ when sampling from a normal distribution with known variance σ^2 is given by $\bar{X} \pm z_{\alpha/2} \dfrac{\sigma}{\sqrt{n}}$, where $z_{\alpha/2}$ is the point of the standard normal distribution such that $\alpha/2$ remains in the right tail.

- Student's t-distribution is a family of symmetrical distributions defined by a single parameter, degrees of freedom.

- A random sample of size n is said to have $n - 1$ degrees of freedom for estimating the population variance, in the sense that there are only $n - 1$ independent deviations from the mean on which to base the estimate.

- The degrees of freedom number for use with the t-distribution is also $n - 1$.

- The t-distribution has fatter tails than the standard normal distribution but converges to the standard normal distribution as degrees of freedom go to infinity.

- A $100(1 - \alpha)\%$ confidence interval for the population mean μ when sampling from a normal distribution with unknown variance (a t-distribution confidence interval) is given by $\bar{X} \pm t_{\alpha/2} \left(s/\sqrt{n} \right)$, where $t_{\alpha/2}$ is the point of the t-distribution such that $\alpha/2$ remains in the right tail and s is the sample standard deviation. This confidence interval can also be used, because of the central limit theorem, when dealing with a large sample from a population with unknown variance that may not be normal.

- We may use the confidence interval $\bar{X} \pm z_{\alpha/2} \left(s/\sqrt{n} \right)$ as an alternative to the t-distribution confidence interval for the population mean when using a large sample from a population with unknown variance. The confidence interval based on the z-statistic is less conservative (narrower) than the corresponding confidence interval based on a t-distribution.

- Three issues in the selection of sample size are the need for precision, the risk of sampling from more than one population, and the expenses of different sample sizes.

- Sample data in investments can have a variety of problems. Survivorship bias occurs if companies are excluded from the analysis because they have gone out of business or because of reasons related to poor performance. Data-mining bias comes from finding models by repeatedly searching through databases for patterns. Look-ahead bias exists if the model uses data not available to market participants at the time the market participants act in the model. Finally, time-period bias is present if the time period used makes the results time-period specific or if the time period used includes a point of structural change.

PRACTICE PROBLEMS FOR READING 10

1. Peter Biggs wants to know how growth managers performed last year. Biggs assumes that the population cross-sectional standard deviation of growth manager returns is 6 percent and that the returns are independent across managers.

    A. How large a random sample does Biggs need if he wants the standard deviation of the sample means to be 1 percent?

    B. How large a random sample does Biggs need if he wants the standard deviation of the sample means to be 0.25 percent?

2. Petra Munzi wants to know how value managers performed last year. Munzi estimates that the population cross-sectional standard deviation of value manager returns is 4 percent and assumes that the returns are independent across managers.

    A. Munzi wants to build a 95 percent confidence interval for the mean return. How large a random sample does Munzi need if she wants the 95 percent confidence interval to have a total width of 1 percent?

    B. Munzi expects a cost of about $10 to collect each observation. If she has a $1,000 budget, will she be able to construct the confidence interval she wants?

3. Assume that the equity risk premium is normally distributed with a population mean of 6 percent and a population standard deviation of 18 percent. Over the last four years, equity returns (relative to the risk-free rate) have averaged −2.0 percent. You have a large client who is very upset and claims that results this poor should *never* occur. Evaluate your client's concerns.

    A. Construct a 95 percent confidence interval around the population mean for a sample of four-year returns.

    B. What is the probability of a −2.0 percent or lower average return over a four-year period?

4. Compare the standard normal distribution and Student's t-distribution.

5. Find the reliability factors based on the t-distribution for the following confidence intervals for the population mean (df = degrees of freedom, n = sample size):

    A. A 99 percent confidence interval, df = 20.

    B. A 90 percent confidence interval, df = 20.

    C. A 95 percent confidence interval, n = 25.

    D. A 95 percent confidence interval, n = 16.

6. Assume that monthly returns are normally distributed with a mean of 1 percent and a sample standard deviation of 4 percent. The population standard deviation is unknown. Construct a 95 percent confidence interval for the sample mean of monthly returns if the sample size is 24.

7. Ten analysts have given the following fiscal year earnings forecasts for a stock:

Forecast (X_j)	Number of Analysts (n_j)
1.40	1
1.43	1

Forecast (X_i)	Number of Analysts (n_i)
1.44	3
1.45	2
1.47	1
1.48	1
1.50	1

Because the sample is a small fraction of the number of analysts who follow this stock, assume that we can ignore the finite population correction factor. Assume that the analyst forecasts are normally distributed.

A. What are the mean forecast and standard deviation of forecasts?

B. Provide a 95 percent confidence interval for the population mean of the forecasts.

8. Thirteen analysts have given the following fiscal-year earnings forecasts for a stock:

Forecast (X_i)	Number of Analysts (n_i)
0.70	2
0.72	4
0.74	1
0.75	3
0.76	1
0.77	1
0.82	1

Because the sample is a small fraction of the number of analysts who follow this stock, assume that we can ignore the finite population correction factor.

A. What are the mean forecast and standard deviation of forecasts?

B. What aspect of the data makes us uncomfortable about using t-tables to construct confidence intervals for the population mean forecast?

9. Explain the differences between constructing a confidence interval when sampling from a normal population with a known population variance and sampling from a normal population with an unknown variance.

10. An exchange rate has a given expected future value and standard deviation.

A. Assuming that the exchange rate is normally distributed, what are the probabilities that the exchange rate will be at least 2 or 3 standard deviations away from its mean?

B. Assume that you do not know the distribution of exchange rates. Use Chebyshev's inequality (that at least $1 - 1/k^2$ proportion of the observations will be within k standard deviations of the mean for any positive integer k greater than 1) to calculate the maximum probabilities that the exchange rate will be at least 2 or 3 standard deviations away from its mean.

11. Although he knows security returns are not independent, a colleague makes the claim that because of the central limit theorem, if we diversify across a large number of investments, the portfolio standard deviation will eventually approach zero as n becomes large. Is he correct?

12. Why is the central limit theorem important?

13. What is wrong with the following statement of the central limit theorem?

> ***Central Limit Theorem.*** "If the random variables $X_1, X_2, X_3, ..., X_n$ are a random sample of size n from any distribution with finite mean μ and variance σ^2, then the distribution of $\bar{X}$ will be approximately normal, with a standard deviation of $\sigma/\sqrt{n}$."

14. Suppose we take a random sample of 30 companies in an industry with 200 companies. We calculate the sample mean of the ratio of cash flow to total debt for the prior year. We find that this ratio is 23 percent. Subsequently, we learn that the population cash flow to total debt ratio (taking account of all 200 companies) is 26 percent. What is the explanation for the discrepancy between the sample mean of 23 percent and the population mean of 26 percent?

   A. Sampling error.

   B. Bias.

   C. A lack of consistency.

15. Alcorn Mutual Funds is placing large advertisements in several financial publications. The advertisements prominently display the returns of 5 of Alcorn's 30 funds for the past 1-, 3-, 5-, and 10-year periods. The results are indeed impressive, with all of the funds beating the major market indexes and a few beating them by a large margin. Is the Alcorn family of funds superior to its competitors?

16. A pension plan executive says, "One hundred percent of our portfolio managers are hired because they have above-average performance records relative to their benchmarks. We do not keep portfolio managers who have below-average records. And yet, each year about half of our managers beat their benchmarks and about half do not. What is going on?" Give a possible statistical explanation.

17. Julius Spence has tested several predictive models in order to identify undervalued stocks. Spence used about 30 company-specific variables and 10 market-related variables to predict returns for about 5,000 North American and European stocks. He found that a final model using eight variables applied to telecommunications and computer stocks yields spectacular results. Spence wants you to use the model to select investments. Should you? What steps would you take to evaluate the model?

18. Hand Associates manages two portfolios that are meant to closely track the returns of two stock indexes. One index is a value-weighted index of 500 stocks in which the weight for each stock depends on the stock's total market value. The other index is an equal-weighted index of 500 stocks in which the weight for each stock is 1/500. Hand Associates invests in only about 50 to 100 stocks in each portfolio in order to control transactions costs. Should Hand use simple random sampling or stratified random sampling to choose the stocks in each portfolio?

19. Give an example of each of the following:

   A. Sample-selection bias.

   B. Look-ahead bias.

   C. Time-period bias.

20. What are some of the desirable statistical properties of an estimator, such as a sample mean?

21. An analyst stated that as degrees of freedom increase, a t-distribution will become more peaked and the tails of the t-distribution will become less fat. Is the analyst's statement correct with respect to the t-distribution:

	becoming more peaked?	tails becoming less fat?
A.	No	Yes
B.	Yes	No
C.	Yes	Yes

22. An analyst stated that, all else equal, increasing sample size will decrease both the standard error and the width of the confidence interval. The analyst's statement is correct in regard to:

A. both the standard error and the confidence interval.

B. the standard error, but incorrect in regard to the confidence interval.

C. the confidence interval, but incorrect in regard to the standard error.

SOLUTIONS FOR READING 10

1. **A.** The standard deviation or standard error of the sample mean is $\sigma_{\bar{X}} = \sigma/\sqrt{n}$. Substituting in the values for $\sigma_{\bar{X}}$ and σ, we have $1\% = 6\%/\sqrt{n}$, or $\sqrt{n} = 6$. Squaring this value, we get a random sample of $n = 36$.

   B. As in Part A, the standard deviation of sample mean is $\sigma_{\bar{X}} = \sigma/\sqrt{n}$. Substituting in the values for $\sigma_{\bar{X}}$ and σ, we have $0.25\% = 6\%/\sqrt{n}$, or $\sqrt{n} = 24$. Squaring this value, we get a random sample of $n = 576$, which is substantially larger than for Part A of this question.

2. **A.** Assume the sample size will be large and thus the 95 percent confidence interval for the mean of a sample of manager returns is $\bar{X} \pm 1.96 s_{\bar{X}}$, where $s_{\bar{X}} = s/\sqrt{n}$. Munzi wants the distance between the upper limit and lower limit in the confidence interval to be 1 percent, which is

   $$\left(\bar{X} + 1.96 s_{\bar{X}}\right) - \left(\bar{X} - 1.96 s_{\bar{X}}\right) = 1\%$$

   Simplifying this equation, we get $2\left(1.96 s_{\bar{X}}\right) = 1\%$. Finally, we have $3.92 s_{\bar{X}} = 1\%$, which gives us the standard deviation of the sample mean, $s_{\bar{X}} = 0.255\%$. The distribution of sample means is $s_{\bar{X}} = s/\sqrt{n}$. Substituting in the values for $s_{\bar{X}}$ and s, we have $0.255\% = 4\%/\sqrt{n}$, or $\sqrt{n} = 15.69$. Squaring this value, we get a random sample of $n = 246$.

   B. With her budget, Munzi can pay for a sample of up to 100 observations, which is far short of the 246 observations needed. Munzi can either proceed with her current budget and settle for a wider confidence interval or she can raise her budget (to around $2,460) to get the sample size for a 1 percent width in her confidence interval.

3. **A.** This is a small-sample problem in which the sample comes from a normal population with a known standard deviation; thus we use the z-distribution in the solution. For a 95 percent confidence interval (and 2.5 percent in each tail), the critical z-value is 1.96. For returns that are normally distributed, a 95 percent confidence interval is of the form

   $$\mu + 1.96 \frac{\sigma}{\sqrt{n}}$$

   The lower limit is $X_1 = \mu - 1.96 \dfrac{\sigma}{\sqrt{n}} = 6\% - 1.96 \dfrac{18\%}{\sqrt{4}} = 6\% - 1.96(9\%) = -11.64\%$.

   The upper limit is $X_u = \mu + 1.96 \dfrac{\sigma}{\sqrt{n}} = 6\% + 1.96 \dfrac{18\%}{\sqrt{4}} = 6\% + 1.96(9\%) = 23.64\%$.

   There is a 95 percent probability that four-year average returns will be between –11.64 percent and +23.64 percent.

   B. The critical z-value associated with the –2.0 percent return is

   $$Z = \frac{\bar{X} - \mu}{\sigma/\sqrt{n}} = \frac{-2\% - 6\%}{18\%/\sqrt{4}} = \frac{-8\%}{9\%} = -0.89$$

   Using a normal table, the probability of a z-value less than –0.89 is $P(Z < -0.89) = 0.1867$. Unfortunately, although your client is unhappy with the investment result, a four-year average return of –2.0 percent or lower should occur 18.67 percent of the time.

4. (Refer to Figure 1 to help visualize the answer to this question.) Basically, only one standard normal distribution exists, but many t-distributions exist—one for every different number of degrees of freedom. The normal distribution and the

t-distribution for a large number of degrees of freedom are practically the same. The lower the degrees of freedom, the flatter the *t*-distribution becomes. The *t*-distribution has less mass (lower probabilities) in the center of the distribution and more mass (higher probabilities) out in both tails. Therefore, the confidence intervals based on *t*-values will be wider than those based on the normal distribution. Stated differently, the probability of being within a given number of standard deviations (such as within ±1 standard deviation or ±2 standard deviations) is lower for the *t*-distribution than for the normal distribution.

5. **A.** For a 99 percent confidence interval, the reliability factor we use is $t_{0.005}$; for df = 20, this factor is 2.845.

 B. For a 90 percent confidence interval, the reliability factor we use is $t_{0.05}$; for df = 20, this factor is 1.725.

 C. Degrees of freedom equals *n* – 1, or in this case 25 – 1 = 24. For a 95 percent confidence interval, the reliability factor we use is $t_{0.025}$; for df = 24, this factor is 2.064.

 D. Degrees of freedom equals 16 – 1 = 15. For a 95 percent confidence interval, the reliability factor we use is $t_{0.025}$; for df = 15, this factor is 2.131.

6. Because this is a small sample from a normal population and we have only the sample standard deviation, we use the following model to solve for the confidence interval of the population mean:

$$\bar{X} \pm t_{\alpha/2}\frac{s}{\sqrt{n}}$$

where we find $t_{0.025}$ (for a 95 percent confidence interval) for df = *n* – 1 = 24 – 1 = 23; this value is 2.069. Our solution is 1% ± 2.069(4%)/$\sqrt{24}$ = 1% ± 2.069(0.8165) = 1% ± 1.69. The 95 percent confidence interval spans the range from –0.69 percent to +2.69 percent.

7. The following table summarizes the calculations used in the answers.

Forecast (X_i)	Number of Analysts (n_i)	$X_i n_i$	$(X_i - \bar{X})$	$(X_i - \bar{X})^2$	$(X_i - \bar{X})^2 n_i$
1.40	1	1.40	−0.05	0.0025	0.0025
1.43	1	1.43	−0.02	0.0004	0.0004
1.44	3	4.32	−0.01	0.0001	0.0003
1.45	2	2.90	0.00	0.0000	0.0000
1.47	1	1.47	0.02	0.0004	0.0004
1.48	1	1.48	0.03	0.0009	0.0009
1.50	1	1.50	0.05	0.0025	0.0025
Sums	10	14.50			0.0070

A. With $n = 10$, $\bar{X} = \sum_{i=1}^{10} X_i/n = 14.50/10 = 1.45$. The variance is

$s^2 = \left[\sum_{i=1}^{10}(X_i - \bar{X})^2\right]/(n-1) = 0.0070/9 = 0.0007778$. The sample standard deviation is $s = \sqrt{0.0007778} = 0.02789$.

B. The confidence interval for the mean can be estimated by using $\bar{X} \pm t_{\alpha/2}(s/\sqrt{n})$. For 9 degrees of freedom, the reliability factor, $t_{0.025}$, equals 2.262 and the confidence interval is

$$1.45 \pm 2.262 \times 0.02789/\sqrt{10} = 1.45 \pm 2.262(0.00882)$$
$$= 1.45 \pm 0.02$$

The confidence interval for the population mean ranges from 1.43 to 1.47.

8. The following table summarizes the calculations used in the answers.

Forecast (X_i)	Number of Analysts (n_i)	$X_i n_i$	$(X_i - \bar{X})$	$(X_i - \bar{X})^2$	$(X_i - \bar{X})^2 n_i$
0.70	2	1.40	−0.04	0.0016	0.0032
0.72	4	2.88	−0.02	0.0004	0.0016
0.74	1	0.74	0.00	0.0000	0.0000
0.75	3	2.25	0.01	0.0001	0.0003
0.76	1	0.76	0.02	0.0004	0.0004
0.77	1	0.77	0.03	0.0009	0.0009
0.82	1	0.82	0.08	0.0064	0.0064
Sums	13	9.62			0.0128

A. With $n = 13$, $\bar{X} = \sum_{i=1}^{13} X_i/n = 9.62/13 = 0.74$. The variance is

$$s^2 = \left[\sum_{i=1}^{13}(X_i - \bar{X})^2\right]/(n-1) = 0.0128/12 = 0.001067.$$ The sample standard deviation is $s = \sqrt{0.001067} = 0.03266$.

B. The sample is small, and the distribution appears to be bimodal. We cannot compute a confidence interval for the population mean because we have probably sampled from a distribution that is not normal.

9. If the population variance is known, the confidence interval is

$$\bar{X} \pm z_{\alpha/2}\frac{\sigma}{\sqrt{n}}$$

The confidence interval for the population mean is centered at the sample mean, $\bar{X}$. The population standard deviation is σ, and the sample size is n. The population standard deviation divided by the square root of n is the standard error of the estimate of the mean. The value of z depends on the desired degree of confidence. For a 95 percent confidence interval, $z_{0.025} = 1.96$ and the confidence interval estimate is

$$\bar{X} \pm 1.96\frac{\sigma}{\sqrt{n}}$$

If the population variance is not known, we make two changes to the technique used when the population variance is known. First, we must use the sample standard deviation instead of the population standard deviation. Second, we use the t-distribution instead of the normal distribution. The critical t-value will depend on degrees of freedom $n - 1$. If the sample size is large, we have the alternative of using the z-distribution with the sample standard deviation.

10. A. The probabilities can be taken from a normal table, in which the critical z-values are 2.00 or 3.00 and we are including the probabilities in both tails. The probabilities that the exchange rate will be at least 2 or 3 standard deviations away from the mean are

$$P(|X - \mu| \geq 2\sigma) = 0.0456$$
$$P(|X - \mu| \geq 3\sigma) = 0.0026$$

B. With Chebyshev's inequality, the maximum probability of the exchange rate being at least k standard deviations from the mean is $P(\mid X - \mu \mid \geq k\sigma) \leq (1/k)^2$. The maximum probabilities of the rate being at least 2 or 3 standard deviations away from the mean are

$$P\left(\mid X - \mu \mid \geq 2\sigma \right) \leq \left(1/2 \right)^2 = 0.2500$$

$$P\left(\mid X - \mu \mid \geq 3\sigma \right) \leq \left(1/3 \right)^2 = 0.1111$$

The probability of the rate being outside 2 or 3 standard deviations of the mean is much smaller with a known normal distribution than when the distribution is unknown and we are relying on Chebyshev's inequality.

11. No. First the conclusion on the limit of zero is wrong; second, the support cited for drawing the conclusion (i.e., the central limit theorem) is not relevant in this context.

12. In many instances, the distribution that describes the underlying population is not normal or the distribution is not known. The central limit theorem states that if the sample size is large, regardless of the shape of the underlying population, the distribution of the sample mean is approximately normal. Therefore, even in these instances, we can still construct confidence intervals (and conduct tests of inference) as long as the sample size is large (generally $n \geq 30$).

13. The statement makes the following mistakes:

- Given the conditions in the statement, the distribution of $\bar{X}$ will be approximately normal only for large sample sizes.

- The statement omits the important element of the central limit theorem that the distribution of $\bar{X}$ will have mean μ.

14. A is correct. The discrepancy arises from sampling error. Sampling error exists whenever one fails to observe every element of the population, because a sample statistic can vary from sample to sample. As stated in the reading, the sample mean is an unbiased estimator, a consistent estimator, and an efficient estimator of the population mean. Although the sample mean is an unbiased estimator of the population mean—the expected value of the sample mean equals the population mean—because of sampling error, we do not expect the sample mean to exactly equal the population mean in any one sample we may take.

15. No, we cannot say that Alcorn Mutual Funds as a group is superior to competitors. Alcorn Mutual Funds' advertisement may easily mislead readers because the advertisement does not show the performance of all its funds. In particular, Alcorn Mutual Funds is engaging in sample selection bias by presenting the investment results from its best-performing funds only.

16. The question raises the issue of whether above-average money management performance is the result of skill or luck. Assembling a group of above-average portfolio managers can be an attempt to exploit survivorship bias. We attempt it by hiring only managers with above-average records and by firing any managers that have below-average records. If past successful performance is a function of skill that can be repeated, then managers with above-average records will perform better than average in the future. An explanation for what is going on in the statement may be that past superior performance has resulted not from skill but from luck.

Say we assume that performance is a matter of luck. Suppose there is a 0.5 chance for a manager to beat his or her benchmark. If we start out with 100 managers and define success as two benchmark-beating years in a row, we will have about 25 successful managers. Their successful track records will not predict future success if performance is random. If performance is random, no matter how we pick our managers, future performance will be above average about half the time and below average about half the time. If we wish to appraise skill, we must discount results that would happen by chance.

17. Spence may be guilty of data mining. He has used so many possible combinations of variables on so many stocks, it is not surprising that he found some instances in which a model worked. In fact, it would have been more surprising if he had not found any. To decide whether to use his model, you should do two things: First, ask that the model be tested on out-of-sample data—that is, data that were not used in building the model. The model may not be successful with out-of-sample data. Second, examine his model to make sure that the relationships in the model make economic sense, have a story, and have a future.

18. Hand Associates should use stratified random sampling for its portfolio that tracks the value-weighted index. Using 50–100 stocks to track 500 means that Hand will invest in all or almost all of the largest stocks in the index and few of the smallest. In addition to size, the stocks may be grouped by industry, riskiness, and other traits, and Hand Associates may select stocks to represent each of these groups or strata. For the equal-weighted index, Hand can use simple random sampling, in which each stock is equally likely to be chosen. Even in this case, however, Hand could use stratified random sampling to make sure it is choosing stocks that represent the various factors underlying stock performance.

19. **A.** An example of sample-selection bias is the failure to include the returns of delisted stocks in reporting portfolio returns. Because delisted stocks frequently are troubled stocks with poor returns, ignoring their returns will bias upwards the returns of portfolios that do not include them.

    B. An example of look-ahead bias is a statistician using data that were not yet available at the time a decision was being made. If you are building portfolios on January 1 of each year, you do not yet have the financial results for fiscal years ending on December 31. So, you do not know this information when you make investment decisions. Suppose a statistician is studying historical portfolio returns and has used annual accounting results to make portfolio selections at the beginning of each year. She is using a statistical model that assumes information is available several weeks before it is actually available. The results of such a model are biased.

    C. One kind of time-period bias is an investment manager reporting the results from a short time period that give an inaccurate picture of the investment performance that might be expected over a longer time period. Time-period bias exists when a test is carried out for a time period that may make the results time-period specific. Another type of time-period bias arises with long time series. Long time series may give a more accurate picture of true investment performance than short time series, but they have the potential of including structural changes that would result in two different return distributions within the long period.

20. An estimator should have several desirable properties, including the following:

    ● Unbiasedness: The expected value of the estimator is equal to the population parameter.

    ● Efficiency: An efficient estimator is unbiased and has a smaller variance than all other unbiased estimators.

- Consistency: A consistent estimator tends to produce more accurate estimates of the population parameter as sample size increases.

21. C is correct. As degrees of freedom increase, the t-distribution will more closely resemble a normal distribution, becoming more peaked and having less fat tails.

22. A is correct. All else equal, a larger sample size will decrease both the standard error and the width of the confidence interval. In other words, the precision of the estimate of the population parameter is increased.

Product		
Seoul		
Tokyo (Comp.)		-11.1%
Mumbai		
Singapore		-4.5%
Sydney		-4.7%
Shanghai B	29710	1.1%	-10.5%
Hong Kong	46446	0.9%	-6.9%
Toronto	316.8	0.7%	-4.2%
Stockholm	22,700.9	0.5%	4.1%
Mexico City	13,524.8	0.1%	

11

Hypothesis Testing

by Richard A. DeFusco, CFA, Dennis W. McLeavey, CFA, Jerald E. Pinto, CFA, and David E. Runkle, CFA

LEARNING OUTCOMES

Mastery	The candidate should be able to:
☐	**a** define a hypothesis, describe the steps of hypothesis testing, describe and interpret the choice of the null and alternative hypotheses, and distinguish between one-tailed and two-tailed tests of hypotheses;
☐	**b** explain a test statistic, Type I and Type II errors, a significance level, and how significance levels are used in hypothesis testing;
☐	**c** explain a decision rule, the power of a test, and the relation between confidence intervals and hypothesis tests;
☐	**d** distinguish between a statistical result and an economically meaningful result;
☐	**e** explain and interpret the p-value as it relates to hypothesis testing;
☐	**f** identify the appropriate test statistic and interpret the results for a hypothesis test concerning the population mean of both large and small samples when the population is normally or approximately distributed and the variance is 1) known or 2) unknown;
☐	**g** identify the appropriate test statistic and interpret the results for a hypothesis test concerning the equality of the population means of two at least approximately normally distributed populations, based on independent random samples with 1) equal or 2) unequal assumed variances;
☐	**h** identify the appropriate test statistic and interpret the results for a hypothesis test concerning the mean difference of two normally distributed populations;
☐	**i** identify the appropriate test statistic and interpret the results for a hypothesis test concerning 1) the variance of a normally distributed population, and 2) the equality of the variances of two normally distributed populations based on two independent random samples;
☐	**j** distinguish between parametric and nonparametric tests and describe the situations in which the use of nonparametric tests may be appropriate.

INTRODUCTION

Analysts often confront competing ideas about how financial markets work. Some of these ideas develop through personal research or experience with markets; others come from interactions with colleagues; and many others appear in the professional literature on finance and investments. In general, how can an analyst decide whether statements about the financial world are probably true or probably false?

When we can reduce an idea or assertion to a definite statement about the value of a quantity, such as an underlying or population mean, the idea becomes a statistically testable statement or hypothesis. The analyst may want to explore questions such as the following:

- Is the underlying mean return on this mutual fund different from the underlying mean return on its benchmark?

- Did the volatility of returns on this stock change after the stock was added to a stock market index?

- Are a security's bid-ask spreads related to the number of dealers making a market in the security?

- Do data from a national bond market support a prediction of an economic theory about the term structure of interest rates (the relationship between yield and maturity)?

To address these questions, we use the concepts and tools of hypothesis testing. Hypothesis testing is part of statistical inference, the process of making judgments about a larger group (a population) on the basis of a smaller group actually observed (a sample). The concepts and tools of hypothesis testing provide an objective means to gauge whether the available evidence supports the hypothesis. After a statistical test of a hypothesis we should have a clearer idea of the probability that a hypothesis is true or not, although our conclusion always stops short of certainty. Hypothesis testing has been a powerful tool in the advancement of investment knowledge and science. As Robert L. Kahn of the Institute for Social Research (Ann Arbor, Michigan) has written, "The mill of science grinds only when hypothesis and data are in continuous and abrasive contact."

The main emphases of this reading are the framework of hypothesis testing and tests concerning mean and variance, two quantities frequently used in investments. We give an overview of the procedure of hypothesis testing in the next section. We then address testing hypotheses about the mean and hypotheses about the differences between means. In the fourth section of this reading, we address testing hypotheses about a single variance and hypotheses about the differences between variances. We end the reading with an overview of some other important issues and techniques in statistical inference.

HYPOTHESIS TESTING

Hypothesis testing, as we have mentioned, is part of the branch of statistics known as statistical inference. Traditionally, the field of statistical inference has two subdivisions: **estimation** and **hypothesis testing**. Estimation addresses the question "What is this parameter's (e.g., the population mean's) value?" The answer is in the form of a confidence interval built around a point estimate. Take the case of the mean: We build a confidence interval for the population mean around the sample mean as a point estimate. For the sake of specificity, suppose the sample mean is 50 and a 95 percent confidence interval for the population mean is 50 ± 10 (the confidence interval runs from 40 to 60). If this confidence interval has been properly constructed, there is a 95 percent probability that the interval from 40 to 60 contains the population mean's value.[1] The second branch of statistical inference, hypothesis testing, has a somewhat different focus. A hypothesis testing question is "Is the value of the parameter (say, the population mean) 45 (or some other specific value)?" The assertion "the population mean is 45" is a hypothesis. A **hypothesis** is defined as a statement about one or more populations.

This section focuses on the concepts of hypothesis testing. The process of hypothesis testing is part of a rigorous approach to acquiring knowledge known as the scientific method. The scientific method starts with observation and the formulation of a theory to organize and explain observations. We judge the correctness of the theory by its ability to make accurate predictions—for example, to predict the results of new observations.[2] If the predictions are correct, we continue to maintain the theory as a possibly correct explanation of our observations. When risk plays a role in the outcomes of observations, as in finance, we can only try to make unbiased, probability-based judgments about whether the new data support the predictions. Statistical hypothesis testing fills that key role of testing hypotheses when chance plays a role. In an analyst's day-to-day work, he may address questions to which he might give answers of varying quality. When an analyst correctly formulates the question into a testable hypothesis and carries out and reports on a hypothesis test, he has provided an element of support to his answer consistent with the standards of the scientific method. Of course, the analyst's logic, economic reasoning, information sources, and perhaps other factors also play a role in our assessment of the answer's quality.[3]

We organize this introduction to hypothesis testing around the following list of seven steps.

- **Steps in Hypothesis Testing.** The steps in testing a hypothesis are as follows:[4]

  1. Stating the hypotheses.
  2. Identifying the appropriate test statistic and its probability distribution.
  3. Specifying the significance level.
  4. Stating the decision rule.
  5. Collecting the data and calculating the test statistic.
  6. Making the statistical decision.
  7. Making the economic or investment decision.

We will explain each of these steps using as illustration a hypothesis test concerning the sign of the risk premium on Canadian stocks. The steps above constitute a traditional approach to hypothesis testing. We will end the section with a frequently used alternative to those steps, the *p*-value approach.

The first step in hypothesis testing is stating the hypotheses. We always state two hypotheses: the null hypothesis (or null), designated H_0, and the alternative hypothesis, designated H_a.

- **Definition of Null Hypothesis.** The null hypothesis is the hypothesis to be tested. For example, we could hypothesize that the population mean risk premium for Canadian equities is less than or equal to zero.

The null hypothesis is a proposition that is considered true unless the sample we use to conduct the hypothesis test gives convincing evidence that the null hypothesis is false. When such evidence is present, we are led to the alternative hypothesis.

---

1 We discussed the construction and interpretation of confidence intervals in the reading on sampling and estimation.

2 To be testable, a theory must be capable of making predictions that can be shown to be wrong.

3 See Freeley and Steinberg (1999) for a discussion of critical thinking applied to reasoned decision making.

4 This list is based on one in Daniel and Terrell (1986).

- **Definition of Alternative Hypothesis.** The alternative hypothesis is the hypothesis accepted when the null hypothesis is rejected. Our alternative hypothesis is that the population mean risk premium for Canadian equities is greater than zero.

Suppose our question concerns the value of a population parameter, θ, in relation to one possible value of the parameter, θ_0 (these are read, respectively, "theta" and "theta sub zero").[5] Examples of a population parameter include the population mean, μ, and the population variance, σ^2. We can formulate three different sets of hypotheses, which we label according to the assertion made by the alternative hypothesis.

- **Formulations of Hypotheses.** We can formulate the null and alternative hypotheses in three different ways:

   1. $H_0: \theta = \theta_0$ versus $H_a: \theta \neq \theta_0$ (a "not equal to" alternative hypothesis)
   2. $H_0: \theta \leq \theta_0$ versus $H_a: \theta > \theta_0$ (a "greater than" alternative hypothesis)
   3. $H_0: \theta \geq \theta_0$ versus $H_a: \theta < \theta_0$ (a "less than" alternative hypothesis)

In our Canadian example, $\theta = \mu_{RP}$ and represents the population mean risk premium on Canadian equities. Also, $\theta_0 = 0$ and we are using the second of the above three formulations.

The first formulation is a **two-sided hypothesis test** (or **two-tailed hypothesis test**): We reject the null in favor of the alternative if the evidence indicates that the population parameter is either smaller or larger than θ_0. In contrast, Formulations 2 and 3 are each a **one-sided hypothesis test** (or **one-tailed hypothesis test**). For Formulations 2 and 3, we reject the null only if the evidence indicates that the population parameter is respectively greater than or less than θ_0. The alternative hypothesis has one side.

Notice that in each case above, we state the null and alternative hypotheses such that they account for all possible values of the parameter. With Formulation 1, for example, the parameter is either equal to the hypothesized value θ_0 (under the null hypothesis) or not equal to the hypothesized value θ_0 (under the alternative hypothesis). Those two statements logically exhaust all possible values of the parameter.

Despite the different ways to formulate hypotheses, we always conduct a test of the null hypothesis at the point of equality, $\theta = \theta_0$. Whether the null is $H_0: \theta = \theta_0$, $H_0: \theta \leq \theta_0$, or $H_0: \theta \geq \theta_0$, we actually test $\theta = \theta_0$. The reasoning is straightforward. Suppose the hypothesized value of the parameter is 5. Consider $H_0: \theta \leq 5$, with a "greater than" alternative hypothesis, $H_a: \theta > 5$. If we have enough evidence to reject $H_0: \theta = 5$ in favor of $H_a: \theta > 5$, we definitely also have enough evidence to reject the hypothesis that the parameter, θ, is some smaller value, such as 4.5 or 4. To review, the calculation to test the null hypothesis is the same for all three formulations. What is different for the three formulations, we will see shortly, is how the calculation is evaluated to decide whether or not to reject the null.

How do we choose the null and alternative hypotheses? Probably most common are "not equal to" alternative hypotheses. We reject the null because the evidence indicates that the parameter is either larger or smaller than θ_0. Sometimes, however, we may have a "suspected" or "hoped for" condition for which we want to find supportive evidence.[6] In that case, we can formulate the alternative hypothesis as the statement that this condition is true; the null hypothesis that we test is the statement that this condition is not true. If the evidence supports rejecting the null and accepting the alternative, we have statistically confirmed what we thought was true. For example, economic theory suggests that investors require a positive risk premium on stocks

5 Greek letters, such as σ, are reserved for population parameters; Roman letters in italics, such as s, are used for sample statistics.
6 Part of this discussion of the selection of hypotheses follows Bowerman and O'Connell (1997, p. 386).

(the **risk premium** is defined as the expected return on stocks minus the risk-free rate). Following the principle of stating the alternative as the "hoped for" condition, we formulate the following hypotheses:

H_0: The population mean risk premium on Canadian stocks is less than or equal to 0.

H_a: The population mean risk premium on Canadian stocks is positive.

Note that "greater than" and "less than" alternative hypotheses reflect the beliefs of the researcher more strongly than a "not equal to" alternative hypothesis. To emphasize an attitude of neutrality, the researcher may sometimes select a "not equal to" alternative hypothesis when a one-sided alternative hypothesis is also reasonable.

The second step in hypothesis testing is identifying the appropriate test statistic and its probability distribution.

■ **Definition of Test Statistic.** A test statistic is a quantity, calculated based on a sample, whose value is the basis for deciding whether or not to reject the null hypothesis.

The focal point of our statistical decision is the value of the test statistic. Frequently (in all the cases that we examine in this reading), the test statistic has the form

Test statistic

$$= \frac{\text{Sample statistic} - \text{Value of the population parameter under } H_0}{\text{Standard error of the sample statistic}} \qquad (1)$$

For our risk premium example, the population parameter of interest is the population mean risk premium, μ_{RP}. We label the hypothesized value of the population mean under H_0 as μ_0. Restating the hypotheses using symbols, we test H_0: $\mu_{RP} \leq \mu_0$ versus H_a: $\mu_{RP} > \mu_0$. However, because under the null we are testing $\mu_0 = 0$, we write H_0: $\mu_{RP} \leq 0$ versus H_a: $\mu_{RP} > 0$.

The sample mean provides an estimate of the population mean. Therefore, we can use the sample mean risk premium calculated from historical data, $\bar{X}_{RP}$, as the sample statistic in Equation 1. The standard deviation of the sample statistic, known as the "standard error" of the statistic, is the denominator in Equation 1. For this example, the sample statistic is a sample mean. For a sample mean, $\bar{X}$, calculated from a sample generated by a population with standard deviation σ, the standard error is given by one of two expressions:

$$\sigma_{\bar{X}} = \frac{\sigma}{\sqrt{n}} \qquad (2)$$

when we know σ (the population standard deviation), or

$$s_{\bar{X}} = \frac{s}{\sqrt{n}} \qquad (3)$$

when we do not know the population standard deviation and need to use the sample standard deviation s to estimate it. For this example, because we do not know the population standard deviation of the process generating the return, we use Equation 3. The test statistic is thus

$$\frac{\bar{X}_{RP} - \mu_0}{s_{\bar{X}}} = \frac{\bar{X}_{RP} - 0}{s/\sqrt{n}}$$

In making the substitution of 0 for μ_0, we use the fact already highlighted that we test any null hypothesis at the point of equality, as well as the fact that $\mu_0 = 0$ here.

We have identified a test statistic to test the null hypothesis. What probability distribution does it follow? We will encounter four distributions for test statistics in this reading:

■ the t-distribution (for a t-test);

■ the standard normal or z-distribution (for a z-test);

- the chi-square (χ^2) distribution (for a chi-square test); and
- the F-distribution (for an F-test).

We will discuss the details later, but assume we can conduct a z-test based on the central limit theorem because our Canadian sample has many observations.[7] To summarize, the test statistic for the hypothesis test concerning the mean risk premium is $\bar{X}_{RP}/s_{\bar{x}}$. We can conduct a z-test because we can plausibly assume that the test statistic follows a standard normal distribution.

The third step in hypothesis testing is specifying the significance level. When the test statistic has been calculated, two actions are possible: 1) We reject the null hypothesis or 2) we do not reject the null hypothesis. The action we take is based on comparing the calculated test statistic to a specified possible value or values. The comparison values we choose are based on the level of significance selected. The level of significance reflects how much sample evidence we require to reject the null. Analogous to its counterpart in a court of law, the required standard of proof can change according to the nature of the hypotheses and the seriousness of the consequences of making a mistake. There are four possible outcomes when we test a null hypothesis:

1. We reject a false null hypothesis. This is a correct decision.
2. We reject a true null hypothesis. This is called a **Type I error**.
3. We do not reject a false null hypothesis. This is called a **Type II error**.
4. We do not reject a true null hypothesis. This is a correct decision.

We illustrate these outcomes in Table 1.

Table 1	Type I and Type II Errors in Hypothesis Testing	
	True Situation	
Decision	H_0 **True**	H_0 **False**
Do not reject H_0	Correct Decision	Type II Error
Reject H_0 (accept H_a)	Type I Error	Correct Decision

When we make a decision in a hypothesis test, we run the risk of making either a Type I or a Type II error. These are mutually exclusive errors: If we mistakenly reject the null, we can only be making a Type I error; if we mistakenly fail to reject the null, we can only be making a Type II error.

The probability of a Type I error in testing a hypothesis is denoted by the Greek letter alpha, α. This probability is also known as the **level of significance** of the test. For example, a level of significance of 0.05 for a test means that there is a 5 percent probability of rejecting a true null hypothesis. The probability of a Type II error is denoted by the Greek letter beta, ß.

Controlling the probabilities of the two types of errors involves a trade-off. All else equal, if we decrease the probability of a Type I error by specifying a smaller significance level (say 0.01 rather than 0.05), we increase the probability of making a Type II error because we will reject the null less frequently, including when it is false. The only way to reduce the probabilities of both types of errors simultaneously is to increase the sample size, n.

---

[7] The central limit theorem says that the sampling distribution of the sample mean will be approximately normal with mean μ and variance σ2/n when the sample size is large. The sample we will use for this example has 103 observations.

Quantifying the trade-off between the two types of error in practice is usually impossible because the probability of a Type II error is itself hard to quantify. Consider H_0: $\theta \leq 5$ versus H_a: $\theta > 5$. Because every true value of θ greater than 5 makes the null hypothesis false, each value of θ greater than 5 has a different ß (Type II error probability). In contrast, it is sufficient to state a Type I error probability for $\theta = 5$, the point at which we conduct the test of the null hypothesis. Thus, in general, we specify only α, the probability of a Type I error, when we conduct a hypothesis test. Whereas the significance level of a test is the probability of incorrectly rejecting the null, the **power of a test** is the probability of *correctly* rejecting the null—that is, the probability of rejecting the null when it is false.[8] When more than one test statistic is available to conduct a hypothesis test, we should prefer the most powerful, all else equal.[9]

To summarize, the standard approach to hypothesis testing involves specifying a level of significance (probability of Type I error) only. It is most appropriate to specify this significance level prior to calculating the test statistic. If we specify it after calculating the test statistic, we may be influenced by the result of the calculation, which detracts from the objectivity of the test.

We can use three conventional significance levels to conduct hypothesis tests: 0.10, 0.05, and 0.01. Qualitatively, if we can reject a null hypothesis at the 0.10 level of significance, we have *some evidence* that the null hypothesis is false. If we can reject a null hypothesis at the 0.05 level, we have *strong evidence* that the null hypothesis is false. And if we can reject a null hypothesis at the 0.01 level, we have *very strong evidence* that the null hypothesis is false. For the risk premium example, we will specify a 0.05 significance level.

The fourth step in hypothesis testing is stating the decision rule. The general principle is simply stated. When we test the null hypothesis, if we find that the calculated value of the test statistic is as extreme or more extreme than a given value or values determined by the specified level of significance, α, we reject the null hypothesis. We say the result is **statistically significant**. Otherwise, we do not reject the null hypothesis and we say the result is not statistically significant. The value or values with which we compare the calculated test statistic to make our decision are the rejection points (critical values) for the test.[10]

- **Definition of a Rejection Point (Critical Value) for the Test Statistic.** A rejection point (critical value) for a test statistic is a value with which the computed test statistic is compared to decide whether to reject or not reject the null hypothesis.

For a one-tailed test, we indicate a rejection point using the symbol for the test statistic with a subscript indicating the specified probability of a Type I error, α; for example, z_α. For a two-tailed test, we indicate $z_{\alpha/2}$. To illustrate the use of rejection points, suppose we are using a z-test and have chosen a 0.05 level of significance.

- For a test of H_0: $\theta = \theta_0$ versus H_a: $\theta \neq \theta_0$, two rejection points exist, one negative and one positive. For a two-sided test at the 0.05 level, the total probability of a Type I error must sum to 0.05. Thus, $0.05/2 = 0.025$ of the probability should be in each tail of the distribution of the test statistic under the null. Consequently, the two rejection points are $z_{0.025} = 1.96$ and $-z_{0.025} = -1.96$. Let z represent the calculated value of the test statistic. We reject the null if we find that $z < -1.96$ or $z > 1.96$. We do not reject if $-1.96 \leq z \leq 1.96$.

- For a test of H_0: $\theta \leq \theta_0$ versus H_a: $\theta > \theta_0$ at the 0.05 level of significance, the rejection point is $z_{0.05} = 1.645$. We reject the null hypothesis if $z > 1.645$. The value of the standard normal distribution such that 5 percent of the outcomes lie to the right is $z_{0.05} = 1.645$.

---

8 The power of a test is, in fact, 1 minus the probability of a Type II error.

9 We do not always have information on the relative power of the test for competing test statistics, however.

10 "Rejection point" is a descriptive synonym for the more traditional term "critical value."

■ For a test of H_0: $\theta \geq \theta_0$ versus H_a: $\theta < \theta_0$, the rejection point is $-z_{0.05} = -1.645$. We reject the null hypothesis if $z < -1.645$.

Figure 1 illustrates a test H_0: $\mu = \mu_0$ versus H_a: $\mu \neq \mu_0$ at the 0.05 significance level using a z-test. The "acceptance region" is the traditional name for the set of values of the test statistic for which we do not reject the null hypothesis. (The traditional name, however, is inaccurate. We should avoid using phrases such as "accept the null hypothesis" because such a statement implies a greater degree of conviction about the null than is warranted when we fail to reject it.)[11] On either side of the acceptance region is a rejection region (or critical region). If the null hypothesis that $\mu = \mu_0$ is true, the test statistic has a 2.5 percent chance of falling in the left rejection region and a 2.5 percent chance of falling in the right rejection region. Any calculated value of the test statistic that falls in either of these two regions causes us to reject the null hypothesis at the 0.05 significance level. The rejection points of 1.96 and −1.96 are seen to be the dividing lines between the acceptance and rejection regions.

Figure 1	**Rejection Points (Critical Values), 0.05 Significance Level, Two-Sided Test of the Population Mean Using a z-Test**

Figure 1 affords a good opportunity to highlight the relationship between confidence intervals and hypothesis tests. A 95 percent confidence interval for the population mean, μ, based on sample mean, $\bar{X}$, is given by $\bar{X} - 1.96 s_{\bar{X}}$ to $\bar{X} + 1.96 s_{\bar{X}}$, where $s_{\bar{X}}$ is the standard error of the sample mean (Equation 3).[12]

Now consider one of the conditions for rejecting the null hypothesis:

$$\frac{\bar{X} - \mu_0}{s_{\bar{X}}} > 1.96$$

Here, μ_0 is the hypothesized value of the population mean. The condition states that rejection is warranted if the test statistic exceeds 1.96. Multiplying both sides by $s_{\bar{X}}$, we have $\bar{X} - \mu_0 > 1.96 s_{\bar{X}}$, or after rearranging, $\bar{X} - 1.96 s_{\bar{X}} > \mu_0$, which we can also write

---

11 The analogy in some courts of law (for example, in the United States) is that if a jury does not return a verdict of guilty (the alternative hypothesis), it is most accurate to say that the jury has failed to reject the null hypothesis, namely, that the defendant is innocent.

12 Just as with the hypothesis test, we can use this confidence interval, based on the standard normal distribution, when we have large samples. An alternative hypothesis test and confidence interval uses the t-distribution, which requires concepts that we introduce in the next section.

as $\mu_0 < \bar{X} - 1.96\,s_{\bar{X}}$. This expression says that if the hypothesized population mean, μ_0, is less than the lower limit of the 95 percent confidence interval based on the sample mean, we must reject the null hypothesis at the 5 percent significance level (the test statistic falls in the rejection region to the right).

Now, we can take the other condition for rejecting the null hypothesis:

$$\frac{\bar{X} - \mu_0}{s_{\bar{X}}} < -1.96$$

and, using algebra as before, rewrite it as $\mu_0 > \bar{X} + 1.96\,s_{\bar{X}}$. If the hypothesized population mean is larger than the upper limit of the 95 percent confidence interval, we reject the null hypothesis at the 5 percent level (the test statistic falls in the rejection region to the left). Thus, an α significance level in a two-sided hypothesis test can be interpreted in exactly the same way as a $(1 - \alpha)$ confidence interval.

In summary, when the hypothesized value of the population parameter under the null is outside the corresponding confidence interval, the null hypothesis is rejected. We could use confidence intervals to test hypotheses; practitioners, however, usually do not. Computing a test statistic (one number, versus two numbers for the usual confidence interval) is more efficient. Also, analysts encounter actual cases of one-sided confidence intervals only rarely. Furthermore, only when we compute a test statistic can we obtain a p-value, a useful quantity relating to the significance of our results (we will discuss p-values shortly).

To return to our risk premium test, we stated hypotheses H_0: $\mu_{RP} \leq 0$ versus H_a: $\mu_{RP} > 0$. We identified the test statistic as $\bar{X}_{RP} / s_{\bar{X}}$ and stated that it follows a standard normal distribution. We are, therefore, conducting a one-sided z-test. We specified a 0.05 significance level. For this one-sided z-test, the rejection point at the 0.05 level of significance is 1.645. We will reject the null if the calculated z-statistic is larger than 1.645. Figure 2 illustrates this test.

Figure 2	Rejection Point (Critical Value), 0.05 Significance Level, One-Sided Test of the Population Mean Using a z-Test

The fifth step in hypothesis testing is collecting the data and calculating the test statistic. The quality of our conclusions depends not only on the appropriateness of the statistical model but also on the quality of the data we use in conducting the test. We first need to check for measurement errors in the recorded data. Some other issues to be aware of include sample selection bias and time-period bias. Sample selection bias refers to bias introduced by systematically excluding some members of the population according to a particular attribute. One type of sample selection bias is survivorship bias. For example, if we define our sample as U.S. bond mutual funds currently operating and we collect returns for just these funds, we will systematically exclude funds that have not survived to the present date. Nonsurviving funds are likely to have underperformed surviving funds, on average; as a result the performance reflected in the sample may be biased upward. Time-period bias refers to the possibility that when we use a time-series sample, our statistical conclusion may be sensitive to the starting and ending dates of the sample.[13]

To continue with the risk premium hypothesis, we focus on Canadian equities. According to Dimson, Marsh, and Staunton (2002) as updated to the end of 2002,[14] for the period 1900 to 2002 inclusive (103 annual observations), the arithmetic mean equity risk premium for Canadian stocks relative to bond returns, $\bar{X}_{RP}$, was 5.1 percent per year. The sample standard deviation of the annual risk premiums was 18.6 percent. Using Equation 3, the standard error of the sample mean is $s_{\bar{X}} = s/\sqrt{n} = 18.6\%/\sqrt{103} = 1.833\%$. The test statistic is $z = \bar{X}_{RP}/s_{\bar{X}} = 5.1\%/1.833\% = 2.78$.

The sixth step in hypothesis testing is making the statistical decision. For our example, because the test statistic $z = 2.78$ is larger than the rejection point of 1.645, we reject the null hypothesis in favor of the alternative hypothesis that the risk premium on Canadian stocks is positive. The first six steps are the statistical steps. The final decision concerns our use of the statistical decision.

The seventh and final step in hypothesis testing is making the economic or investment decision. The economic or investment decision takes into consideration not only the statistical decision but also all pertinent economic issues. In the sixth step, we found strong statistical evidence that the Canadian risk premium is positive. The magnitude of the estimated risk premium, 5.1 percent a year, is economically very meaningful as well. Based on these considerations, an investor might decide to commit funds to Canadian equities. A range of nonstatistical considerations, such as the investor's tolerance for risk and financial position, might also enter the decision-making process.

The preceding discussion raises an issue that often arises in this decision-making step. We frequently find that slight differences between a variable and its hypothesized value are statistically significant but not economically meaningful. For example, we may be testing an investment strategy and reject a null hypothesis that the mean return to the strategy is zero based on a large sample. Equation 1 shows that the smaller the standard error of the sample statistic (the divisor in the formula), the larger the value of the test statistic and the greater the chance the null will be rejected, all else equal. The standard error decreases as the sample size, n, increases, so that for very large samples, we can reject the null for small departures from it. We may find that although a strategy provides a statistically significant positive mean return, the results are not economically significant when we account for transaction costs, taxes, and risk. Even if we conclude that a strategy's results are economically meaningful, we should explore the logic of why the strategy might work in the future before actually implementing it. Such considerations cannot be incorporated into a hypothesis test.

Before leaving the subject of the process of hypothesis testing, we should discuss an important alternative approach called the *p*-value approach to hypothesis testing. Analysts and researchers often report the *p*-value (also called the marginal significance level) associated with hypothesis tests.

■ **Definition of *p*-Value.** The *p*-value is the smallest level of significance at which the null hypothesis can be rejected.

---

13 These issues are discussed further in the reading on sampling.
14 Updated by communication dated 19 May 2003 to the authors.

For the value of the test statistic of 2.78 in the risk premium hypothesis test, using a spreadsheet function for the standard normal distribution, we calculate a p-value of 0.002718. We can reject the null hypothesis at that level of significance. The smaller the p-value, the stronger the evidence against the null hypothesis and in favor of the alternative hypothesis. The p-value for a two-sided test that a parameter equals zero is frequently generated automatically by statistical and econometric software programs.[15]

We can use p-values in the hypothesis testing framework presented above as an alternative to using rejection points. If the p-value is less than our specified level of significance, we reject the null hypothesis. Otherwise, we do not reject the null hypothesis. Using the p-value in this fashion, we reach the same conclusion as we do using rejection points. For example, because 0.002718 is less than 0.05, we would reject the null hypothesis in the risk premium test. The p-value, however, provides more precise information on the strength of the evidence than does the rejection points approach. The p-value of 0.002718 indicates that the null is rejected at a far smaller level of significance than 0.05.

If one researcher examines a question using a 0.05 significance level and another researcher uses a 0.01 significance level, the reader may have trouble comparing the findings. This concern has given rise to an approach to presenting the results of hypothesis tests that features p-values and omits specification of the significance level (Step 3). The interpretation of the statistical results is left to the consumer of the research. This has sometimes been called the p-value approach to hypothesis testing.[16]

HYPOTHESIS TESTS CONCERNING THE MEAN

3

Hypothesis tests concerning the mean are among the most common in practice. In this section we discuss such tests for several distinct types of problems. In one type (discussed in Section 3.1), we test whether the population mean of a single population is equal to (or greater or less than) some hypothesized value. Then, in Sections 3.2 and 3.3, we address inference on means based on two samples. Is an observed difference between two sample means due to chance or different underlying (population) means? When we have two random samples that are independent of each other—no relationship exists between the measurements in one sample and the measurements in the other—the techniques of Section 3.2 apply. When the samples are dependent, the methods of Section 3.3 are appropriate.[17]

3.1 Tests Concerning a Single Mean

An analyst who wants to test a hypothesis concerning the value of an underlying or population mean will conduct a t-test in the great majority of cases. A **t-test** is a hypothesis test using a statistic (t-statistic) that follows a t-distribution. The t-distribution is

---

15 We can use spreadsheets to calculate p-values as well. In Microsoft Excel, for example, we may use the worksheet functions TTEST, NORMSDIST, CHIDIST, and FDIST to calculate p-values for t-tests, z-tests, chi-square tests, and F-tests, respectively.

16 Davidson and MacKinnon (1993) argued the merits of this approach: "The P value approach does not necessarily force us to make a decision about the null hypothesis. If we obtain a P value of, say, 0.000001, we will almost certainly want to reject the null. But if we obtain a P value of, say, 0.04, or even 0.004, we are not *obliged* to reject it. We may simply file the result away as information that casts some doubt on the null hypothesis, but that is not, by itself, conclusive. We believe that this somewhat agnostic attitude toward test statistics, in which they are merely regarded as pieces of information that we may or may not want to act upon, is usually the most sensible one to take." (p. 80)

17 When we want to test whether the population means of more than two populations are equal, we use analysis of variance (ANOVA). We introduce ANOVA in its most common application, regression analysis, in the reading on correlation and regression analysis.

a probability distribution defined by a single parameter known as degrees of freedom (df). Each value of degrees of freedom defines one distribution in this family of distributions. The t-distribution is closely related to the standard normal distribution. Like the standard normal distribution, a t-distribution is symmetrical with a mean of zero. However, the t-distribution is more spread out: It has a standard deviation greater than 1 (compared to 1 for the standard normal)[18] and more probability for outcomes distant from the mean (it has fatter tails than the standard normal distribution). As the number of degrees of freedom increases with sample size, the spread decreases and the t-distribution approaches the standard normal distribution as a limit.

Why is the t-distribution the focus for the hypothesis tests of this section? In practice, investment analysts need to estimate the population standard deviation by calculating a sample standard deviation. That is, the population variance (or standard deviation) is unknown. For hypothesis tests concerning the population mean of a normally distributed population with unknown variance, the theoretically correct test statistic is the t-statistic. What if a normal distribution does not describe the population? The t-test is **robust** to moderate departures from normality, except for outliers and strong skewness.[19] When we have large samples, departures of the underlying distribution from the normal are of increasingly less concern. The sample mean is approximately normally distributed in large samples according to the central limit theorem, whatever the distribution describing the population. In general, a sample size of 30 or more usually can be treated as a large sample and a sample size of 29 or less is treated as a small sample.[20]

■ **Test Statistic for Hypothesis Tests of the Population Mean (Practical Case— Population Variance Unknown).** If the population sampled has unknown variance and either of the conditions below holds:

1. the sample is large, or

2. the sample is small but the population sampled is normally distributed, or approximately normally distributed,

then the test statistic for hypothesis tests concerning a single population mean, μ, is

$$t_{n-1} = \frac{\overline{X} - \mu_0}{s/\sqrt{n}} \tag{4}$$

where

t_{n-1} = t-statistic with $n - 1$ degrees of freedom (n is the sample size)
$\overline{X}$ = the sample mean
μ_0 = the hypothesized value of the population mean
s = the sample standard deviation

The denominator of the t-statistic is an estimate of the sample mean standard error, $s_{\overline{X}} = s/\sqrt{n}$.[21]

---

18 The formula for the variance of a t-distribution is df/(df – 2).

19 See Moore and McCabe (1998). A statistic is robust if the required probability calculations are insensitive to violations of the assumptions.

20 Although this generalization is useful, we caution that the sample size needed to obtain an approximately normal sampling distribution for the sample mean depends on how non-normal the original population is. For some populations, "large" may be a sample size well in excess of 30.

21 A technical note, for reference, is required. When the sample comes from a finite population, estimates of the standard error of the mean, whether from Equation 2 or Equation 3, overestimate the true standard error. To address this, the computed standard error is multiplied by a shrinkage factor called the finite population correction factor (fpc), equal to $\sqrt{(N-n)/(N-1)}$, where N is the population size and n is the sample size. When the sample size is small relative to the population size (less than 5 percent of the population size), the fpc is usually ignored. The overestimation problem arises only in the usual situation of sampling without replacement (after an item is selected, it cannot be picked again) as opposed to sampling with replacement.

In Example 1, because the sample size is small, the test is called a small sample test concerning the population mean.

Example 1

Risk and Return Characteristics of an Equity Mutual Fund (1)

You are analyzing Sendar Equity Fund, a midcap growth fund that has been in existence for 24 months. During this period, it has achieved a mean monthly return of 1.50 percent with a sample standard deviation of monthly returns of 3.60 percent. Given its level of systematic (market) risk and according to a pricing model, this mutual fund was expected to have earned a 1.10 percent mean monthly return during that time period. Assuming returns are normally distributed, are the actual results consistent with an underlying or population mean monthly return of 1.10 percent?

1. Formulate null and alternative hypotheses consistent with the verbal description of the research goal.

2. Identify the test statistic for conducting a test of the hypotheses in Part 1.

3. Identify the rejection point or points for the hypothesis tested in Part 1 at the 0.10 level of significance.

4. Determine whether the null hypothesis is rejected or not rejected at the 0.10 level of significance. (Use the tables in the back of this book.)

Solution to 1:

We have a "not equal to" alternative hypothesis, where μ is the underlying mean return on Sendar Equity Fund—H_0: $\mu = 1.10$ versus H_a: $\mu \neq 1.10$.

Solution to 2:

Because the population variance is not known, we use a t-test with $24 - 1 = 23$ degrees of freedom.

Solution to 3:

Because this is a two-tailed test, we have the rejection point $t_{\alpha/2,n-1} = t_{0.05,23}$. In the table for the t-distribution, we look across the row for 23 degrees of freedom to the 0.05 column, to find 1.714. The two rejection points for this two-sided test are 1.714 and −1.714. We will reject the null if we find that $t > 1.714$ or $t < -1.714$.

Solution to 4:

$$t_{23} = \frac{1.50 - 1.10}{3.60/\sqrt{24}} = \frac{0.40}{0.734847} = 0.544331 \text{ or } 0.544$$

Because 0.544 does not satisfy either $t > 1.714$ or $t < -1.714$, we do not reject the null hypothesis.

The confidence interval approach provides another perspective on this hypothesis test. The theoretically correct $100(1 - \alpha)\%$ confidence interval for the population mean of a normal distribution with unknown variance, based on a sample of size n, is

$$\bar{X} - t_{\alpha/2}s_{\bar{X}} \text{ to } \bar{X} + t_{\alpha/2}s_{\bar{X}}$$

where $t_{\alpha/2}$ is the value of t such that $\alpha/2$ of the probability remains in the right tail and where $-t_{\alpha/2}$ is the value of t such that $\alpha/2$ of the probability remains in the left tail, for $n - 1$ degrees of freedom. Here, the 90 percent confidence interval runs from 1.5 − (1.714)(0.734847) = 0.240 to 1.5 + (1.714)(0.734847) = 2.760, compactly [0.240, 2.760]. The hypothesized value of mean return, 1.10, falls within this confidence interval, and we see from this perspective also that the null hypothesis is not rejected. At a 10 percent level of significance, we conclude that a population mean monthly return of 1.10 percent is consistent with the 24-month observed data series. Note that 10 percent is a relatively high probability of rejecting the hypothesis of a 1.10 percent population mean monthly return when it is true.

Example 2

A Slowdown in Payments of Receivables

FashionDesigns, a supplier of casual clothing to retail chains, is concerned about a possible slowdown in payments from its customers. The controller's office measures the rate of payment by the average number of days in receivables.[22] FashionDesigns has generally maintained an average of 45 days in receivables. Because it would be too costly to analyze all of the company's receivables frequently, the controller's office uses sampling to track customers' payment rates. A random sample of 50 accounts shows a mean number of days in receivables of 49 with a standard deviation of 8 days.

1. Formulate null and alternative hypotheses consistent with determining whether the evidence supports the suspected condition that customer payments have slowed.

2. Identify the test statistic for conducting a test of the hypotheses in Part 1.

3. Identify the rejection point or points for the hypothesis tested in Part 1 at the 0.05 and 0.01 levels of significance.

4. Determine whether the null hypothesis is rejected or not rejected at the 0.05 and 0.01 levels of significance.

Solution to 1:

The suspected condition is that the number of days in receivables has increased relative to the historical rate of 45 days, which suggests a "greater than" alternative hypothesis. With μ as the population mean number of days in receivables, the hypotheses are H_0: $\mu \leq 45$ versus H_a: $\mu > 45$.

Solution to 2:

Because the population variance is not known, we use a t-test with 50 − 1 = 49 degrees of freedom.

Solution to 3:

The rejection point is found across the row for degrees of freedom of 49. To find the one-tailed rejection point for a 0.05 significance level, we use the 0.05 column: The value is 1.677. To find the one-tailed rejection point for a 0.01 level of significance, we use the 0.01 column: The value is 2.405. To summarize, at a 0.05 significance level, we reject the null if we find that $t > 1.677$; at a 0.01 significance level, we reject the null if we find that $t > 2.405$.

---

22 This measure represents the average length of time that the business must wait after making a sale before receiving payment. The calculation is (Accounts receivable)/(Average sales per day).

Solution to 4:

$$t_{49} = \frac{49-45}{8/\sqrt{50}} = \frac{4}{1.131371} = 3.536$$

Because 3.536 > 1.677, the null hypothesis is rejected at the 0.05 level. Because 3.536 > 2.405, the null hypothesis is also rejected at the 0.01 level. We can say with a high level of confidence that FashionDesigns has experienced a slowdown in customer payments. The level of significance, 0.01, is a relatively low probability of rejecting the hypothesized mean of 45 days or less. Rejection gives us confidence that the mean has increased above 45 days.

We stated above that when population variance is not known, we use a t-test for tests concerning a single population mean. Given at least approximate normality, the t-test is always called for when we deal with small samples and do not know the population variance. For large samples, the central limit theorem states that the sample mean is approximately normally distributed, whatever the distribution of the population. So the t-test is still appropriate, but an alternative test may be more useful when sample size is large.

For large samples, practitioners sometimes use a z-test in place of a t-test for tests concerning a mean.[23] The justification for using the z-test in this context is twofold. First, in large samples, the sample mean should follow the normal distribution at least approximately, as we have already stated, fulfilling the normality assumption of the z-test. Second, the difference between the rejection points for the t-test and z-test becomes quite small when sample size is large. For a two-sided test at the 0.05 level of significance, the rejection points for a z-test are 1.96 and −1.96. For a t-test, the rejection points are 2.045 and −2.045 for df = 29 (about a 4 percent difference between the z and t rejection points) and 2.009 and −2.009 for df = 50 (about a 2.5 percent difference between the z and t rejection points). Because the t-test is readily available as statistical program output and theoretically correct for unknown population variance, we present it as the test of choice.

In a very limited number of cases, we may know the population variance; in such cases, the z-test is theoretically correct.[24]

- **The z-Test Alternative.**

  1. If the population sampled is normally distributed with known variance σ^2, then the test statistic for a hypothesis test concerning a single population mean, μ, is

     $$z = \frac{\bar{X} - \mu_0}{\sigma/\sqrt{n}} \tag{5}$$

  2. If the population sampled has unknown variance and the sample is large, in place of a t-test, an alternative test statistic (relying on the central limit theorem) is

     $$z = \frac{\bar{X} - \mu_0}{s/\sqrt{n}} \tag{6}$$

---

23 These practitioners choose between t-tests and z-tests based on sample size. For small samples ($n < 30$), they use a t-test, and for large samples, a z-test.

24 For example, in Monte Carlo simulation, we prespecify the probability distributions for the risk factors. If we use a normal distribution, we know the true values of mean and variance. Monte Carlo simulation involves the use of a computer to represent the operation of a system subject to risk; we discuss Monte Carlo simulation in the reading on common probability distributions.

In the above equations,

σ = the known population standard deviation

s = the sample standard deviation

μ_0 = the hypothesized value of the population mean

When we use a z-test, we most frequently refer to a rejection point in the list below.

- **Rejection Points for a z-Test.**

  A. Significance level of $\alpha = 0.10$.

    1. $H_0: \theta = \theta_0$ versus $H_a: \theta \neq \theta_0$. The rejection points are $z_{0.05} = 1.645$ and $-z_{0.05} = -1.645$.

      Reject the null hypothesis if $z > 1.645$ or if $z < -1.645$.

    2. $H_0: \theta \leq \theta_0$ versus $H_a: \theta > \theta_0$. The rejection point is $z_{0.10} = 1.28$.

      Reject the null hypothesis if $z > 1.28$.

    3. $H_0: \theta \geq \theta_0$ versus $H_a: \theta < \theta_0$. The rejection point is $-z_{0.10} = -1.28$.

      Reject the null hypothesis if $z < -1.28$.

  B. Significance level of $\alpha = 0.05$.

    1. $H_0: \theta = \theta_0$ versus $H_a: \theta \neq \theta_0$. The rejection points are $z_{0.025} = 1.96$ and $-z_{0.025} = -1.96$.

      Reject the null hypothesis if $z > 1.96$ or if $z < -1.96$.

    2. $H_0: \theta \leq \theta_0$ versus $H_a: \theta > \theta_0$. The rejection point is $z_{0.05} = 1.645$.

      Reject the null hypothesis if $z > 1.645$.

    3. $H_0: \theta \geq \theta_0$ versus $H_a: \theta < \theta_0$. The rejection point is $-z_{0.05} = -1.645$.

      Reject the null hypothesis if $z < -1.645$.

  C. Significance level of $\alpha = 0.01$.

    1. $H_0: \theta = \theta_0$ versus $H_a: \theta \neq \theta_0$. The rejection points are $z_{0.005} = 2.575$ and $-z_{0.005} = -2.575$.

      Reject the null hypothesis if $z > 2.575$ or if $z < -2.575$.

    2. $H_0: \theta \leq \theta_0$ versus $H_a: \theta > \theta_0$. The rejection point is $z_{0.01} = 2.33$.

      Reject the null hypothesis if $z > 2.33$.

    3. $H_0: \theta \geq \theta_0$ versus $H_a: \theta < \theta_0$. The rejection point is $-z_{0.01} = -2.33$.

      Reject the null hypothesis if $z < -2.33$.

Example 3

The Effect of Commercial Paper Issuance on Stock Prices

Commercial paper (CP) is unsecured short-term corporate debt that, like U.S. Treasury bills, is characterized by a single payment at maturity. When a company enters the CP market for the first time, how do stock market participants react to the announcement of the CP ratings?

Nayar and Rozeff (1994) addressed this question using data for the period October 1981 to December 1985. During this period, 132 CP issues (96 industrial and 36 non-industrial) received an initial rating in Standard & Poor's *CreditWeek* or Moody's Investors Service *Bond Survey*. Nayar and Rozeff categorized ratings as superior or inferior. Superior CP ratings were A1+ or A1 from Standard & Poor's and Prime-1 (P1) from Moody's. Inferior CP ratings were A2 or lower from Standard & Poor's and Prime-2 (P2) or lower from Moody's. The publication day of the initial ratings was designated $t = 0$. The researchers found, however, that companies themselves often disseminate the rating information prior to publication in *CreditWeek* or the *Bond Survey*. The reaction of stock price was studied on the day before publication, $t - 1$, because that date was closer to the actual date of information release.

If CP ratings provide *new* information useful for equity valuation, the information should cause a change in stock prices and returns once it is available. Only one component of stock returns is of interest: the return in excess of that predicted given a stock's market risk or beta, called the abnormal return. Positive (negative) abnormal returns indicate that investors perceive favorable (unfavorable) corporate news in the ratings announcement. Although Nayar and Rozeff examined abnormal returns for various time horizons or event windows, we report a selection of their findings for the day prior to rating publication ($t - 1$).

All CP Issues ($n = 132$ issues). The null hypothesis was that the average abnormal stock return on day $t - 1$ was 0. The null would be true if stock investors did not find either positive or negative information in the announcement.
   Mean abnormal return = 0.39 percent.
   Sample standard error of the mean of abnormal returns = 0.1336 percent.[25]

Industrial CP Issues with Superior Ratings ($n = 72$ issues). The null hypothesis was that the average abnormal stock return on day $t - 1$ was 0. The null would be true if stock investors did not find either positive or negative information in the announcement.
   Mean abnormal return = 0.79 percent.
   Sample standard error of the mean of abnormal returns = 0.197 percent.

Industrial CP Issues with Inferior Ratings ($n = 24$ issues). The null hypothesis was that the average abnormal stock return on day $t - 1$ was 0. The null would be true if stock investors did not find either positive or negative information in the announcement.
   Mean abnormal return = −0.57 percent.
   Sample standard error of the mean of abnormal returns = 0.38 percent. The researchers chose to use z-tests.

1. With respect to each of the three cases, suppose that the null hypothesis reflects the belief that investors do not, on average, perceive either positive or negative information in initial ratings. State one set of hypotheses (a null hypothesis and an alternative hypothesis) that covers all three cases.

2. Determine whether the null hypothesis formulated in Part 1 is rejected or not rejected at the 0.05 and 0.01 levels of significance for the *All CP Issues* case. Interpret the results.

3. Determine whether the null hypothesis formulated in Part 1 is rejected or not rejected at the 0.05 and 0.01 levels of significance for the *Industrial CP Issues with Superior Ratings* case. Interpret the results.

4. Determine whether the null hypothesis formulated in Part 1 is rejected or not rejected at the 0.05 and 0.01 levels of significance for the *Industrial CP Issues with Inferior Ratings* case. Interpret the results.

---

25 This standard error was calculated as a sample standard deviation over the 132 issues (a cross-sectional standard deviation) divided by the square root of 132. Other standard errors were calculated similarly.

Solution to 1:

A set of hypotheses consistent with no information in CP credit ratings relevant to stock investors is

H_0: The population mean abnormal return on day $t - 1$ equals 0.

H_a: The population mean abnormal return on day $t - 1$ does not equal 0.

Solution to 2:

From the information on rejection points for z-tests, we know that we reject the null hypothesis at the 0.05 significance level if $z > 1.96$ or if $z < -1.96$, and at the 0.01 significance level if $z > 2.575$ or if $z < -2.575$. Using the z-test, $z = (0.39\% - 0\%)/0.1336\% = 2.92$ is significant at the 0.05 and 0.01 levels. The null is rejected. The fact of CP issuance itself appears to be viewed as favorable news.

Because it is possible that significant results could be due to outliers, the researchers also reported the number of cases of positive and negative abnormal returns. The ratio of cases of positive to negative abnormal returns was 80:52, which tends to support the conclusion of positive abnormal returns from the z-test.

Solution to 3:

Using the z-test, $z = (0.79\% - 0\%)/0.197\% = 4.01$ is significant at the 0.05 and 0.01 levels. Stocks earned clearly positive abnormal returns in response to the news of a superior initial CP rating. Investors may view rating agencies as certifying through a superior rating that a company's future prospects are strong.

The ratio of cases of positive to negative abnormal returns was 48:24, which tends to support the conclusion of positive abnormal returns from the z-test.

Solution to 4:

Using the z-test, $z = (-0.57\% - 0\%)/0.38\% = -1.50$ is not significant at either the 0.01 or 0.05 levels. In the case of inferior ratings, we cannot conclude that investors found either positive or negative information in the announcements of initial CP ratings.

The ratio of cases of positive to negative abnormal returns was 11:13 and tends to support the conclusion of the z-test, which did not reject the null hypothesis.

Nearly all practical situations involve an unknown population variance. Table 2 summarizes our discussion for tests concerning the population mean when the population variance is unknown.

Table 2	Test Concerning the Population Mean (Population Variance Unknown)	
	Large Sample ($n \geq 30$)	**Small Sample ($n < 30$)**
Population normal	t-Test (z-Test alternative)	t-Test
Population non-normal	t-Test (z-Test alternative)	Not Available

3.2 Tests Concerning Differences between Means

We often want to know whether a mean value—for example, a mean return—differs between two groups. Is an observed difference due to chance or to different underlying values for the mean? We have two samples, one for each group. When it is reasonable to believe that the samples are from populations at least approximately normally distributed and that the samples are also independent of each other, the techniques of this section apply. We discuss two t-tests for a test concerning differences between the means of two populations. In one case, the population variances, although unknown, can be assumed to be equal. Then, we efficiently combine the observations from both samples to obtain a pooled estimate of the common but unknown population variance. A pooled estimate is an estimate drawn from the combination of two different samples. In the second case, we do not assume that the unknown population variances are equal, and an approximate t-test is then available. Letting μ_1 and μ_2 stand, respectively, for the population means of the first and second populations, we most often want to test whether the population means are equal or whether one is larger than the other. Thus we usually formulate the following hypotheses:

1. $H_0: \mu_1 - \mu_2 = 0$ versus $H_a: \mu_1 - \mu_2 \neq 0$ (the alternative is that $\mu_1 \neq \mu_2$)
2. $H_0: \mu_1 - \mu_2 \leq 0$ versus $H_a: \mu_1 - \mu_2 > 0$ (the alternative is that $\mu_1 > \mu_2$)
3. $H_0: \mu_1 - \mu_2 \geq 0$ versus $H_a: \mu_1 - \mu_2 < 0$ (the alternative is that $\mu_1 < \mu_2$)

We can, however, formulate other hypotheses, such as $H_0: \mu_1 - \mu_2 = 2$ versus $H_a: \mu_1 - \mu_2 \neq 2$. The procedure is the same.

The definition of the t-test follows.

- **Test Statistic for a Test of the Difference between Two Population Means (Normally Distributed Populations, Population Variances Unknown but Assumed Equal).** When we can assume that the two populations are normally distributed and that the unknown population variances are equal, a t-test based on independent random samples is given by

$$t = \frac{\left(\bar{X}_1 - \bar{X}_2\right) - \left(\mu_1 - \mu_2\right)}{\left(\dfrac{s_p^2}{n_1} + \dfrac{s_p^2}{n_2}\right)^{1/2}} \qquad (7)$$

where $s_p^2 = \dfrac{\left(n_1 - 1\right)s_1^2 + \left(n_2 - 1\right)s_2^2}{n_1 + n_2 - 2}$ is a pooled estimator of the common variance.

The number of degrees of freedom is $n_1 + n_2 - 2$.

Example 4

Mean Returns on the S&P 500: A Test of Equality across Decades

The realized mean monthly return on the S&P 500 Index in the 1980s appears to have been substantially different than the mean return in the 1970s. Was the difference statistically significant? The data, shown in Table 3, indicate that assuming equal population variances for returns in the two decades is not unreasonable.

Table 3	S&P 500 Monthly Return and Standard Deviation for Two Decades		
Decade	Number of Months (n)	Mean Monthly Return (%)	Standard Deviation
1970s	120	0.580	4.598
1980s	120	1.470	4.738

1. Formulate null and alternative hypotheses consistent with a two-sided hypothesis test.

2. Identify the test statistic for conducting a test of the hypotheses in Part 1.

3. Identify the rejection point or points for the hypothesis tested in Part 1 at the 0.10, 0.05, and 0.01 levels of significance.

4. Determine whether the null hypothesis is rejected or not rejected at the 0.10, 0.05, and 0.01 levels of significance.

Solution to 1:

Letting μ_1 stand for the population mean return for the 1970s and μ_2 stand for the population mean return for the 1980s, we formulate the following hypotheses:

$$H_0 : \mu_1 - \mu_2 = 0 \text{ versus } H_a : \mu_1 - \mu_2 \neq 0$$

Solution to 2:

Because the two samples are drawn from different decades, they are independent samples. The population variances are not known but can be assumed to be equal. Given all these considerations, the t-test given in Equation 7 has $120 + 120 - 2 = 238$ degrees of freedom.

Solution to 3:

In the tables (Appendix B), the closest degrees of freedom to 238 is 200. For a two-sided test, the rejection points are ±1.653, ±1.972, and ±2.601 for, respectively, the 0.10, 0.05, and 0.01 levels for df = 200. To summarize, at the 0.10 level, we will reject the null if $t < -1.653$ or $t > 1.653$; at the 0.05 level, we will reject the null if $t < -1.972$ or $t > 1.972$; and at the 0.01 level, we will reject the null if $t < -2.601$ or $t > 2.601$.

Solution to 4:

In calculating the test statistic, the first step is to calculate the pooled estimate of variance:

$$s_p^2 = \frac{(n_1 - 1)s_1^2 + (n_2 - 1)s_2^2}{n_1 + n_2 - 2} = \frac{(120-1)(4.598)^2 + (120-1)(4.738)^2}{120 + 120 - 2}$$

$$= \frac{5{,}187.239512}{238} = 21.795124$$

$$t = \frac{(\overline{X}_1 - \overline{X}_2) - (\mu_1 - \mu_2)}{\left(\dfrac{s_p^2}{n_1} + \dfrac{s_p^2}{n_2}\right)^{1/2}} = \frac{(0.580 - 1.470) - 0}{\left(\dfrac{21.795124}{120} + \dfrac{21.795124}{120}\right)^{1/2}}$$

$$= \frac{-0.89}{0.602704} = -1.477$$

The t value of −1.477 is not significant at the 0.10 level, so it is also not significant at the 0.05 and 0.01 levels. Therefore, we do not reject the null hypothesis at any of the three levels.

In many cases of practical interest, we cannot assume that population variances are equal. The following test statistic is often used in the investment literature in such cases:

■ **Test Statistic for a Test of the Difference between Two Population Means (Normally Distributed Populations, Unequal and Unknown Population Variances).** When we can assume that the two populations are normally distributed but do not know the population variances and cannot assume that they are equal, an approximate t-test based on independent random samples is given by

$$t = \frac{\left(\bar{X}_1 - \bar{X}_2\right) - \left(\mu_1 - \mu_2\right)}{\left(\dfrac{s_1^2}{n_1} + \dfrac{s_2^2}{n_2}\right)^{1/2}}$$

(8)

where we use tables of the t-distribution using "modified" degrees of freedom computed with the formula

$$df = \frac{\left(\dfrac{s_1^2}{n_1} + \dfrac{s_2^2}{n_2}\right)^2}{\dfrac{\left(s_1^2/n_1\right)^2}{n_1} + \dfrac{\left(s_2^2/n_2\right)^2}{n_2}}$$

(9)

A practical tip is to compute the t-statistic before computing the degrees of freedom. Whether or not the t-statistic is significant will sometimes be obvious.

Example 5

Recovery Rates on Defaulted Bonds: A Hypothesis Test

How are the required yields on risky corporate bonds determined? Two key factors are the expected probability of default and the expected amount that will be recovered in the event of default, or the recovery rate. Altman and Kishore (1996) documented for the first time the average recovery rates on defaulted bonds stratified by industry and seniority. For their study period, 1971 to 1995, Altman and Kishore discovered that defaulted bonds of public utilities and chemicals, petroleum, and plastics manufacturers experienced much higher recovery rates than did other industrial sectors. Could the differences be explained by a greater preponderance of senior debt in the higher-recovery sectors? They studied this by examining recovery rates stratified by seniority. We discuss their results for senior secured bonds. With μ_1 denoting the population mean recovery rate for the senior secured bonds of utilities and μ_2 denoting the population mean recovery rate for the senior secured bonds of other sectors (non-utilities), the hypotheses are H_0: $\mu_1 - \mu_2 = 0$ versus H_a: $\mu_1 - \mu_2 \neq 0$.

Table 4 excerpts from their findings.

Table 4	Recovery Rates by Seniority					
	Industry Group			**Ex-Utilities Sample**		
Industry Group/ Seniority	**Number of Observations**	**Average Price[a]**	**Standard Deviation**	**Number of Observations**	**Average Price[a]**	**Standard Deviation**
Public Utilities						
Senior Secured	21	$64.42	$14.03	64	$55.75	$25.17

[a]This is the average price at default and is a measure of recovery rate.
Source: Altman and Kishore (1996), Table 5.

Following the researchers, assume that the populations (recovery rates of utilities, recovery rates of non-utilities) are normally distributed and that the samples are independent. Based on the data in the table, address the following:

1. Discuss why Altman and Kishore would choose a test based on Equation 8 rather than Equation 7.
2. Calculate the test statistic to test the null hypothesis given above.

3. What is the value of the test's modified degrees of freedom?

4. Determine whether to reject the null hypothesis at the 0.10 level.

Solution to 1:

The sample standard deviation for the recovery rate on the senior secured bonds of utilities ($14.03) appears much smaller than the sample standard deviation of the comparable bonds for non-utilities ($25.17). Properly choosing not to assume equal variances, Altman and Kishore employed the approximate t-test given in Equation 8.

Solution to 2:

The test statistic is

$$t = \frac{\left(\bar{X}_1 - \bar{X}_2\right)}{\left(\dfrac{s_1^2}{n_1} + \dfrac{s_2^2}{n_2}\right)^{1/2}}$$

where

$\bar{X}_1$ = sample mean recovery rate for utilities = 64.42
$\bar{X}_2$ = sample mean recovery rate for non-utility sectors = 55.75
s_1^2 = sample variance for utilities = 14.03^2 = 196.8409
s_2^2 = sample variance for non-utilities = 25.17^2 = 633.5289
n_1 = sample size of the utility sample = 21
n_2 = sample size of the non-utility sample = 64

Thus, t = (64.42 − 55.75)/[(196.8409/21) + (633.5289/64)]$^{1/2}$ = 8.67/(9.373376 + 9.898889)$^{1/2}$ = 8.67/4.390019 = 1.975. The calculated t-statistic is thus 1.975.

Solution to 3:

$$\text{df} = \frac{\left(\dfrac{s_1^2}{n_1} + \dfrac{s_2^2}{n_2}\right)^2}{\dfrac{\left(s_1^2/n_1\right)^2}{n_1} + \dfrac{\left(s_2^2/n_2\right)^2}{n_2}} = \frac{\left(\dfrac{196.8409}{21} + \dfrac{633.5289}{64}\right)^2}{\dfrac{\left(196.8409/21\right)^2}{21} + \dfrac{\left(633.5289/64\right)^2}{64}}$$

$$= \frac{371.420208}{5.714881} = 64.99 \text{ or } 65 \text{ degrees of freedom}$$

Solution to 4:

The closest entry to df = 65 in the tables for the t-distribution is df = 60. For α = 0.10, we find $t_{\alpha/2}$ = 1.671. Thus, we reject the null if t < −1.671 or t > 1.671. Based on the computed value of 1.975, we reject the null hypothesis at the 0.10 level. Some evidence exists that recovery rates differ between utilities and other industries. Why? Altman and Kishore suggest that the differing nature of the companies' assets and industry competitive structures may explain the different recovery rates.

3.3 Tests Concerning Mean Differences

In the previous section, we presented two t-tests for discerning differences between population means. The tests were based on two samples. An assumption for those tests' validity was that the samples were independent—i.e., unrelated to each other. When we want to conduct tests on two means based on samples that we believe are dependent, the methods of this section apply.

The t-test in this section is based on data arranged in **paired observations**, and the test itself is sometimes called a **paired comparisons test**. Paired observations are observations that are dependent because they have something in common. A paired comparisons test is a statistical test for differences in dependent items. For example, we may be concerned with the dividend policy of companies before and after a change in the tax law affecting the taxation of dividends. We then have pairs of "before" and "after" observations for the same companies. We may test a hypothesis about the mean of the differences (mean differences) that we observe across companies. In other cases, the paired observations are not on the same units. For example, we may be testing whether the mean returns earned by two investment strategies were equal over a study period. The observations here are dependent in the sense that there is one observation for each strategy in each month, and both observations depend on underlying market risk factors. Because the returns to both strategies are likely to be related to some common risk factors, such as the market return, the samples are dependent. By calculating a standard error based on differences, the t-test presented below takes account of correlation between the observations.

Letting A represent "after" and B "before," suppose we have observations for the random variables X_A and X_B and that the samples are dependent. We arrange the observations in pairs. Let d_i denote the difference between two paired observations. We can use the notation $d_i = x_{Ai} - x_{Bi}$, where x_{Ai} and x_{Bi} are the ith pair of observations, $i = 1, 2, \ldots, n$ on the two variables. Let μ_d stand for the population mean difference. We can formulate the following hypotheses, where μ_{d0} is a hypothesized value for the population mean difference:

1. $H_0: \mu_d = \mu_{d0}$ versus $H_a: \mu_d \neq \mu_{d0}$
2. $H_0: \mu_d \leq \mu_{d0}$ versus $H_a: \mu_d > \mu_{d0}$
3. $H_0: \mu_d \geq \mu_{d0}$ versus $H_a: \mu_d > \mu_{d0}$

In practice, the most commonly used value for μ_{d0} is 0.

As usual, we are concerned with the case of normally distributed populations with unknown population variances, and we will formulate a t-test. To calculate the t-statistic, we first need to find the sample mean difference:

$$\bar{d} = \frac{1}{n}\sum_{i=1}^{n} d_i \tag{10}$$

where n is the number of pairs of observations. The sample variance, denoted by s_d^2, is

$$s_d^2 = \frac{\sum_{i=1}^{n}\left(d_i - \bar{d}\right)^2}{n-1} \tag{11}$$

Taking the square root of this quantity, we have the sample standard deviation, s_d, which then allows us to calculate the standard error of the mean difference as follows:[26]

$$s_{\bar{d}} = \frac{s_d}{\sqrt{n}} \tag{12}$$

■ **Test Statistic for a Test of Mean Differences (Normally Distributed Populations, Unknown Population Variances).** When we have data consisting of paired observations from samples generated by normally distributed populations with unknown variances, a t-test is based on

$$t = \frac{\bar{d} - \mu_{d0}}{s_{\bar{d}}} \tag{13}$$

with $n - 1$ degrees of freedom, where n is the number of paired observations, $\bar{d}$ is the sample mean difference (as given by Equation 10), and $s_{\bar{d}}$ is the standard error of $\bar{d}$ (as given by Equation 12).

---

26 We can also use the following equivalent expression, which makes use of the correlation between the two variables: $s_{\bar{d}} = \sqrt{s_A^2 + s_B^2 - 2r\left(X_A, X_B\right)s_A s_B}/\sqrt{n}$ where s_A^2 is the sample variance of X_A, s_B^2 is the sample variance of X_B, and $r(X_A, X_B)$ is the sample correlation between X_A and X_B.

Table 5 reports the quarterly returns from 1997 to 2002 for two managed portfolios specializing in precious metals. The two portfolios were closely similar in risk (as measured by standard deviation of return and other measures) and had nearly identical expense ratios. A major investment services company rated Portfolio B more highly than Portfolio A in early 2003. In investigating the portfolios' relative performance, suppose we want to test the hypothesis that the mean quarterly return on Portfolio A equaled the mean quarterly return on Portfolio B from 1997 to 2002. Because the two portfolios shared essentially the same set of risk factors, their returns were not independent, so a paired comparisons test is appropriate. Let μ_d stand for the population mean value of difference between the returns on the two portfolios during this period. We test $H_0: \mu_d = 0$ versus $H_a: \mu_d \neq 0$ at a 0.05 significance level.

Table 5	Quarterly Returns on Two Managed Portfolios: 1997–2002		
Quarter	Portfolio A (%)	Portfolio B (%)	Difference (Portfolio A – Portfolio B)
4Q:2002	11.40	14.64	−3.24
3Q:2002	−2.17	0.44	−2.61
2Q:2002	10.72	19.51	−8.79
1Q:2002	38.91	50.40	−11.49
4Q:2001	4.36	1.01	3.35
3Q:2001	5.13	10.18	−5.05
2Q:2001	26.36	17.77	8.59
1Q:2001	−5.53	4.76	−10.29
4Q:2000	5.27	−5.36	10.63
3Q:2000	−7.82	−1.54	−6.28
2Q:2000	2.34	0.19	2.15
1Q:2000	−14.38	−12.07	−2.31
4Q:1999	−9.80	−9.98	0.18
3Q:1999	19.03	26.18	−7.15
2Q:1999	4.11	−2.39	6.50
1Q:1999	−4.12	−2.51	−1.61
4Q:1998	−0.53	−11.32	10.79
3Q:1998	5.06	0.46	4.60
2Q:1998	−14.01	−11.56	−2.45
1Q:1998	12.50	3.52	8.98
4Q:1997	−29.05	−22.45	−6.60
3Q:1997	3.60	0.10	3.50
2Q:1997	−7.97	−8.96	0.99
1Q:1997	−8.62	−0.66	−7.96
Mean	1.87	2.52	−0.65

Sample standard deviation of differences = 6.71

The sample mean difference, $\bar{d}$, between Portfolio A and Portfolio B is −0.65 percent per quarter. The standard error of the sample mean difference is $s_{\bar{d}} = 6.71/\sqrt{24} = 1.369673$. The calculated test statistic is $t = (−0.65 − 0)/1.369673 = −0.475$ with $n − 1 = 24 − 1 = 23$ degrees of freedom. At the 0.05 significance level, we reject the null if $t > 2.069$ or if $t < -2.069$. Because -0.475 is not less than -2.069, we fail to reject the null. At the 0.10 significance level, we reject the null if $t > 1.714$ or if $t < -1.714$. Thus the difference in mean quarterly returns is not significant at any conventional significance level.

The following example illustrates the application of this test to evaluate two competing investment strategies.

Example 6

The Dow-10 Investment Strategy

McQueen, Shields, and Thorley (1997) examined the popular investment strategy of investing in the 10 stocks with the highest yields (rebalancing annually) in the Dow Jones Industrial Average, compared with a buy-and-hold strategy in all 30 stocks of the DJIA. Their study period was the 50 years from 1946 to 1995.

Table 6	Annual Return Summary for Dow-10 and Dow-30 Portfolios: 1946 to 1995 ($n = 50$)	
Strategy	**Mean Return**	**Standard Deviation**
Dow-10	16.77%	19.10%
Dow-30	13.71	16.64
Difference	3.06	6.62[a]

[a]Sample standard deviation of differences.
Source: McQueen, Shields, and Thorley (1997, Table 1).

From Table 6 we have $\bar{d} = 3.06\%$ and $s_d = 6.62\%$.

1. Formulate null and alternative hypotheses consistent with a two-sided test that the mean difference between the Dow-10 and Dow-30 strategies equals 0.
2. Identify the test statistic for conducting a test of the hypotheses in Part 1.
3. Identify the rejection point or points for the hypothesis tested in Part 1 at the 0.01 level of significance.
4. Determine whether the null hypothesis is rejected or not rejected at the 0.01 level of significance. (Use the tables in the back of this volume.)
5. Discuss the choice of a paired comparisons test.

Solution to 1:

With μ_d as the underlying mean difference between the Dow-10 and Dow-30 strategies, we have $H_0: \mu_d = 0$ versus $H_a: \mu_d \neq 0$.

Solution to 2:

Because the population variance is unknown, the test statistic is a t-test with $50 - 1 = 49$ degrees of freedom.

Solution to 3:

In the table for the t-distribution, we look across the row for 49 degrees of freedom to the 0.005 column, to find 2.68. We will reject the null if we find that $t > 2.68$ or $t < -2.68$.

Solution to 4:

$$t_{49} = \frac{3.06}{6.62/\sqrt{50}} = \frac{3.06}{0.936209} = 3.2685 \text{ or } 3.27$$

Because 3.27 > 2.68, we reject the null hypothesis. The authors concluded that the difference in mean returns was clearly statistically significant. However, after adjusting for the Dow-10's higher risk, extra transaction costs, and unfavorable tax treatment, they found that the Dow-10 portfolio did not beat the Dow-30 economically.

Solution to 5:

The Dow-30 includes the Dow-10. As a result, they are not independent samples; in general, the correlation of returns on the Dow-10 and Dow-30 should be positive. Because the samples are dependent, a paired comparisons test was appropriate.

4   HYPOTHESIS TESTS CONCERNING VARIANCE

Because variance and standard deviation are widely used quantitative measures of risk in investments, analysts should be familiar with hypothesis tests concerning variance. The tests discussed in this section make regular appearances in investment literature. We examine two types: tests concerning the value of a single population variance and tests concerning the differences between two population variances.

4.1 Tests Concerning a Single Variance

In this section, we discuss testing hypotheses about the value of the variance, σ^2, of a single population. We use σ_0^2 to denote the hypothesized value of σ^2. We can formulate hypotheses as follows:

1. $H_0: \sigma^2 = \sigma_0^2$ versus $H_a: \sigma^2 \neq \sigma_0^2$ (a "not equal to" alternative hypothesis)
2. $H_0: \sigma^2 \leq \sigma_0^2$ versus $H_a: \sigma^2 > \sigma_0^2$ (a "greater than" alternative hypothesis)
3. $H_0: \sigma^2 \geq \sigma_0^2$ versus $H_a: \sigma^2 < \sigma_0^2$ (a "less than" alternative hypothesis)

In tests concerning the variance of a single normally distributed population, we make use of a chi-square test statistic, denoted χ^2. The chi-square distribution, unlike the normal and t-distributions, is asymmetrical. Like the t-distribution, the chi-square distribution is a family of distributions. A different distribution exists for each possible value of degrees of freedom, $n - 1$ (n is sample size). Unlike the t-distribution, the chi-square distribution is bounded below by 0; χ^2 does not take on negative values.

■ **Test Statistic for Tests Concerning the Value of a Population Variance (Normal Population).** If we have n independent observations from a normally distributed population, the appropriate test statistic is

$$\chi^2 = \frac{(n-1)s^2}{\sigma_0^2} \tag{14}$$

with $n - 1$ degrees of freedom. In the numerator of the expression is the sample variance, calculated as

$$s^2 = \frac{\sum\limits_{i=1}^{n}\left(X_i - \bar{X}\right)^2}{n-1} \qquad (15)$$

In contrast to the t-test, for example, the chi-square test is sensitive to violations of its assumptions. If the sample is not actually random or if it does not come from a normally distributed population, inferences based on a chi-square test are likely to be faulty.

If we choose a level of significance, α, the rejection points for the three kinds of hypotheses are as follows:

- **Rejection Points for Hypothesis Tests on the Population Variance.**

  1. "Not equal to" H_a: Reject the null hypothesis if the test statistic is greater than the upper $\alpha/2$ point (denoted $\chi^2_\alpha/2$) or less than the lower $\alpha/2$ point (denoted $\chi^2_{1-\alpha/2}$) of the chi-square distribution with df = $n - 1$.[27]

  2. "Greater than" H_a: Reject the null hypothesis if the test statistic is greater than the upper α point of the chi-square distribution with df = $n - 1$.

  3. "Less than" H_a: Reject the null hypothesis if the test statistic is less than the lower α point of the chi-square distribution with df = $n - 1$.

Example 7

Risk and Return Characteristics of an Equity Mutual Fund (2)

You continue with your analysis of Sendar Equity Fund, a midcap growth fund that has been in existence for only 24 months. Recall that during this period, Sendar Equity achieved a sample standard deviation of monthly returns of 3.60 percent. You now want to test a claim that the particular investment disciplines followed by Sendar result in a standard deviation of monthly returns of less than 4 percent.

1. Formulate null and alternative hypotheses consistent with the verbal description of the research goal.

2. Identify the test statistic for conducting a test of the hypotheses in Part 1.

3. Identify the rejection point or points for the hypothesis tested in Part 1 at the 0.05 level of significance.

4. Determine whether the null hypothesis is rejected or not rejected at the 0.05 level of significance. (Use the tables in the back of this volume.)

Solution to 1:

We have a "less than" alternative hypothesis, where σ is the underlying standard deviation of return on Sendar Equity Fund. Being careful to square standard deviation to obtain a test in terms of variance, the hypotheses are H_0: $\sigma^2 \geq 16.0$ versus H_a: $\sigma^2 < 16.0$.

Solution to 2:

The test statistic is chi-square with $24 - 1 = 23$ degrees of freedom.

---

27 Just as with other hypothesis tests, the chi-square test can be given a confidence interval interpretation. Unlike confidence intervals based on z- or t-statistics, however, chi-square confidence intervals for variance are asymmetric. A two-sided confidence interval for population variance, based on a sample of size n, has a lower limit $.\text{L} = (n-1)s^2/\chi^2_{\alpha/2}$ and an upper limit $\text{U} = (n-1)s^2/\chi^2_{1-\alpha/2}$. Under the null hypothesis, the hypothesized value of the population variance should fall within these two limits.

Solution to 3:

The lower 0.05 rejection point is found on the line for df = 23, under the 0.95 column (95 percent probability in the right tail, to give 0.95 probability of getting a test statistic this large or larger). The rejection point is 13.091. We will reject the null if we find that chi-square is less than 13.091.

Solution to 4:

$$\chi^2 = \frac{(n-1)s^2}{\sigma_0^2} = \frac{23 \times 3.60^2}{4^2} = \frac{298.08}{16} = 18.63$$

Because 18.63 (the calculated value of the test statistic) is not less than 13.091, we do not reject the null hypothesis. We cannot conclude that Sendar's investment disciplines result in a standard deviation of monthly returns of less than 4 percent.

4.2 Tests Concerning the Equality (Inequality) of Two Variances

Suppose we have a hypothesis about the relative values of the variances of two normally distributed populations with means μ_1 and μ_2 and variances σ_1^2 and σ_2^2. We can formulate all hypotheses as one of the choices below:

1. $H_0: \sigma_1^2 = \sigma_2^2$ versus $H_a: \sigma_1^2 \neq \sigma_2^2$
2. $H_0: \sigma_1^2 \leq \sigma_2^2$ versus $H_a: \sigma_1^2 > \sigma_2^2$
3. $H_0: \sigma_1^2 \geq \sigma_2^2$ versus $H_a: \sigma_1^2 < \sigma_2^2$

Note that at the point of equality, the null hypothesis $\sigma_1^2 = \sigma_2^2$ implies that the ratio of population variances equals 1: $\sigma_1^2/\sigma_2^2 = 1$. Given independent random samples from these populations, tests related to these hypotheses are based on an F-test, which is the ratio of sample variances. Suppose we use n_1 observations in calculating the sample variance s_1^2 and n_2 observations in calculating the sample variance s_2^2. Tests concerning the difference between the variances of two populations make use of the F-distribution. Like the chi-square distribution, the F-distribution is a family of asymmetrical distributions bounded from below by 0. Each F-distribution is defined by two values of degrees of freedom, called the numerator and denominator degrees of freedom.[28] The F-test, like the chisquare test, is not robust to violations of its assumptions.

- **Test Statistic for Tests Concerning Differences between the Variances of Two Populations (Normally Distributed Populations).** Suppose we have two samples, the first with n_1 observations and sample variance s_1^2, the second with n_2 observations and sample variance s_2^2. The samples are random, independent of each other, and generated by normally distributed populations. A test concerning differences between the variances of the two populations is based on the ratio of sample variances

$$F = \frac{s_1^2}{s_2^2}$$

(16)

---

[28] The relationship between the chi-square and F-distributions is as follows: If χ_1^2 is one chi-square random variable with m degrees of freedom and χ_2^2 is another chi-square random variable with n degrees of freedom, then $F = (\chi_1^2/m)/(\chi_2^2/n)$ follows an F-distribution with m numerator and n denominator degrees of freedom.

with $df_1 = n_1 - 1$ numerator degrees of freedom and $df_2 = n_2 - 1$ denominator degrees of freedom. Note that df_1 and df_2 are the divisors used in calculating s_1^2 and s_2^2, respectively.

A convention, or usual practice, is to use the larger of the two ratios s_1^2/s_2^2 or s_2^2/s_1^2 as the actual test statistic. When we follow this convention, the value of the test statistic is always greater than or equal to 1; tables of critical values of F then need include only values greater than or equal to 1. Under this convention, the rejection point for any formulation of hypotheses is a single value in the righthand side of the relevant F-distribution. Note that the labeling of populations as "1" or "2" is arbitrary in any case.

- **Rejection Points for Hypothesis Tests on the Relative Values of Two Population Variances.** Follow the convention of using the larger of the two ratios s_1^2/s_2^2 and s_2^2/s_1^2 and consider two cases:

  1. A "not equal to" alternative hypothesis: Reject the null hypothesis at the α significance level if the test statistic is greater than the upper $\alpha/2$ point of the F-distribution with the specified numerator and denominator degrees of freedom.

  2. A "greater than" or "less than" alternative hypothesis: Reject the null hypothesis at the α significance level if the test statistic is greater than the upper α point of the F-distribution with the specified number of numerator and denominator degrees of freedom.

Thus, if we conduct a two-sided test at the $\alpha = 0.01$ level of significance, we need to find the rejection point in F-tables at the $\alpha/2 = 0.01/2 = 0.005$ significance level for a one-sided test (Case 1). But a one-sided test at 0.01 uses rejection points in F-tables for $\alpha = 0.01$ (Case 2). As an example, suppose we are conducting a two-sided test at the 0.05 significance level. We calculate a value of F of 2.77 with 12 numerator and 19 denominator degrees of freedom. Using the F-tables for 0.05/2 = 0.025 in the back of the volume, we find that the rejection point is 2.72. Because the value 2.77 is greater than 2.72, we reject the null hypothesis at the 0.05 significance level.

If the convention stated above is not followed and we are given a calculated value of F less than 1, can we still use F-tables? The answer is yes; using a reciprocal property of F-statistics, we can calculate the needed value. The easiest way to present this property is to show a calculation. Suppose our chosen level of significance is 0.05 for a two-tailed test and we have a value of F of 0.11, with 7 numerator degrees of freedom and 9 denominator degrees of freedom. We take the reciprocal, 1/0.11 = 9.09. Then we look up this value in the F-tables for 0.025 (because it is a two-tailed test) with degrees of freedom reversed: F for 9 numerator and 7 denominator degrees of freedom. In other words, $F_{9,7} = 1/F_{7,9}$ and 9.09 exceeds the critical value of 4.82, so $F_{7,9} = 0.11$ is significant at the 0.05 level.

Example 8

Volatility and the Crash of 1987

You are investigating whether the population variance of returns on the S&P 500 changed subsequent to the October 1987 market crash. You gather the data in Table 7 for 120 months of returns before October 1987 and 120 months of returns after October 1987. You have specified a 0.01 level of significance.

Table 7	500 Returns and Variance before and after October 1987		
	n	Mean Monthly Return (%)	Variance of Returns
Before October 1987	120	1.498	18.776
After October 1987	120	1.392	13.097

1. Formulate null and alternative hypotheses consistent with the verbal description of the research goal.

2. Identify the test statistic for conducting a test of the hypotheses in Part 1.

3. Determine whether or not to reject the null hypothesis at the 0.01 level of significance. (Use the F-tables in the back of this volume.)

Solution to 1:

We have a "not equal to" alternative hypothesis:

$$H_0: \sigma^2_{\text{Before}} = \sigma^2_{\text{After}} \text{ versus } H_a: \sigma^2_{\text{Before}} \neq \sigma^2_{\text{After}}$$

Solution to 2:

To test a null hypothesis of the equality of two variances, we use $F = s_1^2 / s_2^2$ with $120 - 1 = 119$ numerator and denominator degrees of freedom.

Solution to 3:

The "before" sample variance is larger, so following a convention for calculating F-statistics, the "before" sample variance goes in the numerator: $F = 18.776/13.097 = 1.434$. Because this is a two-tailed test, we use F-tables for the 0.005 level (= 0.01/2) to give a 0.01 significance level. In the tables in the back of the volume, the closest value to 119 degrees of freedom is 120 degrees of freedom. At the 0.01 level, the rejection point is 1.61. Because 1.434 is less than the critical value 1.61, we cannot reject the null hypothesis that the population variance of returns is the same in the pre- and postcrash periods.

Example 9

The Volatility of Derivatives Expiration Days

In the 1980s concern arose in the United States about the triple occurrence of stock option, index option, and futures expirations on the same day during four months of the year. Such days were known as "triple witching days." Table 8 presents evidence on the daily standard deviation of return for normal days and options/futures expiration days during the period 1 July 1983 to 24 October 1986. The tabled data refer to options and futures on the S&P 100, a subset of the S&P 500 that includes 100 of the most liquid S&P 500 stocks on which there are traded options.

| Table 8 | Standard Deviation of Return: 1 July 1983 to 24 October 1986 |

Type of Day	n	Standard Deviation (%)
Normal trading	115	0.786
Options/futures expiration	12	1.178

Source: Based on Edwards (1988), Table I.

1. Formulate null and alternative hypotheses consistent with the belief that triple witching days displayed above-normal volatility.
2. Identify the test statistic for conducting a test of the hypotheses in Part 1.
3. Determine whether or not to reject the null hypothesis at the 0.05 level of significance. (Use the F-tables in the back of this volume.)

Solution to 1:

We have a "greater than" alternative hypothesis:

$$H_0: \sigma^2_{\text{Expirations}} \leq \sigma^2_{\text{Normal}} \text{ versus } H_a: \sigma^2_{\text{Expirations}} > \sigma^2_{\text{Normal}}$$

Solution to 2:

Let σ^2_1 represent the variance of triple witching days, and σ^2_2 represent the variance of normal days, following the convention for the selection of the numerator and the denominator stated earlier. To test the null hypothesis, we use $F = s^2_1/s^2_2$ with $12 - 1 = 11$ numerator and $115 - 1 = 114$ denominator degrees of freedom.

Solution to 3:

$F = (1.178)^2/(0.786)^2 = 1.388/0.618 = 2.25$. Because this is a one-tailed test at the 0.05 significance level, we use F-tables for the 0.05 level directly. In the tables in the back of the volume, the closest value to 114 degrees of freedom is 120 degrees of freedom. At the 0.05 level, the rejection point is 1.87. Because 2.25 is greater than 1.87, we reject the null hypothesis. It appears that triple witching days had above-normal volatility.

OTHER ISSUES: NONPARAMETRIC INFERENCE

5

The hypothesis-testing procedures we have discussed to this point have two characteristics in common. First, they are concerned with parameters, and second, their validity depends on a definite set of assumptions. Mean and variance, for example, are two parameters, or defining quantities, of a normal distribution. The tests also make specific assumptions—in particular, assumptions about the distribution of the population producing the sample. Any test or procedure with either of the above two characteristics is a **parametric test** or procedure. In some cases, however, we are concerned about quantities other than parameters of distributions. In other cases, we may believe that the assumptions of parametric tests do not hold for the particular data we have. In such cases, a nonparametric test or procedure can be useful. A **nonparametric test** is a test that is not concerned with a parameter, or a test that makes minimal assumptions about the population from which the sample comes.[29]

We primarily use nonparametric procedures in three situations: when the data we use do not meet distributional assumptions, when the data are given in ranks, or when the hypothesis we are addressing does not concern a parameter.

The first situation occurs when the data available for analysis suggest that the distributional assumptions of the parametric test are not satisfied. For example, we may want to test a hypothesis concerning the mean of a population but believe that neither a t-test nor a z-test is appropriate because the sample is small and may come from a markedly non-normally distributed population. In that case, we may use a nonparametric test. The nonparametric test will frequently involve the conversion of observations (or a function of observations) into ranks according to magnitude, and sometimes it will involve working with only "greater than" or "less than" relationships (using the signs + and – to denote those relationships). Characteristically, one must refer to specialized statistical tables to determine the rejection points of the test statistic, at least for small samples.[30] Such tests, then, typically interpret the null hypothesis as a thesis about ranks or signs. In Table 9, we give examples of nonparametric alternatives to the parametric tests we have discussed in this reading.[31] The reader should consult a comprehensive business statistics textbook for an introduction to such tests, and a specialist textbook for details.[32]

Table 9	Nonparametric Alternatives to Parametric Tests	
	Parametric	**Nonparametric**
Tests concerning a single mean	t-test	Wilcoxon signed-rank test
	z-test	
Tests concerning differences between means	t-test Approximate t-test	Mann–Whitney U test
Tests concerning mean differences (paired comparisons tests)	t-test	Wilcoxon signed-rank test Sign test

We pointed out that when we use nonparametric tests, we often convert the original data into ranks. In some cases, the original data are already ranked. In those cases, we also use nonparametric tests because parametric tests generally require a stronger measurement scale than ranks. For example, if our data were the rankings of investment managers, hypotheses concerning those rankings would be tested using nonparametric procedures. Ranked data also appear in many other finance contexts. For example, Heaney, Koga, Oliver, and Tran (1999) studied the relationship between the size of Japanese companies (as measured by revenue) and their use of derivatives.

---

29 Some writers make a distinction between "nonparametric" and "distribution-free" tests. They refer to procedures that do not concern the parameters of a distribution as nonparametric and to procedures that make minimal assumptions about the underlying distribution as distribution free. We follow a commonly accepted, inclusive usage of the term nonparametric.

30 For large samples, there is often a transformation of the test statistic that permits the use of tables for the standard normal or t-distribution.

31 In some cases, there are several nonparametric alternatives to a parametric test.

32 See, for example, Hettmansperger and McKean (1998) or Siegel (1956).

The companies studied used derivatives to hedge one or more of five types of risk exposure: interest rate risk, foreign exchange risk, commodity price risk, marketable security price risk, and credit risk. The researchers gave a "perceived scope of risk exposure" score to each company that was equal to the number of types of risk exposure that the company reported hedging. Although revenue is measured on a strong scale (a ratio scale), scope of risk exposure is measured on only an ordinal scale.[33] The researchers thus employed nonparametric statistics to explore the relationship between derivatives usage and size.

A third situation in which we use nonparametric procedures occurs when our question does not concern a parameter. For example, if the question concerns whether a sample is random or not, we use the appropriate nonparametric test (a so-called runs test). Another type of question nonparametrics can address is whether a sample came from a population following a particular probability distribution (using the Kolmogorov–Smirnov test, for example).

We end this reading by describing in some detail a nonparametric statistic that has often been used in investment research, the Spearman rank correlation.

5.1 Tests Concerning Correlation: The Spearman Rank Correlation Coefficient

In many contexts in investments, we want to assess the strength of the linear relationship between two variables—the correlation between them. In a majority of cases, we use the correlation coefficient described in the readings on probability concepts and correlation and regression. However, the t-test of the hypothesis that two variables are uncorrelated, based on the correlation coefficient, relies on fairly stringent assumptions.[34] When we believe that the population under consideration meaningfully departs from those assumptions, we can employ a test based on the **Spearman rank correlation coefficient**, r_s. The Spearman rank correlation coefficient is essentially equivalent to the usual correlation coefficient calculated on the *ranks* of the two variables (say X and Y) within their respective samples. Thus it is a number between -1 and $+1$, where -1 ($+1$) denotes a perfect inverse (positive) straight-line relationship between the variables and 0 represents the absence of any straight-line relationship (no correlation). The calculation of r_s requires the following steps:

1. Rank the observations on X from largest to smallest. Assign the number 1 to the observation with the largest value, the number 2 to the observation with second-largest value, and so on. In case of ties, we assign to each tied observation the average of the ranks that they jointly occupy. For example, if the third- and fourth-largest values are tied, we assign both observations the rank of 3.5 (the average of 3 and 4). Perform the same procedure for the observations on Y.

2. Calculate the difference, d_i between the ranks of each pair of observations on X and Y.

3. Then, with n the sample size, the Spearman rank correlation is given by[35]

$$r_s = 1 - \frac{6\sum_{i=1}^{n} d_i^2}{n(n^2 - 1)}$$

(17)

---

33 We discussed scales of measurement in the reading on statistical concepts and market returns.

34 The t-test is described in the reading on correlation and regression. The assumption of the test is that each observation (x, y) on the two variables (X, Y) is a random observation from a bivariate normal distribution. Informally, in a bivariate or two-variable normal distribution, each individual variable is normally distributed and their joint relationship is completely described by the correlation, ρ, between them. For more details, see, for example, Daniel and Terrell (1986).

35 Calculating the usual correlation coefficient on the ranks would yield approximately the same result as Equation 17.

Suppose an investor wants to invest in a U.S. large-cap growth mutual fund. He has narrowed the field to 10 funds. In examining the funds, a question arises as to whether the funds' reported three-year Sharpe ratios are related to their most recent reported expense ratios. Because the assumptions of the t-test on the correlation coefficient may not be met, it is appropriate to conduct a test on the rank correlation coefficient.[36]

Table 10 presents the calculation of r_s.[37] The first two rows contain the original data. The row of X ranks converts the Sharpe ratios to ranks; the row of Y ranks converts the expense ratios to ranks. We want to test H_0: $\rho = 0$ versus H_a: $\rho \neq 0$, where ρ is defined in this context as the population correlation of X and Y after ranking. For small samples, the rejection points for the test based on r_s must be looked up in Table 11. For large samples (say $n > 30$), we can conduct a t-test using

$$t = \frac{(n-2)^{1/2}\,r_s}{\left(1 - r_s^2\right)^{1/2}} \qquad\qquad (18)$$

based on $n - 2$ degrees of freedom.

Table 10	The Spearman Rank Correlation: An Example

	\multicolumn{10}{c}{**Mutual Fund**}

	1	**2**	**3**	**4**	**5**	**6**	**7**	**8**	**9**	**10**
Sharpe Ratio (X)	−1.08	−0.96	−1.13	−1.16	−0.91	−1.08	−1.18	−1.00	−1.06	−1.00
Expense Ratio (Y)	1.34	0.92	1.02	1.45	1.35	0.50	1.00	1.50	1.45	1.50
X Rank	6.5	2	8	9	1	6.5	10	3.5	5	3.5
Y Rank	6	9	7	3.5	5	10	8	1.5	3.5	1.5
d_i	0.5	−7	1	5.5	−4	−3.5	2	2	1.5	2
d_i^2	0.25	49	1	30.25	16	12.25	4	4	2.25	4

$$r_s = 1 - \frac{6\sum d_i^2}{n\left(n^2 - 1\right)} = 1 - \frac{6(123)}{10(100 - 1)} = 0.2545$$

In the example at hand, a two-tailed test with a 0.05 significance level, Table 11 gives the upper-tail rejection point for $n = 10$ as 0.6364 (we use the 0.025 column for a two-tailed test at a 0.05 significance level). Accordingly, we reject the null hypothesis if r_s is less than −0.6364 or greater than 0.6364. With r_s equal to 0.2545, we do not reject the null hypothesis.

---

36 The expense ratio (the ratio of a fund's operating expenses to average net assets) is bounded both from below (by zero) and from above. The Sharpe ratio is also observed within a limited range, in practice. Thus neither variable can be normally distributed, and hence jointly they cannot follow a bivariate normal distribution. In short, the assumptions of a t-test are not met.

37 The data for the table are based on statistics reported in Standard & Poor's Mutual Fund Reports for actual large-cap growth funds for the three-year period ending in the first quarter of 2003. The negative Sharpe ratios reflect in part declining U.S. equity markets during this period.

Table 11	Spearman Rank Correlation Distribution Approximate Upper-Tail Rejection Points		
Sample Size: n	$\alpha = 0.05$	$\alpha = 0.025$	$\alpha = 0.01$
5	0.8000	0.9000	0.9000
6	0.7714	0.8286	0.8857
7	0.6786	0.7450	0.8571
8	0.6190	0.7143	0.8095
9	0.5833	0.6833	0.7667
10	0.5515	0.6364	0.7333
11	0.5273	0.6091	0.7000
12	0.4965	0.5804	0.6713
13	0.4780	0.5549	0.6429
14	0.4593	0.5341	0.6220
15	0.4429	0.5179	0.6000
16	0.4265	0.5000	0.5824
17	0.4118	0.4853	0.5637
18	0.3994	0.4716	0.5480
19	0.3895	0.4579	0.5333
20	0.3789	0.4451	0.5203
21	0.3688	0.4351	0.5078
22	0.3597	0.4241	0.4963
23	0.3518	0.4150	0.4852
24	0.3435	0.4061	0.4748
25	0.3362	0.3977	0.4654
26	0.3299	0.3894	0.4564
27	0.3236	0.3822	0.4481
28	0.3175	0.3749	0.4401
29	0.3113	0.3685	0.4320
30	0.3059	0.3620	0.4251

Note: The corresponding lower tail critical value is obtained by changing the sign of the upper-tail critical value.

In the mutual fund example, we converted observations on two variables into ranks. If one or both of the original variables were in the form of ranks, we would need to use r_S to investigate correlation.

5.2 Nonparametric Inference: Summary

Nonparametric statistical procedures extend the reach of inference because they make few assumptions, can be used on ranked data, and may address questions unrelated to parameters. Quite frequently, nonparametric tests are reported alongside parametric tests. The reader can then assess how sensitive the statistical conclusion is to the assumptions underlying the parametric test. However, if the assumptions of the parametric test are met, the parametric test (where available) is generally preferred to the nonparametric test because the parametric test usually permits us to draw sharper conclusions.[38] For complete coverage of all the nonparametric procedures that may be encountered in the finance and investment literature, it is best to consult a specialist textbook.[39]

---

38 To use a concept introduced in an earlier section, the parametric test is often more powerful.
39 See, for example, Hettmansperger and McKean (1998) or Siegel (1956).

SUMMARY

In this reading, we have presented the concepts and methods of statistical inference and hypothesis testing.

- A hypothesis is a statement about one or more populations.

- The steps in testing a hypothesis are as follows:
  1. Stating the hypotheses.
  2. Identifying the appropriate test statistic and its probability distribution.
  3. Specifying the significance level.
  4. Stating the decision rule.
  5. Collecting the data and calculating the test statistic.
  6. Making the statistical decision.
  7. Making the economic or investment decision.

- We state two hypotheses: The null hypothesis is the hypothesis to be tested; the alternative hypothesis is the hypothesis accepted when the null hypothesis is rejected.

- There are three ways to formulate hypotheses:
  1. $H_0: \theta = \theta_0$ versus $H_a: \theta \neq \theta_0$
  2. $H_0: \theta \leq \theta_0$ versus $H_a: \theta > \theta_0$
  3. $H_0: \theta \geq \theta_0$ versus $H_a: \theta < \theta_0$

  where θ_0 is a hypothesized value of the population parameter and θ is the true value of the population parameter. In the above, Formulation 1 is a two-sided test and Formulations 2 and 3 are one-sided tests.

- When we have a "suspected" or "hoped for" condition for which we want to find supportive evidence, we frequently set up that condition as the alternative hypothesis and use a one-sided test. To emphasize a neutral attitude, however, the researcher may select a "not equal to" alternative hypothesis and conduct a two-sided test.

- A test statistic is a quantity, calculated on the basis of a sample, whose value is the basis for deciding whether to reject or not reject the null hypothesis. To decide whether to reject, or not to reject, the null hypothesis, we compare the computed value of the test statistic to a critical value (rejection point) for the same test statistic.

- In reaching a statistical decision, we can make two possible errors: We may reject a true null hypothesis (a Type I error), or we may fail to reject a false null hypothesis (a Type II error).

- The level of significance of a test is the probability of a Type I error that we accept in conducting a hypothesis test. The probability of a Type I error is denoted by the Greek letter alpha, α. The standard approach to hypothesis testing involves specifying a level of significance (probability of Type I error) only.

- The power of a test is the probability of correctly rejecting the null (rejecting the null when it is false).

- A decision rule consists of determining the rejection points (critical values) with which to compare the test statistic to decide whether to reject or not to reject the null hypothesis. When we reject the null hypothesis, the result is said to be statistically significant.

- The $(1 - \alpha)$ confidence interval represents the range of values of the test statistic for which the null hypothesis will not be rejected at an α significance level.

- The statistical decision consists of rejecting or not rejecting the null hypothesis. The economic decision takes into consideration all economic issues pertinent to the decision.

- The p-value is the smallest level of significance at which the null hypothesis can be rejected. The smaller the p-value, the stronger the evidence against the null hypothesis and in favor of the alternative hypothesis. The p-value approach to hypothesis testing does not involve setting a significance level; rather it involves computing a p-value for the test statistic and allowing the consumer of the research to interpret its significance.

- For hypothesis tests concerning the population mean of a normally distributed population with unknown (known) variance, the theoretically correct test statistic is the t-statistic (z-statistic). In the unknown variance case, given large samples (generally, samples of 30 or more observations), the z-statistic may be used in place of the t-statistic because of the force of the central limit theorem.

- The t-distribution is a symmetrical distribution defined by a single parameter: degrees of freedom. Compared to the standard normal distribution, the t-distribution has fatter tails.

- When we want to test whether the observed difference between two means is statistically significant, we must first decide whether the samples are independent or dependent (related). If the samples are independent, we conduct tests concerning differences between means. If the samples are dependent, we conduct tests of mean differences (paired comparisons tests).

- When we conduct a test of the difference between two population means from normally distributed populations with unknown variances, if we can assume the variances are equal, we use a t-test based on pooling the observations of the two samples to estimate the common (but unknown) variance. This test is based on an assumption of independent samples.

- When we conduct a test of the difference between two population means from normally distributed populations with unknown variances, if we cannot assume that the variances are equal, we use an approximate t-test using modified degrees of freedom given by a formula. This test is based on an assumption of independent samples.

- In tests concerning two means based on two samples that are not independent, we often can arrange the data in paired observations and conduct a test of mean differences (a paired comparisons test). When the samples are from normally distributed populations with unknown variances, the appropriate test statistic is a t-statistic. The denominator of the t-statistic, the standard error of the mean differences, takes account of correlation between the samples.

- In tests concerning the variance of a single, normally distributed population, the test statistic is chi-square (χ^2) with $n - 1$ degrees of freedom, where n is sample size.

- For tests concerning differences between the variances of two normally distributed populations based on two random, independent samples, the appropriate test statistic is based on an F-test (the ratio of the sample variances).

- The F-statistic is defined by the numerator and denominator degrees of freedom. The numerator degrees of freedom (number of observations in the sample minus 1) is the divisor used in calculating the sample variance in the numerator. The denominator degrees of freedom (number of observations in the sample minus 1) is the divisor used in calculating the sample variance in the denominator. In forming an *F*-test, a convention is to use the larger of the two ratios, s_1^2/s_2^2 or s_2^2/s_1^2, as the actual test statistic.

■ A parametric test is a hypothesis test concerning a parameter or a hypothesis test based on specific distributional assumptions. In contrast, a nonparametric test either is not concerned with a parameter or makes minimal assumptions about the population from which the sample comes.

■ A nonparametric test is primarily used in three situations: when data do not meet distributional assumptions, when data are given in ranks, or when the hypothesis we are addressing does not concern a parameter.

■ The Spearman rank correlation coefficient is calculated on the ranks of two variables within their respective samples.

PRACTICE PROBLEMS FOR READING 11

1. Define the following terms:

    A. Null hypothesis.

    B. Alternative hypothesis.

    C. Test statistic.

    D. Type I error.

    E. Type II error.

    F. Power of a test.

    G. Rejection point (critical value).

2. Suppose that, on the basis of a sample, we want to test the hypothesis that the mean debt-to-total-assets ratio of companies that become takeover targets is the same as the mean debt-to-total-assets ratio of companies in the same industry that do not become takeover targets. Explain under what conditions we would commit a Type I error and under what conditions we would commit a Type II error.

3. Suppose we are testing a null hypothesis, H_0, versus an alternative hypothesis, H_a, and the p-value for the test statistic is 0.031. At which of the following levels of significance—$\alpha = 0.10$, $\alpha = 0.05$, and/or $\alpha = 0.01$—would we reject the null hypothesis?

4. Identify the appropriate test statistic or statistics for conducting the following hypothesis tests. (Clearly identify the test statistic and, if applicable, the number of degrees of freedom. For example, "We conduct the test using an x-statistic with y degrees of freedom.")

    A. $H_0: \mu = 0$ versus $H_a: \mu \neq 0$, where μ is the mean of a normally distributed population with unknown variance. The test is based on a sample of 15 observations.

    B. $H_0: \mu = 0$ versus $H_a: \mu \neq 0$, where μ is the mean of a normally distributed population with unknown variance. The test is based on a sample of 40 observations.

    C. $H_0: \mu \leq 0$ versus $H_a: \mu > 0$, where μ is the mean of a normally distributed population with known variance σ^2. The sample size is 45.

    D. $H_0: \sigma^2 = 200$ versus $H_a: \sigma^2 \neq 200$, where σ^2 is the variance of a normally distributed population. The sample size is 50.

    E. $H_0: \sigma_1^2 = \sigma_2^2$ versus $H_a: \sigma_1^2 \neq \sigma_2^2$, where σ_1^2 is the variance of one normally distributed population and σ_2^2 is the variance of a second normally distributed population. The test is based on two independent random samples.

    F. H_0: (Population mean 1) − (Population mean 2) = 0 versus H_a: (Population mean 1) − (Population mean 2) $\neq$ 0, where the samples are drawn from normally distributed populations with unknown variances. The observations in the two samples are correlated.

    G. H_0: (Population mean 1) − (Population mean 2) = 0 versus H_a: (Population mean 1) − (Population mean 2) $\neq$ 0, where the samples are drawn from normally distributed populations with unknown but assumed equal variances. The observations in the two samples (of size 25 and 30, respectively) are independent.

Practice Problems and Solutions: 1-15 taken from *Quantitative Methods for Investment Analysis,* Second Edition, by Richard A. DeFusco, CFA, Dennis W. McLeavey, CFA, Jerald E. Pinto, CFA, and David E. Runkle, CFA. Copyright © 2004 by CFA Institute. All other problems and solutions copyright © CFA Institute.

5. For each of the following hypothesis tests concerning the population mean, μ, state the rejection point condition or conditions for the test statistic (e.g., $t >$ 1.25); n denotes sample size.

   A. $H_0: \mu = 10$ versus $H_a: \mu \neq 10$, using a t-test with $n = 26$ and $\alpha = 0.05$

   B. $H_0: \mu = 10$ versus $H_a: \mu \neq 10$, using a t-test with $n = 40$ and $\alpha = 0.01$

   C. $H_0: \mu \leq 10$ versus $H_a: \mu > 10$, using a t-test with $n = 40$ and $\alpha = 0.01$

   D. $H_0: \mu \leq 10$ versus $H_a: \mu > 10$, using a t-test with $n = 21$ and $\alpha = 0.05$

   E. $H_0: \mu \geq 10$ versus $H_a: \mu < 10$, using a t-test with $n = 19$ and $\alpha = 0.10$

   F. $H_0: \mu \geq 10$ versus $H_a: \mu < 10$, using a t-test with $n = 50$ and $\alpha = 0.05$

6. For each of the following hypothesis tests concerning the population mean, μ, state the rejection point condition or conditions for the test statistic (e.g., $z >$ 1.25); n denotes sample size.

   A. $H_0: \mu = 10$ versus $H_a: \mu \neq 10$, using a z-test with $n = 50$ and $\alpha = 0.01$

   B. $H_0: \mu = 10$ versus $H_a: \mu \neq 10$, using a z-test with $n = 50$ and $\alpha = 0.05$

   C. $H_0: \mu = 10$ versus $H_a: \mu \neq 10$, using a z-test with $n = 50$ and $\alpha = 0.10$

   D. $H_0: \mu \leq 10$ versus $H_a: \mu > 10$, using a z-test with $n = 50$ and $\alpha = 0.05$

7. Identify the theoretically correct test statistic to use for a hypothesis test concerning the mean of a single population under the following conditions:

   A. The sample comes from a normally distributed population with known variance.

   B. The sample comes from a normally distributed population with unknown variance.

   C. The sample comes from a population following a non-normal distribution with unknown variance. The sample size is large.

8. Willco is a manufacturer in a mature cyclical industry. During the most recent industry cycle, its net income averaged $30 million per year with a standard deviation of $10 million ($n = 6$ observations). Management claims that Willco's performance during the most recent cycle results from new approaches and that we can dismiss profitability expectations based on its average or normalized earnings of $24 million per year in prior cycles.

   A. With μ as the population value of mean annual net income, formulate null and alternative hypotheses consistent with testing Willco management's claim.

   B. Assuming that Willco's net income is at least approximately normally distributed, identify the appropriate test statistic.

   C. Identify the rejection point or points at the 0.05 level of significance for the hypothesis tested in Part A.

   D. Determine whether or not to reject the null hypothesis at the 0.05 significance level.

The following information relates to Questions 9–10

	Performance in Forecasting Quarterly Earnings per Share		
	Number of Forecasts	**Mean Forecast Error (Predicted – Actual)**	**Standard Deviations of Forecast Errors**
Analyst A	101	0.05	0.10
Analyst B	121	0.02	0.09

9. Investment analysts often use earnings per share (EPS) forecasts. One test of forecasting quality is the zero-mean test, which states that optimal forecasts should have a mean forecasting error of 0. (Forecasting error = Predicted value of variable – Actual value of variable.)

    You have collected data (shown in the table above) for two analysts who cover two different industries: Analyst A covers the telecom industry; Analyst B covers automotive parts and suppliers.

    A. With μ as the population mean forecasting error, formulate null and alternative hypotheses for a zero-mean test of forecasting quality.

    B. For Analyst A, using both a t-test and a z-test, determine whether to reject the null at the 0.05 and 0.01 levels of significance.

    C. For Analyst B, using both a t-test and a z-test, determine whether to reject the null at the 0.05 and 0.01 levels of significance.

10. Reviewing the EPS forecasting performance data for Analysts A and B, you want to investigate whether the larger average forecast errors of Analyst A are due to chance or to a higher underlying mean value for Analyst A. Assume that the forecast errors of both analysts are normally distributed and that the samples are independent.

    A. Formulate null and alternative hypotheses consistent with determining whether the population mean value of Analyst A's forecast errors (μ_1) are larger than Analyst B's (μ_2).

    B. Identify the test statistic for conducting a test of the null hypothesis formulated in Part A.

    C. Identify the rejection point or points for the hypothesis tested in Part A, at the 0.05 level of significance.

    D. Determine whether or not to reject the null hypothesis at the 0.05 level of significance.

11. Altman and Kishore (1996), in the course of a study on the recovery rates on defaulted bonds, investigated the recovery of utility bonds versus other bonds, stratified by seniority. The following table excerpts their findings.

Recovery Rates by Seniority

Industry Group/ Seniority	Industry Group			Ex-Utilities Sample		
	Number of Observations	Average Price[a]	Standard Deviation	Number of Observations	Average Price[a]	Standard Deviation
Public Utilities						
Senior Unsecured	32	$77.74	$18.06	189	$42.56	$24.89

[a]This is the average price at default and is a measure of recovery rate.
Source: Altman and Kishore (1996, Table 5).

Assume that the populations (recovery rates of utilities, recovery rates of non-utilities) are normally distributed and that the samples are independent. The population variances are unknown; do not assume they are equal. The test hypotheses are $H_0: \mu_1 - \mu_2 = 0$ versus $H_a: \mu_1 - \mu_2 \neq 0$, where μ_1 is the population mean recovery rate for utilities and μ_2 is the population mean recovery rate for non-utilities.

    A. Calculate the test statistic.

B. Determine whether to reject the null hypothesis at the 0.01 significance level without reference to degrees of freedom.

C. Calculate the degrees of freedom.

12. The table below gives data on the monthly returns on the S&P 500 and small-cap stocks for the period January 1960 through December 1999 and provides statistics relating to their mean differences.

Measure	S&P 500 Return (%)	Small-Cap Stock Return (%)	Differences (S&P 500–Small-Cap Stock)
January 1960–December 1999, 480 months			
Mean	1.0542	1.3117	−0.258
Standard deviation	4.2185	5.9570	3.752
January 1960–December 1979, 240 months			
Mean	0.6345	1.2741	−0.640
Standard deviation	4.0807	6.5829	4.096
January 1980–December 1999, 240 months			
Mean	1.4739	1.3492	0.125
Standard deviation	4.3197	5.2709	3.339

Let μ_d stand for the population mean value of difference between S&P 500 returns and small-cap stock returns. Use a significance level of 0.05 and suppose that mean differences are approximately normally distributed.

A. Formulate null and alternative hypotheses consistent with testing whether any difference exists between the mean returns on the S&P 500 and small-cap stocks.

B. Determine whether or not to reject the null hypothesis at the 0.05 significance level for the January 1960 to December 1999 period.

C. Determine whether or not to reject the null hypothesis at the 0.05 significance level for the January 1960 to December 1979 subperiod.

D. Determine whether or not to reject the null hypothesis at the 0.05 significance level for the January 1980 to December 1999 subperiod.

13. During a 10-year period, the standard deviation of annual returns on a portfolio you are analyzing was 15 percent a year. You want to see whether this record is sufficient evidence to support the conclusion that the portfolio's underlying variance of return was less than 400, the return variance of the portfolio's benchmark.

A. Formulate null and alternative hypotheses consistent with the verbal description of your objective.

B. Identify the test statistic for conducting a test of the hypotheses in Part A.

C. Identify the rejection point or points at the 0.05 significance level for the hypothesis tested in Part A.

D. Determine whether the null hypothesis is rejected or not rejected at the 0.05 level of significance.

14. You are investigating whether the population variance of returns on the S&P 500/BARRA Growth Index changed subsequent to the October 1987 market crash. You gather the following data for 120 months of returns before October 1987 and for 120 months of returns after October 1987. You have specified a 0.05 level of significance.

Time Period	n	Mean Monthly Return (%)	Variance of Returns
Before October 1987	120	1.416	22.367
After October 1987	120	1.436	15.795

A. Formulate null and alternative hypotheses consistent with the verbal description of the research goal.

B. Identify the test statistic for conducting a test of the hypotheses in Part A.

C. Determine whether or not to reject the null hypothesis at the 0.05 level of significance. (Use the F-tables in the back of this volume.)

15. You are interested in whether excess risk-adjusted return (alpha) is correlated with mutual fund expense ratios for U.S. large-cap growth funds. The following table presents the sample.

Mutual Fund	1	2	3	4	5	6	7	8	9
Alpha (X)	−0.52	−0.13	−0.60	−1.01	−0.26	−0.89	−0.42	−0.23	−0.60
Expense Ratio (Y)	1.34	0.92	1.02	1.45	1.35	0.50	1.00	1.50	1.45

A. Formulate null and alternative hypotheses consistent with the verbal description of the research goal.

B. Identify the test statistic for conducting a test of the hypotheses in Part A.

C. Justify your selection in Part B.

D. Determine whether or not to reject the null hypothesis at the 0.05 level of significance.

16. All else equal, is specifying a smaller significance level in a hypothesis test likely to increase the probability of a:

	Type I error?	Type II error?
A.	No	No
B.	No	Yes
C.	Yes	No

17. All else equal, is increasing the sample size for a hypothesis test likely to decrease the probability of a:

	Type I error?	Type II error?
A.	No	Yes
B.	Yes	No
C.	Yes	Yes

SOLUTIONS FOR READING 11

1. **A.** The null hypothesis is the hypothesis to be tested.

    B. The alternative hypothesis is the hypothesis accepted when the null hypothesis is rejected.

    C. A test statistic is a quantity, calculated on the basis of a sample, whose value is the basis for deciding whether to reject or not reject the null hypothesis.

    D. A Type I error, also called alpha, occurs when we reject a true null hypothesis.

    E. A Type II error, also called beta, occurs when we do not reject a false null hypothesis.

    F. The power of a test is the probability of correctly rejecting the null hypothesis (rejecting the null hypothesis when it is false).

    G. The rejection point (critical value) is a value against which a computed test statistic is compared to decide whether to reject or not reject the null hypothesis.

2. If we rejected the hypothesis of the equality of the mean debt-to-total-assets ratios of takeover target companies and non-takeover-target companies when, in fact, the means were equal, we would be committing a Type I error.

    On the other hand, if we failed to reject the equality of the mean debt-to-total-assets ratios of takeover target companies and non-takeover-target companies when the means were different, we would be committing a Type II error.

3. By the definition of p-value, 0.031 is the smallest level of significance at which we can reject the null hypothesis. Because 0.031 is smaller than 0.10 and 0.05, we can reject the null hypothesis at the 0.10 and 0.05 significance levels. Because 0.031 is larger than 0.01, however, we cannot reject the null hypothesis at the 0.01 significance level.

4. **A.** The appropriate test statistic is a t-statistic with $n - 1 = 15 - 1 = 14$ degrees of freedom. A t-statistic is theoretically correct when the sample comes from a normally distributed population with unknown variance. When the sample size is also small, there is no practical alternative.

    B. The appropriate test statistic is a t-statistic with $40 - 1 = 39$ degrees of freedom. A t-statistic is theoretically correct when the sample comes from a normally distributed population with unknown variance. When the sample size is large (generally, 30 or more is a "large" sample), it is also possible to use a z-statistic, whether the population is normally distributed or not. A test based on a t-statistic is more conservative than a z-statistic test.

    C. The appropriate test statistic is a z-statistic because the sample comes from a normally distributed population with known variance. (The known population standard deviation is used to compute the standard error of the mean using Equation 2 in the text.)

    D. The appropriate test statistic is chi-square (χ^2) with $50 - 1 = 49$ degrees of freedom.

    E. The appropriate test statistic is the F-statistic (the ratio of the sample variances).

    F. The appropriate test statistic is a t-statistic for a paired observations test (a paired comparisons test), because the samples are correlated.

    G. The appropriate test statistic is a t-statistic using a pooled estimate of the population variance. The t-statistic has $25 + 30 - 2 = 53$ degrees of freedom. This statistic is appropriate because the populations are normally distributed with unknown variances; because the variances are assumed equal, the observations can be pooled to estimate the common variance. The requirement of independent samples for using this statistic has been met.

5. A.   With degrees of freedom (df) $n - 1 = 26 - 1 = 25$, the rejection point conditions for this two-sided test are $t > 2.060$ and $t < -2.060$. Because the significance level is 0.05, $0.05/2 = 0.025$ of the probability is in each tail. The tables give one-sided (one-tailed) probabilities, so we used the 0.025 column. Read across df = 25 to the $\alpha = 0.025$ column to find 2.060, the rejection point for the right tail. By symmetry, -2.060 is the rejection point for the left tail.

B.   With df = 39, the rejection point conditions for this two-sided test are $t > 2.708$ and $t < -2.708$. This is a two-sided test, so we use the $0.01/2 = 0.005$ column. Read across df = 39 to the $\alpha = 0.005$ column to find 2.708, the rejection point for the right tail. By symmetry, -2.708 is the rejection point for the left tail.

C.   With df = 39, the rejection point condition for this one-sided test is $t > 2.426$. Read across df = 39 to the $\alpha = 0.01$ column to find 2.426, the rejection point for the right tail. Because we have a "greater than" alternative, we are concerned with only the right tail.

D.   With df = 20, the rejection point condition for this one-sided test is $t > 1.725$. Read across df = 20 to the $\alpha = 0.05$ column to find 1.725, the rejection point for the right tail. Because we have a "greater than" alternative, we are concerned with only the right tail.

E.   With df = 18, the rejection point condition for this one-sided test is $t < -1.330$. Read across df = 18 to the $\alpha = 0.10$ column to find 1.330, the rejection point for the right tail. By symmetry, the rejection point for the left tail is -1.330.

F.   With df = 49, the rejection point condition for this one-sided test is $t < -1.677$. Read across df = 49 to the $\alpha = 0.05$ column to find 1.677, the rejection point for the right tail. By symmetry, the rejection point for the left tail is -1.677.

6.   Recall that with a z-test (in contrast to the t-test), we do not employ degrees of freedom. The standard normal distribution is a single distribution applicable to all z-tests. You should refer to "Rejection Points for a z-Test" in Section 3.1 to answer these questions.

A.   This is a two-sided test at a 0.01 significance level. In Part C of "Rejection Points for a z-Test," we find that the rejection point conditions are $z > 2.575$ and $z < -2.575$.

B.   This is a two-sided test at a 0.05 significance level. In Part B of "Rejection Points for a z-Test," we find that the rejection point conditions are $z > 1.96$ and $z < -1.96$.

C.   This is a two-sided test at a 0.10 significance level. In Part A of "Rejection Points for a z-Test," we find that the rejection point conditions are $z > 1.645$ and $z < -1.645$.

D.   This is a one-sided test at a 0.05 significance level. In Part B of "Rejection Points for a z-Test," we find that the rejection point condition for a test with a "greater than" alternative hypothesis is $z > 1.645$.

7. A.   When sampling from a normally distributed population with known variance, the correct test statistic for hypothesis tests concerning the mean is the z-statistic.

B. When sampling from a normally distributed population with unknown variance, the theoretically correct test statistic for hypothesis tests concerning the mean is the t-statistic.

C. When the sample size is large, the central limit theorem applies. Consequently, the sample mean will be approximately normally distributed. When the population variance is not known, a test using the t-statistic is theoretically preferred. A test using the z-statistic is also sufficient when the sample size is large, as in this case.

8. A. As stated in the text, we often set up the "hoped for" or "suspected" condition as the alternative hypothesis. Here, that condition is that the population value of Willco's mean annual net income exceeds $24 million. Thus we have H_0: $\mu \leq 24$ versus H_a: $\mu > 24$.

B. Given that net income is normally distributed with unknown variance, the appropriate test statistic is t with $n - 1 = 6 - 1 = 5$ degrees of freedom.

C. In the t-distribution table in the back of the book, in the row for df = 5 under $\alpha = 0.05$, we read the rejection point (critical value) of 2.015. We will reject the null if $t > 2.015$.

D. The t-test is given by Equation 4:

$$t_5 = \frac{\bar{X} - \mu_0}{s/\sqrt{n}} = \frac{30 - 24}{10/\sqrt{6}} = \frac{6}{4.082483} = 1.469694$$

or 1.47. Because 1.47 does not exceed 2.015, we do not reject the null hypothesis. The difference between the sample mean of $30 million and the hypothesized value of $24 million under the null is not statistically significant.

9. A. H_0: $\mu = 0$ versus H_a: $\mu \neq 0$.

B. The t-test is based on $t = \dfrac{\bar{X} - \mu_0}{s/\sqrt{n}}$ with $n - 1 = 101 - 1 = 100$ degrees of freedom. At the 0.05 significance level, we reject the null if $t > 1.984$ or if $t < -1.984$. At the 0.01 significance level, we reject the null if $t > 2.626$ or if $t < -2.626$. For Analyst A, we have $t = (0.05 - 0)/(0.10/\sqrt{101}) = 0.05/0.00995 = 5.024938$ or 5.025. We clearly reject the null hypothesis at both the 0.05 and 0.01 levels.

The calculation of the z-statistic with unknown variance, as in this case, is the same as the calculation of the t-statistic. The rejection point conditions for a two-tailed test are as follows: $z > 1.96$ and $z < -1.96$ at the 0.05 level; and $z > 2.575$ and $z < -2.575$ at the 0.01 level. Note that the z-test is a less conservative test than the t-test, so when the z-test is used, the null is easier to reject. Because $z = 5.025$ is greater than 2.575, we reject the null at the 0.01 level; we also reject the null at the 0.05 level.

In summary, Analyst A's EPS forecasts appear to be biased upward—they tend to be too high.

C. For Analyst B, the t-test is based on t with $121 - 1 = 120$ degrees of freedom. At the 0.05 significance level, we reject the null if $t > 1.980$ or if $t < -1.980$. At the 0.01 significance level, we reject the null if $t > 2.617$ or if $t < -2.617$. We calculate $t = (0.02 - 0)/(0.09/\sqrt{121}) = 0.02/0.008182 = 2.444444$ or 2.44. Because 2.44 > 1.98, we reject the null at the 0.05 level. However, 2.44 is not larger than 2.617, so we do not reject the null at the 0.01 level.

For a z-test, the rejection point conditions are the same as given in Part B, and we come to the same conclusions as with the t-test. Because 2.44 > 1.96, we reject the null at the 0.05 significance level; however, because 2.44 is not greater than 2.575, we do not reject the null at the 0.01 level.

The mean forecast error of Analyst B is only $0.02; but because the test is based on a large number of observations, it is sufficient evidence to reject the null of mean zero forecast errors at the 0.05 level.

10. A. Stating the suspected condition as the alternative hypothesis, we have

$$H_0 : \mu_1 - \mu_2 \leq 0 \text{ versus } H_a : \mu_1 - \mu_2 > 0$$

where

μ_1 = the population mean value of Analyst A's forecast errors

μ_2 = the population mean value of Analyst B's forecast errors

B. We have two normally distributed populations with unknown variances. Based on the samples, it is reasonable to assume that the population variances are equal. The samples are assumed to be independent; this assumption is reasonable because the analysts cover quite different industries. The appropriate test statistic is t using a pooled estimate of the common variance. The number of degrees of freedom is

$$n_1 + n_2 - 2 = 101 + 121 - 2 = 222 - 2 = 220 .$$

C. For df = 200 (the closest value to 220), the rejection point for a one-sided test at the 0.05 significance level is 1.653.

D. We first calculate the pooled estimate of variance:

$$s_p^2 = \frac{(n_1 - 1)s_1^2 + (n_2 - 1)s_2^2}{n_1 + n_2 - 2} = \frac{(101 - 1)(0.10)^2 + (121 - 1)(0.09)^2}{101 + 121 - 2}$$

$$= \frac{1.972}{220} = 0.008964$$

Then

$$t = \frac{(\bar{X}_1 = \bar{X}_2) - (\mu_1 - \mu_2)}{\left(\frac{s_p^2}{n_1} + \frac{s_p^2}{n_2}\right)^{1/2}} = \frac{(0.05 - 0.02) - 0}{\left(\frac{0.008964}{101} + \frac{0.008964}{121}\right)^{1/2}}$$

$$= \frac{0.03}{0.01276} = 2.351018$$

or 2.35. Because 2.35 > 1.653, we reject the null hypothesis in favor of the alternative hypothesis that the population mean forecast error of Analyst A is greater than that of Analyst B.

11. A. The test statistic is

$$t = \frac{\bar{X}_1 - \bar{X}_2}{\left(\frac{s_1^2}{n_1} + \frac{s_2^2}{n_2}\right)^{1/2}}$$

where

$\bar{X}_1$ = sample mean recovery rate for utilities = 77.74

$\bar{X}_2$ = sample mean recovery rate for non-utility sectors = 42.56

s_1^2 = sample variance for utilities = 18.06^2 = 326.1636

s_2^2 = sample variance for non-utilities = 24.89^2 = 619.5121

n_1 = sample size of the utility sample = 32

n_2 = sample size of the non-utility sample = 189

Therefore, $t = (77.74 - 42.56)/[(326.1636/32) + (619.5121/189)]^{1/2} = 35.18/(10.192613 + 3.277842)^{1/2} = 35.18/3.670212 = 9.585$. The calculated t-statistic is thus 9.585.

B. Usually, we need to know degrees of freedom to determine whether a t-statistic is significant. The magnitude of the t-statistic is so large that in this case, there is actually no doubt about its significance even at the 0.01 level. For a two-sided test at the 0.01 level of significance, we look under the 0.005 column (0.01/2 = 0.005). For all but the very first two entries, for 1 and 2 degrees of freedom, the calculated test statistic is larger than the indicated rejection point (critical value). Clearly, with samples of size 32 and 189, there are more than 2 degrees of freedom.

C. This question confirms that we can calculate the degrees of freedom for the test, if needed:

$$df = \frac{\left(\dfrac{s_1^2}{n_1} + \dfrac{s_2^2}{n_2}\right)^2}{\dfrac{\left(s_1^2/n_1\right)^2}{n_1} + \dfrac{\left(s_2^2/n_2\right)^2}{n_2}} = \frac{\left(\dfrac{326.1636}{32} + \dfrac{619.5121}{189}\right)^2}{\dfrac{\left(326.1636/32\right)^2}{32} + \dfrac{\left(619.5121/189\right)^2}{189}}$$

$$= \frac{181.453139}{3.30339} = 54.93 \text{ or } 55 \text{ degrees of freedom.}$$

12. A. We test $H_0: \mu_d = 0$ versus $H_a: \mu_d \neq 0$.

B. This is a paired comparisons t-test with $n - 1 = 480 - 1 = 479$ degrees of freedom. At the 0.05 significance level, we reject the null hypothesis if either $t > 1.96$ or $t < -1.96$. We use df = ∞ in the t-distribution table under $\alpha = 0.025$ because we have a very large sample and a two-sided test.

$$t = \frac{\bar{d} - \mu_{d0}}{s_{\bar{d}}} = \frac{-0.258 - 0}{3.752/\sqrt{480}} = \frac{-0.258}{0.171255} = -1.506529 \text{ or } -1.51$$

At the 0.05 significance level, because neither rejection point condition is met, we do not reject the null hypothesis that the mean difference between the returns on the S&P 500 and small-cap stocks during the entire sample period was 0.

C. This t-test now has $n - 1 = 240 - 1 = 239$ degrees of freedom. At the 0.05 significance level, we reject the null hypothesis if either $t > 1.972$ or $t < -1.972$, using df = 200 in the t-distribution tables.

$$t = \frac{\bar{d} - \mu_{d0}}{s_{\bar{d}}} = \frac{-0.640 - 0}{4.096/\sqrt{240}} = \frac{-0.640}{0.264396} = -2.420615 \text{ or } -2.42$$

Because −2.42 < −1.972, we reject the null hypothesis at the 0.05 significance level. During this subperiod, small-cap stocks significantly outperformed the S&P 500.

D. This t-test has $n - 1 = 240 - 1 = 239$ degrees of freedom. At the 0.05 significance level, we reject the null hypothesis if either $t > 1.972$ or $t < -1.972$, using df = 200 in the t-distribution tables.

$$t = \frac{\bar{d} - \mu_{d0}}{s_{\bar{d}}} = \frac{0.125 - 0}{3.339/\sqrt{240}} = \frac{0.125}{0.215532} = 0.579962 \text{ or } 0.58$$

At the 0.05 significance level, because neither rejection point condition is met, we do not reject the null hypothesis that for the January 1980–December 1999 period, the mean difference between the returns on the S&P 500 and small-cap stocks was zero.

13. A. We have a "less than" alternative hypothesis, where σ^2 is the variance of return on the portfolio. The hypotheses are $H_0: \sigma^2 \geq 400$ versus $H_a: \sigma^2 < 400$, where 400 is the hypothesized value of variance, σ_0^2.

B. The test statistic is chi-square with $10 - 1 = 9$ degrees of freedom.

C. The rejection point is found across degrees of freedom of 9, under the 0.95 column (95 percent of probability above the value). It is 3.325. We will reject the null hypothesis if we find that $\chi^2 < 3.325$.

D. The test statistic is calculated as

$$\chi^2 = \frac{(n-1)s^2}{\sigma_0^2} = \frac{9 \times 15^2}{400} = \frac{2{,}025}{400} = 5.0625 \text{ or } 5.06$$

Because 5.06 is not less than 3.325, we do not reject the null hypothesis.

14. A. We have a "not equal to" alternative hypothesis:

$$H_0: \sigma^2_{Before} = \sigma^2_{After} \text{ versus } H_a: \sigma^2_{Before} \neq \sigma^2_{After}$$

B. To test a null hypothesis of the equality of two variances, we use an F-test:

$$F = \frac{s_1^2}{s_2^2}$$

C. The "before" sample variance is larger, so following a convention for calculating F-statistics, the "before" sample variance goes in the numerator. $F = 22.367/15.795 = 1.416$, with $120 - 1 = 119$ numerator and denominator degrees of freedom. Because this is a two-tailed test, we use F-tables for the 0.025 level (df = 0.05/2). Using the tables in the back of the volume, the closest value to 119 is 120 degrees of freedom. At the 0.05 level, the rejection point is 1.43. (Using the Insert/Function/Statistical feature on a Microsoft Excel spreadsheet, we would find FINV(0.025, 119, 119) = 1.434859 as the critical F-value.) Because 1.416 is not greater than 1.43, we do not reject the null hypothesis that the "before" and "after" variances are equal.

15. A. We have a "not equal to" alternative hypothesis:

$$H_0: \rho = 0 \text{ versus } H_a: \rho \neq 0$$

B. We would use the nonparametric Spearman rank correlation coefficient to conduct the test.

C. Mutual fund expense ratios are bounded from above and below, and in practice there is at least a lower bound on alpha (as any return cannot be less than –100 percent). These variables are markedly non-normally distributed, and the assumptions of a parametric test are not likely to be fulfilled. Thus a nonparametric test appears to be appropriate.

D. The calculation of the Spearman rank correlation coefficient is given in the following table.

Mutual Fund	1	2	3	4	5	6	7	8	9
Alpha (X)	−0.52	−0.13	−0.60	−1.01	−0.26	−0.89	−0.42	−0.23	−0.60
Expense Ratio (Y)	1.34	0.92	1.02	1.45	1.35	0.50	1.00	1.50	1.45
X Rank	5	1	6.5	9	3	8	4	2	6.5
Y Rank	5	8	6	2.5	4	9	7	1	2.5
d_i	0	−7	0.5	6.5	−1	−1	−3	1	4
d_i^2	0	49	0.25	42.25	1	1	9	1	16

$$r_s = 1 - \frac{6\sum d_i^2}{n(n^2-1)} = 1 - \frac{6(119.50)}{9(81-1)} = 0.0042$$

We use Table 11 to tabulate the rejection points for a test on the Spearman rank correlation. Given a sample size of 9 in a two-tailed test at a 0.05 significance level, the upper-tail rejection point is 0.6833 (we use the 0.025 column). Thus we reject the null hypothesis if the Spearman rank correlation coefficient is less than −0.6833 or greater than 0.6833. Because r_s is equal to 0.0042, we do not reject the null hypothesis.

16. B is correct. Specifying a smaller significance level decreases the probability of a Type I error (rejecting a true null hypothesis), but increases the probability of a Type II error (not rejecting a false null hypothesis). As the level of significance decreases, the null hypothesis is less frequently rejected.

17. C is correct. The only way to avoid the trade-off between the two types of errors is to increase the sample size; increasing sample size (all else equal) reduces the probability of both types of errors. From the reading on sampling and estimations, all else equal, a larger sample size will decrease both the standard error and the width of the confidence interval. In other words, the precision of the estimate of the population parameter is increased.

Technical Analysis

by Barry M. Sine, CFA and Robert A. Strong, CFA

LEARNING OUTCOMES

Mastery	The candidate should be able to:
☐	**a** explain the principles of technical analysis, its applications, and its underlying assumptions;
☐	**b** describe the construction of and interpret different types of technical analysis charts;
☐	**c** explain the uses of trend, support, resistance lines, and change in polarity;
☐	**d** identify and interpret common chart patterns;
☐	**e** describe common technical analysis indicators: price-based, momentum oscillators, sentiment, and flow of funds;
☐	**f** explain the use of cycles by technical analysts;
☐	**g** describe the key tenets of Elliott Wave Theory and the importance of Fibonacci numbers;
☐	**h** describe intermarket analysis as it relates to technical analysis and asset allocation.

INTRODUCTION

1

Technical analysis has been used by traders and analysts for centuries, but it has only recently achieved broad acceptance among regulators and the academic community. This reading gives a brief overview of the field, compares technical analysis with other schools of analysis, and describes some of the main tools in technical analysis. Some applications of technical analysis are subjective. That is, although certain aspects, such as the calculation of indicators, have specific rules, the interpretation of findings is often subjective and based on the long-term context of the security being analyzed. This aspect is similar to fundamental analysis, which has specific rules for calculating ratios, for example, but introduces subjectivity in the evaluation phase.

TECHNICAL ANALYSIS: DEFINITION AND SCOPE

Technical analysis is a form of security analysis that uses price and volume data, which is often graphically displayed, in decision making. Technical analysis can be used for securities in any freely traded market around the globe. A freely traded market is one in which willing buyers trade with willing sellers without external intervention or impediment. Prices are the result of the interaction of supply and demand in real time. Technical analysis is used on a wide range of financial instruments, including equities, bonds, commodity futures, and currency futures.

The underlying logic of technical analysis is simple:

- Supply and demand determine prices.
- Changes in supply and demand cause changes in prices.
- Prices can be projected with charts and other technical tools.

Technical analysis of any financial instrument does not require detailed knowledge of that instrument. As long as the chart represents the action in a freely traded market, a technician does not even need to know the name or type of the security to conduct the analysis. Technical analysis can also be applied over any time frame—from short-term price movements to long-term movements of annual closing prices. Trends that are apparent in short-term charts may also appear over longer time frames. Because fundamental analysis is more time consuming than technical analysis, investors with short-term time horizons, such as traders, tend to prefer technical analysis—but not always. For example, fundamental analysts with long time frames often perform technical analysis to time the purchase and sale of the securities they have analyzed.

2.1 Principles and Assumptions

Technical analysis can be thought of as the study of collective investor psychology, or sentiment. Prices in any freely traded market are set by human beings or their automated proxies (such as computerized trading programs), and price is set at the equilibrium between supply and demand at any instant in time. Various fundamental theorists have proposed that markets are efficient and rational, but technicians believe that humans are often irrational and emotional and that they tend to behave similarly in similar circumstances.

Although fundamental data are key inputs into the determination of value, these data are analyzed by humans, who may be driven, at least partially, by factors other than rational factors.[1] Human behavior is often erratic and driven by emotion in many aspects of one's life, so technicians conclude that it is unreasonable to believe that investing is the one exception where humans always behave rationally. Technicians believe that market trends and patterns reflect this irrational human behavior. Thus, technical analysis is the study of market trends or patterns. And technicians believe the trends and patterns tend to repeat themselves and are, therefore, somewhat predictable. So, technicians rely on recognition of patterns that have occurred in the past in an attempt to project future patterns of security prices.

Another tenet of technical analysis is that the market reflects the collective knowledge and sentiment of many varied participants and the amount of buying and selling activity in a particular security. In a freely traded market, only those market participants who actually buy or sell a security have an impact on price. And the greater the volume of a participant's trades, the more impact that market participant

---

1 Fundamental analysts use a wide variety of inputs, including financial statements, legal documents, economic data, first-hand observations from visiting the facilities of subject companies, and interviews with corporate managers, customers, suppliers, and competitors.

will have on price. Those with the best information and most conviction have more say in setting prices than others because the informed traders trade higher volumes. To make use of their information, however, they must trade. Technical analysis relies on knowledgeable market participants putting this knowledge to work by trading in the market, thereby influencing prices and volume. Without trading, the information is not captured in the charts. Arguably, although insider trading is illegal for a variety of reasons, it improves the efficiency of technical analysis.

Trades determine volume and price. The impact occurs instantaneously and frequently anticipates fundamental developments correctly. So, by studying market technical data—price and volume trends—the technician is seeking to understand investor sentiment. The technician is benefiting from the wide range of knowledge of market participants and the collective conclusion of market participants about a security. In contrast, the fundamental analyst must wait for the release of financial statements to conduct financial statement analysis, so a time lag occurs between the market's activities and the analyst's conclusions.

Charles Dow, creator in 1896 of what is now known as the Dow Jones Industrial Average, described the collective action of participants in the markets as follows:

> The market reflects all the jobber knows about the condition of the textile trade; all the banker knows about the money market; all that the best-informed president knows of his own business, together with his knowledge of all other businesses; it sees the general condition of transportation in a way that the president of no single railroad can ever see; it is better informed on crops than the farmer or even the Department of Agriculture. In fact, the market reduces to a bloodless verdict all knowledge bearing on finance, both domestic and foreign.

A similar notion was expressed by George A. Akerlof and Robert J. Shiller:

> To understand how economies work and how we can manage them and prosper, we must pay attention to the thought patterns that animate people's ideas and feelings, their animal spirits. We will never really understand important economic events unless we confront the fact that their causes are largely mental in nature.[2]

Market participants use many inputs and analytical tools before trading. Fundamental analysis is a key input in determining security prices, but it is not the only one. Technical analysts believe that emotions play a role. Investors with a favorable fundamental view may nonetheless sell a financial instrument for other reasons, including pessimistic investor sentiment, margin calls, and requirements for their capital—for example, to pay for a child's college tuition. Technicians do not care why market participants are buying or selling, just that they are doing so.

Some financial instruments have an associated income stream that contributes to the security's intrinsic value. Bonds have regular coupon payments, and equity shares may have underlying cash flows or dividend streams. A fundamental analyst can adjust these cash flows for risk and use standard time value of money techniques to determine a present value. Other assets, such as a bushel of wheat, gallon of crude oil, or ounce of silver, do not have underlying financial statements or an income stream, so valuation models cannot be used to derive their fundamental intrinsic values. For these assets, technical analysis is the only form of analysis possible. So, whereas fundamental analysis is widely used in the analysis of fixed-income and equity securities, technical analysis is widely used in the analysis of commodities, currencies, and futures.

---

2 Akerlof, George A., and Robert J. Shiller. *Animal Spirits: How Human Psychology Drives the Economy, and Why It Matters for Global Capitalism*. Princeton University Press, 2009.

Market participants attempt to anticipate economic developments and enter into trades to profit from them. Technicians believe that security price movements occur before fundamental developments unfold—certainly before they are reported. This belief is reflected in the fact that stock prices are one of the 12 components of the National Bureau of Economic Research's Index of Leading Economic Indicators. A key tenet of technical analysis is that the equity market moves roughly six months ahead of inflection points in the broad economy.

2.2 Technical and Fundamental Analysis

Technical analysis and fundamental analysis are both useful and valid, but they approach the market in different ways. Technicians focus solely on analyzing markets and the trading of financial instruments. Fundamental analysis is a much wider field, encompassing financial and economic analysis as well as analysis of societal and political trends. Technicians analyze the result of this extensive fundamental analysis in terms of how it affects market prices. A technician's analysis is derived solely from price and volume data, whereas a fundamental equity analyst analyzes a company and incorporates data that are external to the market and then uses this analysis to predict security price movements. As the quotation from Dow in Section 2.1 illustrates, technical analysis assumes that all of the factors considered by a fundamental analyst are reflected in the price of a financial instrument through buying and selling activity.

A key distinction between technical analysis and fundamental analysis is that the technician has more concrete data, primarily price and volume data, to work with. The financial statements analyzed by fundamental analysts are not objective data but are the result of numerous estimates and assumptions that have been added together to arrive at the line items in the financial statements. Even the cash line on a balance sheet is subject to corporate management's opinion about which securities are liquid enough to be considered "cash." This opinion must be agreed to by auditors and, in many countries, regulators (who sometimes differ with the auditors). Financial statements are subject to restatements because of such issues as changes in accounting assumptions and even fraud. But the price and volume data used in technical analysis are objective. When the data become subject to analysis, however, both types of analysis become subjective because judgment is exercised when a technician analyzes a price chart and when a fundamental analyst analyzes an income statement.

Fundamental analysis can be considered to be the more theoretical approach because it seeks to determine the underlying long-term (or intrinsic) value of a security. Technical analysis can be considered to be the more practical because a technician studies the markets and financial instruments as they exist, even if trading activity appears, at times, to be irrational. Technicians seek to project the level at which a financial instrument *will* trade, whereas fundamental analysts seek to predict where it *should* trade.

Being a fundamental analyst can be lonely if the analyst is the first to arrive at a fundamental conclusion, even though it is correct, because deviations from intrinsic value can persist for long periods. The reason these deviations may persist is that it takes buying activity to raise (or lower) the price of a security in a freely traded market.

A drawback of technical analysis is that technicians are limited to studying market movements and do not use other predictive analytical methods, such as interviewing the customers of a subject company, to determine future demand for a company's products. Technicians study market trends and are mainly concerned with a security's price trend: Is the security trading up, down, or sideways? Trends are driven by collective investor psychology, however, and can change without warning. Additionally, it can take some time for a trend to become evident. Thus, technicians may make wrong calls and have to change their opinions. Technicians are better at identifying market moves after the moves are already under way.

Moreover, trends and patterns must be in place for some time before they are recognizable, so a key shortcoming of technical analysis is that it can be late in identifying changes in trends or patterns. This shortcoming mirrors a key shortcoming of fundamental analysis in that securities often overshoot fundamental fair values in an uptrend and undershoot fundamental fair values in a downtrend. Strictly relying on price targets obtained by fundamental analysis can lead to closing profitable investment positions too early because investors may irrationally bid securities prices well above or well below intrinsic value.

Fundamental analysis is a younger field than technical analysis because reliable fundamental data are a relatively new phenomenon. In contrast, the first recorded use of technical analysis was in Japan in the 1700s, where it was used to analyze trading in the rice market. The Japanese developed a detailed field of technical analysis with their own chart design and patterns. These tools were translated and widely understood outside Japan only in the 1980s.

Western use of technical analysis was pioneered by Dow, who was also the first editor of the *Wall Street Journal*, in the 1890s. At the time, publicly traded companies were under no requirement to release their financial information even to shareholders, and insider trading was common and legal. Dow created the Dow Jones Industrial Average and the Dow Jones Railroad Average (now the Transportation Average) as a proxy to gauge the health of the economy, because fundamental data were not available. By his logic, if industrial stocks were doing well, industrial companies themselves must be doing well and if railroad stocks were doing well, railroad companies must be doing well. And if both manufacturers and the companies that transported goods to market were prospering, the economy as a whole must be prospering.

Not until the Securities Exchange Act of 1934 were public companies in the United States required to regularly file financial statements that were available to the public. In that year, Benjamin Graham published his seminal work, *Security Analysis*, and three years later, he and several others founded one of the first societies devoted to fundamental analysis, the New York Society of Security Analysts.[3] Fundamental analysis quickly overtook technical analysis in terms of acceptance by practitioners, regulators, and academics.

Acceptance of technical analysis by practitioners was revived in the 1970s with the creation of the Market Technicians Association in New York and the International Federation of Technical Analysts a few years later. Only in the last decade, however, has the field started to achieve widespread acceptance by regulators and academics. An important impediment to acceptance by academics is the difficulty of capturing the subjectivity involved in technical analysis. The human brain can recognize, analyze, and interpret technical information that is difficult for statistical computer models to recognize and test.

Although technical analysis can be applied to any freely traded security, it does have its limits. In markets that are subject to large outside manipulation, the application of technical analysis is limited. For example, the central banks of many countries intervene in their currency markets from time to time to maintain exchange rate stability. Interestingly, traders claim to have been able to successfully predict interventions in some countries, especially those where the central bank is itself using technical analysis. Technical analysis is also limited in illiquid markets, where even modestly sized trades can have an inordinate impact on prices. For example, in considering a thinly traded American Depositary Receipt (ADR), analyzing the more heavily traded local security frequently yields a better analysis.[4] Another example of when technical

---

3 The New York Society of Security Analysts was a successor to the New York Society of Financial Statisticians, which was founded in 1916.

4 An American Depositary Receipt is a negotiable certificate issued by a depositary bank that represents ownership in a non-U.S. company's deposited equity (i.e., equity held in custody by the depositary bank in the company's home market).

analysis may give an incorrect reading is in the case of a company that has declared bankruptcy and announced that its shares will have zero value in a restructuring. A positive technical trend may appear in such cases as investors who hold short positions buy shares to close out their positions.

A good example of when technical analysis is a superior tool to fundamental analysis is in the case of securities fraud, such as occurred at Enron Corporation and WorldCom. These companies were issuing fraudulent financial statements, but many fundamental analysts continued to hold favorable views of the companies' equity securities even as the share prices declined. Simultaneously, a small group of investors came to the opposite view and expressed this view through high-volume sales of the securities. The result was clearly negative chart patterns that could then be discerned by technical analysis.

TECHNICAL ANALYSIS TOOLS

The primary tools used in technical analysis are charts and indicators. Charts are the graphical display of price and volume data, and the display may be done in a number of ways. Charts are then subjected to various analyses, including the identification of trends, patterns, and cycles. Technical indicators include a variety of measures of relative price level—for example, price momentum, market sentiment, and funds flow. We will discuss charts first.

3.1 Charts

Charts are an essential component of the technical analyst's toolkit. Charts provide information about past price behavior and provide a basis for inferring likely future price behavior. A variety of charts can be useful in studying the markets. The selection of the chart to use in technical analysis is determined by the intended purpose of the analysis.

3.1.1 Line Chart

Line charts are familiar to all types of analysts and are a simple graphic display of price trends over time. Usually, the chart is a plot of data points, such as share price, with a line connecting these points. Line charts are typically drawn with closing prices as the data points. The vertical axis (y-axis) reflects price level, and the horizontal axis (x-axis) is time. Even though the line chart is the simplest chart, an analyst can quickly glean information from this chart.

The chart in Exhibit 1 is a quarterly chart of the FTSE 100 Index from 1984 through mid-2009. Up years and down years are clearly evident. The strong rally from 1984 through 1999 and the market decline from late 1999 to late 2002 are also clearly visible. The 2003–2007 rally did not exceed the high reached in 1999, which suggests that investors were not willing to pay as high a price for stocks on the London Stock Exchange during that rally as they were in the prior rally. This information provides a broad overview of investor sentiment and can lead to further analysis. Importantly, the analyst can access and analyze this information quickly. Collecting and analyzing the full array of data normally incorporated in fundamental analysis would take much longer.

Exhibit 1	Line Chart: FTSE 100 Quarterly Price Data, 1984–2009 (Price Measured in British Pounds Sterling)

3.1.2 *Bar Chart*

A line chart has one data point per time interval. A **bar chart**, in contrast, has four bits of data in each entry—the high and low price encountered during the time interval plus the opening and closing prices. Such charts can be constructed for any time period, but they are customarily constructed from daily data.

As Exhibit 2 shows, a vertical line connects the high and low price of the day; a cross-hatch to the right indicates the closing price, and a cross-hatch to the left indicates the opening price. The appeal of this chart is that the analyst immediately gets a sense of the nature of that day's trading. A short bar indicates little price movement during the day; that is, the high, low, and close were near the opening price. A long bar indicates a wide divergence between the high and the low for the day.

Exhibit 2	Bar Chart Notation

Exhibit 3 shows daily performance of the Brazilian Bovespa Index (BVSP) from late 2007 through late 2009. The top part provides the price open, close, high, and low; the bottom part shows volume, which will be discussed in section 3.1.6. The downturn in the second half of 2008 is obvious, but also notable are the extreme price movements in the fourth quarter of 2008. There were 40 trading days from 29 September to 24 November. On 20 of those days, the closing value of the index changed from the previous close by at least 4 percent, a huge move by historical standards. During the same period, the average daily price range (high to low) was 7 percent, compared with 3.7 percent in the previous two months. This potentially important information would not be captured in a line chart.

Exhibit 3	Bar Chart: Bovespa Index, November 2007–November 2009 (Price in Brazilian Reais)

3.1.3 *Candlestick Chart*

Candlestick charts trace their roots to Japan, where technical analysis has been in use for centuries. Like a bar chart, a **candlestick chart** also provides four prices per data point entry: the opening and closing prices and the high and low prices during the period. As shown in Exhibit 4, a vertical line represents the range through which the security price traveled during the time period. The line is known as the wick or shadow. The body of the candle is shaded if the opening price was higher than the closing price, and the body is clear if the opening price was lower than the closing price.

Exhibit 4	Construction of a Candlestick Chart

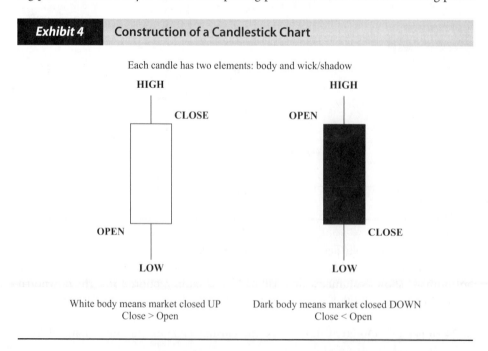

Exhibit 5 shows a weekly candlestick chart for Companhia Vale do Rio Doce for the period 1 January through 15 June 2009.

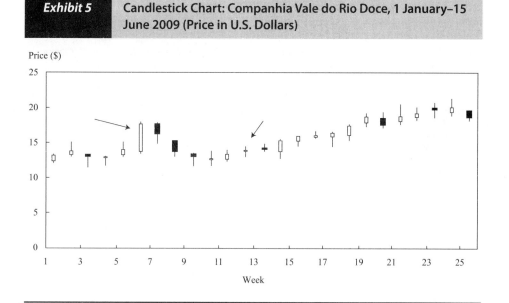

Exhibit 5   Candlestick Chart: Companhia Vale do Rio Doce, 1 January–15 June 2009 (Price in U.S. Dollars)

The advantage of the candlestick chart over the bar chart is that price moves are much more visible in the candlestick chart, which allows faster analysis. The bar chart indicates market volatility only by the height of each bar, but in candlestick charts, the difference between opening and closing prices and their relationship to the highs and lows of the day are clearly apparent. Compare the sixth candle with the twelfth in Exhibit 5. In the sixth candle, the analyst can see significant volatility because the high of the day and low of the day are so far apart. The stock opened near the low of the day and closed near the high, suggesting a steady rally during the day. In contrast, the twelfth candle shows no difference between the high and low, and the shares opened and closed at the same price, creating a cross-pattern. In Japanese terminology used in candlestick charting, this pattern is called a doji. The doji signifies that after a full day of trading, the positive price influence of buyers and the negative price influence of sellers exactly counteracted each other, which tells the analyst that this market is in balance. If a doji occurs at the end of a long uptrend or downtrend, it signals that the trend will probably reverse.

3.1.4 *Point and Figure Chart*

Point and figure charts were widely used in the United States in the early 1900s and were favored because they were easy to create and update manually in the era before computers. As with any technical analysis tool, these charts can be used with equities, fixed-income securities, commodities, or foreign exchange.

Who originated the **point and figure chart** is unclear; they are referred to in a number of books in the United States dating back to 1898. The methodology evolved until 1934 when the first book was published on the topic: *The Point and Figure Method of Anticipating Stock Price Movements* by Victor de Villiers and Owen Taylor. With the advent of powerful charting software and internet websites, complex chart types, such as the candlestick chart, have become more popular. But point and figure charts still offer tremendous value if one knows their limitations and their advantages. The key reason this knowledge is necessary, as explained below, is that point and figure charts are constructed differently from other charts; they have a clear focus on entry and exit levels but no focus on holding periods.

As illustrated in Exhibit 6, a point and figure chart is drawn on a grid and consists of columns of X's alternating with columns of O's. Neither time nor volume are represented on this type of chart, and *the horizontal axis represents the number of changes in price, not time.* Movement along the horizontal axis does reflect the passage of time, but not in any uniform fashion. The analyst makes entries on a point and figure chart only when the price changes by the "box size," which is explained below. This lack of a normal time dimension is perhaps the most unusual characteristic of a point and figure chart.

Exhibit 6	Point and Figure Chart: Wharf Holdings Daily Price Chart, 2007–2009 (in Hong Kong Dollars)

Note: The box size is HK$1, and the reversal size is three.

To construct a point and figure chart, the analyst must determine both the box size and the reversal size. Box size refers to the change in price represented by the height of each box (boxes are generally square, but the width has no meaning). In Exhibit 6, the box size is HK$1. The reversal size is used to determine when to create a new column. In Exhibit 6, the reversal size is three, meaning a reversal in price of three or more boxes.

Although a point and figure chart can be constructed in several ways, these charts are always drawn on graph paper to facilitate seeing the "columns and rows" nature of the data. The vertical axis measures *discrete increments of price.* For example, an analyst in Europe might draw a €1 chart, a €2 chart, or any other increment. In a €1 chart, boxes would be €1 apart (e.g. €40, €41, €42), whereas in a €2 chart they would be €2 apart (€40, €42, €44). The most commonly used box size is 1 unit of currency, which is used when prices range from 20 to 100 per share of the currency.

The next decision the technician needs to make is the reversal size. The most common size is three, meaning a reversal in price of three or more boxes (€3 in the case of a box size of €1). This use of a multibox reversal helps eliminate "noise" in the price data. (*Noise* refers to short-term trading volatility that does not alter the long-term trend of the security.)

In a point and figure chart, X represents an increase in price and O represents a decline in price. In constructing a chart, the technician draws an X in a column of boxes every time the security price closes up by the amount of the box size. (Ideally, all security prices are considered on an intraday basis, but this practice has given way to using closing prices only.) If the price increases by twice the box size, the technician draws two X's to fill in two boxes, one on top of the other. The technician fills in more boxes for larger price moves. The resulting column starts at the opening price level and extends to the closing price level. As long as the security keeps closing at higher prices, the technician keeps filling in boxes with X's, which makes the column higher and higher. If the price does not increase by at least the box size, no indication is made on the chart. Thus, in some cases, the chart is not updated for long periods, but no indication of this passage of time is made on the chart.

The reversal size determines when to create a new column. In the case of a €1 box size, and three-box reversal size, a decline of €3 or more would result in the technician shifting to the next column over and beginning a column of O's. The first box to be filled in is to the right and below the highest X in the prior column. The technician then fills in an O to bring the column down to the price level at the close. Again, each filled-in box (if the box size is €1) represents a €1 decline in the security price. As long as the downtrend continues, without a €3 increase in price, the technician continues adding O's to the column below the prior O's. A reversal in the downtrend by at least the amount of the reversal size prompts the technician to move to the next column and begin drawing a series of X's again. Computer technology makes the process easy, but many technicians prefer to keep point and figure charts on their wall and update them manually because doing so provides a vivid reminder of the market trend.

Point and figure charts are particularly useful for making trading decisions because they clearly illustrate price levels that may signal the end of a decline or advance. They also clearly show price levels at which a security may frequently trade. In using the point size and reversal size to make trading decisions, for uptrends, or columns of X's, the practitioner would maintain long positions. The reversal size could be considered the amount of loss that would prompt the closing of a long position and the establishment of a new short position. The larger the reversal size, the fewer columns in the chart and the longer uptrends and downtrends will run.

The box size can be varied in relation to the security price. For a security with a very low price—say, below €5—a €1 box size might mean few or no updates on the chart because the price would only rarely change by this amount. Thus, the technician could reduce the box size to cents. For highly priced securities, much larger box sizes could be used. The reversal size is a multiple of the box size, so if the box size is changed, the reversal size changes. Practitioners who want fewer columns or trade signals can use a large reversal size.

Analysis of a point and figure chart is relatively straightforward as long as the technician understands its construction and limitations. The chart is relatively simple, and repeated high and low prices are evident. Congestion areas, where a security trades up and down in a narrow range, are evidenced by a series of short columns of X's and O's spanning roughly the same price range. Major, sustained price moves are represented by long columns of X's (when prices are moving up) or O's (when prices are moving down).

3.1.5 *Scale*

For any chart—line, bar, or candlestick—the vertical axis can be constructed with either a **linear scale** (also known as an arithmetic scale) or a **logarithmic scale**, depending on how you want to view the data. With a logarithmic scale, equal vertical distances on the chart correspond to an equal percentage change. A logarithmic scale is appropriate when the data move through a range of values representing several orders of magnitude (e.g., from 10 to 10,000); a linear scale is better suited for narrower ranges (e.g., prices from $35 to $50.) The share price history of a particular company, for instance, is usually best suited to a linear scale because the data range is usually narrow.

The horizontal axis shows the passage of time. The appropriate time interval depends on the nature of the underlying data and the specific use of the chart. An active trader, for instance, may find 10-minute, 5-minute, or even tick-by-tick data useful, but other technical analysts may prefer daily or weekly data. In general, the greater the volatility of the data, the greater the likelihood that an analyst can find useful information in more-frequent data sampling.

Consider Exhibits 7 and 8, which both show the yearly history of the Dow Jones Industrial Average (DJIA) from 1928 to 2010. Plotting the index on a linear scale, as in Exhibit 7, makes it difficult to gather much information from the first 50 years of the data series. Analysts can see a slight uptrend but not much else. The eye is drawn to the bull market of the 1980s, the subsequent dot-com bubble, and the recent era of the subprime crisis. When plotted on a logarithmic scale, as in Exhibit 8, however, many people would find that the data tell a more comprehensive story. The Great Depression of the 1930s stands out, but over the following 75 years, the data follow a relatively stable upward trend.

Exhibit 7   Dow Jones Industrial Average on Linear Scale, 1928–2010 (in U.S. Dollars)

| Exhibit 8 | Dow Jones Industrial Average on Logarithmic Scale, 1928–2010 (in U.S. Dollars) |

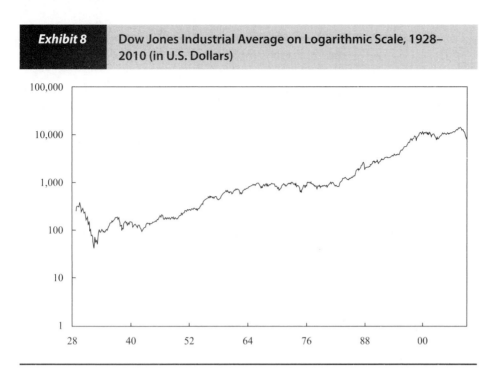

3.1.6 *Volume*

Volume is an important characteristic that is included at the bottom of many charts; see, for example Exhibit 3. Volume is used to assess the strength or conviction of buyers and sellers in determining a security's price. For example, on a daily price chart, below the price section would be a column chart showing the volume traded for that day.

Some technicians consider volume information to be crucial. If volume increases during a time frame in which price is also increasing, that combination is considered positive and the two indicators are said to "confirm" each other. The signal would be interpreted to mean that over time, more and more investors are buying the financial instrument and they are doing so at higher and higher prices. This pattern is considered a positive technical development.

Conversely, if volume and price diverge—for example, if a stock's price rises while its volume declines—the implication is that fewer and fewer market participants are willing to buy that stock at the new price. If this trend in volume continues, the price rally will soon end because demand for the security at higher prices will cease. Exhibit 9 shows a chart for Toronto-Dominion Bank (TD Bank) with volume displayed separately.

Exhibit 9	Daily Candlestick Price Chart and Volume Bar Chart: TD Bank, November 2007–November 2009 (Price in Canadian Dollars)

3.1.7 Time Intervals

Most of the chart examples in this reading are daily price charts in that they show the price and volume on a daily basis. Daily frequency is not required, however, because charts can be constructed by using any time interval. For short-term trading, the analyst can create charts with one-minute or shorter intervals. For long-term investing, the analyst can use weekly, monthly, or even annual intervals. The same analytical approach applies irrespective of the time interval. Using long intervals allows the analyst to chart longer time periods than does using short time intervals for the simple reason that long intervals contain fewer data points, so a longer time frame can be presented on the chart. Using short intervals allows the analyst to see more detail. A useful step for many analysts is to begin the analysis of a security with the chart for a long time frame, such as a weekly or monthly chart, and then construct charts with shorter and shorter time intervals, such as daily or hourly charts.

3.1.8 Relative Strength Analysis

Relative strength analysis is widely used to compare the performance of a particular asset, such as a common stock, with that of some benchmark—such as, in the case of common stocks, the FTSE 100, the Nikkei 225, or the S&P 500 Index—or the performance of another security. The intent is to show out- or underperformance of the individual issue relative to some other index or asset. Typically, the analyst prepares a line chart of the ratio of two prices, with the asset under analysis as the numerator and with the benchmark or other security as the denominator. A rising line shows the asset is performing better than the index or other stock; a declining line shows the opposite. A flat line shows neutral performance.

Suppose a private investor is researching two investment ideas she read about. Harley-Davidson Motor Company (HOG) is a well-known motorcycle company; Rodman and Renshaw (RODM) is a small investment bank. The investor wants to determine which of these two has been the stronger performer (relative to the S&P 500) over the past few months. Exhibit 10 shows relative strength lines for the two stocks for the first six months of 2009. Each point on the relative strength plot is simply the ratio of a share price to the S&P 500. For example, on 9 March 2009, HOG closed at US$8.42 and the S&P 500 closed at $676.53. The relative strength data point is, therefore, 8.42/676.53, or 0.0124. On 27 April, HOG closed at US$19.45, with the S&P 500 at $857.51. The relative strength value is 19.45/857.51, or 0.0227, nearly double the 9 March value.

Exhibit 10	Relative Strength Analysis: HOG vs. the S&P 500 and RODM vs. the S&P 500, January–June 2009

The units on the vertical axis are not significant; the ratio is a function of the relative prices of the assets under consideration. The important information is how the ratio has changed. This type of chart allows an analyst to make a visual determination of that change. As Exhibit 10 illustrates, Harley-Davidson was a strong performer in March and April but lagged the index beginning in May. In contrast, the stock of Rodman and Renshaw began a significant rise in mid-May that outperformed the market average.

3.2 Trend

The concept of a **trend** is perhaps the most important aspect of technical analysis. Trend analysis is based on the observation that market participants tend to act in herds and that trends tend to stay in place for some time. A security can be considered to be in an upward trend, a downward trend, a sideways trend, or no apparent trend. Not all securities are in a trend, and little useful forecasting information can be gleaned from technical analysis when a security is not in a trend. Not every chart will have obvious or clear implications, so the analyst must avoid the temptation to force a conclusion from every chart and thus reach a wrong interpretation.

An uptrend for a security is when the price goes to higher highs and higher lows. As the security moves up in price, each subsequent new high is higher than the prior high and each time there is a **retracement**, which is a reversal in the movement of the security's price, it must stop at a higher low than the prior lows in the trend period. To draw an uptrend line, a technician draws a line connecting the lows of the price chart. Major breakdowns in price, however, when the price drops through and below the trendline by a significant amount (many technicians use 5–10 percent below the trendline) indicate that the uptrend is over and may signal a further decline in the price. Minor breakthroughs below previous lows simply call for the line to be moderately adjusted over time. Time is also a consideration in trends: The longer the security price stays below the trendline, the more meaningful the breakdown is considered to be.

In an uptrend, the forces of demand are greater than the forces of supply. So, traders are willing to pay higher and higher prices for the same asset over time. Presumably, the strong demand indicates that investors believe the intrinsic value of the security is increasing.

A downtrend is when a security makes lower lows and lower highs. As the security moves down in price, each subsequent new high must be lower than the prior high and each time there is a retracement, it must stop at a lower low than the prior lows in the trend period. To draw a downtrend line, a technician draws a line connecting the highs of the price chart. Major breakouts above the downtrend line (e.g., 5–10 percent) indicate that the downtrend is over and a rise in the security's price may occur. And as with an uptrend, the longer the security price stays above the trendline, the more meaningful the breakout is considered to be.

In a downtrend, supply is overwhelming demand. Over time, sellers are willing to accept lower and lower prices to exit long positions or enter new short positions. Both motives of the sellers generally indicate deteriorating investor sentiment about the asset. However, selling may be prompted by factors not related to the fundamental or intrinsic value of the stock. For example, investors may be forced to sell to meet margin calls in their portfolios. From a purely technical standpoint, the reason is irrelevant. The downtrend is assumed to continue until contrary technical evidence appears. Combining fundamental analysis with technical analysis in such a case, however, might reveal a security that has attractive fundamentals but a currently negative technical position. In uptrends, however, a security with an attractive technical position but unattractive fundamentals is rare because most buying activity is driven by traders who expect the security price to increase in the future. The rare exception is covering short positions after a sizable decline in the share price.

A security may trade in a fairly narrow range, moving sideways on the price chart without much upward or downward movement. This pattern indicates a relative balance between supply and demand. A technical analyst may not expect to profit from long or short trades in such securities but might devise profitable option strategies for short-term investors with the ability to accept the risks.

Exhibit 11 shows the application of trend analysis. Depicted is an uptrend line for the shares of China Mobile Limited. Note that through late 2007, every rally took the shares to a new high, whereas sell-offs stopped at increasingly higher levels. The first sign of trouble came in the spring of 2008 when the rally terminated at a lower price point than the prior rally, of late 2007. This movement was followed by the shares breaking through the trendline.

Exhibit 11	Trend Analysis: China Mobile Weekly Price Chart, 2002–2010 (Prices in Hong Kong Dollars)

The chart in Exhibit 11 covers roughly seven years and would most likely be used by investors with a long time horizon. Investors with a shorter horizon might use a chart with a shorter time frame and would thus obtain a different trendline as well as a different trendline breakdown.

Two concepts related to trend are support and resistance. **Support** is defined as a low price range in which buying activity is sufficient to stop the decline in price. It is the opposite of **resistance**, which is a price range in which selling is sufficient to stop the rise in price. The psychology behind the concepts of support and resistance is that investors have come to a collective consensus about the price of a security. Support and resistance levels can be sloped lines, as in trendlines, or horizontal lines.

A key tenet of support and resistance as a part of technical analysis is the **change in polarity principle**, which states that once a support level is breached, it becomes a resistance level. The same holds true for resistance levels; once breached, they become support levels. For example, if the price of a security never rises above SFr10 over a long period of time and begins to decline each time it reaches this level but then finally breaks through this level by a significant amount, the point to which the price rises becomes a support level.

Support and resistance levels are commonly round numbers. Support indicates that at some price level, investors consider a security to be an attractive investment and are willing to buy, even in the wake of a sharp decline (and for resistance, at some level, investors are not willing to buy, even in an uptrend). The fact that these price points tend to be round numbers strongly suggests that human sentiment is at work.

One of the most widely publicized examples of support and resistance is when the DJIA broke through the 10,000 mark in 1999, shown in Exhibit 12. Previously, 10,000 had been viewed as a resistance line, but from 1999 through the end of the chart in 2001, 10,000 served as a support level.

Exhibit 12 Support Level: DJIA Weekly Price Chart, 1990–2001 (Price in U.S. Dollars ÷100)

3.3 Chart Patterns

Chart patterns are formations that appear in price charts that create some type of recognizable shape. Common patterns appear repeatedly and often lead to similar subsequent price movements. Thus, the identification and analysis of chart patterns is a common aspect of technical analysis used to predict security prices. An important connection to understand is that patterns form as a result of the behavior of market participants and that these patterns represent graphical depictions of the collective psychology of the market at a given time.

The recurring patterns that appear in charts can be used as a basis for market forecasting. The reason chart patterns have predictive value is that they are graphic representations of human trading activity and human behavior is frequently repeated, especially trading activity that is driven by fear (in market sell-offs) or hope and greed (as evidenced in bubbles—that is, rallies that extend well beyond valuation levels that would be derived by fundamental values). An example of a rally driven by greed is the recent real estate bubble, which took home prices to unsustainably high levels. This bubble started a few years after the internet stock bubble of the 1990s, which also took prices to unsustainably high levels. In bubbles, investors, driven by hope and greed, drive the price of an asset to irrationally high levels, in the expectation that another buyer will be willing to pay an even higher price for the asset. The housing bubble was notable because it so closely followed the internet stock bubble, despite all that had been written about the "irrational exuberance" of the internet bubble of the 1990s.

Chart patterns can be divided into two categories: **reversal patterns** and **continuation patterns**. These terms refer to the trend for the security in question prior to the formation of the pattern. The most important concept to understand in using chart patterns is that without a clear trend in place prior to the pattern, the pattern has no predictive value. This aspect is frequently forgotten by investors who are so eager to identify and use patterns that they forget the proper application of charts.

3.3.1 *Reversal Patterns*

As the name implies, a reversal pattern signals the end of a trend, a change in direction of the financial instrument's price. Evidence that the trend is about to change direction is obviously important, so reversal patterns are noteworthy.

3.3.1.1 Head and Shoulders   Perhaps the most widely recognized reversal pattern is the **head and shoulders pattern**. The pattern consists of three segments. Volume is an important characteristic in interpreting this pattern. Because head and shoulders indicates a trend reversal, a clear trend must exist prior to the formation of the pattern in order for the pattern to have predictive validity. For a head and shoulders pattern, the prior trend must be an uptrend. Later, we will discuss the *inverse* head and shoulders pattern (preceded by a downtrend).

Exhibit 13 depicts a head and shoulders pattern for Marvell Technology Group during 2006. The three parts of the pattern are as follows:

■ Left shoulder: This part appears to show a strong rally, with the slope of the rally being greater than the prior uptrend, on strong volume. The rally then reverses back to the price level where it started, forming an inverted V pattern, but on lower volume.

■ Head: The head is a more pronounced version of the left shoulder. A rally following the first shoulder takes the security to a higher high than the left shoulder by a significant enough margin to be clearly evident on the price chart. Volume is typically lower in this rally, however, than in the one that formed the first, upward side of the left shoulder. This second rally also fails, with price falling back to the same level at which the left shoulder began and ended. This price level is called the neckline. This price level also will be below the uptrend line formed by connecting the low prices in the uptrend preceding the beginning of the head and shoulders pattern. This head pattern is the first signal that the rally may be coming to an end and that a reversal may be starting.

■ Right shoulder: The right shoulder is a mirror image (or close to a mirror image) of the left shoulder but on lower volume, signifying less buying enthusiasm. The price rallies up to roughly the same level as the first shoulder, but the rally reverses at a lower high price than the rally that formed the head.

| **Exhibit 13** | Head and Shoulders Pattern: Marvell Technology Daily Price Chart, June 2005–June 2006 (Price in U.S. Dollars ÷100) |

Rarely will an analyst see a perfectly formed head and shoulders pattern; variations include two tops on the shoulders or on the head. The head, however, should rise to a higher price level than either shoulder, whereas the shoulders should be roughly symmetrical. In terms of the neckline price level, the first rally should begin at this level and the left shoulder and head should also decline to roughly this level. But necklines may not always form exactly horizontal lines. These imperfect variations make this (and other) technical patterns difficult for quantitative analysts or academicians to model, but the human brain can detect the pattern even if it is imperfectly formed.

Volume is important in analyzing head and shoulders patterns. A new high in price at the top of the head without a new high in volume signals fewer bullish market participants. When one indicator is making a new high (or low) but another is not, this situation is called **divergence**. In divergence, the right shoulder will have even lower volume, signaling that buying interest or demand is tapering off and will soon be overwhelmed by supply. The result will be a price decline.

Once the head and shoulders pattern has formed, the expectation is that the share price will decline down through the neckline price. Technicians tend to use filtering rules to make sure that a clear breakdown of the neckline has occurred. These rules may take the form of waiting to trade until the price falls to a meaningful level below the neckline (3 percent or 5 percent are commonly used) and/or a time limit for the price to remain below the neckline before trading; when a daily price chart is used, the rule may be several days to a week. Prices commonly rebound to the neckline levels, even after a decline has exceeded the filter levels. Prices generally stop, however, at or around the neckline. The neckline was a support level, and under the change in polarity principle, once a support level is breached, it becomes a resistance level.

3.3.1.2 Inverse Head and Shoulders

The head and shoulders pattern can also form upside down and act as a reversal pattern for a preceding downtrend. The three parts of the inverse head and shoulders are as follows:

- Left shoulder: This shoulder appears to show a strong decline, with the slope of the decline greater than the prior downtrend, on strong volume. The rally then reverses back to the price level where it started, forming a V pattern, but on lower volume.

- Head: The head is a more pronounced version of the left shoulder. Another decline follows but on diminishing volume, which takes the price to a lower low than the prior shoulder by a significant enough margin that it is clearly evident on the price chart. This second decline also reverses, with price rising to the same level at which the left shoulder began and ended. This price level, the neckline, will also be above the uptrend line formed by connecting the high prices in the downtrend preceding the beginning of the inverse head and shoulders pattern. This pattern is the first signal that the decline may be coming to an end and that a reversal may be near.

- Right shoulder: The right shoulder is roughly a mirror image of the left shoulder but on lower volume, signifying less selling enthusiasm. The price declines down to roughly the same level as the first shoulder, but the rally reverses at a higher low price than the rally that formed the head.

3.3.1.3 Setting Price Targets with Head and Shoulders Pattern

As with all technical patterns, the head and shoulders pattern must be analyzed from the perspective of the security's long-term price trend. The rally that happened before the formation of the pattern must be large enough for there to be something to reverse. The stronger and more pronounced the rally was, the stronger and more pronounced the reversal is likely to be. Similarly, once the neckline is breached, the security is expected to decline by the same amount as the change in price from the neckline to the top of the head. If the preceding rally started at a price higher than the neckline, however, the correction is unlikely to bring the price lower than the price level at the start of the rally. Because a head and shoulders formation is a bearish indicator (i.e., a technician would expect the previously established uptrend to end and a downtrend to commence), a technician would seek to profit by shorting the security under analysis. When attempting to profit from the head and shoulders pattern, a technician will often use the price differences between the head and the neckline to set a price target, which is the price at which the technician anticipates closing the investment position. The price target for the head and shoulders pattern is calculated as follows:

$$\text{Price target} = \text{Neckline} - (\text{Head} - \text{Neckline})$$

For example, in Exhibit 14, the high price reached at the top of the head is roughly $37 and the neckline formed at roughly $27 for a difference of $10. So a technician would expect the price to decline to a level $10 below the neckline, or to $17; that is,

$$\text{Price target} = \$27 - (\$37 - \$27) = \$17$$

| **Exhibit 14** | Calculating Price Target: Marvell Technology Daily Price Chart, June 2005–November 2006 (Price in U.S. Dollars) |

Example 1

Determining a Price Target from a Head and Shoulders Pattern

Danielle Waterhouse is the technical analyst at Kanektok Securities. One of the companies her firm follows is LPA Petroleum. Waterhouse believes that a graph of LPA's share prices over the past six months reveals a classic head and shoulders pattern. The share price peaked at US$108, and she estimates the neckline at US$79. At today's close, the shares traded at US$78. Based on the head and shoulders pattern, what price target should Waterhouse estimate?

Solution:

Waterhouse estimates the neckline at US$79, which is US$108 minus US$79, or US$29 lower than the head. Her price target is thus US$79 minus US$29, which is US$50. Waterhouse would attempt to sell LPA short at today's price of US$78 and anticipate closing the position at US$50 for a profit of US$28 per share (not accounting for transaction costs).

3.3.1.4 Setting Price Targets with Inverse Head and Shoulders Pattern   Calculating price targets for inverse head and shoulders patterns is similar to the process for head and shoulders patterns, but in this case, because the pattern predicts the end of a downtrend, the technician calculates how high the price is expected to rise once it breaches the neckline. Exhibit 15 illustrates an inverse head and shoulders pattern.

| Exhibit 15 | Calculating Price Target for Inverse Head and Shoulders Pattern: DJIA Daily Price Chart, February 2002–January 2004 (Price in U.S. Dollars ÷100) |

For an inverse head and shoulders pattern, the formula is similar to a head and shoulders pattern:

$$\text{Price target} = \text{Neckline} + (\text{Neckline} - \text{Head})$$

For example, in the price chart in Exhibit 15, the low price reached at the bottom of the head is roughly US$7,197 and the neckline formed at roughly US$9,050. The target can thus be found as $9,050 + (9,050 − $7,197) = $10,903. In this case, a technician might have taken a long position in the summer of 2003 with the hope of eventually exiting the position at about US$10,903 for a profit.

3.3.1.5 Double Tops and Bottoms   A **double top** is when an uptrend reverses twice at roughly the same high price level. Typically, volume is lower on the second high than on the first high, signaling a diminishing of demand. The longer the time is between the two tops and the deeper the sell-off is after the first top, the more significant the pattern is considered to be. Price targets can be calculated from this pattern in a manner similar to the calculation for the head and shoulders pattern. For a double top, price is expected to decline below the low of the valley between the two tops by at least the distance from the valley low to the high of the double tops.

Example 2

Determining a Price Target from a Double-Top Pattern

Richard Dupuis is a technician who trades Eurodollar futures for his own account. He analyzes charts based on one-minute time intervals looking for short-term trading opportunities. Eurodollar futures contracts have been trending upward most of the morning, but Dupuis now observes what he believes is a double-top pattern: After peaking at US$97.03, the futures contract price fell to US$96.42, climbed again to US$97.02, and then started a decline. Because of the double top, Dupuis anticipates a reversal from the uptrend to a downtrend. Dupuis decides to open a short position to capitalize on the anticipated trend reversal. What price target should Dupuis estimate for closing the position?

Solution:

Dupuis estimates the price target as $96.42 – ($97.02 – $96.42) = $95.82.

Double bottoms are formed when the price reaches a low, rebounds, and then sells off back to the first low level. Exhibit 16 depicts a double-bottom pattern for Time Warner. Technicians use the double bottom to predict a change from a downtrend to an uptrend in security prices. For double bottoms, the price is expected to appreciate above the peak between the two bottoms by at least the distance from the valley lows to the peak.

Exhibit 16	Double-Bottom Pattern: Time Warner Daily Price Chart, November 2007–October 2009 (Price in U.S. Dollars)

The reason these patterns are significant is that they show that at some price point, investors step in to reverse trends that are under way. For an uptrend, a double top implies that at some price point, enough traders are willing to either sell positions (or enter new short positions) that their activities overwhelm and reverse the uptrend created by demand for the shares. A reasonable conclusion is that this price level has been fundamentally derived and that it represents the intrinsic value of the security that is the consensus of investors. With double bottoms, if a security ceases to decline at the same price point on two separate occasions, the analyst can conclude that the market consensus is that at that price point, the security is now cheap enough that it is an attractive investment.

3.3.1.6 Triple Tops and Bottoms   **Triple tops** consist of three peaks at roughly the same price level, and **triple bottoms** consist of three troughs at roughly the same price level. A triple top for Rockwell Automation during 1999 is shown in Exhibit 17.

Exhibit 17	Triple-Top Pattern: Rockwell Automation Daily Price Chart, 1999 (Price in U.S. Dollars)

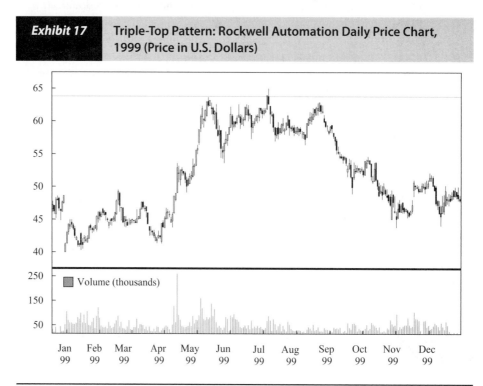

One of the challenges in double-top and triple-top patterns, and one of the valid criticisms of technical analysis in general, is that an analyst cannot know which pattern will result until after the fact. For example, after the broad equity market sell-off in the first quarter of 2009, a number of investment professionals were quoted as calling for a "retest of the lows"—in technical terms, a double bottom.

There is no evidence that market corrections (or rallies) must end with a double bottom (or double top in the case of an uptrend), and there is no generally accepted technical theory that predicts whether a low will be repeated once or even twice before a reversal occurs. A double bottom is considered to be a more significant pattern than a single bottom because traders have stepped in on two occasions to halt declines. However, traders have no way to determine whether a double top or bottom will be followed by a third top or bottom. Triple tops and triple bottoms are rare, but when they occur, they are more significant reversal patterns than double tops or double bottoms. On three separate occasions, traders stepped in to sell or buy shares with enough volume to end a rally or decline under way at the time. Nevertheless, the greater the number of times the price reverses at the same level, and the greater the time interval over which this pattern occurs, the greater the significance of the pattern.

3.3.2 *Continuation Patterns*

A **continuation pattern** is used to predict the resumption of a market trend that was in place prior to the formation of a pattern. From a supply-and-demand standpoint, a continuation pattern indicates a change in ownership from one group of investors to another. For example, if a positive trend was in place prior to a pattern and then one group of investors begins selling, the negative impact on price is quickly offset by other investors buying, so the forces of supply and demand go back and forth in terms of their impact on price. But neither has an overwhelming advantage. This type of pattern is often called "a healthy correction" because the long-term market trend does not change and because while one set of investors is seeking to exit, they are replaced by another set of investors willing to take their positions at roughly the same share price.

3.3.2.1 Triangles   **Triangle patterns** are a type of continuation pattern. They come in three forms, symmetrical triangles, ascending triangles, and descending triangles. A triangle pattern forms as the range between high and low prices narrows, visually forming a triangle. In old terminology, triangles were referred to as "coils" (which was also synonymous with "springs") because a triangle was considered analogous to a spring being wound up tighter and tighter and storing energy that would at some point be released. In a triangle, a trendline connects the highs and a trendline connects the lows. As the distance between the highs and lows narrows, the trendlines meet, forming a triangle. In a daily price chart, a triangle pattern usually forms over a period of several weeks.

In an ascending triangle, as shown in Exhibit 18, the trendline connecting the high prices is horizontal and the trendline connecting the low prices forms an uptrend. What this pattern means is that market participants are selling the stock at the same price level over a period of time, putting a halt to rallies at the same price point, but that buyers are getting more and more bullish and stepping in at increasingly higher prices to halt sell-offs instead of waiting for further price declines. An ascending triangle typically forms in an uptrend. The horizontal line represents sellers taking profits at around the same price point, presumably because they believe that this price represents the fundamental, intrinsic value of the security. The fact that the rally continues beyond the triangle may be a bullish signal; it means that another set of investors is presumably willing to buy at an even higher price because their analysis suggests the intrinsic value of the security is higher. Alternatively, the fundamental facts themselves may have changed; that is, the security's fundamental value may be increasing over time. The technician does not care which explanation is true; the technician is relying solely on the information conveyed by the security price itself, not the underlying reason.

Exhibit 18	**Ascending Triangle Pattern**

In the descending triangle, shown in Exhibit 19, the low prices form a horizontal trendline and the high prices form a series of lower and lower highs. Typically, a descending triangle will form in a downtrend. At some point in the sell-offs, buyers appear with enough demand to halt sell-offs each time they occur, at around the same price. Again, this phenomenon may be the result of fundamental analysts believing that the security has reached a price where it represents a significant discount to its intrinsic value and these analysts step in and buy. As the triangle forms, each rally ceases at a lower and lower high price point, suggesting the selling demand is exerting greater price influence than buying demand.

Exhibit 19	Descending Triangle

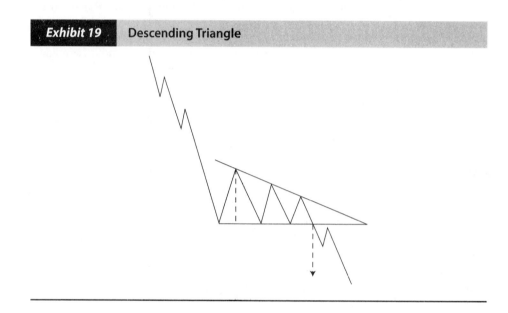

In a symmetrical triangle, the trendline formed by the highs angles down and the trendline formed by the lows angles up, both at roughly the same angle, forming a symmetrical pattern. Exhibit 20 contains a symmetrical triangle formed by the price for Transocean in early 2000. What this triangle indicates is that buyers are becoming more bullish while, simultaneously, sellers are becoming more bearish, so they are moving toward a point of consensus. Because the sellers are often dominated by long investors exiting positions (as opposed to short sellers creating new short positions), the pressure to sell diminishes once the sellers have sold the security. Thus, the pattern ends in the same direction as the trend that preceded it, either uptrend or downtrend.

Exhibit 20	Symmetrical Triangle Pattern: Transocean Weekly Price Chart, June 1999–June 2000 (Price in U.S. Dollars)

The term "measuring implication" refers to the height of a triangle, as illustrated with a dark vertical bar in Exhibit 20. The measuring implication is derived by calculating the difference in price from the two trendlines at the start of the triangle. Once the pattern is broken and the price breaks through one of the trendlines that form the triangle, the analyst expects the price to move by at least the amount of the breakthrough above or below the trendline. Typically, price breaks out of a triangle pattern between halfway and three-quarters of the way through the pattern. The longer the triangle pattern persists, the more volatile and sustained the subsequent price movement is likely to be.

3.3.2.2 Rectangle Pattern   A rectangle pattern is a continuation pattern formed by two parallel trendlines, one formed by connecting the high prices during the pattern, and the other formed by the lows. Exhibit 21 shows two rectangle patterns. As is the case with other patterns, the rectangle pattern is a graphical representation of what has been occurring in terms of collective market sentiment. The horizontal resistance line that forms the top of the rectangle shows that investors are repeatedly selling shares at a specific price level, bringing rallies to an end. The horizontal support line forming the bottom of the rectangle indicates that traders are repeatedly making large enough purchases at the same price level to reverse declines. The support level in a bullish rectangle is natural because the long-term trend in the market is bullish. The resistance line may simply represent investors taking profits. Conversely, in a bearish rectangle, the support level may represent investors buying the security. Again, the technician is not concerned with why a pattern has formed, only with the likely next price movement once the price breaks out of the pattern.

Exhibit 21	Rectangle Patterns

Bullish Rectangle   Bearish Rectangle

3.3.2.3 Flags and Pennants

Flags and **pennants** are considered minor continuation patterns because they form over short periods of time—on a daily price chart, typically over a week. They are similar to each other and have the same uses. A flag is formed by parallel trendlines, in the same way that most countries' flags are rectangular and create a parallelogram. Typically, the trendlines slope in a direction opposite to the trend up to that time; for example, in an uptrend, they slope down. A pennant formation is similar except that the trendlines converge to form a triangle, similar to the pennants of many sports teams or pennants flown on ships. The key difference between a triangle and pennant is that a pennant is a short-term formation whereas a triangle is a long-term formation.

The expectation for both flags and pennants is that the trend will continue after the pattern in the same direction it was going prior to the pattern. The price is expected to change by at least the same amount as the price change from the start of the trend to the formation of the flag or pennant. In Exhibit 22, a downtrend begins at point A, which is $104. At point B, which is $70, a pennant begins to form. The distance from point A to point B is $34. The pennant ends at point C, which is $76. The price target is $76 minus $34, which is $42, the line labeled D.

| Exhibit 22 | Pennant Formation: China Mobile ADR, November 2006–July 2009 (Price in U.S. Dollars) |

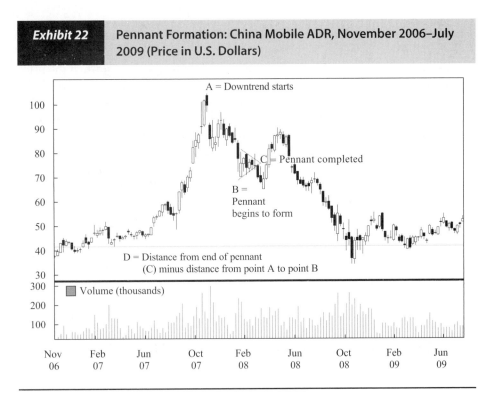

3.4 Technical Indicators

The technical analyst uses a variety of technical indicators to supplement the information gleaned from charts. A technical indicator is any measure based on price, market sentiment, or funds flow that can be used to predict changes in price. These indicators often have a supply-and-demand underpinning; that is, they measure how potential changes in supply and demand might affect a security's price.

3.4.1 Price-Based Indicators

Price-based indicators somehow incorporate information contained in the current and past history of market prices. Indicators of this type range from simple (e.g., a moving average) to complex (e.g., a stochastic oscillator).

3.4.1.1 Moving Average   A **moving average** is the average of the closing price of a security over a specified number of periods. Moving averages smooth out short-term price fluctuations, giving the technician a clearer image of market trend. Technicians commonly use a simple moving average, which weights each price equally in the calculation of the average price. Some technicians prefer to use an exponential moving average (also called an exponentially smoothed moving average), which gives the greatest weight to recent prices while giving exponentially less weight to older prices.

The number of data points included in the moving average depends on the intended use of the moving average. A 20-day moving average is commonly used because a month contains roughly 20 trading days. Also, 60 days is commonly used because it represents a quarter year (three months) of trading activity.

Moving averages can be used in conjunction with a price trend or in conjunction with one another. Moving averages are also used to determine support and resistance.

Because a moving average is less volatile than price, this tool can be used in several ways. First, whether price is above or below its moving average is important. A security that has been trending down in price will trade below its moving average, and a security that has been trending up will trade above its moving average. Second, the distance between the moving-average line and price is also significant. Once price begins to move back up toward its moving-average line, this line can serve as a resistance level. The 65-day moving-average line is commonly cited in the press, and when the price approaches the moving-average line, many investors become concerned that a rally will stall, so they sell the security.

Two or more moving averages can be used in conjunction. Exhibit 23 shows the price chart of Gazprom SP European Depositary Receipts (EDRs) on the Frankfurt Stock Exchange overlaid with 20-day and 60-day EDR moving averages for late 2007 to mid-2009.[5] Note that the longer the time frame used in the creation of a moving average, the smoother and less volatile the line. Investors often use moving-average crossovers as a buy or sell signal. When a short-term moving average crosses from underneath a longer-term average, this movement is considered bullish and is termed a **golden cross**. Conversely, when a short-term moving average crosses from above a longer-term moving average, this movement is considered bearish and is called a **dead cross**. In the case shown in Exhibit 23, a trading strategy of buying on golden crosses and selling on dead crosses would have been profitable.

Exhibit 23	**Daily Price Chart with 20-Day and 60-Day Moving Averages: Gazprom EDR, November 2007–August 2009 (Price in Euros)**

Moving averages are easy to construct, and simple trading rules can be derived for using them. Computers can optimize what time lengths to set when using two moving averages. This optimization may take the form of changing the number of days included in each moving average or adding filter rules, such as waiting several days after a trade signal is given to make a trade. Reasons for optimization include the desire to manage capital drawdowns, to maximize gains, or to minimize losses. Once the moving average is optimized, even if a profitable trading system is devised for that security, the strategy is unlikely to work for other securities, especially if they are dissimilar. Also, as market conditions change, a previously optimized trading system may no longer work.

---

5 A European Depositary Receipt is a negotiable certificate issued by a depositary bank in one country against equity that is traded on the stock exchange of another country.

3.4.1.2 Bollinger Bands   Market veteran John Bollinger combined his knowledge of technical analysis with his knowledge of statistics to create an indicator called **Bollinger Bands**. Bollinger Bands consist of a moving average plus a higher line representing the moving average plus a set number of standard deviations from average price (for the same number of periods as used to calculate the moving average) and a lower line that is a moving average minus the same number of standard deviations. Exhibit 24 depicts Bollinger Bands for the Gazprom EDR.

Exhibit 24	Bollinger Band Using 60-Day Moving Average and Two Standard Deviations: Gazprom EDR Daily Price Chart, November 2007–August 2009 (Price in Euros)

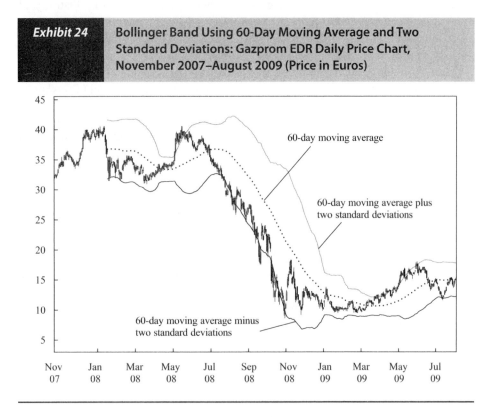

The more volatile the security being analyzed becomes, the wider the range becomes between the two outer lines or bands. Similar to moving averages, Bollinger Bands can be used to create trading strategies that can be easily computerized and tested. A common use is as a contrarian strategy, in which the investor sells when a security price reaches the upper band and buys when it reaches the lower band. This strategy assumes that the security price will stay within the bands.

This type of strategy is likely to lead to a large number of trades, but it also limits risk because the trader can quickly exit unprofitable trades. In the event of a sharp price move and a change in trend, however, a contrarian strategy based on Bollinger Bands would be unprofitable. So, long-term investors might actually buy on a significant breakout above the upper boundary band because a major breakout would imply a change in trend likely to persist for some time. The long-term investor would sell on a significant breakout below the lower band. In this strategy, significance would be defined as breaking above or below the band by a certain percentage (say, 5 percent or 10 percent) and/or for a certain period of time (say, a week for a daily price chart). Again, such rules can easily be computerized and tested.

3.4.2 *Momentum Oscillators*

One of the key challenges in using indicators overlaid on a price chart is the difficulty of discerning changes in market sentiment that are out of the ordinary. **Momentum oscillators** are intended to alleviate this problem. They are constructed from price data, but they are calculated so that they either oscillate between a high and low (typically 0 and 100) or oscillate around a number (such as 0 or 100). Because of this construction, extreme highs or lows are easily discernible. These extremes can be viewed as graphic representations of market sentiment when selling or buying activity is more aggressive than historically typical. Because they are price based, momentum oscillators also can be analyzed by using the same tools technicians use to analyze price, such as the concepts of trend, support, and resistance.

Technicians also look for **convergence** or **divergence** between oscillators and price. Convergence is when the oscillator moves in the same manner as the security being analyzed, and divergence is when the oscillator moves differently from the security. For example, when price reaches a new high, this sign is considered bullish, but if the momentum oscillator being used does not also reach a new high at the same time, this pattern is divergence. It is considered to be an early warning of weakness, an indication that the uptrend may soon end.

Momentum oscillators should be used in conjunction with an understanding of the existing market (price) trend. Oscillators alert a trader to **overbought** or **oversold** conditions. In an overbought condition, market sentiment is unsustainably bullish. In an oversold condition, market sentiment is unsustainably bearish. In other words, the oscillator *range* must be considered separately for every security. Some securities may experience wide variations, and others may experience only minor variations.

Oscillators have three main uses. First, oscillators can be used to determine the strength of a trend. Extreme overbought levels are warning signals for uptrends, and extreme oversold levels are warning signals for downtrends. Second, when oscillators reach historically high or low levels, they may be signaling a pending trend reversal. For oscillators that move above and below 0, crossing the 0 level signals a change in the direction of the trend. For oscillators that move above and below 100, crossing the 100 level signals a change in the direction of the trend. Third, in a non-trending market, oscillators can be used for short-term trading decisions—that is, to sell at overbought levels and to buy at oversold levels.

3.4.2.1 Momentum or Rate of Change Oscillator   The terms *momentum oscillator* and *rate of change oscillator* are synonymous. "Rate of change" is often abbreviated ROC. The ROC oscillator is calculated by taking the most recent closing price, subtracting the closing price from a prior date that is a set number of days in the past, and multiplying the result by 100:

$$M = (V - Vx) \times 100$$

where

   M = momentum oscillator value
   V = last closing price
   Vx = closing price x days ago, typically 10 days

When the ROC oscillator crosses zero in the same direction as the direction of the trend, this movement is considered a buy or sell signal. For example, if the ROC oscillator crosses into positive territory during an uptrend, it is a buy signal. If it enters into negative territory during a downtrend, it is considered a sell signal. The technician will ignore crossovers in opposition to the trend because the technician must *always* first take into account the general trend when using oscillators.

An alternative method of constructing this oscillator is to set it so that it oscillates above and below 100, instead of 0, as follows:

$$M = \frac{V}{Vx} \times 100$$

This approach is shown in Exhibit 25 for Toyota Motor Corporation.

Exhibit 25	Momentum Oscillator with 100 as Midpoint: Toyota Motor, May 2008–October 2009 (Price in Japanese Yen)

In Exhibit 25, the calculation method for the ROC oscillator for Toyota stock, traded on the Tokyo Stock Exchange, is for the oscillator to move around 100 and x is 12 days. Note that for this stock, the ROC oscillator tends to maintain a range between ¥85 and ¥115. So episodes when the oscillator moves outside this range are of particular interest to the technician. An extreme high means that the stock has posted its highest gain in any 12-day period at this point, and an extreme low reading means it has posted its greatest loss over any 12-day period. When investors bid up the price of a security too rapidly, the indication is that sentiment may be unduly bullish and the market may be overbought. Exhibit 25 shows that overbought levels of the ROC oscillator coincide with temporary highs in the stock price. So, those levels would have been signals to sell the stock. The other notable aspect of Exhibit 25 is the divergence when the share price hit a new low in December 2008 but the ROC oscillator did not. This divergence would have been a bullish signal and would have been interpreted to mean that, although the share price hit a new low, investor sentiment was actually higher than it had been previously. In itself, this information would not have been enough to warrant buying the shares because a downtrend in price was still in place, but it alerted the technician to the fact that the trend might end soon. The technician could then look for further indication of the trend's end and, with confirmation, might buy the stock.

3.4.2.2 Relative Strength Index

A **relative strength index** (RSI) is computed over a rolling time period.[6] It graphically compares a security's gains with its losses over the set period. The creator of the RSI, Welles Wilder, suggested a 14-day time period,

---

6 This indicator is sometimes called the Wilder RSI.

and this period is generally the period used in most technical analysis software. The technician should understand that this variable can be changed and that the optimal time range should be determined by how the technician intends to use the RSI information. Factors that influence selection of the time period are similar to those that influence the selection of a time period for moving averages. Short time periods (such as 14 days) provide information about short-term price behavior. If 200 days is used, this short-term information will be smoothed out and, perhaps, will not be apparent at all.

RSI is a momentum oscillator and is not to be confused with the charting method called "relative strength analysis," in which the ratio of two security prices is plotted over time. The RSI provides information on whether or not an asset is overbought. The formula for the RSI is not intuitive and is best understood with an example. The formula is:

$$RSI = 100 - \frac{100}{1 + RS}$$

where $RS = \dfrac{\sum(\text{Up changes for the period under consideration})}{\sum(|\text{Down changes for the period under consideration}|)}$

Exhibit 26 shows closing prices for Ford Motor Company during the month of June 2009.

Exhibit 26	Computation of RSI: Ford, June 2009		
Date	**Close**	**Up Changes**	**Down Changes**
6/1/2009	6.13		
6/2/2009	6.41	0.28	
6/3/2009	6.18		−0.23
6/4/2009	6.36	0.18	
6/5/2009	6.36		
6/8/2009	6.38	0.02	
6/9/2009	6.26		−0.12
6/10/2009	6.19		−0.07
6/11/2009	5.98		−0.21
6/12/2009	6.11	0.13	
6/15/2009	5.93		−0.18
6/16/2009	5.67		−0.26
6/17/2009	5.71	0.04	
6/18/2009	5.68		−0.03
6/19/2009	5.72	0.04	
6/22/2009	5.38		−0.34
6/23/2009	5.53	0.15	
6/24/2009	5.63	0.10	
6/25/2009	5.68	0.05	
6/26/2009	5.61		−0.07
6/29/2009	5.78	0.17	
6/30/2009	6.07	**0.29**	
		1.45	−1.51

During this time, markets were still rebounding from the subprime crisis; auto-mobile company stocks were unusually volatile and, to some speculators, presented interesting short-term trading opportunities. Suppose a trader decided to compute an RSI for the month of June. It would be a 22-day RSI with 21 price changes—11 up, 9 down, and 1 unchanged. To calculate the RSI, the trader would sum the 11 up changes, which sum to US$1.45. The down changes total – US$1.51; the absolute value drops the minus sign. The ratio of these two numbers is 0.96, so the RSI is

$$RSI = 100 - \frac{100}{1+0.96} = 100 - 51.02 = 48.98$$

The index construction forces the RSI to lie within 0 and 100. A value above 70 represents an overbought situation. Values below 30 suggest the asset is oversold. Again, as is the case with most technical tools, an analyst cannot simply learn the default settings and use them in every case. The 30–70 range is a good rule of thumb, but because the oscillator is a measure of volatility, less volatile stocks (such as utili-ties) may normally trade in a much narrower range. More volatile stocks (such as small-capitalization technology stocks) may trade in a wider range. The range also does not have to be symmetrical around 50. For example, in an uptrend, one might see a range of 40–80 but in downtrends, a range of 20–60.

The RSI measure often appears at the bottom or top of a price chart. Exhibit 27 shows a candlestick chart of Ford stock in 2009 with the corresponding RSI.

Exhibit 27 **Candlestick Chart with RSI: Ford, January–August 2009 (Price in U.S. Dollars)**

The candlestick chart of Ford stock prices in Exhibit 27 illustrates several aspects of the use of an RSI. For example, because the RSI oscillator was higher than 70 on 23 March so the stock was overbought at that time, a simple reading of the chart might have led to the conclusion that the trader should sell the stock. Doing so, however, would have caused the trader to miss a significant advance in the shares. A more careful technical analysis that took into account the trend would have indicated that the stock was in an uptrend, so RSI readings above 70 could be expected.

Because RSI is a price-based oscillator, the trader can also apply trend lines to analyze it. Note in Exhibit 27 that both the share price and the RSI oscillator were in uptrends from February until April but that the RSI uptrend was broken on 15 April, a potential warning that the uptrend in price might also break downward. In June, the share price broke its uptrend support line.

3.4.2.3 Stochastic Oscillator

The stochastic oscillator is based on the observation that in uptrends, prices tend to close at or near the high end of their recent range and in downtrends, they tend to close near the low end. The logic behind these patterns is that if the shares of a stock are constantly being bid up during the day but then lose value by the close, continuation of the rally is doubtful. If sellers have enough supply to overwhelm buyers, the rally is suspect. If a stock rallies during the day and is able to hold on to some or most of those gains by the close, that sign is bullish.

The stochastic oscillator oscillates between 0 and 100 and has a default setting of a 14-day period, which, again, might be adjusted for the situation as we discussed for the RSI. The oscillator is composed of two lines, called %K and %D, that are calculated as follows:

$$\%K = 100 \left(\frac{C - L14}{H14 - L14} \right)$$

where

C = latest closing price
$L14$ = lowest price in past 14 days
$H14$ = highest price in past 14 days

and

%D = average of the last three %K values calculated daily

Analysts should think about the %D in the same way they would a long-term moving-average line in conjunction with a short-term line. That is, %D, because it is the average of three %K values, is the slower moving, smoother line and is called the signal line. And %K is the faster moving line. The %K value means that the latest closing price (C) was in the %K percentile of the high–low range ($L14$ to $H14$).

The default oversold–overbought range for the stochastic oscillator is based on reading the signal line relative to readings of 20 and 80, but warnings about always using the default range for the RSI oscillator also apply in the case of the stochastic oscillator. In fact, noted technician Constance Brown has coined a term called the "stochastics default club" to refer to neophyte technicians who trade based solely on these defaults.[7] She has reported being able to develop successful trading strategies by using a time frame shorter than the 14-day default to calculate the stochastic oscillator. Apparently, enough traders are basing trades on the defaults to move the market for certain stocks. So, using shorter time frames than the default, she could trade ahead of the traders in the default stochastic club and generate a profit. Of course, other traders might be tempted to use an even shorter time frame, but there is a drawback to using a short time frame; namely, the shorter the time frame is, the more volatile the oscillator becomes and the more false signals it generates.

The stochastic oscillator should be used with other technical tools, such as trend analysis or pattern analysis. If both methods suggest the same conclusion, the trader has convergence (or confirmation), but if they give conflicting signals, the trader has divergence, which is a warning signal suggesting that further analysis is necessary.

---

7 Brown, Constance. *Technical Analysis for the Trading Professional.* McGraw-Hill, 1999.

The absolute level of the two lines should be considered in light of their normal range. Movements above this range indicate to a technician an overbought security and are considered bearish; movements below this range indicate an oversold security and are considered bullish. Crossovers of the two lines can also give trading signals the same way crossovers of two moving averages give signals. When the %K moves from below the %D line to above it, this move is considered a bullish short-term trading signal; conversely, when %K moves from above the %D line to below it, this pattern is considered bearish. In practice, a trader can use technical analysis software to adjust trading rules and optimize the calculation of the stochastic oscillator for a particular security and investment purpose (e.g., short-term trading or long-term investing).

The reason technicians use historical data to test their trading rules and find the optimal parameters for each security is that each security is different. The group of market participants actively trading differs from security to security. Just as each person has a different personality, so do groups of people. In effect, the groups of active market participants trading each security are imparting their personality on the trading activity for that security. As this group changes over time, the ideal parameters for a particular security may change.

Exhibit 28 provides a good example of how the stochastic oscillator can be used together with trend analysis. The exhibit provides the weekly price chart and stochastic oscillator for Petroleo Brasileiro ADRs, which are traded on the New York Stock Exchange, for June 2008 through June 2009. Note that during the downtrend on the left side of the chart the stochastic oscillator often moved below 20. Each time it reached 80, however, it provided a valid sell signal. When the downtrend ended in November 2008 and an uptrend began, the stochastic oscillator was regularly moving above 80, but each time the %K line moved above %D, a valid buy signal was given.

Exhibit 28	**Weekly Price Chart and Stochastic Oscillator: Petroleo Brasileiro ADR, June 2008–July 2009 (Price in U.S. Dollars)**

3.4.2.4 Moving-Average Convergence/Divergence Oscillator The **moving-average convergence/divergence** oscillator is commonly referred to as MACD, which is pronounced Mack Dee. The MACD is the difference between a short-term and a long-term moving average of the security's price. The MACD is constructed by calculating two lines, the MACD line and the signal line:

- MACD line: difference between two exponentially smoothed moving averages, generally 12 and 26 days.
- Signal line: exponentially smoothed average of MACD line, generally 9 days.

The indicator oscillates around zero and has no upper or lower limit. Rather than using a set overbought–oversold range for MACD, the analyst compares the current level with the historical performance of the oscillator for a particular security to determine when a security is out of its normal sentiment range.

MACD is used in technical analysis in three ways. The first is to note crossovers of the MACD line and the signal line, as discussed for moving averages and the stochastic oscillator. Crossovers of the two lines may indicate a change in trend. The second is to look for times when the MACD is outside its normal range for a given security. The third is to use trend lines on the MACD itself. When the MACD is trending in the same direction as price, this pattern is convergence, and when the two are trending in opposite directions, the pattern is divergence.

Exhibit 29 shows a daily price chart of Exxon Mobil (at the top) with the MACD oscillator for March through October of 2005. Note the convergence in the bottoming of both the oscillator and price in May, which provided confirmation of a change in trend. This change was further confirmed by the MACD line crossing above the signal line. A bearish signal was given in September with the change in trend of both price and the oscillator and the crossover of the signal line by the MACD line. The fact that the MACD oscillator was moving up to a level that was unusually high for this stock would have been an early warning signal in September.

Exhibit 29 MACD and Daily Price Chart: Exxon Mobil, March–November 2005 (Price in U.S. Dollars)

3.4.3 *Sentiment Indicators*

Sentiment indicators attempt to gauge investor activity for signs of increasing bull-ishness or bearishness. Sentiment indicators come in two forms—investor polls and calculated statistical indices.

3.4.3.1 Opinion Polls A wide range of services conduct periodic polls of either individual investors or investment professionals to gauge their sentiment about the equity market. The most common of the polls are the Investors Intelligence Advisors Sentiment reports, Market Vane Bullish Consensus, Consensus Bullish Sentiment Index, and Daily Sentiment Index, all of which poll investment professionals, and reports of the American Association of Individual Investors (AAII), which polls individual investors. All but the AAII survey are subscription-based services. *Barron's* magazine publishes data from four of these surveys on a weekly basis.

By regularly polling, compiling these data over time, and presenting it graphically, these services provide technicians with an analyzable snapshot of investor sentiment over time. Technicians look at prior market activity and compare it with highs or lows in sentiment, as well as inflection points in sentiment, as a gauge when they are forecasting the future direction of the market.

The most widely used investor polls are all U.S.-based. One reason is that inter-pretation of the surveys is determined by comparing the survey results with market performance over time. To gauge a survey's usefulness in predicting major market turns, the survey must have been published over several cycles, and each of the surveys mentioned here, based on U.S. data, has been available for several decades.

3.4.3.2 Calculated Statistical Indices The other category of sentiment indicators are indicators that are calculated from market data, such as security prices. The two most commonly used are derived from the options market; they are the put/call ratio and the volatility index. Additionally, many analysts look at margin debt and short interest.

The **put/call ratio** is the volume of put options traded divided by the volume of call options traded for a particular financial instrument. Investors who buy put options on a security are presumably bearish, and investors who buy call options are presumably bullish. The volume in call options is greater than the volume traded in put options over time, so the put/call ratio is normally below 1.0. The ratio is considered to be a contrarian indicator, meaning that higher values are considered bearish and lower values are considered bullish. But, its usefulness as a contrarian indicator is limited except at extreme low or high levels in relation to the historical trading level of the put/call ratio for a particular financial instrument. The actual value of the put/call ratio, and its normal range, differs for each security or market, so no standard definitions of overbought or oversold levels exist. At extreme lows where call option volume is significantly greater than put option volume, market sentiment is said to be so overly positive that a correction is likely. At extreme highs in the put/call ratio, market sentiment is said to be so extremely negative that an increase in price is likely.

The **CBOE Volatility Index** (VIX) is a measure of near-term market volatility cal-culated by the Chicago Board Options Exchange. Since 2003, it has been calculated from option prices on the stocks in the S&P 500. The VIX rises when market partici-pants become fearful of an impending market decline. These participants then bid up the price of puts, and the result is an increase in the VIX level. Technicians use the VIX in conjunction with trend, pattern, or oscillator tools, and it is interpreted from a contrarian perspective. When other indicators suggest that the market is oversold and the VIX is at an extreme high, this combination is considered bullish. Exhibit 30 shows the VIX from March 2005 to December 2009.

Exhibit 30	VIX, March 2005–December 2009

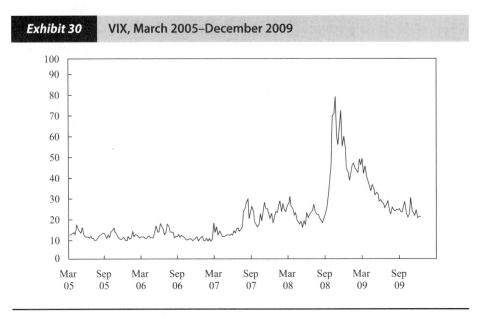

Margin debt is also often used as an indication of sentiment. As a group, investors have a history of buying near market tops and selling at the bottom. When the market is rising and indices reach new highs, investors are motivated to buy more equities in the hope of participating in the market rally. A margin account permits an investor to borrow part of the investment cost from the brokerage firm. This debt magnifies the gains or losses resulting from the investment.

Investor psychology plays an important role in the intuition behind margin debt as an indicator. When stock margin debt is increasing, investors are aggressively buying and stock prices will move higher because of increased demand. Eventually, the margin traders use all of their available credit, so their buying power (and, therefore, demand) decreases, which fuels a price decline. Falling prices may trigger margin calls and forced selling, thereby driving prices even lower.

Brokerage firms must report activity in their customers' margin accounts, so keeping track of borrowing behavior is relatively easy. Exhibit 31 provides a 10-year comparison of margin debt with the S&P 500. The correlation is striking: Rising margin debt is generally associated with a rising index level, and falling margin debt is associated with a falling index level. In fact, for the 113 months shown in Exhibit 31, the correlation coefficient between the levels of margin debt and the S&P 500 is 80.2 percent. When margin debt peaked in the summer of 2007, the market also topped out. Margin debt dropped sharply during the latter part of 2008 as the subprime crisis took the market down. Investors began to use borrowed funds again in the first half of 2009 when heavily discounted shares became increasingly attractive. Margin debt was still well below the average of the last decade, but the upturn would be viewed as a bullish sign by advocates of this indicator.

Exhibit 31	Margin Debt in U.S. Markets vs. S&P 500, 2000–2009

Source: New York Stock Exchange Fact Book.

Short interest is another commonly used sentiment indicator. Investors sell shares short when they believe the share prices will decline. Brokerage firms must report short-sale activity, and these statistics are aggregated and reported by the exchanges and the financial press on a monthly basis. The number of shares of a particular security that are currently sold short is called "short interest." The short interest ratio represents the number of days of trading activity represented by short interest. To facilitate comparisons of large and small companies, common practice is to "normalize" this value by dividing short interest by average daily trading volume to get the short interest ratio:

Short interest ratio = Short interest/Average daily trading volume

Example 3

Short Interest Ratio

At the end of September 2009, *Barron's* reported short interest of 10,936,467 shares in Goldman Sachs, with average daily trading volume of 9,086,174. At the same time, the short interest in TD Bank was 20,420,166 on average trading volume of 1,183,558 shares. Calculate the short interest ratio for both firms.

Solution:

The short interest ratio for Goldman Sachs was 10,936,467 divided by 9,086,174, or 1.2 days. For TD Bank, the short interest ratio was 20,420,166 divided by 1,183,558, or 17.25 days.

There are differences of opinion about how to interpret short interest as an indicator. It is considered to show market sentiment and to be a contrarian indicator. Some people believe that if a large number of shares are sold short and the short interest ratio is high, the market should expect a falling price for the shares because of so much negative sentiment about them. A counter-argument is that, although the short sellers are bearish on the security, the effect of their short sales has already been felt in the security price. The short sellers' next action will be to buy shares back to cover their short positions. When the short sellers cover their positions, those actions will provide a boost to the share price. Therefore, the short interest ratio constitutes future (and known) demand for the shares.

Regardless of the analyst's perspective, in Example 3, the TD Bank short interest ratio of approximately 17 is more noteworthy than the much lower figure for Goldman Sachs.

3.4.4 *Flow-of-Funds Indicators*

Technicians look at fund flows as a way to gauge the potential supply and demand for equities. Demand can come in the form of margin borrowing against current holdings or cash holdings by mutual funds and other groups that are normally large holders of equities, such as insurance companies and pension funds. The more cash these groups hold, the more bullish is the indication for equities. One caveat in looking at potential sources of demand is that, although these data indicate the potential buying power of various large investor groups, the data say nothing about the likelihood that the groups will buy.

On the supply side, technicians look at new or secondary issuance of stock because these activities put more securities into the market and increase supply.

3.4.4.1 Arms Index   A common flow of funds indicator is the **Arms Index**, also called the **TRIN** (for "short-term trading index").[8] This indicator is applied to a broad market (such as the S&P 500) to measure the relative extent to which money is moving into or out of rising and declining stocks. The index is a ratio of two ratios:

$$\text{Arms Index} = \frac{\text{Number of advancing issues} \div \text{Number of declining issues}}{\text{Volume of advancing issues} \div \text{Volume of declining issues}}$$

When this index is near 1.0, the market is in balance; that is, as much money is moving into rising stocks as into declining stocks. A value above 1.0 means that there is more volume in declining stocks; a value below 1.0 means that most trading activity is in rising stocks. Exhibit 32 shows the Arms Index for the S&P 500 on a daily basis for the first six months of 2009. The majority of the points lie above the 1.0 level, suggesting that the market continued to be in a selling mood. Note that the up spikes are associated with large price decreases in the index level and the down spikes reflect the opposite. The trendline shows a slightly negative slope, providing some slight encouragement for the bulls.

---

8 This tool was first proposed by Richard W. Arms, Jr., a well-known technical analyst.

Exhibit 32	Arms Index for the S&P 500, January–July 2009

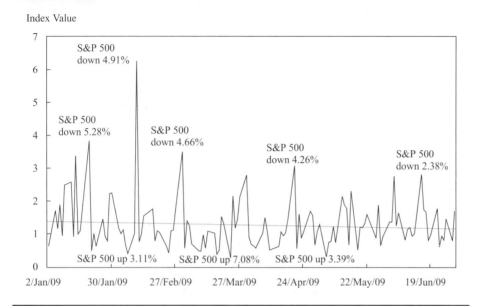

Index Value

Example 4

TRIN Indicator

Sarah Johannson, CFA, recently installed some investment software and is verifying the calculation of some of the statistics it produces. Her screen indicates a TRIN value of 1.02 for the NYSE and 1.80 for the NASDAQ market. These values seem to be unusually far apart to her, and she wonders whether they are both real-time statistics like the other market price data. To check whether they are real-time statistics, a few minutes later, she simultaneously captures the TRIN from her software display (slightly changed to 1.01 for the NYSE and 1.81 for NASDAQ) and on a separate monitor, she does a screen capture of NYSE and NASDAQ data, as follows:

		NYSE	NASDAQ
Number of issues	Advancing	850	937
	Declining	1,982	1,472
Volume	Advancing	76,921,200	156,178,475
	Declining	185,461,042	441,970,884

How does Johannson recalculate and interpret the TRIN value for the NYSE and NASDAQ?

Solution:

Johannson calculates the TRIN values for the NYSE and NASDAQ as follows:

$$\text{TRIN (NYSE)} = \frac{(850 \div 1,982)}{(76,921,200 \div 185,461,042)} = 1.03$$

$$\text{TRIN (NASDAQ)} = \frac{(937 \div 1,472)}{(156,178,475 \div 441,970,884)} = 1.80$$

Johannson concludes that her software is giving her current values and that the NASDAQ is having a much worse day than the NYSE.

3.4.4.2 Margin Debt   The previous section discussed the use of margin debt as an indicator of market sentiment. Margin debt is also widely used as a flow-of-funds indicator because margin loans may increase the purchases of stocks and declining margin balances may force the selling of stocks.

3.4.4.3 Mutual Fund Cash Position   Mutual funds hold a substantial proportion of all investable assets. Some analysts use the *percentage of mutual fund assets held in cash* as a predictor of market direction. It is called the "mutual fund cash position indicator." Mutual funds must hold some of their assets in cash in order to pay bills and send redemption checks to account holders. Cash arrives on a daily basis from customer deposits, interest earned, and dividends received. Cash also increases after a fund manager sells a position and holds the funds before reinvesting them. During a bull market, the manager wants to buy shares as quickly as possible to avoid having a cash "drag" hurt the fund's performance. If prices are trending lower, however, the manager may hold funds in cash to improve the fund's performance.

Exhibit 33 shows year-end mutual fund cash in the United States as a percentage of assets from 1984 through 2008. Over this period, the average cash percentage was 6.8 percent. An analyst's initial intuition might be that when cash is relatively low, fund managers are bullish and anticipate rising prices, but when fund managers are bearish, they conserve cash to wait for lower prices. Advocates of this technical indicator argue exactly the opposite: When the mutual fund cash position is low, fund managers have already bought, and the effects of their purchases are already reflected in security prices. When the cash position is high, however, that money represents buying power that will move prices higher when the money is used to add positions to the portfolio. The mutual fund cash position is another example of a contrarian indicator.

Exhibit 33	Mutual Fund Cash Position, 1984–2008

Some analysts modify the value of the cash percentage to account for differences in the level of interest rates. Cash is not sitting in a desk drawer; it is on deposit somewhere earning interest. When interest rates are low, holding cash can be a substantial drag on the fund's performance if the broad market advances. When interest rates are high, holding cash is less costly.

Example 5

Market Indicators

At the request of a wealthy client, Erik Nielson is preparing a proprietary research report on the shares of a U.S. company. He has completed the part of the report dealing with fundamental analysis and wants to include a section on technical analysis. Nielson has gathered the following information:

Company Information:

- The 20-day moving average of the share price just rose through the 200-day moving average.
- RSI = 40.6.

Market Information:

- TRIN = 1.9.
- Mutual fund cash position = 7.0%

1. How should Nielson interpret each item of information?
2. Do these indicators, in the aggregate, lead Nielson to a buy, hold, or sell recommendation for the company's shares?

Solution to 1:

- Moving average: When a short-term moving average moves above a longer-term moving average, the movement is a golden cross and is a bullish signal.

- RSI: An RSI of 40.6 would be considered neutral. The RSI ranges between 0 and 100. Values greater than 70 are bearish; values below 30 are bullish.

- TRIN: A TRIN value above 1.0 means that there is more volume in declining stocks than in advancing stocks; therefore, a value of 1.9 is bearish.

- Mutual fund cash position: The 7.0 percent figure is near the long-term average, so it is a neutral signal.

Solution to 2:

Of the four indicators, one is bullish, one is bearish, and two are neutral. Most analysts would view this result as "net neutral" and would recommend continuing to hold the stock. An alternative point of view might be that seeing a bullish indicator for the stock while the indicator for the overall market is bearish could be an argument for overweighting the stock.

3.4.4.4 New Equity Issuance   When a company's owners decide to take a company public and offer shares for sale, the owners want to put those shares on the market at a time when investors are eager to buy. That is, the owners want to offer the shares when they can sell them at a premium price. Premium prices occur near market tops. The new equity issuance indicator suggests that as the number of initial public offerings (IPOs) increases, the upward price trend may be about to turn down.

A supply-and-demand effect is also at work. Putting more shares on the market increases the aggregate supply of shares available for investors to purchase. The investment community has a finite quantity of cash to spend, so an increase in IPOs may be viewed as a bearish factor.

3.4.4.5 Secondary Offerings   Technicians also monitor secondary offerings to gauge potential changes in the supply of equities. Although secondary offerings do not increase the supply of shares, because existing shares are sold by insiders to the general public, they do increase the supply available for trading or the float. So, from a market perspective, secondary offerings of shares have the potential to change the supply-and-demand equation as much as IPOs do.

3.5 Cycles

Over the centuries, technicians have noted recurring cycles of various frequencies in the capital markets. The study of cycles in the markets is part of broader cycle studies that exist in numerous fields of study. Many observed cycles, such as one in U.S. equities tied to the cycle of U.S. presidential elections, have an obvious and rational justification. Other cycles do not. However, why cycles in fields seemingly unrelated to finance, such as astronomy or weather patterns, may influence the economy (and thus the capital markets) may have a logical explanation. For example, sun spots affect weather patterns on earth, which in turn affect agriculture and, therefore, capital markets because they are related to agriculture.

3.5.1 *Kondratieff Wave*

The longest of the widely recognized cycles was identified by Nikolai Kondratieff in the 1920s. Kondratieff was an economist in the Soviet Union who suggested that Western economies had a 54-year cycle. He traced cycles from the 1780s to the time he published this theory in the 1920s, and the economic depression of the 1930s was consistent with the cycle he identified. His theory was mainly tied to economic cycles and commodity prices, but cycles can also be seen in the prices of equities during the time of his work.

Kondratieff was executed in a Soviet purge in 1938, but his ideas have come into widespread acceptance, particularly since his works were translated into English in the 1980s. Two economists at the London School of Economics, E. H. Phelps Brown and Sheila Hopkins, identified a 50–52 year economic cycle in the United Kingdom. Together with Kondratieff, credit should be given to two Dutch economists, Jacob van Gelderen and Samuel de Wolff, who wrote about a 50–60 year economic cycle but published their work earlier, in 1913. Their work came to light only recently, however, so the long 54-year economic cycle is known as the **Kondratieff Wave** or K Wave.

3.5.2 *18-Year Cycle*

The 18-year cycle is interesting because three 18-year cycles make up the longer 54-year Kondratieff Wave. The 18-year cycle is most often mentioned in connection with real estate prices, but it can also be found in equities and other markets.

3.5.3 *Decennial Pattern*

The decennial pattern is the pattern of average stock market returns (based on the DJIA) broken down on the basis of the last digit in the year. Years ending with a 0 have had the worst performance, and years ending with a 5 have been by far the best. The DJIA was up every year ending in a 5 from 1885 until 1995, but it declined 0.6 percent in 2005.

3.5.4 *Presidential Cycle*

This cycle in the United States connects the performance of the DJIA with presidential elections. In this theory, years are grouped into categories on the basis of whether they were election years or the first, second, or third year following an election. The third year is the year prior to the next election. The third year shows the best performance;

in fact, the DJIA experienced a positive return in every pre-election year from 1943 through 2007. One explanation for this outcome is that with so many politicians up for re-election, they inject stimulus into the economy in an attempt to improve their chances to be re-elected.[9] Election years are also usually positive years for the stock market, but with less consistency. Post-election years and the so-called midterm year have the worst performance.

These long cycles are important to keep in mind when using other technical analysis tools. However, the long cycles described here and other theories about long cycles present a number of problems. The primary problem is the small sample size. Only 56 presidential elections have been held in the United States, and only 4 completed Kondratieff cycles have occurred in U.S. history. Another problem is that even with the small number of cycles, the data do not always fit the cycle theory, and when they do, that fit may not be obvious.

ELLIOTT WAVE THEORY

4

In a theory proposed by R. N. Elliott in 1938, the market moves in regular, repeated waves or cycles. He identified and categorized these waves and wrote in detail about aspects of market cycles. Elliott was an accountant by training, but in 1929, after he contracted a progressive intestinal illness at age 58 while working in Latin America, he was forced to retire. Then, he turned his attention to a detailed study of equity prices in the United States.

A decade later, in 1938, he published his findings in a book titled *The Wave Principle*. In developing the concept that the market moves in waves, Elliott relied heavily on Charles Dow's early work. Elliott described how the market moved in a pattern of five waves moving up in a bull market in the following pattern: 1 = up, 2 = down, 3 = up, 4 = down and 5 = up. He called this wave the "impulse wave." The impulse wave was followed by a corrective wave with three components: a = down, b = up and c = down.

When the market is a bear market, as defined in Dow Theory—that is, with both of Dow's major indices in bear markets—the downward movements are impulse waves and are broken into five waves with upward corrections broken into three subwaves.

Elliott also noted that each wave could be broken down into smaller and smaller subwaves.

The longest of the waves is called the "grand supercycle" and takes place over centuries. Elliott traced grand supercycles back to the founding of the United States, and his successors have continued his work. Each grand supercycle can be broken down into subcycles until ending with the "subminuette," which unfolds over several minutes. The major cycles are:

- Grand supercycle
- Supercycle
- Cycle
- Primary
- Intermediate
- Minor
- Minute
- Minuette
- Subminuette

---

9 In U.S. presidential election years, the vice presidency, all 435 House of Representatives seats, and 33 of the 100 Senate seats are also up for election.

An important aspect of Elliott's work is that he discovered that market waves follow patterns that are ratios of the numbers in the **Fibonacci sequence**. Leonardo Fibonacci was an 11th century Italian mathematician who explained this sequence in his book *Liber Abaci*, but the sequence was known to mathematicians as far back as 200 BCE in India. The Fibonacci sequence starts with the numbers 0, 1, 1, and then each subsequent number in the sequence is the sum of the two preceding numbers:

0, 1, 1, 2, 3, 5, 8, 13, 21, 34 . . .

Elliott was more interested in the ratios of the numbers in the sequence because he found that the ratio of the size of subsequent waves was generally a Fibonacci ratio. The ratios of one Fibonacci number to the next that Elliott considered most important are the following:

1/2 = 0.50, 2/3 = 0.6667, 3/5 = 0.6, 5/8 = 0.625, 8/13 = 0.6154

He also noticed that the ratio of a Fibonacci sequence number to its preceding number is important:

2/1 = 2, 3/2 = 1.5, 5/3 = 1.6667, 8/5 = 1.600, 13/8 = 1.6250

These ratios converge around 1.618. In mathematics, 1.618 is called the "golden ratio," and it can be found throughout nature—in astronomy, biology, botany, and many other fields. It is also widely used in art and architecture. The ancient Egyptians built the pyramids on the basis of this ratio, and the ancient Greeks used it widely.

As noted, Elliott numbered the impulse waves 1–5 and the corrective waves, a, b and c. Exhibit 34 depicts the impulse and corrective waves in a bull market.

Exhibit 34	Impulse Waves and Corrective Waves

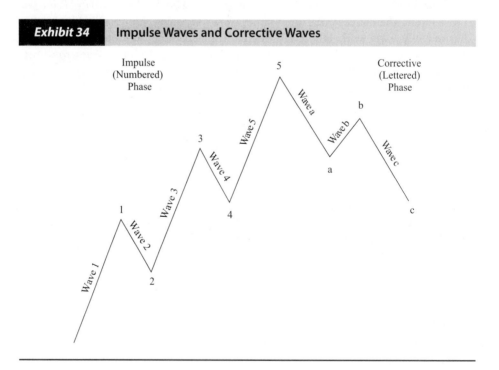

Elliott described the characteristics of each wave. Note the following, as shown in Exhibit 34:

▪ Wave 1 starts as a basing pattern and displays an increase in price, volume, and breadth.[10] Wave 1 consists of five smaller waves.

---

10 Breadth is defined as the ratio of the number of advancing securities in an index or traded on a given stock market to the number of declining issues.

- Wave 2 moves down, retracing much of the gain in Wave 1 but not all of it. Common percentage retracements are Fibonacci ratios, such as 50 percent or 62 percent. Wave 2 never erases all of the gains from Wave 1. Wave 2 consists of three smaller waves.

- Wave 3 moves above the high of the first wave and has strong breadth, volume, and price movement. Most of the price movement in an uptrend typically occurs in Wave 3. Wave 3 consists of five smaller waves. Wave 3 often moves prices 1.68 times higher than the length of Wave 1, which is a Fibonacci ratio.

- Wave 4 is, again, a correction, and the ratio of the change in price during this wave to the price change during the third wave is also generally a Fibonacci ratio. Wave 4 commonly reverses 38 percent of the gain in Wave 3. Wave 5 is also an up wave. Generally, the price movement in Wave 5 is not as great as that in Wave 3. The exception to the rule is that Wave 5 may become extended, as when euphoria overtakes the market. Wave 5 consists of five smaller waves.

After Wave 5 is completed, the market traces out a series of three corrective waves, labeled a, b and c in Exhibit 34.

- Wave a is a down wave in a bull market; Wave a itself breaks down into three waves.

- Wave b is an upward movement and breaks down into five waves. Wave b is a false rally and is often called a "bull trap."

- Wave c is the final corrective wave. In a bull market, it does not move below the start of the prior Wave 1 pattern. Wave c breaks down into three subwaves.

This description of the waves applies to bull markets; in bear markets, the impulse waves are labeled A through E and the corrective waves are labeled 1, 2, and 3. Waves in the direction of the trend consist of five subwaves, and counter-waves consist of three subwaves.

In practice, a good deal of time is required to become proficient with **Elliott Wave Theory**. Wave counts may not become evident at first, and Elliotticians often have to renumber their wave counts on the basis of changes in market trends. This theory is widely used, however, and the patterns Elliott described can still be observed today.

As a technician begins to make initial judgments on wave counts, the next step is to draw lines representing Fibonacci ratios on the charts. These lines alert the technician to the levels at which trends may change in the future and can be used in conjunction with other technical tools for forecasting. Positive price movements generally take prices up by some Fibonacci ratio of prior highs (e.g., 1.5 or 1.62), and price declines generally reverse prices by a Fibonacci ratio (e.g., 0.50 or 0.667). Elliott Wave Theory is used in practice with Dow Theory, trend analysis, pattern analysis, and oscillator analysis to provide a sense of the general trend in the market. As Elliott's nine cycles imply, Elliott Wave Theory can be applied in both very short-term trading as well as in very long-term economic analysis, as is the case with most tools used in technical analysis.

INTERMARKET ANALYSIS   5

Intermarket analysis is a field within technical analysis that combines analysis of major categories of securities—namely, equities, bonds, currencies, and commodities—to identify market trends and possible inflections in a trend. Intermarket analysis also looks at industry subsectors, such as the nine sectors the S&P 500 is divided into, and the relationships among the major stock markets of countries with the largest economies, such as the New York, London, and Tokyo stock exchanges.

Intermarket analysis relies heavily on the field of economic analysis for its theoretical underpinning. The field was pioneered by John Murphy with his 1991 book *Intermarket Technical Analysis*. Murphy noted that all markets are inter-related and that these relationships are strengthening with the globalization of the world economy.[11]

Stock prices are affected by bond prices. High bond prices are a positive for stock prices since this means low interest rates. Lower interest rates benefit companies with lower borrowing costs and lead to higher equity valuations in the calculation of intrinsic value using discounted cash flow analysis in fundamental analysis. Thus rising bond prices are a positive for stock prices, and declining bond prices are a bearish indicator.

Bond prices impact commodity prices. Bond prices move inversely to interest rates. Interest rates move in proportion to expectations to future prices of commodities or inflation. So declining bond prices are a signal of possible rising commodity prices.

Currencies impact commodity prices. Most commodity trading is denominated in US dollars and so prices are commonly quoted in US dollars. As a result, a strong dollar results in lower commodity prices and vice versa.

In intermarket analysis, technicians often look for inflection points in one market as a warning sign to start looking for a change in trend in a related market. To identify these intermarket relationships, a commonly used tool is relative strength analysis, which charts the price of one security divided by the price of another.

Exhibit 35 shows the relative price of 10-year U.S. Treasury bonds compared with the S&P 500. The rise in T-bond price relative to the S&P 500 can be clearly seen. The inflection point in this chart occurs in March 2009. This point would signal that the time had come to move investments from bonds to stocks.

Exhibit 35   Relative Strength of 10-Year T-Bonds vs. S&P 500, September 2008–July 2009

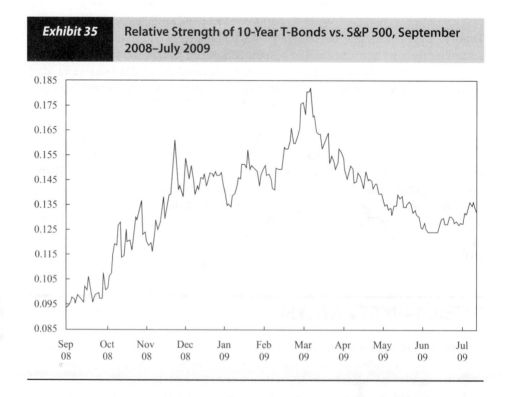

11 Murphy, John J., *Intermarket Technical Analysis: Trading Strategies for the Global Stock, Bond, Commodity, and Currency Markets.* John Wiley & Sons, Inc., 1991.

Exhibit 36 is a relative strength chart depicting the ratio between the S&P 500 and commodity prices. It shows a clear top and reversal of trend in December 2008. This inflection point shows U.S. stocks weakening relative to commodities and would indicate that allocating funds away from the U.S. stocks and into commodities might be appropriate.

Exhibit 36	S&P 500 Index vs. Commodity Prices, November 2007–November 2009

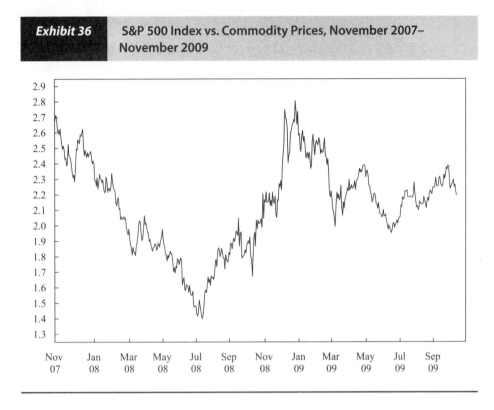

In addition to the preceding comparisons, once an asset category has been identified, relative strength analysis can be used to identify the strongest performing securities in a sector. For example, if commodities look promising, an investor can analyze each of the major commodities relative to a broad commodity index in order to find the strongest commodity.

Intermarket analysis can also be used to identify sectors of the equity market to invest in—often in connection with technical observations of the business cycle at any time. The equities of certain industry sectors tend to perform best at the beginning of an economic cycle. These sectors include utilities, financials, consumer nondurables, and transportation stocks. As an economic recovery gets under way, retailers, manufacturers, health care, and consumer durables tend to outperform. Lagging sectors include those tied to commodity prices, such as energy and basic industrial commodities, and also technology stocks.

Observations based on intermarket analysis can also help in allocating funds across national markets. Certain countries' economies are closely tied to commodities—for example, Australia, Canada, and South Africa. As economies evolve, these relationships change. So, the relationships must be monitored closely. For example, the Chinese equity markets have become much more advanced since 2000, the Chinese economy is much more industrialized than in the past, and its dependence on exports is currently strong.

SUMMARY

- Technical analysis is a form of security analysis that uses price and volume market data, often graphically displayed.

- Technical analysis can be used for any freely traded security in the global market and is used on a wide range of financial instruments, such as equities, bonds, commodity futures, and currency futures.

- Technical analysis is the study of market trends or patterns and relies on recognition of patterns that have worked in the past in an attempt to predict future security prices. Technicians believe that market trends and patterns repeat themselves and are somewhat predictable because human behavior tends to repeat itself and is somewhat predictable.

- Another tenet of technical analysis is that the market brings together the collective wisdom of multiple participants, weights it according to the size of the trades they make, and allows analysts to understand this collective sentiment. Technical analysis relies on knowledgeable market participants putting this knowledge to work in the market and thereby influencing prices and volume.

- Technical analysis and fundamental analysis are equally useful and valid, but they approach the market in different ways. Technical analysis focuses solely on analyzing markets and the trading of financial instruments, whereas fundamental analysis is a much wider ranging field encompassing financial and economic analysis as well as analysis of societal and political trends.

- Technical analysis relies primarily on information gathered from market participants that is expressed through the interaction of price and volume. Fundamental analysis relies on information that is external to the market (e.g., economic data, company financial information) in an attempt to evaluate a security's value relative to its current price.

- The usefulness of technical analysis is diminished by any constraints on the security being freely traded, by large outside manipulation of the market, and in illiquid markets.

- Charts provide information about past price behavior and provide a basis for inferences about likely future price behavior. Various types of charts can be useful in studying the markets: line charts, bar charts, candlestick charts, and point and figure charts.

- Relative strength analysis is based on the ratio of the prices of a security to a benchmark and is used to compare the performance of one asset with the performance of another asset.

- Many technicians consider volume information to be very important and watch for the confirmation in volume of a price trend or the divergence of volume from a price trend.

- The concept of trend is perhaps the most important aspect of technical analysis. An uptrend is defined as a security making higher highs and higher lows. To draw an uptrend line, a technician draws a line connecting the lows of the price chart. A downtrend is defined as a security making lower highs and lower lows. To draw a downtrend line, a technician draws a line connecting the highs of the price chart.

- Support is defined as a low price range in which the price stops declining because of buying activity. It is the opposite of resistance, which is a price range in which price stops rising because of selling activity.

- Chart patterns are formations appearing in price charts that create some type of recognizable shape.

- Reversal patterns signal the end of a trend. Common reversal patterns are the head and shoulders, the inverse head and shoulders, double tops and bottoms, and triple tops and bottoms.

- Continuation patterns indicate that a market trend in place prior to the pattern formation will continue once the pattern is completed. Common continuation patterns are triangles, rectangles, flags, and pennants.

- Price-based indicators incorporate information contained in market prices. Common price-based indicators are the moving average and Bollinger Bands.

- Momentum oscillator indicators are constructed from price data, but they are calculated so that they fluctuate either between a high and low, typically 0 and 100, or around 0 or 100. Some examples are momentum (or rate of change) oscillators, the RSI, stochastic measures, and MACD.

- Sentiment indicators attempt to gauge investor activity for signs of increasing bullishness or bearishness. Sentiment indicators come in two forms—investor polls and calculated statistical indices. Opinion polls to gauge investors' sentiment toward the equity market are conducted by a variety of services. Commonly used calculated statistical indices are the put/call ratio, the VIX, margin debt, and the short interest ratio.

- Flow-of-funds indicators help technicians gauge potential changes in supply and demand for securities. Some commonly used indicators are the ARMS Index (also called the TRIN), margin debt (also a sentiment indicator), mutual fund cash positions, new equity issuance, and secondary equity offerings.

- Many technicians use various observed cycles to predict future movements in security prices; these cycles include Kondratieff waves, decennial patterns, and the U.S. presidential cycle.

- Elliott Wave Theory is an approach to market forecasting that assumes that markets form repetitive wave patterns, which are themselves composed of smaller and smaller subwaves. The relationships among wave heights are frequently Fibonacci ratios.

- Intermarket analysis is based on the principle that all markets are interrelated and influence each other. This approach involves the use of relative strength analysis for different groups of securities (e.g., stocks versus bonds, sectors in an economy, and securities from different countries) to make allocation decisions.

PRACTICE PROBLEMS FOR READING 12

1. Technical analysis relies most importantly on:

    A. price and volume data.

    B. accurate financial statements.

    C. fundamental analysis to confirm conclusions.

2. Which of the following is *not* an assumption of technical analysis?

    A. Security markets are efficient.

    B. The security under analysis is freely traded.

    C. Market trends and patterns tend to repeat themselves.

3. Drawbacks of technical analysis include which of the following?

    A. It identifies changes in trends only after the fact.

    B. Deviations from intrinsic value can persist for long periods.

    C. It usually requires detailed knowledge of the financial instrument under analysis.

4. Why is technical analysis especially useful in the analysis of commodities and currencies?

    A. Valuation models cannot be used to determine fundamental intrinsic value for these securities.

    B. Government regulators are more likely to intervene in these markets.

    C. These types of securities display clearer trends than equities and bonds do.

5. A daily bar chart provides:

    A. a logarithmically scaled horizontal axis.

    B. a horizontal axis that represents changes in price.

    C. high and low prices during the day and the day's opening and closing prices.

6. A candlestick chart is similar to a bar chart *except* that the candlestick chart:

    A. represents upward movements in price with X's.

    B. also graphically shows the range of the period's highs and lows.

    C. has a body that is light or dark depending on whether the security closed higher or lower than its open.

7. In analyzing a price chart, high or increasing volume *most likely* indicates which of the following?

    A. Predicts a reversal in the price trend.

    B. Predicts that a trendless period will follow.

    C. Confirms a rising or declining trend in prices.

8. In constructing a chart, using a logarithmic scale on the vertical axis is likely to be *most useful* for which of the following applications?

    A. The price of gold for the past 100 years.

    B. The share price of a company over the past month.

    C. Yields on 10-year U.S. Treasuries for the past 5 years.

9. A downtrend line is constructed by drawing a line connecting:

    A. the lows of the price chart.

    B. the highs of the price chart.

    C. the highest high to the lowest low of the price chart.

10. Exhibit 1 depicts GreatWall Information Industry Co., Ltd., ordinary shares, traded on the Shenzhen Stock Exchange, for late 2008 through late 2009 in renminbi (RMB).

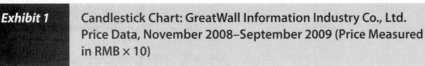

| Exhibit 1 | Candlestick Chart: GreatWall Information Industry Co., Ltd. Price Data, November 2008–September 2009 (Price Measured in RMB × 10) |

Based on Exhibit 1, the uptrend was *most likely* broken at a price level nearest to:

A. 7 RMB.

B. 8.5 RMB.

C. 10 RMB.

11. The "change in polarity" principle states which of the following?

A. Once an uptrend is broken, it becomes a downtrend.

B. Once a resistance level is breached, it becomes a support level.

C. The short-term moving average has crossed over the longer-term moving average.

12. Exhibit 2 depicts Barclays ordinary shares, traded on the London Stock Exchange, for 2009 in British pence.

| Exhibit 2 | Candlestick Chart: Barclays plc Price Data, January 2009– January 2010 (Price Measured in British Pence) |

Based on Exhibit 2, Barclays appears to show resistance at a level nearest to:

A. 50p.

B. 275p.

C. 390p.

13. Exhibit 3 depicts Archer Daniels Midland Company common shares, traded on the New York Stock Exchange, for 1996 to 2001 in U.S. dollars.

Exhibit 3	**Candlestick Chart: Archer Daniels Midland Company, February 1996–February 2001**

Exhibit 3 illustrates *most* clearly which type of pattern?

A. Triangle.

B. Triple top.

C. Head and shoulders.

14. In an inverted head and shoulders pattern, if the neckline is at €100, the shoulders at €90, and the head at €75, the price target is *closest* to which of the following?

A. €50.

B. €110.

C. €125.

15. Which flow-of-funds indicator is considered bearish for equities?

A. A large increase in the number of IPOs.

B. Higher-than-average cash balances in mutual funds.

C. An upturn in margin debt but one that is still below the long-term average.

16. A TRIN with a value of less than 1.0 indicates:

A. the market is in balance.

B. there is more volume in rising shares.

C. there is more volume in declining shares.

17. Bollinger Bands are constructed by plotting:

A. a MACD line and a signal line.

B. a moving-average line with an uptrend line above and downtrend line below.

C. a moving-average line with upper and lower lines that are at a set number of standard deviations apart.

18. Which of the following is *not* a momentum oscillator?

   A. MACD.

   B. Stochastic oscillator.

   C. Bollinger Bands.

19. Which of the following is a continuation pattern?

   A. Triangle.

   B. Triple top.

   C. Head and shoulders.

20. Which of the following is a reversal pattern?

   A. Pennant.

   B. Rectangle.

   C. Double bottom.

21. Which of the following is generally true of the head and shoulders pattern?

   A. Volume is important in interpreting the data.

   B. The neckline, once breached, becomes a support level.

   C. Head and shoulders patterns are generally followed by an uptrend in the security's price.

22. Nikolai Kondratieff concluded in the 1920s that since the 1780s, Western economies have generally followed a cycle of how many years?

   A. 18.

   B. 54.

   C. 76.

23. Based on the decennial pattern of cycles, how would the return of the Dow Jones Industrial Average (DJIA) in the year 2015 compare with the return in 2020?

   A. The return would be better.

   B. The return would be worse.

   C. The answer cannot be determined because the theory does not apply to both of those years.

24. According to the U.S. presidential cycle theory, the DJIA has the best performance during which year?

   A. The presidential election year itself.

   B. The first year following a presidential election.

   C. The third year following a presidential election.

25. What is a major problem with long-term cycle theories?

   A. The sample size is small.

   B. The data are usually hard to observe.

   C. They occur over such a long period that they are difficult to discern.

26. In 1938, R. N. Elliott proposed a theory that equity markets move:

   A. in stochastic waves.

   B. in cycles following Fibonacci ratios.

   C. in waves dependent on other securities.

27. All of the following are names of Elliott cycles *except*:

   A. presidential.

    B. supercycle.

    C. grand supercycle.

28. To identify intermarket relationships, technicians commonly use:

    A. stochastic oscillators.

    B. Fibonacci ratios.

    C. relative strength analysis.

SOLUTIONS FOR READING 12

1. A is correct. Almost all technical analysis relies on these data inputs.

2. A is correct. Technical analysis works because markets are *not* efficient and rational and because human beings tend to behave similarly in similar circumstances. The result is market trends and patterns that repeat themselves and are somewhat predictable.

3. A is correct. Trends generally must be in place for some time before they are recognizable. Thus, some time may be needed for a change in trend to be identified.

4. A is correct. Commodities and currencies do not have underlying financial statements or an income stream; thus, fundamental analysis is useless in determining theoretical values for them or whether they are over- or undervalued.

5. C is correct. The top and bottom of the bars indicate the highs and lows for the day; the line on the left indicates the opening price and the line on the right indicates the closing price.

6. C is correct. Dark and light shading is a unique feature of candlestick charts.

7. C is correct. Rising volume shows conviction by many market participants, which is likely to lead to a continuation of the trend.

8. A is correct. The price of gold in nominal dollars was several orders of magnitude cheaper 100 years ago than it is today (roughly US$20 then versus US$1,100 today). Such a wide range of prices lends itself well to being graphically displayed on a logarithmic scale.

9. B is correct. A downtrend line is constructed by drawing a line connecting the highs of the price chart.

10. B is correct. It is demonstrated in the following chart:

| Exhibit 1 | Candlestick Chart: GreatWall Information Industry Co., Ltd. Price Data, November 2008–September 2009 (Price Measured in RMB × 10) |

11. B is correct.

12. C is correct. As shown in the following chart, Barclays shares traded up to 390p on three occasions, each several weeks apart, and declined thereafter each time.

Exhibit 2	Candlestick Chart: Barclays plc Price Data, January 2009–January 2010 (Price Measured in British Pence)

13. C is correct. The left shoulder formed at around US$18.50, the head formed at around US$20.50, and the second shoulder formed at around US$19.

Exhibit 3	Candlestick Chart: Archer Daniels Midland Company, February 1996–February 2001

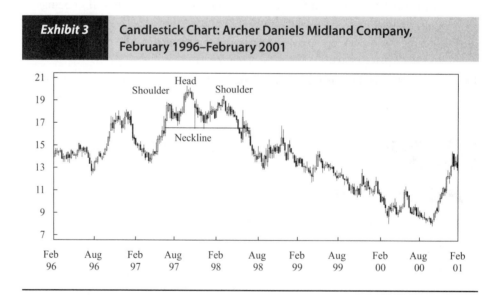

14. C is correct. Target = Neckline + (Neckline – Head): €100 + (€100 – €75) = €125

15. A is correct. A large increase in the number of IPOs increases the supply of equity and if overall demand remains the same, puts downward pressure on equities. Also, companies tend to issue shares of equity when the managers believe they will receive a premium price, which is also an indicator of a market top.

16. B is correct. A value below 1.0 is a bullish sign; it means more volume is in rising shares than in declining ones. The TRIN is calculated as: (Advancing issues/Declining issues)/(Volume of advancing issues/Volume of declining issues).

17. C is correct. Bollinger Bands consist of a moving average and a higher line representing the moving average plus a set number of standard deviations from average price (for the same number of periods as used to calculate the moving average) and a lower line that is a moving average minus the same number of standard deviations.

18. C is correct. Bollinger Bands are price-based indicators, *not* momentum oscillators, which are constructed so that they oscillate between a high and a low or around 0 or 100.

19. A is correct. Triangles are one of several continuation patterns.

20. C is correct. It is one of several reversal patterns.

21. A is correct. Volume is necessary to confirm the various market rallies and reversals during the formation of the head and shoulders pattern.

22. B is correct.

23. A is correct. The decennial pattern theory states that years ending with a 5 will have the best performance of any of the 10 years in a decade and that those ending with a zero will have the worst.

24. C is correct. A possible reason for the superior performance in the third year is that the U.S. presidential election occurs, together with a number of other elections, in a four-year cycle, so the politicians desiring to be reelected inject money into the economy in the third year to improve their chances of winning the following year.

25. A is correct. Long-term cycles require many years to complete; thus, not many cycles are available to observe.

26. B is correct.

27. A is correct. This is the term for a separate cycle theory.

28. C is correct. Relative strength analysis is often used to compare two asset classes or two securities.

Appendices

Appendix A Cumulative Probabilities for a Standard Normal Distribution

$P(Z \leq x) = N(x)$ for $x \geq 0$ or $P(Z \leq z) = N(z)$ for $z \geq 0$

x or z	0	0.01	0.02	0.03	0.04	0.05	0.06	0.07	0.08	0.09
0.00	0.5000	0.5040	0.5080	0.5120	0.5160	0.5199	0.5239	0.5279	0.5319	0.5359
0.10	0.5398	0.5438	0.5478	0.5517	0.5557	0.5596	0.5636	0.5675	0.5714	0.5753
0.20	0.5793	0.5832	0.5871	0.5910	0.5948	0.5987	0.6026	0.6064	0.6103	0.6141
0.30	0.6179	0.6217	0.6255	0.6293	0.6331	0.6368	0.6406	0.6443	0.6480	0.6517
0.40	0.6554	0.6591	0.6628	0.6664	0.6700	0.6736	0.6772	0.6808	0.6844	0.6879
0.50	0.6915	0.6950	0.6985	0.7019	0.7054	0.7088	0.7123	0.7157	0.7190	0.7224
0.60	0.7257	0.7291	0.7324	0.7357	0.7389	0.7422	0.7454	0.7486	0.7517	0.7549
0.70	0.7580	0.7611	0.7642	0.7673	0.7704	0.7734	0.7764	0.7794	0.7823	0.7852
0.80	0.7881	0.7910	0.7939	0.7967	0.7995	0.8023	0.8051	0.8078	0.8106	0.8133
0.90	0.8159	0.8186	0.8212	0.8238	0.8264	0.8289	0.8315	0.8340	0.8365	0.8389
1.00	0.8413	0.8438	0.8461	0.8485	0.8508	0.8531	0.8554	0.8577	0.8599	0.8621
1.10	0.8643	0.8665	0.8686	0.8708	0.8729	0.8749	0.8770	0.8790	0.8810	0.8830
1.20	0.8849	0.8869	0.8888	0.8907	0.8925	0.8944	0.8962	0.8980	0.8997	0.9015
1.30	0.9032	0.9049	0.9066	0.9082	0.9099	0.9115	0.9131	0.9147	0.9162	0.9177
1.40	0.9192	0.9207	0.9222	0.9236	0.9251	0.9265	0.9279	0.9292	0.9306	0.9319
1.50	0.9332	0.9345	0.9357	0.9370	0.9382	0.9394	0.9406	0.9418	0.9429	0.9441
1.60	0.9452	0.9463	0.9474	0.9484	0.9495	0.9505	0.9515	0.9525	0.9535	0.9545
1.70	0.9554	0.9564	0.9573	0.9582	0.9591	0.9599	0.9608	0.9616	0.9625	0.9633
1.80	0.9641	0.9649	0.9656	0.9664	0.9671	0.9678	0.9686	0.9693	0.9699	0.9706
1.90	0.9713	0.9719	0.9726	0.9732	0.9738	0.9744	0.9750	0.9756	0.9761	0.9767
2.00	0.9772	0.9778	0.9783	0.9788	0.9793	0.9798	0.9803	0.9808	0.9812	0.9817
2.10	0.9821	0.9826	0.9830	0.9834	0.9838	0.9842	0.9846	0.9850	0.9854	0.9857
2.20	0.9861	0.9864	0.9868	0.9871	0.9875	0.9878	0.9881	0.9884	0.9887	0.9890
2.30	0.9893	0.9896	0.9898	0.9901	0.9904	0.9906	0.9909	0.9911	0.9913	0.9916
2.40	0.9918	0.9920	0.9922	0.9925	0.9927	0.9929	0.9931	0.9932	0.9934	0.9936
2.50	0.9938	0.9940	0.9941	0.9943	0.9945	0.9946	0.9948	0.9949	0.9951	0.9952
2.60	0.9953	0.9955	0.9956	0.9957	0.9959	0.9960	0.9961	0.9962	0.9963	0.9964
2.70	0.9965	0.9966	0.9967	0.9968	0.9969	0.9970	0.9971	0.9972	0.9973	0.9974
2.80	0.9974	0.9975	0.9976	0.9977	0.9977	0.9978	0.9979	0.9979	0.9980	0.9981
2.90	0.9981	0.9982	0.9982	0.9983	0.9984	0.9984	0.9985	0.9985	0.9986	0.9986
3.00	0.9987	0.9987	0.9987	0.9988	0.9988	0.9989	0.9989	0.9989	0.9990	0.9990
3.10	0.9990	0.9991	0.9991	0.9991	0.9992	0.9992	0.9992	0.9992	0.9993	0.9993
3.20	0.9993	0.9993	0.9994	0.9994	0.9994	0.9994	0.9994	0.9995	0.9995	0.9995
3.30	0.9995	0.9995	0.9995	0.9996	0.9996	0.9996	0.9996	0.9996	0.9996	0.9997
3.40	0.9997	0.9997	0.9997	0.9997	0.9997	0.9997	0.9997	0.9997	0.9997	0.9998
3.50	0.9998	0.9998	0.9998	0.9998	0.9998	0.9998	0.9998	0.9998	0.9998	0.9998
3.60	0.9998	0.9998	0.9999	0.9999	0.9999	0.9999	0.9999	0.9999	0.9999	0.9999
3.70	0.9999	0.9999	0.9999	0.9999	0.9999	0.9999	0.9999	0.9999	0.9999	0.9999
3.80	0.9999	0.9999	0.9999	0.9999	0.9999	0.9999	0.9999	0.9999	0.9999	0.9999
3.90	1.0000	1.0000	1.0000	1.0000	1.0000	1.0000	1.0000	1.0000	1.0000	1.0000
4.00	1.0000	1.0000	1.0000	1.0000	1.0000	1.0000	1.0000	1.0000	1.0000	1.0000

For example, to find the z-value leaving 2.5 percent of the area/probability in the upper tail, find the element 0.9750 in the body of the table. Read 1.90 at the left end of the element's row and 0.06 at the top of the element's column, to give 1.90 + 0.06 = 1.96. *Table generated with Excel.*

Quantitative Methods for Investment Analysis, Second Edition, by Richard A. DeFusco, CFA, Dennis W. McLeavey, CFA, Jerald E. Pinto, CFA, and David E. Runkle, CFA. Copyright © 2004 by CFA Institute.

Appendix A	Continued

x or z	0	0.01	0.02	0.03	0.04	0.05	0.06	0.07	0.08	0.09
0.0	0.5000	0.4960	0.4920	0.4880	0.4840	0.4801	0.4761	0.4721	0.4681	0.4641
−0.10	0.4602	0.4562	0.4522	0.4483	0.4443	0.4404	0.4364	0.4325	0.4286	0.4247
−0.20	0.4207	0.4168	0.4129	0.4090	0.4052	0.4013	0.3974	0.3936	0.3897	0.3859
−0.30	0.3821	0.3783	0.3745	0.3707	0.3669	0.3632	0.3594	0.3557	0.3520	0.3483
−0.40	0.3446	0.3409	0.3372	0.3336	0.3300	0.3264	0.3228	0.3192	0.3156	0.3121
−0.50	0.3085	0.3050	0.3015	0.2981	0.2946	0.2912	0.2877	0.2843	0.2810	0.2776
−0.60	0.2743	0.2709	0.2676	0.2643	0.2611	0.2578	0.2546	0.2514	0.2483	0.2451
−0.70	0.2420	0.2389	0.2358	0.2327	0.2296	0.2266	0.2236	0.2206	0.2177	0.2148
−0.80	0.2119	0.2090	0.2061	0.2033	0.2005	0.1977	0.1949	0.1922	0.1894	0.1867
−0.90	0.1841	0.1814	0.1788	0.1762	0.1736	0.1711	0.1685	0.1660	0.1635	0.1611
−1.00	0.1587	0.1562	0.1539	0.1515	0.1492	0.1469	0.1446	0.1423	0.1401	0.1379
−1.10	0.1357	0.1335	0.1314	0.1292	0.1271	0.1251	0.1230	0.1210	0.1190	0.1170
−1.20	0.1151	0.1131	0.1112	0.1093	0.1075	0.1056	0.1038	0.1020	0.1003	0.0985
−1.30	0.0968	0.0951	0.0934	0.0918	0.0901	0.0885	0.0869	0.0853	0.0838	0.0823
−1.40	0.0808	0.0793	0.0778	0.0764	0.0749	0.0735	0.0721	0.0708	0.0694	0.0681
−1.50	0.0668	0.0655	0.0643	0.0630	0.0618	0.0606	0.0594	0.0582	0.0571	0.0559
−1.60	0.0548	0.0537	0.0526	0.0516	0.0505	0.0495	0.0485	0.0475	0.0465	0.0455
−1.70	0.0446	0.0436	0.0427	0.0418	0.0409	0.0401	0.0392	0.0384	0.0375	0.0367
−1.80	0.0359	0.0351	0.0344	0.0336	0.0329	0.0322	0.0314	0.0307	0.0301	0.0294
−1.90	0.0287	0.0281	0.0274	0.0268	0.0262	0.0256	0.0250	0.0244	0.0239	0.0233
−2.00	0.0228	0.0222	0.0217	0.0212	0.0207	0.0202	0.0197	0.0192	0.0188	0.0183
−2.10	0.0179	0.0174	0.0170	0.0166	0.0162	0.0158	0.0154	0.0150	0.0146	0.0143
−2.20	0.0139	0.0136	0.0132	0.0129	0.0125	0.0122	0.0119	0.0116	0.0113	0.0110
−2.30	0.0107	0.0104	0.0102	0.0099	0.0096	0.0094	0.0091	0.0089	0.0087	0.0084
−2.40	0.0082	0.0080	0.0078	0.0075	0.0073	0.0071	0.0069	0.0068	0.0066	0.0064
−2.50	0.0062	0.0060	0.0059	0.0057	0.0055	0.0054	0.0052	0.0051	0.0049	0.0048
−2.60	0.0047	0.0045	0.0044	0.0043	0.0041	0.0040	0.0039	0.0038	0.0037	0.0036
−2.70	0.0035	0.0034	0.0033	0.0032	0.0031	0.0030	0.0029	0.0028	0.0027	0.0026
−2.80	0.0026	0.0025	0.0024	0.0023	0.0023	0.0022	0.0021	0.0021	0.0020	0.0019
−2.90	0.0019	0.0018	0.0018	0.0017	0.0016	0.0016	0.0015	0.0015	0.0014	0.0014
−3.00	0.0013	0.0013	0.0013	0.0012	0.0012	0.0011	0.0011	0.0011	0.0010	0.0010
−3.10	0.0010	0.0009	0.0009	0.0009	0.0008	0.0008	0.0008	0.0008	0.0007	0.0007
−3.20	0.0007	0.0007	0.0006	0.0006	0.0006	0.0006	0.0006	0.0005	0.0005	0.0005
−3.30	0.0005	0.0005	0.0005	0.0004	0.0004	0.0004	0.0004	0.0004	0.0004	0.0003
−3.40	0.0003	0.0003	0.0003	0.0003	0.0003	0.0003	0.0003	0.0003	0.0003	0.0002
−3.50	0.0002	0.0002	0.0002	0.0002	0.0002	0.0002	0.0002	0.0002	0.0002	0.0002
−3.60	0.0002	0.0002	0.0001	0.0001	0.0001	0.0001	0.0001	0.0001	0.0001	0.0001
−3.70	0.0001	0.0001	0.0001	0.0001	0.0001	0.0001	0.0001	0.0001	0.0001	0.0001
−3.80	0.0001	0.0001	0.0001	0.0001	0.0001	0.0001	0.0001	0.0001	0.0001	0.0001
−3.90	0.0000	0.0000	0.0000	0.0000	0.0000	0.0000	0.0000	0.0000	0.0000	0.0000
−4.00	0.0000	0.0000	0.0000	0.0000	0.0000	0.0000	0.0000	0.0000	0.0000	0.0000

For example, to find the z-value leaving 2.5 percent of the area/probability in the lower tail, find the element 0.0250 in the body of the table. Read −1.90 at the left end of the element's row and 0.06 at the top of the element's column, to give −1.90 − 0.06 = −1.96. *Table generated with Excel.*

Quantitative Methods for Investment Analysis, Second Edition, by Richard A. DeFusco, CFA, Dennis W. McLeavey, CFA, Jerald E. Pinto, CFA, and David E. Runkle, CFA. Copyright © 2004 by CFA Institute.

Appendix B Table of the Student's t-Distribution (One-Tailed Probabilities)

df	p = 0.10	p = 0.05	p = 0.025	p = 0.01	p = 0.005
1	3.078	6.314	12.706	31.821	63.657
2	1.886	2.920	4.303	6.965	9.925
3	1.638	2.353	3.182	4.541	5.841
4	1.533	2.132	2.776	3.747	4.604
5	1.476	2.015	2.571	3.365	4.032
6	1.440	1.943	2.447	3.143	3.707
7	1.415	1.895	2.365	2.998	3.499
8	1.397	1.860	2.306	2.896	3.355
9	1.383	1.833	2.262	2.821	3.250
10	1.372	1.812	2.228	2.764	3.169
11	1.363	1.796	2.201	2.718	3.106
12	1.356	1.782	2.179	2.681	3.055
13	1.350	1.771	2.160	2.650	3.012
14	1.345	1.761	2.145	2.624	2.977
15	1.341	1.753	2.131	2.602	2.947
16	1.337	1.746	2.120	2.583	2.921
17	1.333	1.740	2.110	2.567	2.898
18	1.330	1.734	2.101	2.552	2.878
19	1.328	1.729	2.093	2.539	2.861
20	1.325	1.725	2.086	2.528	2.845
21	1.323	1.721	2.080	2.518	2.831
22	1.321	1.717	2.074	2.508	2.819
23	1.319	1.714	2.069	2.500	2.807
24	1.318	1.711	2.064	2.492	2.797
25	1.316	1.708	2.060	2.485	2.787
26	1.315	1.706	2.056	2.479	2.779
27	1.314	1.703	2.052	2.473	2.771
28	1.313	1.701	2.048	2.467	2.763
29	1.311	1.699	2.045	2.462	2.756
30	1.310	1.697	2.042	2.457	2.750

df	p = 0.10	p = 0.05	p = 0.025	p = 0.01	p = 0.005
31	1.309	1.696	2.040	2.453	2.744
32	1.309	1.694	2.037	2.449	2.738
33	1.308	1.692	2.035	2.445	2.733
34	1.307	1.691	2.032	2.441	2.728
35	1.306	1.690	2.030	2.438	2.724
36	1.306	1.688	2.028	2.434	2.719
37	1.305	1.687	2.026	2.431	2.715
38	1.304	1.686	2.024	2.429	2.712
39	1.304	1.685	2.023	2.426	2.708
40	1.303	1.684	2.021	2.423	2.704
41	1.303	1.683	2.020	2.421	2.701
42	1.302	1.682	2.018	2.418	2.698
43	1.302	1.681	2.017	2.416	2.695
44	1.301	1.680	2.015	2.414	2.692
45	1.301	1.679	2.014	2.412	2.690
46	1.300	1.679	2.013	2.410	2.687
47	1.300	1.678	2.012	2.408	2.685
48	1.299	1.677	2.011	2.407	2.682
49	1.299	1.677	2.010	2.405	2.680
50	1.299	1.676	2.009	2.403	2.678
60	1.296	1.671	2.000	2.390	2.660
70	1.294	1.667	1.994	2.381	2.648
80	1.292	1.664	1.990	2.374	2.639
90	1.291	1.662	1.987	2.368	2.632
100	1.290	1.660	1.984	2.364	2.626
110	1.289	1.659	1.982	2.361	2.621
120	1.289	1.658	1.980	2.358	2.617
200	1.286	1.653	1.972	2.345	2.601
∞	1.282	1.645	1.960	2.326	2.576

To find a critical t-value, enter the table with df and a specified value for α, the significance level. For example, with 5 df, α = 0.05 and a one-tailed test, the desired probability in the tail would be p = 0.05 and the critical t-value would be t(5, 0.05) = 2.015. With α = 0.05 and a two-tailed test, the desired probability in each tail would be p = 0.025 = α/2, giving t(0.025) = 2.571. Table generated using Excel.

Quantitative Methods for Investment Analysis, Second Edition, by Richard A. DeFusco, CFA, Dennis W. McLeavey, CFA, Jerald E. Pinto, CFA, and David E. Runkle, CFA. Copyright © 2004 by CFA Institute.

| Appendix C | Values of χ^2 (Degrees of Freedom, Level of Significance) |

Degrees of Freedom	Probability in Right Tail								
	0.99	0.975	0.95	0.9	0.1	0.05	0.025	0.01	0.005
1	0.000157	0.000982	0.003932	0.0158	2.706	3.841	5.024	6.635	7.879
2	0.020100	0.050636	0.102586	0.2107	4.605	5.991	7.378	9.210	10.597
3	0.1148	0.2158	0.3518	0.5844	6.251	7.815	9.348	11.345	12.838
4	0.297	0.484	0.711	1.064	7.779	9.488	11.143	13.277	14.860
5	0.554	0.831	1.145	1.610	9.236	11.070	12.832	15.086	16.750
6	0.872	1.237	1.635	2.204	10.645	12.592	14.449	16.812	18.548
7	1.239	1.690	2.167	2.833	12.017	14.067	16.013	18.475	20.278
8	1.647	2.180	2.733	3.490	13.362	15.507	17.535	20.090	21.955
9	2.088	2.700	3.325	4.168	14.684	16.919	19.023	21.666	23.589
10	2.558	3.247	3.940	4.865	15.987	18.307	20.483	23.209	25.188
11	3.053	3.816	4.575	5.578	17.275	19.675	21.920	24.725	26.757
12	3.571	4.404	5.226	6.304	18.549	21.026	23.337	26.217	28.300
13	4.107	5.009	5.892	7.041	19.812	22.362	24.736	27.688	29.819
14	4.660	5.629	6.571	7.790	21.064	23.685	26.119	29.141	31.319
15	5.229	6.262	7.261	8.547	22.307	24.996	27.488	30.578	32.801
16	5.812	6.908	7.962	9.312	23.542	26.296	28.845	32.000	34.267
17	6.408	7.564	8.672	10.085	24.769	27.587	30.191	33.409	35.718
18	7.015	8.231	9.390	10.865	25.989	28.869	31.526	34.805	37.156
19	7.633	8.907	10.117	11.651	27.204	30.144	32.852	36.191	38.582
20	8.260	9.591	10.851	12.443	28.412	31.410	34.170	37.566	39.997
21	8.897	10.283	11.591	13.240	29.615	32.671	35.479	38.932	41.401
22	9.542	10.982	12.338	14.041	30.813	33.924	36.781	40.289	42.796
23	10.196	11.689	13.091	14.848	32.007	35.172	38.076	41.638	44.181
24	10.856	12.401	13.848	15.659	33.196	36.415	39.364	42.980	45.558
25	11.524	13.120	14.611	16.473	34.382	37.652	40.646	44.314	46.928
26	12.198	13.844	15.379	17.292	35.563	38.885	41.923	45.642	48.290
27	12.878	14.573	16.151	18.114	36.741	40.113	43.195	46.963	49.645
28	13.565	15.308	16.928	18.939	37.916	41.337	44.461	48.278	50.994
29	14.256	16.047	17.708	19.768	39.087	42.557	45.722	49.588	52.335
30	14.953	16.791	18.493	20.599	40.256	43.773	46.979	50.892	53.672
50	29.707	32.357	34.764	37.689	63.167	67.505	71.420	76.154	79.490
60	37.485	40.482	43.188	46.459	74.397	79.082	83.298	88.379	91.952
80	53.540	57.153	60.391	64.278	96.578	101.879	106.629	112.329	116.321
100	70.065	74.222	77.929	82.358	118.498	124.342	129.561	135.807	140.170

To have a probability of 0.05 in the right tail when df = 5, the tabled value is $\chi^2(5, 0.05) = 11.070$.
Quantitative Methods for Investment Analysis, Second Edition, by Richard A. DeFusco, CFA, Dennis W. McLeavey, CFA, Jerald E. Pinto, CFA, and David E. Runkle, CFA. Copyright © 2004 by CFA Institute.

Appendix D   Table of the *F*-Distribution

Panel A. Critical values for right-hand tail area equal to 0.05

Numerator: df_1 and Denominator: df_2

df2: \ df1:1	1	2	3	4	5	6	7	8	9	10	11	12	15	20	21	22	23	24	25	30	40	60	120	∞
1	161	200	216	225	230	234	237	239	241	242	243	244	246	248	248	249	249	249	249	250	251	252	253	254
2	18.5	19.0	19.2	19.2	19.3	19.3	19.4	19.4	19.4	19.4	19.4	19.4	19.4	19.4	19.4	19.5	19.5	19.5	19.5	19.5	19.5	19.5	19.5	19.5
3	10.1	9.55	9.28	9.12	9.01	8.94	8.89	8.85	8.81	8.79	8.76	8.74	8.70	8.66	8.65	8.65	8.64	8.64	8.63	8.62	8.59	8.57	8.55	8.53
4	7.71	6.94	6.59	6.39	6.26	6.16	6.09	6.04	6.00	5.96	5.94	5.91	5.86	5.80	5.79	5.79	5.78	5.77	5.77	5.75	5.72	5.69	5.66	5.63
5	6.61	5.79	5.41	5.19	5.05	4.95	4.88	4.82	4.77	4.74	4.70	4.68	4.62	4.56	4.55	4.54	4.53	4.53	4.52	4.50	4.46	4.43	4.40	4.37
6	5.99	5.14	4.76	4.53	4.39	4.28	4.21	4.15	4.10	4.06	4.03	4.00	3.94	3.87	3.86	3.86	3.85	3.84	3.83	3.81	3.77	3.74	3.70	3.67
7	5.59	4.74	4.35	4.12	3.97	3.87	3.79	3.73	3.68	3.64	3.60	3.57	3.51	3.44	3.43	3.43	3.42	3.41	3.40	3.38	3.34	3.30	3.27	3.23
8	5.32	4.46	4.07	3.84	3.69	3.58	3.50	3.44	3.39	3.35	3.31	3.28	3.22	3.15	3.14	3.13	3.12	3.12	3.11	3.08	3.04	3.01	2.97	2.93
9	5.12	4.26	3.86	3.63	3.48	3.37	3.29	3.23	3.18	3.14	3.10	3.07	3.01	2.94	2.93	2.92	2.91	2.90	2.89	2.86	2.83	2.79	2.75	2.71
10	4.96	4.10	3.71	3.48	3.33	3.22	3.14	3.07	3.02	2.98	2.94	2.91	2.85	2.77	2.76	2.75	2.75	2.74	2.73	2.70	2.66	2.62	2.58	2.54
11	4.84	3.98	3.59	3.36	3.20	3.09	3.01	2.95	2.90	2.85	2.82	2.79	2.72	2.65	2.64	2.63	2.62	2.61	2.60	2.57	2.53	2.49	2.45	2.40
12	4.75	3.89	3.49	3.26	3.11	3.00	2.91	2.85	2.80	2.75	2.72	2.69	2.62	2.54	2.53	2.52	2.51	2.51	2.50	2.47	2.43	2.38	2.34	2.30
13	4.67	3.81	3.41	3.18	3.03	2.92	2.83	2.77	2.71	2.67	2.63	2.60	2.53	2.46	2.45	2.44	2.43	2.42	2.41	2.38	2.34	2.30	2.25	2.21
14	4.60	3.74	3.34	3.11	2.96	2.85	2.76	2.70	2.65	2.60	2.57	2.53	2.46	2.39	2.38	2.37	2.36	2.35	2.34	2.31	2.27	2.22	2.18	2.13
15	4.54	3.68	3.29	3.06	2.90	2.79	2.71	2.64	2.59	2.54	2.51	2.48	2.40	2.33	2.32	2.31	2.30	2.29	2.28	2.25	2.20	2.16	2.11	2.07
16	4.49	3.63	3.24	3.01	2.85	2.74	2.66	2.59	2.54	2.49	2.46	2.42	2.35	2.28	2.26	2.25	2.24	2.24	2.23	2.19	2.15	2.11	2.06	2.01
17	4.45	3.59	3.20	2.96	2.81	2.70	2.61	2.55	2.49	2.45	2.41	2.38	2.31	2.23	2.22	2.21	2.20	2.19	2.18	2.15	2.10	2.06	2.01	1.96
18	4.41	3.55	3.16	2.93	2.77	2.66	2.58	2.51	2.46	2.41	2.37	2.34	2.27	2.19	2.18	2.17	2.16	2.15	2.14	2.11	2.06	2.02	1.97	1.92
19	4.38	3.52	3.13	2.90	2.74	2.63	2.54	2.48	2.42	2.38	2.34	2.31	2.23	2.16	2.14	2.13	2.12	2.11	2.11	2.07	2.03	1.98	1.93	1.88
20	4.35	3.49	3.10	2.87	2.71	2.60	2.51	2.45	2.39	2.35	2.31	2.28	2.20	2.12	2.11	2.10	2.09	2.08	2.07	2.04	1.99	1.95	1.90	1.84

(continued)

Appendix D   *Continued*

Panel A. Critical values for right-hand tail area equal to 0.05

Numerator: df_1 and Denominator: df_2

df1:1	2	3	4	5	6	7	8	9	10	11	12	15	20	21	22	23	24	25	30	40	60	120	∞
21	4.32	3.47	3.07	2.84	2.68	2.57	2.49	2.42	2.37	2.32	2.28	2.25	2.18	2.10	2.08	2.07	2.06	2.05	2.05	2.01	1.96	1.92	1.87	1.81
22	4.30	3.44	3.05	2.82	2.66	2.55	2.46	2.40	2.34	2.30	2.26	2.23	2.15	2.07	2.06	2.05	2.04	2.03	2.02	1.98	1.94	1.89	1.84	1.78
23	4.28	3.42	3.03	2.80	2.64	2.53	2.44	2.37	2.32	2.27	2.24	2.20	2.13	2.05	2.04	2.02	2.01	2.01	2.00	1.96	1.91	1.86	1.81	1.76
24	4.26	3.40	3.01	2.78	2.62	2.51	2.42	2.36	2.30	2.25	2.22	2.18	2.11	2.03	2.01	2.00	1.99	1.98	1.97	1.94	1.89	1.84	1.79	1.73
25	4.24	3.39	2.99	2.76	2.60	2.49	2.40	2.34	2.28	2.24	2.20	2.16	2.09	2.01	2.00	1.98	1.97	1.96	1.96	1.92	1.87	1.82	1.77	1.71
30	4.17	3.32	2.92	2.69	2.53	2.42	2.33	2.27	2.21	2.16	2.13	2.09	2.01	1.93	1.92	1.91	1.90	1.89	1.88	1.84	1.79	1.74	1.68	1.62
40	4.08	3.23	2.84	2.61	2.45	2.34	2.25	2.18	2.12	2.08	2.04	2.00	1.92	1.84	1.83	1.81	1.80	1.79	1.78	1.74	1.69	1.64	1.58	1.51
60	4.00	3.15	2.76	2.53	2.37	2.25	2.17	2.10	2.04	1.99	1.95	1.92	1.84	1.75	1.73	1.72	1.71	1.70	1.69	1.65	1.59	1.53	1.47	1.39
120	3.92	3.07	2.68	2.45	2.29	2.18	2.09	2.02	1.96	1.91	1.87	1.83	1.75	1.66	1.64	1.63	1.62	1.61	1.60	1.55	1.50	1.43	1.35	1.25
Infinity	3.84	3.00	2.60	2.37	2.21	2.10	2.01	1.94	1.88	1.83	1.79	1.75	1.67	1.57	1.56	1.54	1.53	1.52	1.51	1.46	1.39	1.32	1.22	1.00

With 1 degree of freedom (df) in the numerator and 3 df in the denominator, the critical F-value is 10.1 for a right-hand tail area equal to 0.05.

Appendix D Table of the *F*-Distribution

Panel B. Critical values for right-hand tail area equal to 0.025

Numerator: df_1 and Denominator: df_2

df2:	df1: 1	2	3	4	5	6	7	8	9	10	11	12	15	20	21	22	23	24	25	30	40	60	120	∞
1	648	799	864	900	922	937	948	957	963	969	973	977	985	993	994	995	996	997	998	1001	1006	1010	1014	1018
2	38.51	39.00	39.17	39.25	39.30	39.33	39.36	39.37	39.39	39.40	39.41	39.41	39.43	39.45	39.45	39.45	39.45	39.46	39.46	39.46	39.47	39.48	39.49	39.50
3	17.44	16.04	15.44	15.10	14.88	14.73	14.62	14.54	14.47	14.42	14.37	14.34	14.25	14.17	14.16	14.14	14.13	14.12	14.12	14.08	14.04	13.99	13.95	13.90
4	12.22	10.65	9.98	9.60	9.36	9.20	9.07	8.98	8.90	8.84	8.79	8.75	8.66	8.56	8.55	8.53	8.52	8.51	8.50	8.46	8.41	8.36	8.31	8.26
5	10.01	8.43	7.76	7.39	7.15	6.98	6.85	6.76	6.68	6.62	6.57	6.52	6.43	6.33	6.31	6.30	6.29	6.28	6.27	6.23	6.18	6.12	6.07	6.02
6	8.81	7.26	6.60	6.23	5.99	5.82	5.70	5.60	5.52	5.46	5.41	5.37	5.27	5.17	5.15	5.14	5.13	5.12	5.11	5.07	5.01	4.96	4.90	4.85
7	8.07	6.54	5.89	5.52	5.29	5.12	4.99	4.90	4.82	4.76	4.71	4.67	4.57	4.47	4.45	4.44	4.43	4.41	4.40	4.36	4.31	4.25	4.20	4.14
8	7.57	6.06	5.42	5.05	4.82	4.65	4.53	4.43	4.36	4.30	4.24	4.20	4.10	4.00	3.98	3.97	3.96	3.95	3.94	3.89	3.84	3.78	3.73	3.67
9	7.21	5.71	5.08	4.72	4.48	4.32	4.20	4.10	4.03	3.96	3.91	3.87	3.77	3.67	3.65	3.64	3.63	3.61	3.60	3.56	3.51	3.45	3.39	3.33
10	6.94	5.46	4.83	4.47	4.24	4.07	3.95	3.85	3.78	3.72	3.66	3.62	3.52	3.42	3.40	3.39	3.38	3.37	3.35	3.31	3.26	3.20	3.14	3.08
11	6.72	5.26	4.63	4.28	4.04	3.88	3.76	3.66	3.59	3.53	3.47	3.43	3.33	3.23	3.21	3.20	3.18	3.17	3.16	3.12	3.06	3.00	2.94	2.88
12	6.55	5.10	4.47	4.12	3.89	3.73	3.61	3.51	3.44	3.37	3.32	3.28	3.18	3.07	3.06	3.04	3.03	3.02	3.01	2.96	2.91	2.85	2.79	2.72
13	6.41	4.97	4.35	4.00	3.77	3.60	3.48	3.39	3.31	3.25	3.20	3.15	3.05	2.95	2.93	2.92	2.91	2.89	2.88	2.84	2.78	2.72	2.66	2.60
14	6.30	4.86	4.24	3.89	3.66	3.50	3.38	3.29	3.21	3.15	3.09	3.05	2.95	2.84	2.83	2.81	2.80	2.79	2.78	2.73	2.67	2.61	2.55	2.49
15	6.20	4.77	4.15	3.80	3.58	3.41	3.29	3.20	3.12	3.06	3.01	2.96	2.86	2.76	2.74	2.73	2.71	2.70	2.69	2.64	2.59	2.52	2.46	2.40

(continued)

Appendix D   *Continued*

Panel B. Critical values for right-hand tail area equal to 0.025

Numerator: df_1 and Denominator: df_2

df1: 1	2	3	4	5	6	7	8	9	10	11	12	15	20	21	22	23	24	25	30	40	60	120	∞
16	6.12	4.69	4.08	3.73	3.50	3.34	3.22	3.12	3.05	2.99	2.93	2.89	2.79	2.68	2.67	2.65	2.64	2.63	2.61	2.57	2.51	2.45	2.38	2.32
17	6.04	4.62	4.01	3.66	3.44	3.28	3.16	3.06	2.98	2.92	2.87	2.82	2.72	2.62	2.60	2.59	2.57	2.56	2.55	2.50	2.44	2.38	2.32	2.25
18	5.98	4.56	3.95	3.61	3.38	3.22	3.10	3.01	2.93	2.87	2.81	2.77	2.67	2.56	2.54	2.53	2.52	2.50	2.49	2.44	2.38	2.32	2.26	2.19
19	5.92	4.51	3.90	3.56	3.33	3.17	3.05	2.96	2.88	2.82	2.76	2.72	2.62	2.51	2.49	2.48	2.46	2.45	2.44	2.39	2.33	2.27	2.20	2.13
20	5.87	4.46	3.86	3.51	3.29	3.13	3.01	2.91	2.84	2.77	2.72	2.68	2.57	2.46	2.45	2.43	2.42	2.41	2.40	2.35	2.29	2.22	2.16	2.09
21	5.83	4.42	3.82	3.48	3.25	3.09	2.97	2.87	2.80	2.73	2.68	2.64	2.53	2.42	2.41	2.39	2.38	2.37	2.36	2.31	2.25	2.18	2.11	2.04
22	5.79	4.38	3.78	3.44	3.22	3.05	2.93	2.84	2.76	2.70	2.65	2.60	2.50	2.39	2.37	2.36	2.34	2.33	2.32	2.27	2.21	2.14	2.08	2.00
23	5.75	4.35	3.75	3.41	3.18	3.02	2.90	2.81	2.73	2.67	2.62	2.57	2.47	2.36	2.34	2.33	2.31	2.30	2.29	2.24	2.18	2.11	2.04	1.97
24	5.72	4.32	3.72	3.38	3.15	2.99	2.87	2.78	2.70	2.64	2.59	2.54	2.44	2.33	2.31	2.30	2.28	2.27	2.26	2.21	2.15	2.08	2.01	1.94
25	5.69	4.29	3.69	3.35	3.13	2.97	2.85	2.75	2.68	2.61	2.56	2.51	2.41	2.30	2.28	2.27	2.26	2.24	2.23	2.18	2.12	2.05	1.98	1.91
30	5.57	4.18	3.59	3.25	3.03	2.87	2.75	2.65	2.57	2.51	2.46	2.41	2.31	2.20	2.18	2.16	2.15	2.14	2.12	2.07	2.01	1.94	1.87	1.79
40	5.42	4.05	3.46	3.13	2.90	2.74	2.62	2.53	2.45	2.39	2.33	2.29	2.18	2.07	2.05	2.03	2.02	2.01	1.99	1.94	1.88	1.80	1.72	1.64
60	5.29	3.93	3.34	3.01	2.79	2.63	2.51	2.41	2.33	2.27	2.22	2.17	2.06	1.94	1.93	1.91	1.90	1.88	1.87	1.82	1.74	1.67	1.58	1.48
120	5.15	3.80	3.23	2.89	2.67	2.52	2.39	2.30	2.22	2.16	2.10	2.05	1.94	1.82	1.81	1.79	1.77	1.76	1.75	1.69	1.61	1.53	1.43	1.31
Infinity	5.02	3.69	3.12	2.79	2.57	2.41	2.29	2.19	2.11	2.05	1.99	1.94	1.83	1.71	1.69	1.67	1.66	1.64	1.63	1.57	1.48	1.39	1.27	1.00

Appendix D Table of the F-Distribution

Panel C. Critical values for right-hand tail area equal to 0.01

Numerator: df_1, and Denominator: df_2

df1:	1	2	3	4	5	6	7	8	9	10	11	12	15	20	21	22	23	24	25	30	40	60	120	∞
df2: 1	4052	5000	5403	5625	5764	5859	5928	5982	6023	6056	6083	6106	6157	6209	6216	6223	6229	6235	6240	6261	6287	6313	6339	6366
2	98.5	99.0	99.2	99.2	99.3	99.3	99.4	99.4	99.4	99.4	99.4	99.4	99.4	99.4	99.5	99.5	99.5	99.5	99.5	99.5	99.5	99.5	99.5	99.5
3	34.1	30.8	29.5	28.7	28.2	27.9	27.7	27.5	27.3	27.2	27.1	27.1	26.9	26.7	26.7	26.6	26.6	26.6	26.6	26.5	26.4	26.3	26.2	26.1
4	21.2	18.0	16.7	16.0	15.5	15.2	15.0	14.8	14.7	14.5	14.5	14.4	14.2	14.0	14.0	14.0	13.9	13.9	13.9	13.8	13.7	13.7	13.6	13.5
5	16.3	13.3	12.1	11.4	11.0	10.7	10.5	10.3	10.2	10.1	10.0	9.89	9.72	9.55	9.53	9.51	9.49	9.47	9.45	9.38	9.29	9.20	9.11	9.02
6	13.7	10.9	9.78	9.15	8.75	8.47	8.26	8.10	7.98	7.87	7.79	7.72	7.56	7.40	7.37	7.35	7.33	7.31	7.30	7.23	7.14	7.06	6.97	6.88
7	12.2	9.55	8.45	7.85	7.46	7.19	6.99	6.84	6.72	6.62	6.54	6.47	6.31	6.16	6.13	6.11	6.09	6.07	6.06	5.99	5.91	5.82	5.74	5.65
8	11.3	8.65	7.59	7.01	6.63	6.37	6.18	6.03	5.91	5.81	5.73	5.67	5.52	5.36	5.34	5.32	5.30	5.28	5.26	5.20	5.12	5.03	4.95	4.86
9	10.6	8.02	6.99	6.42	6.06	5.80	5.61	5.47	5.35	5.26	5.18	5.11	4.96	4.81	4.79	4.77	4.75	4.73	4.71	4.65	4.57	4.48	4.40	4.31
10	10.0	7.56	6.55	5.99	5.64	5.39	5.20	5.06	4.94	4.85	4.77	4.71	4.56	4.41	4.38	4.36	4.34	4.33	4.31	4.25	4.17	4.08	4.00	3.91
11	9.65	7.21	6.22	5.67	5.32	5.07	4.89	4.74	4.63	4.54	4.46	4.40	4.25	4.10	4.08	4.06	4.04	4.02	4.01	3.94	3.86	3.78	3.69	3.60
12	9.33	6.93	5.95	5.41	5.06	4.82	4.64	4.50	4.39	4.30	4.22	4.16	4.01	3.86	3.84	3.82	3.80	3.78	3.76	3.70	3.62	3.54	3.45	3.36
13	9.07	6.70	5.74	5.21	4.86	4.62	4.44	4.30	4.19	4.10	4.02	3.96	3.82	3.66	3.64	3.62	3.60	3.59	3.57	3.51	3.43	3.34	3.25	3.17
14	8.86	6.51	5.56	5.04	4.70	4.46	4.28	4.14	4.03	3.94	3.86	3.80	3.66	3.51	3.48	3.46	3.44	3.43	3.41	3.35	3.27	3.18	3.09	3.00
15	8.68	6.36	5.42	4.89	4.56	4.32	4.14	4.00	3.89	3.80	3.73	3.67	3.52	3.37	3.35	3.33	3.31	3.29	3.28	3.21	3.13	3.05	2.96	2.87

(continued)

Appendix D Continued

Panel C. Critical values for right-hand tail area equal to 0.01

Numerator: df_1 and Denominator: df_2

df1:	1	2	3	4	5	6	7	8	9	10	11	12	15	20	21	22	23	24	25	30	40	60	120	∞
16	8.53	6.23	5.29	4.77	4.44	4.20	4.03	3.89	3.78	3.69	3.62	3.55	3.41	3.26	3.24	3.22	3.20	3.18	3.16	3.10	3.02	2.93	2.84	2.75
17	8.40	6.11	5.19	4.67	4.34	4.10	3.93	3.79	3.68	3.59	3.52	3.46	3.31	3.16	3.14	3.12	3.10	3.08	3.07	3.00	2.92	2.83	2.75	2.65
18	8.29	6.01	5.09	4.58	4.25	4.01	3.84	3.71	3.60	3.51	3.43	3.37	3.23	3.08	3.05	3.03	3.02	3.00	2.98	2.92	2.84	2.75	2.66	2.57
19	8.19	5.93	5.01	4.50	4.17	3.94	3.77	3.63	3.52	3.43	3.36	3.30	3.15	3.00	2.98	2.96	2.94	2.92	2.91	2.84	2.76	2.67	2.58	2.49
20	8.10	5.85	4.94	4.43	4.10	3.87	3.70	3.56	3.46	3.37	3.29	3.23	3.09	2.94	2.92	2.90	2.88	2.86	2.84	2.78	2.69	2.61	2.52	2.42
21	8.02	5.78	4.87	4.37	4.04	3.81	3.64	3.51	3.40	3.31	3.24	3.17	3.03	2.88	2.86	2.84	2.82	2.80	2.79	2.72	2.64	2.55	2.46	2.36
22	7.95	5.72	4.82	4.31	3.99	3.76	3.59	3.45	3.35	3.26	3.18	3.12	2.98	2.83	2.81	2.78	2.77	2.75	2.73	2.67	2.58	2.50	2.40	2.31
23	7.88	5.66	4.76	4.26	3.94	3.71	3.54	3.41	3.30	3.21	3.14	3.07	2.93	2.78	2.76	2.74	2.72	2.70	2.69	2.62	2.54	2.45	2.35	2.26
24	7.82	5.61	4.72	4.22	3.90	3.67	3.50	3.36	3.26	3.17	3.09	3.03	2.89	2.74	2.72	2.70	2.68	2.66	2.64	2.58	2.49	2.40	2.31	2.21
25	7.77	5.57	4.68	4.18	3.86	3.63	3.46	3.32	3.22	3.13	3.06	2.99	2.85	2.70	2.68	2.66	2.64	2.62	2.60	2.53	2.45	2.36	2.27	2.17
30	7.56	5.39	4.51	4.02	3.70	3.47	3.30	3.17	3.07	2.98	2.91	2.84	2.70	2.55	2.53	2.51	2.49	2.47	2.45	2.39	2.30	2.21	2.11	2.01
40	7.31	5.18	4.31	3.83	3.51	3.29	3.12	2.99	2.89	2.80	2.73	2.66	2.52	2.37	2.35	2.33	2.31	2.29	2.27	2.20	2.11	2.02	1.92	1.80
60	7.08	4.98	4.13	3.65	3.34	3.12	2.95	2.82	2.72	2.63	2.56	2.50	2.35	2.20	2.17	2.15	2.13	2.12	2.10	2.03	1.94	1.84	1.73	1.60
120	6.85	4.79	3.95	3.48	3.17	2.96	2.79	2.66	2.56	2.47	2.40	2.34	2.19	2.03	2.01	1.99	1.97	1.95	1.93	1.86	1.76	1.66	1.53	1.38
Infinity	6.63	4.61	3.78	3.32	3.02	2.80	2.64	2.51	2.41	2.32	2.25	2.18	2.04	1.88	1.85	1.83	1.81	1.79	1.77	1.70	1.59	1.47	1.32	1.00

Appendix D   Table of the F-Distribution

Panel D. Critical values for right-hand tail area equal to 0.005

df2: \ df1:	1	2	3	4	5	6	7	8	9	10	11	12	15	20	21	22	23	24	25	30	40	60	120	∞
1	16211	20000	21615	22500	23056	23437	23715	23925	24091	24222	24334	24426	24630	24836	24863	24892	24915	24940	24959	25044	25146	25253	25359	25464
2	198.5	199.0	199.2	199.2	199.3	199.3	199.4	199.4	199.4	199.4	199.4	199.4	199.4	199.4	199.4	199.4	199.4	199.4	199.4	199.5	199.5	199.5	199.5	200
3	55.55	49.80	47.47	46.20	45.39	44.84	44.43	44.13	43.88	43.68	43.52	43.39	43.08	42.78	42.73	42.69	42.66	42.62	42.59	42.47	42.31	42.15	41.99	41.83
4	31.33	26.28	24.26	23.15	22.46	21.98	21.62	21.35	21.14	20.97	20.82	20.70	20.44	20.17	20.13	20.09	20.06	20.03	20.00	19.89	19.75	19.61	19.47	19.32
5	22.78	18.31	16.53	15.56	14.94	14.51	14.20	13.96	13.77	13.62	13.49	13.38	13.15	12.90	12.87	12.84	12.81	12.78	12.76	12.66	12.53	12.40	12.27	12.14
6	18.63	14.54	12.92	12.03	11.46	11.07	10.79	10.57	10.39	10.25	10.13	10.03	9.81	9.59	9.56	9.53	9.50	9.47	9.45	9.36	9.24	9.12	9.00	8.88
7	16.24	12.40	10.88	10.05	9.52	9.16	8.89	8.68	8.51	8.38	8.27	8.18	7.97	7.75	7.72	7.69	7.67	7.64	7.62	7.53	7.42	7.31	7.19	7.08
8	14.69	11.04	9.60	8.81	8.30	7.95	7.69	7.50	7.34	7.21	7.10	7.01	6.81	6.61	6.58	6.55	6.53	6.50	6.48	6.40	6.29	6.18	6.06	5.95
9	13.61	10.11	8.72	7.96	7.47	7.13	6.88	6.69	6.54	6.42	6.31	6.23	6.03	5.83	5.80	5.78	5.75	5.73	5.71	5.62	5.52	5.41	5.30	5.19
10	12.83	9.43	8.08	7.34	6.87	6.54	6.30	6.12	5.97	5.85	5.75	5.66	5.47	5.27	5.25	5.22	5.20	5.17	5.15	5.07	4.97	4.86	4.75	4.64
11	12.23	8.91	7.60	6.88	6.42	6.10	5.86	5.68	5.54	5.42	5.32	5.24	5.05	4.86	4.83	4.80	4.78	4.76	4.74	4.65	4.55	4.45	4.34	4.23
12	11.75	8.51	7.23	6.52	6.07	5.76	5.52	5.35	5.20	5.09	4.99	4.91	4.72	4.53	4.50	4.48	4.45	4.43	4.41	4.33	4.23	4.12	4.01	3.90
13	11.37	8.19	6.93	6.23	5.79	5.48	5.25	5.08	4.94	4.82	4.72	4.64	4.46	4.27	4.24	4.22	4.19	4.17	4.15	4.07	3.97	3.87	3.76	3.65
14	11.06	7.92	6.68	6.00	5.56	5.26	5.03	4.86	4.72	4.60	4.51	4.43	4.25	4.06	4.03	4.01	3.98	3.96	3.94	3.86	3.76	3.66	3.55	3.44
15	10.80	7.70	6.48	5.80	5.37	5.07	4.85	4.67	4.54	4.42	4.33	4.25	4.07	3.88	3.86	3.83	3.81	3.79	3.77	3.69	3.59	3.48	3.37	3.26

Numerator: df_1 and Denominator: df_2

(continued)

Appendix D   *Continued*

Panel D. Critical values for right-hand tail area equal to 0.005

Numerator: df_1 and Denominator: df_2

df1: 1	2	3	4	5	6	7	8	9	10	11	12	15	20	21	22	23	24	25	30	40	60	120	∞
16	10.58	7.51	6.30	5.64	5.21	4.91	4.69	4.52	4.38	4.27	4.18	4.10	3.92	3.73	3.71	3.68	3.66	3.64	3.62	3.54	3.44	3.33	3.22	3.11
17	10.38	7.35	6.16	5.50	5.07	4.78	4.56	4.39	4.25	4.14	4.05	3.97	3.79	3.61	3.58	3.56	3.53	3.51	3.49	3.41	3.31	3.21	3.10	2.98
18	10.22	7.21	6.03	5.37	4.96	4.66	4.44	4.28	4.14	4.03	3.94	3.86	3.68	3.50	3.47	3.45	3.42	3.40	3.38	3.30	3.20	3.10	2.99	2.87
19	10.07	7.09	5.92	5.27	4.85	4.56	4.34	4.18	4.04	3.93	3.84	3.76	3.59	3.40	3.37	3.35	3.33	3.31	3.29	3.21	3.11	3.00	2.89	2.78
20	9.94	6.99	5.82	5.17	4.76	4.47	4.26	4.09	3.96	3.85	3.76	3.68	3.50	3.32	3.29	3.27	3.24	3.22	3.20	3.12	3.02	2.92	2.81	2.69
21	9.83	6.89	5.73	5.09	4.68	4.39	4.18	4.01	3.88	3.77	3.68	3.60	3.43	3.24	3.22	3.19	3.17	3.15	3.13	3.05	2.95	2.84	2.73	2.61
22	9.73	6.81	5.65	5.02	4.61	4.32	4.11	3.94	3.81	3.70	3.61	3.54	3.36	3.18	3.15	3.12	3.10	3.08	3.06	2.98	2.88	2.77	2.66	2.55
23	9.63	6.73	5.58	4.95	4.54	4.26	4.05	3.88	3.75	3.64	3.55	3.47	3.30	3.12	3.09	3.06	3.04	3.02	3.00	2.92	2.82	2.71	2.60	2.48
24	9.55	6.66	5.52	4.89	4.49	4.20	3.99	3.83	3.69	3.59	3.50	3.42	3.25	3.06	3.04	3.01	2.99	2.97	2.95	2.87	2.77	2.66	2.55	2.43
25	9.48	6.60	5.46	4.84	4.43	4.15	3.94	3.78	3.64	3.54	3.45	3.37	3.20	3.01	2.99	2.96	2.94	2.92	2.90	2.82	2.72	2.61	2.50	2.38
30	9.18	6.35	5.24	4.62	4.23	3.95	3.74	3.58	3.45	3.34	3.25	3.18	3.01	2.82	2.80	2.77	2.75	2.73	2.71	2.63	2.52	2.42	2.30	2.18
40	8.83	6.07	4.98	4.37	3.99	3.71	3.51	3.35	3.22	3.12	3.03	2.95	2.78	2.60	2.57	2.55	2.52	2.50	2.48	2.40	2.30	2.18	2.06	1.93
60	8.49	5.79	4.73	4.14	3.76	3.49	3.29	3.13	3.01	2.90	2.82	2.74	2.57	2.39	2.36	2.33	2.31	2.29	2.27	2.19	2.08	1.96	1.83	1.69
120	8.18	5.54	4.50	3.92	3.55	3.28	3.09	2.93	2.81	2.71	2.62	2.54	2.37	2.19	2.16	2.13	2.11	2.09	2.07	1.98	1.87	1.75	1.61	1.43
Infinity	7.88	5.30	4.28	3.72	3.35	3.09	2.90	2.74	2.62	2.52	2.43	2.36	2.19	2.00	1.97	1.95	1.92	1.90	1.88	1.79	1.67	1.53	1.36	1.00

| **Appendix E** | Critical Values for the Durbin-Watson Statistic ($\alpha = .05$) |

	K = 1		K = 2		K = 3		K = 4		K = 5	
n	d_l	d_u	d_l	d_u	d_l	d_u	d_l	d_u	d_l	d_u
15	1.08	1.36	0.95	1.54	0.82	1.75	0.69	1.97	0.56	2.21
16	1.10	1.37	0.98	1.54	0.86	1.73	0.74	1.93	0.62	2.15
17	1.13	1.38	1.02	1.54	0.90	1.71	0.78	1.90	0.67	2.10
18	1.16	1.39	1.05	1.53	0.93	1.69	0.82	1.87	0.71	2.06
19	1.18	1.40	1.08	1.53	0.97	1.68	0.86	1.85	0.75	2.02
20	1.20	1.41	1.10	1.54	1.00	1.68	0.90	1.83	0.79	1.99
21	1.22	1.42	1.13	1.54	1.03	1.67	0.93	1.81	0.83	1.96
22	1.24	1.43	1.15	1.54	1.05	1.66	0.96	1.80	0.86	1.94
23	1.26	1.44	1.17	1.54	1.08	1.66	0.99	1.79	0.90	1.92
24	1.27	1.45	1.19	1.55	1.10	1.66	1.01	1.78	0.93	1.90
25	1.29	1.45	1.21	1.55	1.12	1.66	1.04	1.77	0.95	1.89
26	1.30	1.46	1.22	1.55	1.14	1.65	1.06	1.76	0.98	1.88
27	1.32	1.47	1.24	1.56	1.16	1.65	1.08	1.76	1.01	1.86
28	1.33	1.48	1.26	1.56	1.18	1.65	1.10	1.75	1.03	1.85
29	1.34	1.48	1.27	1.56	1.20	1.65	1.12	1.74	1.05	1.84
30	1.35	1.49	1.28	1.57	1.21	1.65	1.14	1.74	1.07	1.83
31	1.36	1.50	1.30	1.57	1.23	1.65	1.16	1.74	1.09	1.83
32	1.37	1.50	1.31	1.57	1.24	1.65	1.18	1.73	1.11	1.82
33	1.38	1.51	1.32	1.58	1.26	1.65	1.19	1.73	1.13	1.81
34	1.39	1.51	1.33	1.58	1.27	1.65	1.21	1.73	1.15	1.81
35	1.40	1.52	1.34	1.58	1.28	1.65	1.22	1.73	1.16	1.80
36	1.41	1.52	1.35	1.59	1.29	1.65	1.24	1.73	1.18	1.80
37	1.42	1.53	1.36	1.59	1.31	1.66	1.25	1.72	1.19	1.80
38	1.43	1.54	1.37	1.59	1.32	1.66	1.26	1.72	1.21	1.79
39	1.43	1.54	1.38	1.60	1.33	1.66	1.27	1.72	1.22	1.79
40	1.44	1.54	1.39	1.60	1.34	1.66	1.29	1.72	1.23	1.79
45	1.48	1.57	1.43	1.62	1.38	1.67	1.34	1.72	1.29	1.78
50	1.50	1.59	1.46	1.63	1.42	1.67	1.38	1.72	1.34	1.77
55	1.53	1.60	1.49	1.64	1.45	1.68	1.41	1.72	1.38	1.77
60	1.55	1.62	1.51	1.65	1.48	1.69	1.44	1.73	1.41	1.77
65	1.57	1.63	1.54	1.66	1.50	1.70	1.47	1.73	1.44	1.77
70	1.58	1.64	1.55	1.67	1.52	1.70	1.49	1.74	1.46	1.77
75	1.60	1.65	1.57	1.68	1.54	1.71	1.51	1.74	1.49	1.77
80	1.61	1.66	1.59	1.69	1.56	1.72	1.53	1.74	1.51	1.77
85	1.62	1.67	1.60	1.70	1.57	1.72	1.55	1.75	1.52	1.77
90	1.63	1.68	1.61	1.70	1.59	1.73	1.57	1.75	1.54	1.78
95	1.64	1.69	1.62	1.71	1.60	1.73	1.58	1.75	1.56	1.78
100	1.65	1.69	1.63	1.72	1.61	1.74	1.59	1.76	1.57	1.78

Note: K = the number of slope parameters in the model.
Source: From J. Durbin and G. S. Watson, "Testing for Serial Correlation in Least Squares Regression, II." *Biometrika* 38 (1951): 159–178. Reproduced by permission of Oxford University Press.

Glossary

A priori probability A probability based on logical analysis rather than on observation or personal judgment.

Abnormal profit Equal to accounting profit less the implicit opportunity costs not included in total accounting costs; the difference between total revenue (TR) and total cost (TC).

Abnormal return The amount by which a security's actual return differs from its expected return, given the security's risk and the market's return.

Absolute dispersion The amount of variability present without comparison to any reference point or benchmark.

Absolute frequency The number of observations in a given interval (for grouped data).

Accelerated book build An offering of securities by an investment bank acting as principal that is accomplished in only one or two days.

Accelerated methods Depreciation methods that allocate a relatively large proportion of the cost of an asset to the early years of the asset's useful life.

Account With the accounting systems, a formal record of increases and decreases in a specific asset, liability, component of owners' equity, revenue, or expense.

Accounting (or explicit) costs Payments to non-owner parties for services or resources they supply to the firm.

Accounting loss When accounting profit is negative.

Accounting profit (income before taxes or pretax income) Income as reported on the income statement, in accordance with prevailing accounting standards, before the provisions for income tax expense.

Accounts payable Amounts that a business owes to its vendors for goods and services that were purchased from them but which have not yet been paid.

Accounts receivable (commercial receivables or trade receivables) Amounts customers owe the company for products that have been sold as well as amounts that may be due from suppliers (such as for returns of merchandise).

Accounts receivable turnover Ratio of sales on credit to the average balance in accounts receivable.

Accrued expenses (accrued liabilities) Liabilities related to expenses that have been incurred but not yet paid as of the end of an accounting period—an example of an accrued expense is rent that has been incurred but not yet paid, resulting in a liability "rent payable."

Accrued interest Interest earned but not yet paid.

Accrued revenue Revenue that has been earned but not yet billed to customers as of the end of an accounting period.

Accumulated depreciation An offset to property, plant, and equipment (PPE) reflecting the amount of the cost of PPE that has been allocated to current and previous accounting periods.

Acid-test ratio A stringent measure of liquidity that indicates a company's ability to satisfy current liabilities with its most liquid assets, calculated as (cash + short-term marketable investments + receivables) divided by current liabilities.

Acquisition method A method of accounting for a business combination where the acquirer is required to measure each identifiable asset and liability at fair value. This method was the result of a joint project of the IASB and FASB aiming at convergence in standards for the accounting of business combinations.

Action lag Delay from policy decisions to implementation.

Active investment An approach to investing in which the investor seeks to outperform a given benchmark.

Active return The return on a portfolio minus the return on the portfolio's benchmark.

Active strategy In reference to short-term cash management, an investment strategy characterized by monitoring and attempting to capitalize on market conditions to optimize the risk and return relationship of short-term investments.

Activity ratio (or participation ratio) The ratio of the labor force to total population of working age.

Activity ratios (asset utilization or operating efficiency ratios) Ratios that measure how efficiently a company performs day-to-day tasks, such as the collection of receivables and management of inventory.

Add-on interest A procedure for determining the interest on a bond or loan in which the interest is added onto the face value of a contract.

Addition rule for probabilities A principle stating that the probability that A or B occurs (both occur) equals the probability that A occurs, plus the probability that B occurs, minus the probability that both A and B occur.

Aggregate demand The quantity of goods and services that households, businesses, government, and foreign customers want to buy at any given level of prices.

Aggregate demand curve Inverse relationship between the price level and real output.

Aggregate income The value of all the payments earned by the suppliers of factors used in the production of goods and services.

Aggregate output The value of all the goods and services produced in a specified period of time.

Aggregate supply The quantity of goods and services producers are willing to supply at any given level of price.

Aggregate supply curve The level of domestic output that companies will produce at each price level.

Aging schedule A breakdown of accounts into categories of days outstanding.

All-or-nothing (AON) orders An order that includes the instruction to trade only if the trade fills the entire quantity (size) specified.

Allocationally efficient Said of a market, a financial system, or an economy that promotes the allocation of resources to their highest value uses.

Allowance for bad debts An offset to accounts receivable for the amount of accounts receivable that are estimated to be uncollectible.

Alternative investment markets   Market for investments other than traditional securities investments (i.e., traditional common and preferred shares and traditional fixed income instruments). The term usually encompasses direct and indirect investment in real estate (including timberland and farmland) and commodities (including precious metals); hedge funds, private equity, and other investments requiring specialized due diligence.

Alternative trading systems   (**electronic communications networks** or **multilateral trading facilities**) Trading venues that function like exchanges but that do not exercise regulatory authority over their subscribers except with respect to the conduct of the subscribers' trading in their trading systems.

American depository receipt   A U.S. dollar-denominated security that trades like a common share on U.S. exchanges.

American depository share   The underlying shares on which American depository receipts are based. They trade in the issuing company's domestic market.

American option   An option that can be exercised at any time until its expiration date.

American-style contracts   An option that can be exercised at any time until its expiration date.

Amortisation   The process of allocating the cost of intangible long-term assets having a finite useful life to accounting periods; the allocation of the amount of a bond premium or discount to the periods remaining until bond maturity.

Amortised cost   The historical cost (initially recognised cost) of an asset, adjusted for amortisation and impairment.

Amortization   The process of allocating the cost of intangible longterm assets having a finite useful life to accounting periods; the allocation of the amount of a bond premium or discount to the periods remaining until bond maturity.

Annual percentage rate   The cost of borrowing expressed as a yearly rate.

Annuity   A finite set of level sequential cash flows.

Annuity due   An annuity having a first cash flow that is paid immediately.

Anticipation stock   Excess inventory that is held in anticipation of increased demand, often because of seasonal patterns of demand.

Antidilutive   With reference to a transaction or a security, one that would increase earnings per share (EPS) or result in EPS higher than the company's basic EPS—antidilutive securities are not included in the calculation of diluted EPS.

Arbitrage   1) The simultaneous purchase of an undervalued asset or portfolio and sale of an overvalued but equivalent asset or portfolio, in order to obtain a riskless profit on the price differential. Taking advantage of a market inefficiency in a risk-free manner. 2) The condition in a financial market in which equivalent assets or combinations of assets sell for two different prices, creating an opportunity to profit at no risk with no commitment of money. In a well-functioning financial market, few arbitrage opportunities are possible. 3) A risk-free operation that earns an expected positive net profit but requires no net investment of money.

Arbitrageurs   Traders who engage in arbitrage (see *arbitrage*).

Arithmetic mean   The sum of the observations divided by the number of observations.

Arms index   A flow of funds indicator applied to a broad stock market index to measure the relative extent to which money is moving into or out of rising and declining stocks.

Asian call option   A European-style option with a value at maturity equal to the difference between the stock price at maturity and the average stock price during the life of the option, or $0, whichever is greater.

Ask   (offer) The price at which a dealer or trader is willing to sell an asset, typically qualified by a maximum quantity (ask size).

Ask size   The maximum quantity of an asset that pertains to a specific ask price from a trader. For example, if the ask for a share issue is $30 for a size of 1,000 shares, the trader is offering to sell at $30 up to 1,000 shares.

Asset allocation   The process of determining how investment funds should be distributed among asset classes.

Asset beta   The unlevered beta; reflects the business risk of the assets; the asset's systematic risk.

Asset class   A group of assets that have similar characteristics, attributes, and risk/return relationships.

Asset utilization ratios   Ratios that measure how efficiently a company performs day-to-day tasks, such as the collection of receivables and management of inventory.

Asset-based loan   A loan that is secured with company assets.

Asset-based valuation models   Valuation based on estimates of the market value of a company's assets.

Assets   Resources controlled by an enterprise as a result of past events and from which future economic benefits to the enterprise are expected to flow.

Assignment of accounts receivable   The use of accounts receivable as collateral for a loan.

At-the-money   An option in which the underlying value equals the exercise price.

Automated Clearing House (ACH)   An electronic payment network available to businesses, individuals, and financial institutions in the United States, U.S. Territories, and Canada.

Automatic stabilizer   A countercyclical factor that automatically comes into play as an economy slows and unemployment rises.

Available-for-sale   Debt and equity securities not classified as either held-to-maturity or held-for-trading securities. The investor is willing to sell but not actively planning to sell. In general, available-for-sale securities are reported at fair value on the balance sheet.

Available-for-sale securities   Debt and equity securities not classified as either held-to-maturity or held-for-trading securities. The investor is willing to sell but not actively planning to sell. In general, available-for-sale securities are reported at fair value on the balance sheet.

Average fixed cost   Total fixed cost divided by quantity.

Average product   Measures the productivity of inputs on average and is calculated by dividing total product by the total number of units for a given input that is used to generate that output.

Average revenue   Quantity sold divided into total revenue.

Average total cost   Total costs divided by quantity.

Average variable cost   Total variable cost divided by quantity.

Back simulation   Another term for the historical method of estimating VAR. This term is somewhat misleading in that the method involves not a *simulation* of the past but rather what *actually happened* in the past, sometimes adjusted to reflect the fact that a different portfolio may have existed in the past than is planned for the future.

Balance of trade deficit   When the domestic economy is spending more on foreign goods and services than foreign economies are spending on domestic goods and services.

Balance sheet (statement of financial position or statement of financial condition) The financial statement that presents an entity's current financial position by disclosing resources the entity controls (its assets) and the claims on those resources (its liabilities and equity claims), as of a particular point in time (the date of the balance sheet).

Balance sheet ratios Financial ratios involving balance sheet items only.

Balanced With respect to a government budget, one in which spending and revenues (taxes) are equal.

Bank discount basis A quoting convention that annualizes, on a 360-day year, the discount as a percentage of face value.

Bar chart A price chart with four bits of data for each time interval—the high, low, opening, and closing prices. A vertical line connects the high and low. A cross-hatch left indicates the opening price and a cross-hatch right indicates the close.

Barter economy An economy where economic agents as house-holds, corporations, and governments "pay" for goods and services with another good or service.

Base rates The reference rate on which a bank bases lending rates to all other customers.

Basic EPS Net earnings available to common shareholders (i.e., net income minus preferred dividends) divided by the weighted average number of common shares outstanding.

Basket of listed depository receipts An exchange-traded fund (ETF) that represents a portfolio of depository receipts.

Behavioral finance A field of finance that examines the psychological variables that affect and often distort the investment decision making of investors, analysts, and portfolio managers.

Behind the market Said of prices specified in orders that are worse than the best current price; e.g., for a limit buy order, a limit price below the best bid.

Bernoulli random variable A random variable having the outcomes 0 and 1.

Bernoulli trial An experiment that can produce one of two outcomes.

Best bid The highest bid in the market.

Best efforts offering An offering of a security using an investment bank in which the investment bank, as agent for the issuer, promises to use its best efforts to sell the offering but does not guarantee that a specific amount will be sold.

Best offer The lowest offer (ask price) in the market.

Beta A measure of systematic risk that is based on the covariance of an asset's or portfolio's return with the return of the overall market.

Bid The price at which a dealer or trader is willing to buy an asset, typically qualified by a maximum quantity.

Bid size The maximum quantity of an asset that pertains to a specific bid price from a trader.

Binomial model A model for pricing options in which the underlying price can move to only one of two possible new prices.

Binomial random variable The number of successes in n Bernoulli trials for which the probability of success is constant for all trials and the trials are independent.

Binomial tree The graphical representation of a model of asset price dynamics in which, at each period, the asset moves up with probability p or down with probability $(1 - p)$.

Block brokers A broker (agent) that provides brokerage services for large-size trades.

Blue chip Widely held large market capitalization companies that are considered financially sound and are leaders in their respective industry or local stock market.

Bollinger Bands A price-based technical analysis indicator consisting of a moving average plus a higher line representing the moving average plus a set number of standard deviations from average price (for the same number of periods as used to calculate the moving average) and a lower line that is a moving average minus the same number of standard deviations.

Bond equivalent yield A calculation of yield that is annualized using the ratio of 365 to the number of days to maturity. Bond equivalent yield allows for the restatement and comparison of securities with different compounding periods.

Bond indenture The governing legal credit agreement, typically incorporated by reference in the prospectus.

Bond market vigilantes Bond market participants who might reduce their demand for long-term bonds, thus pushing up their yields.

Bond option An option in which the underlying is a bond; primarily traded in over-the-counter markets.

Bond yield plus risk premium approach An estimate of the cost of common equity that is produced by summing the before-tax cost of debt and a risk premium that captures the additional yield on a company's stock relative to its bonds. The additional yield is often estimated using historical spreads between bond yields and stock yields.

Bond-equivalent basis A basis for stating an annual yield that annualizes a semiannual yield by doubling it.

Bond-equivalent yield The yield to maturity on a basis that ignores compounding.

Bonus issue of shares A type of dividend in which a company distributes additional shares of its common stock to shareholders instead of cash.

Book building Investment bankers' process of compiling a "book" or list of indications of interest to buy part of an offering.

Book value (or carrying value) The net amount shown for an asset or liability on the balance sheet; book value may also refer to the company's excess of total assets over total liabilities.

Boom An expansionary phase characterized by economic growth "testing the limits" of the economy.

Bottom-up analysis With reference to investment selection processes, an approach that involves selection from all securities within a specified investment universe, i.e., without prior narrowing of the universe on the basis of macroeconomic or overall market considerations.

Break point In the context of the weighted average cost of capital (WACC), a break point is the amount of capital at which the cost of one or more of the sources of capital changes, leading to a change in the WACC.

Breakeven point The number of units produced and sold at which the company's net income is zero (revenues = total costs); in the case of perfect competition, the quantity where price, average revenue, and marginal revenue equal average total cost.

Broad money Encompasses narrow money plus the entire range of liquid assets that can be used to make purchases.

Broker 1) An agent who executes orders to buy or sell securities on behalf of a client in exchange for a commission. 2) *See* Futures commission merchants.

Brokered market A market in which brokers arrange trades among their clients.

Broker–dealer A financial intermediary (often a company) that may function as a principal (dealer) or as an agent (broker) depending on the type of trade.

Budget constraint   A constraint on spending or investment imposed by wealth or income.

Budget surplus/deficit   The difference between government revenue and expenditure for a stated fixed period of time.

Business risk   The risk associated with operating earnings. Operating earnings are uncertain because total revenues and many of the expenditures contributed to produce those revenues are uncertain.

Buy-side firm   An investment management company or other investor that uses the services of brokers or dealers (i.e., the client of the sell side firms).

Buyback   A transaction in which a company buys back its own shares. Unlike stock dividends and stock splits, share repurchases use corporate cash.

Buyout fund   A fund that buys all the shares of a public company so that, in effect, the company becomes private.

CBOE Volatility Index   A measure of near-term market volatility as conveyed by S&P 500 stock index option prices.

CD equivalent yield   A yield on a basis comparable to the quoted yield on an interest-bearing money market instrument that pays interest on a 360-day basis; the annualized holding period yield, assuming a 360-day year.

Call   An option that gives the holder the right to buy an underlying asset from another party at a fixed price over a specific period of time.

Call market   A market in which trades occur only at a particular time and place (i.e., when the market is called).

Call money rate   The interest rate that buyers pay for their margin loan.

Call option   An option that gives the holder the right to buy an underlying asset from another party at a fixed price over a specific period of time.

Callable common shares   Shares that give the issuing company the option (or right), but not the obligation, to buy back the shares from investors at a call price that is specified when the shares are originally issued.

Candlestick chart   A price chart with four bits of data for each time interval. A candle indicates the opening and closing price for the interval. The body of the candle is shaded if the opening price was higher than the closing price, and the body is clear if the opening price was lower than the closing price. Vertical lines known as wicks or shadows extend from the top and bottom of the candle to indicate the high and the low prices for the interval.

Cannibalization   Cannibalization occurs when an investment takes customers and sales away from another part of the company.

Cap   1) A contract on an interest rate, whereby at periodic payment dates, the writer of the cap pays the difference between the market interest rate and a specified cap rate if, and only if, this difference is positive. This is equivalent to a stream of call options on the interest rate. 2) A combination of interest rate call options designed to hedge a borrower against rate increases on a floating-rate loan.

Capacity   The ability of the borrower to make its debt payments on time.

Capital allocation line   (CAL) A graph line that describes the combinations of expected return and standard deviation of return available to an investor from combining the optimal portfolio of risky assets with the risk-free asset.

Capital asset pricing model   (also CAPM) An equation describing the expected return on any asset (or portfolio) as a linear function of its beta relative to the market portfolio.

Capital budgeting   The allocation of funds to relatively long-range projects or investments.

Capital consumption allowance   A measure of the wear and tear (depreciation) of the capital stock that occurs in the production of goods and services.

Capital deepening investment   Increases the stock of capital relative to labor.

Capital expenditure   Expenditure on physical capital (fixed assets).

Capital market expectations   An investor's expectations concerning the risk and return prospects of asset classes.

Capital market line   (CML) The line with an intercept point equal to the risk-free rate that is tangent to the efficient frontier of risky assets; represents the efficient frontier when a risk-free asset is available for investment.

Capital markets   Financial markets that trade securities of longer duration, such as bonds and equities.

Capital rationing   A capital rationing environment assumes that the company has a fixed amount of funds to invest.

Capital stock   The accumulated amount of buildings, machinery, and equipment used to produce goods and services.

Capital structure   The mix of debt and equity that a company uses to finance its business; a company's specific mixture of long-term financing.

Caplet   Each component call option in a cap.

Captive finance subsidiary   A wholly-owned subsidiary of a company that is established to provide financing of the sales of the parent company.

Carrying amount   The amount at which an asset or liability is valued according to accounting principles.

Carrying value   The net amount shown for an asset or liability on the balance sheet; book value may also refer to the company's excess of total assets over total liabilities.

Cartel   Participants in collusive agreements that are made openly and formally.

Cash   In accounting contexts, cash on hand (e.g., petty cash and cash not yet deposited to the bank) and demand deposits held in banks and similar accounts that can be used in payment of obligations.

Cash conversion cycle   (net operating cycle) A financial metric that measures the length of time required for a company to convert cash invested in its operations to cash received as a result of its operations; equal to days of inventory on hand + days of sales outstanding – number of days of payables.

Cash equivalents   Very liquid short-term investments, usually maturing in 90 days or less.

Cash flow additivity principle   The principle that dollar amounts indexed at the same point in time are additive.

Cash flow from operating activities   The net amount of cash provided from operating activities.

Cash flow from operations   The net amount of cash provided from operating activities.

Cash price   The price for immediate purchase of the underlying asset.

Cash settlement   A procedure used in certain derivative transactions that specifies that the long and short parties engage in the equivalent cash value of a delivery transaction.

Central banks   The dominant bank in a country, usually with official or semi-official governmental status.

Change in polarity principle   A tenet of technical analysis that once a support level is breached, it becomes a resistance level. The same holds true for resistance levels; once breached, they become support levels.

Change of control put   A covenant giving bondholders the right to require the issuer to buy back their debt, often at par or at some small premium to par value, in the event that the borrower is acquired.

Character   The quality of a debt issuer's management.

Chart of accounts   A list of accounts used in an entity's accounting system.

Cheapest-to-deliver bond   A bond in which the amount received for delivering the bond is largest compared with the amount paid in the market for the bond.

Classified balance sheet   A balance sheet organized so as to group together the various assets and liabilities into subcategories (e.g., current and noncurrent).

Clawback   A requirement that the GP return any funds distributed as incentive fees until the LPs have received back their initial investment and a percentage of the total profit.

Clearing instructions   Instructions that indicate how to arrange the final settlement ("clearing") of a trade.

Clearinghouse   An entity associated with a futures market that acts as middleman between the contracting parties and guarantees to each party the performance of the other.

Closed-end fund   A mutual fund in which no new investment money is accepted. New investors invest by buying existing shares, and investors in the fund liquidate by selling their shares to other investors.

Coefficient of variation   (CV) The ratio of a set of observations' standard deviation to the observations' mean value.

Coincident economic indicators   Turning points that are usually close to those of the overall economy; they are believed to have value for identifying the economy's present state.

Collateral   The quality and value of the assets supporting an issuer's indebtedness.

Combination   A listing in which the order of the listed items does not matter.

Commercial paper   Unsecured short-term corporate debt that is characterized by a single payment at maturity.

Commercial receivables   **(Trade receivables or accounts receivable)** Amounts customers owe the company for products that have been sold as well as amounts that may be due from suppliers (such as for returns of merchandise).

Committed capital   The amount that the limited partners have agreed to provide to the private equity fund.

Committed lines of credit   A bank commitment to extend credit up to a pre-specified amount; the commitment is considered a short-term liability and is usually in effect for 364 days (one day short of a full year).

Commodity swap   A swap in which the underlying is a commodity such as oil, gold, or an agricultural product.

Common shares   A type of security that represent an ownership interest in a company.

Common stock   See *common shares*.

Common-size analysis   The restatement of financial statement items using a common denominator or reference item that allows one to identify trends and major differences; an example is an income statement in which all items are expressed as a percent of revenue.

Company analysis   Analysis of an individual company.

Comparable company   A company that has similar business risk; usually in the same industry and preferably with a single line of business.

Competitive strategy   A company's plans for responding to the threats and opportunities presented by the external environment.

Complements   Said of goods which tend to be used together; technically, two goods whose cross-price elasticity of demand is negative.

Complete markets   Informally, markets in which the variety of distinct securities traded is so broad that any desired payoff in a future state-of-the-world is achievable.

Complete preferences   The assumption that a consumer is able to make a comparison between any two possible bundles of goods.

Completed contract   A method of revenue recognition in which the company does not recognize any revenue until the contract is completed; used particularly in long-term construction contracts.

Component cost of capital   The rate of return required by suppliers of capital for an individual source of a company's funding, such as debt or equity.

Compounding   The process of accumulating interest on interest.

Comprehensive income   The change in equity of a business enterprise during a period from nonowner sources; includes all changes in equity during a period except those resulting from investments by owners and distributions to owners; comprehensive income equals net income plus other comprehensive income.

Conditional expected value   The expected value of a stated event given that another event has occurred.

Conditional probability   The probability of an event given (conditioned on) another event.

Conditional variances   The variance of one variable, given the outcome of another.

Consistent   With reference to estimators, describes an estimator for which the probability of estimates close to the value of the population parameter increases as sample size increases.

Conspicuous consumption   Consumption of high status goods, such as a luxury automobile or a very expensive piece of jewelry.

Constant maturity treasury   (or CMT) A hypothetical U.S. Treasury note with a constant maturity. A CMT exists for various years in the range of 2 to 10.

Constant returns to scale   The characteristic of constant per-unit costs in the presence of increased production.

Constant-cost industry   When firms in the industry experience no change in resource costs and output prices over the long run.

Constituent securities   With respect to an index, the individual securities within an index.

Consumer choice theory   The theory relating consumer demand curves to consumer preferences.

Consumer surplus   The difference between the value that a consumer places on units purchased and the amount of money that was required to pay for them.

Consumption basket   A specific combination of the goods and services that a consumer wants to consume.

Consumption bundle   A specific combination of the goods and services that a consumer wants to consume.

Continuation patterns   A type of pattern used in technical analysis to predict the resumption of a market trend that was in place prior to the formation of a pattern.

Continuous random variable   A random variable for which the range of possible outcomes is the real line (all real numbers between $-\infty$ and $+\infty$ or some subset of the real line).

Continuous time   Time thought of as advancing in extremely small increments.

Continuous trading market A market in which trades can be arranged and executed any time the market is open.

Continuously compounded return The natural logarithm of 1 plus the holding period return, or equivalently, the natural logarithm of the ending price over the beginning price.

Contra account An account that offsets another account.

Contraction The period of a business cycle after the peak and before the trough; often called a *recession* or, if exceptionally severe, called a *depression*.

Contractionary Tending to cause the real economy to contract.

Contractionary fiscal policy A fiscal policy that has the objective to make the real economy contract.

Contribution margin The amount available for fixed costs and profit after paying variable costs; revenue minus variable costs.

Conventional cash flow A conventional cash flow pattern is one with an initial outflow followed by a series of inflows.

Convergence The tendency for differences in output per capita across countries to diminish over time; in technical analysis, a term that describes the case when an indicator moves in the same manner as the security being analyzed.

Conversion factor An adjustment used to facilitate delivery on bond futures contracts in which any of a number of bonds with different characteristics are eligible for delivery.

Convertible preference shares A type of equity security that entitles shareholders to convert their shares into a specified number of common shares.

Core inflation The inflation rate calculated based on a price index of goods and services except food and energy.

Correlation A number between –1 and +1 that measures the comovement (linear association) between two random variables.

Correlation coefficient A number between –1 and +1 that measures the consistency or tendency for two investments to act in a similar way. It is used to determine the effect on portfolio risk when two assets are combined.

Cost averaging The periodic investment of a fixed amount of money.

Cost of capital The rate of return that suppliers of capital require as compensation for their contribution of capital.

Cost of debt The cost of debt financing to a company, such as when it issues a bond or takes out a bank loan.

Cost of goods sold For a given period, equal to beginning inventory minus ending inventory plus the cost of goods acquired or produced during the period.

Cost of preferred stock The cost to a company of issuing preferred stock; the dividend yield that a company must commit to pay preferred stockholders.

Cost recovery method A method of revenue recognition in which the seller does not report any profit until the cash amounts paid by the buyer—including principal and interest on any financing from the seller—are greater than all the seller's costs for the merchandise sold.

Cost structure The mix of a company's variable costs and fixed costs.

Cost-push Type of inflation in which rising costs, usually wages, compel businesses to raise prices generally.

Counterparty risk The risk that the other party to a contract will fail to honor the terms of the contract.

Cournot assumption Assumption in which each firm determines its profit-maximizing production level assuming that the other firms' output will not change.

Covariance A measure of the co-movement (linear association) between two random variables.

Covariance matrix A matrix or square array whose entries are covariances; also known as a variance–covariance matrix.

Covenants The terms and conditions of lending agreements that the issuer must comply with.

Covered call An option strategy involving the holding of an asset and sale of a call on the asset.

Credit With respect to double-entry accounting, a credit records increases in liability, owners' equity, and revenue accounts or decreases in asset accounts; with respect to borrowing, the willingness and ability of the borrower to make promised payments on the borrowing.

Credit analysis The evaluation of credit risk; the evaluation of the creditworthiness of a borrower or counterparty.

Credit curve A curve showing the relationship between time to maturity and yield spread for an issuer with comparable bonds of various maturities outstanding, usually upward sloping.

Credit migration risk (or downgrade risk) The risk that a bond issuer's creditworthiness deteriorates, or migrates lower, leading investors to believe the risk of default is higher.

Credit risk (or default risk) The risk of loss caused by a counterparty's or debtor's failure to make a promised payment.

Credit scoring model A statistical model used to classify borrowers according to creditworthiness.

Credit-worthiness The perceived ability of the borrower to pay what is owed on the borrowing in a timely manner; it represents the ability of a company to withstand adverse impacts on its cash flows.

Cross-default provisions Provisions whereby events of default such as non-payment of interest on one bond trigger default on all outstanding debt; implies the same default probability for all issues.

Cross-price elasticity of demand The percent change in quantity demanded for a given small change in the price of another good; the responsiveness of the demand for Product A that is associated with the change in price of Product B.

Cross-sectional analysis Analysis that involves comparisons across individuals in a group over a given time period or at a given point in time.

Cross-sectional data Observations over individual units at a point in time, as opposed to time-series data.

Crossing networks Trading systems that match buyers and sellers who are willing to trade at prices obtained from other markets.

Crowding out The thesis that government borrowing may divert private sector investment from taking place.

Cumulative distribution function A function giving the probability that a random variable is less than or equal to a specified value.

Cumulative preference shares Preference shares for which any dividends that are not paid accrue and must be paid in full before dividends on common shares can be paid.

Cumulative relative frequency For data grouped into intervals, the fraction of total observations that are less than the value of the upper limit of a stated interval.

Cumulative voting Voting that allows shareholders to direct their total voting rights to specific candidates, as opposed to having to allocate their voting rights evenly among all candidates.

Currencies Monies issued by national monetary authorities.

Currency option An option that allows the holder to buy (if a call) or sell (if a put) an underlying currency at a fixed exercise rate, expressed as an exchange rate.

Currency swap   A swap in which each party makes interest payments to the other in different currencies.

Current assets   (or liquid assets) Assets that are expected to be consumed or converted into cash in the near future, typically one year or less.

Current cost   With reference to assets, the amount of cash or cash equivalents that would have to be paid to buy the same or an equivalent asset today; with reference to liabilities, the undiscounted amount of cash or cash equivalents that would be required to settle the obligation today.

Current government spending   With respect to government expenditures, spending on goods and services that are provided on a regular, recurring basis including health, education, and defense.

Current liabilities   Short-term obligations, such as accounts payable, wages payable, or accrued liabilities, that are expected to be settled in the near future, typically one year or less.

Current ratio   A liquidity ratio calculated as current assets divided by current liabilities.

Cyclical   See *Cyclical companies.*

Cyclical companies   Companies with sales and profits that regularly expand and contract with the business cycle or state of economy.

Daily settlement   See *Marking to market.*

Dark pools   Alternative trading systems that do not display the orders that their clients send to them.

Data mining   (or data snooping) The practice of determining a model by extensive searching through a dataset for statistically significant patterns.

Data snooping   See *Data mining.*

Date of book closure   The date that a shareholder listed on the corporation's books will be deemed to have ownership of the shares for purposes of receiving an upcoming dividend; two business days after the ex-dividend date.

Date of record   The date that a shareholder listed on the corporation's books will be deemed to have ownership of the shares for purposes of receiving an upcoming dividend; two business days after the ex-dividend date.

Day order   An order that is good for the day on which it is submitted. If it has not been filled by the close of business, the order expires unfilled.

Day trader   A trader holding a position open somewhat longer than a scalper but closing all positions at the end of the day.

Days in receivables   Estimate of the average number of days it takes to collect on credit accounts.

Days of inventory on hand (DOH)   An activity ratio equal to the number of days in the period divided by inventory turnover over the period.

Day's sales outstanding   Estimate of the average number of days it takes to collect on credit accounts.

Dead cross   A technical analysis term that describes a situation where a short-term moving average crosses from above a longer-term moving average to below it; this movement is considered bearish.

Dealers   A financial intermediary that acts as a principal in trades.

Dealing securities   Securities held by banks or other financial intermediaries for trading purposes.

Debit   With respect to double-entry accounting, a debit records increases of asset and expense accounts or decreases in liability and owners' equity accounts.

Debt incurrence test   A financial covenant made in conjunction with existing debt that restricts a company's ability to incur additional debt at the same seniority based on one or more financial tests or conditions.

Debt-rating approach   A method for estimating a company's before-tax cost of debt based upon the yield on comparably rated bonds for maturities that closely match that of the company's existing debt.

Debt-to-assets ratio   A solvency ratio calculated as total debt divided by total assets.

Debt-to-capital ratio   A solvency ratio calculated as total debt divided by total debt plus total shareholders' equity.

Debt-to-equity ratio   A solvency ratio calculated as total debt divided by total shareholders' equity.

Declaration date   The day that the corporation issues a statement declaring a specific dividend.

Decreasing returns to scale   Increase in cost per unit resulting from increased production.

Decreasing-cost industry   An industry in which per-unit costs and output prices are lower when industry output is increased in the long run.

Deductible temporary differences   Temporary differences that result in a reduction of or deduction from taxable income in a future period when the balance sheet item is recovered or settled.

Deep-in-the-money   Options that are far in-the-money.

Deep-out-of-the-money   Options that are far out-of-the-money.

Default risk   (or default probability): The probability that a borrower defaults or fails to meet its obligation to make full and timely payments of principal and interest, according to the terms of the debt security.

Default risk premium   An extra return that compensates investors for the possibility that the borrower will fail to make a promised payment at the contracted time and in the contracted amount.

Defensive companies   Companies with sales and profits that have little sensitivity to the business cycle or state of the economy.

Defensive interval ratio   A liquidity ratio that estimates the number of days that an entity could meet cash needs from liquid assets; calculated as (cash + short-term marketable investments + receivables) divided by daily cash expenditures.

Deferred income   A liability account for money that has been collected for goods or services that have not yet been delivered; payment received in advance of providing a good or service.

Deferred revenue   A liability account for money that has been collected for goods or services that have not yet been delivered; payment received in advance of providing a good or service.

Deferred tax assets   A balance sheet asset that arises when an excess amount is paid for income taxes relative to accounting profit. The taxable income is higher than accounting profit and income tax payable exceeds tax expense. The company expects to recover the difference during the course of future operations when tax expense exceeds income tax payable.

Deferred tax liabilities   A balance sheet liability that arises when a deficit amount is paid for income taxes relative to accounting profit. The taxable income is less than the accounting profit and income tax payable is less than tax expense. The company expects to eliminate the liability over the course of future operations when income tax payable exceeds tax expense.

Defined benefit pension plans   Plan in which the company promises to pay a certain annual amount (defined benefit) to the employee after retirement. The company bears the investment risk of the plan assets.

Defined contribution pension plans Individual accounts to which an employee and typically the employer makes contributions, generally on a tax-advantaged basis. The amounts of contributions are defined at the outset, but the future value of the benefit is unknown. The employee bears the investment risk of the plan assets.

Deflation Negative inflation.

Degree of confidence The probability that a confidence interval includes the unknown population parameter.

Degree of financial leverage (DFL) The ratio of the percentage change in net income to the percentage change in operating income; the sensitivity of the cash flows available to owners when operating income changes.

Degree of operating leverage (DOL) The ratio of the percentage change in operating income to the percentage change in units sold; the sensitivity of operating income to changes in units sold.

Degree of total leverage The ratio of the percentage change in net income to the percentage change in units sold; the sensitivity of the cash flows to owners to changes in the number of units produced and sold.

Degrees of freedom (df) The number of independent observations used.

Delivery A process used in a deliverable forward contract in which the long pays the agreed-upon price to the short, which in turn delivers the underlying asset to the long.

Delivery option The feature of a futures contract giving the short the right to make decisions about what, when, and where to deliver.

Delta The relationship between the option price and the underlying price, which reflects the sensitivity of the price of the option to changes in the price of the underlying.

Demand shock A typically unexpected disturbance to demand, such as an unexpected interruption in trade or transportation.

Demand-pull Type of inflation in which increasing demand raises prices generally, which then are reflected in a business's costs as workers demand wage hikes to catch up with the rising cost of living.

Dependent With reference to events, the property that the probability of one event occurring depends on (is related to) the occurrence of another event.

Depository bank A bank that raises funds from depositors and other investors and lends it to borrowers.

Depository institutions Commercial banks, savings and loan banks, credit unions, and similar institutions that raise funds from depositors and other investors and lend it to borrowers.

Depository receipt A security that trades like an ordinary share on a local exchange and represents an economic interest in a foreign company.

Depreciation The process of systematically allocating the cost of long-lived (tangible) assets to the periods during which the assets are expected to provide economic benefits.

Depression See *contraction*.

Derivative A financial instrument whose value depends on the value of some underlying asset or factor (e.g., a stock price, an interest rate, or exchange rate).

Derivative pricing rule A pricing rule used by crossing networks in which a price is taken (derived) from the price that is current in the asset's primary market.

Derivatives dealers Commercial and investment banks that make markets in derivatives.

Descriptive statistics The study of how data can be summarized effectively.

Development capital Minority equity investments in more mature companies that are looking for capital to expand or restructure operations, enter new markets, or finance major acquisitions.

Diffuse prior The assumption of equal prior probabilities.

Diffusion index Reflects the proportion of the index's components that are moving in a pattern consistent with the overall index.

Diluted EPS The EPS that would result if all dilutive securities were converted into common shares.

Diluted shares The number of shares that would be outstanding if all potentially dilutive claims on common shares (e.g., convertible debt, convertible preferred stock, and employee stock options) were exercised.

Diminishing balance method An accelerated depreciation method, i.e., one that allocates a relatively large proportion of the cost of an asset to the early years of the asset's useful life.

Diminishing marginal productivity Describes a state in which each additional unit of input produces less output than previously.

Direct debit program An arrangement whereby a customer authorizes a debit to a demand account; typically used by companies to collect routine payments for services.

Direct format (direct method) With reference to the cash flow statement, a format for the presentation of the statement in which cash flow from operating activities is shown as operating cash receipts less operating cash disbursements.

Direct method See *direct format*.

Direct taxes Taxes levied directly on income, wealth, and corporate profits.

Direct write-off method An approach to recognizing credit losses on customer receivables in which the company waits until such time as a customer has defaulted and only then recognizes the loss.

Disbursement float The amount of time between check issuance and a check's clearing back against the company's account.

Discount To reduce the value of a future payment in allowance for how far away it is in time; to calculate the present value of some future amount. Also, the amount by which an instrument is priced below its face value.

Discount interest A procedure for determining the interest on a loan or bond in which the interest is deducted from the face value in advance.

Discount rate With reference to U.S. banking, the rate for member banks borrowing directly from the U.S. Federal Reserve System.

Discounted cash flow models Valuation models that estimate the intrinsic value of a security as the present value of the future benefits expected to be received from the security.

Discouraged worker A person who has stopped looking for a job or has given up seeking employment.

Discrete random variable A random variable that can take on at most a countable number of possible values.

Discriminatory pricing rule A pricing rule used in continuous markets in which the limit price of the order or quote that first arrived determines the trade price.

Diseconomies of scale Increase in cost per unit resulting from increased production.

Dispersion The variability around the central tendency.

Display size The size of an order displayed to public view.

Distressed investing Investing in securities of companies in financial difficulties. Private equity funds typically buy the debt of mature companies in financial difficulties.

Divergence In technical analysis, a term that describes the case when an indicator moves differently from the security being analyzed.

Diversification ratio The ratio of the standard deviation of an equally weighted portfolio to the standard deviation of a randomly selected security.

Dividend A distribution paid to shareholders based on the number of shares owned.

Dividend discount model (DDM) A present value model that estimates the intrinsic value of an equity share based on the present value of its expected future dividends.

Dividend discount model based approach An approach for estimating a country's equity risk premium. The market rate of return is estimated as the sum of the dividend yield and the growth rate in dividends for a market index. Subtracting the risk-free rate of return from the estimated market return produces an estimate for the equity risk premium.

Dividend payout ratio The ratio of cash dividends paid to earnings for a period.

Dividend yield Annual dividends per share divided by share price.

Divisor A number (denominator) used to determine the value of a price return index. It is initially chosen at the inception of an index and subsequently adjusted by the index provider, as necessary, to avoid changes in the index value that are unrelated to changes in the prices of its constituent securities.

Double bottoms In technical analysis, a reversal pattern that is formed when the price reaches a low, rebounds, and then sells off back to the first low level; used to predict a change from a downtrend to an uptrend.

Double coincidence of wants A prerequisite to barter trades, in particular that both economic agents in the transaction want what the other is selling.

Double declining balance depreciation An accelerated depreciation method that involves depreciating the asset at double the straight-line rate. This rate is multiplied by the book value of the asset at the beginning of the period (a declining balance) to calculate depreciation expense.

Double top In technical analysis, a reversal pattern that is formed when an uptrend reverses twice at roughly the same high price level; used to predict a change from an uptrend to a downtrend.

Double-entry accounting The accounting system of recording transactions in which every recorded transaction affects at least two accounts so as to keep the basic accounting equation (assets = liabilities + owners' equity) in balance.

Down transition probability The probability that an asset's value moves down in a model of asset price dynamics.

Drag on liquidity When receipts lag, creating pressure from the decreased available funds.

Drawdown A reduction in net asset value (NAV).

DuPont analysis An approach to decomposing return on investment, e.g., return on equity, as the product of other financial ratios.

Duration A measure of an option-free bond's average maturity. Specifically, the weighted average maturity of all future cash flows paid by a security, in which the weights are the present value of these cash flows as a fraction of the bond's price. A measure of a bond's price sensitivity to interest rate movements.

Dutch Book theorem A result in probability theory stating that inconsistent probabilities create profit opportunities.

Earnings per share The amount of income earned during a period per share of common stock.

Earnings surprise The portion of a company's earnings that is unanticipated by investors and, according to the efficient market hypothesis, merits a price adjustment.

Economic costs All the remuneration needed to keep a productive resource in its current employment or to acquire the resource for productive use; the sum of total accounting costs and implicit opportunity costs.

Economic indicator A variable that provides information on the state of the overall economy.

Economic loss The amount by which accounting profit is less than normal profit.

Economic order quantity–reorder point (EOQ–ROP) An approach to managing inventory based on expected demand and the predictability of demand; the ordering point for new inventory is determined based on the costs of ordering and carrying inventory, such that the total cost associated with inventory is minimized.

Economic profit (abnormal or supernormal profit) Equal to accounting profit less the implicit opportunity costs not included in total accounting costs; the difference between total revenue (TR) and total cost (TC).

Economic rent The surplus value that results when a particular resource or good is fixed in supply and market price is higher than what is required to bring the resource or good onto the market and sustain its use.

Economic stabilization Reduction of the magnitude of economic fluctuations.

Economies of scale Reduction in cost per unit resulting from increased production.

Effective annual rate The amount by which a unit of currency will grow in a year with interest on interest included.

Effective annual yield (EAY) An annualized return that accounts for the effect of interest on interest; EAY is computed by compounding 1 plus the holding period yield forward to one year, then subtracting 1.

Efficient market A market in which asset prices reflect new information quickly and rationally.

Elasticity The percentage change in one variable for a percentage change in another variable; a measure of how sensitive one variable is to a change in the value of another variable.

Elasticity of supply A measure of the sensitivity of quantity supplied to a change in price.

Electronic communications networks See *Alternative trading systems.*

Electronic funds transfer (EFT) The use of computer networks to conduct financial transactions electronically.

Elliott wave theory A technical analysis theory that claims that the market follows regular, repeated waves or cycles.

Empirical probability The probability of an event estimated as a relative frequency of occurrence.

Employed The number of people with a job.

Enterprise value A measure of a company's total market value from which the value of cash and short-term investments have been subtracted.

Equal weighting An index weighting method in which an equal weight is assigned to each constituent security at inception.

Equity Assets less liabilities; the residual interest in the assets after subtracting the liabilities.

Equity forward A contract calling for the purchase of an individual stock, a stock portfolio, or a stock index at a later date at an agreed-upon price.

Equity options Options on individual stocks; also known as stock options.

Equity risk premium The expected return on equities minus the risk-free rate; the premium that investors demand for investing in equities.

Equity swap A swap transaction in which at least one cash flow is tied to the return to an equity portfolio position, often an equity index.

Estimate The particular value calculated from sample observations using an estimator.

Estimation With reference to statistical inference, the subdivision dealing with estimating the value of a population parameter.

Estimator An estimation formula; the formula used to compute the sample mean and other sample statistics are examples of estimators.

Eurodollar A dollar deposited outside the United States.

European option An option that can only be exercised on its expiration date.

European-style contracts An option that can only be exercised on its expiration date.

European-style option (or European option) An option that can only be exercised on its expiration date.

Event Any outcome or specified set of outcomes of a random variable.

Ex-date The first date that a share trades without (i.e. "ex") the dividend.

Ex-dividend date The first date that a share trades without (i.e. "ex") the dividend.

Excess kurtosis Degree of peakedness (fatness of tails) in excess of the peakedness of the normal distribution.

Exchange for physicals (EFP) A permissible delivery procedure used by futures market participants, in which the long and short arrange a delivery procedure other than the normal procedures stipulated by the futures exchange.

Exchanges Places where traders can meet to arrange their trades.

Execution instructions Instructions that indicate how to fill an order.

Exercise The process of using an option to buy or sell the underlying.

Exercise price The fixed price at which an option holder can buy or sell the underlying.

Exercise rate The fixed rate at which the holder of an interest rate option can buy or sell the underlying.

Exercise value The value obtained if an option is exercised based on current conditions.

Exercising the option The process of using an option to buy or sell the underlying.

Exhaustive Covering or containing all possible outcomes.

Expansion The period of a business cycle after its lowest point and before its highest point.

Expansionary Tending to cause the real economy to grow.

Expansionary fiscal policy Fiscal policy aimed at achieving real economic growth.

Expected inflation The level of inflation that economic agents expect in the future.

Expected loss Default probability times loss severity given default.

Expected value The probability-weighted average of the possible outcomes of a random variable.

Expenses Outflows of economic resources or increases in liabilities that result in decreases in equity (other than decreases because of distributions to owners); reductions in net assets associated with the creation of revenues.

Experience curve A curve that shows the direct cost per unit of good or service produced or delivered as a typically declining function of cumulative output.

Externality An effect of a market transaction that is borne by parties other than those who transacted.

Extra dividend A dividend paid by a company that does not pay dividends on a regular schedule, or a dividend that supplements regular cash dividends with an extra payment.

FIFO method The first in, first out, method of accounting for inventory, which matches sales against the costs of items of inventory in the order in which they were placed in inventory.

FX swap The combination of a spot and a forward FX transaction.

Face value The amount of cash payable by a company to the bondholders when the bonds mature; the promised payment at maturity separate from any coupon payment.

Factor A common or underlying element with which several variables are correlated.

Fair value The amount at which an asset could be exchanged, or a liability settled, between knowledgeable, willing parties in an arm's-length transaction; the price that would be received to sell an asset or paid to transfer a liability in an orderly transaction between market participants.

Fed funds rate The U.S. interbank lending rate on overnight borrowings of reserves.

Federal funds rate The U.S. interbank lending rate on overnight borrowings of reserves.

Fiat money Money that is not convertible into any other commodity.

Fibonacci sequence A sequence of numbers starting with 0 and 1, and then each subsequent number in the sequence is the sum of the two preceding numbers. In Elliott Wave Theory, it is believed that market waves follow patterns that are the ratios of the numbers in the Fibonacci sequence.

Fiduciary call A combination of a European call and a risk-free bond that matures on the option expiration day and has a face value equal to the exercise price of the call.

Fill or kill See *Immediate or cancel order*.

Financial flexibility The ability to react and adapt to financial adversities and opportunities.

Financial leverage The extent to which a company can effect, through the use of debt, a proportional change in the return on common equity that is greater than a given proportional change in operating income; also, short for the financial leverage ratio.

Financial leverage ratio A measure of financial leverage calculated as average total assets divided by average total equity.

Financial risk The risk that environmental, social, or governance risk factors will result in significant costs or other losses to a company and its shareholders; the risk arising from a company's obligation to meet required payments under its financing agreements.

Financing activities Activities related to obtaining or repaying capital to be used in the business (e.g., equity and long-term debt).

First lien debt Debt secured by a pledge of certain assets that could include buildings, but may also include property and equipment, licenses, patents, brands, etc.

First mortgage debt Debt secured by a pledge of a specific property.

First-degree price discrimination Where a monopolist is able to charge each customer the highest price the customer is willing to pay.

Fiscal multiplier The ratio of a change in national income to a change in government spending.

Fiscal policy The use of taxes and government spending to affect the level of aggregate expenditures.

Fisher effect The thesis that the real rate of interest in an economy is stable over time so that changes in nominal interest rates are the result of changes in expected inflation.

Fisher index The geometric mean of the Laspeyres index.

Fixed charge coverage A solvency ratio measuring the number of times interest and lease payments are covered by operating income, calculated as (EBIT + lease payments) divided by (interest payments + lease payments).

Fixed costs Costs that remain at the same level regardless of a company's level of production and sales.

Fixed price tender offer Offer made by a company to repurchase a specific number of shares at a fixed price that is typically at a premium to the current market price.

Fixed rate perpetual preferred stock Nonconvertible, noncallable preferred stock that has a fixed dividend rate and no maturity date.

Flags A technical analysis continuation pattern formed by parallel trendlines, typically over a short period.

Float In the context of customer receipts, the amount of money that is in transit between payments made by customers and the funds that are usable by the company.

Float factor An estimate of the average number of days it takes deposited checks to clear; average daily float divided by average daily deposit.

Float-adjusted market-capitalization weighting An index weighting method in which the weight assigned to each constituent security is determined by adjusting its market capitalization for its market float.

Floor A series of put options on an interest rate, with each option expiring at the date on which the floating loan rate will be reset, and with each option having the same exercise rate. A floor in general can have an underlying other than the interest rate.

Floor traders Market makers that buy and sell by quoting a bid and an ask price. They are the primary providers of liquidity to the market.

Floorlet Each component put option in a floor.

Flotation cost Fees charged to companies by investment bankers and other costs associated with raising new capital.

Foreign currency reserves Holding by the central bank of non-domestic currency deposits and non-domestic bonds.

Foreign exchange gains (or losses) Gains (or losses) that occur when the exchange rate changes between the investor's currency and the currency that foreign securities are denominated in.

Forward contract An agreement between two parties in which one party, the buyer, agrees to buy from the other party, the seller, an underlying asset at a later date for a price established at the start of the contract.

Forward rate The fixed price or rate at which the transaction scheduled to occur at the expiration of a forward contract will take place. This price is agreed on at the initiation date of the contract.

Forward rate agreement (FRA) A forward contract calling for one party to make a fixed interest payment and the other to make an interest payment at a rate to be determined at the contract expiration.

Fractile A value at or below which a stated fraction of the data lies.

Fractional reserve banking Banking in which reserves constitute a fraction of deposits.

Free cash flow The actual cash that would be available to the company's investors after making all investments necessary to maintain the company as an ongoing enterprise (also referred to as free cash flow to the firm); the internally generated funds that can be distributed to the company's investors (e.g., shareholders and bondholders) without impairing the value of the company.

Free cash flow to equity (FCFE) The cash flow available to a company's common shareholders after all operating expenses, interest, and principal payments have been made, and necessary investments in working and fixed capital have been made.

Free cash flow to the firm (FCFF) The cash flow available to the company's suppliers of capital after all operating expenses have been paid and necessary investments in working capital and fixed capital have been made.

Free float The number of shares that are readily and freely tradable in the secondary market.

Free-cash-flow-to-equity models Valuation models based on discounting expected future free cash flow to equity.

Frequency distribution A tabular display of data summarized into a relatively small number of intervals.

Frequency polygon A graph of a frequency distribution obtained by drawing straight lines joining successive points representing the class frequencies.

Full price The price of a security with accrued interest.

Fundamental analysis The examination of publicly available information and the formulation of forecasts to estimate the intrinsic value of assets.

Fundamental value (also **intrinsic value**) The underlying or true value of an asset based on an analysis of its qualitative and quantitative characteristics.

Fundamental weighting An index weighting method in which the weight assigned to each constituent security is based on its underlying company's size. It attempts to address the disadvantages of market-capitalization weighting by using measures that are independent of the constituent security's price.

Funds of funds Funds that hold a portfolio of hedge funds.

Future value (FV) The amount to which a payment or series of payments will grow by a stated future date.

Futures commission merchants (FCMs) Individuals or companies that execute futures transactions for other parties off the exchange.

Futures contract A variation of a forward contract that has essentially the same basic definition but with some additional features, such as a clearinghouse guarantee against credit losses, a daily settlement of gains and losses, and an organized electronic or floor trading facility.

GDP deflator A gauge of prices and inflation that measures the aggregate changes in prices across the overall economy.

Gains   Asset inflows not directly related to the ordinary activities of the business.

Game theory   The set of tools decision makers use to incorporate responses by rival decision makers into their strategies.

Gamma   A numerical measure of how sensitive an option's delta is to a change in the underlying.

General partner   The partner that runs the business and theoretically bears unlimited liability.

Geometric mean   A measure of central tendency computed by taking the nth root of the product of n non-negative values.

Giffen good   A good that is consumed more as the price of the good rises.

Gilts   Bonds issued by the U.K. government.

Giro system   An electronic payment system used widely in Europe and Japan.

Global depository receipt   A depository receipt that is issued outside of the company's home country and outside of the United States.

Global minimum-variance portfolio   The portfolio on the minimum-variance frontier with the smallest variance of return.

Global registered share   A common share that is traded on different stock exchanges around the world in different currencies.

Gold standard   With respect to a currency, if a currency is on the gold standard a given amount can be converted into a prespecified amount of gold.

Golden cross   A technical analysis term that describes a situation where a short-term moving average crosses from below a longer-term moving average to above it; this movement is considered bullish.

Good-on-close   (market on close) An execution instruction specifying that an order can only be filled at the close of trading.

Good-on-open   An execution instruction specifying that an order can only be filled at the opening of trading.

Good-till-cancelled order   An order specifying that it is valid until the entity placing the order has cancelled it (or, commonly, until some specified amount of time such as 60 days has elapsed, whichever comes sooner).

Goodwill   An intangible asset that represents the excess of the purchase price of an acquired company over the value of the net assets acquired.

Greenmail   The purchase of the accumulated shares of a hostile investor by a company that is targeted for takeover by that investor, usually at a substantial premium over market price.

Gross domestic product   The market value of all final goods and services produced within the economy in a given period of time (output definition) or, equivalently, the aggregate income earned by all households, all companies, and the government within the economy in a given period of time (income definition).

Gross margin   Sales minus the cost of sales (i.e., the cost of goods sold for a manufacturing company).

Gross profit   Sales minus the cost of sales (i.e., the cost of goods sold for a manufacturing company).

Gross profit margin   The ratio of gross profit to revenues.

Grouping by function   With reference to the presentation of expenses in an income statement, the grouping together of expenses serving the same function, e.g. all items that are costs of goods sold.

Grouping by nature   With reference to the presentation of expenses in an income statement, the grouping together of expenses by similar nature, e.g., all depreciation expenses.

Growth cyclical   A term sometimes used to describe companies that are growing rapidly on a long-term basis but that still experience above-average fluctuation in their revenues and profits over the course of a business cycle.

Harmonic mean   A type of weighted mean computed by averaging the reciprocals of the observations, then taking the reciprocal of that average.

Head and shoulders pattern   In technical analysis, a reversal pattern that is formed in three parts: a left shoulder, head, and right shoulder; used to predict a change from an uptrend to a downtrend.

Headline inflation   The inflation rate calculated based on the price index that includes all goods and services in an economy.

Hedge funds   Private investment vehicles that typically use leverage, derivatives, and long and short investment strategies.

Held for trading   (trading securities) Debt or equity financial assets bought with the intention to sell them in the near term, usually less than three months; securities that a company intends to trade.

Held-to-maturity   Debt (fixed-income) securities that a company intends to hold to maturity; these are presented at their original cost, updated for any amortization of discounts or premiums.

Herding   Clustered trading that may or may not be based on information.

Hidden order   An order that is exposed not to the public but only to the brokers or exchanges that receive it.

High water marks   The highest value, net of fees, which a fund has reached. It reflects the highest cumulative return used to calculate an incentive fee.

Histogram   A bar chart of data that have been grouped into a frequency distribution.

Historical cost   In reference to assets, the amount paid to purchase an asset, including any costs of acquisition and/or preparation; with reference to liabilities, the amount of proceeds received in exchange in issuing the liability.

Historical equity risk premium approach   An estimate of a country's equity risk premium that is based upon the historical averages of the risk-free rate and the rate of return on the market portfolio.

Historical simulation   Another term for the historical method of estimating VAR. This term is somewhat misleading in that the method involves not a *simulation* of the past but rather what *actually happened* in the past, sometimes adjusted to reflect the fact that a different portfolio may have existed in the past than is planned for the future.

Holder-of-record date   The date that a shareholder listed on the corporation's books will be deemed to have ownership of the shares for purposes of receiving an upcoming dividend; two business days after the ex-dividend date.

Holding period return   The return that an investor earns during a specified holding period; a synonym for total return.

Holding period return (HPR)   The return that an investor earns during a specified holding period; a synonym for total return.

Holding period yield (HPY)   The return that an investor earns during a specified holding period; holding period return with reference to a fixed-income instrument.

Homogeneity of expectations   The assumption that all investors have the same economic expectations and thus have the same expectations of prices, cash flows, and other investment characteristics.

Horizontal analysis   Common-size analysis that involves comparing a specific financial statement with that statement in prior or future time periods; also, cross-sectional analysis of one company with another.

Horizontal demand schedule   Implies that at a given price, the response in the quantity demanded is infinite.

Household   A person or a group of people living in the same residence, taken as a basic unit in economic analysis.

Hurdle rate   The rate of return that must be met for a project to be accepted.

Hypothesis   With reference to statistical inference, a statement about one or more populations.

Hypothesis testing   With reference to statistical inference, the subdivision dealing with the testing of hypotheses about one or more populations.

IRR rule   An investment decision rule that accepts projects or investments for which the IRR is greater than the opportunity cost of capital.

Iceberg order   An order in which the display size is less than the order's full size.

If-converted method   A method for accounting for the effect of convertible securities on earnings per share (EPS) that specifies what EPS would have been if the convertible securities had been converted at the beginning of the period, taking account of the effects of conversion on net income and the weighted average number of shares outstanding.

Immediate or cancel order   (fill or kill) An order that is valid only upon receipt by the broker or exchange. If such an order cannot be filled in part or in whole upon receipt, it cancels immediately.

Impact lag   The lag associated with the result of actions affecting the economy with delay.

Imperfect competition   A market structure in which an individual firm has enough share of the market (or can control a certain segment of the market) such that it is able to exert some influence over price.

Implicit price deflator for GDP   A gauge of prices and inflation that measures the aggregate changes in prices across the overall economy.

In-the-money   Options that, if exercised, would result in the value received being worth more than the payment required to exercise.

Incentive fee (or performance fee)   Funds distributed by the general partner to the limited partner(s) based on realized profits.

Income   Increases in economic benefits in the form of inflows or enhancements of assets, or decreases of liabilities that result in an increase in equity (other than increases resulting from contributions by owners).

Income constraint   The constraint on a consumer to spend, in total, no more than his income.

Income elasticity of demand   A measure of the responsiveness of demand to changes in income, defined as the percentage change in quantity demanded divided by the percentage change in income.

Income statement   (statement of operations or profit and loss statement) A financial statement that provides information about a company's profitability over a stated period of time.

Income tax paid   The actual amount paid for income taxes in the period; not a provision, but the actual cash outflow.

Income tax payable   The income tax owed by the company on the basis of taxable income.

Income trust   A type of equity ownership vehicle established as a trust issuing ownership shares known as units.

Increasing marginal returns   Where the marginal product of a resource increases as additional units of that input are employed.

Increasing returns to scale   Reduction in cost per unit resulting from increased production.

Increasing-cost industry   An industry in which per-unit costs and output prices are higher when industry output is increased in the long run.

Incremental cash flow   The cash flow that is realized because of a decision; the changes or increments to cash flows resulting from a decision or action.

Independent   With reference to events, the property that the occurrence of one event does not affect the probability of another event occurring.

Independent and identically distributed (IID)   With respect to random variables, the property of random variables that are independent of each other but follow the identical probability distribution.

Independent projects   Independent projects are projects whose cash flows are independent of each other.

Index of Leading Economic Indicators   A composite of economic variables used by analysts to predict future economic conditions.

Indexing   An investment strategy in which an investor constructs a portfolio to mirror the performance of a specified index.

Indifference curve   A curve representing all the combinations of two goods or attributes such that the consumer is entirely indifferent among them.

Indifference curve map   A group or family of indifference curves, representing a consumer's entire utility function.

Indirect format   (indirect method) With reference to cash flow statements, a format for the presentation of the statement which, in the operating cash flow section, begins with net income then shows additions and subtractions to arrive at operating cash flow.

Indirect format   With reference to cash flow statements, a format for the presentation of the statement which, in the operating cash flow section, begins with net income then shows additions and subtractions to arrive at operating cash flow.

Indirect method   See *indirect format.*

Indirect taxes   Taxes such as taxes on spending, as opposed to direct taxes.

Industry   A group of companies offering similar products and/or services.

Industry analysis   The analysis of a specific branch of manufacturing, service, or trade.

Inelastic   Insensitive to price changes.

Inelastic supply   Said of supply that is insensitive to the price of goods sold.

Inflation   The percentage increase in the general price level from one period to the next; a sustained rise in the overall level of prices in an economy.

Inflation Reports   A type of economic publication put out by many central banks.

Inflation premium   An extra return that compensates investors for expected inflation.

Inflation rate   The percentage change in a price index—that is, the speed of overall price level movements.

Inflation uncertainty   The degree to which economic agents view future rates of inflation as difficult to forecast.

Information cascade   The transmission of information from those participants who act first and whose decisions influence the decisions of others.

Information-motivated traders   Traders that trade to profit from information that they believe allows them to predict future prices.

Informationally efficient   A market in which asset prices reflect new information quickly and rationally.

Informationally efficient market   A market in which asset prices reflect new information quickly and rationally.

Initial margin   The amount that must be deposited in a clearinghouse account when entering into a futures contract.

Initial margin requirement   The margin requirement on the first day of a transaction as well as on any day in which additional margin funds must be deposited.

Initial public offering   (IPO) The first issuance of common shares to the public by a formerly private corporation.

Installment method   With respect to revenue recognition, a method that specifies that the portion of the total profit of the sale that is recognized in each period is determined by the percentage of the total sales price for which the seller has received cash.

Installment sales   With respect to revenue recognition, a method that specifies that the portion of the total profit of the sale that is recognized in each period is determined by the percentage of the total sales price for which the seller has received cash.

Intangible assets   Assets lacking physical substance, such as patents and trademarks.

Interest   Payment for lending funds.

Interest coverage   A solvency ratio calculated as EBIT divided by interest payments.

Interest rate   A rate of return that reflects the relationship between differently dated cash flows; a discount rate.

Interest rate call   An option in which the holder has the right to make a known interest payment and receive an unknown interest payment.

Interest rate cap   A series of call options on an interest rate, with each option expiring at the date on which the floating loan rate will be reset, and with each option having the same exercise rate. A cap in general can have an underlying other than an interest rate.

Interest rate collar   A combination of a long cap and a short floor, or a short cap and a long floor. A collar in general can have an underlying other than an interest rate.

Interest rate floor   A series of put options on an interest rate, with each option expiring at the date on which the floating loan rate will be reset, and with each option having the same exercise rate. A floor in general can have an underlying other than the interest rate.

Interest rate forward   See *Forward rate agreement*.

Interest rate option   An option in which the underlying is an interest rate.

Interest rate put   An option in which the holder has the right to make an unknown interest payment and receive a known interest payment.

Interest rate swap   A swap in which the underlying is an interest rate. Can be viewed as a currency swap in which both currencies are the same and can be created as a combination of currency swaps.

Intergenerational data mining   A form of data mining that applies information developed by previous researchers using a dataset to guide current research using the same or a related dataset.

Intermarket analysis   A field within technical analysis that combines analysis of major categories of securities—namely, equities, bonds, currencies, and commodities—to identify market trends and possible inflections in a trend.

Internal rate of return   (IRR) The discount rate that makes net present value equal 0; the discount rate that makes the present value of an investment's costs (outflows) equal to the present value of the investment's benefits (inflows).

Interquartile range   The difference between the third and first quartiles of a dataset.

Interval   With reference to grouped data, a set of values within which an observation falls.

Interval scale   A measurement scale that not only ranks data but also gives assurance that the differences between scale values are equal.

Intrinsic value   See *Fundamental value*.

Inventory   The unsold units of product on hand.

Inventory blanket lien   The use of inventory as collateral for a loan. Though the lender has claim to some or all of the company's inventory, the company may still sell or use the inventory in the ordinary course of business.

Inventory investment   Net change in business inventory.

Inventory turnover   An activity ratio calculated as cost of goods sold divided by average inventory.

Investing activities   Activities which are associated with the acquisition and disposal of property, plant, and equipment; intangible assets; other long-term assets; and both long-term and short-term investments in the equity and debt (bonds and loans) issued by other companies.

Investment banks   Financial intermediaries that provide advice to their mostly corporate clients and help them arrange transactions such as initial and seasoned securities offerings.

Investment opportunity schedule   A graphical depiction of a company's investment opportunities ordered from highest to lowest expected return. A company's optimal capital budget is found where the investment opportunity schedule intersects with the company's marginal cost of capital.

Investment policy statement   (IPS) A written planning document that describes a client's investment objectives and risk tolerance over a relevant time horizon, along with constraints that apply to the client's portfolio.

Investment property   Property used to earn rental income or capital appreciation (or both).

January effect   (also turn-of-the-year effect) Calendar anomaly that stock market returns in January are significantly higher compared to the rest of the months of the year, with most of the abnormal returns reported during the first five trading days in January.

Joint probability   The probability of the joint occurrence of stated events.

Joint probability function   A function giving the probability of joint occurrences of values of stated random variables.

Just-in-time (JIT) method   Method of managing inventory that minimizes in-process inventory stocks.

Keynesians   Economists who believe that fiscal policy can have powerful effects on aggregate demand, output, and employment when there is substantial spare capacity in an economy.

Kondratieff wave   A 54-year long economic cycle postulated by Nikolai Kondratieff.

Kurtosis   The statistical measure that indicates the peakedness of a distribution.

LIFO layer liquidation (LIFO liquidation) With respect to the application of the LIFO inventory method, the liquidation of old, relatively low-priced inventory; happens when the volume of sales rises above the volume of recent purchases so that some sales are made from relatively old, low-priced inventory.

LIFO method The last in, first out, method of accounting for inventory, which matches sales against the costs of items of inventory in the reverse order the items were placed in inventory (i.e., inventory produced or acquired last are assumed to be sold first).

Labor force The portion of the working age population (over the age of 16) that is employed or is available for work but not working (unemployed).

Labor productivity The quantity of goods and services (real GDP) that a worker can produce in one hour of work.

Laddering strategy A form of active strategy which entails scheduling maturities on a systematic basis within the investment portfolio such that investments are spread out equally over the term of the ladder.

Lagging economic indicators Turning points that take place later than those of the overall economy; they are believed to have value in identifying the economy's past condition.

Laspeyres index A price index created by holding the composition of the consumption basket constant.

Law of diminishing returns The smallest output that a firm can produce such that its long run average costs are minimized.

Law of one price The condition in a financial market in which two equivalent financial instruments or combinations of financial instruments can sell for only one price. Equivalent to the principle that no arbitrage opportunities are possible.

Lead underwriter The lead investment bank in a syndicate of investment banks and broker–dealers involved in a securities underwriting.

Leading economic indicators Turning points that usually precede those of the overall economy; they are believed to have value for predicting the economy's future state, usually near-term.

Legal tender Something that must be accepted when offered in exchange for goods and services.

Lender of last resort An entity willing to lend money when no other entity is ready to do so.

Leptokurtic Describes a distribution that is more peaked than a normal distribution.

Level of significance The probability of a Type I error in testing a hypothesis.

Leverage In the context of corporate finance, leverage refers to the use of fixed costs within a company's cost structure. Fixed costs that are operating costs (such as depreciation or rent) create operating leverage. Fixed costs that are financial costs (such as interest expense) create financial leverage.

Leveraged buyout (LBO) A transaction whereby the target company management team converts the target to a privately held company by using heavy borrowing to finance the purchase of the target company's outstanding shares.

Liabilities Present obligations of an enterprise arising from past events, the settlement of which is expected to result in an outflow of resources embodying economic benefits; creditors' claims on the resources of a company.

Life-cycle stage The stage of the life cycle: embryonic, growth, shakeout, mature, declining.

Likelihood The probability of an observation, given a particular set of conditions.

Limit down A limit move in the futures market in which the price at which a transaction would be made is at or below the lower limit.

Limit move A condition in the futures markets in which the price at which a transaction would be made is at or beyond the price limits.

Limit order Instructions to a broker or exchange to obtain the best price immediately available when filling an order, but in no event accept a price higher than a specified (limit) price when buying or accept a price lower than a specified (limit) price when selling.

Limit order book The book or list of limit orders to buy and sell that pertains to a security.

Limit up A limit move in the futures market in which the price at which a transaction would be made is at or above the upper limit.

Limitations on liens Meant to put limits on how much secured debt an issuer can have.

Limited partners Partners with limited liability. Limited partnerships in hedge and private equity funds are typically restricted to investors who are expected to understand and to be able to assume the risks associated with the investments

Line chart In technical analysis, a plot of price data, typically closing prices, with a line connecting the points.

Linear interpolation The estimation of an unknown value on the basis of two known values that bracket it, using a straight line between the two known values.

Linear scale (or arithmetic scale) A scale in which equal distances correspond to equal absolute amounts.

Liquid market Said of a market in which traders can buy or sell with low total transaction costs when they want to trade.

Liquidating dividend A dividend that is a return of capital rather than a distribution from earnings or retained earnings.

Liquidation To sell the assets of a company, division, or subsidiary piecemeal, typically because of bankruptcy; the form of bankruptcy that allows for the orderly satisfaction of creditors' claims after which the company ceases to exist.

Liquidity The ability to purchase or sell an asset quickly and easily at a price close to fair market value. The ability to meet short-term obligations using assets that are the most readily converted into cash.

Liquidity premium An extra return that compensates investors for the risk of loss relative to an investment's fair value if the investment needs to be converted to cash quickly.

Liquidity ratios Financial ratios measuring the company's ability to meet its short-term obligations.

Liquidity risk The risk that a financial instrument cannot be purchased or sold without a significant concession in price due to the size of the market.

Liquidity trap A condition in which the demand for money becomes infinitely elastic (horizontal demand curve) so that injections of money into the economy will not lower interest rates or affect real activity.

Load fund A mutual fund in which, in addition to the annual fee, a percentage fee is charged to invest in the fund and/or for redemptions from the fund.

Locals Market makers that buy and sell by quoting a bid and an ask price. They are the primary providers of liquidity to the market.

Lockbox system A payment system in which customer payments are mailed to a post office box and the banking institution retrieves and deposits these payments several times a day, enabling the company to have use of the fund sooner than in a centralized system in which customer payments are sent to the company.

Locked limit   A condition in the futures markets in which a transaction cannot take place because the price would be beyond the limits.

Lockup period   The minimum period before investors are allowed to make withdrawals or redeem shares from a fund.

Logarithmic scale   A scale in which equal distances represent equal proportional changes in the underlying quantity.

London Interbank Offered Rate (LIBOR)   The Eurodollar rate at which London banks lend dollars to other London banks; considered to be the best representative rate on a dollar borrowed by a private, high-quality borrower.

Long   The buyer of a derivative contract. Also refers to the position of owning a derivative.

Long position   A position in an asset or contract in which one owns the asset or has an exercisable right under the contract.

Long-lived assets   (or long-term assets) Assets that are expected to provide economic benefits over a future period of time, typically greater than one year.

Long-run average total cost curve   The curve describing average total costs when no costs are considered fixed.

Long-run industry supply curve   A curve describing the relationship between quantity supplied and output prices when no costs are considered fixed.

Long-term contract   A contract that spans a number of accounting periods.

Long-term equity anticipatory securities   (also LEAPS) Options originally created with expirations of several years.

Longitudinal data   Observations on characteristic(s) of the same observational unit through time.

Look-ahead bias   A bias caused by using information that was unavailable on the test date.

Loss severity   Portion of a bond's value (including unpaid interest) an investor loses in the event of default.

Losses   Asset outflows not directly related to the ordinary activities of the business.

Lower bound   The lowest possible value of an option.

M²   A measure of what a portfolio would have returned if it had taken on the same total risk as the market index.

Macaulay duration   The duration without dividing by 1 plus the bond's yield to maturity. The term, named for one of the economists who first derived it, is used to distinguish the calculation from modified duration. (See also *modified duration*.)

Maintenance covenants   Covenants in bank loan agreements that require the borrower to satisfy certain financial ratio tests while the loan is outstanding.

Maintenance margin   The minimum amount that is required by a futures clearinghouse to maintain a margin account and to protect against default. Participants whose margin balances drop below the required maintenance margin must replenish their accounts.

Maintenance margin requirement   The margin requirement on any day other than the first day of a transaction.

Management buy-ins   Leveraged buyout in which the current management team is being replaced and the acquiring team will be involved in managing the company.

Management buyout   (MBO) An event in which a group of investors consisting primarily of the company's existing management purchase all of its outstanding shares and take the company private.

Management fee   (or base fee) A fee based on assets under management or committed capital, as applicable.

Manufacturing resource planning (MRP)   The incorporation of production planning into inventory management. A MRP analysis provides both a materials acquisition schedule and a production schedule.

Margin call   A notice to deposit additional cash or securities in a margin account.

Margin loan   Money borrowed from a broker to purchase securities.

Marginal cost   The cost of producing an additional unit of a good.

Marginal probability   The probability of an event *not* conditioned on another event.

Marginal product   Measures the productivity of each unit of input and is calculated by taking the difference in total product from adding another unit of input (assuming other resource quantities are held constant).

Marginal propensity to consume   The proportion of an additional unit of disposable income that is consumed or spent; the change in consumption for a small change in income.

Marginal propensity to save   The proportion of an additional unit of disposable income that is saved (not spent).

Marginal rate of substitution   The rate at which one is willing to give up one good to obtain more of another.

Marginal revenue   The change in total revenue divided by the change in quantity sold; simply, the additional revenue from selling one more unit.

Marginal revenue product   The amount of additional revenue received from employing an additional unit of an input.

Marginal value curve   A curve describing the highest price consumers are willing to pay for each additional unit of a good.

Mark-to-market   The revaluation of a financial asset or liability to its current market value or fair value.

Market   A means of bringing buyers and sellers together to exchange goods and services.

Market anomaly   Change in the price or return of a security that cannot directly be linked to current relevant information known in the market or to the release of new information into the market.

Market bid–ask spread   The difference between the best bid and the best offer.

Market float   The number of shares that are available to the investing public.

Market liquidity risk   The risk that the price at which investors can actually transact—buying or selling—may differ from the price indicated in the market.

Market model   A regression equation that specifies a linear relationship between the return on a security (or portfolio) and the return on a broad market index.

Market multiple models   Valuation models based on share price multiples or enterprise value multiples.

Market order   Instructions to a broker or exchange to obtain the best price immediately available when filling an order.

Market structure   The competitive environment (perfect competition, monopolistic competition, oligopoly, and monopoly).

Market value   The price at which an asset or security can currently be bought or sold in an open market.

Market-capitalization weighting   (or value weighting) An index weighting method in which the weight assigned to each constituent security is determined by dividing its market capitalization by the total market capitalization (sum of the market capitalization) of all securities in the index.

Market-on-close An execution instruction specifying that an order can only be filled at the close of trading.

Marketable limit order A buy limit order in which the limit price is placed above the best offer, or a sell limit order in which the limit price is placed below the best bid. Such orders generally will partially or completely fill right away.

Marking to market A procedure used primarily in futures markets in which the parties to a contract settle the amount owed daily. Also known as the *daily settlement*.

Markowitz efficient frontier The graph of the set of portfolios offering the maximum expected return for their level of risk (standard deviation of return).

Matching principle The accounting principle that expenses should be recognized when the associated revenue is recognized.

Matching strategy An active investment strategy that includes intentional matching of the timing of cash outflows with investment maturities.

Matrix pricing In the fixed income markets, to price a security on the basis of valuation-relevant characteristics (e.g. debt-rating approach).

Maturity premium An extra return that compensates investors for the increased sensitivity of the market value of debt to a change in market interest rates as maturity is extended.

Maturity value The amount of cash payable by a company to the bondholders when the bonds mature; the promised payment at maturity separate from any coupon payment.

Mean absolute deviation With reference to a sample, the mean of the absolute values of deviations from the sample mean.

Mean excess return The average rate of return in excess of the risk-free rate.

Mean–variance analysis An approach to portfolio analysis using expected means, variances, and covariances of asset returns.

Measure of central tendency A quantitative measure that specifies where data are centered.

Measure of location A quantitative measure that describes the location or distribution of data; includes not only measures of central tendency but also other measures such as percentiles.

Measure of value A standard for measuring value; a function of money.

Measurement scales A scheme of measuring differences. The four types of measurement scales are nominal, ordinal, interval, and ratio.

Median The value of the middle item of a set of items that has been sorted into ascending or descending order; the 50th percentile.

Medium of exchange Any asset that can be used to purchase goods and services or to repay debts; a function of money.

Menu costs A cost of inflation in which businesses constantly have to incur the costs of changing the advertised prices of their goods and services.

Mesokurtic Describes a distribution with kurtosis identical to that of the normal distribution.

Mezzanine financing Debt or preferred shares with a relationship to common equity due to a feature such as attached warrants or conversion options and that is subordinate to both senior and high yield debt. It is referred to as mezzanine because of its location on the balance sheet.

Minimum efficient scale The smallest output that a firm can produce such that its long run average cost is minimized.

Minimum-variance portfolio The portfolio with the minimum variance for each given level of expected return.

Minsky moment Named for Hyman Minksy: A point in a business cycle when, after individuals become overextended in borrowing to finance speculative investments, people start realizing that something is likely to go wrong and a panic ensues leading to asset sell-offs.

Mismatching strategy An active investment strategy whereby the timing of cash outflows is not matched with investment maturities.

Modal interval With reference to grouped data, the most frequently occurring interval.

Mode The most frequently occurring value in a set of observations.

Model risk The use of an inaccurate pricing model for a particular investment, or the improper use of the right model.

Modern portfolio theory (MPT) The analysis of rational portfolio choices based on the efficient use of risk.

Modified duration A measure of a bond's price sensitivity to interest rate movements. Equal to the Macaulay duration of a bond divided by one plus its yield to maturity.

Momentum oscillators A graphical representation of market sentiment that is constructed from price data and calculated so that it oscillates either between a high and a low or around some number.

Monetarists Economists who believe that the rate of growth of the money supply is the primary determinant of the rate of inflation.

Monetary policy Actions taken by a nation's central bank to affect aggregate output and prices through changes in bank reserves, reserve requirements, or its target interest rate.

Monetary transmission mechanism The process whereby a central bank's interest rate gets transmitted through the economy and ultimately affects the rate of increase of prices.

Money A generally accepted medium of exchange and unit of account.

Money creation The process by which changes in bank reserves translate into changes in the money supply.

Money market The market for short-term debt instruments (oneyear maturity or less).

Money market The market for short-term debt instruments (one-year maturity or less).

Money market yield A yield on a basis comparable to the quoted yield on an interest-bearing money market instrument that pays interest on a 360-day basis; the annualized holding period yield, assuming a 360-day year.

Money multiplier Describes how a change in reserves is expected to affect the money supply; in its simplest form, 1 divided by the reserve requirement.

Money neutrality The thesis that an increase in the money supply leads in the long-run to an increase in the price level, while leaving real variables like output and employment unaffected.

Money-weighted rate of return The internal rate of return on a portfolio, taking account of all cash flows.

Moneyness The relationship between the price of the underlying and an option's exercise price.

Monopolist Said of an entity that is the only seller in its market.

Monopolistic competition Highly competitive form of imperfect competition; the competitive characteristic is a notably large number of firms, while the monopoly aspect is the result of product differentiation.

Monopoly In pure monopoly markets, there are no substitutes for the given product or service. There is a single seller, which exercises considerable power over pricing and output decisions.

Monte Carlo simulation An approach to estimating a probability distribution of outcomes to examine what might happen if particular risks are faced. This method is widely used in the sciences as well as in business to study a variety of problems.

Moving average The average of the closing price of a security over a specified number of periods. With each new period, the average is recalculated.

Moving-average convergence/divergence oscillator (MACD) A momentum oscillator that is constructed based on the difference between short-term and long-term moving averages of a security's price.

Multi-factor model A model that explains a variable in terms of the values of a set of factors.

Multi-market indices Comprised of indices from different countries, designed to represent multiple security markets.

Multi-step format With respect to the format of the income statement, a format that presents a subtotal for gross profit (revenue minus cost of goods sold).

Multilateral trading facilities See *Alternative trading systems*.

Multiplication rule for probabilities The rule that the joint probability of events A and B equals the probability of A given B times the probability of B.

Multiplier models Valuation models based on share price multiples or enterprise value multiples.

Multivariate distribution A probability distribution that specifies the probabilities for a group of related random variables.

Multivariate normal distribution A probability distribution for a group of random variables that is completely defined by the means and variances of the variables plus all the correlations between pairs of the variables.

Mutual fund A professionally managed investment pool in which investors in the fund typically each have a pro-rata claim on the income and value of the fund.

Mutually exclusive projects Mutually exclusive projects compete directly with each other. For example, if Projects A and B are mutually exclusive, you can choose A or B, but you cannot choose both.

n Factorial For a positive integer n, the product of the first n positive integers; 0 factorial equals 1 by definition. n factorial is written as n!.

NDFs See *Nondeliverable forwards*.

NPV rule An investment decision rule that states that an investment should be undertaken if its NPV is positive but not undertaken if its NPV is negative.

Narrow money The notes and coins in circulation in an economy, plus other very highly liquid deposits.

Nash equilibrium When two or more participants in a non-coop-erative game have no incentive to deviate from their respective equilibrium strategies given their opponent's strategies.

National income The income received by all factors of production used in the generation of final output. National income equals gross domestic product (or, in some countries, gross national product) minus the capital consumption allowance and a statistical discrepancy.

Natural rate of unemployment Effective unemployment rate, below which pressure emerges in labor markets.

Neo-Keynesians A group of dynamic general equilibrium models that assume slow-to-adjust prices and wages.

Net book value The remaining (undepreciated) balance of an asset's purchase cost. For liabilities, the face value of a bond minus any unamortized discount, or plus any unamortized premium.

Net income The difference between revenue and expenses; what remains after subtracting all expenses (including depreciation, interest, and taxes) from revenue.

Net operating cycle An estimate of the average time that elapses between paying suppliers for materials and collecting cash from the subsequent sale of goods produced.

Net present value (NPV) The present value of an investment's cash inflows (benefits) minus the present value of its cash outflows (costs).

Net profit margin (**profit margin** or **return on sales**)An indicator of profitability, calculated as net income divided by revenue; indicates how much of each dollar of revenues is left after all costs and expenses.

Net realizable value Estimated selling price in the ordinary course of business less the estimated costs necessary to make the sale.

Net revenue Revenue after adjustments (e.g., for estimated returns or for amounts unlikely to be collected).

Net tax rate The tax rate net of transfer payments.

Netting When parties agree to exchange only the net amount owed from one party to the other.

Neutral rate of interest The rate of interest that neither spurs on nor slows down the underlying economy.

New Keynesians A group of dynamic general equilibrium models that assume slow-to-adjust prices and wages.

New classical macroeconomics An approach to macroeconomics that seeks the macroeconomic conclusions of individuals maximizing utility on the basis of rational expectations and companies maximizing profits.

New-issue DRP Dividend reinvestment plan in which the company meets the need for additional shares by issuing them instead of purchasing them.

No-load fund A mutual fund in which there is no fee for investing in the fund or for redeeming fund shares, although there is an annual fee based on a percentage of the fund's net asset value.

Node Each value on a binomial tree from which successive moves or outcomes branch.

Nominal GDP The value of goods and services measured at current prices.

Nominal rate A rate of interest based on the security's face value.

Nominal risk-free interest rate The sum of the real risk-free interest rate and the inflation premium.

Nominal scale A measurement scale that categorizes data but does not rank them.

Non-accelerating inflation rate of unemployment Effective unemployment rate, below which pressure emerges in labor markets.

Non-cumulative preference shares Preference shares for which dividends that are not paid in the current or subsequent periods are forfeited permanently (instead of being accrued and paid at a later date).

Non-current assets Assets that are expected to benefit the company over an extended period of time (usually more than one year).

Non-current liability An obligation that broadly represents a probable sacrifice of economic benefits in periods generally greater than one year in the future.

Non-cyclical A company whose performance is largely independent of the business cycle.

Non-participating preference shares Preference shares that do not entitle shareholders to share in the profits of the company. Instead, shareholders are only entitled to receive a fixed dividend payment and the par value of the shares in the event of liquidation.

Non-renewable resources Finite resources that are depleted once they are consumed, such as oil and coal.

Non-satiation The assumption that the consumer could never have so much of a preferred good that she would refuse any more, even if it were free; sometimes referred to as the "more is better" assumption.

Nonconventional cash flow In a nonconventional cash flow pattern, the initial outflow is not followed by inflows only, but the cash flows can flip from positive (inflows) to negative (outflows) again (or even change signs several times).

Noncurrent assets Assets that are expected to benefit the company over an extended period of time (usually more than one year).

Nondeliverable forwards Cash-settled forward contracts, used predominately with respect to foreign exchange forwards.

Nonparametric test A test that is not concerned with a parameter, or that makes minimal assumptions about the population from which a sample comes.

Nonsystematic risk Unique risk that is local or limited to a particular asset or industry that need not affect assets outside of that asset class.

Normal distribution A continuous, symmetric probability distribution that is completely described by its mean and its variance.

Normal profit The level of accounting profit needed to just cover the implicit opportunity costs ignored in accounting costs.

Notching Ratings adjustment methodology where specific issues from the same borrower may be assigned different credit ratings.

Notes payable Amounts owed by a business to creditors as a result of borrowings that are evidenced by (short-term) loan agreements.

Notice period The length of time (typically 30 to 90 days) in advance that investors may be required to notify a fund of their intent to redeem.

Number of days of inventory An activity ratio equal to the number of days in a period divided by the inventory ratio for the period; an indication of the number of days a company ties up funds in inventory.

Number of days of payables An activity ratio equal to the number of days in a period divided by the payables turnover ratio for the period; an estimate of the average number of days it takes a company to pay its suppliers.

Number of days of receivables Estimate of the average number of days it takes to collect on credit accounts.

Objective probabilities Probabilities that generally do not vary from person to person; includes a priori and objective probabilities.

Offer The price at which a dealer or trader is willing to sell an asset, typically qualified by a maximum quantity (ask size).

Official interest rate (or official policy rate, policy rate) An interest rate that a central bank sets and announces publicly; normally the rate at which it is willing to lend money to the commercial banks.

Official policy rate An interest rate that a central bank sets and announces publicly; normally the rate at which it is willing to lend money to the commercial banks.

Offsetting A transaction in exchange-listed derivative markets in which a party re-enters the market to close out a position.

Oligopoly Market structure with a relatively small number of firms supplying the market.

One-sided hypothesis test A test in which the null hypothesis is rejected only if the evidence indicates that the population parameter is greater than (smaller than) θ_0. The alternative hypothesis also has one side.

One-tailed hypothesis test A test in which the null hypothesis is rejected only if the evidence indicates that the population parameter is greater than (smaller than) θ_0. The alternative hypothesis also has one side.

Open market operations Activities that involve the purchase and sale of government bonds from and to commercial banks and/or designated market makers.

Open-end fund A mutual fund that accepts new investment money and issues additional shares at a value equal to the net asset value of the fund at the time of investment.

Open-market DRP Dividend reinvestment plan in which the company purchases shares in the open market to acquire the additional shares credited to plan participants.

Operating activities Activities that are part of the day-to-day business functioning of an entity, such as selling inventory and providing services.

Operating breakeven The number of units produced and sold at which the company's operating profit is zero (revenues = operating costs).

Operating cash flow The net amount of cash provided from operating activities.

Operating cycle A measure of the time needed to convert raw materials into cash from a sale; it consists of the number of days of inventory and the number of days of receivables.

Operating efficiency ratios Ratios that measure how efficiently a company performs day-to-day tasks, such as the collection of receivables and management of inventory.

Operating leverage The use of fixed costs in operations.

Operating profit (operating income) A company's profits on its usual business activities before deducting taxes.

Operating profit margin (operating margin) A profitability ratio calculated as operating income (i.e., income before interest and taxes) divided by revenue.

Operating risk The risk attributed to the operating cost structure, in particular the use of fixed costs in operations; the risk arising from the mix of fixed and variable costs; the risk that a company's operations may be severely affected by environmental, social, and governance risk factors.

Operational independence A bank's ability to execute monetary policy and set interest rates in the way it thought would best meet the inflation target.

Operationally efficient Said of a market, a financial system, or an economy that has relatively low transaction costs.

Opportunity cost The value that investors forgo by choosing a particular course of action; the value of something in its best alternative use.

Option (option contract) A financial instrument that gives one party the right, but not the obligation, to buy or sell an underlying asset from or to another party at a fixed price over a specific period of time. Also referred to as contingent claims.

Option contract See *option*.

Option premium The amount of money a buyer pays and seller receives to engage in an option transaction.

Option price The amount of money a buyer pays and seller receives to engage in an option transaction.

Order A specification of what instrument to trade, how much to trade, and whether to buy or sell.

Order precedence hierarchy   With respect to the execution of orders to trade, a set of rules that determines which orders execute before other orders.

Order-driven markets   A market (generally an auction market) that uses rules to arrange trades based on the orders that traders submit; in their pure form, such markets do not make use of dealers.

Ordinal scale   A measurement scale that sorts data into categories that are ordered (ranked) with respect to some characteristic.

Ordinary annuity   An annuity with a first cash flow that is paid one period from the present.

Ordinary shares   (common stock or common shares) Equity shares that are subordinate to all other types of equity (e.g., preferred equity).

Other comprehensive income   Items of comprehensive income that are not reported on the income statement; comprehensive income minus net income.

Other receivables   Amounts owed to the company from parties other than customers.

Out-of-sample test   A test of a strategy or model using a sample outside the time period on which the strategy or model was developed.

Out-of-the-money   Options that, if exercised, would require the payment of more money than the value received and therefore would not be currently exercised.

Outcome   A possible value of a random variable.

Overbought   A market condition in which market sentiment is thought to be unsustainably bullish.

Oversold   A market condition in which market sentiment is thought to be unsustainably bearish.

Owner-of-record date   The date that a shareholder listed on the corporation's books will be deemed to have ownership of the shares for purposes of receiving an upcoming dividend; two business days after the ex-dividend date.

Owners' equity   (shareholders' equity) The excess of assets over liabilities; the residual interest of shareholders in the assets of an entity after deducting the entity's liabilities.

Paasche index   An index formula using the current composition of a basket of products.

Paired comparisons test   A statistical test for differences based on paired observations drawn from samples that are dependent on each other.

Paired observations   Observations that are dependent on each other.

Pairs arbitrage trade   A trade in two closely related stocks involving the short sale of one and the purchase of the other.

Panel data   Observations through time on a single characteristic of multiple observational units.

Parameter   A descriptive measure computed from or used to describe a population of data, conventionally represented by Greek letters.

Parametric test   Any test (or procedure) concerned with parameters or whose validity depends on assumptions concerning the population generating the sample.

Pari passu   On an equal footing.

Participating preference shares   Preference shares that entitle shareholders to receive the standard preferred dividend plus the opportunity to receive an additional dividend if the company's profits exceed a pre-specified level.

Passive investment   A buy and hold approach in which an investor does not make portfolio changes based on short-term expectations of changing market or security performance.

Passive strategy   In reference to short-term cash management, it is an investment strategy characterized by simple decision rules for making daily investments.

Payable date   The day that the company actually mails out (or electronically transfers) a dividend payment.

Payment date   The day that the company actually mails out (or electronically transfers) a dividend payment.

Payments system   The system for the transfer of money.

Payoff   The value of an option at expiration.

Payout   Cash dividends and the value of shares repurchased in any given year.

Payout policy   A company's set of principles guiding payouts.

Peak   The highest point of a business cycle.

Peer group   A group of companies engaged in similar business activities whose economics and valuation are influenced by closely related factors.

Pennants   A technical analysis continuation pattern formed by trendlines that converge to form a triangle, typically over a short period.

Per capita real GDP   Real GDP divided by the size of the population, often used as a measure of the average standard of living in a country.

Per unit contribution margin   The amount that each unit sold contributes to covering fixed costs—that is, the difference between the price per unit and the variable cost per unit.

Percentage-of-completion   A method of revenue recognition in which, in each accounting period, the company estimates what percentage of the contract is complete and then reports that percentage of the total contract revenue in its income statement.

Percentiles   Quantiles that divide a distribution into 100 equal parts.

Perfect competition   (also price taker) A market structure in which the individual firm has virtually no impact on market price, because it is assumed to be a very small seller among a very large number of firms selling essentially identical products.

Performance appraisal   The evaluation of risk-adjusted performance; the evaluation of investment skill.

Performance evaluation   The measurement and assessment of the outcomes of investment management decisions.

Performance measurement   The calculation of returns in a logical and consistent manner.

Period costs   Costs (e.g., executives' salaries) that cannot be directly matched with the timing of revenues and which are thus expensed immediately.

Permanent differences   Differences between tax and financial reporting of revenue (expenses) that will not be reversed at some future date. These result in a difference between the company's effective tax rate and statutory tax rate and do not result in a deferred tax item.

Permutation   An ordered listing.

Perpetuity   A perpetual annuity, or a set of never-ending level sequential cash flows, with the first cash flow occurring one period from now.

Personal consumption expenditures   All domestic personal consumption; the basis for a price index for such consumption called the PCE price index.

Personal disposable income   Equal to personal income less personal taxes.

Personal income   A broad measure of household income that includes all income received by households, whether earned or unearned; measures the ability of consumers to make purchases.

Plain vanilla swap An interest rate swap in which one party pays a fixed rate and the other pays a floating rate, with both sets of payments in the same currency.

Planning horizon A time period in which all factors of production are variable, including technology, physical capital, and plant size.

Platykurtic Describes a distribution that is less peaked than the normal distribution.

Point and figure chart A technical analysis chart that is constructed with columns of X's alternating with columns of O's such that the horizontal axis represents only the number of changes in price without reference to time or volume.

Point estimate A single numerical estimate of an unknown quantity, such as a population parameter.

Point of sale (POS) Systems that capture transaction data at the physical location in which the sale is made.

Policy rate An interest rate that a central bank sets and announces publicly; normally the rate at which it is willing to lend money to the commercial banks.

Population All members of a specified group.

Population mean The arithmetic mean value of a population; the arithmetic mean of all the observations or values in the population.

Population standard deviation A measure of dispersion relating to a population in the same unit of measurement as the observations, calculated as the positive square root of the population variance.

Population variance A measure of dispersion relating to a population, calculated as the mean of the squared deviations around the population mean.

Portfolio company In private equity, the company that is being invested in.

Portfolio demand for money The demand to hold speculative money balances based on the potential opportunities or risks that are inherent in other financial instruments.

Portfolio planning The process of creating a plan for building a portfolio that is expected to satisfy a client's investment objectives.

Position The quantity of an asset that an entity owns or owes.

Position trader A trader who typically holds positions open overnight.

Posterior probability An updated probability that reflects or comes after new information.

Potential GDP The level of real GDP that can be produced at full employment; measures the productive capacity of the economy.

Power of a test The probability of correctly rejecting the null—that is, rejecting the null hypothesis when it is false.

Precautionary money balances Money held to provide a buffer against unforeseen events that might require money.

Precautionary stocks A level of inventory beyond anticipated needs that provides a cushion in the event that it takes longer to replenish inventory than expected or in the case of greater than expected demand.

Preference shares (or preferred stock) A type of equity interest which ranks above common shares with respect to the payment of dividends and the distribution of the company's net assets upon liquidation. They have characteristics of both debt and equity securities.

Preferred stock See *Preference shares*.

Premium The amount of money a buyer pays and seller receives to engage in an option transaction.

Prepaid expense A normal operating expense that has been paid in advance of when it is due.

Present value (PV) The present discounted value of future cash flows: For assets, the present discounted value of the future net cash inflows that the asset is expected to generate; for liabilities, the present discounted value of the future net cash outflows that are expected to be required to settle the liabilities.

Present value models (or discounted cash flow models) Valuation models that estimate the intrinsic value of a security as the present value of the future benefits expected to be received from the security.

Pretax margin A profitability ratio calculated as earnings before taxes divided by revenue.

Price The market price as established by the interactions of the market demand and supply factors.

Price discovery A feature of futures markets in which futures prices provide valuable information about the price of the underlying asset.

Price elasticity of demand Measures the percentage change in the quantity demanded, given a percentage change in the price of a given product.

Price index Represents the average prices of a basket of goods and services.

Price limits Limits imposed by a futures exchange on the price change that can occur from one day to the next.

Price multiple A ratio that compares the share price with some sort of monetary flow or value to allow evaluation of the relative worth of a company's stock.

Price priority The principle that the highest priced buy orders and the lowest priced sell orders execute first.

Price relative A ratio of an ending price over a beginning price; it is equal to 1 plus the holding period return on the asset.

Price return Measures *only* the price appreciation or percentage change in price of the securities in an index or portfolio.

Price return index (or price index) An index that reflects *only* the price appreciation or percentage change in price of the constituent securities.

Price stability In economics, refers to an inflation rate that is low on average and not subject to wide fluctuation.

Price takers Producers that must accept whatever price the market dictates.

Price to book value A valuation ratio calculated as price per share divided by book value per share.

Price to cash flow A valuation ratio calculated as price per share divided by cash flow per share.

Price to earnings ratio (P/E ratio) The ratio of share price to earnings per share.

Price to sales A valuation ratio calculated as price per share divided by sales per share.

Price weighting An index weighting method in which the weight assigned to each constituent security is determined by dividing its price by the sum of all the prices of the constituent securities.

Price-to-earnings ratio (also P/E) The ratio of share price to earnings per share.

Priced risk Risk for which investors demand compensation for bearing (e.g. equity risk, company-specific factors, macroeconomic factors).

Primary capital markets (primary markets) The market where securities are first sold and the issuers receive the proceeds.

Primary market The market where securities are first sold and the issuers receive the proceeds.

Prime brokers Brokers that provide services including custody, administration, lending, short borrowing, and trading.

Principal   The amount of funds originally invested in a project or instrument; the face value to be paid at maturity.

Principal business activity   The business activity from which a company derives a majority of its revenues and/or earnings.

Principal value   The amount of cash payable by a company to the bondholders when the bonds mature; the promised payment at maturity separate from any coupon payment.

Prior probabilities   Probabilities reflecting beliefs prior to the arrival of new information.

Priority of claims   Priority of payment, with the most senior or highest ranking debt having the first claim on the cash flows and assets of the issuer.

Private equity securities   Securities that are not listed on public exchanges and have no active secondary market. They are issued primarily to institutional investors via non-public offerings, such as private placements.

Private investment in public equity   An investment in the equity of a publicly traded firm that is made at a discount to the market value of the firm's shares.

Private placement   When corporations sell securities directly to a small group of qualified investors, usually with the assistance of an investment bank.

Probability   A number between 0 and 1 describing the chance that a stated event will occur.

Probability density function   A function with non-negative values such that probability can be described by areas under the curve graphing the function.

Probability distribution   A distribution that specifies the probabilities of a random variable's possible outcomes.

Probability function   A function that specifies the probability that the random variable takes on a specific value.

Producer price index   Reflects the price changes experienced by domestic producers in a country.

Production function   Provides the quantitative link between the level of output that the economy can produce and the inputs used in the production process.

Production opportunity frontier   Curve describing the maximum number of units of one good a company can produce, for any given number of the other good that it chooses to manufacture.

Productivity   The amount of output produced by workers in a given period of time–for example, output per hour worked; measures the efficiency of labor.

Profit   The return that owners of a company receive for the use of their capital and the assumption of financial risk when making their investments.

Profit and loss (P&L) statement   A financial statement that provides information about a company's profitability over a stated period of time.

Profit margin   An indicator of profitability, calculated as net income divided by revenue; indicates how much of each dollar of revenues is left after all costs and expenses.

Profitability ratios   Ratios that measure a company's ability to generate profitable sales from its resources (assets).

Project sequencing   To defer the decision to invest in a future project until the outcome of some or all of a current project is known. Projects are sequenced through time, so that investing in a project creates the option to invest in future projects.

Promissory note   A written promise to pay a certain amount of money on demand.

Property, plant, and equipment   Tangible assets that are expected to be used for more than one period in either the production or supply of goods or services, or for administrative purposes.

Prospectus   The document that describes the terms of a new bond issue and helps investors perform their analysis on the issue.

Protective put   An option strategy in which a long position in an asset is combined with a long position in a put.

Pseudo-random numbers   Numbers produced by random number generators.

Pull on liquidity   When disbursements are paid too quickly or trade credit availability is limited, requiring companies to expend funds before they receive funds from sales that could cover the liability.

Pure discount instruments   Instruments that pay interest as the difference between the amount borrowed and the amount paid back.

Pure-play method   A method for estimating the beta for a company or project; it requires using a comparable company's beta and adjusting it for financial leverage differences.

Put   An option that gives the holder the right to sell an underlying asset to another party at a fixed price over a specific period of time.

Put/call ratio   A technical analysis indicator that evaluates market sentiment based upon the volume of put options traded divided by the volume of call options traded for a particular financial instrument.

Putable common shares   Common shares that give investors the option (or right) to sell their shares (i.e., "put" them) back to the issuing company at a price that is specified when the shares are originally issued.

Put–call parity   An equation expressing the equivalence (parity) of a portfolio of a call and a bond with a portfolio of a put and the underlying, which leads to the relationship between put and call prices.

Quantile   (or fractile) A value at or below which a stated fraction of the data lies.

Quantitative easing   An expansionary monetary policy based on aggressive open market purchase operations.

Quantity   The amount of a product that consumers are willing and able to buy at each price level.

Quantity demanded   The amount of a product that consumers are willing and able to buy at each price level.

Quantity equation of exchange   An expression that over a given period, the amount of money used to purchase all goods and services in an economy, $M \times V$, is equal to monetary value of this output, $P \times Y$.

Quantity theory of money   Asserts that total spending (in money terms) is proportional to the quantity of money.

Quartiles   Quantiles that divide a distribution into four equal parts.

Quasi-fixed cost   A cost that stays the same over a range of production but can change to another constant level when production moves outside of that range.

Quick assets   Assets that can be most readily converted to cash (e.g., cash, short-term marketable investments, receivables).

Quick ratio   A stringent measure of liquidity that indicates a company's ability to satisfy current liabilities with its most liquid assets, calculated as (cash + short-term marketable investments + receivables) divided by current liabilities.

Quintiles   Quantiles that divide a distribution into five equal parts.

Quote-driven market   A market in which dealers acting as principals facilitate trading.

Quoted interest rate   (also stated annual interest rate) A quoted interest rate that does not account for compounding within the year.

Random number An observation drawn from a uniform distribution.

Random number generator An algorithm that produces uniformly distributed random numbers between 0 and 1.

Random variable A quantity whose future outcomes are uncertain.

Range The difference between the maximum and minimum values in a dataset.

Ratio scales A measurement scale that has all the characteristics of interval measurement scales as well as a true zero point as the origin.

Real GDP The value of goods and services produced, measured at base year prices.

Real income Income adjusted for the effect of inflation on the purchasing power of money.

Real interest rate Nominal interest rate minus the expected rate of inflation.

Real risk-free interest rate The single-period interest rate for a completely risk-free security if no inflation were expected.

Realizable (settlement) value With reference to assets, the amount of cash or cash equivalents that could currently be obtained by selling the asset in an orderly disposal; with reference to liabilities, the undiscounted amount of cash or cash equivalents expected to be paid to satisfy the liabilities in the normal course of business.

Rebalancing Adjusting the weights of the constituent securities in an index.

Rebalancing policy The set of rules that guide the process of restoring a portfolio's asset class weights to those specified in the strategic asset allocation.

Recession A period during which real GDP decreases (i.e., negative growth) for at least two successive quarters, or a period of significant decline in total output, income, employment, and sales usually lasting from six months to a year.

Recognition lag The lag in government response to an economic problem resulting from the delay in confirming a change in the state of the economy.

Record date The date that a shareholder listed on the corporation's books will be deemed to have ownership of the shares for purposes of receiving an upcoming dividend; two business days after the ex-dividend date.

Redemptions Withdrawals of funds by investors.

Refinancing rate A type of central bank policy rate.

Regulatory risk The risk associated with the uncertainty of how derivative transactions will be regulated or with changes in regulations.

Relative dispersion The amount of dispersion relative to a reference value or benchmark.

Relative frequency With reference to an interval of grouped data, the number of observations in the interval divided by the total number of observations in the sample.

Relative price The price of a specific good or service in comparison with those of other goods and services.

Relative strength analysis A comparison of the performance of one asset with the performance of another asset or a benchmark based on changes in the ratio of the securities' respective prices over time.

Relative strength index A technical analysis momentum oscillator that compares a security's gains with its losses over a set period.

Renewable resources Resources that can be replenished, such as a forest.

Rent Payment for the use of property.

Reorganization Agreements made by a company in bankruptcy under which a company's capital structure is altered and/or alternative arrangements are made for debt repayment; U.S. Chapter 11 bankruptcy. The company emerges from bankruptcy as a going concern.

Repo rates Short-term collateralized lending rates.

Repurchase agreement The sale of securities together with an agreement for the seller to buy back the securities at a later date at a higher price; often called a repo. Typically a short-term agreement; if long term, called a term repo.

Reserve requirement The requirement for banks to hold reserves in proportion to the size of deposits.

Residual claim The owners' remaining claim on the company's assets after the liabilities are deducted.

Resistance In technical analysis, a price range in which selling activity is sufficient to stop the rise in the price of a security.

Restricted payments A bond covenant meant to protect creditors by limiting how much cash can be paid out to shareholders over time.

Retail method An inventory accounting method in which the sales value of an item is reduced by the gross margin to calculate the item's cost.

Retracement In technical analysis, a reversal in the movement of a security's price such that it is counter to the prevailing longerterm price trend.

Return on assets (ROA) A profitability ratio calculated as net income divided by average total assets; indicates a company's net profit generated per dollar invested in total assets.

Return on equity (ROE) A profitability ratio calculated as net income divided by average shareholders' equity.

Return on sales An indicator of profitability, calculated as net income divided by revenue; indicates how much of each dollar of revenues is left after all costs and expenses.

Return on total capital A profitability ratio calculated as EBIT divided by the sum of short- and long-term debt and equity.

Return-generating model A model that can provide an estimate of the expected return of a security given certain parameters and estimates of the values of the independent variables in the model.

Revaluation model The process of valuing long-lived assets at fair value, rather than at cost less accumulated depreciation. Any resulting profit or loss is either reported on the income statement and/or through equity under revaluation surplus.

Revenue The amount charged for the delivery of goods or services in the ordinary activities of a business over a stated period; the inflows of economic resources to a company over a stated period.

Reversal patterns A type of pattern used in technical analysis to predict the end of a trend and a change in direction of the security's price.

Reverse stock split A reduction in the number of shares outstanding with a corresponding increase in share price, but no change to the company's underlying fundamentals.

Revolving credit agreements The strongest form of short-term bank borrowing facilities; they are in effect for multiple years (e.g., 3–5 years) and may have optional medium-term loan features.

Rho The sensitivity of the option price to the risk-free rate.

Ricardian equivalence An economic theory that implies that it makes no difference whether a government finances a deficit by increasing taxes or issuing debt.

Risk averse The assumption that an investor will choose the least risky alternative.

Risk aversion   The degree of an investor's inability and unwillingness to take risk.

Risk budgeting   The establishment of objectives for individuals, groups, or divisions of an organization that takes into account the allocation of an acceptable level of risk.

Risk management   The process of identifying the level of risk an entity wants, measuring the level of risk the entity currently has, taking actions that bring the actual level of risk to the desired level of risk, and monitoring the new actual level of risk so that it continues to be aligned with the desired level of risk.

Risk premium   An extra return expected by investors for bearing some specified risk.

Risk tolerance   The amount of risk an investor is willing and able to bear to achieve an investment goal.

Robust   The quality of being relatively unaffected by a violation of assumptions.

Rule of 72   The principle that the approximate number of years necessary for an investment to double is 72 divided by the stated interest rate.

Safety stock   A level of inventory beyond anticipated needs that provides a cushion in the event that it takes longer to replenish inventory than expected or in the case of greater than expected demand.

Safety-first rules   Rules for portfolio selection that focus on the risk that portfolio value will fall below some minimum acceptable level over some time horizon.

Sales   Generally, a synonym for revenue; "sales" is generally understood to refer to the sale of goods, whereas "revenue" is understood to include the sale of goods or services.

Sales returns and allowances   An offset to revenue reflecting any cash refunds, credits on account, and discounts from sales prices given to customers who purchased defective or unsatisfactory items.

Sales risk   Uncertainty with respect to the quantity of goods and services that a company is able to sell and the price it is able to achieve; the risk related to the uncertainty of revenues.

Salvage value   (or residual value) The amount the company estimates that it can sell the asset for at the end of its useful life.

Sample   A subset of a population.

Sample excess kurtosis   A sample measure of the degree of a distribution's peakedness in excess of the normal distribution's peakedness.

Sample kurtosis   A sample measure of the degree of a distribution's peakedness.

Sample mean   The sum of the sample observations, divided by the sample size.

Sample selection bias   Bias introduced by systematically excluding some members of the population according to a particular attribute—for example, the bias introduced when data availability leads to certain observations being excluded from the analysis.

Sample skewness   A sample measure of degree of asymmetry of a distribution.

Sample standard deviation   The positive square root of the sample variance.

Sample statistic   A quantity computed from or used to describe a sample.

Sample variance   A sample measure of the degree of dispersion of a distribution, calculated by dividing the sum of the squared deviations from the sample mean by the sample size minus 1.

Sampling   The process of obtaining a sample.

Sampling distribution   The distribution of all distinct possible values that a statistic can assume when computed from samples of the same size randomly drawn from the same population.

Sampling error   The difference between the observed value of a statistic and the quantity it is intended to estimate.

Sampling plan   The set of rules used to select a sample.

Say's law   Named for French economist J.B. Say: All that is produced will be sold because supply creates its own demand.

Scalper   A trader who offers to buy or sell futures contracts, holding the position for only a brief period of time. Scalpers attempt to profit by buying at the bid price and selling at the higher ask price.

Scenario analysis   Analysis that shows the changes in key financial quantities that result from given (economic) events, such as the loss of customers, the loss of a supply source, or a catastrophic event; a risk management technique involving examination of the performance of a portfolio under specified situations. Closely related to stress testing.

Scrip dividend schemes   Dividend reinvestment plan in which the company meets the need for additional shares by issuing them instead of purchasing them.

Seasoned offering   An offering in which an issuer sells additional units of a previously issued security.

Seats   Memberships in a derivatives exchange.

Second lien   A secured interest in the pledged assets that ranks below first lien debt in both collateral protection and priority of payment.

Second-degree price discrimination   When the monopolist charges different per-unit prices using the quantity purchased as an indicator of how highly the customer values the product.

Secondary market   The market where securities are traded among investors.

Secondary precedence rules   Rules that determine how to rank orders placed at the same time.

Sector   A group of related industries.

Sector indices   Indices that represent and track different economic sectors—such as consumer goods, energy, finance, health care, and technology—on either a national, regional, or global basis.

Secured debt   Debt in which the debtholder has a direct claim—a pledge from the issuer—on certain assets and their associated cash flows.

Security characteristic line   A plot of the excess return of a security on the excess return of the market.

Security market index   A portfolio of securities representing a given security market, market segment, or asset class.

Security market line   (also SML) The graph of the capital asset pricing model.

Security selection   The process of selecting individual securities; typically, security selection has the objective of generating superior risk-adjusted returns relative to a portfolio's benchmark.

Self-investment limits   With respect to investment limitations applying to pension plans, restrictions on the percentage of assets that can be invested in securities issued by the pension plan sponsor.

Sell-side firm   A broker or dealer that sells securities to and provides independent investment research and recommendations to investment management companies.

Semi-strong-form efficient market   A market in which security prices reflect all publicly known and available information.

Semideviation The positive square root of semivariance (sometimes called semistandard deviation).

Semilogarithmic Describes a scale constructed so that equal intervals on the vertical scale represent equal rates of change, and equal intervals on the horizontal scale represent equal amounts of change.

Semivariance The average squared deviation below the mean.

Seniority ranking Priority of payment of various debt obligations.

Sensitivity analysis Analysis that shows the range of possible outcomes as specific assumptions are changed.

Separately managed account (SMA) An investment portfolio managed exclusively for the benefit of an individual or institution.

Settlement date The date on which the parties to a swap make payments.

Settlement period The time between settlement dates.

Settlement price The official price, designated by the clearinghouse, from which daily gains and losses will be determined and marked to market.

Share repurchase A transaction in which a company buys back its own shares. Unlike stock dividends and stock splits, share repurchases use corporate cash.

Shareholder wealth maximization To maximize the market value of shareholders' equity.

Shareholder-of-record date The date that a shareholder listed on the corporation's books will be deemed to have ownership of the shares for purposes of receiving an upcoming dividend; two business days after the ex-dividend date.

Shareholders' equity Assets less liabilities; the residual interest in the assets after subtracting the liabilities.

Sharpe ratio The average return in excess of the risk-free rate divided by the standard deviation of return; a measure of the average excess return earned per unit of standard deviation of return.

Shelf registration A registration of an offering well in advance of the offering; the issuer may not sell all shares registered in a single transaction.

Short The seller of a derivative contract. Also refers to the position of being short a derivative.

Short position A position in an asset or contract in which one has sold an asset one does not own, or in which a right under a contract can be exercised against oneself.

Short selling A transaction in which borrowed securities are sold with the intention to repurchase them at a lower price at a later date and return them to the lender.

Short-run average total cost curve The curve describing average total costs when some costs are considered fixed.

Short-run supply curve The section of the marginal cost curve that lies above the minimum point on the average variable cost curve.

Shortfall risk The risk that portfolio value will fall below some minimum acceptable level over some time horizon.

Shutdown point The point at which average revenue is less than average variable cost.

Simple interest The interest earned each period on the original investment; interest calculated on the principal only.

Simple random sample A subset of a larger population created in such a way that each element of the population has an equal probability of being selected to the subset.

Simple random sampling The procedure of drawing a sample to satisfy the definition of a simple random sample.

Simulation Computer-generated sensitivity or scenario analysis that is based on probability models for the factors that drive outcomes.

Simulation trial A complete pass through the steps of a simulation.

Single-step format With respect to the format of the income statement, a format that does not subtotal for gross profit (revenue minus cost of goods sold).

Skewed Not symmetrical.

Skewness A quantitative measure of skew (lack of symmetry); a synonym of skew.

Solvency With respect to financial statement analysis, the ability of a company to fulfill its long-term obligations.

Solvency ratios Ratios that measure a company's ability to meet its long-term obligations.

Sovereign yield spread An estimate of the country spread (country equity premium) for a developing nation that is based on a comparison of bonds yields in country being analyzed and a developed country. The sovereign yield spread is the difference between a government bond yield in the country being analyzed, denominated in the currency of the developed country, and the Treasury bond yield on a similar maturity bond in the developed country.

Spearman rank correlation coefficient A measure of correlation applied to ranked data.

Special dividend A dividend paid by a company that does not pay dividends on a regular schedule, or a dividend that supplements regular cash dividends with an extra payment.

Special purpose entity (special purpose vehicle or variable interest entity) A non-operating entity created to carry out a specified purpose, such as leasing assets or securitizing receivables; can be a corporation, partnership, trust, limited liability, or partnership formed to facilitate a specific type of business activity.

Special purpose vehicle See *Special purpose entity*.

Specific identification method An inventory accounting method that identifies which specific inventory items were sold and which remained in inventory to be carried over to later periods.

Speculative demand for money (or portfolio demand for money) The demand to hold speculative money balances based on the potential opportunities or risks that are inherent in other financial instruments.

Speculative money balances Monies held in anticipation that other assets will decline in value.

Speculative value The difference between the market price of the option and its intrinsic value, determined by the uncertainty of the underlying over the remaining life of the option.

Sponsored A type of depository receipt in which the foreign company whose shares are held by the depository has a direct involvement in the issuance of the receipts.

Spot markets Markets that trade assets for immediate delivery.

Spot price The price for immediate purchase of the underlying asset.

Spread risk Bond price risk arising from changes in the yield spread on credit-risky bonds; reflects changes in the market's assessment and/or pricing of credit migration (or downgrade) risk and market liquidity risk.

Stackelberg model A prominent model of strategic decision-making in which firms are assumed to make their decisions sequentially.

Stagflation When a high inflation rate is combined with a high level of unemployment and a slowdown of the economy.

Standard cost   With respect to inventory accounting, the planned or target unit cost of inventory items or services.

Standard deviation   The positive square root of the variance; a measure of dispersion in the same units as the original data.

Standard normal distribution   The normal density with mean (μ) equal to 0 and standard deviation (σ) equal to 1.

Standardizing   A transformation that involves subtracting the mean and dividing the result by the standard deviation.

Standing limit orders   A limit order at a price below market and which therefore is waiting to trade.

Stated annual interest rate   (also quoted interest rate) A quoted interest rate that does not account for compounding within the year.

Statement of cash flows   (cash flow statement) A financial statement that reconciles beginning-of-period and end-of-period balance sheet values of cash; provides information about an entity's cash inflows and cash outflows as they pertain to operating, investing, and financing activities.

Statement of changes in equity   (statement of owners' equity) A financial statement that reconciles the beginning-of-period and end-of-period balance sheet values of shareholders' equity; provides information about all factors affecting shareholders' equity.

Statement of financial condition   The financial statement that presents an entity's current financial position by disclosing resources the entity controls (its assets) and the claims on those resources (its liabilities and equity claims), as of a particular point in time (the date of the balance sheet).

Statement of financial position   The financial statement that presents an entity's current financial position by disclosing resources the entity controls (its assets) and the claims on those resources (its liabilities and equity claims), as of a particular point in time (the date of the balance sheet).

Statement of operations   A financial statement that provides information about a company's profitability over a stated period of time.

Statement of owners' equity   (Statement of changes in shareholders' equity) A financial statement that reconciles the beginning of-period and end-of-period balance sheet values of shareholders' equity; provides information about all factors affecting shareholders' equity.

Statement of retained earnings   A financial statement that reconciles beginning-of-period and end-of-period balance sheet values of retained income; shows the linkage between the balance sheet and income statement.

Statistic   A quantity computed from or used to describe a sample of data.

Statistical inference   Making forecasts, estimates, or judgments about a larger group from a smaller group actually observed; using a sample statistic to infer the value of an unknown population parameter.

Statistically significant   A result indicating that the null hypothesis can be rejected; with reference to an estimated regression coefficient, frequently understood to mean a result indicating that the corresponding population regression coefficient is different from 0.

Statutory voting   A common method of voting where each share represents one vote.

Stock dividend   A type of dividend in which a company distributes additional shares of its common stock to shareholders instead of cash.

Stock-out losses   Profits lost from not having sufficient inventory on hand to satisfy demand.

Stop order   (or stop-loss order) An order in which a trader has specified a stop price condition.

Stop-loss order   See *Stop order.*

Store of value   The quality of tending to preserve value.

Store of wealth   Goods that depend on the fact that they do not perish physically over time, and on the belief that others would always value the good.

Straight-line method   A depreciation method that allocates evenly the cost of a long-lived asset less its estimated residual value over the estimated useful life of the asset.

Strategic analysis   Analysis of the competitive environment with an emphasis on the implications of the environment for corporate strategy.

Strategic asset allocation   The set of exposures to IPS-permissible asset classes that is expected to achieve the client's long-term objectives given the client's investment constraints.

Strategic groups   Groups sharing distinct business models or catering to specific market segments in an industry.

Stress testing   A set of techniques for estimating losses in extremely unfavorable combinations of events or scenarios.

Strike   The fixed price at which an option holder can buy or sell the underlying.

Strike price   The fixed price at which an option holder can buy or sell the underlying.

Strike rate   The fixed rate at which the holder of an interest rate option can buy or sell the underlying.

Striking price   The fixed price at which an option holder can buy or sell the underlying.

Strong-form efficient market   A market in which security prices reflect all public and private information.

Structural (or cyclically adjusted) budget deficit   The deficit that would exist if the economy was at full employment (or full potential output).

Structural subordination   Arises in a holding company structure when the debt of operating subsidiaries is serviced by the cash flow and assets of the subsidiaries before funds can be passed to the holding company to service debt at the parent level.

Structured note   A variation of a floating-rate note that has some type of unusual characteristic such as a leverage factor or in which the rate moves opposite to interest rates.

Subjective probability   A probability drawing on personal or subjective judgment.

Subordinated debt   A class of unsecured debt that ranks below a firm's senior unsecured obligations.

Substitutes   Said of two goods or services such that if the price of one increases the demand for the other tends to increase, holding all other things equal (e.g., butter and margarine).

Sunk cost   A cost that has already been incurred.

Supernormal profit   Equal to accounting profit less the implicit opportunity costs not included in total accounting costs; the difference between total revenue (TR) and total cost (TC).

Supply shock   A typically unexpected disturbance to supply.

Support   In technical analysis, a price range in which buying activity is sufficient to stop the decline in the price of a security.

Survey approach   An estimate of the equity risk premium that is based upon estimates provided by a panel of finance experts.

Survivorship bias   The bias resulting from a test design that fails to account for companies that have gone bankrupt, merged, or are otherwise no longer reported in a database.

Sustainable growth rate The rate of dividend (and earnings) growth that can be sustained over time for a given level of return on equity, keeping the capital structure constant and without issuing additional common stock.

Sustainable rate of economic growth The rate of increase in the economy's productive capacity or potential GDP.

Swap An agreement between two parties to exchange a series of future cash flows.

Swap contract An agreement between two parties to exchange a series of future cash flows.

Swap spread The difference between the fixed rate on an interest rate swap and the rate on a Treasury note with equivalent maturity; it reflects the general level of credit risk in the market.

Swaption An option to enter into a swap.

Synthetic call The combination of puts, the underlying, and riskfree bonds that replicates a call option.

Synthetic put The combination of calls, the underlying, and riskfree bonds that replicates a put option.

Systematic risk Risk that affects the entire market or economy; it cannot be avoided and is inherent in the overall market. Systematic risk is also known as non diversifiable or market risk.

Systematic sampling A procedure of selecting every kth member until reaching a sample of the desired size. The sample that results from this procedure should be approximately random.

t-Test A hypothesis test using a statistic (t-statistic) that follows a t-distribution.

TRIN A flow of funds indicator applied to a broad stock market index to measure the relative extent to which money is moving into or out of rising and declining stocks.

Tactical asset allocation The decision to deliberately deviate from the strategic asset allocation in an attempt to add value based on forecasts of the near-term relative performance of asset classes.

Target balance A minimum level of cash to be held available— estimated in advance and adjusted for known funds transfers, seasonality, or other factors.

Target capital structure A company's chosen proportions of debt and equity.

Target independent A bank's ability to determine the definition of inflation that they target, the rate of inflation that they target, and the horizon over which the target is to be achieved.

Target semideviation The positive square root of target semivariance.

Target semivariance The average squared deviation below a target value.

Tax base The amount at which an asset or liability is valued for tax purposes.

Tax expense An aggregate of an entity's income tax payable (or recoverable in the case of a tax benefit) and any changes in deferred tax assets and liabilities. It is essentially the income tax payable or recoverable if these had been determined based on accounting profit rather than taxable income.

Tax loss carry forward A taxable loss in the current period that may be used to reduce future taxable income.

Taxable income The portion of an entity's income that is subject to income taxes under the tax laws of its jurisdiction.

Taxable temporary differences Temporary differences that result in a taxable amount in a future period when determining the taxable profit as the balance sheet item is recovered or settled.

Technical analysis A form of security analysis that uses price and volume data, which is often displayed graphically, in decision making.

Technology The process a company uses to transform inputs into outputs.

Tenor The original time to maturity on a swap.

Terminal stock value (or terminal value) The expected value of a share at the end of the investment horizon—in effect, the expected selling price.

Terminal value The expected value of a share at the end of the investment horizon—in effect, the expected selling price.

Termination date The date of the final payment on a swap; also, the swap's expiration date.

Theory of the consumer The branch of microeconomics that deals with consumption—the demand for goods and services—by utility-maximizing individuals.

Theory of the firm The branch of microeconomics that deals with the supply of goods and services by profit-maximizing firms.

Theta The rate at which an option's time value decays.

Third-degree price discrimination When the monopolist segregates customers into groups based on demographic or other characteristics and offers different pricing to each group.

Time to expiration The time remaining in the life of a derivative, typically expressed in years.

Time value The difference between the market price of the option and its intrinsic value, determined by the uncertainty of the underlying over the remaining life of the option.

Time value of money The principles governing equivalence relationships between cash flows with different dates.

Time-period bias The possibility that when we use a time-series sample, our statistical conclusion may be sensitive to the starting and ending dates of the sample.

Time-series data Observations of a variable over time.

Time-weighted rate of return The compound rate of growth of one unit of currency invested in a portfolio during a stated measurement period; a measure of investment performance that is not sensitive to the timing and amount of withdrawals or additions to the portfolio.

Top-down analysis With reference to investment selection processes, an approach that starts with macro selection (i.e., identifying attractive geographic segments and/or industry segments) and then addresses selection of the most attractive investments within those segments.

Total comprehensive income The change in equity during a period resulting from transaction and other events, other than those changes resulting from transactions with owners in their capacity as owners.

Total costs The summation of all costs, where costs are classified according to fixed or variable.

Total factor productivity A scale factor that reflects the portion of growth that is not accounted for by explicit factor inputs (e.g. capital and labor).

Total fixed cost The summation of all expenses that do not change when production varies.

Total probability rule A rule explaining the unconditional probability of an event in terms of probabilities of the event conditional on mutually exclusive and exhaustive scenarios.

Total probability rule for expected value A rule explaining the expected value of a random variable in terms of expected values of the random variable conditional on mutually exclusive and exhaustive scenarios.

Total product   The aggregate sum of production for the firm during a time period.

Total return   Measures the price appreciation, or percentage change in price of the securities in an index or portfolio, plus any income received over the period.

Total return index   An index that reflects the price appreciation or percentage change in price of the constituent securities plus any income received since inception.

Total return swap   A swap in which one party agrees to pay the total return on a security. Often used as a credit derivative, in which the underlying is a bond.

Total revenue   Price times the quantity of units sold.

Total variable cost   The summation of all variable expenses.

Tracking error   The standard deviation of the differences between a portfolio's returns and its benchmark's returns; a synonym of active risk.

Tracking risk   (tracking error) The standard deviation of the differences between a portfolio's returns and its benchmark's returns; a synonym of active risk.

Trade credit   A spontaneous form of credit in which a purchaser of the goods or service is financing its purchase by delaying the date on which payment is made.

Trade payables   Amounts that a business owes to its vendors for goods and services that were purchased from them but which have not yet been paid.

Trade receivables   (commercial receivables or accounts receivable) Amounts customers owe the company for products that have been sold as well as amounts that may be due from suppliers (such as for returns of merchandise).

Trading securities   (held-for-trading securities) Securities held by a company with the intent to trade them.

Traditional investment markets   Markets for traditional investments, which include all publicly traded debts and equities and shares in pooled investment vehicles that hold publicly traded debts and/or equities.

Transactions money balances   Money balances that are held to finance transactions.

Transactions motive   In the context of inventory management, the need for inventory as part of the routine production–sales cycle.

Transfer payments   Welfare payments made through the social security system that exist to provide a basic minimum level of income for low-income households.

Transitive preferences   The assumption that when comparing any three distinct bundles, A, B, and C, if A is preferred to B and simultaneously B is preferred to C, then it must be true that A is preferred to C.

Treasury Inflation-Protected Securities   A bond issued by the United States Treasury Department that is designed to protect the investor from inflation by adjusting the principal of the bond for changes in inflation.

Treasury shares   Shares that were issued and subsequently repurchased by the company.

Treasury stock   Shares that were issued and subsequently repurchased by the company.

Treasury stock method   A method for accounting for the effect of options (and warrants) on earnings per share (EPS) that specifies what EPS would have been if the options and warrants had been exercised and the company had used the proceeds to repurchase common stock.

Tree diagram   A diagram with branches emanating from nodes representing either mutually exclusive chance events or mutually exclusive decisions.

Trend   A long-term pattern of movement in a particular direction.

Treynor ratio   A measure of risk-adjusted performance that relates a portfolio's excess returns to the portfolio's beta.

Triangle patterns   In technical analysis, a continuation chart pattern that forms as the range between high and low prices narrows, visually forming a triangle.

Trimmed mean   A mean computed after excluding a stated small percentage of the lowest and highest observations.

Triple bottoms   In technical analysis, a reversal pattern that is formed when the price forms three troughs at roughly the same price level; used to predict a change from a downtrend to an uptrend.

Triple tops   In technical analysis, a reversal pattern that is formed when the price forms three peaks at roughly the same price level; used to predict a change from an uptrend to a downtrend.

Trough   The lowest point of a business cycle.

Trust receipt arrangement   The use of inventory as collateral for a loan. The inventory is segregated and held in trust, and the proceeds of any sale must be remitted to the lender immediately.

Turn-of-the-year effect   Calendar anomaly that stock market returns in January are significantly higher compared to the rest of the months of the year, with most of the abnormal returns reported during the first five trading days in January.

Two-fund separation theorem   The theory that all investors regardless of taste, risk preferences, and initial wealth will hold a combination of two portfolios or funds: a risk-free asset and an optimal portfolio of risky assets.

Two-sided hypothesis test   A test in which the null hypothesis is rejected in favor of the alternative hypothesis if the evidence indicates that the population parameter is either smaller or larger than a hypothesized value.

Two-tailed hypothesis test   A test in which the null hypothesis is rejected in favor of the alternative hypothesis if the evidence indicates that the population parameter is either smaller or larger than a hypothesized value.

Two-week repo rate   The interest rate on a two-week repurchase agreement; may be used as a policy rate by a central bank.

Type I error   The error of rejecting a true null hypothesis.

Type II error   The error of not rejecting a false null hypothesis.

Unanticipated (unexpected) inflation   The component of inflation that is a surprise.

Unbilled revenue   (accrued revenue) Revenue that has been earned but not yet billed to customers as of the end of an accounting period.

Unclassified balance sheet   A balance sheet that does not show subtotals for current assets and current liabilities.

Unconditional probability   The probability of an event *not* conditioned on another event.

Underemployed   A person who has a job but has the qualifications to work a significantly higher-paying job.

Underlying   An asset that trades in a market in which buyers and sellers meet, decide on a price, and the seller then delivers the asset to the buyer and receives payment. The underlying is the asset or other derivative on which a particular derivative is based. The market for the underlying is also referred to as the spot market.

Underwritten offering   An offering in which the (lead) investment bank guarantees the sale of the issue at an offering price that it negotiates with the issuer.

Unearned fees   Unearned fees are recognized when a company receives cash payment for fees prior to earning them.

Unearned revenue (**deferred revenue** or **deferred income**) A liability account for money that has been collected for goods or services that have not yet been delivered; payment received in advance of providing a good or service.

Unemployed People who are actively seeking employment but are currently without a job.

Unemployment rate The ratio of unemployed to the labor force.

Unexpected inflation The component of inflation that is a surprise.

Unit labor cost The average labor cost to produce one unit of output.

Unit normal distribution The normal density with mean (μ) equal to 0 and standard deviation (σ) equal to 1.

Units-of-production method A depreciation method that allocates the cost of a long-lived asset based on actual usage during the period.

Univariate distribution A distribution that specifies the probabilities for a single random variable.

Unlimited funds An unlimited funds environment assumes that the company can raise the funds it wants for all profitable projects simply by paying the required rate of return.

Unsecured debt Debt which gives the debtholder only a general claim on an issuer's assets and cash flow.

Unsponsored A type of depository receipt in which the foreign company whose shares are held by the depository has no involvement in the issuance of the receipts.

Up transition probability The probability that an asset's value moves up.

Utility function A mathematical representation of the satisfaction derived from a consumption basket.

Utils A unit of utility.

Validity instructions Instructions which indicate when the order may be filled.

Valuation The process of determining the value of an asset or service.

Valuation allowance A reserve created against deferred tax assets, based on the likelihood of realizing the deferred tax assets in future accounting periods.

Valuation ratios Ratios that measure the quantity of an asset or flow (e.g., earnings) in relation to the price associated with a specified claim (e.g., a share or ownership of the enterprise).

Value at risk (VAR) A money measure of the minimum value of losses expected during a specified time period at a given level of probability.

Variable costs Costs that fluctuate with the level of production and sales.

Variance The expected value (the probability-weighted average) of squared deviations from a random variable's expected value.

Variation margin Additional margin that must be deposited in an amount sufficient to bring the balance up to the initial margin requirement.

Veblen good A good that increases in desirability with price.

Vega The relationship between option price and volatility.

Venture capital Investments that provide "seed" or start-up capital, early-stage financing, or mezzanine financing to companies that are in the early stages of development and require additional capital for expansion.

Venture capital fund A fund for private equity investors that provides financing for development-stage companies.

Vertical analysis Common-size analysis using only one reporting period or one base financial statement; for example, an income statement in which all items are stated as percentages of sales.

Vertical demand schedule Implies that some fixed quantity is demanded, regardless of price.

Volatility As used in option pricing, the standard deviation of the continuously compounded returns on the underlying asset.

Voluntarily unemployed A person voluntarily outside the labor force, such as a jobless worker refusing an available vacancy.

Vote by proxy A mechanism that allows a designated party—such as another shareholder, a shareholder representative, or management—to vote on the shareholder's behalf.

Warehouse receipt arrangement The use of inventory as collateral for a loan; similar to a trust receipt arrangement except there is a third party (i.e., a warehouse company) that supervises the inventory.

Weak-form efficient market hypothesis The belief that security prices fully reflect all past market data, which refers to all historical price and volume trading information.

Wealth effect An increase (decrease) in household wealth increases (decreases) consumer spending out of a given level of current income.

Weighted average cost method An inventory accounting method that averages the total cost of available inventory items over the total units available for sale.

Weighted average cost of capital A weighted average of the aftertax required rates of return on a company's common stock, preferred stock, and long-term debt, where the weights are the fraction of each source of financing in the company's target capital structure.

Weighted mean An average in which each observation is weighted by an index of its relative importance.

Weighted-average cost of capital A weighted average of the aftertax required rates of return on a company's common stock, preferred stock, and long-term debt, where the weights are the fraction of each source of financing in the company's target capital structure.

Wholesale price index Reflects the price changes experienced by domestic producers in a country.

Winsorized mean A mean computed after assigning a stated percent of the lowest values equal to one specified low value, and a stated percent of the highest values equal to one specified high value.

Working capital The difference between current assets and current liabilities.

Working capital management The management of a company's short-term assets (such as inventory) and short-term liabilities (such as money owed to suppliers).

Yield The actual return on a debt security if it is held to maturity.

Yield spread The difference between the yield on a bond and the yield on a default-free security, usually a government note, of the same maturity. The yield spread is primarily determined by the market's perception of the credit risk on the bond.

Yield to maturity The annual return that an investor earns on a bond if the investor purchases the bond today and holds it until maturity.

Zero-cost collar A transaction in which a position in the underlying is protected by buying a put and selling a call with the premium from the sale of the call offsetting the premium from the purchase of the put. It can also be used to protect a floating-rate borrower against interest rate increases with the premium on a long cap offsetting the premium on a short floor.

Index			2011
Japan (Nikkei)			
Seoul			-11.1%
Taiwan (Taipei)			-4.5%
Mumbai			-4.7%
Singapore			
Sydney			
Shanghai B	2971.0	0.1%	-10.5%
Hong Kong	4644.0	0.9%	-6.9%
Toronto	316.8	0.7%	-4.2%
Stockholm	22,700.9	0.5%	4.1%
Mexico City	13,524.8	0.1%	

Index

Standard & Poor's (S&P) 500 Index
  arithmetic mean and standard
    deviation of returns, 374
  Arms index, 642–643
  CBOE Volatility Index, 639
  Chebyshev's inequality for, 371–372
  consensus current P/E, 344
  cumulative relative frequency and
    relative frequency of, 338
  and data mining, 535
  equity market returns, 369
  expected value from, 350
  frequency distribution for holding
    period returns, 328–333
  frequency polygon, 336–337
  histogram, 335–336
  as indicator, 513
  intermarket analysis, 649–651
  margin debt vs., 640–641
  mean returns on, 569–570
  modal interval, 346
  portfolio expected return and variance
    of return, 433, 434, 436, 437
  range, 361
  relative strength analysis, 614–615
  Sharpe ratio, 375
  skewness and kurtosis, 381
  and S&P 100, 580
  weighted mean, 349n.20
Standard & Poor's Insurance Brokers
    Index, 391
Standards of Practice Council (SPC),
    9–10
Standards of Practice Handbook, 3,
    5–7, 10
  revisions to, 6
  tenth edition, 7, 9–10
Standards of Professional Conduct,
    5–179. see also Asset Manager
    Code of Professional Conduct
    (AMC)
  adoption of, 8–9
  and applicable law, 20
  conflicts of interest [Standard VI],
    118–133
    disclosure of conflicts [Standard
      VI(A)], 16, 118–125
    priority of transactions [Standard
      VI(B)]4, 16, 125–130
    referral fees [Standard VI(C)], 16,
      130–133
    text of, 16
  duties to clients [Standard III], 61–87
    fair dealing [Standard III(B)], 15,
      68–75
    loyalty, prudence, and care [Standard
      III(A)], 7, 15, 61–68
    performance presentation [Standard
      III(D)], 15, 81–84
    preservation of confidentiality
      [Standard III(E)], 15, 84–87
    suitability [Standard III(C)], 15,
      75–81
    text of, 15
  duties to employers [Standard IV],
    87–103
    additional compensation
      arrangements [Standard IV(B)], 16,
      95–96

  loyalty [Standard IV(A)], 15, 87–95
  responsibilities of supervisors
    [Standard IV(C)], 16, 97–103
  text of, 15–16
evolution of, 6
and importance of ethics, 10–13
integrity of capital markets [Standard
    II], 47–61
  market manipulation [Standard
    II(B)], 15, 57–61
  material nonpublic information
    [Standard II(A)], 14, 47–57
  text of, 15
investment analysis, recommendations,
    and actions [Standard V], 103–118
  communication with clients and
    prospective clients [Standard V(B)],
    16, 111–116
  diligence and reasonable basis
    [Standard V(A)], 16, 103–111
  record retention [Standard V(C)], 16,
    116–118
  text of, 16
notification of, 94–95
practice problems, 145–154
and Professional Conduct Program, 8
professionalism [Standard I], 19–47
  independence and objectivity
    [Standard I(B)], 14, 27–37
  knowledge of the law [Standard I(A)],
    14, 19–27
  misconduct [Standard I(D)], 14,
    45–47
  misrepresentation [Standard I(C)],
    14, 37–45
  text of, 14
responsibilities of CFA members and
    candidates [Standard VII], 133–144
  conduct of CFA candidates/members
    [Standard VII(A)], 17, 133–138
  reference to CFA Institute,
    designation and Program [Standard
    VII(B)], 17, 138–144
  text of, 17
solutions to problems, 155–162
and Standards of Practice Council,
    9–10
in Standards of Practice Handbook, 3,
    5–7
text of, 14–17
and values of CFA Institute, 13–14
stated annual interest rate, 247
stated rates, for single cash flow,
    253–254
statements of account information, 64
statistical inference, 325, 523, 552
statistical significance, 557
statistics, 323–410. see also test statistic
  about, 324
  defined, 324
  dispersion, 361–377
    Chebyshev's inequality, 371–372
    coefficient of variation, 372–374
    mean absolute deviation, 362–363
    population variance and standard
      deviation, 363–366
    range, 361
    sample variance and standard
      deviation, 366–369

  semivariance and semideviation,
    369–370
  Sharpe ratio, 374–377
frequency distributions, 327–334
  construction of, 328–330, 333–334
  defined, 327
  and holding period formula, 327–328
  and relative frequency, 330–333
graphic presentations of data, 335–338
  frequency polygons and cumulative
    frequency distributions, 336–338
  histograms, 335–336
kurtosis, 383–386
measurement scales, 325–327
  identifying, 326–327
  types of scales, 326–327
measures of central tendency, 339–355
  arithmetic mean, 339–343
  geometric mean, 350–354
  harmonic mean, 354–355
  median, 343–345
  mode, 346–347
  weighted mean, 347–350
nature of, 324–325
populations and samples, 325
practice problems, 391–397
quantiles, 355–361
  calculating, 356–359
  in investment practice, 359–361
  types of, 355–359
sample, 325, 514, 515
solutions to problems, 398–410
symmetry, 377–382
using geometric and arithmetic means,
    386–388
status, client, 85
stochastic oscillator, 636–637
stock ownership, 121, 122
stock price
  as Bernoulli random variable, 468–469
  binomial model, 476–477
  and commercial paper issuance,
    566–568
  lognormal distribution for, 491
stock screens, 421–422
stratified random sampling, 515–517
stratum, 516
stress testing, 489
Student's t-distribution. see
    t-distribution
sub-advisors
  defined, 212
  Disclosure (GIPS Section I.4), 181, 183
  Fundamentals of Compliance (GIPS
    Section I.0), 176
  selecting, 105
subjective probability, 414
submanagers, 80, 108–109
subminuette, Elliott wave, 647
Suez, 357
suitability, 80–81
  for entire portfolio, 79
  for investor risk profile, 78–81
Suitability [Standard III(C)], 75–81
  application of the standard, 78–81
  compliance procedures, 78
    investment policy statements, 78
    regular updates, 78
    suitability test policies, 78

Index